W9-BGV-508

MEDITERRANEAN SEA

Siwa Oasis

WESTERN DESERT

Baharīya Oasis

Dakhla Oasis

Kharga Oasis

FAIYUM BASIN

Medinet el-Fayum
Hawara

Memphis
el-Lisht

LOWER EGYPT

Oxyrhynchus

Illahun
Herakleopolis

Meidum

Hermopolis Magna
el-Ashmunein

Tuna el-Gebel

Meir

Asyut

Cusae

Hatnub

Bersheh
Antinoöpolis
Beni Hasan

Zawyet el-Amwat

el-Amarna

EASTERN DESERT

Abydos

Badari

Antaeopolis

Diospolis Parva

Akhmim

Valley of
the Kings

Naqada

Dendera

Armant
Mo'alla

Thebes (Luxor)

Coptos

Gebelein

Esna

Hierakonpolis

Edfu

Elkab

UPPER EGYPT

Gebel es-Silsila

Kom Ombo

RED SEA

ARABIA

Gulf of Suez

Gulf of Aqaba

SINAI

Wadi Mughara

PALESTINE

Gaza

Joppa

Jerusalem

Dead Sea

THE OXFORD ENCYCLOPEDIA OF ANCIENT EGYPT

THE OXFORD ENCYCLOPEDIA OF

ANCIENT

EGYPT

DONALD B. REDFORD

EDITOR IN CHIEF

VOLUME 3

OXFORD

UNIVERSITY PRESS

2001

OXFORD
UNIVERSITY PRESS

Oxford   New York
Athens   Auckland   Bangkok   Bogotá   Buenos Aires   Calcutta
Cape Town   Chennai   Dar es Salaam   Delhi   Florence   Hong Kong   Istanbul
Karachi   Kuala Lumpur   Madrid   Melbourne   Mexico City   Mumbai
Nairobi   Paris   São Paulo   Shanghai   Singapore   Taipei   Tokyo   Toronto   Warsaw

and associated companies in
Berlin   Ibadan

Library of Congress Cataloging-in-Publication Data
The Oxford Encyclopedia of Ancient Egypt / Donald B. Redford, editor in chief.
p.   cm.
Includes bibliographical references and index.
ISBN 0-19-510234-7 (set)—ISBN 0-19-513821-X (v. 1) —
ISBN 0-19-513822-8 (v. 2)—ISBN 0-19-513823-6 (v. 3)
1. Egypt—Civilization—To 332 B.C.—Encyclopedias.
2. Egypt—Civilization—332 B.C.–638 A.D.—Encyclopedias.
3. Egypt—Antiquities—Encyclopedias.
I. Redford, Donald B.
DT58 .O94   2001
932—dc21   99-054801

The photographs and line drawings used herein were supplied by contributors to the work,
members of the Editorial Board, major museums, and by commercial photographic archives.
The publisher has made every effort to ascertain that necessary permissions to reprint materials have
been secured. Sources of all photographs and line drawings are given in captions to illustrations.

EDITORIAL AND PRODUCTION STAFF
Commissioning Editor: Christopher Collins
Project Editor: Eugene Romanosky
Development Editors: Donald B. Spanel, Marion Osmun
Copy Chief: Martha Goldstein
Copyeditors: Jane McGary, Martin Ahermaa, Betty Leigh Hutcheson,
Mark La Flaur, Wendy Raver
Proofreaders: Karen Fraley, Ellen Thorn, Walter Saxon, Carol Wengler
Translators: Julia Harvey, Susan Romanosky, Elizabeth Schwaiger,
Sabine H. Seiler, Robert E. Shillenn, Jennifer Worth
Bibliographic Researcher: Melinda Hartwig
Photo Researcher: Elena Pischikova
Indexers: Carol Roberts and Kay Wosewick
Cartographer: Bill Nelson
Book Designer: Joan Greenfield

Publisher: Karen Casey

P

PAINTING was used in ancient Egypt from the Predynastic era through the Roman period. It enhanced almost every surface in Egyptian art: tomb and temple walls; mud-brick structures such as palaces, domestic shrines, and houses; sculpture and relief; coffins, sarcophagi, and cartonnage; cosmetic objects, furniture, leather, linen, ostraca, papyri, pottery and tomb models. Painting added detail to carved, sculpted, and molded images and in the case of flat surfaces, created the form and design itself. The color of paint identified, and codified with its symbolic value, information about the image. Specific styles, techniques, representational types, and ateliers are revealed in painted images and scenes, which were crafted in response to the political, social, and religious demands of their time. Any discussion of painting must of course be limited, given the wide range of surfaces that carried painted decoration in ancient Egypt. For our purposes, a general study of painting will be followed by a chronological survey of flat painting with figural decoration, focusing on the largest category of painting, that on tomb walls.

Typology and Techniques. The Egyptian palette was composed of white *(ḥḏ)*, black *(km)*, red *(dšr)*, blue *(ḥsbḏ)*, green *(wꜣḏ)*, and yellow *(nwb or ḳnit)*. A number of other colors were formed by mixing the above colors to form blue-red *(ṯms)*, turquoise-green *(mfkꜣt)*, yellow-orange-red *(kt)*, gray *(dḥt?)*, gray-blue, brown, and pink, among others. In the Old Kingdom, the basic palette consisted of black, white, red, green, yellow, blue, and gray. By the Middle Kingdom, red tones were expanded to form brown and pink; and later in the New Kingdom, additional shades of blue, yellow, and red were added. This palette continued through the remainder of Egyptian painting, becoming more pastel in the Ptolemaic and Roman periods.

In painting, color had a symbolic and classificatory meaning to the ancient Egyptians. Black, the color of the fertile earth, symbolized fertility, renewal, and the underworld. Red symbolized fire, blood, the desert, and chaos; it was the skin color of the male figure in art. Yellow was a solar color connoting the sun, the flesh and bones of the gods; it was the skin tone of the female figure in art. White implied purity; green, growth, vigor, and resurrection. Blue, associated with water and the heavens, was frequently found in the bodies, beards, and wigs of deities; in the post-Amarna period it became associated with the skin color of Amun-re.

The colors came from naturally occurring substances. White came from calcium carbonate (whiting) or calcium sulphate (gypsum). Huntite white was first employed during the Middle Kingdom and became more common in the New Kingdom, when it was used as a contrast to whitewash or as a base to bring out the luminosity of the overlaid pigments. Black was carbon from charcoal or deposited soot. Ochers, ranging from yellow to red to dark brown, originated from naturally occurring iron oxides. Beginning in the Middle Kingdom, yellow was also obtained from orpiment, which appeared as bright yellow. A lighter yellow was derived from jarosite. Realgar red was used in the New Kingdom and appeared as a bright orange-red. Introduced in the fifth dynasty, the color blue was composed originally of azurite (copper carbonate) from the Sinai and Eastern Desert; later it was manufactured from a frit compound of heated quartz, lime, and alkalis (natron or plant ash), ground malachite, and calcium carbonate. Green was made of naturally occurring powdered malachite or a mixture of malachite and calcium carbonate. Sometimes ocher yellow was mixed with a blue frit to produce green. Varnish (tree resin or beeswax) was also added or applied to color. Varnish, first used in the Predynastic period in tomb painting; was also applied on vessels, coffins, minor art objects, and statuary eyes.

To make those minerals and compounds suitable for application, they were first ground into a powder. Natural gum, derived from indigenous trees such as the acacia or from glue, was combined with the colored particles. The pigment was then applied with a brush to stone, wood, plaster, linen, papyrus, leather, clay, or a wall prepared with gypsum plaster, which had been allowed to dry before receiving paint, in a technique known as tempera. In some cases, rapid execution or heavily trodden areas necessitated applying paint to a wet plaster surface, as can be seen on some of the royal palace floors at Tell el-Amarna during the reign of Amenhotpe IV in the eighteenth dynasty. In the case of tomb walls of poor-quality stone, the wall received a mixture of Nile mud and hacked straw, sometimes reinforced with limestone chips, to create a level surface, which was finished with several layers of gypsum plaster and smoothed before painting. Walls

1

of good stone were dressed, patched with gypsum plaster, smoothed, and coated with a thin plaster wash. Walls in mud-brick buildings, such as palaces and houses, were plastered before they received painted decoration. To produce the so-called Faiyum portraits, encaustic was utilized; pigment was mixed with wax that was gently heated for easy application, and the mixture was applied to primed wood with the help of a palette knife *(cestrum)* or a brush. Brushes from all periods were made from a common Egyptian rush *(Juncus maritimus)*, palm ribs, or wood, which were cut, bruised into bristles, and bound together with a string. The thickness of the brush determined the thickness of the line. From the third century BCE on, the marsh reed *Phragmites communis* was used as a type of quill pen.

In wall compositions, scenes and figures were often constructed with the help of a system of guide lines. First the boundaries of the wall and the register lines were marked by a string dipped in red paint, which artisans stretched across the wall and snapped at intervals. Within this, a system of lines was drawn to aid the artist in building figures and scenes. Sometimes the draftsman drew forms freehand without the help of guide lines: After the sketch was correctly drawn, background wash was applied of white, gray; pale blue-gray or yellow around the figures and objects; individual colors were then painted in, and the forms were outlined again with the details delineated with a fine brush. Rows and columns were also drawn and the hieroglyphs painted in; when required, a final background wash was applied. Procedural exceptions exist—for example, in the Hall of Barks in the Temple of Sethy I at Abydos, where the background wash was applied last. Where the image was to be carved, the corrected sketch was chiseled into sunk or raised relief and then painted. Lighting for painters working in dimly lit areas was provided by lamps filled with oil and floating wicks that produced minimal smoke.

In sculpture, relief, and the minor arts, color enhanced the surface and indicated detail. In the case of soft stone and wood sculpture and objects, a layer of plaster was applied and then painted; sometimes color was painted directly on wood or hard stone. Raised and sunk relief often received plaster to even out defects in the stone before color was brushed on. Linen funerary and votive cloths were plastered and painted. Cartonnage, or alternating layers of shaped linen and plaster, was decorated with colorful vignettes. Funerary papyri made of strips of pressed papyrus reed laid in transverse layers were painted with scenes and texts, and then rolled to form "books" like the *Book of Going Forth by Day* (*Book of the Dead*). On Predynastic vessels, designs were painted in monochrome using a yellow-white calcareous clay slip (White Cross-lined Ware) or a red to purple-brown ocher (Decorated Ware). In the New Kingdom, polychrome decoration appeared on pots, executed with mineral pigments such as ochers, frits, calcium, soot, and cobalt blue. Egyptian faience, the heated mixture of quartz sand with lime and alkalis (natron or plant ash) covered with a glaze, had details added in black or brown slurry (glazing powder) or paint. Bone and ivory contained designs incised and filled with color.

Paint was applied in washes of solid colors placed side by side, which sometimes ran into one another, creating gradations of color. The deliberate use of shading and shadowing was infrequent. The Egyptian word "variegated" *(s3b)* described the use of color to indicate textures such as fur, feathers, or scales. Color was also manipulated to create an illusion of depth in compositions with overlapping figures and objects, where near and far figures were rendered in alternating tones.

Political, Religious, and Social Aspects. Beginning in the Early Dynastic era, specific royal iconography was developed to express the tenets of kingship and the strength of the state. Scenes of the king interacting with the gods and maintaining the order of the universe in painted temples and palaces displayed royal power to the people. The elite, who were legitimized by and governed for the king, showed their privileged position through the content and the quality of the decoration in their tombs and funerary equipment. The owner's titles, name, and chosen subject matter established his or her identity and status, and the style of painting revealed access to royal workshops and artists. The content and quality of the painted images of royalty and the elite proclaimed to the governed in visual terms the stability of the state, various ideologies, and the order of the universe. Painted scenes expressed the relationship between the living and the world of the gods and the dead. In temples, the beauty of the decoration would persuade the gods to reside there so that they would maintain the established order of the universe and continue the existence of the world. Scenes and commentaries in royal tombs identified the dead king with the sun god and his perpetual regeneration. Nonroyal tomb-chapels were places of assembly for family members and other visitors.

Certain representations occurred in specific contexts. Gods' temples were decorated with scenes such as the king performing ritual acts before the gods, or deities embracing and giving gifts to the ruler. Decoration was organized into lower, middle, and upper horizontally stacked bands corresponding to subjects of terrestrial, divine, and celestial nature, respectively. Palace floors at the eighteenth dynasty royal cities of Tell el-Amarna and Malqata were painted with pools of water teeming with fish, rimmed with plants and animals; ceilings were decorated with birds flying overhead. Palace throne daises and floors

PAINTING. *Detail from a hunting scene, showing birds flying over a papyrus marsh.* This wall painting is from the eighteenth dynasty private tomb of Menna at Thebes. (Courtesy Dieter Arnold)

found at Tell el-Amarna, Kom al-Samak (Malqata), and the nineteenth dynasty palace of Merenptah at Memphis were also decorated with images of bound prisoners over which the king, the preserver of order, would walk, symbolically subduing Egypt's foes. Scenes in royal funerary temples emphasized the king's offering cult and position in the cosmos and depicted events from his or her reign. Vignettes in the royal tombs were drawn from various "books" representing the solar cycle, the underworld, and the *Book of Going Forth by Day,* as well as showing the ruler in the presence of the gods.

Objects and monuments intended for private patrons contained representations of deities and depictions concerned with supplying the deceased with food, as well as information to ensure his or her safe passage and rebirth in the next world. Coffins, designed to protect the body and act as a home for the *ka,* were decorated with a false door, offerings, and offering scenes, and later with gods and funerary scenes. Funerary papyri and linen were painted with texts and vignettes from funerary "books." Figures of protective deities like Bes embellished household altars and walls, and goddesses such as Hathor adorned votive linens. Stelae were decorated with figures of the deceased before offerings, the king or deities; these were placed either in the tomb to provide magically for the owner in the next life, or in temples where the patron would be linked with the gods and the temple rituals. Tomb chapels with scenes of offering and images derived from funerary books or the patron's life ensured that he or she would not only be supplied with food and safe passage to the beyond but also be remembered by the living who would celebrate the funerary cult.

Images known as "scenes of daily life" were painted on walls and objects, and reflect real events from the life of the owner as well as ideal, ritual concepts. Motifs in tombs, such as the dead banqueting with family and friends or inspecting the fields, were ideal images that operated magically, to guarantee their provisioning; they also may record situations that occurred in life. Scenes of the dead fishing and fowling, or the production and bringing of foodstuffs, were meant to function allegorically to supply them with sustenance in the hereafter. Daily life scenes also displayed the deceased's family and social position in life, thereby linking the dead eternally to their personal and professional roles and guaranteeing them continued life and high status in the hereafter.

A visual image and style was established for each king, and its essence was transferred to the painted figural representations of gods and men. The style of painting revealed the identifying features of the king, based on the artistic synthesis of his or her essential characteristics, idealized and expressed in proportions that were standardized for easy identification. Images of elite officials were done either in the likeness of their ruler, or sometimes in a more individual style. Painted portraits of non-royal people occurred in isolated instances; these can be identified by their variance from stylistic and typological norms, or their individuality, as in the case of the later so-called Faiyum portraits. Where exceptions to the perfected human form existed in painting, they often represented standard characterizations of rank and culture, such as fatness, leanness, age, sensuality, or the uncultivated commoner or foreigner. An exceptional break from the ideal royal form occurred during the Amarna period, when the distorted image of Amenhotpe IV and his family as the objects of worship along with the Aten betrayed a new ideology of kingship that was codified in art. In some periods, kings modeled the style of their art on previous models to ally themselves with the political ideals of former times. An example is offered by Montuhotep I, who consciously copied the decorative programs of Old Kingdom pyramid complexes in the painted relief decoration in the anterior of his eleventh dynasty mortuary temple at Deir el-Bahri. Presumably, painters themselves also drew from earlier models in order to perfect their art or satisfy their patrons.

During the Early Dynastic period, anonymous craftsmen and their products, previously created for the community, came under the patronage and control of the king and the state, who set the cultural norms, developed the canonical human form, and standardized artistic training. Painters worked in teams with other painters, sculptors, or craftsmen; they depended on their employers to supply them with commissions, materials, and the money or goods to pay for their work. Teams of workmen personalized images and texts for the patron within conventional scenes and motifs. Biographical texts, the use of details and themes specific to the patron, suggest that the client (or his successor or delegate) selected the program of decoration. Mass-produced coffins, papyri, and stelae had blanks left for the purchaser's name, which implies that the subject matter was crafted in advance, without a specific person in mind. In all painted works, the execution of the decoration was the artist's responsibility within the prescribed rules of figural portrayal, decorum, and placement of key elements (e.g., the false door) on the object or in the tomb. The artist's specific rendition of scenes, even with stock themes, attests to his individual contribution to the final painting.

In all periods, painted relief was the preferred method of decoration in temples and tombs because of its permanence and durability. Where painting and relief follow within the same monument, the more important, prominently placed scenes are executed in relief. In the case of limited time, money, or access to resources, sketches originally intended to be cut into relief were completed in painting, presumably so they could act as effective images and function ritually within the monument. Flat painting was used in contexts where the rock was inadequate for carving, and in mud-brick constructions like palaces, houses, and shrines that could not support carved relief. Painting tended to be preferred in nonroyal contexts; where royal and sacred monuments of stone carried flat painting, it often seems to have been a quick alternative to relief. Perhaps flat painting was preferred because of its low cost and because it could be rapidly achieved by a team of workmen. Painting also allowed a more spontaneous artistic conception of form that could be exploited more readily in nonsacred monuments.

Chronology. Flat painting appeared early in the Predynastic period on pottery known as White Cross-lined Ware. From the Naqada I period to early Naqada II (4000–3400 BCE); designs were painted on the surface of the vessel with a fiber brush before firing. Images of the hunt, the flora and fauna of the Nile Valley, and geometric patterns embellish the exterior of these vessels, often with little consideration of their shape. The painted images on the succeeding Decorated Ware of the Naqada II to III periods (3500–3100 BCE) represent the world of man and perhaps historical events, arranged in groups of related figures. Potters painted Nile scenes composed of boats at the center of the jar, bounded by trees and birds along the riverbank, with desert animals beyond. Some of these pots are adorned with the large figure of a woman standing on a boat cabin with her arms raised, attended by smaller male figures. This female figure has been identified as a goddess, a mourner, or a dancer.

The reportory of scenes found on Decorated Ware also

PAINTING. *Detail from a harvest scene, including a depiction of two fighting girls.* This wall painting is from the eighteenth dynasty private tomb of Menna at Thebes. (Courtesy Dieter Arnold)

occurs on linen from Gebelein and on a wall in tomb 100 at Hierakonpolis. Dating to Naqada IIc, the painting in tomb 100 introduces new motifs and representational devices, such as the base line, which later would become a major device for ordering compositions. The plastered mud-brick wall is painted in yellow, red, green, white, and black on a light yellow background, with themes of hunting, ferrying, fighting, ritual running or dancing, and a chieftain subduing foes. The entire composition places traditional pictures of the hunt on the upper part of the wall and motifs of combat and triumph below, in an arrangement that focuses on the hereditary and divine nature of kingship. This representational cycle, found in what may have been a ruler's tomb, shows the beginning of royal and religious imagery that will be fully exploited in later royal monuments.

In the first and second dynasties, the exteriors of *mastaba* tombs are decorated with geometric designs that imitate hanging mats, painted in black, white, red, blue-green, and yellow on a white gesso ground. During the third dynasty, painted decoration moves inside the *mastaba*. In the corridor chapel of Hesire at Saqqara, an elite official from the reign of Djoser (c.2687–2669 BCE), depictions of funerary gifts are painted on the walls to reinforce

magically the objects actually buried in the tomb. The tomb also has painted fragments of men with cattle and a crocodile, once part of an early example of a "daily life scene" on the marsh. From the reign of Sneferu (c.2632–2608), the tomb chapel of Nefermaat and Atet at Meidum introduces a new technique of paste inlay. Colored mineral pastes were mixed with resin and set into a specific type of sunk relief composed of undercut edges and raised grids that held the color in place. The method aimed at permanence and even merited special description in Atet's chapel: "He made his gods in writing which cannot be erased." The famous masterpiece, the "Geese of Meidum" (Cairo, Egyptian Museum, JE 34571), was also found in the chapel of Atet, where it was part of a larger scene of the owner fowling with a clap net. The geese were painted in tempera with the palette of the Old Kingdom, which was expanded by overlaying colors and mixing hues to produce browns and grays. The solid color of the birds was enhanced by skillful brushwork which created textures such as stippling, feathering, and mottling.

Painted relief was the preferred mode of decoration in monuments of the Old Kingdom, although flat painting was occasionally utilized. Painting appears as the dominant form of decoration in the sixth dynasty tombs of officials in the provincial towns outside the capital of Memphis. The Old Kingdom artistic tradition is clear in the composition, coloring, and execution of paintings in tombs as far south as Naga ed-Deir, but the hallmarks of a later painting style also appear. This style, with its conventions of representing attenuated figures with large eyes and ears, may have begun in Memphite art of the fifth dynasty and moved out into the provinces, where it continues into the art of the First Intermediate Period, particularly in Upper Egypt. In the First Intermediate Period, painting is not rendered in any one uniform style, but rather is characterized by an influx of local styles. Generally, the best examples of what previous art surveys have termed "First Intermediate Period style" are the paintings found in the Upper Egyptian elite tombs at Thebes, el-Moalla, Gebelein, and Aswan. These tombs lay in the Theban domain, well out of reach of the Herakleopolitans, the inheritors of Memphite conventions and artists. In general, detail in Upper Egyptian painting is rendered as a series of patterns with colors laid in dissonant and often strident combinations. Principal figures are depicted unusually larger than the subsidiary figures who are scattered across the picture surface, with or without register lines. Paintings at sites in Herakleopolitan territory, like Bersheh, Assiut, and Beni Hasan, are executed in a more traditional Memphite manner with local style overlays.

Painted stone stelae from First Intermediate Period sites reflect both the classic Memphite manner and particular local styles. Stone stelae began as niche stones in the second dynasty when they were inset at the back of the southern niche of elite *mastabas*. They are decorated with painted relief scenes of the deceased seated facing a table of offerings and a hieroglyphic list. By the First Intermediate Period, some stone stelae are decorated in flat painting and placed on the walls of the rock-cut offering chambers marking the offering place and close to the burials. Stelae are composed of a horizontal line of text above, and an image of the deceased holding a staff and scepter facing a pile of offerings—an image borrowed directly from relief-carved Old Kingdom false door jambs.

The local variants in painting during the First Intermediate Period and the freedom expressed in them led to the innovation and technical proficiency of Middle Kingdom elite tomb painting. The floating register lines of the First Intermediate Period developed into the wavy lines of the desert hills, as rendered, for example, in the tomb of Senet at Thebes (tomb 60). Inventive scenes in the twelfth dynasty painted tomb of Ukhhotep III at Meir (C1) show women laboring on the land and fowling, activities traditionally performed by men. These scenes build on similar themes that appeared in the First Intermediate Period tomb of Ankhtifi at el-Moalla. Local officials' practice of borrowing royal prerogatives in the First Intermediate period was imitated in the twelfth dynasty. In the tombs of Ukhhotep III (Meir nr. C1) and Khnemhotpe II (Beni Hasan nr. 3), royal symbols are appropriated; and the nomarch Wahka II in his tomb at Qaw el-Kebir shows the Nile god presenting him with offering gifts as if he were a king. In tombs and on other objects, the polychrome palette of the First Intermediate Period is a legacy to the twelfth dynasty.

Generally, elite tomb painting at the beginning of the Middle Kingdom appears stiff and awkward; later, during the reigns from Senwosret II to Amenemhet III, it exhibits a greater sense of artistry and innovation. Consciously archaizing and innovative motifs contributed to the development of Middle Kingdom painting. In the twelfth dynasty tombs at Meir, artists borrowed the subject matter from the accessible sixth dynasty tombs but rendered their figures in the style of the Middle Kingdom. The sophisticated painting in the First Intermediate Period tombs at Beni Hasan inspired the virtuosity of painting seen in later twelfth dynasty tombs. Images of mythological creatures (snake-necked panther, winged griffin), scenes of manufacturing flint knives, spinning, weaving, and wrestling were introduced into Middle Kingdom tomb repertories.

Wooden coffins, which appeared with dynastic times, are at first largely undecorated except for the palace façade design. During the sixth dynasty, painted rows of text run down the center and sides of the rectangular box, with *wedjat*-eyes on the exterior and a false door on the interior next to the face of the mummy. Sarcophagi of the First Intermediate Period and twelfth dynasty add more decoration to the sixth dynasty type. During this time, the Coffin Texts, descended from the Pyramid Texts of the Old Kingdom, are introduced into the sarcophagus interior. Offering piles, an offering list, and object friezes are painted in the interior of the casket in bright, clear colors. The cedar coffin of Djehutynakht IV from Bersheh (Boston, MFA 20.1822–1826) illustrates the technical excellence of painting at this time. The outer coffin is painted on the interior with a false door, an offering scene, and object friezes. The paintings show exquisite manipulation of color tones and texture layering, the use of a varied palette applied on white underpainting, and the suppression of defining outlines. Later in the twelfth dynasty, interior decoration on coffins vanishes, and the outer casing is painted with a cavetto cornice, and a false door or offering piles on the side of the box. Images of Isis and Nephthys, the two goddesses associated with the resurrection of Osiris, sometimes appear at the foot and head of the coffin, respectively. These goddesses are among the first deities to decorate nonroyal objects; through their association with the god Osiris, they acted to identify the deceased with Osiris and aid his or her rebirth in the next world. Painted funerary masks made of cartonnage were also utilized during the Middle Kingdom and were fitted on the wrapped mummy itself. During the twelfth dynasty, a new type of coffin was introduced, made of wood or cartonnage in a human form. This developed into the *rishi*-coffin of the seventeenth dynasty, named after the Arabic word for "feather," made manifest in the pair of folded, stylized wings that decorate the anthropoid casket from shoulder to toe. These wings may symbolize the wings of Isis spread in protection over the deceased.

At the beginning of the New Kingdom, Thebes was the center of elite and royal burial. Elite chapels, cut into the hillside, take the form of a "T" with a transverse front hall, and an inner passage leading back to an offering niche decorated with statues or a stela. The subterranean sarcophagus chamber of the tomb is reserved for the burial and inaccessible. The entrance of the chapel is decorated with images of the deceased going in (toward the setting sun or Osiris) and out of the tomb (toward the rising sun). In the broad hall, ideally, the small walls contained a painted autobiographical stela on one wall and a false door, the contact point between the living and the dead, on the other. The decoration of the long walls was variable and could contain scenes of offering and banqueting before the deceased or the tomb owner fulfilling his official duties before the king. The painted scenes on the back walls of the broad hall, which were immediately visible upon entering the tomb, were particularly important for the self-presentation of the tomb owner. The longitudinal corridor was painted with mortuary images, such as the funeral procession or the Opening of the Mouth ritual. During the reign of Amenhotpe IV (1382–1365 BCE), the decoration shifted to painted relief in elite tombs at Tell el-Amarna, and focused on the king and his family. Late in the eighteenth dynasty, Theban tomb chapels returned to painted scenes of "daily life," but scenes of a religious nature increased. By the nineteenth and twentieth dynasties, the chapel acted as a type of funerary temple with decoration drawn largely from the *Book of Going Forth by Day*. The false door disappears, the stela is moved to the façade of the tomb, and the decorative program stresses the tomb owner venerating the gods. The end of the New Kingdom brought a decline in the number of painted monumental tombs, and images of the hereafter were transferred to coffins and papyri, which subsequently led to the flowering of papyrus and sarcophagus painting.

Early eighteenth dynasty Theban tomb painting relies on Middle Kingdom style, which in turn was patterned on Old Kingdom models. The Old and Middle Kingdom elite tombs that dot the Theban landscape may have been examples for painters who sought the prestige of earlier periods by appropriating their style of painting. In the elite tombs of the early eighteenth dynasty, the style of painting is stiff and depends on the basic color palette. Beginning in the reign of Thutmose III (1504–1452 BCE) and reaching full expression in the reigns of Thutmose IV (1419–1410) and Amenhotpe III (1410–1382), painting is freed, gestures are varied, the color palette expands, and line becomes fluid; the sense of space is enhanced by overlapping; and compositions are organized around groups. During the reigns of these last two kings, the style of painting and motifs vary according to the tomb owner's institutional group and appear to commemorate specific social concerns and ideologies. In the late eighteenth dynasty and the Ramessid period, elite tomb painting retains the expressiveness of the Amarna era, but it gradually becomes rigid under religious reformation and the return to the canonical ideal of the perfect type. Painted scenes continue to be organized in horizontal registers on the wall as in the eighteenth dynasty, but Ramessid tombs expand and extend them beyond the borders of the wall like a film-strip. Scenes are organized vertically, with images of the hereafter in the upper bands and mortuary cult representations in the lower bands. At Saqqara during the late eighteenth dynasty, flat painting is used in the side chapels and statue rooms of elite tombs.

Elite coffins proliferated in a number of different styles during the New Kingdom. Until the reign of Thutmose III, *rishi*-coffins continue to be employed, as well as painted funerary masks of cartonnage. Early in the eighteenth dynasty, another anthropoid coffin which was composed of painted and plastered wood came into use; texts are arranged in four evenly spaced vertical bands crossed by bands running across the lid, and a central band of text spreads from below the collar to the feet of the sarcophagus. Early in the dynasty, funerary and offering scenes fill the spaces between the bands, followed later by images such as the Four Sons of Horus, Anubis, and Thoth. The image of a vulture with outstretched wings, placed on the chest of the coffin, was replaced in the reign of Amenhotpe III with the winged goddess Nut. Until the reign of Thutmose III, the decoration is executed in polychrome on a white background that imitates the white linen of a mummy shroud. Later, black (the color of resurrection) serves as the background, which is decorated with gold leaf or gold paint (colors of the flesh of the gods and the sun). A new anthropoid coffin was introduced in the late eighteenth dynasty, with decoration rendered in gem colors (red, light and dark blue) on a yellow-gold background that is covered by a layer of varnish.

In the Middle Kingdom there appeared wooden toilet and canopic chests plastered and decorated with figural scenes. Beginning in the eighteenth dynasty, chests for *shawabti*s (substitute laborers for the deceased) and other types of chests were introduced. The wooden box of King

PAINTING. *Painted wooden chest of Tutankhamun, showing the king in a battle against Syrian enemies.* This eighteenth dynasty chest is now in the Egyptian Museum, Cairo. (Scala / Art Resource, NY)

Tutankhamun in the Egyptian Museum, Cairo (JE 61467), which held royal sandals, a gilt headrest, and cloth bundles, is plastered and painted with four scenes of the king in his chariot. On the long sides, the pharaoh at the center wages war against Syrians and Nubians, the traditional enemies of Egypt who signified the chaotic forces that must be subdued by the king. The same theme is echoed on the lid, which depicts the king hunting in the desert. The idea of order is symbolized visually by the register lines and symmetrical ranks of soldiers and horses, and chaos is implied by the tumbling mass of foreigners and animals. The short sides are painted with the heraldic symbol of Tutankhamun as a sphinx trampling the northern and southern enemies of Egypt.

Flat painting decorated the walls of eighteenth dynasty royal tombs in the Valley of the Kings from the reign of Thutmose I until that of Horemheb, when painted relief again became the dominant form of decoration for the king's sepulchre. The iconography in these royal tombs was chosen from various funerary books which were transferred onto the wall like an unfurled scroll of papyrus; the yellow background color in the royal tombs emulated its hue. The *Book of That Which Is in the Underworld,* later known as *Amduat,* was the sole book that decorated the walls of the royal burial chamber. This book aimed at initiating the king into the underworld by describing the ways and functions of the beyond and explaining, hour by hour, the nightly voyage of the sun. When painted relief

became the preferred method of decoration in the royal tombs, the number of funerary books expanded; in the tomb of Ramesses VI, all the known books of the underworld and the sky, and an abundance of scenes from the *Book of Going Forth by Day* and scenes of divinities, adorn the walls.

The painted decoration of the royal tombs in the Theban necropolis was the responsibility of the artisans who resided in the village at Deir el-Medina during the New Kingdom. Founded early in the eighteenth dynasty on the west bank at Thebes, Deir el-Medina housed craftsmen, including carpenters, stonecutters, relief sculptors, and painters, who painted the royal tombs and their own tombs as well. Their chapels draw from the same pool of iconography as elite Theban tombs; however, the style of the tombs and the themes used in their burial chambers occasionally borrows from the royal sphere. Walls are painted yellow, figures mirror the royal figural style, and rarely, scenes found in the royal tombs occur in painters' sepulchers. A special group of tombs are painted with a palette of yellow, black, and red on a white background, in a style described as "monochromatic" by Bernard Bruyère *(Tombes thébaines de Deir el-Médineh à décoration monochrome,* Cairo, 1952). These monochromatic tombs may have been painted by a distinct group of painters who also appeared in the scenes. The workmanship of specific Deir el-Medina artisans has been identified by comparing their signed drawings on flakes of limestone (ostraca) with

PAINTING. *Thutmose III standing and pouring a libation before Amun-Re.* This eighteenth dynasty mural is from the shrine of Hathor at Hatshepsut's temple in Deir el-Bahri. It is now in the Egyptian Museum, Cairo. (Scala / Art Resource, NY)

paintings in royal tombs. Ostraca, the ancient equivalent to notepaper, are preserved from the earliest times until the Roman period, with one of largest caches coming from the village of Deir el-Medina. Ostraca illustrate aspects of the everyday world of the ancient Egyptians and candidly reveal the artistic process. Forms outlined in black, or sometimes painted with the basic color palette, depict small-scale studies of larger compositions, votive gifts with images of a deity, portions of animal fables, or motifs from house paintings.

Figural painting in the New Kingdom appears on polychrome and blue-painted pottery and faience. On polychrome pottery, the use of motifs of humans, animals, and plant life (also found on other media like furniture, textiles, and wall paintings), led to the development of large, wide jars with funnel or bulbous necks to provide large spaces for decoration. Blue-painted pottery, with its predominant use of a pale blue color derived from cobalt aluminate spinel, is decorated with images such as men or women on a skiff in the marsh and the figure of Bes. Details are executed in red and black, with occasional additions of white, yellow, and green. Polychrome pottery has

a wide range of colors that include thick applications of red, black, yellow orpiment, green, and blue frits on a white gypsum or calcium carbonate background. New Kingdom faience is decorated with figural scenes; images concerned with Hathoric activities, such as female musicians and aquatic themes associated with rebirth, often adorn these objects.

In temples, certain features and sometimes entire scene cycles are executed in flat paint. A couple of fans rendered in color from a relief-cut bark procession on the north wall of the Hypostyle Hall of the temple of Amun at Karnak prove that some details were rendered only in paint. A small temple of Amenhotpe III at Wadi el-Sebua in Nubia is decorated completely in paint with traditional temple scenes. In the funerary temple of Sety I at Abydos, painting appears alongside relief in the Hall of Barques, where it was intended to replace the carved decoration. The execution of the painting is more careful than the "freer" style found in elite Theban tombs, which reflects the ritual formality of temple decoration. The unfinished Ptolemaic temple of Thoth at Kasr el-Agouz on the west bank at Thebes contains painted decoration, notably in a scene that represents the king dedicating the chapel to the principal deities of the temple.

Mud-brick royal palaces, houses, and shrines were embellished with paintings. From the Middle Kingdom and Second Intermediate Period site of Tell ed-Dab'a, palace paintings are believed to have been completed by Minoan artists. From this period and the early eighteenth dynasty, the walls of the north palace at Deir el-Ballas (opposite Coptos) include painted images of armed men wielding battle-axes. Found in the entrance corridor, these forms invoke the king's domination over foreigners and act as talismans to guard the palace from the entry of chaotic forces. Other wall compositions depict royal life and ritual: the daughters of Amenhotpe IV sit on cushions beside the now lost representations of their parents from the King's House at Tell el-Amarna (Ashmolean Museum, Oxford 1893.1); and from the Great Palace at Tell el-Amarna, images of servants remain from a destroyed scene of Amenhotpe IV returning to the palace after a ceremonial visit. Palace floors at Tell el-Amarna and Malqata painted with images of flora and fauna show rich detail and fluid improvisation, accomplished without pre-drawing. Although earlier remains of decorative painting exist—for example, from mud-brick houses at the Middle Kingdom site of Illahun (Kahun)—the majority of examples come from the New Kingdom. At Tell el-Amarna, the decoration of elite houses follows the same cosmic divisions as royal palaces. Houses are embellished with various motifs, such as sky-blue roofs, ceiling moldings of floral collars, and shrine-shaped pendant friezes, and lower walls rimmed with papyrus plants. Paintings of household gods (Bes and Taweret) and women in various poses from private houses at Deir el-Medina and the workman's village at Tell el-Amarna may have been prophylactic, focusing on childbirth and other concerns of the female occupants. Private chapels associated with funerary and religious cults in the workman's village at Tell el-Amarna and Deir el-Medina are adorned with paintings of gods, humans, plants, and abstract patterns.

A substantial portion of Third Intermediate and Late period tomb decoration is achieved in painted relief; however, flat painting appears in the tombs at the Ramesseum and the Theban necropolis, the Bahriya Oasis, and Coptos. Associated with the Third Intermediate burials, particularly at the Ramesseum, are wooden funerary stelae which were plastered and brightly painted. Instead of the traditional stela scene of the deceased seated before the offering table accompanied by family members, these wooden stelae are decorated with a single scene of the deceased adoring a deity. Where earlier stelae were primarily donated by men and set up in memorial or tomb chapels, the new stelae were donated by men or women and were placed in burials beside the body. Wooden stelae continued to be produced through the twenty-first and twenty-second dynasties and into the Ptolemaic period. An example of a wooden stela donated by a woman (Paris, Louvre E 52) dates from the Third Intermediate Period; on the front, it represents the "mistress of the house, Taperet" adoring the god Re-Horakhty, from whose solar disk stylized rays of lily flowers extend toward the face of the adorer. The two symbolic plants of Egypt, the papyrus on the left and the lotus to the right, emerge from the heads of the god of the earth and the god of the horizon and hold up the sign of the sky, which is painted blue. The cosmic setting and painted offerings of the stela symbolize Taperet's provisioning by the gods, which would guarantee her life in the next world.

Limited remains of papyri with figural painting are preserved from the Middle Kingdom. By the New Kingdom, papyri were abundant and included not only painted funerary books but also oracle and magical papyri, illustrated ancient animal fables, architectural sketches, and maps. The most popular funerary papyrus, the *Book of Going Forth by Day*, was an essential component in New Kingdom burials, where it was placed near the mummy for easy reference by the deceased. This is a body of spells, hymns, prayers, and accompanying scenes that allowed the deceased to come and go from the tomb without accident, receive offerings left by visitors, make use of his or her senses, pass the judgment of the weighing of the heart, and celebrate with the gods in paradise. The formulae, written in black with chapter headings and titles in red, are accompanied by illustrated vignettes, beautifully colored in the New Kingdom, and later developed into finely crafted, uncolored outlines. Some papyri were mass-produced, with blanks left for the purchaser's name and titles; others were products of the patron's compositional specifications. At the end of the twenty-first dynasty and the beginning of the twenty-second, vignette papyri with numerous illustrations and few texts were created from excerpts of a number of funerary works such as the *Book of That Which Is in the Underworld*, the *Litany of Re*, and the *Book of Going Forth by Day*, with new depictions. After a hiatus, the last of these reappeared during the twenty-sixth dynasty in a revised, standardized form of 165 spells with illustrations, continued into the Ptolemaic and Roman period.

During the Third Intermediate Period, inner coffins were decorated with new scenes that reflected the passage into the underworld and the daily course of the sun, which associated the deceased with the cycle of transformation and eternal life. Coffin interiors show a variety of motifs, like the *djed*-pillar (the backbone of Osiris), deities, deified kings, and images of the deceased offering before solar or underworld gods, executed in polychrome on a red or yellow background. During the reign of Osorkon

PAINTING. *Stela showing the noblewoman Taperet before the god Re-Horakhty, who radiates beneficial rays toward her.* This twenty-second dynasty stela is from Lower Egypt, now in the Louvre, Paris. (Giraudon / Art Resouce, NY)

II, coffins composed of one to three caskets plus a cartonnage case were painted in polychrome on a light background. Texts were shortened and images moved away from vignettes from funerary books and included instead simplified motifs of rebirth and symbols of protection. The depiction of the sky goddess Nut moved from the lid onto the floor of the coffin, where her outstretched arms enfolded the mummy, identifying the deceased with the sun which was born from her each day. Coffins of the Late Period abandoned the cartonnage case of the twenty-second and twenty-third dynasties and introduced a

wooden coffin that represented the deceased as a statue on a pedestal with a raised backpillar. Vignettes and long texts from the *Book of Going Forth by Day* were restored, and the winged goddess Nut reappeared on the chest lid. Decoration of the inner and outer coffins was painted in bright colors on a white or yellow background made of plastered linen on wood. Also revived from the Third Intermediate Period were coffins composed of a wooden rectangular outer box with four corner posts decorated with falcons or jackals holding up a vaulted lid. This outer box was painted in clear colors with scenes of deities in shrines divided by texts, or occasionally with an archaizing scene of the deceased seated before a table of offerings at either end. Images of the daily-nightly solar boats decorated the lid, which symbolized the sky.

Votive and funerary linen cloths, shirts, and leather hangings remain from the New Kingdom, decorated either in ink or with multicolored drawings or paintings. Some royal burials of the seventeenth and eighteenth dynasties included linen sheets illustrating vignettes from the *Book of Going Forth by Day*. In workman's tombs at Deir el-Medina, linen cloths were found with painted representations of priests offering to the deceased, or the dead before an offering table. During the eighteenth and nineteenth dynasties, votive textiles—adorned with scenes of the living donor and family making an offering to Hathor—were presented as cult offerings in the goddess's shrine at Deir el-Bahri. An unusual leather hanging, also from this shrine (New York, Metropolitan Museum of Art 31.3.98), is painted with a harpist and erotic dancer and may depict an ancient fertility rite associated with Hathor worship. Other deities adorned linen shrouds: Taweret, Osiris, or in the case of female burials, Amentet, the Goddess of the West. In the Late period, the practice was revived of adorning linen strips with texts and illustrations selected from funerary books. During the Roman period, specially prepared portraits of the deceased were pasted on to mass-produced cloths decorated with figures of Anubis or Osiris.

Painting during the Ptolemaic and Roman periods merged Egyptian thought and technique with the influence of the Hellenistic world. Ptolemaic and Roman tombs at Tuna el-Gebel (the cemetery of Hermopolis in Middle Egypt) and Alexandria, and Roman tombs at Panopolis, depict the deceased in the Greek manner, but in compositions with Egyptian details that may have been organized intentionally. For example, the outer room of the chapel in the family tomb of Petosiris (tp. Phillip Arrhideaus, 323–317 BCE) is decorated with "daily life scenes" in a Hellenistic style, while the inner, more sacred room contains funerary scenes executed in an Egyptianizing style. Paintings of deities of the Ptolemaic and Roman pantheon adorn temples in Theadelphia and Karanis. Paintings of the genies of Pharbaïthos (genies connected with the protection of the body of Osiris) decorate the Osirian "catacombs" in the temple of Amun at Karnak, from the reign of Ptolemy IV. In the Dakhla Oasis, the temples of Ismant el-Kharab, dating to the Roman emperor Hadrian, are painted in both the Egyptian and classical Roman styles.

Beginning in the early twenty-sixth dynasty and common by the Ptolemaic period, linen mummy shrouds were decorated with painted panels of cartonnage that covered the head, chest, lower rib cage, stomach, legs, and feet of the deceased; a funerary mask and footpiece were fitted over the head and feet, respectively. Blanks left for the deceased's name suggest they were not commissioned for a particular individual. The body cartonnage consisted of traditional funerary motifs, and the face often was gilded to identify the deceased with the golden color of the flesh of the gods and the sun god who guaranteed eternal life. From the first to the fourth century CE, funerary portraits were adopted by the Ptolemaic and Roman population. Termed "Faiyum portraits" after the region southwest of Cairo where they were first discovered, these painted panels were also found in Memphis, Thebes, and Antinoë in Middle Egypt. The Faiyum portraits are composed of rectangular panels of cypress, cedar, linden, lime, or fig wood, primed and painted with encaustic or tempera. Some representations were commissioned during the life of the patron, who sat for the portrait and hung it inside his or her house. Later Faiyum portraits exhibit few variations and appear to have been mass-produced. These portraits may have functioned as domestic art, ancestral portraits, commemorative objects in the living cult of the patron, or solely for burial. At death, the portraits were cut out of their frame and fitted into the wrappings over the head of the mummy. A few Faiyum portraits are evidently individual portraits, but most appear to capture the general likeness of the patron.

[*See also* Artists and Artisans; Grid Systems; Portraiture; *and* Royal Tomb Painting]

BIBLIOGRAPHY

Arnold, Dorothea, and Janine Bourriau, eds. *An Introduction to Egyptian Pottery*. SDAIK, 17. Mainz, 1993. An introduction to the techniques, traditions, clays, fabric, and decoration of ancient Egyptian pottery.

Baines, John. "Techniques of Decoration in the Hall of Barques of the Temple of Sethos I at Abydos." *Journal of Egyptian Archaeology* 75 (1989), 13–30. A discussion of decorative procedures in a temple context.

Bierbrier, Morris L., ed. *Portraits and Masks: Burial Customs in Roman Egypt*. London, 1997. Essays from the 1995 colloquium on burial customs in ancient Egypt, concerning the material factors and social, archaeological, and spiritual contexts of "Faiyum Portraits."

Davies, W. V., ed. *Colour and Painting in Ancient Egypt*. London, forthcoming. The most current treatment of the technical and artistic aspects of color and painting with essays by leading Egyptologists and conservators.

Hartwig, Melinda K. "Institutional Patronage and Social Commemoration in private Theban Tomb Painting during the Reigns of Thutmose IV (1419–1410 B.C.) and Amenhotep III (1410–1382 B.C.)." Ph.D. diss. New York University, forthcoming. A study of the social, ideological and rhetorical purposes of tomb painting and its patronage by specific institutional groups.

Helck, Wolfgang, Eberhard Otto, and Wolfhart Westendorf, eds. *Lexikon der Ägyptologie*. Vols. 1–6. Wiesbaden, 1975–1986. Entries "Farben," "Grabdekoration," "Harz," "Leichentuch," "Malerei," "Mumienporträts," "Nefermaat," "Rischi-Sarg," "Sarg AR und MR," "Sarg NR-SpZt," "Stele," "Wachs," are concise summaries with excellent bibliographies.

Hornung, Erik. *The Valley of the Kings: Horizon of Eternity*. New York,

1990. A survey of the development of art, architecture, iconography, and religious symbolism in the royal tombs in the Valley of the Kings.

James, T. G. H. "Painting and Drawing." In *The Dictionary of Art*, edited by Jane Turner, vol. 9, pp. 897–906. New York, 1996. A chronology of wall painting, drawing, and papyrus illustration in Egypt from the Predynastic to Ptolemaic period.

Keller, Catherine A. "Royal Painters: Deir el-Medina in Dynasty XIX." In *Fragments of a Shattered Visage: The Proceedings of the International Symposium of Ramesses the Great*, edited by Edward Bleiberg and Rita Freed, pp. 50–86. Memphis, 1993. An exploration of the training, methods, materials, work process, tomb decoration, and identification of the Ramessid painters at Deir el-Medina.

Lacovara, Peter. *The New Kingdom Royal City*. London, 1997. A study of the development of the royal city of Deir el-Ballas.

Lucas, A. *Ancient Egyptian Materials and Industries*. Edited by J. R. Harris. 4th ed. London, 1962. A reference manual that although slightly out of date is still the best comprehensive treatment (a new version is currently being compiled).

Mekhitarian, Arpag. *Egyptian Painting*. New York, 1954. The classic publication on the stylistic development of tomb painting, with particular reference to the New Kingdom, amply illustrated with superb photos.

Peck, William H. *Egyptian Drawings*. New York, 1978. A summary of the conventions, materials, use, and subjects of Egyptian drawing on tombs walls, ostraca, linen, papyri, and faience.

Pinch, Geraldine. *Votive Offerings to Hathor*. Oxford, 1993. A study of the types, decoration, and components of painted textiles, pottery, faience, and stelae votive offerings.

Robins, Gay. *The Art of Ancient Egypt*. Cambridge, Mass., 1997. An accessible up-to-date survey of Egyptian art and painting that focuses on its context as well as the underlying social and religious structures that influenced it. Excellent discussions on coffin and papyri decoration; abundantly illustrated.

Schulz, Regine, and Matthias Seidel, eds. *Egypt: The World of the Pharaohs*. Cologne, 1998. English edition of a German compilation of essays on ancient Egyptian art and society chronologically arranged and well illustrated; with invaluable treatments on private and royal tomb decoration.

Tefnin, Roland, ed. *La Peinture Égyptienne Ancienne. Un Mond de Signes à Préserver*. Monumenta Aegyptiaca, 7. Brussels, 1997. A collection of papers on the analysis of images with references to a semiological approach; includes methods of conservation in tomb and temple painting.

MELINDA K. HARTWIG

PALACES. From the Early Dynastic period until the late New Kingdom, Egyptian palaces, temples, and royal tombs are closely related through the concepts of the divine nature of the king and the cosmological aspect of royal dominion.

Early Dynastic Period and Old Kingdom. The form of the Early Dynastic palaces of the kings of Upper Egypt, known as *pr-wr* ("great house"), can be traced back to reed structures of Predynastic times. Early in the historic period, *pr-wr* became the word for "sanctuary" in Upper Egypt. A related term for "palace," *pr-ʿ3* (also "great house") was extended to the ruler himself and is the source of "pharaoh." The decorated high palace façade surmounted by the Horus falcon (originally *srḥ*, "lordly, exalted [building]") became the emblem of the divine ruler. The word *ʿḥ* (originally "shrine") occurs in the terms for both "royal palace" *(ʿḥ-nswt)* and "palace (or fortress) of the gods" *(ʿḥ-nṯr)*. The palaces, temples, and monumental royal tombs of the early dynasties are models of the cosmos, and all are surrounded by paneled enclosure walls.

In this early period, temples and tombs were built wholly of mud brick, with the exception of the doorways and sometimes the floors. Beginning in the third dynasty, tombs were built of durable stone; later, temples too were of stone. Palaces, however, being domestic buildings for earthly life, were constructed of brick throughout Egyptian history.

The hieroglyphic sign for *ʿḥ*, based on the early structural form, looks much like a donjon or keep, the heavily fortified inner tower of medieval European castles, within a similarly fortified enclosure. An example of such a structure of first dynasty date is the fortress on the island of Elephantine. It was abandoned and replaced by a more extensive complex to the west of the town which was dominated by a small, massive step pyramid; this building, called "The Headband of King Huny," was a kind of fortified tower which was perhaps topped by the royal pavilion. Another early remnant has been discovered at the ancient royal residence of Upper Egypt, Hierakonpolis: the foundations of a richly paneled monumental gate to a royal palace or temple.

A palace of the first dynasty at Memphis is mentioned on sealings of Adj-ib. This has not been found, but the name of the early residence town and palace, Inebu-hedj ("White Fortress"), suggests the paneled façades of the large first dynasty *mastaba*s on the northern cliffs of Saqqara and the magnificent white limestone enclosure of Djoser's funerary palace. A palace-like structure was unearthed by an expedition of the German Archaeological Institute in the early dynastic layers at Tell el-Fara'in, or Buto, the ancient royal residence of Lower Egypt. This may have been a provincial palace of the king; it includes all the typical secular elements—king's house, harem, gardens and pools, administrative center, armory, storehouses, and workshops.

Every pyramid town had a palace where the king resided while overseeing the construction of his pyramid and its complex. Czech excavators have found traces of column bases near the pyramid of Sahure (fifth dynasty), confirming textual mention of a columned entrance hall in Sahure's palace. The fifth dynasty royal architect Senedjem-ib-Inti was praised by his king, Djedkare Izezi, for designing and building a large (126 × 630 meters/400 × 2,000 feet) royal palace, "Lotus Flower of Djedkare," within the king's pyramid precinct at Saqqara South. A monumental brick wall on a solid foundation of basalt blocks, discovered in 1994 about 1,250 meters (4,000 feet) east of the Great Pyramid, may have been the eastern enclosure of the palace or pyramid town of Khufu.

In the late 1990s, a large palace complex of about 2,500 square meters was being excavated by an expedition of the French Archaeological Institute at Ain Asil in the oasis of Dakhla. It was the residence of the Egyptian governors of the oasis. It includes residential and administrative buildings with porticos, columned halls, warehouses, silos, and even shrines dedicated to the memory of the governors. Parts of a late sixth dynasty palace of a governor of the first Upper Egyptian nome have been found at Elephantine; it also included a memorial chapel to a governor, probably Hekaib.

Middle Kingdom. During the Middle Kingdom, the various functions of the royal palace seem to separate and be relocated in more specialized buildings. Thus, a palace of Senwosret I at Thebes is named "Senwosret Is Observing the Primeval Hill," undoubtedly an indication that it was a ritual structure attached to a temple that, like the one at Medamud, incorporated a mound representing the site of first creation. The eleventh dynasty kings Antef and Montuhotpe may have had palaces near the temple of Karnak, at Medamud or el-Tod, or on the west bank of the Nile near the modern village of el-Taref, where the large *saff*-tombs of these kings were cut into the desert hillside.

From the thirteenth dynasty, we have an account book detailing deliveries and expenses at the palace at Thebes during visits of the royal court over a period of several months; because this papyrus was found in Dra Abul Naga on the western side of Thebes, the palace was probably situated there on the hillside in front of Dra Abul Naga or Taref. The permanent royal residence and administrative center of the twelfth and thirteenth dynasties, however, was established by Amenemhat I at Itjtawy near modern Lisht. Poetic descriptions of the costly decoration of its state rooms appear in the *Instructions of Amenemhat* and in the *Story of Sinuhe*.

Other royal palaces must have existed in the pyramid towns in Dahshur and the Faiyum. The acropolis of the pyramid town of Illahun, the only such community of the Middle Kingdom to have been excavated, is dominated by a large and spacious palace area and storage areas which could easily have accommodated the king's household, court, and administration for a long period.

An extensive Middle Kingdom palace complex has been excavated at Bubastis, an important town and cult center of the goddess Bastet, near modern Zagazig. In view of the extensive palace complex built earlier by the governors at Dakhla Oasis, it is possible that the Bubastis complex was that of the governors of this rich and important province. Statues of officials found in one of its main rooms suggests that cult chapels for deceased governors may have existed here. However, a large lintel and frag-

ments of door jambs and threshold depicting royal figures and the titulary of Amenemhet III indicate that the palace also accommodated the king on his visits to the temple of Bastet and the administrative center of the eastern Delta.

Another palace, dating to the early twelfth dynasty, is found farther to the northeast in the area of Khata'ana; it is attested by a monumental gate with the names of Amenemhet I, renewed by Senwosret III. This same region has a palace from the early thirteenth dynasty, with a large garden; it may have belonged to a governor or even to a local ephemeral king.

Shortly after the thirteenth dynasty, the Nile Delta was taken over by Middle Eastern settlers who proclaimed themselves kings. They were succeeded by powerful rulers, the so-called Hyksos (fifteenth dynasty), who established their capital at Avaris (modern Tell ed-Dab'a), with a strongly fortified palace. This has recently been excavated by an Austrian team. Only the substructures and the platform on which this mighty palace once stood survived destruction by the Thebans, who used Avaris as a staging point for their campaigns against the successors of the Hyksos in southern Palestine. Thousands of fragments of murals featuring Cretan styles and motifs—probably the work of Cretan artists—evidence far-reaching relations and cultural interaction at this period. The architecture of the palace differs considerably from any of previous periods: whereas the typical earlier palace covers a large area with a series of rooms and large, columned halls without much variation in elevation, the Hyksos palace is characterized by a high platform built on massive brick casemates surrounded by columned halls and monumental staircases leading to a still higher platform, on which the royal apartments probably stood.

At the end of the seventeenth dynasty, the Upper Egyptian rivals of the Hyksos kings erected near Ballas (ancient Ombos, the "Gold Town") two very similar palaces from which they launched their campaigns against the Lower Egyptian overlords. These palaces, comprising several platforms built on casemates, with surrounding columned halls and monumental staircases, are reminiscent of Minoan palaces on Crete and Thera. This type of palace is restricted to the period of transition to the New Kingdom, but it was resumed at the end of the twenty-sixth dynasty in the palace of Apries at Memphis, which may have been influenced by Greek palace architecture.

New Kingdom. Of the Theban royal palaces of the New Kingdom, only the palace complex of Amenhotpe III at Malqata has yet been discovered. The rest have been either buried under cultivated land or destroyed during later construction. Even their location is disputed. An obvious hypothesis is that the royal palace was situated south of Karnak between the temples of Karnak and Luxor, and excavations in this area, near the village of el-

PALACES. *Detail of the twelfth-dynasty coffin of Khnumnakhte.* On the right is an eye panel. Below the eyes is a so-called palace façade, a painted imitation of a house exterior, complete with niches in the wall, reed matting, and a door with two leaves and a bolt. (The Metropolitan Museum of Art, Rogers Fund, 1915. [15.2.2])

Goud, have indeed brought to light evidence of dense habitation from the Middle Kingdom to the Late period, with town houses but no traces of a palace. A palace on the north side of the temple of Amun at Karnak is known from the records of Hatshepsut on the Red Chapel, but textual evidence from the time of Hatshepsut and Thutmose III clearly places the official Theban palace on the western side. The word used for the official royal palace is *ḏ₃dw* ("columned hall of appearance"), a word that also appears in Old Kingdom texts. The designation *ḥft-ḥr-nb-s* ("Opposite to Its Lord," i.e., the temple of Amun) points to an area directly across from Karnak, on the western bank, on the hillside of Dra Abul Naga and Taref. This is approximately the same area where the palace of the early Middle Kingdom may have stood.

This palace was surely rather moderate, in accordance with the straitened circumstances of the early eighteenth dynasty, and could not be compared with the large palaces of the eastern Delta. Therefore, when Thebes under Amenhotpe III became a rich and glorious metropolis, a new palace city had to be created south of the city at Malqata. It had a large artificial lake—the modern Birket Habu—which served as a harbor for the royal fleet, a place of leisure and entertainment for the beloved queen, Tiye, and a stage for the celebration of the king's *sed-*festival. This enormous palace city (about 350,000 square meters) included several state and residential palaces, an audience hall, temples for the *sed-*festival commemorating the king's thirtieth year of reign, and the necessary kitchens, storehouses, wine cellars, and workshops, as well as administrative buildings and, probably, residences for the highest officials. The king's private apartments and the harem were probably on terraces on the hillside above the artificial lake, affording the royal family a view of western Thebes and cooling breezes. The palace area has been only partly excavated and not well published, and, sadly, the last remnants of its walls—painted with geometric designs and vivid desert hunting scenes—are eroding and falling apart.

During the Amarna period, the Theban palaces were temporarily abandoned, but they might still be used during royal visits at the beginning of the nineteenth dynasty. They must have fallen into ruin soon thereafter, during the later years of Ramesses II, when the king no longer visited Thebes. To provide housing during visits there, his successor Ramesses III enlarged his mortuary temple by the addition of two large palace buildings, the so-called High Gates. The one on the eastern side served as a temporary royal residence for the king, and that on the western for his harem.

Amarna Period. Akhenaten, the heretic son of Amenhotpe III, decided in his fifth year of reign to build a new royal city on virgin ground near modern Tell el-Amarna, far from the old centers of traditional religion. He built his city, called Akhetaten ("Horizon of Aten"), in great haste, and in almost equal haste it was abandoned after his death, never to be inhabited again. Therefore, the ground plan of its temples, palace, and residences are exceptionally well preserved. More information about the buildings comes from the decoration of the rock-cut tombs in the ridge to the west of the city.

The main axis of Akhetaten was a long, wide avenue several kilometers long—the Royal Road—flanked on both sides by temples of Aten and palaces. The avenue began in the North City, which enclosed the North Riverside Palace, a fortified complex with a residential palace built on terraces on the cliffs, a large administrative building, barracks for the royal bodyguard, and large warehouses and granaries; in addition, there are some large houses, perhaps the residences of courtiers close to Akhenaten. Farther to the south lay the North Palace, another royal residence, with official reception halls and a suite of courts, gardens, and living rooms painted with bright scenes from nature. According to inscriptions found there, this was the palace of Princess Meritaten, Akhenaten's eldest daughter and heiress, who was married to his chosen successor, Smenkhkare.

After passing the Great Aten Temple, the avenue reached the Central City, with the Great State Palace on the riverside and the King's House across the avenue from it. The center of the Great Palace was an enormous courtyard surrounded on all four sides by colossal statues of Akhenaten, and having a suite of large halls and open courts. These were the state apartments, where the king performed the rituals of royal regeneration and received dignitaries and foreign envoys: an impressive background for royal propaganda. At the southern end of the Great Palace an extension for Smenkhkare was added at a later date, consisting of a huge hall with 544 painted brick columns and walls encrusted with glazed tiles. A brick bridge led across the Royal Road from the Great Palace to a smaller palace, the King's House; this was also a building of state, with the "Window of Appearance" where the king appeared to his courtiers, accompanied by his family, to give daily orders and distribute rewards. Adjacent to this palace was a personal royal chapel, the Small Aten Temple, a *ka*-house or mortuary temple of the king with royal statues.

The plan of the palaces and temples and their arrangement along a processional avenue is an accurate copy of the grand processional avenues connecting the temples of Amun at Thebes in the time of Amenhotpe III, modified to the requirements of Akhetaten, where the various royal palaces replaced the temples and the royal family moved in procession instead of the barks of the gods. It is therefore not surprising that this arrangement was not repeated in the following Ramessid period.

The boy-king Tutankhamun resided in the old palace of Thutmose I at Memphis, and probably also in Malqata at Thebes. Sety I began the construction of a residential city and palace near the old Hyksos residence, Avaris, at Qantir in the eastern Delta, the origin of the Ramessid family. Inlays of faience and glazed tiles with his name are evidence for his building activities. His glorious son, Ramesses II, chose this place for his famous residence, Piramesse. Its splendor is echoed in glazed tiles and faience inlays from door frames, throne pedestals, and decorated windows—perhaps a window of appearance. Only traces of the walls have yet been identified, but we know that large stables, storehouses, and workshops for the production of weapons and faience were added to the palace. According to poetic descriptions, the palace was the center of the royal residence, with temples of the great gods lying north, east, west, and south of it. Gigantic colossi more than twenty meters in height adorned the temple pylons facing the palace.

Piramesse served for nearly two centuries as the residence of the powerful rulers of the nineteenth and twentieth dynasties. When this glorious city was finally abandoned at the beginning of the twenty-first dynasty, much of its building stone was transported to the new residence at Tanis, and the brickwork was left to decay. The palace district at Tanis has not yet been discovered.

Temple Palaces. This distinct type of palace has long been known from Western Thebes. The best-preserved example was excavated to the south of the mortuary temple of Ramesses III at Medinet Habu. Foundations of similar buildings have been found on the southern side of the Ramesseum and, more recently, in the southern court of the mortuary temple of Sety I at Qurna and near that of Merenptah. These palaces were built of mud brick against the southern sides of the temple courts, which, as is typical of temple components, are of stone. The temple palaces exhibit small-scale versions of the main features of royal palaces: a columned reception hall, richly decorated and painted; a throne room with two to four columns and a throne pedestal; rooms for sleeping and rest on both sides of the throne room; and behind these rooms, small apartments for attendants (not the harem). A significant feature of all these palaces is the "Window of Appearance" in the middle of the palace façade; the entrances are near the corners of the façade.

These small palaces have long been regarded as temporary royal residences for kings visiting from their Delta residences to participate in the Theban festivals. However, a close examination reveals that they could never have served as residences, even for a short stay. There are no kitchens; the bathrooms have no functioning water drainage, and because the palaces are within the sacred precincts, this sort of service utility must have been prohibited on grounds of ritual purity. Large false doors carved on the roof of the throne room in Medinet Habu and in the rear wall of the Qurna palace indicate that these buildings were intended for the use of the king in the afterworld. They were probably "inhabited" by portable statues of the deified kings which appeared in the "Window of Appearance" and were carried in the processions and feasts of the necropolis.

Similar palaces are attested by decorated architectural fragments that are beside other temples near important cult centers. At Memphis a rather large and sumptuous temple palace of Merenptah was uncovered, part of the larger complex of temples and palaces of the Memphite residence. At Tell el-Yehudiyya, glazed tiles of a palace of Ramesses III were found. The powerless kings of the twenty-first and twenty-second dynasties took over the temple palace of Ramesses III at Medinet Habu and transformed it into an official state palace. They probably lived in the eastern High Gate, which was large enough for their modest rituals and state appearances.

It was not until the twenty-sixth dynasty, under the Saite kings, that sumptuous palaces were again built. Regrettably, the palaces of the residence at Sais have wholly disappeared, but at Buto parts of a large palace have recently been excavated. The best-preserved palace of this period was that of Apries at Memphis; today, however, only towering substructures and casemates bear witness to the glorious palaces of this ancient capital.

BIBLIOGRAPHY

Assman, Jan. "Palast oder Tempel." *Journal of Near Eastern Studies* 31 (1972), 143–155.

Bietak, M. *Eine Palastanlage aus der Zeit des späten Mittleren Reichs und andere Forschungsergebnisse aus dem östlichen Nildelta (Tell ed-Dabʿa, 1979–1984)*, pp. 325–332. Vienna, 1985.

Kemp, Barry J. "The Palace of Apries at Memphis." *Mitteilungen des Deutschen Archäologischen Instituts, Abteilung Kairo* 33 (1977), 101–108.

Kemp, Barry J. "The Harim-Palace at Medinet el-Ghurab." *Zeitschrift für Ägyptische Sprache und Alterumskunde* 105 (1978), 122–133.

O'Connor, David. "City and Palace in New Kingdom Egypt." *Sociétés urbaines et Égypte et au Soudan*, pp. 73–87. Cahier de recherches de l'Institut de papyrologie et d'égyptologie de Lille, 11. Lille, 1989.

O'Connor, David. "Mirror of the Cosmos: The Palace of Merenptah." In *Fragments of a Shattered Visage*, edited by Edward Bleiberg and Rita Freed, pp. 167–197. Memphis, Tenn., 1993.

Stadelmann, Rainer. "Tempelpalast und Erscheinungsfenster in den Thebanischen Totentempeln." *Mitteilungen des Deutschen Archäologischen Instituts, Abteilung Kairo* 29 (1973), 221–242.

Uphill, Eric P. "The Concept of the Egyptian Palace as a 'Ruling Machine.'" In *Man, Settlement and Urbanism*, edited by P. Ucko, pp. 721–734. London, 1972.

RAINER STADELMANN

PALERMO STONE. *See* King Lists.

PALETTES. Objects characteristic of early Nile cultures, palettes also appear in the Near East as imports or local imitations. Traces of dyes indicate that they were used to grind and mix mineral pigments. Ocher, malachite, galena, pyrolusite, and hematite were ground and then mixed with resins, oils, and fats. The mixtures were used as body paints and cosmetics; powdered ocher was used to tint ceramic vessels, and in a funeral context it was sprinkled in grave pits or used to paint certain containers for human remains.

Typologically, the origin of palettes is in Late Paleolithic grinders. In the Early Khartoum period (7400–4900 BCE), flat gneiss plates were also used for grinding ocher. In the Early Khartoum Neolithic (4900–3800 BCE), round, oval, and nearly rectangular palettes of sandstone, diorite, and porphyry appear in elite burials and in settlements. Similar objects have been found in sites of the Late Khartoum Neolithic (3800–2700 BCE). Farther to the north, sandstone palettes stained with ocher appear in Epipaleolithic cultures (e.g., Abkan, Elkabien).

Palettes reached their zenith of popularity in the Egyptian Predynastic period; they are especially common in the South, though the oldest examples come from the North. In Faiyum A, several shapeless or roughly oval limestone and diorite palettes have been found. A shield-shaped palette and several fragments in siltstone, basalt, and granite come from Merimde. El-Omari has provided two examples of calcite palettes, one tetragonal and one oval. Several Upper Egyptian rhomboid or rectangular palettes of siltstone—one ornamented with a schematic drawing that may be a dog—are known from Maadi; tetragonal or unshaped local palettes of limestone are infrequent; some have schematic representations of unidentifiable animals or geometric patterns.

Most Upper Egyptian palettes were found in men's, women's, and children's graves, frequently near the face of the deceased. In Southern cultures, the five oldest examples come from Tasa (limestone or calcite [Egyptian alabaster], in geometric shapes). During the Badari culture, siltstone (earlier labeled as schist) becomes the dominant material, and two types of palettes occur: one is rectangular, with the long sides straight or slightly convex, and the short sides concave or with triangular indentation; the other is oval-pointed, sometimes with incisions on the points.

Palettes are common in the Nubian A-Group and above all in the Naqada culture. Typological and chronological development is similar in both. The Naqada I phase is characterized by rhomboid palettes. Some are decorated on the top with stylized birds or horns; others are ornamented with schematically outlined, engraved animal figures (e.g., a crocodile or an elephant), or with signs (harpoon, horns) reminiscent of the later so-called nome standards. The most beautiful is the Stockholm Palette, decorated with a representation of a hippopotamus hunt: a man in a small boat, and before him a hippopotamus, joined to the hunter by a broken line, symbolizing the harpoon rope; behind appear other animals (hippopotamus, two herbivores). Toward the end of Naqada I (Phase Ic) there appear zoomorphic palettes: fish, tortoises, and the "pelta-shaped"—in fact, a stylized representation of a boat, with the ends sometimes modeled into schematic bird heads.

During the Naqada II phase, the rhomboid palettes decrease, though examples still occur. Shield-shaped palettes are popular. Pelta-shaped and zoomorphic (fish, tortoise, elephant, hippopotamus, ram, horned animals) continue to occur. A particular subgroup comprises waterfowl. Birds or bird heads often decorate the tops of palettes, especially those that are shield-shaped. On these, there also occur signs ("Min's emblem" on the el-Amra Palette), figures (a stylized cow's head and five stars on the el-Gerzeh Palette), and scenes. One of the oldest (Phase IIc) decorated with a relief is the Manchester Palette, depicting a man stalking a flock of ostriches. The identical shapes of the man's and the birds' heads may indicate that a masked hunter is depicted, and that the palette is associated with hunting magic.

The period of Naqada III is marked by geometrization of palettes (square, rectangular, and round). The edges are frequently decorated with a simple geometric design forming a sort of frame. Other shapes are rare. Characteristic is the change in function of certain types: the geometrical palettes are utilitarian; the shield-shaped form are ceremonial palettes, and their decoration is connected with certain ideas. The latter were probably used in rites and rituals involving chiefs and rulers. The group of ceremonial palettes is comprised of two basic types: one type is decorated with zoomorphic and anthropomorphic scenes; the other is adorned only with so-called heraldic

and coronation animals, sculpted in full relief. There are presently about twenty-five such palettes and fragments known, the majority of uncertain provenance, dated primarily to Naqada III. Some of them have round dishes in the center, invoking the primeval function of the palettes, but not related to the sun cult, as has been claimed.

The most significant in the first group is the Oxford Palette, found at the Hierakonpolis Main Deposit. It is shield-shaped; from the midpoints of the sides, sculpted in high relief, extend the figures of two wild dogs (*Lycaon pictus*), with their heads in full sculpture. On the obverse appear two scenes. The upper, occupying two-thirds of the surface, shows two fantastic animals—serpopards—whose long necks surround the dish. These creatures are licking a dead antelope, above which is a long-necked bird (ostrich?). Behind the serpopards' necks and below the dish there are three wild dogs. In the lower scene, three domesticated dogs in collars are attacking a herd of herbivores, symbolized by four animals. On the reverse, the proportions are reversed: in the upper scene (one-third of the surface), two lions attack animals identical to the dead antelope on the obverse. The lower portion is again a hunt: predators (a panther and a wild dog) and fantastic animals (a serpopard and a griffin) attack a herd of herbivores. At the bottom there is a man playing a flute (?), wearing an animal mask and a tail on his belt, with a giraffe next to him.

The Oxford Palette is the only known example to contain such elaborate zoomorphic scenes. This group also includes objects (e.g., the Louvre Palette) decorated with a few figures, which are probably an abbreviation (legible to the ancients) of the more detailed scenes described. The animals seen on these palettes include wild dogs, serpopards, lions, birds, oryx, and ibex. Not all the figures are unambiguously legible to us, which results in differences in interpretation and numerous controversies regarding the symbolism and meaning of this group.

The scenes and figures described above have been interpreted as chaotic and symbolizing "power," or as symbols associated with life and death, peace and struggle; the heraldic animals have been read as images of the divinities to whom the palette is dedicated, and the scenes themselves have been thought to be connected with the divine myth. Others interpret the palettes with zoomorphic decoration as the first manifestation of the cult of the Divine Eye (the sun), and the animals as symbolizing particular mythological figures. A more likely explanation of the symbolism in this group of palettes is that they are connected with hunting magic. The hunting theme occurs very generally in predynastic art, initially in the same pictures as other subjects (cf. the Hierakonpolis painting). Later, perhaps because of the limited space for decoration, the subjects were separated. Still, the early chiefs and rulers were still the "first hunters" for their subjects, and so magical operations were needed to aid them in performing this function and to ensure success in the hunt—a success also enjoyed by other members of society through the mediation of the king. This is also indicated by palettes that depict domestic dogs sucking the teats of heraldic wild dogs (Metropolitan Museum Palette, Muna-gat fragment). The magical intention was probably for the dogs to acquire the characteristics of wild nature. To the same categories of hunting magic we may also assign arti-facts in which the function of the heraldic animals is served by herbivorous hunt victims (e.g., the White Oryx Palette).

One of the more controversial motifs found on several palettes is a palm flanked by two giraffes. Its relatively frequent occurrence indicates that it is not coincidental. It has been regarded as a Near Eastern motif of adoration for the holy tree; as the symbol of long years of peace (the palm), observed by two "seers" (the giraffes); as the seat of the sun (the palm), and the props of heaven (the gi-raffes); or as a substitute for the pharaoh, similar to the *srḫ*. Since the motifs in question also occur on other Pre-dynastic artifacts, though often separately, none of these theories would seem fully correct. Although the palm may be a symbol associated with the state and authority, it is not a substitute for the pharaoh, but rather for the state, in both the territorial and ideological senses; the giraffes may incarnate primeval forces friendly to man, symboliz-ing at the same time a certain part of the country.

The decoration of the Hunters' Palette (Phase IIIa/b?) stands on the borderline between zoomorphic and an-thropomorphic decoration. Its center is occupied by a representation of hunting. On both sides appear two rows of hunters dressed in kilts, with animal tails fastened to their belts and feathers in their long hair. Armed with bows, lances, maces, and knives, they are hunting lions and herbivorous animals. There is a striking lack of heral-dic or fantastic animals; yet nome standards appear in the hands of some hunters, as well as obvious hieroglyphic signs—the *pr-nw* shrine and the double *protoma* of a bull. This artifact, too, has been the subject of much controversy, serving for example as the foundation for a theory on dual-ism in Egyptian thought—an interpretation that should be subjected to criticism. Probably its subject matter is hunt-ing with beaters, interrupted by the sudden appearance of lions, while in the hieroglyphic characters we may discern the symbol for the king or the kingdom.

The obverse of the Battlefield Palette (Phase IIIb?) is yet another on which animals have the dominant role. In con-trast to the preceding example, however, the animals here are either an express incarnation of the ruler (the lion), or

they benefit from his victory: predatory birds and a canine predator on the Lucerne fragment. People are depicted here as defeated naked prisoners, or as corpses lying on the battlefield. Only one human figure, dressed in a long cloak (preserved fragmentarily), clearly belongs to the victors. An important role is played here by the nome standards (ibis, falcon), holding the captives with human hands. Standards serve a similar function on the fragmentary Bull Palette, perhaps the artistic masterpiece of this genre, which shows the figure of the victor-ruler in the shape of a bull. The re-verse of the Battlefield Palette is decorated with the palm-and-giraffes motif. The fragment of the Libyan Palette is decorated on one side with registers containing rows of bulls, asses, rams, and trees. Next to the last is the hiero-glyph *Ṯḥ*. On the other side, seven fortresses are being de-stroyed or built by animals holding hoes in their hands.

The most famous is the Narmer Palette, found near the Main Deposit of the Hierakonpolis temple. On the side without a dish, under the symbols of Bat or Hathor and the royal *srḫ*, are two scenes. In the first, the king, wearing the White Crown and accompanied by a sandal-bearer, is about to smite a kneeling enemy with a mace; beside him is a pair of hieroglyphs (his name?). Facing the king is an emblem-atic group: a falcon with one human arm, leading a personi-fied land sign by a rope, and perching on six papyrus stems that sprout from the sign. The second scene shows two na-ked dead enemies and the hieroglyphic markings of for-tresses. On the other side are three registers. First, the pha-raoh in the Red Crown inspects ten beheaded prisoners; before him are four standards and a high official (vizer, scribe, or priest); after him, a sandal-bearer. Above the corpses is something that is most likely the caption of a door leaf with a falcon behind it, and a boat with a falcon on a harpoon hovering above. Second, serpopards are held in bonds by two men; the dish is framed by the entwined necks of the animals. Third, a bull, symbolizing the pha-raoh, is destroying a fortress and trampling an enemy.

The Narmer Palette has been the object of much specu-lation and various, sometimes fantastic, theories. Among the most important are those that treat it as evidence of the victory of King Narmer over the following: the Delta and the unification of the country; the Northern rebellion, the last Lower Egyptian dynasty; or the Canaanites. Others treat it as a year-names tablet. The theory most nearly in ac-cordance with the present state of research is that the pal-ette constitutes the ritual confirmation of expansion, was used in magical rites preceding further expeditions or in rituals involving the ruler during his coronation or during holidays commemorating that event (the Appearance of the King of Upper and Lower Egypt), or for a *sed* jubilee.

All the palettes under discussion may have some links with the cult and rituals surrounding the rulers of the day.

We should probably agree with John Baines (1995) in asserting that "although the reliefs look like propaganda, correlates in the everyday world would have had to be in living ceremonial, in what was proclaimed about the king, and in the architecture of palaces. The reliefs, however, must be interpreted on their own terms, as objects with a very small audience who were deeply involved with their meaning and creation," and not as part of a lost repertoire.

In later periods, the function of the palette was limited to the utilitarian. Examples from the dynastic periods are rare, and are typically rectangular with a trapezoidal cross section.

[*See also* Ceremonial Mace Heads.]

BIBLIOGRAPHY

Asselberghs, Henri. *Chaos en beheersing: Documenten uit aeneolithish Egypte.* Leiden, 1961. Corpus of predynastic art, with extensive English summary.

Baines, John. "Origins of Egyptian Kingship." In *Ancient Egyptian Kingship,* edited by D. O'Connor and D. Silverman, pp. 95–156. Leiden, 1995.

Ciałowicz, Krzysztof M. *Les palettes égyptiennes aux motifs zoomorphes et sans décoration.* Etudes de l'art prédynastique. Kraków, 1991. Typology of Naqada palettes and an analysis of zoomorphic scenes on ceremonial palettes.

Hoffman, Michael A. *Egypt before the Pharaohs.* 2d ed. London, 1991. Predynastic Egypt through the perspective of archeological discoveries.

Kantor, Helen J., "The Relative Chronology of Egypt and its Foreign Correlations before the Late Bronze Age." In *Chronologies in Old World Archaeology,* edited by R. Ehrich, pp. 1–46. 3d rev. ed. Chicago, 1992. Chronological foundations of the predynastic period against the background of neighboring countries.

Kemp, Barry. *Ancient Egypt: Anatomy of a Civilisation.* London and New York, 1989. An original approach to the origins of the Egyptian state.

Needler, Winifred. *Predynastic and Archaic Egypt in the Brooklyn Museum.* New York, 1984. Catalog containing an exhaustive discussion of particular categories of artifacts.

Payne, Joan Crowfoot. *Catalogue of the Predynastic Egyptian Collection in the Ashmolean Museum.* Oxford, 1993. Catalog containing an exhaustive discussion of particular categories of artifacts.

Petrie, W. M. Flinders. *Corpus of Prehistoric Pottery and Palettes.* London, 1921.

Petrie, W. M. Flinders. *Ceremonial Slate Palettes.* London, 1953.

Quibell, J. E., and F. Green. *Hierakonpolis II.* London, 1902. Artifacts from Hierakonpolis as seen by their discoverers.

Regner, Christina. *Schminkpaletten.* Bonner Sammlung von Aegyptiaca 2. Wiesbaden, 1996. Catalog containing a discussion of the typology, occurrence, and meaning of palettes.

Ridley, R. T. *The Unification of Egypt.* Deception Bay, 1973. Corpus containing the majority of the decorated artifacts from the end of the predynastic period.

Vandier, J. *Manuel d'archéologie égyptienne I.* Paris, 1952. A collection of basic information on predynastic Egypt, including earlier theories, with extensive passages devoted to art.

Williams, Bruce B. *Decorated Pottery and the Art of Naqada III.* Münchner Ägyptologischen Studien, 45. Berlin, 1988. Brief discussion and analysis of late Predynastic art.

KRZYSZTOF M. CIAŁOWICZ

PALM. *See* Flora.

PAN-GRAVE PEOPLE. The Middle Bronze Age in Nubia was roughly coeval with the Middle Kingdom and the Second Intermediate Period in Egypt (c.2061–1569 BCE). The various cultural affiliations, the developmental phases, and the subphases of the Nubian peoples that lived in this era have only been broadly defined; they are still undergoing the process of redefinition. Of particular interest, however, is a population belonging to the Lower Nubian tradition—but also found in the deserts bordering the Nile River and in other parts of Egypt—that was designated by early archaeologists as the Pan-Grave culture. The name was derived from their shallow round or oval graves (0.5–2 meters in depth [1.5–6 feet]), which resembled European baking or cooking pans.

The Pan-Grave burials can be associated with the Medjay, the fierce Nubian bowmen mentioned in ancient Egyptian texts; the term is also found in the toponym *Mg3*, and both may derive from the Egyptian term for "the one who moves about," testifying to their nomadism. The Medjay were attested to have been employed as mercenaries, as an expeditionary force in Egypt, at least as early as the Old Kingdom. They have also been associated with a group of mercenaries resident at Gebelein during the First Intermediate Period. The fortresses built in the Second Cataract region seem, at least in part, to have been needed to protect the area from incursions by this group. The fort at Serra was named "repelling the Medjay," and the Semna dispatches recorded efforts to keep these peoples within their desert boundaries.

The confines of the Pan-Grave peoples in the desert margins has been borne out archaeologically. Cemeteries of this population were often found to be on the perimeter of Nubian C-Group or even Egyptian cemeteries that were positioned closer to the Nile. Whereas the Pan-Grave ceramic assemblage included incised and black-top pottery, these ceramics differed considerably from Nubian C-Group ceramics made at that time. For example, Pan-Grave black-topped "luxury wares" were very finely finished with bodies having a distinct, level black rim; the incised wares were often of similar exceptional quality. The Pan-Grave burial customs and material culture were similar to those of the Nubian Kerma culture of that time. The oval tumulus graves of the Pan-Grave people resembled those of the Kerma culture, as did their practice of decorating the graves with the painted skulls of horned cattle, sheep, or goats.

Daggers and axes have been frequently included in Pan-Grave burials, attesting to an owner's possible role as a mercenary. Distinctive Pan-Grave costume included sets of armlets or sashes made of rectangular mother-of-pearl

White   Black

Patinated
surface of stone   Yellow

Red   Dark red

PAN-GRAVE PEOPLE. *Drawing of a stela from Gebelein depicting a Nubian bowman in traditional costume with his Egyptian wife and family.* The stela is now in the Museum of Fine Arts, Boston. (Courtesy Peter Lacovara; after Henry G. Fischer, "The Nubian Mercenaries of Gebelein" *KUSH* 9, 1961.)

plaques that were bored at both ends for stringing. Other elements of costume included beaded leather kilts, leather sandals, bead and shell necklaces, and wire torques.

The range of the Pan-Grave people has been established as north to Middle Egypt and south to the Third Cataract of the Nile. Attestations of their presence as far south as Khartoum, however, may have resulted from some misidentification of ceramic types. As for the Pan-Grave peoples who migrated into Egyptian territory and were employed as military guards and bowmen, Janine Bourriau (1991) has suggested that this group was acculturated into Egypt throughout the course of the Middle Kingdom. For example, a gradual evolution has been noted in some of the Pan-Grave cemeteries in Egypt, in which a segregated area with burials that follow a strictly Lower Nubian tradition give way to tombs found within Egyptian necropoli. This evidence substantiates Egyptianization. Bourriau has also suggested that the Pan-Grave mercenary soldiers for the Egyptian army were replaced, during the Second Intermediate Period, by recruits from the Kerma culture. In fact, early excavators had actually confused the Kerma burials in Egyptian cemeteries with those of the true Pan-Grave people who had also been buried there.

[*See also* C-Group; *and* Kerma.]

BIBLIOGRAPHY

Bietak, Manfred. "The C-Group and the Pan-Grave Culture in Nubia." In *Nubian Culture: Past and Present*, main papers presented at the Sixth International Conference for Nubian Studies, Uppsala, 11–16 August, 1986, edited by Tomas Hägg, pp. 1–17. Stockholm, 1987. A thorough discussion of the differences between these two contemporaneous cultures.

Bourriau, Janine. "Relations between Egypt and Kerma in the Middle and New Kingdoms." In *Egypt and Africa: Nubia From Pre-History to islam*, edited by W. V. Davies, pp. 129–144. London, 1991. A discussion of the composition of the Medjay switch—from the Pan-Grave to the Kerma culture—in the later Second Intermediate Period.

Fischer, Henry G. "The Nubian Mercenaries of Gebelein during the First Intermediate Period." *KUSH* 9 (1961), 44–80.

Hodge, Carleton T. "The Medjay/*misri.*" *Language Sciences* 8 (1969), 11–12. A review of the derivation and significance of the term.

Hoffman, Inge. "Bietrag zur Herkunft der Pfannengräber-Leute." *Zeitschrift der Deutschen Morgenländischen Gesellschaft,* Suppl. 3 (1969), 1113–1135. A concise review of the literature on the subject, with an extensive bibliography.

Wainwright, G. A. *Balabish*. London, 1920.

PETER LACOVARA

PAPYRUS. As a writing material, papyrus was in use in Egypt from at least 3000 BCE until as late as the tenth century CE. It was manufactured from the papyrus plant, (*Cyperus papyrus*), which grew along the Nile River. This plant is only one of some six hundred species with the genus *Cyperus,* which all belong to the far larger family of sedges (Cyperaceae). In antiquity, the papyrus plant was widespread in the Nile Valley, but it was overused and so nearly disappeared from there before modern times; it now flourishes chiefly in eastern and central Africa. It grows best in marshland, prefers shallow and still or relatively slow-moving water, or soil that is at the least waterlogged. A number of modern subspecies have been identified; it is not clear how these relate to the plant that was exploited in antiquity and then removed in making way for agricultural land.

Ancient Egyptian terms for the "papyrus plant" were *w3ḏ, twfy,* and *ḏt,* the last two also being used for "papyrus marsh." The most common term for the writing material made from the plant stem was *ḏmꜥ,* which could also signify a "manufactured roll," an "inscribed book," or a "document," as well as a papyrus employed to make other objects. A term for "bookroll" or "scroll" was *ꜥrt,* used of both papyrus and leather rolls, and for inscribed rolls, both literary and documentary.

The Greeks referred to the writing material as either *bublos* (later *biblos*) or *papuros.* The latter term is generally explained as deriving from an Egyptian expression *p3-pr-ꜥ3,* which might mean "the [thing] belonging to Pharaoh," and might indicate that papyrus was perceived to be the chief Egyptian product, or export, under royal control. No such phrase is actually attested in Egyptian, however, and the adoption by the Greeks of an Egyptian-language term (even if it had been borrowed indirectly) would suggest that it was first in common use among Egyptians. The derivation is thus problematic.

The question remains as to whether or not the cultivation of papyrus and the manufacture of the writing material was in fact under state control. For dynastic times, we have scarcely any evidence. We know that papyrus could be bought and sold. It is argued that, during dynastic times, the sheer quantity of papyrus that we may deduce was consumed by the bureaucracy would rule out both the possibility of small-scale production to meet local needs, and that of a single, central "state factory." Large-scale production at many locations all over Egypt is generally guessed to be the most likely. Modern attempts at papyrus manufacture have in recent years begun to be able to rival the quality of the ancient product. They suggest that considerable skill and experience is required, that discrimination is needed in the harvesting of the plant, which may well have needed to be cultivated, and that probably only freshly gathered papyrus can be used. All this hints that small-scale, *ad hoc* manufacture is unlikely to have been successful or common.

For Greco-Roman times, we have some documentary evidence concerning papyrus manufacture. There are indications of widespread factories in the Nile Delta, but there is no reason to suppose that papyrus was not made elsewhere in the Nile Valley. The trade in papyrus seems to have been centered upon Alexandria, on the Mediterranean coast. We have no decisive evidence as to whether the manufacture and trade were state operated. If they were entirely state owned, it would be a little surprising that our sources did not reveal this. For the Ptolemaic period, our knowledge of the general methods of the administration would suggest at least that close state supervision would be likely. Some papyrus was available only from "royal sales offices," but there was patently no complete royal monopoly on sales.

Our evidence for the process of manufacturing papyrus as a writing material is very restricted. From dynastic times, a few tomb scenes depict its harvesting. They are often associated with scenes of building papyrus boats, however, and there is no representation of making the writing material. Inferences about manufacture can be drawn from the examination of surviving papyri, and damaged fragments can be more revealing than well-preserved rolls. A special case of this is fragments recovered from cartonnage, scrap pieces of papyrus formed with the aid of gesso and glue into molded mummy casings, especially during Ptolemaic times. The various wet processes used to extract the papyrus from the cartonnage—both outmoded methods employing acid and present-day enzyme techniques—can reveal the structure of the material. Modern experiments in papyrus manufacture have led to several advances in understanding. They have particularly helped in considering the way in which papyrus strips bond together, and what details of the processing may encourage or impede the binding.

From the Greco-Roman period, a description of the

making of papyrus sheets and rolls was recorded by Pliny the Elder. His account is extremely difficult to follow, and it remains disputed how Pliny obtained his information, how fully he understood it, and to what extent the surviving manuscripts may present a garbled text. Some details, however, seem plausible, and Pliny's account cannot be completely ignored.

The stalk of the papyrus plant is triangular in cross section. It has a tough outer rind, which was discarded in papyrus manufacture. This encloses a soft, spongy, white pith, given a degree of strength by many so-called fibers (fibrovascular bundles), which run the entire length of the stalk and are very visible in the finished papyrus. The process probably proceeded by slicing or peeling the pith into thin strips, about 1 to 3 centimeters (0.5 to 1.25 inches) wide. A series of these was laid down side by side. Sometimes they were arranged to be very slightly overlapping, and sometimes just touching each other. Modern experience in manufacture shows that with care the latter arrangement can be achieved without the risk that gaps may subsequently appear. A second, similar layer of strips was then laid down upon the first, with the strips running at right angles to those of the first layer. The resulting sheet was then consolidated by pressing or by careful beating and was allowed to dry. The component cells of the spongy matter of the pith (parenchyma cells) physically interlock, and the two layers of papyrus are held firmly together by this bond.

Evidently, the practice was to have the sheets made into rolls, and we have no evidence that single sheets as manufactured were available. A writer needing a simple sheet of papyrus cut what was required from a roll with a sharp knife, either before or after writing the text. Rolls were made by pasting a series of sheets together with a starch paste, each sheet overlapping its neighbor by 1 to 3 centimeters (0.5 to 1.25 inches). There is good evidence that a roll of twenty sheets was the standard length. The user could cut the roll to obtain a shorter length, or paste rolls or parts of rolls together for a longer text. A few papyrus rolls from dynastic Egypt are of extraordinary length (the longest known measures 42 meters/130 feet), but these are funerary books or other works that were not meant for routine consultation. Literary or administrative rolls were much more commonly only a few meters in length.

Another dimension that varied was the width of the roll. The papyrus roll was normally used lying horizontally across the lap of the writer or reader. Egyptian scripts run from right to left, and so the roll was unrolled progressively from the left hand into the right hand. The width of the roll corresponded to the height of the individual pages of writing and is usually referred to as the "height" of the roll. This dimension varied greatly according to the kind of text, and from period to period.

Thus a late New Kingdom literary text might typically be written on a roll only 10 to 12 centimeters (4 to 6 inches) high, whereas an account roll of the same period might measure over 40 centimeters (15 inches) in height. The latter would be a complete roll as manufactured, but the former would be made by the user, who sliced through the roll to produce two, three, or four rolls of lesser height.

In the classical world, papyrus exported from Egypt was regarded as the chief writing material. The earliest papyri from Egypt written in Greek date to the fourth century BCE, but papyrus was evidently already widely used in Greece in the sixth century BCE, when, for example, papyrus rolls were depicted in vase paintings. How early papyrus began to be exported to Greece is uncertain (and evidence for the use of writing is not evidence for the use of papyrus). Suggestions that it may already have been known in the Bronze Age Aegean remain unsubstantiated, although it was no doubt utilized in the Levant throughout the first millennium BCE.

Papyrus ceased to be used, in Europe as in Egypt, around 1000 CE. Some papyrus documents have survived in the papal and other chancelleries. Carbonized papyri from Herculaneum, one of the towns buried by lava from Vesuvius, in Italy, were Greek philosophical texts, and they began to be studied as early as the eighteenth century. Throughout the nineteenth century, some accidental finds of Greek papyri in Egypt came onto the antiquities market. In the 1870s, expansions in Egypt's agriculture led to the large-scale extraction of fertile soil from the abandoned sites of ancient towns. There, great quantities of papyrus—chiefly in Greek, Coptic, and Arabic—began to come to light in the rubbish dumps of former Greco-Roman towns, principally in the Faiyum but also, for example, at Hermopolis and Herakleopolis. The Greek papyri, in particular, were eagerly acquired by foreign museums and libraries. For example, about 70,000 Greek papyri from the Faiyum are now in the Vienna library's collection. In the 1890s, excavations began to be financed with the specific aim of discovering papyri. The most productive were the seasons at Oxyrhynchus in Middle Egypt, beginning in 1896. Sites became progressively denuded by the removal of fertile soil, but the era of excavations in search of papyri did not come to an end until the 1930s.

BIBLIOGRAPHY

Bierbrier, M. L. *Papyrus: Structure and Usage.* London, 1986.

Černý, Jaroslav. *Paper & Books in Ancient Egypt.* London, 1952; repr. Chicago, 1977. Deals with books and scribal practice in dynastic times.

Leach, Bridget, and John Tait. "Papyrus." In *Ancient Egyptian Materials and Technology,* edited by Ian Shaw and Paul Nicholson. Cambridge, 1999.

Lewis, N. *Papyrus in Classical Antiquity.* Oxford, 1974.

Lewis, N. *Papyrus in Classical Antiquity: A Supplement.* Brussels, 1989.

Lucas, A. *Ancient Egyptian Materials and Industries*. 4th ed., rev. by J. R. Harris. London, 1962.

Parkinson, Richard, and Stephen Quirke. *Papyrus*. London, 1995.

Ragab, H. *Le Papyrus*. Cairo, 1980.

Turner, E. G. *Greek Papyri: An Introduction*. Oxford, 1968.

BRIDGET LEACH AND JOHN TAIT

PAPYRUS RYLANDS IX, one of a group of nine Demotic papyri discovered at el-Hiba (ancient Teudjoi) on the eastern bank of the Nile River in Middle Egypt. They are all concerned with the affairs of a priestly family who lived there during the sixth and seventh centuries BCE. The text, twenty-five columns in length, is a draft copy of a complaint addressed by one member of the family, Petiese, to the chief finance minister of Egypt in the reign of the Persian king Darius I, concerning the injustices which he and his relatives suffered at the hands of other priests in their native town.

Petiese's complaint is divided into four parts. The first narrates the circumstances leading to its submission. In the ninth year of the reign of Darius, a certain Ahmose came to Teudjoi and claimed a priestly stipend, which he said was owed him. This could not be paid because the temple finances were in such parlous condition. Seeking an explanation for this state of affairs, Ahmose was directed to the temple scribe, who happened to be the writer of the complaint, Petiese. As the latter recounts, he blamed the temple clergy, with whom he was in dispute, for its financial woes. These priests learned of his accusation and sought to exact revenge. Lucky to escape with his life, Petiese fled to Memphis and asked the chief finance minister to take up his case and see that justice was done. That official instructed him to write a full history of his difficulties with the priests and how they arose, and it is to this account that the second part of the complaint is devoted.

According to Petiese, his great-great-grandfather had been inspector of a large tract of Egyptian territory extending from Memphis in the North to Aswan in the South. Finding the temple of Amun at Teudjoi with its staff depleted, and struggling under a heavy burden of taxation, he arranged for its taxes to be remitted and restored it to its former prosperity, erecting a stela and two statues of himself there to commemorate his pious deed. As a reward, he was given the stipend of the prophet of Amun of Teudjoi and other benefices as well. Subsequently, he raised a second stela on which his various priestly offices were enumerated.

The stipends of Petiese's ancestor were inherited by his son and grandson. However, when the latter, Petiese's grandfather, was sent to accompany the king on a journey to Asia, his benefices were confiscated by the other priests and divided among them. After his death, his son, Petiese's father, refused to renounce his claim to the stipend of the prophet of Amun and was therefore forced to flee from Teudjoi with his family. In his absence, the priests demolished his house, defaced one of the stelae set up by his ancestor, and threw his statues into the river. Petiese, acting on behalf of his father, was able to obtain a small financial compensation from them; he rebuilt the house and moved the family back into it. At the time when his petition was drawn up, however, the priestly stipend that he claimed was still being denied him.

The third part of Petiese's complaint purports to give copies, in Hieratic, of the texts on the two stelae erected by his great-great-grandfather in the temple of Teudjoi. The fourth part comprises three hymns which condemn the wickedness of evildoers and extol the righteousness of the god Amun, who avenges the ones whom they have wronged. Plainly, Petiese's opponents are destined for divine retribution.

Papyrus Rylands IX is important for the insights that it provides into Egyptian economic affairs, social and political history, temple administration, and legal procedure during the sixth and seventh centuries BCE. One has to exercise caution in using it as a source of evidence, since the text is written in a tendentious manner and some of the statements made in it are contradicted by contemporary documents. Nevertheless, employed with due care, it has much to offer. Regrettably, the outcome of Petiese's complaint is unknown. The papyrus in which it is preserved is the latest of the texts in the family archive to which it belongs. Thereafter, the affairs of Petiese and his relatives are a closed book.

BIBLIOGRAPHY

Griffith, F. Ll. *Catalogue of the Demotic Papyri in the John Rylands Library, Manchester*. Manchester and London, 1909. Vol. 1, plates 23–47; vol. 2, plates 21–42; vol. 3, pp. 60–112 and 218–53. Original edition of text, including photographs, hand copies and glossary. Still not entirely superseded.

Vittmann, Günter. *Der demotische Papyrus Rylands 9*. Ägypten und Altes Testament, 38. Wiesbaden, 1998. Most recent edition, with comprehensive commentary and bibliography.

MARK SMITH

PAPYRUS WESTCAR. The document known as Papyrus Westcar (P. Berlin 3033, named after its collector) preserves the only extant copy of the *Tales of the Court of King Khufu*. Its provenance is unknown; the manuscript is usually dated to the Second Intermediate Period on the basis of the Hieratic hand, but it may be slightly later. The date of composition is uncertain but is perhaps at the end of the Middle Kingdom.

Twelve columns survive, of around twenty-six lines

each, and there are probably at least two columns missing from the start. The extant text opens with a series of tales set in various Old Kingdom courts (Djoser, Nebka, Sneferu), which are being told to King Khufu by his sons. The first tale is lost apart from Khufu's response, but it was probably preceded by a narrative prologue in which the king requested entertainment to avoid boredom. Each of the tales involves a magical wonder performed by a lector-priest, such as the movement of a body of water.

Instead of a fourth tale, there is a narrative about wonders done in the presence of Khufu himself by a commoner called Djedi, in which Khufu's behavior is less than ideal. Khufu is seeking some esoteric information for use in his great pyramid, but he is told that access to this is possible only for the eldest of three children of the sun god, who will be born to a woman and who will succeed Khufu's dynasty. After this comes an account of the birth of the first three kings of the fifth dynasty. The end of the tale is lost; the manuscript breaks off in the middle of the episode recounting the events following the triplets' birth. The manuscript is incomplete, although the lost final portion may have been short.

The royal characters are historical (although the identity of one prince, Bauefre, is problematic). With one exception, the nonroyal characters are otherwise unknown and are presumably fictional: the actual mother of the first two fifth dynasty kings was Khentkawes, while in the *Tales* the mother is the wife of a priest, Rudjdjedet. The *Tales* rewrite history, but apparently in order to entertain rather than for propagandistic motives.

The *Tales* are usually analyzed as prose, but they are probably loosely structured verse; the extant text comprises around 530 metrical lines. The language and style suggest a later date than that of other Middle Egyptian fictional narratives, such as the *Story of Sinuhe*, but the looser structure and the "lower," more frivolous tone may represent a contemporaneous tradition of narrative art that was more culturally peripheral, and that is otherwise attested only in small fragmentary papyri. Many elements of parody have been detected, including allusions to the royal birth-cycle of kings, rituals of the goddess Hathor, and royal commemorative inscriptions. Nevertheless, the *Tales* also include the themes of good as opposed to bad kings, and of true as opposed to false wonders, although the serious aspects of these are not fully developed. In many respects, the *Tales* can be seen as a forerunner of the Ramessid late Egyptian stories.

BIBLIOGRAPHY

Blackman, A. M. *The Story of King Kheops and the Magicians: Transcribed from Papyrus Westcar, Berlin Papyrus 3033.* Edited by W. V. Davies. Reading, 1988. Standard edition of the text.
Goedicke, H. "Thoughts about the Papyrus Westcar." *Zeitschrift für ägyptische Sprache und Alterumskunde* 120 (1992), 23–36.
Parkinson, R. B. *The Tale of Sinuhe and Other Ancient Egyptian Poems 1940–1640 BC.* Oxford, 1997. Recent translation, pp. 102–127.
Simpson, William K. "Pap. Westcar." In *Lexikon der Ägyptologie*, 4: 744–746. Wiesbaden, 1982.

R. B. PARKINSON

PARADISE. In Western culture the word "paradise" usually refers to a location: first, the Garden of Eden, where the first human beings lived in perfect harmony with their maker and with the rest of his creation, then the abode of the blessed dead where this primeval harmony has been restored and where they live forever in bliss. Comparably well-defined and more or less permanent locations did not exist in ancient Egyptian religion. This does not mean, however, that the concept of an ideal world at the beginning of time did not exist. The opening lines of the *Book of the Heavenly Cow* describe it as follows: "Once upon a time it happened that Re, the god who created himself, arose after he had held the kingship and men and gods were still united. Then mankind began to plan a rebellion against Re, for His Majesty had become old." Other texts also allude to this primeval world, the "era of Re" (*rk R*ᶜ) or the "era of the god" (*rk nṯr*), and king lists often begin with a dynasty of gods, headed by either Re or Ptah, which comes before the dynasties of the human pharaohs. During this era gods and humans lived together in an undivided world, and it was humankind's fault that this harmonious situation came to an end. According to the version of the myth recorded in the *Book of the Heavenly Cow*, Re initially decided to annihilate all human beings, but after a great many of them had been killed, he eventually took pity on them; instead of continuing the massacre, he withdrew to the back of the Heavenly Cow and retired from his duties, leaving the day-to-day running of affairs to his deputy, the god Thoth. One of the earliest references to this myth is found in the Coffin Texts (Spell 1130), where the Lord of All says, "I made everyone equal to his fellow, and I told them not to do evil, but it was their hearts which disobeyed what I had said." In chapter 175 of the *Book of Going Forth by Day*, the creator god asks Thoth for advice after the Children of Nut—i.e., the first generation of humanity—have rebelled against him, and Thoth replies: "You should not witness evil, you should not suffer it. Let their years be shortened and their months be curtailed, for they have corrupted the hidden things in everything you have created." Human beings have destroyed the perfect order of creation; as a result, death comes into the world and "paradise" is lost.

A model of the original ideal world is found in the Egyptian temple with its perpetual cycle of rituals, the aim of which was the reigning maintenance of the perfect cosmic and social order (*maat*) established at creation. Only the reigning king, who was himself a god among men and a man among the gods and who was therefore able to act as the deputy of the gods on earth, had access to the inner temple; in everyday cultic practice, however, he was replaced by priests who acted on his behalf. Ordinary human beings had no access to the gods in the temple. Only after death were they reunited with the gods, whom they would then be able to worship directly, without a royal intermediary, as is shown by numerous representations on tomb walls and funerary objects, especially after the Amarna period.

The abode of the dead can hardly be described as Paradise, however. The spell from the *Book of Going Forth by Day* (or *Book of the Dead*, BD) quoted above contains a dialogue between Osiris, the god of the dead with whom the deceased himself is identified, and Atum, the creator god: "O my lord Atum, why is it that I have to travel to the district of silence, where there is no water and no air, which is so deep, so dark and so impenetrable?—You will live there in peace of mind.—But one cannot even have sex there!—I have given blessedness instead of water, air and sexual pleasure, and peace of mind instead of bread and beer, so says Atum." Clearly the idea of being trapped forever in the realm of the dead provoked mixed feelings in the Egyptians, and although at death everyone who successfully passed the final judgment became an Osiris, most funerary texts put emphasis on the identification of the deceased with the sun god, who is not restricted in his movements but enters the netherworld at night, only to be reborn and resurrected in the morning. The mummified body of the deceased rests in its tomb in the underworld, but his *ba*, represented as a bird with a human head, is able to move in and out of the tomb. The *ba* joins Re on his eternal journey along the sky and through the realm of the dead: at sunrise, when Re is reborn, the *ba* leaves the tomb, and at night, when Re travels through the underworld, where he temporarily unites with the body of Osiris, the *ba* returns to the mummified body in the tomb.

At first sight, the idea of a perpetual cycle would seem to be difficult to reconcile with the concept of a permanent locality such as Paradise. There is, however, a particular stretch of the daily journey of the sun god, and of the deceased with him, that has sometimes been called the Egyptian equivalent of the Greek Elysian Fields. Egyptian texts use two different names for this abode: the Field of Offerings (*sḫt ḥtpw*), and the Field of Rushes (*sḫt iꜣrw*). They are mentioned together as early as the Old Kingdom Pyramid Texts, and it remains unclear whether these names refer to two different locations or whether they are two names for one and the same place; obviously, they are closely related. Although they are occasionally said to be in the northern sky, most texts agree that they are situated in the east, at the place of sunrise: "the gate . . . from which Re goes out into the east of the sky" is "in the middle of the Field of Rushes" (BD 149). In chapters 109 and 110 of the *Book of Going Forth by Day*, which describe and even depict these fields, the Field of Rushes is called "the City of the God" (i.e., Re); it is inhabited by the "Eastern Souls" and by Re-Horakhty (the rising sun) and the Morning Star (visible only in the eastern sky). Despite the term "city" used here, the Field of Rushes is really an inundated marshland divided by lakes and canals; according to the Pyramid Texts, the sun god purifies himself in the morning in the Lake of the Field of Rushes. In BD 109 and 149 it is described as follows: "Its walls are of iron, its barley stands 5 cubits high, with ears of 2 and stalks of 3 cubits, and its emmer stands 7 cubits high, with ears of 3 and stalks of 4 cubits; it is the blessed, each of them 9 cubits tall, who reap them alongside the Eastern Souls." This idealized farmland stands in stark contrast to the gloomy abode of Osiris, which is airless and without food, drink, and sexual pleasures, totally different from the picture that emerges from the opening lines of chapter 110: "Beginning of the spells of the Field of Offerings and the spells of going out into the day, entering and leaving the necropolis, attaining the Field of Rushes, dwelling in the Field of Offerings, the Great City, the Mistress of Air, being in control there, being a blessed one there, plowing and harvesting there, eating and drinking there, making love there, and doing everything that one was used to do on earth." In the vignette illustrating this chapter, the deceased, often accompanied by his wife, is shown paddling across the waterways of these fields in his boat and plowing, sowing, reaping, and threshing, often dressed in beautiful white linen garments which demonstrate that all of this hard labor should not be taken too literally: in actual fact, it is carried out by the deceased's substitutes, the *ushabti* statuettes which were an essential part of his or her funerary equipment.

The deceased spend only part of their lives after death in this place of abundance, however. When the sun goes down below the horizon and Re enters the underworld, they too return to their tombs. The next morning they will rise from the sleep of death again, bathe in the waters of the Field of Rushes, and provide for their daily sustenance there. The food offerings that they receive every day along with the daily rituals carried out by their relatives or their funerary priests, are the earthly equivalent of the products of the Field of Offerings and the Field of Rushes. One of the most common scenes in Egyptian tombs from all periods is that of the deceased seated at an offering table stacked with tall loaves of bread. From the sixth dynasty onward, these loaves are often replaced by the reed-leaves which in the hieroglyphic script spell the word *sḫt* ("field"), and in later texts and representations the offering tables are expressly labeled "the Fields of Offerings."

[*See also* Afterlife; Hell; *and* Judgment of the Dead.]

BIBLIOGRAPHY

Bayoumi, Abbas. *Autour du champ des souchets et du champ des offrandes.* Cairo, 1941. Deals with both the Field of Rushes and the Field of Offerings, which are considered to be two separate areas. Based almost exclusively on the Pyramid Texts and the *Book of Going Forth by Day.* Both this work and that of R. Weill are now somewhat dated, but so far they have not been superseded.

Hornung, Erik. *Der ägyptische Mythos von der Himmelskuh: Eine Ätiologie des Unvollkommenen.* Orbis Biblicus et Orientalis, 46. Freiburg and Göttingen, 1982; 2d ed., 1991. Edition with translation and commentary of the *Book of the Heavenly Cow.* Contains excursus on the dynasty of gods and on the rebellion of mankind and their punishment.

Kees, Hermann. "Earu-Gefilde." *Reallexikon der ägyptischen Religionsgeschichte,* edited by Hans Bonnet, pp. 161–162. Berlin, 1952. Short article on the Field of Rushes and the Field of Offerings, which are considered to be virtually identical.

Leclant, Jean. "Earu-Gefilde." In *Lexikon der Ägyptologie,* 1: 1156–1160. Wiesbaden, 1975. An up-to-date summary of what is known about the Field of Rushes; it also deals with the Field of Offerings.

Lesko, Leonard H. "The Field of Ḥetep in Egyptian Coffin Texts." *Journal of the American Research Center in Egypt* 9 (1971–1972): 89–101. Annotated translation of the earliest version of chapter 110 of the *Book of Going Forth by Day.*

Luft, Ulrich. *Beiträge zur Historisierung der Götterwelt und der Mythenschreibung.* Studia Aegyptiaca, 4. Budapest, 1978. Study of the "Era of the God" and of the dynasty of gods which preceded those of the human kings.

Mercer, Samuel A. B. *The Pyramid Texts in Translation and Commentary.* Vol. 4. New York, 1952. Pp. 65–68 give a useful excursus entitled "Marsh of Reeds and Marsh of Offerings in the Pyramid Texts."

Munro, Peter. "Brothälften und Schilfblätter." *Göttinger Miszellen* 5 (1973): 13–16. On the interpretation of the offering table as the "Field of Offering."

Weill, Raymond. *Le champ des roseaux et le champs des offrandes dans la religion funéraire et la religion générale.* Paris, 1936. More comprehensive than Bayoumi's study, but even more dated, especially from a methodological point of view. Funerary texts, and the Pyramid Texts in particular, are considered to reflect a rivalry between the theologies of Osiris and Re, a view few Egyptologists would subscribe to nowadays. Weill opts for a sharp distinction between the two Fields, situating the Field of Rushes in the east and the Field of Offerings, undoubtedly wrongly, in the west.

Worsham, Charles E. "A Reinterpretation of the So-Called Bread Loaves in Egyptian Offering Scenes." *Journal of the American Research Center in Egypt* 16 (1979): 7–10. Covers much the same ground as Munro's article.

JACOBUS VAN DIJK

PATRIARCHY. *See* Gender Roles.

PEOPLE. Tracking the movements and establishing the identity of peoples in the archaeological and historical records is a difficult and often ambiguous project. Physical anthropology is the best source of identification, but the early misuse of the "race concept" created overly simplistic definitions driven more by colonialism and racism than by science. Modern studies based on population genetics are much more complex and yield more ambiguous results. Historical linguistic evidence, especially names, is also used to establish group identities where historical records exist, as is often the case in Egypt and the surrounding regions. Archaeological data have been used to reconstruct the identity of ethnic groups in two ways: by characterizing artifact assemblages as culture areas, without necessarily establishing that they belong to a historically known group; and by matching groups identified in texts with an artifact assemblage. Unlike physical anthropology and linguistics, archaeological evidence is abundant and relatively easy to analyze, but all studies of this kind rest on the important assumption that a given artifact assemblage does in fact represent a cultural identity, rather than a sphere of cultural influence or culture contact—and this may or may not be true. Radical diffusionists in the late nineteenth and early twentieth centuries favored massive movements of peoples as the engine of cultural change. Thus W. M. Flinders Petrie's "Dynastic Race" concept linked cultural achievement with racial identity in the origins of pharaonic civilization. These models have, unfortunately, been revived by some Afrocentric scholars, who otherwise rightly emphasize Egypt's African origins. Diffusion and population movements did exist in the past, but they must be carefully demonstrated. For example, the identity of Uruk colonies (c.3500 BCE) in southern Anatolia was established by using a combination of architecture, material culture, and textual evidence. In a similar way, a combination of archaeology, text, and art history has documented an Egyptian colonial presence and the diffusion (and subsequent adaptation) of certain aspects of Egyptian iconography, ideology, and institutions in Nubia and in Syria-Palestine.

Race of the Ancient Egyptians. The race and origins of the ancient Egyptians have been a source of considerable debate. Scholars in the late and early twentieth centuries rejected any consideration of the Egyptians as black Africans by defining the Egyptians either as non-African (i.e., either Near Eastern or Indo-Aryan), or as members of a separate brown (as opposed to black) race, or as a mixture of lighter-skinned peoples with black Africans. In the latter half of the twentieth century, Afrocentric scholars have countered this Eurocentric and often racist perspective by characterizing the Egyptians as black and African. A common feature of all of these approaches, including the last, is the connection of race to cultural achievement. At the same time, however, modern physical anthropologists have increasingly challenged the entire notion of race, replacing it with the more complex and scientifically based population genetics.

The origins of the modern conception of race derive from the work of nineteenth-century anthropologists like L. H. Morgan and E. B. Tylor, who developed "scientific" unilinear evolutionary models for the development of human beings from "savagery" to "civilization." This model profoundly influenced early Egyptological views of race. Racial groups were ranked by evolutionary categories linked to supposed intellectual capacities based on elaborate cranial measurements, allegedly providing causal links among phenotypic traits, mental capacity, and sociopolitical dominance. This methodology, not coincidentally, reinforced the existing Euro-American domination of Third World peoples with the claim of scientifically "objective" methodologies based on race and evolution. Thus, the great achievements of ancient Egypt could not flow from black Africans, since theirs was an inferior race; so the "Dynastic Race" must have been white, or at least brown.

As early as 1897, Franz Boas challenged this racial ideology, in particular the argument for connections among language, culture, and biology (i.e., race). Boas demonstrated that supposedly distinctive core racial indicators could change quickly in response to clothing styles, nutrition, and cultural and environmental factors. Ashley Montague, a student of Boas, played a key role in developing and disseminating this concept; he argued in *Man's Most Dangerous Myth: The Fallacy of Race* (New York, 1942) that the old paradigm of static races should be replaced by dynamic populations with overlapping characteristics. Far from being absolute, genetic traits are distributed in clines, or continuously varying distributions of traits inconsistent with racial categories. Modern physical anthropology has demonstrated that 94 percent of human variation is found within human populations, rather than between the major populations traditionally labeled races. Biological characteristics affected by natural selection, migration, or drift are distributed in geographic gradations. These encompass all the features used to define racial physical "phenotypes," including facial form, hair texture, blood type, and epidermal melanin (the chemical determining darkness of skin). These physical features cross alleged racial boundaries as if they were nonexistent, leading to the inevitable conclusion that there are no biological races, just clines. Physical anthropologists are increasingly concluding that racial definitions are the culturally defined product of selective perception and should be replaced in biological terms by the study of populations and clines. Consequently, any characterization of the race of the ancient Egyptians depends on modern cultural definitions, not scientific study. Thus, by modern American standards it is reasonable to characterize the Egyptians as "black," while acknowledging the scientific evidence for the physical diversity of Africans.

Origins of the Egyptians in Northeastern Africa. In spite of the evidence against scientific race, both Egyptologists and Afrocentric scholars often continue attempts to define the Egyptians as members of an essentialist racial category, usually attempting to link them either to a supposed "Caucasoid" or "Negroid/Africoid" phenotype. Such models imply that the founders of pharaonic Egypt came from sub-Saharan Africa, western Asia, or Europe/Transcaucasus. While there was some immigration from all these areas, physical anthropology has demonstrated the fundamental continuity of ancient and modern Egyptian populations. The evidence also points to linkages to other northeastern African peoples, not coincidentally approximating the modern range of languages closely related to Egyptian in the Afro-Asiatic group (formerly called Hamito-Semitic). These linguistic similarities place ancient Egyptian in a close relationship with languages spoken today in northeastern Africa as far west as Chad and south to Somalia. Archaeological evidence also strongly supports an African origin. A widespread northeastern African cultural assemblage, including distinctive multiple barbed harpoons and pottery decorated with dotted wavy line patterns, appears during the early Neolithic (also known as the Aqualithic, a reference to the mild climate of the Sahara at this time). Saharan and Sudanese rock art from this time resembles early Egyptian iconography. Strong connections between Nubian (Sudanese) and Egyptian material culture continue in the later Neolithic Badarian culture of Upper Egypt. Similarities include black-topped wares, vessels with characteristic ripple-burnished surfaces, a special tulip-shaped vessel with incised and white-filled decoration, palettes, and harpoons. The presence of formative pharaonic symbolism in the Lower Nubian A-Group royal burials at Qustul has led Bruce Williams to posit a common Egyptian-Nubian pharaonic heritage, although this notion has been much disputed. Other ancient Egyptian practices show strong similarities to modern African cultures, including divine kingship, the use of headrests, body art, circumcision, and male coming-of-age rituals, all suggesting an African substratum or foundation for Egyptian civilization (rather than diffusion from sub-Saharan Africa, as claimed by some Afrocentric scholars).

Other Peoples in Egypt. Throughout pharaonic Egypt's long history, peoples from surrounding areas interacted with Egyptians. Many of them settled in the Nile Valley, where they assimilated to, and sometimes exerted some influence on, Egyptian culture. We can identify a number of these groups from Egyptian records, although it must be remembered that their depiction was often colored by the stereotypes of state ideology (see below). The main emphasis will be placed on groups who lived in or came to the Nile Valley in large numbers.

Nubians. Nubian–Egyptian trade flourished during the late Predynastic period through the first dynasty, presumably accompanied by small numbers of expatriate traders and perhaps envoys. The Early Dynastic period raids that destroyed the Lower Nubian A-Group culture

brought Nubians to Egypt as slaves and perhaps mercenaries. During the Old Kingdom, archaeological evidence
from the Egyptian colonial settlement at Buhen at the
Second Cataract reveals a population of impoverished
Nubians, presumably slaves. Nubians are attested as soldiers and administrators during the late Old Kingdom,
and large numbers of Nubian mercenaries were used during the civil wars of the First Intermediate Period. A group
of these Egyptianized soldiers settled at Gebelein, where
funerary stelae depict them as prosperous members of
the local community. A statue of the Middle Kingdom
founder Nebhepetre Mentuhotep with black skin may
point to Nubian ancestry, although the use of black may
simply reflect the statue's Osirian symbolism. Artistic and
physical evidence suggests that his wives Ashayit, Hen-
henit, Kemsit, and Sadeh were probably Nubian. Nubian-
style tattoos were found on women in elite burials of the
period. Nubians are featured in Middle Kingdom tombs
at Beni Hasan and Meir. Later images showing a black-
skinned queen Ahmose Nefertari, wife and sister or half-
sister of the New Kingdom's founder, Ahmose, may
indicate Nubian ancestry, although, again, black may
symbolize the deceased's connection with Osiris.

Vegetation in the Eastern Desert of Egypt and the Sudan could support a sizable seminomadic pastoral population. These people are identified in Egyptian sources as
the Medja, who were grouped along with Nubians and depicted with the same physical appearance and dress. They
have been identified archaeologically with the so-called
Pan-Grave culture, whose characteristic cemeteries are
found as far north as 27° north latitude in southern Upper
Egypt and range into Sudanese Nubia. Archaeologically,
they are related to the Lower Nubian C-Group and Upper
Nubian Kerma cultures, but they represent a distinct tradition. Papyrus Boulaq records the visit of the Medja chief
to the Egyptian court at Thebes in the thirteenth dynasty,
attesting to close relations. Medja mercenaries were employed extensively during the Second Intermediate Period, in the seventeenth dynasty Theban campaigns to
wrest control of Egypt from the Nile Delta–based Hyksos
fifteenth dynasty. The characteristic Pan-Grave assemblage was found at the palace and town of Ballas, which
may have served as a key staging area for the Egyptian
reconquest of northern Upper Egypt and of Lower Egypt.
Many Medja settled in Egypt and assimilated into Egyptian society during the Second Intermediate Period and
New Kingdom. During the New Kingdom, the word
"Medja" lost its ethnic connotation, becoming synonymous with "police," attesting to the Medja's considerable
reputation as soldiers. The Lower Nubian princes of
Egypt's New Kingdom colonial administration may have
been drawn from acculturated Medja elite. Other Egyptianized Nubians, whether of the C-Group, Medja, or (less

likely) Kerman, entered New Kingdom society, often rising to prominent positions in the government.

Egypt lost control of Nubia at the end of the New Kingdom, and by about 850 BCE a new power arose at Napata
in Upper Nubia. By about 750 BCE, the Nubian pharaoh
Piya gained control of southern Upper Egypt and had his
daughter Amenirdis installed as heir to the key post of
"Divine Wife of Amun" at Thebes; at the death of the
twenty-third dynasty "Divine Wife," Shepenwepet, Amer-
nirdis assumed the title and functions. In Year 21 of his
reign, Piya defeated the Libyan prince Tefnakht, establishing the twenty-fifth dynasty as rulers over all of Egypt. A
number of Nubians no doubt settled in Egypt during this
period, intermarrying with Egyptians. Although Piya and
his successors depicted themselves as the "saviors" of
Egyptian civilization, their Egyptianization was not as
comprehensive as royal ideology indicates. Monumental
and presumably administrative texts were written in
Egyptian, but they kept their Nubian names (possibly in
a Nilo-Saharan language, suggesting an origin in central
Africa), mode of succession, and elements of dress and
regalia. Although Egyptian gods were adopted, temples
renovated or built, and pyramid tombs adopted, these features were not slavishly copied but were adapted to suit
Napatan needs and perceptions. After the Assyrian conquest, Kushite pharaonic culture continued to flourish in
the South, becoming a prominent source of Egyptian influence in sub-Saharan Africa until the early centuries CE.

Puntites. The earliest mention of Punt is on the Palermo Stone, which notes an expedition mounted under
the reign of the fifth dynasty king Sahure. Contact continued sporadically until the New Kingdom. Visits to the
land of Punt are not mentioned in Egyptian sources after
the reign of Ramesses III (c.1150 BCE). The scene of an
expedition to Punt from Queen Hatshepsut's mortuary
complex at Deir el-Bahri shows Puntites with red skin and
facial features similar to Egyptians, long or bobbed hair,
goatee beards, and kilts. The so-called queen of Punt is
represented as steatopygous. These same reliefs show the
Puntites as a settled people, with houses placed on stilts.
The flora and fauna shown indicate a location in coastal
Sudan or Eritrea. At least some Puntites visited Egypt
with their families, but it is unlikely that many settled
there.

Pygmies. A few references from the Old Kingdom seem
to refer to the people known today as Pygmies. Small
numbers of Pygmies were brought to Egypt as sacred
dancers. They are found in the Pyramid Texts, involved in
the frenetic mortuary dance. The safe arrival of a dancing
Pygmy is a matter of concern to young Pepy II in a letter
to the expedition leader Harkhuf, recorded in his tomb at
Aswan. These references imply that Pygmies danced especially for the king, just as the king dances before the god.

If necessary, a dwarf could substitute, suggesting that Pygmies were a great rarity and never present in large numbers. Today Pygmies live in the rain forests of central Africa, although there is considerable debate regarding the antiquity of their occupation there.

Libyans. Although groups from Libya (such as the Tjemech) probably interacted with Egypt from early times, they do not reach prominence in Egyptian records until the New Kingdom. Libyans are depicted at Akhenaten's court as emissaries or mercenaries. During the nineteenth and twentieth dynasties, Libyans were identified as Tjehenu and became one of four essential peoples or "races" depicted in the solar theology (see below). Egyptian texts mention two main groups, the Meshwesh and Libu. Slight differences in dress and appearance between the two groups may indicate a cultural distinction. Libyan incursions into the western Nile Delta were a serious problem for Ramessid kings. Accounts of military campaigns mounted against them indicate large numbers of cattle and sheep taken as booty, implying a significant pastoral component. The same texts mention towns, implying an urban civilization. Their most likely origin lies in Cyrenaica (coastal Libya), although the region is still relatively unknown archeologically. Some texts imply that they also ranged through the northern oases and Sahara. Archaeologically, the oases have a distinct material culture, often mixed with Egyptian pottery and artifacts reflecting contact and conquest at various periods. Several ongoing archaeological projects should permit a better definition of these groups. Libyans settled in large numbers in the Nile Delta, eventually founding the Bubastite twenty-second dynasty, based at Tanis. The third-century BCE Egyptian historian Manetho refers to Sheshonq I as the first of a series of Libyan chiefs who ruled Egypt for two hundred years. Theban records refer to him as "Great Chief of all the Meswesh," who had been used as police during the New Kingdom. The kings of the Bubastite dynasty were at least partly Libyan, and the Saite dynasty rulers may well have had some Libyan ancestry.

Near Easterners (Asiatics). Evidence of contact with the Near East goes back to the Predynastic period. Although some scholars favoring diffusionist models have argued for a massive influx through the Nile Delta or the Wadi Hammamat via the Red Sea, the consensus today is for increasing contact and interaction focused on the Nile Delta and the Sinai. There is ample textual evidence in the form of names for the presence of Syrian-Palestinians in Egypt's public institutions and private houses. For example, the Middle Kingdom Brooklyn Papyrus lists seventy-seven servants of the lady Senebtisi, forty-eight of whom have Near Eastern names. Other texts show that new generations of families like these received Egyptian names, gradually assimilating into Egyptian society. Several stelae from this period depict servants labeled as Near Easterners, but with Egyptian names, dress, and hairstyles. Some may have come to Egypt as captives from military campaigns, although there was considerable movement of peoples going both ways for trade and diplomacy.

Egypt gradually became more engaged with Near Eastern peoples during the later Middle Kingdom, through the establishment of a major point of immigration at Tell ed-Dab'a in the eastern Nile Delta. This site has all the hallmarks of a trade diaspora, an expatriate settlement serving as an interface between the two trading partners. Excavations document a gradual increase in the numbers and influence of Syrian-Palestinians at Dab'a over the course of the thirteenth dynasty. By the late thirteenth dynasty, Middle Bronze Age pottery makes up 40 percent of the assemblage, "warrior" tombs with typical weaponry and associated equid burials appear with great frequency, and monumental temples in the standard Middle Bronze Age layout rival those of sites in Syria-Palestine. A complex settlement hierarchy developed in Palestine during this period, anchored by major trade "gateways" at Tell ed-Dab'a in the south and Hazor in the north. At the end of the thirteenth dynasty, Tell ed-Dab'a became the capital of the Syrian-Palestinian fifteenth dynasty, the Hyksos, which established direct control over the northern half of Egypt and forced the Upper Egyptian seventeenth dynasty to accept a role as a vassal state. The Hyksos only partly assimilated to Egyptian culture, although it is likely that many of their descendants remained in the Delta after Egypt's "expulsion" of the early eighteenth dynasty, thereby becoming part of Egyptian New Kingdom society.

Substantial numbers of Near Eastern peoples, mostly Syrian-Palestinians but including individuals from Mitanni (Syria) and Hatti (Anatolia), were captured during the great military campaigns of the New Kingdom, which ranged as far as northern Syria. Others came as tribute from vassal states controlled by Egypt or as free traders, craftsmen, and scribes. Most prisoners were assigned to various royal and temple estates to provide labor in the fields, although some were parceled out as rewards to valorous warriors. Skilled Near Eastern craftsmen were employed in Egyptian workshops, and others were employed as servants in elite and royal households. Literate elites from the Near East were often employed in the Egyptian bureaucracy, where their linguistic skills proved valuable to the conduct of international trade and diplomacy; the ambitious might rise to high positions. The Canaanite Ben-ozen became chief of the department of alimentation and beverage and chief royal herald under Ramesses II. The chief draftsman in the temple of Amun, Pas-Ba'al, was possibly taken prisoner under Thutmose III, and his descendants occupied his office for six generations. An individual with the Canaanite name Aper-El became vizier under Amenhotpe III, and Chancellor Bey became a virtual kingmaker at the end of the nineteenth dynasty. Egyptians intermarried with Near Easterners, and slaves were sometimes adopted into Egyptian families. Although most Near Easterners assimilated to some degree, the cultural influence was not unidirectional. Levantine mythical and literary motifs, loan words, and deities such as Ba'al, Astarte, and Reshep all entered into the Egyptian cultural sphere during the New Kingdom.

Mediterranean peoples. Archaeological, historical, and artistic evidence point to limited interactions among Egypt, Minoan Crete, and Mycenean Greece during the Bronze Age. Pottery and other artifacts from the Aegean appear in Egypt during the Middle and New Kingdoms. Egyptian objects also appear in the Aegean during this period. Minoan-style architectural frescoes from the beginning of the eighteenth dynasty at Tell ed-Dab'a in the Nile Delta suggest the presence of artisans from Crete in Egypt. Scenes of Aegean emissaries and traders, like those from the tomb of Rekhmire, vizier under Thutmose III, provide further evidence of interaction in the New Kingdom. A fragmentary list of Aegean place names from the mortuary temple of Amenhotpe III points to an Egyptian embassy for Mycenean Greece. It is not likely, however, that many of these Aegean peoples settled in Egypt.

The "Sea Peoples" is a term used to encompass the movements of Mediterranean peoples by both sea and land at the end of the Late Bronze Age (c.1200–1100 BCE). The disruptions caused by this massive migration through the Anatolian Plateau and down the eastern Mediterranean coast brought down the great Hittite Empire and such coastal Levantine trading centers as Ugarit. Some captive groups were turned into mercenaries in the Egyptian army, most notably the fierce Sherden, who became elite royal bodyguards under Ramesses II. The Harris Papyrus notes that captive Peleset, Shardana, Weshesh, Denyen, and Shekelesh were used as garrison forces and mercenaries under Ramesses III. The exact origin of each of these groups is a matter of considerable debate; the consensus favors the Aegean and western Anatolia as the origin of most of them. Some soldiers and their families were settled in coastal Palestine, where they are identified archaeologically with the Philistines. Others settled in Egypt. Papyrus Wilbour, a tax roll of farms in the Faiyum area, lists several Shardana as landholders.

Greeks and Carians began to be used as Egyptian mercenaries in the Late period, settling at sites like Naukratis in the Nile Delta. Trade with the Mediterranean expanded during the Saite twenty-sixth dynasty, bringing other peoples from the Mediterranean shores to Egypt. The Persian king Cambyses II conquered Egypt in 525 BCE, but only small numbers of Persians actually came to Egypt,

with most of the nation's bureaucracy remaining in Egyptian hands. More Greeks came into Egypt during the struggles of native dynasts against Persian rule, and with the conquest of Egypt by Alexander of Macedon in 332 BCE. These immigrants founded several new cities in the Nile Delta, the most important being the port city of Alexandria. Its population numbered 300,000 Greek citizens and another 200,000 Egyptians, living in crowded mansions and tenements. The Macedonian elite established cities modeled on the Greek concepts of *polis* and tribe, with strict citizenship rules to keep out the "barbarian" Egyptian rabble. The royal family, the Ptolemies, remained to the end very Macedonian; Cleopatra VII was the first even to speak Egyptian. Temples with priesthoods of Greek origin were set up syncretizing Egyptian and Greek deities: like Dionysus with Osiris, Hathor with Aphrodite, and Amun with Zeus.

Royal Ideology and the Depiction of Foreigners. Different peoples were separated on the basis of culture, language, and physical appearance in both the royal ideology and more prosaic sources. Unlike modern racist thinkers, the Egyptians recognized these features as separate categories; thus, an acculturated Nubian like the "Royal Fan-bearer" (a military title) Mahirper was acknowledged and depicted as culturally Egyptian, but with Nubian dark skin, facial features, and curled hair. Egyptian ideology separated the world's peoples into four groups: Egyptians, Near Easterners, Libyans, and Nubians. New Kingdom royal tombs provide idealized portraits of these different peoples. Egyptians have red-brown skin, black shoulder-length hair, simple white kilts, and small trimmed beards. Nubians are represented with black skin, scarification on the cheeks and brow similar to that still practiced in the Nubian Sudan today, short trimmed hair in braids or ringlets, hoop earrings, and decorated leather sashes and aprons worn over white Egyptian-style kilts. Libyans are shown with light skin and geometric tattoos, braided or ringleted hair with curled side lock(s?) and two ostrich feathers; they wear a loincloth(?) under a long leather cloak showing the natural patterns of the cow's hair. Near Easterners are depicted as Syrian-Palestinians with yellow skin, black bobbed hair with a headband tied at the back, elaborately decorated kilts, and ample (sometimes pointed) beards and mustaches. In other scenes, different hairstyles, dress, and facial features are used to differentiate other Near Eastern peoples—like the Anatolian Hittites or Syrian Mitanni—from the Syrian-Palestinians.

Egypt's ideological view of foreigners reflects goals and perceptions different from the administrative realities of dealing with diplomacy, trade, and empire. Antonio Loprieno has characterized the Egyptian view of the various peoples in *Topos und Mimesis: Zum Ausländer in der ägyp-*

tischen Literatur (Wiesbaden, 1988). *Topos* represents an idealized view of the world that serves a rhetorical, not necessarily a literal, end; *mimesis* reflects the reality of daily experience, if ultimately filtered through Egyptian cultural perceptions.

The ideological *topos* applied to foreign peoples in Egypt reflects a propagandistic manipulation of reality aimed at an inner audience. In the celebrative central ideology, often expressed in monumental art and architecture, Egypt becomes the center of the universe, and all the foreign lands bow down to the pharaoh, regardless of their actual relationship. Foreigners represent chaotic, uncivilized threats to the inner order, ultimately disposed of by the ruler. The role of foreigners in the Egyptian foreigner topos is in opposition to *maat* (order, harmony, rightness). *Maat* exists in opposition to *isfet* (disorder, chaos), which constantly tries to upset the heavenly and earthly order. One of the most potent forces of *isfet* is the traditional foreign enemies of Egypt. Thus, foreigners are depicted as strangers and generalized as an ethnic group with negative qualities. They are not really people and are often compared with animals—their speech is unintelligible, like the jabbering of baboons. The characteristic dress and physical appearance described above emphasizes each group's otherness in the foreigner *topos*. On an even more abstract level, the traditional enemies of Egypt are referred to as the "Nine Bows." This *topos* appears iconographically as actual bows, sometimes combined with topical images of captive Near Easterners and Nubians. Footstools, statue and throne bases, processional ways, and even sandals carry the Nine Bows motif, so that the king would constantly trample underfoot the enemies of Egypt. The application of this principle reaches an extreme in the formal Presentation of Tribute, where loyal native officials in Egypt's colonial administration appear in the *topos* of "pacified Nubian" described above, while at the same time their tombs, grave goods, and other monuments show that they were completely Egyptianized.

A more realistic portrayal occurs in texts reflecting mimesis. Foreigners are treated as individuals, not as stereotypes. They are identified by name, can speak Egyptian like a "real" person, and thus are incorporated into the Egyptian cultural framework. Unlike the topical foreigner, they can act in a positive way. In everyday life, foreign influences and even deities were tolerated in Egypt. For example, despite state ideological representations of Near Easterners as uncivilized enemies, Levantine mythical and literary motifs, loan words, and deities such as Ba'al, Astarte, and Reshep, had all entered into the Egyptian cultural sphere by the New Kingdom. Although no indisputably Nubian deities appear in Egypt, elite military dress and accouterments, including leather kilts and hairstyles, were borrowed from Nubia.

[*See also* Afrocentrism; Foreigners; *and* Race.]

BIBLIOGRAPHY

Bernal, Martin. *Black Athena.* New Brunswick, N.J., 1987. Bernal provides a good critique of the racist biases of the late nineteenth and early twentieth centuries that minimized Egypt's African-ness and denied interactions with the Aegean. Unfortunately, he goes on to revive seriously flawed radical diffusionist approaches that posit massive migrations and influence of Egyptians on the development of Classical civilization.

Boas, Franz. *Race, Language and Culture.* Chicago, 1940. A seminal work refuting the connection of biology (race) and culture.

Celenko, Theodore, ed. *Egypt in Africa.* Indianapolis, 1996. The companion volume for an innovative exhibit exploring ancient Egypt's African roots, juxtaposing images from Egypt and other African cultures. Each section is accompanied by essays from Egyptologists and Africanist scholars, exploring related themes.

Curtin, Phillip. *Cross Cultural Trade in World History.* Cambridge, 1984. Curtin draws on insights from anthropology and economic history to documents a broad and diverse group of trading relationships in the ancient and modern world, including the movement of peoples in the creation of trade diasporas, an expatriate settlement serving as an interface between the two trading partners.

Diop, Cheikh Ante. *The African Origin of Civilization.* Chicago, 1974. A highly influential work that rightly points out the African origins of Egyptian civilization, but reinforces the methodological and theoretical foundations of colonialist theories of history, embracing racialist thinking and simply reversing the flow of diffusionist models.

Keita, S. O. Y., and Rick Kittles. "The Persistence of Racial Thinking and the Myth of Racial Divergence." *American Anthropologist* 99 (1997), 534–544. An excellent summary of the evidence against race as a scientific concept, with particular reference to the ancient Egyptians.

Kemp, Barry J. "Imperialism in New Kingdom Egypt (c.1575–1087 B.C.)." In *Imperialism in the Ancient World*, edited by P. D. A. Garnsey and C. R. Whittaker, pp. 7–57, 283–297. Cambridge, 1978. An excellent consideration of Egypt's Nubian and Syrian-Palestinian empires, including an extensive discussion of foreigners in Egyptian ideology.

Leahy, Anthony. *Libya and Egypt, c.1300–750 B.C.* London, 1990.

Liverani, Mario. *Prestige and Interest: International Relations in the Near East ca. 1600–1100 B.C.* Padua, 1990. Provides a perceptive, wide-ranging comparison of Egypt and the great powers of the Near East, contrasting ideological pronouncements emphasizing the internal prestige of the ruler with diplomatic correspondence reflecting political and economic interest.

O'Connor, David. *Ancient Nubia: Egypt's Rival in Africa.* Philadelphia, 1993. Provides an excellent general introduction to the civilizations of ancient Nubia and their relationship with Egypt, including a number of case studies which employ new analyses of the University of Pennsylvania's early excavations.

Redford, Donald B. *Egypt, Canaan, and Israel in Ancient Times.* Princeton, 1992. A comprehensive survey of Egypt's interactions with Syro-Palestine, including discussions of the role of Near Easterners in Egypt.

Sadr, Karim. *The Development of Nomadism in Ancient Northeast Africa.* Philadelphia, 1991.

Sanders, N. K. *The Sea Peoples.* London, 1987. Discusses the origins of the Sea Peoples and their impact on the eastern Mediterranean and Egypt.

Säve-Söderbergh, Torgny, and Lana Troy. *New Kingdom Pharaonic Sites.* Uppsala, 1991. A thorough report on the excavation of several Nubian cemeteries important to understanding the acculturation of Lower Nubians in the New Kingdom and the origins and role of the Lower Nubian princes.

Silverman, David. "Pygmies and Dwarves in Old Kingdom Egypt." *Serapis* 1 (1989), 53–55.

Smith, Stuart T. "State and Empire in the Middle and New Kingdoms." In *Anthropological Analysis of Ancient Egypt,* edited by Judy Lustig, pp. 66–89. Sheffield, 1997. Contrasts the economic and social dynamics of Egypt's empire with the portrayal and role of foreigners in Egyptian ideology.

Vogel, Joseph O., ed. *Encyclopedia of Precolonial Africa.* Walnut Creek, 1997. Includes numerous surveys of various aspects of northeast African history and culture, including human origins, pastoralism, rock art, and the rise of Neolithic culture and origins of the ancient Egyptians. See especially articles by Holl on Pan-Africanism and Afrocentrism; Ehret on African languages; and Williams, Hassan, Wettestrom, and Fattovich on the origins of Egyptian civilization and its connections to adjacent areas.

STUART TYSON SMITH

PEPINAKHT HEQAIB, whose "good (or familiar) name" was Heqaib ("ruler of my heart"), was a major official at Elephantine, an island in the Nile River near Aswan, during the reign of Pepy II. His principal title was "Overseer of Foreigners" (i.e., mercenaries). A rather bellicose "autobiographical" inscription in his tomb at Qubbet el-Hawa (Aswan) indicates that he was primarily responsible for controlling the military situation in Nubia and the Eastern Desert at a time when the attacks—presumably by the new C-Group population—on Egyptian expeditions to the south and east were increasing. The king dispatched him to devastate ("hack up") the Lower Nubian districts of Wawat and Irtjet, and Pepinakht reports killing numbers of Nubians and bringing back some unspecified number of captives, along with their cattle as booty. On another campaign, he claims to have brought back the chiefs of these districts, their children, and members of their entourages. Subsequently, Pepinakht was sent to the Red Sea coast to recover the bodies of an expedition leader named Ankhty and his men, who, while building a boat there for a trip to the land of Punt (on the Somali coast), had been murdered by the locals. Pepinakht drove off the tribesmen, trumpeting that he had "set the fear of Horus [i.e., the king] in the foreign countries," thereby pacifying them. In addition to his military activities, Pepinakht Heqaib performed administrative functions in the pyramid complexes of both King Merenre and King Pepy II.

Pepinakht Heqaib appears to have enjoyed a considerable reputation in the Aswan region, for at some time after his death, he was deified and became the object of a cult among the officials at Elephantine that lasted until the Middle Kingdom. Excavations carried out principally by Labib Habachi and inscriptions in the tombs of later officials indicate that a series of shrines, complete with altars and statues, had been built on Elephantine Island in Heqaib's honor.

BIBLIOGRAPHY

Habachi, L. "Heqaib." In *Lexikon der Ägyptologie,* 2:1120–1122. Wiesbaden, 1974.

Martin-Pardey, E. "Pepinacht." In *Lexikon der Ägyptologie,* 4:929. Wiesbaden, 1982.

Zibelius-Chen, K. *Die ägyptische Expansion nach Nubien.* Wiesbaden, 1988.

GERALD E. KADISH

PEPY I (ruled c.2354–2310 BCE), a king of the sixth dynasty, Old Kingdom. It is tempting to describe Pepy's reign as the zenith of the Old Kingdom, considering all his achievements, particularly the number of his architectural constructions and the quality of the works of art of his time. Despite some important recent discoveries, there are still many uncertainties regarding his reign. He was the son of Teti (r. 2374–2354 BCE) and of the queen Ipout. His titulature designated him as the Horus *Meritawy* ("beloved of the Two Lands"), "the son of Re, Pepy," the King of Upper and Lower Egypt *Meryre* ("beloved of Re"), with the prenomen *Nefersahor* ("excellent is the protection of Horus"). This titulature is attested by diverse documents (such as vestiges of cartouches in his own tomb and inscriptions at Tomas, in Nubia). His reign was so long that historians disagree about its duration. A census of cattle was taken twenty-five times during his reign (meaning that he reigned for at least fifty years—and the Manethonian sources attribute fifty-three regnal years to him). [*See* Manetho.]

Pepy I was a great builder. His name is found at Bubastis, Abydos, Dendera (confirming his attachment to the cult of the goddess Hathor), and in Elephantine; he sent expeditions to the Wadi Hammamat and the copper mines of the Sinai; his presence is known at Tomas, at Abydos, and throughout Nubia. As the great inscription of Unas at Abydos shows, the army of Pepy I intervened in the Palestinian confines. The provincial administration grew very powerful during his reign. His *sed*-festival was celebrated in his thirty-sixth year, as attested by a number of documents, some of which are beautiful calcite (Egyptian alabaster) vases. A small statue of the seated king, also in calcite (Egyptian alabaster), has been found, as has another in schist, in which he is kneeling in the pose of one making an offering. Especially notable are fragments of a metal statue found at Hierakonpolis, expressing a natural grandeur.

Pepy I's funerary complex, situated to the south of the middle part of the necropolis at Saqqara, has been the object of a long process of clearing. The French Archaeological Mission at Saqqara (MAFS) has gathered from the site many statues of kneeling prisoners, arms linked in front, their expressive faces presenting a striking ethnographical gallery of the peoples of Africa and the Near East. His pyramid was called *Men-nefer-Pepy* ("Pepy is

PEPY I. *The ruined mortuary temple of Pepy I at Saqqara.* (Courtesy Dieter Arnold)

stable and perfect"); this name, *Men-nefer,* is the origin of the designation of the nearby capital, transcribed by the ancient Greeks as Memphis. The pyramid was originally 50 meters (160 feet) in height, and so was easily visible from the valley. Today, however, it has been reduced to a mound only 10 meters (32 feet) high, since it was stripped away on all sides (each of which was 76 meters/240 feet long). During the clearing away of the funerary chamber, almost three thousand blocks and fragments of many dimensions were gathered, and by matching adjacent pieces the walls could therefore be put in place again. Their hieroglyphs are magnificently engraved, often retaining their painting, which is in an eternally fertile green. These reliefs furnish long sequences of the Pyramid Texts, the most ancient funerary compositions of humanity, intended for the resurrection of the pharaoh.

Several wives of Pepy I have been attested. There was a queen who was put aside after a harem conspiracy (and whose name has remained unknown). There were also two sisters from a noble family of Abydos, who were both named Ahkhesenpepy (or Ankhesenmerire). Through the excavations led by the MAFS to the immediate south of the king's pyramid, additional queens of Pepy I became known: Noubounet, Inenek/Inti (who carried the title of vizier), and Mehaa, the mother of a prince Horneterykhet.

The continuing excavation should bring further discoveries.

BIBLIOGRAPHY

Orientalia (Rome). Reports about the excavations of the MAFS in the funerary complexes of the king and his queens have been published regularly in the journal.
"Pepy I." In *Lexikon der Ägyptologie,* 6:926–927. Wiesbaden, 1982.

JEAN LECLANT
Translated from French by Susan Romanosky

PEPY II (ruled c.2300–2206 BCE), last important king of the sixth dynasty, Old Kingdom. According to traditional historiography, Pepy II was Horus *Neter-Khâou* ("deity of apparitions"), the "son of Re" *Neferkare* ("the *ka* of Re is perfect"), the King of Upper and Lower Egypt *Pepy.* After his reign, a poorly known period of Egyptian history began, leading into the First Intermediate Period. Possibly the increasing status of the governors of the nomes resulted from a weakening of the royal power brought about by the advanced age of Pepy II. Admittedly, though, many of the facts necessary to understand the fall of the Old Kingdom are missing.

Pepy II was only six years old when his predecessor Merenre Antyemsaf died; a magnificent statue in the

PEPY II. *The Pyramid of Pepy II at Saqqara.* (Courtesy Dieter Arnold)

Brooklyn Museum shows, in exceptional fashion, the very young king seated on the knees of his mother. He was traditionally thought to have reigned until his hundreth year, thereby enjoying the longest reign in world history. New readings of the documents, however, significantly lower the duration. In fact, only one date is known, the "thirty-third census year," which would be the sixty-sixth year of his reign.

Many famous inscriptions date from this period. Horkhuf, in his rock-cut tomb at Aswan, tells the story of the trade missions that he led to the South, as far as the country of Yam, in order to bring back "all kinds of rare and excellent products"; he also brought back a pygmy (from the forests of Central Africa) for the pleasure of his sovereign. Soon, Egypt's relations with the countries to its south became difficult. The prince and chancellor Mehu was killed there; his remains were brought back by his son Sabni in the course of another mission. In another direction, to the northwest of Egypt, signs of Pepy II are present in the oasis of the Libyan desert. At Byblos, to the northeast in Syria-Palestine, vases with his name attest to the pursuit of active commercial exchanges there.

The funerary complex of Pepy II, situated at South Saqqara, was excavated in the 1930s and published by the Swiss archaeologist Gustave Jéquier; the sanctuary is decorated with some excellent bas-reliefs. The pyramid, called *Men-ankh-Pepy* ("Pepy endures and lives"), had concealed in its funerary chamber many passages of the Pyramid Texts, which are also present in the remains of the pyramids of three of his queens: Neith, Ipuit (Apuit), and Wedjebten.

BIBLIOGRAPHY

Beckerath, Jürgen von "Pepy II." In *Lexikon der Ägyptologie*, 6:927–929. Wiesbaden, 1982.
Jéquier, Gustave. *Les pyramides des reines Neit et Apouit.* Cairo, 1933.
Jéquier, Gustave. *Le monument funéraire de Pépi II.* 3 vol. Cairo, 1936–1940.

JEAN LECLANT
Translated from French by Susan Romanosky

PERFUME. *See* Toiletries and Cosmetics.

PERSIA. In 529 BCE, the Greek general of mercenaries, Phanes of Halicarnassus, betrayed the Egyptian pharaoh Amasis (r. 570–526 BCE). Thus the Persian king Cambyses II was able to threaten the Egyptian frontier. After Amasis died, his successor, Psamtik III, was conquered and captured by Cambyses in the battle of Pelusium (525 BCE).

Egypt then became, with Cyprus and Phoenicia, the sixth satrapy of the Achaemenid Empire. With Cambyses II, the First Persian Occupation began Egypt's twenty-seventh dynasty, and it includes Darius I (r. 521–486 BCE), Xerxes (r. 486–465 BCE), Artaxerxes I (r. 465–424 BCE), Darius II (r. 423–405 BCE), and Artaxerxes II (405–359 BCE). The Greek historian Herodotus traveled in Egypt about 450 BCE, so the Egypt he described was a Persian satrapy.

Memphis continued as the capital (as it had been under the previous Saite dynasty) and was soon the residence of the Persian satrap, who headed Egypt's entire administration. Various officials and numerous scribes were employed, and among these were Egyptian scribes for reports in their native language, while the official language became Aramaic. The garrison posts continued to be situated in Mareotis, Daphnis, and Elephantine, yet everywhere in the Nile Valley, between the Delta and Nubia, there was a presence of Near Eastern foreigners, merchants, and soldiers—Phoenicians, Ionians, and Carians—from all of the satrapies throughout the Achaemend Empire.

The First Persian Occupation began with Cambyses, who undertook an "Africa" policy, with three unsuccessful expeditions against Carthage on the Mediterranean, against the oasis of the Libyan Desert, and against Nubia. Cambyses assumed a pharaonic guise, as indicated by autobiographical texts of Wedjahorresenet, a high official and court doctor. The texts are engraved on his naophorus statue (now in the Vatican Museum), a basalt statute brought from Egypt and discovered at Tivoli in the ruins of Hadrian's villa. Wedjahorresenet served under Amasis, Cambyses, and Darius I. For Cambyses Wedjahorresenet created the epithet *mswty-R‘* ("Born of Re"). Cambyses was interested in removing the "foreigners" (evidently members of the army of occupation) from the temple of Neith at Sais, to purify the temple, to return to the goddess her annuity, and to reestablish the priests, ceremonies, and processions as they had been before.

Ruin and oppression certainly could have occurred throughout Egypt during the violence of the conquest; but the evidence for the ferocity and impiety of Cambyses in Egypt, referred to by the Greek historians, is not supported by contemporary Egyptian documents. A stela from the Serapeum (the underground catacombs where the Apis bulls were buried at Saqqara) dated from the sixth year of the Cambyses rule, testifies that Cambyses did not kill Apis, but that instead, the sacred bull, born in Year 27 of Amasis, received solemn obsequies and was buried in a sarcophagus donated by the same Cambyses, and that the succeeding Apis, born during the reign of Cambyses, died of natural causes in Year 4 of Darius I (as is shown by another stela from the Serapeum). To understand the foundation of the anti-Cambyses tradition, it is worth considering the resentment on the part of the Egyp-

tian priesthood, which had been stung by Cambyses' decree that drastically limited royal subsidies to the Egyptian temples previously in effect.

The posthumous persecutions of Amasis by Persian conquerors is suggested by the Cambyses legend related by the Greek and Roman historians. In it, Cambyses, a grandson of Apries, took revenge against the usurper Amasis and reclaimed the throne of his grandfather. In 522 BCE, on the return trip home to Persia, Cambyses died from a leg infection incurred while in Syria. There, in the court circle of Susa, the rebellion broke out of the sorcerer Gaumata, claimant to the legitimate succession of Cyrus. The circumstances of the death (a dagger wound to the thigh that became gangrenous) are related by Herodotus as proof of divine punishment—since the wound was in the same spot that would have resulted from an attack on the Apis bull by Cambyses. According to Diodorus Siculus, Cambyses' death is punishment for his impiety. He is contrasted with the piety of his successor Darius I, who was generous toward the temples of the Egyptian gods and revoked Cambyses' decree.

Darius I (522–486 BCE) was the son of Istaspe, satrap of Hyrcania; Darius was a tolerant and strong ruler who restored order in the empire and conquered a new province, India. According to Diodorus, Darius I was the sixth and last law-giver of Egypt, as confirmed by the Demotic papyrus mentioned above. In his third year of rule, Darius ordered his satrap in Egypt to convene the learned among the soldiers, the priests, and the scribes so as to codify the laws in use to Year 44 of the reign of Amasis. His committee of wise men sat for sixteen years, until Darius's nineteenth year. Between his nineteenth and twenty-seventh year, the committee was reunited at Susa and the laws were transcribed on papyrus in Aramaic and Demotic. Such a juridical guide for Egypt was needed by the administration of that satrapy, since they were generally Persian or Babylonian and their official language was Aramaic.

The protection accorded to Egyptian temples and priests by Darius I was extended to the construction of a grand temple to Amun-Re, in the Kharga Oasis (an archive of Persian-era Demotic ostraca was recently found at Deir Manawir). Darius I's building activities in Egypt are also known from the hieroglyphic inscriptions in the quarries of Wadi Hammamat, from blocks with Darius' cartouche found at Elkab, and from those at Busiris in the Delta. A large number of the Saqqara Serapeum stelae have dates between the third and fourteenth year of Darius I. A small stela from the Faiyum (now in the Berlin Museum) is dedicated to Darius I in the form of the falcon-god Horus. The Vatican naophorus statue of Wedjahorresnet reveals that Darius ordered restoration work at the "House of Life" at Sais.

Yet rebellion against the Persians was constant. Aryan-des, the first satrap of Egypt, was deposed by Darius I after rebelling. Pherendates succeeded him in 492 BCE and was the satrap to whom Peteese of Teudjoi referred his petition in Year 9 of Darius I, to obtain justice (Demotic Papyrus Rylands IX). To intensify contact with the Egyptian satrapy, Darius I accomplished an objective imagined but never carried out by Necho II—the opening of a navigable route from the Nile to the Red Sea. This was accomplished by means of a canal 45 meters wide and 5 meters deep (130 by 15 feet) that could be traveled for some 84 kilometers (52 miles), enabling navigation from Bubastis at Lake Timsah by the Bitter Lakes (Gulf of Heroonpolita) to the Red Sea in four days. Along the route of the canal were erected commemorative stelae of large dimensions—over 3 meters (10 feet) in height and 2 meters (6 feet) in width—in the three languages of the empire: Elamite, Akkadian, and Old Persian; they were located at Suez, at Chaluf or Kebret, at the Serapeum, and at Pithom (Tell el-Maskhuta). The waterway, which tended to silt up in the southern part, was put back into use under Ptolemy II (according to the stela discovered at Pithom) and also under the Roman emperor Hadrian. From as early as Cambyses, the Persian kings resorted to Egyptian sculptors and stonemasons, who are often mentioned on the Elamite foundation tablets of Persepolis. Many learned Egyptians, especially doctors, resided at the Court of Susa.

Trade with Persia was important to Egypt. An Aramaic text, recovered by B. Porten and A. Yardeni, contains the accounts of many colonies and of maritime traffic for a port (probably Memphis) during Year 11 of Xerxes I (475 BCE). The captains of the ships—which brought gold, silver, wine, oil, and lumber—are indicated as Ionians and have Greek names (e.g., Simonides, Moskhos, Tymokledes, Mikkos, Iokles, Phanes', etc.); other ships' captains are perhaps Phoenician. The boats returned loaded with Egyptian natron (sodium carbonate), highly valued in antiquity for the manufacture of glass.

From 404 to 343 BCE, the recovered independence of Egypt included the twenty-eighth, twenty-ninth, and thirtieth dynasties. The rulers of the thirtieth dynasty defended Egypt from Persia's attempts at reconquest, even resorting to alliances with the Greeks. Nektanebo I secured the support of the priesthood by a maneuver that consisted of a customs tax on merchandise that arrived at Naukratis in the Nile Delta (the Greek emporium from the time of the Saite kings), allotting 10 percent of the tax to the temple of Neith at Sais. Nektanebo's son Tachos (or Teos; r. 362–360 BCE) intervened militarily in an anti-Persian role in Syria, but his uncle, the general Tjahapimu, who was kept in Egypt as regent, took advantage by placing his own son, Nektanebo, by the Queen Udjashu, on the throne. This change was favored because of the discord incurred by the financial measures that Tachos

took. He limited the priests' revenues and a tax was imposed on housing and on the grain to be offered to Atria, in addition to the tenth due on ships and crafts. Tachos, betrayed by the Spartan general Agesilaos, fled Egypt, took refuge at Sidon, and then at the Persian court at Susa.

Nektanebo II (r. 361/60–343 BCE) repelled two Persian invasions: one in 358 BCE, by the army of Prince Artaxerxes; the second in 351 BCE, led by the same man, now Artaxerxes III Ochus. When he retook Cyprus and Sidon, he was able to land at Pelusium in the Nile Delta. From Pelusium, the Persians then took the other cities of the Delta and as far south as Memphis. Nektanebo II escaped to Nubia with his treasure. Classical sources accuse Artaxerxes III of violence and brutality even more subtle than that ascribed to Cambyses. Then in 338 BCE, the eunuch Bagoas murdered Artaxerxes; in 336 BCE, he also killed the king's son and successor Xerxes. Under Darius III, the satrap Sabace fought and died at Issus. The last Persian satrap, Mazaces, lost Egypt to Alexander the Great of Macedon in 332 BCE. The Achaemenid Empire had ended, and Egypt had become a province once more. After Alexander, the Ptolemies and then the Romans became the masters of the Nile Valley, which was governed by foreign rulers until after World War II.

[See also Achaemenids; and Late Period, *the overview article and the article on the* Thirty-first Dynasty.]

BIBLIOGRAPHY

Briant, P. *Histoire de l'Empire perse.* Paris, 1996.
Curtis, John. *Ancient Persia.* London, 1988.
Dandamaev, M. *A Political History of the Archaemenid Empire.* Leiden, 1989.
Erich, Robert W., ed. *Chronologies in Old World Archaeology.* 3d ed. Chicago, 1992.
Nissen, Hans J. *The Early History of the Ancient Near East, 9000–2000 B.C.* Chicago, 1988.
Sherwin-White, Susan M., and Amélie Kuhrt. *From Sardis to Samarkand.* London, 1993.
Young, T. Cuyler, Jr., et al., eds. *The Hilly Flanks and Beyond: Essays on the Prehistory of Southwestern Asia Presented to Robert J. Braidwood.* Studies in Ancient Oriental Civilization, 36. Chicago, 1983.

EDDA BRESCIANI
Translated from Italian by Jennifer Worth

PERSIAN PERIOD. *See* Late Period, *overview article.*

PETAMENOPHIS. The most extensive private tomb constructed at any Egyptian site during the pharaonic era belonged to a little-known chief lector-priest, Petamenophis, who lived from the late twenty-fifth into the early twenty-sixth dynasties. Although that title was the highest rank recorded on his tomb, the tomb's massive size indicated that he was one of the most influential individuals in Upper Egypt at that time. Probably constructed during the earliest decades of the twenty-sixth dynasty, his tomb was located within a series of monuments built for local officials in the Asassif region of the Theban plain, dating from about 700–540 BCE. Sometimes considered an expression of an "Archaic revival," the tombs actually follow a four hundred year hiatus of tomb building; yet they incorporate features from nearby private tombs and mortuary temples of the preceding periods, rather than recalling elements of much earlier dynasties. These tombs are conspicuous for their size and complexity, as well as for their shared features, such as the massive mud-brick superstructures, the dramatic subterranean courtyards, the innovative use of architectural sculpture, and the multilevel burial chambers.

The inscriptions from one of the seven known statues of Petamenophis indicate that he was consecrated as lector-priest in 662–661 BCE. Most probably, he achieved the rank of chief lector priest in following years. He lived during the era that coincided with Mentuemhet's term of office as governor of Upper Egypt, yet the mention of any king or "Divine Adoratress" (a female relative of a Nubian king, installed as religious leader at Thebes) is noticeably absent from Petamenophis' tomb. Anthes (1937) speculated that such an omission would be more likely during a period of foreign rule (during the rule of the Nubians of the twenty-fifth dynasty, rather than that of the twenty-sixth dynasty). Petamenophis' name does not appear on the Saite Oracle Papyrus, dated to 651 BCE, with Mentuemhet and other Theban high officials of the early twenty-sixth dynasty. Nor is there any other evidence that Petamenophis lived far into the twenty-sixth dynasty. Mentuemhet clearly did, and perhaps he was a younger, regional contemporary of Petamenophis.

BIBLIOGRAPHY

Anthes, R. "Der Berliner Hocker des Petamenophis." *Zeitschrift für ägyptische Sprache und Altertumskunde* 73 (1937), 29.

Bianchi, Robert Steven. "Petamenophis." In *Lexikon der Ägyptologie*, 4: 991–992. Wiesbaden, 1982. Good additional bibliography.

Eigner, Diethelm. *Die Monumentalen Grabbauten der Spätzeit in der Thebanischen Nekropole*. Vienna, 1984. Provides a comprehensive overview of the Theban Late period tombs.

Loukianoff, Grégoire. "Les statues et les objects funéraires de Peduamonapet," *Annales du Service des Antiquités de l'Égypte* 37 (1937), 219–232. Identifies objects bearing Petamenophis' name and titles, although some have been disregarded (see Bianchi, 1982).

Porter, Bertha, and Rosalind L. B. Moss. *Topographical Bibliography of Ancient Egyptian Hieroglyphic Texts, Reliefs, and Paintings*, vol. I, 1, 2d ed., pp. 50–56. Oxford, 1960. References, plans, wall scenes, texts, and finds from Theban tomb 33.

Thomas, Nancy Katherine. "A Typological Study of Saite Tombs at Thebes." Ph.D. diss., Univ. of California, Los Angeles, 1980. Discusses the chronology of Late period tomb owners and the development of tombs.

NANCY THOMAS

PETOSIRIS, (Eg., *p3-di-wsir*, "he whom Osiris has given"; also called *Khapakhonsu*) was high priest of Thoth and *lesonis*-priest (*oikonomos*, head of finance) of the temple of Thoth at Hermopolis during the second half of the fourth century BCE. He is famous today for the well-preserved family chapel that he erected at Tuna el-Gebel.

The family of Petosiris had been protégés and appointees of the thirtieth dynasty. His father Es-shu had administered the temple at royal behest, probably under Nektanebo II, and it was one of Es-shu's younger sons, Petosiris, who eventually took over his father's estate as "Master of All His Property," and "Greatest of the Five, Controller of the Cult-seats," priestly titles of the fifteenth (Hermopolitan) nome of Upper Egypt. With priesthoods at Horwer and Nefrusi, as well as the sacerdotal functions for Thoth and Amun-Re, Petosiris received his inheritance just when Egypt was about to endure the second Persian occupation, by the army of Artaxerxes III in 342 BCE. His vivid account of the devastation caused by this invasion—it cannot be dated later—is now graphically supported by the excavations at Mendes, which show the fury and methodical demolition of the site by the Persians:

> I have been faithful to the lord of Hermopolis since I was born, and his every counsel was in my heart. [He] selected me to administer his temple . . . and I passed seven years as *lesonis*-priest of this god, adminstering his income . . . when all the while a foreign ruler was *dominus* over Egypt, and nothing was in its former place. For war had broken out in Egypt: the South raged and the North was in uproar, and people went about bewildered. No temple had its staff, and the priests were dispersed(?); there was no telling what might happen therein in the future.

Petosiris shepherded his nome through this period of crisis and was later revered as a leading man of his city, "with many dwellings and fields and cattle without number."

For the art historian, the tomb and family chapel loom large because they reflect the first impact of Greek art and culture on Egypt. Petosiris survived the arrival of Alexander in Egypt and witnessed the early influx of Greek settlers and their influence. Together with his son and successor, Tachos, he erected the bipartite tomb chapel, with an inner chamber over the sarcophagus dedicated to his ancestors, and an outer transverse hall provided an intercolumnar screen celebrating himself. While the inner chamber is decorated in the traditional Egyptian canon, the outer chamber features scenes from the traditional Egyptian repertoire of agriculture, animal husbandry, and viticulture, rendered under the strong influence of the classical Greek canon. Some aspects, such as the use of profile, echelon, and stance, hark back to a Nilotic past, but the musculature, individual likeness, irregular spac-

PETOSIRIS. *Relief from the tomb of Petosiris at Tuna el-Gebel.* (Courtesy Donald B. Redford)

ing, and costume point to the advent of a classical Greek style. The reliefs are important in demonstrating how, at the beginning of Ptolemaic period, in contrast to what was to come later, even a provincial city such as Hermopolis, far from the Nile Delta, was open to external influence.

BIBLIOGRAPHY

Briant, P. *Histoire de l'Empire perse de Cyrus à Alexandre.* Paris, 1996.
Lefebvre, G. *Le tombeau de Petosiris.* Paris, 1924.

DONALD B. REDFORD

PETRIE, WILLIAM MATTHEW FLINDERS

(1853–1942), archaeologist, born at Charlton, Kent, on 17 June 1853. His father, William Petrie, was a civil engineer and surveyor; his mother, Anne, was the daughter of Matthew Flinders, the navigator and explorer. Petrie was a delicate child, educated by his parents at home. His mother taught him music, history, and French, and encouraged him in her own hobbies, geology and coin-collecting, while his father schooled him in mathematics and science and taught him surveying. Together they measured Stonehenge, and Petrie surveyed ancient earthworks in the West Country. In 1880 he went to Egypt to test the theory that the Great Pyramid had been built by divine inspiration. He surveyed the whole pyramid field, and his careful measurements refuted the theories of the "British Israelites," which brought him to the attention of scholars. Distressed at the destruction of the monuments by careless excavators and treasure-hunters, he eagerly accepted the suggestion of Amelia Edwards, secretary of the newly founded Egypt Exploration Society, that he should excavate at Tanis in the Nile Delta. In his first season (1883–1884), he laid down new principles of scientific excavation in Egypt: careful recording of all finds, even broken objects unfit for museum display, and personal supervision of his workmen, whom he rewarded for what they found. Pottery and potsherds, until then discarded as rubbish, became valuable for relative dating purposes. In the following year, Petrie discovered two Greek cities in the Delta, Naukratis and Daphne; a wealth of Greek pottery confirmed their identities.

When he left the Egypt Exploration Society in 1886, Edwards helped him find private sponsorship. In the Faiyum Depression, to the west of the Nile, he opened two brick pyramids, found a number of mummies of the Roman period with painted portraits, and excavated a Middle Kingdom town. In 1890, he was persuaded to dig in Palestine; at Tell el-Hesy he cut a section through the mound, dating the levels there using recovered pottery from Egypt, with which he was familiar; for this he has been called "the father of Palestinian archaeology." At Tell el-Amarna, one winter, he found the palace of Akhenaten, with its painted pavement, and Aegean pottery, which established a chronological link with the Mycenaean world. In 1892, Edwards died; she left money to found a chair of Egyptology at University College, London and wanted the new professor to excavate in Egypt and train students. She made it clear that Petrie was her choice. In 1905, he left the Egypt Exploration Society for good and founded the British School of Archaeology in Egypt; his wife Hilda (Urlin), whom he had married in 1896, acted as its secretary and main fundraiser for the rest of their lives, besides helping him in the field.

One of Petrie's most important contributions to archaeological science was his system called Sequence Dating. Another was his discovery of the royal tombs of the first dynasty at Abydos (1899–1903). *Methods and Aims in Archaeology* (London, 1904) was to become a textbook for his students, many of whom, having survived the spartan regime of a Petrie camp, became archaeologists of the next generation. Petrie set an example with the prompt publication of his excavation reports; a number of popular books; the journal *Ancient Egypt* (which he edited); and lectures that fostered public interest in Egyptology. Elected a Fellow of the Royal Society in 1902 and a Fellow of the British Academy in 1904, he was knighted in 1923. In 1935, he moved to Palestine; his last fieldwork was on large tells near the Egyptian frontier. He died on 29 July 1942, and he is buried in Jerusalem, his last home.

Petrie's "Journals" and letters from the field (from 1880 to 1926) are in the Griffith Institute, Oxford; copies of these, and his notebooks and diaries, are in the Petrie Museum at University College, London.

BIBLIOGRAPHY

Drower, M. S. *Flinders Petrie: A Life in Archaeology.* London, 1985; reprinted, Madison, 1995.

Petrie, W. M. F. *Seventy Years in Archaeology.* London, 1931.

Uphill, E. P. "Bibliography: W. M. F. Petrie." *Journal of Near Eastern Studies* 31 (1942), 356–379.

MARGARET S. DROWER

PETUABASTIS, a name given to several kings of the Third Intermediate Period and Late period, meaning "gift of Bast."

Petuabastis I (r. 813–c.773 BCE) first king of the twenty-third (Tanite or Libyan) dynasty of the Third Intermediate Period. The third-century BCE Egyptian historian Manetho called the dynasty *Tanite*, pinpointing the city of Tanis, in the eastern Nile Delta, as the place of family origin (not its capital), implying that it was an offshoot of the

twenty-second dynasty. The relationship of Petuabastis I to Sheshonq III is unknown, although they may have been brothers. The seat of the twenty-third dynasty, however, is not certain. Its last ruler, Iuput II, was named after Petuabastis I's coregent Iuput I, who reigned at Leontopolis (Tell Moqdam) as Piya's victory stela indicates; the burial of a Queen Kama(ma), mother of Osorkon III(?), was found at Tell Moqdam. Petuabastis I and his entire line probably reigned at Tell Moqdam, other monuments of theirs are known from the Nile Delta and Memphis and not only from Thebes, where it has been suggested that the dynasty may have reigned. In his fifteenth and sixteenth years of reign, Petuabastis I had a short-lived coregent, Iuput I. The separate regime of Petuabastis I enabled the rebellious Thebans to withdraw recognition of the twenty-second dynasty kings in favor of the new line.

Petuabastis II. This local king in Tanis is known from inscriptions at Tanis, an unfinished statue at Memphis, and blocks at the museum in Copenhagen. Petuabastis II was encountered in Tanis by Assurbanipal, king of Assyria, in 667–666 BCE, and dethroned by him in 665 BCE. He recurred in later Egyptian tradition in four of six Demotic tales in the *Inaros–Petuabastis Cycle.* The known manuscripts are of Greco-Roman date; one of them also names Esarhaddon of Assyria.

Petuabastis III. A minor rebel king of the First Persian Occupation, or twenty-seventh dynasty, Late period, Seheribre Petuabastis III had a reign of uncertain date. He may have been in power as early as the end of the reign of either Cambyses, who ruled from 525 to 522 BCE, or Darius I, who ruled from 521 to 486 BCE.

BIBLIOGRAPHY

Habachi, Labib. "Three Monuments of the Unknown King Sehetepibre Pedubastis." *Zeitschrift für Ägyptische Sprache und Altertumskunde* 93 (1966), 69–74.

Kitchen, K. A. *The Third Intermediate Period in Egypt (1100–650 BC).* 2d ed. with suppl. Warminster, 1996. Gives essential references with discussions.

KENNETH A. KITCHEN

PHARAOH. *See* Kingship.

PHILADELPHIA. *See* Faiyum.

PHILAE, an island at the First Cataract of the Nile (24°02′N, 32°59′E), on the southern frontier of Ancient Egypt. It is the site of the most beautiful of all ancient Egyptian temples. In the 1970s, the architectural structures of the original island were moved to their present

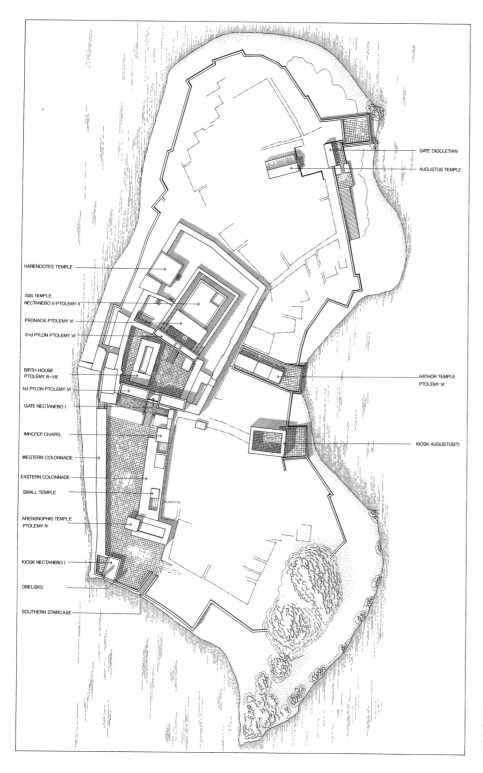

HARENDOTES TEMPLE

ISIS TEMPLE
NECTANEBO II/PTOLEMY II

PRONAOS PTOLEMY VI

2nd PYLON PTOLEMY VI

BIRTH HOUSE
PTOLEMY III–VIII

1st PYLON PTOLEMY VI

GATE NECTANEBO I

IMHOTEP CHAPEL

WESTERN COLONNADE

EASTERN COLONNADE

SMALL TEMPLE

ARENSNUPHIS TEMPLE
PTOLEMY IV

KIOSK NECTANEBO I

OBELISKS

SOUTHERN STAIRCASE

GATE DIOCLETIAN

AUGUSTUS TEMPLE

HATHOR TEMPLE
PTOLEMY VI

KIOSK AUGUSTUS(?)

PHILAE. *Plan of the island of Philae in Roman times.* (From Dieter Arnold, *Temples of the Last Pharaohs.* Oxford University Press, 1999.)

position on the island of Agilkia, to the northwest, when Philae was about to become permanently flooded by the construction of the Aswan High Dam. The new location was carefully landscaped to make it resemble Philae as much as possible.

In Egyptian religious thought, islands and hills were regarded as sources of creative power, a concept which goes far to explain the cultic importance of a number of islands in the First Cataract area. Philae and the neighboring island of Biga to the west formed an integrated religious complex devoted to the cult of Osiris. The ritual focus was Biga, the site of the *abaton*, one of the alleged tombs of Osiris; Philae was dedicated preeminently to Isis, his sister-wife, who became the epitome of the divine wife and mother and thus the most popular of all Egyptian goddesses in the Late and Greco-Roman periods. Although Isis was the major deity of the Philae, the site's location on the frontier between Egypt and Nubia meant that the cults of Nubia also featured on the island, where they were represented by significant cult buildings.

The monuments are dominated by the great temple of Isis and its associated structures, which are concentrated in the west and center of the island on, or adjacent to, a granite outcrop which must have been chosen originally as an embodiment of the primeval hill on which the holy-of-holies of all Egyptian temples was claimed to rest. There is some evidence at Philae of cult activity in honor of Amun in the time of the Nubian pharaoh Taharqa who ruled Egypt between 689 and 664 BCE. These meager traces might well mean that the rise of this frontier religious center owed something to the kings of the Nubian twenty-fifth dynasty, to which Taharqa belonged; however, the earliest known cult building in honor of Isis was a small shrine erected in the Saite period by Psamtik II. This was followed by a further small temple on the granite outcrop, erected by Amasis. Therefore, it now seems that the Saite kings introduced the cult of Isis into this area and laid the foundations for her subsequent glorification on the island.

The next evidence of building dates to the thirtieth dynasty and takes the form of a kiosk of Nektanebo I, which is now situated at the southwestern end of the main temple, and a gate of the same king embedded in the first pylon of the main temple. The gateway clearly formed part of a thirtieth dynasty enclosure wall, but all these features should be regarded as embellishments to the preexisting Saite temple enclosure, because there seems to be no trace of a substantial temple of thirtieth dynasty date.

The building work in the main Isis temple area is overwhelmingly Ptolemaic and forms part of the well-documented Ptolemaic policy of promoting the Isis cult throughout the kingdom and beyond, although a substantial amount of the decoration was added in the Roman period. The core of the Isis temple—everything north of the vestibule—was built by Ptolemy II just behind the ancient shrine of Amasis, which was then demolished. Its decoration, as is normal at this and similar sites, was added sporadically for a long time. This temple was surrounded by a brick girdle wall which almost certainly followed the line of that of the thirtieth dynasty and showed the undulating pattern in laying the brick courses, which was typical of such late structures. This feature may have been used for entirely practical reasons, but it has also

been claimed that it imitates the waves of the primeval ocean surrounding the primeval hill on which all temples were claimed to rest.

The temple shows an intriguing ground plan in that the main building has two axes: the main cult area accessed by the second pylon is skewed northeastward in relation to the court to the south. This feature probably arose from the interaction of several factors: the preexistence of the temple of Amasis; a determination to maintain the granite outcrop as the center of cult activity; and the configuration of the island itself—that is, any expansion of the central shrine to the south would have to be skewed to fit the available space. The temple in its final form is a much expanded structure that is entered by the first pylon (Ptolemy V–VI), which gives access to a court flanked on the left by a *mammisi*, probably begun by Ptolemy III but expanded and completed by Ptolemy VIII. This structure, typical of late temples, was, for ritual purposes, the site of the birth of Harpocrates, the son of Isis and Osiris. On the eastern side there stands a colonnade probably built by Ptolemy VIII. The much smaller second pylon, probably completed by Ptolemy VI, leads via a court and vestibule to the sanctuary dedicated to Isis and her son Harpocrates. Throughout the main temple area there are many examples of work added during the Roman period: for example, the birth-house contains reliefs dating to the reigns of Augustus and Tiberius, who feature alongside Antoninus in the inner part of the temple; the temple is accessed from the west via a gate associated with the emperors Hadrian, Marcus Aurelius, and Lucius Verus; and the enclosure also contained, to the north, a Claudian temple dedicated to Harendotes, the son of Osiris as champion and protector of his father. In the mid-sixth century CE the island of Isis was Christianized, and a number of churches were dedicated there, including one to the Virgin Mary and one to Saint Stephen, the former being the standard Christian substitute for Isis and the second a highly appropriate replacement for Harendotes. This cultic change brought with it the usual rash of mutilations to the pagan monuments.

The buildings of the Isis enclosure are supplemented by numerous subsidiary structures. To the south lies the long Outer Court, which now forms the main point of access to the temple enclosure. At its southern entrance stands the kiosk of Nektanebo I, removed there no later than the reign of Ptolemy XII and flanked by colonnades of Roman date on the western and eastern sides. In addition, the eastern colonnade embodies the remains of a temple of the Nubian god Arensnuphis (Ptolemaic with some Roman decoration), a well-preserved shrine of Imhotep (Ptolemy V), and a further cult-place often ascribed on quite inadequate evidence to the Nubian deity Mandulis.

PHILAE. *Antique depiction of the temple area at Philae.*

There are numerous other buildings to the north, east, and south which are more loosely connected with the enclosure. At the water's edge on the northeastern section of the island stands a spectacular Roman-period gate, which was probably a triumphal arch of Emperor Diocletian. There are also a temple dedicated to the cult of Rome and Augustus and two Coptic churches, as well as the remains of a Coptic monastery. To the east of the great enclosure wall lies a temple of Hathor (Ptolemy VI/VIII and early Roman), a deity with close affinities with Isis who was associated, in particular, with the neighboring island of Biga. Finally, to the south of Hathor's temple and overlooking the Nile stands a beautiful but unfinished kiosk often ascribed to Trajan; it certainly received such decoration as it has in his reign, but the building itself may well be earlier.

In addition to these major structures, the original island of Philae also contained mud-brick settlement remains on the northern part of the island and to the east and southeast. These areas would originally have housed the staff that served the temple, but the remains that were extant until the floodwaters destroyed them are described in the literature as Roman and Christian.

It is difficult to overrate the importance of the religious complex at Philae. It provides us with a major late cult center which is exceptionally well-preserved. Beginning in the Saite period and continuing into the thirtieth dynasty, it underwent a spectacular flowering in the Greco-Roman period, and, becuase of the circumstances of its dismantling and removal, there is possible a unique insight into its architectural evolution until and including its conversion to a Christian center. In addition, the voluminous texts and iconography yield much information on the last centuries of pharaonic religious thought and practice. In fact, Philae was the last bastion of ancient Egyptian culture, and it is no coincidence that the latest datable hieroglyphic inscription (24 August 394 CE) comes from Philae.

BIBLIOGRAPHY

Bernand, A. *Les inscriptions grecques de Philae.* Vol. 1, *Epoques ptolémaiques.* Vol. 2, *Haut et Bas Empire.* Paris, 1969. This collection includes inscriptions from the Ptolemaic period to the late Roman Empire.

Giammarusti, Antonio, and Alessandro Roccati. *File, storia e vita di un santuario egizio.* Rome, 1980. Good, well-illustrated survey of the history and salvage of the site.

Haeny, Gerhard. "A Short Architectural History of Philae." *Bulletin de l'Institut Français d'Archéologie Orientale* 18 (1985), 197–233. An invaluable short account of the archaeological data gleaned from moving the temple to its new site.

Iversen, E. *Obelisks in Exile: The Obelisks of Istanbul and England.* Copenhagen, 1972. Contains a discussion of the Philae obelisk now in Kingston Lacy, Dorset.

Lyons, H. G. *A Report on the Island Temples of Philae.* Cairo, 1896. Like the following citation, an important early survey of the monuments on the site that is still of great value.

Lyons, H. G. *A Report on the Island Temples of Philae.* Cairo, 1908.

Porter, Bertha, and Rosalind L. B. Moss. *Topographical Bibliography of Ancient Egyptian Hieroglyphic Texts, Reliefs and Paintings.* Vol. 6, *Upper Egypt: Chief Temples.* Oxford, 1939–1970, pp. 202–256. Minutely detailed but not quite up-to-date guide to the site.

Vassilika, Eleni. *Ptolemaic Philae.* Orientalia Lovaniensia Analecta, 34. Leuven, 1989. A pioneering study of the architecture, iconography, and work methods employed in the Ptolemaic buildings.

Žabkar, L. V. *Hymns to Isis in Her Temple at Philae.* Hanover, N.H., and London, 1987. Analysis of eight early Ptolemaic hymns, with much useful discussion of Isis theology.

ALAN B. LLOYD

PHOENICIA. *See* Lebanon.

PIETY. The concept of piety in ancient Egypt could be defined as a personal, individual expression of faith in and devotion to a deity, as opposed to institutionalized religious practice, which was traditionally the preserve of the king. The monarch was responsible for the maintenance of *maat*—the order of the universe, both cosmic and social, as established by the creator at creation—which included the maintenance of the relationship between the gods and humankind. This was achieved via the temple rituals conducted, in theory, by the king, but in practice by priests who acted for him. The ordinary person had no role in this activity.

Historical Developments. Evidence for personal religion prior to the New Kingdom is limited. Some personal names, which in ancient Egyptian are often theophoric, hint at a personal relationship between the deity and the bearer of the name. These names are particularly common in the Late period: for example, *Padiese*, "he, whom Isis gave" (Greek, *Isidore*). Yet some are attested from earliest times: for example, *Shed-netjer*, "whom the god rescues" (from the first dynasty); from the Old Kingdom there were the names *Khui-wi-Ptah* (or *-Re, -Horus, -Khnum,* or *-Sobek*), "may Ptah (or Re, Horus, etc.) protect me." A few texts of the Middle Kingdom also make brief references to personal worship.

The paucity of evidence for personal religion prior to the New Kingdom can be explained by the limits set by what John Baines (1985) defined as "decorum," a set of rules regarding what could and could not be expressed in image and/or text in certain contexts. These guidelines can be illustrated in the way deities appeared on nonroyal monuments. Until the Middle Kingdom, decorum excluded the possibility for nonroyal persons to depict deities on their monuments; they appeared only in texts, almost exclusively of a funerary nature, or in the form of their emblems. Not until the end of the Middle Kingdom were the first representations of nonroyal persons worshiping a deity inscribed on nonroyal stelae. Even there, a barrier usually in the form of a column of inscription and/or an offering table separated the worshiper from the deity. Not until the early New Kingdom and onward did images of deities regularly appear on nonroyal monuments.

Personal religion was encouraged by New Kingdom developments that contributed to a gradual breaking down of the barriers that separated individual and deity, such as the evolution and growth of festival processions of the deities. During the New Kingdom, evidence survives for a burgeoning of such processions, when the divine images were brought out of the seclusion of their temples and carried in a portable boat-shrine along a processional way. Although the images were hidden from view in the cabins of the boats (or barks, as they are often called), the ordinary person could approach them and seek the advice of the deity on all manner of personal issues, through an oracle.

Among the earliest literary evidence for personal piety in the New Kingdom are limestone *ostraca*, dated paleographically to the pre-Amarna period, which carry short prayers addressed to the god Amun. These *ostraca* may have been placed along the processional way taken by the god, and they bear some of the earliest sentiments of love and devotion to a deity: "Amun-Re, you are the beloved one, you are the only one!"

The growth of personal piety was accompanied by a diminution of the exclusive role of the king and official religion. As Jan Assmann (1984) has pointed out, one of the aims of King Akhenaten was to reverse that trend and restore to the monarch the central role in religion, as the mediator between the one god Aten and the people. His reform failed, indeed it succeeded in achieving the exact opposite—people were not prepared to abandon their old deities, and, since the official cults of the old gods were proscribed by the king, people were forced to turn to them directly. This situation probably explains the explosion of evidence for personal piety in both post-Amarna and Ramessid times, the latter dubbed by James H. Breasted in 1912 "the age of personal piety."

The trauma of the Amarna period and its aftermath doubtless also contributed to the atmosphere of uncertainty that is evident in the following historical period. That uncertainty was illustrated by theophoric names, which contain the verb *šd* ("rescue," "save"), names such as Shed-su-Amun ("may Amun save him"). Although sporadically met in earlier periods, such names were most frequently used in the New Kingdom (Ranke 1935, p. 330 f.). The letter of the scribe Butehamun to the captain of the bowmen Shed-su-Hor ("may Horus save him") also reflected this phenomenon (Wente 1990, p. 196), as did the emergence of the god Shed, the personification of the concept of the rescuing activity of a deity demonstrated in the study of Hellmut Brunner (1958, pp. 17–19). The inscriptions of Si-mut Kiki (Wilson 1970) provide a particularly good example of some of the perceived dangers and illustrate the concept of a chosen personal deity, to whom the devotee was particularly attached and from whom protection was sought, a well-attested phenomenon of piety that made its first appearance at that time.

As Assmann pointed out (1989, p. 75 ff.), a further religious development in the New Kingdom generated a change in the role of *maat*. Whereas it was previously held that one's fate depended on one's behavior (if one lived a life in accordance with the principles of *maat* then one would perforce flourish; if one transgressed against it one would be punished—the king being the one who upheld *maat* and meted out punishment), instead one came to be seen as directly responsible to the deity, who personally intervened in the individual's life and punished wrongdoing. The misfortunes from which people then needed to be saved were not only those of an impersonal kind but also included divine wrath, meted out as punishment for perceived wrongdoing.

Sources. Archaeological sources for the practice of piety have survived in the form of shrines and votive offerings, but for a proper understanding of the phenomenon we are dependent on literary sources. These are varied, including biographical inscriptions, hymns, inscriptions on scarabs, Wisdom Literature and, in particular, the prayers (often penitential) of individuals. A very good example in a hymn may be found in those to Amun in the Leiden Papyrus (Prichard 1969, p. 369). The most important Wisdom teaching is that of Amenemope (Lichtheim 1976, pp. 146–163). The prayers of individuals, inscribed on stelae dedicated to the deity as votive offerings, are very similar to the biblical penitential psalms expressing sorrow for wrongdoing and thanks for forgiveness. The bulk of our evidence comes from the Deir el-Medina, in Western Thebes, from the village of the workmen who built the tombs of the kings. This bias is due primarily to the chance of good preservation of the site, rather than to any unique religious development that may have taken place there, although the fact that Thebes probably suffered from the excesses of the Amarna period more than other places may also have been a factor. Ashraf Sadek (1987) presented the evidence from other locations, among which the Wepwawet sanctuary at Assyut (where more than six hundred small stelae were discovered) was particularly significant.

The Elements of the Prayers. The following themes and terminology are regularly encountered in the prayers, hymns, and votive offerings:

1. The introductory words of praise and appeal to the deity often include a description of the deity who is said to be "one who hears petitions *(nḥwt),*" "who comes at the voice of the poor *(nmḥw)* in need," "who comes at the voice of him who calls to him."

2. In the description of the transgressor, the writer claims to be a "silent one," that is, a devout person *(gr);* a poor, humble person *(nmḥw).* By way of apology, the claim is made to be ignorant and senseless *(iwty ḥȝty),* to be one who does not know good *(nfr)* from evil *(bin).*

3. The writer confesses to having committed an act of transgression *(sp n thi),* to having done what is abhorrent or "taboo" *(btȝ or bwt),* to having sworn falsely *(ˤrk m ˤdȝ)* by the deity.

4. The deity punishes the transgression, often with sickness; very frequent is the expression "seeing darkness by day," an image for separation from the deity.

5. A promise is made to proclaim the might of the deity to all the world, to "son and daughter, the great and small, generations not yet born," to "the fish in the water and the birds in the air," to "the foolish and the wise."

6. An account is given of answer to prayer—the deity is said to respond to the pleas of the petitioner and "to come as a sweet breeze" to be "merciful" *(ḥtp)* to "turn" *(ˤn)* to the petitioner "in peace" *(ḥtp).*

The Deities. There was a range of deities, from the major gods and goddesses worshiped throughout Egypt (such as Amun-Re, Ptah, Hathor, Thoth, Osiris, Wepwawet, Horakhty and Haoeris) to local deities (such as Meretseger, the personification of the western mountain, "the Peak," at Thebes). Also worshipped were deified kings, such as Amenhotpe I and less commonly, mortals, such as Amenophis, Son of Hapu, an official of Amenhotpe III. Amun was popularly worshiped in his forms *pȝ rhn nfr* ("the goodly ram") and *smn nfr n ʾImn* ("the goodly goose of Amun"). The prevalence of the former was based on his animal symbol, the ram, being the most public form of the god. It decorated the prow and stern of his portable bark, and the avenues leading to his temples in Thebes were lined with statues of rams. The god Thoth, patron of scribes, was favored by this profession, and prayers to him appear in the Ramessid schooling literature.

The Petitioners. One of the terms by which petitioners regularly referred to themselves in the penitential prayers was *nmḥw,* "a poor, humble person." This does not mean that piety was a religion of the poor, since they would not have had the means to commission the monuments that provide us with our data. The people from Deir el-Medina who called themselves *nmḥw* were relatively well-situated artisans, and most of the dedications found in the shrines around the Great Sphinx at Giza are by people of middle, lower-middle, or low rank, but even the viceroy of Nubia Huy, addressed a prayer of personal piety to his master, the king Tutankhamun. The king was also involved in this movement: Ramesses II's record of the Battle of Kadesh, inscribed on temple walls and pylons, did on a massive scale what the small votive stelae of the ordinary person did more modestly. In the prayer of Ramesses III to Amun at Karnak, sentiments and expressions are found that parallel those of the nonroyal prayers.

Other terms used to designate the ideal god-fearing pious person were *mꜣʿty, "* a just one," comparable to the *sadiq,* "just," of the biblical tradition; *ḳbḥw,* "the cool, quiet one"; and *gr* or *gr mꜣʿ,* "the silent one" or "the one who is justly silent." Their antithesis is *šm* or *šm rꜣ,* "the hot or hot-mouthed one." The term "the silent one" is found in prayers of personal piety but is even better known from the wisdom teachings; it refers to those who do not assert themselves but who place their trust in the divine, recognize the supreme free will of a deity, and are totally submissive to that will. That attitude is succinctly summarized in chapter 25 of the *Instructions of Amenemope*: "For man is clay and straw, God is his builder; he pulls down, he builds in a moment. He makes a thousand insignificant as he wishes, he makes a thousand people overseers when he is in his hour of life. Happy is he who reaches the West [i.e., the grave] being safe in the hand of god." There, worldly success—once seen as the result of correct behavior, of a life lived in accordance with *maat*—is held to be totally in the gift of a god; not success, then, but rather an unbroken relationship with a god, was the true mark of a successful life. The model frequently used for the relationship between the individual and a deity is that of servant *(bꜣk)* and master *(nb);* as does a servant his master, so the devout person "follows" *(šms)* and is "loyal" to *(šms ḥr mw/mtn)* a deity.

The confessions of fault in the penitential prayers refer to "actual sin"; the reference is always to some concrete, individual act or an inner thought or personal attitude. A concept of "general sin" is not found (i.e., the concept of the existence of a barrier between humankind and the divine that is not the result of an individual deed or thought but of the general condition of humankind—the Christian concept of "original sin"). The closest to the latter would be the statement on the stela of Nebra, that "the servant is disposed to do evil" (Lichtheim 1976, p. 106).

Locations of Cults. Ashraf Sadek (1987) has collected the evidence for the locations of cults of personal piety. They include nonofficial shrines (such as the small chapels erected by groups of individuals at Deir el-Medina or the tiny shrines set up along the path from Deir el-Medina to the Valley of the Kings), as well as places provided at official cult centers (such as the eastern temple at Karnak, dedicated to Amun and "Ramesses who hears petitions," or the monumental eastern gateway at Deir el-Medina, with its relief of "Ptah who hears petitions"). At the Tenth Pylon at Karnak, two individuals—Amenhotep, son of Hapu, and Piramesse—set up statues of themselves to act as mediators between the great god Amun and petitioners. The regular festival processions of the deities were also important occasions for the practice of personal religion; the promise in many of the penitential prayers—to make a public proclamation of the experienced greatness and mercy of the deity—was most probably fulfilled at such processions. The stela of Pataweret (Brunner 1958, pp. 6–12) from the Wepwawet sanctuary at Asyut provides valuable data on this aspect of personal religion. Divided into three registers, the bottom one depicts Pataweret's experience of the saving intervention of Wepwawet, called "the savior," who rescued him from being taken by a crocodile. The other two registers show where he expressed his thanks to the god. In the middle one he is shown alone, praying before an image of the god at a shrine. In the top register he is shown publicly praising the god during a procession.

Although compositions comparable to those of personal piety in the Ramessid era are not known from later periods, many of the sentiments found in them appear in later biographical texts, and their formulas of piety live on in some of the Greco-Roman temple inscriptions.

[*See also* Cults; Ethics and Morality; Hymns; *and* Religion.]

BIBLIOGRAPHY

Assmann, Jan. *Ägyptische Hymnen und Gebete.* Zurich, 1975. The most comprehensive collection of translations into a modern language of ancient Egyptian hymns and prayers; those dealing with piety are on pages 349–417.

Assmann, Jan. *Ägypten: Theologie und Frömmigkeit einer frühen Hochkultur.* Stuttgart, 1984. An excellent treatment of ancient Egyptian religion, including piety.

Assmann, Jan. "State and Religion in the New Kingdom." In *Religion and Philosophy in Ancient Egypt,* James P. Allen, et al., pp. 55–88. Yale Egyptological Studies, 3. New Haven, 1989. A stimulating study on religious developments in the New Kingdom.

Baines, John. *Fecundity Figures.* Warminster, 1985.

Baines, John. "Society, Morality, and Religious Practice." In *Religion in Ancient Egypt: Gods, Myths, and Personal Practice,* edited by Byran E. Shafer, pp. 123–200. Ithaca, 1991. Considers piety within the larger context of ancient Egyptian society.

Breasted, James H. *The Development of Religion and Thought in Ancient Egypt.* New York, 1912.

Brunner, Hellmut. "Eine Dankstele an Upuaut." *Mitteilungen des Deutschen Archäologischen Instituts, Abteilung Kairo* 16 (1958), 5–19; reprinted in Hellmut Brunner, *Das Hörende Herz,* pp. 173–188. Orbis biblicus et orientalis, 80. Freiburg and Göttingen, 1988. An important study on piety in the New Kingdom, which also traces the development of the god Shai, the personification of divine rescue.

Brunner, Hellmut. "Persönliche Frömmigkeit." In *Lexikon der Ägyp-*

tologie, 4: 951–963. Wiesbaden, 1982. A detailed article providing comprehensive references to sources on piety.

Lichtheim, Miriam. *Ancient Egyptian Literature: A Book of Readings.* Vol. II, *The New Kingdom.* Berkeley, 1976. A modern and reliable translation of Egyptian texts, including a selection dealing with piety.

Prichard, J. B., ed. *Ancient Near Eastern Texts Relating to the Old Testament.* Princeton, 1979.

Ranke, Hermann. *Die Ägyptischen Personennamen.* Vols. 1–2. Glückstadt, 1935 and 1952. Volume I gives a dictionary of names. Volume II is a comprehensive study of the meaning of ancient Egyptian names.

Sadek, Ashraf Iskander. *Popular Religion in Egypt during the New Kingdom.* Hildesheim, 1987. A comprehensive study of all aspects of personal religion in Egypt.

Wente, Edward. *Letters from Ancient Egypt.* Atlanta, 1990.

Wilson, John A. "The Theban Tomb (No. 49) of Si-Mut, Called Kiki," *Journal of Near Eastern Studies* 29 (1970), 187–192.

BOYO OCKINGA

PIGS. Although much has been written about the relationship between people and "pigs" (*š3j, rr(t),* and *jph*) in pharaonic Egypt, it is only in recent decades that some longstanding misconceptions have been exposed. It is now generally accepted that the local breed of domestic pig *(Sus domesticus)* descended from an indigenous progenitor, the wild boar *(Sus scrofa),* which formerly abounded in the Nile Delta, the Wadi Natrun, the Faiyum, and elsewhere. It became extinct around 1900, as a result of over-hunting.

The oldest domestic pig remains presently known in Egypt come from the large settlement site of Merimda Beni Salama (western Delta), initially occupied in the early fifth millennium BCE. That pork formed an important element in the diet of some Predynastic Egyptians is confirmed by the presence of pig remains at sites throughout the country, particularly in Lower Egypt. In the Predynastic and Early Dynastic cemetery at Manshiyet Abu Omar (eastern Delta), burials of the poor frequently contain pig bones, while those of the elite have cattle bones. Pig meat may always have been regarded in ancient Egypt as table fare for those of humble station.

A small number of votive pig figurines, of first dynasty date, have been recovered from several temple sites. Textual and zooarchaeological evidence indicates that pig-farming continued to be practiced during the Old and Middle Kingdoms. Swine are, however, conspicuously absent from the panoramic scenes of daily life decorating the tomb-chapels of the privileged classes of these epochs, nor are they mentioned in their extensive offering-list menus. Pigs were evidently regarded as an unclean food for the pious dead who sought to keep ritually pure in the beyond. The origin of this prohibition is obscure, but the pig's legendary associations with grubbing, dirt, and filth may have prompted its lowly status, especially in religious and funerary contexts. This taboo varied over time, was probably never absolute, and may have applied exclusively to a certain segment of society, such as priests, or only at particular times of the year. It appears to have escalated sharply during the Late Dynastic period and beyond; the ancient Greek historian Herodotus (II, 47) also remarked on Egypt's underclass of swineherds.

In the New Kingdom, information on pigs in Egyptian animal husbandry expands considerably. Inscriptions indicate that temples and wealthy citizens maintained large numbers of them on their country estates. The tomb-chapels of several notables of the first half of the eighteenth dynasty illustrate swine alongside other farmyard beasts. Pigs are also portrayed being driven over newly sown fields, treading seed into the muddy soil, a practice still current a thousand years later when Herodotus (II, 14) visited the country. Excavations during the 1980s in the workers' village at Akhenaten's capital at Tell el-Amarna have revealed an extensive pig-farm. Other evidence suggests the widespread consumption of pork, at least among the less affluent. Pig-breeding continued to be a relatively important economic activity in Egypt through the Greco-Roman period.

In Egyptian mythology, the male pig was regarded as a symbol of evil. In Spell 157 of the Coffin Texts, and later in the *Book of Going Forth by Day* (*Book of the Dead*, chapter 112), the typhonic god Seth transforms himself into a black boar in his conflict with the sky god Horus. Reliefs on Horus's Ptolemaic period temple at Edfu show him triumphing over Seth, who is in the form of a large boar. Many scholars have interpreted this myth as the underlying cause for the selective shunning of pig meat in ancient Egypt. Conversely, beginning in the Third Intermediate Period, delightful statuettes and amulets in the shape of a rooting sow nursing her litter of piglets were popular; they represent the sky goddess, Nut, although some identify them with Isis. These objects were thought to endow their owners with fecundity.

BIBLIOGRAPHY

Bonneau, Danielle. "La sacrifice du porc et Liloïtion en Pachôn." *Chronique d'Égypte* 66 (1991), 330–340. Discusses the pig as a rare sacrificial animal, and the question of pork consumption in ancient Egypt.

Firmage, Edwin. "Zoology (Fauna)." In *The Anchor Bible Dictionary,* edited by David Noel Freedman, vol. 6, pp. 1109–1167. New York and London, 1992. A thorough review of pigs in the ancient Near East, including Egypt, with special attention to pork prohibition.

Hecker, H. M. "A Zooarchaeological Inquiry Into Pork Consumption in Egypt from Prehistoric to New Kingdom Times." *Journal of the American Research Center in Egypt* 19 (1982), 59–71. Survey of zooarchaeological evidence for pigs in ancient Egypt.

Helck, Wolfgang. "Ein Verlorenes Grab in Theben-West TT 145 des Offiziers Neb-Amun unter Thutmosis III." *Antike Welt: Zeitschrift für Archäologie und Kulturgeschichte* 27.2 (1996), 73–85. Includes an excellent overview of the pig in pharaonic civilization, with many references.

Houlihan, Patrick F. *The Animal World of the Pharaohs.* London and New York, 1996. The chapter devoted to farmyard animals includes swine; extensive bibliography.

Ikram, Salima. *Choice Cuts: Meat Production in Ancient Egypt.* Orientalia Lovaniensia Anacleta, 69. Leuven, 1995. Stresses that the archaeological and textual records prove that pigs were readily consumed in ancient Egypt, despite Herodotus's report.

Miller, Robert L. "Hogs and Hygiene." *Journal of Egyptian Archaeology* 76 (1990), 125–140. Important study on the value of pigs in the subsistence economy of the workmen's villages at Deir el-Medina and Tell el-Amarna.

Redding, R. W. "The Role of the Pig in the Subsistence System of Ancient Egypt: A Parable on the Potential of Faunal Data." In *Animal Use and Culture Change*, edited by Pam J. Crabtree and Kathleen Ryan, pp. 20–30. MASCA Research Papers in Science and Archaeology 8, Supplement. Philadelphia, 1991. Survey of pig use in ancient Egypt and its relationship to political centralization.

Simoons, Frederick J. *Eat Not This Flesh: Food Avoidances from Prehistory to the Present.* 2d. ed. Madison, 1994. Interesting discussion on pork avoidance in the ancient Near East, including Egypt.

te Velde, Herman. "Some Egyptian Deities and Their Piggishness." In *Intellectual Heritage of Egypt: Studies Presented to László Kákosy by Friends and Colleagues on the Occasion of His 60th Birthday,* edited by Ulrich Luft, pp. 571–578. Studia Aegyptiaca, 14. Budapest, 1992. The author studies the "piggishness" of the gods and the associations of the pig with Seth and other deities.

PATRICK F. HOULIHAN

PIRAMESSE. From the early days of Egyptology, continuing attempts were made to locate the position of the Ramessid capital called "The House of Ramesses Beloved of Amun Great of Victories." It was believed to be identical with the biblical city called "Ramesses," from which the Israelites departed Egypt on their Exodus. In the Nile Delta, the vast ruins of Tanis, the region around Pelusium, and the frontier forts of Sile, Tell el-Maskhuta and Tell el-Rotaba, all situated on the eastern edge of the Nile Delta, were in turn identified and then dismissed as Piramesse. The French archeologist Pierre Montet insisted that Tanis was indeed the only Ramessid city that could be considered a candidate, because of the enormous numbers of Ramessid architectural fragments that he had uncovered there. Excavations in the vicinity of the modern village of Qantir, led by the Egyptian Egyptologists Mahmoud Hamza (1928) and Labib Habachi (1940–1943), uncovered parts of palaces as well as dwellings of high Ramessid officials and brought the region of Qantir into focus. This work was continued, with a detailed evaluation of archeological remains within the region's topography, by the Austrian Egyptologist Manfred Bietak (since 1966). With further progress of the excavations at Tanis and Qantir, all data led to the final localization of the Ramessid capital in the region between Qanti and el-Khata'na,

which has come to be generally accepted. Qantir/Piramesse, the central area of which covers more than 10 square kilometers, is about 100 kilometers (65 miles) northeast of Cairo and about 80 kilometers (50 miles) west of Ismailia, not far from Faqus, in Sharkijeh province.

In cooperation with the Egyptian Antiquities Organization and in collaboration with the Austrian mission, the Pelizaeus Museum initiated intensive work in the endangered archeological zone. Francis L. I. Griffith, the British scholar, could still note on an inspection of the area in 1886 that one finds at Qantir a low tell (settlement mound), which continues without interruption as far south as el-Khata'na, more than 2 kilometers (1.5 miles) to the south of Qantir. Today the area is almost completely leveled and prepared for agricultural exploitation, except for very limited remains at Tell ed-Dab'a. Already in antiquity, specifically during the twenty-first dynasty, most of the stone masonry, statues, obelisks, and the like had been removed from Piramesse to build new residences in such sites as Tanis and Bubastis.

During the course of nineteen field seasons since 1980, five excavation sites have been opened; two of these were labeled Q I and Q IV, respectively. Both major sites contain, from top to bottom, badly damaged remains of cemeteries, followed by a more or less preserved habitation level; beneath this is a chariot garrison with attached multifunctional workshops and extensive horse stables; and below that is a foundry with installations for the industrial production and casting of bronze (Q I) and glass (Q IV). The latest excavations have revealed the remains of a palace-like structure below the royal stud (Q IV), comprising further stables, pillared halls, and a room with a polychrome stucco floor, including gold-plating. These latter elements can be dated to the reign of Ramesses II by inscriptions and are most likely connected to the systematic building activities of the new residence. They may also reflect a technological transfer in regard to metal processing.

Evidence for this is provided by vast installations that demonstrate the melting of bronze by heating open crucibles from above, and the use of specialized furnaces for heating large-scale casting molds. Those installations cover an area well over 30,000 square meters and are unique in antiquity for their high-temperature technology and size.

Altogether, the strata represent a period of a more than three hundred years of settlement history, from about 1300 BCE to the beginning of the first millennium, from the latter part of the eighteenth dynasty to the early twentieth. Earlier occupation levels (Middle Kingdom and Second Intermediate Period) are to be found at Tell ed-Dab'a.

Traces of connections to foreign cultures and countries of the eastern Mediterranean are well documented at Piramesse. Particularly interesting in this regard is the occupation level labeled the Chariot Garrison. Three large contemporary functional units may be distinguished. The north of site Q I contains a peristyle court lined with octagonal pillars which protected polychrome wall paintings from the frequent, sometimes violent rainstorms. The pillars show on their four principal sides the royal protocol of Ramesses II in a version that dates its erection to his first *sed*-festival in regnal Year 30. The clearest indication of the use of this court for chariotry, in addition to the numerous objects recovered, is the prints of horses' hooves in parts of the courtyard floor.

The second functional unit—multifunctional workshops with intra-craft and cross-craft specialization—is situated within the south part of Q I. These include fireplaces of various types, crucibles of various types, tyeres, layers of ashes and burnt clay, slag, charcoal, casting molds, scrap metal, and recycled bronze objects, all of which indicate the presence of foundries in which not just bronze but also gold, silver, and glass were being produced or worked. Regional concentrations of humus layers, dunghills, and latrines, in combination with stone and bronze knives, hatchets, scrapers, and sickle blades, point to the processing of organic materials such as wood, leather, or reeds. Stone detritus such as flakes and nodules of flint, blue chalcedony, different varieties of carnelian and agate, fragments of alabaster still bearing saw marks, smashed pieces of desert boulders, drill cores from rock crystal, pressure stones of bow-drills and their crescents, ball-hammers, and anvils suggest a wide spectrum of raw materials, techniques, and occupations. A specialized area served for the working of animal bones, receiving some of its raw material from a nearby zoo in which elephants, lions, gazelles, and other wild animals were kept. Taken as a whole, this cross-craft workshop reveals an interrelated web of dependent processes, linked together like a modern assembly line to repair and produce chariots and their equipment as well as bronze and glass.

The third functional unit at site Q IV comprises within an area of more than fifteen thousand square meters six rows of twelve rectangular rooms each, a column hall being situated at the western end of each row. The function of this architectural complex, which has no known parallel, can be inferred from the whitewashed floors, tethering stones, and "toilets" built of limestone inside these rooms: all of them—column halls as well as the slender rectangular rooms—are to be designated as "stable rooms," the whole being a royal stud housing a minimum of almost 460 horses and their grooms. Finds of chariot finials include yoke saddle knobs and yoke knobs, mainly carved of alabaster, limestone, or marble. Similarly numerous planoconvex discs, made of the same materials, once decorated the terminal ends of the wooden frame of the chariot's

floor frame. Gold-plated bronze buttons, nailheads covered with gold leaf, punched gold bands, and rivets, together with a once-gilded linchpin, reveal that in addition to standard chariot types, lavishly decorated parade chariots were also manufactured and used here.

This conclusion can be further verified by the recovery of a functioning pair of horse bits along with a nave cap made of bronze. Numerous weapons—short swords, arrows, javelins, and lance heads—as well as pieces of scaled body armor belonging to helmets and cuirasses, complete the picture of the charioteers' armory. Correlating the information gained by excavations to ancient Egyptian texts, we can recognize the architecture and its contents as the "armory" and at the same time the "headquarters of thy (the king's) chariotry," described in the hymns of Piramesse.

Within the workshop we note limestone molds for embossing metal sheets, which are unparalleled in the cultural record of the ancient Near East. The identification of the designs engraved into these slabs is possible through Egyptian reliefs depicting Hittite soldiers carrying a shield whose outline exactly resembles the design and proportion of the motif found on the limestone slabs; it is comparable also to the orthostats found at Zencirli, on which the Hittite weather god wears the horned crown and is armed with a lance, a short sword, and the same Hittite figure-eight shield. The Amarna Letters contain lists of gifts sent by Tusratta, king of Mitanni, to Amenhotpe III, naming alongside other costly items, "nine leather shields, the *urukmannu* of which are of bronze." Therefore I identify the Hurrian word *urukmannu* with those metal parts that were produced by embossing bronze sheets using the above described molds, hammers, and punches, also found at Piramesse. Their presence within this metropolis can only be understood as proof that Egyptians and Hittites worked peacefully, side by side. This holds true also for the motif on the back side of the molds, depicting a highly stylized head of a bull, symbol of the Hittite weather god.

The most likely explanation for the peaceful presence of Hittites in Egypt's Ramessid capital is the occasion of the diplomatic marriage between Ramesses II and the eldest daughter of the Hittite king Hattusili III, Maat-hor-nofru-re, which took place in regnal Year 34 of Ramesses II. In several texts, particular emphasis is placed on the friendly encounter of the formerly hostile troops, enabling the ancient historians to state that "both lands had become one (and the same) land." The shield molds with the Hittite motifs must have been used to maintain the shields of the Hittites who served as a palace or body guard for the queen in the Ramessid residence, an outward expression of the friendly union between the two superpowers of the day.

Finds from the Mycenaean world are also present in abundance, most of them in the form of pottery; there is also a scale of a Mycenaean boar's-tusk helmet. We also have evidence for the cults of several foreign deities, such as a relief depicting a statue of Astarte, the ancient Near Eastern goddess of war and love and protectress of the royal horse team, mounted on horseback; in addition, the name of the ancient Near Eastern god of war, Resheph, was found on a limestone door post. The former object is the archeological manifestation of a passage in one of the hymns of Piramesse, telling us that "Astarte [is situated] in her (the city's) east." Since the hieroglyphic name of Astarte is also preserved on one of the palmiform columns of the stable, it may be assumed that the stable at least was protected by this goddess. Altogether, we have more than circumstantial proof that the hymns on Piramesse are accurate in describing its splendor, contents, layout, and size, comparing Piramesse to other Egyptian cities such as Thebes, Memphis, and Heliopolis.

Since 1996, the size and layout of the Ramessid metropolis has been further investigated in cooperation with the Bayerisches Landesamt für Denkmalpflege, Munich, using a caesium magnetometer (SMART SM4G). With this device, sun-dried mud-brick walls, foundation pits filled with sand, and similar features of lower magnetism are clearly to be differentiated from cultural layers with higher magnetism. This enables us not only to measure but also to draw the outlines of individual buildings as well as the ground plans of city districts. Covering an area of almost 100 hectares, the investigated fields contain a palace area, vast living quarters consisting of villas and houses of the Amarna type, with courtyards, gardens, streets, avenues, channels, and perhaps parts of a harbor. Several official buildings of still unknown function, one of them resembling in part the North Palace of Tell el-Amarna, and another one comparable to the so-called Foreign Office depicted in the tomb of Tjai at Thebes, are situated to the south of Q I and Q IV. It is hoped that the continuation of the magnetic investigation will lead to a map covering at least the city center with its area of more than 10 square kilometers.

BIBLIOGRAPHY

Bietak, Manfred. *Avaris and Piramesse*, 2d ed. Oxford, 1986.
Hayes, W. C. *Glazed Tiles from a Palace of Ramesses II at Kantir.* New York, 1937.
Pusch, Edgar B. "Ausländisches Kulturgut in Qantir-Piramesse." In *Akten München 1985*, edited by S. Schoske pp. 249–256. Hamburg, 1989.
Pusch, Edgar B. "Bericht über die sechste Hauptkampagne in Qantir' Piramesse-Nord herbst 1988." *Göttinger Miszellen* 112 (1989), 67–90.
Uphill, Eric P. *The Temples of Per Ramesses.* Warminster, 1984.

EDGAR B. PUSCH

PITHOM. Modern Tell el-Maskhuta was known anciently as Per Atum (hence biblical Pithom), Tukw ("The Estate of Atum in Tkw" [biblical Sukkoth]), Greek Heronpolis (Eroöpolis, Heroön), and Roman Ero (Hero). This multicomponent stratified site (30°33′N, 32°60′E) in the Wadi Tumilat region of the eastern Nile Delta was occupied during the last two-thirds of the seventeenth century BCE, and again from around 610 BCE to perhaps the early fourth century CE. It experienced brief periods of decline in the fifth century BCE and again in the first century BCE through the first century CE. Probably founded in connection with overland trade to southern Arabia during the Hyksos period, it was a control point and entrepôt on the sea-level canal of Necho II, which ran from the Nile to the head of the Red Sea via the Wadi Tumilat and the Bitter Lakes region.

Tell el-Maskhuta was the first site excavated by the Egypt Exploration Society (Édouard Naville, 1883). Prior to World War I, Jean Clédat conducted excavations, apparently largely in the temple precincts, which yielded numerous museum specimens but little of scholarly substance. More recently, the Egyptian Antiquities Organization, now the Supreme Council of Antiquities, has conducted numerous excavations in the northern cemetery, along the Ismailia Canal, and in a number of areas in and on the margins of the modern village. Most current knowledge of the site derives from a major series of surveys and excavations conducted by a multidisciplinary University of Toronto team directed by John S. Holladay, Jr.

Second Intermediate Period Occupation. During the Second Intermediate Period (Middle Bronze IIB), a small—roughly 2 hectares—unfortified village with strong Near Eastern or Hyksos characteristics occupied the center of what was to become the fortified site. It was essentially a self-subsistent entity, with numerous silos and, in the earlier strata, entombments within individual ownership plots (much as at Tell ed-Dab'a during the earlier occupational periods). Judging from plant remains preserved in cooking-fire ashes, the village was seasonal, with no occupation during the summer months. Farming (wheat and barley) and animal husbandry (cattle, sheep and goats, pigs, donkeys, and at least one horse) formed a major part of the local economy, although they were not, apparently, the major reason for the site's existence.

Hunted animals included a small hartebeest, ostriches, and gazelle, reflecting a semi-arid savanna setting; and a variety of migratory waterfowl, indicating the regional presence of small lakes or swamps. At least some pottery—the local pottery constituted a subset of the Tell ed-Dab'a repertory—was made on site, and there is evidence for other industrial pursuits, such as weaving on the (non-

Egyptian) warp-weighted loom, and secondary copper-smelting. Flint blades (mostly segmented sickle blades) apparently arrived at the site fully formed; they were locally hafted or rehafted.

That the inhabitants were not simple peasant farmers seems most evident from the burials, which were rich and mostly in tombs. These followed Near Eastern patterns, including ass burials outside of early "warrior" tombs, and were characterized by strong age and sex patterns in the distribution of grave goods. Bronze daggers, a battle-axe, knives, toggle-pins, and other items characterized most adult burials, with amulets being reserved for juveniles. Gold and silver headbands and armbands, earrings, rings, and scarab mounts were not uncommon. Amethyst beads and an amethyst scaraboid probably were looted from twelfth dynasty tombs.

It appears that Pithom, and other Near Eastern sites in the Wadi Tumilat, existed as adjuncts—with Tell el-Maskhuta perhaps being a major reception point—for long-distance overland trade in high-value commodities with southern Arabia and the Horn of Africa. Presumably the need for such a difficult overland route arose during a period in which the Nile no longer was accessible to traffic bound for Avaris/Tell ed-Dab'a (Holladay 1997b).

Eighteenth and Nineteenth Dynasties. The site was unoccupied from the eighteenth dynasty through the early twenty-sixth—a conclusion that could not have been reached by Naville, working prior to the development of a critical chronology of Egyptian and foreign pottery. Naville (1903, pp. 2–5) and others found significant monuments of the reigns of Ramesses II, Sheshonq I, and Osorkon II, misleading Naville to declare that "the founder of the city, the king who gave to Pithom the extent and the importance we recognize, is certainly Ramesses II. . . . It is he who built the enclosure and the storehouses. . . . We find here confirmation of the evidence derived from other monuments that he is the Pharaoh of the Oppression, as he built Pithom and Raamses, the site of which last is still uncertain" (1903, p. 13).

Conclusive evidence against this theory lies in the fact that in deposits from the end of the Hyksos occupation of Tell el-Maskhuta until the building of the canal and new settlement under Necho II, the Wadi Tumilat Project found not a single fragment of eighteenth or nineteenth dynasty pottery out of the hundreds of thousands of sherds and intact vessels surveyed or excavated and studied at the site. As at Tanis, these earlier monuments were all transported easily by canal to the site, for the same purpose of enhancing the reputations of later kings.

Late Saite through Early Roman Period. Locational and historical analysis, together with inferences from archaeological data, allow the firm conclusion that Tell el-Maskhuta was founded in connection with Necho II's building of the Nile-to-Red Sea canal early in his reign. Following the Hyksos settlement and its immediate aftermath, the earliest succeeding construction made widespread use of "gleyed" soils excavated from below the Wadi's permanent water table. This building period was preceded by four burials northeast of the temple site, in a very limited excavation area, of entire young bulls—one the first short-horned cow yet identified by skeletal elements in Egypt. Unquestionably there were a great many more of these currently unique "foundation sacrifices." Almost immediately afterward, some of the early houses were razed to make way for a massive 8–9-meter (27-foot) thick fortification wall. This suggests a turn in military fortunes, such as that ensuing on Necho's expulsion from the Near East in 605 BCE (Holladay 1982, pp. 19–23 and Fig. 13). Soon afterward, the site underwent massive destruction, presumably at the hands of Nebuchadrezzer II in 601 BCE. Other destructions occurred around 568, 525, and 487 BCE.

About 13 percent of the fortified area was excavated by the University of Toronto team. Evidence was discovered for Saite and Persian domestic complexes, the latter possibly those of servitors of the temple of Atum. Within the Saite and early Persian period settlement areas, it appears that the primary socio-economic structure was the household-based small estate, with beehive-shaped granaries enclosed within a square one-story housing. Evidence for baking and cooking on more than a nuclear-family basis characterized enough of these and later granaries to suggest that this was probably the norm throughout. A ruined shrine gave evidence of a small Phoenician presence in the town, presumably the local equivalent of the "Camp of the Phoenicians" at Memphis.

Large long-room Persian and Hellenistic granaries, at least two mass bakeries, and (apparently) temple-related industrial installations, including a stonecarver's workshop, a potter's workshop, and more than one site of secondary copper-smelting were found. Somewhat later, massive late Hellenistic storehouses were built at the site. Those surveyed by Naville were north of the temple area, and the Toronto group excavated similar remains. Naville attributed his to the Israelites, quoting Villiers Stuart to the effect that they had been "built of bricks *without straw*" (1903, pp. 11–12; cf. *Exodus* 5.6–19), although he also (correctly) associated them with the Ptolemies.

Where modern excavations were conducted, these storehouses seem to date, with frequent wholesale replacement, from the late third century to the last quarter of the second century BCE, but the little-explored northwestern ones, including those excavated by Naville, may begin as early as the reign of Ptolemy II. In that case, the

PITHOM. *Field Q at Pithom, from the tomb of Ptolemy II.* This picture shows four of a row of
ten or more bread ovens in a walled-in court to the east of a six-room granary (left). Three of
the granary rooms were small and separated by transverse walls from three typically long rooms
comprising the remainder of the structure. An earlier two-room granary of similar design,
reused in this period at least in part as a potter's shed, appears in the top left of the photograph.
(WTP Photo M81 B50:28. Courtesy Wadi Tumilat Project)

smaller granary of the same date near the eastern enclosure wall must have been intended—with its bakery—primarily as a rations facility for a group of laborers or
craftsmen. The very large storehouses must be linked to
the site's canal-based importance and socioeconomic
function, which is illuminated by the great "Pithom Tablet," or stela, of Ptolemy II, discovered by Naville.

Outside the northern enclosure wall, evidence for a
blocked-up Persian well and a later water-sweep suggest
that agricultural activities—or a much more dispersed
settlement pattern—may have obtained immediately outside the fortified townsite. Nearby, traces of dozens of
small cooking circles on the ground surface adjacent to
the enclosure wall probably suggest the presence of non-
urban client peoples, whether sojourners, local traders, or
field-workers.

A large Persian tomb and a separate shaft tomb with a
massive limestone coffin were discovered by the Egyptian Antiquities Organization, together with store facilities and other large building remains, in an extramural
area near the present village, southwest of the Atum temple. Part of another limestone coffin of probably Hellenistic type was dredged up during the clearance of the canal
to the north of the present site, and a third, anthropomorphic and probably Hellenistic, was found in the excavation of a nine-room tomb near the canal. These coffins,
together with the large temple, its accompanying *naos*
and statues, and the large Pithom Tablet indicate the presence of important Persian and Ptolemaic officials. For the
Persian period, this conclusion is strengthened by the discovery of a burnt bulla of Artaxerxes I and a calcite (Egyptian alabaster) bowl with the cartouche of Artaxerxes I.
Considerably to the west of the enclosure area, between
the village and the present schoolhouse, an area of dense
housing remains has been uncovered.

Severely disturbed Roman remains (with frog lamps
but lacking African Red-Slip ware and lamps with molded
disks) overspread much of the site (Holladay 1982, pls.

31–35), which, together with very slender coin information, suggests a terminal date before or during the early fourth century CE. Several square, domed tombs were excavated in a necropolis about 250 meters (800 feet) east of the fortified area. Though robbed, the remains showed injuries and an age curve consistent with a military population. Some inhumations, including children in amphora burials, were Christian, to judge from orientation and epigraphic data.

Trade-related Aspects of the Saite–Roman Town.
Whereas Herodotus (*Persian Wars* II, 158–159; Rawlinson 1952, pp. 197–198), the Periplus of the Erythrean Sea (Casson 1989), and the "Pithom Tablet" (Naville 1903, pp. 18–21, pls. 8–10) give more than usual attention to "mere commerce" involving the sea-level canal, the archaeological record of Tell el-Maskhuta yields an astonishing view of the body of traffic moved along the canal. For example, the very large percentage of foreign—particularly Phoenician—amphoras during the Saite and Persian periods; Greek amphoras during all periods; a small Phoenician shrine during the Saite Period, probably destroyed by the Persian invaders; and the four great stelae of Darius the Great, which began near Maskhuta and marched on down to Suez all describe how he completed the canal and caused oceangoing ships to go to Persia. The Persian and Ptolemaic periods were characterized by numerous incense altars (for South Arabian incense) and some minute Himarytic coins, presumably also South Arabian, as well as the Tell el-Maskhuta Bowls (Rabinowitz 1956), probably a trade gift to Hathor ("the lady," cf. Holladay 1992, p. 591), and literally thousands of Athenian tetradrachma coins, presumably also trade gifts to the temple, but possibly merchant-bankers' hoards, found at the site. Similarly, quite apart from the Great Stele erected at Maskhuta by Ptolemy II, which lists the imports from his great African expedition, the huge storehouses of the Ptolemaic period would have no function in a town divorced from the means of moving large masses of materials on a routine basis. During the late Ptolemaic and early Roman periods, large "top" or "carrot"-shaped Egyptian amphoras, some apparently made at Naukratis (Coulson and Leonard 1981) became the container of choice and were exceedingly common. During this period, Roman and Palestinian amphoras were present, but not common.

Ultimately, apart from the historical, archaeological, and (quantified) socioeconomic illumination afforded upon Hyksos activities in the Wadi Tumilat (Holladay 1997b) and the operation of the sea-level Saite and later canal, the site's most lasting contributions to Egyptian archaeology will lie in the extensive quantified publication of its stratified pottery assemblages (see Holladay 1982, pls. 1–35; 1997b, pls. 7.1–18; Paice 1987). These include Paice's stratigraphically derived chronology of Phoenician amphoras, the publication of the plans of stratified domestic and industrial structures and installations, as well as their accompanying artifactual assemblages (for houses of the Second Intermediate Period at Maskhuta, see Paice, Holladay, and Brock 1996).

BIBLIOGRAPHY

Abdalla Ali, Mahrous. "A Marble Sarcophagus from Tell el-Maskhuta." *Journal of the Society for the Study of Egyptian Antiquities* 19 (1989), 48–49.
Casson, Lionel. *The Periplus Maris Erythraei*. Princeton, 1989.
Coulson, William, and Albert Leonard. *Cities of the Delta*, Part 1: *Naukratis*. American Research Center in Egypt Reports, 4. Malibu, Calif. 1981.
Holladay, John S., Jr. *Cities of the Delta*, Part 3: *Tell el-Maskhuta*. American Research Center in Egypt Reports, 6. Malibu, Calif., 1982.
Holladay, John S., Jr. "Maskhuta, Tell el-." In *The Oxford Encyclopedia of Archaeology in the Near East*, edited by Eric M. Meyers, vol. 3, pp. 432–437. New York, 1997.
Holladay, John S., Jr. "The Eastern Nile Delta during the Hyksos and Pre-Hyksos Periods: Toward a Systemic/Socioeconomic Understanding." In *The Hyksos: New Historical and Archaeological Perspectives*, edited by Eliezer D. Oren, pp. 183–252. Philadelphia, 1997.
Naville, Édouard. *The Store-City of Pithom and the Route of the Exodus*. London, 1903.
Oren, Eliezer D. "The 'Kingdom of Sharuhen' and the Hyksos Kingdom." In *The Hyksos: New Historical and Archaeological Perspectives*, edited by Eliezer D. Oren, pp. 253–283. Philadelphia, 1997.
Paice, Patricia. "A Preliminary Analysis of Some Elements of the Saite and Persian Period Pottery at Tell el-Maskhuta." *Bulletin of the Egyptological Seminar* 8 (1986/1987), 95–107.
Paice, Patricia. "Persians." In *Encyclopedia of the Archaeology of Ancient Egypt*, edited by Kathryn A. Bard, pp. 611–615. London, 1999.
Paice, Patricia, John S. Holladay, Jr., and Edwin C. Brock. "The Middle Bronze Age/Second Intermediate Period Houses at Tell el-Maskhuta." In *Haus und Palast im alten Ägypten: Internationales Symposium 8. bis 11 April 1992 in Kairo*, edited by Manfred Bietak, pp. 159–173. Vienna, 1996.
Redford, Donald B. "Pithom." In *Lexikon der Ägyptologie*, 4: 1054–1058. Wiesbaden, 1983.
Rabinowitz, I. "Aramaic Inscriptions of the Fifth Century B.C.E. from a North-Arab Shrine in Egypt." *Journal of Near Eastern Studies* 15 (1956), 1–9.

JOHN S. HOLLADAY, JR.

PIYA (ruled c. 735–712 BCE), third king of the twenty-fifth or Kushite, dynasty, Late period. Piya, also known as Piankhy, was the first ruler of the Kushite kingdom to attempt to control all of Egypt; he is therefore to be viewed as the real founder of the twenty-fifth dynasty. His activities are known mainly from his monumental stela erected at the site of Napata (Gebel Barkal). Piya's first attempts to involve himself in affairs to the north of his southern kingdom of Kush (now in Sudan) led him into immediate conflict with the various princes and dynasts of a divided Egypt. In particular, he claims to have moved north to the ancient center of Amun worship, Thebes, in an effort to exert political and religious influence over that region. He first installed his sister Amunirdis as "God's Wife of Amun" at Karnak, and he appears to have received the tacit submission of Middle Egypt, where various garrisons held by local potentates blocked his way. On his famous stela of victory, dated to the twenty-first year of his reign, Piya is described as focusing particular attention on the city Hermopolis, led by Namlot, who subsequently betrayed him.

Egypt at this time was nominally held by a weak and ineffective pharaoh, Takelot III (r. 750–720 BCE), who effectively ruled only his center in the eastern Nile Delta, Bubastis. Real control over the land was held by numerous monarchs, among the most powerful of whom was Tefnakhte, prince of Sais in the western Delta (r. 724–717 BCE). It was Tefnakhte who organized the resistance to Piya after the Kushite ruler had effectively gained control of Hermopolis and, hence, of all Upper Egypt. After recounting the fall of Hermopolis in his stela, Piya then explains in detail his march to regain control of the old capital of Memphis and its final capture through another siege. At this point, the war became more complicated for the Kushite ruler. Although Piya claimed pharaonic jurisdiction over the entire Nile Valley—a theological claim as well as a political one—and although he had received approval from the priesthood at Heliopolis, Piya faced organized resistance from the western Delta.

For more than a century, the northwest portions of Egypt had been assimilated by a series of Libyan military men, who eventually consolidated their power at the ancient commercial city of Sais. At the time of Piya's move to the North of Egypt, the leader of this center, Tefnakhte, was pharaoh in name and deed, and he effectively controlled all of the Delta northwest of el-Lisht. It was Tefnakhte who initiated opposition to Piya's control over Middle Egypt after Namlot, the ruler of Hermopolis, had switched his allegiance from Piya to the Saite ruler, and after other major cities in the vicinity also opposed the Kushite pharaoh. This political move was the effective cause of Piya's march north, eventually to capture all of Egypt and subsequently to take Memphis itself. Piya returned to his ancestral kingdom of Kush and erected his stela of victory in his twenty-first regnal year (c.715 BCE). Nonetheless, Tefnakhte was not deposed, and soon thereafter Sais resumed its opposition to the Kushites.

Known mainly from the lengthy and detailed inscription on his victory stela as well as from decorated blocks at Thebes, Piya remains a shadowy figure, especially in contrast to his successors. He was not a native Egyptian and, as such, was vehemently opposed by the native rulers. They organized the resistance against him and the subsequent Kushite rulers. Nevertheless, Piya's religious piety—or at least his conservatism—was one of his hall-marks, and there is little doubt that his adherence to the long-standing Amun cult of Thebes, stressed in his stela of victory, was a primary reason why Thebes remained firmly under his control during his reign.

BIBLIOGRAPHY

Grimal, Nicolas-Christophe. *La stele triomphale de Pi('ankh)y au Musée du Caire, JE 48862 et 47086–47089.* Cairo, 1981. The most recent study of Piya's victory stela; contains an up-to-date translation with a detailed historical analysis.

Kitchen, K. A. *The Third Intermediate Period in Egypt (1100–650 BC).* Warminster, 1973. An extremely detailed and significant work which covers the reign of this pharaoh in some detail.

Spalinger, Anthony J. "The Military Background of the Campaign of Piye (Piankhy)." *Studien zur Altägyptisachen Kultur* 7 (1979), 273–301. A detailed analysis of Piya's campaign in Egypt.

Yoyotte, Jean. "Les principautés du Delta au temps de l'anarchie libyenne." *Mélanges Maspero* 4.1 (1961), 121–191. A seminal study of the Delta at the time of Piya's invasion that has not been surpassed.

ANTHONY J. SPALINGER

PLUTARCH (c.46–120 CE), a greek historian and philosopher. Born in Chaeronea in Boeotia, Plutarch was educated in Athens, mainly by the Platonist Ammonius, who had an Egyptian name and came to Athens from Egypt. Plutarch spent some time in Rome and also in Alexandria, but the small town of Chaeronea remained his permanent home. There, he filled various public posts and was a priest at nearby Delphi. His family life was very happy; his wife Timoxena bore him five children, while a circle of friends and pupils acted as a little academy under his lead.

Plutarch was a prolific writer, and his many biographical works included *Parallel Lives*, about Greeks and Romans. His *Moral Essays* covered a wide variety of themes, such as greed, flattery, loquacity, superstition, education, and marriage; his style was popular, being both lively and instructive. In other essays a more ambitious approach appeared, in that themes were tackled that interested Stoics, Epicureans, and Platonists. As an avowed Platonist, Plutarch was in some ways open to Stoic influence; for example, in his emphasis on Providence.

His intense interest in religious beliefs and practices in addition to his vast reading on the whole field have led to the considered claim by Jean Hani (1976) that Plutarch is antiquity's best historian of religions. The claim is strongly supported by Plutarch's superb treatise *On Isis and Osiris* (the *De Iside et Osiride*—although written in Greek, the *Moral Essays* are traditionally called by their Latin titles). In this work, a distinction should be made between the accounts given of myths and rites and the often added interpretations. The accounts showed, on the whole, a remarkable reliability when compared with the evidence of the Egyptian sources; the interpretations, in contrast, were often colored by Pythagorean, Platonic, Stoic, Gnostic, and even Iranian ideas; in chapters 46, 47, and 48 the dualistic basis of Zoroastrianism was presented in an exposé, which has often been quoted as authoritative.

For evidence on the contemporary cult of the Egyptian deities, Plutarch relied to some extent on his friend Clea, who held a double priesthood at Delphi—that of Isis and that of Dionysus. His book is dedicated to Clea. (It is possible, though not certain, that Plutarch was also an initiated devotee of Isis.) On a wide range of information about Egyptian religion, Plutarch was greatly indebted to a large number of Greek writers, whose compilations he probably used. Their quality varied, but most important among them to Plutarch was Manetho, a bilingual Egyptian and a high priest at Heliopolis under the first two kings of the Ptolemaic dynasty.

BIBLIOGRAPHY

Brenk, Frederick E. *In Mist Apparelled: Religious Themes in Plutarch's Moralia and Lives.* Suppl. Mnemosyne, 48. Leiden, 1977. An able overview of Plutarch's approach to religion; perhaps the role of demonology is underrated.

Griffiths, John Gwyn. *Plutarch's De Iside et Osiride.* Cardiff, 1970.

Griffiths, John Gwyn. "Plutarch of Chaeronea." In *Lexikon der Ägyptologie,* 2: 1065–1067. Wiesbaden, 1982.

Hani, Jean. *La Religion Égyptienne dans la pensée de Plutarque.* Paris, 1976. Not a line-by-line commentary, but a thorough discussion, arranged thematically, of the many remarks on Egyptian religion in the *De Iside et Osiride* and also in parts of Plutarch's other works.

Hopfner, Theodor. *Plutarch über Isis und Osiris,* part 1: *Die Sage* and part 2:, *Die Deutungen der Sage.* Monographien des Archiv Orientalni,9. Prague, 1940 and 1941. The two parts were republished in one volume by Georg Olms (Hildesheim, Zurich, and New York, 1991). Only in part 1 does Hopfner provide a Greek text (based mainly on that of Sieveking [Teubner, 1935]); but he provides a translation throughout and a detailed commentary, which is enhanced by his thorough knowledge of the comparative literary material in Greek and Latin, as well as of the Greek magical papyri. He was not equipped, however, to deal properly with the Egyptian sources.

Jones, C. P. "The Teacher of Plutarch." *Harvard Studies in Classical Philology* 71 (1966), 205–213. The role of Ammonius in Plutarch's *Dialogues* is examined in some detail.

Russell, D. A. *Plutarch.* New York, 1973. Probably the best introduction to Plutarch's life and letters, with a full guide to all the writings and an attractive appreciation of their unique charisma.

J. GWYN GRIFFITHS

POETRY. *See* Hymns; Literature; *and* Lyric.

POLYGAMY. *See* Marriage and Divorce.

PORTRAITURE. The origins of portraiture in ancient Egypt no doubt lie in the belief in eternal life. In the early phases of Egyptian history known collectively as the Predynastic period, there were attempts to preserve the body. In the Old Kingdom, the cadaver was wrapped in linen that was stiffened with resin or plaster. Lifelike details were molded or modeled, creating a sculpture from the body. Throughout Egyptian history, the ever-increasing elaboration of funerary equipment reveals the desire to prepare the deceased for eternity; tomb sculptures represent a personal ideological imperative that preserves the identity of the deceased as a self-presentation of a virtuous life, both to the deities and to humans.

The ancient Egyptians required abstract qualities or physical correspondence, and often both, in their portraiture, which was limited almost exclusively to sculpture. A pensive or contemplative expression, for example, is a frequent component of a lifelike rendering. Still more than outward appearance, the virtue of the individual represented his or her reality. Foremost in the Egyptian value system was a principle known as *maat* ("harmony, cosmic equilibrium"), which all persons were expected to preserve. Idealizing statues must have been portraits because they created a necessary fiction; they revealed the admirable qualities, especially the adherence to *maat*, by which the deceased wished to be remembered. They are the three-dimensional equivalents of the paintings of the judgment of the dead found on cartonnages and sarcophagi. In both sculpture and painting, the deceased is always represented as a sinless, upstanding individual. Unlike later artists, the Egyptian sculptor had little opportunity for personal expression or deviation from convention. Many strictures, including the patron's wishes, controlled the portrait's content.

Tomb sculptures were private and directed primarily toward the deities. Public statues, particularly of royalty, were erected in and around temples and palaces to serve as the official images or self-presentations to both mankind and the theological pantheon. Although the context and purpose of public sculpture often explain the variation in facial types, especially in royal statues, the aspects or character traits were not necessarily different between private and public statues. Furthermore, the official image of a ruler was but one element of the ideological program of his sculptures, regardless of context. His dress, insignias, and crowns—even the dazzling paint or luster of the highly polished stone—were critical elements in the dramatic presentation of his stature.

A few scholars deny the existence of portraiture in Egyptian art, claiming that idealizing sculptures cannot possibly be realistic and that lifelike sculptures are formulaic or pastiches. Others insist that any lifelike attributes, particularly in the facial features, qualify a sculpture as portraiture. To be a portrait, the reasoning goes, an image must be recognizable and unable to be confused with the representations of other individuals. Advocates of this argument do not necessarily require complete verisimilitude. They admit stylistic conventions—a unique configuration of the eyebrow or the outlines of the eye—as markers of identity, along with more specific details such as facial musculature. The problem with this interpretation is that it implicitly requires a physical correspondence between the subject and the sculpture. It also precludes a common means of association by an individual with a group or, in the case of royal portraits, with an earlier ruler. The genealogy of portraiture and the association of an individual with an earlier period contain a very specific political, social, or theological message. Therefore, the continuation of a portrait type may indicate a desire to be associated with a previous person or era rather than being proof of physical similarity. Despite the denial of an individual's "real" appearance, sculptures—as well as paintings and reliefs—of this type are portraits because they reveal the qualities by which the person wished to be known.

There are other factors that must be taken into account when considering a historical portrait in isolation. For example, a statue can be identified with a particular individual in several ways. In its original context or through an identifying inscription, the identity would have been clear, regardless of the stylization, idealization, or similarity to earlier representations. Then again, the great majority of Egyptians would not have seen the pharaoh; hence, the degree of realism of a royal statue would have been lost on them. Furthermore, most sculptures have by now been removed from their settings, and many either are uninscribed or have lost their original identifying text. Because the facial features of so many of these sculptures are non-individualized, they remain anonymous. Many sculptures were appropriated by later persons and transported to distant locations. Sometimes they were recut and reinscribed for the new owner, but occasionally they were simply reinscribed. Because the original face was left untouched, the recognition factor seems irrelevant. The new inscription gave the sculpture a new identity; hence, its inner qualities now applied to the new owner. Even when naturalistic details appear, the identity is often difficult to determine without an inscription. Although these works seem idealized, stylized, or formulaic to us, to the ancient Egyptians they were portraits because they conformed to the prevailing style that was appropriate for expressing the inner character of individuals or the role that they fulfilled.

Thus, three different types of portrait are found in ancient Egyptian art: idealized and realistic portraits of real individuals and depictions of fictitious or nonspecific individuals, such as a "foreigner." The third category combines the first two types because it is a "study" of a more general nature, often with a seemingly realistic appearance. Realism does not consist of surface appearance; otherwise, any photograph would be a portrait. What makes a portrait is the artist's elucidation of an emotional, psychological, or intellectual component, an inner life that transcends physical correspondence. Those components are not always recognizable; artists often transmit them in a personal code decipherable by no one else. In modern times, the artist's perception becomes the defining element of the portrait. This luxury of personal interpretation, however, was a freedom that the ancient Egyptian artist did not enjoy.

That portraiture resists a single, all-purpose definition is not surprising, because it encompasses at least four sometimes opposing impulses: the public's expectations, the subject's wishes, the artist's vision, and artistic conventions. Despite the difficulties of interpretation, in very simple terms a portrait is a character study. It probes beneath the surface and reveals not the full range of the individual's psyche but one or a few aspects, which differ according to the needs that the portrait satisfies. Frequently a portrait is a labored or artificial study, especially when it serves an official or public purpose. Most often, a portrait captures a passing but revelatory mood and transfixes it for all time. Because the artist, subject, and viewer have different perceptions of the finished product, some scholars have rightly questioned the validity of the specific label "portraiture" and have suggested simply "representation" or "approximation" as alternatives. "Likeness" is another option, if it includes works that evoke the psychological or intellectual qualities of the individual and not merely the physiognomic details.

Consequently, portraiture is one of the most confusing, ill-defined, and controversial terms in the study of ancient Egyptian art. Part of the problem is the overemphasis on and misunderstanding of realism, which generally conforms to the modern expectation of anatomical verisimilitude. Realism, however, remains the greatest obstacle to the understanding of portraiture and is the focus here. Before the importance of realism to the Egyptological controversy can be assessed, some general observations on portraiture are necessary.

The style or type of portrait varies according to the intended audience. A portrait created for public display relies heavily on physiognomy. Because the portrait is an official image, however—most often of government, business, and academic persons—the artist acquiesces to formulaic exigencies and endows the representations with heroic qualities, such as the abilities to lead, make difficult decisions, and endure crises. Individual qualities are subordinated to expected roles, and it is sometimes questionable whether correspondence exists. Realism thus serves an ideal or an expectation, but it does not necessar-

PORTRAITURE. *Red quartzite bust of Akhenaten, eighteenth dynasty.* The bust is 12 centimeters (4.75 inches) high. (The Metropolitan Museum of Art, Rogers Fund, 1911. [11.150.26])

ily portray the individual. Realism is not an objective quality; it is subjective and mutable. The realism of a portrait depends on the viewers for whom it was created and the function that it served.

Correspondence is perhaps more evident in portraits intended for the subject's personal enjoyment because something of the individual's inner qualities appear. Nonetheless, uncertainty about the realism remains. The artist may defer to the patron's vanity by subduing some features and emphasizing others. The subject may specify the qualities to be expressed or the manner of representation. The descendants of an illustrious ancestor sometimes commission a flattering portrait, as if to create an official image.

Because the majority of human representations in Egyptian art appear to contemporary sensibilities as idealizing, generalizing, or even formulaic—slim, youthful, physically appealing figures devoid of lifelike features—they are not often regarded as portraits. By contrast, the slightest personal flourish—a furrowed brow, a pensive look, a distinctive nose—supposedly makes the representation the genuine item. Quite apart from the unwarranted primacy accorded to realism, this reductive reasoning is unfortunate on at least two counts. It omits the many nuances of realism, and it completely overlooks an intriguing related issue. Why are lifelike human representations generally confined to sculptures of men? Although numerous exceptions exist, Egyptian paintings and reliefs of both men and women are usually not individualizing, or fall within the category discussed above. Not until the Ptolemaic period do individualizing sculptures of women appear with any regularity, and even then the artist depends heavily on iconographic attributes to portray the

identity of an individual queen. Before then, that women are generally depicted in all three media as beautiful, svelte, young, and flawless may seem an enlightened aesthetic, but an equally valid interpretation is darker and pessimistic: the individuality of women was unimportant. The lack of evidence for individualizing portraits of women is as much a social as an artistic commentary because it demonstrates that their role was limited and minimal. The sculptures and reliefs of Hatshepsut illustrate this point well; this female pharaoh is typically portrayed in the guise of a male. The only compromise that convention allowed is Hatshepsut's very occasional portrayal in female form in some of her portraits.

The third portrait type is the most intensely personal, a representation intended neither as an official image nor as a private commission, but as an independent work. It is a category that either did not exist or was rare in ancient Egypt. The artist is free of constraints and expectations and endows the portrait with whatever qualities and sensations come to mind. Because these images are occasionally unflattering to the individual, they may seem more honest and realistic. For example, caricatures, especially the political and social varieties, are freighted with prejudice. Nonetheless, the majority of "independent" portraits are more benign, and on first consideration they are ostensibly the most important of the three types because they represent a personal, unbound, and therefore objective response; but they are no more realistic than portraits commissioned as official images or as more private and personal works. The representations of the same individual are subjective aesthetic responses that may differ from one artist to the next. Which portrait is the most realistic? Whether physical or internal, realism in portraiture is not an empirical, objective quality grounded in consensus. It is an ethos, a preference, or an interpretation, an ever-shifting variable, whose validity and expression depend on the audience, the subject, and the artist.

Few ancient Egyptian portraits are free of stylization. The best illustration consists of the plaster masks found in the workshop of the sculptor Thutmose at Tell el-Amarna, the capital of the eighteenth dynasty pharaoh Akhenaten. Some of the masks seem unretouched, but the majority are reworked or stylized to fit the prevailing artistic style. Although part of the individual's outward appearance is preserved, the alterations suggest that realism was not as important as the assimilation of the individual with the pharaoh by adopting his official style.

Stylization occurs in even the most seemingly realistic portraits. From the fourth dynasty come numerous sculptures known as "reserve heads," which display highly individualizing features. Among the most "realistic" of all Old Kingdom artistic works, these sculptures are regarded as true portraits. In one case, evidence exists for their anatomical veracity: the hooked nose on the head of Prince Nofer, now in the Museum of Fine Arts, Boston, recurs among his tomb reliefs. The function of the reserve heads has been debated, but it is generally agreed that they preserve the deceased's vital character. Interestingly enough, that character or inner life is less in evidence than the meticulous surface treatment. However, on a related sculpture, the bust of Ankhkhaef, also in Boston, both the internal and external aspects are revealed. The significant point is that on all these realistic heads, stylization is also crucial. The eyes and the eyebrows are rendered in an artificial manner that is not lifelike but is a traditional aesthetic style. The awkward proportions of some of the heads, the peculiar treatment of their mouths, and their overall ungainly appearance indicates stylization or at least suggests that the heads are not completely lifelike.

Because the mummies of numerous kings survive, a comparison between their heads and their artistic representations is often instructive. The aquiline noses of the mummies of the nineteenth dynasty pharaohs Sety I and Ramesses II are prominent throughout not only their sculptures but also their paintings and reliefs, which are among the most individualizing royal representations in these two media. Nonetheless, they display the same stylization around the eyes found in the reserve heads.

Even the most anatomically detailed Egyptian representations can be deceptive, sometimes they are almost caricatures. The idealizing images of the deceased as slim and athletic have their counterpart in remarkably corpulent figures such as the renowned Old Kingdom statues of Kaiaperu in the Egyptian Museum, Cairo, and of Hemiunu in the Pelizaeus Museum, Hildesheim. Although physical correspondence is a possibility, these statues may have been shaped by a class distinction. Both persons held important positions that freed them from need and from hard manual labor. Their dramatic bodily presence may have been a visual conceit manifesting their affluence. At the opposite extreme, the depictions in painting and relief of pot-bellied fishermen, emaciated and lame cowherds, bald and bewhiskered laborers, and carefully observed foreigners are probably more genre figures born of social commentary than actual individuals. The famous relief of the queen of Punt from Hatshepsut's temple at Deir el-Bahri and the innumerable scenes of other foreigners are meticulous in their detail; yet it is the peculiarity of the subject matter, its non-Egyptian otherness, that captured the artist's attention. The image of the queen of Punt may seem at first to be extraordinarily realistic, but it could well be a caricature. Unless the artist accompanied Hatshepsut's expedition to Punt, he would have relied on eyewitness reports, which no matter how reliable would have resulted in exaggeration and stylization. Likewise, for all their ostensible realism, the representations

of foreigners surely served as conventions or stereotypes; they are not necessarily realistic portraits of actual, historical foreigners simply because they seem to be individualizing.

Still, not every secondary character is formulaic. From the tomb of Horemheb at Saqqara come several reliefs depicting stock figures such as mourners, some of whom have anatomical details (receding hairlines, everted navels) that are unparalleled in similar scenes and probably indicate actual persons. These surprising individual flourishes in ancillary figures provide much of the liveliness of Egyptian art and serve as reminders of the profit to be gained from close study of even the most formulaic or repetitive phenomena.

Realism can be misleading also among representations of historical persons. The well-known statues of Senwosret III and his late twelfth dynasty successors in various collections, for example, have very lifelike, careworn faces, lacking the usual stylization of the eyebrows and eyes. Most remarkably, indications of advanced age are manifest in these statues as never before. Nonetheless, their expressions and appearances seem to be idealizations, evincing a quality or aspect of the king that was part of his official image, his self-presentation to deities and the public. Although the rulers of the waning twelfth dynasty may have had family resemblances that were accurately rendered in their sculptures, the close similarities between the sculptures of Senwosret III and his successors indicate that more than genealogy is at work. Actually, the rudiments of the style successfully exploited by Senwosret III first appear in the reign of Senwosret II. A new ideology expresses itself in the ponderous, haggard faces, which have their analogy in several pensive didactic texts related to kingship.

The phenomenon of appropriation is the clearest indication that physical correspondence was not essential for portraiture. In the thirteenth dynasty and about a millennium later in the twenty-fifth dynasty, private persons followed the late twelfth dynasty royal style. The physiognomy of these nonroyal persons obviously had no importance in their self-presentation. Their borrowing or adaptation of the official image of earlier kings allowed them to share some of the ideological aspects inherent in the royal sculptures. Similarly, portraits of the early Ptolemaic rulers are often hard to distinguish from those of the thirtieth dynasty. This similarity may have been a deliberate royal policy to link the Ptolemies with Egypt's past or, alternatively, the continuation of a stylistic convention. The type was then copied by private individuals, who commissioned portraits that demonstrated a desire to be associated with the royal house.

Exactly the same process recurs throughout Egyptian art, royal and nonroyal, not only in sculpture but also in painting and relief. Once a new official royal style was established, it became the archetype among kings and commoners, who made their own modifications through successive generations. Among many examples, there are a Thutmosid and a Ramessid style. Sometimes the official image had an antiquarian aura. Because Ahmose and Amenhotpe I, the first two kings of the eighteenth dynasty, restored native rule after the Hyksos domination and saw themselves as the heirs of Nebhepetre Montuhotpe, the late eleventh dynasty pharaoh who reunified the country after a period of civil strife, they depicted themselves in his image. Many pharaohs, particularly Ramesses II of the nineteenth dynasty, appropriated the sphinxes and other sculptures of much earlier kings; sometimes the only alterations were not to the face but to the identifying cartouche.

In many respects, portraits filled a general role. It was not necessarily just the facial features of an individual that mattered, but rather the role that was fulfilled. When the pharaoh died, the portrait could be reused acceptably by his successor because it represented the ideals of kingship and not merely the actual features of the individual ruler. New portrait types developed in order to show a ruler's desire—such as association with the previous pharaoh and the promotion of a dynasty—rather than his features. The representation of women in Egyptian art follows a similar pattern: their continual idealization indicates the limited social role of the eternally youthful, slim, beautiful woman.

Portraiture enabled the Egyptians to promote themselves to their deities and their fellows alike in a desired or prescribed manner. The evidence for "realistic" representations of individuals needs to be treated with the utmost caution, because they potentially account for the most stylized type. Idealizing images at least portray an individual in a specific role, and as a consequence they should not be misleading to the modern onlooker.

[See also Reserve Heads.]

BIBLIOGRAPHY

Ashton, Sally-Ann. "Ptolemaic Royal Sculptures from Egypt: Greek and Egyptian Traditions and Their Interaction." Ph.D. diss., King's College, University of London, 1999.

Assmann, Jan. "Preservation and Presentation of Self in Ancient Egyptian Portraiture." In *Studies Presented to William Kelly Simpson*, edited by Peter Der Manuelian, vol. 1, pp. 55–81. Boston, 1996.

Bianchi, Robert S. "The Pharaonic Art of Ptolemaic Egypt." In *Cleopatra's Egypt: Age of the Ptolemies*, edited by Robert S. Bianchi et al., pp. 55–80. Brooklyn, 1988.

Breckenridge, James D. *Likeness: A Conceptual History of Ancient Portraiture.* Evanston, Ill., 1968.

Spanel, Donald B. *Through Ancient Eyes: Egyptian Portraiture.* Birmingham, Ala., 1988.

Vandersleyen, Claude. "Porträt." In *Lexikon der Ägyptologie*, 4: 1074–1080. Wiesbaden, 1982.

SALLY-ANN ASHTON
AND DONALD B. SPANEL

POTTERY. *See* Ceramics.

POULTRY. Taking full advantage of the abundance of avian life in their country, the ancient Egyptians' diet was enriched by birds, especially delicious and highly nutritious migratory waterfowl. Just how plentiful and comparatively easy water birds are to obtain in Egypt can be seen from the fact that from 1979 to 1986, by a conservative estimate, between 260,000 and 374,000 of them were taken annually without firearms in the Nile Delta alone, using essentially ancient technology. Moreover, there is sound ecological and other evidence indicating that four or five thousand years ago, the available wildlife was far richer. [See Birds.]

By the middle of the first dynasty, as shown by a representation on a gaming disc found in the tomb (no. 3035) of the chancellor Hemaka at Saqqara, and now in the Egyptian Museum, Cairo, fowlers had perfected the technique of employing large, rectangular clapnets to capture huge numbers of these migrants. Most of this hunting presumably took place in the then-extensive swamplands of the Delta, but probably also in the Faiyum. Those birds not immediately killed when caught were fattened, even force-fed, and kept in a semidomesticated state until needed for food or sacrifice. Members of the aristocracy maintained, as did individual temples, substantial stocks of poultry on their domains. These birds had considerable economic importance. The vast repertoire of scenes from daily life decorating the walls of tomb-chapels belonging to the elite from the Old Kingdom onward routinely include the activities of busy poultry yards and aviaries. These places are shown teeming with various kinds of ducks, geese, cranes, and doves, and frequently have captions giving the birds' names and numbers. The famous fifth dynasty *mastaba* (tomb 60) of the high-ranking court official Tiy at Saqqara, for example, is noteworthy for its wide assortment of vibrant aviculture and fowling compositions. Such birds must have been so esteemed as table fare, that tomb owners evidently wished to eat them throughout eternity. Generous numbers of waterfowl are carried as offerings by bearers featured in tomb-chapels and temples spanning all eras, they appear among the piles of victuals heaped before the deceased, are put on funerary tables, are named in their extensive menus for the beyond, and are mentioned in temple offering lists. There is some textual evidence from the New Kingdom that birds were affordably priced in ancient Egypt. However, the specially raised and force-fed poultry on view in tomb scenes were undoubtedly reserved for the wealthy. Curiously, the eggs seem to be absent as food in funerary contexts, probably owing to a taboo.

When images are carefully executed and paint is still extant, it is sometimes possible to recognize the precise

POULTRY. *A mixed flock of waterbirds being trapped with clap-nets, including some pintails and European teal.* This is a tempera copy of a detail from a wall painting in the tomb of the twelfth dynasty nomarch Khnumhotep III at Beni Hasan. (Reproduced from I. Rosellini, *I monumenti dell'Egitto e della Nubia: Monumenti civili.* Pisa, 1834)

species depicted. Some of these fowl also appear as standard hieroglyphs. Frequently identified table birds are bean goose (*Anser fabalis*) or graylag goose (*Anser anser*), *r3* and *sr;* white-fronted goose (*Anser albifrons* and *Anser erythropus*), *trp;* Egyptian goose (*Alopochen aegyptiacus*), *smn;* ruddy shelduck (*Tadorna ferruginea*), *bsbs*?; pintail (*Anas acuta*), *zt* and *ḥp;* turtle dove (*Streptopelia turtur*) and palm dove (*Streptopelia senegalensis*), *mnwt* and *'b3,* common crane (*Grus grus*), *ḏ3t,* *'jw,* and *g3,* and demoiselle crane (*Anthropoides virgo*), *wḏ'.* Other valuable birds sometimes kept for food include swan (*Cygnus* sp.), *dnḏn*?; wigeon (*Anas penelope*), *wš3t;* European teal (*Anas crecca*), probably *sr* and *s;* quail (*Coturnix coturnix*), *p'rt;* coot (*Fulica atra*), *wḥ't;* and possibly pigeons (*Columba* sp.). Pigeon cotes, a customary feature of the Upper Egyptian landscape well into the present century, probably did not exist during dynastic times, and are first attested in the archaeological record during the Greco-Roman period.

The impression one derives from pictorial and written sources of which kinds of poultry were viewed as desirable for dining is confirmed through zooarchaeological studies on bones from cemeteries and settlement sites. Burials of well-to-do people often had mummified victuals. A sumptuous funerary repast prepared for Tutankhamun during the eighteenth dynasty, found near his tomb (no. 62) in the Valley of the Kings, consisted of one brant goose (*Branta bernicla*), one white-fronted goose, two bean geese, four teals, two shovelers (*Anas clypeata*), one gadwall (*Anas strepera*), and two ducks that were not identified. In the intact eighteenth dynasty tomb of the architect Kha at Thebes (tomb 8), the deceased was interred with a large amphora filled with eviscerated poultry, reportedly preserved with salt. Theban tomb paintings show birds being processed in this manner and stored in similar tall jars.

Although Egyptian aviculturalists doubtless experienced some success breeding these birds, owing to the sheer abundance of waterfowl in the wild and ease of obtaining them, there was not a strong incentive for captive propagation. Nevertheless, the growing demand for table geese eventually led to the complete domestication of a goose, probably the graylag, by the time of the New Kingdom. The Egyptian goose occasionally appears in avicultural scenes, but only during the Old and Middle Kingdoms. By the early eighteenth dynasty, this large indigenous duck had risen in distinction, becoming sacrosanct to Amun, the powerful god of the city of Thebes. It was surely for this reason that this species was kept as a pet by some Theban notables, and is displayed quietly sitting near them in their decorated tomb-chapels, even accompanying them on fowling expeditions, despite the bird's infamously aggressive behavior. Otherwise, domestic poultry evidently played a small role in Egyptian religious belief.

Today's most characteristic farmyard bird, the chicken (or red jungle fowl, *Gallus gallus*), was unknown to the ancient Egyptians until the nineteenth dynasty, and then only as a marvel imported from Southeast Asia by way of the Near East. The chicken did not become commonplace along the banks of the Nile until at least the Ptolemaic period. Classical writers, such as Diodorus Siculus (I, 74), in the middle of the first century BCE, mention the large-scale artificial incubation of poultry eggs by Egyptian aviculturalists. Presumably, the practice of constructing hatcheries first developed during the Late period. It is also possible that the eggs of other species, such as the sacred ibis (*Threskiornis aethiopicus*), were incubated to supply the popular and burgeoning animal-cult industry with birds used as votive offerings. The earliest archaeological evidence for these installations comes from the sixth century CE. Hatcheries like this were still being used in some small villages of Upper Egypt as recently as the late 1950s.

BIBLIOGRAPHY

Boessneck, Joachim. *Die Tierwelt des alten Ägypten. Untersucht anhand kulturgeschichtlicher und zoologischer Quellen.* Munich, 1988. This volume provides an authoritative discussion of poultry in ancient Egypt, based primarily upon zooarchaeological findings.

Darby, William J., Paul Ghalioungui, and Louis Grivetti. *Food: The Gift of Osiris.* Vol. 1. London and New York, 1977. In this extensive survey of food in pharaonic Egypt, considerable space is devoted to birds. While valuable information is presented, numerous errors occur and mar the book's reliability.

Houlihan, Patrick F. *The Birds of Ancient Egypt.* Warminster, 1986. The only comprehensive study of the birds represented in Egyptian art and hieroglyphs, and includes an examination of those species maintained for food consumption; contains lengthy bibliography.

Houlihan, Patrick F. *The Animal World of the Pharaohs.* London and New York, 1996. This handsomely illustrated book aimed at a general audience includes a chapter devoted to avifauna and its role in ancient Egypt.

Ikram, Salima. *Choice Cuts: Meat Production in Ancient Egypt.* Orientalia Lovaniensia Analecta, 69 Leuven, 1995. The author offers some interesting remarks about the processing and preserving of poultry using salt, and victual bird mummies.

Mahmoud, Osama. *Die wirtshaftliche Bedeutung der Vögel im Alten Reich.* Frankfurt and Bern, 1991. Study of the role of birds, particularly poultry keeping, in the economy of the Old Kingdom.

Vandier, Jacques. *Manuel d'archéologie égyptienne.* Vol. 5. Paris, 1969. Presents a superb overview and interpretation of the scenes of daily life relating to keeping poultry.

PATRICK F. HOULIHAN

PREDYNASTIC PERIOD. Toward the end of the Upper Paleolithic, some important changes occurred in the cultures of Nubia and Upper Egypt, in which tools were made from blades and from geometric microliths on flakes in Mesolithic settlement camps that were larger than the hunting camps of the Paleolithic. Many grinding stones found in sites of the Afian culture in the Kom Ombo region (c.12,000 BCE) were worn from constant use; these, and microlithic sickle blades with lustrous edges were also discovered in the northern Nubian Qadanian (12,000–9000 BCE). The oldest cemetery in the Nile Valley (Gebel Sahaba) is associated with this culture. There, fifty-nine skeletons in contracted position (on the left side, with the head to the east) were unearthed. Some had flint points embedded in the bones as a result of a battle or a ritual. The Esnian Culture (11,000–10,000 BCE) was characterized by large camps, with numerous grinding stones and sickle blades. Around 9000 BCE, similar cultures waned, from climatic change, and the basis of human life in the Nile Valley became hunting and fishing until the end of the sixth millennium BCE.

The Early Khartoum culture occupied central Sudan (c.7400–4900 BCE). Found there were some seasonal camps and associated cemeteries (e.g., Khartoum Hospital, Saqqai) used by hunting-fishing-gathering groups; also stone tools, bone tools, and the oldest pottery in Africa (Wavy Line, Dotted Wavy Line). Later (c.4900–3800 BCE) in this same area, the Early Khartoum Neolithic (Kadero, Shaheinab) was based on animal husbandry (under Western Desert influence), although cultivation was unknown.

In the Nile Valley (6000–5000 BCE), the origins of a farming economy resulted from the joining of local traditions with outside influences that came from the Near East and the Sahara. Near Eastern influences include the appearance of cultivated wheat, flax, oats, and goats. Saharan influences include domesticated cattle and the cultivation of barley. Egyptian pottery of the time, like the flint technology, also shows influence from both directions. Movement into the Nile Valley from the adjacent desert is most probably explained by the drought periods of the Middle Holocene, which put pressure on the inhabitants of the Western and the Eastern Egyptian deserts, and even the Negev, to move toward the Nile, with all its swampy, miasmic problems.

Early Predynastic Period. Both Upper Egypt, near Nubia, and Lower Egypt, near the Nile Delta and the Mediterranean, have yielded cultural materials of note.

Faiyum A. In Lower Egypt, the oldest Predynastic culture (c.5200–4500 BCE), discovered by Gertrude Caton-Thompson (1934), became the subject of many research expeditions. Seasonal camps were localized on the banks of Lake Moeris and traces of Faiyuman habitation construction were found, with numerous fireplaces preserved, concentrated in the central part of the camps. Silos were dug into the ground lined with basketry, since the economy was based on cultivation: wheat, three varieties of barley, and flax (oldest evidence in Egypt). Animal husbandry (with some cattle, sheep, goats, pigs, and dogs) was less significant. Fishing in shallow flood basins had great importance, and a variety of animals was hunted. Simple wooden sickles with several blades, hollow-based arrowheads, numerous axes (made from flint, chert, dolerite, and limestone), grinders, scrapers, rubbers, and bone items (harpoons, pins, needles, awls) are known. Undecorated pottery was used, of red or black surface (smooth, rarely polished) and simple forms—hemispherical bowls, large ovoid vessels, flat plates, and small pots. Rare personal ornaments included Red Sea mussel and amazonite beads. Burials are unknown.

Merimde Beni Salama. At Merimde, another Predynastic culture (c.5000–4500 BCE) was found, at the southwestern edge of the Delta, by H. Junker (1929–1939) and J. Eiwanger (1977–1983). Junker distinguished two main phases and one transitional; Eiwanger three phases (within five layers), emphasizing that their continuity is unclear. Phase I was related to the Palestinian Neolithic A, but a flake industry pointed to a local Epi-Paleolithic heritage. Well-fired pottery was made from untempered silt, polished dark pink, with incised herringbone decoration; a lighter smooth pottery was made with characteristic thick walls and some diversity of form (hemispherical bowls, plates, cups). Flint tools were made of blades and flakes with unifacial or, rarely, bifacial flaking (scrapers, borers, axes, and small arrowheads similar to Near Eastern patterns). There were also numerous grinders and rubbers. According to many scholars, the ceramic and flint-working technologies, the anthropomorphic and scarce zoomorphic figurines, and the domesticated animals point to Near Eastern roots for the first inhabitants. Phase II, despite continuity in many areas, offered numerous African characteristics. Phase III represents a regional culture similar to Faiyum A. The uninterrupted succession of layers indicate the development of single society. Numerous animal enclosures and small oval huts with fireplaces were partially dug into the ground. Techni-

cal advancement in ceramics and stoneworking and the presence of a workshop suggest craft specialization. There were also numerous products from bone, horn, ivory, terracotta, and shell. In Merimde, graves were found: small oval pits with contracted skeletons on their right sides, with heads to the south, wrapped in mats or skin. The economy was the same in all phases, with animal husbandry (cattle predominating from Phase II on; also sheep, pigs, goats, and dogs) and crop cultivation (wheat, probably barley, and sorghum), both still supplemented by hunting and gathering.

El Omari. Known from a large site, the El Omari culture (c.4600–4400 BCE) is at the outlet of the Wadi Hof, north of Helwan. It was named after its discoverer and was investigated by P. Bovier-Lapierre and F. Debono. Oval, round, and irregular pits were found, dug out from the wadi deposit or cut into the cliff and lined with mats, clay, and wicker. The economy was based on the cultivation of wheat, barley, broad beans, peas, and flax; animal husbandry was based on cattle, goats, sheep, and especially pigs. Fishing was important but hunting and gathering less so. Red pottery from two kinds of local clays was straw-tempered, polished, and smoothed, showing similarity to Palestinian Neolithic A and B.

Moerian. Distinguished by B. Ginter and J. K. Kozlowski, the Moerian culture was a later phase of the Neolithic in the Faiyum (c.4400–3800 BCE). It is characterized by a flint industry on blades and bladelets that were struck from small concretions, affiliated with the Epi-Paleolithic technological tradition of the Western Desert. Two-thirds of the tools are backed blades, micro-retouched blades and bladelets, retouched blades, and perforators. Pottery, tempered with organic material and sand, includes hemispherical bowls, S-profile vessels, and pots with cylindrical necks. The Moerian economy was based on animal husbandry, hunting, and fishing.

Lower Egyptian or Maadi culture. The oldest phase (c.3800–3500 BCE) parallels the Naqada I culture, represented by the Naqada settlement (a suburb of Cairo) and the early graves from Wadi Digla investigated in 1930–1953. The economy was based on agriculture (wheat, barley, and flax); animal husbandry (cattle, sheep, goats, pigs, dogs, and donkeys—used as a means of transportation—the oldest example of this in Egypt); and trade, supplemented by hunting and fishing. Three types of buildings occur: dwellings showing some similarities with the Chalcolithic stage of Beersheba culture. Possibly, the structures were built by arrivals from Palestine. The funerary rites differ from those of Upper Egypt, and animal burials were found (dogs, goats, and lambs). The material culture shows both Egyptian and Palestinian influences. Copper was important. Besides adornments, there were copper tools—fish-hooks, pins, needles, chisels, and axes/adzes—

which probably played an important role (as in Palestine). Raw materials were imported, from Wadi Araba in the Sinai, in the form of ingots—three were found, of uniform weight—and ore. Trade, especially with Sinai and Palestine, included pottery, basalt vessels, copper, flint rocks, Canaanite flint blades, Red Sea shells, pigments, resins, oils, cedar wood(?), and asphalt. Exports included pottery, basalt vessels, flint objects, shells, and Nile fishes.

Upper Egyptian cultures. With the complexity of the cultural succession in this southern region, several systems of relative chronology have been proposed by Egyptologists. W. M. Flinders Petrie (1901) divided the Predynastic period into 80 Sequence Datings (S.D.): 1–29 were reserved for earlier cultures that were not known at that time; 30–37 were identified by the term Amratian; 38–62 were called Gerzean; and 63–76 were Semainean. The lack of uniform typological criteria, the incorrect evaluation of Wavy-handled pottery, and the failure to take horizontal stratigraphy into account, caused eventual criticism. W. Kaiser (1957) then offered his system, based on the horizontal distribution of pottery classes and types of objects within Cemetery 1400–1500 at Armant; emphasizing the evolutionary character of the Naqada culture, he divided it into three periods, within which he distinguished eleven (later fifteen) subperiods. Based on a larger number of cemeteries, S. Hendrickx (1996) has proposed a modification of the system—taking into account the local differentiation—and extending his modification to the second dynasty.

Tasa-Badari. Discovered by G. Brunton, the paucity of data made it impossible to determine whether Tasa was a separate culture, a preliminary phase, or a mutation of the Badarian culture (c.4300–3700 BCE). Its originality was manifested in the simple pottery (deep bowls and pots) of brown and grey-black; black or brownish-black polished beakers, decorated with incised lines filled with a white paste, constitute a special group. Tasa may have occupied part of central and southern Egypt to the Armant region, whereas the Badari essentially occupied the northern part of Upper Egypt (Matmar-Qau); some sites in the South, in the Wadi Hammamat, and on the Red Sea coast may indicate that the Badarian were relatively mobile. The economy was based on crops (wheat and barley), animal husbandry (goats, cattle, and sheep), and hunting. In Hemmamiya are found pear-shaped grain silos (3 meters/10 feet deep), lined with mats or baskets, and nearby are huts, fireplaces, and animal enclosures. The best-known artifactual inventory comes from the graves of the extramural cemeteries, where, besides pottery, hollow-based arrowheads were found, as well as saw-edged sickle blades, stone axes, bone needles, pins, awls, and combs; ivory bracelets, beads, rings, vessels, spoons, and combs; cosmetic palettes, shell and stone beads, ear

and nose studs, amulets, and clay boat models. Copper was rare but the presence of turquoise and seashells indicates trade contacts along the Red Sea coast. The origin of the Badarian culture is unknown, but some features can be traced to Palestine (ceramic decoration called "rippling," crop cultivation, animal husbandry), the Western Desert oases (flint-tool techniques, animal husbandry), and Nubia (pottery decorations, animal husbandry). The Badarians seem to have combined various local traditions in forming the first stage of Upper Egyptian culture.

Naqada I (Amratian; c.3900–3550 BCE). The region of Naqada-Mashasna, beyond the range of Badari, was the core area with the oldest finds and the largest population density (e.g., Ballas, Diospolis Parva, el-Amra, Abydos). Naqada I and Badari had coexisted, but in a later phase, the Amratian formed the first culture that spread over all of Upper Egypt. The majority of the information on this culture derives from its cemeteries, since its settlements are poorly preserved. Agriculture and animal husbandry had developed, but they were still supplemented by hunting and fishing. The funerary rituals were similar to those of Badari, but the average graves were richer and all status levels were still buried together. Gradually, at Hierakonpolis, only the few wealthy had larger, and richer, graves. In Hemmamiya, houses and the first aboveground granaries were found.

The existence of a Lower Egyptian kingdom at this period is not probable, but head coverings similar to the Red Crown of Lower Egypt were worn by some figures in rock engravings and paintings (from both the Eastern and Western Deserts); they may be local chiefs. From this period come the first attempts at Egyptian faience and there was some slight increase in copper objects—pins, needles, beads, bracelets, awls, and rings. Models made from cheap materials were deposited in graves (mace heads, knives, boats). Trade intensified in all directions but objects characteristic of Naqada I have been found mostly to the south in Nubia, very rarely to the northern region of the Delta and Sinai. The increase in trade was accompanied by social stratification, still progressing slowly, and the development of local elites.

Middle Predynastic Period

Lower Egyptian culture (Maadi-Buto; c.3500–3200 BCE). The second phase of Lower Egyptian culture includes the last period at Maadi, the youngest graves at Wadi Digla, the cemetery at Heliopolis, and the oldest layer at Buto; the third phase occurs only at Buto. Among the most important finds from archaeological work in Buto were the discoveries associated with the expansion of the Naqada culture. In the first layer (contemporary to Naqada IIB), structures had walls of wattle and daub. Pottery consisted of vessels typical of the Delta and others of clearly foreign provenience. Layer III a was transitional, containing constructions and artifacts characteristic of Lower Egyptian Culture and the beginning of Naqada II D2. Layers III b–f and IV had exclusively Naqadian materials (II D2–first dynasty).

Naqada II (Gerzean; c.3550–3200 BCE). The most important sites are Hierakonpolis, Naqada, el-Amra, Mahasna, Abydos, Matmar, Gerza, and Minshat Abu Omar. Most characteristic of this phase is the expansion to the north—Naqada II, emerging from the regions of Naqada I, gradually led to the cultural unification of all Egypt. The expansion into the northern part of Middle Egypt began in Naqada IIC; the expansion into the Delta was no later than Naqada II D1. It was primarily a territorial occupation, secondarily securing trade routes to the east. The basic principles of the equipment of Egyptian graves originated in this period, with the quantity and quality of grave goods reflecting the growing Naqada culture's social stratification. Separate necropolises appeared, containing exclusively large and rich graves. Graves of the elite are known from Abydos, Minshat Abu Omar, Diospolis Parva, and Hierakonpolis, testifying about social development and the creation of centers of authority. Although buildings are not well known from the period, the models of houses discovered in graves depict rectangular brick buildings, with wooden beams (lintels) over the doors. New kinds of pottery were made of tempered silt. Decorated pottery had scenes of birds and animals, triangles symbolizing the desert, and plants. Others with the portrayal of boats with human figures may point to the existence of rituals that involve the leaders/chiefs of clans/tribes. The oldest preserved Egyptian wall painting, at Hierakonpolis, may therefore be confirmed, since it shows hunting, triumph, and rites associated with boats. Such scenes in a grave context suggest the beginnings of the custom of "taking" symbolic and real events of life into the next world.

Conical mace heads were replaced by pear-shaped mace heads, which, beginning in mid-Naqada II, become symbols of authority—one of the attributes of power in Egypt's royal iconography. The production of copper increased in importance, as did that of gold and silver. In general, metal was sought after, probably a sign of status. Flint was still the most important material for tool production, but techniques had advanced; in addition to traditional tools made from flakes, a new technique appeared—production of long blades, later processed by bifacial retouching (ripple-flake). The number of personal adornments of bone, ivory, and semiprecious stones increased markedly, as did bracelets, rings, beads, pendants, and amulets. The rich material culture indicates that groups of highly specialized craftsmen existed. Centers of production, such as Hierakonpolis, plus a relatively small number of workshops distributed products throughout Egypt.

The first Egyptian cities developed as the residences of the elite. There, the majority of craftsmen also lived. The cities soon played a central role for the larger surrounding territory. For example, Naqada (Eg., *Nubt*, "city of gold") developed significantly in this period, based on trade in gold and copper from mines in the Eastern Desert. Changes in the environment and in society also transformed Hierakonpolis (Eg., *Nekhen*), regarded by the ancients as the capital of the Upper Egyptian state, into a major political and economic center. Naqada is equidistant (about 100 kilometers/64 miles in a straight line) from Hierakonpolis and Abydos, and other important population centers were grouped in their immediate vicinity. Strong economic centers of local authority arose and trade was conducted in every direction. Contacts with the Levant are indicated by small quantities of Palestinian pottery in Upper Egypt, as well as by the presence of Naqada II products in the Palestine region. Contacts with Sumer and Elam are yet debatable. Although raw materials (obsidian, lapis lazuli), products (cylinder seals), and certain art motifs (a hero strangling a lion) of Mesopotamia or Elam appeared, their presence in Egypt may be the result of a series of indirect trade contacts, not from regular exchange. Sources have been identified, other than those previously supposed, for at least some of the imported goods. For example, obsidian tools were regarded as proof of connections between the Nile Valley and the Near East, but new analyses have shown beyond a doubt that that obsidian was acquired in Ethiopia. Contacts to the south are better confirmed: found in Upper Egypt was pottery characteristic of Nubian Group A (made of silt, with a large number of admixtures, and decorated with ornaments filled with white). Many Gerzean period products were also found in Nubia.

Late Predynastic (Protodynastic) Period. Naqada III culture (c.3200–3050 BCE) was characterized by the abandonment or reduction in significance of certain population centers in Egypt's South (e.g., Matmar, Mahasna), the maintenance or even growth in significance of others (e.g., Hierakonpolis, Abydos), and the foundation of yet others (e.g., Elkab, Tarkhan, Tura). Social changes were of increasing importance, yet despite a certain variance in material culture, this period was a direct continuation of the Gerzean. A major settlement move from the desert to the vicinity of the Nile was necessary in Naqada III. Ecological changes that began in Naqada II were intensified, bringing with them a relative cessation in herding in favor of agriculture. Changes in the material culture indicate an accompanying alteration in the spiritual realm. Some objects were modified in shape, while their basic function was preserved; others, while their shape was preserved, had their functions changed—from utility to ritual-cult-symbolic (e.g., palettes). Pottery included decorated wares, cylindrical jars, cups, and large transport-storage jars, often with engraved and painted *serekhs*, indicating that the contents were intended for the royal court. The production of flint artifacts relatively decreased—due mainly to the expanded use of metal tools. The use of jewelry also increased, as did the role of sculpture and relief. In Coptos, no later than Narmer's time, three colossal statues of Min (4 meters/13 feet high) and three statues of lions (1.5 meters/4 feet long) were erected. Many items have elaborate scenes: palettes, ceremonial mace heads, and knife handles. In temple deposits at Hierakonpolis, Abydos, and Elephantine, a number of figurines—prisoners, children, women, scorpions, baboons—were made of various materials, some votive but some fragments of larger objects and furniture. They indicate development of the ritual-symbolic sphere—that associated with the centralization of authority.

Glyptics and writing became increasingly important, clearly developed under the influence of impulses from the Near East, passing through a brief phase of imitation, then ultimately containing typically Egyptian motifs and inscriptions. The role of long-distance trade, conducted in all the traditional directions, increased considerably. Contacts with Palestine and the Sinai intensified, showing the importance of this nearby northeastern region and its goods (wine, oil, resin, timber, copper). The Protodynastic colonization of northern Sinai and southern Canaan lasted until the mid-first dynasty. The kings known from this period ruled over all of Egypt—"Uj," Iry-Hor(?), Ka, "Scorpion," and Narmer—have been dated to Naqada IIIB–IIIC1 (c.3150–3050 BCE). Toward the end of the Protodynastic Dynasty "0," probably in the reign of Narmer, the kingdom of the pharaohs was established, more or less in the form known from the Early Dynastic (Archaic) period. The gradual (not by conquest) formation of an Egyptian state was therefore the last stage, not the first, from which the civilization of the Nile Valley grew.

BIBLIOGRAPHY

Adams, Barbara. *Prednyastic Egypt.* Shire Egyptology, 7. Aylesbury, 1988.
Adams, Barbara, and Krzysztof M. Ciałowicz. *Protodynastic Egypt.* Shire Egyptology, 25. Buckinghamshire, 1997. Civilization and art from the last years of Naqada II to the middle of the first dynasty.
Brink, Edwin C. M. van den, ed. *The Nile Delta in Transition. 4th–3rd Millennium B.C.* Tel Aviv, 1992. The Nile Delta in the light of new excavations and theories.
Caton-Thompson, Gertrude, and Eleanor Gardner. *The Desert Fayum.* London, 1934.
Debono, Fernand, and Bodil Mortensen. *El Omari. A Neolithic Settlement and Other Sites in the Vicinity of Wadi Hof, Helwan.* Archäologische Veröffentlichungen, 82. Mainz, 1990. The first comprehensive publication and analysis of materials from the Omari culture.
Ginter, Bolesław, and Janusz K. Kozłowski. *Predynastic Settlement near Armant.* Heidelberg, 1994. Results of the investigations by an expedition in Upper Egypt from the Institute of Archeology, Jagiellonian University.
Hendrickx, Stan. *Elkab V. The Naqada III Cemetery.* Brussels, 1994.
Hendrickx, Stan. "The Relative Chronology of the Naqada Culture: Problems and Possibilities." In *Aspects of Early Egypt,* edited by Jeffrey Spencer, pp. 36–69. London 1996. Important and documented modification of the relative chronology of the Naqada complex.
Hoffman, Michael A. *Egypt before the Pharaohs.* Austin, 1991. Predynastic Egypt in the perspective of archeological discoveries.
Kaiser, Werner. "Zur Entstehung des gesamtägyptischen Staates." *Mitteilungen Des Deutschen Archäologischen Instituts Abt. Kairo* 46 (1990), 287–297. The emergence of the Egyptian state and the modification of the relative chronology proposed in 1957.
Kemp, Barry J. *Ancient Egypt. Anatomy of a Civilisation.* London and New York, 1989. An original approach to the origins of the Egyptian state.
Krzyżaniak Lech, Karla Kroeper, and Michał Kobusiewicz, eds. *Interregional Contacts in the Later Prehistory of Northeastern Africa.* Studies in African Archaeology, 5. Poznań, 1996. The fourth volume of papers from one of the most important cyclical conferences on Predynastic Egypt.
Midant-Reynes, Béatrix. *Préhistoire de l'Égypte. Des premiers hommes aux premiers pharaons.* Paris, 1992. Exhaustive discussion of the material culture and social development of the prehistoric period in Egypt, against the background of the adjacent regions.
Needler, Winifred. *Predynastic and Archaic Egypt in The Brooklyn Museum.* New York, 1984. Catalog discussing these categories of artifacts.
Payne, Joan Crowfoot. *Catalogue of the Predynastic Egyptian Collection in The Ashmolean Museum.* Oxford, 1993. Another exhaustive discussion of these categories of artifacts.
Spencer, A. J. *Early Egypt. The Rise of Civilisation in the Nile Valley.* London, 1993.
Vercoutter, Jean. *L'Egypte et la vallée du Nil.* vol. I: *Des origines à la fin de l'Ancien Empire.* Paris, 1992. The beginnings of Egyptian civilization, taking into account the development of art.
Wendorf, Fred, and Romuald Schild, eds. *Prehistory of the Nile Valley.* New York, 1976.

KRZYSZTOF M. CIAŁOWICZ

PRICES AND PAYMENT. These are a key feature of the commercial, market economy. The ancient Egyptian economy, based on redistribution and reciprocity, set prices in units of value that referred directly to commodities, rather than to the abstract concept of money. For the purpose of exchange and trade, the Egyptians first calculated the value of goods and services in units that were directly related to the necessities of life and, later, they calculated in terms of the weights of metals. Yet the Egyptians never fully abstracted the idea of money—goods and services, as well as metals, were valued concretely for what they were.

Sources for the study of prices and payments do not survive from all periods of Egyptian history. Information about wages and rations are best known from documents of the Old, Middle, and New Kingdoms, while commodity prices are best preserved from the Ramessid period. Wage payments in the Old Kingdom are known from the Abusir Papyri. For the Middle Kingdom, there are temple documents, biographies, and archaeological data. New Kingdom wages are known from Deir el-Medina and from documents pertaining to shipping. All the sources indicate that wage payments were made in rations of bread, beer, grain, meat, and cloth, which were the daily necessities of life.

Rations were expressed most frequently in units of bread and beer, the two staples of an Egyptian diet. Most likely, the lowest salaries, which were close to subsistence level, were actually paid in bread and beer. Just as modern coins are guaranteed to contain standard amounts of metal, each loaf of bread was baked from a standard recipe, using equal amounts of ingredients, and had a standard nutritional value. Uniformity was assured through a system called *pfs*, translated as "baking value." *pfs* could also be used by the employer to ensure that a predictable number of loaves would be baked from a known amount of grain. The baking value was based on the number of loaves or beer jars produced from a set measure of grain; the higher the value, the smaller would be the loaves, the weaker the beer, or the smaller the jars. Most wage lists assumed that a standard *pfs* was used in baking and brewing.

Uniformity was also assured through the use of tokens or tallies. During the Middle Kingdom at Uronarti, ceramic tallies have been discovered in the shape of a standard loaf of bread. Presumably that tally could be used to check whether a worker's wages in bread loaves were all the same size. Beer jars were also of a roughly standard size. The standard basic wage was ten loaves of bread and one-third to two full jugs of beer per day (Egyptian beer was much less alcoholic than modern brews and higher in calorie content). That was the ration of the lowest paid staff members. Others were paid in multiples of the standard wage, varying from twice to fifty times the standard wage for highly paid people. Various methods could be used for apportioning wages. For example, documentation exists for a particular ship's crew in which the captain and other officials received twice the ration of the ordinary sailors. In another case, the highest paid official received thirty-eight one-third loaves while the lowest paid worker received one and one-third loaves.

In an example from the Middle Kingdom the staff of a temple received a commission on all the goods that came to the temple. One inscription describes the way the staff was paid in "temple days":

> As for a temple day, it is 1/360 part of a year. Now, you shall divide everything which enters this temple—bread, beer, and meat—by way of the daily rate. That is, it is going to be 1/360 of the bread, the beer, and of everything which enters this temple for [any] one of these temple days which I have given you.

In that temple, the regular staff received 2/360 of the total revenue of the temple, while the chief priest received 4/360.

In another case from the Middle Kingdom, an expedition leader received five hundred loaves a day as his "ration." Large sums like that were probably not paid out in actual loaves of bread or jars of beer. It is unlikely that an expedition leader could take his ever-increasing number of loaves of bread—fifteen thousand loaves after a month—with him on an extended trip into the desert or that he could eat that much, even with a large family and servants to support. Thus it seems possible that five hundred loaves of bread was actually a unit for measuring out commodities, approximating the modern idea of a unit of money, a practice that allowed the ancient Egyptians to save and also to draw against an account of bread and beer.

Because the standard measures for bread loaves and beer jars vary from place to place and time to time, it is difficult to calculate how much people had to eat and to determine how well people lived. The caloric value of the soldier's ration at Uronarti was about one-third kilo (0.5 pound) of barley per day. Baked into bread, this is the equivalent of 1,458 calories from bread each day. If these soldiers did any physical work, they must have received at least an additional fifteen hundred calories from beer and/or vegetables just to maintain their weight.

The New Kingdom craftsmen at Deir el-Medina received all the necessities of life from their employer: their houses were owned by the state, food and clothing rations were given to them, as well as most of the other necessities, including water, fuel for their ovens, and the tools they needed to perform their duties. Yet the robust trade that they conducted among themselves indicates that those workers required additional goods and services that the state had not provided.

Information about the prices of commodities was derived from Deir el-Medina. Prices were recorded on a few papyri and on numerous ostraca that date to a 150-year period during the nineteenth and twentieth dynasties. Many problems with the interpretation of those texts must be overcome, however, before commodity prices can be determined. The ostraca were written in the cursive Hieratic script by nonprofessional scribes who did not write as legibly as did professional scribes. The ostraca were often broken in antiquity and ink has faded during storage in museums. Moreover, the texts were never intended for others to read, but were personal notes, so that many details that would have been known to the original reader were not recorded. Among the details that were often excluded was the date of when it was written. Such omission often makes it difficult to compare prices, although scholars have determined which ostraca are roughly contemporary by comparing the people named in them. This process has its own difficulties, because the small number of families living in the village drew on a limited stock of personal names, making it difficult, for example, to pinpoint the generation of a particular Pentaweret. Another difficulty in determining prices was the lack of description of the goods that were priced. Clearly, some variation in the price of two chairs was based on the quality of the workmanship, although the variation is almost never described in the ostraca. Finally, the precise meanings of words used to describe the commodities is often not understood. Sometimes, only the general category of the good can be determined from the writing. In spite of these difficulties, scholars have isolated four units of value that were used to price commodities: the *deben* (*dbn*), the *senyu* (*snjw*, originally called *š'tj* [*shaty*]), the *hin* (*hnw*), and the *khar* (*ẖȝr*).

The *deben* is a measure of weight used for gold, silver, and, most commonly, copper. One *deben* of copper weighs ninety-one grams. It was divided into ten *kite*. Copper weights seem never to be lower than five *kite* or one-half *deben*, while the more precious metals are found with weights of less than five *kite*. It is sometimes difficult to determine whether the actual weight of the metal is being described or its value in *deben*—or, indeed, whether the Egyptians made such a distinction. In the Cairo Ostracon 25242 *verso*, for example, twenty *deben* of copper was added to four *deben* as the value of a basket, demonstrating that the actual weight was difficult to separate from the idea of its value. *Deben* of copper and bronze were not distinguished by the Egyptians. Both were valued as one *kite* of silver. Silver *deben* were rarely mentioned in the ostraca, but are more common in the papyri. Papyrus, of course, was used to record official and thus more expensive transactions, while the ostraca were used by the villagers to record private, smaller transactions. This practice ensures that gold *deben* are never mentioned in the ostraca but appear occasionally in the papyri; it must be assumed that when the word *deben* is used alone on ostraca, copper *deben* should be understood.

The *senyu* ("piece"?) is the second unit of value used by the Egyptians. It is a weight in silver equal to 1/12 *deben* or 7.6 grams. Its value is calculated as five *deben*, but that calculation does not always hold true (see below). The *senyu* is found as a weight or value only in the nineteenth dynasty and early twentieth dynasty up to the first half of the reign of Ramesses III. The *senyu* could be used to express a value in the same column of figures with *deben*. The Berlin Ostracon 1268 states the value of objects in *senyu* but the total of the column in *deben* of copper. The Varille Ostracon 25 totals a razor valued at one *deben*, with a donkey valued at seven *senyu*.

The *hin*, a third unit of value, is a measure of volume equal to 0.48 liters (about one-half quart). Its value is 1/6 *senyu*, but other calculations show that it was also equal to one copper *deben*. The value of the *hin* is probably based on the value of one *hin* of sesame oil, said to be equal to one copper *deben*. *Mrḥt*-oil and *'d*-fat were also measured in *hin*, but their values seem to vary in relation to *deben*, both more and less than one *deben*. Thus the value of one *hin* equal to one *deben* is based on sesame oil.

The *khar* is a measure of the volume of grain, either emmer or barley, equal to 76.88 liters (about 80 quarts), which is divided into four *oipe*. The *khar* is translated as "sack" and was valued at two *deben*. *Deben*, *senyu*, and *khar* are all found together in documents ranging from the time of Ramesses II (*Hieratic Ostraca* 65) through Ramesses V (*Hieratic Ostraca* 28). The *khar* is most commonly found as a unit of value for baskets, both because the volume of a basket was equal to its value and because baskets are relatively inexpensive. The same principle is at work in the Cairo Ostracon 25242, in which a bed is valued in *deben* while its legs are valued in *oipe*. Ostracon Deir el-Medina 21 also differentiates between expensive items in *deben* and cheaper items in *oipe*.

The rough equivalent values among *deben*, *senyu*, *hin*, and *khar*, as given above, reveal the difficulty of calculating precise values for commodities, as well as fixed ratios among the four different units of value. One document values a basket at one-quarter *senyu* for a volume of one-half *khar*. Since one *khar* is equal in value to two *deben*, the logical conclusion would be that one *senyu* equals four copper *deben* in value. Yet another example shows that one *senyu* of *mss*-garments is equal to five copper *deben*. Finally, another document values one *hin* of oil at 1/6 *senyu*. Since one *hin* is equal to one *deben*, the logical conclusion is that one *senyu* is equal to six *deben*. Clearly modern ideas about money and prices were not at work in ancient Egypt. Modern conceptions of money would not allow one *senyu* to be equal to either four, five, or six *deben*, yet this was the actual state of affairs in Deir el-Medina.

Perhaps the real difficulty in interpreting prices and payments is that modern scholars are attempting to systematize a procedure which was actually determined on a case by case basis. All of the prices discussed above were derived from specific barter agreements. Barter prices were much more fluid than the fixed prices in present-day western markets. Barter prices were set by the strength of each individual's desire to conclude an exchange and each individual's skill at arriving at a good price, in addition to some abstract idea of value based on weight or volume. Use value was probably more important than abstract value and all the commodities exchanged at Deir el-Medina were valued according to actual use: grain was for eating; silver was a raw material for making an object. The value of a good grew according to the need for it.

Because the prices were set by barter, prices tended to cluster in amounts that are multiples of five, especially for amounts over ten *deben*. Numbers, then, were usually rounded to the nearest five. J. J. Janssen (1988) illustrated that principle by the following example. The Ostracon Deir el-Medina 72 verso described the purchase of a coffin in the following way:

> Given to him in exchange for the coffin: eight and one-half *deben* of copper; again five *deben* of copper; one pig made five *deben;* one goat made two *deben;* two logs of sycamore wood made two *deben*. Total: twenty-five and one-half *deben*.

There, the value of the coffin was first agreed to be approximately twenty-five *deben*. Then values were established for the individual items brought to the exchange. The coffinmaker would decide how much use he could make of the two lots of copper, the animals, and the wood before determining the value he would assign to them. It is unlikely that those goods were accepted for resale at a profit, since that concept seems to be unknown to the Egyptians. The actual desire to own these items becomes much more important than the abstract value assigned to them in *deben*.

There is evidence for inflation and price fluctuation during the course of the Ramessid period. During the reign of Ramesses II, one *deben* of silver was valued as one-hundred *deben* of copper. By the reign of Ramesses IX, one *deben* of silver was valued at sixty *deben* of copper. Janssen (1988) believed this change occurred by the reign of Ramesses III, when a typical *mss*-garment was valued at five *deben* or one *senyu*. Thus the silver-to-copper ratio would be 1:60. It seems unlikely, though not impossible, that the government would have intervened in setting prices of this sort. Clearly, the Egyptian state regulated the standard measures of length and volume so that the basic ratio of one sack of grain to one *deben* of copper seems not to have varied.

The best source for our knowledge of loans is also Deir el-Medina. There are two kinds of loans attested from the village: one type is made with a fixed date for repayment and a penalty if that date is missed; a second type appears not to have a repayment date and is more likely to reflect an obligation for reciprocity between the lender and debtor. There is limited evidence that loans with fixed repayment dates were made from people of higher social status to those of lower social status, while reciprocal loans were made between people of more equal status.

In sum, the Egyptians were able to conduct business in a way that met their needs without ever fully abstracting the concept of money from their units of exchange value. An often robust economy ran smoothly, using various means of valuing labor and commodities without either money or true markets.

[*See also* Coinage; Trade and Markets; *and* Weights and Measures.]

BIBLIOGRAPHY

Bleiberg, Edward. "Debt, Credit, and Social Solidarity at Deir el-Medina." In *Deir el-Medina in the Third Millennium AD*. Leiden (forthcoming). Attempts to explain the two different methods of lending found in the village.

Janssen, J. J. *Commodity Prices from the Ramessid Period: An Economic Study of the Village of Necropolis Workmen at Thebes*. Leiden, 1975. Groundbreaking study of the Deir el-Medina ostraca, which established the values for most commodities in ancient Egypt.

Janssen, J. J. "On Prices and Wages in Ancient Egypt." *Altorientalische Forschungen* 15 (1988), 10–23. An important essay on the Egyptian concept of value.

Janssen, J. J. "Debts and Credit in the New Kingdom." *Journal of Egyptian Archaeology* 80 (1994), 129–136. A consideration of reciprocal loans.

Kemp, Barry. "The Birth of Economic Man." In *Ancient Egypt: Anatomy of a Civilization*, pp. 232–260. London, 1989. An account of the economy that gives less weight to redistribution and reciprocity.

Menu, Bernadette. "Le prêt en droit égyptien ancien." In *Recherches sur l'histoire juridique, economique, et sociale de l'ancienne Egypte*, pp. 230–272. Versailles, 1982.

EDWARD BLEIBERG

PRIESTESSES. *See* Priesthood.

PRIESTHOOD. For much of ancient Egyptian history, there was no class of full-time professional priests. The king served as Egypt's archetypal high priest of all divine cults, and is the only individual shown carrying out cultic activities in the temples. Until the New Kingdom, most priests served on a part-time basis while continuing to hold other administrative positions in the state or local government. Priestly service was prestigious, since the practitioner of cultic duties was filling an essentially royal role, acting as a liaison between humanity and the gods. It was also potentially lucrative, as priests on duty received a portion of the offerings presented to the gods and deceased kings in whose cults they served.

Yet there is relatively little firm evidence regarding the qualifications for priesthood. The Egyptians attributed all priestly appointments to the king himself. Private "autobiographies," such as that of the Middle Kingdom chief priest at Abydos, Wepwawet-aa, describe the official's promotion to the priesthood as taking place within the royal palace—in the case of Wepwawet-aa, this was perhaps a ceremonial palace used by the king on visits to the sanctuary of Osiris. In actual practice, highly ranked priests and officials (other than the king) must also have played an active role in selecting priests, just as they did in the performance of cult rituals in the gods' temples. In the Old and Middle Kingdoms, local officials served as priests, often apparently inheriting the role, as did the local governor (*ḥзty-ʿ*), who acted as the chief priest. In the New

Kingdom, when Tutankhamun restored the temples following the Amarna period, he stated that he selected the sons of prominent dignitaries as priests. By the Late period, according to the ancient Greek historian Herodotus, many priestly titles were inherited.

Categories of Priests. Numerous categories of priests existed in Egypt, varying with different cults, regions, and historical periods. Among the earliest documented and longest-lived categories of priest were the *ḥmw-nṯr* (hem; "god's servants" or "prophets"), who are first attested in the first dynasty. Associated primarily with temples rather than funerary cults, these priests performed rituals, prepared offerings, and participated in the economic activities of the temples, including the maintenance of temple estates. They were among the limited number of people who had access to the innermost parts of the temple and to the hidden cult image, the tangible manifestation of the deity. In temples of local deities, particularly during the Old and Middle Kingdoms, the overseer of *hem*-priests (*imy-r ḥmw-nṯr*) was almost invariably the local governor of the district.

A lower-ranked class of priests, the *w'bw* (wab; "pure priests") assisted the *hem*-priests in the maintenance of the temple and the performance of cultic activities. Priests in this category had apparently been initiated into the priesthood, but had not yet advanced to the rank of *hem*-priest; biographies refer to *wab*-priests being promoted to the office of *hem*-priest later in their careers. While *wab*-priests were not permitted to enter the temple's innermost sanctuary, or come face to face with the god's image, they did handle sacred objects and cult instruments. They were therefore required to observe strict rules of purity, and they can be identified in some representations by their shaved heads. In New Kingdom temples, *wab*-priests are shown carrying the god's image in processions.

In temples, the *ḫntiw-š*, often viewed as secular officials associated with the temple, appear to have performed many of the same functions as the *hem*- and *wab*-priests, at least during the Old Kingdom, although they did not enter the sanctuary or see the god's cult statue. In ceremonies and rituals, including funerals, another priest, designated as the *imy-ḫnt* ("the one who is in front"), appears to have led the activities.

The priest who actually recited the spells and rites, both in temple ceremonies and at funerals, was a "lector-priest" (*ḥry-ḥbt*). Priests of this category are recognizable by their characteristic attire of a kilt and wide sash, worn diagonally over the shoulder, and they are often depicted holding or reading from a papyrus scroll. Lector-priests are first attested in the Old Kingdom cult of Re at Heliopolis. Although the earliest holders of the title were members of the royal family, by the Middle Kingdom, any literate official seems to have been able to serve in this capacity. Egyptian literature often portrays lector-priests as wise men and sages who can foresee coming events. In the *Tale of King Khufu and the Magicians*, for example, lector-priests perform miraculous feats, and are privy to secret knowledge, unknown even to the king. The Middle Kingdom prophet Neferti, who warns of disaster, followed by salvation, is also said to be a lector-priest. Owing to their knowledge of the appropriate spells, lector-priests were among the principal practitioners of magic and medicine. They also took part in funerals, reading the necessary spells and assisting in the Opening of the Mouth ceremony. The significance of chief lector-priests in researching and preserving ancient religious texts is demonstrated by evidence such as the twenty-fifth dynasty tomb of the chief lector-priest Petamenophis, who revived the long-dead Pyramid Texts, along with the Coffin Texts, the *Book of Going Forth by Day* (*Book of the Dead*), and the *Amduat* (royal Underworld Books).

From the Old Kingdom, *sem*-priests (*smw*) were associated with the Opening of the Mouth ceremony. In mortuary religion, they played the role of Horus in the funeral ceremonies, while the deceased was cast in the role of Osiris. Originally members of a high-ranking class of priests associated with the Memphite funerary deity, Ptah-Sokar, *sem*-priests came to be relatively common. From the end of the Old Kingdom onward, they are depicted in tomb scenes showing mortuary rituals. In the New Kingdom, they regularly take part in funeral ceremonies shown in the *Book of Going Forth by Day* and on tomb walls, especially in the Ramessid period, where they can be identified by their panther-skin robes. *Sem*-priests were the first priests to wear robes of this type, although by the New Kingdom, they were worn by high-ranking priests of Amun and others as well. Another attribute sometimes associated with *sem*-priests is the sidelock, a sign of youth that identifies them with Horus.

Women in the Priesthood. During the Old Kingdom, women frequently held priestly titles, a practice that declined appreciably in the Middle Kingdom, and then reappeared later, in the Third Intermediate Period. Among the titles commonly held by elite Old Kingdom women was *ḥmt-nṯr* ("god's servant" or "priestess") of Hathor, or less often of Neith. Queens and princesses also served in this capacity in the mortuary cults of their fathers and husbands.

Although no female *wab*-priests have been identified during the Old Kingdom, the Abusir Papyri (see below) refer to women carrying out some of the duties of the *wab*-priest and receiving the same pay as their male counterparts. Two Middle Kingdom stelae identify women holding the title of *w'bt*. By the New Kingdom, when the priesthood developed into a full-time profession, women rarely played a role other than as musicians. Rare excep-

PRIESTHOOD. *A priest throwing grain to the fire, and a priestess with a flute.* This wall painting is from the tomb of Amennakht at Deir el-Medina. (Boromeo / Art Resource, NY)

tions do exist, however, including a female second prophet of Amun and a female second prophet of Mut. At no period did women serve as overseers of priests (*imy-r ḥmwt-nṯr*).

Upper-class women served as singers and musicians in the temple cults of a variety of deities from the Old Kingdom onward, and many of the priestesses of Hathor may have been involved in musical performances during religious festival and other rites. From the Middle Kingdom until the end of the New Kingdom, the role of singer was almost the sole priestly activity of women. The *ḥnr* ("musical troupe") included women who danced and played music under the leadership of a woman identified as the *wrt-ḥnr* (the "chief of the musical troupe"). Prior to the New Kingdom, the usual term for a woman serving as a singer in the temple was *ḥsyt*. The term *šmꜥyt* was first used in reference to individual singers during the New Kingdom, at which time it became one of the most frequently attested feminine titles. In addition to singing, temple chantresses apparently played a variety of musical instruments. In many instances, they are shown holding a sistrum or a *menat* (a type of necklace sacred to the goddess Hathor), which was shaken to create music.

Three Middle Kingdom women are known to have borne the title of "god's wife" (*ḥmt-nṯr*) of a deity, serving in the cults on Min, Amun, and Ptah. Although the duties associated with this title during the Middle Kingdom are unclear, by the early New Kingdom the title of "God's Wife of Amun" had taken on considerable importance, the earliest examples being associated specifically with the queen. The first queen to hold the title was Ahmose-Nefertari, the wife of Ahmose and first queen of the eighteenth dynasty. Ahmose-Nefertari had served as the second prophet of Amun, an exceptional rank for a woman, but arranged by contract to exchange the title for the position of god's wife. Following her death, she was succeeded by Hatshepsut and her daughter Neferure, and, from the reign of Thutmose III on, by a series of lesser-known women, who seem to have been related to the royal family only by marriage. New Kingdom "God's Wives" are shown taking part in temple rituals at Luxor and elsewhere, and sometimes bear the additional titles of "Divine Adoratrix" (*dwꜣt-nṯr*) and "Hand of the God" (*drt-nṯr*). In the Late period, "God's Wives" rose in significance to become the principal priests of the cult of Amun at Thebes (see below).

Temple Priests. Temple reliefs typically portray the king as the sole practitioner of all divine cults, the quintessential high priest of every god's temple. Although the king presumably performed cultic activities on special occasions at major temples, a hierarchy of local priests was responsible for performing the daily cultic rituals in temples throughout Egypt. These rituals, recorded in scenes from a number of temples (notably the temple of Sety I at Abydos), were performed three times per day in major temples. These ceremonies involved: the ceremonial breaking of the sanctuaries' seals; the recitation of prayers and offering of incense; the awakening of the cult statue and its removal from the shrine by the *hem*-priest; the undressing, cleansing, anointing, and reclothing of the cult image; the performance of the Opening of the Mouth to revivify the deity; the offering of food and other gifts; and, ultimately, the return of the cult statue, wrapped in clean linen, to its shrine. The Opening of the Mouth was perhaps the most vital element of the ritual, since it enabled the deity to act through his or her statue. Priests utilized a number of implements in this ceremony, one of the most characteristic being the *psškf,* a blade with which the officiating priest touched the mouth of a statue or of the mummy, thereby animating it. Finally, the priest backed out of the sanctuary, sweeping away his footprints behind him, and the shrine was resealed.

During festivals, the priests at major temples were responsible for carrying the cult statue from the temple in a bark or palanquin and bringing it into public view. Because the priests themselves are rarely labeled in scenes of these activities, it is not clear whether those who conducted the divine image were particularly important members of the priesthood or the priests who happened to be on duty at the time. From the New Kingdom onward, chief priests were also instrumental in interpreting oracles—when asked a question, the god would answer by directing his portable bark, carried by priests, in the direction of the written response it chose.

At least three institutions associated with the temple were devoted to storing and disseminating information and skills required for specialized categories of priests. In the "House of Gold" (*ḥwt nbw*), master craftsmen put the finishing touches on cult statues, which were then transformed into suitable residences for the deity by ceremonies, including the Opening of the Mouth. The "House of Books" (*pr mdȝt*) housed the manuscripts of sacred texts, such as transfiguration spells, litanies of gods' names, religious treatises, and instructions for rituals. The "House of Life" (*pr ʿnḫ*) not only housed the texts of rituals, including those for crowning the king and mummifying the dead, but also served as a point of reference for both priests and royalty, thus preserving ancient ceremonies and cult practices for future generations of priests.

Funerary and Mortuary Cult Priests. Although stelae and tomb scenes usually show burial offerings being brought by family members, professional mortuary priests are documented serving in private memorial cults as early as the first dynasty. A class of specifically funerary priests included the servants of the *ka* (*ḥmw-kȝ*), who provided for the immortal life force of the deceased person. Scenes in tombs from the Old Kingdom onward show priests participating in the funeral—*wab*-priests pour libation offerings, while lector-priests read aloud the funerary texts critical to transforming the deceased person into an immortal being. Lector-priests also perform the *int-rd* ceremony, sweeping away the footprints of the celebrants after the ceremony has been completed.

Mortuary literature, from the Pyramid Texts on, provides evidence that the funeral ceremony included not only the reading of religious texts, but also the performance of acts such as playing the role of deities associated with the myth of Osiris. The Coffin Texts, for example, include directions for those taking part in the ceremony, along with texts that must have been spoken aloud, presumably by a lector-priest. Women, who had served as funerary priests (*ḥmwt-kȝ*) during the Old Kingdom, thereafter acted as *dry*-mourners, impersonating the grieving Isis and Nephthys.

Sem-priests are identifiable by the end of the Old Kingdom, after which they are shown offering incense and performing the Opening of the Mouth ceremony on the mummy of the deceased. Beginning in the New Kingdom,

scenes of the funeral accompany several chapters of the *Book of Going Forth by Day*, and form an increasingly significant part of tomb decoration. A priest wearing a mask of the god Anubis is shown preparing the mummy for burial, and supporting the upright coffin in front of the tomb entrance, while the Opening of the Mouth takes place. The heir of the deceased is typically shown performing this ritual, touching the mouth with a ceremonial implement, such as an adze tipped with iron or flint.

Wealthy and influential officials established mortuary endowments in the same way as kings, to perpetuate their memorial cults and to provide for mortuary priests. Several Abydene stelae refer to contractual arrangements with mortuary priests, and the twelfth dynasty tomb of the vizier Djefai-hapi I at Asyiut preserves the complete text of his mortuary contracts. According to the contracts, the priests are responsible for delivering offerings of bread and other items to the vizier's statues in the local temple, in exchange for being paid a portion of the offerings dedicated in the temple.

Domestic Cult and Magic Priests. Many domestic cults, aimed in large part on protecting the home and its inhabitants from harm, required literate or learned individuals to perform the appropriate rites. Hence, priests were often called upon to serve in this capacity. Lector-priests, with their specialized knowledge of religious texts, were the principal practitioners of apotropaic magic. They also appear to have been consulted in times of medical emergencies, as the Old Kingdom biography of Washptah attests. A group of men identified as *ḥkȝw* ("magicians") appears in association with the House of Life. Both lector-priests and physicians (*swnw*) also held specialized titles associated with specific types of magic, such as "Scorpion Charmer." Along with written and spoken prayers, these priests were familiar with, and able to produce, the correct amulets for protection and talismans for blessing.

Organization. Among the best preserved evidence for the organization of the priesthood during the Old Kingdom are the archives of the royal cult temples of the fifth-dynasty king, Neferirkare Kakai, at Abusir. According to the carefully recorded temple accounts, the priests and other temple staff worked on a rotating basis, serving full-time in the temple for one month in every five-month period. Some staff members were employed on the temple estates in other capacities during the remainder of the year. The priests on duty were organized into workgroups, or "phyles." Each phyle was in turn subdivided into two subgroups, each headed by a *shd*, ("inspector"). The temple's inventory, income, and expenditures were meticulously registered at the end of each watch.

During the Old Kingdom, while local rulers headed the temples of their own provinces, the chief priests of the state-sponsored temples of major deities were often members of the royal family, sons, or sons-in-law of the king. This pattern suggests a strong degree of royal control over the temples during this period. Certain deities and cult centers had specific titles for their chief priests: at Heliopolis, the chief priest of Ra was known as the "Greatest of Seers," while the chief priest of Ptah at Memphis was the "Greatest of Directors of Craftsmen," in recognition of Ptah's role as the god of craftsmen. The chief priest of Thoth at Hermopolis was the "Great One of the Five," referring to the creator god and the four pairs of deities that made up the Hermopolitan Ogdoad.

In the Middle Kingdom, the local governor continued to serve as the chief priest of the local temple, although in many cases these men were now appointed by the king. The excavations at Illahun, the town built for the priests maintaining the mortuary cult of King Senwosret II, produced a series of papyri, including the archives of the temple scribe, Horemsaf, who recorded both the temple's accounts and the correspondence of the chief priest. As in the Old Kingdom, priests served in rotating watches, but the number of watches was now reduced to four. The records document the distribution of offerings to several categories of priests, indicating their relative rank. The chief priest (*imy-r ḥmw-nṯr*) was the highest-paid, followed by the chief lector-priest (*ḥry-ḥbt ḥbt ḥry-tp*), the lector-priests, the phyle regulator (*mty m s3*), the *wab*-priests and other priests associated with offerings and cult maintenance, and finally the temple scribe. The homes of the priests, and the layout of the town itself, corroborate the written evidence of the organization of the priestly community and relative status of the priests. At Abydos, the state constructed a town of similar structures to house the priests associated with the cult of Senwosret III, whose temple and cenotaph lie nearby.

No temple archives of the New Kingdom has survived to provide evidence similar to that of the Abusir or Illahun material. Nevertheless, the priesthood is reasonably well documented, owing to the better overall preservation of temples and private tombs. Although secular administrators continued to serve as priests of many cults (at least early in the period), the priesthood emerged during the New Kingdom as a full-time profession. During the first half of the eighteenth dynasty, the old title for the chief *hem*-priest was replaced by a new one, the "first prophet" (*ḥm-nṯr tpi*). At first, this new, full-time position was held exclusively by members of the royal family, but soon thereafter by other officials appointed directly by the king. The first prophet enjoyed considerable authority in the major divine cults, particularly that of Amun at Thebes, and his wife typically served as the leader of temple musicians and dancers. In the largest cult centers, such as Thebes, a series of full-time second, third, and occasionally fourth prophets assisted with the running of the temple.

The first prophet of Amun at Karnak, responsible for the cult and revenues of Egypt's largest temple complex, was one of New Kingdom Egypt's most important officials. A pair of inscriptions dedicated by the priest Bakenkhons record the progress of his career, stating that fourteen years of schooling and public service preceded his appointment to the rank of *wab*-priest. Thereafter, he served as "god's father," third prophet, and second prophet—a process that took nearly four decades—before he received the title of first prophet. In the early part of the eighteenth dynasty, the first prophet at Karnak also held the title of chief prophet of Upper and Lower Egypt, and with it the duty of supervising, on the king's behalf, the affairs of all the temples in Egypt. During the reign of Thutmose IV, this office was transferred to another official, often the chief priest of Ptah, serving in Memphis. The first prophet of Amun became extraordinarily influential by the end of the New Kingdom, by which time the office had come to be hereditary.

Also serving a crucial role in New Kingdom temple rituals was the chief lector-priest (*ḥry-ḥbt ḥry-tp*), who, as in previous periods, oversaw the preservation and recitation of the texts, prayers, and rituals. In the larger temples, he was now assisted by a second, third, and sometimes fourth lector-priest. Lector-priests are also documented announcing the verdicts of the oracles that took place at festivals. *Wab*-priests continued to function on a rotating basis as earlier, with four phyles of priests serving a one-month term. The "God's Father" (*it-nṯr*), occasionally attested in the Old Kingdom, became a regular priestly title in the New Kingdom. Among other responsibilities, "God's Fathers" led the processions held at festivals. The wives of priests, organized into phyles as were their husbands, served as temple musicians.

Although the classes of priests continued essentially unchanged into the Third Intermediate Period and the Late period, the status of the priesthood of Amun skyrocketed. At the end of the twentieth dynasty, generals used the title of first prophet to take actual political control over southern Egypt, contributing to the disintegration of Egypt's central government. Some additional changes in the temple administration also took place during this time. The full-time priests were now assisted by part-time *hem*-priests, arranged in phyles and serving on a rotating basis, resuming a priestly title that had gone out of use early in the New Kingdom. Most priestly offices by this period had become hereditary.

When Egypt was reunited under the Saite and Kushite dynasties, the volatile office of first prophet of Amun was eliminated, and the "God's Wife of Amun" became the highest priestly title in Thebes. Although earlier "God's

Wives" had clearly married and had children, those of the Late period were celibate, unmarried daughters of the ruler or a powerful priest, who adopted their successors. Their chosen successors eventually came to be known as the first prophets of Amun. In the twenty-fifth dynasty, the Kushite ruler Kashta enlisted the "God's Wife of Amun," Shepenwepet I, to adopt his daughter Amenirdis as her successor, thus solidifying his own claim to power in Thebes. Amenirdis was in turn followed by Shepenwepet II and Amenirdis II, during whose term of office Psamtik I expelled the Kushites to found the twenty-sixth dynasty. In order to establish his own rule, Psamtik, with the aid of the "Overseer of Upper Egypt," Montuemhat, arranged for his own daughter, Nitocris, to be adopted as heiress. The stela recording her installment as god's wife describes the elaborate ceremony involved, and lists the enormous endowment allotted to the office during this period. The invasion of Cambyses and the Persians brought the significance of the "God's Wives" to an end; although the title continued to exist in later times, it never regained its political importance.

During the Greco-Roman period, the full-time clergy of major cults continued to be assisted by part-time priests, divided into four phyles; until 238 BCE, when Ptolemy III reorganized the system, adding a fifth phyle. Virtually all offices were hereditary. The highest-ranking member of the priesthood in this period was the high priest of Ptah at Memphis, although the priests of Amun at Thebes retained significant status. Several categories of priest below the rank of prophet included (among others): the sacred scribes known as *hierogrammates* (of which Manetho was one); the *hierostolistes*, who tended the cult statue; the *horologoi*, astronomers who maintained the calendar of festivals; and the *pastophoroi*, who carried the gods' shrines in processions. "God's Wives" continue to function, albeit in a reduced role, and female *wab*-priests and *hem*-priests are also documented.

[See also Administration, *article on* Temple Administration; Cults; Economy, *article on* Temple Economy; Funerary Ritual; Offerings; *and* Temples.]

BIBLIOGRAPHY

David, A. Rosalie. *Religious Ritual at Abydos.* Warminster, 1973. Discusses in detail the daily temple ritual.

Fischer, Henry G. "Priesterin." In *Lexikon der Ägyptologie,* 4: 1100–1105. Wiesbaden, 1982. Provides a summary, in English, of the evidence regarding priestesses and their roles.

Gitton, Michel, and Jean LeClant. "Gottesgemahlin." In *Lexikon der Ägyptologie,* 2: 792–812. Wiesbaden, 1974. Gives the fullest available summary, in German, of the title "God's Wife," with reference to individual holders of the title.

Helck, Wolfgang. "Priester." In *Lexikon der Ägyptologie,* 4: 1084–1097. Wiesbaden, 1982. A comprehensive summary, in German, of the major categories of priests and their organization.

Pinch, Geraldine. *Magic in Ancient Egypt.* Austin, 1994. An informative and easily readable account of Egyptian magical practices and practitioners.

Quirke, Stephen. *Ancient Egyptian Religion.* London, 1992. An excellent survey of Egyptian religious practices accessible to the general reader, as well as the student or scholar, including a full discussion of the organization of the priesthood, the role of priests, and the development of their offices.

Robins, Gay. *Women in Ancient Egypt.* Cambridge, Mass., 1993. An excellent survey of the role of women in Egyptian society, with a chapter dedicated to their position in the temple and their role in cultic activities.

Roth, Ann Macy. *Egyptian Phyles in the Old Kingdom.* Chicago, 1991. A full scholarly study of the organization of temple phyles in the Old Kingdom, with a discussion of evidence for phyle organization in Middle Kingdom.

Sauneron, Serge. *The Priests of Ancient Egypt.* New York and London, 1960. One of the most complete available works in English regarding the function and activities of Egyptian priests, with reference to original sources and to events of individual priests documented in Egyptian texts.

Shafer, Byron, ed. *The Temple in Ancient Egypt.* Ithaca, 1998. A thorough summary of the major categories of priests and their organization, along with an excellent study of historical developments in the priesthood.

DENISE M. DOXEY

PROPERTY. *See* Landholding.

PSAMMETICHUS. *See* Psamtik I.

PSAMTIK I (664–610 BCE), first ruler of the twenty-sixth or Saite dynasty, Late period. Psamtik I's origins in the eastern Nile Delta indicate that he belonged to a group of powerful local potentates who had previously opposed the attempts of the Kushite (twenty-fifth dynasty) kings to dominate the whole of Egypt. With probable tacit support from the Assyrians, led by Assurbanipal, Psamtik I consolidated his control over the North of Egypt, with a capital in Sais, before moving south to Thebes in 656 BCE. The inherent weakness of the Kushite dynasts meant that Psamtik's annexation of Upper Egypt was accomplished more by diplomacy than by force of arms. During his long reign, Egypt was once more unified. With a perspicacious talent for solidifying his kingdom, Psamtik set up a series of garrison posts at the various borders of Egypt (northern, western, and southern), and also hired foreign mercenaries, especially Carians and other Greeks. Owing to that policy, Psamtik I became well known to the Greeks, who called him Psammetichus.

At the beginning of his second decade of reign, Psamtik attacked his Libyan neighbors in the northwest, in an effort to diminish their traditional influence in the Delta region. During the same time, a major Jewish quarter was founded at Elephantine, an island in the Nile near the Kushite border in the South. Close to the end of his life, Psamtik aligned his nation with Assyria, possibly through clever diplomacy; then, fearing no opposition from this declining empire, Psamtik marched north into Syria-Palestine. By the close of Psamtik's life, Egypt met the rising Neo-Babylonian Empire on the battlefield (616 and 610 BCE). It is probable that, at his death, Psamtik effectively controlled the shores of Palestine while exercising some commercial influence in Lebanon. Connected with this military activity was his development of a navy.

Psamtik was the son of Necho I, a minor Saite king, who died on the battlefield opposing the Kushites, and who was married to a daughter of the high priest of Heliopolis, making Psamtik's northern ancestry evident. His most famous daughter, Nitokris, was appointed to be the "God's Wife of Amun" at Thebes in 656 BCE, nine years after he took control of the western Delta region. The events of the trip to the religious capital of the South, recorded on a monumental stela, indicate Psamtik's peaceful moves into Upper Egypt, as well as his adherence to the religious norms of Egypt's traditional religious center, Thebes, and of the temple of Amun in particular.

BIBLIOGRAPHY

Caminos, Ricardo A. "The Nitocris Adoption Stela." *Journal of Egyptian Archaeology* 50 (1964), 71–100. The standard study of Psamtik I's daughter's voyage to Thebes in 656 BCE.

Kitchen, K. A. *The Third Intermediate Period in Egypt (1100–650 BC).* Warminster, 1973. An extremely detailed and significant work which covers the reign of this pharaoh in some detail.

Parker, Richard A. *A Saite Oracle Papyrus from Thebes.* Providence, 1962. A useful study of a papyrus connected to Psamtik's domination over Thebes.

ANTHONY J. SPALINGER

PTAH. The god Ptah was one of the major deities of Egypt, yet surprisingly little is known about his early history. With few exceptions, the major textual sources date from the New Kingdom or later, when Egyptian religion had long been shaped according to the dominating theology of Heliopolis. Nevertheless, Ptah is known to have been worshiped as early as the Early Dynastic period, the date of his image on a stone vessel found at Tarkhan, south of el-Lisht. There he is shown in his usual anthropoid form without indication of limbs—a form that he shares with some other ancient gods such as Min and Osiris—that was later interpreted as the form of a mummy. Wearing a tight-fitting skullcap, he stands on a pedestal in an open shrine, holding a scepter. Later representations usually show him with a straight beard; the scepter is almost invariably a *was*-scepter, which from the New Kingdom on is often combined with *ankh* and *djed* symbols. Occasionally the god is shown seated.

The evidence from the Old Kingdom is sparse and consists mainly of personal names and a few titles. Theophoric names composed with the name of Ptah appear at the end of the fourth dynasty and seem to have suddenly become very popular during the fifth, suggesting that the god had begun to play an important role on the level of personal piety. By contrast, royal names of the same period ignore Ptah, and he is virtually absent from royal inscriptions. In the Pyramid Texts, Ptah occurs only two or three times, always in connection with the provision of food for the deceased king. From the end of the fourth dynasty, titles referring to the priesthood of Ptah confirm the existence of a temple in the capital city, Memphis. Most of the holders of these titles are also connected with the royal workshops, particularly with the making of jewelry. Some of them also bear the title "Chief Controller of Craftsmen" *(wr ḥrp ḥmwt)*, which soon becomes the title of the high priest of Ptah in Memphis. Clearly Ptah was associated early on with arts and crafts. Perhaps he was originally a local god who assumed the role of divine craftsman and patron deity of artists, craftsmen, and builders when Memphis became the capital of Egypt and, therefore, the location of the royal workshops. It is equally possible that he had been associated with the royal workshops even before these were transferred to Memphis. In any case, Ptah was the chief god of Memphis throughout Egyptian history, and the name of his temple—*Ḥwt-k3-Ptḥ* ("Temple of the *ka* of Ptah")—became the name of the city of Memphis and ultimately of the whole country (*Hikuptah* > Gr. *Aigyptos*, "Egypt"). Little remains of this temple, but it is thought to have been even larger than the vast complex of Amun-Re at Karnak. Some of the god's epithets also refer to Memphis: "South of his Wall" means "having a temple south of the (White) Wall" (i.e., Memphis), or perhaps "whose (enclosure) wall is in the south (of Memphis)"; "who is upon the Great Throne" refers to the Great Temple in Memphis; and "Lord of Ankhtawy" probably refers to the area on the west bank of the Nile between the city and the necropolis in the desert. Other common epithets of the god include "Lord of *Maat*" (the principle of world order), "Great of Strength," and "Benevolent of Face," an epithet that is often wrongly said to be restricted to gods depicted in human form.

At an early date, Ptah was linked with Sokar, another Memphite god, who was chiefly a god of the dead; as Ptah-Sokar (later Ptah-Sokar-Osiris), he plays a role in many funerary texts. Other deities worshiped in Memphis were the lion goddess Sekhmet and the lotus god Nefertum, with whom Ptah forms a triad (father-mother-child) from the New Kingdom on. He is also associated with the Memphite form of Hathor, the "Lady of the Southern Sycamore," who had a temple in the southern part of the city. From the eighteenth dynasty on, the sacred Apis bull of

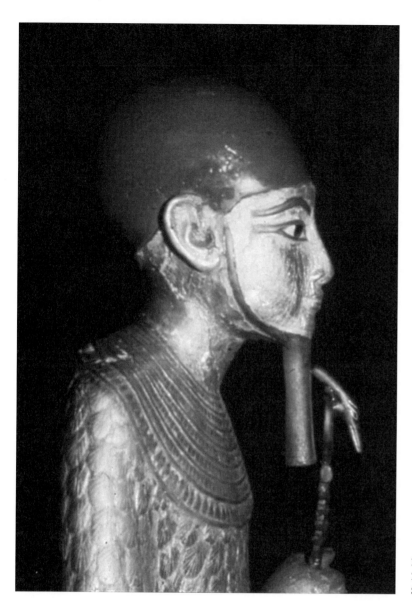

PTAH. *Statue of Ptah from the Treasury of the tomb of Tutankhamun, eighteenth dynasty.* (Courtesy David P. Silverman)

Memphis, originally an independent god, was viewed as the living manifestation of Ptah. In the Late period, the deified mortal Imhotep was regarded as his son. According to the ancient Greek historian Herodotus, the temple of Memphis also contained a statue of Ptah as a dwarf (Gr., *pataikos*), and images of Ptah in this form have been found.

The meaning of the name *Ptah* is not known. An etymology found in the Coffin Texts (Spell 647) connects it with a verb *pth* ("to fashion"), but although this would obviously agree well with his role of divine craftsman, it is also possible that the verb is actually derived from the god's name rather than the other way round. The same spell also contains the first allusions to Ptah as a creator god, but these are already cast in Heliopolitan terms. Texts from the New Kingdom further expand this idea, in

particular the Memphite Theology—long thought to date back to the Old Kingdom, now shown to be much later, probably the Ramessid period of the New Kingdom—and a series of hymns to Ptah in a papyrus in Berlin. These texts equate him with the primeval god Atum, who created the world at the beginning of time through his "heart" (thought) and "tongue" (word); this god manifests himself as the earth god Tatenen, the Primeval Mound, who is embodied in Ptah, the divine sculptor who forms a concept of creation in his mind and then realizes it materially. As primeval creator god, Ptah, or Ptah-Tatenen, as he is often called, he becomes one of the three state gods of Egypt, along with Amun of Thebes and Re of Heliopolis. One famous text says that all the gods are forms of this trinity: "Three are all the gods: Amun, Re, and Ptah, there is none like them. Hidden is his identity as

Amun. He is visible as Re. His body is Ptah." In another text, the sun god Re is said to be his own Ptah or "fashioner" who casts his body of gold. In late texts Ptah is even depicted as the father of the Ogdoad of Hermopolis, the primeval elements from which the ordered universe developed. As primeval god he encompasses the whole world: his feet are on the earth, his head is in the sky, his eyes are sun and moon, his breath is the air, and the liquid of his body is the water. Images of Ptah as a sky god show him with a blue skullcap and a body covered in feathers. This universal god is also a god of destiny, who decides between life and death and determines the length of the king's reign and of every individual's lifetime. As "Ptah who hears prayers," he played an important role in the personal religion of many ordinary Egyptians.

Outside Memphis, Ptah was worshiped in many places where artists and craftsmen were active, such as Deir el-Medina and the Sinai. He had cults in all of Egypt's important temples, including those of Karnak, Western Thebes, Abydos, Piramesse, and Nubia.

BIBLIOGRAPHY

Allen, James P. *Genesis in Egypt: The Philosophy of Ancient Egyptian Creation Accounts.* Yale Egyptological Studies, 2. New Haven, 1988. Excellent discussion of Ptah as creator god, with translations of some of the key documents, pp. 38–47.

Begelsbacher-Fischer, Barbara L. *Untersuchungen zur Götterwelt des Alten Reiches im Spiegel der Privatgräber der IV. und V. Dynastie.* Orbis Biblicus et Orientalis, 37. Freiburg and Göttingen, 1981. On Ptah in the Old Kingdom as reflected by personal names, priestly titles, and names of institutions, see pp. 126–151.

Bonnet, Hans. *Reallexikon der ägyptischen Religionsgeschichte.* Berlin, 1952. This famous work contains a detailed entry on Ptah (pp. 614–619), which however relies heavily on the Memphite Theology, which Bonnet dates to the Early Dynastic period.

Erichsen, W., and Siegfried Schott. *Fragmente memphitischer Theologie in demotischer Schrift (Pap. demot. Berlin 13603).* Akademie der Wissenschaften und der Literatur, Abhandlungen der geistes- und sozialwissenschaftlichen Klasse, Jahrgang 1954, Nr. 7. Mainz and Wiesbaden, 1954. Edition and translation of an important late Ptolemaic text dealing with Ptah as creator god.

Junge, Friedrich. "Zur Fehldatierung des sog. Denkmals memphitischer Theologie, oder Der Beitrag der ägyptischen Theologie zur Geistesgeschichte der Spätzeit." *Mitteilungen des Deutschen Archäologischen Instituts Abteilung Kairo* 29 (1973), 195–204. Concludes mainly on linguistic grounds that the Memphite Theology does not represent a copy of an Old Kingdom original, but was newly composed as a pseudo-ancient text by order of King Shabaka of the twenty-fifth dynasty.

Lichtheim, Miriam. *Ancient Egyptian Literature: A Book of Readings,* vol. 1. Berkeley, 1973. See pp. 51–57 for a complete modern translation of the Memphite Theology, which is still assigned an Old Kingdom date. The introduction contains a bibliography of earlier publications and discussions of this important text.

Sandman Holmberg, Maj. *The God Ptah.* Lund, 1946. A fundamental work which offers a comprehensive discussion of all aspects of the god. Like all the literature predating the 1970s, it puts a great deal of emphasis on Shabaka's Memphite Theology, still thought to date from the Old Kingdom. Includes a bibliography.

Schlögl, Hermann Alexander. *Der Gott Tatenen nach Texten und Bildern des Neuen Reiches.* Orbis Biblicus et Orientalis, 29. Freiburg and Göttingen, 1980. Monograph on the god Tatenen, who from the New Kingdom onward was considered a form of Ptah. In an excursus (pp. 110–117), the Memphite Theology is dated to the nineteenth dynasty on historico-religious grounds.

Stolk, Martinus. *Ptah: Ein Beitrag zur Religionsgeschichte des Alten Aegyptens.* Berlin, 1911. An early monograph on Ptah, now largely superseded but still useful as a succinct survey of the data. Contains a list of personal names from all periods of Egyptian history composed with the name of Ptah.

Velde, Herman te. "Ptah." In *Lexikon der Ägyptologie,* 4: 1177–1180. Wiesbaden, 1982. The most up-to-date summary of what is known about Ptah, and the only one to take into account the late date of Shabaqa's Memphite Theology.

Wolf, Walther. "Der Berliner Ptah-Hymnus (P 3048, II–XII)." *Zeitschrift für Ägyptische Sprache und Altertumskunde* 64 (1929), 17–44. Translation and commentary of a series of hymns to Ptah dating from the end of the twentieth dynasty, which were sung or recited during the rituals in the temple.

JACOBUS VAN DIJK

PTOLEMAIC PERIOD. The Ptolemaic period is the entire epoch of Hellenistic Egypt, beginning with Alexander the Great's arrival in Egypt in 332 BCE and ending with the Roman conquest in 30 BCE. Within these three centuries, there is a differentiation between the period under the kings of the Macedonian dynasty (332–304 BCE) and that of the Ptolemaic pharaohs (304–30 BCE, the Ptolemaic period in the strict sense). The sequence of the Ptolemaic kings used here follows that established by Otto and Bengston (1938), although the latest research shows that between Ptolemy VI and VIII, no other king ruled with an autonomous government.

Political and Dynastic History. Following his victory over Darius III in the battle of Issus (late in 332 BCE), Alexander the Great pushed on into Egypt. The Persian satrap Mazakes ceded the country to him without a struggle. Alexander's actions primarily belong to the sphere of religious politics and ideological history. He founded the port city of Alexandria, begun in 331 BCE, before departing to conquer the Persian Empire, and never returned to Egypt. The settlement of Babylon (323 BCE) established Arrhidaeus Philip III (Alexander's incompetent half-brother) and his son, Alexander IV, as coregents of the Alexandrian empire, but they appear in Egyptian documents as successive pharaohs (323–316 BCE and 316–304 BCE, respectively). In the wake of Alexander the Great's death his empire was split into parts, ruled by his generals, the so-called Diadochi. Ptolemy I (born in 367/6 BCE, the son of Lagus, and a successful comrade-in-arms of Alexander) seized de facto power over Egypt as satrap.

Ptolemy I Soter. Satrap (323–306/304 BCE) and king (r. 306/304–283/282 BCE), the founder of the dynasty conquered Cyrenaica (Libya) in 322/321 BCE. By bringing the

PTOLEMAIC PERIOD. *Limestone plaque of a Ptolemaic king.* (University of Pennsylvania Museum, Philadelphia. Neg. # S35–139361:1)

body of Alexander the Great to Egypt, he precipitated the First Diadoch War (c.321/320 BCE) against the state administrator Perdikkas, who pushed forward into the Nile Delta, lost two battles, and was murdered by his own officers. In the settlement of Triparadeisos (321/320 BCE), Ptolemy I was confirmed ruler of Egypt and Libya. He participated in subsequent Diadoch Wars (319–315 BCE and 314–311 BCE), with campaigns in Syria and Phoenicia. He ruled Cyprus from 313 to 306 BCE, and in 309 BCE, he conquered several cities in Caria and Lycia (Asia Minor). In the meantime, Philip III was assassinated (317 BCE) and Alexander IV was murdered in Macedonia (in 310/309 BCE, but his regnal years were counted until 304 BCE). In late summer or fall of 306 BCE, Ptolemy I assumed the Hellenistic royal title of *basileus*, following the example of the Diadoch Antigonus Monophthalmos, thus renewing personal kingship in the Macedonian tradition for his domain, and forging a link from him to Alexander the Great. Henceforth the dates on Greek documents for the years of Ptolemy I's reign are counted retroactively from Alexander's death. Other Diadochi followed suit and assumed the title of king. In the fall of 306 BCE, Ptolemy I repelled an invasion led by Antigonus and his son Demetrius. At the beginning of 304 BCE, he became pharaoh (Egyptian documents date from year 305/4 BCE [regnal Year 1] onward). During the fourth Diadoch War (303–301) Ptolemy I occupied western Syria and Phoenicia (Coele-Syria) and illegally kept possession of the province

after the battle of Ipsos (301), with the acquiescence of the Diadoch Seleucus I. In 295/294 BCE, Ptolemy I finally added Cyprus and the Phoenician cities of Sidon and Tyre to his empire.

Ptolemy II Philadelphus (r. 283/282–246 BCE), son of Ptolemy I and his third wife Berenice I, had been coregent since 285/284 BCE. Ptolemy II was married at first to Arsinoe I, daughter of the Diadoch Lysimachus of Thrace. Then, around 279/278, he wed his sister, Arsinoe II, widow of the same Lysimachus, who would become the first reigning woman in the Ptolemaic dynasty at the side of her brother-husband. Soon after 280, Ptolemy II conquered Samos and other cities in southwest Asia Minor; in 278 Ptolemaic rule over Pamphylia is attested. Magas, the half-brother of Ptolemy II and governor of Cyrene, broke free of Alexandrian dominance and assumed the title of king. Around 175, Ptolemy II expanded his rule to northern Lower Nubia (Twelve Mile Land). Victories in the first Syrian War (274–271 BCE) against the Seleucid King Antiochus I, successor to Seleucus I, are not proved. The Alexandrian court poet, Theocritus (Idyll XVII: 86–90) enumerated the Ptolemaic territories in Anatolia (c. 270), mentioning Pamphylia, Cilicia, Lycia, and Caria. Around 270/269, Ptolemy II commissioned the restoration of the canal leading from the Nile to the Red Sea. In the following years, numerous strongholds were built between the Gulf of Suez and the road of Bab el-Mandeb. During the so-called Chremonideic War (267–261; named after Chremonides, an Athenian who called for an alliance between the Ptolemaic Empire, Athens, and Sparta against the Macedonian king, Antigonus Gonatas), the Ptolemaic admiral Patroclus, a Macedonian by birth, founded permanent Ptolemaic bases in the Aegean Itanos (East Crete), Thera, Methana/Arsinoe (in the Peloponnesus), and Chios (in the Cyclades). Ephesus was Ptolemaic from 262 to approximately 255. During the Second Syrian War (260–253) against the third Seleucid king, Antiochus II, Ptolemaic influence waned in the Cyclades, and Ionia, Pamphylia and Cilicia became Seleucid domains. After the peace accord, Antiochus II married a daughter of Ptolemy II called Berenice (252). Around 250, Magas died in Cyrene, after he had come to a settlement with Ptolemy II, and had engaged his daughter, also called Berenice (that is, Berenice II), to the heir to the throne in Alexandria, Ptolemy III.

Ptolemy III Euergetes (r. 246–222/221 BCE) regained the province of Libya through his marriage to Berenice II. The catalyst for the Third Syrian War (246–241) was a conflict after the death of Antiochus II, when his widow, Berenice, as well as his first wife, Laodice, each claimed the Seleucid throne for her own son. Ptolemy III came to the aid of his sister Berenice, and marched into Seleucia in Pieria and into Antiochia along the Orontes. Although his sister had been murdered, in the meantime, he conquered Syria all the way to the Euphrates (246). The first insurrection by the Egyptians against the Ptolemaic regime forced him to retreat in 245. With the acquisition of Seleucia in Pieria, Cilicia, Pamphylia, Ionia (especially Ephesus and Samos), and the Hellespont and southern Thrace (including the island of Samothrace), the Ptolemaic Empire reached its greatest extent.

Ptolemy IV Philopator (r. 221–204 BCE), the son of Ptolemy III and Berenice II, married his sister Arsinoe III soon after coming to power. In the Fourth Syrian War (219–217) against the Seleucid king Antiochus III, Coele-Syria was lost at first but then regained in the Battle of Raphia (22 June 217). Soon after, northern Egypt was the scene of many insurrections, initially supported by the new Egyptian military state that had been created in the wake of arming the populace against Antiochus III. Toward the end of Ptolemy IV's reign, the rebellions turned into a peasants' war. From 206 to 186, local pharaohs ruled in Thebes with varying degrees of success (Herwennefer, 206–200, Ankhwennefer, 200–186), in part with the support of Nubian troops. This allowed the neighbor to the south, Meroë, to reclaim Lower Nubia. Ergamenes II and Adikhalamani appear as pharaohs on the temple reliefs of Philae, Debod, and Dakka.

Ptolemy V Epiphanes (r. 204–180 BCE), born 9 October 210, was the son of Ptolemy IV and Arsinoe III. He was subject to the guardianship of a series of regents. Arsinoe III had been assassinated immediately after the death of Ptolemy IV. The dynastic, military, and economic weaknesses of the Ptolemaic Empire sparked the Fifth Syrian War (202–195). Antiochus III conquered Coele-Syria in 198, and by 197 he had also taken Ptolemaic Asia Minor. Philip V of Macedonia annexed Ptolemaic Thrace in 200. After making peace with Antiochus, Ptolemy V married his daughter Cleopatra I (194/3). The rebels in northern Egypt were suppressed in 197 and 185. The Theban pharaoh, Ankhwennefer, was overthrown in August of 186 by Komanos, the epistrategos ("commander of troops") of the Chora (the land outside Alexandria). On 9 October 186, Ptolemy V declared a general amnesty (the Philanthropa Decree), together with an appeal to the refugees to return to their home villages (a measure against the so-called Anachoresis). In the spring of 180, Ptolemy V was poisoned by his generals.

Ptolemy VI Philometor (r. 180–145 BCE). Cleopatra I reigned on behalf of her young son, Ptolemy VI Philometor until her death in 176; she was succeeded in her role as guardian by two courtiers of nonroyal descent. These guardians wed Ptolemy VI in the spring of 175 to his sister, Cleopatra II. From the fall of 170 an official tripartite reign of the Ptolemaic siblings was in force: Ptolemy VI, Cleopatra II and Ptolemy VIII. In the Sixth Syrian War (170/169–168), the Seleucid king Antiochus IV, Cleopatra I's brother and the uncle of the Ptolemaic kings, conquered Cyprus and the Egyptian Chora in two campaigns, during which he even issued *prostagmata* (royal decrees) in his role as *basileus*. He was prevented from taking Alexandria by a Roman envoy, C. Popilius Laenas, and was forced to retreat from the Ptolemaic Empire ("Day of Eleusis" in July 168). There were uprisings soon after in Alexandria, in the Faiyum, and in the region of Thebes. Ptolemy VIII held absolute power in Alexandria for a short period (164/3), which was followed by the joint rule (the first for a Ptolemaic royal couple) of Ptolemy VI and Cleopatra II (from the summer of 163 onward). Cleopatra II was named queen, following her husband, in Egyptian and Greek documents. Ptolemy VIII was given the province of Libya and lived in Cyrene. The Romans were repeatedly drawn into the struggle between the brothers. Ptolemy VIII in 155 BCE even deeded his part of the empire to them, in the event that he died without legitimate heirs (the so-called Testament of Euergetes, preserved on a stela discovered in the Apollo temple at Cyrene in 1929). In the late 160s, Ptolemy VI allowed a large number of Jewish emigrants to enter from Palestine; he placed Onias IV (son of the high priest Onias III) in an influential position in the army and permitted the construction of a Yahweh temple in Leontopolis (Tell el-Yehudiyya). By about 150, the strategos Boëthos had established Ptolemaic dominance in the Thirty Mile Land

PTOLEMAIC PERIOD. *Antique photograph (c.1885) of the Bab el-'Abd of Ptolemy III, a monumental gate in the Precinct of Montu at Karnak.* The decoration of the gate was completed under Ptolemy IV. Photograph by the Bonfils family. (University of Pennsylvania Museum, Philadelphia. Neg. # ST2–987c)

(that is, all of Lower Nubia, possibly all the way to the Second Cataract of the Nile at Wadi Halfa). From 150 to 145, Ptolemy VI intervened in the Syrian (Seleucid) throne struggles and wed his daughter, Cleopatra Thea, in succession to each of the opposing pretenders to the throne, Alexander Balas and Demetrios II. Ptolemy VI accepted the "Diadem of Asia" in Antiochia in the spring of 145 but later limited Ptolemaic claims to Coele-Syria. Although he defeated Alexander Balas in the battle of Oinoparas in July 145, he himself was mortally wounded.

Ptolemy VIII Euergetes II (r. 145–116 BCE) was immediately brought to Alexandria from Cyrene. He married his brother's widow in 145/144, who was also his own sister, Cleopatra II. At the same time, he killed her youngest son, whose father was Ptolemy VI Philometor. (This youngest son has been erroneously ascribed a separate reign between Ptolemy VI and VIII as Ptolemy VII). Ptolemy VIII then lashed out brutally against the Jews and the Greek intelligentsia in Alexandria, but at the same time

he tried to gain the goodwill of the Egyptian priests and the populace by signing amnesty decrees. As late as 145, he surrendered the last strongholds in the Aegean (Itanos, Thera, and Methana). In 141/140, Ptolemy VIII married Cleopatra III, the younger daughter of Ptolemy VI and Cleopatra II by an additional marriage. The two wives were officially on the same hierarchical level, and were listed below Ptolemy VI in the latter's official documents. Around 139, a Roman delegation led by the younger Scipio visited Egypt. During the civil war with Cleopatra II (132–124), Ptolemy VIII was forced to flee to Cyprus with Cleopatra III (fall of 131). Cleopatra II then proclaimed herself to be the sole ruler in Alexandria as Thea Philometor Soteira. At the same time, Harsiese (the last Egyptian to hold the title of pharaoh) led a revolt in Thebes, whence he was rapidly expelled, although there is proof of his presence in el-Hiba in November of 130. Having returned in the spring of 130, Ptolemy VIII was able to prevent intervention by the Seleucid king, Demetrius

II, in support of his mother-in-law, Cleopatra II, and forced her to flee to Syria. In 127/126 he took Alexandria; the city was then the scene of a bloody purge. The embattled Ptolemaic factions reconciled in 124. Around 122, the high priest of Ptah at Memphis married Psenptah II, a Berenice, probably directly related to the royal house. In 118, Ptolemy VIII published his great amnesty decree (see below). He died on 28 June 116.

Ptolemy IX Soter II and Ptolemy X Alexander I (together, r. 116–81 BCE), were sons of Ptolemy VIII and Cleopatra III. In the fall of 116 there was a short tripartite rule shared by Cleopatra II, Cleopatra III, and Ptolemy IX, followed (after the death of the elder Cleopatra) by the joint rule of Cleopatra III and Ptolemy IX (116–107). The queen mother had absolute governing power and appears in administration records above the name of the king. Ptolemy X became strategos of Cyprus, where he proclaimed himself king in 114/113. In 107, Ptolemy IX fled from his mother to Cyprus, where he ruled independently (106/105–88). Ptolemy X (in Egypt, 107–88) returned to Alexandria and became coregent to Cleopatra III, whom he supported in her war in Syria (103–101) against Ptolemy IX, and whom he then killed in 101. Ptolemy X married Cleopatra Berenice III (daughter of Ptolemy IX) who became the new coregent, and who once again appears after the king in all documents. From 100 onward, Ptolemy Apion (son of Ptolemy VIII and an unknown woman) was king of Cyrene; prior to his death (in 96), he deeded his empire to the Romans, who initially took possession of the "Royal Land" and liberated the Greek cities. (The Roman province of Cyrene was founded as late as 75/74 BCE). Ptolemy X was forced to flee Alexandra in 88 and died in the attempt to reconquer Cyprus (87), after he, too, had deeded his empire to the Romans (but his will, which was met with internal resistance in Rome, was not executed). From 88 until his death at the end of 81, Ptolemy IX once again ruled in Alexandria, and Cleopatra Berenice III remained coregent.

Ptolemy XI Alexander II. After the death of Ptolemy IX, Cleopatra Berenice III took over as sole ruler at the beginning of 80 BCE. In June, Ptolemy XI Alexander II (the son of Ptolemy X's first marriage to an unidentified woman) came from Italy to Alexandria and married the queen (who was his stepmother), then killed her a few days later. Ptolemy XI was then assassinated by the Alexandrians.

Ptolemy XII Neos Dionysos (r. 80–51 BCE), son of Ptolemy IX and an unidentified woman, was brought to the throne by the Alexandrians, and his brother was made king of Cyprus (Ptolemy of Cyprus). Ptolemy XII married his sister Cleopatra VI Tryphaina, who gave birth to (Cleopatra) Berenice IV. In 76 BCE, Ptolemy XII was crowned pharaoh by the fourteen-year-old high priest of Ptah,

Psenptah III. Toward the end of the decade, Ptolemy XII married an Egyptian woman, probably a noblewoman and relative of the family of high priests of Memphis, which had close links to the royal house. She became the mother of Cleopatra VII, Ptolemy XIII and XIV, and Arsinoe IV. Cleopatra VI fell into disgrace in 69/68 BCE. Caesar confirmed Ptolemy XII as king in 59, thereby renouncing the Roman inheritance to Egypt. Cyprus, by contrast, was annexed in 58 by Rome according to Ptolemy X's testament. Ptolemy of Cyprus then committed suicide. Ptolemy XII was exiled from Alexandria because of his inactivity (58–55) and pursued his case for repatriation in Rome by paying enormous bribes. In the meantime, Alexandria was ruled by Berenice IV. In the spring of 55, A. Gabinius restored Ptolemy XII as king in Alexandria with the support of the Roman army. The Roman troops, the Gabiniani, were stationed in Egypt and they henceforth protected Ptolemy XII. The Roman banker C. Rabirius Postumus was given the office of *dioicete* (see below), which gave him the legal right to oversee the collection of the king's debts. Owing to the general animosity that resulted from his attaining this office, he soon had to leave the country. During the last year of Ptolemy XII's reign (he died at the beginning of 51 BCE), Cleopatra VII was his coregent.

Cleopatra VII. The last two decades of the Ptolemaic empire (under Cleopatra VII and her coregents Ptolemy XIII–XV) were characterized by dynastic discord and constant intervention from Rome. Ptolemy XII had designated Cleopatra VII and Ptolemy XIII as coregents in his will, and made Rome the executor of this succession. Cleopatra VII soon reigned on her own, but she was pushed aside in 49 by the supporters of Ptolemy XIII. In the summer of 48, Pompey came to the coast near Pelusium after his defeat in the battle of Pharsalus. There the courtiers of Ptolemy XIII had him assassinated. Julius Caesar entered Alexandria, and soon settled the dispute in accordance with Ptolemy XII's will. He also declared Ptolemy XIV and Arsinoe IV kings of Cyprus, which once again became Ptolemaic. Caesar fell in love with Cleopatra VII. The powers at the Ptolemaic court unleashed the Alexandrian War against Caesar (48/47), which Caesar won through the timely arrival of reinforcements. Ptolemy XIII died in battle; Arsinoe IV, who had been proclaimed queen by her army (that is, in opposition to Cleopatra), was captured. Cleopatra VII was given governing power by Caesar, with Ptolemy XIV as coruler. Egypt was a Roman protectorate (47–44 BCE) by virtue of the three legions that remained behind after Caesar's departure. On 23 June 47, Ptolemy XV Caesar was born, the son of Cleopatra and Julius Caesar; the Alexandrians gave him the patronymic "Caesarion" (son of Caesar). From 46 to 44, Cleopatra VII and Ptolemy XIV lived with Caesar in

Rome. Soon after Caesar's death, Cleopatra VII returned to Alexandria and murdered her brother Ptolemy XIV (44 BCE). At the same time, she raised Ptolemy XV Caesar to be her coregent. Thus, in official documents, the heads of the state were once again a mother and her son. During the Roman civil war, the legions stationed in Egypt decided to defect to Cassius in 43 BCE, with the Ptolemaic satrap of Cyprus following suit. In 41, Cleopatra VII had to defend her case in front of Mark Antony in Tarsus; she won his affection and convinced him to order the assassination of Arsinoe IV, who was living in exile in Ephesus. In the winter of 41/40, Mark Antony visited Cleopatra VII in Alexandria and joined Ptolemaic Cyprus to Roman Cilicia: Cleopatra VII gave birth to twins (in 40 BCE), whose father was Mark Antony: they were named Alexander Helios and Cleopatra Selene. Cleopatra VII spent the winter of 37/36 with Antony in Antiochia; subsequent to Antony's political reorganization of the Near East, Cleopatra received areas of Lebanon, near Jericho, and regions of the Nabataean realm, as well as Cyrene and landholdings on Crete. In 36, Ptolemy Philadelphus, the third child of Mark Antony and Cleopatra, was born. In the fall of 34, Mark Antony celebrated his triumph as New Dionysos in Alexandria. Soon after, he legalized his union with Cleopatra VII in marriage, a bigamous marriage (in the tradition of Hellenistic rulers), which had no legitimacy in Roman law since he was still married to Octavia (Octavian's sister). In view of the propaganda war between Mark Antony and Octavian, Cleopatra VII was seen as a threat to Rome and to the world, and she was declared an enemy of the state in Rome (32 BCE). On 2 September 31, Antony lost the battle of Actium. On 1 August 30, Octavian conquered Alexandria, and two days later made Egypt a Roman province. Mark Antony and Cleopatra then committed suicide. Ptolemy XV Caesar was beaten to death. Octavia raised the children of Mark Antony and Cleopatra VII in Rome; Cleopatra Selene married Juba II of Mauritania in 20 BCE; their son, Ptolemy of Mauretania, ruled that country as the last Ptolemy, from 23 to 40 CE.

Like Alexander the Great, who was often imitated in Roman times, Cleopatra VII had her greatest fame after her death. As late as 373 CE, a Cleopatra statue was plated in gold by a priest of Philae. Her mystique lives on in the works of Shakespeare and George Bernard Shaw, and in films.

Ideology and Religious Culture. The Egyptian pharaoh was the central figure in Egyptian religion and the divine representative on Earth. The belief that the deeds of Egypt's ruler were cult actions that guaranteed world order and all life inspired Egyptian priests and Macedonian kings alike to legitimize Alexander the Great's seizure of power, according to the ancient Egyptian royal ideology. By putting an end to the detested Persian rule,

Alexander had fulfilled the primary mythic task of a pharaoh: ending chaos and restoring order. By making offerings to the gods of Heliopolis and Memphis, especially to the royal deity, Apis, the Macedonian simultaneously declared his ascension to the throne as Egyptian king. Furthermore, at the beginning of 331 BCE, Alexander traveled to the Amun temple in the Siwa Oasis with a group of chosen friends (among them Ptolemy I), for confirmation from a king's oracle that he was the son of Zeus-Ammon and thus the legitimate successor to the indigenous pharaohs. In the New Kingdom, occasionally oracles had been used to legitimize the ascension of a new king to the throne, by recognizing the king as the chosen and beloved son of Amun-Re (corresponding to Zeus-Ammon of Siwa), and thus recognizing him as the heir of the gods in the office of King. The bark sanctuary in the temple of Luxor and another sanctuary in the Karnak temple have reliefs and inscriptions that date from the period of Alexander the Great. Alexander's function as pharaoh was passed on successively to Philip III (recorded in the bark sanctuary in Karnak) and to Alexander IV (see the gate of the Khnum temple on the island of Elephantine). At the same time, the satrap Ptolemy sought to grow into the pharaonic role. On the Satrap Stela of 311 BCE, he confirms temple lands to the priests of Buto and appears as the returning victor from Asia, bearing images of gods that the Persians were believed to have stolen—a theme that was often used to legitimize the Ptolemies as devout pharaohs during the entire third century BCE. In January 304, Ptolemy I became pharaoh, about a year and a half after having taken the Hellenistic title of *basileus*. The victory over the insurgents Antigonus and Demetrius could be taken as proof of his ability to hold the divine office. Henceforth the Ptolemaic king would embody two different kingships: the Hellenistic, personal kingship as *basileus*, and the national Egyptian kingship as the pharaoh. Hence we find both Greek and Egyptian statues of the Ptolemies and their wives, depending on their specific goals; the pharaonic statues wear the Egyptian royal headcloth or the double crown and other Egyptian elements, but the face is either stylized in the native Egyptian manner or displays some degree of naturalistic Greek influence.

The two kingdoms of the Ptolemies corresponded to the two large population groups of the empire, Greeks and Egyptians. Therefore the religious politics and the development of religion on the whole continued in two currents. The cult of Alexander as a national god in Alexandria was aimed at the Greek population. The office of priest for this cult, founded around 290 BCE, was the highest in the Hellenistic world. There is no proof of an Egyptian ever having held it. The subsequent Ptolemaic royal couples were integrated over time into the Alexander cult so that it developed into a Ptolemaic dynastic cult. Out of this, a Ptolemaic family charisma developed over the course of the third century BCE, which promulgated the divinity of individual members of the Ptolemaic family. From the second century BCE onward, this family charisma would compensate for the victorious quality now missing but once an essential feature of the *basileus*. By the end of the second century BCE, the office of the Alexander priest was held by the kings Ptolemy IX and X, and even in 105/104 BCE, by Cleopatra III. Furthermore, numerous state priestly offices were founded, first to venerate deceased members of the dynasty and later for living ones, in Alexandria and in Ptolemaïs of Upper Egypt. These priests and priestesses are mentioned in the documents much like the Alexander priests (termed "eponymous priests"). This type of official Greek cult of the king reached its late, exaggerated peak toward the end of the second century BCE, when five eponymous priesthoods existed for the living Cleopatra III in Alexandria.

Toward the Egyptians, the Ptolemies pursued a successful religious policy within the framework of the Egyptian cults, and they could count on the cooperation of the high priest of Ptah of Memphis. The latter represented all Egyptian priests and was responsible for the royal titulary of the Ptolemaic kings and for the crowning of the pharaoh. From the reign of Ptolemy II onward, the Ptolemies were included in the old Egyptian cult of kings.

The main area of interaction and cooperation between priests and kings was, as it had always been, the prolific building of temples. The great Ptolemaic projects began with the new construction of the Isis temple at Philae under Ptolemy II. The best-preserved temple in the old Egyptian style is the Horus temple of Edfu, which was started in 237 BCE, and continued to be built well into the middle of the fifth decade of the first century CE. It is a complete complex with a classic Ptolemaic ground plan: behind the pylon is a large courtyard, followed by the first large *pronaos*, and then the somewhat narrower and lower second *pronaos* ("Hall of Appearance"). Subsequently, along the temple axis are the offering hall, the "Hall of the Ennead," and the single-room sanctuary (surrounded by chapels), which is designed as an autonomous architectural element. A Thoth temple was begun under Ptolemy IV in Nubia at Dakka; construction continued during the revolt in Upper Egypt (from 206 BCE onward) under the patronage of the Meroitic king, Ergamenes II, who is portrayed there as pharaoh. Temple construction flourished under Ptolemy VI and Ptolemy VIII. Of special note is the double-temple for Haroëris and Sobek in Kom Ombo and the temple house of the large Khnum temple in Esna (the great *pronaos* is Roman). The last Ptolemaic construction project on a large scale was the Hathor temple in Dendera, begun under Ptolemy XII and continued under Cleopatra VII, into which the goddess could officially enter in the first year of Augustus Caesar. Egyptian temple construction continued in the Roman period.

Egyptian royal ideology was adapted to the actual history of the dynasty; especially the increasingly political role of the queen was transposed into the world of religious monuments in accordance with the status given her in administrative documents. This led to the formation of a female pharaoh beside and finally in front of the male pharaoh—in contrast to earlier female pharaohs, who had reigned on their own, such as Hatshepsut and Tawosret. Arsinoe was posthumously given a throne name, and Berenice II received a titulary composed of a Horus- and a birth-name in her lifetime. From this period onward, the king's wife is shown in temple reliefs performing rituals equal to her husband. Ptolemy VIII is depicted with one or two pharaonic female companions behind him, depending on the political circumstances (Cleopatra II and III, for example, in Kom Ombo). In Tod, expressions such as "the two Horuses" or "the masters of the two lands" were coined for the joint rule of Ptolemy VIII and Cleopatra II. Cleopatra III and VII, during whose reigns the female element in the dynasty reached its peak, appear in some reliefs in front of their royal sons, or even acting alone during cult ceremonies.

During the Ptolemaic period, numerous actions within the sphere of religious policy were carried out to unite the complex and varied population of the empire. Even during his early years as a satrap, Ptolemy I founded a Hellenistic cult of Serapis for the Memphite Osiris-Apis, in consultation with the famed Egyptian priest and historian, Manetho. He also created the Serapeum on the Rhakotis hill in Alexandria (the large Hellenistic building, with a science library, dates from the reign of Ptolemy III). After her death in 270 BCE, Ptolemy II raised Arsinoe II to the status of a full Egyptian and Greek goddess (on the Mendes Stela). Egyptian and Greek temples were consecrated to her (Arsinoeia), and she was honored in the Egyptian temples as a guest goddess and was identified with other goddesses, especially Isis and Aphrodite. In Memphis, the high priest of Ptah himself acted as priest for the goddess Arsinoe during the third century BCE. The Egyptian high clerics met repeatedly during the reigns of Ptolemy II to VI to formulate a uniform approach to Ptolemaic kingship. The clerics would take stock of various beneficial royal deeds and invariably honor the king (or royal couple) with cult ceremonies, statues, and celebrations. Of these so-called priest decrees, usually published in hieroglyphic, Demotic, or Greek inscriptions, the most important are: the Canopus Decree (238 BCE), which introduced a leap year of 366 days every four years—an idea that, however, did not take hold; the Raphia Decree (217 BCE), which celebrated the victory after the Battle of Raphia, and is the first occurrence of the hieroglyphic royal title transposed into Greek; the Rosetta Stone (196 BCE), which commemorated the crowning of Ptolemy V as pharaoh; and the Philensis Decrees (186 and 185 BCE), which marked the suppression of the large uprising in Upper Egypt. The Dionysian worldview that had risen to prominence with Alexander the Great and had been increasingly supported by the dynasty since Ptolemy IV could be understood from the Egyptian perspective by equating Dionysus with Osiris (the title of Ptolemy XII; the name "Neos Dionysos" is written in hieroglyphs as "young Osiris").

Government. Ptolemaic kings ruled with absolute power and the assistance of close advisers (*philoi*). At the top of the administrative hierarchy in Alexandria were the royal secretary for diplomatic affairs (*epistolographos*), the chancellor (*hypomnematographos*), the author of royal edicts, the top generals, and the *dioicete*, who oversaw civil administration. This position, which was likely a parallel of the *sntj* office created by Amasis, was adopted from the Egyptian past. The most famous *dioicete* was Apollonios of Caria (approximately 262–245 BCE), whose secretary, Zenon of Kaunos (also in Caria), compiled the most significant Hellenistic archives at that time. The *dioicete* was head of local civil administration; the geographical division of the country by nomes (districts) of varying number was maintained; under Ptolemy II, the Faiyum became a separate nome (Arsinoites). The nomarch supervised the agricultural production of the nome. The *oikonomos* was head of finance. The *basilicus grammateus* ("royal scribe") was charged with administering and registering land properties. As commander of troops, the district *strategon* rose to the top of the entire province administration under Ptolemy III, while the nomarch was gradually relegated to the status of a lowly finance official. The office of *epistrategos* was probably created in the wake of suppressing the revolt in Upper Egypt in 187. The *epistrategos* resided in Ptolemaïs in Upper Egypt, exercising supreme military as well as civil authority throughout the Chora. While the high officials were exclusively Greek during the third century BCE, the domain of local civil administration tended to remain in Egyptian hands. Only from Ptolemy VIII onward could Egyptians rise to the highest offices of the land. General Paos was *epistrategos* of the Chora from 129 BCE onward, Phommous likewise 115–110 BCE; both were awarded the highest title at the Ptolemaic court, *syngenes* ("blood relative").

In theory, as in the past, the king was owner of the entire land. Therefore all land that was not "royal land" and farmed by half-free royal tenants was seen as "loaned land." To this belonged the large estates of temple lands, the land of Greek cities (Naukratis, Alexandria, and Ptolemaïs), and royal feudal and private lands all fell into this category. The king deeded large estates to deserving officials (*doreai*; for example, the 2,750-hectare *dorea* of the *dioicete* Apollonios in the Faiyum); soldiers in active service (*cleruch*s) were given smaller holdings (*Kleroi*) to support their families. From the second century BCE, the *cleruchs* were divided into the *stratiotai* (usually Greeks or descendants of the Macedonian occupation army) and the poorer *maximoi*, who were mostly members of the Egyptian peasantry. From the time of Ptolemy II onward, there is documented evidence of Jewish *cleruchs*, especially in the Faiyum. In 165/164 BCE, the *maximoi* complained successfully about a royal decree, "On Agriculture," which forced farmers to cultivate land released at reduced lease rates (compulsory lease). The *anachoresis* ("flight from the landholding" which a farmer was forced to cultivate) worsened as a result of taxes and forced obligations. Consequently, the office of the *idios logos* was created during the first half of the second century BCE. This official was charged with finding profitable use for the abandoned and confiscated farms, which were usually appropriated by the state as fallow land.

From the early Hellenistic period, in the Faiyum, arable land had been increased enormously through irrigation along the edge of the desert, resulting in some thirty to forty new towns, which developed into centers of Greek culture. The greatest achievement in water management (probably under Ptolemy II) was the creation of an artificial lake with a surface area of 114 square kilometers and a capacity of 275 million cubic meters. The lake was used to irrigate an arable area of approximately 150 square kilometers for a second harvest in spring. Zenon, among others, was responsible for increasing agricultural production, especially the repeated sowing wheat.

The king was also a legislator and supervised the judiciary in the country through his highest judge (*archidikastes*). Egyptian and Greek law had equal validity; the jurisdiction of the Egyptian and Greek courts of law were reorganized in the amnesty decrees of 118 BCE.

The large temple lands occupied a position of their own within the overall organization of the country, and their structure remained virtually unchanged from the New Kingdom until the reorganization under Amasis, and into the Ptolemaic period. The high clergy of the so-called "god's house" of the supraregional deity, along with the adjacent "house of life" (the school for the training of priests), and the lands belonging to it, were not subject to the "law of pharaoh," but to a "law of Thoth" handed down by Re. They were also exempt from taxation. The same temple area would contain the various royal cult institutions and their economic institutions and fields, which were supervised by the state administration and operated by *wab*-priests, who were dependent on the king and were paid a wage (*syntaxis*). Higher Greek officials also exerted influence on the state-owned areas of temples (for example, the *dioicete* Apollonios on the Serapeum of Memphis). The temple administration and the temple economy, as well as state administration and state economy, were thus closely linked. Alexander the Great and Ptolemy I went to great lengths to secure the property of temples, which accumulated even more through donations from later kings (especially from Ptolemy II). Probably the greatest donation was the transfer of tax income from the Twelve Mile Land to the Isis temple of Philae. The temples were the centers of public life, sciences, and the arts, as well as large economic entities.

In addition to the trade in the Mediterranean (Rhodes was one of the most important trading posts), trade to the south and southeast was an important factor in the Ptolemaic economy. Relations with the empire of Meroë and trading posts on the Red Sea coast were maintained to trade for products from central Africa and the purchase of elephants for military purposes. To protect the incense route in the second century BCE, which reached the Mediterranean via Gaza (Ptolemaic in the third century BCE), the state collaborated with the southern Arabian Minaeans and the Sabaeans. Tensions soon developed with the Nabataeans, who controlled the northern section of the trade route—or rather with Nabatean pirates, with whom the Ptolemies fought battles in the Red Sea from the second century BCE onward. A shorter shipping route was probably found, making partial use of monsoon winds.

Elements of Greek education and culture were widespread in urban and (during the Ptolemaic period) also in village *gymnasia*. The peak, however, was reached with the School of Alexandria and its two centers, the Museion and the Serapeum. The foundation of the Museion and its rapidly growing library, which soon contained several hundred thousand papyrus scrolls, most likely dates from the time of Demetrius of Phaleron, an Athenian statesman who had become advisor to Ptolemy I in 297 BCE. In the third century BCE, the king called the most eminent scholars of the Greek world to the Museion as professors, researchers, and directors of the library. They included Zenodotos of Ephesos, one of the teachers of Ptolemy II; Apollonius of Rhodes, teacher of Ptolemy III; the physicians Praxagoras of Kos and Herophilos of Chalcedon; the mathematicians and geometricians Euclid (who died c.270 BCE) and Konon of Samos; the astronomer Aristarchus of Samos (c.310–230 BCE), who was famous for his heliocentric system; and the scholar Erathosthenes of Cyrene (c.284–202 BCE), who calculated the circumference of the Earth, and taught Ptolemy IV. The court poets Theocritus of Syracuse and Callimachus of Cyrene served the Ptolemaic royal ideology. The Septuagint is thought to have been begun under the government of Ptolemy II,

with the collaboration of the royal court, and to have been completed near the middle of the second century BCE. During the second century BCE, the Homeric scholars Aristophanes of Byzantium and Aristarchus of Samothrace served as directors of the Museion library.

[*See also* Alexander; Alexandria; *and* Cleopatra VII.]

BIBLIOGRAPHY

General Works
Bianchi, Robert S., et al. *Cleopatra's Egypt: Age of the Ptolemies.* New York, 1988. Catalog created for an extensive exhibition on Ptolemaic Egypt (in part also for Egypt under Roman rule), with short introductory articles on Ptolemaic-Roman relations, on the ethnic and cultural relationship between Greeks and Egyptians, on Egyptian priests and Egyptian adoration of Ptolemaic queens as well as on pharaonic art in Egypt under the Ptolemies. Includes a large bibliography.
Bowman, Alan K. *Egypt after the Pharaohs, 332 BC–AD 642 from Alexander to the Arab Conquest.* Oxford, 1986. General introduction to the organizational, religious and cultural development of Egypt during the period indicated in the title.
Fraser, Peter M. *Ptolemaic Alexandria.* 3 vols. Oxford, 1972. Comprehensive presentation of topics relating to Hellenistic Alexandria (topography, history, religion, art and science).
Hölbl, Günther. *A History of the Ptolemaic Kingdom.* London, 2000. Rev. ed. *Geschichte des Ptolemäerreiches,* Darmstadt, 1994. Focuses on the history of ideology and the history of temple construction; extensive bibliography.
Otto, W. and H. Bengston. *Zur Geschicte Neiderganges des Ptolemäerrriches.* Munich, 1938.
Schneider, Thomas. *Lexikon der Pharaonen.* Zürich, 1994. Pp. 205–225 give detailed individual biographies of the Ptolemies, based on Hölbl (1994).
Thompson, Dorothy J. *Memphis under the Ptolemies.* Princeton, 1988. Excellent presentation of the topographical, ethnic and religious conditions in Ptolemaic Memphis.

Political and Dynastic History
Bagnall, Roger S. *The Administration of the Ptolemaic Possessions outside Egypt.* Leiden, 1976. Detailed information on the history and organization of all regions under Ptolemaic rule outside of Egypt.
Beyer-Rotthoff, Brigitte. *Untersuchungen zur Aussenpolitik Ptolemaios' III.* Bonn, 1993. The political history of Ptolemy III, geographically categorized (Seleucid kingdom, Greek, the Occident) as well as an overview of Ptolemaic control at sea and domestic politics; excellent study of sources.
Ellis, Walter M. *Ptolemy of Egypt,* London, 1994. History of Ptolemy I.
Grainger, John D. *Hellenistic Phoenicia.* Oxford, 1991. Excellent overview of the political history of Ptolemaic Syria and Phoenicia.
Huss, Werner. *Untersuchungen zur Aussenpolitik Ptolemaios' IV.* Munich, 1976. Presentation of the foreign policy under Ptolemy IV, based on a detailed study of sources and categorized by geographical areas, with an emphasis on the Fourth Syrian War.
Pestman, P. W. "Haronnophris and Chaonnophris, Two Indigenous Pharaohs in Ptolemaic Egypt (205–186 BC)." In *Hundred-Gated Thebes,* edited by S. P. Vleeming, pp. 101–137. Leiden, 1995. Comprehensive study of the great revolt in Upper Egypt.
Schrapel, Thomas. *Das Reich der Kleopatra: Quellenkritische Untersuchungen zu den "Landschenkungen" Mark Antons.* Trier, 1996. The territorial reorganization of the Ptolemaic empire in the 30s of the first century BCE.
Sullivan, Richard D. *Near Eastern Royalty and Rome, 100–30 BC.* To-

ronto, 1990. Pp. 81–95, 229–279, history of the Ptolemaic Empire in connection to Rome under Ptolemy IX until Roman conquest.

Whitehorne, John. *Cleopatras*. London, 1994. Biographies of the most important female Hellenistic figures named Cleopatra.

Religion and Ideology

Huss, Werner. *Der makedonische König und die ägyptischen Priester.* Stuttgart, 1994. Very detailed and extensively annotated presentation of the relationship (cooperation and opposition) between the Egyptian clergy and the Ptolemaic king.

Huss, Werner. "Die in ptolemaiischer Zeit verfassten Synodaldekrete der ägyptischen Priester." *Zeitschrift für Papyrologie und Epigraphik* 88 (1991), 189–208. Overview of decrees issued by priests.

Onasch, Christian. "Zur Königsideologie der Ptolemäer in den Dekreten von Kanopos und Memphis (Rosettana)." *Archiv für Papyrusforschung* 24–25 (1976), 137–155. Study of the problem of creating a universal Ptolemaic royal ideology from Ptolemy III to V.

Smith, R. R. R. *Hellenistic Royal Portraits.* Oxford, 1988. Contains a critical study of the different influences found in Ptolemaic royal sculpture as well as an annotated catalogue and photographs.

Sauneron, Serge, and Henri Stierlin. *Edfou et Philae: Derniers temples d'Égypte.* Paris, 1975. General introduction to architecture and cult traditions (everyday traditions and special celebrations) of the most important temple sites in Ptolemaic Egypt.

Organization

Clarysse, Willy, and Katelijn Vandorpe. *Zenon, un homme d'affaires grec à l'ombre des pyramides.* Louvain, 1995. Introduction to the history and content of the papyri of the Zenon archives, with text examples (Greek and French) and cultural-historic commentary.

Goudriaan, Koen. *Ethnicity in Ptolemaic Egypt.* Amsterdam, 1988. Definition and characterization of ethnic groups "Hellenic" and "Egyptian."

Grzybek, Erhard. *Du calendrier macédonien au calendrier ptolémaïque. Problèmes de chronologie hellénistique.* Basel, 1990. Macedonian and Egyptian calendars during the reign of Ptolemy II, but contestable hypotheses.

Lewis, Naphtali. *Greeks in Ptolemaic Egypt: Case Studies in the Social History of the Hellenistic World.* Oxford, 1986. On the fate of individual Greeks in Ptolemaic Egypt.

Samuel, Alan E. *From Athens to Alexandria: Hellenismus and Social Goals in Ptolemaic Egypt.* Louvain, 1983. On the Greek impact on the economy, technology, culture, and society of Ptolemaic Egypt.

Thomas, J. David. *The Epistrategos in Ptolemaic and Roman Egypt, 1. The Ptolemaic Epistrategos.* Opladen, 1975. Responsibilities and importance of the Ptolemaic epistrategos, as well as biographies of well-known individuals who held this office.

GÜNTHER HÖLBL
Translated from German by Elizabeth Schwaiger

PUNISHMENT. *See* Crime and Punishment.

PUNT. For about two thousand years (c.2600–600 BCE), Punt appeared in Egyptian sources as a real geographical and political entity. Later, it featured as merely an antiquated entry in Greco-Roman period name lists. The phrase "God's Land" serves as a partial synonym for Punt in literary sources, but it covered a large area—almost anything northeast, east, or southeast of Egypt. In its heyday (c.2400–1170 BCE), Punt served the pharaonic government and temples primarily as a source of aromatics (*'ntyw* and *sntr*, normally understood as myrrh and incense), and also of gold, electrum (a natural silver and gold alloy), panther skins, and other exotica. Most of those goods reached Egypt through indirect trade by a chain of middlemen, except when the pharaohs dispatched occasional major expeditions to conduct direct trade with Punt. In the latter case, high officials from the court would, on occasion, lead the intended expedition as far as its Red Sea departure point, while a lesser royal envoy commanded it out to Punt and back. Then, the responsible higher official (like Chief Treasurer Nehesi under Hatshepsut) would present the results to the sovereign at court. Barter was the normal means of trade. In the case of Hatshepsut's expedition, the royal envoy in command brought Egyptian food products for his Puntite hosts, and "all kinds of things from the Palace." These were brought officially for Hathor (the goddess for places outside Egypt), for whom a shrine was set up in Punt, but perhaps in practice they were goods to be exchanged for products sought by the Egyptians. Geopolitically, Punt consisted of a series of local chiefdoms (Egyptian references are to "chiefs," in the plural). It is not clear whether (in Hatshepsut's time) Parehu, "chief of Punt," was an overlord, or merely one ruler among many. Some chiefs of Punt returned to Hatshepsut's court with her expedition. Military action in Punt was probably logistically unrealistic, and could offer no advantage over peaceful trade. Mutual cultural influence, whether in ideas or artifacts, is not discernible—direct archaeological evidence is lacking.

The location of Punt was long disputed, having been first sought in South Arabia until the discovery of the Punt-reliefs of Queen Hatshepsut (c.1470 BCE), which showed Punt with African flora and fauna. After that find, it was often suggested to have been situated in Somalia (an East African country with well-known aromatic sources). A fresh study of all features was published by Rolf Herzog, in his *Punt* (Glückstadt, 1968), in which he made a strong case for locating Punt in eastern Sudan and northeastern Ethiopia. Through a misunderstanding of some Egyptian sources, however, Herzog failed to recognize the reality of Egyptian seafaring expeditions to Punt down the Red Sea—that the eastern Sudan/Eritrean coastline had also belonged to Punt (Kitchen 1971). The East African location is shown by the occurrence of giraffes in Hatshepsut's scenes, the symbiosis of dom palms with hamadryas baboons, and the depiction of the rhinoceros (thereby India and eastward being excluded); then, too, part of the Puntite population was negroid, and pile-dwellings were in use. Likewise, a mention during the Saite period (c.600 BCE) of the rain on the mountain of Punt draining into the Nile, requires an Ethiopian/eastern

Sudanese setting, and rules out Somalia completely. Two pygmies brought from tropical Africa down the Nile to Egypt, in one case explicitly via Punt, in the fifth and sixth dynasties (c.2400 and c.2300 BCE, respectively), also serve to locate Punt. The gold of Amau reached Egypt by trade through Punt in one direction and by the Third and Fourth Cataract region of her own Nubian empire in another. This also points to an Ethiopian/eastern Sudanese location for Punt if Amau included part of the gold-bearing mountainous area of northeasternmost Sudan, east of the Fourth and Fifth Cataracts of the Nile and just north of Punt. The "mining region of Punt" may have adjoined the Amau deposits. In this situation, Egypt's access to Punt (and vice versa) could have occurred by two routes: the Nile Valley or the Red Sea. Egypt's great official expeditions to Punt clearly traveled by the Red Sea route—as shown by depictions in Hatshepsut's mortuary temple, in which Red Sea/Indian Ocean fishes swim below her ships. The route of Ramesses III's expedition went via the Wadi Hammamat to the Red Sea and back. Middle Kingdom inscriptions in the Wadi Hammamat (linking the Nile and Red Sea) and a harbor on the Red Sea near Quseir (with inscriptions there mentioning visits to Punt) confirm this route. In the New Kingdom, about 1450 BCE, Puntites in turn visited Egypt with their products, most likely by the Red Sea, but possibly using the Nile.

BIBLIOGRAPHY

Bradbury, Louise. "*Kpn*-Boats, Punt Trade, and a Lost Emporium." *Journal of the American Research Center in Egypt* 33 (1996), 37–60. Advocates the Nile route for Puntite traders visiting Egypt; for some reservations, see Kitchen (1998) below.

Fattovich, Rodolfo. "The Problem of Punt in the Light of Recent Fieldwork in the Eastern Sudan." In *Akten des vierten internationalen Ägyptologen Kongresses München 1985*, 4, edited by Sylvia Schoske, pp. 257–272. Hamburg, 1991. A valuable summary survey of local archaeology and interconnections in eastern Sudan, within terrain possibly part of ancient Punt.

Kitchen, K. A. "Punt and How to Get There." *Orientalia NS* 40 (1971), 184–207.

Kitchen, K. A. "The Land of Punt." In *The Archaeology of Africa, Food, Metals and Towns*, edited by Thurstan Shaw, Paul Sinclair, Bassey Andah, and Alex Okpoko, pp. 587–608. London/New York, 1993. A concise, documented survey from the Egyptian sources, including most of the ancient Egyptian pictures of Punt, Puntites and expeditions; with prior bibliography.

Kitchen, K. A. "Further Thoughts on Punt and its Neighbours." In *Egyptology Studies*, edited by J. W. Tait, Egypt Exploration Society London, 1999. Seeks to define the bounds of Punt and its neighbors; reviews recent developments.

Naville, E. H., ed. *The Temple of Deir el-Bahari*, vol. 3. London, 1898. The primary publication, in line drawings and color, of all the Punt expedition scenes of Queen Hatshepsut in her Deir el-Bahri temple.

Smith, William Stevenson. "The Land of Punt." *Journal of the American Research Center in Egypt* 1 (1962), 59–61, with figure. Presents a fuller restoration of Queen Hatshepsut's depiction of the land of Punt than attained by Naville.

KENNETH A. KITCHEN

PYGMIES. *See* People.

PYLON. The Greek word *pylon* (Eg., *bḫnt*) refers to the massive portals characteristic of Egyptian temples, from at least as early as the Middle Kingdom, but pylons are best known from the temples of New Kingdom to Roman times. The pylon was usually seen as the entrance to the temple or, in the case of multiple pylons, to areas of the temple complex. There seems to have been no set number of pylons for a given temple; the number depended on such factors as the size of the structure and its architectural history. Some buildings had but one or two such gateways, but the Karnak temple of Amun in its final form had ten pylons, six on the east–west axis and four running southward from the main structure; all but one was constructed by succeeding pharaohs, in the course of about two centuries, during the eighteenth dynasty. The earliest known pylon of the Karnak temple was built at the behest of Thutmose I.

The pylon normally consisted of two large towers with sloping sides, connected at about mid-height by a large doorway. The shape of the pylon is believed to symbolize the horizon, and it imitates the hieroglyph for the horizon (*3ḫt*). The pylon is built on a rectangular ground plan, but the front face of the structure is usually battered (i.e., it slopes backward as it rises in height). Scenes on a number of Egyptian monuments indicate that the two-to-four battered recesses (at Amarna even more) in the front face of the pylon were used for flagstaffs, from which pennants flew above the level of the tops of the pylon. This was perhaps usual on occasions when the god's statue was engaged in some ritual activity, either within the temple or in procession to some other temple. The edges of the pylon were trimmed with torus moldings, and there were cornices at the top. A number of the known pylons have staircases within, as well as small windows. In Ptolemaic-era examples, there are sometimes auxiliary doorways cut through the pylon.

Most of the shell of the pylon—commonly of stone, but some of mud bricks—was filled with rubble or with crudely hewn blocks of stone. At Karnak, restoration efforts at the site have disclosed that many of the interior blocks of the Third Pylon consisted of reused material from the chapels of Senwosret I (of the twelfth dynasty) and of Amenhotpe I, Queen Hatshepsut, and Thutmose IV (all of the eighteenth dynasty). An extraordinary example of such pylon construction, using building materials from earlier edifices, was revealed when the south-axis pylons (Nine and Ten) of Horemheb were dismantled for restoration purposes; thousands of blocks of a size a worker could carry on his shoulder (called *talatat*) had been taken

PYLON. *South view of the pylon of the Khons Temple at Karnak.* (Courtesy Dieter Arnold)

directly from the East Karnak temples of Akhenaten, carried to the Horemheb construction site, and reused.

Access to the first pylon of a temple was usually by means of a road, one sometimes lined with ram-headed sphinxes. In the case of Karnak, a canal from the Nile River led to a quay at one end of the avenue of sphinxes. In instances of two or more pylons, they were sometimes joined by side walls that formed an enclosed courtyard, as in the case of the court before the Seventh Pylon, added in the Ramessid era. The creation of some courts, as at the funerary temple of Ramesses III at Medinet Habu, resulted in the impression that the pylon transsected the side walls of the court.

The pylons were usually covered with carved reliefs—originally brilliantly painted—showing a variety of scenes. Most common are scenes of the king ceremonially executing captured enemy leaders in the presence of his divine father and sponsor, Amun-Re. Other examples show rows of divinities receiving offerings from the king and/or bestowing various gifts on him. Still others show the king engaged in the hunting of such animals as wild bulls. For unknown reasons, the First Pylon of the Karnak temple was left undecorated by its builder, apparently Nektanebo I (380–363 BCE).

BIBLIOGRAPHY

Badawy, A. *A History of Egyptian Architecture*, vol. 3. Berkeley, 1968.
Baines, J., and J. Málek. *Atlas of Ancient Egypt*. Oxford, 1980.
Jaroš-Deckert, B. "Pylon." In *Lexikon der Ägyptologie*, 4:1202–1205. Wiesbaden, 1982.
Spencer, P. A. *The Egyptian Temple: A Lexicographical Study*. London, 1984.

GERALD E. KADISH

PYRAMID. The monument that to many symbolizes ancient Egypt was originally a royal tomb in the form of a pyramid—a structure with a square base and four triangular sides sloping to a single apex—symbolizing the primeval hill that emerged from the waters during the creation of the world and on which life arose. Such a concept represents a rationalization of the primitive grave, capped by a mound of earth or sand, which gave rise to the *mastaba*, the boxlike tomb superstructure developed in the first dynasty.

The origin of the word "pyramid" remains obscure. Sometimes it has been considered to derive from the word *pr-m-ws*, a geometrical term for the height of a pyramid. Nor do we know exactly how many pyramids were built: the estimate is approximately one hundred. Many

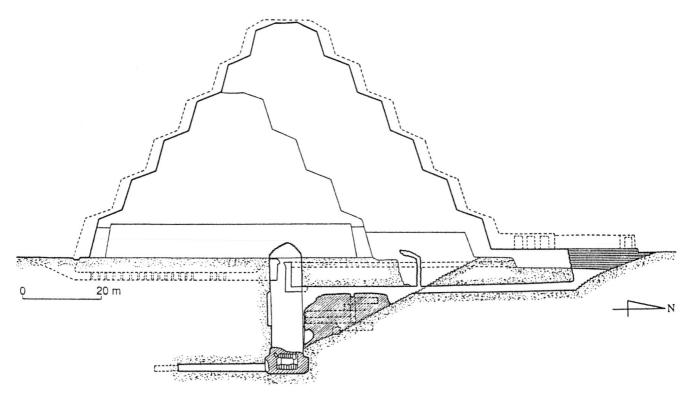

PYRAMID. *North–south cross section of the Pyramid of Djoser at Saqqara, third dynasty.* (Courtesy Miroslav Verner)

pyramids mentioned in written records have not yet been discovered, and others may have been wholly destroyed.

History and Development. The period during which the Egyptian kings regularly built these tombs is often called the "Age of the Pyramid Builders." It extends from the beginning of the third dynasty to the beginning of the eighteenth. Subsequently, the pyramid—significantly reduced in size and of steeper slope—appeared with private tombs as a part of the above-ground shrine. There it symbolized not only the primeval hill but also the rising solar deity, as well as recalling the royal tombs. From the Late period onward, the pyramid became again a favorite form of a royal tomb, this time among Nubian rulers from Napata and Meroë.

The oldest pyramids date from the third dynasty; they are stepped and are surrounded by a complex of other buildings of a religious-symbolic character. The basic orientation of the whole pyramid complex, enclosed by a high wall on a rectangular groundplan, is roughly north to south. The shape of the pyramid has most often been interpreted as a stylized primeval hill and, at the same time, a gigantic stairway to heaven. In fact, the Egyptian term for "pyramid" (*mr*) has been derived from a root *i'i* ("to ascend"), thus giving "place of ascent." The orientation of the complex has therefore been connected to the idea that the pharaoh's soul was supposed to become one of the "immortal" circumpolar stars.

The oldest pyramid of all is the Step Pyramid of Netjerikhet (better known under his later name, Djoser) at Saqqara. Djoser's burial complex consists of an extensive set of buildings circumscribed by a huge enclosure wall (c.278 × 545 meters/c.850 × 1,700 feet) and surrounded by a trench (the so-called Dry Moat) 40 meters (125 feet) wide. The dominant feature is the six-step pyramid, 62.5 meters (200 feet) high; it is the only known pyramid that does not have a square ground plan, but rather a rectangular one (109 × 121 meters/350 × 375 feet). The original plan for a stylized primeval hill was twice extended and finally changed into a step pyramid in two additional building phases; the reasons for the changes of plan are still the subject of discussion.

The burial chamber, made of red granite, is situated under the pyramid and is accessible by a staircase from the north; it is surrounded by a complicated system of underground galleries. Eleven burial shafts for members of the pharaoh's family lie under the pyramid's eastern part.

The mortuary temple stood at the northern foot of the pyramid. One remarkable feature of the complex is a structure known as the "South Tomb," in which the underground part is a faithful copy of the substructure of the Step Pyramid. It may have been a symbolic representation of the ruler's tomb in southern Egypt. The complex also includes a columned entrance hall, a broad courtyard, and buildings of symbolic importance, such as a series of dummy shrines for celebrations of the royal jubilee (the *sed*-festival), the government palaces of Upper and Lower Egypt, granaries and stores, and so on. All this was intended for use by the deceased king throughout eternity, as an afterlife projection of the pharaonic center.

The whole complex (except for a few details) is of limestone and arouses wonder at the monumentality of its architecture, the bizarre forms arising from the transfer to stone of elements of light Early Dynastic architecture that had mainly used plant materials, and the perfection of craftsmanship in the execution of every detail. Its builder (possibly Djoser's son Imhotep, the subsequently venerated sage) was probably inspired in many respects by the actual royal residence in nearby Memphis.

The second pyramid complex of the third dynasty, built also at Saqqara and belonging to Djoser's successor Sekhemkhet, was never completed. It remains a mystery why the sealed calcite (Egyptian alabaster) sarcophagus in the burial chamber was empty. Another unfinished stepped pyramid, which has been named the Layer Pyramid owing to its core of inclined layers, lies in Zawiyet el-Aryan. It may have belonged to Khaba, a third dynasty king.

At the beginning of the fourth dynasty, the stepped form gave way to the true pyramid, and the surrounding buildings were arranged in what became a largely standard pattern. A complete complex consists of a pyramid with burial chamber, a valley (lower) temple, a causeway, and a mortuary (upper, or pyramid) temple. The pyramid and the mortuary temple at its eastern foot were surrounded by a huge enclosure wall. The valley temple on the edge of the desert served as both a harbor and as a monumental gate. The causeway joined the two temples. Later, the so-called northern chapel would emerge as a feature placed above the entrance to the underground section in the northern wall of the pyramid. The so-called cult pyramid close to the southeastern corner of the pyramid has a simple burial chamber in which there is never any trace of a burial. Its significance has not yet been fully explained, but it may have been a symbolic representation of the ruler's tomb in southern Egypt. Trenches with funerary boats were also sometimes parts of the complex.

The orientation of the complex was changed from north–south to east–west (the entrance to the pyramid, however, remained on the north). This was evidently connected to the victory of the solar cult.

The first ruler of the fourth dynasty, Sneferu, was the greatest builder of pyramids in history; he built four, with an overall volume of masonry of around 3.7 million cubic meters. The pyramid at Meidum, where Sneferu's original residence was situated, was initially constructed as a seven-step and then eight-step pyramid, but it was ultimately rebuilt into a "true" pyramid. It is a rare piece of evidence showing the transition between the two types. The first phase of its building was formerly attributed to the last pharaoh of the third dynasty, perhaps named Huny.

Sneferu moved his residence to Dahshur and then had two pyramids built there, the so-called Bent and Red pyramids. The Bent Pyramid was planned from the beginning as a true pyramid. During building, however, its geological foundation proved unstable, and so the volume was reduced from the level at roughly half its completed height, giving the pyramid its unique shape. The infrastructure consists of two systems of chambers and corridors linked by a tunnel cut into the masonry of the pyramid. The chambers have false vaults. At the eastern foot of the pyramid lay the humble site of the mortuary cult, with an altar and two stelae. Fragments of relief decoration and statues of the pharaoh were discovered in the valley temple. Sneferu was actually buried in yet another pyramid at Dahshur, the Red Pyramid, although this complex was not fully completed (it lacks a valley temple, causeway and other elements).

The smallest of Sneferu's pyramids is situated in Sila, on the eastern edge of the Faiyum Oasis. Similar pyramids, the significance of which has not yet been fully explained, are spread throughout the Nile Valley from Sila to Elephantine. They have no burial chambers or adjacent buildings of a cult nature, and they are not precisely oriented to the four cardinal points. They are usually dated to the end of the third dynasty and beginning of the fourth and have most often been interpreted as state-cult constructions symbolizing the authority of the pharaoh.

Sneferu's son Khufu chose Giza for the site of his pyramid and established a new royal cemetery there. The pyramids of Giza became the symbol of the power of the state and authority of the pharaoh at its height. Khufu's pyramid, regarded from antiquity as one of the Seven Wonders of the World, is rightly called the "Great Pyramid": its side was approximately 230.35 meters (750 feet) long; the angle of incline of the walls was approximately 50°50'35''; and the original height was approximately 146.50 meters (450 feet).

Research has shown that the core of this pyramid, though made up mostly of compacted stone masonry, contains also irregular chambers filled with sand. This technique would have accelerated construction substantially, made it significantly cheaper, and at the same time much increased its stability in earthquakes.

A complex system of chambers and corridors lies inside the pyramid and beneath it. The question of whether this was constructed according to a gradually developed or previously established plan is still debated.

The original entrance to the pyramid was in the northern face. From there a descending corridor led to an unfinished chamber perhaps 30 meters (96 feet) underground. Just above the foundation of the pyramid, a second, ascending corridor breaks away from the first. This opens into the so-called Great Gallery, the ceiling of which consists of a false vault. One use of the gallery was as a temporary storage place for the granite blocks that were supposed to block the bottom part of the ascending corridor; the workmen could escape via the so-called service shaft leading into the underground part of the descending corridor.

A horizontal passage leads from the lower end of the Great Gallery to the so-called Queen's Chamber. The latter's significance is not entirely clear, but it is possible that at a certain phase of construction it served as a reserve burial chamber.

Khufu was ultimately buried in what is known as the King's Chamber, linked to the upper end of the Great Gallery by a corridor with a portcullis made of three huge slabs of red granite. The whole chamber is constructed out of the same material, including the ceiling and the sarcophagus by the western wall. A relieving construction consisting of five other compartments (four with flat ceilings, and the highest with a saddle ceiling) was built above the chamber out of huge limestone and granite blocks. This was designed to distribute the pressure of the pyramid's masonry on the King's Chamber and to increase the stability of the whole building, not only as a precaution against earthquakes but also because the chamber does not lie precisely on the axis of the pyramid.

In the King's Chamber (as in the Queen's) there are small shafts opening in the north and south walls and leading diagonally upward to the surface of the pyramid. Their significance is unclear: some experts believe that these were made to allow the pharaoh's soul to ascend to the heavens, while others believe them to be ventilation shafts.

By the eastern foot of the pyramid there was a mortuary temple with a large open forecourt and a pillared hall. This was linked with the valley temple, not yet excavated, by a causeway. In front of the eastern side and along the southern side of the pyramid, five funerary boats were placed in trenches; two of them have been discovered undamaged. Near the southeastern corner stood a cult pyramid and the three small pyramids attributed to the ruler's mother Hetepheres I and his wives Meretites and Henutsen.

Khufu's successor Djedefre built his pyramid complex at Abu Rawash. It was formerly believed that the pyramid possessed steep walls that had never been finished, and that the ruler's statues in the mortuary temple had been deliberately destroyed. New excavations have shown, however, that Djedefre's pyramid was completed in standard form, but later, mainly in the Roman period, it was devastated by unusually intensive stone quarrying.

From a distance, Khafre's pyramid appears to be the highest in the Giza cemetery, because it was built on a more elevated site than the Great Pyramid; in fact, it was originally probably 3 meters (10 feet) lower than Khufu's. The relative simplicity of the substructure is balanced by the greater complexity and grandeur of the overall plan of pyramid complex, especially the valley and mortuary temples. The complex includes the Great Sphinx, a colossal statue of a lion with a human head (possibly a likeness of Khafre, but sometimes attributed to Khufu). This protective deity symbolically guarded the entrance to the whole kingdom of the underworld. Later, the Sphinx was worshiped as the solar deity Horemakhet ("Horus on the Horizon").

The valley temple of Khafre's complex is considered one of the milestones in the development of ancient Egyptian architecture. In addition to limestone, red granite and alabaster are extensively used in its construction. The assurance with which the builders subjected the stone to geometrical form is remarkable, as is the overall harmonious impression made by the architecture of the temple. In Khafre's complex, too, the mortuary temple was surrounded by five burials of boats. The unfinished pyramid (perhaps Baka's), also known as the Great Pit in Zawiyet el-Aryan, is usually dated to the period just after Khafre.

The smallest of the Giza pyramids belongs to Khafre's son Menkaure. It has a complicated substructure and the extensive use of red granite on the casing of the lower part. Three small pyramids belonging to the queens were situated by its southern side. The causeway and valley temple, where numerous statues of the ruler were found during excavations, were completed by Menkaure's successor, the last known fourth dynasty pharaoh, Shepseskaf. Perhaps because there was no suitable site left at Giza (and perhaps also for dynastic and political reasons), Shepseskaf had his own tomb built in South Saqqara near Sneferu's pyramids at Dahshur. Surprisingly, this tomb is not in the form of a pyramid, but of a large *mastaba* or sarcophagus. The reasons for this deviation from previous practice are more likely to have been economic than religious.

The beginning of the fifth dynasty saw several significant changes in the pattern of royal tombs. These mainly involved changes in the design of the mortuary temple, the extension of relief decoration in the complex, a reduction in the size of the pyramid, and a standardization of its substructure. One development related to the new conception is the building of the sun temples, which were

PYRAMID. *Ceiling of the crypt of the Pyramid of Meidum, third–fourth dynasty.* (Courtesy Dieter Arnold)

supposed to link the solar cult, then at its height, to the royal mortuary cult. The first sun temple was built by Userkaf, and more such temples were built by his successors Sahure, Neferirkare, Neferefre, Newoserre, and Menkauhor. So far only two have been found—Userkaf's at Abusir and Newoserre's at Abu Ghurob.

Userkaf's pyramid complex is to some extent atypical in both layout and location. Political reasons were probably behind Userkaf's decision to squeeze it into the larger precinct of Djoser's complex at Saqqara. The siting of the mortuary temple south of the pyramid and several other peculiarities are clearly results of this decision. A small pyramid for the queen, with its own mortuary temple, was included in the complex.

Sahure's complex at Abusir represents another important achievement in the development of the royal tomb. A causeway in the form of a corridor connects the valley temple, which has two landing ramps, with the mortuary temple. The latter's standardized design includes an entrance hall, an open columned courtyard, and a transverse corridor separating off the intimate part of the temple, with its shrine of five niches for statues of the ruler, an offering hall, and two groups of storage chambers.

The pyramid is not large; its core is made up of low-quality limestone placed in horizontal layers. The underground part includes an access corridor sloping down from the north. This is equipped with a granite portcullis and opens into an anteroom situated roughly on the vertical axis of the pyramid. South of the anteroom lies the burial chamber, which has a three-layer saddle ceiling.

Sahure's pyramid complex is distinguished by the harmony of its overall plan, its use of different colored stones, and, especially, its brilliant relief decoration. In the entrance part of the complex, the apotropaic character of the ornamentation scheme (i.e., motifs for warding off evil) was intended to deflect any potential danger threatening the peace of the pharaoh's tomb. The causeway is also decorated with scenes relating to the building of the complex and the ceremonies and festivals linked to its completion. The decoration of the mortuary temple emphasized, in addition to offering scenes, the mythological role of the pharaoh, his victory over the enemies of Egypt, his hunting prowess, his multiplication of the riches of the land, and his meeting with the gods.

Sahure's successors Neferirkare Kakai, Raneferef (Neferefre), and Newoserre Any likewise built their pyramid complexes at Abusir, but each reflects a particular set of circumstances. Neferirkare's pyramid was originally designed as a step pyramid; it was later converted to a true pyramid but never completed. Its mortuary temple was finished later and so were the trenches with funerary boats by the northern and southern sides of the pyramid.

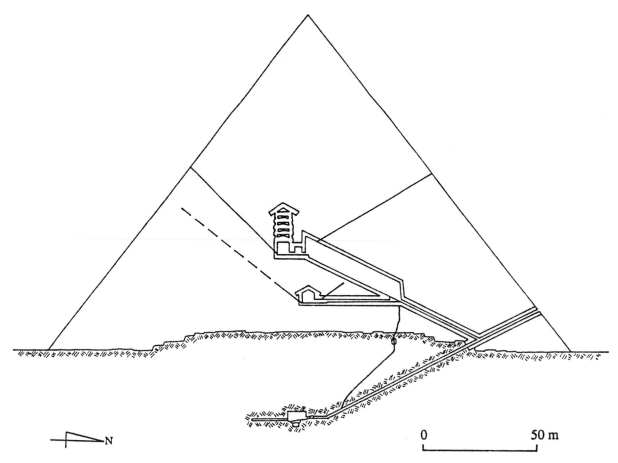

PYRAMID. *North–south cross section of the Pyramid of Khufu at Giza, fourth dynasty.* (Courtesy Miroslav Verner)

The small pyramid of the pharaoh's wife Khentkaus II was situated south of the pyramid.

Raneferef only managed to build the first step of the core of his pyramid, which after his premature death was hastily changed into a square-shaped *mastaba*. This change also affected the form of the mortuary temple erected for Raneferef by his younger brother Newoserre Any. No valley temple and causeway were ever built. Lack of a suitable site forced Newoserre Any to modify his own complex. The element most affected was the mortuary temple. Among other novel features in its design, we find a small square room with a column (the so-called *antichambre carrée*). Newoserre Any also appropriated Neferirkare Any's incomplete valley temple and causeway. The two small pyramid complexes that probably belonged to Newoserre Any's wives had to be built as far away as the southern edge of the Abusir pyramid field. The pyramid of Newoserre Any's successor Menkauhor has not yet been discovered. Sometimes it has been identified with the so-called Headless Pyramid in North Saqqara, and at other times with the ruins near the Red Pyramid in Dahshur.

Djedkare Izezi's pyramid complex, although situated in South Saqqara, does not deviate from the basic pattern of fifth dynasty royal tombs. The massive tower buildings in the façade of the mortuary temple, however, regarded as prototypes of pylons, represent a new element, as does the extension of the underground spaces of the pyramid to include the storeroom with three recesses, which are found repeated in subsequent pyramids of the fifth and sixth dynasties. The adjoining complex of the queen is remarkable for its size and ground plan.

Although standard in form, the pyramid complex of the last fifth dynasty pharaoh, Unas, represents another achievement in the development of the royal tomb. It is the first in which the religious inscriptions known as the Pyramid Texts are carved in the corridor, antechamber, and burial chamber. They occur in subsequent pyramids (even those of queens) of the sixth through eighth dynasties. Their order and content, which incorporate in part the mortuary liturgy, have been linked by some to the layout of the funerary complex. Two trenches for funerary boats are also parts of Unas's complex.

Teti's pyramid complex of the sixth dynasty in North Saqqara follows the same design as that of Unas, but in the courtyard of the mortuary temple, for example, there are pillars instead of columns (as found in later complexes of the sixth dynasty). North of Teti's pyramid are the two small pyramid complexes of his wives, Iput I and Khuit. The most striking peculiarity of the essentially standard complex of his successor Pepy I is the large number of small pyramids and mortuary temples of queens. Four have so far been discovered, and there may well be more.

In contrast to Merenre Antyemsaf's pyramid in South Saqqara, which still awaits full excavation, the nearby pyramid complex of Pepy II has been fully cleared. This possesses, apart from some minor peculiarities (such as a large valley temple with two landing ramps, or the three chambers in front of the entrance hall of the mortuary temple), the basic features already established in earlier development. Near the pyramid lay the three small pyramid complexes of the pharaoh's queens, Neith, Iput II, and Udjebten. Close to the causeway stands the small pyramid of King Aba, which is chronologically the last pyramid in which Pyramid Texts have been found.

The tombs of the rulers of the First Intermediate Period have still to be discovered, but some of them may have the form of pyramids. Near Dara there is a large building of uncertain type and date. It may have been built during the First Intermediate Period and was probably a local ruler's (step?) *mastaba* rather than a pyramid.

At the beginning of the Middle Kingdom, the unifier of Egypt, Montuhotep I had a terraced tomb complex built in Deir el-Bahri. This combines a pyramid complex with elements of the so-called *saff*-tomb (a rock-cut tomb with a façade made up of a row of pillars) of his Upper Egyptian ancestors. According to one theory, the terraced building of the mortuary temple was crowned by a small pyramid, but another theory suggests that this was a cubic structure symbolizing the primeval mound. Besides the real burial chamber, Mentuhotep's complex contains a symbolic tomb of the king (the so-called *Bab el-hossan*).

The founder of the twelfth dynasty, Amenemhet I, returned to the pyramid complex type of tomb. It stands near el-Lisht, which was probably also the site of the new capital Itjtawy. The core of the pyramid is made of fragments of low-quality limestone. The mortuary temple is reduced in size, and numerous tombs of members of the royal family are within the complex.

Changes are also visible in the neighboring complex of Amenemhet's son Senwosret I. The core of his pyramid consists of a diagonal framework of solid stone walls. The space between them is filled with pieces of low-quality limestone. The pyramid of the king was surrounded with small pyramids of queens and princesses. The mortuary temple resembles a sixth dynasty design. It includes an entrance hall, an open pillared courtyard, a transverse corridor, a shrine with five niches, an *antechambre carrée*, an offering hall, and two groups of storage rooms. The causeway was decorated with standing statues of Senwosret I.

In the construction of the core of the pyramid of Amenemhet II in Dahshur, as in the pyramids of his successors, mud bricks are used instead of limestone. This yet largely unexcavated complex was made famous by the treasures found in the tombs of the princesses Ita and Khnemet.

The substructures of the pyramids of Amenenhet I and Senwosret I have been submerged in groundwater for a long time, and detailed information is therefore lacking. We do not know to what extent they may already reflect a change evident in later twelfth dynasty pyramids. The design of the substructure, recalling a labyrinth, was intended to resemble the tomb of Osiris, god of the dead, whose cult became the major influence on the plan of the royal tombs. This is very clear in the pyramid of Senwosret II at Illahun in the Faiyum Oasis. The entrance to the underground part no longer leads from the north; it is actually situated outside the pyramid. Near its valley temple, a large residential area for workmen, officials, and priests has been discovered.

The substructure of the pyramid of Senwosret III at Dahshur, accessible from the west, is relatively simple. It contains a red granite burial chamber and an antechamber. The southern part of the additionally expanded, north–south oriented complex includes a large mortuary temple. This pyramid is also famous for the treasures discovered in the adjoining tombs of the princesses Sithathor and Merit.

Amenemhet III originally built himself a Dahshur pyramid complex similar in design to those of his predecessors. Here, also, is a labyrinth of corridors and chambers, an obvious attempt to imitate the mythic pattern of the tomb of Osiris and to create an underworld "island" for the king's sarcophagus. An unstable, waterlogged clay foundation threatened the stability of the pyramid, so the pharaoh decided to build himself another pyramid complex at Hawara in the Faiyum Oasis. The burial chamber there has been hollowed out of a single huge block of quartzite and has a triple ceiling. The first, lowest ceiling is flat and made of huge quartzite blocks; above this, there is a saddle ceiling constructed from huge blocks of limestone; and above this, a brick vault 7 meters (22 feet) high. The large mortuary temple in front of the southern side of the pyramid, with its intricate layout, was regarded by classical travelers as the Labyrinth of legend.

The pyramids from the end of the twelfth dynasty and the thirteenth dynasty have as yet been only partly exca-

PYRAMID. *The Black Pyramid of Amenemhet III at Dahshur, twelfth dynasty.* (Courtesy Dieter Arnold)

vated. It is not known, for example, to whom the two pyramids at Mazghuna belonged. The pyramid of Khendjer in South Saqqara, another nameless pyramid nearby, and the pyramid of Ameny Qemau in South Dahshur have all been dated to the thirteenth dynasty. The builders of these rather small pyramids, which are constructed out of poor-quality materials, were in many respects inspired by the complexes of the later twelfth dynasty. It is believed that further undiscovered pyramids from this period lie in South Saqqara and Dahshur.

No one has yet managed to find the tombs of the rulers of the fourteenth through sixteenth dynasties, and it is unclear whether these were pyramids, especially in the case of the Hyksos rulers. The situation is also obscure in the case of the badly damaged tombs of the pharaohs of the seventeenth dynasty at Thebes, near Dra Abul Naga. Some written sources and the isolated find of a pyramidion suggest that they might have been pyramids. Also in this necropolis are fragments of a small pyramid complex attributed to Ahmose I, the first pharaoh of the eighteenth dynasty. If the attribution is correct, then this is the last Egyptian royal pyramid to be constructed.

All known pyramids had been robbed in ancient times. Many were used as quarries. In some (Djoser, Raneferef, Djedkare Izezi, Merenre Antyemsaf, and others) remains of mummies have been found, the identity and dating of which are the subject of discussion.

Construction. As far as structure and construction methods are concerned, research has shown that each pyramid has two basic parts (aside from the substructure). These are a core and a casing, which could both be built in various ways. The core was usually made of poorer quality, very roughly worked limestone or mud bricks, while the casing was always constructed from very high-quality white limestone.

The core of the Step Pyramid is made of limestone ashlars (square-cut blocks) placed in layers inclined inward so that the resulting pressure is directed toward the center of the building. The core of the Great Pyramid is constructed in a combination of compact stone masonry placed in accretion layers and probably also chambers filled with sand. In the fifth dynasty, the cores were built in horizontal layers of coarse stone blocks, with careful construction only on the outside; the inside was filled with waste material. There followed a period in which cores were made from small irregular pieces of stone stuck together with clay-lime mortar. From the twelfth dynasty, there was the adoption of core construction using mud bricks, with a skeleton of limestone walls radiating from the vertical axis of the pyramid. It is believed that the casing was usually constructed at the same time as the core, but this was not the case with some pyramids, such as those of Sneferu in Meidum or Neferirkare Kakai's.

No detailed answer can yet be given to the question of the engineering construction of the Egyptian pyramids. For that, it would be necessary to take them apart, investigate them fully, and put them together again, since research has shown that no universal method existed. Instead, at different times and at different places, pyramids were made using various materials and plans.

Even in antiquity, authors were suggesting two basic methods: the use of wooden machines (suggested by Herodotus) or the use of ramps (suggested by Diodorus Siculus). It is likely that the pyramids were built up to approximately half their projected height (perhaps 80 percent of the volume of masonry), mainly by using a system of ramps, part of which would be integrated into the core. In the next phase, more use was probably made of simple machines—wooden levers, rollers, stone false pulleys, ropes, and so on.

It has been estimated that the total work force in the construction of the Great Pyramid, including provisioning, quarries, and transport of materials, was perhaps thirty-five thousand people. In the building of small pyramids such as those of the fifth dynasty, fewer than ten thousand may have been employed. Both textual and graphic evidence show that haulage was accomplished either by gangs of men or by teams of oxen.

The work, from the quarrying of stone to the completion of the casing, was perfectly organized. The degree of coordination of individual tasks and the skill and productivity of the stoneworking were extraordinary. These may be the simplest secrets of the pyramid builders, but perhaps the greatest.

[*See also* Giza; Saqqara; *and* Tombs, *article on* Royal Tombs.]

BIBLIOGRAPHY

Arnold, Dieter. *Building in Egypt: Pharaonic Stone Masonry*. New York, 1991.

Arnold, Dieter. "Zur Zerstörungsgeschichte der Pyramiden. Ein Vortrag." *Mitteilungen des Deutschen Archäologischen Instituts, Abteilung Kairo* 47 (1991), 21–28.

Bennet, John. "Pyramid Names." *Journal of Egyptian Archaeology* 52 (1966), 174–176.

Edwards, I. E. S. *The Pyramids of Egypt*. Rev. ed. Harmondsworth, 1985.

Formicone, L. "Das Gerät für die Konstruktion der Pyramide." *Göttinger Miszellen* 153 (1996), 33–44.

Goyon, G. *Le secret des bâtisseurs des grandes pyramides*. "Khéops." Paris, 1977.

Lauer, J.-P. *Les Pyramides de Sakkarah*. 5th ed. Bibliothèque Général, 31. Cairo, 1977.

Lauer, J.-P. "Le problème de la construction de la Grande Pyramide." *Revue de l'Égypte* 40 (1989), 91–111.

Lehner, Mark. *The Complete Pyramids*. New York, 1997.

Stadelmann, Rainer. *Die Ägyptischen Pyramiden: Vom Ziegelbau zum Weltwunder*. 2d ed., rev. & enl. Mainz, 1991.

Verner, Miroslav. *Die Pyramiden*. Hamburg, 1998.

MIROSLAV VERNER

PYRAMID TEXTS, a collection of funerary rituals and spells first inscribed on the sarcophagi and subterranean walls of nine Old Kingdom pyramids: those of Unas, last pharaoh of the fifth dynasty; his sixth dynasty successors Teti, Pepy I, Merenre Antyemsaf, and Pepy II; three queens of Pepy II (Neith, Iput, and Wedjebteni); and the eighth dynasty pharaoh Ibi.

The pyramid of Unas, which preserves the most complete Old Kingdom corpus, contains 236 spells (sometimes called "Utterances"), varying in length from a few words to several pages in translation. The pyramids of Unas's successors have yielded another 750 spells, bringing the total to nearly one thousand. The exact number of spells in the Pyramid Texts cannot be determined, since most of the subterranean walls in the pyramids of Unas's successors have been damaged, with large portions lost.

Copies of the Pyramid Texts were also inscribed on the sarcophagi, coffins, and tomb walls of nonroyal burials from the First Intermediate Period onward. The most important of these later sources is the twelfth dynasty tomb of Senwosret at el-Lisht, which contains a nearly complete copy of the collection of Unas, with some additions. Copies of Pyramid Texts that were made later than the Old Kingdom generally reproduce the texts of Unas, although a number of spells from the later Old Kingdom pyramids were also used, primarily in Middle Kingdom sources.

In the First Intermediate Period and Middle Kingdom, the Pyramid Texts were re-edited and expanded with additional spells, known as Coffin Texts. Both Pyramid Texts and Coffin Texts are often interspersed in later sources, indicating that they were considered a single genre. Although many Coffin Texts can be identified as newer creations, on the basis of content and differences in language, others are composed with the same grammar as that of the Pyramid Texts and may actually have been a part of the original corpus. At least six spells that were initially identified by scholars as Coffin Texts have since been found among the fragmentary texts of Tety and his successors, whereas others are essentially the same as older Pyramid Texts.

Despite their large number, the spells of the Pyramid Texts may be grouped into a few distinct assemblages, on the basis of their content and location within the pyramids. The tombs of Unas and his sixth dynasty successors each have the same basic interior arrangement; these consist of a sarcophagus chamber, an antechamber to its east,

PYRAMID TEXTS. *Portion of the Pyramid Texts from the Pyramid of Unas at Saqqara, fifth dynasty.* (Courtesy Donald B. Redford)

and a corridor leading from the northern wall of the antechamber to the pyramid's northern face. The Pyramid Texts occupy the walls of those rooms in a specific arrangement that reflects their function and that of the rooms themselves.

The northern wall of the sarcophagus chamber is devoted to the Offering Ritual, designed to provide the deceased with the means of daily life; it consists mostly of short spells of one or two sentences each, spoken to the deceased as the offerings were presented. The spells in the southern half of the sarcophagus chamber are fewer and longer. Addressed to the deceased and the gods, they form the text of the Resurrection Ritual, designed to arouse the king's spirit from the sarcophagus and send it to new life

among the gods. It begins with the words "You have not gone away dead: you have gone away alive"; it concludes with the assurance that "your name will live on among people even as your name comes to be with the gods."

In the pyramid of Unas these two rituals occupy nearly the entire wall space of the sarcophagus chamber, with the exception of the western gable above the sarcophagus. That gable wall is devoted to a third set of spells, meant to protect the sarcophagus and its contents from the danger of snakes and other harmful beings. In later pyramids, the wall to the west of the sarcophagus contains spells addressed to the sky goddess Nut.

The walls of the antechamber and corridor are inscribed with a fourth set of spells, designed to aid the deceased's passage from the night of the tomb to the day of new life outside the pyramid. Originally written in the first person, these were meant to be recited by the spirit itself during its nightly journey and were "personalized" for each tomb, by substituting the name of the deceased for the first person.

In their content and arrangement, the Pyramid Texts reflect a vision of the afterlife modeled on the nightly journey of the sun through the Duat (the netherworld) on its way to rebirth at dawn. As the sun received the power of new life by joining with the body of Osiris in the depths of the Duat, the deceased's spirit gained the same power by uniting each night with its Osiris, the deceased's mummy, in its Duat, the sarcophagus chamber. This "solar" concept of daily resurrection constituted the primary vision of the afterlife for most of Egyptian history. The Pyramid Texts, however, also contain evidence of an earlier "stellar" concept, in which the deceased's spirit became one of the "imperishable stars" in the northern sky. Perhaps, for that reason, the corridor leading from the tomb emerges in the pyramid's northern face, rather than on the eastern (the direction of sunrise).

From grammatical evidence, the composition of most Pyramid Texts can be dated to no later than the mid-fifth dynasty. The specific subterranean architecture associated with the Pyramid Texts is first attested in the late fourth dynasty tomb of the pharaoh Shepseskaf, although it is prefigured in that of his predecessor, Menkaure; this association suggests a date of composition that is no earlier than Menkaure's reign, although some of the Pyramid Texts' "stellar" passages may well be older.

The spread of Pyramid Texts to nonroyal burials after the Old Kingdom has long been viewed by Egyptologists as a "democratization of the hereafter." Nonroyal tombs of the Old Kingdom, however, depict funeral rites analogous to those of the Pyramid Texts; they also contain lists of offerings identical in content and order to those of the Pyramid Texts' Offering Ritual—both of which suggest that Pyramid Texts were already recited during nonroyal burials of the Old Kingdom.

BIBLIOGRAPHY

Allen, James P. "Reading a Pyramid." In *Hommages à Jean Leclant*, edited by Catherine A. Berger et al., vol. 1: *Études pharaoniques*, pp. 5–28. Bibliothèque d'étude, 106. Cairo, 1994. A study of the sequence and meaning of the Pyramid Texts of Unas and Senwosretankh and their relationship to tomb architecture.

Faulkner, Raymond O. *The Ancient Egyptian Pyramid Texts*. Oxford, 1969. Complete translation. A companion volume by the same author, *Supplement of Hieroglyphic Texts* (Oxford, 1969), includes some of the hieroglyphic texts from the pyramids of Pepy II and his queen Neith.

Lichtheim, Miriam. *Ancient Egyptian Literature: A Book of Readings*. Berkeley, 1973. Includes a translation of some Pyramid Texts.

Mercer, Samuel A. B. *The Pyramid Texts in Translation and Commentary*. 4 vols. New York, 1952. An unreliable translation, but it includes some valuable essays on aspects of the Pyramid Texts by other scholars.

Piankoff, Alexandre. *The Pyramid of Unas*. Bollingen Series, 40. Egyptian Religious Texts and Representations, 5. Princeton, 1968. Complete photographic record and translation of the Pyramid Texts of Unas; the only primary publication of Old Kingdom Pyramid Texts generally available.

Sethe, Kurt. *Die altägyptischen Pyramidentexte*. 4 vols. Leipzig, 1908–1922; reprint, Hildesheim, 1960. Primary scholarly publication of Pyramid Texts from the pyramids of Unas and the sixth dynasty pharaohs; does not include the texts of Ibi, Pepy II's queens, or many of the texts discovered since 1922. (These later texts were published, in part, in a series of volumes by Gustave Jéquier and in journal articles by Jean Sainte-Fare Garnot and by Jean Leclant.) The complete Pyramid Texts of Tety, Pepy I, and Merenre await final publication.

Sethe, Kurt. *Übersetzung und Kommentar zu den Altägyptischen Pyramidentexten*. 2d ed., 6 vols. Hamburg, 1962. Translation of Spells 213–582, with extensive philological commentary.

JAMES P. ALLEN

Q

QANTIR. *See* Piramesse.

QEBEHSENUEF. *See* Four Sons of Horus.

QUARRIES AND MINES. The quarrying of stone in the Nile Valley began at least as early as 40,000 years ago, when the Middle Palaeolithic inhabitants of Middle Egypt were quarrying and working cobbles of chert along the limestone terraces on either side of the Nile. The earliest Palaeolithic chert quarries consisted of pits and trenches for surface extraction, but there are Upper Palaeolithic quarries at Nazlet Khater 4, on the western bank of the Nile, midway between Asyut and Sohag, which include vertical shafts and subterranean galleries (providing a foretaste of the quarrying methods of pharaonic times). The excavations at Nazlet Khater 4 yielded many large hammerstones, used for the roughest stages of quarrying, as well as several of the picks used for finer work, which were carved from the horns of the gazelle and hartebeest.

Egyptian exploitation of the minerals in the cliffs and deserts on either side of the Nile Valley, and in the Sinai Peninsula, can be traced back to prehistoric times, with some of the earliest known items of jewelry made from Eastern Desert carnelian and sard. Copper slag is known from the vicinity of the Predynastic mines at Bir Nasib in southern Sinai, and turquoise miners were likely exploiting the nearby region of Serabit el-Khadim in the Chalcolithic period. The prehistoric workings were relatively small in scale compared with the massive royal expeditions that were sent to Sinai and Nubia during the first two dynasties. Some of the inscriptions and graffiti associated with the mining and processing sites provide information on the dates of the expeditions, lists of various types of workmen, and—in rarer instances—detailed narrative accounts of specific expeditions.

A great deal of archaeological and textual information has survived concerning mining expeditions in pursuit of building stone, copper, gold, turquoise, malachite, and a variety of other gemstones. Copper mining and smelting sites included Wadi Dara, Buhen, and Qubban, while numerous pharaonic gold-mining sites in the Eastern Desert of both Egypt and Nubia have been identified and surveyed during the 1980s and 1990s. Turquoise was mined at Wadi Mughara and Serabit el-Khadim, amethyst at Wadi el-Hudi and Gebel el-Asr (the so-called Khephren diorite quarries), galena at Gebel el-Zeit, and natron at the Wadi Natrun. The rough limestone for the interiors of pyramid complexes and *mastaba*s in the Memphite necropolis was obtained from local quarries, while the much finer material for the outer casing of pyramids was quarried at Tura and Ma'sara on the opposite side of the Nile. Most of the sandstone for the temples at Thebes and other Upper Egyptian towns was obtained from the Gebel es-Silsila quarries, midway between Luxor and Aswan.

The Archaeology of Quarries and Mines. Pharaonic quarrying and mining sites were of prime importance to the prosperity and stability of Egypt's economy. Since the 1980s, a number of archaeologists have begun to study the Egyptian quarries and mines, with approaches ranging from the scientific provenancing of stones and metals to the experimental replication of the technology employed in extracting and working the various minerals.

The granite quarries at Aswan, which were first exploited at least as early as the beginning of pharaonic times, are still in use in the twentieth century; thus a great deal of evidence concerning the ancient extraction and working of this extremely hard stone derives from the extensive archaeological remains to the southeast of the modern city. On the basis of surviving buildings and other monuments, it has been estimated that 45,000 cubic meters of stone were removed from the Aswan quarries during the Old Kingdom, although at that time, the quarrying would have largely comprised the prying up of loose boulders scattered across its surface. Probably by the New Kingdom, the largest quantities of granite were quarried, including the many eighteenth and nineteenth dynasty colossal statues and obelisks.

The so-called unfinished obelisk is a useful piece of evidence for the quarrying and working techniques of the New Kingdom, when large numbers of obelisks were carved for the temples at Thebes and elsewhere. An eighteenth dynasty monument, it measures nearly 42 meters (128 feet) long; it was abandoned, no doubt reluctantly, at an advanced stage in the process of extraction. Clearly, the quarriers first removed the weathered upper layers of the granite, then excavated a trench, marking out the shape of the obelisk, which was still attached to the bedrock. The 0.75-meter (2.5-foot)-wide trench was divided into a number of 0.6-meter (2-foot)-wide working areas, marked out by vertical red lines down the side of the trench, which might well have contained as many as fifty workmen around the obelisk at any one time. The marks made by the quarry overseers still survive on the trench faces, showing that the depth of each trench was periodically measured by lowering a cubit rod into it and marking the top of the rod with a triangle. Once the trench had reached the necessary depth, the workers would gradually undercut the block, a process which was just beginning in the case of the unfinished obelisk. Finally, to move the quarried obelisk from its matrix, it had to be pushed out horizontally—a considerably easier task than attempting to pull it vertically, upward, out of the hole.

Quarrying and mining sites of differing dates and geographical locations show the Egyptians' ability to adapt their strategies to changing contexts and circumstances. Just as with the design of their functionally and topographically variable Middle Kingdom fortresses and garrisons in Nubia, there was much flexibility and spontaneity in the Egyptian procurement of stone and metals. Some ancient workers' settlements have been found near mineral sources, which are close to present-day cities, substantial towns, or villages, as in the cases of Aswan (granite and sandstone), Gebel es-Silsila (sandstone), and Tura (limestone). At these worker sites, only minimal accommodation was required, since the quarriers were near permanent settlements. Sites situated in more remote locations included not only the traces of quarrying or mining but also the remains of settlements or encampments, facilities for the provision of water, tracks and roads linking the sites with the Nile Valley, evidence of processing and manufacturing activities, textual and pictorial memorials of the expeditions, and, in some cases, ritualistic and religious remains (ranging from rough cairns and alignments of standing stones at Hatnub to the extensive temples of Hathor at Serabit el-Khadim and Timna).

One of the first quarrying sites to be studied in any detail was the Old Kingdom quarry for the relatively soft stone gypsum (2 on Mohs Scale of Hardness) at Umm el-Sawwan, at the northern edge of the Faiyum region, which were surveyed and excavated in 1928 by Gertrude Caton-Thompson and Dorothea Gardner. The quarriers had been accommodated in a large, sprawling settlement of at least 250 small stone-built structures and considerable evidence was found for the local production of flint tools for quarrying and for vase making. Some of the gypsum seems to have been carved into small funerary items for private tombs, but large amounts were probably also ground into mortar for large-scale state-sponsored building purposes in the Saqqara necropolis (only about 20 kilometers/13 miles to the northeast). In the same way, Egyptian alabaster (travertine, a calcite; 3 on Mohs Scale

of Hardness) at Hatnub and Wadi Gerrawi was quarried not only for small vessels, statuettes, and offering tables but also for royal purposes, such as colossal statuary and architectural elements.

The Gebel el-Zeit galena (lead ore) mines, located on the Gulf of Suez coast, about 50 kilometers (32 miles) to the south of Ras Gharib, were studied by Georges Castel and Georges Soukiassian in the early 1980s. The mines date from the Middle Kingdom to the Ramessid era (i.e., most of the second millennium BCE), and they incorporated hundreds of shafts and about thirty gallery mines. The site had numerous dry-stone shelters, votive structures, and a small sanctuary, evidently dating from the Middle Kingdom to the nineteenth dynasty. No large-scale commemorative inscriptions and carvings survived at Gebel el-Zeit, but the sanctuary contained a cache of votive objects, including small stone and faience portable stelae, some of which bear depictions of kings making offerings to "Horus Master of the Deserts" and "Hathor Mistress of Galena" (suggesting at least a degree of official involvement in the galena mining). One stela was dedicated by Minemhat, a seventeenth dynasty governor of the province of Coptos, traditionally the center for quarrying and mining in the Eastern Desert. Gebel el-Zeit would have been the northernmost outpost for expeditions sponsored by seventeenth dynasty kings (c.1674–1567 BCE), whose power base was at Thebes.

Three basic types of settlement housed the miners and quarriers of pharaonic times. First, primarily in the Old Kingdom and First Intermediate Period, dense concentrations of drystone huts were often located on a high point and surrounded by an enclosure wall (e.g., the turquoise miners' settlement at Wadi Mughara and the eleventh dynasty amethyst miners' hilltop settlement at Wadi el-Hudi in Lower Nubia). Second, substantial rectangular walled settlements were built of drystone or mud brick, with varying degrees of fortification (e.g., the twelfth dynasty amethyst miners' fortress at Wadi el-Hudi). Third, and most frequently, there were the wide scatters of rough stone shelters and windbreaks (e.g., those at the calcite [Egyptian alabaster] quarries of Hatnub, the gypsum quarries of Umm el-Sawwan, and the galena mines of Gebel el-Zeit). Many quarries—for example, Wadi Mughara, Wadi el-Hudi, and Hatnub—comprise a combination of two or three of these settlement types. Changes in settlement type can sometimes be correlated with the nature and date of the quarrying expeditions. At the Hatnub quarries, some 17 kilometers (11 miles) southeast of Tell el-Amarna, in the Eastern Desert, the Old and Middle Kingdom drystone shelters often comprised extensive, carefully constructed multiroomed huts, which presumably housed many gangs of workmen. The New Kingdom encampment at Hatnub, in contrast, consisted mainly of

QUARRIES AND MINES. *Sandstone quarry at Gebel es-Silsila.* (Courtesy Donald B. Redford)

one-room shelters, hastily and loosely assembled from large limestone slabs and boulders. This contrast between the two chronological phases mirrors the textual evidence at the site—the state-sponsored Old and Middle Kingdom expeditions left numerous inscriptions and graffiti in the quarries, whereas the New Kingdom quarriers, whose encampment shows far fewer signs of bureaucratic or organizational backing from the local or national government, left only one inscription on the quarry walls.

The nature of quarrying and mining settlements can also be used as an indication of the degree of threat experienced (or perceived) by workers at various locations. The dispersed structures and lack of communal protective measures at Hatnub and Umm el-Sawwan suggest a relative lack of concern about attacks from the desert, whereas the Old Kingdom hilltop settlement at Wadi Mughara and the twelfth dynasty fortress at Wadi el-Hudi indicate that forays into the Sinai and to Lower Nubia were presumably regarded, at least in the Old and Middle Kingdoms, as somewhat more dangerous than those into more familiar areas of either the Western or the Eastern Desert. There are also major differences between Old and Middle Kingdom mining inscriptions in the Sinai mines. During the Old Kingdom, mention was made of naval personnel and lists of particular sets of troops; such military references were far less common in the Middle Kingdom in-

scriptions. It seems likely, therefore, that Early Dynastic and Old Kingdom mining expeditions into the Sinai Peninsula were militarized, whereas Middle and New Kingdom mining took place in a context of more peaceful cooperation with the non-Egyptian inhabitants of the central and southern Sinai.

Quarrying Tools. The types of tools used for the quarrying of soft stones (Mohs 1–5) during pharaonic times has not been definitively determined. Judging from the marks preserved on quarry walls, some type of axe or pointed pick was probably used in the Old and Middle Kingdoms, whereas a pointed chisel hammered with mallet was evidently employed from the New Kingdom onward. The wide grooves on the surfaces of a few stone blocks suggest that a very large stone chisel may sometimes have been used. Some Egyptologists have argued that most of the tool marks were made by soft copper chisels in the Old and Middle Kingdoms and harder copper or bronze chisels from the New Kingdom onward (with characteristic patterns possibly deriving from specific chronological phases); others have pointed out that harder alloys would already have been available during the Old Kingdom. Those chisels that have survived at ancient construction sites usually have a broad, flat cutting edge rather than a point. Chert and flint (Mohs 7) tools were also used for stoneworking.

As far as the extraction of such hard stones as granite (Mohs 6–7) is concerned, it was once assumed—because of the many surviving groups of rectangular wedge holes at Aswan—that the rock was removed by inserting wet wooden wedges into holes and levering the blocks away from the bedrock. It has been pointed out, however, that even wooden wedges soaked in water would generally not have been strong enough to break the granite, and that no wedge holes have yet been securely dated to pharaonic times. Iron wedges could have been used to extract hard stones from the Ptolemaic period onward. Various experimental studies and analyses of the quarries at Aswan suggest that the actual process of extraction in pharaonic times involved the excavation of opencast quarries, by means of hammerstones, gradually removing the desired stone from the surface downward. In the quartzite quarry at Gebel Gulab (on the western bank at Aswan), a broken obelisk inscribed with the name of the nineteenth dynasty ruler Sety I survives *in situ* near the quarry face from which it was extracted. The nearby quarry face shows definite traces of the use of stone pounders. Pounder marks have also been found at Qau el-Kebir, in a limestone quarry of unusually dense and hard rock (limestone may be soft [Mohs 3], medium [Mohs 4], or dense and hard [Mohs 5]). Further evidence for the extraction of stone by pounding has survived in the form of a set of marks in the siltstone quarry of the Wadi Hammamat, which may well date to pharaonic times.

Transporting Stone and Metal. A number of variations of the Old Kingdom titles "Master of the Roads" and "Official of the Masters of the Roads" have been found both in the Memphite necropolis and in the mining areas of the Wadi Hammamat and Wadi Abbad (in the Eastern Desert), suggesting that the coordination and maintenance of land routes through the desert was a high priority for the Egyptian administration. Many archaeological traces of specially constructed roads have been found in the areas surrounding mines, quarries, and major structures.

In the case of mineral resources exploited regularly for long periods, considerable amounts of time and energy were spent on the building of roads, the nature of each route being determined primarily by such factors as the bulk and quantities of the minerals, the nature of the topography, and the materials locally available for road-building. Thus the Old Kingdom quarries at Hatnub are linked with the Nile Valley by a drystone causeway extending for some 17 kilometers (11 miles), two small stretches of which are built up to a height of several meters, to allow stone blocks to be dragged across deep wadis. A paved road employing slabs of sandstone and fossil (petrified) wood conects the Gebel Qatrani basalt quarries with the site of Qasr el-Sagha at the northern end of the Faiyum region, covering a distance of about 10 kilometers (6 miles).

The longest known Egyptian quarry road is an 80-kilometer (50-mile) route in Lower Nubia, linking the diorite-gabbro and anorthosite gneiss quarries of the Old and Middle Kingdoms, near Gebel el-Asr, with the closest Nile embarkation point (at the former Tushka, now because of the new Aswan High Dam, covered by Lake Nasser). In the 1930s, Reginald Engelbach undertook a detailed examination of the ancient road, which was not a built structure (like the roads to Hatnub and Gebel Qatrani) but instead appears to have been simply a cleared track through the desert, with occasional scatters of stone or pottery.

An important indication of the degree to which ancient Egyptians planned and organized their quarrying and mining expeditions has survived in the form of the Turin Mining Papyrus. This document—the earliest surviving Egyptian map—is an annotated record of an expedition to the mines and quarries of the Wadi Hammamat in the Eastern Desert in the mid-twelfth century BCE. The area depicted in the map has been identified with the archaeological site at Bir Umm Fawakhir, where there are still extensive remains of a Byzantine gold-mining settlement.

Control and Organization of Expeditions. Throughout pharaonic times, the procurement of stone and metals was an integral part of the social and economic contract between the pharaoh and his high officials (and also between such officials and their subordinates). Since the products of mining and quarrying were the raw materials from which essential items of religious and funerary architecture and equipment were made, the large-scale quarrying of stone has been interpreted by many Egyptologists as a rough index of fluctuations in royal power and social stability at different dates. Royal officials relied on the king to provide them with the necessary labor and raw materials for their own funerary equipment. A good example of this is the sixth dynasty inscription of Weni at Abydos, which not only describes the quarrying expeditions that he organized for the king but also mentions that the king presented him with a fine limestone sarcophagus from the quarries at Tura.

Although most major expeditions were evidently sent by kings or nomarchs, there is good evidence for the involvement of temples in the procurement of stone and metal. Mineral deposits are often listed among the assets of funerary estates or temples. Thus, an inscription on the walls of a rock-cut temple of the early thirteenth century BCE in the Wadi Abbad, in Upper Egypt, announces that the gold mines in the vicinity were owned by the temple of Sety I at Abydos. The text makes it clear that this endowment included not only the mineral rights but also the means to exploit them, comprising a team of miners, their settlement, and a well dug on the king's orders.

Archaeologists can often distinguish between instances of low-level exploitation of mineral resources by individuals and the higher level of organization and visibility associated with large-scale expeditions, such as those designed to acquire stone or metals for the king and his high officials. Some sites—Hatnub, Umm el-Sawwan, and Gebel el-Zeit—suggest that certain raw materials were the object of intermittent private exploitation throughout pharaonic times (perhaps sometimes following in the footsteps of the major state expeditions); others—the turquoise mines in the Sinai and the amethyst mines at Wadi el-Hudi—were almost certainly visited only by royal workmen. Which raw materials were subject to royal monopoly is not clear, but the difficult and expensive logistics of many quarrying and mining expeditions would have prevented private individuals from undertaking them without royal support.

Sending expeditions out to the remote mining areas in the deserts was based on a king's (or a nomarch's) ability to provide the necessary workforce. The numbers of workers sent on quarrying and mining expeditions were probably comparable with those sent on military campaigns. An inscription in the Wadi Hammamat quarries in the Eastern Desert describes the dispatching of an expedition of seventeen thousand workers in the thirty-eighth year of the reign of the twelfth dynasty ruler Senwosret I. If the figures are taken at face value, the scale of that expedition was comparable with the twenty thousand Egyptian troops who are said to have fought at the Battle of Qadesh during the reign of Ramesses II. More quarry workers probably returned home than those in the fighting force, although quarrying and mining were also dangerous assignments and many lives were lost.

There are few surviving indications, either textual or archaeological, of the extent to which the various expedition members were given training for their specific tasks. Many of the workers appear to have been press-ganged into quarrying by means of a corvée system that was operated in the various regions of Egypt and Nubia—in the same way that workers were obtained for large-scale, state-organized agricultural, hydraulic, or architectural projects. The detailed descriptions of personnel that were carved on the walls of quarries often list the geographical origins of various groups of recruits. They would have made up the bulk of the workforce and engaged in such laborious nonskilled duties as digging and transportation (as well as the related tasks of providing military escorts in dangerous terrain). These manual laborers are often described as "stone-cutters," and two inscriptions in the Sinai mines record the presence of two hundred such workers. Each mining or quarrying expedition must also have included at least a small group of professionals, and we can occasionally catch glimpses of these in the inscrip-

tions. Possibly, such men as *smnt3w* ("prospectors," the hieroglyphic determinative for which was a figure of a man holding a bag or stick) and *ikyw* (possibly professional miners/quarriers) might have been more permanent state employees. One prospector, a "reckoner of gold" called Thuthotep, left a graffito in the vicinity of the Abrak well, in the Nubian Eastern Desert, about 240 kilometers (156 miles) southeast of Aswan.

Some of the most detailed descriptions of expeditions have survived in the form of inscriptions at the Wadi el-Hudi amethyst mines, the Wadi Hammamat *bḫn*-stone (siltstone) quarries, and the Sinai copper/turquoise/malachite mines. They provide a good opportunity to study the composition of the mining workforces. Whereas Early Dynastic and early Old Kingdom quarry inscriptions tended to concentrate on the recitation of royal names and titles, from the sixth dynasty onward, the texts provided more of the names and titles of the actual leaders and members of the expedition. For most of pharaonic times, the overall controller of the expedition usually held the title *sḏ3wty-nṯr* ("God's Treasurer"), although the less specific rank of *imy-r mš'* ("Commander of the Expedition/army") is also sometimes used. In one early twelfth dynasty inscription at Wadi el-Hudi, the lower ranks were clearly recruited mainly from local towns, some fourteen hundred of whom were supervised by about one hundred officials from the north. Similarly, the eleventh dynasty stela of Intef at Wadi el-Hudi describes the expedition members as "thousand after thousand" of local Nubians. Smaller numbers of workers were recorded at the Serabit el-Khadim turquoise mines, where the Middle Kingdom expeditions ranged from 168 to 734 men, usually accompanied by a similar number of donkeys (an average expedition comprising approximately three hundred men and four hundred animals).

The names of about a tenth of the officials organizing quarrying and mining expeditions tend to recur over certain periods of time, and a considerable amount of analysis can be undertaken into the changing ranks of officialdom. During the late twelfth dynasty reign of Amenemhet III, for example, most of the repetitions of names of high officials involved in expeditions to the Sinai take place within periods of less than ten years, and it is noticeable that the individuals have usually been promoted to some extent by the time their name reappears. Low-ranking quarrying officials (e.g., doctors, foremen, and workmen) were sent on a larger number of successive expeditions than their superiors. The low-ranked officials were also less likely to be promoted; higher officials, such as treasury representatives and scribes, were less likely to return but more likely to have been promoted if they did so. This continuous process of change in personnel, especially in the higher ranking jobs, must have been caused by the unpopularity of the task and the fact that the king may have been deliberately preventing any officials from gaining control of the quarries. The control over precious raw materials could be as powerful a tool for ambitious officials as it was for the king.

[*See also* Calcite; Copper; Diorite and Related Rocks; Eastern Desert and Red Sea; Gems; Gold; Limestone; Minerals; Quartzite; Sandstone; *and* Silver.]

BIBLIOGRAPHY

Anthes, Rudolf. *Die Felseninschriften von Hatnub.* Leipzig, 1928.

Arnold, Dieter. *Building in Egypt: Pharaonic Stone Masonry.* New York and Oxford, 1991.

Aston, Barbara G., James A. Harrell, and Ian Shaw. "Stone." In *Ancient Egyptian Materials and Technology,* edited by P. T. Nicholson and I. Shaw. Cambridge, 2000.

Castel, Georges, and Bernard Mathieu. "Les mines de cuivre du Wadi Dara." *Bulletin de l'Institut français d'archéologie orientale* 92 (1992), 51–65.

Castel, Georges, and Georges Soukiassian. *Gebel el-Zeit I: Les mines de galène (Egypte, IIe millénaire av. J.-C.).* Cairo, 1989. Includes extensive color photographs and detailed diagrams of mine shafts and galleries.

Couyat, J., and Pierre Montet. *Les inscriptions hiéroglyphiques et hiératiques du Quâdi Hammâmât.* Cairo, 1912–1913.

Drenkhahn, Rosemarie. "Artisans and Artists in Pharaonic Egypt." In *Civilizations of the Ancient Near East,* edited by J. Sasson, vol. 1, pp. 331–343. New York, 1995.

Eyre, Christopher. "Work and Organisation of Work in the Old Kingdom/New Kingdom." In *Labor in the Ancient Near East,* edited by M. A. Powell, pp. 5–48, 167–222. New Haven, 1987. Discusses the major texts relating to such factors as the personnel and seasonal nature of quarrying and mining expeditions.

Fakhry, Ahmed. *The Inscriptions of the Amethyst Quarries at Wadi el-Hudi.* Cairo, 1952.

Gardiner, Alan, T. Eric Peet, and Jaroslav Černý. *The Inscriptions of Sinai.* 2d ed. London, 1955.

Harrell, James A. "An Inventory of Ancient Egyptian Quarries." *Newsletter of the American Research Center in Egypt* 146 (1989), 1–7.

Harrell, James A., and V. M. Brown. "The Oldest Surviving Topographical Map from Ancient Egypt: Turin Papyri 1879, 1899 and 1969." *Journal of the American Research Center in Egypt* 29 (1992), 81–105.

Klemm, D. D., and R. Klemm. *Steine und Steinbrüche im alten Ägypten.* Berlin, 1993.

Klemm, R., and D. D. Klemm. "Evolution of Methods for Prospection, Mining and Processing of Gold in Egypt." In *Proceedings of the First International Conference on Ancient Egyptian Mining and Metallurgy and Conservation of Metallic Artifacts,* edited by Feisal Esmael, pp. 341–354. Cairo, 1998.

Lucas, Alfred. *Ancient Egyptian Materials and Industries.* 4th ed., rev. by J. R. Harris. London, 1962.

Petrie, W. M. Flinders, and C. T. Currelly. *Researches in Sinai.* London, 1906.

Rothenberg, Beno. *The Egyptian Mining Temple at Timna.* London, 1988.

Sadek, Ashraf I. *The Amethyst Mining Inscriptions of Wadi el-Hudi.* 2 vols. Warminster, 1980–1985.

Seyfried, Karl-Joachim. *Beiträge zu den Expeditionen des Mittleren Reiches in die Ost-Wüste.* Pelizaeus Museum. Hildesheimer Ägyptologische Beiträge, 15. Hildesheim, 1981.

Shaw, Ian. "A Survey at Hatnub." In *Amarna Reports,* edited by B. J. Kemp, pp. 189–212. London, 1986.

Shaw, Ian. "Pharaonic Quarrying and Mining: Settlement and Procurement in Egypt's Marginal Areas." *Antiquity* 68 (1994), 108–119.

Shaw, Ian. "Exploiting the Desert Frontier: The Logistics and Politics of Ancient Egyptian Mining Expeditions." In *Social Approaches to an Industrial Past: The Archaeology and Anthropology of Mining,* edited by Bernard Knapp, pp. 242–258. London, 1998.

Shaw, Ian, and Robert Jameson. "Amethyst Mining in the Eastern Desert: A Preliminary Survey at Wadi el-Hudi." *Journal of Egyptian Archaeology* 79 (1993), 81–98.

IAN SHAW

QUARTZITE, the hardest and toughest stone normally encountered in nature (7 on Mohs Scale of Hardness). The Egyptian variety is a sedimentary stone, correctly termed an "orthoquartzite" (to distinguish it from the metamorphic quartzites). Quartzite is composed of quartz (a crystalline form of silica) grains solidly cemented with chemical silica—so the cement and the grains are of the same material. Silica cement interlocks the grains and fills in the pore spaces, making a dense, compact stone of great strength.

Egyptian quartzite quarries are located at Gebel Ahmar near Cairo, at Gebel Gulab, and at Gebel Tingar near

QUARTZITE. *Quartzite bust of a twelfth dynasty king.* (The Metropolitan Museum of Art, Gift of J. Pierpont Morgan, 1912. [12.183.6])

Aswan (within the Oligocene Gebel Ahmar Formation). Other sites occur within silicified Upper Cretaceous Nubia Group sandstones (the Umm Barmil Formation). Egyptian quartzite is usually white, with reddish, yellow, and orange varieties, the colors being produced by iron oxides. It was often used for sarcophagi, statues, and portcullis stones. Quartzite behaves much like large quartz masses (also 7 on Mohs Scale of Hardness) and can be worked with little concern for breakage or cleavage—but it was not ordinarily used as an architectural stone. Nonetheless, some examples include pillars in Pepy II's pyramid court at Saqqara; the burial chamber of Amenemhet III at Harawa; the Thutmose III Chapelle Rouge blocks at Luxor; and included here for their immense size, the so-called Colossi of Memnon at Luxor. These colossal statues were sculpted from single quartzite blocks of 21.3 meters (64 feet). Since quartzite occurs mainly in Lower Egypt, the transport of such large stones upriver must have been a serious consideration.

For sculpture, quartzite takes a fine polish and the colors can be used for pleasing effects. Examples include the head of Nefertiti and the wonderful figures of Amenhotpe III. Betsy Bryan (Kozloff and Bryan 1992) states that quartzite was chosen as "an indicator of the solar devotion, for red, yellow, and gold tones were considered the sun colors."

Quartzite was far harder than the metal tools (copper, bronze) available, so it must have been worked with tools fabricated from other forms of quartz—chert (flint)—as well as quartz fragments. The final finishing would have been done by polishing with rubbing blocks and quartz sand. This extreme hardness may have made quartzite a "status" stone for statuary.

Quartzite was known to ancient Egyptians as *nmti, nmtt, bỉꜣyt, bỉꜣt, ỉnr-n-dw, ỉnr-n-bnwt, ỉnr-nfr-n -bỉꜣt-ꜥꜣt, ỉnr-n-rwḏt nt-ḏw-dsr,* and *ỉnr-n-bnwt.*

BIBLIOGRAPHY

Aston, Barbara G. "Ancient Egyptian Stone Vessels." *Studien zur Archäologie und Geschichte Altägyptens,* 5. Heidelberg, 1994.

Erman, Adolf, and Hermann Grapow. *Wörterbuch der Aegyptischen Sprache.* 6 vols. Berlin, 1982.

Harrell, James A. "An Inventory of Ancient Egyptian Quarries." *Newsletter of the American Research Center in Egypt,* 146 (1989), 1–7, plus cover photo.

Harris, J. R. *Lexicographical Studies in Ancient Egyptian Minerals.* Deutsche Akademie der Wissenschafter zu Berlin Institut für Orientforschung, 54. Berlin, 1961.

Kozloff, Arielle P., and Betsy M. Bryan. *Egypt's Dazzling Sun. Amenhotep III and His World.* Bloomington, 1992.

CLAIR R. OSSIAN

QUBBET EL-HAWA. *See* Aswan.

QUEENS. The ruler of Egypt was usually male; because the succession ideally passed from father to son, kings married to obtain heirs. There were, therefore, within the king's immediate circle a number of royal women, which included his mother, his wives, and his daughters. In addition to their role in producing royal offspring, the king's mother and his principal wife were bearers of divine queenship, which complemented the divine aspect of kingship. In English, "queen" can refer to a queen consort, a queen mother, or a female ruler. Ancient Egyptian has no single term that corresponds to queen in all these meanings, but it does have specific designations for these roles. From the third dynasty the king's consort was called *ḥmt nsw* ("king's wife"). Because kings were polygynous (having several wives), the more descriptive title *ḥmt nsw wrt* ("great wife of the king") was introduced in the later Middle Kingdom to distinguish the principal wife of the king from his secondary wives, who were also called *ḥmt nsw.* The queen mother was given the title *mwt nsw* ("king's mother"), attested from as early as the first dynasty. On the rare occasions that female rulers occupied Egypt's throne, they held the same titles and fivefold titulary as male rulers, the only difference being that they often, although by no means always, used feminine grammatical forms. In what follows, the term *queen* will be used to refer only to a king's principal wife and to a king's mother, but not to secondary wives or female rulers.

The sources available to us for the study of royal women are, in the main, monumental or, less frequently, administrative. Because of their impersonal nature, they tell us little about royal women as individuals, but rather they provide information on their various roles and the concept of queenship. They also show that over the three millennia of recorded ancient Egyptian civilization, there were many changes relating to royal women; for example, in their titles, their insignia, the contexts in which they were depicted, and the way in which they were buried. What follows is, therefore, a broad overview.

The earliest titles for queens of the first dynasty related them to the king in his aspect of Horus or Seth, and titles of this type continued through the Old Kingdom, and occurred sporadically into the New Kingdom as archaisms. During the sixth dynasty the title *jrjt-pꜥt* was added. Although it was to remain part of queens' titularies into the Ptolemaic period, its significance is unclear; it is the feminine form of an important ranking title for male officials. It was rarely used by nonroyal women and when present, usually at the beginning of a long string of titles, it signified that the individual was a queen.

Old Kingdom queens are attested with the titles of priestess of Hathor, of various other deities, and of deceased kings. From the Middle Kingdom onward the commonest titles used by queens were "king's (principal) wife," "king's mother," and "king's daughter," all of which defined their relationship to the current or previous king. Priestly titles that connected the queen to specific cults were rare at that time. Some royal women of the eighteenth dynasty held the title "god's wife of Amun" which signified a priestly role in the cult of Amun-Re at Thebes, but that office was distinct from the role of queen and could also be performed by king's daughters. Other queens' titles, first occurring in the twelfth dynasty but most common from the eighteenth dynasty onward, related the holder to the Two Lands and reflected a common kingly designation: "mistress of the Two Lands," "lady of the Two Lands," and "mistress of Upper and Lower Egypt." During the twenty-first and twenty-second dynasties, queens often bore priestly titles that related them to the cults of various deities, including the goddesses Hathor and Mut and the child god Khons. Ptolemaic-era queens adopted the title *ḥq3t*, the female form of *ḥq3* ("ruler"), used by the king and embodied in the *ḥq3*-scepter, the crook carried by the king as part of his insignia.

The insignia used by queens increased in complexity with time. The first images of queens are dated to the Old Kingdom. In three-dimensional sculpture, they sat on a special type of "box" throne; however, they do not wear anything that marks them as queens. In the fifth dynasty, queens began wearing a vulture headdress. The body of the bird forms a cap and its wings spread downward against the side of the queen's head; its head and tail stick out in front and behind, respectively. The headdress relates to the Upper Egyptian vulture goddess Nekhbet, and it was clearly meant to associate or even identify the queen with her. Nekhbet formed a close pair with Wadjet, the Lower Egyptian cobra goddess; when Wadjet was shown in human form, she took over Nekhbet's vulture headdress but replaced the vulture head with a cobra's head, or *uraeus*. This form of headdress is attested for queens of the sixth dynasty, presumably associating them with Wadjet. The *uraeus* was also worn alone by royal women beginning in the fifth dynasty. In addition to relating them to Wadjet, it mirrored the king's use of a single *uraeus* and marked the bearer as sharing in the divine nature of the king. Other goddesses adopted the *uraeus* as well as the vulture headdress, so their general use by queens firmly related the queens to female deities. From the eighteenth dynasty onward, queens were shown with a double *uraeus*. In some examples, the snakes wear the crowns of Upper and Lower Egypt, making it explicit that they refer to Nekhbet and Wadjet. In others, especially during the Amarna period, they wore instead the disk and horns of Hathor, which related to the solar aspect of the *uraeus* and the dual nature of Hathor as the eye of the sun god Re.

In the thirteenth dynasty, a crown consisting of two tall, straight falcon feathers was first worn by queens, and from the eighteenth dynasty it became one of their most important items of insignia. The two feathers were worn by the male deities Min, Amun, and Montu, and occasionally by some Middle Kingdom kings. Texts equate the double feathers with "the two *uraei* that were on the head of his father Atum" and with the eyes of the sun god. Since the *uraeus* was the solar eye, the two feathers embodied a feminine duality that was parallel to the double *uraeus*. In the reign of Amenhotpe III, the solar aspect of the crown was stressed by the addition of the solar disk and the horns of Hathor, first shown worn by Queen Tiy at the *sed*-festival, perhaps a corollary of the king's own rejuvenation and solarization. Hathor is one of the goddesses who, as the daughter of Re, represents the duality of the solar eye in its raging and pacified aspects. The combination of the double feathers with the horns and disk remained an item of queenly insignia into the Ptolemaic period. The queen was also represented as carrying the *ankh*-sign, symbolizing "life." Life was something that belonged to the deities, which they give to the king. That it was also given to the queen associated her with the king, and it stressed her complementary role.

From the fifth dynasty onward, king's mothers and king's consorts were distinguished by their use of insignia that associated or identified them with various goddesses and the transformational power within them; they were the bearers of divine queenship, and they probably played a ritual role to complement that of the king. In temple decoration, the king was shown interacting with deities on a cosmic stage, an interaction reflected in the performance of ritual within the temple, although on most occasions that ritual was enacted by priests appointed to deputized for the king. In a small minority of temple scenes, the king was accompanied by a queen, perhaps indicating that on some of the occasions, when the king performed the ritual in person, the queen also had a role to play. The king was most likely to conduct ritual at important festivals, and the queen was present at the annual Opet Festival at Thebes, when the divine aspect of the king was renewed. She is also shown in depictions of the Min-festival at Thebes. The only queen shown regularly in temple scenes with the king was Nefertiti, during the atypical Amarna period; her ubiquitous presence may be related to the absence of goddesses at that time. The king's mother had a special status not shared with his consort, and that resulted from her role in the myth of the king's divine birth. When a king came to the throne, this event revealed that his mother—whether the previous king's principal wife or merely a secondary wife—had on the occasion of his conception been impregnated by the god (Amun-)Re.

The equivalence between the king's mother and his principal wife—displayed by their shared titles, insignia, and presence in similar ritual scene types—was not acci-

QUEENS. *Limestone statue of a seventeenth dynasty queen, from Thebes.* (The Metropolitan Museum of Art, Rogers Fund, 1916. [16.10.224])

provided with an independent income and a group of potentially loyal officials to serve their interests. By contrast, most secondary wives together with the royal children were grouped in larger living and administrative units. Without question, royal women had potential access to the highest authority in the land and, even if they had no official authority, probably played an unofficial role through their influence on the king. Queens who acted as regent for a young king would have exercised authority officially on his behalf.

The temptation to manipulate the succession probably always existed, although few traces of such intrigues have survived. For example, a papyrus from the twentieth dynasty reveals a plot to assassinate Ramesses III and replace the legitimate heir by another prince. The prime mover was the prince's mother. If she had been successful, she would have achieved the important position of king's mother, and no doubt she and her son would have rewarded their followers well.

Many kings married their (half-)sisters and had offspring by them. It was once thought that they took this action because the right to the throne passed through the female line although royal power was exercised by the man married to the current royal "heiress"; according to this hypothesis, every king, even if the son of the previous king, had to legitimize his rule by marrying the "heiress," who was normally his (half-)sister. If this hypothesis were true, it should be possible to trace an unbroken line of kings' consorts in descent from one another; yet such a line does not exist. Further, not all kings married royal women, but no distinction exists between those who did so and those who did not. In other words, the "heiress" hypothesis was not supported by the evidence, so it is necessary to look elsewhere for an explanation of brother–sister marriage among kings. Little evidence exists for such marriages among the king's subjects, while a number of such examples exist for the divine world—presumably, the king would be stressing his divine aspect by taking the divine world as his model.

Some of our evidence concerning queens and other royal women has come from their burials, although not one burial has survived intact and the majority of burials remains unknown. Presumably, the king was responsible for the burial arrangements of his family members. In the Early Dynastic period, some royal women were buried in subsidiary graves that surrounded the king's tomb at Abydos; others, such as Meritneith at Abydos and Hetepwyneith at Naqada, had large, independent tombs. In the Old Kingdom, some queens were provided with burials in *mastabas*, while others were buried in subsidiary pyramids, a practice that also occurred in the twelfth dynasty. In the New Kingdom, during the eighteenth dynasty, a number of royal women were buried in rock-cut tombs in desert wadis (the so-called southwest valleys) on the

dental. Together the two women represented the divine mother–consort as embodied in the sky goddess. Through her, the sun god perpetually renewed himself, by impregnating her at night as he set and by being born of her as he rose in the morning. On earth, the king represented the sun god, but when the divine parallel of renewal was transferred to the human sphere, the mother and consort could no longer be physically embodied as a single being; then, the role had to be divided between the king's mother and his principal wife. Secondary wives, by contrast, did not use queenly insignia and titles; nor did they appear in temple scenes, and they seem to have had no ritual role.

Despite their ritual role, it is unclear whether queens had any institutionalized authority in the political system. Individual queens were usually given their own estates together with a staff of male officials, so that they were western bank of the Nile River at Thebes. Because these tombs were undecorated, and they are all now plundered, the occupant can only be identified if some object or fragment has survived with her name. Such a tomb was prepared for Hatshepsut, wife of Thutmose II and mother of Thutmose III, when she was queen and, probably, also one for her daughter Neferure. Amenhotpe III included in his own tomb, in the Valley of the Kings, rooms for the burials of his principal wife Tiy and his daughter Satamun, whom he married; Akhenaten (Amenhotpe IV) did the same for Nefertiti and his daughter Meketaten in his tomb at Amarna. The Valley of the Queens, most famous for the decorated tomb of Nefertari, the wife of Ramesses II, was used for burials of royal family members—princes as well as women—during the nineteenth and twentieth dynasties. Some New Kingdom royal women were almost certainly buried at sites other than Thebes. The "harem" palace of Miwer, at Medinet el-Ghurob, had an associated cemetery, where most of the royal inhabitants were presumably buried; a tomb belonging to a king's son is known from there, as well as a number of female burials. After the New Kingdom, even less is known of the burials of royal women, although some items of burial equipment exist for several twenty-sixth dynasty queens. Queens of the Ptolemaic era were buried at Alexandria, in Hellenistic-style tombs, but none have survived.

Although kingship was regarded as a male office, and the king was identified with the male god Horus and as the son of the sun god Re and of other deities, nevertheless a few female rulers are known. Since they stand in contrast to the several hundred male kings who ruled during the three millennia of ancient Egypt's recorded history, clearly female rulers were anomalies—it was not the norm for a woman to ascend to the throne.

The historians Herodotus and Manetho, as well as the Turin Canon, all referred to a female ruler called Nitokris in Greek or Nitiqret in Egyptian. Manetho placed her as the last ruler of the sixth dynasty, while the Turin Canon put her after Merenra. She is not known from monuments or contemporary documents. In contrast, the female king Sobekneferu, the last ruler of the twelfth dynasty, is known from a number of contemporary monuments; she is attested with the full fivefold titulary of a king, and a regnal date of Year 3. A fragmentary quartzite statue, now in the Louvre, Paris, shows her in a combination of female dress and male royal costume, wearing the *nemes*-headdress of a king; she may have been the daughter of Amenemhet III and the consort of Amenemhet IV before becoming the ruler.

Hatshepsut is the female king about whom we know most. She was the daughter of the third king of the eighteenth dynasty, Thutmose I, and of his principal wife Ahmose. Hatshepsut married her half-brother Thutmose II,

as his principal wife, and on his death became queen regent for his young son and heir Thutmose III. In that capacity, some of her actions were kingly, such as commissioning a pair of obelisks for the temple of Karnak and having herself represented in temple relief, offering directly to Amun-Re, rather than accompanying a king who performed the ritual. The titles and insignia used by Hatshepsut were, however, related to her roles as king's principal wife and as god's wife in the cult of Amun at Thebes. At some point, at the latest by the seventh year of Thutmose III's reign, she became king and ruled as coregent, adopting a full king's titulary and kingly insignia. A few statues and reliefs show her as king but wearing female dress, yet on the majority of her monuments, her image is that of a male king wearing traditional male dress. Although we do not know what happened to Hatshepsut in the end, by his Year 22, Thutmose III was ruling alone, and Hatshepsut had disappeared from the scene. Although Hatshepsut never ruled alone during her reign, she was clearly the dominant partner in the coregency, which lasted at least fourteen years. She ruled at a time of prosperity and built prolifically for the gods, especially at Thebes, where she constructed her great funerary temple at Deir el-Bahri, with her tomb in the Valley of the Kings. The first depictions of the Opet festival come from her reign, which seems to have been innovative in many ways. After her death, Thutmose III ruled for another three decades. At some point, he ordered Hatshepsut's names and images to be removed from the monuments, and the later temple king lists that relate to rituals for the royal ancestors omitted her name.

At the end of the nineteenth dynasty, Twosret, who had been the consort of Sety II, became queen regent for the young king, Siptah. During that time, she began the construction of a tomb for herself in the Valley of the Kings. On Siptah's death, she became king, presumably with a full kingly titulary, although we do not know her *nebty* and golden Horus names; she is not well attested as king, and her reign was short, brought to an end with the successful bid for the throne made by Sethnakhte, the first king of the Twentieth Dynasty. Twosret's fate is not known, but Sethnakhte took over her tomb and adapted it for his own burial.

Probably the most famous female ruler of Egypt is Cleopatra VII, the last member of the Greek Ptolemaic dynasty to govern Egypt. Although the Ptolemies were not only Greek by origin but also by culture, they adopted from the Egyptians the custom of royal brother–sister marriage. A number of Ptolemaic queens were very powerful women.

Cleopatra VII was the daughter of Ptolemy XII. In 51 BCE, she succeeded her father together with her brother Ptolemy XIII. For the next twenty years, she ruled Egypt, first with Ptolemy XIII, then with her next brother, Ptolemy XIV, and finally with her son, Ptolemy Caesar (by the Roman emperor Julius Caesar). She was politically ambitious and strove to extend her own influence, and that of Egypt, by associating herself successively with two powerful Roman generals, first Julius Caesar and then Mark Antony; her aim was always to keep Egypt independent of Rome. However, her defeat with Mark Antony at the Battle of Actium in 31 BCE, followed by their deaths in 30 BCE, gave Egypt into the hands of Octavian, who became the emperor Augustus.

Little is known about Cleopatra from Egyptian sources, so most of our information comes from Greek and Roman writers who were hostile to her. Clearly, she was an intelligent woman, highly educated in Greek literature, music, and science. She was reputedly good at languages, and she may have been the only Ptolemy who learned to speak Egyptian.

[*See also* Ahmose-Nefertari; Cleopatra VII; Hatshepsut; Nefertiti; *and* Sobekneferu.]

BIBLIOGRAPHY

Beckerath, Jürgen von. "Sobeknofru." In *Lexikon der Ägyptologie,* 5: 1050–1051. Wiesbaden, 1984.

Berman, Lawrence M., and Bernadette Letellier. *Pharaohs: Treasures of Egyptian Art from the Louvre.* Cleveland, 1996. Includes part of a statue of Sobekneferu as ruler.

Bierbrier, Morris L. "How Old was Hatshepsut?" *Göttinger Miszellen* 144 (1995), 15–18. Discusses the problem of Hatshepsut's age at the death of her husband, Thutmose II.

Bryan, Betsy M. "In Women Good and Bad Fortune Are on Earth: Status and Roles of Women in Egyptian Culture." In *Mistress of the House, Mistress of Heaven: Women in Ancient Egypt,* edited by Anne K. Capel and Glenn E. Markoe, pp. 25–36. New York, 1996. Includes a discussion of women who became rulers of ancient Egypt.

de Buck, Adriaan. "The Judicial Papyrus of Turin." *Journal of Egyptian Archaeology* 23 (1937), 152–164. Publication of a papyrus documenting an attempt by a secondary wife of Ramesses III to put her son on the throne, instead of the legitimate heir.

Carter, Howard. "A Tomb Prepared for Queen Hatshepsut and Other Recent Discoveries at Thebes." *Journal of Egyptian Archaeology* 4 (1917), 107–118. Report on the rock-cut tomb and sarcophagus prepared for Hatshepsut before she became queen; also a tomb possibly belonging to her daughter, Neferura.

Goedicke, Hans, and Gertrude Thausing. *Nofretari: Eine Dokumentation der Wandgemälde ihres Grabes.* Graz, 1971. A photographic record of the tomb of Nefertari, queen of Ramesses II, in the Valley of the Queens.

Jánosi, Peter. "The Queens of the Old Kingdom and Their Tombs." *Bulletin of the Australian Centre for Egyptology* 3 (1992), 51–57.

Kemp, Barry J. "The Harim-Palace at Medinet el-Ghurab." *Zeitschrift für Ägyptische Sprache und Altertumskunde* 105 (1978), 122–23. Discusses the palace at Medinet el-Ghurab, the ancient harem of Merwer/She, founded by Thutmose III.

Kitchen, Kenneth A. "Tausret." In *Lexikon der Ägyptologie,* 6: 244–245. Wiesbaden, 1986.

Martin, Geoffrey Thorndike. *The Royal Tomb at el-Amarna,* vol. 2. London, 1989. The royal tomb includes a set of rooms, probably prepared for Nefertiti, and a second smaller set, used for the burials of Princess Meketaten and a secondary wife of Akhenaten.

McDonald, John K. *House of Eternity: The Tomb of Nefertari.* Los Angeles, 1996. An illustrated guide to the tomb of Nefertari, the queen of Ramesses II, in the Valley of the Queens.

Newberry, Percy E. "Queen Nitocris of the Sixth Dynasty." *Journal of Egyptian Archaeology* 29 (1943), 51–54.

Robins, Gay. "A Critical Examination of the Theory that the Right to the Throne of Ancient Egypt Passed Through the Female Line in the 18th Dynasty." *Göttinger Miszellen* 52 (1983), 67–77. Challenges the established view that the kingship of ancient Egypt passed through the female line of the royal family and that kings could only legitimize themselves by marrying the royal "heiress."

Robins, Gay. *Women in Ancient Egypt,* pp. 21–55. London and Cambridge, Mass., 1993. Includes a discussion of royal women and queenship, based mainly on New Kingdom evidence.

Schulman, Alan. "Diplomatic Marriage in the Egyptian New Kingdom." *Journal of Near Eastern Studies* 38 (1979), 177–193. Discusses marriages between Egyptian kings and the daughters of foreign rulers.

Seipel, Wilfried. "Hatschepsout I." In *Lexikon der Ägyptologie,* 2: 1045–1051. Wiesbaden, 1977.

Troy, Lana. *Patterns of Queenship in Ancient Egyptian Myth and History.* Uppsala, 1986. A study of the role of royal women and divine queenship.

Winlock, H. E. *The Treasure of the Three Princesses.* New York, 1948. Burial of three secondary wives of Thutmose III, in a small rock-cut tomb at Thebes.

Zivie, Christiane. "Nitokris." In *Lexikon der Ägyptologie,* 4: 513–514. Wiesbaden, 1982.

GAY ROBINS

QURNA, the main private cemetery in the center of the Theban necropolis (25°44′N, 32°36′E). The name is an abbreviated version of the toponym Ilwet el-Sheikh Abd el-Qurna ("the hill of Sheikh Abd el-Qurna") that refers to a sheikh of the modern village, which still covers an unknown number of tombs on the hill. The term *Qurna* seems to be a derivation of el-Qurn ("the peak"), which may refer to the mountain that is 482 meters (1,450 feet) above sea level, overlooking the Theban necropolis. In older terminology, Qurna referred to the area in the northwestern part of the necropolis, around and including the mortuary temple of Sety I (the Temple of Qurna), which is now occasionally called "Old Qurna," as opposed to Qurna ("the hill") or New Qurna (the modern village designed and built by the Egyptian architect Hassan Fathy, some 3 kilometers [2 miles] east of the necropolis and close to the Fadiya Canal).

Qurna is the central part of the New Kingdom private necropolis in Thebes. It consists of the hill proper and the plain east of it, which is defined as the area southwest of Khokha and north of the mortuary temple of Ramesses II (the Ramesseum). In the hillside and the plain, there are far more than 150 decorated tombs, more than half of which date to the eighteenth dynasty. Of the remaining tombs, between twenty and thirty date to the eleventh and early twelfth dynasties, with the rest dating to the Ramessid (nineteenth and twentieth dynasties) or to the Saite period (twenty-sixth dynasty). Many of the tombs of Qurna were known to early travelers, and selected tomb-wall scenes and inscriptions had been copied by members of the Napoleonic expedition (1798–1799).

Today, exact figures or statistical analyses of the spatial and chronological distribution of the tombs in Qurna are still difficult to determine, since the majority of them have not been investigated thoroughly. In addition, since their original construction and decoration, many tombs had been extensively remodeled, redecorated, or otherwise reused. Yet the immense importance of the tombs in Qurna is based on the large number that still have substantial parts of their original decoration (painting on plaster, or relief, or both) well preserved. The decoration has provided abundant information both on aspects of daily life and on religious ceremonies, allowing for detailed studies of the development of style and iconography. The tomb inscriptions have shed light on theological conceptions, social stratigraphy, administration, and the family relationships of those buried in the tombs.

Studies have revealed that, contrary to previous conclusions, there are patterns by which the site for a tomb was chosen, the manner in which it was decorated, and the way that the burials were equipped. At times, especially during the eighteenth dynasty, certain areas were used for the construction of tombs by members of the same social class. Sometimes elements of decoration and/or the textual program of one tomb were slightly remodeled and used in another. Generally speaking, the private tombs in Qurna belong to the elite of the eighteenth dynasty. Among the tomb owners are viziers (the highest nonroyal position in the administration), high priests of Amun and other high-ranking members of the clergy, overseers of the granaries of the Two Lands, mayors of Thebes, high-ranking military officers, and royal stewards. The Qurna hill has yielded some of the best-known private tombs of Western Thebes and thus of ancient Egypt.

The tomb of the vizier under Thutmose III, Rekhmire (tomb 100 in Western Thebes), is halfway up the hill. It is considered to be the best example of the T-shaped tomb type and is the most completely decorated extant tomb of the eighteenth dynasty. It also shows the general distribution of the wall scenes and texts of the time most clearly: the broad hall (corresponding to the horizontal stroke of a T) mainly contains the daily life scenes, which depict various activities in which the vizier was involved during his lifetime. The scenes and texts of the passage, or transverse hall, are mainly devoted to topics of the netherworld, oriented toward representations of gods and goddesses, which are depicted on the western end of the hall.

The subterranean burial chamber of the tomb of Sennefer (a mayor of Thebes during the time of Amenhotpe II; tomb 96) is well known for its unique ceiling decoration, of vine leaves. The tombs of Nakht (tomb 52) and Menna (tomb 69) were built for middle-class officials under the reign of Thutmose IV and are vivid examples of smaller tombs with painted decoration.

Another vizier and mayor of Thebes at the end of the eighteenth dynasty, Ramose (tomb 55), had his tomb built in the plain of Qurna during the reigns of Amenhotpe III and Amenhotpe IV. His tomb contains one of the finest examples of wall decoration, in raised relief, in New Kingdom times. It also shows the drastic change of style that took place after Amenhotpe IV changed his name to Akhenaton and moved to his new city at Amarna. Some of the walls in Ramose's tomb were decorated in the new, Amarna style.

Today, the Qurna hill remains one of the primary targets of Egyptological investigation. Since the end of the nineteenth century, numerous projects were dedicated to the excavation, recording, and documentation of the tombs of Qurna. To a certain extent, the history of archaeological and epigraphic research in the tombs of Qurna parallels the history of Egyptology; and every major Egyptological institution has, one way or another, contributed to their investigation. This part of the Theban necropolis is still far from being thoroughly investigated, however. Almost every year, new tombs have been discovered and long-known tombs have been reinvestigated under the new, scientific-scholarly approach.

BIBLIOGRAPHY

Assmann, Jan, ed. *Theben*, vols. 1–13. Mainz, 1983–1996. Publication series in German of mostly Ramessid private tombs in the Theban necropolis.

Davies, Norman de Garis. *The Tomb of the Vizier Ramose*. London, 1941.

Davies, Norman de Garis. *The Tomb of Rekh-mi-Re at Thebes*. Egyptian Expedition, publications of The Metropolitan Museum of Art, 11. New York, 1943.

Dorman, Peter F. *The Tombs of Senenmut: The Architecture and Decoration of Tombs 71 and 353*. Egyptian Expedition, publications of The Metropolitan Museum of Art, 24. New York, 1991.

Guksch, Heike. *Die Gräber des Nacht-Min und des Men-cheper-Ra-seneb. Theben Nr. 87 und 79*. Archäologische Veröffentlichungen, Deutsches Archäologisches Instituts Abteilung, Kairo, 34. Mainz, 1995.

Kampp, Friederike. *Die Thebanische Nekropole*. Theben, 13. Mainz, 1996. Standard publication of the private tombs of Thebes with up-to-date bibliography.

Polz, Daniel. *Das Grab des Hui und des Kel: Theben Nr. 54*. Archäologische Veröffentlichungen Deutschen Archäologisches Instituts, Abteilung, Kairo, 74. Mainz, 1997.

Porter, Bertha, and Rosalind L. B. Moss. *Topographical Bibliography of Ancient Egyptian Hieroglyphic Texts, Reliefs and Paintings*, vols. I and II. Oxford, 1960–1972.

DANIEL C. POLZ

R

RACE. The concept of race in human beings has come under considerable debate during the twentieth century. Recent surveys show that approximately half the anthropologists in the United States reject any scientific basis for race among humans. The American Anthropological Association characterizes racial categories as both arbitrary and subjective. This disfavor reflects both the inability to create consistent scientific definitions for supposed human racial groups and the misuse of the race concept in models of cultural evolution in the late nineteenth and early twentieth centuries. The latter led to the use of "scientific" race to support racist and colonial ideologies of superiority and inferiority. As a cultural, not scientific, construct, the concept of race can reveal key insights into the worldview of different cultures, particularly the ways they see themselves vis-à-vis the groups who surround them. This article will review modern views of race, followed by a comparison with and consideration of ancient Egyptian notions of race.

Modern Conceptions of Race. The origins of the modern conception of race derive from the work of nineteenth-century anthropologists like L. H. Morgan and E. B. Tylor, who developed "scientific" unilinear evolutionary theoretical models for the development of human beings from "savagery" to "civilization." Racial groups were ranked by evolutionary categories, linked to intellectual capacities, based on elaborate cranial measurements; supposedly, this provided causal links between phenotypic (observable) traits, mental capacity, and sociopolitical dominance. This model not coincidentally reinforced the existing European-American domination of third-world peoples with the claim of scientifically "objective" methodologies based on race and evolution.

The unilinear evolutionary model did influence some early Egyptologists. W. M. Flinders Petrie used it to develop his notion of the "Dynastic Race," to explain the rapid development of Egyptian civilization. In part this was based on prevailing models of culture change that emphasized migration as an explanation for cultural change, but, ultimately, racist notions drove the model. The implication was that Egypt had a "white" or "brown" ruling class dominating a native "black" African underclass who supplied the labor to build Egypt's great monuments. Petrie's model was never enthusiastically accepted by the Egyptological community as a whole, although the idea persisted through a few enthusiasts. James Henry Breasted echoed the sentiments of most contemporary Egyptologists in seeing the Egyptians as indigenous, but as a brown rather than black race, related to other northeastern Africans. It is interesting to note that the Egyptians became "white" for a classroom textbook, presumably reflecting the racism of the day. The last serious argument in support of the Dynastic Race theory appeared in Walter Emery's *Archaic Egypt* (New York, 1961). In the context of his discussion, it is ironic that some Afrocentric scholars seeking to undo the legacy of late nineteenth- and early twentieth-century racist scholarship have revived the concept of race, often employing the same diffusionist arguments linking race to cultural achievement.

As early as 1897, the anthropologist Franz Boas challenged this racial ideology, in particular the argument for connections among language, culture, and biology (i.e., race). His observations contradicted the notion of races as biologically fixed natural groupings of physical traits ranked by proximity to the apes. Boas demonstrated that supposedly distinctive "core" racial indicators could change quickly in response to clothing styles, nutrition, and cultural and environmental factors. He still, however, recognized biological races, but he argued forcefully for the separation of culture and language from race and against the inherent racism of earlier evolutionary models. Boas and his influential student Ruth Benedict argued that culture was the most important explanation of human variation. Race's role was minimal and carefully circumscribed.

Further tainted by Nazism's use of genocide in the name of racial purity, the biological concept of race was gradually replaced by population genetics from the 1930s to the 1950s. Instead, micro-evolutionary theory focused on breeding populations with a collective set of genetic traits. Ashley Montague, another student of Boas, played a key role in developing and disseminating this concept, arguing in *Man's Most Dangerous Myth: The Fallacy of Race* (New York, 1942) that "the character of these populations must lie in the study of the frequency distribution of the genes which characterize them—and not in the study of entities [racial categories] which are purely imaginary" (p. 36). Dynamic populations with overlapping characteristics replaced the old paradigm of static races.

Far from being absolute, genetic traits are distributed in clines, that are continuously varying distributions of traits inconsistent with racial categories.

In spite of the evidence, race is still a powerful interpretive model in modern society. As Kamala Visweswaran (1998) concludes, "Races certainly exist, but they have no biological meaning outside the social significance we attach to biological explanation itself. . . . In other words, to say that race has no biological meaning is not to say race lacks meaning." In other words, race is culturally constructed, and it is applied in modern societies in both positive and negative (i.e., racism) ways. Modern popular views of race still cling to supposed "phenotypic" traits (e.g., skin color, nose shape, and hair color and texture) that mark a small number of distinct races.

Ancient Egyptian Concept of Race. Race and culture were often linked in Egyptian royal ideology in a scheme that recognized Egyptians as civilized superiors to their barbaric foreign counterparts with different skin color, dress, and speech. Unlike modern essentialist racial models, however, the Egyptians separated language and culture (costume, hairstyle, etc.) from race (skin color, facial features/phenotype), acknowledging that foreigners could act in positive ways and be incorporated into the civilized sphere. The solar theology explicitly acknowledges different racial groups: "You made the earth as you wished . . . you set every man in his place, you supply their needs; everyone has his food, his lifetime is counted. Their tongues differ in speech, their characters likewise; their skins are distinct, for you distinguished the peoples" (Hymn to the Aten, Lichtheim, 1973, pp. 131–132).

This is rendered artistically in scenes from the tombs of Ramesses III and Sety I showing the basic divisions of humankind. These depictions separated humankind into four peoples or races, each with stereotypical skin color, coiffure, and dress. The Egyptians (rmṯ "people") are shown with red-brown skin, black shoulder-length hair, a simple white kilt, and small trimmed beard (only men are represented). Near Easterners ("Asiatics"; ʿȝmw, specifically Syrian-Palestinians), appear with yellow skin, a black bobbed hairstyle with headband tied at the back, elaborately decorated kilts, and ample, sometimes pointed, beards and mustaches. Nubians (Nḥsiw) are shown with black skin, broad, flat noses, short hair in trimmed ringlets, hoop earrings, and decorated leather sashes over white Egyptian-style kilts. Finally, Libyans (Ṯḥnw) appear as very light-skinned, with geometric tattoos, braided or ringletted hair with sidelocks and two ostrich feathers; they wear a loincloth under a long leather cloak showing the natural patterns of the cow's hair.

Although these ideologically charged racial stereotypes approached modern racism in the context of state dogma, on a practical level the Egyptians did not engage in the kind of racial prejudice seen in modern times. Modern racism revolves largely around differences in skin color; in particular, dark skin color was (and with some groups still is) a sign of inferiority, regardless of individual achievement and sophistication. Miscegenation, or racial intermarriage, is often considered immoral. At its worst, skin color distinguished between slaves and free people, in general, in the pre–Civil War American South. The ancient Egyptians, and indeed ancient Mediterranean peoples did not generally make skin color a definitive criterion for racial discrimination. Slavery was not connected to race or even class. Thus, while Nubians were depicted with black skin, Nubians like the soldier and royal confidant Mahirper achieved high position in Egyptian society as long as they assimilated to Egyptian cultural norms. Similarly, a man of Near Eastern ancestry like Aper-El could achieve the highest office in the land. Nubians, Near Easterners, and other peoples married freely with Egyptians, and slaves were sometimes adopted into Egyptian families, at least among the elite. It was the cultural identity of immigrants to Egypt that mattered to their success in Egyptian society, not their skin color or ancestry. Thus, we may regard the Egyptians more as cultural chauvinists than as racists.

Race and foreigners in Egyptian literature. Egypt's ideological view of foreigners, expressed in the basic racial divisions discussed above, reflects different goals and perceptions from the administrative realities of diplomacy, trade, and empire. Antonio Loprieno (1988) has characterized the Egyptian view of different peoples through a distinction between *topos* and *mimesis*, reflected in Egyptian literature. Topos represents an idealized view of the world, which serves a rhetorical but not necessarily literal end; mimesis reflects the reality of daily experience, if ultimately filtered through Egyptian cultural perceptions.

The ideological topos applied to foreign peoples in Egypt reflects a propagandistic manipulation of reality aimed at an inner audience. In the celebrative central ideology, often expressed in monumental art and architecture, Egypt becomes the center of the universe, and all the foreign lands bow down to the pharaoh regardless of their actual relationship. Foreigners represent chaotic, uncivilized threats to the inner order, ultimately disposed of by the ruler. The role of foreigners in the Egyptian foreigner topos stands in opposition to *maat* ("order, harmony, rightness"). *Maat* exists in opposition to *isfet* ("disorder, chaos"), which constantly tries to upset the heavenly and earthly order. The sun god Re appoints the king as the upholder of *maat* on Earth. Without the king and his constant struggle for *maat*, the whole world would fall into chaos and decay and would no longer be habitable. One of the most potent forces of *isfet* is the traditional foreign enemies of Egypt. Thus, foreigners appear as chaotic masses threatening Egypt's inner order. They are depicted as strangers and generalized as an ethnic group with negative qualities. The particular dress and physical appearance of each ethnic group emphasizes their otherness in the foreigner topos. Several literary themes characterize the foreigner topos. In a military context, foreigners are cowards, instantly defeated by the king, often without a fight. Thus, the boundary stela of Senwosret III (c.1850 BCE), set up at Semna just south of the Second Cataract, reads:

> Since the Nubian listens to the word of mouth,
> To answer him is to make him retreat.
> Attack him, he will turn his back,
> Retreat, he will start attacking.
> They are not people one respects,
> They are wretches, craven-hearted. (Lichtheim, 1976, p. 119)

The *Instructions for Merikare* adopt a similar theme:

> Lo the miserable Asiatic,
> He is wretched because of the place he's in:
> Short of water, bare of wood,
> Its paths are many and painful because of mountains.
> He does not dwell in one place,
> Food propels his legs,
> He fights since the time of Horus,
> Not conquering nor being conquered,
> He does not announce the day of combat,
> Like a thief who darts about a group . . .
> The Asiatic is a crocodile on its shore,
> It snatches from a lonely road,
> It cannot seize from a populous town.
>   (Lichtheim, 1976, pp. 103–104)

Other texts take the foreigner topos a step farther. Not only are foreigners wretched cowards, they are not really people *(rmt)*; they are compared with animals, their speech unintelligible, like the jabbering of baboons. In the *Admonitions of Ipuwer*, everything in Egypt is topsy-turvy: the poor man is rich, the servant is served by a former master. Not surprisingly, even foreigners are treated like people:

> Foreigners have become people everywhere.
> Foreign bowmen have come into Egypt.
> Lo, [break]
> There are no people anywhere.
>   (Lichtheim, 1976, pp. 151–152)

The *Prophecy of Neferti* is usually attributed to Amenemhet I's reign (c.1950 BCE), although the theme below is better suited as a reference to the Hyksos domination of the Nile Delta in the Second Intermediate Period. In any case, the author takes up the theme of foreigner as animal, comparing Near Eastern immigrants with a flock of rapacious birds descending on Egypt:

> A strange bird will breed in the Delta marsh,
> Having made its nest beside the people
> The people letting it approach by default.
> Then perish those delightful things,
> The fishponds full of fish-eaters,
> Teeming with fish and fowl.
> All happiness has vanished,
> The land is bowed down in distress,
> Owing to those feeders,
> Asiatics who roam the land.
> Foes have risen in the East,
> Asiatics have come down into Egypt.
>   (Lichtheim, 1976, p. 141)

The New Kingdom *Instructions of Anii* likens Near Easterners and Nubians directly to various animals, dismissing them as mere beasts:

> There's nothing [superfluous in] our words,
> Which you say should be reduced.
> The fighting bull who kills in the stable,
> He forgets and abandons the arena;
> He conquers his nature,
> Remembers what he's learned . . .
> The monkey carries the stick,
> Though its mother did not carry it.
> The goose returns from the pond,
> When one comes to shut it in the yard.
> One teaches the Nubian to speak Egyptian,
> The Syrian and other strangers too.
> Say: "I shall do like all the beasts,"
> Listen and learn what they do. (Lichtheim, 1973, p. 144)

A more realistic portrayal occurs in texts reflecting mimesis. Foreigners are treated as individuals, not as stereotypes. They are identified by name and can speak Egyptian like a "real" person, and thus are incorporated into the Egyptian cultural framework. The fact that they are foreigners does not preclude the possibility that they can act in a positive way. Foreign influences and even deities are tolerated. For example, despite state ideological representations of Near Easterners as uncivilized enemies, Levantine mythical and literary motifs, loanwords, and deities such as Ba'al, Astarte, and Reshep all entered into the Egyptian cultural sphere during the New Kingdom. Although no indisputably Nubian deities appear in Egypt, elite military dress and accouterments, including leather kilts and hairstyles, were borrowed from Nubia.

The Middle Kingdom *Tale of Sinuhe* tells of a court official who flees Egypt upon the assassination of Amenemhet I to live in northern Palestine (Lebanon). A number of Near Easterners who help Sinuhe are depicted in very positive light, and he brags about his service to Ammu-nenshe, the ruler of Upper Retenu:

> When Asiatics conspired to attack the Rulers of Hill-Countries, I opposed their movements. For this ruler of Retenu made me carry out numerous missions as commander of his troops . . . I won his heart and he loved me, for he recognized my valor. He set me at the head of his children, for he saw the strength of my arms. (Lichtheim, 1976, p. 227)

When a champion comes to challenge Sinuhe, he recognizes that his position is unusual, and that as a stranger he is regarded as inferior to local princes, a concept entirely foreign to the state topos:

> I am indeed like a stray bull in a strange herd, whom the bull of the herd charges, whom the longhorn attacks. Is an inferior beloved when he becomes a superior? No Asiatic makes friends with a Delta-man. And what would make papyrus cleave to that mountain? (Lichtheim, 1976, p. 227)

Not surprisingly, in the end the story is still biased towards things Egyptian, but the following passage represents more a cultural chauvinism than an expression of modern racism:

> I was put in the house of a prince. In it were luxuries: a bathroom and mirrors. In it were riches from the treasury; clothes of royal linen, myrrh, and the choice perfume of the king and of his favorite courtiers were in every room. Every servant was at his task. Years were removed from my body. I was shaved; my hair was combed. Thus was my squalor returned to the foreign land, my dress to the Sand-farers. I was clothed in fine linen; I was anointed with fine oil. I slept on a bed. I had returned the sand to those who dwell in it, the tree-oil to those who grease themselves with it. (Lichtheim, 1976, p. 233)

Foreigner topos in art and archeology. Egypt's rich artistic and archaeological records shed further light on the ancient Egyptian view of foreigners in both the state ideology and everyday life. Both the foreigner topos and mimesis are reflected in pictorial representations of foreigners in Egyptian art. Topical depictions of foreigners as stereotypes appear prominently on large-scale monuments. The foreigner topos is also reflected strongly in the architectural setting and accouterments connected with kings that show foreigners as defeated enemies, with the stereotypical racial features mentioned above. These architectural elements and objects reflect the orthodoxy of the king's topical role as subduer of the traditional enemies of Egypt, who threaten *maat*, the eternal order of things. On the other hand, evidence from more private contexts reflects a mimetic viewpoint in the broader society, depicting foreigners as real people within an Egyptian cultural framework.

Objects from Tutankhamun's tomb show that the king was surrounded by imagery reflecting the foreigner topos.

The elaborate battle scene on the painted box from the antechamber shows the king, larger than life, defeating a chaotic and disorganized mass of Near Easterners on one side, Nubians on the other. The ends of the box show Tutankhamun as a sphinx trampling a topical Near Easterner and Nubian with the stereotypical racial features of the foreigner topos (costume, skin color, and facial features). Similar bound prisoners decorate many of the objects from the tomb. In a text from one of his chariots, the king is "the Perfect God who appears in [*maat*] and who smites the nobles of all the foreign lands, who carries off millions and chops down thousands, (all) brought together beneath his sandals." This symbolism is repeated over and over in the king's accouterments and the architectural setting for his appearances. The trampling motif is very common, often acting as sympathetic magic against Egypt's enemies. Thus, Tutankhamen's royal footstool has representations of topical Near Easterners and Nubians on which the king could rest the royal feet, and bound prisoners shown on the soles of the king's sandals allowed him to trample his enemies with each step he took. His walking staff had similar figures on the base, so that the king would drag his enemies in the dust. Foreigners were also depicted on the royal throne dais, the "window of appearances" where loyal followers were rewarded in state ceremonies, and on the bases of royal statues, which often listed conquered cities. Whenever the king made a public appearance, his own accouterments and surroundings emphasized his role as defender of *maat* and enemy of *isfet*—the topical foreign enemies of Egypt.

In contrast to state art, private tombs often represent a more mimetic view of foreigners, especially when an acculturated immigrant owns the tomb. Nubian mercenaries settled at Gebelein in the First Intermediate Period are represented as Egyptians on their stelae, except for stereotypical Nubian facial features and dark skin color. Mahirper, who was given the honor of burial in the Valley of the Kings, is shown in his copy of the *Book of Going Forth by Day* as an Egyptian noble, but with Nubian features, military hairstyle, and dark skin. Egyptianized Nubian princes of Egypt's Lower Nubian empire, like Djehutyhotep of Tehkhet and Hekanefer of Miam (Aniba), are shown as Egyptian officials in their tombs, which have the same repertory of scenes and assemblage of grave goods as a typical elite tomb in Egypt. The same can be said of acculturated Near Eastern immigrants like Aper-El, vizier under Amenhotpe III, whose tomb at Saqqara is completely Egyptian in style and grave goods.

The Theban tomb of the viceroy of Kush Huy, the Egyptian official in charge of Egypt's Nubian colony, shows Nubians in the Presentation of *Inw*. The term *inw* is usually translated as "tribute," but it really reflects a combination of tribute and gift exchange that reinforced social relationships. The ceremony was highly symbolic, stressing the topical role of the king as subduer of Egypt's enemies. As a result, the depiction of Nubians lies somewhere between topos and mimesis, depending on their role in the event. The Lower Nubian chiefs are depicted with the topical Nubian racial features, but they are surrounded by family members shown almost entirely as Egyptians. Huy names their leader, Hekanefer, prince of Miam (Aniba). As noted above, his tomb at Toshka East depicts him as a normal Egyptian official, reflecting a more mimetic view. The tomb of Djehutyhotep, prince of Tehkhet (the area around Fadrus and Serra) in the reign of Thutmose III, is better preserved, including several scenes depicting him as entirely Egyptian.

The "tribute" scene of Huy may actually represent a fairly accurate portrayal of the performance of the foreigner topos during this ceremony. Topos required that the Nubians bearing the "tribute" of Wawat and Kush appear in the racial stereotype of "southern foreigner," with the typical ethnic costume, coloring, and facial features. Beneath the native trappings, however, the Lower Nubian participants wear the dress of the Egyptian elite, reflecting the fact that by this period their society was completely egyptianized. The subsidiary princelings, whom topos apparently did not require to wear foreign costumes, are shown in almost completely Egyptian outfits. These great ceremonies, recorded in the tomb of Huy and elsewhere, must have made an impressive display of royal power and authority. A New Kingdom model letter describes this event:

> Think about the day when the tribute is sent, and you are brought into the presence (of the king) under the Window (of Appearances), the Nobles to either side in front of his Majesty, the Princes and the Envoys of every foreign land standing, looking at the tribute . . . tall *Trk*-people in their garments, with fans of gold, high (feathered?) hairstyles, and their jewelry of ivory, and numerous Nubians of all kinds.

This text emphasizes the racial stereotypes, providing a good match to the tomb scenes. By including officials otherwise unconnected with the event, the king and central authority gained added prestige within an important segment of Egyptian society. These carefully organized events showed that the king could command people from a far-off land, wearing exotic costumes and bearing exotic and valuable gifts like gold, ivory, ebony, panther skins, even live giraffes and panthers. The use of racial stereotypes in the portrayal of foreigners was thus closely tied to the ideological legitimization of the king, which reinforced his authority both at home and abroad. The foreigner topos transformed the reality of Egyptian–Nubian relations to suit political purposes. On a cosmological level, they reinforced the role of the king in the mainte-

nance of *maat*. This concept provided a powerful integrating force in Egyptian society and government, legitimizing the king's authority over the entire nation. The depiction of the king as the subduer of foreign lands established an ideological footing for Egypt's external relationships, emphasizing how the king brought order from chaos and vigorously subdued *isfet*, personified by the "rebellious" and inherently "chaotic" foreigners who might threaten Egypt and thus *maat*.

[*See also* Afrocentrism; Foreigners; *and* People.]

BIBLIOGRAPHY

Benedict, Ruth. *Race: Science and Politics.* New York, 1940.

Bernal, Martin. *Black Athena.* New Brunswick, N.J., 1987. A good critique of the racist biases of the late nineteenth and early twentieth centuries that minimized Egypt's African-ness and denied interactions with the Aegean. Unfortunately, he goes on to revive seriously flawed radical diffusionist approaches that posit massive migrations and influence of Egyptians on the development of classical civilization.

Boas, Franz. *Race, Language and Culture.* Chicago, 1940. A seminal work refuting the connection of biology (race) and culture.

Celenko, Theodore, ed. *Egypt in Africa.* Indianapolis, 1996. The companion volume for an innovative exhibit exploring ancient Egypt's African roots, juxtaposing images from Egypt and other African cultures. Each section is accompanied by essays from Egyptologists and Africanist scholars exploring related themes.

Davies, Nina de Garis, and Alan H. Gardiner. *The Tomb of Huy Viceroy of Nuiba in the Reign of Tut'ankhamun (No. 40).* London, 1926. Excellent documentation of this important tomb with its representations of Nubian and Near Eastern "tribute," emphasizing the artistic stereotypes of the foreigner topos.

Diop, Cheikh Ante. *The African Origin of Civilization.* Chicago, 1974. A highly influential work that rightly points out the African origins of Egyptian civilization, but reinforces the methodological and theoretical foundations of colonialist theories of history, embracing racialist thinking and simply reversing the flow of diffusionist models.

Keita, S. O. Y., and Rick Kittles. "The Persistence of Racial Thinking and the Myth of Racial Divergence." *American Anthropologist* 99 (1997), 534–544. An excellent summary of the evidence against race as a scientific concept, with particular reference to the ancient Egyptians.

Kemp, Barry J. "Imperialism in New Kingdom Egypt (c.1575–1087 B.C.)." *In Imperialism in the Ancient World,* edited by P. D. A. Garnsey and C. R. Whittaker, pp. 7–57, 283–297. Cambridge, 1978. An excellent consideration of Egypt's Nubian and Syrian-Palestinian empires, including an extensive discussion of foreigners in Egyptian ideology.

Lichtheim, Miriam. *Ancient Egyptian Literature.* Vol. 1, *The Old and Middle Kingdoms.* Los Angeles, 1976.

Lichtheim, Miriam. *Ancient Egyptian Literature.* Vol. 2, *The New Kingdom.* Los Angeles, 1983.

Liverani, Mario. *Prestige and Interest: International Relations in the Near East ca. 1600–1100 B.C.* Padua, 1990. A perceptive, wide-ranging comparison of Egypt and the great powers of the Near East, contrasting ideological pronouncements that emphasize the internal prestige of the ruler, with diplomatic correspondence reflecting political and economic interest.

Loprieno, Antonio. *Topos und Mimesis: Zum Ausländer in der ägyptischen Literatur.* Wiesbaden, 1988.

Redford, Donald B. *Egypt, Canaan, and Israel in Ancient Times.* Princeton, 1992. A comprehensive survey of Egypt's interactions with Syria-Palestine, including discussions of the role of Near Easterners in Egypt.

Säve-Söderbergh, Torgny, and Lana Troy. *New Kingdom Pharaonic Sites.* Uppsala, 1991. A thorough report on the excavation of several Nubian cemeteries, important to understanding the acculturation of Lower Nubians in the New Kingdom and the origins and role of the Lower Nubian princes.

Smith, Stuart T. "State and Empire in the Middle and New Kingdoms." *In Anthropological Analysis of Ancient Egypt,* edited by Judy Lustig, pp. 66–89. Sheffield, 1997. Contrasts the economic and social dynamics of Egypt's empire with the portrayal and role of other peoples in Egyptian ideology.

Snowden, Frank. *Before Color Prejudice.* Cambridge, Mass., 1983. Contrasts modern and ancient views of race, arguing that modern color prejudice did not exist in antiquity.

Visweswaran, Kamala. "Race and the Culture of Anthropology." *American Anthropologist* 100 (1998), 70–83.

Vogel, Joseph O., ed. *Encyclopedia of Precolonial Africa.* Walnut Creek, Calif., 1997. Includes numerous surveys of various aspects of northeastern African history and culture, including human origins, pastoralism, rock art, the rise of Neolithic culture, and the origins of the ancient Egyptians. See especially articles by Holl on Pan-Africanism and Afrocentrism, with particular reference to Diop; Ehret on African languages; and Williams, Hassan, Wettestrom, and Fattovich on the origins of Egyptian civilization and its connections to adjacent areas.

STUART TYSON SMITH

RAMESSES I (r. 1315–1314 BCE), first king of the nineteenth dynasty, New Kingdom. Of nonroyal birth, Ramesses was the son of a troop commander named Sety, probably from the eastern part of the Nile Delta. Ramesses first appears in the historical record as general, then vizier, during the reign of the preceding pharaoh, Horemheb. During this period, Ramesses commissioned a statue at Karnak and two sarcophagi, which were later reused for the burial of one of his great-grandsons. Ramesses is probably depicted in the tomb of Horemheb at Memphis, constructed before that pharaoh came to the throne. Sitre, the wife of Ramesses and the mother of his successor, Sety I, was also of nonroyal birth. Ramesses was probably advanced in age at his accession, and he ruled for less than two years. He may actually have served for most of his reign as coruler—first with Horemheb, then with his son, Sety I.

Ramesses I modeled his titulary on that of Ahmose, founder of the eighteenth dynasty, and he clearly intended his rule to mark the beginning of a new dynastic tradition. Inscriptions from his reign testify to the dedication of temples in Nubia and Palestine, as well as building activity throughout Egypt. His most ambitious building project was undertaken at Karnak, where he began work on the second pylon and hypostyle hall. Like most of his other projects, those monuments were completed by, and in the name of, his successors.

Ramesses I was buried in a small tomb in the Valley of the Kings opposite that of Horemheb. His mummy was later removed to the Royal Cache but has not been identified among the bodies from that find. His most well-known monument is the small mortuary chapel erected for him at Abydos by Sety I (now in The Metropolitan Museum of Art in New York).

Ramesses I's major accomplishment was the founding of a vigorous new dynasty, for which he was honored by later generations.

BIBLIOGRAPHY

Kitchen, Kenneth A. *Pharaoh Triumphant: The Life and Times of Ramesses II, King of Egypt.* Warminster, 1982. Includes a popularized account of the family and reign of Ramesses I.

Winlock, Herbert E. *The Temple of Ramesses I at Abydos.* New York, 1937. Publication, translation, and discussion of the mortuary chapel of Ramesses I.

JAMES P. ALLEN

RAMESSES II, king of Egypt for sixty-six years and some months, c.1304–1237 (or 1279–1213) BCE, third ruler of the nineteenth dynasty, New Kingdom. He came from a family of military origin, from the eastern Nile Delta. His father Sety I appointed the young Ramesses as prince-regent (not coregent), with all the attributes of kingship (including a harem), except his own regnal years. Prince Ramesses participated in some of his father's wars (plus a minor Nubian raid of his own) and in the supervision of his father's building works. When he became sole ruler, Ramesses II made his mark in four ways: with his ambitious wars and peace treaty; as an unequalled builder of temples; as a family man; and as an innovator in religious and other spheres. The memory of his reign and deeds also impacted on later epochs.

War and Peace. His first campaign, in the fourth year of his reign, took Ramesses up the coasts of Canaan and Phoenicia, probably to conquer Irqata by siege (Amara West temple scene), then on his return journey, leaving inscriptions at Byblos, Tyre, Adhlun(?), and Nahr el-Kalb. His second campaign in Year 5 was a pincer-movement attack on Kadesh in southern Syria. The king and main army took the inland route, while a support force took the coast route, to rendezvous northwest of Kadesh—just in time to help the king fight his way out of the military trap laid by the Hittite king, Muwatallis II. On the day, Ramesses won, but ultimately Egypt lost, as Kadesh was never regained, and the Egyptian-held, southern Syrian zone of Upe was temporarily lost to the Hittites. In about Year 7, Ramesses invaded north again, in Moab and

Edom (Jordan), before returning north in future campaigns. In Year 8 and 10, Ramesses attacked towns in central Syria, bypassing Kadesh to do so, but these he could not hold against Hittite opposition, so he seems to have given up a futile struggle there. The stela from Beth-Shan (northern Canaan) of Year 18 may reflect a political crisis between Egypt and the Hittites over the custody of the young Hittite king, Urhi-Tesup (Mursil III), who had fled to Egypt some time after being dethroned by Hattusilis III. Yet within three years, facing worse problems with Assyria, Hattusilis was happy to make a peace treaty with Ramesses II (also war-weary) in Year 21. When the alliance matured into friendship, Hattusilis III married off two of his daughters to Ramesses II, the first in Year 34 and the second a decade or so later, with great celebrations and poetical inscriptions. In the meantime, Egyptian physicians served regularly at the Hittite court, attending the Hittite royal family.

To the south, in Nubia, trouble in Irem (a land to the south of the Third Cataract of the Nile and Napata) led to a punitive campaign in about Year 40, conducted by two of Ramesses II's sons, along with Setau, viceroy of Nubia. In Year 44, with the forces available, Setau also conducted a raid into a neighboring oasis, bringing back and enslaving its inhabitants, to build the temple at Wadi es-Sebua. Inscriptions from the western forts of Ramesses II, on his Libyan border, suggest that there may also have been a campaign in that quarter; but no definite facts are reported, still less a plausible date for any such conflict.

Great Builder. Between gateways built in Byblos and Joppa in the Levant and a temple at Napata (Gebel Barkal) in the Sudan, the intervening 1900 kilometers (1,200 miles) have yielded more buildings and monuments of Ramesses II than of any other pharaoh. Preeminent are the eastern Delta capital Piramesse (Khataana-Qantir), a string of forts on Egypt's Libyan borders, major work and several obelisks at Heliopolis, the Great West Hall and minor shrines at Memphis, temples at Herakleopolis and later Antinoe, and an entire memorial temple at Abydos (plus major works in the temples of Sety I and Osiris). At Thebes, he completed the Great Hypostyle Hall in the Karnak temple and added an entire forecourt (with pylon and obelisks) to the Luxor temple. On the western bank of the Nile, he built his own memorial temple, known as the Ramesseum, and the shrine for Queen-mother Tuya, with tombs for her and the queens Nefertari, Istnofret (now lost), Bint-Anath, Meritamun, and Nebt-tawy in the Valley of Queens, as well as his own great tomb and a vast mausoleum for his offspring in the Valley of Kings. In Nubia, the temples at Aksha, Amara West, Beit el-Wali, Gerf Husein, Wadi es-Sebua, Derr, and two at Abu Simbel are all his works. Chronologically, during Years 1–20 of

RAMESSES II. *Statue of Ramesses II, now in the Museo Egizio, Turin.*

his reign, he erected the main buildings at Piramesse, the memorial temple at Abydos, the Karnak Great Hypostyle Hall, the Luxor forecourt, the Ramesseum, the tombs of the king, his offspring, and Queens Tuya and Nefertari, and the temples at Beit el-Wali (regency/Year 1), Aksha, Abu Simbel and the early work at Amara West. Years 21–32 included the Derr temple and other ongoing work (for example, in the Valley of Queens). In Year 33 and onward, he produced the temples at Gerf Husein and Wadi es-Sebua, the jubilee hall at Piramesse, and he added texts to the Luxor obelisks. Most of his other works cannot be dated specifically.

Family Man. From the beginning, Ramesses II had two principal queens, Nefertari and Istnofret, who bore his principal sons and daughters. The two Hittite princesses were added in the thirties and forties of the reign, as were his daughters, the princess-queens Bint-Anath, Merita-mun, Nebt-tawy, and probably Hentmire. His known off-spring number forty-eight or fifty sons and between thirty-eight and fifty-four daughters; these are undoubt-edly minimum figures. Four sons were successively crown prince and heir: Amenhirkhopshef and Ramesses (his two eldest), Khaemwaset (the fourth son), and Merenptah (the thirteenth), his successor. Khaemwaset became a priestly scholar in the temple of Ptah at Memphis, interested in Egypt's past. He "labelled" the pyramids with texts, list-ing offerings in the names of their original owners. From his "excavations," he placed a statue of a fourth dynasty prince in the temple of Ptah. The sixteenth son, Merya-tum, was high priest of Re at Heliopolis. Some of the rest had military or civil administration careers.

Innovator. Ramesses II took the unprecedented step of tunneling a vast mausoleum of offering rooms and burial chambers for many of his sons in the Valley of Kings, ex-tended in direction toward his own tomb, so that father and sons would be close in death as in life. In the Valley of the Queens, he inaugurated a whole set of decorated tombs for his queens (four out of six are known) and queen-mother. In the North, Prince Khaemwaset began a mausoleum of corridors with burial cells for the Apis Bulls, sacred to the god Ptah, which saw extended use for a thousand years thereafter. In art, the celebratory texts and the huge graphic scenes of the Battle of Kadesh form a unique presentation in records of Egyptian warfare. On the literary level, stelae inscribed with poems on his prow-ess had the texts so designed that his royal cartouches formed a zigzag pattern clear to anyone glancing at the text. Mainly in Nubia, he alone made serious use of temples partly built and partly cut into the living rock ("hemi-speos"). There and in Egypt, he promoted royal statue-cults of his kingship to a level far beyond the begin-nings of such usage in the eighteenth dynasty.

Afterglow. Having reigned in much outward splendor for more than sixty years, marked by large and enduring monuments, Ramesses II made a lasting impact on pos-terity. In Egypt, nine later kings adopted his personal name completely (Ramesses III–XI), and two others more briefly (Ramesses-Siptah and Ramesses-Psusennes). More than three centuries after his death, some dignitaries bore a title "King's Son of Ramesses," while several kings of the Libyan dynasties used his prenomen, Usimare. In the fourth century BCE, Theban priests of the god Khons adapted the tradition about Ramesses II's physicians heal-ing people at the Hittite court, and they wove a story, the *Princess of Bakhtan*, about their god's acting similarly at the court of the king of the mysterious land of Bakhtan. In the Roman period, Prince (Setne) Khaemwase became the magician-hero of popular tales. Outside Egypt, the land and town of Rames(s)es appear in the Bible (e.g., *Gn.* 47.11; *Ex.* 1.11; 12.37). The Greek traveler Herodotus (c.450 BCE) knew tales of a Rhampsinitus and saw his buildings at Memphis. Some four centuries later, using writings by Hecataeus and others, Diodorus spoke of the temple, the great statues and the war scenes of the Rames-seum as "the tomb of Ozymandias" (Usimare, the preno-men of Ramesses II); he also knew the name "Remphis." Pliny named "Rhamseseis," and Tacitus mentioned the campaigns of Rhamses. Thus this pharaoh's repute en-dured in shadowy form for more than a millennium, into Roman times, and on into modern knowledge, down to Shelley's poem "Ozymandias" of 1817, written before the discoveries of modern Egyptology. With the 1960s flood-ing of Nubia by the High Dam at Aswan, and the publicity at the time to "save Abu Simbel," the monumental figures of Ramesses II fronting that temple have now become part of the popular images of ancient Egypt, along with the Pyramids, mummies, and the treasures of Tutankh-amun.

[*See also* Battle of Kadesh.]

BIBLIOGRAPHY

Desroches Noblecourt, Christiane. *Ramsès II, la véritable histoire.* Paris, 1996. Recent account of the reign, complementing that of Kitchen (1982), particularly on the Nubian temples.

Edel, Elmar. *Die ägyptisch-hethetische Korrespondenz aus Boghazköi in babylonischer und hethetischer Sprache.* Opladen, 1994. Gives a full edition of the known correspondence in cuneiform between Ramesses II and the Hittites.

Edel, Elmar. *Der Vertrag zwischen Ramses II. von Ägypten und Hattus-ili III. von Hatti.* Berlin, 1997. A virtually definitive, full edition of both the Egyptian and cuneiform versions of the treaty of Ramesses II with Hattusil III, with detailed discussion.

Habachi, Labib. *Features of the Deification of Ramesses II.* Glückstadt, 1969. A good account of the known statue-cults established by Ramesses II, presenting the monumental evidence.

Kitchen, K. A. *Pharaoh Triumphant, The Life and Times of Ramesses II.* Warminster, 1982. A convenient, readable outline of the reign (illustrated), with bibliography.

Kitchen, K. A. *Ramesside Inscriptions Translated & Annotated.* 2 vols. Oxford, 1996 and 1998. A full English translation of most of the royal and official texts from the reign of Ramesses II. Gives basic bibliographies, introductions, and some detailed notes.

Porter, Eliot, and Wilma Stern. *Monuments of Egypt.* Albuquerque, 1990. Color photographs of the monuments of Ramesses II.

KENNETH A. KITCHEN

RAMESSES III (r. 1198–1166 BCE), second king of the twentieth dynasty, New Kingdom. He was the son of King Sethnakht and Queen Tiy-Merenaset. His two main wives, Isis, the daughter of a foreign lady called Hemdjeret, and the other a queen whose name is not known bore him at least ten sons, including the future kings Ramesses IV,

RAMESSES III. *Painting of Ramesses III and Isis, from the tomb of Amunherkhepeshef, a son of Ramesses III, in the Valley of the Queens.* (Courtesy Donald B. Redford)

VI, and VIII. The main historical sources for the reign are the inscriptions of the king's funerary temple at Medinet Habu (in Western Thebes) and the pseudo-autobiographical history of the reign known as Papyrus Harris I.

Until the fifth year of his reign, apart from the pacification of Nubia, Egypt was at peace, allowing the king to establish his power and to start building Medinet Habu (not completed before Year 12). Then, from Year 5 to 11, he fought three attempted invasions of Egypt: in Year 5, the Libu people of Cyrenaica; in Year 8, the Proto-Hellenic Sea Peoples, who had wrought destruction across the Near East; in Year 11, the coalition of Libyan tribes led by the Meshwesh. Whether a Syrian campaign took place before the Libyan is a matter of conjecture. The wars brought Egypt a new prosperity. After the temple estates had been audited in Year 15 by a countrywide inspection, they received workers, cattle, and all kinds of riches. About Year 20, three expeditions brought back myrrh and incense from Punt, copper from the mines of Timna', north of Eilat, and turquoise from Serabit el-Khadim, in

western Sinai. The Timna' expedition included a battle with Edom. New temples were then built throughout the country, the best preserved being the station temple of the king at Karnak and the neighboring Khonsu temple.

On the thirtieth anniversary of his accession to the throne, the king celebrated his *sed*-festival at Memphis. This solemn display of the king's powers was accompanied by some dissatisfaction: in Year 29, the workmen of Deir el-Medina went on strike four times to obtain their monthly wages in grain, which the state's administration, then overworked by the festival's preparation, failed to deliver in time. A year later, a party of high officials, probably prompted by the impending death of the king, plotted with a secondary queen, Tiye, to give the crown to her son Pentaweret instead of to the legitimate heir, Prince Ramesses (the future Ramesses IV). The view that the king fell victim to this "harem conspiracy" remains unsubstantiated. Nevertheless, the conspirators were exposed and about forty people were put to death, revealing a division between the dynasty and the governing class, ominous for any future power. Ramesses IV's idea, to publish at his father's death an apologetical account of that reign (the Papyrus Harris I), was hence obviously calculated to inspire his subjects' gratitude to the dynasty, and to turn that gratitude into loyalty toward himself.

Ramesses III was buried in his tomb in the Valley of the Kings, although his mummy would be discovered in the Deir el-Bahri cache. As none of his eight successors, Ramesses IV to XI, achieved anything memorable, he is justly considered the last significant king of the New Kingdom.

BIBLIOGRAPHY

Edgerton, William F., and John A. Wilson. *Historical Records of Ramses III, The Texts in* Medinet Habu *Volumes I and II.* Studies in Ancient Oriental Civilization, 12. Chicago, 1936. An excellent translation of the historical inscriptions of the Medinet Habu temple.

Grandet, Pierre. *Ramsès III, Histoire d'un règne.* Paris, 1993. A history of the reign, with all necessary references to other literature.

Grandet, Pierre. *Le Papyrus Harris I (BM 9999). Traduction et commentaire.* Bibliothèque d'étude, 109. Cairo, 1994. An annotated translation of one of the main historical sources for the reign.

Kitchen, Kenneth A. *Ramesside Inscriptions: Historical and Biographical,* vol. 5. Oxford, 1983. Addenda in vol. 7. Oxford, 1989. A collection of all the sources for the reign (except Papyrus Harris I) in their original hieroglyphic script.

Kitchen, Kenneth A. *Ramesside Inscriptions: Translated and Annotated,* vol. 5. Oxford, forthcoming. An annotated translation of all the sources for the reign.

Peden, Alexander J. *Egyptian Historical Inscriptions of the Twentieth Dynasty.* Documenta Mundi. Ægyptiaca, 3. Jonsered, 1994. An anthology of various sources on the twentieth dynasty.

PIERRE GRANDET

RAMESSES IV (r. 1166–1160 BCE), third king of the twentieth dynasty, New Kingdom. This Ramessid king was probably the eldest surviving son of Ramesses III by one of his principal spouses, Isis-Tahemdjert. Following the death of his father Ramesses III (who perhaps succumbed to an assassination plot at Thebes), Ramesses IV succeeded him as pharaoh and immediately began a building program. Major quarrying and mining expeditions were sent to the Wadi Hammamat in the Eastern Desert for prized building stone, and to Serabit el-Khadim and Timna in the Sinai Peninsula for turquoise and copper. Ventures to exploit the natural resources outside of the Nile Valley were matched by a vigorous building program within Egypt proper; the king's ambitions, however, were thwarted by the brevity of his reign. While it is clear that he hoped to erect large monuments of his own, for the most part Ramesses IV left only his names and titles (at a considerable number of sites) in brief wall texts, on statues, and on other small objects. His tally of substantial monuments is meager; the most notable is a planned vast memorial temple on the western bank at Thebes. Among

those that do exist are two great stelae from Abydos that may reveal the king's theological attitudes. An Egyptian presence was maintained in Nubia and the southern Levant under the fourth Ramesses, but there is no firm evidence of large-scale military conflict at that time. Ramesses IV died (apparently from natural causes) in the seventh year of his reign, at some fifty years of age. Ramesses IV was buried at Western Thebes in a small but splendidly decorated tomb near the modern entrance to the Valley of the Kings. He left a son who became Ramesses V.

BIBLIOGRAPHY

Haring, A. *Bibliotheca Orientalis* 54 (1997), col. 632.

Helck, W. "Ramses IV." In *Lexikon der Ägyptologie,* 5: 120–123. Wiesbaden, 1983. An excellent survey of the reign [in German] with detailed references to the main historical documents and sources.

Keller, C. A. "Speculations Concerning Interconnections between the Royal Policy and Reputation of Ramesses IV." In *For His Ka: Essays Offered in Memory of Klaus Baer,* edited by D. P. Silverman, pp. 145–157. Chicago, 1994.

Peden, A. J. *The Reign of Ramesses IV.* Warminster, 1994. A concise and convenient review of this reign with modern English translations of some of the key historical texts of the period.

Vandersleyen, C. *L'Égypte et la vallée du Nil. Tome II: De la fin de l'Ancien Empire à la fin du Nouvel Empire,* pp. 619–626. Paris, 1995. A very reliable and up-to-date account (in French) of Ramesses IV's Egypt.

ALEX J. PEDEN

RAMESSES VI (r. 1156–1149 BCE), fifth king of the twentieth dynasty, New Kingdom. Probably a son of Ramesses III, this king was buried in the Valley of the Kings at Thebes (tomb 9), which appears to have been begun under Ramesses V, who probably occupied the same tomb. It was apparently robbed within twenty years of the death of Ramesses VI, if it is correct that the robbery of a royal tomb described in Papyrus Mayer B refers to it. In any event, the construction of the tomb was responsible for the preservation of the tomb of Tutankhamun (tomb 62), the entrance of which was hidden by the construction of huts for the workmen of tomb 9.

Under Ramesses VI, Egypt still had some influence on, or connections with, the outer reaches of its empire; a statue base of Ramesses VI is known from Megiddo in Palestine, and the king's cartouches are known from the area of the Third Cataract of the Nile in Nubia. Ramesses VI appears to have been the last New Kingdom pharaoh under whom copper-mining expeditions were sent to the Sinai.

Ramesses VI is otherwise known from the tomb of his mother, Isis, who was buried in tomb 51 of the Valley of the Queens. He is also attested on a number of statues and minor inscriptions in Karnak, Coptos, and Bubastis.

BIBLIOGRAPHY

Dodson, A. "The Sons of Ramesses III." *KMT. A Modern Journal of Ancient Egypt* 8.1 (1997), 29–43.

Kitchen, K. A. "Ramses V–XI." In *Lexikon der Ägyptologie*, 5.1: 124–128. Wiesbaden, 1983.

STEVE VINSON

Vandersleyen, C. *L'Égypte et la vallée du Nil.* Vol. 2, *De la fin de l'Ancien Empire à la fin du Nouvel Empire.* Paris, 1995. An instructive and up-to-date survey of Ramesses IX's regime and its troubles, pp. 636–642.

ALEX J. PEDEN

RAMESSES IX (r. 1139–1120 BCE), eighth king of the twentieth dynasty, New Kingdom. The highest attested date for Ramesses IX is regnal Year 19. His family background and parentage are uncertain, but he appears to have been a grandson of Ramesses III and to have ascended the throne after his father (probably a junior son of Ramesses III) predeceased him and after his putative uncle, Ramesses VIII, died without surviving male issue. His reign was overshadowed by political, social, and economic problems; most notable among these were the growing powers of the high priests of Amun at Thebes, the movements of hostile Libyan tribesmen or mercenaries through the Western Desert, and soaring grain prices (at least in Thebes). The last mentioned seems to have encouraged large-scale looting in the Theban necropolis. Most of the crucial evidence for these troubles comes not from Ramesses IX's surviving building works (which are scarce for a reign of almost two decades, indicating a deterioration of royal finances), but from a number of administrative papyri. Despite these distressing conditions, however, there was gold prospecting in the Eastern Desert, mining for galena, and even a minor police action against troublesome desert tribesmen. Outside the Nile Valley, all remaining Egyptian garrisons in the Levant had almost certainly been withdrawn by the era of Ramesses IX, but an Egyptian presence was still maintained in Nubia. At his death, Ramesses IX was interred in a hastily completed tomb in the Valley of the Kings at Western Thebes. He was probably the last New Kingdom pharaoh to establish a Theban memorial temple (Helck, 1961). His successor, Ramesses X, may have been his eldest surviving son, although this remains conjectural.

BIBLIOGRAPHY

Dodson, A. "The Sons of Rameses III." *KMT. A Modern Journal of Ancient Egypt* 8.1 (1997), 29–43. A useful outline (with references) of the latest research into the family background of Ramesses III and his successors, including Ramesses IX.

Helck, W. *Materialien zur Wirtschaftsgeschichte des Neuen Reiches.* Wiesbaden, 1961. See part 1, p. 115.

Kitchen, K. A. "Family Relationships of Ramesses IX and the Late Twentieth Dynasty." *Studien zur Altägyptischen Kultur* 11 (1984), 127–134.

Kitchen, K. A. "Ramses V–XI." In *Lexikon der Ägyptologie*, 5.1: 124–128. Wiesbaden, 1983. Includes a detailed summary of the known historical facts of Ramesses IX's reign by a leading authority on the Ramessids.

RAMESSES XI (r. 1111–1081 BCE), tenth king of the twentieth dynasty, New Kingdom. This pharaoh had the prenomen Menmare-Setepenre, and the nomen Khaemwaset-Ramesses. His highest documented regnal Year is 27 (on an Abydos votive stela), but he is generally thought to have ruled for twenty-nine years. His familial relationship with the preceding members of the twentieth dynasty, if any, remains uncertain. In many ways he ushered in the Third Intermediate Period.

His reign was marked by considerable disarray, much of which had its origins in previous reigns. To restore order, Ramesses XI was compelled to appoint a number of powerful individuals, who eventually overshadowed him. The Theban region appears to have become particularly unsafe as a result of civil unrest and constant incursions of marauding Libyans. Early in his rule, the high priest of Amun at Thebes, Amenhotep, was apparently suppressed, presumably during the turmoil later remembered as the "Year of the Hyenas." In response to this state of affairs, the viceroy of Nubia, Panehsy, was given additional powers over all of Upper Egypt, but he apparently overstepped his authority.

This situation prevailed until Ramesses XI's year 19, when the "Renaissance" (*wḥm-mśwt*, literally, "repeating-of-births") was instituted. Herihor, a military leader, replaced Panehsy in Upper Egypt and Nubia, while Smendes, perhaps Herihor's eldest son, ruled on Ramesses XI's behalf in the North at Tanis. In addition to his military responsibilities, Herihor assumed the title "High Priest of Amun." The circumstances behind this change in leadership are unknown, but it probably reflects the continuing weakness of Ramesses XI's rule. Henceforth, most official documents were dated according to the Renaissance rather than by Ramesses XI's regnal year. Now largely a figurehead, Ramesses XI resided rather than ruled at Memphis, performing largely ceremonial functions, such as the burial of the Apis bull.

The division of power between Herihor (as High Priest of Amun and military leader in the South) and Smendes (who was effectively the ruler of the North) set the pattern for Egypt's governance, which was to carry over into the early part of the Third Intermediate Period, following Ramesses XI's death. In the first two years of the Renaissance, the people who had robbed the Theban temples and royal tombs were tried and, in several instances, executed. Herihor may even have acted briefly as king or

Ramesses XI's coregent at Thebes, a kingship attested only within the Khonsu Temple at Karnak. After Herihor's death, sometime in the sixth or seventh year of the Renaissance, scribes continued to date according to the Renaissance, probably until the end of Ramesses XI's reign.

BIBLIOGRAPHY

Beckerath, J. von. "Zur Chronologie der XXI. Dynastie." In *Gedenkschrift für Winfried Barta*, edited by D. Kessler and R. Schulz, pp. 49–55. Frankfurt, 1995. A detailed refutation of key aspects of Jansen-Winkeln's proposals for a revision of late twentieth dynasty history.

Černý, J. "Egypt: From the Death of Ramesses III to the End of the Twenty-first Dynasty." In *Cambridge Ancient History*, vol. 2, pp. 606–657. 3rd edn. Cambridge, 1975. Somewhat out of date, but reliable on most of its major points.

Goelet, O. "A New 'Robbery' Papyrus. Rochester MAG 51.346.1." *Journal of Egyptian Archaeology* 82 (1996), 107–127. Publication of a recent papyrus that reveals thefts at the Karnak temple, which probably would have led to the discrediting of the Theban hierarchy and the subsequent installation of Herihor at the beginning of the "Renaissance."

Jansen-Winkeln, K. "Das Ende des Neuen Reiches." *Zeitschrift für Ägyptische Sprache und Altertumskunde* 119 (1992), 22–37. A detailed but controversial study of the events and personalities at the end of the twentieth dynasty.

Kitchen, K. A. *The Third Intermediate Period in Egypt (1100–650 BC)*. 2d ed. Warminster, 1995. Recently updated, and by far the most comprehensive and accurate source for the history, genealogies, and dating systems of the late twentieth dynasty.

OGDEN GOELET

RAMESSES–HATTUSILIS CORRESPONDENCE.

With the exception of three interesting but relatively uninformative letters from the Tell el-Amarna archive, nearly all the extant correspondence between the Hittite and Egyptian royal courts consists of cuneiform letters found at the capital of Hattusas (modern Bogazköy), dating to the reigns of Hattusilis III and Ramesses II. Approximately a hundred letters have been found, some of them quite fragmentary. Nearly all these letters are written in a dialect of the "diplomatic" Akkadian cuneiform that had become the language of international relations in the Bronze Age. Although the archive overwhelmingly represents the point of view of the Hittite recipients, the Bogazköy material also preserves a few preliminary draft letters in Hittite, which presumably were later translated into Akkadian before transmission to the Egyptian court. Since the Ramessid capital at Qantir is in a poor state of preservation, it seems unlikely that this site will yield any Egyptian communications.

Not only did the two monarchs write each other, occasionally their wives and other family members exchanged letters as well. The topics of this correspondence are wide-ranging: the exchange of gifts, marriage arrangements, medical problems, treaty negotiations, and perhaps even a proposed visit of Hattusilis to Egypt. The epistolography reflects the stilted diplomatic language of the times: after effusive greetings, the writer inquires after the health of the king and his family, his houses, chariots, and even horses. A major concern throughout is the exchange of gifts, a critical affirmation of friendship in the diplomatic practice of that era.

Although they are not letters *sensu stricto*, perhaps the most important of these documents are three copies in Akkadian of the Hittite version of the treaty of Ramesses' regnal Year 21, all of which differ in several aspects from the hieroglyphic version in the Karnak temple. When supplemented by a number of letters concerned with the drafting of the final versions of the pact on silver tablets, these copies reveal a great deal about the international relations and negotiations leading to this pivotal event.

Urhi-teshub, Hattusilis's half-brother, whom he had managed to depose, is the subject of several of these letters, most of which were written while he was an exile in Egypt. As a claimant to the throne, Urhi-teshub remained a potentially unsettling factor in Egyptian-Hittite relations until the treaty had been concluded. By the time of the marriage correspondence some thirteen years later, the Urhi-teshub problem had apparently been defused.

The later group of letters is concerned with the marriage of a Hittite princess to Ramesses, doubtless as a means of cementing the treaty ties between the two royal houses. In this correspondence especially, Pudukhepa, the Hittite queen, wields such remarkable influence that during the marriage negotiations Ramesses would sometimes send parallel letters both to her and to Hattusilis, addressing her as "sister."

BIBLIOGRAPHY

Beckman, G. *Hittite Diplomatic Texts*, edited by H. A. Hofner, Jr. SBL Writings from the Ancient World, Series 7. Atlanta, Ga., 1996. Contains a good selection from Hittite treaties and diplomatic correspondence, not only with Egypt but also with other contemporary countries.

Edel, E. *Die ägyptisch-hethitische Korrespondenz aus Boghazköi in babylonischer und hethitischer Sprache*. Vol. 1, *Umschriften und Übersetzungen*; vol. 2, *Kommentar*. Abhandlungen der Rheinsch-Westfälischen Akademie der Wissenschaften, 77. Opladen, 1994. Now the fundamental study of the Ramesses–Hattusilis correspondence; contains copies of the cuneiform tablets, transcriptions, translations, and extensive commentaries of the documents.

Goetze, A. "The Struggle for the Domination of Syria (1400–1300 B.C.)." In *The Cambridge Ancient History*, vol. 2, part 2, pp. 1–20. Cambridge, 1975. A good description of the history and society of the Hittite Empire for this period.

Murnane, W. J. *The Road to Kadesh: A Historical Interpretation of the Battle Reliefs of King Sety I at Karnak*. 2d ed. Chicago, 1990. A wide-ranging study, primarily concerned with the Amarna correspondence, which also describes the diplomatic and military background of the ancient Near East leading up to the battle of Kadesh.

OGDEN GOELET

RE AND RE-HORAKHTY. Re is the sun god. His Egyptian name, *r'*, is usually written with the sun disk. He is often called "Re-Horakhty" ("Re [is] Horus of the Horizon"); this should be understood as a surname describing the character of the god. Re was the most important god of the Egyptian pantheon because he created the world. The awe of him was based on the fact that the cosmic dimension of the sun surpasses the comprehension of man. An Old Kingdom text describes him as "glorious, shining, besouled, strong, mighty, far-reaching, far-striding."

For the Egyptians, the course of the sun was the measurement of time. After its nightly absence, it rose again on the horizon with absolute regularity. The rising sun was the symbol for the creation of the world, and the daily course of the sun the symbol of the world's cyclical renewal; hence the paramount importance of Re as creator and master of life.

The second factor in Re's importance was his unbreakable link with the king. The master of earth and the master of the universe were of the same nature; one was a mirror image of the other. In ancient Egypt, theology and political theory were interdependent: the figure of the king was always the center of attention, and the status of a god or of a mortal was measured by his or her proximity to the king.

The sun god is an interesting case in the history of religion because he is absent from the early historical sources. Between the late second dynasty and the fifth, we can observe the way his image developed as an analogy of that of the king. From the beginning, the king appeared as a god and a human at once. His divine aspect was embodied in a falcon named Horus. In the fourth dynasty the reigning king was called "the son of Re," thus defining the relationship between pharoah and sun god. A relationship was also established between the royal falcon and Re, by uniting both in the symbol of the winged sun disk, an image that remained a constant in temples and religious monuments as the omnipresent complement of the king, until the end of Egyptian history. The earliest depictions of the sun god as a man with a falcon's head and with a sun disk are preserved in the royal pyramid temples.

The kings of the fifth dynasty erected solar temples next to their pyramids in the necropolis of Abusir, and these structures differ from other temples of the time in that they feature a large, open courtyard at the center of which rises an obelisk on top of a tall pedestal; in front of this is a large offering altar. Unlike other deities, Re never has a sanctuary with a cult statue; his image is the sun itself, which rises daily over the tip of the obelisk. The pyramidion and several types of pillars also appear as symbols of Re. The most significant solar temple, that at

Heliopolis (now completely destroyed), was probably erected during this period. The hieroglyph for that city's Egyptian name, Iwn, contains a pillar resembling an obelisk.

The most important early source for the sun god is the Pyramid Texts of the Old Kingdom, a collection of spells describing the fate of the deceased king in the underworld which are carved on the walls of royal tombs of the late fifth and sixth dynasties. The protagonist is once again the king, who in death has become one with his heavenly father, Re. The texts witness a highly developed theology. The sun god is not a clearly defined individual, but instead has several names and images. His multiplicity is a reflection of his many capabilities. The Pyramid Texts describe Re as the sun that rises on the eastern horizon in the morning in the shape of a scarab beetle whose name is Khepri ("the Emerging One"). The scarab in his bark is lifted by the personified primordial waters, or Nun. During the day Re traverses the sky in the bark, accompanied by a large entourage of gods; at sunset he becomes Atum, the "All-Lord." No one can halt his course. Every evening he is swallowed by the sky goddess Nut, who gives birth to him anew each morning, and thus the cycle continues. Crowns and the throne associate Re with kingship.

Creative force is the sun god's central characteristic. Although the Pyramid Texts do not relate extensive myths, they contain mythic elements, referring to the creation of the world. In the beginning there was Re under his name Atum, who came into being. He rose in the shape of a *benben* stone, or obelisk-like pillar, in the temple of the Benu-Phoenix in Heliopolis, city of the pillar. Then he spit forth Shu and Tefnut, the first divine couple, personifying air and moisture. They begot Geb and Nut (earth and sky), and the latter in turn bore two divine couples—Osiris and Isis, and Seth and Nephthys. This completed the Ennead of gods, and the world was able to function.

Re, as creator, is in dialogue with his opposite, death, from the very beginning. In the Pyramid Texts we read that death is not the end of life, but rather its original source. Death is personified by Osiris who is murdered by his brother, Seth, and subsequently resurrected by Re to rule over the dead. The link between Re and Osiris is the deceased king who, in the afterlife identifies with both gods. Unlike most other deities, Re does not have a family; however, he has his eye, the sun disk, to give birth to other creatures. These offspring include (among others) his son, the king, and the goddess Hathor, who embodies the feminine creative principle, giving birth to her creatures and nourishing them with milk; as a sign of her connection with Re, she bears the sun disk on her head. Re's closest ally is the goddess Maat, the embodiment of order and truth; she represents the unimpeachable principle of his rule.

RE AND RE-HORAKHTY. *Funerary stela of the priest Diefankh on the right and Re on the left, mummiform and with the sun disk and uraeus-serpent on his head, holding a scepter.* Diefankh raises his arms in adoration, and between the two figures is an offering stand with a lotus. This plastered and painted wood stela is from the Ramesseum at Thebes and dates from the twenty-second or twenty-third dynasty. (University of Pennsylvania Museum, Philadelphia. Neg. # S8–73219)

In the Middle Kingdom we encounter a new image of Re. Several hymns to the sun god tell how he created the world solely for humankind. Human beings are made in his image, and he provides them with everything they need for life. Evil, however, does not come from the god but from mortals' own rebellious hearts, and for this they are judged in the underworld. With his rays, which penetrate each body, Re supervises and controls human beings, rewarding the obedient and destroying the disobedient. On earth, the king does this in his stead.

The relationship between Re and Osiris is newly defined at this time. All mortals now change into Osiris in death, a concept already discernible by the end of the Old Kingdom. Re gives Osiris his power by bestowing on him his crown, and he also guards him while he travels through the underworld at night. The phase of the daily rebirth of the sun in the form of a scarab is now symbolized by an amulet in that form, which soon becomes the most popular and widespread symbol of good fortune. In an expanded political theology, the names of several other deities with roles as creator or ruler are combined with that of Re, especially as Amun-Re; in this composite form, Re expands his own potential through the incorporation of other deities into his own being.

Re worship reaches its height in the New Kingdom. The walls of its royal tombs are decorated with images of the Underworld Books which describe the nightly journey of the sun. The nocturnal Re in his bark is depicted as a human with a ram's head. In the fifth hour, the god is united with his corpse, which at this time is Osiris. This is the moment when the sun suffers death, which at the same time generates new life. In the sixth hour, Apophis, a serpent embodying evil, is killed. Then in the twelfth hour, Re is newly born as a scarab. Among the new texts is The Litany of Re, which describes how the king identifies with the seventy-five nocturnal figures of Re, and how Re and Osiris become one in the depth of night.

In the tombs of officials, Re appears in very different form. At the entrance are inscriptions of the solar hymns describing Re's creation deeds. The deceased wants to be free to leave the tomb during the day to see the sun, for gazing on Re will rejuvenate him daily through eternity. However, there is also a perception that the sun god could destroy his creation at the end of eternity; this aspect adds a philosophical dimension to the theology.

Papyri recounting Re myths exist primarily from the New Kingdom. They focus on two themes. In one, Re becomes elderly and tired, and therefore organizes the world in a way that it no longer requires his personal intervention; he transfers his power to Horus or to the king. In the other, Re conceives the heir to the throne as his physical son.

Some New Kingdom temples feature an open courtyard with an altar to Re. There a specific sun cult was celebrated: at the turn of each hour, a priest—ideally, the king—recited one of twelve poetic hymns predicting the victorious course of the sun. On the temple walls, the newborn sun is now sometimes depicted as a crouching infant, and the adult sun god in human form. In the time of Amenhotpe III, the reigning king is not merely the son of Re, but identifies so strongly with Re that he calls himself "the dazzling sun." Amenhotpe IV, also called Akhenaten, even instituted a monotheistic religion centered on the sun. He declared the physical embodiment of the sun, the solar disk or Aten, to be the only existing god. After Akhenaten's death, his idea was abandoned, and the theologians restored the traditional beliefs. Thereafter, however, Amun-Re was a "universal god," all-encompassing, who maintained life for sky, earth, gods, and humans.

From the end of the New Kingdom, the royal Underworld Books were democratized, and excerpts appear as late as the early Ptolemaic period in tombs, on papyri, and on sarcophagi. Now anyone could take the journey in Re's nocturnal bark. In addition, a new image of the king emerges: on painted coffins of the Third Intermediate Period, Re-Horakhty-Atum appears in the mummiform shape of Osiris, and the owner of the tomb worships him as the ruler of the underworld. This is the merger of Re and Osiris recognized by ordinary mortals; in the royal funerary belief it had already been accomplished in the New Kingdom in a mummiform image of the god with a ram's head. The magical-mythical papyri, intended to protect both living and dead, rely heavily on solar symbolism: they often depict the sun's course in a single image that combines the travel of Re by day and by night, with his rebirth in the morning. Thus the believers ensure their own regeneration. The Litany of Re is further developed by adding new, often grotesque figures to the existing figures of Re. Also new are lists describing the twelve images of Re for the hours of the day.

Among the amulets placed on the mummy to protect the dead, we now find several solar symbols: the sun-in-the-horizon, the sun disk, the celestial bark, the double lion, and the obelisk. The Egyptians also used the hypocephalus, a disk depicting Re's nocturnal form with four ram's heads. Taking many shapes and possessing several heads increased the power of the god. Eventually, however, Re became less important over the course of the first millennium, as the kingship was weakened under a succession of foreign rulers.

Even in the Greco-Roman period, however, new magical-mythical papyri were created, offering a new interpretation of the sun's path. The *Book of Faiyum* tells how Re enters the body of Sobek, the crocodile god, and swims across the Faiyum lake during the twelve hours of the night. In the magical texts, Re continues to be the highest power, upon whom a magician may call if he proves the depth of his knowledge. Hence, the listing of the twelve manifestations of the diurnal sun plays an important role, as does the list of the figures that issued from Re during the act of creation as Khepri, the morning sun.

Re played a dominant role in the large Horus temple at Edfu because he was identified with Horus of Edfu and with his main symbol, the winged sun. On the ceiling of a chapel are depicted the twelve figures of Re as diurnal sun and, as a new aspect, the fourteen *ka*-powers of Re. The sun god is even the protagonist of a dramatic tale about the victory of the winged sun over the enemies of creation. However, since the kings of the Greco-Roman period were foreigners, the theology of Re had become a purely academic pursuit, limited to priests and no longer part of the living faith of the people.

[*See also* Hymns, *article on* Solar Hymns; *and* Myths, *article on the* Solar Cycle.]

BIBLIOGRAPHY

Assmann, Jan. *Ägyptische Hymnen und Gebete.* Zurich and Munich, 1975. The great majority of the approximately 250 hymns collected, edited, and interpreted by the author over more than two decades are dedicated to the sun god. An indispensable sourcebook.

Assmann, Jan. *Egyptian Solar Religion in the New Kingdom: Re, Amun and the Crisis of Polytheism.* Translated by A. Alcock. London, 1995. The development of the solar theology through the New Kingdom, discussing the growing tension between traditional polytheism and the concept of Re as the unique, one and only, or universal god. The chief sources are the numerous solar hymns collected by the author in the Theban private tombs.

Faulkner, Raymond O. *The Ancient Egyptian Pyramid Texts Translated into English.* Warminster, 1969.

Faulkner, Raymond O. *The Ancient Egyptian Coffin Texts.* 3 vols. Warminster, 1973–1978. Excellent translations of two of the most difficult text corpora, making them accessible to those interested in the history of religion, with indexes of divinities, localities, etc.

Faulkner, Raymond O. *The Ancient Egyptian Book of the Dead.* Edited by Carol Andrews. Rev. ed. London, 1985. With a glossary and very fine illustrations from the best *Book of the Dead* papyri in the British Museum, though without index.

Habachi, Labib. *The Obelisks of Egypt: Skyscrapers of the Past.* Cairo, 1984. The meaning and the production of obelisks, with a description of extant temple obelisks.

Hornung, Erik. *Conceptions of God in Ancient Egypt: The One and the Many.* Translated by John Baines. Ithaca, 1982. Darmstadt, 1971. Describes the fundamental concepts of Egyptian religious thinking, some of them pertaining to the complex aspects of the sun god.

Hornung, Erik. *Die Unterweltsbücher der Ägypter.* New ed. Zurich and Munich, 1992. Complete translation of all the royal books or guides to the underworld from the New Kingdom, describing the journey of the sun god through the twelve hours of the night. The illustrations that are an integral part of these compositions are reproduced in line drawings, the introduction giving a summary of the contents.

Hornung, Erik. *Valley of the Kings: Horizon of Eternity.* Translated by D. Warburton. New York, 1990. A collection of texts and pictures pertaining to the sun god as found in the royal tombs of the New Kingdom. The author explains the main concepts in a systematic order, elucidating the often strange mode of Egyptian expression.

Kozloff, Arielle P., and Betsy M. Bryan, with Lawrence M. Berman. *Egypt's Dazzling Sun: Amenhotep III and His World.* Cleveland, 1992. The relation of this king with the sun god, the new and imaginative ways of identification with his divine partner, are a major theme.

Lichtheim, Miriam. *Ancient Egyptian Literature.* Vol. 1, *The Old and Middle Kingdoms.* Berkeley and Los Angeles, 1973. Translations of the key sources of the Middle Kingdom: king Wahankh Intef II's hymns to Re and Hathor, the hymn to the sun god in the *Instructions for Merykare,* the hymn to Amenemhat III on the stela of Sehetep-ib-re, the building inscription of Senwosret I from his temple at Heliopolis, and the tale of *The Birth of the Royal Children.*

Lichtheim, Miriam. *Ancient Egyptian Literature.* Vol. 2, *The New Kingdom.* Berkeley and Los Angeles, 1976. Contains the main mythological texts relating to the sun god: *The Destruction of Mankind, The Two Brothers,* Horus and *Seth.*

Quirke, Stephen. *Ancient Egyptian Religion.* London, 1992. A brief history of Re's career from the second dynasty to Roman times, mentioning all the important textual and iconographical sources; a sober, clear interpretation.

MAYA MÜLLER

REBIRTH. *See* Afterlife.

REDISTRIBUTION. *See* Economy.

REFERENCE WORKS. Although the comprehensive study of all civilizations is formidable because it involves familiarity with so many areas—history, art, language, religion, economy, and many other aspects of culture and society—scholars of antiquity encounter an especially daunting obstacle in the incomplete and equivocal nature of what exists. Spotty and ambiguous documentation is part of a larger and ironic problem that particularly besets Egyptology: although ancient Egypt lasted a very long time and produced countless material remains, no one can hope to understand all aspects of its culture and history, because the data for all their abundance are inadequate and perplexing. Nonetheless, with the exception of classical studies, Egyptology has a richer variety of reference works and research tools than any other study of ancient cultures. Furthermore, with the proliferation of computer-based technology, access to that information has never been easier.

Almost from the beginning, Egyptology has witnessed a passion for meticulous documentation. Not long after the discovery of the Rosetta Stone in July 1799, Napoleon Bonaparte dispatched a scientific expedition to record the topography, flora, fauna, and antiquities of Egypt. Published over two decades, the nineteen-volume report was the first reference work—*Description de l'Égypte ou Recueil des observations et des recherches qui ont été faites en Égypte pendant l'expédition de l'armée française, publié par les ordres de Sa Majesté l'empereur Napoléon le Grand* (Paris, 1809–1828). Not to be outdone, a German scientific team produced an even greater report in a mere ten years and in only twelve volumes—Karl Richard Lepsius, *Denkmäler aus Aegypten und Aethiopen nach den Zeichnungen der von Seiner Majestät dem Könige von Preussen Friedrich Wilhelm IV, nach diesen Ländern gesendeten und in den Jahren 1842–1845 ausgeführten wissenschaftlichen Expedition auf Befehl Seiner Majestät* (Berlin, 1849–1859). The scholarly range and the elephant-folio format of both the French and the German tomes make them works of massive intellectual and physical proportions.

Newer publications are decidedly smaller but are available much more quickly. Because of the computer and computer-based hieroglyphic fonts, publication costs (but not retail prices) and production time have declined remarkably. Ironically, however, in proportion to the vast Egyptological literature, few comprehensive reference works exist. Therefore, it is necessary to consult either specialized or general studies to conduct research on most topics. Those two contrary distinctions recur in the list below. Furthermore, any enumeration of research volumes is selective and subjective. The following bibliography has curious inclusions and, no doubt, egregious omissions; at least, it provides a basis for improvement.

General

Atiya, Aziz S., ed. *The Coptic Encyclopedia.* 8 vols. New York, 1991. Extensive but uneven documentation of all aspects of the Copts, ancient and modern.

Beinlich-Seeber, Christine. *Bibliographie Altägypten, 1822–1946.* 3 vols. Ägyptologische Abhandlungen, 61. Wiesbaden, 1998. A superbly cross-indexed resource for all earlier Egyptological publications, beginning with the first years. To be used with the two works by Ida Pratt (1925, 1942) and the *Annual Egyptological Bibliography.*

Bratton, Fred G. *A History of Egyptian Archaeology.* New York, 1968.

Dawson, Warren R., and Eric P. Uphill. *Who Was Who in Egyptology.* 3d ed., revised by Morris L. Bierbrier. London, 1995. Capsule biographies and bibliographies for deceased Egyptologists and many other persons connected (often peripherally) to Egyptology.

Deutsche Orient-Gesellschaft Mitgliederverzeichnis. Addresses of German Egyptologists and other scholars of the ancient Near East.

Donadoni, Sergio, et al. *Egypt from Myth to Egyptology.* Milan, 1990. Popular and well-illustrated history of Egyptology, particularly in Italy.

Helck, H. Wolfgang, et al., eds. *Lexikon der Ägyptologie.* 7 vols. Wiesbaden, 1975–1992. As the monumental Pauly-Wissowa-Kroll, *Realencyclopädie der classischen Altertumswissenschaft* is the standard reference work for all aspects of classical studies, the *LÄ,* although of much smaller scope, is the most comprehensive resource for Egyptology. Articles in German, French, and English.

Informationsblatt der deutschsprachigen Ägyptologie. 1971–. Addresses of all Egyptological faculty and students in Germany, Austria, and parts of Switzerland; lists of M. A., Ph.D., and *Habilitationen* topics; news of lectures and courses; information about museum permanent collections and temporary exhibitions; news from special research institutions (such as the Berlin *Wörterbuch* project, the German Archaeological Institute in Cairo) and from lesser-known collections.

Informatique et Egyptologie. Paris, 1988–. Egyptology and computers.

Janssen, J. M. A., et al., eds. *Annual Egyptological Bibliography.* Leiden, 1948–. The standard reference work for all Egyptological literature as of 1948.

Newsletter of the International Association for Coptic Studies. Rome, 1977–. Addresses of members; lists of current doctoral dissertations, recent publications, works in progress; information about museum permanent collections and temporary exhibitions.

Newsletter of the International Assocation of Egyptologists. Hildesheim, 1981–. Addresses of museums and other collections; information about temporary exhibitions.

Pratt, Ida A. *Ancient Egypt: Sources of Information in the New York Public Library.* New York, 1925. *Ancient Egypt: 1925–1941.* New York, 1942. Until the publication of Christine Beinlich-Seeber's three volumes, this was the essential work for publications that antedate coverage by the *Annual Egyptological Bibliography.*

Putnam, James. *Egyptology: An Introduction to the History, Art, and Culture of Ancient Egypt.* London, 1990. An excellent guide.

Säve-Söderbergh, Torgny. *Pharaohs and Mortals.* Translated by Richard E. Oldenburg. Indianapolis, 1961. Useful history of Egyptology, primarily in Europe.

Sasson, Jack, ed. *Civilizations of the Ancient Near East.* 4 vols. New York, 1995. Contains many useful entries on ancient Egypt.

Thomas, Nancy, ed. *The American Discovery of Ancient Egypt.* 2 vols. Los Angeles and New York, 1996. Consisting of an exhibition catalog and a separate volume of essays, this work provides an in-depth discussion of the emergence of Egyptology in the United States, as illustrated by important objects in American museums.

Wilson, John A. *The Culture of Ancient Egypt.* Chicago, 1956. First published in 1951 as *The Burden of Egypt,* this essay is a dated but still very useful introduction.

Wilson, John A. *Signs and Wonders upon Pharaoh: A History of American Egyptology.* Chicago, 1964. Should be read with Thomas (1996).

Wortham, John D. *British Egyptology.* Newton Abbot, England, 1971.

Archaeology

Archéologia. A popular-format French magazine, with excellent coverage of excavations in Egypt as well as news from European museums and universities.

Bard, Kathryn, ed. *Encyclopedia of the Archaeology of Ancient Egypt.* New York, 1999.

Bolletino d'Informazioni. Serie Archeologica, Istituto Italiano di Cultura del Cairo. Cairo, 1964–1979. Apparently defunct, this publication is a valuable record of past activity of all foreign archaeological missions in Egypt.

Egyptian Archaeology. Published by the Egypt Exploration Society (EES), one of the oldest Egyptological research groups devoted specifically to archaeology, this popular-format magazine provides in-depth information about excavations and news from the EES and from museums and universities in Great Britain.

KMT. A copiously illustrated American popular magazine

with engaging accounts on a wide variety of Egypto-logical subjects, *KMT* is an excellent source of information about excavations, past and current.

Leclant, Jean. "Fouilles et travaux en Egypte et au Soudan." First published in *Orientalia* 19 (1950) and appearing in every issue to the present, this continually updated account constitutes the longest-running series in any Egyptological topic by the same author. Originally focused on excavations in Egypt, the articles now cover the Sudan as well. The best comprehensive reference for all current archaeological work.

Vandier, Jacques. *Manuel d'archéologie égyptienne.* 6 vols. Paris, 1952–1978. Although out of date in parts, a well-illustrated scholarly reference and a still invaluable reference to Egyptian art and archaeology.

Architecture

Arnold, Dieter. *Building in Egypt: Pharaonic Stone Masonry.* New York, 1991.

Arnold, Dieter. *Lexikon der ägyptischen Baukunst.* Munich and Zurich, 1994.

Badawy, Alexander. *A History of Egyptian Architecture.* 3 vols. Berkeley and Los Angeles, 1966. Volumes 1 and 2 cover through the New Kingdom; volume 3 is a synthesis, *A Study of the Harmonic System; A History of Egyptian Architecture: The Empire (the New Kingdom)—From the Eighteenth Dynasty to the End of the Twentieth Dynasty (1580–1085 B.C.).* Berkeley and Los Angeles, 1968.

de Cenival, Jean-Louis. *Living Architecture: Egyptian.* New York, 1964.

Edwards, I. E. S. *The Pyramids of Egypt,* rev. ed. Harmondsworth, England, 1986.

Maragioglio, Vito, and Celeste Rinaldi. *L'architettura delle piramide menfite.* 8 vols. Turin and Rapallo, 1962–1977. In English and Italian.

Smith, William S. *The Art and Architecture of Ancient Egypt.* 2d ed. by William K. Simpson. New Haven, 1998.

Stadelmann, Rainer. *Die ägyptischen Pyramiden: Vom Ziegelbau zum Weltwunder.* Kulturgeschichte der Antiken Welt, 30 Mainz, 1985.

Art

Aldred, Cyril. *Middle Kingdom Art in Ancient Egypt, 2300–1590 B.C.* London, 1950.

Aldred, Cyril. *New Kingdom Art in Ancient Egypt during the Eighteenth Dynasty, 1590–1315 B.C.* 2d ed. London, 1961.

Aldred, Cyril *Old Kingdom Art in Ancient Egypt.* 2d ed. London, 1968.

Aldred, Cyril. *The Development of Ancient Egyptian Art from 3200 to 1315 B.C.* 3d ed. London, 1973.

Aldred, Cyril. *Egyptian Art in the Days of the Pharaohs. 3100–320 B.C.* London, 1980.

Hornemann, Bodil. *Types of Ancient Egyptian Statuary.* 7 vols. Copenhagen, 1951–1969.

Leclant, Jean, ed. *Le monde égyptien: Les pharaons,* vol. 1: *Les temps des Pyramides: De la Préhistoire aux Hyksos (1560 av. J.-C.).* Paris, 1978.

Leclant, Jean, ed. *Le monde égyptien: Les pharaons,* vol. 2: *L'Empire des Conquérants: L'Égypte au Nouvel Empire (1560–1070 B.C.).* Paris, 1979.

Leclant, Jean, ed. *Le monde égyptien: Les pharaons,* vol. 3: *L'Égypte du crépuscule: De Tanis à Méroé (1070 av. J.C.-IVᵉ siècle apr. J.-C.).* Paris, 1980.

Robins, Gay. *The Art of Ancient Egypt.* Cambridge, Mass., 1997.

Schaefer, J. Heinrich. *Principles of Egyptian Art.* Translated and edited by John R. Baines. Rev. ed. by Emma Brunner-Traut. Oxford, 1986.

Smith, William S. *A History of Egyptian Sculpture and Painting in the Old Kingdom,* 2d ed. Boston, 1949.

Vandersleyen, C., et al. *Das alte Ägypten.* Propyläen Kunstgeschichte, 15. Berlin, 1975.

For an extensive bibliography of Egyptian collections in various museums, see Smith (1998) in the Architecture section above. Of special importance is the so-called Catalogue Générale (CG), a series of almost one hundred catalogs from the Egyptian Museum, Cairo; despite its extent, the CG by no means covers the full inventory of the world's most extensive collection of ancient Egyptian antiquities.

History and Chronology

Beckerath, Jürgen von. *Handbuch der ägyptischen Königsnamen.* Münchner Ägyptologische Studien, 20. Munich, 1984. Not as detailed as Gauthier's *Livre des rois* (1907–1917), *see below,* but a more convenient list of all the Egyptian kings. Covers through the Roman period.

Cambridge Ancient History. 13 vols. Cambridge, 1970–1998. The most complete reference in English, spanning the entire spectrum of ancient Egyptian history, from the Predynastic period through the Roman domination.

Gauthier, H. *Le livre des rois d'Égypte: Recueil de titres et protocoles royaux, noms propres de rois, reines, princes et princesses, noms de pyramides et de temples solaires.* 5 vols. Mémoires publiés par les Membres de l'Institut Français d'Archéologie Orientale du Caire, 17–21. Cairo, 1907–1917. A still-valuable resource for the titularies of not only all pharaohs and the royal persons but also the Ptolemies and the Roman emperors.

Grimal, Nicolas. *A History of Ancient Egypt.* Translated by Ian Shaw. Oxford and Cambridge, Mass., 1993.

Parker, Richard. *The Calendars of Ancient Egypt.* Studies in Ancient Oriental Civilization, 26. Chicago, 1950.

Philology, Grammars

Allen, James P. *Middle Egyptian: An Introduction to the Language and Culture of Hieroglyphs.* Cambridge and New York, 2000. The best grammar of Middle Egyptian in English since Gardiner's *Egyptian Grammar.*

Černý, Jaroslav, and Sarah Israelit-Groll. *A Late Egyptian Grammar.* Studia Pohl, Series Major, 4. Rome, 1975. Standard grammar of Late Egyptian.

Edel, Elmar. *Altägyptische Grammatik.* 2 vols. Rome, 1955–1964. Standard grammar for Old Kingdom Egyptian.

Erman, Adolf. *Neuägyptische Grammatik,* 2d ed. Leipzig, 1933. The first grammar of Late Egyptian. Still useful.

Frandsen, Paul J. *An Outline of the Late Egyptian Verbal System.* Copenhagen, 1974. An essential concomitant to Černý and Groll (1975).

Gardiner, Alan H. *Egyptian Grammar: Being an Introduction to the Study of Hieroglyphs.* 3d ed., rev. Oxford, 1957. The standard English-language grammar for Middle Egyptian (the classical stage of Egyptian), and one of the most widely consulted Egyptological reference works.

Grandet, P., and Mathieu, B. *Cours d'Égyptien hiéroglyphique.* 2 vols. Paris, 1990–1995.

Johnson, Janet H. *The Demotic Verbal System.* Studies in Ancient Oriental Civilization 38. Chicago, 1978.

Johnson, Janet H. *Thus Wrote Onchsheshonqy: An Introductory Grammar of Demotic.* Studies in Ancient Oriental Civilization, 45 Chicago, 1986.

Korostotsev, Mikhail A. *Grammaire du neo-égyptien.* Moscow, 1973.

Lambdin, Thomas O. *Introduction to Sahidic Coptic.* Macon, Ga., 1983.

Layton, Bentley. *Sahidic Coptic Grammar.* Rome, forthcoming. [Promises to be the best Coptic grammar ever, incorporating all major scholarship in the Coptic verbal system.]

Mallon, Alexis. *Grammaire copte: Bibliographie, chrestomathie, vocabulaire.* 4th ed. Beirut, 1956.

Spiegelberg, Wilhelm. *Demotische Grammatik.* Heidelberg, 1925.

Till, Walter C. *Koptische Grammatik.* 4th ed. Lehrbücher für das Studium der Orientalischen und Afrikanischen Sprache, 1 Leipzig, 1970. The standard grammar for the Sahidic dialect of Coptic.

Although hieroglyphic fonts are not reference works, they are essential tools and deserve mention. Of the several computer-based hieroglyphic fonts that exist, two excellent programs are to be recommended: Glyph for Windows and MacScribe for the Macintosh. There is also Inscribe (to date, for Windows only) from Saqqara Technology. The World Wide Web URL (universal resource locater) for Glyph and MacScribe is http://www.ccer.ggl.ruu.nl, which is at the Center for Computer-Aided Egyptological Research at the University of Utrecht in The Netherlands. The URL for Inscribe is http://www.saqqarat.co.uk.

Literature

Biedenkopf-Ziehner, Anne, et al. "Koptologische Literaturübersicht." *Enchoria* 2 (1972), 103–136, 3 (1973), 81–152; 4 (1974), 141–156; 5 (1975), 151–180; 6 (1976), 93–120; 8 (1978), 51–72; and 10 (1980), 151–184.

Bresciani, Edda. *Letteratura e poesia dell'antico Egitto.* Turin, 1969.

Erman, Adolf. *The Ancient Egyptians.* Translated by Aylward M. Blackman, rev. ed. by William K. Simpson. New York, 1966.

Lefebvre, Gustave. *Romans et contes de l'époque pharaonique.* Paris, 1949.

Lichtheim, Miriam. *Ancient Egyptian Literature.* 3 vols. Berkeley and Los Angeles, 1973–1980. A judicious selection of texts, of various content, from the Old Kingdom through the Late period. The only English-language survey of Egyptian documents that includes Demotic.

Murnane, William J. *Texts from the Amarna Period in Egypt.* Society of Biblical Literature, Writing from the Ancient World, 5. Atlanta, 1995.

Parkinson, Richard B. *Voices from Ancient Egypt: An Anthology of Middle Kingdom Writings* London, 1991. A sensitive and well-annotated translation of many of the greatest of ancient Egyptian literary works.

Roccati, Alessandro. *La littérature historique sous l'ancien empire égyptien.* Paris, 1982.

Simon, Jean. "Bibliographie copte." *Or* 18 (1949), 100–120, 216–246; 19 (1950), 187–201, 295–327; 20 (1951), 291–305, 423–442; 21 (1952), 339–357; 22 (1953), 39*–63*; 23 (1954), 70*–97*; 24 (1955), 54*–76*; 25 (1956), 49*–73*; 26 (1957), 116*–139*; 27 (1958), 48*–67*; 28 (1959), 91*–114*; 29 (1960), 45*–69*; 30 (1961), 62*–88*; 31 (1962), 51*–77*; 32 (1963), 114*–136*; 33 (1964), 124*–145*; 34 (1965), 215*–252*; and 35 (1966), 139*–168*. Covers Coptic studies in many categories, such as philological, historical, literary, theological, and hagiographical.

Simpson, William K., ed. *The Literature of Ancient Egypt: An Anthology of Stories, Instructions, and Poetry.* rev. ed. New Haven, 1973. A useful one-volume collection of all the important ancient Egyptian literary texts.

Thissen, Heinz-Josef, and Heinz Felber. "Demotistische Literaturübersicht." *Enchoria* 1 (1971), 57–72; 2

(1972), 96–102; 3 (1973), 71–80; 4 (1974), 83–94; 5 (1975), 127–134; 6 (1976), 83–92; 7 (1977), 180–190; 8 (1978), 39–50; 9 (1979), 125–134; 10 (1980), 141–150; 11 (1982), 99–108; 12 (1984), 155–186; 13 (1985), 173–200; 14 (1986), 135–154; 15 (1987), 181–196; 16 (1988), 101–118; 17 (1990), 133–152; 18 (1991), 153–174; 19–20 (1992–1993), 181–214; 21 (1994), 107–127; 22 (1995), 182–217; and 23 (1996), 150–176.

Wente, Edward. *Letters from Ancient Egypt.* Society of Biblical Literature, Writing from the Ancient World, 1. Atlanta, 1990. Invaluable collection of nonliterary texts that allow glimpses into the private lives of the ancient Egyptians.

Philology, Dictionaries, and Lexicography

Andreu, G., and S. Cauville. "Vocabulaire absent du *Wörterbuch.*" *Revue d'Egyptologie* 29 (1977), 5–13; *Revue d'Egyptologie* 30 (1978), 10–21.

Beinlich, Horst, et al. "The Beinlich Word List: An Internet-Searchable Database." An extensive World Wide Web–based archive of Egyptian words in transliteration, with German translation and cross references to the Erman-Grapow *Wörterbuch* and/or more recent publications. The URL (universal resource locater) for the word list is http://www.newton.cam.ac.uk/egypt/test/beinlich.html.

Crum, Walter E. *A Coptic Dictionary.* Oxford, 1929.

Černý, Jaroslav. *Coptic Etymological Dictionary.* Cambridge, 1976.

Dakin, Alec N., et al. "Index of Words, etc., Discussed, vols. 1–25." *Journal of Egyptian Archaeology.* 25 (1931), 243–267, *Journal of Egyptian Archaeology* 40 (1954), 14–23.

Erman, Adolf, and H. Grapow. *Wörterbuch der Ägyptischen Sprache.* 12 vols. Leipzig and Berlin, 1926–1963. The standard dictionary. Extensive lists of words omitted from the *Worterbüch,* additional nuances of meanings, and the most recent updates from the *Worterbüch* project in Berlin are available (see the other works cited in this section and below under Internet addresses).

Faulkner, Raymond O. *A Concise Dictionary of Middle Egyptian.* Oxford, 1962. Well titled.

Hannig, Rainer. *Die Sprache der Pharaonen: Grosses Handwörterbuch Ägyptisch-Deutsch (2800–950 v. Chr.).* Kulturgeschichte der Antiken Welt, 64 Mainz, 1995. Less complete than the Erman-Grapow *Wörterbuch* but an invaluable reference work nonetheless.

Kasser, Rodolphe. *Compléments au dictionnaire copte de Crum.* Bibliothèque d'Etudes Coptes, 7. Cairo 1964.

Meeks, Dmitri. *L'année philologique.* 3 vols. Paris, 1977–1979. Planned as an ongoing work, this excellent series was of short duration. It consists of lengthy lists of words, with useful citations to textual occurrences and to scholarly discussions that elucidate nuances of meaning.

Shennum, David. *English–Egyptian Index of Faulkner's Concise Dictionary of Middle Egyptian.* ARTANES, 1 Malibu, Calif., 1977.

Religion

Bonnet, Hans. *Reallexikon der ägyptischen Religionsgeschichte.* Berlin, 1952. Dated but useful scholarly discussions of many Egyptian deities.

Černý, Jaroslav. *Ancient Egyptian Religion.* London, 1952.

Hornung, Erik. *Conceptions of God in Ancient Egypt. The One and the Many.* Translated by John R. Baines, Ithaca, N.Y., 1982.

Morenz, Siegfried. *Egyptian Religion.* Translated by Ann E. Keep. Ithaca, N.Y., 1973.

O'Connor, David B., and David Silverman. *Ancient Egyptian Kingship.* Probleme der Ägyptologie, 9. Leiden, 1995.

Quirke, Stephen. *Ancient Egyptian Religion.* London, 1992. The best overview.

Sites, Topography, and Geography

Amélineau, Émile. *La géographie de l'Égypte à l'époque copte.* Paris, 1893.

Aufrère, Sydney, et al. *L'Égypte restituée.* 3 vols. Paris, 1991–1997. Sites, temples, and pyramids from Upper, Lower, and Middle Egypt.

Baines, John R., and Jaromír Málek. *Atlas of Ancient Egypt.* New York, 1980.

Kees, Hermann. *Ancient Egypt: A Cultural Topography.* Translated by Ian D. Morrow. Edited by T. G. H. James. Chicago, 1977.

Porter, Bertha, Rosalind L. B. Moss, and Jaromír Málek. *Topographical Bibliography of Ancient Egyptian Hieroglyphic Texts, Reliefs, and Paintings.* 7 vols. Oxford, 1927–. First published in 1927 and continually updated, this series is the one of the basic reference works in Egyptology. The title does not reveal the wealth of information inside; the bibliographies for every Egyptian site cover architecture and objects of all sorts. An eighth volume, for monuments with no provenance, is planned.

Wreszinski, Walter. *Atlas zur altägyptischen Kulturgeschichte.* 3 vols. Leipzig, 1923–1954.

Internet Addresses

Because Internet addresses, for both e-mail and the World Wide Web, often change or cease functioning, the selection below is limited to well-established venues, all providing numerous links to other locations; however, even the addresses in this small sample may change.

http://www.egyptology.com—An essential portal, this address offers access to many other sites of scholarly and general interest.

http.//www.harrassowitz.de—Otto Harrassowitz Buchhandlung, POB 2929 Taunusstr. 5, 65019, Wiesbaden, Germany. Both a publisher and a vendor of scholarly books in many different disciplines, Harrassowitz is the best source anywhere for difficult-to-find Egyptological items. For years, its catalog has been the most comprehensive list of Egyptological books in print, including newly reprinted items. If a selection is not listed, Harrassowitz will readily order it from the publisher or seek a used copy, if the work is out of print.

http://www.leila-books.com—Leila Books, 39 Sharia Qasr el Nil, 2d Floor, Office 12, Cairo, Egypt. An invaluable source for books published in Egypt, especially the volumes from the Institut Français d'Archéologie Orientale.

http://www.newton.cam.ac.uk/egypt/—Second only to Abzu (*see below*) in importance, this site at Cambridge University has rich documentation about computers and Egyptology, recent publications, excavations, and items of general interest. Perhaps its most often downloaded archive is the list of e-mail addresses for Egyptologists.

http://www.oi.uchicago.edu/OI/DEPT/RA/ABZU/ABZU_REGINDX_EGYPT.HTML—Commonly known as Abzu, this URL (universal resource locater) at the Oriental Institute, University of Chicago, is the most important scholarly Web address in Egyptology because it provides links to an almost limitless spectrum of Egyptological subjects. The nine categories covered by Abzu are archaeological sites; art; Egyptological institutions; imaging—site reconstruction; museums and collections; papyrology; philology—texts—translations; travel and miscellaneous; and resources listed alphabetically by author. Among its innumerable offerings, Abzu offers access to lists of Egyptological dissertation topics (both recently completed and in progress) at the University of Chicago; the online catalogs of several libraries with extensive Egyptological holdings; important online archives of Hieratic, Demotic, Coptic, Greek, and Latin papyri (such as those at Duke University and the University of Michigan at Ann Arbor); book reviews and news of recent publications; the digitized slip archive of the Berlin *Wörterbuch;* and announcements of museum exhibitions.

majordomo@oi.uchicago.edu—This e-mail address provides access to the Ancient Near East (ANE) bulletin board, another critical resource pioneered by the Oriental Institute, University of Chicago. The geographical and historical parameters are from the Indus River to the Nile and from the beginnings of human habitation to the rise of Islam, respectively. There are two bulletin boards: the news list and the open-discussion forum. The news list relays official items sometimes found nowhere else: announcements of conferences, recent publications, and obituaries of scholars; wire-service reports from the Middle East about archaeological discoveries; and postings of academic and museum positions. The open-discussion forum provides both this information and an opportunity for discussion of any topic pertinent to the study of the ancient Near East. The value of the second option is that it allows nonspecialists to read up-to-the minute news items and to pose questions, which Egyptologists occasionally answer. Unfortunately, the questions and the responses can be tedious. There are two types of subscriptions for either the news or the open-discussion list: instantaneous receipt of individual items as they are posted to the bulletin board or delayed receipt in batch or digest form. To subscribe to the news list for either method of receipt, send a note with the simple text SUBSCRIBE ANENEWS or SUBSCRIBE ANENEWS-DIGEST; likewise, for the open-discussion bulletin board, send either of the two notes SUBSCRIBE ANE or SUBSCRIBE ANE-DIGEST.

[*See also* Journals.]

DONALD B. SPANEL

REKHMIRE, vizier during the reigns of Thutmose III (c.1504–1452 BCE) and Amenhotpe II (c.1454–1419 BCE). Rekhmire was a scion of a distinguished family of administrators, having been preceded as vizier by his grandfather Aametju and his uncle Amunuser. His father, Neferweben, may have served briefly in the same office, but the evidence for this is extremely meager. Rekhmire's chief monument is the funerary chapel that he built in Western Thebes (tomb 100), the decoration of which sheds important light on his life and on the civil administration of Egypt.

First mentioned as vizier in an account papyrus dated to the thirty-fourth year of the reign of Thutmose III, Rekhmire recorded in his funerary chapel a version of the text known as the "Duties of the Vizier," which describes the primary official functions of pharaoh's chief deputy: personnel management, internal security, and the dispensation of justice. Scholarly debate since the 1980s has focused on the original date of composition of this remarkable text. It is a matter of dispute whether certain grammatical features reflect the Middle Kingdom or the early eighteenth dynasty, and therefore whether the text reflects a governmental organization original to the twelfth or thirteenth dynasties rather than the New Kingdom, furthermore, it is not certain whether, during the reign of Thutmose III, there was a single vizier or two such officers representing Upper and Lower Egypt, as was the case later in the dynasty (Kruchten 1991).

Rekhmire's funerary chapel is renowned for its detailed portrayals of foreigners from the lands north and south of Egypt, shown bringing to the royal court precious gifts and rare animals such as elephants, bears, and giraffes. A highlight of these tribute processions is one of the earliest portrayals of Minoans, distinguished by their curled tresses, who are depicted wearing striped and tasseled kilts and carrying objects of Aegean manufacture. Other scenes include a comprehensive sequence of mortuary rituals from the Opening of the Mouth ceremony, conducted before the mummy of the deceased prior to burial. Still another section of the chapel is devoted to detailing the various crafts that Rekhmire must have supervised in the course of his duties; there are lively portrayals of craftsmen at work in their ateliers—sculptors, carpenters, bricklayers, brewers, bakers, stonemasons, lapidaries, leather-workers, and metal-workers. The transition to the reign of Amenhotpe II is marked by a depiction of Rekhmire's triumphant return home after a visit to the king, during which he was confirmed in the office of vizier.

The funerary chapel of Rekhmire contains no burial chamber, suggesting that he was interred in a separate location in the Theban necropolis. No statues of Rekhmire are known, and other attestations are scarce. His name occurs on an ostracon with the appended title "Overseer of Works at Djeser-akhet," at the temple Thutmose III built at Deir el-Bahri. The quartzite funerary stela from his chapel is presently in the Louvre (C 74) in Paris.

BIBLIOGRAPHY

Davies, Norman de Garis. *Paintings from the Tomb of Rekh-mi-Reʿ at Thebes.* Publications of the Metropolitan Museum of Art Egyptian Expedition, 10. New York, 1935. Details in color of several of the more magnificent scenes from Theban Tomb 100.

Davies, Norman de Garis. *The Tomb of Rekh-mi-Reʿ at Thebes.* Publications of the Metropolitan Museum of Art Egyptian Expedition, 11. New York, 1943. Complete drawings and a description of the decoration of Theban Tomb 100.

Kruchten, Jean-Marie. *Biblioteca Orientalis* 48 (1991), pp. 821–831.

Newberry, Percy. *The Life of Rekhmara.* London, 1900. An early account, now somewhat outdated, of Rekhmire's life, based on the information contained in his Theban tomb.

van den Boorn, Guido. *The Duties of the Vizier.* London, 1988. A detailed analysis of the text describing the responsibilities of the vizier, based largely on the version in Rekhmire's tomb, compared with parallels in the tombs of User (Theban Tomb 131), Amenemope (TT 29), and Paser (TT 109).

PETER DORMAN

RELIEF SCULPTURE. The most important and most widespread artistic medium used by the ancient Egyptians was sculpture in relief. It came into being at the dawn of historical time, toward the end of the fourth millennium BCE, at the same time as writing in its earliest form. Actual relief sculpture, as the Egyptians understood it, served for the decoration of the walls of monumental stone structures. Its use was restricted to sacred buildings, since only temples and tombs were built of stone, while the residences and palaces were built of mud brick. Egyptian relief sculpture has a distinctive appearance, found only in the Nile Valley and nowhere else in the ancient world. It is uncommonly flat—the depth of a relief rarely exceeds a few millimeters—and it is usually colorfully painted. Invariably, Egyptian relief sculpture consists of an image and an inscription. It covers the whole wall, with the exception of a small area at the base, and not only individual architectural features or sections of the wall. Buildings began to be decorated with relief sculptures in the fourth dynasty, and through time these reliefs took over all the walls of a room and all the rooms of a building, inside and outside, including the door frames, columns, architraves, and ceilings. In the temples, only reliefs are found and, although reliefs are very frequently found in tombs, sometimes there are wall paintings instead of reliefs. From the beginning of the Old Kingdom, sacred architecture was inconceivable without reliefs. Over the course of Egyptian history, there came to be such a number of reliefs that if they were stood side by side they would extend for many kilometers/miles. Reliefs constitute a compendium of the Egyptian religion, but reading it presupposes the knowledge of the Egyptian theologians, and these reliefs are therefore difficult for us to interpret today.

The kings' tombs and temples were residences of the gods, in which the deceased king dwelled as a god along with all the other divinities. The message of the relief and its inscriptions are primarily directed to the owner; they were not a medium of communication with the general population. The building inscription of Edfu says that priests and scholars should come to look at the temple and to admire the accomplishment of the king. As to the direct function of the relief, Egyptologists are not certain. What is clear, however, is that the reliefs make a political-theological statement about the king as the leader of the world. The reliefs show that it is the king, not the gods, who holds the main role: he conquers enemies, performs every conceivable ritual and symbolic act, celebrates festivals, and acts as a priest. In all this, the gods lovingly support the king. It is impossible to separate politics and theology in ancient Egypt, because the ruler is at the same time a god. Many scenes describe rituals that were per-

RELIEF SCULPTURE. *Drawing of a relief of Perneb receiving offerings.* The fifth dynasty relief is from Perneb's *mastaba* in Saqqara. (The Metropolitan Museum of Art, Gift of Edward S. Harkness, 1913. [13.183.3])

formed in the temple. Many reflect a highly developed theological understanding about the events that are being played out in a higher sphere between the gods and the king—events that serve to keep the world in existence. The reliefs clearly confirm the consensus of the upper class as to the role of the king as the preserver of creation. Overall, the buildings are a demonstration of the power and greatness of the ruler.

The tombs of nonroyal individuals are their residences for the afterlife. The rooms above ground, where the reliefs and autobiographical texts are found, were accessible to relatives and visitors. The pictures focus especially on the work of the lower class, which is initiated and controlled by the owner of the tomb, including the production of foodstuffs and other goods and the repro-

duction of the cattle. The tomb is intended to make the name of its owner live on and to perpetuate his beneficial activity.

The earliest reliefs appear on large votive offerings set up in the temples, such as cosmetic palettes and mace-heads of "Dynasty 0" (about 3100 BCE). In the Early Dynastic period, the first stelae appear. These are personal memorials that belong to the tombs, and later, in increasing numbers, also to the temples. They are the most important supports for reliefs, besides the walls of buildings. From the third dynasty, the walls of royal pyramid complexes, temples of the gods, and tombs of officials began to be covered with relief sculptures. From around this same time have been found reliefs on stone cliffs, like those seen in the mines and quarries on the Sinai Peninsula, in the Eastern Desert, and in Nubia. They represent the rule of Egypt even at the edge of the civilized world. Large stone pieces of furniture in the temples, such as altars, shrines, obelisks, and pyramidia may be adorned with relief sculptures, and in the tombs the sarcophagi are also thus decorated. The statues carry reliefs on the pedestal and the rear support; beginning in the eleventh century BCE, representations are even chiseled into the figure itself. Small luxury household items, such as boxes, containers, and furniture, may have relief carvings in wood, faience, or metal.

Great effort was required to produce a wall relief. A relief sculpture always requires teamwork, in which at least three specialized craftsmen take part. First, one artist, using a fine brush and ink, draws the preliminary sketch onto a wall. Then the sculptor goes to work, chiseling out the depictions and inscriptions. Finally, the painter paints the picture as thoroughly as though it were a wall painting. Today, however, the color has been preserved on only a very few examples. Relief sculpture was done using two different techniques. One kind is raised relief, in which the figures are raised and stand out several millimeters from the background. The other kind is sunk relief, used on the outside walls of buildings. Here the outline of the figures is sunk several millimeters into the background. When the light strikes the image, bold shadows appear in the areas that have been hollowed out. Little information has come down to us about the work sites. The most important sites were always located where the king resided, because he was the one who commissioned work on the temples and the royal tomb complex. And where the king lived, there the highest officials also lived, and it was they who commissioned work on their tombs. Relief sculpture, which requires significant resources to be produced, is an art form typically associated with kingly courts, and a decrease in quality can often been detected in the provinces and when those who commissioned the work had less wealth.

Few of the names of the artists who worked in relief sculpture have come down to us, and there were very rarely any individual stylistic features. This would have required a highly developed notion of individuality, a view that emerged for the first time with the ancient Greeks. Instead, Egyptian sculpture is characterized by a strong attachment to tradition. The rules of the art were developed at the beginning of the historical period and were handed down in the workshops to each new generation as a precious heritage. Therefore, between the first dynasty and the Roman period, there was only a gradual, barely perceptible change in style. The initiative for innovation belonged completely to the king. Thus it happened that under each new king, a variation in style was developed. Differences in style between reliefs from the same period

tend to be connected to the nature of the commission given to the workshop. In other words, the work proceeded differently according to the function of the building, the size of the relief sculpture, or the kind of stone that was used. Only rarely can a particular style be attributed to a specific place.

Already with the appearance of the first relief sculptures in Dynasty "0," the conventions for representation have largely been set. The relief sculpture is practically two-dimensional and does not reflect knowledge of perspective. The human form, as well as those of animals, plants, and objects, is represented according to fixed rules, which were to change only insignificantly over three millennia. Equally regulated is the manner in which several figures are placed together in a joint action or scene and how a wall is subdivided. What we see here is a unique product of the Egyptian mind and one of the most striking visual features of this culture. In the beginning, the proportions of the figures are still unsure, but by the third dynasty the system is fully developed. If we look at a standing figure of a king, a god, or the owner of a tomb (of which there are thousands from all periods), we see that the figure is a silhouette cut with minimal depth, while extremely fine layering within a few millimeters gives it its modeling. The body is very slender, but proportioned naturally. The angles of vision from which the individual parts of the body are viewed vary greatly. The head is viewed from the side, but the eye is viewed from the front, and the trunk from the armpits downward is viewed somewhat from the side, as are the arms and legs. However, the observer does not realize that the parts of the body are contradictory in their positions, because the body is represented as practically flat and mostly without the contours of bones and muscles.

The structure of the figure makes it clear that the Egyptian artists had a relationship to reality, that is to say, to space and time, completely different from that of European artists from classical antiquity onward. The body is not developed in space and assumes no depth; rather, all its parts lie equally parallel to the surface. As a result of this two-dimensional composition, the contour lines result in geometric figures. The upper body forms a triangle, and the same is true for the legs and the pelvis. Thus, the body is structured according to two contradictory principles: it combines the natural proportions with a symmetrical double triangle. This combination is what conveys the "typically Egyptian" impression.

The figures are placed together in groups of several people who are doing something together. Frequently, the figures are all standing on one horizontal line. Since there is no third dimension of depth, the figures can be arranged only from left to right, or vice versa. Two means are used to place the figures into relation to one another:

RELIEF SCULPTURE. *Eighteenth dynasty relief of Thutmose IV from his Festival Hall at Karnak.*
(Courtesy Donald B. Redford)

overlapping and symmetry. In many cases, the figures overlap so much that they form a narrow ladder shape. There are two main kinds of symmetry encountered: translational symmetry, in which one figure or one motif is repeated several times while it is shifted sideways, and axial symmetry, in which a group of figures or a motif consists of two halves that are mirror images of each other. Often both kinds of symmetry are combined. The illusion of movement is created through the arrangement of the figures or their extremities in a diagonal direction, and even parallel to one another. The composition of the group is ornamental in character. What is characteristic is a beautiful harmony of the lines, a masterfully crafted consonance of regular forms—a harmony that flows from the symmetry.

A wall is usually subdivided into several sections that are separated by horizontal lines. This order is repeatedly interrupted, however, because gods, kings, and the owners of the tomb are represented as far larger than ordinary people and bring together several series of small scenes. Scenes that are particularly important are repeated twice in mirrorlike fashion, and very frequently alongside a door.

The relief sculpture, since it is little more than two-dimensional, portrays "space and time" reality only to a very limited extent. The geometry and symmetry operating here make visible an unchanging world that transcends time. The Egyptians were little interested in ephemeral events; they focused instead on the fixed patterns of behavior, a harmonic order. The system of representation proves this: Little development takes place, but people are certain that the world, as it is, is in order and will always remain so.

As for the development of style between the Old Kingdom and the eighteenth dynasty it is primarily the proportions of the figures that change. However, significant change in style is characteristic of the Amarna period. Everything is overtaken by a great dynamism. Only present-day actions of the king and of the owners of the tombs are portrayed, which take place at specific places such as the temples and palaces of the city of Tell el-Amarna. In the twenty-sixth dynasty, an amazing phenomenon of historicism appears: in the tombs of rich, educated officials there are relief sculptures in the styles of several earlier periods. From the thirtieth dynasty into the Roman period we find a mixed Hellenistic-Egyptian style. A final real change in style can be observed in the temples of the Ptolemaic period. The relief is somewhat higher and the

RELIEF SCULPTURE. *Deep-sunk relief, nineteenth dynasty.* A red granite doorjamb from a temple of Ramesses II at Thebes. (The Metropolitan Museum of Art, Gift of Edward S. Harkness, 1913. [13.183.2])

figures present somewhat more corporeality, since they are more roundly modeled. The free space around the figures is filled with intricately detailed decoration. Very typical is the arrangement of the scenes on the walls into a uniform system of rectangles, which produces a stiff and lifeless effect.

In the early Old Kingdom, under King Sneferu, about 2,500 BCE, for the first time there appear a series of continuous relief sculpture scenes on the walls in the royal pyramid complex. The decoration concept, which was to remain in effect from then on, is already very much present: the base area of the wall contains a series of Nile gods, which represent the fruitfulness of the earth watered by the Nile. On the strips of depictions above this is a series of scenes, each showing the king performing a ritual act, either alone or with a god. The king may be standing beside a symbolic object, or he may be running a course while holding symbolic objects in his hands. He is raising a mace in order to slay an enemy lying on the ground, or he is standing in a boat in the papyrus marsh, hunting birds. Often he is standing beside a divinity who is embracing and kissing him. Or he may be simply standing, facing the divinity, and both hold a scepter; or the two of them are performing the ritual for the founding of a temple, driving rods into the ground. Above the king there often hovers a falcon or a vulture, both protective powers with which he is allied. On the top, the wall is finished off with a narrow band covered with stars that represents the heavens. The king is wearing a short apron—which appears in several variants, from the belt of which there always hangs the tail of an animal—and several types of crowns. When he is draped in a short or long mantle, it means he is celebrating the jubilee of his coronation.

Concerning scenes that first appear in the fifth dynasty, a few should be mentioned that show what the gods do for the king: a goddess is standing and nursing the king, who is depicted as a large child. In one large scene depicting homage being given, the king is seated on a throne between two gods who bestow life on him, while long rows of gods and courtiers hail him. Elsewhere the ruler appears in the shape of a sphinx who tramples his enemies. The divinities are depicted as men and women and often bear a crownlike symbol on their heads. Some gods have the head of an animal or a body shaped as a mummy. The manner in which the gods and the king behave with one another shows that the king is fully integrated into his divine family. Moreover, the king is also depicted so often that it will be clear that he is the most important and most active partner. The characteristics of the king and the divinities mentioned above—elements of clothing, insignia, heads of animals, and crowns—may occur in many different combinations and form a complex system of symbols which tells something about the character, rank, and function of the wearer in a specific context. Egyptology is still far from having completely deciphered this system.

From the Middle Kingdom onward there was an increase in depictions of sacrificial scenes in which the king offers the divinity a gift; in such representations the

RELIEF SCULPTURE. *Limestone relief of the face of a man, probably from the twenty-sixth dynasty.* In this relief from Mit Rahina, the facial features are subtly molded within a sharply cut, deep outline. (University of Pennsylvania Museum, Philadelphia. Neg. # S4–143064)

king is shown in the role of priest. From the New Kingdom onward, rituals such as the daily care of the cult image were thoroughly depicted as a sequence of many scenes. In addition, there were processions, festivals, and mythical events. Finally, even historical events came to be shown, particularly wars that Pharaoh had won. The scenes of conquests and battles demonstrate the power of the divine king to annihilate all the enemies of Egypt, and so these depictions form a magical wall of protection around the temple. What is striking about the Ptolemaic period is that the temples are consecrated to a divine mother or father whose child brings about the salvation of the world; his birth is the most important feast of the year. Beginning in the New Kingdom, the ceiling of the temple is decorated as the heavens, with flying birds and constellations. The temple with its relief sculptures is an image of the world and of everything done by the king and other divinities in order to keep the world alive and periodically to renew it.

The earliest scene that appears in tombs of nonroyal individuals shows the owner of the tomb, whether man or woman, sitting at a table laden with food. Through all periods this scene remained the most important one because of the Egyptians' belief that the body was necessary for life in the next world and that it must be nourished. To this nucleus, beginning in the fourth dynasty, are added large standing figures of the owner of the tomb and his family. Later there are also depictions of men and women bringing foodstuffs, piles of food, and offering lists. During the fourth and fifth dynasties there developed a basic set of scenes depicting the reproduction of plants and animals and the production of goods for daily consumption. The scenes are always dominated by a large figure of the tomb owner, standing or sitting, who watches over the various labors, depicted on several small strips that are densely packed with figures. For these kinds of work in farming, animal husbandry, fishing and bird-catching, crafts, and transportation, a fixed repertory of formulations was developed from which several could be chosen and combined in new ways. The only scenes in which the tomb owner himself appears as active are those of the hunt in the papyrus marsh or in the desert. Their great importance is emphasized in the way they are presented as very large and often in axial symmetrical repetition. The fourth important complex was the burial ritual, which can consist of many scenes. In the Old and Middle Kingdoms, divinities, kings, or religious scenes are practically never depicted in the tombs of officials.

In the New Kingdom, important changes were introduced in the themes. Now the king is frequently depicted, in particular as the tomb owner liked to show how he was rewarded by the king for his merits. The religious scenes that describe the afterlife become more and more common and finally displace all other scenes. Occasionally there are scenes that otherwise are found only in temples, such as the coronation jubilee of the king, or the king making sacrifice to a god. In the necropolis of Thebes, more than half of the tombs are painted. In many cases these are smaller tombs that belonged to less wealthy people. In this period, however, painting is artistically more innovative and alive than the severe relief sculpture.

During the first millennium BCE it was common for artists to study historical monuments in order to copy scenes from all sources: the mythological scenes from the afterlife were taken from the tombs of kings; from the nonroyal tombs came the scenes of daily life, the funeral ritual, and interaction with the gods of the dead. The latest relief sculptures are found in Roman Alexandria in catacomb tombs, where the king is shown offering a sacrifice before a divinity, a depiction that traditionally was customary only in temples. In this scene the deceased himself can be the god in his appearance as Osiris.

The Egyptians felt a strong need to express their religion in images and to clarify these images through inscriptions. In the center there stands the king in his capacity as a god who, along with the other gods, keeps the world going, and in addition there were depictions of the afterlife of the ruler as well as of the members of the upper class who were related to him. Flat relief sculpture was the perfect means for making visible and perpetuating the activities of the king and of the gods.

Egyptian images are always composed of both figures and writing, while the hieroglyphs themselves are also small pictures that are integrated into the large picture. Only drawing and word together could make a valid statement. The relief sculptures of temples and tombs do not tell stories, and thus they are fundamentally different from what we are accustomed to in later cultures, particularly Christian culture in the West. Egyptian relief sculpture instead records symbolic actions from the life of the king, the gods, and the members of the upper class, and also scenes of work from the life of farmers, craftsmen, priests, scribes, servants, and soldiers. It is always a fictitious world that is presented to us: the gods speak in loving relationship with the king, all enemies collapse and die, all people are equally young and beautiful, the harvests are abundant, the herds of cattle are without number, and all predatory animals are slain. However, the fictitious world becomes reality through the fact that the figures and inscriptions are hewn into the stone wall. The Egyptians attributed to the images and the written words the power to bring into being the things they described. The temples and tombs with their relief sculptures that cover the walls, their cults, and their sacrifices all had an effect on life by regenerating it. Therefore the images and words had to be held fast in stone, which would never cease to exist.

[*See also* Grid Systems; *and* Painting.]

BIBLIOGRAPHY

Aldred, Cyril. *Egyptian Art in the Days of the Pharaohs, 3100–320* BC. London, 1980. History of Egyptian art from the first to thirtieth dynasty; bibliography, index, and glossary.

Eaton-Krauss, Marianne. *Ancient Egyptian Art*. Oxford, 1999. Complete history of Egyptian art, including relief; emphasizes precise analysis of development of style and the meaning of the representations.

Freed, Rita. "Relief Styles of the Nebhepetre Montuhotep Funerary Temple Complex." In *Chief of Seers. Egyptian Studies in Memory of Cyril Aldred*, edited by Elizabeth Goring et al. London and New York, 1997. Thorough study of the innovative early eleventh dynasty, which was decisive for the development of Middle Kingdom relief sculpture.

Lauer, Jean-Philippe. *Saqqara, the Royal Cemetery of Memphis Excavations and Discoveries since 1850*. London, 1978. Brief description of the most important tombs of kings and high officials, mainly from the Old Kingdom.

Leclant, Jean. *Recherches sur les monuments thébains de la XXVᵉ dynastie dite éthiopienne*. Bibliothèque d'Étude, 36. Cairo, 1965. Inventory of buildings of the twenty-fifth dynasty and their relief sculptures, with study of the iconography of gods, kings, and divine consorts.

Martin, Geoffrey T. *The Hidden Tombs of Memphis: New Discoveries from the Time of Tutankhamun and Ramesses the Great*. London, 1991. Introduces a group of marvelously decorated tombs from the end of the eighteenth dynasty, discovered in Saqqara from 1975 onward and of great significance for Egyptian art.

Robins, Gay. *The Art of Ancient Egypt*. London, 1997. A general art history, with particular attention to the function and context of ancient artworks, and explanation of working techniques.

Robins, Gay. *Egyptian Painting and Relief*. Shire Egyptology, 3. Princes Risborough, 1986. Brief explanation of the principles of representation, including the squared grid system used to obtain proportions of major human figures.

Smith, William Stevenson. *The Art and Architecture of Ancient Egypt*. 2d edn., revised by W. K. Simpson. Harmondsworth, 1981. Art history from the late prehistoric period to end of the dynastic period; considers style and the meaning of representations, and discusses some unusual motifs.

Vandier, Jacques. *Manuel d'archéologie égyptienne*. 6 vols. Paris, 1952–1978. The only handbook with a general iconography of nonroyal tomb art, including scenes of daily life; one chapter covers the technique of relief sculpture and its conventions.

Vergnieux, Robert. *Recherches sur les monuments thébains d'Amenhotep IV à l'aide d'outils informatiques Methodes et resultats*. Geneva, 1999. New reconstruction of scenes from the temples of Akhenaten in Karnak, before he founded Tell el-Amarna; very well illustrated.

MAYA MÜLLER

Translated from German by Robert E. Shillenn

RELIGION. Herodotus' statement that the Egyptians "are religious to a higher degree than any other people" (Book II, 37) eulogizes Egypt to an uncommon degree. About six centuries later, in the *Perfect Discourse*, Hermes Trismegistos summed up the spirit of Egyptian religious beliefs for his disciple, Asclepius, in a striking metaphor: Egypt "has become the image of heaven, and what is more, the resting-place of heaven and all the forces that are in it. If we should tell the truth: our land has become the temple of the world" (*Codex Nag Hammadi* VI, 70, 5–10). About the same time, Lucian mocked the Egyptian gods who had infiltrated the assembly of the Olympian gods (*Deorum concilium*, 10–11). The quoted texts, mainly those of the third century CE, give evidence of the prestige and the power Egyptian religion had in Greek thought.

Polytheism. Egyptian religion was polytheistic from beginning to end. In the Early Dynastic period, fetishes, animals (for example, on the mace head of King "Scorpion," the Battlefield Palette, and the Narmer Palette), and human beings are attested everywhere in religious representations (Hoffman 1984, 306–347; Hornung 1983). The gods working for the king never appear on standards, but the divine fetishes and animals in the service of the king do. Hence, the divine signs on the standards symbolize the connection of a god with a specific town.

Animal representations of gods like Wepwawet, Thoth, or the various falcon gods, which appear in animal shape in dynastic times as well, or fetish representations of gods like Min, who has usually taken a human shape by then, make one cautious about tracing a historical development from fetishism to zoolatry and the cult of anthropomorphic gods. Gods of animal or human shape are also mentioned in the early onomasticon, such as Apis, Neith, and others, indicated by the common god hieroglyph (*ntr*) ("god"), which may stand for a specific god. It is difficult to trace the development of the fetishes and most of the animals commonly associated with the cult of a specific god from the predynastic period through dynastic times (e.g., the relation of the Abydos fetish to Osiris, first apparent in the Middle Kingdom). Baines (1995, 113) proposes another interpretation of the predynastic animals: they were embedded into the context of the king as representations of royal power; he also refers to the general absence of entirely human representations in depictions of gods and kings.

Ucko (1968, 427–434) investigated the so-called idols of the Badarian culture and dismissed the existence of anthropomorphic gods. However, it is difficult to detect features in predynastic human figures that would challenge their interpretation as deities. The scarcity of human figures from predynastic times suggests that the figures of bearded men and dancing or naked women were intended as divinities.

The gods could assume many different shapes (Assmann 1991, 57–58; Hornung 1983). Their appearance was therefore unpredictable, though a certain pattern had developed by dynastic times.

The *ba*. The manner in which sacred animals and fetishes were connected with the gods was formulated by the Egyptians themselves in later times. The gods were rarely present because they dwelt in distant territories that could be described only vaguely. The sun god, Re, continually traversed the sky and the netherworld, and thus had no specific dwelling-place in Egypt. Since the Old Kingdom, Re was attached to Heliopolis by being syncretized with Atum. The remote gods could "enter into the statues" provided for them in the temples (*Memphite Theology*, 60) or, according to the theology of the Late period, they could enter this world as *ba* (*b3*), the active spirit or personality of gods and men (Assmann 1991, 67). The god could choose among the various "vessels" that Egyptians prepared for him.

The kings set up cult statues in the temples to be at the disposal of the gods. With the decline of royal power after the New Kingdom, the gods could take over this task themselves (*Memphite Theology*, 60). According to the Palermo stone, statues were created by royal acts. All statues (including mummies) were animated by the Opening of the Mouth ceremony; the statue then became the potential restingplace for the divine *ba*. The prevention of free access of the god to his image endangered his efficacy in the world. Sorcerers used to threaten the gods with this restriction, in a practice documented as early as the Pyramid Texts. The *Perfect Discourse* refers to Egypt as "the restingplace of the gods" but adds that the gods can leave Egypt forever—a concept that was also formulated in the myth of the Heavenly Cow, recorded in royal tombs since the end of the eighteenth dynasty (Hornung 1982).

The divine *ba* (creative power) could rest in a variety of places. It was therefore important that the *ba* stayed with the dead: "Your *ba* belongs to your innermost properties" (Spells 753a and 413a of the Pyramid Texts; Morenz 1973, 157–158; for the concept of the *ba* see Žabkar 1968). The plural of *ba* also means "dangerous divine power" in later periods (for example, British Museum Papyrus 10251 r° (19); Edwards 1960). In the Old Kingdom, people had names evoking the positive divine power, for example, *Ḫꜥ-bꜣ.w-ptḥ* ("the power of Ptah has arisen"). In the Coffin Texts, the god and his *ba* are clearly distinguished (Spell 333), while animals appear as manifestations of different divine powers (Hornung 1982; Assmann 1979, 7–42).

The sacred animals can be regarded as living cult images: chief representatives of a sacred species were kept at the temples, and fetish animals were kept in homes (Kessler 1989). The first group was evident in cults—the Apis bull attached to Osiris, the Buchis and Mnevis bulls attached to the sun god, and even the beetle Khepri (the resurrecting form of the sun god). *Ba* was incorporated in these living images just as the god Horus appeared in the living king. The gods could also appear in various animals—baboon, ibis, snake, frog, kite, or falcon—which were given the actual names of their divine masters.

The ka. In contrast to the active *ba*, the sacred images prepared for the gods were called the *ka* (*kꜣ* "double"). The Egyptians thought that the *ka* was the creative force that accompanies people in life (Schweitzer 1956). Double statues of the Old and the Middle Kingdoms represent the person with his double. In Spell 1623a of the Pyramid Texts, Geb, the father of Osiris, is "the *ka* of every god"; that is, he is the representative and the "vessel" of all gods. Horus, the king, has a *ka* that is joined with the royal cenotaphs or *ka*-mansions (documented since the sixth dynasty), showing the divine force of the king established throughout Egypt. Several Old Kingdom pyramids belonging to one king—for example, Sneferu—may be interpreted as *Ka*-mansions. During the Middle Kingdom the "soul" mansions—the proper Egyptian name is not recorded—probably fulfilled this function for the nobility. The royal *ka*-mansion disappeared in the eighteenth dynasty, and was replaced by the "house of millions of years" erected also in multiples for a single king (Arnold 1996, 139).

Inscriptions of the Hathor temple in Dendera clearly describe the connection of the gods to the statue (*ka*). The cult statue of the goddess was transferred onto the roof of the temple where, defended against the profane gaze by a wall, it was deposited in a little kiosk on New Year's Eve. In the morning, the divine power (*ba*) of the goddess descended with the rays of the rising sun and united with her statue (*ka*).

Local Dimension of the Gods. The Egyptian gods of dynastic times can be understood in terms of their cults, in terms of their cosmic dimensions, and also in terms of the language used to characterize them (Assmann 1991). The cult was not locally fixed, but it had local aspects, though some scholars have overestimated the extent of these (Kees 1956). Most of the major gods, such as Amun, Re, Osiris, and Thoth, obviously had roots in more than

one settlement. Most gods had cult places in many Egyptian temples, and in addition one or two cult centers, where the honored god was called "lord" (for example, Khnum in Elephantine, Kom Ombo, Edfu, Esna, Thebes, Dendera, Hypsele, Antinoöpolis, and Herakleopolis; Gardiner 1947; Badawi 1937). In most temples, however, one god was linked with other gods; this is clearly demonstrated by their composite names.

Toward the Late period, the connection of a god with a settlement became more important. Greek toponyms such as Hermopolis, Heliopolis, and Crocodilopolis conclusively prove this. In the toponyms of pharaonic times, such divine names were used only in connection with the chapels and temples situated there. The toponym of Memphis (*Mn-nfr w-ppy*, "Pepy's beauty rests"), known since the New Kingdom, is the name of the funerary temple of King Pepy I of the sixth dynasty; *ꜥnḫ-tꜣ.wy* ("the revival of the two lands") or *Ḥw.t-kꜣ-ptḥ* ("the *ka*-mansion of Ptah") are the occasional toponyms of the town from the Old Kingdom onward. This is also true of the toponym Dendera, in which the name of a goddess is joined to the sacred pillar (*iwn.t*).

The temple was the resting place of the gods, where they could visit and accept the offerings presented to them. The temple was imagined as the image of the cosmos with the god's house at its core on the highest point of the structure, that is, the primeval hill. Temples were hidden from public view by walls. The best-preserved Egyptian temples belong to the Ptolemaic and Roman periods, and all these features were present in them.

Gods in Time and Space. Gods were tied to time and space. They grew old, faded away, and were resurrected. This feature belongs mainly to the sun god, Re, who was "born" every morning and "died" every night. Connected with the birth of gods, mainly the child members of divine triads, were special buildings (*mammisi*) adjacent to temples, erected in the Ptolemaic and Roman periods. The conceptual antecedent of this structure is the representations of the king's divine birth, frequent since the eighteenth dynasty. However, its origin clearly dates back to the time of the Pyramid Texts (for example, Spell 632).

The Egyptians did not define the death of Osiris, lord of the underworld. Osiris was always regarded as a dead god, despite the late custom of the corn mummy, which is often taken as a sign of his resurrection. New life generally arises out of the dead part of the god (mummy, soil). Hence, the comparison of Osiris with gods of resurrection in the ancient Near East should be treated with caution. The birth of the divine son, Horus (also the "beloved son"), was interpreted in two ways: the dead Osiris sired the son on his sister-consort, Isis; or the sun god conceived his son with a mortal queen.

The lifetime of the gods defined the boundaries of existence. Gods were tied to a structured creation, in contrast to a formless chaos. Eschatological texts show some ambiguity concerning the end of the world. Chapter 175 of the *Book of Going Forth by Day* (*Book of the Dead*) reveals the end of existence in the primeval waters. The text continues: "How prosperous will be what I have done for Osiris, elevated before all gods [that is, the dead ones]. I have given him government over the desert. His son Horus is the heir of my seat on the Island of Flame." The catastrophe is not total, however. Osiris's rule over the desert and Horus's inherited dominion on the Island of Flame do not end. The topic of this spell may be the same as that of the myth of the Heavenly Cow, where the aged creator withdraws from government on earth into heaven. What is left of the world resembles chaos more than well-ordered Egypt. The Egyptians did not reflect on this inevitable catastrophe; instead, they always looked for ways and means to maintain order (*maat*).

Creation of the Gods. Creation is one of the main topics of Egyptian theology. Several concepts are known, each tied to a specific town—Heliopolis, Hermopolis, or Memphis. The first matter to appear in the primeval waters was usually believed to have been a hill bearing the primeval egg, which a primeval wind would fertilize, according to a tradition of the Late period. The egg could also be associated with Re (Spell 292 of the Coffin Texts). In another concept, a lotus flower grew on the primeval hill, and in it the child-god Nefertum appeared (Frankfort 1948, 151–159). Although chaos is formless, the Egyptians called the primeval waters Nun (*Nny, Nww*), who was both the creator and the most ancient element of creation. According to a more elaborate concept, from Hermopolis, there were eight primordial gods, in four pairs, all with negative significance. They are *Nny* and *Nnit* ("water abyss"), *Kky* and *Kkit* ("darkness"), *Ḥhy* and *Ẉhy* ("infinity"), and *Imn* and *Imnt* ("invisibility"). The positive elements are "sacred water" (for example, the sacred lakes of the temples), "light" (for example, the sun, the moon, and the stars), "limitation" (linked to the expression *drw*, "boundary"), and "observation" (that is, Amun comes forth from invisibility). The pairs were shaped as frogs or frog-headed human beings. That is why the goddess of birth has the shape of a frog. Apart from these pairs, the Egyptians had another group of five gods: four primeval gods presided over by Thoth.

The Heliopolitan and Memphite theologies also concentrated on the creation of the world. According to the Heliopolitan system, the creator, Atum, masturbated to generate the first pair of gods—Shu (*Šw*, "emptiness filled with air") and Tefnut, the goddess of humidity (*Tfnw.t*), who remains rather dim beside her male counterpart. According to another version, Atum spit them out (1653a–b of the Pyramid Texts). The creation of the next genera-

tion—Geb, the god of the earth (*Gbw*) and his consort, Nut, the goddess of the sky (*Nw.t*)—is not well documented in texts. This cosmic pair became the parents of the next four gods: Osiris (*Wsir*), Isis (*3.t*), Seth (*Stḫ, Stš*), and Nephthys (*Nb.t-ḥw t*, "mistress of the chapel"). A dividing line is to be drawn between the first two pairs, the cosmic gods, and the four of the next generation; the latter have to do with kingship. Osiris and Isis generate the living king (*Ḥrw*, Horus, "the far one"). Seth opposes the young royal heir of Egypt. The existence of his consort makes the imagining of pairs a structural necessity. The system focuses on the generation of the king as the guarantor of creation. The notion of the king's divine kinship was gradually expanded through Egyptian history.

Memphite theologians thought creation was done through words. The heart and tongue of Ptah formed the center of the Memphite system. Contrary to the Memphite view, the Heliopolitan Atum generated the gods in a sexual way. Still important, however, is the division between cosmic and political divine spheres. The main topic of reflection in Memphis was the establishment of the kingdom after the cosmogony was accomplished.

The Egyptians did not dwell on the moment when the first thing emerged from chaos into being. The epithet *ḫpr ds.f* ("the self-created") was attached to all gods whom Egyptians chose to consider as creators. In the Middle Kingdom, the primordial existence of a god who did not belong to a specific theological system is often stressed (for example, the god *Ḥk3*, "Magician" in Spell 261 of the Coffin Texts), though the connection sometimes seems to be contrary to the god's origins. Egyptian thought tends to start with the explanation of what to call the created world, probably under the influence of Memphite thinking. The first instances of divine concern may be found in 1695a of the Pyramid Texts: "They create (*sḫpr*) this NN like Re in this his name of Creating (*ḫprr*)." Literary works did not appear before the Middle Kingdom, but the acts of the gods are mentioned in the Pyramid Texts.

Besides the major cosmological systems, there were also minor cosmogonies, known to us from quotations in texts. These systems have no unique features because they syncretized other known systems; for example, the theology of Amun used the cosmogony of Re-Atum (Sethe 1929).

The Egyptians conceived the leading god of a cult center as the head of a triad, which consisted of the god, his consort, and their child. This concept was widespread in Egypt from the Old Kingdom, when the god-child was usually the king, to the Late period, when he was the king's divine substitute. If there was no local goddess at hand, the Egyptians created one for the triad (for example, *Nḥm.t-ꜥw3y* "Savior of the robbed one," in Hermopolis). Prominent triads are known in Thebes (Amun-Mut-Khonsu), Memphis (Ptah-

Sakhmet-Nefertum), Elephantine (Khnum-Satis-Anukis), and everywhere in a general connection with kingship (Osiris-Isis-Horus). Other triads may be detected in several places, but written or archaeological evidence is scarce.

Syncretism and Personification. The term "syncretism" has a special usage in Egyptology, designating the coexistence or perhaps cooperation of two or more gods. Coexistence could be of a theological or political nature. This feature first appeared in the fourth dynasty with Atum-Re of Heliopolis. Prominent examples from the Middle Kingdom are Amun-Re of Thebes and Ptah-Sokar of Memphis, as well as less permanent linkages like Sobek-Re and those of minor gods with important gods, where the lesser may claim the cultic attributes of the greater. One of the most disputed of these relationships is the Ramessid triad Amun-Re-Ptah, which signifies an amalgamation of the powers of the three gods in one entity. Another important, long-lived syncretism (starting in the Old Kingdom) occured between Re and Osiris, that is, the fusion of the living god with the dead one. Statements like "this certain Osiris is arisen as Re" (*in Wsir mn pn ḫʿy m Rʿ*, Coffin Texts, I, 191g–192a) support this view. "Re unifies with his mummy Osiris in the sixth hour" of the *Book of That Which Is in the Underworld* (*Amduat*) was a phrase used in kings' tombs since the eighteenth dynasty. The *unio mystica* ("mystical union," as Hornung has called it), clearly shows that syncretism was a temporary unification in which each god kept his own characteristics. "It is Re who rests in Osiris, Osiris rests in Re," was written in the nineteenth dynasty next to the ram-headed, mummiform Re in the tomb of Nefertari (tomb sixty-six in the Valley of the Queens). This is also of the fusions that represented attempts to connect king and gods more closely. Toward the Late period the number of syncretized gods increased without reference to kingship, the divine nature of which was steadily waning.

The Egyptians created personified conceptions and emblems, too, but these were always joined with a god or used as decorations (Baines 1985). The feature can be observed already in predynastic times, when standards represented gods. It is doubtful, however, that animated standards of other objects were actually venerated as deities. The Inundation (*Ḥʿpy*, Hapy) and the Magician (*Ḥkз*, Heka) should be excepted because they already had cults.

Gods in Narrative. The mythic dimension of language in Egypt is closely bound to literacy. Texts known since the third dynasty make reference to the activities of the gods, usually within accounts of relations between nobles and the king. Narrative literature did not appear before the Middle Kingdom, but myths certainly existed in oral tradition long before. Allusions to the deeds of gods are inserted in early ritual texts, such as the Pyramid Texts.

Late in Egyptian history, myths often have an etiological character, like the Horus myth of Edfu. Most of the known Egyptian myths concern the origins and nature of kingship as the central topic of interest.

Hymns (*dwзw*) and litanies were used in the cults. Hymns seemed to be addressed to both gods and kings, and were also incorporated in the Pyramid Texts. The Middle Kingdom hymn to the crocodile god, Sobek, that equates the beast with the king is a striking example of connecting the king to a god. The powers of the king are revealed in the crocodile god, and the powers of the god in the king (Papyrus Ramesseum VI, 11. 62. 95. 107). Numerous hymns to Re, Osiris, Thoth, Amun, Khnum, and other minor gods were created for ritual purposes. Toward the last days of Egyptian religion, a strict daily schedule seems to have evolved, which consisted of hymns, litanies, and rituals taken from the theologies of every period (for example, at the temple of Khnum at Esna; Sauneron, 1962).

A litany enumerates the names of the god in a cultic context (*wdn*). Elaborate litanies could have an explanatory text, like the *Litany of Re* (Hornung, 1975–1976). Essentially, the litany mirrors the multiplicity of forms of one god in different cult centers.

The idea of divinity developed as a result of long and intensive reflection. The theology of Amun evolved between the Old and Middle Kingdoms, well before Amun appeared at Thebes in the Middle Kingdom. Yet the concepts of kingship are fully formed in the Pyramid Texts, which mark a *terminus ante quem* of their origin (for example, Spell 606). Scholars date the origin of these concepts to the Early Dynastic period. The Memphite system appears to have developed in various stages, with many textual deviations like (Morenz 1973, 155; Assmann 1996, 392–395). The evolution of these concepts can also be shown in royal mortuary texts (Pyramid Texts, *Book of That Which Is the Underworld*), or the texts of nonroyal burials (Coffin Texts, or *Book of Going Forth by Day*).

Monotheism and Henotheism. Several attempts have been made to explain Egyptian religion in terms of monotheism (Hornung 1983). Scholars of the nineteenth century, steeped in the Christian tradition, tended to find traces of monotheism in Egyptian beliefs. The main evidence put forward was the anonymous god to whom Egyptians prayed in literary and wisdom texts. Now, however, the anonymous god is understood to represent a way of invoking any divine power (*ba*) emanating from any gods. It was only the eighteenth dynasty religious reforms of Amenhotpe IV (Akhenaten) that tried to introduce and promote a single god, the Aten. Akhenaten did not succeed; the reform was supported only by the young intellectuals of his court, and even his adherents did not completely accept his monotheism, as representations of other gods found in their tombs prove. After the intermezzo of Amarna, the Egyptians abandoned monotheism for good.

Several researchers have applied the concept of henotheism to Egyptian religion. This religious practice focuses on one god addressed in a particular time of worship. The believer unites all known divine powers in his favorite god. Henotheistic practices have been documented as early as the Old Kingdom, and may have been theologically connected with the notion of the anonymous god.

Cult. The center of the Egyptian cult was the temple, a sacred area enclosed by a wall, that excluded the profane. The temple could be called a "house" (*pr*), or a "chapel" (*ḥw.t*), or a "chapel of the god" (*ḥw.t-nṯr*), which includes section of the temple devoted to worldly needs. Inside was the cult statue, consecrated ("born") by a royal act, which served as dwelling for the divinity. The king (or his priestly substitute) had to care for the cult statue during the daily ritual. In depictions of cultic performance, it is always the king who acts in front of the god. The kings (and later, nobles) are represented holding a relic or a cult object, a convention demonstrating reverence.

An early exception seems to be the worship of Osiris, known from many stelae in the Middle Kingdom, in which the dead person worships the god. The deceased became Osiris, as only the dead king did in the Old Kingdom, and could perform the cult rituals before the god of the dead. After a certain point in history, nobles were allowed by the king to set up their statues in the local temple or in sacred areas like Abydos, and could thus share in the rituals performed for the deity there at any time.

The cult ritual was a dialogue between gods (Assmann 1991, 60), and thus the king (or his representative) acted in the divine performance as a god. Until the Middle Kingdom, the spheres of administration and cult were not separated, but in the eighteenth dynasty, a special priesthood was established. Hence, the administrators acquired access to the cult sanctuary, acting on behalf of the king. It is doubtful that the general population were ever admitted into this activity.

The offering list was a ritual document that originated in the Old Kingdom and persisted until the end of Egyptian antiquity. This list consists of such things as animals, cereals, food, and garments. Animals like gazelles or birds frequently signify the enemies of Osiris. Bulls, however, represent the power of kings and gods. Therefore, the offering has a protective and a nutritive significance, that is, the annihilation of the god's enemies and the sustenance of the gods by the meal made of the sacrificial bull. The offerings often allude (by speaking of the eye of Horus or the testicles of Seth) to the myth of Horus and Seth, which was closely connected with kingship from the Old

Kingdom onward. By the Late period, this connection became rather complicated (if not incomprehensible), but the myth of kingship remained at the core.

The King. The king represented Egypt before the gods. He worshipped the gods in standing, kneeling, and crawling positions while presenting offerings to them. One of the statues of the Luxor cache shows King Horemheb kneeling in front of Atum. The symbolism of the offerings shows their significance: he must secure order (*mꜣꜤ.t* "maat"), which is compulsory for gods as well as kings. The sense of offering is not merely to give in order that the god will give in return (Hornung 1983); it reminds the deity that order must be maintained. Disorder and chaos attack order when the sun god traverses the underworld by night, and the people could revolt against the aged god (*Book of That Which Is in the Underworld, Myth of the Heavenly Cow*).

The king was the single link between the divine and the profane. He was the representative of god on Earth, or his image from the thirteenth dynasty on. The doctrine of the king as the image of god is one of the awkward features of Egyptian religion. Recorded since the Second Intermediate Period, the doctrine attempts to explain how a living being can acquire divine status. The concept was first formulated in the Coffin Texts, and had perhaps been used earlier in the Pyramid Texts. It may have originated in the union of the dead king with Osiris, or that of the living king with Horus.

The first title of the king is Horus. There is a close connection of deity and king since late predynastic times, in that the god Horus appears in the royal person. This basic concept was maintained during all periods, although in various royal representations, the proportions of the king to the god were eventually changed in favor of the god: the falcon sits, hardly visible, on the neck of the fourth dynasty king Khafre; the king bears plumage covering the back of his head down to his waist in several eighteenth dynasty representations; and a giant Horus falcon protects King Nektanebo II of the thirtieth dynasty. In a statue of the Luxor cache found in 1988, King Horemhab stands in the last position in front of Amun; he represents Amun, who protects him, for his people.

Doubts have been expressed about the divine nature of the king. His divine status has been explained by reference to his two natures (Silverman 1995, 65). The king became an offspring of the god (son of Re) in the fourth dynasty (886a–887b of the Pyramid Texts). This has been viewed as a loss of divine power. This feature could be interpreted as a way of embedding the king into the Heliopolitan system. This new concept defined the status of the dead king as Osiris, and that of the living king as son of Re. In mortuary texts, taking Re as the principle of life and Osiris as the principle of death, the title "Son of Re" demonstrates the affiliation of the ruling king to the sphere of life, while "Son of Osiris" can also be applied to the same ruling king. This can be supported by the construction of solar temples together with the "Osirian" pyramids in the fifth dynasty, which also shows the close connection of Re and Osiris with kingship.

The permanent co-presence of king and gods at every place in Egypt was clearly impossible. The king thus had to deputize members of the royal family (in the Old Kingdom), and later, nobles of his court to represent him. Priestly ranks were closely connected to administrative ranks in the Old and Middle Kingdoms, and an independent priesthood with its own titles developed only during the New Kingdom. The clerical and administrative hierarchy was organized into groups called "phyles" (s3). High priests were appointed at all great temples from the local administration, while officials were entrusted with informal tasks in temples, which could include the temporary leadership of the local phyle (Stela Louvre C 13). At the beginning of the eighteenth dynasty, the temple hierarchy grew stronger and began to influence the king. The origins of this special relationship between gods (through the priests) and kings go back as far as the Middle Kingdom. The god is said to elevate the king before millions (*Instructions for Merikare* 116), thus legitimizing the king. In the New Kingdom, the dominant god, Amun-Re, often intervened in politics (electing the king, or conducting campaigns) through his priesthood. The designation of priests by the king became a formality, though the king retained the right to appoint high priests. In the Ramesside Period the god could even appropriate this task (the appointment of the high priest of Amun, *Nb-wnn*, in the reign of Ramesses II). Near the end of the eighteenth dynasty, Akhenaten attempted to restore the original relationship of king to god. The king became the exclusive partner of the god, the only intermediary between the one god and the people (Redford 1995, 177–178). The clerical challenge to kingship may have motivated King Akhenaten.

The male-dominated Egyptian society did not concede any important cultic position to women. Though priestesses existed since the Old Kingdom, their number and their importance were always limited, and in most cases they served female gods. Many women seem to have been involved in the so-called harem (*ḥnr*) as chantresses or as dancers, as shown by reliefs in the Old Kingdom tombs, textual evidence from the Middle Kingdom archives of Illahun, and in large numbers of Theban and other temples of the New Kingdom. Apart from the minor positions that women held during all periods, the rank of the "god's wife of Amun" eventually acquired the highest political influence (in the first half of the first millennium BCE). It was inaugurated in the First Intermediate Period, when a "god's wife of Min" is first mentioned, and thus the rank was not limited to servants of Amun.

The idea of an intermediary relation between kings and gods seems to be displayed in the recently found two-sided relief statue of King Amenhotpe III in Luxor. On the front, the king stands on a sledge, which emphasizes his exceptional status as the god Horus, while on the back, the king kneels, in holy discourse with and makes an offering to Amun, Lord of Karnak (Silverman 1995, 62–63). Both representations reflect Horus's position in the divine hierarchy as the offspring of the gods. Thus, royal statues took part in the cult as intermediaries, and were themselves divine in the New Kingdom, particularly in the Ramessid period. The king making an offering in front of the king's cult statue needs additional explanation. In the Old Kingdom, the divinity appears in a dual role—as a heavenly and an earthly god. But the royal Horus title does not automatically signify the heavenly Horus. He can, however, instill his divine power into the king. Similarly, Osiris represents two gods: Osiris, the ruler of the underworld, and Osiris, the dead king, specified by name; these attributes are evident already in the early Middle Kingdom. Hence the king, as the potential receiver of the divine power (*ba*), also divides into cult statue and living king.

In the New Kingdom, the Egyptian who was not part of the priesthood could not directly participate in the rituals or enter the temple. He saw only the veiled figures of the gods during outdoor processions, and could only participate in the cult of gods during festivals. Herodotus makes some reference to those events, but he is cautious about the details. A glance at the Theban festival calendar of the New Kingdom and those of the Ptolemaic and Roman temples clearly show that everywhere in Egypt celebrations were held in a great number throughout the year, and especially on New Year's Day, when order (*maat*) was restored.

Egyptians could not always pray directly to the gods. A "personal piety" movement developed from the Middle Kingdom onward, in which Egyptians could directly address the gods and seek a divine answer. Evidently in the early eighteenth dynasty, the gods could resolve political questions through oracles and also had the power to pardon human sins. Since creation was not perfect, misguided people would sin against order (*maat*, Spell 125 of the *Book of Going Forth by Day*); gods and kings had to prevent chaos. The creator formed mankind in his own image—not just his physical appearance, but also the free will that seduced humans from the correct course of order. For the same reason, people could hope for divine salvation if they took the god into their hearts.

Egyptian religion had great appeal in Hellenistic times. The cult of the goddess Isis spread throughout the Roman Empire. The nature of her cult was by then more Hellenistic than Egyptian, but Isis never lost her Egyptian identity, and her temple in Philae was not closed until the sixth century CE.

[*See also* Ba; Cults; Deities; Divinity; Hymns; Ka; Kingship; Monotheism; Myths; Piety; *and* Royal Roles.]

BIBLIOGRAPHY

Arnold, Dieter. *Die Tempel Ägyptens.* Augsburg, 1996.

Assmann, Jan. *Ägypten: Eine Sinngeschichte.* Munich, 1996.

Assmann, Jan. *Ägypten: Theologie und Frömmigkeit einer frühen Hochkultur.* 2d ed. Stuttgart, 1991.

Baines, John. *Fecundity Figures: Egyptian Personification and the Iconology of a Genre.* Warminster, 1985.

Baines, John. "Origins of Egyptian Kingship." In *Ancient Egyptian Kingship*, edited by D. O'Connor and D. P. Silverman, pp. 95–156. Leiden, 1995.

Brunner, Hellmut. *Grundzüge der altägyptischen Religion.* Darmstadt, 1983.

Edwards, I. E. S. *Hieratic Papyri in the British Museum.* 4th series, *Oracular Amuletic Decrees of the Late New Kingdom.* London, 1960.

Frankfort, Henry. *Kingship and the Gods: A Study of Ancient Near Eastern Religion as the Integration of Society and Nature.* Chicago, 1948.

Gardiner, Alan M. *Ancient Egyptian Onomastica.* Oxford, 1947.

Hoffman, Michael. *Egypt Before the Pharaohs.* London, 1984.

Hornung, Erik. *Buch von der Anbetung des Re.* Aegyptiaca Helvetica, 1–2. Geneva, 1975–1976.

Hornung, Erik. *Conceptions of God in Ancient Egypt: The One and the Many.* Translated by J. Baines. London, 1983.

Hornung, Erik. *Der ägyptische Mythos von der Himmelskuh: Eine Ätiologie des Unvollkommenen.* Göttingen, 1982.

Junker, Hermann. *Die Götterlehre von Memphis.* Berlin, 1940.

Junker, Hermann. *Die politische Lehre von Memphis.* Berlin, 1941.

Kees, Hermann. *Der Götterglaube im alten Ägypten.* 2d rev. ed. Berlin, 1956.

Morenz, Siegfried. *Egyptian Religion.* Translated by Ann E. Keep. London, 1973.

Redford, Donald B. "The Concept of Kingship during the Eighteenth Dynasty." In *Ancient Egyptian Kingship*, edited by D. O'Connor and D. P. Silverman, pp. 157–183. Leiden, 1995.

Sauneron, Serge. *Les fêtes religieuses d'Esna aux derniers siècles du paganisme.* Cairo, 1962.

Schweitzer, Ursula. *Das Wesen des Ka im Diesseits und Jenseits der alten Ägypter.* Hamburg, 1956.

Sethe, Kurt. *Amun und die acht Urgötter von Hermopolis.* Berlin, 1929.

Silverman, David P. "The Nature of Egyptian Kingship." In *Ancient Egyptian Kingship*, edited by D. O'Connor and D. P. Silverman, pp. 49–92. Leiden, 1995.

te Velde, Herman. *Seth, the God of Confusion.* Probleme der Ägyptologie, 6. Leiden, 1967.

Tobin, Vincent A. *Theological Principles of Egyptian Religion.* American University Studies, 7/59. New York, 1989.

Ucko, Peter J. *Anthropomorphic Figurines of Predynastic Egypt and Neolithic Crete.* London, 1968.

Žabkar, Louis V. *A Study of the Ba Concept in Ancient Egyptian Texts.* Chicago, 1968.

ULRICH H. LUFT

RESERVE HEADS. Among the private statuary of the Old Kingdom is a group called reserve heads or portrait heads (Ger., *Ersatzköpfe* or *Porträtköpfe* Fr., *têtes de remplacement* or *de réserve*). The label "magical heads" seems more accurate, because it expresses the contradictory functions of these objects, as revealed by recent inquiry.

At this writing, thirty-three magical heads have been discovered, as well as eight isolated ears separately carved and initially stuck with plaster. The Giza head presented to the media in 1992 is not to be counted as a magical head: the beginning of the shoulder and the irregular break of the neck clearly demonstrates that this head was part of a statue. However, a small unfinished head (unpublished), found in 1989 by the Lisht expedition of The Metropolitan Museum of Art, in a twelfth dynasty stratum, may tentatively be considered a late resurgence of this type of object.

Typological Features. Reserve heads are metonymical objects: a head and its neck, without the shoulders. The neck section is flat-bottomed so that the head does not need any further support. When the head is posed on the flat section, its gaze is much higher than the horizon line and the gaze of complete statues (except in very rare exceptions). The famous Nefertiti bust and the other composite statues of Tell el-Amarna have nothing in common with these heads, nor do the busts emerging from false doors in some Old Kingdom *mastaba*s (e.g., Neferseshem-ptah and Idw, Giza, sixth dynasty). The bust of the vizier Ankh-haf (reign of Khafre, fourth dynasty) is however an exception, since it shares some features with the magical heads, such as the ablation of the ears.

For the private statuary of the Old Kingdom, a smaller scale than life-size was usually preferred, but, except for one late occurrence, the magical heads are all life-size. They are always monochrome, unlike other statuary of the Old Kingdom. The heads usually have the color of their material, a white limestone; two examples in grey siltstone from the Nile have been found. In three cases, tiny traces of paint have been discovered (two red and one black).

The most characteristic feature of the magical heads is that they present at least one, and frequently more, of the four following types of marks, produced by a clumsy hand certainly after the finishing touch of the sculptor: a circle around the neck, a little higher than its base; a groove running from the skull to the nape; the ears destroyed, unstuck, or omitted; and a clumsy outline of the edge of the close-shaven hair. None of these features appears on any private statues except the magical heads.

Geographical Situation. The origin of these heads (and ears) is the area around Memphis in the broadest sense of the term (except for a head from a private collection in Belgium and one at University College, London, of which the provenance is not certain). The vast majority of them have been found in Giza. A few isolated examples come from Abusir, Dahshur, and Abu Roash.

Chronological Situation. The most ancient magical head, found in Dahshur (Cairo CG 519), can be dated to Sneferu's reign (beginning of the fourth dynasty). It is during this period that the magical heads ritual seems to have appeared. The ritual came into particular favor under Khufu (the majority of the heads come from the G4000 cemetery of Giza). The heads are also well attested in Khafre's cemetery, G7000. The latest examples (fifth and sixth dynasties), isolated in time as in space, are characterized by poor stylistic quality. This stylistic decay seems to be parallel to the progressive extinction of the specific ritual practice.

Situation in the Tomb. H. Junker, the Austrian archaeologist who led excavations in the Giza necropolis at the beginning of this century, concluded from his observations that the heads were fixed into the masonry of the wall separating the funerary chamber from the bottom of the shaft, behind a monolithic portcullis. Since the chamber invariably opened to the north, the heads then looked in the direction of the circumpolar stars. While destroying the blockage, tomb-robbers let the heads roll to the bottom of the shaft or inside the chamber. It can be concluded from these observations that the magical heads belonged to the underworld, a context that differentiates them from other private sculpture of the Old Kingdom, which was always placed in close contact with the living (in *serdab*s or in offering chapels). This specific situation must be related to the marks described above.

Significance. When first discovered, the heads were believed to be prosthesis heads to replace magically the head of the dead, if it were damaged. This theory was largely developed by H. Junker (1914) who came to suggest, after his excavations in the fourth dynasty necropolis of Giza, an identity of function between the realization of the magical heads, the practice of mummification, the creation of plaster masks, and even private statuary in general. This interpretation does not attribute to these heads any specific meaning inside the semantic field of the image as a substitute of the dead. The mutilating marks, for instance, are not taken into account; their meaning could be of some importance, however, because this kind of mark is never found on any other type of substitute, whether mummies, masks, or normal statues. Incomplete though it might prove to be, Junker's theory became a dogma accepted by almost all Egyptologists.

In contrast to the idea of the heads being substitutes come A. L. Kelley's (1974) and N. B. Millet's (1981) theories. In their two short articles, they suggest that these heads were models for sculptors, used in the making of the funerary masks or of plaster casts. The breaking of the ears and the damage to the nape would have been caused during the unmolding of the head. This theory has major flaws. First, it does not take into account the particular situation of the head within the tomb. Second, we may wonder why a head should have been so carefully carved just to produce one funerary mask. Third, the idea of sculptors making a funerary mask using such a technique is irrelevant: the heads should have been bigger than life-size, so that the masks would fit over the thick linen wrapping the head of the deceased. Fourth, it is unlikely that an Egyptian artist would be unable to unmold a mask without damaging the original. Finally, if these heads were sculptor's models, how can we explain the fact that no normal private statue has been found belonging to the important individuals who had a magical head set among their funerary furniture?

The most recent study on the subject (Tefnin 1991) is based on a thorough reading of the archaeological documents, on the historiographical analysis of the previous theories, and on connecting the heads to the magical and religious literature. There is, however, a serious methodological problem linked to the late date of the texts (eighteenth dynasty at the earliest for the *Book of Going Forth by Day* [*Book of the Dead*] and the ritual of the Opening of the Mouth; Greco-Roman period for the rituals of Apophis' destruction). There does not exist any text contemporary with the heads. Because of the scarcity of texts from the fourth, fifth, and sixth dynasties, two choices appear: either we decide to ignore any explanation, or we agree to extrapolate, knowing the traditional character of Egyptian thought and myth.

Thus, the circle around the neck, which could not have been made by the hand of a sculptor, evokes the vast semantic field of decapitation, attested in some prehistoric cemeteries, well known in pharaonic law and used to punish Apophis (enemy of Osiris) in the late magical texts (Papyrus Bremner-Rhind, Papyrus Jumilhac). It can also be connected with execration plaques buried in the Giza necropolis during the eighteenth dynasty, studied by G. Posener. Dangerous dead persons were stamped on these plaques in the guise of prisoners; their throats were then cut by a line of red paint, certainly during the performance of a ritual. As in the case of the magical heads, we thus discern two distinctive moments: first, the fashioning of the figure by a trained artist or craftsman; subsequently, a violent and destructive gesture performed by a nonartist, certainly a ritual specialist. The deep groove at the back of the head represents a fracture of the skull, with blood gushing as in the A14 hieroglyph of a wounded prisoner, meaning "the enemy" or "the dead." The magical plaques of Giza, mentioned above, show the same bleeding wound, painted in red on top of the stamped figure during the performance of a violent ritual. This ritual action can be connected with a rather enigmatic moment of the well-known ritual of Opening of the Mouth, a moment of extreme tension between the *sem*-priest (eldest son or priest representing the family), the sculptor who is asked to create a likeness of the father, and a craftsman called "polisher" (?) who has to take the father's head and hit it despite the priest's opposition. This one says: "I am Horus-Seth, I shall not allow you to make my father's head become white (*shd*)." Is not this head "made white," bleeding white, in the text of the ritual, exactly equivalent to the white limestone magical head, deeply grooved at the back? And does not the text suggest admirably the double nature of these heads: first a naturalistic sculpture made by a master sculptor, and then violently hit during the ritual?

The texts are not so clear about the mutilation of the ears, sculpted as a whole or stuck to the head with plaster, and then cut off with a wooden blade or a metallic chisel, or even omitted in late occurrences. Those marks are so evident that we cannot avoid the idea of a ritual deafening of the dead, imprisoning him in the *igrt*, the world of silence, and reducing him to sensorial impotence, like Apophis's punishment. The clumsy outlining of the hair is also evident and specific for this group of heads. No text explains clearly that ritual practice, so that we may only appeal to anthropology, which provides many examples of an association between hair and life.

From the contrast between the perfection of the carving and the clumsiness of the ritual marks there arises a semantic ambiguity: these heads were meant to be beautifully carved, even bearing resemblance to the deceased—as may be suggested by the words of the Opening of the Mouth—but they were also magical objects that could become dangerous when placed close to the dead, and that had therefore to be ritually "canceled." The same superstitious fear led, as is well known, to mutilation of the hieroglyphs eventually written in the underground part of the tomb (but never the signs written in the funerary chapel, which belonged to the world of the living). However, there remains a major mystery: Why did the eminent individuals of that short period in the Old Kingdom not all have such magical heads in their tombs? The idea of royal favor must be rejected. It remains the hypothesis that certain dead persons were potentially more dangerous than others, owing perhaps to the circumstances of the death (e.g., drowning, violent death in general, or an ill-fated day of death). Nevertheless, it seems that the link between these magical heads and execration rituals cannot be denied.

BIBLIOGRAPHY

Junker, Herman. *Giza.* Vols. 1, 7, 8, 12. Vienna, 1929–1955. These volumes of the monumental excavation reports of the Austrian team at Giza contain all information on the conditions of discovery of the heads in the cemeteries near the pyramids of Khufu and Khafre.

Junker, Herman. "The Austrian Excavations, 1914." *Journal of Egyptian Archaeology* 1 (1914), 250–253. Brief account of the excavations mentioned above, already containing the major elements of Junker's interpretation.

Kelley, A. L. " 'Reserve Heads': A Review of the Evidence for their Placement and Function in the Old Kingdom Tombs." *Journal of the Society for the Study of Egyptian Antiquities* 5 (1974), 6–12.

Millet, N. B. "The Reserve Heads of the Old Kingdom." In *Studies in Ancient Egypt: Essays in Honor of Dows Dunham.* Boston, 1981. These two studies propose an alternative to the theory of the reserve heads: they are described as models of sculptor and/or models for plaster masks.

Smith, W. S. *A History of the Egyptian Sculpture and Painting in the Old Kingdom.* 2d ed. Boston, 1949. In this monumental book, the author reviews Junker's theories and adds precious information extracted from the excavations of G. A. Reisner (Harvard-Boston Expedition) in the same necropolis. Excellent illustrations.

Tefnin, Roland. *Art et magie au temps des Pyramides: L'énigme des têtes dites "de remplacement."* Monumenta Aegyptiaca, 5. Brussels, 1991. Not opposed to Junker's conclusions but completing them, emphasizing the mutilation inflicted on the heads, not taken into account in the earlier theory. Also offers a detailed, illustrated catalog of all known heads and fragments, with bibliography.

ROLAND TEFNIN
Translated from French by Angélique Corthals

RHINOCEROSES. There are only two species of the rhinoceros known to have lived on the African continent during historical times: the black rhinoceros (*Diceros bicornis*) and the white rhinoceros (*Ceratotherium simum*). The number and range of wild rhinoceroses has been in steady decline for many centuries but both existed in southern Sudan until recent decades. From a Predynastic rock drawing of game animals being chased by a hunter with bow and arrows on a cliff face near Silwa Bahri in Upper Egypt, probably dating from the Amratian (Naqada I) period, it is reasonably certain that rhinoceros distribution extended as far north as Egypt.

Accurate ceramic models of rhinoceros horns were discovered in an elite first dynasty tomb at Saqqara (tomb 3357), placed there, perhaps, as apotropaic devices. The rhinoceros, called in Egyptian *ȝbw* and *škb*, became locally extinct or uncommon by the end of the Early Dynastic period; its appearance seems to be recalled once or twice in figures during the Old and Middle Kingdoms, though these could well be elephants. No positively identifiable representations occur again until the New Kingdom's eighteenth dynasty, when one is pictured as a native of the land of Punt in Hatshepsut's mortuary temple at Deir el-Bahri. Thutmose III boasts, on a stela erected at the temple of Montu at Armant, that he shot one while campaigning in Nubia. During the nineteenth dynasty, likely during the reign of Ramesses II, a live rhinoceros is depicted among Nubian booty carved on a pylon, also at Armant, and it is being restrained by a gang of men using ropes. It is surrounded by a series of inscriptions, which give its various measurements, including the length of the horn. Assyrian sources report that Takelot II of the twenty-second dynasty sent a diplomatic gift of a live rhinoceros to Shalmaneser III, the king of Assyria. An Ethiopian rhinoceros took part in the grand procession of Ptolemy II Philadelphus, held in Alexandria during the early 270s BCE.

BIBLIOGRAPHY

Boessneck, Joachim. *Die Tierwelt des alten Ägypten: Untersucht anhand kulturgeschichtlicher und zoologischer Quellen.* Munich, 1988. Includes authoritative observations on the rhinoceros in ancient Egypt.

Gowers, William. "The Classical Rhinoceros." *Antiquity* 24 (1950), 61–71; 25 (1951), 155. Survey of rhinoceroses in the classical world; includes the principal Egyptian material.

Houlihan, Patrick F. *The Animal World of the Pharaohs.* London and New York, 1996. Handsomely illustrated book aimed at a general audience; useful information is given on the rhinoceros in pharaonic Egypt.

Osborn, Dale J., with Jana Osbornova. *The Mammals of Ancient Egypt.* Warminster, 1998. Includes much useful information on the rhinoceros in ancient times.

Störk, L. *Die Nashörner.* Hamburg, 1977.

PATRICK F. HOULIHAN

RIFEH. *See* Asyut.

ROMAN OCCUPATION. The occupation of Egypt by the Roman Empire began in 30 BCE. The Ptolemaic dynasty that had begun after the conquest by Alexander the Great of Macedon ended with the death of Cleopatra VII in 30 BCE, upon Octavian's arrival; Egypt then became a province of the Roman Empire administered by prefects, the equestrian governors appointed by the emperor. With only brief intermissions, Egypt was ruled by a Roman or Byzantine government until its loss to the Arabs spreading Islam in 641 CE. [*This article will treat the period up to 395 CE; the Late Antique period in Egypt, from 395 to 641 CE, usually referred to as Coptic, will be discussed in the article on Copts.*]

Chronology. The Roman occupation marked an important change in Egypt's fortunes; although it remained under foreign rule, it was no longer an independent country, as it had been under the Greeks. The chronological framework for Roman Egypt is thus based on Roman dynastic history, although little of that history involved Egypt directly and only a few of the emperors took a direct interest in the province. In 395 CE, the effective separation of Rome's Eastern and Western Empires began, with Egypt following the fortunes of the Eastern Empire ruled from Constantinople. The year 395 CE is only one of the points sometimes used in ending the period, and corresponds to no particular event in Egypt itself.

Octavian, given the title Augustus, ruled the Roman Empire until his death in 14 CE. His successors, related in various ways, formed the Julio-Claudian dynasty, which ended in 68 with the death of Nero. The Flavians (r. 69–96) disappeared with the death of Domitian; with Nerva (r. 96–98) began almost a century of rule by a sequence of emperors who, in the main, adopted their successors. Their reigns were viewed in antiquity, as by the nineteenth-century British historian Edward Gibbon, as the high point of the empire's history. The last of those emperors, the less-praised Commodus, was killed in 192, and after a time of turmoil the Severan dynasty (r. 193–235) took power, which was succeeded by a turbulent period with numerous rulers and pretenders, ending with the recovery of central control by Diocletian (r. 284–305) and his associates and successors. The most successful of these, Constantine, gained control of Egypt by defeating Licinius in 324; his son Constantius died in 361 and, after the dramatic interlude of Julian "the apostate," the house of Valentinian ruled to the end of the period discussed here.

Political History. By the standards of most of the Roman Empire, Egypt had an uneventful history—usually at peace, rarely on the front lines, and only occasionally visited by an emperor. The southern frontier, with Nubia and the Red Sea, had some military unrest under the first few Augustan governors but was then quiet until the mid-third century, when trouble with the Blemmyes and other tribes produced a flurry of activity; Diocletian, however, obtained peace with subsidies. Egypt itself was for the first three centuries of Roman rule undisturbed by invasion, but there was episodic violence in the Mediterranean seaport of Alexandria and an occasional revolt. Most important, the increasing conflict in Alexandria between the large Jewish population and their gentile neighbors produced mob violence in the years 38, 41, and 66 CE, and finally the massive Egyptian and Cyrenaean rebellion of 115–117 that ended in large-scale slaughter of the Jewish population, but only after the Romans brought in additional forces. For imperial campaigns, the garrison of Egypt, in turn, contributed at various points to concentrations of troops in Judaea, Arabia, and points east. Another internal revolt, in which again imperial military forces suffered temporary defeat, occurred in regnal year c.171/2, that of the so-called Boukoloi, in the Nile Delta—in the wake of a severe plague under Marcus Aurelius; the dam-

age and depopulation were significant. In 215, Alexandria suffered severely from Caracalla's soldiers. In 269, the Palmyrene queen Zenobia took Egypt and, in 270, Alexandria, which were then recovered by Aurelian (r. 270–275), but only after substantial damage. A revolt by L. Domitius Domitianus in regnal year 296/7 led to an eight-month siege of Alexandria by Diocletian, ultimately successful for him but disastrous for the city. After this, the major military actions of the fourth century were mainly played out in other parts of the empire. Alexandrian political life remained volatile, and the city became much diminished in extent and condition from what it had been in the second century.

Despite these and lesser troubles, Roman Egypt was usually left in peace under its governing prefects. After taking over the Greek empire, the Romans had inherited a land of villages and towns in Egypt, with few self-governing cities. This resulted from the policy of the Ptolemaic kings, who had founded only one such city, Ptolemais in Upper Egypt, which was added to the city of Naukratis and to Alexander the Great's creation, Alexandria. The Romans also founded just one, Antinoöpolis, the creation of Hadrian in 130 CE, in memory of his lover Antinous, who drowned in the Nile. The Romans, however, set about the development of local ruling elites in the chief towns of the nomes (provinces) and Septimius Severus, in 201 CE, granted those local elites their own governing councils. The third century saw enormous physical, cultural, and institutional development in those cities, which came to resemble other cities of the Greek

East much more closely than before. (Hardly anything is known of their political histories.)

The Roman emperors visited Egypt only occasionally, apart from the interventions already mentioned. Vespasian had been acclaimed there in 69 CE, by the troops of the prefect Tiberius Iulius Alexander; Vespasian's son, Titus, had also passed through the province. After suppressing the revolt of the Boukoloi, Avidius Cassius had been proclaimed emperor in 175 at Syene but was soon killed; Marcus Aurelius then visited Egypt in 176 and pardoned the Alexandrians for their support of Avidius Cassius. A long visit by Septimius Severus led to considerable physical and institutional benefits, but the Alexandrians' hostility to his son, Caracalla, ferociously reciprocated, led to the massacre of 215 CE and extensive damage to Alexandria.

Military Administration. In the absence of serious outside military threats, the Roman army in Egypt was focused largely on internal security, achieved with one major troop concentration at Nikopolis, outside Alexandria, and many small detachments spread throughout the length of the valley and along the roads of the Eastern Desert that led to quarries, mines, and ports. Total forces were modest. The Roman legions had been diminished from three under Augustus to two under Tiberius, then to one after Hadrian. The auxiliary forces occasionally fluctuated in number but seem usually to have included ten to thirteen units, about a third of which were cavalry. The total garrison has been estimated from as much as twenty-one thousand early in the reign of Augustus to as little as twelve thousand in most of the third century.

From the Ptolemies, the Romans inherited a complex system of centrally directed administration that had been controlled from Alexandria, although at least in the relatively remote districts the late Ptolemaic governors sometimes seemed like powerful theocratic barons, combining priesthoods with royal functions. Much of this structure the Romans retained; the country's division into the districts called nomes remained basic, with governors still called *strategoi* in charge of them. The nomes were divided into toparchies, each with a number of villages (averaging perhaps eight to fifteen villages per toparchy), with officials at village and toparchy level reported to the *strategos*. The character of the system was drastically overhauled, however. The *strategoi* came from outside the nomes of appointment, where they served for only a few years; at first they were Alexandrians, then from the early second century CE, increasingly from the elites of the nome capitals. The central administration in Alexandria, led by equestrians, also saw regular turnover and was part of a career track rather than a permanent assignment. Despite their presence, Alexandria was allowed a significant measure of self-administration.

In the lower ranks of the administration, too, major changes were made by the Romans, who gradually replaced career professionals with short-term (often one-year) appointments of private citizens, serving in rotation. Such uncompensated service eventually became obligatory (those appointments are called "liturgies"), although the pace at which compulsion was introduced has not yet become clear. The system seems to have been essentially complete by the time of Hadrian. The more responsible positions, particularly in tax collection, were given to men of property, who could be held liable for shortfalls. Required labor in the humble tasks, such as keeping irrigation channels clear, was distributed more broadly. The villagers had to supply most of their own officials, while nome-level appointees came from the upper strata of the nome capitals, or *metropoleis*, and only the *metropoleis* were encouraged to develop a political identity.

Under the Romans, the development of an urban upper class was not a quick process, but it had clearly begun by the time of Augustus and proceeded deliberately. The Romans left most land controlled by private individuals under grants from the Ptolemaic kings in the hands of the possessors and thus allowed much land to pass into full private ownership—which had not been a significant practice under the kings. Those who could trace their ancestry to Greek settlers, to the satisfaction of the new Roman government, became part of a privileged elite, who paid lower taxes and were given some role in the running of their cities, although not yet full self-government. That step came with Septimius Severus and opened an era of urban growth and activity, as competitive elites constructed buildings and held festivals and games similar to those of their counterparts elsewhere in the Eastern Empire. With their privileges went ever-increasing responsibility for local administration, and the new city councils of the third century became the main administrative organs of the nomes.

With the political changes, Egypt came to resemble fully other Roman provinces in administrative structure. The changes introduced by Diocletian and his successors were equally reflected in Egypt, including the subdivision of provinces into smaller units, the separation of civil and military authority, and the imposition on the cities of centrally appointed officials, such as the "curator" (*logistes*), the "exactor" (*ekdikos*), and the "defensor" (*syndikos*). Such officials were, however, sometimes drawn from the local elites rather than being outsiders, like the *strategoi* (who slowly disappeared in favor of the new exactor in the fourth century). The new regional provinces, which changed boundaries and names on occasion, brought paid imperial bureaucrats closer to the localities, but the numbers of such officials were still small by any modern standard.

ROMAN OCCUPATION. *Funerary mask of a woman's head.* The mask, made of painted plaster, with inlaid glass eyes, is from Balansura. It dates from the Roman period, second century CE. (University of Pennsylvania Museum, Philadelphia. Neg. # S8–31437)

Economy. Only a tiny fraction of Egypt is cultivable, the rest being mainly desert. In ancient times, however, the Nile Valley and Delta had been so productive that their approximately 23,000-square-kilometer cultivated area was the richest agricultural area of the Mediterranean world, regularly shipping wheat surpluses to Rome and later to Constantinople. Part of this grain was collected by the government in the land tax, but part was private surplus sold on the open market, which came to Rome through trade. By the Roman period, the dominance of bread wheat was complete over the emmer wheat com-

mon in Egypt before the arrival of the Ptolemies. A wide array of other field crops was grown, including barley, many legumes, oil-bearing seed plants, and vast quantities of fodder crops that were fed as clover or dry as hay (the gasoline of ancient Egypt, as it has been called, the staple food of donkeys). Vineyards and orchards increased in quantity in the Ptolemaic period but even more so under Roman rule; land not inundated annually by the Nile was needed for the fruit crops, which had to be irrigated by raising water to their levels. The Faiyum and the western oases succeeded in cultivating vines and olives, the quality of which elsewhere in Egypt was mediocre. [*See* Trade and Markets.]

Egypt's agricultural wealth undoubtedly employed and supported most of its population in Roman times. The production of crops was carried out through a wide variety of structures, including much direct cultivation by smallholders, extensive leasing to peasants of land owned by the government and by large landowners, and some farming by salaried laborers or contractors of capital-intensive enterprises such as vineyards. The government's role was limited mainly to taxation and the shipping of grain collected as tax, along with the provisioning of the army through requisitions and purchases. As the pre-Roman cities (Alexandria and Memphis, particularly) were joined by the *metropoleis* that grew into full-fledged cities, however, they created larger populations less directly tied to farming. There were extensive craft-based industries in some cities, particularly in the area of textiles; linen was an Egyptian specialty in this period, as later. The cities also developed a considerable services sector. As the urban population in the Roman period, including that at Alexandria, probably amounted to somewhere between a sixth and a quarter of the population, its consumption needs both directed rural production and stimulated urban specialization.

Rome's system of taxation also had large effects on Egypt's production. The bulk of the taxes was collected in wheat, levied at low fixed rates on private land but at higher, more variable rates on public (government-owned) land. There were cash taxes due on nonarable crops, and many cash taxes due that were unrelated to land, including a poll tax and the several capitation taxes usually collected with it. Those amounted altogether to a sizable part of a family's income, but they were charged only on adult males (ages fourteen to sixty-two). There were also monthly levies on all manner of trades and crafts. There was not, however, any general income tax, in the modern sense. These cash-taxes lost their importance in the course of the third century CE, and most of them disappeared around the last quarter of that century, if not earlier; whether that development was related to the substantial depreciation in the currency of the time is as yet unclear. Some levies in gold and silver bullion were introduced in the fourth century, almost always charged on land, like the wheat taxes, and taxation on the trades and crafts survived in an altered form. Broad capitation taxes disappear from our evidence in the late empire. The number of attested taxes is very large, but many of them seem to have had limited impact or short duration. The taxation system after Diocletian was generally simpler than in earlier centuries and, except in times of crisis, had fairly low rates, considering Egypt's productivity.

Only the lack of evidence from Alexandria limits our sense of Egypt as a trading center in the Roman period. It was, however, the key link in the trade to India, through caravan routes across the desert to the Red Sea ports of Myos Hormos and Berenike. Yet Alexandria and Pelusium played much larger roles, exporting Egypt's agricultural produce, its distinctive manufactures like papyrus and linen, and no doubt many items for which little evidence survived. Although tax grain dominated the Roman-era documentary record, the export of private surpluses was at least as important. [See Taxation.]

Society. Ptolemaic Egypt had included Greco-Macedonian military settlers, civilians of Greek descent, official Greeks of Egyptian or mixed descent, and Egyptians essentially untouched by the presence of foreigners. Official ethnicity had thus moved from representing the national origin of the head of the household to being a heritable status, and from that to being an acquirable status. Inheriting a situation of this complexity, the Romans took an entirely different approach, one rooted in their own categories of legal status. Greeks and Egyptians were no longer opposites; instead, Hellenes were to be a subcategory of Egyptians.

In the Roman class structure of Egypt there were several strata. The top stratum included the holders of Roman citizenship. The second stratum included the citizens of the three, later four, Greek cities of Egypt: non-Romans, but citizens. Of those cities, Alexandria occupied a somewhat higher niche than Ptolemais, Naukratis, or Antinoöpolis, but the majority of the citizens of all four were recognizably Greeks by any definition. The Romans did not call those people Hellenes; however; they were identified collectively as "citizens," astoi in Greek. The third stratum included Egyptians, peregrine noncitizens in Roman terms, but all the inhabitants of the country except for the two citizen groups already mentioned. Within the Egyptian stratum, the Romans distinguished a privileged group of residents of the metropoleis (the chief towns of the nomes), who were variously called metropolitai or Hellenes. The gulf between Alexandrians and Egyptians was considerable, and the Romans sought by legislation to keep it so, penalizing intermarriage.

The growth of private landownership contributed, in time, to the development of a complex economic structure that partly corresponded to the legal divisions but did not entirely coincide with them. Not all metropolitans were wealthy landowners—indeed, only a minority were—but many more had medium-sized holdings, capable of providing them with a comfortable income or supplementing other means. In the villages, there was a sizable middle stratum of independent landowners with enough property to support themselves adequately and bear the burdens of mid-level local self-administration; the small group that had larger holdings furnished the village with its elite, and they rotated the top administrative liturgies among themselves.

The Roman transformation of Egyptian society brought a greater measure of hierarchy, and particularly of relationships of patronage, than had the Ptolemies. Under Rome, a wealthy urban landowner would typically have both a free and slave urban staff, probably a country staff, and a host of peasant tenant farmers, many of whom would also be dependent on him for loans of money or grain, to provide working capital for the growing season. Even less grand personages, like substantial village proprietors, would through leasing and credit attract dependents. Those ties did not run only in one direction, for the urban landowners depended on reliable tenants to obtain an income from their properties and, sometimes, made considerable concessions to keep them. [See Social Stratification.]

The effects on women of the Roman transformation were diverse. Egyptian women had been traditionally and legally more independent than Greek women, both in owning and managing property and in controlling their personal lives. On the whole, Roman law tended to reinforce only some of these traits; the increased stratification of society gave the benefits of such liberal legal provisions mainly to women of the upper class, where most property owned by them was concentrated. The growth of slavery under the Romans, particularly in the cities, affected women more than men, since perhaps two-thirds of slaves were female. Unwanted female babies tended to be abandoned, and many of them were salvaged to fill the ranks of the slaves. In a society where average life expectancy was low (less than twenty-five years), women fared even less well than men, surviving infancy in smaller numbers and dying younger. [See Women.]

Languages and Literature. Under Rome, the most widely spoken language of Egypt remained Egyptian, as it would until well after the Arab conquest of the seventh century. Its spoken form is poorly known, because all the forms in which it was written were, to some degree, deliberate creations for particular purposes. The Romans had little use for Demotic, the cursive form that prevailed from the Saite period onward, and after a century of Roman rule it dwindled to remnant status. Coptic, which used the Greek alphabet plus supplementary characters from Demotic, appeared in mature form only in the third century CE, after many experiments with writing Egyptian in Greek characters. The regional phonological variations of Coptic indicate a complex array of dialects. [*See* Coptic *and* Demotic.]

Unlike the Ptolemies, who—although Greek speakers themselves—allowed Egyptian a significant role in their administration, the Romans operated the province almost entirely in Greek. The Romans' own language, Latin, had only a limited place in the military, in the upper administration, and in the legal life of Roman citizens, who used it for some documents, like wills. Compared to Greek, Latin was a minor presence, and Greek texts from Egypt outnumber Latin texts by about fifty to one. After the early first century CE, virtually all contracts, correspondence, accounts, reports, petitions, court documents, and the like were written in Greek, no matter what languages the parties may have spoken. An inference of bilingualism from the documents is debatable, but it seems certain that in the cities both Greek and Egyptian were commonly used; the village elites could certainly use Greek, and many of their poorer neighbors undoubtedly spoke at least a little of the language of power. The basic knowledge of written Greek, traditionally beginning with the letter shapes, was taught in many of the villages; more advanced education, in most cases, required going to the larger centers.

Traditional Egyptian literature was preserved in Demotic at least through the second century CE in some temples, especially in the Faiyum. Substantial portions of libraries from Tebtunis and Soknopaiou Nesos have survived, giving an idea of the range of works that were still copied. There is virtually no evidence, however, to suggest that there was a circulation of those works outside the priestly milieu. By contrast, several thousand papyri with works of Greek literature have been found in a wide variety of places, although the cities were the major sources; Oxyrhynchus, in particular, has yielded a rich array of literary papyri, of both the staples of Greek literature (known to us from manuscripts copied by medieval monks) and of works that did not survive in that way. The great bulk of those papyri were of a relatively small group of popular authors prominent in Greek education, above all Homer; his *Iliad* dominated the scene, although his *Odyssey* was not uncommon. Menander, none of whose plays had come to us from the Middle Ages, was also extremely popular, and his work has been recovered from the papyri. Along with the works common in the schools and widely read, small numbers of the texts of many more authors have become known from the papyri. A limited circle of the erudite acquired, read, and passed around those texts,

sometimes annotating them. Their culture was uncompromisingly Hellenic and hardly reflective of the Egyptian setting. Egypt also produced many learned writers in the Roman period. Perhaps most emblematic was Athenaeus of Naukratis, whose *Deipnosophistai* contained a treasury of Greek learning but has little about Egypt. [*See* Demotic Literature.]

Physical Environment and the Arts. Under the Romans, the juxtaposition and complex intertwining of Greek, Roman, and Egyptian elements—identifiable in domains as diverse as language and bureaucracy—had their counterparts in the arts, the architecture, and the urban organization of space. Except for Egyptian temples, the public buildings of the cities were largely Greek in character, and they were connected by a skeleton of colonnaded streets, arches, and *tetrastyla* that were characteristic of Roman cities everywhere. The participation of the cities in the metropolitan culture of the empire was thus visible on the surface. The domestic and commercial quarters of most of the cities—which are still poorly known—were more reminiscent of Egyptian villages, although with a higher density. Alexandria, as one might expect, was less Egyptian in this respect than the nome capitals.

Egyptian temples continued to be built and decorated in traditional style during the first two centuries of Roman rule, just as they had been throughout the Ptolemaic period. The priests, who controlled the architectural and decorative programs, continued to innovate in their expressions of the liturgy and theology of the old cults, but to the eyes of most viewers these temples can hardly be distinguished from those of the New Kingdom; and few have been able to make any sense out of the hieroglyphic inscriptions of the Roman era. The pace of such construction and decoration, however, dropped severely after the mid-second century CE, and little new work was done after the early third century.

In painting and sculpture the situation is yet more complex. As long as Egyptian religion was a vital force, many arts connected with it continued to be produced in traditional style—not only the relief sculpture on temples but also the decoration of mummies and coffins, for example, retained their Egyptian forms. At the same time, many works of art in standard metropolitan forms, particularly in sculpture, were produced by artists trained in Greco-Roman traditions.

The interaction of the two traditions and the form it took has been sharply debated in recent years, with one school of thought seeing substantial Greek influence on Egyptian art, other scholars seeing hardly any at all. [*A corresponding controversy about Coptic art is discussed in the article on Copts.*] Perhaps both traditions borrowed motifs from each other as they found it desirable. The so-called Faiyum portraits, for example, are

ROMAN OCCUPATION. *Late Roman basilica at Hermopolis.* (Courtesy Donald B. Redford)

largely Greek in their naturalistic character and metropolitan imperial in their hairstyles, clothing, and jewelry, yet they were inserted after death into mummies prepared and decorated in purely Egyptian style. The patrons who commissioned them were certainly predominantly Greek-speaking people of means, but at the same time they saw themselves as Greeks of Egypt. The statue of Horus dressed as a Roman soldier (now in the British Museum) represents, by contrast, the use of Egyptian material in an essentially Roman context. Certainly the classes who could commission art patronized many genres that drew from both the Greek and the Egyptian traditions.

Religion. The decline of the temples under the Romans has already been mentioned, but its sources are not well documented. Both a decline in government support and a withdrawal of interest on the part of the local elites must have played a part. Similar declines, although not all on quite the same schedule, were found in other pointers to the role of traditional religion, such as mentions of festivals and occurrences of names formed on the traditional gods, both Egyptian and Greek; in part, the process may reflect the growth of popular cults, less grounded in the major temples than were the cults of the major figures of the pantheon. The veneration of Shaï, as a god of (good) fortune, is an example. Except in names

and in the minor arts, these cults have left less tangible evidence of their presence than did the worship of the old gods. Despite this decline, Egyptian cults remained vital presences through the first 250 years of Roman rule; yet the same may not be true of the cults imported by the Greek settlers under the Ptolemies. For example, syncretistic identification of deities makes it difficult to know whether a cult of Apollo represents that god or an Egyptian equivalent, such as Horus. At the same time, however, Roman Capitoline cults made at least some impression in the cities; and Egyptian cults—especially of Isis, Osiris, Sarapis, Harpokrates, and Anubis—acquired great popularity in many parts of the Roman world outside Egypt, during the same period that their decline in Egypt was beginning.

In the first 150 years of Roman rule, the Jewish population played a large role in Egypt, not only in Alexandria but in the countryside, right up the Nile Valley. What is known of the religious side of this presence, however, comes mainly from Alexandria. The effective genocide with which the Romans quelled the rebellion of the Jews in their own homelands during the emperor Trajan's reign (r. 98–117 CE) wiped Judaism out as a significant force in Egypt for some time to come; only in the second half of the third century does it again make any showing, and no doubt it took slow immigration over centuries to rebuild the Egyptian Jewish community that we learn about from the Cairo Geniza documents that date to after the Arab conquest.

The early history of Christianity in Egypt is poorly known; it has been surmised that it was closely linked to the Jewish community, thereby suffering from that community's destruction. Only in the third century did an organized Christian church become visible, and yet by that century's end there was a well-developed episcopal organization throughout the province of Egypt. The explosive growth of the fourth-century church was probably built on foundations now hard to discern from the limited evidence for the period before Constantine. The degree to which Christianity in this period represented either a unitary phenomenon or a cluster of different groups has been much debated; Platonic thought in various forms played an important and distinctive role throughout the Alexandrian theological tradition, but the relationship of the so-called Gnostic texts to other lines of development remains much debated. [*For more discussion of theological controversies, see* Copts.] Also in the third century, Manichaeism came into Egypt, spreading considerably in the fourth; it existed for a time in an uneasy relationship with the Christian church and even considered itself part of that church.

Sources. Information from ancient authors about Roman Egypt is vital in some respects but limited in quantity; Strabo provided an extremely valuable account from the Augustan period, but there was no later equivalent. Philo was an important source for data on Jewish society and philosophy in first-century CE Alexandria. There has been no systematic study of the numerous scholars and writers in Roman Egypt. Alexandria was a major center of Christianity from the third century onward, and a large volume of Christian literature there illuminated many aspects of Egypt; saints' lives and monastic literature, such as the *Lives of the Desert Fathers*, have been of particular value for social history.

The tens of thousands of documentary papyri and ostraka (all potsherds in this period) have been the largest source of information on most of the subjects treated in this article. Many texts are still unpublished and many of those published have been inadequately studied. Most are in Greek, a few in Latin; from the early Roman period, a number of Demotic Egyptian texts have survived (many unpublished), and from the fourth century onward the volume of Coptic documents, especially letters, has been substantial. Particularly valuable are the archives and dossiers of related texts, which range in size from a handful to many hundreds. Although the typicality of such archives may be difficult to assess, they give a depth of information about particular families, offices, or places that

scattered texts cannot offer. By contrast, most of Egypt's cities have produced relatively few surviving inscriptions on stone, compared to the numerous and informative inscriptions known from the cities of Asia Minor for the same period. Even gravestones are comparatively few. It is unclear how much this situation results from the hazards of survival.

Archaeology has contributed less to the knowledge of Roman Egypt than expected, but excavations in recent years have given a new impetus to the field, and large numbers of objects await study. Roman city sites are poorly preserved and have received little systematic attention, although excavations in Hermopolis, Antinoöpolis, and Alexandria have been informative. Karanis is the best-known village excavation, but several other Faiyum villages have had recent digging (e.g., Tebtunis, Narmouthis, Bacchias), and Kellis (in the Dakhleh Oasis) is proving productive. In the Eastern Desert, excavations at the Mons Claudianus quarry camp and associated sites have also been rewarding. Habitation sites located in Egypt's cultivated area have generally been badly preserved, even lost to shifts in the course of the Nile over the millennia; and Alexandria's remains have been buried under deep deposits from subsequent ages. These factors account for the dominance of desert sites in the archaeology of Egypt.

[*See also* Alexandria; Hermopolis; *and* Ptolemaic Period.]

BIBLIOGRAPHY

Alston, Richard. *Soldier and Society in Roman Egypt: A Social History.* London, 1995. A broad treatment, arguing that the army was neither socially isolated, economically prominent, nor unpopular.

Bagnall, Roger S. *Egypt in Late Antiquity.* Princeton, 1993. Offers a comprehensive discussion of Egyptian society, economy, and culture in the period from the accession of Diocletian to the middle of the fifth century.

Bagnall, Roger S. *Reading Papyri, Writing Ancient History.* London, 1995. A survey of the kinds of uses to which historians can put the papyri.

Bailey, Donald M., ed. *Archaeological Research in Roman Egypt,* Proceedings of the Seventeenth Classical Colloquium of the Department of Greek and Roman Antiquities, British Museum held on 1–14 December, 1993. *Journal of Roman Archaeology, Supplementary series,* no. 19. Ann Arbor, 1996. A collection of conference papers giving a good survey of the state of archaeological work on the Roman period.

Bowman, Alan K. *Egypt after the Pharaohs.* 2d ed. London, 1996. A well-illustrated and readable survey of Egypt from Alexander to the Arab conquest, with good bibliography.

Bowman, Alan K. and Dominic Rathbone. "Cities and Administration in Roman Egypt." *Journal of Roman Studies* 82 (1992), 107–127. Shows how the early Roman emperors transformed Egypt from Hellenistic kingdom to Roman province.

Doxiadis, Euphrosyne. *The Mysterious Fayum Portraits: Faces from Ancient Egypt.* London, 1995. A comprehensive study, from a painter's perspective, with many excellent color plates.

Dunand, Françoise and Christiane Zivie-Coche. *Dieux et hommes en Égypte 3000 av. J.-C. 395 apr. J.C.:* Anthropologiereligieuse. Paris,

1991. Diachronic survey of Egyptian religion from the earliest times to the coming of Christianity.

Johnson, Allan Chester. *Roman Egypt to the Reign of Diocletian*, vol. 21. In *An Economic Survey of Ancient Rome*, ed. Tenney Frank. Baltimore, 1936. Largely a collection of data, including translations of primary texts, concerning the economy of Egypt; still very useful, although obsolete in some respects.

Kehoe, Dennis P. *Management and Investment on Estates in Roman Egypt during the Early Empire.* Papyrologische Texte und Abhandlungen, 40. Bonn, 1992. Explores the symbiotic relationship of large landlords and their tenants.

Lewis, Naphtali. *Life in Egypt Under Roman Rule.* Oxford, 1983. An accessible survey topically organized.

Modrzejewski, Joseph Mélèze. *The Jews of Egypt from Rameses II to Emperor Hadrian.* Translated from the French by Robert Corman. Philadelphia, 1995. Includes discussions of the turbulent history of the Alexandrian Jews from Gaius to the great revolt.

Modrzejewski, Joseph Mélèze. *Droit impérial et traditions locales dans l'Égypte romaine.* Aldershot, 1990. A fundamental collection of papers on legal status and institutions in Egypt under Roman rule.

Montserrat, Dominic. *Sex and Society in Graeco-Roman Egypt.* London, 1996. An examination of sexuality and gender based on a wide range of sources, including magical and astrological texts.

Rathbone, Dominic W. *Economic Rationalism and Rural Society in Third-Century A.D. Egypt: The Heroninos Archive and the Appianus Estate.* Cambridge, 1991. A detailed examination of the largest papyrus archive from Roman Egypt, leading to broad conclusions about the agricultural economy.

Rowlandson, Jane L. *Landowners and Tenants in Roman Egypt: The Social Relations of Agriculture in the Oxyrhynchite Nome.* Oxford, 1996. A major study of the land-tenure system, the land market, and the use of leasing to manage estates.

Rupprecht, Hans-Albert. *Kleine Einführung in die Papyruskunde.* Darmstadt, 1994. The most recent systematically arranged bibliography of works on the papyri and Greco-Roman Egypt.

Turner, Erich G. *Greek Papyri: An Introduction*, rev. ed. Oxford, 1980. The standard introduction in English to the subject, with valuable discussions of literary culture in Roman Egypt.

ROGER S. BAGNALL

ROPEMAKING. *See* Basketry, Matting, and Cordage.

ROSETTA STONE. The Rosetta Stone is named from its find-place, a village in the western Egyptian Nile Delta, known locally as el-Rashid but Europeanized as Rosetta. The village is situated a few kilometers from the sea on the Bolbitine (Rosetta) branch of the Nile. Tradition recounts that the stone was discovered in mid-July 1799, built into an old wall being demolished for an extension to Fort Julien. It had not originated from Rosetta but, like other locally used pharaonic blocks, had been brought from some nearby ancient site, probably Naucratis. The demolition detail and its officer, a lieutenant of engineers named Pierre Bouchard, were members of Napoleon's expedition to Egypt.

By mid-August, the stone was in Cairo, the center of interest for the scholars whom Napoleon had brought with him. In spring of 1801, when Cairo was threatened by British Army successes, the stone was taken for safety to Alexandria, but its surrender was compelled by article XVI of the Capitulation of Alexandria at the end of August 1801. It reached England on HMS *L'Égyptienne* in February 1802 and was deposited with the Royal Society of Antiquaries in London; copies of its texts were then dispatched to centers of scholarship throughout Europe. Late in 1802, it was removed to the British Museum and immediately exhibited as registered Egyptian Antiquity 24.

The Rosetta Stone is an inscribed slab of granitoid stone still measuring 114 centimeters (3 feet, 9 inches) in height, 72 centimeters (2 feet, 4.5 inches) in width, and 28 centimeters (11 inches) in thickness; it weighs about 762 kilograms (0.75 ton). It lacks a large part of the upper left corner, a narrow section of the upper right edge and the lower right corner. Originally, it would have had a rounded top containing the winged sun disk and a scene of the king before various deities.

The Rosetta Stone is important because its inscription is bilingual. It is written in three scripts (hieroglyphs, De-

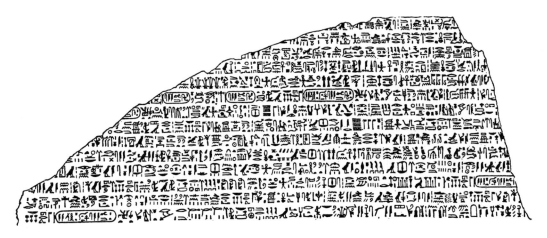

ROSETTA STONE. *Drawing of the hieroglyphic portion of the Rosetta Stone.*

motic, and Greek) but only two languages (Egyptian and Greek), of which the latter could be read. The Greek section is a copy of a decree passed by a council of Egyptian priests meeting at Memphis on 27 March 196 BCE to celebrate the first anniversary of the coronation of the pharaoh Ptolemy V Epiphanes, who, like all the Ptolemaic rulers of Egypt, was a Macedonian Greek. The text is a mere catalog of priestly privileges, especially those of an economic nature, and a list of the honors bestowed on Ptolemy V in return for his services to Egypt, at home and abroad. It ends, however, with the information that the decree is to be written in the sacred and native and Greek characters: in other words, the Greek section is a translation of the two sections written in hieroglyphs and Demotic, scripts that had been unread for more than thirteen centuries.

The Rosetta Stone is popularly believed to have provided the key to the decipherment of hieroglyphs. In fact, the breakthrough, based on the correct reading of the name Ptolemy in its cartouches, could only be made by reference to other texts.

[*See also* Decipherment; *and the biographical entry on Champollion.*]

BIBLIOGRAPHY

Andrews, Carol. *The Rosetta Stone.* London, 1981.
Quirke, Stephen, and Andrews, Carol. *The Rosetta Stone: Facsimile Drawing.* London, 1988. With introduction and full translations.

CAROL A. R. ANDREWS

ROYAL CULTS. See Cults, *article on* Royal Cults.

ROYAL FAMILY. Among ordinary mortals in ancient Egypt, the basic family pattern was not very different from our concept of the nuclear family. Among royalty, however, although the king was seen to be the son of his father and mother—usually the previous king and one of his wives—his mythological and political parentage lay elsewhere. The ancient Egyptian myth-makers developed a system to reconcile these contradictory ideas.

As Lana Troy (1986) has said in her fundamental study on the role of the feminine principle in ancient Egyptian kingship, "Kingship is a manifestation of the creator, placed in the context of a mortal sovereign. The Egyptians . . . insist upon the androgynous identity of the creator and thus, as an analogous power, the kingship is a composite of male and female elements." It is within this framework that the royal family must be seen and distinguished from the nonroyal family pattern.

Before discussing the various members of the royal family, it is essential to understand that, however individual they may have been as persons, they were first and foremost seen as participants in a mythic play of the regeneration and perpetuation of kingship. These ideas, highly sophisticated for an early civilization, were expressed in words and pictures in a variety of ways. The Egyptians were masters in the art of giving their ideas visual form; we must now learn to decode and interpret the messages they conveyed.

From the very beginning of Egyptian history, kings and queens were projections of concepts that had their origins in a divine precedent referring to the act of creation and to a perpetual continuation of this act. The former concept was given mythic shape in the story of Re-Atum impregnating himself, and the latter in the relationship of Re and his female counterpart and daughter Hathor, who encloses within her womb the solar child. Kingship was eternal; eternity was conceived as a repetition of events, no doubt inspired by the regular cycle of the annual inundation, germination, and fruition, a pulse that must have been innate in all Egyptians.

As a representative of the deity who initiated this rhythm of continuity by uniting the male and female qualities in his person, the king personified such perpetuity. But because of the nature of human biology, his own person was insufficient: a female counterpart was required in order to effectuate the process of impregnation, the precondition for continuation of life. The role of the female members of the royal family was to make this feminine element available. Only then would the king be able to reenact the creation as it had been set in motion by "the complete one," Atum, who impregnated himself and created the first pair of deities, Shu (male) and Tefnet (female)—at least according to one of the creation myths.

Kinship terms in the royal family center around the king: mother of the king, wife of the king, sister of the king, son of the king, daughter of the king, and children of the king. But the designations are flexible, in that "sister" may also mean "wife," "father" may mean "ancestor," "brother" may mean "nephew." As applied, the terms should not always be taken literally; they are often to be seen as a designation of rank rather than affiliation.

From the fourth dynasty on, the king was "Son of Re," the creator sun god. In the eighteenth dynasty, Amun in the form of Amun-Re was his father. In addition to these clear indications of divine parentage, the king was Horus, and therefore for the duration of his life on earth he also considered Osiris his father. As Horus, he was a reincarnation of Osiris, king of the dead, with whom he would himself be identified in the afterlife. As so often in Egyptian thought, one must become accustomed to a multiplicity of approaches; several answers to a problem are not mutually exclusive, and each contributes an aspect of the

ROYAL FAMILY. *Eighteenth dynasty sculpted head of a princess, a daughter of Akhenaten.* It was found at Tell el-Amarna and is now in the Cairo Museum. (Courtesy David P. Silverman)

truth. The king played his different parts according to ritual and political requirements.

Where the king had a choice of fathers, the identity of his mortal mother was certain. In the days before modern blood testing and gene technology, visual evidence was irrefutable, and the identity of the mother would never be in doubt; that of the father was a matter of trust—or of mythology. In the descriptions of theogamy, the divine wedding between the mother of a ruler and Amun-Re, the mortal father, usually the reigning king, was not entirely denied a part in the process: when Amun-Re made his way toward the queen's bedroom, he came in the guise of the king. The scent of the divine seed, however, revealed his true identity. The description of the union between the god and the queen is the closest we get to a report of cohabitation, the Egyptian written sources on these topics being usually very discreet or veiled in symbolic imagery. Commemorated on temple walls, first in the New Kingdom, theogamy is depicted in the illustrations as if made in heaven; but the vocabulary used in the narrative is extremely graphic and leaves little to the imagination.

In the Amarna period, when certain otherwise obscure references are suddenly elucidated by being indicated in an unconventional manner, the union of the royal couple is rendered in no uncertain terms. The king, playing the part of Aten, the sun god, is depicted before the marital bed in the company of Nefertiti; they also appear in situations of intimate foreplay. The crucial sexual union between the male and the female, the basis of all regeneration, is in Amarna iconography more publicly displayed than anywhere else. The difference between this presentation and "theogamy" is the temporal viewpoint: King Akhenaten refers to himself and acts as the sun god on Earth; "theogamy" descriptions refer to the ruler's parents. In Akhenaten's universe, the ultimate union of the male and the female was further expressed as existing in his own person. It was as it had been in the beginning, when the creator god created the world.

Although the mother of the king was frequently of royal birth herself, this does not seem to have been a prerequisite. In the Early Dynastic period and the Old Kingdom, only three of some fifteen kings' mothers had any other royal titles, and they became incorporated in the mythology only at the coronation of their sons. There are numerous examples from later periods in which the king's mother was not his father's chief wife. In the case of Akhenaten's mother, her parentage was well publicized; although she came from a family of officials, she became the chief queen of Amenhotpe III, who emphasized her nonroyal parentage.

In the Old Kingdom, the queen was "the one who sees Horus"; that is, she had the privilege of seeing the king in his true, divine, and virile form. Her role was then, as it remained, to provide the female element required to arouse the king. A king usually had more than one queen, and they were differentiated in rank by titles accumulating as they progressed in their own life cycle. A "king's daughter" could become "king's wife" and finally, if she bore a son and lived long enough to see him don the crowns of Egypt, also "king's mother." In the Middle Kingdom, the chief queen was singled out by the title "Great Royal Wife," a designation that continued in use throughout the New Kingdom. The ritual and official role of a queen was not necessarily dependent on whether she had given birth to the heir.

In the eighteenth dynasty, the kings began to marry close relatives—if not a full sister, then a half-sister who became "Great Royal Wife." It is as if there was a trend toward making myth come true and finding new ways of modeling the current representative of the god and his situation on the divine precedent. By having a father or mother in common, the king and the queen themselves became equivalent to the first pair in the world: Like Shu and Tefnet, they were sister and brother, husband and wife.

This virtual equality in status of the male and female principles reached its height in the Amarna period, when Nefertiti is portrayed as taking active part in public life with the king, exceeding the conventional role of royal companion and performing male tasks. Her figure is depicted on equal terms with that of Akhenaten, or she is there as his double, in artistic terms rendered as "layering," as a silhouette behind the king, indistinguishable from him. Her role as mother of the following generation is emphasized on house altars and in tombs, and by the fact that the couple's daughters are said to be hers, with no mention of the identity of their father. When she is shown vanquishing foreign enemies and taking active part in offerings on her own, without the king, it is once more the Amarna myth-makers emphasizing a point that is elsewhere only suggested.

Toward the end of the eighteenth dynasty, even the multigenerational process of creation in the myth of Re and Hathor found a parallel in real life when Amenhotpe III elevated his daughter to "Royal Wife." Again, in the message presented to the public, Akhenaten apparently took this idea one step further by producing offspring by two of his daughters—children who by having their mother's names, followed by "the little," are a reduplication of the previous generation.

The position and role of the daughters of the king is an issue that was taken up once more in the case of Ramesses II and two of his daughters. The attitude of this king to himself as a divine being, reminiscent of that of Akhenaten, is perhaps the reason for this explicit multi-

generational union, which ensured the continuity of kingship.

In spite of all these precautions, in the Late period artificial relationships had to replace the duality of queenship. A mother/daughter situation was now contrived with regard to the priestess's title of "God's Wife," which had been given to queens since the early eighteenth dynasty. By adopting a successor the generational continuum was assured.

With regard to the male members of the royal family other than the king, kinship terms are again to be taken with some caution. In the fourth dynasty, "King's Son" becomes a title designating rank rather than filiation. The biological son is distinguished by the addition of the phrase "of his body." The "eldest king's son," often holding the office of vizier, was still the king's offspring. In the Middle Kingdom, the prince designated to succeed his father is singled out by becoming coregent. In the New Kingdom, "King's Son" remains a rank, in particular carried by the nonroyal viceroy of Nubia, known as "King's Son of Kush."

By being singled out in myth and tradition, the royal family symbolized the aspiration of all Egyptians for the repetition of events that was eternity. The feminine element in kingship was essential, and it found its spatial reference in the extensive quarters of the royal households known as the harem. Described in literature and depicted in art, the harem with its inhabitants—chief queen, minor queens, foreign princesses, and their young offspring—provided a storehouse for the seed that guaranteed the future in mundane terms as well as on a mythological level.

[*See also* Queens.]

BIBLIOGRAPHY

Helck, Wolfgang and Wolfhart Westendorff, eds. *Lexikon der Ägyptologie*, 3: 461–661. Wiesbaden, 1980. The following articles by various scholars on the royal family contain full bibliographies to 1979: "König-Gott-Verhältnis," "Königin," "Königinnentitel," "Königsberufung," "Königsbezeichnung," "Königsideologie," "Königsmutter," "Königssohn," "Königssohn von Kusch," "Königstochter."

Redford, Donald. *Akhenaton, the Heretic King*. Princeton, 1987. An excellent summary of the period.

Silverman, David. "The Nature of Kingship." In *Ancient Egyptian Kingship*, edited by David O'Connor and David Silverman, pp. 49–92. Leiden, 1995. For a brief treatment of the familial relationship during the Amarna period with a full bibliography.

LISE MANNICHE

ROYAL ROLES. The theological foundations of Egyptian royalty changed over time, despite the durable character of pharaonic system. Although the Egyptians wrote no histories, because of their iterative concept of events and their tendency to see facts in isolation, they were not ignorant of history. Their awareness of the passage of time is demonstrated in their long genealogies and king-lists, their annals, their organization of tasks and days according to the height of the annual Nile flood, their astronomic observations of a changing sky, and their political vicissitudes. In all this they had the realism and the intellectual flexibility to adapt their doctrines and their expression to the contingencies of history.

Historical Fluctuations of the Theological Concept of Power. In the Predynastic period (c.3000 BCE), kings "Scorpion" and Narmer were closely linked to Horus, god of Hierakonpolis. Horus, initially the dominant falcon god gliding across the distant sky, is ever more identified as the posthumous son of Osiris by Isis. The king "born as Horus living in the horizon" (Pyramid Texts) sits on "the throne of Horus of the living" in his role as heir, dedicated to the promise of eternity. Against this background, the royal ideology borrows at the same time from the theology of Heliopolis, and kings since Djedefre (fourth dynasty, c.2560 BCE) bear the title "Son of Re." The references to Horus, Osiris, and the sun underscore the emancipation of the king from the grip of the earth, the fundamental act of power; the paternity of Re also signals the historic influence on royalty of the Heliopolitan clergy. The symbiosis of king and falcon is sculpturally introduced in the images of Khafre, a foreshadowing of composite images to come, much as the Osirian cycle forms separate episodes in the Pyramid Texts, and as the legend of the solar parentage and miraculous birth of the first three kings of the fifth dynasty is composed several centuries later. In this period of the Old Kingdom, the king, in issuing decrees, speaks neither of himself nor of what he does; without any need for explanation, the "son of Re" ignores the constraints of autobiography.

Breaking away from the concept of a divinely sired king—previously unknown in references to royalty [see the articles *Instructions for Merikare* and *Instructions of Amenemhet*]—and that of a distant king seeking refuge in silence, the First Intermediate Period (c.2180–2040 BCE) sees references to the negative (though correctible) aspects of the royal role. Evoking the opponents of power and the sacrilege of undisciplined royal troops who, in attacking the dead, transform a military victory into a political setback, the instructions of King Akhtoy for Merikare paint a lucid and severe picture of the royal institution. Stripped of its divine dress, royalty is presented as a powerful but not oppressive institution, a regime of liberation and protection "to support the spine of weak man." Despite the insignificance or the nonexistence of numerous holders of power (seventy kings in seventy days in Dynasty 7 of Manetho), the monarchic idea survived and created a framework all its own, as is demonstrated by its autonomy from the realities of political power.

From the Middle Kingdom onward (c.2040–1780 BCE), continuing what had been begun before their time, the new sovereigns adapted royalty to the current reality while restoring the idea of monarchy through the novel means of a controlled literature which the king used to address his subjects (e.g., *Story of Sinuhe, Instructions of Amenemhet*) or which spontaneously expressed loyalist sentiments *(Instructions of Sehtepibre)*. Royal phraseology eulogizes the king: his powers and qualities are gathered into a repertory and then analyzed in reference to various deities; it also celebrates loyalty in order to bring the king closer to those who had been cut from his service in the aftermath of the anarchy and rivalries of the preceding period. Henceforth, ideology and the practice of power are in proportion, and the royal eulogies are composed in reference to particular events. Certain later kings—Neferhotpe (thirteenth dynasty) and Montuhotpe (perhaps seventeenth dynasty)—were reluctant to compose general eulogies, and rather more prone to sing their own praises in a specific circumstance: that of the kings "leaning on" the city of Thebes. By contrast, the kings of the New Kingdom (c.1560–1070 BCE) were voluble in the praise of their own virtues in a time when Egyptian imperialism reached its highest point. At the same time, kings of overpowering character (Hatshepsut at Deir el-Bahri, Amenhotpe III at Luxor, and Ramesses II at the Ramesseum) returned to the liturgical sources of royalty. The *Ritual of Royal Birth* is used to refine in text and image the divine parentage or theogamy, the birth and nursing of the royal child. Thus, through a focus on the king's childhood and youth, emphasis is put on the king's capacity for eternal renewal. The royal child is he in whom divine nature resides, and only he can make it manifest, at the end of a process characterized in terms that stress the stages of physical transformation, and which he translates by means of his exceptional personal qualities. The themes of royal predestination and multiple filiation reinforce royal legitimacy. In particular, the increasing emphasis on filiation to Isis reflects the growing influence of the Osirian cycle.

Nevertheless, by the end of the New Kingdom, there is a profound perturbation. After the reflux of imperialism, decreased means of subsistence had led to a propensity for corruption in certain state institutions. Under these conditions, some individuals turned to the gods to resolve their personal affairs, and the door was opened for a new concept of political power—theocracy. Amun, "king of the South and king of the North," exercised power through his oracles, consulted by the king, who continued to perform the rites. One perceives the difficulty in keeping intact two opposing images: a royal interlocutor who in the rites is on the same level as the deity, and a "common" king who is on the same level as his subjects when, to manage his personal destiny, he seeks the oracle's approval of decisions on the management of the Egyptian state. The resulting "crisis of values" led to a temporary ideological mutation.

When the Libyan kings ascended to the throne around 945 BCE, the priesthood adapted the content of its ideology to the foreign kings. To begin with, the Egyptian priests, while reprising the theme of Isiac filiation, defined the Libyan and Ethiopian kings by comparing them to Horus, son of Isis, and reserving identification with the sun god for their indigenous predecessors (with the exception of upstarts like Ahmose, founder of the New Kingdom, or atypical rulers like Queen Hatshepsut). In particular, the tendency of royal titles from the twenty-second dynasty on to reflect the childhood of Horus—a means of ensuring a future in uncertain times—is in direct correlation to the rise of young gods in the Mediterranean and increasing contact between Egypt and that region. With the Persian conquest, then the Macedonian and the Roman, Egyptian theology adjusted to the disappearance of national kings, replaced by distant rulers. A shift occurred from the theology of the child-king identified as a specific king born of a queen of royal blood, the great royal spouse, to a theology of a child-god who was assimilated to the foreign king born of a goddess who varies according to location. The elements of mammisiac ritual (from *mammisi*, "house of birth") borrow from the model of the former theogamies but let only the divine actors intervene. The royal Egyptian doctrine became a structure that functioned independently of its protagonists: the logic of its forms carried it on to a logic of qualities, and royalty became an almost empty signifier. It preserved some traits that maintained its identity: the Achaemenids, the Ptolemies, and the Caesars were represented as pharaohs, bearing Egyptian titles and integrated into an ideology in which the theme of the birth of the king-god guaranteed the continued institutional presence of the pharaoh. Nevertheless, several aspects alert one to changes: in addition to the idea of the Egyptian god-son, the Alexandrine sovereigns imposed their own deification; royal cartouches are sometimes empty, awaiting an "absent king"; in the temple of Duch, only the walls seen by the officiating king as he entered the temple are decorated, while the opposite sides visible from the sanctuary where the god who receives his guest resided, remain anepigraphic, as if the ritual apparatus, emptied of substance, were merely *trompe-l'oeil*.

Royal Functions. In his role as demiurge, interlocutor between the divine and human realms, the pharaoh is responsible to humankind. It is important to remember that what we are describing are ideological images and mechanisms and not the attributes of any actual sovereign.

As "Master of Performing Rituals," the king alone ensures, in theory, the daily upkeep of a god whose biological rhythm, like of man, can tire. In order to prevent the deity from abandoning his land, the King maintains divine energy by offering products manufactured by man. The king's compensation consists of divine provision in the form of abstract principles, according to a reciprocity of well-understood interests. The notion of a circuit between the king and the gods is physically, textually, and iconographically confirmed by accolades and embracements.

Maat, the principle of human order promoted by the king, is the offering *par excellence*. To offer *maat* to the god, when he has given it to the king, reinforces the divine action. The monarchy, the continuation of the creator god on Earth, is fortified by rituals that mark stages in the royal career: the legitimizing ritual of theogamy, and the more institutional rituals of crowning and the *sed*-festival; the former relates to the King's establishment as royal, and the latter is a verification of royal competencies. The alliance between the vigor of the monarchy and the renewal of the divine force is complete.

The panegyric of the *Instructions of Sehtepibre*, the oldest copy of which dates from the period of Amenemhet III, is composed according to the process of establishing equivalences between the king and various deities, such as personifications of concepts, followed by explanations:

> He is Sia (= discernment) in the hearts . . .
> He is Re with whose rays one sees . . .
> His ardor burns stronger than the flame of a brazier . . .
> He makes verdant more than a great Nile (= Hapy) . . .
> The king is sustenance, his mouth is plenty . . .
> He is Atum for the one who attaches the necks . . .
> He is Khnum for everybody,
> The begetter who creates mankind.
> He is Bastet, who protects the two lands . . .
> He is Sekhmet against the violator of his order.

The qualities and powers of the sovereign thus enumerated pertain, with respect to humans, to his role as creator and nurturer of mankind (Khnum and Hapy), to the prudent and charitable practice of the government of Egypt (Sia and Atum), and to his role of power (peaceable and defensive like Bastet, but also formidable like Re and Sekhmet).

Although the regulation of water is not part of the origin of the pharaonic institution, since artificial irrigation dating back to the Predynastic epoch took over from natural irrigation practiced by the Neolithic farmers, the Nile flood to which the pharaoh compares himself, and which he optimizes, is the source of the provisions of Egypt. King "Scorpion" is shown holding a hoe to dig a system of waterways for plants, and Menes drains the future site of Memphis by building a dam. Depicted as spirits of the marsh weighed down by the plants and fishes of the Nile, the kings are also a stone dam holding back the flood and collecting water. A bulwark against famine and hunger, Amenemhat I secures for his people a well-nourished, settled existence, in opposition to the nomadic one of starving peoples. Of Ramesses II, it is said that the "his speech creates nourishment," a phrase that reveals the mode of royal action through the word, and the blessings of the organization follow from the forecast; Sety I is "he who fills the stores, who enlarges the granaries." These royal virtues reflect an economic organization that takes advantage of the central control which regulates the production of goods and commodities from lands whose ultimate owner is the king. He also owns its subterranean resources, and turquoise in particular is linked to the exaltation of the monarchic principle. Guarantor of nourishment, the king ensures the perpetuation of humanity. Queen Hatshepsut, transcending her nature as a woman, is integrated into the virile model of fecundity: "The Two Lands are filled with your children's children, the quantity of your seed is great"; temple walls are engraved with lists of royal children in impressive numbers; kings give proof of their fecundity in a family setting and, by extension, their capacity to people the kingdom. Practically speaking, the assimilation of Hapy and Khnum translates the food obsession in marginal subsistence economy and reflects the need to ensure the continuation of generations in a context of demographic fragility. From the point of view of royal ideology, on the other hand, the eulogies and reliefs celebrate a prolific Egypt and king.

In the administration of the kingdom, the sources of decision-making power are speech and writing, while the modalities of organizational power are laws and decrees. If the speech of the king is creative speech (ḥw), as well as that of the demiurge, the eloquence he uses in the exercise of power is threefold. The king utters magical formulas or spells (ṯsw), deadly to enemies and rebels. By contrast, discourse (mdt) is a learned work modeled on ancient writings. When used appropriately, they serve as advice and ensure the superiority of the king over the savage form of discourse represented by the speech of the demagogue inciting a crowd. A third form of speech, sayings (ḏdt), are the acts of enunciation by which the king governs. The power of the word is made concrete in writing, which arises with the birth of cities and pharaonic power. Having "the strength of proof," writing can be seen as a technique of managing and controlling people. Writing is the daily technique of state continuity in that it makes it possible to name, classify, and enumerate. Thus, writing does not support the spirit of dispute.

The practical modalities of royal power make it possible for the intentions of the king to become acts. The king regulates the operation of the kingdom by issuing "orders" (wḏ nsw) and by composing "laws" (hpw). The laws characterize the organization of Egyptian society. The king is the source of the law that is at the heart of the tradition of the legislating king (Herodotus, II., 136, 137, 177; Diodorus Siculus I., 65, 94, 95): he "promulgates" laws, "applies" them, "reaffirms" them, "perfects" them. The written laws of Egypt are neither put into a system nor classified into categories of civil, penal, administrative, or institutional law. There is no code of pharaonic laws, nor a constitution of the kingdom. The content of the laws is known through the royal decrees, which include all writings of the king, from a letter to an individual to an act establishing a decision of the executive power with general or particular implication. A decree may announce a new reign, relate to public health, command the digging of a canal, ordain a nomination or dismissal, and so on.

The theme of the pharaonic victory over all other countries is a necessary convention. As representative of the demiurge on Earth, the king cannot be defeated. Trampling and slaughtering the enemies thrown at his feet, the king sends them into oblivion whence they will never return. The theme of the king as chief of war and of the hunt perhaps originates in a much earlier period when man and animal were not seen as entirely separate. Hunting and warfare, capture and putting to death represent taming wildness in the realm or giving gifts to the gods in the form of sacrifices, which are seen less as the suppression of living beings sprung from creation than as the suppression of ill-omened forces. These are undoubtedly indications of anxiety as well as an expression of the harmony that man maintains with his environment; this relativistic concept of man does not isolate him in the universe. On the other hand, the Egyptians rarely use agricultural images to convey mass destruction of enemies, like stalks of wheat mown down in a field. The agricultural activities, more recent factors in the accumulation of riches, are not given the same symbolic weight as predatory activities. The themes of the king as shepherd and nurturer have less prestige in the symbolic frame of the sphere of power, perhaps implying a lack of adaptation to the new means of subsistence.

Although war is initially not a geographical concept for the Egyptians, it is nevertheless connected to space. To begin with, one notes the paradox of the absence of maps: in this highly developed visual world, the kings had no visual record of their kingdom or of their conquered territories. Text therefore came to fulfill the function of maps and topography. Indeed according to the cosmogonic texts "the spatial nature of the world is negated"; space is perceived as the future, and it is the king's task to complete that which is incomplete and to expand the boundaries by giving existence to that which is latent. In this context, the king's wars are never acts of aggression but of reaction to provocation from those who are "nonexistent," or simple defense against those who cross Egypt's boundaries.

Finally, writing about means of war is very distinct from acting on those means. The ritual and rhetorical appearance of the king does not rely on a Machiavellian catalogue of deceits. Rather, societal values and aspirations are incarnated in a man with whom the group identifies. The body of the king, in some way captured by the collectivity of the subject who make him king, is not reducible to a single sign. This multivalent quality of the sovereign is ritualized and becomes the object of many identifications in narratives of battle: with meteorological phenomena (rain, wind, storm), the elements of the world (sun, flame, shade, mountain, sky, stars), defensive arms (wall, shield), and above all animals, including composites (griffin and sphinx) that define him as a being of excess. War rhetoric is a discourse of discussion, one among other tools of intellectual persuasion, such as magic, diplomacy, theocratic affirmation of royal might, reflection, and composure.

[See also Kingship.]

BIBLIOGRAPHY

Assmann, Jan. Der König als Sonnenpriester. Glückstadt, 1970.
Blumenthal, Elke. Untersuchungen zum ägyptischen Königtum der Mittleren Reiches, I. Phraseologie. Abhandlungen der sächsischen Akademie der Wissenschaften zu Leipzig, 61. Berlin, 1970.
Bonhême, Marie-Ange, and Annie Forgeau. Pharaon: Les secrets du pouvoir. Paris, 1988.
Brunner, Hellmut. Die Gerburt der Gottkönigs: Studien zur Uberlieferung eines altägyptischen mythos. Ägyptologische Abhandlungen, 10. Wiesbaden, 1964.
Daumas, François. Les Mammisis des temples égyptiens. Annales de l'Université de Lyon, 32. Paris, 1958.
Derchain, Philippe. "Le rôle du roi d'Égypte dans le maintien de l'ordre cosmique." In Le pouvoir et le sacré, pp. 61–73. Annales du Centre d'Étude des Religions, 1. Brussels, 1962.
Grimal, Nicolas. Les termes de la propagande royale égyptienne de la XIXe dynastie à la conquête d'Alexandre. Mémoires de l'Académie des Inscriptions et des Belles-Lettres, n.s., 6. Paris, 1986.
Hornung, Erik. "Zur geschichtlichen Rolle des Königs in der 18. Dynastie." Mitteilungen des Deutschen Archäologischen Instituts, Abteilung Kairo 15 (1967), 120–133.
Jacobsohn, H. Die Dogmatische Stellung des Königs in der Theologie der alten Ägypter. Ägyptologische Forschungen, 8. Glückstadt, 1939.
Johnson, Janet H. "The Demotic Chronicle as a Statement of a Theory of Kingship." Journal of the Society for the Study of Egyptian Antiquities 13 (1984), 61–72.
Kaplony, P. "Bemerkungen zum ägyptischen Königtum vor allen in der Spätzeit." Chronique d'Égypte 47 (1971), 250–274.
Kruchten, Jean-Marie. Le décret d'Horemheb. Brussels, 1981. On the king as lawgiver.
O'Connor, D., and D. Silverman, eds. Kingship in Ancient Egypt. Leiden, 1997.
Posener, Georges. L'enseignement loyaliste: Sagesse égyptienne du Moyen Empire. Centre de recherches d'histoire et de philologie de la IVe section de l'École Pratique des Hautes Études, 2. Hautes études orientales, 5. Geneva, 1976. Text, translation, and commentary of a wisdom text containing a Eulogy of the King.
Spalinger, Anthony J. "The Concept of the Monarchy during the Saite Epoch: An Essay of Synthesis." Orientalia 47 (1978), 12–36.

MARIE-ANGE BONHÊME
Translated from French by Elizabeth Schwaiger

ROYAL TOMB PAINTING. Every ancient Egyptian aspired to the afterlife and one of the means to attain it was by preparing a proper burial, which only a small elite including the king, members of the royal family, and officials could afford, as commoners were interred in modest pit tombs. A strict hierarchy, with the king's tomb at its apex, determined the type of tombs individuals could build. While royal funerary complexes grew increasingly elaborate, both in plan and in decoration, it is not until the New Kingdom that the actual tombs displayed a full-fledged decorative program.

Pre–New Kingdom Tombs. The earliest surviving example of painted-tomb decoration comes from a Predynastic tomb at Hierakonpolis, in Upper Egypt, which showed motifs randomly painted on the wall surface. These motifs of boats, animals, and stick figures dancing, fighting, or about to smite enemies were similar to those found on the pottery of the period, but the smiting motif later became a fundamental symbol of kingship.

Following the mastabas (from the Arabic term for "bench") of the Early Dynastic period, the royal pyramids of the Old Kingdom (the Step Pyramid of Djoser at Saqqara, in Lower Egypt), grew distinct from the elite burials, as they affirmed through their architecture and symbolic decoration, the king's unique role in society and his special position in relation to the cosmos. Until Djoser, the decoration inside the royal tombs consisted essentially of geometric patterns (of either multicolored paint or blue tiles) imitating natural materials such as reed mats found in houses. With Djoser, however, the decoration in the pyramid substructure began to expand beyond the blue-colored tiles lining the walls and niches of the passageways to include limestone relief panels that proclaimed the king's power and authority under the divine protection. The panels showed Djoser wearing the insignia of his royal office, symbolically striding over the territory delimited by markers, as he performed the "ritual of kingship." Above him hovered the Horus falcon or the Nekhbet vulture, holding the hieroglyphic sign for eternity as a symbol of divine protection, while behind him personified hieroglyphs offered him life. Stylistically, the boldly carved outlines, the modeling hinting at the musculature

ROYAL TOMB PAINTING. *A mummy on a funerary bed with various divinities.* This nineteenth dynasty wall painting is from the tomb of Nefertari in the Valley of the Queens. (Giraudon / Art Resource, NY)

and bone structure underneath the surface, made the royal figure appear forceful (in contrast with the lean figures of the contemporary private individuals).

With the advent of the fourth dynasty, the layout of the royal funerary complexes was radically modified and consisted of the actual tomb, now in the shape of a true pyramid, an upper structure (the mortuary temple) and a lower structure (the valley temple) joined by a causeway, oriented east–west, as opposed to the earlier north–south orientation. Both the new orientation of the complex and the tomb's pyramidal shape related to the sun god Re, whose prominence was increasing. The king was believed to be his earthly manifestation and to join him at death on his perpetual cycle, while he was also an earthly manifestation of the god Horus, the son born to the original king, Osiris, with whom he was identified at death.

The funerary complexes of Sneferu (at Dahshur), of Khufu, Khafre, and Menkaure (at Giza) displayed an elaborate decorative program with painted relief scenes focusing on the king's privileged position in the cosmos and relationship with the gods (either under their protection or embraced by them), as well as scenes relating to his mortuary cult (i.e., processions of female personifications of estates bearing offerings), and to the festival of renewal. By contrast, the actual tombs were left undecorated.

In the following fifth and sixth dynasties, royal pyramids continued to be built at Abusir, in the North, according to the basic architectural and artistic models of the previous period, but on a much smaller scale (Pepy II's complex was the last one to be built on a large scale). In the pyramid of Unas, the last king of the fifth dynasty, however, wall decoration in the form of blue hieroglyphic inscriptions carved in vertical columns was introduced inside the burial chamber. The Pyramid Texts, the earliest known mortuary texts, were designed (like the monument in which they were found) for the sole benefit of the deceased king in his passage from this world into the next. The Pyramid Texts were used in the pyramids of the Old and Middle Kingdoms until the New Kingdom, when they were replaced by new funerary books.

The Old Kingdom ended with the collapse of the central government and, after a period of turmoil called the First Intermediate Period, Nebhepetre Montuhotep I reunified the country and began the Middle Kingdom. Montuhotep's funerary complex at Thebes, in Upper Egypt, had a radically new layout of terraced structures and pillared passages, but its decoration showed traditional scenes of royal ideology such as the king defeating the forces of chaos (i.e., enemies in battle, wild beasts in the desert, fishing and fowling in the marshes), ritual processions of boats, and cult scenes. The king was also depicted in his ritual role, offering to the gods or embraced by them. In an effort to stress the return to a strong government, Montuhotep deliberately modeled his monuments after the Memphite artistic tradition of the Old Kingdom. The emulation of earlier models—using artistic forms from the past—which occurred at several other times in Egyptian history, is called "archaism" (see discussion below).

During the twelfth dynasty, Egypt enjoyed a period of strong government and prosperity. The capital was moved again to the North, to a new site called Itjtawy, and the royal cemetery was established at nearby el-Lisht, where the kings returned to the Old Kingdom tradition of pyramid complexes. Due to poorer construction, however, these are badly preserved. The fragmentary decoration of the pyramid complex of Senwosret I depicted the traditional motifs relating to the king's ability to abolish chaos, the provisioning of his cult, as well as new panel representations emblematically proclaiming the king's name and guaranteeing his supply of offerings.

By the thirteenth dynasty, however, the gradual infiltration of immigrants from Syria-Palestine eventually caused the king to move his residence to Thebes, leaving the foreigners, later known as the Hyksos, to take control of the North from their capital in the Nile Delta, Avaris. With the political power and economic resources divided between the North and the South, the country went again through a period of instability called the Second Intermediate Period. Very little survives from this complex and poorly understood period, during which small royal tombs were built.

New Kingdom Tombs. Following the expulsion of the Hyksos and the reunification of Egypt under Ahmose in the eighteenth dynasty, a new age began, which is called the New Kingdom. After a series of successful military campaigns in the early part of the dynasty, Egypt became an empire and reached an unprecedented level of prosperity, evidenced by the refined artistic production of the period. Although the kings resided mostly in the North, virtually all were buried at Thebes, in the place now called the Valley of the Kings. In contrast to the conspicuous royal burials of the preceding periods, those of the New Kingdom were built with a concern for privacy and security, as they were cut deeply into the Theban mountain, separate from the funerary temples located in the valley, on the edge of cultivation.

Typically, a royal tomb consisted of a series of sloping corridors alternating with stairs, pillared halls, and chambers that became increasingly higher and larger, as each king made his tomb greater than his predecessor by adding to the plan. After Ramesses III, however, this expansion trend was reversed. Just like the architectural plan, the decorative program grew progressively elaborate. As the ideological focus changed, new themes were added to the decorative repertoire, and the thematic distribution throughout the tomb changed as well. Thus, the minimal wall decoration in the form of hieroglyphic inscriptions in the burial chamber of the earlier royal tomb gave way to a flourishing of decoration in the form of texts and im-

ages. Unlike the earlier royal Pyramid Texts, the New Kingdom books of the netherworld were increasingly illustrated, as they described the next world in minute detail.

As care was taken in selecting the books according to their location within the tomb, the idea that the royal tomb served as both a gateway between this world and the next and a visual map of the beyond was articulated through spatial, iconographical, and textual symbolism. Thus, in the early eighteenth dynasty, as the beyond was perceived as the underworld, the tomb was built with a sharply bent axis in imitation of the underworld's crooked topography (depicted in the Middle Kingdom *Book of Two Ways* and the New Kingdom *Book of That Which Is In the Underworld* [*Amduat*]), and the decoration representing the sun god's journey beneath the earth was limited to the deepest part and focal point of the tomb, namely, the burial chamber. Given its shape, buff-colored background, stick figures, and cursive hieroglyphs, Re's nightly voyage was recounted as if on a papyrus unrolled on the wall. From Thutmose III on, the decoration began to extend to the walls of specific focal points, namely, the shaft, the antechamber, and the pillars of the burial chamber, and to show images of the king in the company of deities. Generally, when not shown on equal footing with the latter, the king was depicted in the subordinate position, since he was similar to but not equal to them. The corridors were usually left undecorated. The ceilings were painted with either yellow or white stars on a blue or black background representing the night sky.

The tomb of King Akhenaten, who attempted to impose a form of monotheism through an innovative theological reform, at his new capital Akhetaten (modern Tell el-Amarna) in Middle Egypt, represents an exception in the development of royal tomb decoration. Although similar in plan to its Theban precedents, the tomb displayed a radically new decorative program, of which little remains following the destruction perpetrated against the heretic king's monuments in an effort to expunge his memory from the records. Thus, instead of the traditional scenes of the sun's journey through the beyond and of the king in company of the funerary gods, new scenes were introduced, focusing on the public and private life of the royal family, for example, ritually offering to the solar disk, the royal couple at the "window of appearance" rewarding officials, traveling through the city, in mourning, and playing with their daughters.

In the nineteenth dynasty, as the beyond came to be understood as also comprising the heavens and the emphasis lay on the sun's progression from morning to night, or from the tomb entrance (symbolizing the east) to the burial chamber (symbolizing the west), the tomb was built in a nearly straight axis, while the decoration extended to the entire tomb (as first seen in that of Sety I). The decorative motifs followed a clear distribution pattern, with the dividing point being the first pillared hall, where the Osiris shrine was depicted. Hence, the upper half of the tomb, closest to the entrance, was dominated by images of the sun god Re, while the lower half of the tomb was dominated by images of the underworld god Osiris and other earth gods. From Ramesses II, images of the king greeting the falcon-headed sun god, Re-Horakhty, accompanied with texts related to the sun's daily and nightly cycle, such as the *Litany of Re,* were placed typically near the entrance, while the solar disk containing the nocturnal manifestation of the sun god, as the ram-headed deity, and his morning manifestation, as the scarab beetle, appeared on the façade above the entrance. As a way to evoke the sun's westward progression from morning to night, the solar disk was painted yellow on the exterior to represent the daytime sun and red within the tomb for the nighttime sun. The symbolic orientation was also reinforced by the presence of deities associated with the cardinal points, such as the goddesses Isis (symbolizing the south, on the left) and Nephthys (symbolizing the north, on the right), as well as the goddess Maat shown kneeling on a basket supported by the heraldic plants of Upper and Lower Egypt.

In the twentieth dynasty, this thematic division was abandoned and, as solar and Osirian themes merged, Re's journey through the heavens and the lowest reaches of the earth was combined. The fusion of both phases of the solar cycle was expressed by the straighter axiality of the tomb plan. In the tomb of Ramesses VI, which marked the last step in the development of royal decoration, most known funerary texts were profusely depicted, as was Re's supremacy. The Ramessid ceiling decoration varied according to the space and showed, in addition to stars, such creatures as vultures, winged serpents, scarabs, and falcons, flying into the tomb to protect the dead king from hostile forces; these elements were replaced by astronomical texts and scenes, and in the tomb of Ramesses VI, the sky goddess Nut stretched over the heaven. By the late New Kingdom, the royal tomb thus embodied the complete cosmos, visually, textually, as well as spatially through the symbolic location of its images.

Just as the iconography became increasingly elaborate, so did the style. The decoration was at first drawn in black outlines, except for the painting in color of the background and details such as the red solar disks or the royal insignia. Then with the tomb of Thutmose IV, the divine scenes were painted entirely in color, and from the tomb of Horemheb, the decoration was done in painted reliefs. The use of colors was not only limited (black, white, yellow, red, blue, and green) but also governed by conventions. Typically, the wall background was white, except

briefly in the tombs of Horemheb and Ramesses I, where it was blue-gray, and in Sety I's tomb, where yellow was introduced in the burial chamber.

In the main, although artists drew from the same repertories, the decoration of each tomb varied in style, iconography, and quality, reflecting possibly the owner's preferences, the time allowance, and the artists' skills.

Post–New Kingdom Tombs. Following the New Kingdom, the Third Intermediate Period was another time of instability. To Thebes, the kings of the twenty-first and twenty-second dynasties preferred Tanis, in the eastern Delta, as their new burial grounds. Located in the city, within the precinct of the temple of Amun, the tombs did not survive well. They represented a new type called *temenos* and consisted of a small underground burial chamber, possibly surmounted by a funerary chapel. Their decoration essentially continued the themes of the New Kingdom royal tombs.

From the Late period onward, Egypt fell periodically under foreign rule. Despite the many changes brought on by foreign occupation, Egypt maintained its indigenous artistic tradition well into Roman times. Yet, either because the rulers were not native to Egypt and, as foreigners, were buried in their homeland, or because the later royal tombs, probably located in the North, within a temple precinct, were destroyed in antiquity, little remains of the tradition of royal funerary painting of this later period.

The Royal Family. While the royal tomb sought to stress the king's unique role in the cosmos that set him apart from the rest of the population, the members of the royal family built tombs that identified them in relation to the king. In the Old Kingdom the spatial proximity to the royal tomb was ideologically paramount, and members of the royal family and high officials were buried as close as possible to the king's tomb in the hope of partaking in the latter's eternal destiny. The chief queens lay in subsidiary pyramids, next to the royal pyramids, while the rest of the royal entourage was buried in *mastaba*s in the cemeteries surrounding the pyramids. Despite their royal connection, the superstructures or chapels of these tombs were decorated with scenes found in nonroyal tombs, such as the deceased receiving ritual offerings and scenes of so-called everyday life (e.g., the tomb of Khufu's granddaughter, Queen Meresankh III). In the late Old Kingdom, however, as provincial cemeteries developed and spatial proximity to the king's burial became much less important, the gap between the king and the elite began to lessen.

Although principally reserved as a burial ground for the ruling kings, the Valley of the Kings was occasionally used for members of the royal family and high officials, particularly during the early New Kingdom. Despite the

ROYAL TOMB PAINTING. *Queen Nefertari surrounded by deities.* Another nineteenth dynasty wall painting from the tomb of Nefertari in the Valley of the Queens. (Giraudon / Art Resource, NY)

honor that such burials would confer on their owners, certain measures against the full use of royal prerogatives were taken in an effort to maintain the strict social hierarchy characteristic of Egyptian society. In this way, the early New Kingdom tombs were simplified, yet undecorated, versions of the king's tomb.

As time went on, however, the distinction between royal and nonroyal tombs became less apparent as more privileges were appropriated by the elite. In the nineteenth dynasty, the members of the immediate royal family began to be buried systematically in what is now called the Valley of the Queens. While many of these burials were undecorated pit tombs, some displayed their semi-royal nature through decoration. The partial use of royal privileges in these tombs is perhaps nowhere better illustrated than in the recently restored tomb of Ramesses II's queen, Nefertari. Although the tomb maintained smaller proportions than the king's and used the commoners' *Book of Going Forth by Day* (*Book of the Dead*) as funerary text, it displayed royal iconography that included images of the queen alone facing the gods.

Unlike the queens, who were conceded the high royal privilege of interacting directly with the gods, the princes were shown in their own tombs accompanied by their royal father, except when represented as adults, such as the son of Ramesses IX, Prince Montuherkhepeshef, who wore the sidelock, characteristic of children, over a wig. The sidelock stressed his filial relationship to the king and the wig his adult status.

Furthermore, in his own tomb, the king did not appear in the company of his earthly family—except at Tell el-Amarna, where Akhenaten's family constituted the main iconographic theme in both the king's tomb and those of his courtiers—or generally in the private tombs, where the deceased's relatives were portrayed. Beginning in the New Kingdom, the elite could also be in the presence of both deities and the king in their tombs.

Royal Portraiture. The question of portraiture in ancient Egyptian art remains perplexing to the modern Western viewer, for whom physical resemblance to the model defines a portrait. Egyptian art was first and foremost idealizing, with occasional forays in naturalism. Typically, both men and women, royal and nonroyal, were shown as youthful and in accordance with conventions appropriate to their social role. While their communal identity was thus asserted by the degree to which they conformed to set ideological principles, their personal identity was revealed through the inscriptions accompanying the representations.

In his tomb, the king's cosmic role influenced not only the choice of images but also the way in which the ruler was represented. What typically identified the king was not his personal physiognomy (despite the occasional presence of individualizing features, such as the nose of Thutmose III and Sety I) but a number of formal clues that visually signaled his persona. In this way, the king was always shown wearing the insignia of his kingly office, such as the headdress and the scepter, regardless of the particular style or degree of elaboration of the representation. Moreover, unlike the commoners, the king alone appeared, both literally and figuratively, in the company of and on equal footing with the gods—in the same composition, on the same scale, and directly interacting with the divine sphere. Thus, the king's status as mediator between the divine world and the human sphere was conveyed through the composition or context. Yet what identified the king in specific terms were the inscriptions, which were part of the images. Thus, even in his own tomb, namely, the point where he met his eternal destiny, the king's personal physiognomy was subordinated to the funerary ideology. Representations focused exclusively on the king's ritual role, bypassing his earthly ties.

Nevertheless, the kings occasionally exhibited marked physiognomical traits or signature elements, such as the aging, grave, and discontented expressions of Senwosret III and Amenemhet III in the twelfth dynasty, or the body curves of Akhenaten in the eighteenth dynasty, which not only appeared as individualizing, but also identified these kings easily. Yet it has been observed that episodes of naturalism in art tended to coincide with cultural changes and that these images may instead have represented visually coded responses to particular situations. A case in point is that of Akhenaten and his family, whose unorthodox, even androgynous features—large head, long neck, slender torso, high small of the back, belly fold, short lower legs, and large buttocks and thighs—are thought to have been devised to promote the king's religious concepts rather than to render a pathological condition afflicting the monarch, as has been hypothesized by some scholars. Thus, the radically new images functioned as symbols for the new ideas advocated by the king in the same way that traditional royal images were visual formulas of the concept of kingship. Similarly, Queen Hatshepsut, who proclaimed herself king, was shown (although not in her tomb, which was left undecorated) mostly as a male king in traditional male regalia, whereas in the texts, she was identified as a woman.

What mattered, therefore, was not the physical reality, but the visual impact produced by the images designed to convey ideas beyond words. Whether idealizing or naturalizing, royal representations could not be dissociated from their propagandistic, political, and religious functions, as they made visual statements about kingship and the king's position in the cosmos. Even when presenting idiosyncratic physical traits, they were the cumulative expression of conventions that were harnessed in the service of kingship and the king's cosmic role.

Furthermore, the gods and members of the court were often shown resembling the king. The practice of emulating certain features of the king's face or a likeness (however remote) may have been politically motivated, designed to show loyalty toward the ruler and to flatter him. Such practice also weakens the assumption of portraiture, in the Western sense of individual resemblance.

Gender-Based Distinctions. Traditionally, in royal and private monuments alike, gender was distinguished by the use of such artistic conventions as size, skin color, costume, and hairstyle, as well as by composition. Images of women were generally idealized and their costumes remained more conservative than the men's. In this way, female deities were shown wearing the tight-fitting sheath dresses, an early type of garment throughout pharaonic history, as a sign of conformity to the world order established at creation. In contrast, queens were shown wearing the sheath dresses until the mid-eighteenth dynasty, when they began to be depicted in contemporary fashionable dress. Among the royal women, distinctions were made between queens and princesses. Queens, whose status may have been partially divine, were shown wearing insignia that were either originally divine (vulture headdress of the goddess Nekhbet) or royal (*uraeus*); they also held symbols, such as the sign of life, like the king and the gods. Although princesses were potential queens, they were represented as nonroyal women, without divine and royal attributes.

Even in their own tombs, women typically occupied a secondary position in relation to men, and the members of the royal family were identified in relation to the king, just as a nonroyal woman was identified in relation to her spouse or to another male figure. Although the king appeared in his tomb without his earthly consort, interacting solely with the gods, the same was not true of the queen until the New Kingdom, when she was shown alone before the gods. The absence of the king's image in the queens' tombs of the New Kingdom indicated a loosening of the rules of decorum that resulted from the appropriation of certain royal prerogatives.

Archaism. Over the course of history, kings have used artistic forms from the past for their own monuments. Although copied, the earlier forms were never borrowed wholesale; instead they reinterpreted the past in new versions. That practice is called "archaism," and the reasons for kings to resort to reusing earlier forms in defining their own art had little to do with antiquarianism or nostalgia. The practice tended to occur in such periods of cultural change following turmoil as the twelfth and eighteenth dynasties. Moreover, the forms used as models typically came from periods of strong government and economic prosperity. By returning to the art connected to past golden eras, the king associated himself with those reigns and thereby sought to legitimize his own. Archaism in art was part of a strategy whereby the ruler presented himself as the heir to a particular reign in order to gain the authority necessary to rule.

Conclusion. As the point of contact where the king would join Re and travel through the cosmos, the royal tomb in the New Kingdom re-created the cosmos through the symbolic use of its architectural layout and wall decoration in order to help the king reach his destiny in eternity. Since it was exclusively funerary, the imagery included scenes of the sun god's perpetual journey, the netherworld, and the king interacting with the gods; it excluded references to either historical events or highlights in the king's personal life, as were found in the officials' tombs. The officials' explicitly commemorative appearance, owing to decorum, however, implicitly helped the individual to reach the afterlife by proclaiming his or her adherence to proper behavior in this world. Thus, unlike the royal tomb of the earliest periods, when the king stood at the center of the universe, relying less explicitly on the divine for his eternal voyage and more explicitly on his monument for power in this world, the New Kingdom royal tomb was a ritualistic vehicle designed to enact the king's union with the divine.

BIBLIOGRAPHY

Assmann, Jan. "Preservation and Presentation of Self in Ancient Egyptian Portraiture." In *Studies in Honor of William Kelly Simpson*, vol. 1. Boston, 1996. Excellent discussion of the two functions of portraiture in society.

Baines, John. *Fecundity Figures. Egyptian Personification and the Iconology of a Genre.* Warminster, 1985. Detailed study of the application of the system of decorum as illustrated by fecundity figures.

Baines, John. "Trône et dieu: aspects du symbolisme royal et divin des temps archaïques." *Bulletin de la Société Française d'Égyptologie.* 118 (1990), 5–37. Discussion of early royal and divine symbolism.

D'Auria, Sue, et al. *Mummies and Magic: The Funerary Arts of Ancient Egypt.* Boston, 1988. Exhibition catalog for the Museum of Fine Arts, Boston. Chronological survey of the various types of funerary artifacts, with useful introductory essays and an extensive bibliography.

Hornung, Erik. *Conceptions of God in Ancient Egypt: The One and the Many.* Translated by J. Baines. Ithaca, N.Y., 1982. Excellent analysis of the ancient conceptions of the divine; translated from the German *Der Eine und die Vielen* (Darmstadt, 1971).

Hornung, Erik. *The Valley of the Kings: Horizon of Eternity.* Translated by D. Warburton. New York, 1990. Classic survey of the Theban royal necropolis, offers a detailed discussion of the funerary ideology, with ample illustrations.

McDonald, John K. *House of Eternity: The Tomb of Nefertari.* Los Angeles, 1996. Illustrated account of the recent restoration project of the queen's tomb by the Getty Conservation Institute and the J. Paul Getty Museum, Los Angeles.

Reeves, Nicholas, and Richard H. Wilkinson. *The Complete Valley of the Kings: Tombs and Treasures of Egypt's Greatest Pharaohs.* London, 1996. Good introduction to the royal necropolis from the historical and archaeological perspective; includes the history of its discovery, a brief description of each tomb, and many illustrations.

Robins, Gay. *Women in Ancient Egypt.* Cambridge, Mass., 1993. Study of the status and the role of women from various sources, including art.

Robins, Gay. *The Art of Ancient Egypt.* Cambridge, Mass., 1997. Up-to-date illustrated survey, with an extensive bibliography.

Romer, John. *Valley of the Kings.* New York, 1981. Survey of the royal necropolis, with a focus on the history of the tombs and of the travelers and scholars who studied them.

Simpson, William Kelly. "Egyptian Sculpture and Two-dimensional Representation as Propaganda." *Journal of Egyptian Archaeology* 68 (1982), 266–71. Summary discussion of the propagandistic elements and their motives in Egyptian art.

Spanel, Donald. *Through Ancient Eyes: Egyptian Portraiture.* Birmingham, 1988. Exhibition catalog prepared for the Birmingham Museum of Art, Birmingham, Alabama, in 1988; useful introductory essay reviews the issues relating to portraiture.

Wilkinson, Richard H. "Symbolic Location and Alignment in New Kingdom Royal Tombs and their Decoration." *Journal of the American Research Center in Egypt* 31 (1994), 79–86. Study of the relationship between the symbolic orientation of the royal tombs and their decorative schemes.

PATRICIA A. BOCHI

S

SACRED ANIMALS. *See* Cults, *article on* Animal Cults.

SACRED BARKS. In antiquity, boats represented the ultimate mode of travel in the Nile Valley, and they played a crucial role in Egyptian religious practice and belief from prehistory onward. The sun god was believed to traverse the sky by day and the underworld by night in his sacred bark (*wiȝ*). Paintings on Naqada II pottery depict large ceremonial boats decorated with sacred emblems and figures. In dynastic times, both full-sized navigable craft and portable models—dragged or carried by priests—featured prominently in rituals and in festivals, when they were used to transport cult statues. Although no actual examples survive, their history can be traced in reliefs and inscriptions.

Among the most ancient examples was the Memphite god Soker's *Ḥnw*-boat. Although the earliest known representations date to the New Kingdom, its iconography suggests that it dates back to earliest times. The *Ḥnw*-boat resembles figures on Naqada II pottery, featuring a bank of oars along the front half of its impossibly curved hull. The cabin shrine has two mummiform falcons similar to the archaic gold and copper example found at Hierakonpolis, one projecting from the roof and the other from the front of the cabin. Its hull is supported by four pairs of posts attached to a sledge, with a rope secured to the front and sides of the sledge and running underneath the hull. A second rope, tied to the front of the sledge, was used to drag it in procession. Later, in Ramesses III's temple at Medinet Habu, the *Ḥnw*-boat was transported on carrying poles.

Other primitive barks, mounted on sledges with towropes, are shown in later reliefs. Some bear enthroned statues of the king or of Hathor as a cow with the king standing before her and again kneeling beneath her udders to suckle, with examples from Deir el-Bahri and Luxor and in Ramesses II's Abydos temple. These sledge-mounted barks predate those carried by priests on a platform with carrying poles. In New Kingdom barks, such carrying platforms are still represented in the form of the now obsolete sledge, an anachronism which betrays the original method of locomotion.

Another early bark, the *Nšmt*-boat of Osiris, is known from the twelfth dynasty at Abydos, where certain officials oversaw its construction. These texts probably refer to a large river-going craft rather than to a processional one, but later, in the temple of Sety I, a model vessel with carrying poles is depicted. The prow is decorated with a figurehead of the god emerging from a lotus stem, while the reliquary of Osiris protrudes from the top of the cabin shrine. A number of other sacred barks, rarely seen elsewhere, grace the walls of Sety I's Abydos temple, including those of Ptah, Re-Horakhty, Isis, and Horus.

From New Kingdom times onward, portable barks, heavily gilded and fitted at prow and stern with emblems of the gods and supported by carrying poles, became the standard form of processional shrine, the best-known example being that of Amun-Re of Thebes. From reliefs dating between the early eighteenth dynasty and the Ptolemaic era, it is possible to trace the Amun bark's iconographic development. The earliest datable representation comes from the alabaster bark chapel of Amenhotpe I at Karnak, but it is possible that this form existed earlier. A fragmentary relief from the temple of Nebhepetre-Montuhotpe II at Deir el-Bahri shows its prow, but this relief is a post-Amarna restoration dating to the Ramessid period. Still, it is most likely a replacement of an original relief depicting the bark. A pair of reused blocks from Karnak depict the craft's prow and cabin shrine. These could belong to a monument of Amenhotpe I or to the twelfth dynasty, as they are similar in style to that found on reliefs on blocks of Senwosret I. The evidence is sketchy, but it is likely that Amun's processional bark existed in the Middle Kingdom, perhaps as early as the eleventh dynasty.

Originally, the iconography of the vessel was simple; its slim hull was slightly upturned at prow and stern, each end having ram-headed figureheads with cobras emerging from their foreheads. The cabin, in the form of the Upper Egyptian *pr-wr* shrine, was decorated with a frieze of uraei along the top of its side panels, with two friezes of alternating pairs of *ḏd* and *tit* amulets below; the lower half was undecorated. The cabin was protected by a light canopy roof supported by poles. Otherwise, the decoration and fittings were quite sparse. A pair of oars and their steering columns had falcon-headed terminals. A sphinx on a standard was placed behind the prow.

Dozens of blocks from Hatshepsut's Red Chapel indicate that by her reign, the bark sported a veil partly

SACRED BARKS. *A relief depicting a sacred bark, from the eighteenth dynasty Red Chapel of Hatshepsut at Karnak.* (Courtesy Peter Brand)

shrouding the cabin shrine, to which it was attached by a large clasp in the form of a vulture with outstretched wings. The pattern of decoration on the exposed part of the cabin now consisted of two friezes of uraei supported on *nb*-baskets and wearing *3tf*-crowns; a *šn*-sign protruding from its chest separated each cobra from its neighbor. The ram figureheads fore and aft had aegises in the form of *wsḫ*-collars with falcon-head terminals. The deck was peopled with a number of figurines, including ones of Hathor and Maat standing near the prow; in front of the cabin shrine were a statuette of a kneeling king proffering *nw*-jars, and a royal sphinx with human arms extending a *nmst*-jar. The four poles supporting the canopy over the cabin shrine were each steadied by a kneeling king. Finally, another royal figure acting as helmsman stood behind the oarlocks, steering by means of a tiller in the form of a uraeus. Other embellishments included a *wḏ3t*-eye near the front of the hull and two clasps on each side of the hull in the form of winged scarabs that secured it to the carrying platform. The iconography of the bark remained largely the same before the Amarna period, but under Thutmose IV, *šbyw*-collars, consisting of two strands of biconical beads, were placed on the ram figureheads.

Since the bark was perhaps the most visible avatar of Amun-Re's cult, Akhenaten's partisans systematically expunged representations of it wherever such images appeared. Doubtless the gilded icon itself was likewise destroyed, since Tutankhamun's Restoration Edict dwells at length on the replacement of this costly and prestigious cult object. He claims to have refashioned it on thirteen carrying poles (*nb3w*), whereas formerly it had been on eleven. This statement has been puzzling to scholars, since there is no room in the confined inner recesses of the temples to accommodate so many carrying poles and their bearers. In fact, no more than five poles could have fit, even this increase being made possible only by a widening of the doorways in various temples and shrines. Although it has been thought that the larger bark with five poles appeared under Thutmose III, it is more likely that Tutankhamun was responsible. The reference to thirteen poles is probably hyperbole.

In the wake of the Amarna heresy, embellishments to the bark became increasingly complex. The figureheads were fitted with *3tf*-crowns, large floral *w3ḫ*-collars and triple-stranded *šbyw*-collars; kneeling figurines of the king and the souls of Nekhen and Pe making jubilation and standing ones of the "*Mrt*-goddess" were set along the runners of the carrying platform. The formerly plain veil was now encrusted with hieroglyphic appliques forming parts of the royal titulary, arranged in rebus patterns. Two Maat goddesses with interlocking wings protecting a rebus of Tutankhamun's prenomen were most prominent among these.

This practice of incorporating titulary rebuses on the veil, and later on the exposed upper part of the cabin shrine, continued well into the Ramessid period and beyond. Certain elements, such as the winged goddesses, were retained for centuries. Others, specific to an individual king's titulary, were either discarded or altered so that they no longer referred explicitly to that king. Under Sety I, for example, the winged Maat figures knelt on *mn*-boards and had sun disks on their heads, thereby rendering his prenomen Menmaatre. In later reigns, rebuses were modified to depict the names of other kings, but temple reliefs indicate that some of these *mn*-signs, distinctive of Sety's name, were retained until the reign of Ramesses III. In this way, the rich iconography of the veil and cabin shrine underwent a continuous but gradual evolution.

Amun-Re also had a huge river barge called the Amun-Userhet, or "Amen-is-Mighty-of-Prow." Under Ramesses III, it was 130 cubits long (about 70 meters/224 feet). The barge itself closely resembled the processional bark, having elaborate ram-headed aegises, huge oars and steering columns, and even large versions of the crew of statues populating its deck. Its great cabin served as a floating temple complete with flagstaves and obelisks on its façade. All these fittings were plated with gold; from Amenhotpe III's reign on, even the hull was clad to the waterline with large gold sheets embossed with ritual scenes. During Theban religious celebrations, such as Opet and the Festival of the Valley, this dazzling floating temple was towed by ships and by men pulling dozens of tow ropes from shore, along canals and up the river, along with Amun's consort Mut and their son Khonsu, who were provided with river barges of their own as early as Tutankhamun's reign. Other gods had similar barges, but none are as well known as those of the Theban triad.

BIBLIOGRAPHY

Calverley, A. M. and M. F. Broome. *The Temple of King Sethos I at Abydos.* 2 vols. London, 1933, 1958.

Epigraphic Survey. *The Festival Procession of Opet in the Colonnade Hall.* Reliefs and Inscriptions at Karnak, 1. Chicago, 1994.

Epigraphic Survey. *Ramses III's Temple within the Great Enclosure of Amon.* Reliefs and Inscriptions at Karnak, 1–2. Chicago, 1936.

Foucart, G. *Une temple flottant: Le vaissuau d'or d'Amon-Râ.* Fondation Piot, Monuments et mémoires publiés par l'Académie des Inscriptions et Belles-Lettres, 25. 1921–1922. See pp. 143–169.

Górski, H. J. "La barque d'Amon dans la décoration du temple de Thoutmosis III à Deir el-Bahari." *Mitteilungen des Deutschen Archäologischen Instituts, Abteilung Kairo* (1990), 99–112.

Nelson, H. H. *The Great Hypostyle Hall at Karnak.* Vol. 1, part 1, *The Wall Reliefs.* Edited by W. J. Murnane. Chicago, 1981.

Karlshausen, C. "L'évolution de la barque Processionnelle d'Amon à la 18ᵉ Dynastie." *Revue d Égyptologie* 46 (1995), 119–137.

Lacau, P., and H. Chevrier. *Une chapelle d'Hatshepsout à Karnak.* 2 vols. Cairo, 1977.

Murnane, W. J. "The Bark of Amun on the Third Pylon at Karnak." *Journal of the American Research Center in Egypt* 16 (1979), 11–27.

Murnane, W. J. "Tutankhamun on the Third Pylon at Karnak." *Varia Aegyptiaca* 1 (1985), 59–68.

Traunecker, C., F. Le Saout, and O. Masson. *La chapelle d'Achôris à Karnak.* 2 vols. Recherche sur les grandes civilisations, 5. Paris, 1981.

PETER BRAND

SAIS, Greek name for the ancient Egyptian *S3w* and present-day Sa el-Hagar, located on the eastern bank of the Rosetta branch of the Nile River (30° 58′N, 30° 46′E). In pharaonic times, Sais was the capital of the fifth Lower Egyptian nome and the main cult center of the warrior goddess Neith, as well as a center for science and the arts. Sais was first mentioned in inscriptions of the Archaic period. Its political importance grew, particularly during the Late period, and by the eighth Tefnakht and Bocchoris fought against the Kushites, and formed the twenty-fourth dynasty. One of their successors, Necho I, appointed by the Assyrian king, Esarhaddon, after his conquest of Egypt in 671 BCE, extended his jurisdiction over the Delta and Memphis. His son Psamtik I succeeded in reuniting the whole of Egypt, thus founding the twenty-sixth dynasty; subsequently kings of this dynasty enlarged and embellished Sais. The goddess Neith, considered to be mother of Re, supplanted Amun as patroness of the dynasty. Further building activities took place in Sais, in the thirtieth dynasty and in the Ptolemaic period. In Greco-Roman times, many objects were removed from the temples of Sais; some were later found by archaeologists in Alexandria and in various sites along the Rosetta branch of the Nile, as well as in Italy.

Sais was better known from historical sources and descriptions of travelers, both ancient (Herodotus, Strabo, Athenagoras) and modern (Carsten Niebuhr's *Description de l'Egypte,* 1776) than from archaeological excavations. Although much sculpture originating from Sais is in museums worldwide, the site was never subject to systematic archaeological research. Small-scale excavations were completed by August Mariette in the mid-nineteenth century and by Georges Daressy in 1901. Excavations by the Egyptian Antiquities Organization in 1988 and 1989 and the Tanta University uncovered remains that from the Late period and from Greco-Roman times. Remains

SAIS. *Drawing of a relief depicting the front of the temple of Neith at Sais. The relief is on a statue from the early twenty-seventh dynasty.* (Courtesy Karol Myśliwiec; after R. El-Sayed, *Documents relatifs à Sais et ses divinitiés*)

burial rites in pharaonic Egypt was the funeral procession from a place called Sais to a place called Buto.

Besides Neith and Osiris, many other deities were worshipped in Sais—among them Re, Atum, Sobek, Horus, Amun, Min, Nekhbet, Isis, Hathor, Wadjet, and Selket. In the Late period, Neith was identified with the Greek goddess Athena (and in 1989 some bronze figurines of Athena were found at the site). At the beginning of the Christian era, Sais became the seat of a bishopric.

[*See also* Late Period; Neith; *and* Osiris.]

BIBLIOGRAPHY

El-Sayed, Ramadan. *Documents relatifs à Saïs et ses divinités*. Bibliothèque d'études, 69. Cairo, 1975. Detailed study of the most important hieroglyphic texts concerning Sais.

El-Sayed, Ramadan. *La déesse Neith de Saïs*. Bibliothèque d'études, 86. 1–2. Cairo, 1982. Monograph on the main divinity of Sais, based on hieroglyphic texts.

KAROL MYŚLIWIEC

SAITE PERIOD. *See* Late Period, *article on* Twenty-sixth Dynasty.

known from the nineteenth-century plans and drawings comprise huge brick walls that form an extensive enclosure, which probably surrounded the temples and the royal necropolis. The discovery of many sarcophagi at Kawadi, to the northeast of this enclosure, seems to indicate the necropolis of the nobles. A large depression and a fragment of a monumental stone wall beside it constitute the central part of the still-visible structures.

Much information concerning the Late period temples of Sais has been derived from inscriptions on statues and stelae. The most important Late period sanctuaries were dedicated to Neith and Osiris and the enclosure of the great temple comprised four sanctuaries as was mentioned repeatedly in those texts. Two sanctuaries, namely Res-Net and Meh-Net, were connected with the weaving of linen, for which Sais and the goddess Neith were famous. At Sais, linen was associated with the mummy of Osiris, whose local incarnation was called Hemag, "the wrapped." The wrapping of the god was performed at Hut Hemag (the "Palace of Hemag"), part of a larger sanctuary called the Hut-Bit ("The Palace of the King of Lower Egypt"), which emphasized the royal aspect of his nature and the divine aspect of the kingship. The Hut-Bit was probably located in the northern part of the great enclosure, behind the temple of Neith. Believed by the ancient Egyptians to be the place of the tomb of Osiris, Sais played an important part in Lower Egypt's sepulchral beliefs and rituals. An essential episode of the traditional

SANDSTONE, a soft, easily worked sedimentary rock, composed of rounded to angular grains (1/16–2 millimeters/0.0025–0.08 inch) of cemented calcium carbonate, quartz, iron oxides, and sometimes chlorite. In Egypt, the grains are mostly quartz and the color can vary widely: white, gray, reddish, brown, or yellow. Egyptian quarries generally mined the Nubia Group of the Upper Cretaceous era, from the Duwi, Quseir, Umm Barmil, and Timsah formations; collectively these units are commonly referred to as "Nubian sandstone" (Harrell 1989).

Important quarries are to be found along the Nile Valley margins, to the north of Aswan near Hierakonpolis, at el-Mahamid village near Elkab, at Gebel es-Silsila, from the Sidi el-Hasan tomb to Ezbet Ali Amer village in the Gharb el-Gaafra district, at Wadi el-Shatt el-Rigal and near Nag el-Hosch village. Other large quarries are to the south of Aswan, near Qertassi, the sandstone source for temples at Philae and Qertassi. Farther south, into Nubia (northern Sudan), the stone steadily decreases in quality.

Sandstone is an important architectural material, owing to its relative ease in quarrying, shaping, and decorating. Its initial use in major construction began during the New Kingdom, for the great temples at Luxor and Karnak. Before that, limestone was the construction favorite. Yet for general use, for small-scale construction, sandstone was chosen through much of Egyptian history. Sandstone generally supports longer horizontal free spans than does limestone, allowing for more impressive open

SANDSTONE. *Quarry at Gebel es-Silsila.* (Courtesy Donald B. Redford)

spaces. The choice of sandstone for the large temples of Middle Egypt may have originally been based on ease of access to local quarries. The new material quickly proved its value, since unlike limestone, Nubian sandstone splits easily into horizontal depositional bedding planes, facilitating removal from the quarry.

Although much statuary in sandstone is known, the sculptor's inability to produced highly polished surfaces limited its appeal. Even when smoothed and painted, sandstone statues tend to look unfinished. Examples include the statue of Montuhotep I (eleventh dynasty, 2061–2011 BCE), a seated man of the thirteenth dynasty (1783–1633 BCE), Amun Horemakhet and Djedasetiufankh (both c.690–650 BCE). The most impressive sandstone sculptures ever produced are the four seated statues of Ramesses II at Abu Simbel, each 20 meters (65 feet) tall. Color does not appear to have been an important factor in selecting sandstone for sculpture, although many examples of reddish sandstone statues are known; perhaps reddish sandstones were generally used to indicate skin tones, as in painted scenes, or perhaps they indicated links to solar worship.

Ancient Egyptian words for sandstone include: *s wḏt, inr ḥd n r wḏt, inr ḥd nefer n rwḏt, r wḏt, biꜣt,* and *rwḏ.*

BIBLIOGRAPHY

Erman, Adolf, and Hermann Grapow. *Wörterbuch der Aegyptischen Sprache.* 6 vols. Berlin, 1982.

Faulkner, Raymond O. *A Concise Dictionary of Middle Egyptian.* Oxford, 1962.

Harrell, James A. "An Inventory of Ancient Egyptian Quarries." *Newsletter of the American Research Center in Egypt* 146 (1989), 1–7, plus cover photo.

Harris, J. R. *Lexicographical Studies in Ancient Egyptian Minerals.* Deutsche Akademie der Wissenschafter zu Berlin Institut für Orientforschung, 54. Berlin, 1961.

Lesko, Leonard H., and Barbara Switalski, eds. *A Dictionary of Late Egyptian.* 4 vols. Berkeley, 1982.

Russman, Edna R. *Egyptian Sculpture—Cairo and Luxor.* Austin, 1989.

CLAIR R. OSSIAN

SAQQARA, the site of the principal cemetery at Memphis (20°50–53′N, 31°13′E). Its name seems to derive from that of the god of the necropolis, Sokar, which was later applied to the nearby village. Spreading over 6.2 kilometers (3.7 miles) on the western plateau, some 40 kilometers (25 miles) to the south of present-day Cairo, Saqqara is part of a series of necropolises along the Nile River, extending from Abu Rowash in the north to Dahshur in the south, all serving the ancient Egyptian capital. The uniqueness of Saqqara is based on continuous use, from the first dynasty (c.3050–2850 BCE) through the early Christian era (fifth century CE). The development of Saqqara is of prime interest because it contains clues to the history of Memphis as a political, economic, and religious center.

According to the ancient Greek historian Herodotus, Menes (who may be identified with the first two historical kings, c.3000 BCE, Narmer and Aha) was the founder of Memphis. The associated Early Dynastic (Archaic) cemetery, with monumental brick *mastaba*s, was built on the verge of the plateau, so as to be seen from the royal residence in the valley. The English archaeologist Walter B. Emery, who cleared thirteen *mastaba*s between 1936 and 1956 on behalf of the Service des Antiquités de l'Égypte (Cairo) and then for the Egypt Exploration Society (London), was convinced that they were the tombs of the kings of the first dynasty. After much debate, the site of the royal necropolis of that time is considered to be at Abydos, with the Saqqara tombs—rivaling in size, complexity, and wealth those of kings—belonging to high-ranking officials of the early Memphite administration. Those brick *mastaba*s, rectangular in plan and decorated with a system of intricate recesses in the brickwork (usually referred to as palace-façade), show the elaboration of the funerary practices during that formative period. Until the reign of Den (fifth king of the first dynasty) the funerary apartments, sunk into the bedrock and covered by a timber ceiling, were sealed by a brick superstructure partitioned into storage magazines, which contained the remains of a rich material culture (copper tools, stone and pottery vessels, ivory furniture, etc.). Later, underground storerooms were cut into the rock, and the burial chamber was reached by a stairway on its eastern side; the brick framework of the superstructure was then filled with rubble. Those tombs present architectural elements found in the later royal funerary monuments of the Old Kingdom: the stepped core within the superstructure; access to the burial chamber

from the north blocked with granite portcullis; recessed palace-façade enclosure walls; a cult place on the northern side; a model estate; and a solar bark. Although those elements were not limited to the necropolis of Saqqara, their combination appears to be the result of a Memphite architectural tradition.

The Early Dynastic period cemetery of the second and third dynasties, mainly excavated between 1910 and 1912 by James Quibell, then chief inspector at Saqqara, covers the northwestern part of the plateau. The most elaborate tombs, those with brick superstructures, also have extensive interiors that were cut deep in the rock; they feature such elements of domestic architecture as bedrooms and latrines. The first royal tombs on the plateau, farther to the south, are those of Hotepsekhemwy (r. 2850–2820 BCE) and Ninuter (r. 2790–2754 BCE), kings of the second dynasty, and of these only a series of extensive underground apartments was found. The grand funerary complex of Djoser (r. 2687–2668 BCE), first king of the third dynasty, is best known as the first monument built in dressed stone and the first of the Egyptian pyramids. It was originally conceived as a symbol of the union of the Two Lands, within the palace-façade enclosure, two tombs were built for him—a *mastaba*, in the northern part of the complex (covering a granite burial chamber surrounded by galleries and rooms decorated with faience plaques that imitated matting) and a southern tomb that duplicated the northern setting but was intended for the royal *ka*. To the east was built a network of dummy administrative and religious buildings that presented the insignia of both the northern and the southern kingdoms—the Two Lands. In the middle of Djoser's complex is the courtyard of the *sed*-festival (the jubilee during which the king won divine approbation for a continued reign and symbolically united the two kingdoms), as was depicted on carved panels inside the funerary apartments of his tomb. Djoser's tomb is best known as the Step Pyramid, the six steps, or courses, of which cover the original *mastaba* and still rise to 140 meters (425 feet). The vizier-architect Imhotep was credited with having invented that feature, as well as the use of limestone, which sometimes imitated Predynastic structures of reed matting and wood. The clearing of the monument, started in 1924 by C. M. Firth, is still being carried out by the French architect, Jean-Philippe Lauer, who has devoted his life to its study and preservation. Other kings of the third dynasty followed Djoser's example before Saqqara was temporarily abandoned.

Shepseskaf (r. 2523–2519 BCE), last known pharaoh of the fourth dynasty, returned to South Saqqara to build a coffin-shaped tomb, the *mastaba* Faraoun, cleared by the French archaeologist Gustave Jequier in 1924. Userkaf (r. 2513–2506 BCE), first king of the fifth dynasty, mixed tradition and innovation in constructing his pyramid next to

SAQQARA. *The causeway of Unas.* (Courtesy Dieter Arnold)

the complex of Djoser; he adopted its orientation, with a satellite pyramid and a temple on the south, and he originated a new type of monument, a sun temple, farther to the north in the necropolis of Abusir. There, at least three of his successors chose to complete their funerary complexes. King Izezi (r. 2436–2404 BCE) of the fifth dynasty restored Saqqara as the site of the royal necropolis; while his pyramid is mostly unexplored, those of his successors, Unas (r. 2404–2374 BCE), last king of the fifth dynasty, and all the kings of the sixth dynasty are famous because the walls of their corridors and burial chambers are inscribed with the Pyramid Texts. The French Archaeological Mission at Saqqara under the direction of Jean Leclant has undertaken a major architectural and epigraphic project in the funerary complexes of Unas, Teti (r. 2374–2354 BCE), Pepy I (r. 2354–2310 BCE), and Merenre Antyemsaf (r. 2310–2300 BCE), that reveals a complex architectural network, which includes the funerary temples and satellite pyramids for the queens. The modern name of Memphis was directly derived from *Mn-nfr,* the name given to the pyramid of Pepy I, which demonstrates the impact that his monument had on the local economy.

Because of the uninterrupted work of the Egyptian Antiquity Service in the private necropolis of the Old Kingdom, conducted by such archaeologists as Auguste Mariette in 1858, James Quibell from 1905 to 1914, and Selim Hassan in 1937 and 1938, hundreds of *mastaba*s and rock-cut tombs that date from the fifth and sixth dynasties have been discovered; yet little is known of the structure and development of the private necropolis. The existence of clusters of officials' tombs around royal funerary complexes has been reassessed by the recent excavations around the pyramids of Unas and Teti. Those display a variety of forms and arrangements, from simple brick tombs with one chapel to complex, monumental, fully decorated *mastaba*s of limestone, akin to what is seen throughout the necropolis. By the sixth dynasty, because the provision of a tomb was the sole responsibility of its owner, its size, complexity, and achievement as a monument reflected more the wealth of the official than his position within the administration (as illustrated by the tomb of Khentika, vizier under Teti, which is four times smaller than that of his predecessor Kagemni). The modesty of the tombs of the kings' sons also reflected the reorganization of the administration, in which they held relatively insignificant positions (Neferseshem-seshet's tomb is a simple brick *mastaba*, while Raemka usurped the tomb of another official. In both cases, their tombs were separated from their respective father's funerary complexes).

Both the increase in the number of officials and the lack of space in the crowded necropolis at Memphis led to the clustering of tombs within family compounds. Either near a royal sepulcher (Mereruka, Ankhmahor) or in peripheral areas (Ti, Ptahhotep/Akhethotep), the *mastabas* were established like houses—with vestibules, courtyards, storerooms, pillared halls, and private apartments—in which the household members shared the benefit of the funerary cult, either with the patriarch or independently through individual chapels. The decoration of those multiroomed tombs elaborated on the existing themes—offerings, funerary rituals, banquets, the marsh and other outdoor scenes—which derived from the royal context. Similarities in the organization, content, and style of the decoration indicates both the indigenous development of the necropolis of Saqqara and a local artistic tradition.

With the transfer of the royal residence to the south, around Dahshur, during the Middle Kingdom, Saqqara lost its status as royal necropolis, although activity persisted or was resumed at some Old Kingdom pyramids. Perhaps by royal decree, the mortuary cult of Pepy I was restored, as suggested by an inscription on a statue of Amenemhet-ankh, son of Amenemhet II (r. 1929–1895 BCE). Similarly attesting a continuity in the funerary activity of that complex was the establishment of the tombs of the inspectors of the pyramids of Teti, Ihy, and Hetep.

This importance of Memphis as a major administrative center during the New Kingdom is constantly reasserted by new discoveries. Since 1980, Alain Zivie's project has cleared tombs of high officials of the early eighteenth dynasty, in the escarpment south of Teti's pyramid. The sepulchers of Nehesi, treasurer under Hatshepsut (r. 1502–1482 BCE), Aper-El, vizier under both Amenhotpe III (r. 1410–1372 BCE) and Akhenaten (r. 1372–1355 BCE), and the recently discovered tomb of Maia, nurse of Tutankhamun (r. 1355–1346 BCE), confirm the high status of Memphis—even during the reign of Akhenaten, when the royal residence was established at Amarna. Those tombs were cut in poor limestone and extend on several levels, connected by shafts, with pillared halls and decorated chambers. This cluster, still in use during the Ramessid period, extends towards the pyramid of Teti on the plateau, where free-standing tombs of the late eighteenth dynasty, now destroyed, were documented by Victor Loret and J. Firth in the 1920s and 1930s.

The main late eighteenth and nineteenth dynasty cemetery is situated on the plateau to the south of Unas's causeway. While trying to relocate the tomb of Maya, treasurer under Tutankhamun, the expedition directed by Geoffrey T. Martin uncovered, in 1975, the tomb built by the army commander Horemheb before he became king (in 1343 BCE) and those of other high officials, surrounded by the smaller tombs of their dependants. The superstructure of those free-standing tombs followed a basic pattern, which included at the west, a cult chamber (occasionally supported by columns), crowned by a small pyramid (sometimes set behind), flanked by chapels opening onto a courtyard. The most elaborate monuments developed into templelike tombs with a pylon entrance on the east, a series of paved courtyards (some with porticoes), statue rooms, and storage magazines. The brick walls, lined with limestone blocks, were decorated with scenes of the owner's life, funerary rites, offering bearers, and divine adoration. A shaft opening in the floor of the courtyard led to a series of underground chambers, cut on several levels, for the deceased and his family.

The deification of Horemheb and the establishment of a cult chapel in his tomb during the Ramessid period may have provided the impetus for the construction of the tombs of the sister of Ramesses II (r. 1304–1237 BCE) and for other high officials, which are expected to be found either in Piramesse, the capital, or in Thebes, where some held office. The location in North Saqqara of the chapel of Khaemwaset, son of Ramesses II (credited with having restored numerous monuments), and the numerous decorated blocks found throughout the necropolis suggest a much larger distribution for the New Kingdom necropolis than what is known. Later, intrusive burials attest to continuing funerary activity at Saqqara during the Late period. The twenty-sixth dynasty (664–525 BCE) provided a revival, since its high officials had their tombs cut in the escarpment north of the Unas causeway. For example, Bakenrenef, vizier of Psamtik I (r. 664–610 BCE), opened an extensive rock-cut tomb; it had a pillared hall preceded by a courtyard and a pylon entrance and was continuously used as a familial burial place for ten centuries, until the second century CE.

Installations for the cult of sacred animals flourished in Saqqara until the end of the Ptolemaic era. During the Late period, the northern part of the cemetery was progressively transformed into a sacred animal necropolis. Northwest of the pyramid of Djoser, Auguste Mariette discovered in 1851 the Serapeum—a series of galleries where the Apis bulls were buried—from the New Kingdom reign of Amenhotpe III to Roman times. Numerous votive stelae, both private and royal and dedicated to the Apis, attest to the continuity of that cult. So, too, do the successive alterations made at the complex, such as the processional alley flanked by sphinxes leading to the entrance pylon, restored by Nektanebo I (r. 380–363 BCE), or the Greek "hemicycle of the philosophers," in which seated statues of Xenophon, Plato, Aristotle, and others were erected. In the valley that slopes to the north toward Abusir, excavations led by Walter B. Emery between 1964 and 1971 and later by Geoffrey T. Martin and Harry S. Smith have revealed temples and associated catacombs containing thousands of mummies of baboons, falcons, and ibises. Nothing remains of the temple of Bastet, but the conversion of New Kingdom rock-cut tombs in the escarpment of the Bubasteion into catacombs for cat-mummies similarly attests to the vigor of that cult during the Late period.

[See also Pyramid.]

BIBLIOGRAPHY

Emery, Walter B. *Archaic Egypt.* Baltimore, 1961.

Lauer, Jean-Philippe. *Saqqara: The Royal Cemetery of Memphis, Excavations and Discoveries since 1850.* New York, 1976.

Lehner, Mark. *The Complete Pyramids.* London, 1997.

Mariette, Auguste. *Le Sérapéum de Memphis,* edited by G. Maspero. Paris, 1882.

Mariette, Auguste. *Les Mastabas de l'Ancien Empire,* edited by G. Maspero. Paris, 1889 and New York, 1976.

Martin, Geoffrey T. *The Sacred Animal Necropolis at North Saqqâra: The Southern Dependencies of the Main Temple Complex.* London, 1981.

Martin, Geoffrey T. *The Hidden Tombs of Memphis: New Discoveries from the Time of Tutankhamun and Ramesses the Great.* London, 1991.

Munro, Peter. *Das Unas-Friedhof Nord-West: topographisch-historische Einleirung.* Mainz, 1993.

Saqqara. Aux origines de l'Égypte pharaonique. Les Dossiers d'Archéologie, 146–147. Dijon, 1990.

Smith, Harry S. "Saqqara. Late Period." In *Lexikon der Ägyptologie,* 5: 412–428. Wiesbaden, 1984.

Spencer, Alan J. "Researches on the Topography of North Saqqâra." *Orientalia* 43 (1974), 1–11.

Stadelmann, Rainer. "Origins and Development of the Funerary Complex of Djoser." *Studies in Honor of William Kelly Simpson,* edited by P. der Manuelian. Boston, 1996.

Zivie, Alain-Pierre, ed., *Memphis et ses nécropoles au Nouvel Empire.* Paris, 1988.

Zivie, Alain-Pierre, *Découverte à Saqqarah: le vizir oublié.* Paris, 1990.

VIOLAINE CHAUVET

SARCOPHAGI. *See* Coffins, Sarcophagi, and Cartonnages.

SATIRE. *See* Humor and Satire.

SCARABS. The ancient Egyptian model for the sacred scarab is a dung beetle *Scarabaeus sacer,* which functions within the ecosystem of North Africa and Egypt by disposing of the dung of large herbivores. The scarab utilizes dung both as a source of nourishment for itself and its young as well as for their protection. In the wild, the scarab can be observed crafting dung balls into two distinctive shapes with mechanical precision by using its legs and mouth parts. The first of these, termed a brood ball, is a pear-shaped pellet of sheep dung into which the female lays her eggs. As the larvae develop they feed on the fecal matter of the nest. Meanwhile, the female continuosly attends the brood ball by removing molds and fungi until the larvae emerge from their incubation as adults. The second ball, of cattle dung, is a perfectly shaped sphere used for food. The scarab rolls this nourishment with its hind legs across the landscape and into an underground chamber, which is reached via a vertical shaft and horizontal passage! It was the dung beetle's association with the food ball that prompted the ancient Egyptians to develop several visual conceits, but those conceits, while based on nature, were artificial constructs often ignoring or fundamentally altering entomological reality.

Foremost among those conceits was the ancient Egyptian creation of a mythological beetle which propelled the sun disc across the heavens by using its forelegs, not its hind legs. By associating the sun, via the model of the food ball, with the sacred scarab, the Egyptians suggested that the beetle was spontaneously generated from it, ignoring the reality of the brood ball. The dung beetle's elaborate underground tunnel system into which the food ball was maneuvered served as another model for the Egyptians. It was reminiscent of their developing concept of the architectural plans of tombs from the Old Kingdom. Nature, thus modified, provided the ancient Egyptians with a powerful visual image for the diurnal course of the sun which, as one of their most dynamic cosmic cycles, could be readily applied to myths involving creation, and by extension, resurrection. In fact, the ancient Egyptian word for the "scarab" is *ḫpr,* from a verbal root connoting concepts such as "to be created" and "to come into being," and as the noun meaning "form" or "manifestation." The scarab was, therefore, considered to be the embodiment of the creator god who was self-engendered.

The gradual merging of the characteristics of the creator and sun gods led in the Old Kingdom to the development of Khepri, the god of the rising sun often depicted in the form of a male with an entire beetle set onto his shoulders to serve as a head. That image was in contrast to the depictions of other composite deities, which relied on the combination of an animal head on a human body. Because he represented the emergence of the sun from the darkness of night, Khepri was depicted in funerary scenes from the *Book of That Which Is in the Underworld* as a symbol of the resurrection of the deceased into the hereafter.

The earliest appearance of the scarab in the ancient Egyptian cultural record dates to the prehistoric period of the fourth millennium BCE, when pottery vases containing dung beetles were intentionally interred within tombs. It was not until some two thousand years later, during the sixth dynasty of the Old Kingdom, that crafted scarabs first appeared in ancient Egypt. After the inception of that form, hundreds of thousands of scarabs were manufactured over the course of Egypt's long history in almost every known material, from glazed steatite and faience to glass and semiprecious stones of jasper, carnelian, and lapis lazuli. The oval space formed by the underside of the scarab provided the ancient Egyptians with a convenient surface on which inscriptions and designs could be displayed. These designs vary but may be conveniently grouped into geometric designs, hieroglyphic signs, and figures of both humans and animals.

Geometric designs are generally confined in time to the Middle Kingdom and Second Intermediate Period and can be divided into four general categories: spiral scrolls, concentric circles, coiled cord patterns, and cross patterns. Scarabs bearing mottos in hieroglyphs are attested in different periods, their messages often containing prophylactic formulas or expressions of good fortune. These appear to be introduced during the course of the eighteenth dynasty and continue in use until the Late period. Among the sentiments expressed are "lots of good luck" and "may your name endure and may you be blessed with children." Names of divinities are also found in such mottos for the same purposes. Here one reads, "may the god Khonsu be my protection," "stable is the city which the god Amun loves," and "the god Amun-Re is the strength of the individual." These same functions are inherent in designs representing animals and human figures, both human and divine. Consequently, the types of scarabs might be employed simultaneously as amulets for the dead as well as for the living, each group requiring talismans drawn from a common repertory of motifs and mottos.

Scarabs might also have served officials as seals, a practice which gained wider currency from the time of the First Intermediate Period, although it is only from the twelfth dynasty of the Middle Kingdom that signet rings in the form of scarabs are first attested. Those continued in use into the Second Intermediate Period, and they provide historians with important historical documents. For example, more than sixty of the two thousand known examples inscribed with the names and titles of officials have been found in the Palestine region. The data contained in such texts enables scholars to explore the interconnections between Egypt and the Levant during the Bronze Age. The presence of such Egyptian scarabs may have been the impetus for the local production of Egyptianizing scarabs in the Levant, the existence of which is confirmed by the archaeological excavation of unfinished examples in Canaanite sites.

The earliest scarabs of the sixth dynasty were summarily crafted and probably served as amulets because of their blank undersides. Scarabs inscribed with the names of kings of the Old Kingdom known to have ruled before the sixth dynasty are now regarded as posthumous creations, intended to protect their owners from harm because of the omnipotence of the pharaoh. A similar function was fulfilled by numerous other scarabs of all periods that simply contained royal epithets, such as "The King of Upper and Lower Egypt," "The Lord of the Two Lands," "The Good God," and the like.

One of the most common types of amulets is termed a *heart scarab*, usually inscribed with a version of Spell 30B of the *Book of Going Forth by Day* (*Book of the Dead*). Heart scarabs were primarily made of green stone, anciently termed *nmḥf* and tentatively identified as green jasper (a quartz), although the majority of that classification appear to be crafted of any number of similarly colored stones, including feldspar, serpentine, and basalt. The earliest examples date from the eighteenth dynasty and replace the head of the scarab with that of a human. Although the spell cited above specifies that the heart scarab replaces the deceased's heart, in practice the heart scarabs appear to have been placed at random anywhere on or within the mummy's torso. Their purpose was to insure that the heart, regarded as the seat of intellect and conscience, would not bear false witness against the deceased in the hall of judgment, as the opening lines "Oh my heart, oh my mother . . . stand not up against me as a witness," reveal. Heart scarabs were also incorporated into the design of a pectoral, a chest ornament of rectangular shape that imitated the façade of an ancient Egyptian temple.

Another classification of scarabs is the *commemorative*. Those created during the reign of Amenhotpe III of the eighteenth dynasty are justifiably the most famous because of the number of themes into which they can be divided. More than sixty examples bearing ten lines of hieroglyphs mentioning the pharaoh and Tiye, his queen, are termed the *marriage scarabs*, although the precise occasion for their issuance has not been determined. Some six others commemorated his marriage to Gilukhepa, a princess of the Mitanni, whereas a dozen others celebrated the creation of a pleasure lake, the Birket Habu in Western Thebes, constructed in honor of Queen Tiye. Amenhotpe III was an avid hunter who issued two additional series of commemorative scarabs, to recount his bagging of 96 wild bulls and 102 lions, respectively. Each group of those scarabs revealed differences in both their manufacture and text, suggesting that they were made in different workshops and were awarded to favored courtiers at home and abroad, to glorify the monarch. His son and successor Amenhotpe IV, called Akhenaten, also issued a series of commemorative scarabs early in his reign, of which less than half a dozen examples have survived. Those were of glazed steatite (soapstone), modeled on the scarabs issued by his father, and they seem to commemorate a jubilee.

Related to the scarabs are a classification termed *scaraboids*, which, while retaining the oval bottom of the surface for either inscriptions and/or designs, replaced the body of the scarab proper with that of another animal—cats, ducks, frogs, hedgehogs, rams' heads, and the like—designed to conform to the general configuration of that insect.

The image of the sacred scarab transcended the borders of ancient Egypt and imitations were created far and wide around the Mediterranean in the first millennium BCE by such diverse cultures as the Greeks, Etruscans, and Phoenicians. The popularity of the scarab has not diminished. In the wake of Napoleon's epoch-making campaign to Egypt in 1799, the scarab became a motif incorporated into European jewelry, particularly in the Victorian era, and it is still encountered as a popular fashion accessory to this day.

The ancient Egyptians' fascination with the beetle did not end with the *Scarabaeus sacer*, because other beetles were found within the record of their material culture. For example, the elaterid beetle (*Agrypnus notodonta*) may have served as the model for images on two reliefs from the first dynasty, as well as for pendants of a necklace from the fourth dynasty. It has been suggested that the symbol of the goddess Neith is a design incorporating two head-to-head elaterids, flanked by their respective abdomens.

Buprestids are beetles, perhaps to be identified as *Steraspis squamosa*, of outstanding visual appeal because of their color. An examination of one of the canes from the tomb of Tutankhamun revealed that crushed buprestid elytra (anterior wings) were employed as a pigment. Furthermore, buprestid femurs (legs) were strung together as elements of an ancient Egyptian necklace. Crafted amulets in the form of buprestids are also known, and those were made of a variety of materials, including gold. Perhaps the most remarkable example of the buprestid as a motif in ancient Egyptian art appears crawling up one of the posts of the bed canopy of Queen Hetepheres of the fourth dynasty. The insect was, however, also functional, because its body served to conceal a dowel within the canopy construction.

The larva of the buprestid beetle bore into the tamarisk (a desert shrub or tree), to pupate under the bark until the adult emerged from the small hole. That characteristic may have been regarded, anciently, as a regenerative cycle, linking the buprestid to the cycle of Osiris, god of the dead.

BIBLIOGRAPHY

Andrews, Carol. *Amulets of Ancient Egypt*. Austin, 1994.

Angier, Natalie. "In Recycling Waste, the Noble Scarab Is Peerless." *The New York Times* 10 December 1991, C1, C12.

Ben-Tor, Daphna. *The Scarab: A Reflection of Ancient Egypt*. Jerusalem, 1989.

Blankenberg-Van Delden, C. *The Large Commemorative Scarabs of Amenhotep III*. Leiden, 1969.

Hornung, E. and E. Stähelin, eds. *Skarabäen und andere Siegelamulette aus Basler Sammlungen*. Mainz, 1977.

Kritsky, Gene. "Beetle Gods of Ancient Egypt." *American Entomologist* (Summer, 1991), 85–89.

Malaise, M. *Les scarabées de coeur dans l'Égypte ancienne:* Brussels, 1978.

Martin, G. T. *Scarabs, Cylinders, and Other Ancient Egyptian Seals: A Checklist of Publications*. Warminster, 1985.

ROBERT STEVEN BIANCHI

SCEPTERS. *See* Insignias.

SCIENCE. There is no generic word for "science" in the language of ancient Egypt. *Rḫ* ("to know") comes closest and had a wide range of meanings. For simplicity's sake, this article focuses on our modern concept of "science," with its many disciplines. The ancient Egyptians would not have used the same categories, and probably no such categories existed. Science was the domain of the god Thoth.

Artifacts, tomb paintings, inscriptions, and papyri inform on the Egyptians' knowledge of science. Our study of their hand-crafted objects, tools, and buildings offers insight about their techniques and, indirectly, suggests the knowledge required to develop such techniques. There is, however, no proof about the degree of knowledge reflected in those artifacts. Images of craftsmen at work, for example, have illustrated manufacturing processes and some applied techniques; these illustrations are often accompanied by short explanatory texts and sometimes contain specific terminology. The greatest significance is given, however, to those Egyptian texts that are regarded as "scientific" literature in the broadest sense. Since the preserved material is only a small percentage of the original, our holdings are incomplete and our knowledge of Egyptian science somewhat sketchy.

Scientific Disciplines. The following sciences are documented for ancient Egypt:

- Anatomy (for art)
- Astronomy and astrology (the two disciplines being inseparably linked in ancient Egypt)
- Biology and veterinary medicine
- Chemistry
- Geography
- Geology

- History
- Law
- Linguistics
- Mathematics, including geometry
- Medicine
- Mineralogy
- Pedagogy (education)
- Philosophy
- Physics (above all mechanics)
- Sociology (the rules for social life)
- Theology

Historical Development. From prehistoric times, the inhabitants of the Nile Valley had to make sense of the world around them. Gathering and storing foods, selecting materials for shelters, making tools, struggling against disease and disorder—such concerns and others would have led them to acquire and pass on a wide range of knowledge. As their social structure became more complex, some tasks grew more specialized, so only certain groups knew or used certain kinds of specialized information. Toward the end of the fourth millennium BCE, Egypt was unified under one king into an empire that stretched from Aswan in the South to the Mediterranean coast. This sociopolitical development advanced Egyptian science, since the state provided an administration to manage labor and goods. Without writing, this would have been extremely difficult to achieve, but with the beginning of writing, about 3000 BCE, a new profession became important—that of the scribe. With both specialization and writing, Egypt had the basis for scientific expansion. Later the Egyptians themselves recognized this period as a golden era in science, the arts, and technology.

From the Old Kingdom, examples of historical records are known, including lists of annals. Theology and magic are represented by extensive collections (e.g., the Pyramid Texts). In copies made during later periods, some Wisdom Literature is also contained. Just how specialized individual disciplines could be in ancient Egypt is best understood when considering medicine. From tomb monuments specialized physicians are known (e.g., eye doctors). The remains of the Middle Kingdom, an era whose attitudes were influenced by the dissolution of the Old Kingdom, give evidence for other sciences. Onomastica (lists) show the efforts undertaken to create an encyclopedic record of the world. In mathematics, there were, for example, a good approximation for, and a method of calculating the surfaces and volumes of, the various geometric shapes. Astronomy, until then scarcely evident, was represented in separate texts, albeit strongly integrated into religion. This was also the beginning of the Bronze Age in ancient Egypt, after the adoption and widespread use of bronze.

In the course of the Second Intermediate Period, the Hyksos kings, Near Eastern rulers over the Delta region, seem to have been very interested in Egyptian science; the Rhind Papyrus on mathematics, for example, has been dated to the time of the Hyksos king Apophis. The Hyksos, as later the Persians, tried to ingratiate themselves as popular rulers by taking an interest in Egyptian culture.

During the New Kingdom, when Egypt expanded into the Near East and south into Nubia, the knowledge of foreign lands seems to have enriched Egyptian science—seen most clearly in the foreign plant and animal illustrations within the temple of Karnak, the "Botanical Garden" of Thutmose III. The Onomastica and the teaching texts of this period list many foreign location names, but foreign contacts were by no means restricted to military or diplomatic efforts. Near Easterners began to reside in Egypt, and some advanced to high administrative office. Then, too, Egyptian physicians resided at various royal and princely courts in the Near East. How much foreign expertise was learned is difficult to say, but the scientific texts in Babylonian cuneiform script found in Amarna point to relevant contacts. Even the technique used in applying plant dyes to fabric came to Egypt from Palestine during the New Kingdom.

In the Late period, Egypt was ruled by foreign kings but always maintained and developed its own culture. The Late period was characterized both by a deliberate focus on the Egyptian culture of the distant past, as well as by the adoption of new ideas. The Persian king Darius I (r. 521–486 BCE), who had absorbed Egypt into his empire, was recognized in Egyptian sources as an expert on Egyptian magic, a patron of Egyptian science, and for having commissioned a compilation of Egyptian law; evidence also exists to show that knowledge was transferred from Mesopotamia to Egypt during the Persian era. The expertise acquired by the Egyptians was mostly in areas that were then more advanced in Mesopotamia or then completely unknown in Egypt. Egyptian astronomy, astrology, and mathematics gained the most from contacts with the Mesopotamian tradition. Omina (which foretold the future by observation of the sun and the moon and on which the Babylonian calendar is based) were used in Egypt from the sixth century BCE onward. The zodiac, also originating in Mesopotamia, was introduced to Egypt as late as the third century BCE, and from that time forward it played an important role in Egyptian astronomy and astrology. Not yet known exactly are when the Pythagorean theorem (known in Mesopotamia since the second millennium BCE), the approximation formula for the root of irrationals (attributed to Hero of Alexandria), and the number 3 as an approximation of π (pi) were brought to Egypt from Babylon.

The Ptolemaic era, during which Egypt was ruled by a

Hellenistic dynasty of Macedonian origin, was a turning-point in Egyptian science in several ways. The new administration operated increasingly in Greek, with the Egyptian language gradually receding into the background of public life. Few career opportunities where Egyptian was used remained available, outside the priesthood. Since the majority of Egyptian scribes were soon among the priesthood—and not, as had been the case, in administration—it meant that representatives of Egyptian science gathered in an ever smaller priestly elite. Perhaps the local priests rejected Greek science as it began to flourish in Egypt because they took great pride in their own ancient traditions. Few documents indicate that Egyptian priests adopted any aspect of Greek or Hellenistic science, whereas ample evidence indicates that the Greeks learned from the Egyptians. The mathematical and geometric theorems mentioned above are a case in point. Greek authors wrote on Egypt and its culture, and they even translated Egyptian literature, law, and scientific texts. Through Hellenistic science and the Museion in Alexandria—a research facility that attained international acclaim at the beginning of the third century BCE—Egyptian knowledge was introduced to Europe. During the Ptolemaic era, scientific texts were written in Egypt in Demotic, a cursive style of script. Notable examples are the Onomasticon Papyrus Cairo CG 31168+31169 and some papyri on mathematics.

In 30 BCE, Egypt fell under Roman rule and the Egyptian language was almost removed from its public life. The Egyptian scripts became known and practiced only by Egyptian priests; numerous scientific texts, however, show the intensity with which they were studied and copied. Some works, such as the "Book of the Temple," have survived in Hieratic and Demotic versions, and even in Greek translation. New copies were made of older works, and some were glossed (above all works on religion and spells) or commentated (the astronomic-cosmological treatises of the Carlsberg Papyri 1 and 1a). Egyptian science reached as far south as the empire of Meroë in Nubia. There, upper-class families knew how to write in Demotic and in hieroglyphs; they also studied Egyptian religion and astronomy, as shown by graffiti on the island of Philae in the Nile.

The impact of Egypt on the Greeks and Romans continued to be of importance. For example, the Egyptian calendar, modified with the introduction of leap years, was introduced in the Roman Empire by Julius Caesar in 46 BCE. Known as the Julian calendar, it remains the basis for the modern Western calendar (the Gregorian calendar), with adjustments made for accuracy in 1582 CE. The enormous effort made by the Egyptians to counteract the downfall of their culture, with a flood of writings—"writing against the tide" so to speak—became futile as Christianity spread across Egypt in the first centuries CE and pagan cults were banned. Thus ended "Egyptian" science, which was by then restricted to the priesthood. The Copts (Christian Egyptians) rejected Egyptian science as pagan and preferred Greek and, later, Arab traditions. (Still, the Hermetic scripts—a collection of Greek works on theology and philosophy, created between the second century BCE and the third century CE—seems to be a continuation of pagan Egyptian works, such as the *Book of Thoth* [Jasnow/Zauzich, in *Proceedings of the Seventh International Congress of Egyptologists Cambridge, 1995.* Leiden, 1998, pp. 607–618]

Principles and Methods. It is difficult to ascertain which mnemonic aids were known to the Egyptians other than (and prior to) writing. Images show that counting from 1 to 10 with the help of the fingers was common, while painted dots were used to calculate greater sums. A finger-counting "rhyme" indicates that verses were used as an aid in memorization. One visual manner of recording information is documented in laundry lists that date from the New Kingdom, where each piece of clothing is illustrated and accompanied by the relevant number of dots (not the number symbols of script). Writing had the greatest role in recording, above all in the area of science. There were fully composed texts as well as lists; both types of text were sometimes visually structured by the use of red ink for headings or subheadings, called "rubrics."

Various techniques were developed for recording scientific texts, although in Egypt they never became canons with a fixed wording. The most conservative approach was to record word by word. The word-by-word transcription into another script of the Egyptian language (e.g., transcribing a Hieratic text into Demotic) was another technique that made it possible to hand down material without changes in content. During Greek and Roman rule, some Egyptian works were also translated into Greek. The reduction of a text to the essential—at times even in the form of keywords or lists—was a more radical treatment, but it had more effect on the form than the content, provided the scribe was still working with the complete text. Conversely, lists could be expanded into full text.

Glosses, created to explain difficult terminology or to clarify a specific context, led to a new kind of text, especially when the glosses were not treated as explanatory notes but as components of the text. This occurred naturally when a glosses was written in the same language and script as the basic text. Since glosses were intended to make the text easy to understand, they were often written in everyday vocabulary and, during Greek and Roman times, frequently in Demotic as the most widespread Egyptian script. Many glosses were written in Greek in the Roman era, especially those recording the exact pronunciation of Egyptian words in scholastic or magic texts—since Greek, in contrast to the Egyptian scripts, contained vowels.

Commentaries were a more detailed form of written explanations, such as the commentaries on medical writings and the Carlsberg Papyri 1 and 1a, which record commentaries on a thousand-year-old astronomy and cosmology text. There were also some collected writings, in which material on related subjects had been gathered from various sources, as found in several of the medical papyri (e.g., Ebers Papyrus, Hearst Papyrus). Texts were created for teaching, in which were posed specific tasks for the student of the material that was being taught; these usually also demonstrated the solution (of all the texts on mathematics, this type is most common).

The following concepts and devices were used—singly or in combination—depending on the branch of science.

- *Analogy:* thinking in complementary sets of two, characteristic for Egypt, was practiced in an approach whereby the two arguments either corresponded with one another or were in opposition. (Thus, for example, from the idea, based in etymology, that humans had been created from the tears of a creator god, an analogy was formed to state that gods were created in his laughter.)
- *Approximation:* deliberate use of approximation in mathematics—for example, during the Middle Kingdom (8/9 of diameter)^2; in Demotic texts, 3 as an approximation of π (pi); the roots of irrationals; and approximation formulae to calculate the area of segments and irregular rectangles.
- *Comparison:* often used in description.
- *Definition:* for medical expressions and special terminology.
- *Description:* for plants, animals, diseases, wounds, gods, and so on—a very important component of Egyptian science texts.
- *Etymology:* plays on words were often used in theology, to help deduce the essential similarities and the relatedness of different things. Using similar words or allusions might explain the origin of names, of sacred sites, and so on. (Thus, the tears of the creator god, *rmt*, ["to weep"] were understood as the origin of human beings [*rmi*]).
- *Rules:* comparatively little evidence exists for universally applicable rules formulated by the Egyptians, who tended to operate with practical values underlying rules.
- *Schematization:* the reduction of complicated facts into simplified schemata, as used in texts on astronomy, among others.

- *Sequences:* found in the so-called 2:*n*-table (of mathematics), where the division of 2 by multiples of certain numbers resulted in unit fractions based on an identical scheme; at times, such calculation patterns were explicitly put forth as rules.
- *Sorting:* by content and, in later periods, alphabetically.
- *Technical language:* each science had its own terminology, to varying degrees, which had an impact not only on the vocabulary as a whole but also on grammar. For example, some verb forms are typical for scientific texts; and these often followed specific patterns of construction, so that a point-form style could be used. Frequently used words were also often abbreviated.
- *Tests:* used explicitly in mathematics to check solutions or to determine the degree of accuracy in approximations.
- *Trial:* to provoke reactions in a patient, which was relevant for diagnosis.
- *Visualization:* sketches for geometric tasks or even maps (of areas in the sky and in the afterlife), sometimes strongly schematized.

The knowledge recorded in texts had been gained in many different ways. Adaptation from other cultures has been mentioned in the historical overview. The ancient Egyptians would sometimes indicate that a god had written a certain book, which was subsequently discovered; other texts were ascribed to earlier kings. In fact, most of the texts (with the exception of the Wisdom texts) were anonymously authored and were obviously understood to be a collective cultural achievement. This cannot have occurred, however, without discoveries made by individuals. Amenemhet, for example, boasted that he had manufactured and developed a new water clock during the reign of Amenhotpe I, stating that in summer the night lasts for twelve hours, whereas in winter it has fourteen hours. Most such realizations were based on observation—the basis of all science. In the case of astronomy, long-term observation was the approach. In general, though, Egyptian science had little empirical thrust; there was no ambition to systematically research the entire world. Thus, although invasive practices were used in mummification, no evidence has been found that corpses were dissected to gain knowledge in anatomy. Expeditions to foreign lands were usually undertaken for military or economic reasons, and not in search of knowledge. The circumnavigation of Africa, an event whose veracity remains contested, is said to have been initiated by Necho II (r. 610–595 BCE) and had likely more to do with the king's naval policy than with a quest for knowledge. The New Kingdom expeditions of Queen Hatshepsut to the land of Punt were undertaken primarily to acquire exotic goods; the detailed paintings in her tomb in Deir el-Bahri do show, however, that foreigners were carefully observed. The depictions of animals and plants in the "Botanical Garden" of Thutmose III in Karnak confirm this impression, yet again they were acquired because of this ruler's war campaigns in the Near East. Next to observation, from which deductions were drawn, speculation played a large role. Those phenomena that could not be observed were especially speculated upon, such as the netherworld, gods, demons, and the creation of the world. Speculation commonly involved drawing analogies to the known world on earth.

Organization. Specialization is one of the most striking features of Egyptian science. As early as the Old Kingdom, there were already specialized physicians. Then the training of scribes, on which scientific recording was based, specialized at an early stage, to prepare the student for his future work. A "basic schooling" of about four years was sufficient for most. The training of scribes focused on Egypt's classic literature. In more advanced studies, students learned how to compose their own letters and how to study the natural sciences. As students were apprenticed to masters early in their training, they gained practical experience in their field and, at the same time, all the specialized training they would need. There is no evidence that a final examination was held at the end of the training years (yet craftsmen were required to pass a special test, as indicated by examination dialogues embedded into religious contexts).

Scribes who did not enter into a specialized profession after their training were devoted to creating purely scientific inscriptions in the House of Life. In the House of Life—each major temple had its own—religious inscriptions were authored, copied, and stored. It was not only a library, scriptorium, and "university" but also a central cult site, where the well-being and flourishing of Egypt and its population was safeguarded, with the help of cult and magic. Inscribing religious and scientific texts was subordinate to that all-important task and helps explain the strong link between science, religion, and magic. Separating the three is the modern approach. Specific houses of life seem to have been held in especially high regard. The priests of Heliopolis, for example, were renowned for their wisdom, as was reverently recorded in Egyptian as well as in classical texts. Centers of scholarship were engaged in a lively exchange of information, since the same texts were known in various locations.

The Egyptian priesthood must have been very organized in creating written records during Roman times, when it alone was responsible for carrying on the Egyptian tradition in science. There seems to be no other explanation for the enormous amount of text produced during that time. The temples, however, seem to have been increasingly short of funds, as is evident in the many manuscripts written on poor quality or recycled papyrus or onto the back pages of Greek administration records. When pagan cults were banned in 392 CE and the temples were closed, Egyptian science lost its organizational basis.

In summary, it is important to emphasize the task-orientation of Egyptian science and its integration into religion. Systematic research and experimentation in a multitude of fields—the pursuit of "pure" knowledge—did not exist in ancient Egypt. Knowledge to the Egyptians was not gained from nature, but found in books. This reflects the importance of script in Egyptian science and the role of essential cultural traditions in the intellectual life of ancient Egypt. Tradition, in turn, was deeply rooted in religion. Hence, Egyptian science served theology or was a component of theology, in an attempt to explain—by means of speculation—that which could not be understood by any other means. To Egyptians, magic was the culmination of knowledge, for with its help one could even coerce the gods.

The conditions and possibilities for scientific pursuits were very different in ancient Egypt than they are today. Yet there was without question a sincere search for knowledge. While the goals and methods were different from today's, this does not mean that they were illogical. Their sophistication in the development of terminology and of principles would make it erroneous to dismiss ancient Egypt as "unscientific." The modern concept of "science" is the product of a developmental sequence which, among other traditions, began in pharaonic Egypt.

Update of Research Interests. Researching Egyptian science is difficult because of the sketchiness of the available material—a difficulty common to all research on ancient Egypt but especially true for the earliest periods. Publication policies pose another problem. The publication of Egyptian texts from the Greco-Roman era [in Egypt] had been neglected, although more resources exist from that period than from more ancient times. Such texts were thought of as works that had been marred by a nascent degeneration in the culture or, conversely, as works that were too strongly influenced by the Greek tradition, having been created during a culturally coopted, barren, or otherwise unproductive period. It was assumed that such factors made texts from that period unworthy of close study. New publications have begun to redress that preconception. The lack of interest in the later period has also had an adverse effect on work needed to revise and include individual texts in collections, which often follows the first edition. Thus, the only complete collection for the Greco-Roman era, with full source references, is a work on astronomical texts. The collected publications on other branches of science either omit the later period—as has been done for the Onomastica—or, instead, focus exclusively on the later period without taking the preceding eras into account (e.g., for mathematics: only the Demotic papyri have been compiled). The study of the way the different branches of science evolved across the millennia in ancient Egypt is, therefore, a task still largely incomplete. There are no era-specific studies, which present the spectrum and the status of science for a specific cultural phase against the intellectual history of Egypt. For that context, it is also vital to research the relevant intercultural contacts; however, that would be possible only for some of the eras, since the material available is still fairly limited. It is also evident that as yet there is no treatise on the all-embracing topic of science in ancient Egypt.

[*See also* Astrology; Astronomy; Mathematics; Medicine; *and* Technology and Engineering.]

BIBLIOGRAPHY

Assman, Jan. *Das kulturelle Gedächtnis. Schrift, Erinnerung und politische Identität in frühen Hochkulturen.* 2d ed. Munich, 1997. A rather philosophical study of the cultural significance of writing, as exemplified in various cultures.

Brunner, Hellmut. *Altägyptische Erziehung.* Wiesbaden, 1957. An investigation, based on primary sources, of the organization, methods, and theories of education in ancient Egypt.

Fischer-Elfert, Hans Werner. "Naturwissenschaften und ihre Behandlung im Unterricht des Alten Ägypten." In *Naturwissenschaftlicher Unterricht und Wissenskumulation. Geschichtliche Entwicklung und gesellschaftliche Auswirkungen,* edited by Johann Georg Prinz von Hohenzollern and Max Liedtke, pp. 50–61. Schriftenreihe zum Bayerischen Schulmuseum Ichenhausen, 7. Bad Heilbrunn, 1988. An overview with brief bibliography.

Gardiner, Alan H. "The House of Life." *Journal of Egyptian Archaeology* 24 (1938), 157–179. An investigation based on material remains.

Lucas, A., and J. R. Harris. *Ancient Egyptian Materials and Industries.* 4th ed. London, 1989.

Osing, Jürgen. *Hieratische Papyri aus Tebtunis I.* 2 vols. Copenhagen, 1998. Publication of several Egyptian compendia.

Schott, Siegfried. "Voraussetzung und Gegenstand altägyptischer Wissenschaft." In *Jahrbuch der Akademie der Wissenschaften und der Literatur, Mainz,* pp. 277–295. Mainz, 1951. A study of Egyptian science from the standpoint of intellectual history; difficult to find.

Spuler, B. *Handbuch der Orientalistik.* Erste Abteilung: *Der Nahe und der Mittlere Osten.* Erster Band: *Ägyptologie.* Zweiter Abschnitt: *Literatur.* 2d ed., pp. 201–225. Leiden and Cologne, 1970. Includes a chapter on scientific literature, transmitted in hieroglyphic and Hieratic script, including texts on astronomy and mathematics, medical literature, dictionaries, reference works, and students' notes. Includes bibliography.

Westendorf, Wolfhart. "Wissenschaft." In *Lexikon der Ägyptologie,* 6: 1278–1279. Wiesbaden, 1986. Brief article on scientific literature.

FRIEDHELM HOFFMANN
Translated by Elizabeth Schwaiger
and Martha Goldstein

SCORPIONS. A venomous animal found in warm climates, the scorpion is an invertebrate belonging to the phylum Arthropoda, class Arachnides. It possesses four pairs of legs for locomotion, two large claws, and a tail ending with a pair of small stingers connected to a gland in which the venom is stored. In Egypt, scorpions range in color from almost white (Buthridas) to yellow and light brown (Scorpionidae), with sizes ranging up to 8–10 cm, not counting the tail. They are extremely hardy and resistant to hunger and thirst. Scorpions are generally found in desert areas, hiding under rocks during the day, but are also known to nest in the bricks of adobe houses.

Well attested as early as the Predynastic and Early Dynastic periods, the scorpion is depicted on various painted vessels and carved on schist palettes, as well as sculpted in the round, often in precious metals. The scorpion, as drawn by the ancient Egyptians, is frequently shown in side or three-quarter view, with the number of legs varying from three to four pairs. When it is drawn in texts or engraved on monuments, it is shown flat, positioned either horizontally or, in later periods, vertically, with two to four pairs of legs. After the Old Kingdom, it is no longer found on vessels, but is often made into a talisman, sculpted in the round.

Several Egyptian names for the scorpion are used, all feminine nouns. From the Old Kingdom to the Late period, *ḏɜrt* is attested, although in the medical papyri—copied in the New Kingdom, but written in the "classical" language—this word appears as the plural form *dɜrw*. From the Middle Kingdom to the Late period, *wḥt* is common. A scorpion called *ḏdbt* also occurs in a magical papyrus. The scorpion is not mentioned in onomastica, with one exception, an Old Kingdom lady who is called *Ḏɜrt*.

Though present everywhere in Egypt, the scorpion is rarely encountered in texts; it is never mentioned in the Pyramid Texts, whereas serpents are frequent. In the Coffin Texts, it serves only as the determinative of the goddess *Ḥḏdt*, perhaps the same goddess that is found later in the Edfu temple. In fact, the scorpion is mentioned mainly in magical texts, in formulas either to repel these arachnids, to conjure away their venom, or to cure their sting: "Formulas to repulse the scorpions" (*rɜ[w] n šnɜt dɜrt*).

The venom of both scorpions and snakes is neurotoxic and results in death by asphyxiation. Ostraca found at Deir el-Medina, on the western bank of the Nile at Thebes, mention workers bitten by scorpions, and thus absent from work. "The scorpion has bitten him—sick" (*psḥ sw tɜ wḥˁt mr*). In the Late period, several Greek funerary stelae mention young people killed by a scorpion's sting.

The magical texts are simultaneously treatises with recipes for curing stings and a collection of incantations that are a psychological means to help the sick person to

SCORPIONS. *Amulet in the form of a scorpion, in the Egyptian Museum, Cairo.* (Courtesy David P. Silverman)

cope with his illness. These incantations are sometimes hidden within mythological events.

A magnificent though incomplete papyrus, recently published, lists the snakes of Egypt, with descriptions, and gives information on how to treat—or decline to treat, because of their high toxicity—their bites. This treatise belongs to the library of the *ḥrp Srḳt,* "the exorcisor of the goddess Serket (variant, Selket)." When the Egyptians went to the turquoise mines in the Sinai—a particularly hot, desert environment—they used to bring with them a *šd wḥ't* ("the one who removes scorpions"), a *s3 Srḳt* and a *ḥrp Srḳt,* servants of the goddess Serket, and specialists in the prevention and cure of scorpion stings and snake bites. If these specialists were not sufficient, the embalmers were also present. The *šd wḥt* was also used to purify (*sw'b*), that is, to clear a temple of these arachnids.

Only a few examples of deified scorpions exist, and they are all personifications of goddesses, mostly a result of syncretism: *Ḥḏdt* (Edfu temple); Isis-*Ḥḏdt* (scorpion-goddess of Edfu); Isis-*wḥ't* (often represented by a scorpion with a human head); Isis-Serket, with two ostrich feathers flanking a scorpion with head down (temple of Sety I at Abydos); and a goddess with a scorpion on her head (or with her head replaced by a scorpion), found on the Horus-on-the-Crocodile stelae—a form of Isis of Tell Tebilleh in the Nile Delta. Most of these goddesses are Nubian in origin. The sovereigns at Meroë liked to wear a headdress surmounted by a scorpion with a human head.

BIBLIOGRAPHY

Goyon, J.-C. "Isis-scorpion et Isis au scorpion." Bulletin de l'Institut Français d'Archéologie Orientale 78 (1978), 439–457.

Jelinkova-Reymond, E. *Les inscriptions de la statue guérisseuse de Djed-Her-le-Sauveur.* Bibliothèque d'Etudes de l'Institut Français d'Archéologie Orientale, 33. Cairo, 1956.

Sauneron, S. *Un manuel égyptien d'ophiologie.* Bibliothèque générale de l'Institut Français d'Archéologie Orientale, 11. Cairo, 1989.

Tod, Marcus N. "The Scorpion in Graeco-Roman Egypt." *Journal of Egyptian Archaeology* 25 (1939), 55–.

FRÉDÉRIQUE VON KÄNEL

SCRIBES. Professional scribes were very important for the operation of the Egyptian state, which was ruled by an efficient administration, organized into various departments, all of which employed scribes. For this reason, the profession was considered one of the noblest and was recommended to young people in *Instructions* and other didactic treatises. These works present a portrait of the scribe as a man who earns a good living and occupies an important place in society.

We do not possess any explicit evidence concerning the organization of scribal schools, their curricula, and their teaching methods. However, from indirect evidence in texts, we can infer that, especially in the third millennium BCE, the primary mode of early instruction was teaching by fathers to sons. Occasional reliefs depict a father carrying scribal instruments, accompanied by his son, also a scribe. Princes and privileged youths were educated at court, as shown by the inscription of Ptahshepses, a private individual who lived during the fifth dynasty and owned a stela, now in the British Museum. Proof of the existence of schools appears in the Middle Kingdom. They were situated near the court, as noted in the "Satire on Trades," which is framed as the remarks of a father who accompanies his child to school at the capital.

Children started their studies at the age of six or seven, and pursued elementary training for at least four years. There followed a long period of apprenticeship preceding entrance into the administration, as reported in the inscriptions of Bekenkhons, a high priest of Amun at Karnak in the time of Ramesses II.

Students started by learning cursive writing (Hieratic). There exist ostraca containing exercises in writing and counting—signs inscribed inside a grid, words repeated many times, or lists of numbers or dates. Their further training utilized the *Instructions* and the classical literary texts, which were memorized by repeating them aloud and were often copied on ostraca or papyri. They also used true manuals, such as the *Kmyt* (*Kemit*), containing assorted sentences, advice useful for scribes, and glorifications of the role of the scribe. Basic education included some knowledge of geography, arithmetic, and geometry. The study of foreign languages was limited, but it surely existed, since we possess bilingual texts, especially from the New Kingdom, when diplomatic language was Akkadian. Scribes had to know at least the most common foreign words and place names, as indicated by the *Satirical Letter*, dating to the nineteenth dynasty. Here a scribe, displaying a mastery of the lexicon, including many Semitic loan words, attacks a colleague in regard to his knowledge of various difficult subjects, including the geography of western Asia.

Young people specialized in various subjects, such as administration, medicine, or theology, and attended schools annexed to the royal palace or to other institutions. Near the temples were situated "Houses of Life," known, for example, from Memphis, Abydos, Amarna, Akhmim, Coptos, Esna and Edfu; these were centers of the scribes' literary activity, where medical or religious texts were written. Young men could eventually enter them as apprentices, but we probably should not regard the "Houses of Life" as a kind of university. Some temples also possessed libraries, containing not only religious but also medical, astronomical, and literary texts.

For their exercises, students and scribes also used onomastica, lists of plants, animals, minerals, place names, and so on, which are known from the Middle Kingdom to Greco-Roman times. In one of these, a document from Tebtunis, different types of documents and scribal instruments are enumerated.

The instruments are shown, tied together, in the hieroglyphic sign *sš*, indicating ideas connected with writing, and attested since the earliest records, often in a very stylized manner. On one side appears a cylindrical holder for reed pens (made of the sedge *Juncus maritimus*); on the other is a rectangular palette with two wells for pigments; and in the middle is a circular leather bag for pigment pellets and sundries. This object, at first colored red because it was made of leather, was later interpreted as a water-pot utilized by scribes to thin their ink. Now colored blue, this became the object usually represented in the middle of the hieroglyph *sš*. Apart from the objects symbolized in the hieroglyphic sign, the essential tools of the scribe are first represented in the Saqqara tomb of Hesyre, dating to the third dynasty. In the fourth dynasty, the equipment is more richly represented in tomb reliefs, which now show, in addition to the previous items, straw baskets or wood cases for papyri, leather or linen rolls, papyri rolled up and fixed with cords, and pots for water, used for thinning ink and rinsing reed pens. The equipment also included small cloths for cleaning, a stone to prepare papyrus, and a small mallet used to smooth it. The first palettes were simple shells (still used in the fourth dynasty and occasionally in the fifth), or the small rectangular palette mentioned above. From the fifth dynasty until the Late period, the rectangular palette was much lengthened (20 to 43 centimeters/6 to 15 inches), always with two wells for black and red pigments (or more wells for colors, if the palette was for a painter) and with a central slot to hold reeds. In Ptolemaic and Roman times, writing materials changed—especially the pen, now rigid and sharpened, made of the stem of a reed (*Phragmites aegyptiaca*). The writing material varied widely: might be stone for monumental inscriptions, but for more common uses papyri (often erased and reused), ostraca—fragments of stone or potsherds, frequently employed for personal use—and wood tablets, often used by students. A nearly complete set of scribal equipment was found by Howard Carter in a tomb from the beginning of the New Kingdom next to the causeway of the Hatshepsut temple on the Theban west bank. It includes, in addition of the above-mentioned objects, a clay figurine of a baboon, the image of Thoth, the god of writing and patron of scribes.

SCRIBES. *Statue of a scribe, in the Brooklyn Museum of Art.* (Courtesy Stephen Phillips)

A relatively small number of people went to school, and among them we must distinguish different degrees of literacy. Most literate people, and most functionaries bearing the simple title of scribe, knew only the Hieratic script. They could probably read only the commonest hieroglyphic signs, such as those forming royal cartouches. Other people, like craftsmen or stonecutters, could carve hieroglyphs, but they could rarely read what they wrote. In regard to arithmetic, a relatively large number of people could perform elementary calculations, but only the most experienced scribes or architects could solve difficult mathematical or geometrical problems. A complete knowledge of hieroglyphics was restricted to a small number of people, such as high dignitaries and lector-priests. The latter title, indicating a very high level of literacy, is often borne by high priests, important officials, doctors,

or even the royal hairdresser, in place of the title of scribe, which they probably held at the beginning of their career.

Some high officials continued nevertheless to bear, in addition to many others, the simple title of scribe, either indicating their presence in the administration or serving as the abbreviation of a composite title such as "scribe of the divine books" or "scribe of the king's documents." Most of these highly literate functionaries, however, did not list among their titles that of scribe; if present in their titulary, it is generally composite or refers to the supervision of scribes in a particular branch of the administration ("scribe of the treasury," "director of scribes of the granary," "inspector of scribes of the king's documents," etc.).

In tombs of high officials, scribes are often mentioned or represented attending to different activities. We possess some of their funerary objects, like statues or offering tables, and their tombs. Although few burials of the lowest-level scribes have been identified, some tombs of some more important scribes, especially supervisors, have survived. In the Old Kingdom at Giza, there are tombs of at least fourteen scribes, already represented with name and title in tombs of high officials, out of 219 attested on reliefs; at Saqqara, where 320 scribes are represented, only five of their tombs are known. Yet a great number of tombs belonging to high-level scribes are known.

In some cases, true "dynasties" of scribes, extending through many generations, are attested. This phenomenon is due to the transmission of the title from father to son, a characteristic of the Egyptian administration. But scribes of modest origin who became important officials are not unknown, especially in the New Kingdom.

We can estimate that less than one percent of Egyptians—at least during the Old Kingdom—were literate. The figure is necessarily approximate; we do not know the exact population of Egypt, the total number of tombs, the level of literacy of the tomb-owners, and other facts. The percentage given is calculated on a population of 1 to 1.5 million people; on the number of tombs that probably existed, which were in most cases owned by literate persons; and on the number of persons represented in tombs bearing title indicating a possible level of literacy. But the question of literacy in Egypt remains open. For certain places and periods, we can postulate a higher and more certain percentage of literacy; this is especially true for Deir el-Medina during the New Kingdom, where literacy probably reached a level of 5 to 7 percent.

Scribes are known not only from tombs and representations, but also from papyri, seals, and graffiti. A very interesting case is represented by scribes mentioned in the archives, the most ancient known having been found in Gebelein and dated to the fourth dynasty. From the site there also comes a beautiful example of a scribe's wooden box, containing papyri, lumps of black and red ink, reeds, and a mortar. Larger archives survive from the temples of Abusir (fifth dynasty), those of Illahun (Middle Kingdom), and the Theban temples of the New Kingdom. The scribes mentioned in these documents may be the authors of the archive files, or personnel of the temple who registered economic data (payments of craftsmen and personnel, records of duties, inventories of the temple's implements and properties, etc.). They might also be responsible for the management of the temple workers. Besides their activities pertinent to writing and recording, supervision was an important occupation of scribes. Graffiti found in necropolises (e.g., Saqqara), in quarries (e.g., the Wadi Hammamat or the Sinai), or in sites far from Egypt (e.g., Buhen) attest to the presence of scribes among work groups or expeditions. The "scribe of the crew," the "scribe of the recruits," and the "scribe of the army" organized and managed the subsistence needs and implements of workers, craftsmen, or soldiers. A relief now in The Metropolitan Museum of Art, New York, confirms this: it shows two squads of recruits followed by a chief holding a lance and a scribe's palette; among the soldiers, another scribe appears.

Many other scribal activities are represented in reliefs or in the models of daily life that are typical of the end of the Old Kingdom and the beginning of the Middle Kingdom. We very often sense a parallelism between the scenes showing scribes and their titles. They most often appear in agricultural scenes, recording the different phases of rural activities up to the filling of the granaries with cereals, when a "scribe of the granary" is always present. They attend to cattle-counting, an activity exemplified by the title "scribe of the cattle"; and they are present in the breeding of birds or the force-feeding of geese or hyenas, as well as at the return of fishermen, to record the quantity of fish caught. Scribes also appear in bakeries and breweries. Their presence is always requisite beside goldsmiths, to control the metals' weight and the quantity of jewels produced; they can appear near weavers or traders, to ensure good work or fair exchange. They also play an important role in the administration of justice, bearing the titles of judge and scribe, and often appearing under a canopy in front of which guilty farmers are forcibly detained. An administrative building of this type, where scribes worked and wrote, was discovered in Balat. Scribes are also shown engaged in the funerary cults of kings and private persons, and may present the deceased with a list of the products of their estates.

The simple title of scribe does not denote high rank, but it represents the condition of entry into the administration, afterward giving access to specialized activities or to different administrative departments. It is attested from the beginning of Egyptian history. In the first three dynasties, there are more than forty mentions of scribes, especially on seals and pots, at Saqqara, Helwan, Beit Khallaf, Abydos, Hierakonpolis, Elephantine, and Byblos. The title, also attested on objects of unknown provenance, may be simple or composed, such as "scribe of divine books" or "scribe of the desert." In the early dynasties the simple title of scribe covered a variety of activities in the administration. Beginning in the fourth dynasty, and increasingly in the following dynasties, we can see a specialization of scribes, accompanied by an increase in their titles, which are often very detailed. Their hierarchy is also well established: there are very rare mentions of under-directors (*imy ḫt*) of scribes; very well attested are directors (*sḫd*); less known are inspectors (*ḥrp*), and always present chiefs (*mr*) of scribes in every department. Exceptionally, chiefs of inspectors (*mr ḥrpw*) of scribes are also attested. Scribes work in all branches of the administration, and may hold modest offices, but they are also very highly placed in temples and at court. An important number of them belong to the king's personal chancery and to the royal archives; others attend to the king's clothing and food, together with specific officials. Numerous scribes work in the central office of the vizier, often charged with judicial tasks or with the recording of judicial acts. The vizier himself is frequently styled "chief of the scribes of royal documents." Scribes might also have a role in the management of economic matters, as shown by their hierarchy in the *pr ḥry wḏb*, a center of redistribution of goods that had a great importance in the Egyptian economy. Simple scribes, with their directors and chiefs, are also attested in the state granary and treasury, as well as in secondary departments of the latter ("scribe of the gold houses," "scribe of the *wˁbt*-workshop," etc.). Furthermore, they work in the fields, where they collect information and taxes for the central government. This activity, already known in the Old Kingdom, is very well attested in the New Kingdom on many papyri. Finally, they play a role in temples, writing religious and administrative texts or managing personnel and economic matters. We know of many priests bearing scribal titles.

The profession of scribe was considered so important that a special type of statue represented this official, sitting cross-legged, holding a papyrus open on his lap, with a reed pen ready to write, and sometimes a palette slung over one shoulder. These statues can be found in temples from the Middle Kingdom to the Late period; they were deposited in tombs during the Old Kingdom. They sometimes appear in burials of men bearing scribal titles, but often the tombs were owned by officials who did not bear the title. Scribes' statues, then, do not necessarily represent an activity carried on by a tomb-owner during his life, but imply the literacy of the owner and the importance of writing in the afterlife.

This last aspect also emerges from the presence in tombs of model scribes' palettes, often made of alabaster or ivory, which were never used in life but could be necessary in the underworld. Some were found in the tomb of Tutankhamun. References to the scribe are also present in religious texts—first in the Pyramid Texts, where allusion is made to the knowledge and practice of writing. This tradition continues in the Coffin Texts.

Evidence is sparse for the existence of female scribes. None is known in the Old Kingdom; the only representation from that period of a woman writing and holding scribe's implements is that of the goddess of writing, Seshat, the feminine counterpart of Thoth. The image, in a Saqqara *mastaba* of the sixth dynasty, of the princess Idut in a boat where scribal instruments are placed, does not mean that she was literate, or a woman scribe; actually, these objects belonged to the first male owner of the tomb, the vizier Ihy. In the Middle and New Kingdoms, the title *sšt* is attested, but its interpretation is controversial. Some scholars consider it not as the title "scribe" in the feminine, but as that of cosmetician. More certain evidence of the title "woman scribe" (*sš sḥmt*) is found in the twenty-sixth dynasty tomb of the lady Ireteru, who was in the service of the divine worshipper Nitokris. If women were therefore exceptionally occupied as scribes, they could be educated to read and write, especially in the highest social strata. Indeed, we possess evidence of documents, letters, and poetic compositions written or dictated by women, and in some New Kingdom Theban tombs, the traditional scribes' implements are represented under a woman's chair, probably as a proud indication of her literacy.

BIBLIOGRAPHY

Baines, John. "Literacy and Ancient Egyptian Society." *Man*, n.s. 18 (1983), 572–599. A very rich article, published in a review of anthropology, illustrating the importance and the role of writing in the Egyptian culture and of literate people in the society.

Baines, John, and Christopher J. Eyre. "Four notes on literacy." *Göttinger Miszellen* 61 (1983), 65–96. A basic article very often mentioned in Egyptological studies, concerning levels and proportions of literacy; literate women; scribes and literate persons of Deir el-Medina.

Brunner, Hellmut. *Altägyptische Erziehung*. Wiesbaden, 1957. The classical study on the organization, methods and aims of teaching in the different periods of Ancient Egyptian history. Contains the principal sources concerning education (funerary inscriptions of scribes or students, *Instructions*, examples of miscellanies, etc.).

Bryan, Betsy M. "Evidence for Female Literacy from Theban Tombs of the New Kingdom." *Bulletin of the Egyptological Seminar* 6 (1984), 17–32. Article considering the spare textual and figurative evidence for female literacy.

Černý, Jaroslav. *Paper and Books in Ancient Egypt. An Inaugural Lecture delivered at University College, London, 29 May, 1947*. London, 1952. An introduction to scribes' instruments and characteristics of papyrus as writing material.

Gardiner, Alan H. "The House of Life." *Journal of Egyptian Archaeology* 24 (1938), 157–179. The author collects and studies all the sources on this institution which was an important center of scribes' activity.

Janssen, Rosalind M. and Jac. J. *Growing up in Ancient Egypt*, pp. 67–89. London, 1990. The chapter on the "Schoolboy" concerns organization of schools, methods and subjects of study, and evidence for female literacy.

Kaplony-Heckel, Ursula. "Schüler und Schulwesen in der ägyptischen Spätzeit." *Studien zur altägyptischen Kultur* 1 (1974), 227–246. On schools and students' exercises in the Late period, with uncommon examples of verbal conjugations.

Leospo, Enrichetta, ed. *La scuola nell'antico Egitto*. Torino, 1997. A volume on school intended for the general public, and available in the Egyptian Museum of Turin. The different aspects of education, didactical texts, writing material, etc. are illustrated with objects of the Egyptian Museum of Turin. Containing some interesting unpublished items.

Parkinson, Richard, and Stephen Quirke. *Papyrus*. London, 1995. A clear treatment of the history, manufacture, and usage of papyrus, with a chapter on the equipment for writing.

Piacentini, Patrizia. "Enquête sur les scribes dans la société égyptienne de l'Ancien Empire (les nécropoles memphites)." Ph.D. diss., Ecole Pratique des Hautes Etudes, IVe Section, Paris, 1997. Includes a prosopography of all the known scribes of the Old Kingdom, a detailed study of their titles and their hierarchy in the administration, and a review of the documents of the third millennium BCE, mentioning scribes (letters, decrees, papyri, seals, graffiti, etc.). It will be published in 2000.

Schlott, A. *Schrift und Schreiber im Alten Ägypten.* Munich, 1989. A general study on different writings used in Egypt and on the figure of the scribe.

Schott, Siegfried. "Schreiber und Schreibgerät im Jenseits." *Journal of Egyptian Archaeology* 54 (1968), 45–50. The author collects and discusses the allusions to the scribe in Pyramid and Coffins Texts.

Scott, Gerry D. "The History and Development of the Ancient Egyptian Scribe Statue." Ph.D. diss. Yale University, 1989. Catalog and detailed study of the statues of scribes from the Old Kingdom to the Late Period.

Vernus, Pascal. "Quelques exemples du type du «parvenu» dans l'Egypte ancienne." *Bulletin de la Société Française d'Égyptologie* 59 (1970), 31–47. On the social success of the scribe, based on his competence; with a choice of translated texts.

Wente, Edward. *Letters from Ancient Egypt: Writings from the Ancient World.* Atlanta, 1990. Contains the up-to-date translation of the *Kemit*, of letters mentioning scribes and of the *Satirical Letter* of the scribe Hori.

Williams, Ronald J. "Scribal Training in Ancient Egypt." *Journal of the American Oriental Society* 92 (1972), 214–221. Article concerning the methods of training of the scribes, illustrated by a number of sources translated and annotated.

PATRIZIA PIACENTINI

SCRIPTS. [*This entry surveys the various types of ancient Egyptian scripts, with reference to each script's evolution, duration, relation to other scripts, and context of use. It comprises six articles:*

An Overview
Hieroglyphs
Cryptography
Hieratic
Demotic
Coptic

For related discussions, see Grammar; *and* Language.]

An Overview

With recent discoveries by German excavators at Abydos, there is now evidence that the ancient Egyptian hieroglyphic script dates back to approximately 3500 BCE. This makes the appearance of hieroglyphs in Egypt a development parallel with the appearance of cuneiform script in Mesopotamia. The long-held theory that the development of Egyptian hieroglyphs was inspired by merchants from Mesopotamia must now be reexamined in favor of the view that the hieroglyphic script and writing itself may have developed independently in Egypt, simultaneously with or even before its counterpart in Mesopotamia. This view allows scholars to understand better the significant differences between the hieroglyphic and cuneiform scripts.

These discoveries are also relevant to the issue of what stimulated the development of writing in Egypt. Most of the finds are texts identified as accounts or receipts for goods—that is, administrative documents. This parallels nicely the formation of cuneiform in Mesopotamia, where the earliest "texts" are of a similar accounting nature. The emergence of writing for business purposes places early Egyptian communities at developmental stages parallel with Mesopotamia, even though the cultural milieu of Egypt was different. If writing started for accounting and other business purposes, then the roles played by the merchant scribes would also be significant for Egyptian society. It is clear from later developments that scribes held an important place in Egyptian society throughout its history, but the same cannot be said of merchants. Why did this division take place? Some have argued that as the Egyptian nation-state developed, the use of hieroglyphs was usurped by the elite for propaganda and religious purposes; thus, writing became associated with power structures and remained a focus and forum for the power elites.

Some scholars have suggested that as the use of hieroglyphs was appropriated by the elite, writing itself became a social status marker. In this view, the use of language was tied closely to the position that the writer held in society. In a clear sense, writing was power. The central elite effectively controlled writing, and thus all aspects of writing were associated with the maintenance of the status quo and the regular functioning of the state. The term used to denote hieroglyphs, *mdw-nṯr* ("god's words"), reinforces this notion. Thus, the elite utilized writing and tagged it as a religious aspect of their power status.

Writing became a mechanism to maintain power relations within the society. In this manner, the seemingly open path to advancement in society through merit was actually a restricted one, in that only those already within the elite classes could take part in that "meritocracy" and improve their status. A curious system then developed in which certain members of the elite were literate but were not expected, in their nominal offices, to write. This would pertain especially to the king and perhaps members of the very highest levels in Egyptian society, for whom writing was an administrative chore best left to those designated as "scribes" actually to carry out.

Within the script itself, the notion of symbolism was adopted by the elite in order to portray specific power relations. The Narmer Palette, it has been argued, represents a wholly symbolic piece in which the king represents the effective, dominant figure in the world. The use of the hieroglyphic script here then becomes a vehicle to affirm the centrality of the king as the ideal figure of human action. The representation of the king and the use of hieroglyphs (i.e., writing) were understood as a single medium, and that medium became the vehicle through which ideology was expressed. That notion might be extended to include the idea that the Narmer Palette could also be representational on a different plane, that of reflecting a historical occurrence. Hieroglyphic script thus held the symbolic potential within the Egyptian world of providing a medium for the elite (especially the king) to represent the prestige of the status quo and thus to affirm cultural values, as well as to represent historical fact.

Two immediate uses dominated the earliest phase of the script. These centered around administrative use and monumental use. The recent finds from Abydos, including hundreds of receipts and other accounting texts, suggest that the hieroglyphic script was developed initially for administrative use. The developmental stage of the script is still poorly understood, but it is thought to have progressed in this elementary stage for several hundred years. Unfortunately, the accidents of preservation prohibit us from understanding the whole story.

Then the script was adapted and reformulated by the power elite for monumental functions, culminating early on in the decoration of symbolic/historical pieces, such as the myriad of decorated mace heads and palettes dating principally to the Predynastic and Early Dynastic periods. A key to understanding monumental representations is to remember that the king is represented not simply as a secular ruler, but also as the divine ruler of Egypt. Thus, from earliest times Egyptian hieroglyphic scripts had a multifaceted nature. Religious and cultural symbolism were simply other aspects of the use of writing as an instrument of control, though the script itself was restricted in nature until it went through additional developmental stages. In the same manner, the Western view of Egyptian hieroglyphic writing as an "art form" can be included within this concept. Hieroglyphs thus have the potential for modern interpretations of symbolic art, but as cultural expressions of power and prestige they remain purely Egyptian.

The two aspects of writing are not, however, to be seen as divergent. Rather, they reinforce the notion of power and prestige that writing represents. An Old Kingdom scene from the tomb of Mereruka showing tax collection, recording of payments, and the punishment of delinquent taxpayers provides a very clear representation of this concept. The tomb setting highlights the religious context of the scene. The use of the hieroglyphic script shows that the scene itself is a text combining "simple" writing with scenes which are themselves "writing" as well. The content of the scene portrays some of the power relations that the tomb owner wished to express. The business aspect of taxation is fitting in the tomb because it expresses not only the administrative nature of Mereruka's social position, but also his power relations over those whom he has

direct control. Monumental and administrative writing thus are aspects of the same process. In a very real sense, the medium itself becomes the message.

This representation also enables the viewer to note the extraordinary capacity of the monumental script to reflect the permanence of these cultural relationships beyond the barriers humans normally associate with death. Writing as a process then transcends human existence in the here and now and incorporates the afterlife as well. We find a number of examples of physical "letters to the dead" left at the tomb for the deceased to read and answer. This may be another reason that the power elite restricted the use of the script, at least in its earliest developmental stages. Over time, however, the symbolism associated with writing changed.

For the king and other members of the elite, certain symbols associated solely with their status—such as decorated mace heads and palettes—declined in use. However, they were replaced in monumental contexts with the script itself, absorbing the representational efficacy of the material and transforming it literally into the power of the written word. Writing hieroglyphs on stone and similarly permanent materials became another mechanism for restricting the use of monumental hieroglyphs to the elite.

The physical location of the writing remained a vital aspect of the elite's use of hieroglyphs. If writing was restricted in use and thus a marker of elite status, one would expect to see its use limited to physical localities associated with the elite, such as temples, palaces, and *mastaba* tombs. It is in precisely these locations that writing has survived. Barring accidents of preservation, the Old Kingdom seems to continue the pattern in which the location of the elite's burial and the writings in their tombs are keyed to the relationship they held with their king.

Another aspect of writing is the relationship that the form of the script had to the types of power relations it symbolized. Out of hieroglyphs there developed a cursive script known as Hieratic. It has been theorized that the principal reason for the development of this script was convenience of use. The drawing and/or carving of hieroglyphic signs would be seen as a potentially difficult task, and this led to developing a cursive script that would be easier to write. Unfortunately, the preservation of Hieratic materials is extremely limited from the Predynastic and Early Dynastic periods, and the arguments derive from a modern reflection of common sense and evidence *ex silentio*. Can one make judgments based on the difficulty one experienced in writing an ancient and unfamiliar script?

During the formative stage of Egyptian hieroglyphs (3500–3100 BCE), the script went through a dynamic period of formulating many of the signs found in the Old Kingdom. Likewise, there was a standardization of orthography, or the manner in which the individual signs were written. This period was one of the coalescence of the "artistic" nature of hieroglyphic orthography, in which the use of blank spaces around signs gradually diminished until a regular square/rectangular matrix was developed and became the standard pattern or arrangement during the Old Kingdom.

What is most intriguing about the late Predynastic period through the Early Dynastic period, with respect to the writing of the Egyptian language, is that many different aspects of the script were developed. Not only was there the development of a syllabary of hundreds of signs, but the regime of the standard orthography was experimented with and normalized. Buried within that script are notions of religious domination (sometimes referred to as "honorific transposition," where the hieroglyphic sign for a god or king is placed in front of other words in sentences or phrases to indicate a position of prominence). Likewise, the symbolic nature of the script—whether in individual signs, words, phrases or sentences—is displayed. Thus, the images (i.e., the signs themselves) take on added meaning and display magical power simply by their existence outside of the simple "translation" of the text. This leads to the practice in later times of drawing or carving hieroglyphs of certain potentially "evil" signs (e.g., snakes) either with knives in the sign or with the sign broken into two or more parts in order to limit the magical efficacy of the sign (a practice known as "graphic mutilation").

The symbolic nature of the script may also explain why the hieroglyphic script was almost never used to write other languages. The script had become so identified with Egypt and the expressions of its culture that it was not possible to apply it to another language. This is in marked contrast to cuneiform, which was adapted for use with a number of different languages from many different cultures over a long time.

The normalization of the script over a relatively short period indicates that the process of writing in ancient Egypt was not a simple matter, but one in which the elite (be they merchants/scribes, religious leaders, or chiefs/ princes) played a significant role. Unfortunately, the archaeological record at this point does not provide enough evidence to allow us to determine whether the process of developing the script was a simple outgrowth of accounting or business needs, or the joint effort of political and religious leaders, or the outcome of military imposition by a dominant political group, or a combination of these factors. As further evidence is uncovered, that problem may be elucidated.

Over a span of roughly four thousand years (3500 BCE– 500 CE), the writing of the Egyptian language went through a series of profound changes. It is safe to say that the hieroglyphic script was the most unchanging of all of the scripts found in Egypt. Up through 394 CE (the date of the last attested hieroglyphic inscription), the forms of the signs remained relatively stable. In line with the above arguments, this suggests a strong pattern of cultural permanence reflected in the script itself. The secondary, related script known as Hieratic was a "simplified," cursive form of the hieroglyphic script, and for the first two millennia of writing in Egypt there appears to have been a close correspondence between individual hieroglyphic signs and cursive Hieratic signs. It appears, however, that the Hieratic script diverged from hieroglyphic in function. Purely administrative texts are normally in Hieratic, as are personal documents such as letters. Through the Old Kingdom, one can hypothesize that there was no obstacle against moving from one script to the other. Thus, on the tomb of Horkhuf, within a monumental inscription, a letter from the king to Horkhuf is reproduced. Presumably the letter was written earlier in Horkhuf's career in Hieratic but was transcribed into hieroglyphs for display on the monument. Likewise, Pyramid Texts found in royal tombs may have been archived in Hieratic and transposed by the craftsmen into hieroglyphs; this assumption is based on later parallels in the production of religious texts on royal tomb walls.

Hieratic, like hieroglyphs, theoretically was an expression of the vernacular. It is clear, however, that the script and spoken language diverged rapidly. The hieroglyphic script was at the greatest variance with the spoken language because the script itself hardly changed to reflect language development over time, nor did it reflect the regional dialects that existed, but which are not expressed well in Egyptian scripts until the rise of Coptic. In addition, the Hieratic script came to diverge from the hieroglyphic in several important ways. First was the development of ligature signs. Theoretically, a ligature was a cursive method of writing common groups of signs, such as man-determinative over plural strokes. Over time additional ligatures developed, representing a variety of sign groups. At the same time, Hieratic went through changes as a separate script. There is then a series of Hieratic scripts roughly grouped by historic period: Old Kingdom, Middle Kingdom, and New Kingdom. In the New Kingdom one begins to see a divergence between the types of Hieratic script used for literary and nonliterary texts. It may be argued that the separation of Hieratic reflects the proficiency of scribes in the types of texts with which they were accustomed to work.

It should also be noted that a sub-script known as "cursive hieroglyphs" was used. This sub-script appears to be closely tied to hieroglyphs, but it utilizes forms that are somewhat reminiscent of Hieratic. Some scholars suggest that this script was restricted in use to official religious texts and the training of scribes. This suggestion has some merit, since this sub-script continued in use up through the New Kingdom; however, one finds examples of it in some contexts, such as graffiti, that suggest more widespread use.

There appears to have been a conscious attempt during the Amarna period to "update" the hieroglyphic and Hieratic scripts to bring them closer in line with the actual spoken language. Numerous monumental hieroglyphic texts are found with "Late Egyptianisms" expressed. In later periods, there were conscious efforts to attempt to re-create the "pure" hieroglyphic forms, but this is to be understood as an aspect of the nationalistic and archaizing tendencies of the Late period.

Out of the New Kingdom syllabary there developed a series of scripts. Hieroglyphs and New Kingdom Hieratic (literary and nonliterary forms) continued, but variations developed. In the Theban area, the Third Intermediate Period saw the rise of a localized script known as Abnormal Hieratic, characterized by the increased use of ligatures and a regionally based variation on the Hieratic script. Soon after this, a new script known as Demotic developed in the north (perhaps in the Nile Delta).

The Demotic script is characterized by very cursive signs and ligatures. Scholars are divided over the relationship between individual Demotic signs and whether they actually represent corresponding hieroglyphic/Hieratic signs. It should be noted that the early Demotic script in its developmental format is very similar to Old Kingdom Hieratic in that it is written in a generally larger hand, and individual signs are slightly more recognizable as derived from hieroglyphic signs. Over time, the Demotic script increasingly adopted cursive signs that bear little or no relationship to hieroglyphic forms—as did Hieratic.

Demotic became the standard writing form of the vernacular. It was used from the seventh century BCE up to 452 CE, when the last Demotic inscription was inscribed on the walls at the temple of Philae. Since it was in use for such a long period of time, Demotic script also went through a series of developmental stages which are roughly equivalent to the Saite-Persian, Ptolemaic, and Roman periods. Scholars of Demotic are divided on the origins and meanings of sign usage in the script. While all agree that there is some relationship to hieroglyphs and Hieratic, they contest the degree of that relationship. Derivations from literary versus nonliterary Hieratic and the relation to Abnormal Hieratic are still questioned. In a great historical anomaly, there survives a Saite dynasty document which contains "witness copies" of a business document written variously in Late New Kingdom style Hieratic, Abnormal Hieratic, and early Demotic. Thus, while the Saite kings were consciously generating monumental hieroglyphic

texts in an archaic style, scribes within Egypt were still attempting to deal with multiple scripts for everyday use. Ultimately Demotic won out, Abnormal Hieratic disappeared, and Hieratic reverted to specialized usages, mainly in religious texts.

Unlike earlier scripts in Egypt, Demotic could be written on a wide variety of surfaces. Whereas hieroglyphs frequently were inscribed in stone or other durable material (reflecting the restrictive use mentioned above) and Hieratic was typically drawn on papyrus (though some Hieratic texts are found painted or carved in stone), Demotic has been found on stone, papyrus, metal, wood, bone, and pottery. It was used for monumental inscriptions, religious texts, scribal training texts, literary documents, letters, graffiti, and magical texts, as well as innumerable business and legal documents.

It is while Demotic was the primary script in Egypt that historic events (e.g., the conquest of Egypt by the Greeks) forced significant cultural and linguistic changes on Egypt. Greek became the language of the ruling class, and Demotic was demoted to the status of a native script. Although Egyptian culture and language continued, this foreign domination spelled the end of true native Egyptian scripts. Contemporary with the gradual christianization of Egypt, the last stage of the Egyptian language, Coptic, developed. This was accompanied by a major break with the traditional written forms, in that the Greek alphabet was now adapted to write the Egyptian language. The Greek alphabetic signs were supplemented by a number of signs used to represent sounds not found in Greek, and these additional signs may have been derived from Demotic sign groups. One also begins to see forms of punctuation and sentence marking, not typical of earlier scripts. The process of adapting the Greek alphabet was not a straightforward leap from Demotic/Greek usage to Greek/Coptic usage; rather, there are a few Proto-Coptic or early Coptic texts in which scribes experiment with the use of Greek alphabetic forms. Coptic was also a major shift in that it was the first time the Egyptian language was written with vowels. There are numerous dialectal variants (such as Sahidic, Bohairic, Fayyumic, or Achmimic) expressed clearly for the first time. Some scholars regard the use of a "foreign" script overlay onto the Egyptian language as an artificial construct, in that the lack of written vowels was a normative feature for native Egyptian scripts, and so the writing of Coptic with a script developed for Greek appears a bit peculiar.

Over time, the symbolic and representational nature of Egyptian hieroglyphs and their concomitant restricted usage changed. What may once have been entirely restricted to the elite eventually broadened to affect more of the population. Interaction with external cultures and their different languages and scripts affected Egypt from a cultural point of view, expanding the Egyptian concept of what could and could not be done with script. This is not to say that external factors caused changes in Egyptian scripts: Egypt may have developed native scripts and used them in a restricted manner internally, but its forced exposure to external cultures having their own scripts provided the conditions for inevitable change.

Most studies of Egyptian literacy have suggested that throughout Egyptian history (basically from unification into the Roman period) there was a literacy rate of approximately 1 percent. This is thought to have varied little over time, so that although the total number of literate persons increased, this was mostly a reflection of a rise in population from one million at unification to about four and a half million by the Roman period. Unfortunately, there is so little factual evidence one can use to make these estimates that an exact figure may never be determined. However, in light of the above discussion, the more significant change that affected Egypt during this time period was the change from a situation where language was power to one where literacy was power. In the former case, the script was a restricted entity controlled by an elite, and it represented certain linguistically institutionalized power relationships within Egyptian culture. In the latter case, there was a restricted minority who were literate and who held power owing to their positions, but script was more openly used within the population (as reflected in the increase in types and contents of written material found throughout society). Thus, the symbolic import of the script changed.

From a historical point of view, some scholars have argued that the continued use of Egyptian script was a cultural statement employed by the Egyptian populace to express their national identity. To be a true Egyptian would thus be confirmed by the use of the traditional language and script. The use of the Greek alphabet for the Coptic stage of the language may be viewed as a means by which Egyptian cultural identity was co-opted. These nationalistic expressions may be understood as a version of "language as power," though not in the same sense as suggested above.

In certain circumstances there arose a need to utilize an even more restricted or symbolic language as part of the script, and to meet this scribes developed an artificial script known as "cryptographic hieroglyphs." This cryptographic usage is restricted mostly to monumental and religious texts and is found most frequently from the Greco-Roman periods. The use of cryptographic signs, however, is found as early as the Old Kingdom. The basic principle of the cryptographic system is acrophony: using a consonantal sound from a regular hieroglyphic sign as a part of another word. For example, the god Khnum (*ẖnm*) could be written using the child-with-hand-to-mouth sign (Gar-

diner sign list A17) three times. The first instance represents the *ẖ* from the word *ẖrd* "child"; the second instance represents the sign used as the *n* from that sign's use in the word *nni* "child"; and finally, the third instance represents *m* from that sign's use in the word *msw* "children." The three signs combined would then represent *ẖnm* "Khnum." By adopting a "secret" script-within-a-script, the Egyptians provided a new layer of symbolic meaning to their writing system.

During periods of interaction with other cultures, notably the end of the Middle Kingdom and throughout the New Kingdom, there was some mutual, direct influence between Egyptian and other scripts. The Proto-Sinaitic inscriptions, found mostly in the Sinai, date from the eighteenth to seventeenth centuries BCE and represent an attempt to use a version of Egyptian hieroglyphic and Hieratic-based signs as alphabetic characters in order to write an early Northwest Semitic language. Only a few such inscriptions have been discovered so far.

On the other hand, increased contact with Syria-Palestine following the Hyksos conquest caused Egyptian scribes to deal on a regular basis with foreign words and foreign personal names in a variety of administrative documents. From the Old through the Middle Kingdom, Egyptian scribes used a system of group writing (also called a syllabic orthography) that provided a consistent means for dealing with written vocalic sounds. Thus, a monoconsonantal sign had a reed-leaf or quail-chick sign added to indicate *i* and *u* vowels. In the New Kingdom, the main innovation was the use of the aleph-vulture to indicate *a* vowels, with additional uses of consonant-vowel and consonant-vowel-consonant combinations and short consonant-vowel groups. The complex system was abandoned only as Egypt's interactions with Syria-Palestine decreased during the Third Intermediate Period and foreign words were encountered less and less by Egyptian scribes.

Perhaps the only other attempt to utilize the Egyptian script for another language was in connection with Meroitic. From the third century BCE through the fourth century CE, some Demotic sign groups were adopted and reinterpreted in Nubia to write the Meroitic language.

A further area of study of the hieroglyphic script steps outside the historical and anthropological realm dealt with so far. This area deals more with the description of the script from a linguistic point of view in an attempt to understood how the Egyptians described and understood the individual sign units. In writing hieroglyphs, the Egyptians developed a system of picture signs that used a variety of signs with specific consonantal meaning. Thus, there is a series of monoconsonantal signs such as the viper (Gardiner [1957] sign list I9) indicating /f/, the owl (G17) indicating /m/, and so on. There are also a number of biconsonantal signs, such as the *senet* board with game pieces (Y5) representing /*mn*/, the eye (D4) representing /*ir*/, and so on; and there are triconsonantal signs, such as the stomach-windpipe (F35) representing /*nfr*/. As a group, these three types of signs are all phonograms—that is, signs that represent specific sounds.

But there are numerous other signs utilized by the Egyptians. Before one examines them individually, it must be noted that the Egyptians were able to represent linguistic signs graphically by the hieroglyphs themselves. An orthographic sign denotes either a mental concept (the signified) or a sound pattern (the signifier). Most alphabetic writing systems denote only sounds, but Egyptian hieroglyphs can represent both. In this terminology, those hieroglyphic signs that represent mental concepts are ideograms, and those that represent sound patterns are phonograms.

With the sun sign (GN5), the sign itself is an ideogram representing the mental concept of "sun." It also has a secondary reference /*rˤ*/, the sound pattern directly connected to the mental concept. Thus, this type of sign was designed to be both an ideogram and a phonogram. Some scholars have used the term "pictogram" as a synonym of "ideogram," but a distinction must be made: a pictogram refers only to the actual script, while an ideogram combines language and script in a single sign.

The other type of sign, the phonogram, carries only the sound pattern portion of meaning and not a mental concept. Egyptian phonograms are to be seen as expressing only part of the sound pattern for a word and not the entire word. Thus, the Egyptians could write the word meaning "sun" utilizing two monoconsonantal signs, the mouth /*r*/ (D21) and the forearm /*ˤ*/ (D36) and combining the two to represent /*rˤ*/ "sun." For the most part, one must assume that the creators of the hieroglyphic script designed phonograms by combining ideograms according to the rebus principle. The phonogram acts independently of the image it represents and is limited to a use as a "sound picture." It transfers the phonetic value of certain words represented by ideograms to an unrelated word. This allows a unique feature of Egyptian hieroglyphs, where by a sign can be used as a phonogram in certain circumstances and as an ideogram in others.

A third type of sign used by the Egyptians is called the "determinative." A determinative may be loosely defined as a sign that specifies the meaning of a more broadly generic word. Thus, a seated-god sign (A40) placed after the phonograms representing /*imn*/ would aid the reader/speaker to know that the word meant "(the deity) Amun." If one replaces the seated-god sign with the man-with-raised-arms (A4), the word group would then mean "secret, hidden." A determinative is thus able to give expression to contextual associations within the script. Some

scholars have suggested the term "semagram," which would include both determinatives and ideograms, but further study is needed before we accept this term.

One must keep in mind that the system of Egyptian hieroglyphs retained its pictographic nature throughout its history. This allowed it to react to changing historical trends but also provided a framework for the development of new signs, and signs with highly idiosyncratic phonetic values. In a general sense, the average scribe would normally use a range of six hundred to seven hundred signs; However, owing to regional and temporal variations, modern scholars have recorded more than four thousand hieroglyphic signs, many of which can be classified as variations on the smaller (six hundred to seven hundred) set.

In studying the Egyptian script, it must be remembered that the evolution of the script (a diachronic study) must be related to the entire writing process (a synchronic study)—to attain a complete understanding of the Egyptian system of writing.

[*See also* Grammar; Language; Literacy; Scribes; Symbols; *and* Vocabulary.]

BIBLIOGRAPHY

Baines, John. "Communication and Display: the Integration of Early Egyptian Art and Writing." *Antiquity* 63 (1983), 471–482.

Baines, John. "Literacy and Ancient Egyptian Society." *Man* (n.s.) 18 (1983), 572–599.

Baines, John, and Christopher Eyre. "Four Notes on Literacy." *Göttinger Miszellen* 61 (1983), 65–96. Contains extensive bibliography.

Bard, Kathryn. "Origins of Egyptian Writing." In *The Followers of Horus: Studies Dedicated to Michael Allen Hoffman 1944–1990*, edited by R. Friedman and B. Adams, pp. 297–306. Oxford and Bloomington, 1992.

Depuydt, Leo. "On the Nature of the Hieroglyphic Script." *Zeitschrift für Ägyptische Sprache* 121 (1994), 17–36.

Eyre, Christopher, and John Baines. "Interactions between Orality and Literacy in Ancient Egypt." In *Literacy and Society*, pp. 91–119. Copenhagen, 1989.

Fischer, Henry G. "The Origin of Egyptian Hieroglyphs." In *The Origins of Writing*, edited by W. Senner, pp. 59–76. Lincoln, 1989. The entire volume contains reasoned discussions on the origins of scripts and alphabets, though some of the ideas may now be outdated.

Gardiner, Alan H. *Egyptian Grammar*. 3d rev. ed. Oxford, 1957. The fundamental study and source of sign lists.

Janssen, Jac J. "Literacy and Letters at Deir el-Medina." In *Texts from Deir el-Medina and Their Interpretation*, edited by R. J. Demaré and A. Egberts, pp. 81–94. Leiden, 1992.

Loprieno, Antonio. *Ancient Egyptian: A Linguistic Introduction*. Cambridge and New York, 1997. See especially chapters 1–4.

Nissen, Hans J., Peter Damerow, and Robert Englund. *Archaic Bookkeeping: Early Writing and Techniques of Economic Administration in the Ancient Near East*. Chicago and London, 1993.

Postgate, Nicholas, et al. "The Evidence for Early Writing: Utilitarian or Ceremonial?" *Antiquity* 69 (1995), 459–480.

Ray, John D. "The Emergence of Writing in Egypt." *World Archaeology* 17 (1986), 307–316.

Ray, John D. "Literacy and Language in Egypt in the Late and Persian

Periods." In *Literacy and Power in the Ancient World*, edited by A. Bowman and G. Woolf, pp. 51–66. Cambridge, 1994.

Schenkel, Wolfgang. "The Structure of Hieroglyphic Script." *Royal Anthropological Institute News*, August 1976, no. 15, pp. 4–7. This article was expanded and updated as "Schrift" in *Lexikon der Ägyptologie*, 5: 713–735. Wiesbaden, 1984.

te Velde, Herman. "Scribes and Literacy in Ancient Egypt." In *Scripta Signa Vocis: Studies about Scripts, Scriptures, Scribes and Languages in the Near East Presented to J. H. Hospers*, edited by H. L. J. Vanstiphout et al., pp. 253–264. Gröningen, 1986.

Vleeming, Sven. "La phase initiale du démotique ancien." *Chronique d'Égyte* 56. 111 (1981), 31–48.

Wente, Edward. "The Scribes of Ancient Egypt." In *Civilizations of the Ancient Near East*, edited by Jack M. Sasson, pp. 2211–2221. New York, 1995.

EUGENE CRUZ-URIBE

Hieroglyphs

Hieroglyphs was the name the ancient Greeks gave to the pictorial script of the ancient Egyptians—*hieroglyphika grammata* ("sacred sculptured letters"). The inscribed texts produced in this script are composed of miniature picture-characters that are cut in high relief and often painted as well. These characters are pictograms: they portray astronomical entities, people, tools, vessels, furniture, animals, parts of humans and animals, plants, and much else. A good many of these hieroglyphic texts have been preserved in Egypt itself; others are found in museums all over the world. Despite their pictorial quality, the hieroglyphs function as an actual script; that is, they embody the words and sounds of the Egyptian language in a visual code. Some of the pictograms should be read iconically, but others carry only phonetic value. During the main period of its use, the script drew on an inventory of about six hundred signs. Though not itself an alphabetic script, it fostered the development of the alphabetic scripts that came later. The hieroglyphic system is, however, above all the most iconic script that we know.

The Egyptians called the hieroglyphs *mdw-nṯr* ("god's words"). An individual hieroglyph was called *tjt* ("sign," "image," or "icon"). Since the drawing and carving of the hieroglyphs demanded a great amount of skill and time, the use of this script was, throughout the history of ancient Egypt, largely restricted to monumental objects: artifacts that were meant to last for all eternity. Accordingly, most of the hieroglyphic inscriptions are found on tomb walls, tomb furniture, temple walls and furnishings.

For everyday writing—on papyrus and ostraca—scribes used a cursive version of the hieroglyphs that also still bears the name the ancient Greeks gave to it, Hieratic. Mostly written in ink, this version of the pictorial script (whose lineage dates back to the earliest hieroglyphs)

shows less regard for the iconicity of its characters. (Figure 1). From the seventh century BCE on, Hieratic gave way to a still more cursive script called Demotic; it is the latter script that was used in daily life throughout the Ptolemaic and Roman periods. Even after the evolution of Demotic, hieroglyphic and Hieratic inscriptions continued to be produced, if only, by and large, in religious contexts. In addition to these three scripts, yet another variety emerged from the Middle Kingdom on; it was employed in the writing of the funerary texts that we now call Coffin Texts and the *Book of Going Forth by Day* (*Book of the Dead*). Such texts, written in ink on wooden coffins and later on papyrus rolls, are in a script that is less pictorial than the hieroglyphs but that maintains the latter's basic iconic features.

Until the beginning of the nineteenth century, the prevailing opinion of scholars was that the hieroglyphs gave symbolic expression to religious and philosophical doctrines. The repeated attempts at their decipherment became a battlefield where many bright minds were defeated. Only after the discovery in 1799 of the Rosetta Stone (a tripartite inscription in hieroglyphs, Demotic, and Greek) was the French scholar Jean-François Champollion able to establish, in 1822, the phonetic principles of the "fantastic script." Once the code had been broken, the way was opened for a new era of studies of Egyptian civilization.

Direction of Writing. Hieroglyphic inscriptions can be written in horizontal lines or in vertical columns. They can be written from right to left (the preferred direction) or from left to right. Signs that have fronts and backs (e.g., birds, reptiles, or humans) indicate the direction of the writing in that they are drawn facing the beginning of the inscription.

Basic Principles. In the Egyptian language every word is founded on a lexical root, an abstract structure made up of a sequence of consonants or glides. The majority of these roots are bi- or triconsonantal. A tier of various vowels is superimposed on the root to create different words and meanings. A clear example is the triconsonantal root *sḏm*, at the base of all words that have to do with hearing; the infinitive "to choose" was probably pronounced /satap/, while the participle "the one who chooses" is best reconstructed as /satip/. The root *sn* sustains similar variation: when pronounced /san/ it signifies "brother," but in /sanu:wew/ the meaning changes to "brothers."

The script pictograms represent the root alone, without the vowel tier. It is a consonantal, vowelless script. In the cases of *sḏm* and *sn*, the decision as to how to construe the root-vowel combination—as noun, participle, singular, plural, infinitive, etc.—is largely context-dependent.

A single pictogram of the Egyptian script can present

the following: a triconsonantal (or triliteral) sign—⌇ *n-f-r;* ⌐ *n-ṯ-r;* ◁ *ḥ-t-p;* 👤 *ḫ-p-r;* a biconsonantal (biliteral) sign—⌇ *s-n;* 🐦 *w-n;* 🦊 *m-r;* or such monoconsonantal (uniliteral) signs as ◯ *r* or 🦉 *m.*

This script actually includes twenty-four monoconsonantal signs, which could easily have obviated the whole cumbersome system of bi- and triconsonantal signs and have led directly to the beginning of a consonantal alphabetic script. The ancient Egyptian scribes, however, simply did not pursue this path, although they early on developed the ability to decompose the multiconsonantal signs into their monoconsonantal elements. In all probability, a mixture of cultural and semiotic considerations discouraged such "alphabetizing" development. Two main cultural reasons suggest themselves: conservatism; and a conscious desire to maintain the complexity of the script to ensure that it remained the exclusive preserve of ancient Egypt's elite, those who held power and the scribes who wrote their service. In the semiotic realm, the closed system of the hieroglyphs may well have furthered ideological indoctrination; moreover, for those sensitive to its intricacies, it is a very beguiling system that is rich in cognitive rewards.

Reading Strategies. There are two routes by which a pictogram of the hieroglyphic system can lead the reader to a meaning (a signified); thus, this system elicits two main reading strategies. First, the pictogram may function mainly through its iconic meaning; the two chief forms of iconic function are the logograms and the determinatives. Second, the pictogram simply signals its phonetic value, and its iconic meaning is to be disregarded; this type of pictogram is generally termed a "phonogram."

Iconic functions: Logograms. With logograms it is generally the case that the pictorial meaning of the sign (the signifier) sends the reader directly to the meaning (the signified); that is, the pictogram is read iconically:

🐕 *ṯzm* = "dog," 👤 *z* = "man," 🐂 *kꜣ* = "bull," ⬜ *pr* = "house," 🟫 *pt* = "sky," 🐎 *ssmt* = "horse," 🐎 *wrrt* = "chariot," ⌇ *ṯbt* = "sandal," 🐊 *msḥ* = "crocodile."

Sometimes the pictorial meaning stands in a metonymic (contiguity) relationship to the signified:

👂 *sḏm* = "hear," 🦵 *iw(j)* = "come," 🖋 *zḫ* = "scribe," 🐦 *dšr* = "red." "Hearing" and "ear," "come" and "legs" stand in the contiguity relationship of organ and activity. "Scribe" and "scribe's palette" stand in the contiguity relationship of owner and tool. The last example, "red," evinces a part-whole relationship; the part, "redness," is represented by the concrete whole—the bird marked by the unique color feature "red." It must, however, be stressed that logograms of any type (sometimes called "ideograms") are "semograms"; that is, they are signs that

signal meanings of specific words through their iconic features. At the same time, for the native reader, this iconic meaning also conveys phonetic information; for example, to the pictogram for "house" the reader also attaches the "name" of this icon, its phonetic value *pr.*

Iconic functions: Determinatives. One of the most compelling and attractive elements of the script lies in the rich development of its system of determinatives. First appearing during the Old Kingdom, this mechanism reaches its full power in the Middle Kingdom. The determinatives are pictographs that are placed after the sometimes ambiguous vowelless roots: they function as reading aids but carry no phonetic value. They mark the ends of words and provide additional information, either semantic or pictorial, about the words. There are four main ways in which a determinative can relate to the word that precedes it.

First, the determinative can provide a "pictorial synonym" for a word that presents itself through phonograms (see below) and not through logograms. In the word *zšn* 🏺 "lotus-shaped cup," the determinative invests the three written monoconsonantal signs with additional visual information about the exact shape of the cup. From *ṯbty* 👡 we learn what typical Egyptian sandals looked like.

Second, the determinative can be an icon that stands in contiguity (metonymic, schematic) relationship to the word. The word *ꜥrryt* 🏠 "gate" takes the "house" determinative, and the word *nꜥ* 🛶 "travel" presents the typical Egyptian travel vehicle, the Nile boat.

Third, the determinative can act as a classifier (taxogram). Here it provides, in pictorial form only, a more inclusive term, in the vertical axis of the category to which the word belongs. Specific gods thus acquire a "general god" 👤, 🦅 determinative. These two prototypical icons of gods (in human and falcon shapes) become the pictorial manifestations of the general idea of divinity. The "human" (male) icon 👤 is appended to proper names and to various terms for social status and occupations. The determinative the Egyptologists call the "bad bird" is especially intriguing; a sparrow 🐦 is appended as a classifier to words that have nothing to do with birds. The meanings conveyed by the words with this bird-determinative create a semantic category in which the central members are "small," "evil" "difficult," "sickness," and "low social classes."

Finally, in a rare but fascinating mechanism, determinatives can stand in a "metaphoric" relationship to the word. Here a simile is created by the combination of the word and the determinative. When the giraffe functions as the determinative of the verb *sr* 🦒 "foretell," it means

"to see before everybody else, like a giraffe"; *qnd* means "to be angry (like a monkey)," and *ȝms* means "to care (like a cow for its calf)."

Phonographic meaning functions. In the *rebus* device (paronomasia, punning), the reader works with only the "name" or the sounds of the written icon. To understand this process, we may imagine the icon of a bee being used to represent the English verb "be," or the word "belief" indicated by the combination of the two concrete icons Bee + LeaF. Since the Egyptian script provides only the consonantal skeleton, the problem of the above examples' vowel discrepancies never arises.

To ensure that the reader does not make false decisions, determinatives are also often employed in phonogramic readings; they mark word ends and can provide additional semantic information. A typical Egyptian example is the word *pr(j)* "come out" . This word shares the consonantal structure of the word *pr* "house." The fact that the "walking legs" classifier appears after the house pictogram—rather than the stroke that usually signifies a "logogram reading"—prompts the reader to discard the iconic meaning "house" and to think instead of a word with the same consonantal structure that involves movement.

The monoconsonantal signs of the script almost always function as phonograms only: as in *bin* "bad" (+ + + "bad bird" determinative). Such signs have yet another, special use. They "complement" biconsonantal and triconsonantal signs by repeating a part or even the whole of their phonetic components. In so doing, they instruct the reader not to interpret the given signs as a logogram but rather as a phonogram. The phonetic information conveyed by the complementary monoconsonantal signs is redundant and should be ignored. For example, "become" should be read only as *ḫpr*, not *ḫprpr*. "be" should be read *wn*, not *wnn*. The word "seeds" should be read *prt*, not *prrt*.

In summary, an individual hieroglyph can be construed in three distinct ways:

1. as a logogram, providing both semantic and phonetic information
2. as a determinative, providing semantic information only
3. as a phonogram, providing phonetic information only

Duration and Evolution. The first hieroglyphs appear during the period in which the Egyptian state was

SCRIPTS: HIEROGLYPHS. *False door with hieroglyphic relief decoration.* This false door is from the late fifth dynasty *mastaba* of Henu at Saqqara. (Courtesy Donald B. Redford)

formed, around 3100 BCE, used for names, titles, and names of institutions. By the time of the Old Kingdom, the hieroglyphs have developed into a full-fledged writing system. Until the Ptolemaic period the script maintains a rather stable repertory of between 750 and 1,000 signs. A hieroglyphic word did not have one "correct" spelling, though strong scribal conventions, especially from the Middle Kingdom on, impose firm orthographic conventions and restrict the number of possible variations. As a mirror of the Egyptian cultural universe, however, the script adds signs that reflect new developments. Among the most salient of these are the horse and chariot.

These were added to the inventory at the beginning of the New Kingdom, a few decades after their appearance in Egyptian life.

During the Ptolemaic period the hieroglyphs cease to be a general communication system and instead come to constitute a form of discourse between the gods and the priestly elites of the various temples. This closure of the system opens the way for much play with the principles of the script: the cultivation of redundancies, use of rare signs, revivification of old forgotten meanings for known signs, and inventions of new meanings based on new rebus games and symbolic readings. During this period the number of signs amount to about five thousand.

This Ptolemaic innovation is, however, rooted in a long-standing tradition. From the Old Kingdom on we encounter sporadic variations of the customary script on both private and royal monuments. Egyptologists term these variations "cryptography." These inscriptions play just as freely with the script's semiotic options as do those of the Ptolemaic period; it is only in their more secular nature that these earlier writing games differ from the liberties taken by the Ptolemaic script. Interestingly, the cryptography of the eighteenth dynasty often gives monoconsonantal representations of words that were traditionally written by triconsonantal or biconsonantal signs.

The latest dated authentic hieroglyphic inscription is found in the temple of Philae and is assigned to 394 CE. With the spread of Christianity throughout Egypt, the tradition of the old writings, long since the exclusive preserve of priestly cases, passed into oblivion. The Coptic script, already common in the third century CE, marks the definitive disappearance of the pictorial script. Coptic is the form of Egyptian written in the Greek alphabet, supplemented by seven special characters that derive from hieroglyphs. All that remains after this are confused and misleading traditions in the works of non-Egyptian writers.

Semiotic Characteristics of Hieroglyphs. The hieroglyphic system was invented on the eve of the Predynastic period; it is only one manifestation of the newly created state ideology that initiated a series of innovative semiotic demonstrations in architecture and the visual arts as well as in writing.

Born of visual art, the hieroglyphs—far more than any later script—played an integral part in the ongoing visual indoctrination carried out by the power-holders at the various levels of Egyptian society. Unlike scripts whose signs are arbitrary, the pictograms of the ancient Egyptian script are miniature pictures and, as such, they strictly obey all the rules of Egyptian pictorial art.

The pictograms have a twofold ideological function. First, they represent the a priori conceptual landscape of their inventors. Second, the same pictorial system reflects on the conceptual world of the reader, and even, to some extent, on that of the nonliterate beholder; for many pictograms were recognizable, even if not always fully understandable, to the uninitiated.

Established as an official aggregate of prototypical images, the script promulgated what the official culture deemed to be the "correct" image for every word: the reader is precluded from choosing his own images. Take, for example, the word *z* 𓀀 "man." The sign is always an Egyptian, never an African or Near Easterner. The combined determinative 𓀀𓁐𓏤𓏤𓏤 (three strokes always convey plurality) appears in words referring to collectives, such

as people of various tribes. In this determinative the man is always the first element, but refreshingly the woman, though second, is of the same height and seated in the same position as the man. Another example is the word *sdr* 𓄂 "spend the night." This sign presents a typical Egyptian bed, but one that was hardly available to most Egyptians. Such details reveal much about the social circles in which the hieroglyphic script was invented and cultivated.

Pictorially, the icons had a life of their own. In funerary contexts, where reality calls forth fear and magic, they are often mutilated. Even when acting as phonograms, the signs for the lion or snake are cut because of the referents' known dangerous nature. Ducks and owls are also cut, most likely to keep them from flying away and thereby magically ruining the inscription and, more important, the dead person's chances for a decent afterlife.

As a semiotic system, the hieroglyphic script is unsurpassed. It imposingly bestrides the crossroads of word and picture—with words that do not *describe* pictures, but are instead *made up* of pictures. They irresistibly transport the reader from literal-iconic meanings to all manner of transposed meanings. The final meaning of a word is often captured in the tangle of associations, connotations, and metaphors suggested by the pictorial.

Legacy of the Hieroglyphs. There is almost universal agreement that the Egyptian script fostered one of humanity's greatest inventions—the alphabetic script, which eventually democratized writing—making literacy possible not only to closed casts of scribes. Until recently, it was believed that the early alphabetic script (called Proto-Sinaitic) came from Canaan, most probably from the Egyptian temple of Serabit el-Khadem in the Sinai peninsula, sometime in the early second millennium BCE. The temple in Serabit el-Khadem was dedicated to Hathor, the Egyptian goddess of turquoise. The temple, which stood in the center of the turquoise mining area, contained numerous hieroglyphic inscriptions, some of which mentioned Canaanites, who were employed by the Egyptians. About a dozen short, crudely made, early alphabetic inscriptions were also found in the temple surroundings. These inscriptions were partially deciphered and include, among other words, the name of the Canaanite goddess Ba'alat. It is very plausible that the Canaanites working in the site identified the Egyptian goddess Hathor with their goddess Ba'alat.

Recently, in Egypt, two very similar crudely inscribed, early alphabetic rock inscriptions were discovered (among hundreds of Egyptian graffiti). They are located in the forlorn Wadi el-Hol, an ancient unused caravan road in the Western Desert, along which soldiers, traders, nomads, and couriers once traveled from Thebes to Abydos. The inscriptions are attributed by their discoverers—according to Egyptian palaeographic considerations—to approximately the same date as the Proto-Sinaitic inscriptions in the Sinai. There are a number of similarities between the two scripts. Both appear in very remote areas, on the fringes of the Egyptian civilization, and in both cases the inscriptions are unrefined, most probably drawn by an untrained hand.

The Proto-Sinaitic script seems to record a West Semitic dialect, and the word Ba'alat, the name of the Canaanite goddess, was identified with certainty. The two inscriptions found in Egypt have not yet been deciphered, but scholars tend to believe that the language recorded in Wadi el-Hol is also a West Semitic dialect. In fact, a nearby Egyptian inscription mentions a military commander of the "Asiatics" (Near Easterners). Both versions of the early alphabet show strong pictorial affinities to Egyptian hieroglyphs (the inscriptions of Wadi el-Hol may be connected to the rock-cut cursive hieroglyphs so abundant in the surrounding area). It is however difficult to reconstruct the circumstances that initiated the invention of the alphabet.

Far more than any other script, Egyptian hieroglyphs are "friendly" to the uninitiated; they seem familiar and inviting to our eyes. While the outsider may recognize in them an entire world, that does not mean that he or she can read them. However attractive and seductive they are, the icons ultimately remain elusive. Only against such a highly charged cognitive background can we recognize the role the hieroglyphs played in the invention of the alphabet.

Those who stood at the threshold of the "house of writing," but still lacked the key to enter it, must have experienced both frustration and creative excitement. The true genius of the "inventor" of the alphabet was the composite ability to recognize the iconic meaning of the hieroglyphs, to select freely among them, and thus to create a qualitatively new system of writing—at once pictorial yet oblivious (objective), to the icon. This new, alphabetic script is acrophonic: its icons (letters) stand only for the *first* consonants of the words they denote. The "inventor" used Semitic (not Egyptian) words for the new "hieroglyphic" icons; "palm (of the hand)," for example, which is *kp* in Semitic, represents the letter *k*; the "head," which is *r's* in Semitic, stands for the letter *r*.

The Proto-Canaanite alphabetic system is both acrophonic and monoconsonantal. It proved much easier to use than the hieroglyphic system because, unlike the latter, it does not burden the reader with a plethora of alternative readings of the icons. Each "hieroglyph" of the early alphabetic script allows one, and only one, reading option. In the new script the icon is, in fact, nothing more than a tool, for its pictorial meaning is nothing more than a mnemonic device; the icon always points beyond itself

to an abstract linguistic unit, the consonant. Thus the iconic meaning becomes redundant—and, in fact, the icon was lost for a schematic sign once the script was adopted by the professional scribes of Phoenicia about 1050 BCE.

What the alphabet does share with the hieroglyphic script is the principle of consonantal representation. Both the Ancient Egyptian and Canaanite languages were consonantal and root-inflected; each could have been properly represented (at least for a native speaker) by this kind of writing system. The crucial resemblance in the two systems has led some scholars to the belief that the "creator(s)" of the early alphabetic inscriptions must have had a knowledge of Egyptian. This conjecture is rendered somewhat improbable by the fact that there is simply no trace of correct Egyptian sign usage in the early alphabetic system. This brilliant invention was possible because its inventor or inventors were probably not hampered by any prior knowledge of any other writing system, including Egyptian.

Since the earliest alphabet was the ancestor of the linear Phoenician alphabet, which fathered the Greek alphabet, which later was made into the Latin alphabet—the hieroglyphs may well be still with us, as *Ur-progenitor* of them all. In every book we read, every letter we write, the legacy of the hieroglyphs lives on.

BIBLIOGRAPHY

General Introductions

Davies, W. V. *Egyptian Hieroglyphs: Reading the Past.* London, 1987. A friendly, up-to-date introduction for the non-specialist; ample illustrations, and basic bibliography.

Fischer, Henry G. "Hieroglyphen." In *Lexikon der Ägyptologie*, 2: 1189–1199. Wiesbaden, 1977. An encyclopedic representation of the system; contains lengthy bibliography. (In English.)

Schenkel, Wolfgang. "Schrift." In *Lexikon der Ägyptologie*, 5: 713–715. Wiesbaden, 1984. A concise representation and scientific discussion; extensive bibliography. (In German.)

Schenkel, Wolfgang. "The Structure of the Hieroglyphic Script." *Royal Anthropological Institute News* 15 (1976), 4–7. A very scholarly, concise introduction for the non-specialist. Few illustrations, new terminology (no bibliography).

Comprehensive Discussions

Champollion, Jean. F. *Principes généraux de l'écriture sacrée égyptienne.* Paris, 1836; Reprint, 1984. A comprehensive edition of Champollion's pioneering work on Egyptian hieroglyphs and grammar, published after his premature death. Although out of date now, the work is still most engaging intellectually and esthetically. It contains magnificent hieroglyphs drawn by Champollion himself.

Schott, Siegfried. *Hieroglyphen: Untersuchungen zum Ursprung der Schrift.* Wiesbaden, 1951. Scholarly book; important data and discussion of the early stages of the script.

Emergence of the Hieroglyphic Script

Bard, Kathryn A. "Origins of Egyptian Writing." In *The Followers of Horus: Studies dedicated to Michael Allen Hoffman 1944–1990*, edited by R. Friedman and B. Adams, pp. 297–306. Oxford, 1992.

Fischer, Henri G. "The Origin of the Egyptian Hieroglyphs." In *The Origins of Writing*, edited by W. M. Senner, pp. 59–76. Lincoln, 1989.

Ray, John. "The Emergence of Writing in Ancient Egypt." *World Archaeology* 17.3 (1986), 307–316.

Sign Lists

Gardiner, Alan H. *Egyptian Grammar.* 3rd rev. ed. Oxford, 1957. This fundamental study of Middle-Egyptian grammar contains the most useful sign list—compiled by an Egyptologist—to date. It includes about 750 signs of frequent use, mostly from the Middle Kingdom and the 18th dynasty. The signs are arranged in categories after their iconic values, e.g., "Man and His Occupation," "Woman and Her Occupation," "Parts of Human Body," "Mammals," "Birds," "Buildings," "Parts of Buildings," "Ships and Parts of Ships," etc. The sign-list is accompanied by various examples for the use of each sign. This list has been recently computerized as the "Macscribe" and "Glyph" systems.

Kahl, Jochem. *Das System der ägyptischen Hieroglyphenschrift in der 0.-3. Dynastie.* Göttinger Orient forschung IV, 29. Wiesbaden, 1994. The lengthy work includes a complete list of hieroglyphs occurring during dynasties 0–3. The list complements Gardiner's list, inserting new subinumeration for early variations that later disappeared and thus do not occur in Gardiner's list. Also contains extensive bibliographical information about the inscriptions.

Semiotic Aspects

Goldwasser, Orly. *From Icon to Metaphor: Studies in the Semiotics of the Hieroglyphs.* Orbis Biblicus et Orientalis, 142. Fribourg and Göttingen, 1995. A study of the hieroglyphic sign with the tools of modern semiotics. Includes chapters on word-determinative relations, and on the formation stage of the script.

Velde, Herman te. "Egyptian Hieroglyphs as Signs, Symbols and Gods." *Visible Religion* 4–5 (1986), 63–72.

Vernus, Pascal. "L'écriture hiéroglyphique: Une écriture duplice?" *Cahiers Confrontation* 16 (1986), 59–66. On the tension within the hieroglyphic sign between iconic and phonetic readings. Interesting examples.

Hieroglyphs—Between Script and Art

Davies, Nina. M. *Picture Writing in Ancient Egypt.* Oxford, 1958. Exquisite drawings of single hieroglyphs.

Fischer, Henri. *L'écriture et l'art de l'Égypte ancienne.* Paris, 1986.

Weeks, Kent. R. "Art, Word, and the Egyptian World View." In *Egyptology and the Social Sciences,* edited by K. Weeks, pp. 59–81. Cairo 1979.

Phonological Aspects

Kammerzell, Frank. "The Sounds of a Dead Language: Reconstructing Egyptian Phonology." *Göttinger Beiträge zur Sprachwissenschaft* 1 (1998), 21–41.

Ptolemaic System

Daumas, François. *Valeurs phonétiques des signes hiéroglyphiques d'époque Gréco-Romaine.* Montpellier, 1988. List of signs used during the Ptolemaic period.

Fairman, H. W. "An Introduction to the Study of Ptolemaic Signs and Their Values." *Bulletin de l'Institut français d'archéologie Orientale* 43 (1945), 51–138. A polemic article, yet the best introduction in English to the subject.

Greek and Later Traditions

Iversen, Erik. *The Myth of Egypt and Its Hieroglyphs in European Tradition.* 2d ed. Princeton, 1993. A comprehensive history of the hieroglyphic script, also for the non-specialist. Description of the system; the Ptolemaic evolution. Emphasis on the classical tradition, Middle Ages, Renaissance and the 17th–18th century. Also decipherment.

van de Walle, B., and Vergote, J. "Traduction des Hieroglyphica d'Horapollon." *Chronique d'Égypte: Bulletin périodique de la Foundation Égyptologique Reine Elisabeth* 35 (1943), 39–889; 199–247. A detailed Egyptological discussion of the Greek *Hieroglyphica* of Horapollo. The *Hieroglyphica* is written in Greek, and it describes in words (it contains no pictures) Egyptian hieroglyphs and their alleged meanings. The text, probably dating from the fourth century CE, reappeared in Europe in the beginning of the fifteenth century, and fueled a widespread fascination with hieroglyphs during the Renaissance era. As Horapollo was not aware (or did not understand) the use of the signs as phonograms, he tried mostly to explain the system on the basis of allegorical interpretations and factitious symbolic readings. Although there is in the greater part of his explanation an element of truth, by ignoring the phonetic functions of the hieroglyphs Horapollo led generations of scholars astray on the wrong path of "fantastic" readings of the signs. (For an English translation of Horapollo, see George Boas, *The Hieroglyphics of Horapollo.* Princeton, 1993.)

Hieroglyphs and the Alphabet

Naveh, Joseph. *Early History of the Alphabet. An Introduction to West Semitic Epigraphy and Palaeography.* 2d ed. Jerusalem, 1987.

Sass, Benjamin. *Studia Alphabetica. On the Origin and Early History of the Norhtwest Semitic, South Semitic, and Greek Alphabets.* Orbis Biblicus et Orientalis, 102. Göttingen, 1991.

ORLY GOLDWASSER

Cryptography

Hieroglyphic signs were based for the most part on observable images, and they represented both the sounds and the generalized ideas that comprised the language of ancient Egypt. In addition to the linguistic properties that these signs possessed, they still were pictographs and had, therefore, an added esthetic dimension. The interconnections between art and writing in ancient Egypt were quite important and widespread. The visual properties of the "letters" allowed ancient Egyptian scribes and artisans to make use of calligraphic processes not possible with other contemporaneous scripts. In some cases, the hieroglyphs could communicate a message beyond the one specified within the text. Such a text can be considered cryptographic, since its secondary communication was not meant to be apparent. Sculptural images in both two and three dimensions can also be considered as cryptograms, if, in addition to their primary visual statement, they have another, less explicit but nonetheless intended communication that certain viewers could understand. For example, the Old Kingdom figure of the official Hesy-Re, which appears in raised relief on a wooden panel from his tomb, grasps an item in each hand; these objects, while part of the scene, also represent an emblematic writing of his full name and serve to identify the individual.

Other instances are not uncommon. In a three-dimensional sculptural composition of the Ramesssid period, the focus is the god Hauron, who dominates the figure of Ramesses as a child, and the sedge plant, the heraldic plant of Upper Egypt. All these components are not only integral to the sculpture but also have significance as hieroglyphs. This secondary meaning may not have been immediately apparent to any but the initiated. The god can be read as "Re," the royal child as the Egyptian word *mes*, meaning "to bear," and the plant as *su*. Together, they comprise the name "Ramesses." The same pharaoh had his name written cryptographically over the entrance to the temple he built at Abu Simbel. At this location, however, the sculptured composition spells out part of his coronation name, User-maat-Re. He also had this name incorporated into his crown on a faience tile, presumably used as decoration for a temple.

Scribes and artisans had the option of using a recognizable sign or devising new ones from images otherwise without hieroglyphic associations. They could also take hieroglyphs known for a particular reading and then manipulate them in such a way as to extend their meaning. The craftsmen who produced the jewelry of Tutankhamun used several techniques when they fashioned the small double cartouche box for the king, decorating it with representations that appear to have hieroglyphic meaning. At the bottom of the composition is the word for "festival," pronounced *ḥl*, but the word *nb*, meaning "lord," which has a similar appearance, undoubtedly was to be read. The figures of the seated king in different costumes in the center of the two cartouches on each side of the box are understood together to mean manifestations, *ḫprw*, and the representation of the sun disk at the top refers to the sun god, Re. The imagery on the obverse and reverse of this object, therefore, depicts the coronation name of the king, Neb-Kheperu-Re, "Re Is the Lord of Manifestations."

Even the orientation of hieroglyphs could play a role in providing double or hidden meanings. Scribes could arrange signs in a text in such a way that they could be read in several directions at once. Such compositions form a sort of Egyptian acrostic or crossword puzzle. The scribes could also devise "sportive" writings by manipulating signs and their order, and thus confound the reader.

Cryptographic writing was most popular in the New Kingdom and later, but embedded messages occurred even prior to the Old Kingdom. The technique allows compositions to have both explicit and implicit messages. In some examples, cryptographic writing masked a message that was to remain hidden. Such may well be the purpose of the group that Ramesses II had sculpted over the entrance to his temple at Abu Simbel. This encrypted writing of his name ensured that the structure would always be associated with him. It is likely that the same motive may account for the fact that many pieces of jewelry that were buried with Tutankhamun contain the name of the king hidden in a similar manner. The name was a significant feature of the personality of the individual, and its survival was essential to ensure the eternal afterlife. Perhaps for this reason, many of the examples of cryptographic writing include names. Hatshepsut, the eighteenth dynasty queen, also had a sculpture produced for her in which the elements of her coronation name, Maatka-Re, were successfully encoded. In this case, the underlying intent of such works is especially important because, while most other representations of Hatshepsut and inscriptions bearing her name were destroyed after her unorthodox reign, this particular sculpture survived.

Hieroglyphs were understood by the Egyptians as the words of the gods, and therefore, by their very nature, they were immortal like the gods. Recording something in these signs was an attempt to perpetuate the message they carried. Encrypting it would enhance the chances of its endurance. The fact that only relatively few people would be able to read these communications once they were able to decode them was probably of little concern to the authors. Once the message was written, and as long as it survived, it would always be recognized in the spiritual dimension. This practice extended beyond the recording of names, and the Egyptians not infrequently embedded longer communications. In a Middle Kingdom pectoral with gold openwork that incorporates inlays and the cartouche of Amenemhet III, the craftsman fashioned a central scene of the smiting pharaoh as a focus. Rather smaller, but nonetheless important, are accompanying hieroglyphs which could be understood as decorative elements that also identify various figures. Taken in the broader context, however, the entire composition can be read as a message attesting to the prowess of the king. Such royal propaganda, whether explicit or implicit, was apparently important to the pharaohs.

Sometimes the ingenuity of the craftsmen who produced the cryptographic writing might inspire a literate visitor to a chapel to recite prayers and thus benefit a tomb or statue owner. In other cases, the purpose of the encryption was to prevent the true meaning of a text from being recognized except by a few select people. Occasionally religious texts were written cryptographically, thus allowing only the initiated to unlock the secrets of the inscription. In the latest periods, this practice became exaggerated to the point that certain texts—for example those in the temple at Esna—consist of several columns depicting only one animal, either a crocodile or a ram, distinguished only by the different crowns the figures wear.

BIBLIOGRAPHY

Drioton, E. "Les principes de la cryptographie égyptienne." *Comptes rendus des séances de l'Académie d'inscriptions et belles-lettres.* 1953. Seminal work on the subject, in which the author gives references to his earlier studies on the topic.

Epigraphic Survey. *The Tomb of Kheruef: Theban Tomb 192.* Oriental Institute Publications, 102. Chicago, 1980. Plates 14–15 illustrate the earliest word square, and a translation appears on pp. 35–36. References to other, later examples and discussions by other scholars are in the accompanying notes.

Fischer, H. G. "Cryptography." In *Lexikon der Ägyptologie* 2: 1196. Wiesbaden, 1977. Most helpful and provides many references.

Fischer, H. G. *L'écriture etell'art de l'Egypte ancienne.* Paris, 1986.

Silverman, David P. "Cryptographic Writing in the Tomb of Tutankhamun." *Studien zur Altägyptischen Kultur* 8 (1980): 233–236. Focuses on the double cartouche box, but gives other examples as well as good bibliography.

Zandee, Jan. *An Ancient Egyptian Crossword Puzzle.* Leiden, 1966.

DAVID P. SILVERMAN

Hieratic

The term "Hieratic" is something of a misnomer. It derives from the Greek expression *grammata hieratika* ("priestly writing"), coined by St. Clement of Alexandria in the second century CE to designate the cursive script that was used for writing religious texts on papyri during the Greco-Roman period. But prior to the sixth century BCE, when Demotic became Egypt's standard script for written communication, Hieratic for more than two thousand years had served to inscribe secular documents, such as letters, accounts, and legal instruments, as well as religious, magical, literary, medical, and mathematical texts. Thus, the range of documents in the Hieratic script was considerably broader than the term "Hieratic" etymologically denotes.

Materials. Hieratic owes its cursive character to the fact that it was executed with a rush brush which deposited a flow of ink whose width depended on the pressure exerted on the brush. Not until the Common Era was Hieratic written with a reed pen. Papyrus was the medium *par excellence* for Hieratic texts. Because of the cost and limited availability of papyrus rolls, owing to seasonal shortages, a scribe frequently erased an older text and used the second-hand papyrus for a new text, creating a palimpsest—a practice especially common when writing letters. Hieratic texts were also written on leather rolls, but only a few have survived. At no cost, scribes obtained limestone flakes or potsherds for inscribing secular documents, as well as literary texts. Thousands of these Hieratic documents, known as ostraca, have been found in the Ramessid workmen's village of Deir el-Medina and its environs. Texts on ostraca are usually relatively brief, but there are some large ostraca containing accounts or long literary texts, such as the *Story of Sinuhe.* Hieratic inscriptions were also written on cloth: for example, an Old Kingdom letter to the dead on linen, dockets on mummy shrouds in the twenty-first dynasty, and chapters of the *Book of Going Forth by Day* (*Book of the Dead*) on mummy bandages in the Ptolemaic and Roman periods.

Wooden tags often bear Hieratic inscriptions, and even a scribe's wooden palette might serve for impromptu jottings. Wooden boards coated with gesso were used by scribes, especially during their education. Ink inscriptions on these boards could be easily erased, permitting reuse by students or by scribes drawing up preliminary records. In the First Intermediate Period and Middle Kingdom, the interiors of wooden coffins were decorated with Hieratic funerary inscriptions, known as the Coffin Texts.

Throughout Egyptian history, Hieratic notations were made on pottery vessels. Wine jar inscriptions, for example, generally indicate the date, vineyard, and vintner. Execration texts were penned in Hieratic on clay figurines and jars that were then ritually smashed. Quite extraordinary are a number of clay tablets bearing Hieratic inscriptions incised with a stubby bone stylus while the clay was still moist. These documents, dating to the late sixth dynasty and discovered at Balat in the Dakhla oasis, include accounts, lists of names, and several letters. The choice of material may reflect the scarcity of papyrus in the oasis.

A scribe, finding himself in an area where an *in situ* surface presented itself, might inscribe a Hieratic graffito with a prayer or text to be read by subsequent passers-by. Thus, Hieratic inscriptions in ink appear in remote locations, such as the Hatnub quarries, or on the walls and columns of temples and tomb chapels that were visited over the years. Hieratic graffiti written overhead on jagged ceilings of rock-cut chambers demanded considerable dexterity on the scribe's part.

Occasionally a person journeying in the desert selected a rock on which to incise a Hieratic inscription. Such inscriptions, which were etched in stone with a pointed spike, approximate the ductus of free-flowing ink from a rush brush. Inscriptions of this nature, dating from the First Intermediate Period and into the Third Intermediate Period, abound in the vicinity of western Thebes. During the twenty-second dynasty, stone donation stelae were regularly carved in Hieratic.

Writing Hieratic. Two types of Hieratic script can be distinguished: the uncial, or book hand, used for literary, scientific, and religious texts, and the more cursive business hand, for secular documents. The cursive hand tends to be most extreme in such documents as accounts and letters. In particular, much-used epistolary formulae might be written extremely cursively, and the repetitive nature of accounts was conducive to abbreviated forms of Hieratic signs.

Throughout the Old Kingdom and into the twelfth dynasty, Hieratic texts were normally written in vertical lines. In the course of the twelfth dynasty, horizontally inscribed Hieratic texts become increasingly frequent, and during the reign of Amenemhet III this practice was regularized. This change from vertical to horizontal may have been instituted to prevent the scribe's hand from smudg-

SCRIPTS: HIERATIC. *Linen mummy bandages inscribed with Hieratic script.* These bandages are from Abu Ghurob and date from the Ptolemaic period. (University of Pennsylvania Museum, Philadelphia. Neg. # S4–143072)

ing lines previously penned, but it is also likely that columns of horizontal lines, forming "pages" on the papyrus scroll, made consultation of the document easier. Also, horizontal lines probably permitted the scribe to increase his writing speed.

Relationship of Hieratic to Hieroglyphs. Although hieroglyphs may be written in either direction, Hieratic, when written horizontally, always proceeds from right to left; and when written vertically, the signs face right, with the lines of text generally being read from right to left. Whereas hieroglyphic signs are always neatly separated, it was possible in writing Hieratic for the scribe to execute two or even three signs without removing his brush from the writing surface, thus creating ligatures. Owing to the decorative nature of hieroglyphic writing, there is greater freedom in the orthography of words than in Hieratic, where words are spelled more consistently, particularly within a single text. Biconsonantal signs in Hieratic generally receive a phonetic complement, which in hieroglyphic writing is more often optional. Some Hieratic signs that would otherwise be identical are differentiated by a diacritic mark or stroke; and in Hieratic a simple slanting line substitutes for some of the more complex hieroglyphs. In hieroglyphic inscriptions there is never any sort of punctuation, but in some Hieratic literary and religious texts, red dots—sometimes called "verse points" by modern scholars—in or above the line serve to indicate a separation of clauses or phrases, and a red line may terminate a section as a sort of paragraph marker.

Hieratic signs can be transcribed into hieroglyphs, but the underlying hieroglyph is generally not readily apparent, so that the relationship between hieroglyphic writing and Hieratic is somewhat analogous to the difference between our printed text and handwriting. Modern transcriptions of Hieratic into hieroglyphs retain the exact disposition of the Hieratic signs. Such transcriptions would have been unacceptable in a well-formulated hieroglyphic inscription, where an esthetic arrangement of signs was sought. This is not to imply that Hieratic texts were devoid of beauty, for some of the book hands reveal calligraphy at its finest. It must be stressed that when a scribe wrote a Hieratic text, he never thought in terms of the underlying hieroglyphs. The Hieratic script was self-sufficient, having developed at a very early stage in the history of Egyptian writing, and its evolution was quite independent of hieroglyphs, so that the reader of a Hieratic document did not transpose the text into hieroglyphs. Although the modern scholar may find it frustrating to decipher highly cursive hands, there never was any intention on the scribe's part to obfuscate matters—his aim was to communicate in writing as effectively as possible.

Many hieroglyphic texts carved on monuments were originally composed in Hieratic: for example, hieroglyphic versions of Old Kingdom royal decrees and letters from the king. One can even point to the occasional influence of Hieratic on hieroglyphic. In the First Intermediate Period, Hieratic forms of signs frequently intrude within hieroglyphic inscriptions, and in Ramessid monumental inscriptions several signs derived from the Hieratic are fairly frequent.

Less common are Hieratic copies of hieroglyphic inscriptions. The eighteenth dynasty Berlin Leather Roll is a copy of a now lost building inscription of Senwosret I, and an early eighteenth dynasty writing board preserves a scribe's Hieratic rendition of a stela of King Kamose, of which only a few fragments have survived. In the latter case, the Hieratic version appears to be a fairly faithful copy of the hieroglyphic original, differing only in the fuller orthography of some words and in the positioning of some of the signs to accord more with Hieratic practice. In contrast, a Hieratic papyrus inscribed with a poem on Ramesses II's Battle of Kadesh diverges sufficiently from the hieroglyphic versions to suggest that there was a distinct original Hieratic version from which Hieratic copies were made. A lengthy Demotic petition of the Persian period includes uncial Hieratic copies of two stone stelae of Psamtek I, and some late Hieratic religious papyri seem to have been transcribed from hieroglyphic originals.

Learning Hieratic. What is known about the educa-
tion of a young Egyptian scribe derives mainly from the copious amount of inscriptional material in Hieratic from the workmen's community of Deir el-Medina. Unlike modern analytical instruction in ancient Egyptian, in which the student is introduced to hieroglyphs before Hieratic, the ancient student learned Hieratic first. Through the laborious process of memorizing the proper Hieratic orthography of individual words in their entirety without really spelling them out sign by sign, the student gradually became acquainted with the orthographies of a large stock of words, which at any given period tended to be written in a fairly consistent manner. The student learned that a group of signs—some of which were indeed phonetic—followed by one or more determinatives was essentially a unit that corresponded to a given spoken word. This procedure is understandable, since the child had grown up from infancy immersed in the spoken language. The pedagogical approach was therefore more holistic than analytical; the student even learned how to write entire sentences without the sort of analytical approach now used in the teaching of ancient Egyptian.

In the New Kingdom, the *Book of Kemit*, which was in epistolary form and included phraseology drawn from the ideal biography, served as a primer. Found recorded on hundreds of ostraca, this early Middle Kingdom composition is characterized by archaic forms of the Hieratic signs, not overly cursive, and was the only text still regularly written in vertical columns. Following this introduction to Hieratic, the student was presented with the *Satire on the Trades* and other Middle Kingdom literary compositions, which he learned to write horizontally from right to left. Henceforth, all Hieratic that he would pen was in horizontal lines. Subsequently in his education, the student was taught to inscribe texts composed in the colloquial language of the New Kingdom, now known as Late Egyptian. The Late Egyptian Hieratic texts used for instructional purposes included literary works as well as samples of documents such as letters. Although the student was not taught to think analytically about the Hieratic writing system, gradually it would have become obvious to him that there was some underlying phonetic system that was operative, as he drew comparisons between the writing of words with similar consonantal structure. Only when the student was eventually introduced to hieroglyphs would he become more analytic in his approach to orthography.

It is uncertain whether scribes learned Hieratic before hieroglyphs during the Old Kingdom, when students were trained on an apprenticeship basis and the center of education was at the Memphite palace, to which even sons of provincial governors were sent to be educated among the princes. The two extant Old Kingdom writing boards, whose didactic role is indicated by their list nature, are inscribed in hieroglyphic, not Hieratic. Since in Old Egyptian the divergence between hieroglyphic and Hieratic orthographies was not as marked as later on, it is possible that hieroglyphs were taught at an earlier stage.

Hieratic through History. The oldest Hieratic inscription is in ink on a jar naming King "Scorpion," just prior to the first dynasty. In addition to the king's name, the vessel's contents are indicated in much the same way as a slightly earlier inscription of King Ka does in ink hieroglyphs. The earliest Hieratic signs bear a close resemblance to contemporary hieroglyphs, but after this initial phase Hieratic underwent its own independent development.

That Hieratic was written on papyrus as early as the first dynasty is inferred from the existence of an uninscribed roll from the tomb of Hemaka at Saqqara. During the first three dynasties, brief Hieratic inscriptions in both black and red ink were penned on pottery and stone vessels as well as wooden labels. Beginning in the early Old Kingdom, quarry marks and other Hieratic inscriptions are found in connection with pyramid complexes; limestone ostraca make their first appearance in the fourth dynasty. From Gebelein in the south of Egypt come the oldest inscribed Hieratic papyri, which are datable to the second half of the fourth dynasty and concern a building project and supplies. The Abusir Papyri of the fifth and early sixth dynasties are extensive, consisting of royal decrees, letters, and numerous accounts pertaining to the operation of funerary temples at Abusir. In all Old Kingdom papyri a continuous text is written in vertical lines, though the accounts, arranged in a grid system, contain entries inscribed horizontally. The Hieratic of the Gebelein and particularly the Abusir Papyri exhibits maturity in the standardization of the cursive forms. From Elephantine in the south, there is a corpus of Old Kingdom Hieratic texts of the late sixth dynasty, principally letters and legal documents; they are generally less cursively written than the Abusir archives. In the nearby late Old Kingdom cemetery at Qubbet el-Hawa, many pottery vessels have been discovered with Hieratic notations giving personal names and identifying the contents.

What is noteworthy about Hieratic inscriptions of the Old Kingdom and most of the First Intermediate Period is the absence of literary texts. This deficiency may simply be due to accident, or it may be indicative of a dearth of creative writing on a broad scale. In the religious realm, there are a number of papyri of probable First Intermediate Period date that contain funerary texts in Hieratic, written in vertical lines. From the same period come several letters to the dead, mostly on pottery but also on papyrus. The script of these documents tends to be quite individualistic or local, perhaps reflective of the breakdown of a uniform educational system during a period of political fragmentation.

What is known about the situation at the beginning of the twelfth dynasty is that there was an imperative necessity to recreate a competent scribal bureaucracy loyal to the king and able to perform effectively the necessary administrative tasks. Therefore, a concerted effort was made to educate young scribes, and to this end new literary compositions were composed to be copied in Hieratic by students in the schools.

From the early twelfth dynasty, there are the Hekanakhte archives, primarily letters and accounts, and the Reisner Papyri, dealing with a building project in Middle Egypt. The Illahun Papyri from the pyramid town and valley temple of Senwosret II and administrative papyri of the thirteenth dynasty reveal through their highly developed cursive hands the success of the educational program. The Middle Kingdom witnessed the development of a marked distinction between the clear uncial script and the more rapidly executed cursive business hand. Under Hyksos domination, good uncial Hieratic is exhibited in the literary Papyrus Westcar and a mathematical treatise.

From the eighteenth dynasty there are medical, literary, and nonliterary texts in Hieratic. In general, the distinction between the book hand and the business hand is less extreme than in the late Middle Kingdom; even in nonliterary documents the signs are generally clearly formed, and the number of ligatures is minimal. During this dynasty, regional variations in the Hieratic script are not readily apparent, but this may be due to the limited amount of material from both the North and the South with which to make valid comparisons.

The Ramessid period presents a wealth of Hieratic texts. With such an abundance of Hieratic documents, it is possible to discern two developments. One is the increasing separation between the uncial and cursive business hands, a distinction that becomes especially marked in the twentieth dynasty in such documents as the Wilbour Papyrus, which displays extreme cursiveness, far removed from the book hands of literary and religious documents. Although the majority of Hieratic inscriptions come from the Theban area, there exist a fair number of documents, both literary and nonliterary, penned in the North, making it possible to identify regional variants in the forms of certain Hieratic signs. The document that most clearly demonstrates regional differentiation in the uncial Hieratic is the Great Harris Papyrus, pieced together from individual sections written by scribes of Thebes, Memphis, and Heliopolis. Such local differences might be attributable to a gradual weakening of the central government located at Piramesse in the eastern Delta and the rising political and religious significance of Thebes.

Following the Ramessid period, the split between the clear uncial Hieratic, used mainly for religious texts, and the extremely cursive script of administrative documents becomes acute, making it difficult to discern the relationship of the two scripts. Religious documents, such as the *Book of Going Forth by Day*, reflect a phase in which the Hieratic is even influenced by hieroglyphic forms—indeed, occasional signs in these texts are quite clearly hieroglyphs. But the administrative documents of the twenty-first dynasty are written in a very cursive Hieratic, which might be regarded as an early phase of Abnormal Hieratic.

Abnormal Hieratic. Once believed to be a version of Demotic, Abnormal Hieratic is a highly cursive version of Hieratic used in the Theban area during the twenty-fifth and twenty-sixth dynasties. Abnormal Hieratic, which derives ultimately from the script of Upper Egyptian administrative documents of the second half of the twentieth dynasty, is represented by about a hundred and fifty legal texts, land leases, letters, and economic texts. A Saite oracular papyrus from Thebes has its main portion in normal Hieratic, whereas some of the witness texts are penned in Abnormal Hieratic.

Demotic, whose origins are to be sought in the poorly attested Hieratic business hand used in the North during the twenty-first through the twenty-fifth dynasties, developed in Middle and Lower Egypt in the seventh century BCE. During the reign of Amasis, Demotic superseded Abnormal Hieratic in the South to become the standard script for secular documents throughout the entire land. Although Demotic became the dominant script in affairs of daily life, the conservative uncial Hieratic continued to be used for religious literature until the second decade of the third century CE.

BIBLIOGRAPHY

Brovarski, Edward. "Two Old Kingdom Writing Boards from Giza." *Annales du Service des Antiquités de l'Égypte* 71 (1987), 27–52. The use of writing boards with lists in a scribe's education.

Brunner, Hellmut. *Altägyptische Erziehung*. Wiesbaden, 1957. Remains the basic work on the Egyptian educational system, including how scribes were trained to write.

Brunner, Hellmut. "Hieratisch." In *Handbuch der Orientalistik*, first series, *Der Nahe und der Mittlere Osten*, vol. 1, Ägyptologie, part 1, *Ägyptische Schrift und Sprache*, pp. 40–47. Leiden and Cologne, 1973. Offers a comprehensive survey of Hieratic.

Gardiner, Alan H. "The Transcription of New Kingdom Hieratic." *Journal of Egyptian Archaeology* 15 (1929), 48–55.

Gasse, Annie. *Données nouvelles administratives et sacerdotales sur l'organisation du domaine d'Amon, XXᵉ–XXIᵉ dynasties, à la lumière des papyrus Prachov, Reinhardt et Grundbuch (avec édition princeps des papyrus Louvre AF 6345 et 6346–7).* 2 vols. Bibliothèque d'Étude, 104. Cairo, 1988. The appendix of this work discusses the highly cursive Hieratic script of late New Kingdom and twenty-first Dynasty administrative documents and provides a paleography of the most characteristic signs.

Goedicke, Hans. *Old Hieratic Paleography.* Baltimore, 1988. An informative discussion of the origin and evolution of Hieratic; provides a comprehensive paleography from the Early Dynastic period through the early twelfth dynasty.

Janssen, Jac. J. "Literacy and Letters at Deir el-Medîna." In *Village Voices: Proceedings of the Symposium "Texts from Deir el-Medîna and their Interpretation" Leiden, May 31–June 1, 1991*, edited by R. J. Demarée and A. Egberts, pp. 81–94. Leiden, 1992. Considers literacy among men and women of the village of Deir el-Medina.

Janssen, Jac. J. "On Style in Egyptian Handwriting." *Journal of Egyptian Archaeology* 73 (1987), 161–167. Explores the delicate issue of identifying the handwriting of individual scribes.

Malinine, Michel. *Choix de textes juridiques en hiératique "anormal" et en démotique.* Paris, 1953. The introduction includes discussion of how northern and southern styles of Hieratic in the New Kingdom led to the development of Demotic and Abnormal Hieratic.

Malinine, Michel. "L'hiératique anormal." In *Textes et langages de l'Égypte pharaonique: Cent cinquante années de recherches, 1822–1972; Hommages à Jean-François Champollion*, vol. 1, pp. 31–35. Cairo, 1973. A general survey of scholarly work on Abnormal Hieratic.

Möller, Georg. *Hieratische Paläographie, die aegyptische Buchschrift in ihrer Entwicklung von der fünften Dynastie bis zur römischen Kaiserzeit.* 3 vols. 2d rev. ed. Leipzig, 1927–1936; reprint, Osnabrück, 1965. This standard, but much dated, paleography of Hieratic from the Old Kingdom to the Roman period contains useful discussions of the sources. Scant attention is paid to the cursive administrative hands of the late New Kingdom and Third Intermediate Period.

Posener, Georges. "L'écriture hiératique." In *Textes et langages de l'Égypte pharaonique: Cent cinquante années de recherches, 1822–1972; Hommages à Jean-François Champollion*, vol. 1, pp. 25–30. Cairo, 1973. A general survey of scholarly contributions to Hieratic paleography.

Posener, Georges. *Littérature et politique dans l'Égypte de la XIIᵉ dynastie.* Paris, 1956. Includes discussion of the role of Hieratic literary texts in education.

Posener-Kriéger, Paula. "Les travaux de l'Institut Français d'Archéologie Orientale en 1986–1987." *Bulletin de l'Institut Français d'Archéologie Orientale* 87 (1987), 299–336. Information about the Hieratic clay tablets from Balat, p. 301.

Posener-Kriéger, Paula. "Travaux de l'IFAO au cours de l'année 1988–1989." *Bulletin de l'Institut Français d'Archéologie Orientale* 89 (1989), 291–341. Information on additional Hieratic tablets from Balat, pp. 294–296.

Vleeming, S. P. "La phase initiale du démotique ancien." *Chronique d'Égypte* 56 (1981), 31–48. Offers a good discussion of the regional origins of Abnormal Hieratic and Demotic.

Wente, Edward F. "The Scribes of Ancient Egypt." In *Civilizations of the Ancient Near East*, edited by Jack M. Sasson, vol. 4, pp. 2211–2221. New York, 1995. A general discussion of scribes, including remarks on their education in Hieratic and literacy.

EDWARD F. WENTE

Demotic

The most cursive script developed by the ancient Egyptians is Demotic, used for more than one thousand years. The oldest known Demotic inscription dates from the middle of the seventh century BCE; the latest dates from the middle of the fifth century CE. The term *Demotic* comes from Greek δημοτικά ("popular"), first used by the historian Herodotus in the fifth century BCE to distinguish it from Egypt's "sacred" Hieratic and hieroglyphic scripts. The Egyptians referred to Demotic as *sḫ n šꜥ.t* ("letter" or "document writing")—more accurately rendered in Greek

ʾεπιστολογραφική by the Roman-period scholar Clement of Alexandria.

Demotic developed from Hieratic and, like Hieratic, was always written from right to left. Most Demotic texts were written in ink using a brush (or, later, reed) on papyrus or on ostraca. Formal documents, those intended to have a longer lifespan, were normally written on papyrus; when formal documents were found written on ostraca, the common assumption was that they were drafts for a final version that would have later been written on papyrus. It has been suggested, however, that the texts from Ain Manawir, in the Kharga Oasis, dating from the Second Persian Occupation (343–333 BCE), may have been written on ostraca because papyrus was not available. In addition to the common use of papyrus and ostraca, Demotic inscriptions were occasionally written on wood, linen, and other materials; when a Demotic inscription was carved in stone or metal, the script became more angular and the orthography (spelling) was occasionally simplified.

Demotic used both ideographic signs, including determinatives, and phonetic signs, including a series of uniliteral or "alphabetic" signs (some of which had different forms when used word-initial than when used word-medial or word-final; some had specific forms to be used when written over or under another sign). The traditional or historic written form of the word (in earlier scripts) formed the basis for Demotic, which reflected historic orthography, not the contemporary pronunciation. The phonetic inventory of Demotic differs only slightly from that of earlier and later stages of the language; thus, /d/ was not distinguished from /t/ but /l/ was regularly distinguished from /r/. Two new transliterations were frequently used: ḥ as distinct from h and ṯ, the latter frequently used to indicate that a final written t is to be pronounced. Individual signs were often schematized and many Demotic signs consisted of ligatures connecting two or more phonetic or ideographic signs. Scribes seem to have learned to read and write by memorizing words as units.

From the twenty-sixth dynasty through the Second Persian Occupation (664–333 BCE), Demotic (or "early Demotic") consisted largely of individual signs or ligatures with clear connections to Hieratic and hieroglyphic signs. Extensive work now identifies the Hieratic and hieroglyphic counterparts and antecedents of early Demotic signs. Yet Demotic soon developed its own orthographic conventions, distinct from those of Hieratic. By the Ptolemaic period (304–30 BCE), Demotic script was considerably smaller in size and more stylized than in its early period, and connections to Hieratic had lost their importance (if they were even recognized by the scribes). There are also distinctions in orthography and paleography that have been attributed to local scribal "schools" (e.g., Memphite versus Theban), to differences in textual genres

(e.g., literary versus administrative versus private), and to the skill and care of individual scribes. (Most of the known texts were probably written by professional scribes; even the literate might hire or employ a professional for the sake of expertise, proper legal terminology, or clarity of handwriting.)

By Roman times (30 BCE–395 CE), Demotic scribes had begun writing with the Greek reed, rather than the Egyptian brush, which led to what has been called a "spidery script," lacking thick and thin strokes. During that period, scribes also frequently added phonetic (usually alphabetic) signs to earlier conventional spellings or replaced conventional historic spellings with "alphabetic" ones, as if they were indicating changes in pronunciation or providing phonetic aids to help in recognizing nonobvious word-groups or ligatures. When a scribe copied a text that had been written much earlier, he normally updated paleography and orthography, but occasionally "archaisms" would be transferred from the older text to the newer. (A Ptolemaic period copy of a legal manual found at Hermopolis includes sporadic early Demotic paleography and calendrical dates for the agricultural cycle, which suggest that the original was written much earlier—early Persian period or earlier.)

Demotic script developed in the North of Egypt, contemporary with the development of Abnormal Hieratic in the South, especially as documented in Thebes from the Third Intermediate Period into the twenty-sixth (Saite) dynasty. The first king of the twenty-sixth dynasty, Psamtik I (r. 664–610 BCE), expanded his power base from the city of Sais in the western Nile Delta to incorporate all the Delta and then all of Upper Egypt. Along with the imposition of Saite rule over Upper Egypt, and the appointment of men from the Delta to certain positions in Upper Egypt, came the spread of Demotic script from the Delta southward. The oldest Demotic papyri, dating to the twenty-first year of the reign of Psamtik I, come from el-Hiba in the Nile Valley, just south of the entrance to the Faiyum. Although both Demotic and Abnormal Hieratic were cursive developments from the contemporary Hieratic, the differences in orthography between the two systems were accompanied by differences in the form or style of the documents and in vocabulary, especially legal terminology and phraseology. The oldest extant inscription reflecting Demotic is a stela from Saqqara that records the sale of a house; although the text is written in Hieratic, both the script and the legal terminology indicate that it is a transcription from a Demotic original. Local scribes in Thebes, the Upper Egyptian scribes about whom there is the most information, gradually converted to Demotic—first adopting bits of orthography, phraseology, and formatting; then converting entirely to Demotic so that, by the reign of Amasis (r. 569–526 BCE) at the end of the twenty-sixth dynasty, Demotic had become Egypt's accepted script for administrative, legal, and economic documents.

Among the more than 150 early Demotic documents written between individuals—many, but not all, of whom have titles connecting them with a religious establishment—there are sales documents (of priestly offices, real estate, farm animals, or self into slavery), land leases, gifts of land, loans, business-partnership agreements, cessions, private letters, and documents establishing economic and inheritance rights between spouses and between parents and children, as well as divorce contracts and transfers of property between heirs. Traditionally, such personal legal documents were written records of declarations made by one party (or group of people acting as a whole), accepted by another party (or group of people), and recorded by a scribe who served as notary, usually on behalf of a temple. Certain types of documents were normally written using the format of letters. Documents of a more official nature included accounts, a temple inventory and tax receipts (usually written by temple scribes concerning land within the domain of the temple; the role of temple scribes in "central" administration is also reflected in the 10 percent transfer tax for selling land, "the 1/10 of the accounting[?] that scribes and/or representatives (of the king)" collected by and for the temples).

That fewer formal administrative than personal documents were preserved in Demotic may reflect the fact that administrative documents would normally have been recycled (e.g., their backs [*verso*] were used for private or literary texts; whole papyri were converted to cartonnages, etc.) when they were no longer needed by the administrative entity for whom they were made. Private documents were retained to prove ownership and were passed along to new owners when property was transferred. Several family archives exist from the period. Those documents reflect an individual's or family's economic interests and transactions and were retained and stored because of their ongoing legal and economic importance. Especially common in the documents and archives are the choachytes (*wзḥ-mw*, "water-pourer"), who carried out rites for the deceased and whose papers may have been preserved more frequently than those of others since they were stored in the tombs where the choachytes worked, not in their homes.

Although most early Demotic texts are clearly documentary in nature, Papyrus Rylands IX, a long petition for redress from a senior (Persian?) official in Memphis under Darius I (521–486 BCE), incorporated certain literary features. In addition, the petition concluded with three columns of hymns to the god Amun in Demotic, although the copies of the dedicatory inscriptions on two private stelae that are quoted in the text are given in Hieratic. Regular use of Demotic for literary (including religious)

texts occurs slightly later. The oldest known literary texts in Demotic—fragments excavated at Saqqara—date from the fourth century BCE and a significant number of new literary compositions are known from Ptolemaic times. The Ptolemaic compositions are new examples of traditional Egyptian literary genres, especially narratives (e.g., the stories involving Setna Khaemwase, the high priest of Ptah at Memphis), mythological texts (e.g., fragments of the story of Horus and Seth), (pseudo-)prophetic texts (e.g., the Demotic Chronicle, in which a theory of legitimate kingship is presented using the kings of the twenty-eight to thirtieth dynasties as good and bad examples of leadership: this text was used to predict or justify a rebellion in Herakleopolis after its actual occurrence), word lists, and Wisdom Literature or didactic texts (e.g., *The Instructions of Ankhsheshonqy*). Some compositions or compilations fall into scientific or reference categories (e.g., mathematical texts, legal manuals presenting a compilation of case law). Although in Ptolemaic times most religious compositions continued to be written in Hieratic (or hieroglyphs), numerous private religious documents were written in Demotic, including funerary stelae, votives, graffiti, letters to gods (the Demotic counterpart of the earlier letters to the dead), and oracle questions; there are also records of dreams, sometimes accompanied by interpretations.

The culmination of Demotic literary production occurred in early Roman times (first and second centuries CE); a massive amount of literary material is known from many literary genres, but much is preserved only fragmentarily. They were composed, copied, and stored in Egyptian temple libraries. Several narrative cycles are also preserved, as well as mythological texts, satire, and Wisdom texts. Some texts are clearly updatings and reworkings of earlier (Hieratic or Demotic) material. Both astronomical and astrological texts appeared for the first time in Demotic in Roman Egypt; other handbooks included medical and dream interpretation manuals. What seem to be magicians' handbooks were among the latest preserved (most exemplars date from the third century CE or later). For the first time, there was also extensive composition of religious texts in Demotic—including ritual books, hymns, and funerary papyri—composed both for private individuals and as new liturgical texts. Massive collections of Roman-era Demotic literary papyri were found at sites in the Faiyum; it has been suggested that they reflect the last updating of temple libraries.

Most of the wide range of documentary texts attested in early Demotic is also preserved from Ptolemaic Egypt, supplemented by several new types. Demotic was also used for private letters, labels, graffiti, and jottings of various kinds. Well attested are formal administrative documents—those prepared by employees of the administra-

SCRIPTS: DEMOTIC. *Papyrus inscribed with Demotic script.* (University of Pennsylvania Museum, Philadelphia. Neg. # S8–80163)

tion (e.g., census lists) and those prepared by institutions recognized by the state (e.g., trial records, rules for cult guilds, or tax receipts for a wide range of new taxes)—as are documents made by individuals to recognized institutions or to employees of the state. Some texts that have been considered literary materials may actually have been administrative (e.g., the legal manuals). The first Ptolemies encouraged Greek literacy in order to staff a Greek-speaking and -writing administration, because so many Egyptians learned to read and write Greek and participated in the administration. The Ptolemaic administration accepted the full legal status of documents written in Demotic, although documents that had to be filed with the central administration eventually had to have a Greek summary, or docket, added, evidently for the benefit of employees literate only in Greek. Bilingual individuals evidently had the right to choose in which language (and, thus, following which legal system) they would have a

document composed. Depending upon the situation, one language (and system) might have been preferable to the other. For example, since Egyptian women could own, buy, and sell real and personal property on their own, in their own names, but Greek women had to be represented in legal documents by men, normally a close male relative, a woman with the option might prefer a Demotic scribe to carry out her business. Through time, as more Egyptians learned Greek and more families became bilingual, many family archives included both Greek and Demotic documents.

When Egypt was incorporated into the Roman Empire (in 30 BCE), the Romans seem to have denied official validity to documents written in Demotic. Only Greek was acceptable. Thus, although there are some contracts in Demotic from early Roman times, the only public documents written in Demotic that occur in large numbers from this period are tax receipts. Nevertheless, Demotic continued to be used in the Egyptian cultural sphere, as indicated by the extensive collection of Roman period Demotic literary texts mentioned above, as well as Demotic funerary stelae. Roman period mummy tags, frequently written in both Demotic and Greek, can be seen not only as identification labels for the mummies but also, with their short religious formulas, as inexpensive versions of funerary stelae. In addition, literate Egyptians wrote letters in Demotic and left Demotic graffiti in quarries, tombs, and temples throughout the Late period. This personal use of Demotic, frequently to express faith in the Egyptian gods, outlasted even the conversion of most of the country to Christianity; the latest dated Demotic text is a graffito, at the temple of Isis on the island of Philae, dated to 452 CE.

Throughout the millennium during which Demotic was used, it was never the sole Egyptian script available. Hieroglyphs were retained especially for formal inscriptions, and Hieratic was used for literary, and especially religious, texts. Demotic was not the official, administrative script during most of the period of its use. Aramaic was used during the Persian occupation, whereas Greek was used in the Ptolemaic and Roman periods. Nonetheless, Egyptians, especially temple personnel, frequently or even regularly used Demotic to communicate with the central administration. This led to varied interactions between the Demotic and the other scripts and languages. From the early Demotic period, there are stelae presenting a hieroglyphic or Hieratic transcription of a contract originally written in Demotic. There are also Hieratic literary texts contemporary with early Demotic, in which the grammar of the text incorporated Demotic features. In later examples, Demotic was used to add notes or glosses to a hieroglyphic or Hieratic text. Some Demotic literary texts appear to be translations of earlier Hieratic or hieroglyphic texts. In other cases, the Hieratic and Demotic were used for different sections of a text; in a handbook describing the process of embalming a deceased Apis bull, Demotic was used in general, but the ritual passages were retained in Hieratic; individual words or signs were occasionally written in Hieratic, even in the very late Demotic magical texts mentioned above. Occasionally the scripts seem to share more equal status. Synodal decrees, issued by the senior Egyptian priesthood in honor of the middle Ptolemies, present the formal decree in Greek, Demotic, and hieroglyphs.

Translation between Demotic and non-Egyptian languages has been well attested, for example, the translations between legal texts in Demotic and contemporary documents in Aramaic during the Persian period and in Greek during the Ptolemaic period. There are also a number of literary texts: the Demotic fragments of the *Story of the Wise Man Ahiqar* were presumably translated from Aramaic; a Greek translation exists of at least a portion of the *Myth of the Sun's Eye* and a section of the legal manual mentioned above. In addition, there are literary texts preserved only in Greek that seem to be translations from Demotic (e.g., the *Dream of Nektanebo*, portions of the *Alexander Romance*, concerning Nektanebo). The extent of the influence of Greek literature and literary forms on Demotic, and vice versa, has been intensively discussed.

During the Ptolemaic period, individual Greek words (names, titles, and professions) could be written in Demotic using the appropriate "alphabetic" signs. Also, one long text in Aramaic was written using a restricted inventory of Demotic "alphabetic" signs and determinatives. Similarly, Egyptian names and other words were written in Greek characters in Greek documents. In early Roman times, Old Coptic—using the Greek alphabet and a more or less consistent set of Demotic "alphabetic" signs for sounds not represented in the Greek alphabet—was developed for transcribing Egyptian into Greek. It could be used for glossing individual words written in a Demotic text or, rarely, as a stand-alone script for writing a text. Old Coptic standardized into the final Coptic alphabet by about the third century CE.

[*See also* Grammar, *article on* Demotic.]

BIBLIOGRAPHY

Depauw, Mark. *A Companion to Demotic Studies.* Papyrologica Bruxellensia, 28. Fondation Égyptologique Reine Élisabeth. Brussels, 1997.

JANET H. JOHNSON

Coptic

In the history of the Egyptian language one comes close to a history, in a nutshell, of the written word itself: a rich history, writ large in stone monuments and small on ceramic amulets and ostraca, papyri and paper. The Egyptian language possesses the longest continuous testimony of inscription of any on earth. It has been written in one form or another, and sometimes several forms simultaneously, for five millennia. The Egyptian language is also among the earliest to be reduced to writing: one finds hieroglyphic labels on stone and ostraca in Egypt on the eve of the third millennium BCE. Only the Sumerian cuneiform of Mesopotamia is an older witness to writing. It would be another millennium before Linear B would appear on Crete, and another half millennium before the Hittites crafted hieroglyphs in Anatolia and Syria. The Chinese, who claim the oldest writing system still in wide use, began developing their classical logograms in 1300 BCE, seventeen hundred years after similar efforts in the Nile Valley.

The history of Egyptian writing is not only long but also varied. Over time, Egyptian scribes developed several writing systems to represent their ancestral language, developments that pressed the limits of orthography. Following Plato's discussion of verbalized concepts, syllables, and letters,—*logoi, syllabai,* and *grammata,* respectively—and their relation to *stoicheia* or elementary sounds, scholars now describe writing systems as logogrammatic, syllabary, or alphabetic. Logogrammatic systems are made up of logograms, conventional graphic signs, often of pictorial origin, that represent concepts. In a syllabary, graphic signs represent phonemes that are vocalic, or combinations of vocalic and consonantal sounds. An alphabet is constituted of letters, graphic signs that represent one phoneme. Most languages use only one writing system; a few—such as Japanese, possessed of both a syllabary and a system of symbols originally derived from Chinese—simultaneously employ two. The Egyptians used all three kinds of writing system variously in antiquity and in the first centuries of the Roman period. About three thousand years after the first monumental inscriptions appeared, the Egyptian language was rendered in an alphabetic script that eventually superseded hieroglyphic writing and its derivatives.

The Egyptian language was first rendered logogrammatically in its famous hieroglyphs. Though many of the ancient Egyptian logograms, their stylization notwithstanding, resemble the objects or ideas they were written to represent, they also had phonetic associations. The Egyptians attached phonetic value to logograms, which they in turn used to represent the sounds of words unrelated in meaning. The ancient language was thus a complex system of logograms and phonograms that were extended rebuses. Some hieroglyphic phonograms represented a single consonant; others stood for two or three. Thus, biconsonantal and triconsonantal graphic signs were a functional syllabary for part of the writing system. Often a logogram would be accompanied by phonogrammatic elements to aid in recognition and, perhaps, pronunciation. This complementation, as Egyptologists call it, was a partial or complete rebus of the logogram with which it was written.

Such was the monumental script of the Egyptians: complex, sophisticated pictures telling stories of empire and immortality. The colorfully painted iconic forms of the first dynastic monuments are more reminiscent of the cave paintings of Lascaux than the cursive ligatures of later Egyptian literati. Hieroglyphic script is indeed a thing of beauty that apparently remained a joy, at least to some literate Egyptians, forever. It remained in use, *mutatis mutandis,* from the first dynasty until the fourth century CE. The stylized pictures that became the first Egyptian script were suited to and perfected for monumental representation. For ancient Egyptian scribes, three discrete but related considerations informed the graphic syntax of their compositions: esthetics, hierarchy, and danger. Hieroglyphic writing was never far from artistic composition; size, proportion, and abhorrence of a vacuum determine the orientation of figures in inscribed space. In a culture for which the pyramid was both the most important architectural structure and the root metaphor for the cosmos, hierarchy is the premier organizing principle. Thus, the names of gods and kings take precedence over other elements of the sentence; in this hierarchical privileging of divine and royal epithets, called "honorific transposition," prestige is a species of syntax. In this way, signifiers are given the honor due those things they signify. Likewise, in hieroglyphs signifiers were also accorded the power of those things they signified. Through graphic art, the power of articulation becomes the power of representation. The figures of writing are more than icons; they are themselves the essence of the power of that which they signify. This is the logic of magic, and this logic further influenced Egyptian writing in the rendering of certain hieroglyphs that were held to be so potent that they were written only in abbreviated or otherwise altered form. The heads of insects, the tails of snakes, even the bodies of some human figures, were sometimes omitted because their full strength threatened the sacral spaces in which they were inscribed. For this reason Apophis, the serpentine enemy of the sun god Re, is often written with daggers piercing its torso.

In the second half of the third millennium BCE, Egyptian scribes coined a shorthand form of hieroglyphics, called Hieratic, to facilitate nonmonumental writing. Hieratic is but the writing of hieroglyphs abbreviated and further stylized, and was no doubt presaged by the cursive hieroglyphic labels of the Predynastic period. It often served as the script for drafts of hieroglyphic texts. The two systems, hieroglyphic and Hieratic, coexisted and even informed each other until the end of the third century CE. Unlike its logogramic predecessor, Hieratic usually reads right to left. In early Hieratic the lines of writing are columnar, but after the twelfth dynasty the script is universally horizontal, one of several orthographic changes that attended the end of the Middle Kingdom and the beginning of the Second Intermediate Period in the second quarter of the second millennium BCE. By the time of the New Kingdom, around 1500 BCE, Hieratic had developed several subspecies of script. A traditional book hand was reserved for literary texts, and a secular, cursive hand was used to record business transactions and the like. During the Third Intermediate Period in the first quarter of the first millennium BCE, the development of the cursive hand followed the fault line of the classic split between the northern and southern regions of the country that had given rise to the ancient pharaonic epithet, "ruler of the two kingdoms." In Upper Egypt, the scribes of the south fashioned the so-called Abnormal Hieratic script, which is more slanted, ligatured, and spare than the script that preceded it. In the North, however, Hieratic was supplanted by a script the Egyptians themselves described as "writing with letters." The Greeks were later to give it the name by which it is known today, Demotic, that is, the "popular" script *(demotika)*. In the Late period, the Northern rulers extended their hegemony over the South, and one of the features of this extension was the use of Demotic as the script of government, business, and law throughout the country. The latest specimen of Demotic is a graffitto from the middle of the fifth century CE.

In the late dynastic period, Egyptians experienced foreign rule for the first time in their long history. Assyrian domination was successfully repelled by the militarily vigorous twenty-sixth dynasty, but Egypt later succumbed to the Persians in the fifth century BCE and again, briefly, in the middle of the fourth. Alexander of Macedon then brought Greek hegemony to Egypt in 332 BCE. The Hellenistic combination of centralized administration and cultural chauvinism was to leave a lasting impression on the Egyptians, especially in the realm of language. In Papyrus Heidelberg 114, from the middle of the third century BCE, there is the oldest specimen of spoken Egyptian transcribed in the Greek alphabet. This script, called Proto-Coptic, was the twilight of alphabetized Egyptian writing.

The transliteration of Egyptian words was attended by orthographic experiments that required at the same time a departure from and a continuation of the Demotic heritage. Egyptian scribes of the Common Era adopted most of the capitals and a few lowercase letters of the Greek alphabet and they included characters from Demotic to convey sounds that occurred in Egyptian but not in Greek. In this phase of alphabetization, called Old Coptic, the Greek letters of the new alphabet were combined with Demotic borrowings. Old Coptic transliteration used more Demotic signs before the dawn of Coptic orthography proper. In Papyrus Bodmer VI, the *Book of Proverbs* is translated into Coptic using Old Coptic letters. At the same time, Demotic letters were being appropriated variously, and other scribes were rendering Coptic in Greek letters without Demotic supplement. The Chester Beatty Isaiah Papyrus is a Greek translation of the *Book of Isaiah* with Coptic glosses, dating from the third century CE. These glosses are written using the Greek alphabet exclusively, without recourse to Demotic characters. In the Delta region of Bashmur, scribes apparently forwent the use of Demotic letters as late as the eighth century CE: perhaps this was a scribal characteristic of what Athanasius, the eleventh-century grammarian and bishop of Kus, speaks of as the Bashmuric dialect.

Magical papyri, dating from the first century CE, also provide short but fully alphabetic texts. In magic, the source of all power is the word fitly spoken: the exactitude of incantation requires that the language be rendered with precision. At the same time, some Egyptian signs had apparently taken on magical significance in and of themselves, and so these appear in amulets and on mummy labels in addition to the seven autochthonous letters that were to become the alphabetic norm. In this way, magicians, sorcerers, and their clients found the alphabetical script congenial to their will to power.

The idiosyncratic transcription of magical formulae, though an important motivation for alphabetic writing in Egypt, was not sufficient impetus for true orthography. The wide adoption of alphabetized Coptic script, and thus the transition from Old Coptic to Coptic proper, is coeval with Christianity in Egypt. Various reports of the importance of biblical literacy among the Copts suggest the widespread existence of at least portions of a Coptic Bible by the middle of the third century CE. Athanasius tells us that the early hero of Egyptian monasticism, Antony, divested himself of all his wealth and became a desert recluse upon hearing the scripture lesson of *Matthew* 19.21, "If you would be perfect, go and sell what you have, and give to the poor." Because Athanasius also says that Antony was illiterate in Greek, one must conclude that Antony heard the life-transforming words of scripture in his mother tongue. The fourth-century church historian Epiphanius reports that a Coptic Christian intellectual named Hieracas, born in the third quarter of the third century CE, commented on the Bible in the Egyptian tongue (*Haer.* lxvii). Even if Hieracas was a glossator of a Greek text of the Bible, his are the first recorded efforts of Coptic exegesis. By the first quarter of the fourth century CE, the monastic rule of Pachomius dictated that aspirants read twenty psalms, two epistles, or some other part of the holy scriptures before being received into the monastic community. Those who were not literate had to know their scriptures by heart. At least the Psalter, Gospels, and Epistles must have been available to the Copts in a written form of their native tongue. Alphabetic writing was thus standardized for Christian literature.

TABLE 1. *The Coptic Alphabet.*

Letter	Letter Name	Greek Letter	Sound
ⲁ	alpha	α	short "a"
ⲃ	beta	B	v
ⲅ	gamma	Γ	g
ⲇ	dalda	Δ	d
ⲉ	ei	ε	short "e"
ⲍ	zeta	Z	z
ⲏ	(h)eta	H	"a" (not a diphthong)

TABLE 1. *The Coptic Alphabet (continued).*

Letter	Letter Name	Greek Letter	Sound
ө	theta	Θ	th
ι	iota	I	long "i" (not a diphthong)
κ	kappa	K	k
λ	lambda	λ	l
м	mi, me	M	m
н	ni, ne	N	n
ӡ	ksi	ξ	ks
о	ou	о	short "o"
п	pi	π	p
р	ro	P	r
с	simma, semma	ς	s
т	tau	τ	t
Υ, ΟΥ	he	Υ	ou, w
ф	phi	φ	ph
χ	chi	χ	ch
ψ	psi	ψ	ps
ω	o	ω	long "o" (not a diphthong)

Autochthonous letters

†	ti		ti
ϛ	bau		"6"
ϣ	shai		sh
ϥ	fai		f
ϩ	hori		h
ь, ꙅ	chai (Bohairic only)		German "ch"
ϩ, ꙍ	(no name recorded; Achmimic only)		German "ch"
x	janjia		j
ϭ	chim(m)a		"ch" of "church"
ⲧ	(no name recorded)		number 900

The resulting Coptic alphabet (Table 1) is made up of twenty-four letters taken over from the Greek and seven derived from Demotic to represent Egyptian sounds. Several letters stand for sounds that are sometimes represented with digraphs. The letter "i," ι, is frequently rendered "ei," ει. The letter † is a Demotic form for the digraph τι the usage of which becomes standard for the spelling of certain words, such as the verb † "give." As in the Greek alphabet, ӡ renders the consonantal blend *ks*, and ⲧ the sound *ps*. Hieroglyphic Egyptian had different signs for the aspirated, laryngeal, and fricative sounds often represented in transliteration by the letter *h*. These consonantal distinctions had become confused by the rise of Demotic, and they collapse into one alphabetic sign rendered differently in different dialects. Two sounds heretofore important in the language—the glottal stop and the guttural, the *aleph* and *ayin* of Semitic philology respectively—have no alphabetic representation in Coptic. They are recognized in alphabetic script only implicitly and discerned in the Coptic lexicon only etymologically in some dialects: glottal stops came over into Coptic as long vowels, and gutturals as doubled long vowels.

In some syllabic combinations, the long vowels *i* and *u* are consonantal—that is, *y* and *w*, respectively—and are sometimes called semi-consonants. When *i* is consonantal, it may be so indicated by a diaeresis, but Coptic scribes observed this orthographic convention neither universally nor consistently. The consonantal *u* may be discerned only by its syllabic context. Coptic scribes used the superlinear stroke or, in some manuscripts, a superlinear accent mark, to indicate syllabification and aid in reading. Though not vocalic markers themselves, these strokes signal to the reader that a syllable comprised of one letter is to be read as the sound of the letter assisted by a semi-vowel—that is, a shortened short *e* sound, the *shwa* of Semitic philology. Superlinear strokes are also used to designate abbreviations and *nomina sacra*, and long superlinear strokes are frequently used in manuscripts to stand for an *n* at the end of a line of writing.

Coptic was written in continuous script with no intervening spaces or marks between syllables, phonemes, or words. Occasionally the full stop was used to divide sentences, and the double stop, less frequently, to mark paragraph divisions. Even this minimal punctuation appears fitfully in manuscripts. The regularity of punctuation in printed Coptic texts, usually borrowed from Greek conventions, is a happy conceit of modern publication. As in much of ancient paleography, the scribe's use of punctuation and other diacritical apparatus was more a prerogative to be exercised than a rule to be followed.

Some diversity in Egyptian writing derived from ancient dialectal differences in pronunciation. Spoken Egyptian no doubt possessed several dialects throughout its long life. The variant pronunciations and usage, and the orthography that gave them regular expression, were manifest in regional forms of literary Coptic. The number of distinguishable Coptic dialects, and the basis of distinction, are debated hotly among scholars. The regional origin and distribution of Coptic dialects is also a matter of dispute. Scholarly consensus recognizes a half-dozen dialects scattered along the Nile Valley. The two most widespread dialects, owing to their use in Coptic Christian literature, are Sahidic and Bohairic. Sahidic, the ubiquitous dialect of the south (Arabic, *aṣ-ṣaʻid*), is also called "Theban" after the ancient upper Egyptian city of Thebes. Sahidic was the dialect of Coptic scripture and liturgy from the third through eleventh centuries CE, and became the classical language of Coptic monasticism through the literary craft of Shenoute and his disciple Besa. Bohairic, so named because it was the dialect of Lower Egypt—that is, of the north (in Arabic, *al-buhairah*)—was apparently native to the western Delta, including Alexandria and Nitria. The *h* sound, written as ϩ in Sahidic, is rendered alphabetically in Bohairic as ь or ꙅ, signs retained for this sound only in this dialect from Old Coptic, in which it was occasionally substituted by the Greek letter *chai* (χ). Bohairic Coptic became the ecclesiastical language of the Coptic Orthodox Church in the third quarter of the eleventh century CE. It remains alive in modern Coptic liturgy and the contemporary poetry of Pisenti Rizkallah.

Less influential were the dialects of Middle Egypt. The Achmimic dialect of southern Middle Egypt takes its name from Akhmim, the premier city of the region. The Achmimic alphabet uses neither the *hori* of Sahidic nor the *chai* of Bohairic, but yet another version of the Demotic sign for the *h* sound, the sign ϩ. Fayyumic was the dialect of northern Middle Egypt, that is, the Faiyum. This dialect is immediately recognizable by the substitution of ⲗ *l*, for ⲣ, *r*, in many of its words, and the use of superlinear dots between letters instead of strokes. The Subachmimic dialect was native to the region south of Akhmim as far as Thebes. It is a dialect of the texts found at Nag Hammadi and of the literature of the Egyptian Manichees, both corpora dating from the fourth and fifth centuries CE. Another dialect, called Middle Egyptian, apparently originated midway between the Nile's northern and southern extremities. This nomenclature, however, is infelicitous, since "Middle Egyptian" is also the name of the classical phase of Egyptian hieroglyphics between 2000 and 1500 BCE. The Coptic dialect called "Middle Egyptian" is found near Oxyrhynchus, ancient capital of the nineteenth nome of Upper Egypt, and is thus also known as Oxyrynchite.

Although the Egyptians started writing with pictures on ostraca and stelae three thousand years before the birth of Christ, later hymns, horoscopes, and hagiography called for shorter and shorter shorthand. With the rise of Christianity and the codex, the Egyptian language underwent changes to accommodate a new communications technology and a new faith. In so doing, ancient Egyptian became Coptic, and the Coptic alphabet became the means by which the people of Egypt wrote new oracles in a new version of the old language of the pharaohs.

[See also Grammar, *article on* Coptic.]

BIBLIOGRAPHY

Crum, W. E. "An Egyptian Text in Greek Characters." *Journal of Egyptian Archaeology* 28 (1942), 20–31.

Crum, W. E. "Coptic Documents in Greek Script." *Proceedings of the British Academy* 25 (1939), 249–271.

Davies, W. V. *Reading the Past: Egyptian Hieroglyphs.* Berkeley and Los Angeles, 1988.

Goodwin, C. W. "On an Egyptian Text in Greek Characters." *Zeitschrift für ägyptische Sprache und Altertumskunde* 6 (1868), 18–24.

Griffith, F. L. "The Date of the Old Coptic Texts, and Their Relation to Christian Coptic." *Zeitschrift für Ägyptische Sprache und Altertumskunde* 34 (1901), 78–82.

Ishaq, Emile Maher. "Coptic Language, Spoken." *The Coptic Encyclopedia,* vol. 2, pp. 604–607. New York, 1991.

Kahle, Paul E. *Bala 'izah.* 2 vols. London, 1954. Vol. 1, pp. 193–268, offers a classic treatment of Coptic dialects and their effect on orthography, with an unparalleled survey of inscriptional, papyrological, and codicological evidence.

Kasser, Rodolphe. "Alphabet in Coptic, Greek." *The Coptic Encyclopedia,* vol. 8, pp. 30–32. "Alphabets, Coptic." *The Coptic Encyclopedia,* vol. 8, pp. 32–41. "Alphabet, Old Coptic." *The Coptic Encyclopedia,* vol. 8, pp. 41–45. New York, 1991.

Layton, Bentley. "Coptic Language." In *Interpreter's Dictionary of the Bible, Supplementary Volume,* pp. 174–179. Nashville, Tenn., 1976.

Metzger, Bruce M. "The Coptic Versions." In *The Early Versions of the New Testament,* pp. 99–152. Oxford, 1977. Excellent overview of the translation of New Testament literature into the Coptic language. His discussion of dialectical evidence is especially helpful.

Plumley, J. Martin. *An Introductory Coptic Grammar.* London, 1948. The first chapter (pp. 1–19) treats the alphabet, providing a good overview with helpful etymological explanations.

Worrell, W. H. *Coptic Sounds.* Ann Arbor, 1934. Still indispensable for helping the scholar of the language make sense of Coptic orthography and dialectical variation.

ALLEN DWIGHT CALLAHAN

SCULPTURE. [*This entry surveys the various types of ancient Egyptian sculpture, with reference to stylistic development, media used, and the contexts and purposes of sculpture. It comprises five articles:*

An Overview
Royal Sculpture
Private Sculpture
Divine Sculpture
Wood Sculpture

For related discussions, see Bronze Statuettes; *and* Relief Sculpture.]

An Overview

Ancient Egypt produced more statuary than has any other civilization in the history of the world. Egypt's longevity, national wealth and stability, and the abundance, variety, and quality of its materials made this possible. The motivation sprang from the profound belief that spirits—both human and divine—needed to be housed, appeased, and nurtured within appropriate sculptures. Each statue provided a permanent body for the earthly habitation of a given god's or deceased individual's spirit. These statues were not considered to be alive, but the spirits residing within were, and according to Egyptian religion they received prayers and offerings and bestowed benefactions with lifelike vigor.

The king controlled sculpture production with two priorities in mind: providing cult statues and temple decorations for the gods, whom he represented on earth, and furnishing himself with images to house his own spirit throughout the afterlife. Once his needs were well on their way to being met, high officials and eventually lesser officials could expect to be favored with portraits, *shawabtis,* or other sculpted offerings of their own. Frequently, these nonroyals' goods are inscribed with the words "A boon which the king gives to [name]."

Pharaoh's control began with the substances from which sculpture was made. The most readily available and easily worked resources—clay and mud brick—were rarely used for sculpture after the Predynastic period, perhaps being too common for such lofty purposes. The finest materials—hard stones, fine metals, precious woods, and ivory—were difficult to obtain and were strictly governed. Gangs of workers overseen by trusted officials went on long journeys to acquire the best stones, organic materials, and metals for statuary. Sculptors themselves traveled to the quarries and carried out much of their work on the spot, thus lightening the stone block for transit. In some highly productive reigns, like that of Amenhotpe III, stylistic differences exist between sculptures in brown quartzite, quarried in the North, and those in granodiorite, coming from the South, suggesting that different sculptors traveled to and worked in each quarry. Faience and glass relied on ubiquitous raw materials, particularly sand; however, the techniques and equipment required to create the finished products resided in the skilled craft shops attached to temples and palaces and were in the domain of pharaoh as ruler and as high priest. Thus, a vast and complex industry evolved to supply Egypt's tombs and temples with sculpture. It included not only the sculptors, but also quarrymen, miners, traders, hunters, transporters, painters, metalworkers, scribes, officials, and overseers.

Each substance was imbued with meaning. Gold, the divine metal that never tarnished, was regarded as the skin of the gods; silver was their bones. Turquoise was sacred to Hathor, since both blue and green symbolized fertility. White equaled purity, making both limestone and calcite (also called travertine or Egyptian alabaster) appropriate for religious and funerary statuary. Wood was sacred to the mother goddesses, Nut, Hathor, and Isis, who were often depicted as trees providing shade and sustenance for the deceased. Red granite had solar significance; black granodiorite stood for Egypt's ancient name, Kemet, "the Black Land," and its fertile, silt-fed soil flanking the Nile. The color black also had underworld associations, and many statues of Osiris were made of black basalt. Quartzite, called *biꜣt* ("wondrous") by the Egyptians, ranged from solar golds to reds, and it glinted appropriately in the sunlight.

Egyptian sculpture was made to last for eternity. The blocky form used throughout the millennia served this purpose well. Backs of figures are often supported by pillars or slabs; arms are clenched closed to the body; legs are attached to chairs or other supporting features. There are no jutting parts to break off. The center of gravity is kept low, so the statue is bottom-heavy and quite stable. For example, where the king is seated on a massive throne, most of the weight is well below the center line of the statue's height. Where a figure stands against pillars or slabs, these are cut thicker toward the bottom.

To fulfill its purpose, statuary had to be recognizable to the appropriate spirit. Thus, the ancient Egyptians invented the *twt ꜥnḫ,* the "perfected likeness." That such images can be and often are true portraiture can best be proved by comparing representations of pharaohs like Ramesses II with their mummies. Further securing a statue's identity was a hieroglyphic inscription identifying the individual by name, title(s), and sometimes lengthy history. This was considered crucial to the statue's ability to function properly, especially when courtiers' portraits often bore the facial features of their pharaoh out of piety, flattery, or, perhaps, familial relationship.

Anthropomorphic images of gods generally bear the features of the pharaoh in whose reign they were sculpted, because he was their representative on earth. They are identified by their attributes—headgear, staves, and other emblems, as well as by inscriptions. Divine animals—Hathor cow, Apis bull, Anubis jackal, Bastet cat, and Horus falcon—appear with each detail of conformation and deportment carefully and realistically recorded. These too are inscribed with the relevant names and epithets.

Sculptors' names never appear on these images, as they did rarely on religious art until recent centuries. Although most records are now lost, it is known that the best Egyptian sculptors were famous in their day, some gaining enough wealth and prominence to have important tombs or large villas. Pharaohs discriminated among craftsmen, elevating particularly worthy individuals in their social standing. Officials close to the king must have vied for the opportunity to avail themselves of these masters' services. For example, Amenhotpe III's vizier, Amenhotep, son of Hapu, and his brother-in-law, the high priest Anen, were among the few nonroyals to be sculpted in granodiorite by the artist who had provided Amenhotpe III himself with his best portraits in that stone.

One may speak of sculptors as individuals, but the production of a statue was a team effort. Most two-dimensional scenes of sculptors at work show several individuals chiseling or polishing different parts of the same statue. Actually, the word "crew" is probably more appropriate, since the master sculptor must have overseen his troops much as an ancient Nile barge captain ran his ship's crew. Texts from Deir el-Medina suggest that the teams of workers who decorated the nineteenth dynasty royal tombs were divided into right and left halves like the crews of Nile rowing ships.

Aesthetically, the composition of Egyptian statuary also relies on a strict division of sides. Frontality is a significant principle of Egyptian statuary, but profile views are equally important—sometimes more so, because the first view of a statue could be from the side rather than from the front. In fact, the hieroglyph for "statue" is the profile view of a (wooden) statue of a man holding a long staff in one hand and a scepter in the other. Three-quarter views of Egyptian statuary are often unsuccessful because there is a point at which the torso and the buttocks of a seated figure do not line up, even though the front view and the side views are perfectly convincing. Animal figures, such as striding bulls, recumbent jackals, perched falcons, and sitting cats, are best viewed in profile, which in each case imitates the appropriate hieroglyph.

To plan their work, sculptors relied on a grid system, traces of which are occasionally visible on unfinished bases and statues. Using grids made it possible to standardize figural proportions during a given period and to change them as successive tastes required. According to the Old Kingdom's classic proportions, the width of a standing man's shoulders equal one-third of his height from floor to hairline. Toward the end of the Old Kingdom, shoulders became narrower, but in the eleventh dynasty they approached the classic form again. Following a narrowing of proportions during the thirteenth dynasty and the Second Intermediate Period, eighteenth dynasty shoulders broadened once again during a period of imperialistic conquest and muscular might; then they narrowed toward the end of the dynasty during a trend toward ease and feminization.

Centuries of destruction, reuse, and dispersal have caused parts of broken statues to become separated. Many modern efforts at reuniting long-lost parts have been successful after narrowing down the possibilities by first studying styles, materials, inscriptions, and proportions, and finally by examining and matching up likely prospects at their breaks.

Historical Analysis. Egypt's great age and relative immutability make it difficult to capsulize its art without taking advantage of vast generalities. Some periods and types of sculpture are thus omitted from the following discussion. Reigns and dynasties were not equally strong in artistic activity. In fact, there are only five great eras of heightened creativity in sculpture: the late Predynastic period and Early Dynastic period, and the fourth, twelfth, eighteenth, and twenty-sixth dynasties, to which one might add the early Ptolemaic period. Each of these epochs is marked by a burst of energy—in terms of imagination, workmanship, and volume—directed at developing new ideas or revisiting latent ones with renewed zeal.

Predynastic period. Most Predynastic sculpture is rather abstract or composed of generalized forms. Hu-

SCULPTURE: AN OVERVIEW. *Fourth dynasty statue of Khafre, now in the Egyptian Museum, Cairo.*

man figures emphasize large, staring eyes and sexual attributes.

The earliest sculpture in the round yet found is a half life-size oval terra cotta head with gouged eyes, nostrils, and slit mouth, unearthed at Merimda at the western edge of the Nile Delta. Dated to the end of the fifth millennium BCE, it recalls earlier Neolithic stone masks found near the Dead Sea. Ivory—both elephant and hippopotamus—was favored for small anthropoid statuettes in the Badarian period (5500–4000 BCE). A buxom female of 14 centimeters (5.5 inches), in the British Museum, stands on athletic-looking legs and has large, staring, incised eyes and a wide, bountifully incised pubic triangle. Dated to the Amratian period (Naqada I, 4000–3500 BCE) and totally different in style is the Louvre's 24-centimeter (9.5 inch) elongated male figure, its tapering legs close together, its genitalia emphasized, and its eyes inlaid. Yet a third style is represented by the Louvre's 6.5 centimeter (3 inch) bearded, robed figure, whose abstract composition resembles a chess pawn. Rather similar Chalcolithic ivory figures have been found near Beersheba in present-day Israel.

Brooklyn's elegant "bird lady" of 33.8 centimeters (13.2 inches) represents a unique type of Egyptian late Predynastic terra cotta female with upflung arms, birdlike head, large breasts, and elongated yet steatopygic, cone-shaped lower body. The first mother-and-child (standing) composition appears at this time.

Animal figures appeared in the form of slate palettes (Naqada I/II) carved bilaterally into silhouettes of hippos, cattle, birds, turtles, jackals, giraffes, and fish. From the same time are flints chipped bifacially to form silhouettes, especially of birds and lizards, as well as the occasional quadruped. Fine stone vessels were also carved in animal form during the fourth millennium.

The first considerable stone sculpture is Oxford's basalt, 39.5 centimeter (15.4 inch) bearded man, wearing a penis sheath, skullcap, and long, broad beard. It is pillar-shaped—nearly cylindrical—with legs clamped together, arms clenched flat to the sides. Although it vaguely resembles some Amratian and Gerzean ivories, its skillful carving suggests a date contemporary with a peak period of stone carving at the end of the Predynastic era and Early Dynastic period, when slate palettes and stone mace heads were in production.

Early Dynastic period. Arch realism is the hallmark of the best Early Dynastic (Archaic) sculpture, whether in a delicate stone vessel carved in the shape of a folded leaf, like one in Cairo, or in the oldest three-dimensional representation of a pharaoh yet found, the British Museum's tiny stoop-shouldered king in ivory. Discovered by W. M. Flinders Petrie at Abydos, the latter depicts a thin-faced, perhaps aged king in white crown and diamond-patterned robe, striding left leg forward, as would become customary for standing male figures for the rest of Egyptian history.

Found at Hierakonpolis's temple are the earliest known stone portraits of a pharaoh, a pair representing the second dynasty's last king Khasekhemwy, enthroned and wearing the White Crown; the pair are now shared by Cairo (graywacke, 56.5 centimeters/22 inches) and Oxford (limestone, 62 centimeters/24 inches). In contrast with Oxford's bearded man, these statues are the earliest examples in stone of what would become Egypt's sculptural rule: four-sided composition wherein the profiles are as strong as the frontal view.

Officials, too, began to have their hard stone statues at this time. They were usually seated, wearing short layered wigs. Their quality, in terms of both composition and workmanship, is inferior to Khasekhemwy's.

A few stone animal sculptures are known from the Early Dynastic period, such as Berlin's 52 centimeter (20 inch) calcite baboon, and Cleveland's 15.4 centimeter (6 inch) calcite frog goddess, Heket. Faience, appearing around 3000 BCE, provided a new material for the creation of small figurines—rather lumpy, poorly articulated animals, along with the occasional human figure. The finest animal carvings from the period are Cairo's ivory lion game pieces, found in a tomb at Abu Rowash and dated to the first dynasty, and the heavily muscled and veined ivory bull-leg furniture supports from Abydos. Unique to the Early Dynastic period are the clay bucrania (bulls' heads) set around the perimeter of royal *mastabas*.

Third Dynasty and Old Kingdom. From the third dynasty to the end of the Old Kingdom, nearly all known human figure sculpture appears to be funerary. As wealth increased, so did the size of royal tombs, the number of private tombs, and the amount of statuary. This dawn of monumental sculpture rose with the powerful and mysterious, over life-size (142 centimeters/55 inches), painted limestone statue of the third dynasty king Djoser from his *serdab* at Saqqara, now in Cairo. Like Khasekhemwy, he is enthroned and robed, with one hand on his thigh and the other across his chest. He is the first pharaoh to be depicted wearing a *nemes*-headcloth, here over a heavy, long wig.

Probably carved by the same sculptor are the earliest known life-size portraits of private persons, the standing limestone statues of the official Sepa and his wife, Nesa, now in the Louvre. Nesa stands erect with her feet together, typical for statues of women. Sepa steps forward onto the left foot. He awkwardly holds a tall staff flat against his chest and leg and a baton against his right arm, so they would not protrude and break. By the fifth dynasty, such items were used only on wooden statuary. On stone statuary a more easily contained roll of cloth replaced them thenceforth.

Egyptian sculpture blossomed during the fourth dynasty. While the only remaining portrait of Khufu, the builder of the Great Pyramid, is a tiny (7.5 centimeters/3 inches) ivory seated figure—the first royal to be shown bare-chested and wearing the short kilt—the magnificent portraits of Djedefre (though fragmentary), Khafre, and Menkaure more than compensate. Egypt's largest and most famous sculpture, the Great Sphinx (70 meters/224 feet long), guarding Khafre's valley temple and causeway, was carved in place from a colossal nodule of hard limestone. The composition of this pharaoh-faced recumbent lion, itself a god named Horemakhet, is so secure and so well developed that one suspects earlier models, but none exist.

Found at his pyramid's valley temple and now in Cairo, Khafre's proud enthroned image is the most majestic of

SCULPTURE: AN OVERVIEW. *Family group statuette, eighteenth dynasty.* This group of two men and a boy may represent three generations of male relatives—or the same person in different stages of life. The statuette dates from the reign of Akhenaten and is of painted limestone. (The Metropolitan Museum of Art, Rogers Fund, 1911. [11.150.21])

all pharaonic portraits. Bare-chested and barefoot, he wears only the short kilt and *nemes.* A falcon protectively clasps the back of the king's head in its wings. Deftly executed on the sides of the throne is a design that would become standard for such statues, the *sm3-t3wy*, representing the unification of Egypt. Khafre's over life-size (168 centimeters/65.5 inches) image is carved in the hardest of Egyptian stones, a black-speckled gray diorite favored by this king.

Most of Menkaure's portraits, found at his valley temple and now in Cairo and Boston, depict him in graywacke groups, either a dyad with his wife, or in triads flanked by deities. In either case, the women reach behind him clasping his far arm with one hand. Both his wife's and the deities' faces resemble his own pudgy face. Below

the neck their physiques are taut and perfect, the female forms clearly visible through the sheer, clinging fabric of their gowns. In the fifth and sixth dynasties, group statues with fairly generic faces become commonplace for officials, who sit or stand next to a relative or wife and sometimes children, often in the same affectionate embrace as Menkaure enjoyed.

While in most periods private portraiture is a clone of royal imagery, the fourth dynasty is exceptional. The best portraits are highly individualized. Some are true masterpieces, like Cairo's brilliantly painted limestone portraits of Rahotep and Nofret (121 centimeters/47 inches), whose quartz and rock crystal eyes give them a particularly lifelike appearance; Hildesheim's ponderous Hemiunu (150 centimeters/58.5 inches) with his narrow eyes, aquiline nose, double chin, and flabby chest; the Louvre's alert, pinch-faced red scribe (whose cross-legged sitting pose became the convention for this profession); and Boston's sensitive life-size bust of the care-worn Ankh-haf. In the best likenesses, sculptors observed the natural asymmetry of the human face and preserved this feature of Egyptian portraiture throughout history.

Ankh-haf's bust is a new type: an image finished from head to chest, not broken from a full statue. It may be related to the so-called reserve heads, realistic, life-size limestone portraits terminating at the base of the neck and without hair or ears, which were placed at the entrances to the subterranean burial chambers of some fourth dynasty *mastaba*s at Giza.

Many wooden statues of private individuals remain from the fifth and sixth dynasties, the favored trees being native acacias and sycamore figs. Ebony was imported from farther south in Africa. Wooden statues were made in pieces attached by the same techniques used in furniture joinery, a fine example being a striding statue of the bald and rotund lector-priest Ka-aper (112 centimeters/60 inches) in Cairo. Inlaid eyes heighten the sense of realism. Some officials' wood statues depict them at various stages of life, such as Brooklyn's three statues of Metjetji, two of which wear youthful faces with rather generic features; the third and finest bears an older, personalized portrait.

Unique to the Old Kingdom is a class of small painted limestone servant images for the tomb. Usually less than 20 centimeters tall, each one depicts a man or a woman working to supply the deceased with the necessities of life in the next world: kneading bread, brewing beer, or making clay pots.

The first large-scale metal sculpture is Cairo's 177-centimeter (69 inch) copper statue of the sixth dynasty pharaoh Pepy I, found at Hierakonpolis with Khasekhemwy's statues. Pepy's statue and a smaller one tucked inside were probably not cast, but rather hammered over a wooden core. The eyes were inlaid. A deftly carved small (21 centimeters/8 inches) calcite statuette of the same king, now in Brooklyn, recalls the robed Khasekhemwy statues, with the addition of a falcon perched sideways on the back of the throne. Pepy II appears as a small child in the earliest known enthroned mother-and-child composition, a calcite statuette in Brooklyn.

After Pepy II's reign, the government of Egypt collapsed, the Memphite families losing control of everything south of Saqqara. The ensuing one hundred and fifty years, known as the First Intermediate Period, saw little in the way of sculpture production.

Middle Kingdom. As Egypt's political epicenter moved from Memphis to Thebes, so the construction of monuments moved away from Giza, Saqqara, and other Old Kingdom sites to Middle Egypt, Upper Egypt, and the Faiyum. Pharaohs began to commission multiple monumental statues in series. Enough sculpture remains from the Middle Kingdom that in many reigns we begin to have a sense of statues not as individual entities but as elements in grand schemes.

Stone sculpture revived under the strong rule of the eleventh dynasty king Montuhotpe II. His stolid, painted sandstone seated portrait of 138 centimeters (54 inches), found ritually buried at his funerary temple at Deir el-Bahri and now in Cairo, wears the Red Crown of Lower Egypt, making it official that this Southerner has conquered the North. Montuhotpe's design for the decoration of his funerary temple included a processional avenue flanked by rows of figures of himself, mummiform as Osiris.

The twelfth dynasty king Senwosret I developed a rich sculptural program for his funerary complex at el-Lisht, including ten nearly identical, over life-size, unpainted white limestone statues of himself enthroned. Two cedarwood statuettes of this same king, also found at el-Lisht and now shared by Cairo and New York, depict the king with a pleasantly round face, large, intelligent eyes, and a perfect physique.

Senwosret III and his son Amenemhet III commissioned more statuary than ever before to fulfill complex decorative schemes for their temples. Some were done in nearly identical multiples, like the group of over life-size granodiorite seated statues of a bare-chested Senwosret wearing kilt and *nemes*, made for the Montu temple at Medamud. The faces are starkly realistic, with sunken eyes, drooping eyelids, protruding cheekbones, hollow cheeks, distinct prognathisms, and huge ears. Some appear aging or indeed old, yet the bodies remain fit and muscular. More than one hundred portraits are known for Senwosret III, the greatest being Kansas City's monumental head in brown quartzite, a stone that was not used before the Middle Kingdom. Amenemhet III erected a pair of colossal 12 meter (38.5 foot) seated statues (now lost), also in the newly favored quartzite, not far from his Faiyum pyramid temple, the famous Labyrinth of Classical authors. An unusual life-size granodiorite double statue of Amenemhet III from Tanis, now in Cairo, shows him as twin images of a Nile god, carved in the same block. Sphinxes continued to be part of pharaonic imagery, and female sphinxes also began to appear.

The technology to smelt and cast bronze developed during this period, perhaps in the Near East, some examples having been found in the Judaean desert. The earliest are copper alloyed with arsenic, as in the magnificent statuettes of Amenemhet III in the George Ortiz collection, Geneva. Most dramatic is the half life-size bust of the king with inlaid eyes, wearing a separately cast *nemes*-headcloth.

During the Middle Kingdom, women began to appear in individual portraits, such as Cairo's large seated granodiorite statue of Senwosret II's queen, Nofret, wearing a banded and curled Hathor wig, and Boston's monumental granodiorite image of Lady Sennuwy, found in the burial of her husband, the governor of Kerma.

High officials were now allowed temple statues, apparently for the first time. Many have been found at Karnak. Officials also set up offering chapels at Abydos and filled them with stelae and sculpture, benefiting from the proximity to the Abydene deities. Hard stones such as granodiorite and quartzite were increasingly used for private individuals. New forms appeared, such as the block statue, wherein the individual squats, with his body—except for head, hands, and feet—enveloped in a robe, providing broad blank fields for long inscriptions. Toward the end of the twelfth dynasty, pair statues with spouses standing hand-in-hand reappear. A variation of this composition has members of a family, sometimes numerous, standing against a stela.

New fashions materialized for both men and women, such as the male cone-shaped, chest-high, calf-length kilt, which provided room for longer inscriptions. The female dress was a tubular skirt suspended from two broad straps over the breasts.

During the First Intermediate Period and through the Middle Kingdom, large wood statues of private individuals continued to be made for tombs at Asyut, probably from local wood. A well-carved, brilliantly painted example with inlaid eyes, representing an official named Nakht, is in the Miho Museum, Misono, Japan. One of the most important life-size wooden statues remaining from Egypt was made toward the end of the thirteenth dynasty for the obscure king Hor. On its head is the carved wood hieroglyph for the word *ka*, suggesting that this is a divine statue for the *ka* of a dead king. Both the design and the execution of this statue are surprisingly fine, considering that it was made during a time of political and economic decline.

Complex genre scenes and figures, carved in wood and then painted, were made to provide necessities for the afterlife. From Mesehti's eleventh dynasty tomb at Asyut, and now in Cairo, are two sets of model soldiers, the figures carved and equipped separately and attached to wooden palettes, each 190 centimeters long. Meketre's eleventh dynasty Theban tomb divulged several models: a group of barges carrying fishermen with nets; a diorama where the deceased sits in a kiosk with friends and family, inspecting twenty variegated cattle herded by a dozen herdsmen; a carpentry shop and a weaver's studio—each populated by ten or more figures contained in small, open-roofed boxes. Other painted wooden tomb companions include female offering bearers, sometimes well over a meter tall, balancing heavy containers on their heads with one hand while carrying an extra vessel or animal in the other.

Also specific to this period are well-modeled, prettily painted faience statuettes made as tomb gifts. Most impressive are turquoise-colored hippopotami with birds, insects, and plants drawn on them. The hippos' jaws and/or legs were broken to render them ritually powerless to destroy the tomb owners' fields during the afterlife. Small white faience jerboa mice may have warded off other rodents from food offerings. Partially or completely nude adolescent girls with truncated legs, also in turquoise faience, may have been fertility figures. This type of figurine continued to be made, though much more crudely, in terra cotta during the Second Intermediate Period.

*Shawabti*s, mummiform servant statuettes inscribed with promises to work in their owners' fields throughout the afterlife, were invented during the Middle Kingdom, as were canopic jars with heads sculpted in human form. Both became standard burial equipment for centuries to come.

New Kingdom. The first images after the Second Intermediate Period, such as London's seated limestone figure (35 centimeters/14 inches) of Tetisheri, mother of King Sekenre Ta'o, were awkward, yet the New Kingdom was to become the most prolific period for Egyptian sculpture. Colossal size, number, and rich materials were emphasized, along with the highest quality of workmanship. Temple statuary increased both for kings and wealthy commoners.

Sculpture production multiplied exponentially during the coregency of Hatshepsut and Thutmose III, in an attempt to exceed all that had been done in the past. Most of Hatshepsut's statuary comes from her funerary complex at Deir el-Bahri. Torn down and thrown into rubbish heaps by her nephew, Thutmose III, who outlived her, these statues have been found and reconstituted by the Metropolitan Museum. They include thirty-eight statues, ranging in height from 264 to 624 centimeters (8.6 to 20.3 feet), of the queen mummiform as Osiris, which were engaged to—that is, built up in courses with—the pillars and walls against which they stood. Those wearing the White Crown stood south of the temple axis; those wearing the Double Crown stood north. Freestanding statues and sphinxes lined the processional avenue used on festival days, while the way to the door of the sanctuary was lined with a variety of statues: sphinxes, freestanding statues of the queen, and kneeling statues. Most of these were in red granite, and many were colossal. The most personal is an over life-size (190 centimeters/74 inches) indurated limestone portrait of a narrow-waisted, small-breasted woman sitting in the *nemes* headdress and short kilt of a king. Her face is thin, with an aquiline nose and a narrow

SCULPTURE: AN OVERVIEW. *Twenty-sixth dynasty statue of Osiris from Saqqara, now in the Egyptian Museum, Cairo.* (Scala / Art Resource, NY)

chin, features which tended to be softened in her more idealized imagery. Separating Hatshepsut's idealized portraits from those of her nephew is often difficult. At times the sculptors may have purposely generalized some portraits, allowing the cartouches added at the end to seal the statues' identities.

Thutmose III's archetypical portrait is Turin's 188-centimeter (73-inch) tall figure in black granodiorite. It sits in Turin close to a similar statue of his grandfather, Thutmose I. Like him, Thutmose III wears the *nemes* and short kilt, his powerful legs slightly spread, the sacred bull's tail visible between them. These statues are more monumental, broader, and more muscular than Middle Kingdom statues, in keeping with their aspirations for and success at international conquest. Thutmose III's favorite types of statuary are illustrated in the tomb of his last and greatest vizier, Rekhmire. They include sphinxes, the king kneeling and holding *nu*-pots, enthroned statues, the king bearing a tray of offerings, and the king kneeling and extending a large vessel. The use of a rare, hard white marble occurred during this reign.

More statuary remains from the reign of Amenhotpe III than from any other pharaoh to his time. His charming facial features—almond eyes, small nose, and thick, sensual lips bent in a constant half-smile—are those of the serene emperor of a secure land. He transformed Thebes on both banks of the Nile with his architectural and sculptural program. In front of his vast funerary temple on the west bank, he placed two colossal (17 meters/54.4 feet), brown quartzite statues, now wrecks. Additional colossi, remains of which are in London, Paris, and Luxor, stood according to their geographic symbolism in one of the courtyards. Perhaps as many as a thousand statues, including stone lions, sphinxes, and crocodiles, decorated the temple.

Across the river, the avenues between Karnak and Luxor were flanked by monumental statues of recumbent rams. Pylons were faced with colossi. Countless statues of the lion-headed female goddess Mut or Sakhmet were commissioned in dark granodiorite to fill her sanctuary between the two great temples. Discovered in a pit in 1989 is the most interesting statue made for the Luxor temple, a life-size red quartzite statue of the king as a statue standing on a sledge. More typical of his oeuvre are the granodiorite enthroned statues, like those in London, New York, and Luxor. Many of these were recut by later kings and are now difficult to recognize. Amenhotpe's renovations stretched a thousand miles south in the Sudan to Soleb, where he supplied temples with processional avenues of statuary, including the great red granite lions now in the British Museum.

The success of both Hatshepsut's and Amenhotpe's sculptural programs undoubtedly owed a great deal to the men who oversaw them, Senenmut and Amenhotep, son of Hapu, respectively. Both were honored with important portraits placed in temples. Senenmut's compositions include new inventions. In some he holds the statue of a deity (in Brooklyn, the serpent goddess, Renenutet), or embraces his queen's small daughter (Cairo). Amenhotep son of Hapu's sculptures are more traditional standing figures or cross-legged scribes, one depicting him as an old man. Other Amenhotpe III officials adopted the new compositions, like Cleveland's Minemheb, who kneels holding a shrine and divine statue, here Thoth's baboon.

Tomb statuary also existed. Some life-size images were carved in the living limestone rock at Thebes, then painted, and some were carved separately, but their quality is inferior to hard stone temple statues. Of fine quality are small hardwood statuettes, sometimes with eyes inlaid in glass. Bronze statuary occurs rarely and more often as small funerary furnishings, such as mirror handles or ceremonial weapons, rather than as royal or official portraits.

Dazzling small sculptures, probably temple gifts, were made in faience (the Metropolitan Museum's sphinx), wood (Berlin's tiny head of Queen Tiye), and glazed steatite statues (the Louvre's Tiy, Durham's Amenhotpe). Red and yellow jasper were used throughout the New Kingdom on composite sculptures, but the most beautiful representative is the yellow fragment with sensuous female lips, now in New York.

During the later eighteenth dynasty, female representations increased greatly in number and importance. Cairo's colossal limestone group from Medinet Habu shows a queen equal in size to her husband, with the royal daughters standing larger than life beside their parents' legs. Women also appear in exquisite small statuettes, such as George Ortiz's 48.5-centimeter (19-inch) tall serpentinite Princess Isis. Feminine dress became much more elaborate during this reign. Dresses were intricately pleated, and often worn with shawls. Wigs for both men and women became quite large and heavy with multiple tresses and braids.

Amarna period and Tutankhamun. In his later portraits Amenhotpe III appears rotund and Queen Tiye's figure sags, the realities of life appearing briefly in pharaonic representations. Their son Akhenaten advanced this realism to its extreme, adopting a wide-hipped, short-limbed, heavy-breasted, effeminate form for his own portraiture, for example on his colossi at East Karnak, now

in Cairo. This body type, coupled with an elongated face, has caused scientists to wonder if the king was diseased. In later years, however, his style was tempered, producing the Louvre's yellow stone statuette (64 centimeters/25 inches) of a well-fed Akhenaten enthroned, wearing the *nemes* and short kilt, a slight paunch spilling out over his belt. He is the first king to be shown almost always with pierced ears.

More female portraits are known from this reign than ever before. The later years produced Berlin's magnificent life-size painted limestone bust (48 centimeters/18.7 inches) of Akhenaten's queen Nefertiti, found in excavations of the workshop of the royal sculptor Thutmose at Tell el-Amarna, along with many other portraits of Nefertiti, royal princesses, and other women, as well as some male portraits.

On his return to Thebes, Tutankhamun carried many of the later Amarna stylistic traits with him, including the long chin, flaccid body, long torso, and short legs, but none of these in the extreme. The sculptures from his tomb represent types and materials otherwise known only from tomb paintings: wood statues in active poses, such as harpooning, and complicated inlaid and painted alabaster sculptural compositions. Highly naturalistic animal figures carved in ivory, such as New York's small gazelle and leaping horse, may also come from this reign.

Later New Kingdom. The nineteenth dynasty, especially the long reign of Ramesses II, called "the Great," was a period of revision and reuse of earlier monuments, as well as the construction of new ones. More colossal statuary remains from Ramesses II than from Amenhotpe III, perhaps because no subsequent king tore apart as many earlier monuments as did Ramesses. His statuary is more remarkable for its size than for its design, which is generally uninventive and academic. His best portrait however, is spectacular. Now in Turin, it is a variation of the traditional enthroned king (190 centimeters/74 inches). Holding a scepter and staff, he wears the *ḫprs*-crown; a long, finely pleated, fringed gown with sleeves; a pleated, fringed shawl over one shoulder, and sandals. The aquiline nose, small eyes, and pointed chin closely resemble the features of his mummy in Cairo. Queen Nefertari stands knee-high beside his leg on the Turin statue. The proportions of both figures are elongated, especially the limbs.

Ramesses the Great left colossal statues at many sites, including both banks of the Nile at Luxor, but nothing is more astonishing than the twin temple complex for himself and his wife at Abu Simbel, where both architecture and statues—pylon colossi, Osirid figures engaged with columns, and cult figures—are carved from the living rock. These figures are more idealized than the Turin portrait and the costume more traditional.

Many of Ramesses' portraits started out as portraits of

earlier kings, which he recut and reinscribed. He did not invent the practice, but he made tremendous use of it. Therefore, some portraits, like the Louvre's seated grano-diorite image, a recut statue of Amenhotpe III, appear awkward and not easily recognizable as Ramesses without his cartouches.

Temple statuary for high officials continue to be common, as did fine hardwood statuary. Private individuals' proportions, like the royals', are elongated, and their costumes and wigs long and elaborate. Canopic jars lids now bear different heads—baboon, jackal, falcon, and human—for the four sons of Horus. A new sculpture type, the limestone "ancestor bust," seems to have been set up in household shrines before eventually being transferred to tombs. The Miho Museum's superb solid silver statuette (41.9 centimeters/16.3 inches) of a falcon-headed god, overlaid with gold and inlaid with stone, probably dates to this period.

The decline after Ramesses II's death lasted through five dynasties until the Kushite revival of the twenty-fifth dynasty. The kings of the Third Intermediate Period, especially the Tanite kings of the twenty-second dynasty, specialized in reusing their predecessors' statues rather than creating new ones. They excelled in metal sculpture, however, such as the tiny gold statuettes—actually jewelry—from the royal tombs at Tanis, like the triad of King Osorkon II flanked by Horus and Isis. Queen Karomama II's portrait (59 centimeters/23 inches) in damascened bronze, acquired by Champollion in Thebes, is one of the finest bronze sculptures from antiquity.

Late period. When they gained power over Egypt and its wealth, the Kushites began to commission grand hard stone statuary for themselves. Berlin's granite sphinx of Princess Shepenupet II (82 centimeters/32 inches), Khartoum's monumental granodiorite King Tanwetamani, and Boston's Khonsu-ir-aa (43.5 centimeters/17 inches) are strong and important sculptures of the period, the first two at least from the Sudan. The finest work of the period, however, was produced for Egypt's central temples, such as Cairo's over life-size portrait of Queen Amenirdas and large statues of the mayor of Thebes, King Taharqa's great official, Mentuemhat, who virtually ruled Egypt. His portraits, especially his statue as an aged man, bear the arch-realism of the Old Kingdom.

Bronze statuary becomes more common and technically finer. Two twenty-fifth dynasty furniture legs, one in Boston and one in Khartoum, incorporate naturalistically modeled, perfectly cast geese with carefully incised feathers, eyes, and bills. Kings and queens become much more commonly portrayed in bronze statuettes, such as the University Museum, Philadelphia's Necho, Berlin's Taharqa, and Athens's Queen Takushit. Soon bronze-casting became a major industry in Egypt, and thousands of statuettes of divinities, both human—Osiris, Amun, Isis,

SCULPTURE: AN OVERVIEW. *Horus-falcon guarding the hypostyle hall of the temple of Horus at Edfu, Ptolemaic period.* (© Photograph by Erich Lessing / Art Resource, NY)

etc.—and animal—Bastet cats, Oxyrhynchus fish, Apis bulls, etc.—were produced to fill the needs of a rising middle class who wished to buy the favors of their gods.

At the same time, faience genre statuettes, such as female figures with monkeys, were produced for magical use within Egyptian folk religion. These were popular outside Egypt as well, in ancient Kush and throughout the Mediterranean, including Greece. During the Ptolemaic period, the production of faience votive statuettes of deities, both anthropomorphic and theriomorphic, moved into high gear, and nearly every Egyptian collection has examples of the fine robin's-egg-blue figures made from the fourth century BCE on.

More portraits of officials than of pharaohs survive from the twenty-sixth dynasty. Favorite poses are block statues and shrine offering statues. Middle Kingdom style was revived, sometimes so successfully that the later versions are difficult to separate from the originals. Much Late period statuary is bland and academic, but the best approaches the realism of Mentuemhat's statue. By the end of the dynasty, temples like Karnak were virtual forests of statuary; the eventual clean-up resulted in burying tens of thousands of stone statues and bronze statuettes in a pit within the temple, where they were found some twenty centuries later.

Persia's defeat of Egypt in 525 BCE nearly finished sculpture production in Egypt, although it revived briefly during the thirtieth dynasty, during which the native kings Nektanebo I and II refurbished temples and commissioned new statuary.

Ptolemaic period. Egypt's Greek rulers continued the sculptural traditions of the Nile Valley even while introducing their own. Discovered in Alexandria Bay in the 1990s were parts of colossal statues, perhaps of Ptolemy II and his queen Arsinoe, which in good pharaonic tradition probably graced temple pylons along with sphinxes, of which many survive. In order to gain favor with Egypt's powerful clergy, the foreign kings had themselves portrayed in traditional pharaonic poses (more standing than enthroned) and wearing the royal *nemes* and kilt, but smiling, slim, and effete, lacking the imperial bearing of their predecessors. Happy queens appear in filmy gowns, virtually nude, holding the *mnit* or other feminine attributes. Hellenistic style breathed a new type of voluptuousness into Ptolemaic women, whose femininity is expressed in large breasts rather than in the wide hips and thighs of Karomama, Nefertiti, and Tiy. Some, perhaps many, of these are recut statues from much earlier periods, such as the Miho Museum's Arsinoe II, a visibly slimmed-down statue of Amenhotpe III's Queen Tiy.

Vestiges of Egypt's traditional sculptural style lasted long after the death of the kingdom in 30 BCE. More than two hundred years later, funerary statues in the Romano-Egyptian catacombs of Alexandria were still being carved in limestone: standing figures, the left leg forward, wearing the traditional kilt, but with portrait and hair in Roman Antonine style. And Emperor Caracalla in the early third century was still depicted wearing the royal *uraeus* on his brow.

[*See also* Archaism; Art; Artists and Artisans; Bronze Statuettes; Funerary Figurines; Grid Systems; Portraiture; Relief Sculpture; *and* Sphinx.]

BIBLIOGRAPHY

Aldred, Cyril. *Akhenaten and Nefertiti.* Brooklyn, 1973. Exhibition catalogue with many examples of Amarna and pre-Amarna sculpture.

Arnold, Dorothea. *The Royal Women of Amarna: Images of Beauty from Ancient Egypt.* New York, 1996. Exhibition catalog with essays on Akhenaten's artistic revolution and the workshop of the sculptor Thutmose.

Arnold, Dorothea, Christiane Ziegler, et al. *Egyptian Art in the Age of the Pyramids.* New York, 1999. Exhibition catalog of Old Kingdom art, with essays on the conception and use of statuary.

Berman, Lawrence M. *Pharaohs: Treasures of Egyptian Art from the Louvre.* Includes nineteen portraits in the round of pharaohs from Djedefre to Nero, and a précis of each.

Bianchi, Robert S. *Cleopatra's Egypt: Age of the Ptolemies.* Brooklyn, 1988. Exhibition catalog analyzing the art of the Ptolemaic and Roman periods, with 140 entries on objects of all media ranging in time from the first Ptolemy to Caracalla.

Bothmer, Bernard V. *Egyptian Sculpture of the Late Period. 700 BC to AD 100.* Brooklyn, 1960; reprinted, New York, 1969. Exhibition catalog with the classic discussions of styles and statue types of the Late period.

Bourriau, Janine. *Pharaohs and Mortals: Egyptian Art in the Middle Kingdom.* Cambridge, 1988. Exhibition catalog with discussions of Middle Kingdom portraits and various types of small statuary and their uses.

Delange, Elisabeth. *Catalogue des statues égyptiennes du moyen empire, 2060–1560 avant J. C.* Paris, 1987. Catalog of the Louvre's Middle Kingdom statuary, with up-to-date discussion of style.

Friedman, Florence Dunn, ed. *Gifts of the Nile: Ancient Egyptian Faience.* Providence, 1998. Exhibition catalog describing the history and techniques of manufacture of faience and related materials, with 200 entries of objects of all periods.

Hayes, William C. *The Scepter of Egypt.* 2 vols. Rev. ed. New York, 1990. A general history of art, based on the Metropolitan Museum collections.

Hornung, Erik. *Idea Into Image: Essays on Ancient Egyptian Thought.* Princeton, 1992. Essays, many of which deal with the ideas behind the creation and use of statuary.

James, T. G. H., and W. V. Davies. *Egyptian Sculpture.* London, 1983. A handbook based on the British Museum's collection.

Kozloff, Arielle P., and Betsy M. Bryan. *Egypt's Dazzling Sun: Amenhotep III and His World.* Cleveland, 1992. Exhibition catalog with discussions of the development of this pharaoh's sculpture program and its meaning, and descriptions of all sizes and types of his statuary and their materials.

Robins, Gay. *Proportion and Style in Ancient Egyptian Art.* Austin, 1994. Explains grids and figural style changes.

Robins, Gay. *The Art of Ancient Egypt.* Cambridge, Mass., 1997. The most up-to-date discussion of the general subject, incorporating recently developed ideas.

Russmann, Edna R., and David Finn. *Egyptian Sculpture: Cairo and Luxor.* Austin, 1989. An overview and stylistic analysis of Egyptian sculpture, based on the Cairo and Luxor collections.

Saleh, Mohammed, and Hourig Sourouzian. *Official Guide: The Egyptian Museum Cairo.* Mainz, 1987. Contains images and discussions of many objects and types of objects discussed here.

Seipel, Wilfried. *Gott, Mensch, Pharao: Viertausend Jahr Menschenbild in der Skulptur des alten Ägypten.* Vienna, 1992. Exhibition catalog of 211 examples of figural sculpture from all periods.

Valbelle, Dominique. "Craftsmen." In the *The Egyptians,* edited by Sergio Donadoni, pp. 31–59. Chicago, 1997. Explores the identities, work ethics, and daily life of the sculptors.

Wildung, Dietrich. *Sudan: Antike Königreiche am Nil.* Munich, 1996. Exhibition catalog of art from all periods in ancient Sudan, including sculpture from the period of the Kushite domination of Egypt.

Ziegler, Christiane. *Les statues égyptiennes de l'Ancien Empire.* Paris, 1997. Catalog of the Louvre's Old Kingdom statuary with up-to-date discussion of style.

ARIELLE P. KOZLOFF

Royal Sculpture

Representations of the pharaohs in Egyptian statuary, known from the Early Dynastic to the Roman period had many functions: propagandistic, religious, didactic, commemorative, magical, and decorative. Found in temples, tombs, palaces and—exceptionally—private homes, they are made of various materials: most frequently stone, and less frequently wood, metals, or faience. The surfaces of the statues were usually painted, or sometimes overlaid with gold foil, but only a few statues now have parts of this coating. Like other cult objects, royal statues were believed to be endowed with life, which was granted through the Opening the Mouth ceremony.

In other domains of Egyptian art, three-dimensional representations of the pharaohs were subject to a canon of iconographic and stylistic patterns, which, however, display a diachronic development. Even the most conservative archetypes change through the centuries, and each epoch introduces new types, which sometimes remain for a long time in the sculptor's repertory.

Anthropomorphic representations of the ruler are most common, although his affinity with certain animals, particularly those that are zoomorphic incarnations of the most important gods, is frequently emphasized in various ways. The most popular type of statue showing the king as a syncretic, half-human and half-animal being is the sphinx, combining the body of a reclining lion with the head of a pharaoh. The oldest known statue of this type is a fragmentarily preserved sphinx of Djedefre (now in the Louvre), and its most monumental version is the Great Sphinx in Giza, from living rock, probably in the time of Khafre. Long rows of uniform sphinx statues bordered the streets leading to the main entrances of many Egyptian temples. A long sequence of sphinxes dating from the reign of Nektanebo I is still preserved in front of the Luxor temple. A particular type of royal sphinx the king's human head with a lion's mane. First recorded in the statuary of Middle Kingdom (a statue attributed to Amenemhet III in the Egyptian Museum, Cairo), it is also found in representations of Hatshepsut (in the Metropolitan Museum) and Taharqa (British Museum). Among the iconographic variations of the sphinx with royal head, there are also figures with two human arms replacing the animal's forefeet and holding a cult object. This pattern is first found in the statuary of Amenhotpe III found in the temple of Monthu at Karnak. Another peculiar version of sphinx figurine, dating from the same reign and now in Cairo, shows the animal with two wings.

Anthropomorphic effigies portray the king either alone or accompanied by one (dyad), two (triad), or more figures. These are members of his family or his ancestors, various gods in their human, half-animal, or zoomorphic shape, or—rarely—other figures of the same king; exceptionally, a nonroyal figure occurs.

The king represented alone more frequently appears seated, standing, or kneeling, and less frequently striding or prostrate. Seated royal statues occur as early as the second dynasty; the first known life-size representation of a king in this attitude is the statue of Djoser (Egyptian Museum, Cairo) found in Saqqara. Monumental versions of this archetype later decorated entrances to Egyptian temples. A pair of colossal seated statues was usually placed in front of the temple, one on each side of the entrance. A classical example of such decoration is the Memnon Colossi in Thebes, which originally adorned the mortuary temple of Amenhotpe III. Being an important instrument of political and religious propaganda, statues showing a sitting king usually bear a decoration in relief that has symbolic value. The heraldic scene depicting the unification of Lower and Upper Egypt usually decorates the outer faces of the lateral panels in the royal throne, and figures of bound foreign captives appear on the base of the statue. Thus, the king is portrayed as the ruler of all Egypt, victorious over the rest of the world.

A representation of the king kneeling and offering two globular wine vessels is first found in the statuary of Khafre (now in the Pelizaeus-Museum, Hildesheim). Besides this classical version of a kneeling king, there are also statues of pharaohs offering various other ritual objects, such as the statuette of a god, a small shrine (Merenptah, in Cairo), or an offering table (Sety II in Karnak, Ramesses III from Tanis). A standing king can also be shown as the bearer of an offering or a cult object. Three statues attributed to Amenemhet III (Egyptian Museum, Cairo; Museo Ludovisi alle Terme, Rome), as well as statues of Thutmose III (Cairo), Amenhotpe III (Cairo), and Osorkon (British Museum, London), represent the king offering fish. A similar statue of Horemheb (British Museum) shows him offering flowers. Several sculptures portray a standing king in the gesture of adoration. The oldest known examples of the latter are statues of Senwosret III (four in the British Museum and in Cairo). A small figurine in Cairo, showing Ramesses IV in the same attitude, is made of faience. Among the iconographic innovations of the long reign of Amenhotpe III, there is a type of statue depicting a standing king as bearer of a standard at his side (Karnak North and Egyptian Museum, Cairo). This pattern became particularly popular in the Rammesid period.

Several artistic innovations occur in the group of statuary showing a standing king. Unique of its kind is a wooden statue (Egyptian Museum, Cairo) representing the *ka* of king Hori (thirteenth dynasty); the nude "double" of the king, wearing the wig and beard of a god,

SCULPTURE: ROYAL SCULPTURE. *Old Kingdom statue of the third dynasty king Djoser, now in the Egyptian Museum, Cairo.* (Courtesy David P. Silverman)

bears two raised arms on his head. Another unique statue from the reign of Amenhotpe III, is a large representation of the king's statue standing on a sledge; found in 1989 in the cache of the Luxor temple and now in the Luxor Museum, and unparalleled in many respects, it belongs among the masterpieces of Egyptian sculpture. Another unusual work is the only monumental representation of a Persian ruler of Egypt, the headless figure of Darius I found in Susa and now in the Iran-Bastam-Museum, Teheran. Its iconography combines Egyptian and Persian elements.

An important group of statues and statuettes shows the king as a mummiform Osiris with hands crossed on his chest. Monumental versions occur in Egyptian temples, on the frontal face of pillars in the façade. The pharaoh holds the usual attributes of Osiris. Small figurines showing a mummiform pharaoh with various tools in his hands are the *shawabtis* belonging to the equipment of royal burials. The largest group of such stone figurines ever found in a royal tomb came from the Taharqa's pyramid at Nuri, Sudan; the largest groups are now in the Archaeological Museum, Khartoum, and the Museum of Fine Arts, Boston.

The oldest statue showing a striding pharaoh (Egyptian Museum, Cairo) dates from the reign of Senwosret I. The attitude of prostration first appears in the statuary of Amenhotpe III (Metropolitan Museum of Art). In the few later versions of this pattern, the pharaoh is represented offering a ritual object, such as socle with one or more heads of gods (Ramesses II, in Cairo), a socle with a scarab (Ramesses IX, collection of C. T. Trechmann, Great Britain), or a stela inscribed with a prayer (Osorkon II, Egyptian Museum, Cairo, and University Museum, Philadelphia), or a sacred barge (Osorkon III, Egyptian Museum, Cairo).

An important group of statues represents the pharaoh as a child. The oldest known example is a representation (Egyptian Museum, Cairo) of Pepy II as a seated nude boy; however, juvenile features do not necessarily represent a king in his youth. Recent studies of the art of Amenhotpe III have proved that Egyptian sculptors endowed his effigies with a boyish facial expression in the last phase of his long life, specifically after his *sed*-jubilee, in order to express the idea of his symbolic regeneration as king. A unique statue of Ramesses II, found in Tanis and now in Cairo, portrays the king as a squatting nude child with various attributes; it is a sophisticated anagram of his name, a cryptographic three-dimensional composition of hieroglyphic signs constituting the name Ra-mes-su. Some other royal statues may also be "read" as anagrams of a king's name.

The oldest known group statues date from the fourth dynasty. The first dyads show Djedefre with his wife, and the first triads represent Menkaure with the goddess Hathor and the personification of one of the nomes of Egypt (Egyptian Museum, Cairo, and Museum of Fine Arts, Boston). Later, particularly in the time of Ramesses II, monumental triads become a popular instrument of political theology, showing the king as a child of an important divine couple or emphasizing his affinity to particular gods shown in his company. In exceptional cases, this propaganda includes other members of royal family or royal ancestors. Thus, Senwosret I is represented with his three predecessors (in a statue at the Egyptian Museum, Cairo), while a statue of Merenptah found in Heliopolis shows him with his father, Ramesses II, and the god Osiris. Another statue of Merenptah (from Bubastis, now in Cairo) portrays him with his son Sety II, while a colossal statue of Amenhotpe III (also in Cairo) depicts him with his wife and their own propaganda; for example, the vizier Panehsy is shown standing behind Merenptah and his wife in a work from Deir el-Medina. A fine, large calcite dyad of Amenhotpe III, showing the king with the crocodile-headed god Sobek, was found in Dahamsha in Upper Egypt and is now in the Luxor Museum.

Dyads and triads represent a group of persons frontally, standing or seated side by side. A specific case of this artistic concept appears in groups composed of two or more figures of the same king; the only visible difference between the parallel figures is in their facial features. The earliest such dyad is a double standing representation (Staatliche Sammlung Ägyptischer Kunst, Munich) of Newoserre Any, which allegedly emphasizes the double—human and divine—nature of the pharaoh. One of the two faces is young, while the other reveals features of advanced age. Next in date are the double royal statues of the Middle Kingdom. One, attributed to Amenemhet III and now in Cairo, shows the ruler as the Nile god offering fish, fowl and lotus plants. A group statue of Ramesses II (Egyptian Museum, Cairo) shows two kings kneeling in front of the god Heh, raising an altar. Unique in Egyptian statuary are the four colossi representing the seated Ramesses II, hewn in the façade of his temple at Abu Simbel. Their differentiated facial features probably express the Egyptian idea of totality symbolized by the sacred number four, which would fit the political megalomania of this king.

Contrasting with the large number of groups of linear composition are the less numerous statues depicting an action between two or more persons. In many cases, their sophisticated, mostly asymmetrical composition appears as a three-dimensional version of scenes that occur repeatedly in Egyptian relief and painting. Although some conventions of this group were copied in subsequent periods, there are many innovative forms. One of the most popular patterns shows a small king seated on the knees of another person, usually a god or one of the king's parents. The king does not always have the features of a child. The oldest known example is a small calcite statue (Brooklyn Museum, New York) showing Pepy II on the knees of his knees of her nurse, Satre (Egyptian Museum, Cairo). Her successor Thutmose III is represented in the same attitude with the goddess Renenutet (also in Cairo). An unfinished limestone statuette from Tell el-Amarna portrays Akhenaten kissing one of his daughters, who is seated on his knees. The theme of a child seated on his mother's knees was more popular outside the royal context. Its purely religious version, showing Isis with her child Horus, is one of the most popular images among Egyptian bronze statuettes; this later became the prototype of a popular representation of the Virgin Mary.

Two types of group statues were particularly popular from the New Kingdom on: scenes of the coronation ceremony, and representations of an offering or adoring king kneeling in front of a seated divinity. In the first case, the god, seated behind the pharaoh, puts his hands on the king's crown and shoulder. Large sculptures showing the coronation ceremony are particularly numerous in the statuary of Tutankhamun; most of them probably constituted an integral part of the decoration of the Luxor temple. An unusual statue, found in Medinet Habu and now in Cairo, shows Ramesses III crowned by two gods, Horus and (probably) Thoth. Associated with the coronation groups is a type of statue showing a divinity striding behind a king and putting hands on him a gesture reminiscent of coronation scenes. This patterns is found, for example, in a large anepigraphic statue from Tanis and now in Cairo, showing a Ramessid king followed by a goddess.

An iconographic invention of the Ramessid period is the three-dimensional version of the scene showing a pharaoh killing an enemy. First occurring in the statuary of Merenptah (Egyptian Museum, Cairo) this pattern was copied for Ramesses IV (Cairo) and Ramesses VI (Cairo, Turin), who appear accompanied by a lion.

Representations of a pharaoh protected by an animal, or a zoomorphic incarnation of a god, are popular from the eighteenth dynasty. They paraphrase the earlier concept of a king protected by a falcon, the animal embodying Horus, the divine original of the pharaohs. In the Old Kingdom, the falcon is shown either folding its wings around the head of the king (first in the statuary (Museum of Fine Arts, Boston) of Khufu—a diorite statue of Khafre from Giza (Egyptian Museum, Cairo) is the type's classical example) or standing transversely behind the king's head. The first pattern was in use at least until the Ramessid period. A specific case is the royal child squatting in the shadow of a falcon, constituting an anagram of the name Ra-mes-su, described above.

Beginning in the reign of Amenhotpe II, who is shown standing before the Hathor cow and the Meretseger snake (both in the Egyptian Museum, Cairo), the type of statue representing a small king in the shadow of a large animal is a standard pattern in royal statuary. Representations of kings protected by sphinxes with the heads of various animals—for example, of rams or falcons—occur particularly often. Several statues showing a falcon as the protector of the king date from the reign of Nektanebo II, the last indigenous pharaoh (e.g., in the Metropolitan Museum of Art, New York).

Some royal sculptures served a magical function. An example is a group statue representing Ramesses III with a goddess (perhaps Isis, the work, from Heliopolis, is lost). The magic formulae engraved on its surface bring to mind the "healing statues" of nonroyal figures popular in the Late period.

The individuality of each royal effigy was achieved not only by rendering specific facial features but also through the king's garments and other attributes. These details emphasize the affinity of the pharaoh with particular gods, define his ritual functions, or commemorate historical events of political or religious significance. Most frequently the king is represented barefoot, wearing a short apron and a broad collar on his nude torso. Some statues, including the oldest known figurine of the Early Dynastic period (British Museum, London), show him wrapped in the temple long overcoat worn by the pharaohs on the occasion of their *sed*-jubilee. Other kinds of long gown

characterize the king celebrating his coronation. A specific kind of dress ("Horus gown"), known since New Kingdom, identifies him with Horus; it looks like a large scalp of a falcon, the head of the animal forming a kind of hood over the king's head. Some statues show a pharaoh wrapped in a panther skin, which brings to mind his function as head priest. In many other cases this function is indicated more symbolically by a panther's head hanging from the king's belt.

Headdress is one of the most diagnostic elements in royal attire. Pharaohs are represented wearing various kinds of kerchiefs, crowns, and wigs. The *nemes*-cloth is the most popular royal headgear in Egyptian statuary of all periods. The most popular crown is the Double Crown composed of two elements symbolizing Lower and Upper Egypt; their combination, expressing the unity of the country, associates the king with the Heliopolitan god Atum, with whom he also shared the epithet "Lord of the Two Lands." Various kinds of feather crowns associated the king with different gods, particularly Osiris, whose most typical crown (the *atef*) often appears in royal iconography, especially in funerary contexts. From the New Kingdom on, many statues show a pharaoh wearing the Blue Crown ḫprs, which has the shape of a high vaulted tiara with sharp edges. The oldest known statues of a standing pharaoh wearing this crown (Brooklyn Museum; Egyptian Museum, Cairo; Pelizaeus-Museum, Hildesheim) date from the reign of Amenhotpe III. Diagnostic primarily of a monarch's military victory, this crown is also associated with the coronation ceremony, as in the fine seated statue of Ramesses II in the Museo Egizio, Turin.

Short wigs are often adorned with a circlet, sometimes with two ribbons hanging behind it. Some types of royal headgear co-occur with an artificial beard of rectangular shape attached to the headdress with lateral bands. A constant element of royal headdress is the *uraeus* set above the king's forehead. Its shape, and specifically the arrangement of its coils, varies according to the type of headdress and the artistic trend of the period, so that it is one of the most useful dating criteria in royal sculpture. Two parallel snakes often appear at the forehead of Kushite kings (twenty-fifth dynasty), whose iconography constitutes a specific chapter in Egyptian art. Another characteristic feature of their effigies is the tightly fitting skullcap, in which one may discern an affinity with the Memphire god Ptah, one of the most venerated divinities of that dynasty. All pharaohs share another common feature with Ptah: the rectangular shape of their artificial beard, contrasting with the beards of all other gods, which are curved forward at the base.

Queens and other members of the royal family appear less frequently than kings in Egyptian statuary. Statues of

SCULPTURE: ROYAL SCULPTURE. *Middle Kingdom statue of the twelfth dynasty king Amenemhet III, now in the Egyptian Museum, Cairo.* (Courtesy David P. Silverman)

various size, made of various materials, show the queen alone. She is usually portrayed in a long, close-fitting dress, with various types of headgear associating her with different goddesses. She often wears a wig, which sometimes supports a crown, frequently a feather crown. The scalp of a vulture seen on the heads of some queens emphasizes their affinity with goddess Nekhbet in their role as mothers.

Like the majority of statues showing nonroyal subjects, most royal effigies are carved in one monolithic block with a back pillar, a rectangular plate at the rear of the statue. The inscription on the pillar usually contains significant information about the subject.

For many reasons, these and other inscriptions found on royal statues may not be a satisfactory criterion in their dating. Many statues were usurped by later rulers, sometimes more than once and their inscriptions were then recarved. Some pharaohs, deified and venerated by their descendants, are known to have posthumous representations that bear their names but belong stylistically to a later epoch. Archaization, the copying of earlier works, as well as other sorts of imitation and artistic inspiration, occurs frequently in royal statuary, which results in controversial attributions and interpretations. Many statues are preserved only fragmentarily, and if a fragment is anepigraphic or bears only a part of its inscription, criteria of style and iconography remain the only tools for its chronological or topographical attribution.

Each period had its particular style. Representations of some rulers display easily identifiable diagnostic features,

SCULPTURE: ROYAL SCULPTURE. *The nineteenth dynasty rock-cut temple at Abu Simbel dedicated to Queen Nefertari and the goddess Hathor.* On each side of the entrance are monumental figures of the queen, flanked on both of her sides by her king Ramesses II. (Courtesy David P. Silverman)

and a diachronic development within a reign may be observed only in exceptional cases. The latter is true of a few pharaohs whose rule was long and whose artistic production is known from many inscribed works (e.g., Amenhotpe III, Ramesses II). In some cases, geographic attribution may be proposed as well. Differences of style prove that various workshops or sculptors were simultaneously active in various parts of the country, and even in the same center or temple. In regard to the rendering of facial features, it seems that Lower Egyptian workshops were generally more open to innovative trends and perhaps more inventive than Upper Egyptian artists. Contrasting with a naturalistic approach to the physiognomy of a king, often found in the work of Lower Egyptian sculptors, is the attachment of Upper Egyptian artists to traditional, classical, conservative patterns, especially after the Amarna period. A late exemplification of such differences may be found in the representations of Nektanebo I.

In spite of the naturalistic trends, it remains an open question, to what extent, if at all, Egyptian sculptors created "portraits" in the modern sense of a direct likeness of the object to its model. On one hand, the existence of gypsum casts of human faces (e.g., from Tell el-Amarna) proves that the desire to preserve the original facial fea-

tures of a person for posterity was present in Egyptian mind. On the other hand, the idealized, impersonal, rather timeless features characterizing the majority of royal sculptures demonstrate that it was much more important to express the king's strength and self-satisfaction than his physical likeness or any particular emotion. However, there are many departures from this general tendency, particularly in the periods of great political and social change. Thus, an unprecedented naturalism may be observed in the representations of some twelfth dynasty kings, such as Senwosret III and Amenemhet III. Their "pessimistic portraits," emphasizing the sadness of their tired faces, sometimes have the impact of psychological studies, bringing to mind the social problems known from this period's literature.

Another period that reveals a naturalistic approach toward royal physiognomy is the "religious revolution" of Akhenaten, which seems to have been the culmination of a long evolution reflecting profound religious and political changes that started with the rule of Hatshepsut and reached their climax in the time of Amenhotpe III. Many representations of Akhenaten and his family endow their physiognomy with exaggerated, almost caricatural features which exceed the notion of "naturalism" to approach a mannerism that must have had a more ideological than artistic motive. Not only the overemphasized dolichocephaly of the king, but also his female characteristics—broad hips, thick thighs, narrow shoulders, thin arms, and the unnatural elongation of the face—characterize the unparalleled individuality of his effigies. The feminine aspects may be a visual expression of the bisexuality of the king in his identification with the primeval god. In spite of an official return to religious and artistic orthodoxy after the fall of Akhenaten, stylistic echoes of his sculpture are clear in many representations of later kings, in both statuary and relief.

Specific iconographic and stylistic features also distinguish the statuary of the Kushite twenty-fifth dynasty. In respect to the physiognomy and attire of these kings, two tendencies may be observed. Besides representations following traditional patterns of pharaonic sculpture, there are statues emphasizing the Negroid facial features and strong musculature of the Kushites. A new type of headdress with a double *uraeus* at the forehead, and a characteristic necklace with small ram's heads, also individualize the representations of these pharaohs.

New trends in the style of royal statuary appear in the time of the last indigeneous thirtieth dynasty. They display rounded faces with protruding cheekbones, almond-shaped eyes with long thin cosmetic lines paralleled by a straight extension of the eyebrow, smiling mouths with slightly raised corners, and the slanting profile of the double chin. This prototype, possibly of Lower Egyptian origin, strongly influenced royal sculpture of the Ptolemaic period, even some effigies that were executed principally in the Greek style.

From the beginning of Egyptian art up to Roman times, royal statuary had an obvious impact on the representations of Egyptian noblemen and gods. Both their facial features and elements of their attire express a homogeneous trend which is also found in relief sculpture of the same period. This proves that royal sculpture and effigies of other subjects were made in the same workshops.

[*See also* Portraiture; *and* Sphinx.]

BIBLIOGRAPHY

Aménophis III, le Pharaon-Soleil. Paris, 1993. Catalog of an important exhibition, with comprehensive documentation and studies on statuary of Amenhotpe III.

Berman, Lawrence Michael, ed. *The Art of Amenhotep III: Art Historical Analysis. Papers Presented at the International Symposium Held at the Cleveland Museum of Art, Cleveland, Ohio, 20–21 November 1987.* Cleveland, 1990. Collection of articles presenting new approaches to the art of one of the most important periods.

Corteggiani, Jean-Pierre. *The Egypt of the Pharaohs at the Cairo Museum.* London, 1987. Modern catalog of chosen masterpieces in the Egyptian Museum, Cairo, including original observations on royal statuary.

Freed, Rita E. *Ramesses the Great.* Memphis, Tenn. 1987. Catalog of an exhibition presenting many statues of Ramesses II.

Hayes, William C. *The Scepter of Egypt: A Background for the Study of Egyptian Antiquities in the Metropolitan Museum of Art.* 2 vols. New York, 1953, 1959. Catalog illustrating and describing many royal statues of the third and second millennia BCE.

Josephson, Jack A. *Egyptian Royal Sculpture of the Late Period, 400–246 B.C.* Sonderschriften des Deutschen Archäologischen Instituts Kairo, 30. Mainz, 1997. A detailed study of royal statuary of the last indigeneous dynasties and the beginning of the Ptolemaic period.

Luxor Museum of Ancient Egyptian Art. *Catalogue,* Cairo, 1979. Presents masterpieces of Egyptian art from the Theban region, including many royal statues.

Myśliwiec, Karol. *Royal Portraiture of the Dynasties XXI–XXX.* Mainz, 1988. First essay of synthesis on royal sculpture from the fall of the New Kingdom to the beginning of the Ptolemaic period.

Russmann, Edna R. *The Representation of the King in the XXVth Dynasty.* Brussels and Brooklyn, 1974. The standard work on royal sculpture of the Kushite dynasty.

el-Saghir, Mohammed. *La découverte de la cachette des statues du temple de Louxor.* Mainz, 1992. Documentation and preliminary interpretation of a group of unusual royal statues found in 1989 in the Luxor temple.

Vandier, Jacques. *Manuel d'archéologie égyptienne.* Vol. 3, *Les grandes époques: La statuaire.* 2 vols. Paris, 1958. Essay on the first classification of royal statuary of Old, Middle, and New Kingdoms, according to chronological and structural criteria.

Wildung, Dietrich. *Sesostris und Amenemhet: Ägypten im Mittleren Reich.* Munich, 1984. A compendium of knowledge on Egyptian art of Middle Kingdom, including royal statuary.

KAROL MYŚLIWIEC

Private Sculpture

Describing the private statuary of ancient Egypt calls for a variety of approaches. The corpus consists of thousands of objects created over a period of more than three thousand years, now displayed in countless museums and private collections. During that surprisingly long period, socioeconomic and political contexts, iconography, and styles clearly altered. Despite these changes, however, it is possible at a glance to distinguish an Egyptian statue from a Greek one.

To fix the limits of Egyptian private statuary as a whole poses two immediate problems. First, there is the question of what is included in "statuary"; and second, within that group, what criteria enable a part of it to be labeled "private." The answers to both questions are less obvious than generally believed.

Let us first consider the term "statuary." In the vocabulary of Western art, the word denotes works sculpted in a tridimensional way. This feature makes them viewable from any angle and differentiates them from high relief, which depends on its material surface as a background. This Western definition applies to the majority of ancient Egyptian wood and bronze works, but not to the majority of stone works, most of which are supported by a pillar or dorsal panel. The most common theory for the use of these supports is that they prevented the stone sculpture from being broken and therefore deprived it of its magical essence. But it is interesting to note that some "block-statues," especially during the Ramessid and Late periods, have these supports when they are not actually required. Many other statues were sculpted within a hollow block, thus forming a niche or *naos*. They could also be sculpted into the wall of the hypogeum itself. Since Egyptian reliefs are always very low, as a rule representing the figure in profile, it could be suggested that two features that allow us to define the whole of Egyptian statuary are the pronounced ledge of the volumes and the frontality of the pose, but it need not be completely in the round.

The definition of the private character of statuary is more complex. Where can the limit between "private" or "official" statuary be drawn? The answer varies according to the criteria that we decide to use.

The most evident distinction takes into account the institutional quality of the person represented: a king is a king, and anyone else is a private person. But consider the queen: from the Middle Kingdom onward, queens wore the *uraeus* and other regalia, emphasizing their specific status, but during the Old Kingdom, except for the inscriptions, nothing differentiates them from nonroyal women.

Is there then a difference in quality of execution or in style depending on whom the statue represents? Certainly not: many statues representing high officials are equal to or even finer than royal statues, and it is now clear that, during certain periods (for example the Middle Kingdom, as demonstrated by Wildung), the stylistic innovations were created by provincial workshops and later adopted by the palace workshops.

This point leads to the problem of local workshops. That workshops existed independently of the court or the great temples cannot be denied, but there is little evidence for their organization. It has been deduced from their inscriptions that some private statues were made in the official workshops as a mark of royal favor. The king granted access to the quarries and authorization to use special stones like red or black granite, Bekhen stone (graywacke), quartzite, diorite, basalt, or fine limestone. Unfortunately, written documents of this custom are very rare, and stylistic analysis does not settle the problem. Moreover, it is possible that private statues, even those executed for commoners in the royal workshops, were made by apprentices, or inversely, that talented royal sculptors also ran local workshops.

Is it possible to distinguish private and royal statuary on a typological basis? On the whole, it is not. From the time of the Old Kingdom, private individuals may be represented standing, seated, or kneeling, the three main poses of Egyptian statuary, equally typical of kings. However, specific types exist: it seems normal that commoners are never represented as sphinxes (a divine and solar metaphor of kingship), but it is more surprising that no king is represented as a squatting scribe (a sign of scholarship), although several of them were highly literate and were even called sons of Thoth ("Thutmose"), the god of scholars. In the beginning of the twelfth dynasty, a new type, called the "block-statue," appeared. Its significance will be discussed later; it should be noted, however, that its pose is strictly private; it is not attested for kings or queens, though it is used for statues of princes, and it does not depict women.

Can we then distinguish private and royal sculpture by their specific location? Here again, the answer cannot be definite. The most ancient *serdab* (a closed room connected only with the place of offerings in the tomb, through a small opening at eye level) belongs to the Step Pyramid of King Djoser (third dynasty). This room allowed the statue, conceived as the magical double of the dead, to be reanimated from the afterworld by the living's gifts. This idea of the *serdab* was soon adopted by the officials of the Old Kingdom: many of their *serdabs* have been discovered, some of them with dozens of statues, usually in various poses. Inside the chapel itself, the dead could appear emerging from the world of the dead, either standing up (e.g., Mereruka) or as a bust (e.g., Ankh-haf, Idw, Nefer-seshemptah). Similarly, royal statuary abounded in the chapels and courtyards of funerary temples. But, as early as the Old Kingdom, statues of commoners could be placed outside the *serdab*s, either in the chapel or at the bottom of the shaft, close to the mortuary chamber itself (e.g., the so-called reserve heads). From the Middle Kingdom into the New Kingdom, private statues became more obviously objects of public contemplation in the temples of the gods, often playing, as the royal statues did, the role of intermediary between gods and humanity. At the end of this evolution, during the Late period, the funerary statues disappeared, and private statues adopted the same locations as royal ones, such as courtyards and chapels of temples.

It is clear only that royal statuary can be recognized by its iconographic regalia, particularly the *uraeus* (but not the *sndt*-loincloth, adopted by noblemen from the First Intermediate Period on and largely worn by civil servants of the Late period). Statues of queens (from the Middle Kingdom) have to be excluded from this study, as well as the statues of the "God's Wives" of the first millennium BCE. However, the statues of king's children need to be taken into consideration because no iconographic features differentiate them.

The association with private statuary of the statuettes called "models" or "servant statues" is rather doubtful. These are anonymous figurines (with some exceptions), displayed in tombs during the end of the Old Kingdom and the Middle Kingdom. Alone or in groups, they represent the various activities of daily life, producing goods for

SCULPTURE: PRIVATE SCULPTURE. *Sixth dynasty painted group statue of the dwarf Seneb, with his wife and children.* This statue is from Giza and is now in the Egyptian Museum, Cairo. (Courtesy David P. Silverman)

tomb's owners in the afterlife. Some represent offering-bearers or even naked women lying on a bed (commonly labeled "concubines to the dead"). Some of these figurines, particularly the standing offering-bearers, have much in common with some private statues, especially those carved in wood. It is possible that they were produced by the same workshops. However, they differ from private statues in that they do not normally represent individuals but rather types of activities, iconographically close to those carved on the walls of mortuary chapels. In short, as far as the artistic and sociological aspects are concerned, the only adequate method to differentiate between a specific group called "private statues" and the others lies in the distinction between works made in official workshops and works produced by private or local workshops. Unfortunately, because of the poor state of the documentation, this sole relevant feature can rarely be determined. Consequently, we must accept the modern Egyptological consensus, even unsatisfactory, and consider that private statuary comprises all statues that do not depict a deity, a king, a queen (except during the Old Kingdom), or a servant.

What were the reasons that led the Egyptians, soon after the rise of the pharaonic state, to produce so many representations of men and women in the round? The first motive is undoubtedly linked to a conception of the afterlife, the everlasting presence of the dead. This conception is fundamentally different from Judeo-Christian thought in which the superiority of a noble, immaterial and eternal soul is glorified, while the physical part of the human being is discounted. By contrast, Egyptian religion did not neglect any part of the individual, who was believed to consist of his vital force *(k3)*, his name *(rn)*, his soul *(b3)*, his body (made eternal by the ritual of the mummifica-

SCULPTURE: PRIVATE SCULPTURE. *Twelfth dynasty serpentine statue of an official.* (University of Pennsylvania Museum, Philadelphia. Neg. # S8–56178)

tion), and even his shadow *(šwyt).* The material body and the spirit that animated it were then linked together metaphysically and indissolubly to reach the afterlife. In this very link resides the reason for the importance of private statuary in Ancient Egypt. It can also explain the humanist tendency of Egyptian art, which manifests itself through various features: typological (the poses), iconographic (costumes are often very simple: the reality of the human being is exalted more than his social appearance), physical (young, "heroic" body, or, on the contrary, marked by the corpulence of prestige), and, finally, physionomic (an attempt at naturalism, if not realism: the anatomy is generally well respected, allowing the expression of the spirit).

The poses used in private statuary are basically restrained, but enriched by many variations in the details. There are five main poses. In the first, the subject is standing, left foot forward and arms held straight by the sides, in later times holding a scroll in the fists (a metonymic representation of a commander's baton). The female counterpart of this type has the hands pressed flat on the thighs, or an arm bent across the chest; most have both feet together, or the left very slightly forward. In the seated pose, the arms lie on the thighs (one arm occasionally bent across the chest). This attitude is not at all passive and does not suggest repose: the psychological tension is perceptible. As the standing pose suggests walking, the seated pose suggests the individual's readiness to stand up and act. The kneeling attitude is attested as early as the third dynasty (statue of Hetepdief). Some occurrences are known during the Old Kingdom (for example, Kaemked), and it became more common during the New Kingdom and the Late period, either in the simple pose (hands flat on the knees), or in a more complex iconographic variation, bearing a *naos,* sistrum, or stela.

Khufu's reign saw the emergence of a very interesting attitude, the cross-legged scribe statue (the most ancient ones were found in the *serdab* of Prince Kawab, son of the king). The man is squatting, his loincloth used as a tablet, an unrolled papyrus on his knees. Though frequent in the Old, Middle, and New kingdoms, this form became rare during the Late period and had completely disappeared at the time of the Ptolemaic kings. The scribe statue is, despite its traditional label, a noble attitude which exalts the intellectual capacities of the individual. Because no king, queen, or common woman is depicted in this pose, there can be little doubt that it was a sign of belonging to the particular social rank of high officials involved in the government of the state.

The first examples of block-statues are two statues of an individual called Hetep, who lived at the very beginning of the twelfth dynasty. Such a statue represents a man seated on the ground, wrapped in his cloak. Like the scribe-statues, the block-statues figure only noblemen— never a king, a queen, or a private woman. The meaning of the pose is uncertain. Some scholars have noted that a similar attitude of rest or waiting is still to be observed among Arabic populations. But this kind of ethnographic comparison has its limits: there is no equivalent of the pose depicted on any Ancient Egyptian relief or painting, where it could have been expected, for instance, in scenes showing the owner watching workmen in his fields. However, wooden models from the First Intermediate Period and the beginning of the Middle Kingdom—the period during which the type of the block-statue was created—depict the same pose: on the deck of a boat, perhaps traveling to Abydos, a crouched dead man is shown wrapped in his shroud. On the other hand, many stone statues of this type were made through the Ptolemaic period, showing a slight difference in the treatment of the feet, which may be meaningful. In some cases they are bare, the cloak stopping at the level of the ankles; in others they are covered by the shroud, as in the royal Osirid pillars. Therefore, some scholars evoke the idea of the reborn dead freeing themselves from the shroud and the tomb in the moment of their resurrection. But this theory fails to account for the block-statues with bare feet that can be found at any period after the twelfth dynasty. In this case, the dress seems to be a normal cloak and not an Osirian shroud. It is important to note that this type of statue offered large flat surfaces for inscriptions, thus making them very useful for religious and biographical accounts, even if they were not principally destined to be so.

Egyptian private statuary does not consist only of isolated statues: an important part of it consists of groups. The simplest example is the husband-and-wife group, or dyad, depicted either seated or standing (the prototype is the parallel statues of Rahotep and Nefert from Meidum, from the beginning of the fourth dynasty). The woman may appear on the left or right side of the husband, and her height can vary slightly: sometimes equal to the man's height, sometimes less. She is often represented beside him, tenderly putting her arm around his shoulders or waist. She can also be shown kneeling, rendered very small-scale, against her husband's leg and touching him with her hand (the oldest example is the fragmentary statue of Radedef and his wife, fourth dynasty). There is an exceptional group of a man represented as a block-statue, with his wife kneeling beside him (twenty-sixth dynasty). In these conjugal groups, different features usually designate the man as more active, such as the left foot placed farther forward or an arm slightly hiding the wife's shoulder. However, many groups are depicted in perfect equality and symmetry; the couples depicted hugging, in particular, can be linked by their arms forming an X. Because of the large number of variations, no typological system can be strictly defined (for a useful enumeration of the variations of pose, clothing, and hair up to the end of the New Kingdom, see Vandier 1958). Children are figured like their mother, either the same size or at a smaller scale, in between or beside their parents' legs. After the New Kingdom, family groups disappear from the repertory of private sculpture.

The meaning of these family groups is obvious, but the

statues called "pseudo-groups," have a more obscure meaning. Often during the Old and the Middle kingdoms, statues show the same individual represented twice, thrice, or even four times, as in the rock-cut chapel of Meresankh III, the wife of Khafre at Giza. Members of the family may accompany the multiplied figure. Furthermore, it often happens that an accompanying figure appears identical in name, size, and physionomy, but differs in clothes, hairstyle, attitude, or titles.

In contrast to royal and divine costumes (*snḏt*-loincloth, feminine frock with braces, and tripartite wigs), which conform to the archaic tradition, private statuary offers us a more accurate idea of the evolution of fashion. However, it would be naive to rely wholly on it, since no Egyptian image is strictly documentary. Wearing a certain piece of clothing could have particular meanings that we fail to understand. Statues depict the male Egyptians of the Old Kingdom, kings or commoners, exclusively wearing the loincloth, while their wives wear a dress to the neck or held by braces. There is no image of any king of the Middle Kingdom wrapped in a cloak, but civil servants wore long skirts and often wrapped themselves in a thick cloak (a fashion which also offers the sculptor the possibility of a large degree of abstraction in the rendering of the human body). The difference between royal and private representations can also be observed during the eighteenth dynasty and the Ramessid period: the images of the Kings (even the woman-king Hatshepsut) wear the traditional loincloth, leaving the torso naked, while the officials develop a more complex fashion based on draperies and pleated dresses, as well as cloaks and shawls made of thin linen. With a very few exceptions, royal (and divine) iconography seems to be purely institutional, in contrast with the more natural representation of nonroyal human beings. The Third Intermediate Period represents a break in this evolution and is characterized by archaistic tendencies: block-statues covered with inscriptions abound; the archaic *snḏt*-loincloth is readopted by commoners; and the scroll in the men's fists recalls the noble and simple attitude of Old Kingdom officials. After the sophisticated fashions of the New Kingdom, austerity returns.

Nudity is another interesting question. The Western mind opposes, as far as moral values are concerned, nudity, perceived as negative, and a normal modest way of dressing. There is no evidence that the Egyptians shared exactly this view. An example shows this fact very clearly: at any period of Egyptian art, images in relief or painting invariably depict women or goddesses wearing a strap-dress which reveals bare bosom, the straps being seen from the front and the breast in profile. However, when the same dress is depicted in statuary, the breast is never visible, but covered by the straps. Statues of women com-

SCULPTURE: PRIVATE SCULPTURE.
Seated statue of Sitepehu, "Overseer of Priests,"
during the reign of Hatshepsut, eighteenth
dynasty. This sandstone statue is from Abydos.
(University of Pennsylvania Museum,
Philadelphia. [Neg. # S8–32892])

pletely naked appear rarely in private statuary (some examples exist from the First Intermediate Period), but the feminine body is often more unveiled than hidden by the sculpted dress. It does not matter whether the gown is straight or pleated: the body seems to be inscribed in the transparent dress, revealing with great precision the shape of the breast, stomach, and thighs, even the hollow of the navel. The neckline is frequently omitted, and the presence of a dress is often suggested only by a slight flare above the feet. Masculine nudity is far from rare; it is especially common between the end of the Old Kingdom and the beginning of the Middle Kingdom, but is limited to tomb statues. Many officials are represented naked, holding a long stick, symbol of their important social and administrative position. The effect, for us, is surprising. In some cases, the naked body may have been wrapped in clothes or in pieces of linen, but this cannot be certain, because the exceptional climate of Egypt has preserved much textile material. Another explanation could be that the dressed statues of men, hiding the anatomic signs of their sexual capacity, might have seemed insufficient to secure the complete restoration of the vital functions in the afterlife. As far as the female's body was concerned, it is evident that the transparency of the dress was sufficient to secure the magical process. Young children, both boys and girls, are usually depicted naked. With a finger in the mouth and often with a special hairdress (a single lock hanging from the right side of the shaven skull), they are either alone or part of a family group. Like statues of private women or family groups, this type is no longer attested during the first millennium BCE.

The question of Egyptian portrait is highly controversial. Were the statues of private individuals intended to be portraits in the modern sense of the word? Did the sculptors seek any resemblance at all? It is, of course, hard to prove, because comparison with mummies gives very few clues. The best approach lies in comparing statues that depict the same individual. But the resemblance of these statues—especially those found in the *serdab*s of the Old Kingdom—might be only the result of the routine work of a master sculptor or of a workshop. On the other hand, we can observe that some important officials are depicted in several statues, all different from one other (Amenhotep, son of Hapu, eighteenth dynasty, or Montuemhat, twenty-fifth to twenty-sixth dynasties). It is also theoretically possible to compare statues and reliefs depicting the same individual. However, besides the methodological problem of comparison between statues in the round and two-dimensional figures, such a double set of representation is very unusual. Two examples are often put forward: a reserve head of Nefer, and a statue of Prince Hemiunu, both from the time of Khufu (fourth dynasty), whose tombs have some fragmentary reliefs depicting them. Unfortunately, in contradiction to frequent claims, the reserve head has clearly been reworked, and the face of Hemiunu is severely damaged, thus making an objective comparison impossible. We must admit that the face of a private statue usually depicts a conventional physiognomy. However, it is clear that certain artists did seek, if not a perfect resemblance, at least a naturalistic expression of the human face (especially of male faces). But "naturalism" does not mean "realism." Several factors do not permit us to talk of a search for realism, as in a modern portrait. The first is that Egyptian statuary of any period clearly prefers to represent not the real age of the individual depicted, but an ideal, middle age, mixing the strength of youth with the intellectual qualities of maturity. Another factor is the influence of the king's physiognomy on his contemporaries, which cannot be ignored, even if it is inappropriate to talk systematically of "mimetism" (the twelfth and eighteenth dynasties offer good examples of this phenomenon). Finally, returns to the past are stylistically and thus physiognomically frequent during the history of Egyptian sculpture, especially after periods of political and economical crisis (beginnings of the Middle and New kingdoms), as well as during the whole Late period. These manifestations of archaistic tendencies sometimes went as far as the reuse of ancient statues, with or without physiognomic alterations. However, the best works of private statuary in periods of political stability were produced by artists anxious to reproduce human reality, taking into account every aspect of the human being, the correct analysis of the anatomical structure of the body, and a strong expression of intellect and spirituality. This humanistic and naturalistic tendency, born at the very beginning of the Old Kingdom, reached a climax during the fourth and fifth dynasties and reappeared under the twelfth dynasty (from local workshop experiments, as the statues of the sanctuary of Heqa-ib at Elephantine tend to prove); then, after a long idealistic phase during the New Kingdom (apart from the aesthetic adventure of Amarna), it came back strongly under the Nubian twenty-fifth dynasty. Finally, it came to an end with masterpieces in the Ptolemaic period, a series of priests' heads carved in hard stones, green or black, splendid works of art which achieve brilliantly a humanist endeavor begun with statues like those of Ankh-haf, Hemiunu, or Kaaper (the "Sheikh el-Beled"), three millennia earlier.

The study of Egyptian art clearly urges us to give up the linear sketch inspired by Greek art: more than a linear evolution, the history of the Egyptian private statuary is a constant fluctuation between an idealized vision and a more concrete approach to the human being, moving back and forth between tradition and innovation.

[See also Portraiture.]

BIBLIOGRAPHY

Freed, R. E. *Egypt's Golden Age: The Art of Living in the New Kingdom. A Picture Book.* Boston, 1981. A sumptuously illustrated book devoted to the artistic perfection of the objects of daily life during the New Kingdom, showing many statuettes and figurines of exquisite quality.

Habachi, L. *Elephantine IV: The Sanctuary of Heqaib.* 2 vols. Mainz, 1985. Heqa-ib was a governor of the First nome of Upper Egypt during the sixth dynasty. His popularity led to his deification. During the twelfth dynasty, a splendid series of private statues was placed in a small sanctuary devoted to him on Elephantine Island.

Hornemann, B. *Types of Ancient Egyptian Statuary.* Copenhagen 1951–1969. Presented as a series of files (in boxes), an extended collection of drawings showing all the typological variations Egyptian statuary offers. Indispensable for any iconographic study.

Malek, J. *In the Shadow of the Pyramids: Egypt during the Old Kingdom.* London, 1986. A interesting general introduction to the arts of the Old Kingdom. Some very beautiful pictures of private statuary.

Smith, W. S. *A History of the Egyptian Sculpture and Painting in the Old Kingdom.* 2d ed. London, 1949. This quite old but still monumental book presents a brilliant synthesis of royal and private statuary of the Old Kingdom. The study is based mainly on the excavations of H. Junker and G. A. Reisner in the cemeteries of Giza. Technical, aesthetic, and symbolic problems are treated; illustrations are numerous and excellent for the time.

Spanel, D. *Through Ancient Eyes: Egyptian Portraiture.* Birmingham, 1988. The introductory pages of this exhibition catalog are probably the best text devoted specifically to the problem of the Egyptian portraiture (royal and private). The author reviews the simple cleavage between the "objective" portrait of Western tradition and the conventional idealization of Egyptian art, demonstrating that the question of objectivity is unsolvable and pointless.

Vandier, J. *Manuel d'archéologie égyptienne. Vol. 3, La statuaire.* Paris, 1958. The indispensable reference book on royal and private statuary from the beginning of the Old Kingdom until the end of the New Kingdom. The theories on stylistic evolution and schools of sculpture are greatly out of date, but this book provides a detailed typological and iconographic account of the statuary (attitudes, clothes, wigs, ornaments; types and variations). It contains a detailed index of the statues, according to their date and museums. Unfortunately, a planned volume on the Late period was never published.

ROLAND TEFNIN
Translated from the French by Angélique Corthals

Divine Sculpture

Divine sculpture housed the spirits of Egypt's myriad gods and goddesses. Although they were not considered to be the deities themselves, the statues were believed to be alive. In fact, each one was brought to life through rituals performed in the sculptor's workshop where it was made. From minuscule to majestic, in stone, metal, or fired materials, these figures were carefully identified images in which the appropriate spirits resided, and from which they bestowed favors.

Some spiritual imagery was inspired by the appearance of the sky: the formations and movements of the sun, moon, and stars. Thus, the Milky Way was believed to arch across the sky as a nude, golden woman through whose body the Sun passed at night to be reborn on the horizon each morning. Other concepts developed from natural forces or from elements of nature on Earth. The divine guardian of the cemetery, Anubis, came to be represented as a jackal, probably because this animal tended to live at the edge of the desert where the Egyptians buried their dead.

Divinities are represented in three different forms: human figures, animal figures, and mixtures of the two, either animals with human heads or humans with animal heads. Some can be represented in either human or animal form. The pure human figures are so generic that they can be distinguished from one another only by their inscriptions and by their crowns or other attributes. For example, the goddesses Isis and Maat, both depicted as slim young women wearing patterned sheath gowns, are individualized only by their headgear—a throne-shaped crown for Isis and a feather for Maat. It is superficially easier to identify those entities depicted as animals, since Egypt's fauna was rich enough to provide a different species for each deity. However, as major cults became more complex and new cults arose, many of the animals developed multiple identities. For example, in the early centuries the falcon almost always represented the sun god Horus. By the late New Kingdom, the falcon-headed human figure could represent Re, Horus the Elder, Horus the Son, Montu, or Ptah-Sokar-Osiris, as well as some other minor deities, depending on which crown it was wearing.

Divine sculpture had several different applications: cult statue, votive statue, temple guardian figure, funerary guardian figure, architectural element, implement or vessel, and personal amulet. Gods and goddesses in human, animal, or mixed form occur in most of these applications.

Cult Statues. The cult statue of a deity inhabited the Holy of Holies, the innermost sanctuary of its temple. The temple's high priest was the only human being with access to the sanctuary, and it was his job to meet the cult statue's personal needs. From the time the priest greeted the statue in the morning (with choirs singing hymns in the background) until he left the sanctuary at the end of the day, removing his footprints with a whiskbroom, he devoted his waking hours to bathing, perfuming, clothing, and feeding the statue. On festival days the cult statue "appeared" to the masses by being carried inside a small, portable shrine on a model boat resting on parallel poles, borne on priests' shoulders along wide processional avenues. People waited along the route in hopes of reading omens in the movements of the boat. Such festivals were crucial to the general faith because they allowed average human beings nearly direct access to their gods.

No statue in the world today can be securely identified as the central cult statue of any ancient Egyptian temple. Because temples were refurbished from time to time, it is possible that a series of cult statues, not just one, served each of Egypt's temples for the centuries they were in use. Some sculptures, however, have the right characteristics to stake claims as cult statues. The earliest, dated to the end of the fifth millennium BCE, is an oval, painted terra cotta human head with hollow eyes, nostrils, and mouth, found in 1982 at Merimda west of the Delta, and now in the Cairo Museum. A hole under the chin suggests that it was once fastened to a post. The tremendous rarity of manufactured sculpture at such an early date favors this being the earliest known cult statue.

One of the most impressive early (c.3200 BCE) full female figures is a 33.8-centimeter (13-inch) tall terra cotta statuette of a semi-nude female with a birdlike head and upflung arms, now in the Brooklyn Museum. She may be the most ancient example of an Egyptian sky goddess, whose form is discussed later in connection with its use on ritual implements.

The earliest known stone example larger than an amulet is the 39.5-centimeter (15-inch) tall (preserved to just below the knees) basalt male figure in the Ashmolean Museum, Oxford. Standing stiffly frontal with arms pressed to its sides, the "MacGregor Man," named after its former

SCULPTURE: DIVINE SCULPTURE. *Statue of the god Ptah of Memphis, eighteenth dynasty.* Dedicated by Amenhotpe III, the statue is now in the Museo Egizio, Turin. (Alinari / Art Resource, NY)

owner, wears a closely cropped hairstyle resembling a skullcap and a long, flat triangular beard reaching nearly to the waist. The face is riveting: large, heavily outlined eyes, thick eyebrows joining in the center, long aquiline nose, and a wide, thin-lipped mouth. The sole item of clothing is a belt holding a large cylindrical penis sheath, which is usually recognized as an item of divine costume in ancient Egypt.

This statue is so startling that some have futilely questioned its authenticity. Its style recalls Predynastic ivory amulets dating to the middle of the fourth millennium BCE, and its rather generic nature suggests that a god rather than a specific individual is represented. Echoes of this figure recur in the Old Kingdom (around 2575 BCE) in a gneiss (diorite) statuette of a god wearing a plain round wig, beard, and penis sheath, now in the Brooklyn Museum; and in the New Kingdom (around 1400 BCE) on a limestone statue of a god wearing a tall plumed crown, long smooth wig, beard, and penis sheath, found at Karnak and now in the Cairo Museum.

Far more glamorous, and probably dating to the early nineteenth dynasty (c.1300 BCE), is a falcon-headed, seated human figure in the Miho Museum in Misono, Japan.

More than 41 centimeters (15.5 inches) tall, it is solid-cast in silver and weighs 16.5 kilograms. It was once entirely covered with sheet gold, pieces of which still adhere to the surface. The eyes are inlaid with rock crystal, and the wig with a precious material called "Egyptian blue," which was manufactured in royal and temple workshops. It recalls an ancient description of a god: "bones of silver, flesh of gold, and hair of real lapis lazuli." The loss of this statue's crown, attributes, and inscriptions prevents us from identifying the divine spirit that inhabited it.

The Miho statue recalls a magnificent, realistically modeled head of a falcon wearing a tall plumed crown (in all, 37.5 centimeters/14.5 inches in height), beaten from heavy sheet gold and inlaid with obsidian eyes. It was probably made to top a now-lost copper cult statue of the sun god Horus. This gold falcon head, now in the Cairo Museum, was excavated in 1897–1898 at the temple at Hierakonpolis, about 75 kilometers (47 miles) south of Luxor, where Horus had been worshiped as patron deity since predynastic times.

Votive Statues. Most of the representations of divinities left to us from ancient Egypt are votive statues, given to temples and shrines by kings, courtiers, scribes, priests, military officers, or even municipalities in the hope of a benefaction from the god or goddess in residence. Most common is the single figure, either standing or enthroned. Among the grandest of these are hundreds of life-size and over life-size hard stone statues created during the eighteenth dynasty reign of Amenhotpe III in honor of his favorite deities—for example, the womanly Nephthys, now in Paris, and her look-alike Neith, now in Marseille, the monumental jackal-headed Anubis, now in Copenhagen, and the huge scarab beetle at the corner of Karnak's sacred lake. The largest series by far comprises the dozens of over life-size statues of the lion-headed goddess Sakhmet, many of which are inscribed with the names of the cities and towns that donated them.

All these statues were made for specific locations in Amenhotpe's temples. Their placement was neither random nor merely decorative. Instead, it followed intricate iconographic schemes relating to Amenhotpe III's concept of the cosmos. Thus, in addition to the individual powers that a given statue had, when it was placed into a specific cosmic grouping, the aggregate performed quite a potent magical function.

The facial features of divine images always resemble those of the king during whose reign they were produced. In some instances, a new king had little time or resources to commission large numbers of divine statuary in his own image. He would simply have the cartouches of earlier kings abraded out of the stone and replaced with his own. Sometimes the results were ridiculous, as when the aged military-man-become-pharaoh, Horemheb, had his name carved onto two huge statues in Karnak temple, one of the god Amun and one of his consort Amunet, in place of the cartouche of the boy king, Tutankhamun, who commissioned them, and whose sweet, youthful features adorn them.

Divine imagery occasionally incorporates more than one figure into a single sculptural block. Menkaure, the builder of the smallest of the three great pyramids at Giza, commissioned a series of triads (three figures side by side in the same block) as gifts for his own funerary temple at the base of the Giza plateau. The goddess Hathor, shown as a woman with her identifying crown of horns and disk, is a key figure in these triads. The third figure in several instances is a deity wearing the headdress of an Egyptian nome (geographic subdivision). This may indicate that these nomes paid at least some of the cost of the statue.

Triads and dyads (two figures side by side in the same block) remained infrequent, but important, compositions for royal displays of devotion. In the Luxor Museum, a monumental and glorious calcite (Egyptian alabaster) dyad of the crocodile-headed god Sobek, enthroned, with his arm around a shoulder-high Amenhotpe III is one of the greatest statues in a reign of superlative sculpture. A nearly life-size granodiorite triad in the Louvre has Osiris flanked and embraced on one side by a Ramessid pharaoh and on the other by Horus.

The theme of a god or goddess in animal form protecting or guiding the pharaoh occurs frequently. A magnificent example is the over life-size diorite portrait of the mighty fourth dynasty king Khafre, found near his valley temple at Giza. An appropriately sized falcon Horus, god of the sky and of the living king, perches behind the king's head, clasping the royal headdress in his wings. Much later, in a nineteenth dynasty sculpture in Cairo, the relative sizes of pharaoh and falcon are nearly reversed. Here, Ramesses II as a young boy crouches on the talons and beneath the beak of a huge falcon, which, the inscription tells us, is not Horus but Hurun, a Near Eastern god. In even less realistic relative size, standing knee-high to a Horus falcon four times his height, is Nektanebo II, the last ruler of the thirtieth dynasty, in a series of sculpted portraits.

It became quite common in the New Kingdom and later for images of important nonroyal officials to be incorporated with divine imagery. One composition involved the deity, in animal form, protecting the individual. For example, a number of small statuettes depict the baboon representing the god of wisdom, Thoth, squatting on his haunches on a shrine watching over a scribe who sits cross-legged below. A rarer type involves Hathor as a striding cow protecting a courtier—for example, the twenty-sixth dynasty official Psamtik—beneath her chin. In the eighteenth dynasty this composition had been reserved for royalty, as in the limestone sculpture from Deir el-Bahri, now in Cairo, where Hathor protects Thutmose III beneath her chin, while his son Amenhotpe II nurses at her udder.

In the New Kingdom, the pharaoh's favorite officials were often given the privilege of commissioning portraits of themselves presenting divine statuary as gifts. In such a composition, the image of the deity becomes a sculpture within a sculpture, as in Brooklyn's statue of Queen Hatshepsut's highest official and consort, Senenmut, who kneels holding an image of the serpent goddess Renenutet before him, or Cairo's statue of the twentieth dynasty official Kenu, who presents a whole triad of the god Amun, his wife Mut, and their son Khonsu as an offering.

During the Late period, as something approaching a middle class arose in Egypt and as bronze became a more widely used commodity, it was possible for large numbers of individuals to commission bronze statuettes or to purchase ready-made ones as personal gifts for shrines and temples. These statuettes, usually no more than 20 or 30 centimeters (6 to 10 inches) tall, were mostly single human or animal figures. Among the few groups are Isis with her little son Horus on her lap, and mother cats, sacred to the goddess Bastet, with their kittens. Since bronze, as well as other precious substances, was controlled by the royal palace, the statuettes are inscribed with the opening line of the traditional offering formula, "A favor which the king gives to [X] so that [the deity] might grant every good thing."

Many of the thousands of votive sculptures, large and small, existing today have been preserved by the housekeeping efforts of priests who periodically gathered up the oversupply of temple gifts and buried them in large pits within the temple precincts. French archaeologists discovered a huge cache of such material—more than seventeen thousand statuettes in bronze alone—at Karnak in the early years of the twentieth century. Many of these have found their way into collections around the world. In 1989, an Egyptian team found twenty-four monumental stone statues from the reign of Amenhotpe III in a pit inside the great court of Luxor temple. They are now housed in a special wing of the Luxor museum.

Guardian Figures. A third major application for divine sculpture was the guardian figure, usually an animal or a human-animal mix. The most famous of these is the great sphinx at Giza, representing the god Harmachis (Horus of the Horizon), which was carved in place from an outcropping of limestone to serve as a sentinel over the funerary structures of Khafre, who built the second-tallest of the nearby pyramids. From the fourth dynasty onward, the crouching lion with the head of a pharaoh, wearing the *nemes*-headcloth, became a favorite guardian figure. Among the largest sphinxes outside Egypt are a red granite Middle Kingdom colossus, now in the Louvre, and a red granite pair commissioned by Amenhotpe III for an unknown site and now in St. Petersburg, Russia.

Amenhotpe III also had divine guardian figures made in pure animal form. The most famous of these are his pair of mirror-image red granite lions representing the moon god Khonsu, from the Soleb temple in Sudan and now in the British Museum. In addition, he furnished the approach to Soleb with an avenue flanked by monumental recumbent rams carved in gray granite, some of which are still in place. Sacred to the god Amun-re, each ram protects a small mummiform figure of Amenhotpe between its bent front legs. Apparently Amenhotpe made red granite versions for Karnak temple. During the nineteenth dynasty the criosphinx, a ram-headed lion representing Amun-Re, became the predominant guardian figure at Karnak, and during the early fourth century BCE, Nektanebo I lined the two-mile-long avenue from the southern gate of Karnak temple to the northern gate of Luxor temple with hundreds of human-lion sphinxes bearing his own portrait. Today many of these still monitor the Theban gates and avenues where believers once stood on festival days waiting to catch a glimpse of the cult statue.

Divine sculpture also served as guardian figures in the funerary sphere. Tutankhamun's tomb provides a full array of beautiful examples. His canopic shrine is guarded

SCULPTURE: DIVINE SCULPTURE. *Statue of the lion goddess Sekhmet, eighteenth dynasty.* The statue, 7 feet (2.13 meters) high, and made of diorite, is one of some six hundred statues of Sekhmet that were placed in the Mut precinct at Karnak. (The Metropolitan Museum of Art, Gift of Henry Walters, 1915. [15.8.3])

on each side by one of four identical goddesses in gilded wood—Isis, Nephthys, Neith, and Selkis—individualized only by their crowns. Another shrine, equipped with wooden carrying poles, is surmounted by the alert figure of Anubis as a jackal-watchdog.

The most ubiquitous of all funerary guardian figures were the Four Sons of Horus, whose names and effigies adorned the jars holding the soft organs of the body, which had to be preserved separately. Until the end of the eighteenth dynasty and in Tutankhamun's burial, the jar lids are in the form of human heads (the pharaoh's with the royal headcloth). Thereafter, the lids are individualized for each of the Four Sons: jackal-headed Duamutef, who guarded the stomach; ape-headed Hapy, the lungs; human-headed Imsety, the liver; and falcon-headed Qebhsenuef, the intestines. These divine guardian figures can be found in nearly every museum collection.

Architectural Elements. Architectural elements—especially columns and pillars—also incorporate divine images. The wrapped mummy shape of Osiris, the god of the dead, suited temple columns and was incorporated by Senwosret I into the pillars of a twelfth dynasty structure at Karnak (later reused at a different part of the same temple), and it appears in the nineteenth dynasty at the Ramesseum, Ramesses II's funerary temple on the west bank of Luxor. Hathor's face with bovine ears topped the columns of many temples built in her honor, for instance at Dendera, where she adorned all four sides of each capital. Actually, these columns were huge enlargements of a type of musical rattle, the sistrum, which was sacred to Hathor.

Vessels and Implements. Other divine forms were shaped perfectly to serve as vessels or implements. The chubby figure of the divine dwarf Bes, god of hearth and home, made a fitting container for perfumes and ointments. The nude, outstretched form of the sky goddess Nut, the embodiment of the Milky Way, was well suited as the handle for a ritual implement often called a cosmetic spoon, which was popular during the eighteenth dynasty. Although they come in a variety of shapes, the spoons' iconography usually represents Nut as she is about to swallow the Sun (her son) at the end of the day, before it passes through her body during the night, so that she may give (re-)birth to it the next morning at dawn.

Amulets. Finally, almost every form of divine sculpture that existed in large scale was also made in the smallest of sizes to be used as personal amulets, charms, or beads. Thus, we find single figures of Sakhmet, Anubis, and other deities; groups of Isis and Horus; triads of Amun-Re, Mut, and Khonsu; ram's heads, cats, baboons, winged scarabs, and all the other sacred avatars were sculpted in semiprecious stone or molded in metal, glass, faience, or Egyptian blue, and fitted with suspension loops or perforations so that they could be worn for good luck and protection both in this life and in the afterlife.

[*See also* Amulets; Canopic Jars; Funerary Figurines; *and* Sphinx.]

BIBLIOGRAPHY

Brunner-Traut, Emma, and Helmut Brunner. *Osiris, Kreuz, und Halbmond: Die Drei Religionen Ägyptens.* Mainz, 1984. Exhibition catalog in which the first 140 entries include many images of divine statues and statuettes as well as implements, vessels, and amulets in divine form.

el-Saghir, Mohammed. *The Discovery of the Statuary Cachette of Luxor Temple.* Mainz, 1991. The official publication of the 1989 discovery of two dozen votive statues from the reign of Amenhotpe III in the great court of Luxor Temple.

Fazzini, Richard, et al. *Ancient Egyptian Art in the Brooklyn Museum.* Brooklyn, 1989. Excellent essays on some of the works cited here.

Hornung, Erik. *Conceptions of God in Ancient Egypt.* Ithaca, 1982. The classic work on this subject.

James, T. G. H. *Ancient Egypt: The Land and Its Legacy.* Austin, 1988. A guidebook to Egypt and its art, including divine sculpture, with special emphasis on the history of discovery and exploration of the monuments.

Josephson, Jack A. *Egyptian Royal Sculpture of the Late Period 400–246 B.C.* Mainz, 1997. Includes illustrations and stylistic discussions of divine images of this period where they join with the royal, including sphinxes.

Kozloff, Arielle P. "Divine Art." In *Searching for Ancient Egypt: Art, Architecture and Artifacts,* edited by David P. Silverman, pp. 39–45. Dallas, 1997. A brief introduction to the spiritual development of the ancient Egyptians and their divine imagery.

Kozloff, Arielle P., and Betsy M. Bryan. *Egypt's Dazzling Sun: Amenhotep III and His World.* Cleveland, 1992. Exhibition catalog with discussions of divine statuary, including animal forms and divine images on ritual implements and vessels.

Morenz, Siegfried. *Egyptian Religion.* Translated by A. E. Keep. Ithaca, 1973. Includes a lengthy discussion of the creation and daily life of the cult statue.

Reeves, Nicholas. *The Complete Tutankhamun: The King, The Tomb, The Royal Treasure.* London, 1990.

Robins, Gay. *The Art of Ancient Egypt.* Cambridge, Mass., 1997. The most up-to-date discussion of the general subject, incorporating recently developed ideas.

Russmann, Edna R., and David Finn. *Egyptian Sculpture: Cairo and Luxor.* Austin, 1989. An insightful history of Egyptian sculpture, including divine sculpture, based almost entirely on the collections of Egypt's two major museums.

Saleh, Mohamed, and Hourig Sourouzian. *Official Guide: The Egyptian Museum Cairo.* Manz, 1987. Contains images and discussions of many of the objects cited here.

Roehrig, Catharine H. "Cult Figure of a Falcon-Headed Deity." In *Miho Museum: South Wing,* edited by Takeshi Umehara et al., pp. 18–21. Misono, 1997. Originally published in *Ancient Art from the Shumei Family Collection* (New York, 1996).

Seipel, Wilfried. *Gott, Mensch, Pharao: Viertausend Jahr Menschenbild in der Skulptur des alten Ägypten.* Vienna, 1992. Exhibition catalog of 211 entries, including many examples of divine sculpture, most of which are votive sculptures or presumed cult statues.

Wildung, Dietrich, and Günter Grimm. *Götter: Pharaonen.* Mainz, 1978. Exhibition catalog of 175 entries, many for divine sculptures.

ARIELLE P. KOZLOFF

Wood Sculpture

Throughout most of the history of ancient Egypt, sculpture in wood has appeared alongside that in stone. The vulnerability of the former material, however, has resulted in a lack of understanding of the frequency of wood sculpture. Conditions that only superficially affect stone sculpture have a far more destructive effect on wood, and many instances are known of wood sculpture being found in a state impossible to preserve or even to record. This is the case, for example, for the Old Kingdom necropolis of Giza, where the majority was found to have been eaten by termites or reduced to pulp. This example underscores how remarkable it is that any wood sculpture has survived at all, let alone in a state that enables Egyptologists to assess stylistic development.

The fact that wood is more vulnerable than stone was known to the ancient Egyptians, too. Nevertheless, they decided that the material was appropriate for carving sculpture and became highly skilled at it. The inscriptions accompanying workshop scenes rarely referred to the statues depicted, but the tools shown are a good indication of the material in question—an adze in the hand of a workman is an indication that the material is wood, whereas hammers and mallets tend to be confined to working stone. The statues are usually shown in a completed state, regardless of the type of tool or action.

Throughout Egyptian history, the majority of wooden sculpture appears to have been made from native timber, that is, from acacia, sycamore, and tamarisk. Imported woods such as cedar and ebony were occasionally used, and in the New Kingdom they were the favored materials for royal sculpture in wood. Few statues have as yet had their material analyzed, so our knowledge of the woods used in ancient Egypt may yet change. As the indigenous woods did not yield sizable lengths of workable timber, statues larger than 30 to 40 centimeters (12 to 16 inches) were usually made from several separately carved pieces joined together by dowels, and mortise and tenon joints. The joins are almost invariably at the shoulders and the fronts of the feet. If the left arm is bent forward to hold a staff then the forearm is a separate piece. Life-size statues are made up of more pieces than smaller ones and patching is common on larger statues. The best-known example is the Sheikh el-Beled in the Cairo Museum. The patching and doweling visible on this statue would not have been evident on the finished product as statues were completely covered in a layer of paint or painted plaster on which many details of costume and jewelery were added. Sadly, this painted layer has usually deteriorated completely, along with much potential information on styles and fashions. The statues from the tomb of Metjetjy (sixth dynasty) are examples where the painted layer is still extant.

As so few statues have survived to our time, it is virtually impossible for scholars to identify individual workshops. In the Old Kingdom, Memphis and its necropolis clearly had its own workshop, with similar ones being set

SCULPTURE: WOOD SCULPTURE. *Statuette of King Senwosret I wearing the Crown of Lower Egypt, twelfth dynasty.* Made of painted cedarwood, the statuette is from the tomb of Imhotep at Lisht. (The Metropolitan Museum of Art, Museum Excavations 1913–1914; Rogers Fund supplemented by contribution of Edward S. Harkness [14.3.17])

up in the provinces as the period progressed. Asyut, Meir, and Beni Hassan were prolific producers of wooden statues during the First Intermediate period and the Middle Kingdom, and it is possible to discern characteristics peculiar to one place or another: for example, the eyes painted on statues from Beni Hassan are generally much larger than elsewhere. The lack of a complete sculptural record, however, invites caution when postulating the existence of stylistic schools. From the New Kingdom onward, series of wooden statues are carved for different locations. The Ahmose-Nefertari statues from Thebes and the kneeling figures holding Ptah shrines from Saqqara, for example, indicate that separate workshops were producing local "lines." The later periods are characterized by a virtual dearth of wooden sculpture, so very little is known about workshops during this time.

In the Old Kingdom, statues were placed in the tomb, first in a *serdab* and toward the end of the period in the burial chambers, to ensure that the *ba* of the deceased had somewhere to return if anything happened to the body. Groups of statues depicting the tomb owner in various guises were popular, particularly during the reigns of Unas (fifth dynasty) and Pepy II (sixth dynasty). These groups often consisted of several wooden statues and a stone one, despite stone being the more durable material. This distribution appears to have more to do with what the ancient Egyptian wanted to achieve in the afterlife than with the relative costs of the materials involved. Important court officials were as likely to have provided themselves with wooden statues as with stone ones; the comparative durability of stone, however, has biased our record of this phenomenon.

Depictions on the walls of Old Kingdom tombs show the tomb owner performing two basic sets of tasks: in one he is a passive participant, receiving offerings or overseeing his servants in the fields or elsewhere; in the other he takes a more active role by striding, hunting, or fishing. The task for artisans was how to convey these two aspects. Stone was ideal for impervious and inanimate form but wood was able to depict naturalistic, lifelike effects and thus convey an active role. In mixed Old Kingdom statue groups the stone statue is virtually always a seated figure, or else a standing figure with pendant arms. The legs are carved either together or with the left only slightly advanced. The wooden statues are striding, the left leg advanced with a staff held in the left hand. Even when the statues have pendant arms, the left leg is almost without exception advanced, thus conveying the idea of movement.

Female statues are invariably passive, standing figures in the Old Kingdom. The statues preserved are confined to the period until the reign of Unas and then from the reign of Merenre forward. The earlier statues are larger in format than later ones, which begin to show a wider variety in wig and dress styles. At the end of the Old Kingdom a female tomb owner was found with wooden statues for the first time. Pair statues also existed but very few have survived. At the beginning of the Old Kingdom, statues

are large (greater than 60 centimeters/23 inches), of high quality, and rare. After the reign of Merenre, quantity increases and the average size of 30 to 50 centimeters (12 to 20 inches) decreases. Statues in different costumes and wigs appear with inscriptions listing different titles, but not enough inscribed groups survive to enable scholars to associate particular costumes with specific titles. The costumes are nearly always a variation on the theme of the short gala kilt or the long, apron-fronted kilt. The former skirt is worn mostly with the staff and scepter pose, the latter with the arms pendant and with the right hand often holding a flap of the skirt. The echelon-curl wig in several variations was the most popular.

The inscriptions on wooden statue bases throughout the Old Kingdom are invariably lists of names and titles. It is not until the very end of the period that the well-known offering formula "for the *ka* of" the deceased appears. During the First Intermediate Period and the Middle Kingdom this becomes an almost invariable part of the inscriptions, and is the reason why wooden statues are often referred to as *ka* statues. The Old Kingdom statues, however, had not yet acquired this specific offering purpose.

At the end of the Old Kingdom, female offering bearers in wood appeared in the tombs for the first time. They are three-dimensional personifications of the funerary estates illustrated on the walls of the tombs. At first appearance, they are far superior to the small servant statues which form part of the scenes of daily life so popular in the First Intermediate period and the Middle Kingdom; the scenes from the tomb of Meketra are true masterpieces of their kind. As the period progresses, however, their special import decreases and their presence seems to become perfunctory. The quality also declines dramatically.

The wooden sculpture of the owners of the tombs and their wives remains of a relatively high quality during the Middle Kingdom, but their overall size decreases after the eleventh dynasty. The range of wigs and costumes for both males and females is much wider than in the Old Kingdom, but the accompanying texts on the bases are more stylized and thus still prevent us from linking the costumes and wigs to specific occupations, with the notable exception of the statue of Yuya in the Metropolitan Museum, who is wearing the vizier's costume. Female statues tend to have very pronounced waistlines and hips as the period progresses; statues from the earlier periods being more true to life in this respect. The techniques of manufacture remained the same as for the Old Kingdom. During this time local workshops in the provinces produced the majority of wooden sculpture, for example, at Asyut, Meir, Beni Hasan, and Dahshur. The earliest extant royal statues in wood date from the twelfth dynasty—two

SCULPTURE: WOOD
SCULPTURE. *Figure of Osiris,
nineteenth–twentieth dynasty, from
a private collection.* (Art Resource,
NY)

splendid statues are attributed to Senwosret I—and from this time on, statues of the king and his consorts became more common. The most magnificent statue in this genre is the *ka* statue of King Awibre Hor of the thirteenth dynasty, now in the Cairo Museum.

Up to this point in time, wooden sculpture follows an unbroken line of development. The quality of the works produced during the First Intermediate Period did not change, nor did the availability of materials. The general impression is one of realism and movement.

There is very little extant wooden material from the period between the Middle and New Kingdoms, making it impossible to trace the line of development between the two, or any effect that the Second Intermediate Period may have had on the production of sculpture. The relatively numerous statues from the first part of the eighteenth dynasty continued to be inspired by the Middle Kingdom and are full of force and character. Model scenes, however, had disappeared as had the female offering bearers. After the reign of Thutmose III statues became far less numerous, but they revived under Amenhotpe III as the first statues to display Amarna traits. The figures are very elegant, but more stylized; their realism decreases. At this time the majority of the statues were female, many of them nude, and there is also a group that probably were originally the handles of mirrors. In the immediate post-Amarna period, statues became relatively numerous again, both males and females, and are generally of a high quality with complicated dress and coiffures. After the reign of Sety I female statues virtually disappear, but male statues continue to be popular through the twentieth dynasty. Two pair statues, both masterpieces, are known from the eighteenth dynasty, and show the tomb owner and his wife seated side by side. Wooden *shawabtis* are known from the Middle Kingdom on, but the best examples date to the New Kingdom.

During the later New Kingdom sculptors were less inclined to innovation and all types of statuary duplicated those made in stone (e.g., standard bearers and naophorous statues). The realism of the earlier periods declined into frozen conventions. Royal sculpture in wood is now relatively common. There are several known statues of Amenhotpe III in ebony, accompanied by Queen Tiye. Royal tombs were supplied with large wooden statues (e.g., Thutmose III, Tutankhamun, Horemheb). Statues of queens are uncommon, especially in the later part of the period, an exception being the statues of the deified Ahmose Nefertari. Royal tombs and temples of the period were provided with resin-coated or gilded wooden statues, which were placed in wooden shrines. With the exception of those from the tomb of Tutankhamun, they are all poorly preserved.

During the later Egyptian periods, private wooden statuary all but disappears. Like most art from that time, the few surviving examples are in an archaizing style imitating Middle Kingdom examples. Divine statuary appeared in the burial chambers of private tombs: kneeling figures of Isis and Nephthys were placed on either side of the sarcophagus; *ba*-birds, falcons and *akhom* figures as well as Anubis jackals were placed on top. Ptah-Sokar-Osiris figures, often with a cavity containing a papyrus roll, were also popular.

[*See also* Models.]

BIBLIOGRAPHY

There are no books that deal specifically with wood sculpture. Some of the more general art books do have sections discussing wood.

Eaton-Krauss, Marianne. *The Representations of Statuary in Private Tombs of the Old Kingdom*. Ägyptologische Abhandlungen, 39. Wiesbaden, 1984. A thorough discussion of two-dimensional representations of tomb statues of both wood and stone in wall scenes in Old Kingdom *mastabas*.

Harvey, Julia. "A Late Middle Kingdom Wooden Statue from Assiut in the Walters Art Gallery." *The Journal of the Walters Art Gallery* 49/50 (1991/92), 1–6. A comparative study of some female wooden statues from the Middle Kingdom.

Harvey, Julia C. "A Typological Study of Egyptian Wooden Statues of the Old Kingdom." Ph.D. diss., University College, London, 1994. (In preparation for publication).

Reeves, Nicholas. *The Complete Tutankhamun: The King, The Tomb, The Royal Treasure*. London, 1990. See in particular the section dealing with ritual figures and magical objects on pp. 130–139 for the wood statues from the tomb. For similar statues from other royal tombs see the relevant sections in:

Reeves, Nicholas and Richard H. Wilkinson. *The Complete Valley of the Kings: Tombs and Treasures of Egypt's Greatest Pharaohs*. London, 1996.

Smith, W. S. *A History of Egyptian Sculpture and Painting in the Old Kingdom*. 2d ed. London, 1949. Fundamental study of Old Kingdom art including wood sculpture.

Tooley, Angela M. J. *Egyptian Models and Scenes*. Shire Egyptology Series, no.22. Princes Risborough, 1995. An introduction for the general reader to models and scenes, including offering bearers, not only in wood but also in stone.

Vandier, J. *Manuel d'archéologie égyptienne*, vol. 3, *les grandes époques: La Statuaire*. Paris, 1958. This is the most comprehensive discussion of Egyptian statuary to date, and is a mine of information and illustrations from the Old Kingdom to the end of the New Kingdom.

JULIA HARVEY

SEAFARING. Clay and stone models from Neolithic sites attest to the early development of river navigation in Egypt. Papyrus, tied in bundles, was used to form rafts or canoe-like craft that let people use the Nile in new ways. Illustrations of boat shapes more suited to wooden construction appear in the late Predynastic period, along with single masts with sails. Because the Nile current flows north to the Delta at up to four nautical miles per hour, and the prevailing wind blows from north to south, journeys on the river were relatively easy once the sail was in use. Portage around the rocky cataracts at Aswan and farther south overcame those obstacles. Major and minor canal works were part of Egyptian state projects from the earliest kings, culminating in a Persian-period canal between the Red Sea and the Nile wide enough to handle two ships passing. At sea, ships probably stayed near the coast on routes identified by landmarks passed on from generation to generation, at least until the Late period.

In the late Predynastic and Early Dynastic periods, evidence for seafaring is mostly indirect. Simple drawings of wooden boats scratched on the walls of the Wadi Hammamat, a resting point on the route between the Nile and the Red Sea, may show vessels being carried across the desert as in later times. First dynasty boat depictions show mostly ceremonial wooden boats, but one label from Abydos differs: two blocky vessels are associated with the words for an imported wood (*mrw*) and Lebanon, leading some scholars to suggest that we are looking at either cargo ships or ships made from imported wood.

Large, long, coniferous timbers and many imported objects in first dynasty and later sites offer evidence for trade with the eastern Mediterranean, where the nearest forests belonged to the ancient Syrian-Palestinian cultures. Inscriptions at Byblos in Lebanon may be linked to the second dynasty ruler Khasekhemwy (c.2714–2687 BCE). Contact with Mesopotamian civilization seems to have come along this northern sea route during the late Predynastic and Early Dynastic periods, because few artifacts can be traced along the proposed southern route through the Persian Gulf and around the Arabian Peninsula to the Red Sea.

The first secure written evidence for Mediterranean seafaring by Egyptians comes from the Palermo Stone, which mentions forty ships, loaded with cedar, in the early fourth dynasty reign of Sneferu. Also from the Old Kingdom is a gold Egyptian ax head found in Lebanon and inscribed "the boat crew 'Pacified-is-the-Two-Falcons-of-Gold' port gang." Both Khufu (fourth dynasty) and Sahure (fifth dynasty) used the "Two Falcons of Gold" epithet. Khufu's name is on vase fragments found at Byblos, and the 43-meter-long (135 feet) royal ship of Khufu is built almost entirely of imported cedar. The earliest detailed portraits of seaworthy ships come from decorated blocks in the mortuary temple for the fifth dynasty ruler Sahure (2458–2446 BCE) at Abusir. Twelve ships are illustrated, with careful attention to construction, rigging, and passengers, who include a mixture of Egyptians and Syrians.

In addition to a strong sewn girdle around the hull's bulwarks, the Sahure vessels include a massive hogging truss, invented to counter the physical stresses of seafaring. The hogging truss, looped around each end of the ship, was tightened with a device known as a Spanish windlass, which kept both ends under tension, thus maintaining the hull's integrity and shape. Like other Old Kingdom boats, this fleet relied on bipod masts—two-legged, fixed masts that spread the force of the sail across the hull. Although the sails are not set in these illustrations, they probably were long and narrow, like those commonly illustrated for river vessels of the same period. Large, forked spars helped spread the fixed sails, and helmsmen used quarter-rudders for steering.

Sahure also sent an expedition to the land of Punt in his thirteenth regnal year. Punt, probably modern Somalia or Eritrea at the southern end of the Red Sea, fed Egyptian appetites for incense, precious woods, and other raw materials. Pepy II (r. 2300–2206 BCE) also recorded an expedition to Punt, and there are stone fragments carved with seagoing ships from the time of Unas (r. 2404–2374). The Sahure text records eighty thousand measures of myrrh alone, so we must imagine fairly large ships with crews able to navigate the reef-lined shores of the Red Sea more than forty-five hundred years ago. These oceangoing, cargo ships were known as *kbn.t* ("Byblos") or *h'w* ships even until the Late period.

In the Middle Kingdom, there are no extant illustrations of seagoing ships, but there are other sources of evidence for seafaring. The cedar Dahshur boats and many fine cedar coffins point to abundant imports from Lebanon, and gold jewelry featuring Red Sea shells is fairly common and has been interpreted as an indication of seafaring. In addition, scraps of boatlike planks and carved limestone anchors at Wadi Gawasis on the Red Sea testify to seagoing activity there. Abdel Monem el-Sayed of the University of Alexandria excavated shrines, anchors, and what seems to be a campsite on the ancient shore. His work shows that this site—rather than Quseir, for which there are no pharaonic finds—was the anchorage for travel to Punt.

In addition to fragments of limestone with the cartouche of Senwosret I (r. 1971–1928 BCE), el-Sayed found anchors, some inscribed with narratives describing voyages to Punt in ships built at "the dockyards of Coptos" and carried, in pieces, across the Eastern Desert by a crew of nearly thirty-eight hundred men. Cedar plank fragments from the site feature mortises and plank dimensions which correspond well with what we know of extant Middle Kingdom watercraft. Other finds show that Mersa Gawasis was used during the reigns of Amenemhet II (Year 28, c.1900 BCE), Senwosret II (Years 1, 5, and 6, c.1897–1891 BCE), and Senwosret III (r. 1878–1843 BCE). Inscriptions suggest that both Punt and perhaps mines in the Sinai were reached by sea from Mersa Gawasis during the twelfth dynasty.

Middle Kingdom texts, particularly the *Instructions of*

Ipuwer from the end of the period, and the *Story of the Shipwrecked Sailor,* deal with seafaring. Comments by Ipuwer indicate unhappiness with the lack of Egyptian ships trading with Byblos for resin and other goods related to rituals, while the Shipwrecked Sailor mixes fact and fantasy about a Red Sea trip to the Sinai that resulted in his spending months on an island with a lapis lazuli and golden snake after his 54-meter-long (180 foot) ship sank. Spells from the *Book of Going Forth by Day* (*Book of the Dead*) also provide us with a glimpse of Nile-based navigation and practice during this time.

Seafaring in the New Kingdom seems a more common occurrence, with refinements in rigging and steering gear traceable through images and models of ships. No physical remains of New Kingdom hulls have been found as yet. The most spectacular images come from the mortuary temple of Hatshepsut (r. 1502–1482 BCE), at Deir el-Bahri where a fleet of *kbn.t* ships sets sail for Punt and returns loaded with all kinds of cargo, including incense trees, monkeys, and natives.

Hatshepsut boasts that she reopened the ways to Punt, and this extraordinary series of illustrations suggests that she invested heavily in the expedition. Five ships with upright bows and curved papyriform sterns, hogging trusses, and single masts with broad sails are shown entering and leaving the anchorage at Punt. Only one includes an illustration of beam ends; otherwise, artistic attention was lavished on the rigging. Fifteen oarsmen shown on the side facing the viewer would have required about a meter of room each, suggesting the ships were at least 22 meters (70 feet) long. We have no indication of width, although the standard reported for Egyptian (and other) cargo ships is three times longer than broad.

Thutmose III's reign provides us with dockyard records that monitored the movement of ships as well as single goatskins and reused timbers, the first use of *menesh* for a ship type (in the expedition to Syria-Palestine, Year 30, c.1474 BCE), and further records of cedar acquired and goods stored at harbors for Egyptian use. An Amarna tablet refers to the king's ships in Tyre, and seagoing ships seem to be illustrated by Ramesses III in the Sea Peoples' battle scene at Medinet Habu. Egyptian grain was exported to Palestine and Anatolian Egyptian vassals, according to cuneiform texts there, but whether Egyptian or local ships were used is not known.

A number of authors argue that the keel was introduced during the New Kingdom, but there is little evidence to support this hypothesis. There are central, longitudinal timbers at the ends of models and in depictions which extend beyond the planked sides of the hulls, but these stop short at the waterline. The Late Bronze Age shipwreck at Uluburun, Turkey (c.1306 BCE) has no frames, and its "keel" provides longitudinal stiffening but protrudes only about 2 centimeters (0.75 inch) beyond the planking on what was undoubtedly a seafaring ship of the highest quality.

During the Late period and on into Roman times, a number of textual references make it clear that there was a continued investment in seafaring by the rulers of Egypt. In addition to trading vessels and warships, Egyptian shipwrights built enormous cargo ships, including obelisk carriers for Roman emperors from Augustus to Constantine. One that was built for Caligula was so immense that Claudius filled it with cement and sank it as a significant part of the foundations for harborworks at Ostia, the port of Rome.

The ancient Egyptians began traveling on the Nile at least seven thousand years ago, and probably had started sea voyages in wooden boats by about fifty-five hundred years ago. Although no seagoing ship has been excavated, abundant evidence for Egyptian routes to the Levant and the Red Sea points to an active merchant fleet and a competent navy for much of Egyptian history, particularly from the New Kingdom onward.

[*See also* Ships and Shipbuilding.]

BIBLIOGRAPHY

Jones, Dilwyn. *A Glossary of Ancient Egyptian Nautical Titles and Terms.* London, 1988. Comprehensive collection and translations.

Jones, Dilwyn. *Egyptian Bookshelf: Boats.* London, 1995. General overview of evidence for Egyptian watercraft.

Kemp, Barry. *Ancient Egypt: Anatomy of a Civilization.* London, 1989.

Landström, B. *Ships of the Pharaohs.* London, 1970. Unsurpassed collection of pictorial evidence for Egyptian watercraft, but the interpretations are dated.

Lipke, P. *The Royal Ship of Cheops.* Oxford, 1984. Detailed report on the reconstruction of the Khufu ship.

Patch, D.C., and C. Ward Haldane. *The Pharaoh's Boat at the Carnegie.* Pittsburgh, 1990. Investigation of the Middle Kingdom Egyptian boat at the Carnegie Museum.

el-Sayed, Abdel Monem A. H. "New Light on the Recently Discovered Port on the Red Sea Shore." *Chronique d'Égypte* 58.115–116 (1983), 23–37. Summary of finds and interpretation of the Mersa Gawasis anchorage.

Vinson, Steve. *Egyptian Boats and Ships.* Buckinghamshire, 1994. Specialist information in an accessible, well-illustrated format.

Ward, Cheryl. *Sacred and Secular: Ancient Egyptian Ships and Boats.* Boston, 1999. This volume for specialists and nonspecialists examines the cultural context and the physical characteristics of twenty ancient rivercraft.

CHERYL WARD

SEALS AND SEALINGS. Sealing was used in Egypt from the Early Dynastic period onward to ensure that documents and the contents of containers or rooms were preserved intact. This sealing was done by pressing a cylinder or stamp seal against a prepared surface of Nile mud, leaving a distinctive impression imprinted on the clay. Although the mud sealing could be broken easily, the seal decoration theoretically could not be reproduced without the seal itself. The primary purpose was to reveal any unauthorized tampering with the contents of the letters, pottery vessels, baskets, boxes, sacks, storerooms, or tombs that had been sealed.

Evidence from the seals themselves and the mud sealings they produce tends to be complementary. Many extant seals come from the antiquity trade or have been excavated in funerary contexts. Dating is complicated by the possibility of seals being heirlooms or objects recovered years after their creation, and again pressed into service. The archaeological context of sealings is a firmer indication of date because, once broken, sealings were not reused. Seals were often worn on necklaces or rings and thus functioned as jewelry or amulets. The presence of sealings is evidence that seals were functional and not merely ornamental. Both sealings and seals provide significant chronological data as well as evidence for reconstructing Egyptian administration and cultural contact with neighboring lands.

Cylinder Seals. The earliest type of seal commonly used in Egypt was cylindrical in shape and was pierced lengthwise for a cord or wire, on which it could be hung from the owner's wrist or neck. Incised decoration or writing was placed on the exterior of the seal; the impression would repeat the same design as long as the seal was rolled across fresh mud placed over jar openings or over cords tying together other goods. This type of sealing was most useful for large objects because the design could be extended indefinitely.

The earliest evidence for cylinder seals comes from the Uruk period (about 3700 BCE) in southwestern Iran and southern Mesopotamia. By the end of the fourth millennium, this type of tubular seal was used throughout the ancient Near East, coming rather late to Egypt. The idea of sealing and the decorative motifs used on the seals could have been transmitted to Egypt through trade goods on which clay sealings had been affixed. The iconography of Predynastic Egyptian cylinder seals with patterns of cross-hatching and fish motifs shows its closest affiliation to be with material from Susa, suggesting southwestern Iran rather than Mesopotamia proper as the source for the seals found in Egypt. While some early cylinder seals were imported from western Asia, others may be Egyptian-made, but of foreign inspiration.

Sealing was not characteristic of the Predynastic period in Egypt; fewer than twenty seals are known from Predynastic cemeteries, and these may have been exotic pieces of jewelry or trade goods. About half of the examples were acquired by purchase or are without clear archaeological context. Excavated cylinder seals have come from Abusir el-Meleq (tomb 1033), Ballas (tomb 307), Nag el-Deir (tomb 7304), Naqada (tombs 1863 and 29), Matmar, and Zawiyet el-Aryan. Predynastic cylinder seals have also been recovered from the Nubian sites of Gerf Hussein, Saras West, and Kashkush. In all cases the archaeological context is of later Gerzean (Naqada II) date. The late Predynastic cylinder seals from Egypt form a coherent group of small (2–3 centimeters/1–2 inches) stone (mostly limestone) seals.

Sealing and writing were both adopted by the central government bureaucracy of a unified Egypt to extend and ensure state control over the country; first dynasty seals and sealings form some of the earliest collections of hieroglyphic writing. Seals and sealings of the new state have been recovered from both Palestine ('En Besor) and from A-Group contexts in Nubia. The tombs of the governing class of Early Dynastic Egypt were full of large jars containing provisions for the afterlife. These were topped by large cone-shaped lumps of clay, often set atop a small saucer placed over the jar opening. A cylinder seal was rolled up one side of this cap and down the other; sometimes this was repeated with a second seal, and the two impressions cross at the top.

The royal names preserved on first and second dynasty sealings are of primary importance in dating and sequencing tombs in the major cemeteries of the period. Emery suggested that many of the Abydos tombs were only cenotaphs (memorials), with the pharaohs actually being buried at Saqqara. The first dynasty Saqqara tombs, however, are better explained as the burial places of the high officials identified in the sealings. Sealings from a number of kings often appear in the same Saqqara tomb, and there are more first dynasty Saqqara tombs than there are pharaohs for this period. Sealed grave goods from royal storehouses would have been assigned as rewards or payment to the officials actually buried in the tombs.

Small cylinder seals belonging to individuals have been found in lower-class Early Dynastic burials, most notably at the site of Nag el-Deir. Most are made of black steatite, but some are made of wood and ivory. They are decorated with hieroglyphic signs that seem to represent the owners' names. Usually these seals have a representation of the human figure seated in front of an offering table, such as is depicted on Old Kingdom false doors and stelae. Thus, these seals seem to be an inexpensive version of the funerary stela, with the primary function of preserving the name of the deceased. There is no evidence that these private Early Dynastic cylinder seals were ever used to seal anything.

Although the private funerary use of cylinder seals did not continue into the third dynasty, the royal and official use of the larger seals with complex designs and texts continued throughout the Old Kingdom (third to sixth dynasties). Seals were such an important part of the state bureaucracy that an official from Meir records in his tomb that his seal of office never spent the night apart from him. Important groups of Old Kingdom sealings have been found at Abusir, Beit Khallaf, Giza, and Buhen in Nubia. They provide evidence for bureaucratic activity, as well as for dating and for identifying officials and tomb-owners. For example, the box sealings in the Giza tomb of Queen Hetepheres show that she was buried in the reign of her son Khufu, rather than that of her husband Sneferu. Sealings in the Giza *mastaba*s were used to seal canopic chests. After being passed around the chest in two directions, a string was tied at the top; the knot was covered with a lump of clay across which a cylinder seal was rolled.

Cylinder seals continued to be made in Egypt throughout the Middle Kingdom, during which period, as the traditional form of seal, they were favored for royal names. Many examples would not have been suitable for use as seals, being made with multiple lobes or having glaze filling up the incised characters of the royal name. By the First Intermediate Period, therefore, cylinders seem to be treated more as a type of amulet rather than as a working badge of office. Cylinders continue to appear as an archaic form in the Second Intermediate Period, New Kingdom, and even later.

Seal Amulets. The use of seals as amulets becomes increasingly important with the introduction of a new type of seal in sixth dynasty Egypt. These seal amulets appear in circular, oval, and rectangular shapes, with a flat base on which a design is carved. A number of these seals have small ring-shanks on the back and thus are referred to as "button seals" (*Knopfsiegel* in German). The backs of many of these seals are simple domes or pyramids. Others are carved in the shape of a wide variety of human and animal figures—crocodile, hippopotamus, frog, lizard, ape, and hawk—sometimes just the head of which is shown. Soon scarab (beetle-shaped) seals, along with cowroid and hemispherical seals, were introduced. Although at first just one form among many, by the end of the First Intermediate Period the scarab had become the dominant Egyptian seal type.

The seal amulets are made of glazed and unglazed steatite, limestone, faience, pottery, bone, ivory, and rock crystal. Their design repertoire consists largely of geometric motifs, linear maze patterns, and magical symbols, but it also includes human, animal, and insect figures done in a linear style. With the introduction of scarab and ovoid seal amulets toward the end of the First Intermediate Period, the geometric designs are replaced by floral motifs with spiral and scroll patterns. This type of decoration is in stark contrast to the traditional hieroglyphic inscriptions found on cylinder seals. Early scholars, such as Petrie and Frankfort, sought to explain this phenomenon through foreign influence from Syria, Anatolia, or the Ae-

gean. Some influence in the choice of seal type and in the geometric or spiral designs may have reached Egypt from abroad, since a steady commerce connected Old Kingdom Egypt with the Phoenician port city of Byblos on the Levantine coast.

Ward (1970) has argued plausibly for a native Egyptian origin of the First Intermediate Period seal amulets. The key factor here is archaeological context; no pottery or other objects with foreign associations have been found in connection with seal amulets. There is no pattern of foreign influence, but rather a clear distinction in the status and social class of the seal owners: the seal amulets are associated with the burials of individuals of relatively low social status and wealth.

The forerunners of the seal amulets may be a series of cylinder seals from the late Old Kingdom described by Fischer (1972). These cylinder seals are decorated with motifs that resemble hieroglyphs but are used in a decorative fashion. Frequently the designs are arranged so that one half faces one way and the other half faces in the opposite direction in a *tête-bêche* (head to foot) arrangement, also found among seal amulet designs. As central control loosened in the sixth dynasty, a more popular taste in seal design came into play; its decorative patterns first emerged with hieroglyphic signs and then came to dominate the seal motif repertoire.

The seal amulets represent a provincial art style rather than the formal art of the pharaonic court. Although small quantities of seal amulets have been found in Lower and Upper Egypt, the vast majority of known seal amulets (399 of 575, by one count) have been recovered from Brunton's excavations in Middle Egypt at the sites of Matmar, Mostagedda, and Qau/Badari, most of them from burials of women and children. For example, Brunton records 229 seals from Qau/Badari, 48 percent of which were found with women, 5 percent with children, and 4 percent with men. The seals accompanying men were often scarabs. The position of these seals is most often at the neck, where they would have been hung from a string, either alone or with beads or other amulets as part of a necklace. In some cases the seals seem to have been placed with other toilet articles in a box near the body. Some seals (mostly scarabs) were found placed in the hands of the deceased. Although fully capable of being used as seals, these objects apparently served rather as protective amulets or had a decorative function as jewelry.

Middle and New Kingdom Sealings. Sealings show that scarabs or ovoids were being used as personal seals in early twelfth dynasty Thebes. These seals were not inscribed with their owners' names and have the same type of decoration as the seal amulets. Two identical sealings found on the Hekanakhte correspondence are decorated with a spiral design and the hieroglyph for "seal." Another impression with C-scroll decoration was recovered from

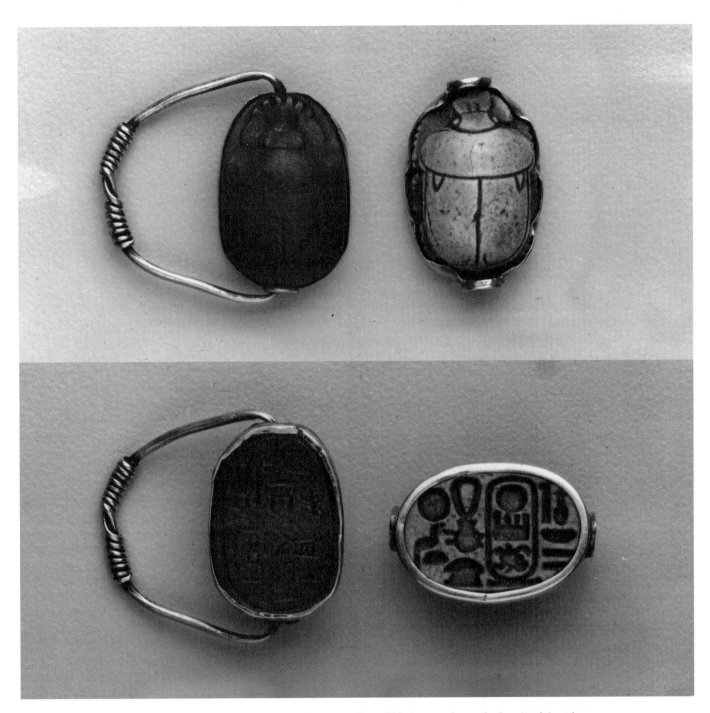

SEALS AND SEALINGS. *Scarab seal rings.* (*Left*) twelfth dynasty, from Abydos; (*Right*) mid-eighteenth to nineteenth dynasty, provenance unknown. (University of Pennsylvania Museum, Philadelphia. Negs. # S4–143066 [*top*]; S4–143067 [*bottom*])

the Theban tomb of Meketre. The great silver scarab of Meketre's estate manager Wah shows the type of seal from which these impressions were made. It is decorated with S-scrolls and such hieroglyphic motifs as cobras and the sign for "life." Further evidence is provided by around fifty seal impressions and hundreds of fragmentary, undeco-

rated clay sealings (*bullae*) recovered from East Karnak in 1991. Along with spirals, scrolls, rosettes, and hieroglyphic emblems, linear and stick figure motifs appear on the East Karnak sealings.

Comparable collections of late twelfth and thirteenth dynasty sealings are known from Lower Egypt (Abu Ghâlib), from a royal mortuary town (Kahun) near the capital, from Upper Egypt (Abydos), and from a number of fortresses in Nubia. The largest number and best-published sealings from this period come from the Nubian fortress of Uronarti; almost five thousand sealings were recovered from this site by Reisner and Wheeler. About half of these were large door or sack sealings that bore the name of the Uronarti storehouse—"Storehouse of the Fortress of *Ḥst-iwnw*." Some of these were overstamped with private seals, indicating that an individual was taking personal responsibility for the security of the goods involved. Often the fingerprints made while pressing down the seal are still visible.

New Kingdom jar sealings are known from palace, funerary temple, village (Deir el-Medina), and tomb contexts at Thebes and other sites in Upper Egypt and Nubia. Important collections from Malqata (reign of Amenhotpe III), Tell el-Amarna (reign of Akhenaten), and the tomb of Tutankhamun show three major types of jar sealings: cylindrical, domed, and cap-shaped. Paintings from Theban tomb 188 (Parennefer) depict the act of impressing the seal against the mud sealing. The sealer holds the seal in the right hand and a bowl in his left, which would have contained water with which to wet or clean off the seal. The stamp seals contain inscriptions identifying the jar contents, such as "honey for the *sed*-festival" or "wine from the estate of the Aten." New Kingdom Theban tombs were generally closed with some form of sealing. Most notable is the seal of the royal necropolis with the figure of the Anubis jackal represented over three rows of three captives each, found in the tomb of Tutankhamun and elsewhere in the Valley of the Kings. The use of scarabs, seals of other shapes, and signet rings to seal papyrus documents continued through the New Kingdom until the Greco-Roman period.

Seals and sealing performed a number of roles throughout ancient Egyptian history. They served as security devices, for both the state bureaucracy and private individuals, for documents, containers, and spaces. Seals were used as protective amulets, funerary labels, and personal ornaments, sometimes in addition to, but often to the exclusion of, their sealing function. Although usually decorated with hieroglyphic inscriptions containing names, titles, and/or protective emblems, Egyptian seals performed many of these same functions with only simple decorative patterns.

[*See also* Amulets; *and* Scarabs.]

BIBLIOGRAPHY

Baines, John, ed. *Stone Vessels, Pottery and Sealings from the Tomb of Tut'ankhamun.* Oxford, 1993. Note articles by Colin Hope ("The Jar Sealings," pp. 87–138) and Olaf E. Kaper ("The Door Sealings and Object Sealings").

Boochs, Wolfgang. *Siegel und Siegeln im Alten Ägypten.* (Kölner Forschungen zu Kunst und Altertum, 4.) St. Augustin, 1982. Concentrates on textual and inscriptional evidence for how seals were used in ancient Egypt.

Brunton, Guy. *Qau and Badari I–III.* (British School of Archaeology in Egypt Publications, 44, 45, 50.) London, 1927–1930. Excavation report of the largest collection of First Intermediate Period seal amulets.

Dunham, Dows. *Second Cataract Forts II: Uronarti, Shalfak, Mirgissa.* Boston, 1967. A fuller treatment of the Uronarti material with the same illustrations appears in George A. Reisner "Clay Sealings of Dynasty XIII from Uronarti Fort," *Kush* 3 (1955), 26f. Dunham also includes seal impressions from Shalfak (pl. 71) and Mirgissa (figs. 9–12).

Fischer, Henry. "Old Kingdom Cylinder Seals for the Lower Classes." *Metropolitan Museum Journal* 6 (1972), 5–16.

Frankfort, Henri. *Cylinder Seals: A Documentary Essay on the Art and Religion of the Ancient Near East.* London, 1939. Classic presentation of the influence of Mesopotamian glyptic on Egypt; see especially pp. 292–300.

Gibson, M., and R. Biggs, eds. *Seals and Sealings in the Ancient Near East.* (Bibliotheca Mesopotamica, 6.) Malibu, 1977. Publication of a symposium concerning the role of seals in ancient Near Eastern society. Note articles by Janet Johnson ("Private Name Seals of the Middle Kingdom," pp. 141–145) and Bruce Williams ("Aspects of Sealing and Glyptic in Egypt before the New Kingdom," pp. 135–138).

Hope, Colin. *Malkata and the Birket Habu Jar Sealings and Amphorae.* Egyptology Today, 5.2. Warminster, 1978. Provides basic typology of New Kingdom jar sealings, including list of depictions of sealed jars in tombs from Tell el-Amarna and Thebes.

Kaplony, Peter. *Die Rollsiegel des Alten Reichs.* (Monumenta Aegyptiaca, 2–3.) 2 vols. Brussels, 1977, 1981. Old Kingdom cylinder seals studied by motif and king's name, with an extensive section on the seals from Abusir.

Martin, Geoffrey T. *Scarabs, Cylinders and Other Ancient Egyptian Seals: A Checklist of Publications.* Warminster, 1985. Extensive bibliography of older material, but does not include excavation reports.

Petrie, W. M. Flinders. *Buttons and Design Scarabs.* (British School of Archaeology in Egypt Publications, 38.) London, 1925. Reprinted by Aris & Phillips in 1974, this seminal publication contains illustrations of seals and scarabs from the Egyptian collection in University College, London.

Pittman, Holly. "Cylinder Seals and Scarabs in the Ancient Near East." In *Civilizations of the Ancient Near East,* edited by Jack M. Sasson, vol. 3, pp. 1589–1603. New York, 1994. General survey useful for placing Egypt in its Near Eastern context.

Podzorski, Patricia V. "Predynastic Egyptian Seals of Known Provenience in the R. H. Lowie Museum of Anthropology." *Journal of Near Eastern Studies* 47 (1988), 259–268.

Reisner, George A., and W. S. Smith. *A History of the Giza Necropolis II: The Tomb of Hetep-heres the Mother of Cheops.* Cambridge, Mass., 1955. Chapter 6, "The Mud Impressions," covers the sealings from the tomb of Hetepheres and other seal impressions recovered by the Harvard-Boston Expedition to Giza.

Reisner, George A., and N. F. Wheeler. "The Art of Seal Carving in Egypt in the Middle Kingdom." *Bulletin of the Museum of Fine Arts, Boston* 28 (1930), 47–55. Good general introduction, with emphasis on the socio-economic context of the Uronarti sealings.

Ward, William A. *Egypt and the East Mediterranean World 2200–1900 B.C.: Studies in Egyptian Foreign Relations during the First Intermediate Period.* Beirut, 1971. Reviews interconnections between Minoan glyptic art and Egyptian seal amulets, arguing for the native Egyptian development of spiral decoration.

Ward, William A. "The origin of Egyptian Design-Amulets." *Journal of Egyptian Archaeology* 56 (1970), 65–80.

STEVEN BLAKE SHUBERT

SEA PEOPLES. This evocative name has been adopted by modern historians from occasional Egyptian usage in order to describe neatly a number of different groups involved in a bewildering migration around and across the Mediterranean Sea over a period of at least fifty years in the later twelfth and early eleventh centuries BCE. This was accompanied by widespread destruction of individual settlements and the collapse of wider political entities from Greece to the Levant. Its causes are still poorly understood, but there is no doubt that it ranks among the most significant and formative episodes in the history of the eastern Mediterranean, since it marked the end of the Bronze Age and the beginning of the Iron Age. Egypt, on the southern periphery of this movement, was affected less than more northerly areas. Although the attempted invasions of the country by the Sea Peoples presented a major challenge to the pharaohs of the nineteenth and twentieth dynasties, and the successful repulsion of them was recorded in detail, the impact of the Sea Peoples on Egypt in the longer term was insignificant compared to that of the Libyan tribes with whom they were at times allied.

Our knowledge of the Sea Peoples, insofar as Egypt is concerned, derives primarily from the textual and pictorial records carved in the reigns of Merenptah (c.1237–1226 BCE) and Ramesses III (c.1198–1166 BCE). This can be supplemented by scattered references in other inscriptions and papyri, notably Ramesses II's accounts of the Battle of Qadesh and a literary text, the *Story of Wenamun*. For the wider picture, we rely on texts from the Hittite kingdom in Anatolia and from Ugarit in Syria, as well as on an increasing body of archaeological data from the whole of the eastern Mediterranean. The Homeric epics may also have a contribution to make to our understanding, but the historical relevance of much of their subject matter remains controversial, particularly in chronological terms.

The Egyptian inscriptions are mostly official accounts created as part of a scheme of temple decoration in which the primary aim was to exemplify a particular king's performance of his role as protector of Egypt. They are triumphal in tone and naturally present the outcome of battles as overwhelming victories for the pharaoh. They list enemies killed or captured but make no reference to Egyptian casualties. They are nonetheless important for the detail they give of the direction and composition of the attacks on Egypt, and for the pictorial evidence they provide on the appearance, costume, and weaponry of the Sea Peoples. The Peleset, for instance, are characterized by feathered headdresses and short tasseled kilts, and the Sherden by horned helmets. The letters from Ugarit, written in the last days of the city's existence, offer a quite different and touching insight. They show a population bewildered by the speed and unexpectedness of the attacks and unable to protect themselves because their own fighting forces had been sent to help allies faced by the same problem.

Although the possibly quite diverse origins of the different groups that made up the Sea Peoples are not known with any certainty, there is a broad consensus that they came mainly from the Aegean and Anatolia, and archaeological discoveries increasingly suggest that upheavals in the Mycenaean world lay behind their abandonment of their native countries. The following names—which occur in various combinations in Egyptian texts—are generally regarded as coming under the umbrella term "Sea Peoples": Denyen, Ekwesh, Lukka, Peleset, Sherden, Shekelesh, Teresh, Tjeker, and Weshesh. These are not exact renderings of the names because the Egyptian script did not record vowels, and so, by a different convention, the Denyen appear in some modern books as Danuna, the Ekwesh as Akawasha, the Sherden as Shardana, and so on. Attempts to relate them to particular geographical areas rely largely on resemblances between the names they bear in Egyptian texts and names known from other, especially Hittite and Classical, sources. For example, the Sherden/Shardana have been linked with Sardinia—either as their original homeland or as the place where some of them eventually settled—on the basis of the similar consonantal structure of the two words, but a connection with Sardis has also been mooted. It is likewise proposed that the island of Sicily got its name from the Shekelesh. Connections with the Greek world have been reinforced by suggestions that the Akawasha are Achaeans, while the Denyen should be equated with the Danaoi, or mainland Greeks. Such identifications are inevitably conjectural—often there are two or more equations that are equally plausible phonetically—and, since no written languages can currently be associated with any of these peoples, they are likely to remain so. We can be certain only that the Peleset, wherever they came from originally, settled in the Levant as the people we know today as the Philistines. For this group alone among the Sea Peoples has it been possible through archaeology—and despite the derogatory caricature of them created in early Israelite texts—to reconstruct their sophisticated material culture.

Precisely what caused this enormous upheaval is also unknown. Famine has often been invoked by way of explanation, and prolonged crop failure certainly could have led to wholesale migration in search of food. A short-

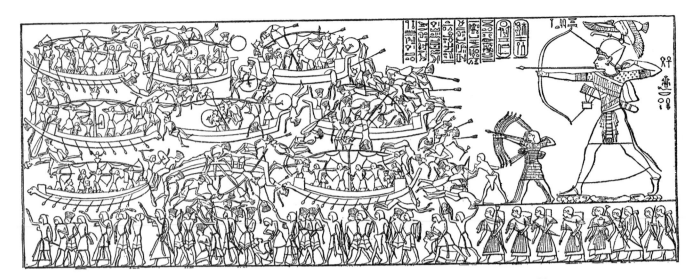

SEA PEOPLES. *Depiction of battle with the Sea Peoples.* On the right, Ramesses III and his soldiers fight on the shore, the king standing on corpses of the enemy. Below them, Egyptian officers lead away bound prisoners.

age in Anatolia seems to be indicated by Merenptah's sending of grain to the Hittites, although this might only have been a temporary measure. A marked rise in the price of grain in Egypt in the twentieth dynasty has also been noted in this context. Again, this is an insufficient basis from which to extrapolate a crop failure in regions far distant, and the price rise in any case postdates the invasions of the Sea Peoples. Another idea recently mooted is that a volcanic explosion in Iceland may have played a part, but the tree-ring dating of this eruption to 1159 BCE—probably just after the reign of Ramesses III had ended—would seem to make this also too late to have been a major factor. In fact, archaeological evidence for widespread climatic change is largely lacking, and political and military strife in the Mycenaean world may well have been the main catalyst. Fine questions of cause and effect depend to a large extent on still unresolved questions of relative chronology between the different areas involved.

The two actual invasions of Egypt that are known to us occurred about forty years apart, in Year 5 of Merenptah's reign and Year 8 of Ramesses III. Since these were separated by a civil war lasting some twenty years, it is quite possible that there were others, which went unrecorded or the record of which has not survived. However that may be, the Egyptians had certainly had contact with some groups among the Sea Peoples long before the period at which the hostile and destructive coalition associated with the name in Egyptian sources is likely to have come into being. The Lukka are mentioned as marauders from the sea in the Amarna Letters, dating to the reign of Amenhotpe III, 150 years earlier, and Sherden warriors

were already serving in the Egyptian army under Ramesses II, as the many temple records of the Battle of Qadesh attest. In the subsequent battles against the Sea Peoples, some soldiers from the same geographical and ethnic background fought on the Egyptian side against their compatriots. Allegiances doubtless changed easily enough in the circumstances.

Some fragments of painted papyrus, excavated in 1936 but only recently published, contain rare and tantalizing scenes. They were found at Tell el-Amarna and hence presumably date to the reign of Akhenaten. Very unusually for the medium, these show episodes of a battle, including Libyans in the act of killing an Egyptian. Another scene depicts a group of running infantry in which soldiers of Egyptian appearance are mixed with others whose headgear strongly resembles the boars'-tusk helmets of the Mycenaeans. No text survives on the fragments to explain their significance, but, given the long-standing Egyptian predilection for the use of foreign troops, it is a reasonable inference that warriors from the Mycenaean world were already part of the armies of pharaoh in the late eighteenth dynasty.

This would not be surprising in the light of the intensification of the relationship between Egypt and the Aegean that is apparent in the reign of Akhenaten's father, Amenhotpe III. This is epitomized notably by faience plaques bearing the king's name that have been found on the Greek mainland, and by a "geographical list" of Aegean place names inscribed on the base of a royal statue found in his mortuary temple at Thebes. The carving of the list beneath the king's feet was a traditional device of sympathetic magic to prevent these countries from harming

Egypt; it need not imply that the actual relationship was anything other than amicable. Visitors had been coming to the Egyptian court from Crete and the Greek mainland since the reign of Hatshepsut, as is shown by paintings in Theban tombs. These depict Minoan and later Mycenaean figures—probably both envoys and traders—bringing expensive gifts to the Egyptian court. Remarkable discoveries of fresco fragments, Minoan in style, content, and technique, made recently at Tell ed-Dabʿa in the Delta and now dated by the excavator to the reign of Amenhotpe I, show that there were already significant contacts between the Theban kings and their Aegean counterparts still earlier, in the sixteenth century BCE.

Whatever the reality of the Libyan danger hinted at by the papyrus fragments from Tell el-Amarna, recognition of a threat to Egypt from the west can be inferred from the campaign of Sety I into Libya, recorded on the north wall of the hypostyle hall at Karnak. This was followed under Ramesses II by the construction of a series of forts along the western edge of the Delta and on the Mediterranean coast. Recent excavations at one of the latter, Zawiyet Umm el-Rakkham, about 300 kilometers (200 miles) west of Alexandria, have begun to show the site's other role as an important trading station, accessible to marine traffic bound in either direction along the coast, but also well positioned at the African end of the route from Crete. Non-Egyptian items predominate among the pottery, which has yielded many examples of storage and transport jars typical of the Late Bronze Age eastern Mediterranean. Routes to Egypt used for peaceful trading could easily become a means of entry for hostile forces, and it was essential to protect them.

A sense of impending danger from the west may have been among the factors that prompted Ramesses II to secure his northeastern frontier by coming to terms with the Hittites after the indecisive Battle of Qadesh early in his reign. A peace treaty and marriage alliance followed, which must have left both great powers feeling free to exercise control over the small city-states within their respective spheres of influence without challenge. This idyllic situation was not to last long. Inscriptions in the temple of Amun at Karnak reveal that in Year 5 of Merenptah, several of the Sea Peoples approached Egypt from the west as part of a Libyan force. The largest contingent seems to have been the Ekwesh, while Sherden, Teresh, Shekelesh, and Lukka were also present. After a six-hour battle near Buto in the northwestern Delta, the Egyptians claimed victory. If the numbers of the enemy dead and captured are a reliable guide, the Sea Peoples made up about one-third of the invaders. Following the usual practice, the male prisoners were incorporated into Merenptah's own army.

In the next Sea Peoples' assault on Egypt, in Year 8 of Ramesses III, the Libyans were not involved, although they attacked separately in Years 5 and 11. Instead, the onslaught came from the northeast, partly by land and partly from the sea, and was the work of a coalition that had previously attacked the Hittites, Cilicia, Syria, and Cyprus. The conflict is vividly described in reliefs on the walls of the mortuary temple of Ramesses III at Medinet Habu. On this occasion, the peoples named are the Tjeker, the Shekelesh, the Weshesh, the Denyen, and the Peleset. Again, the Egyptians gained an overwhelming victory. The scenes show that, on this occasion at least, the foreigners included women and children in carts, and there can be no doubt that what we see is not just a military force but a population on the move. The upshot of this campaign was the settlement of the Peleset, and also some of the Tjeker and Sherden, on the coastal plain just north of Egypt.

The impact of the Sea Peoples movement outside Egypt was immense. Egypt's principal adversary for the role of great power in the eastern Mediterranean, the Hittite kingdom, was destroyed, as were many of the rich cities of the Levant over which the Egyptian and Hittite kings had earlier fought. Trade routes were inevitably disrupted. New populations settled over much of the eastern Mediterranean, notably on Cyprus and in the coastal regions of Syria and Palestine. Of these, the Peleset seem best to have preserved a distinctive identity.

The effects on Egypt are less easy to gauge. In contrast to the substantial settlement of Libyans, only the Sherden among the Sea Peoples remain visible to any significant extent. Their continuing military importance is shown by the fact that, in the historical retrospective that closes the Harris Papyrus, a summary of the reign of Ramesses III, they are explicitly named among those to whom the king's report is addressed. Numerous Sherden, mostly with Egyptian names, are recorded as settled in Middle Egypt in the land survey from the reign of Ramesses V recorded in the Wilbour Papyrus. They had presumably been given plots of land in return for their military service, had doubtless intermarried, and were in the process of being assimilated to native ways. There are also several passing references to individual Sherden in the late twentieth dynasty archive from Deir el-Medina known as the Late Ramessid Letters. Thereafter, even they disappear from sight.

The effort needed to resist the incursions of both the Libyans and the Sea Peoples must, however, have weakened the authority of the later Ramessid kings. The country's resources were probably seriously depleted, and any hope of reviving imperial glories beyond Egypt's frontiers had vanished. The kings' preoccupation with military affairs in the north must also have fostered a growing sense of independence and of hereditary right in the Theban priesthood. The Sea Peoples can thus be said to have contributed to the division of Egypt at the end of the New Kingdom. Political relationships changed internally and externally. The *Story of Wenamun*, describing events at the end of the twentieth dynasty, depicts the Tjeker continuing to behave in a piratical fashion. Wenamun himself, as envoy of the Theban priesthood in search of cedar for a new sacred boat for the god Amun, but also as a representative of a weakened Egypt, is shown seeking to establish commercial and diplomatic relations with the country's new neighbors.

BIBLIOGRAPHY

Barnett, R. D. "The Sea Peoples." In *Cambridge Ancient History*, vol. 2, part 2. 3d ed. Cambridge, 1975. Still useful review of the main sources.

Cline, Eric. *Sailing the Wine-Dark Sea: International Trade and the Late Bronze Age Aegean*. Oxford, 1994. A comprehensive treatment of a topic that offers important background to the migrations.

Davies, W. V., and Louise Schofield, eds. *Egypt, the Aegean and the Levant*. London, 1995. Important collection of essays on eastern Mediterranean interrelationships in the second millennium BCE.

Dothan, Trude. *The Philistines and Their Material Culture*. Rev. ed. Jerusalem, 1982. Classic account of this much vilified people.

Dothan, Trude, and Moshe Dothan. *People of the Sea: The Search for the Philistines*. New York, 1992. More popular treatment of the same subject as the previous entry.

Drews, Robert. *The End of the Bronze Age: Changes in Warfare and the Catastrophe ca. 1200 B.C.* Princeton, 1993. Regards developments in weaponry and methods of warfare as particularly important in explaining events in this period.

Edgerton, W. G., and J. A. Wilson. *Historical Records of Ramesses III*. Chicago, 1936. Translations of the Medinet Habu inscriptions.

Gitin, Seymour, et al., eds. *Mediterranean Peoples in Transition, Thirteenth to Early Tenth Centuries BCE, in Honor of Trude Dothan*. Jerusalem, 1998. Publication of a symposium dedicated to one of the leading authorities on the Philistines, which contains a very wide range of stimulating papers offering fresh evidence and new perspectives both geographically and thematically.

James, Frances W., Patrick E. McGovern, and Anne G. Bonn. *The Late Bronze Egyptian Garrison at Beth Shan: A Study of Levels VII and VIII*. Philadelphia, 1974. Detailed report on the excavation of one of the forts constructed to protect the northeastern frontier of Egypt against invasion by land.

Moran, W. *The Amarna Letters*. Baltimore and London, 1992. Authoritative translations of the correspondence which forms one of the most important sources for international relations in the fourteenth century BCE.

Redford, Donald B. *Egypt, Canaan, and Israel in Ancient Times*. Princeton, 1992. Chapter 9; the author is rather more confident of precise identifications of names of Sea Peoples with specific places than are many other scholars.

Sandars, N. K. *The Sea Peoples: Warriors of the Ancient Mediterranean*. Rev. ed. London, 1985. A good introduction to the complexities of the subject; adopts a broad geographical perspective and integrates textual and archaeological evidence.

ANTHONY LEAHY

SEASONS. *See* Calendars.

SECOND INTERMEDIATE PERIOD. In Egyptian history, the term "Intermediate" denotes periods between those of political unity, a criterion affecting control of material and human resources. An aspect of mass human relations, unity may be perceived and expressed variously by individuals or groups, or by later commentators, according to context. This fluidity qualifies precise borders in time and space.

The Second Intermediate Period may be summarized as follows—from the end of the Middle Kingdom to the start of the New Kingdom. There were three centers: Itjtawy, the residence founded by Amenemhet I south of Memphis; Tell ed-Dabʻa, the largest settlement excavated in the eastern Nile Delta; and Thebes, the focus of Upper Egypt. Groups of kings are identified with "dynasties" in the king lists of the third-century BCE historian Manetho and with groups of kings in the sole surviving cursive pharaonic king list, the Ramessid-era's Turin Canon. The Second Intermediate Period is omitted in the two surviving hieroglyphic Ramessid-era king lists from Abydos.

During the last phase of the Middle Kingdom, all Egypt was ruled by a series of short-reigning kings (thirteenth dynasty) based at Itjtawy, of unknown relation to the family of Amenemhet I (twelfth dynasty) and, in nearly all cases, to each other. Tell ed-Dabʻa was then a large site with a substantial Levantine population. Thebes was the administrative center for Upper Egypt and occupied Nubia, as in the twelfth dynasty. The Second Intermediate Period may be divided into three phases.

In phase 1, the thirteenth dynasty ruled from Itjtawy, with Thebes as their southern administrative center. Eastern Delta sources include kingly titles for at least two of a series of rulers, probably based at Tell ed-Dabʻa (fourteenth dynasty). These two local "kings" indicate an end to unity, at least in some aspects.

In phase 2, Itjtawy is no longer attested as a capital; the series of kings with Egyptian names continued, but only in southern Upper Egypt and based at Thebes (seventeenth dynasty). A series of foreign kings (the "Hyksos") dominated Egypt, probably based at Tell ed-Dabʻa (fifteenth dynasty). Contemporary sources attest to no separate group or groups of rulers in either Upper or Lower Egypt; "Dynasty 16" in Manetho may reflect later interpretations of royal names.

Phase 3 was characterized by warfare between the fifteenth and seventeenth dynasties, attested only for the reign of the Hyksos king Apophis against the Theban rulers Sekenenre Taʻo, his immediate successor Kamose, and his son and second successor Ahmose. The last expelled the Hyksos, reuniting Egypt; his reign thus straddles the Second Intermediate Period and the start of the New Kingdom. The seventeenth dynasty royal palace, settlement, and fort at Deir el-Ballas, south of Dendera, are exactly coeval with this period and perhaps served as strategic headquarters for the Theban military operations.

The break in the record leaves historians to rely on the later king lists in attempts to reconstruct the sequences of rulers. At present there is no clear sequence, or even total number, of kings for any dynasty, although for the first half of the thirteenth dynasty the sequence seems well preserved in the Turin Canon. Surviving seventeenth dynasty burial equipment and the description of a series of tombs in the twentieth dynasty Tomb Robbery Papyri provide, if not a possible sequence, one (perhaps incomplete) group of kings.

Historians disagree on the point within the thirteenth dynasty when unity ended at the secession of the eastern Delta. Foreign sculpture appears in early thirteenth dynasty archaeological levels at Tell ed-Dab'a, indicating a non-Egyptian elite expressing different traditions in monumental form soon after the end of the twelfth dynasty. Yet the thirteenth dynasty brother kings Neferhotpe I and Sobekhotpe IV are attested in the eastern Delta and, significantly, at Byblos in Lebanon. The pyramidion of king Merneferre Aya is the latest thirteenth dynasty monument found in the Delta, and his reign also seems last in a group of kings attested from distinctive royal scarabs. Byblos may have provided a model for thirteenth dynasty relations with Tell ed-Dab'a, with a foreign governor in control of a local population but acknowledging his nonroyal status before the Egyptian king. On available evidence, Nehesy was the first Delta ruler to claim kingship, marking a visible end to the unity of the Middle Kingdom. The relation of these early Delta kings (fourteenth dynasty) to the Hyksos (fifteenth dynasty) is unclear, as is the manner in which the first Hyksos became king. Likewise, the transformation of the thirteenth dynasty at Itjtawy into the seventeenth at Thebes is not documented. There is no contemporary evidence for or against later tales of foreign invasions and military election of the first Hyksos; New Kingdom and Hellenistic accounts may unite elements from a wide variety of sources, from displaced references to other periods or kings, to literary tales originally without historical reference. During the last phase of the Middle Kingdom and phase 1 of the Second Intermediate Period, eastern Delta sites became Near Eastern in material culture. Precise dating and causes of the population overspill from the Levant are uncertain, but already in the mid-twelfth dynasty, an inscription of Amenemhet II records among booty from the sack of two foreign places 1,554 Near Eastern captives. Influx by war might have been compounded by economic migration, with establishment of foreign trading emporia in the eastern Delta in the early thirteenth dynasty. Salable ("slave") status of Near Easterners in late Middle Kingdom legal documents may reflect origins as war captives, in which case it would

not necessarily extend to all Near Easterners. At least thirty-six funerary monuments, in addition to documentary papyri, attest to Near Eastern estate workers in Egypt. In papyri, Near Eastern names may be used for identification, with Egyptian second names. On funerary monuments, Egyptian names generally replace Near Eastern and often refer to the owner of the deceased, such as Senebhenutes "may her mistress be well"; sometimes name forms stress alien identity, such as Iunertaer ("we come to our land") and Tepnefer ("good start [to a campaign]"). Owners of such slaves ranged from viziers to middle-ranking officials, and their attested professions are food and textile producers, house servants, and temple doorkeepers. For thirteenth dynasty Thebes, Papyrus Brooklyn 35.1446 records an estate dominated by Near Eastern textile workers, but this seems to belong to a vizier, and so may not be typical of their proportion in Upper Egyptian households. Abydos stelae may also record the personnel of estates around the royal residence, rather than in Upper Egypt. Therefore, geographical distribution of such workers is difficult to assess from the texts, in contrast to the large-scale eastern Delta influx attested in settlement and burial sites.

In material culture, phase 1 of the Second Intermediate Period continues the late Middle Kingdom pattern; even the notable increase in foreign pottery within Egypt may have begun under Amenemhet III of the twelfth dynasty. Titles in the administration follow the model of precision evident since the reign of Senwosret III; and there continued to be occupation of Lower Nubia and some presence at Byblos and Gebel Zeit, if not at Sinai. By phase 3, however, every area of life had been affected by major changes. These may be ascribed to the Hyksos directly, as rulers of foreign origin, or indirectly as a result of the new position for Egypt in eastern Mediterranean and Levantine trading contacts.

A new content in trade can be deduced from the appearance of small closed forms of export pottery, called "Tell el-Yahudiyya ware"; in the late Middle Kingdom, examples of this Levantine invention ("Lisht juglets") were already common on Egyptian sites. The small-scale closed Levantine vessels contrast with earlier forms and imply a trade in such precious liquids as scented oils, prefiguring the Late Bronze Age distribution of the Mycenaean stirrup jar. Like the latter, Levantine juglets fostered local imitations on a large scale in Egypt and elsewhere. The distribution of Late Middle Kindom and Second Intermediate Period phase 1 Tell el-Yahudiyya ware indicates strong Egyptian-Syrian contact, whereas production and distribution in phase 2 suggests greater focus on the southern Levant. This coincides with the development of massive fortified urban centers in that area, and the history of Egypt under the Hyksos must be seen against this background in trade and neighboring settlement patterns. Substantial platforms in the eastern Delta have been ascribed to the Hyksos, though their date and function are as yet uncertain.

In warfare, texts relating to the Second Intermediate Period's campaigns during phase 3 attest to the introduction of horses and chariotry. Also related to war, tin-copper alloys of bronze generally replace arsenical copper alloys by the New Kingdom, ushering in the Late Bronze Age. These and other advances in technology, such as the vertical loom, are generally ascribed to the Near East, and foreign kings within Egypt might have accelerated their import. Still, some northern Levantine/Mesopotamian techniques might have been blocked rather than helped by the strength of the Hyksos and the southern Levant, particularly as regards luxury court products. For example, glassy faience scarabs are attested in the late Middle Kingdom, but core-molded glass vessels first appear in Egypt only under Thutmose III in the expansionist phase of the early New Kingdom. Most imports of technology have yet to be dated with precision from laboratory analyses, and several features ascribed to Hyksos rule may not have arrived in Egypt until the early New Kingdom (vertical loom, certain weapon types, spread in use of tin-copper alloys of bronze). Minoan-style frescoes uncovered at Tell ed-Dabʿa derive from rubble, and their original context remains debated; they may belong to an eighteenth rather than fifteenth dynasty structure. In either event, they help to account more concretely for Aegean elements in the Ahhotep treasure at Thebes (the Aegean sphinx and the gallop pose).

For phase 3 of the Second Intermediate Period, the frescoes confirm a Mediterraenan circuit that included the Aegean civilizations, with shipping and the corresponding importance of the storm in religion. The principal deity of the fourteenth and fifteenth dynasties was Seth, associated with foreign lands and ungovernable weather; a Ramessid-era stela marks the four hundred years of his dominance in the eastern Delta, as if mythologizing a continuity from the time of Avaris to the time of its successor Piramesse, the Delta residence of the Ramessid kings. Late Middle Bronze Age Syrian cylinder seals celebrate a storm god of the sea allied with the motif of the bull; the Minoan fresco technique has also been discovered at Levantine sites. The international web of storm god, bull-leaping, and fresco-painted rooms reflects, on the religious plane, a new economic and political world common to the Hyksos and the reunifying Theban kings. It did not remove from Tell ed-Dabʿa traditional motifs of royal titulary and the devotion of kings to established Egyptian deities; the Hyksos kings styled themselves "Son of Re" and included the name of the sun god in their throne names.

Evidence for literacy among the Hyksos is ambiguous. The greatest surviving mathematical manual from Egypt, the Rhind Mathematical Papyrus, opens with a formula identifying the copyist as a subject of the Hyksos king Apophis as Son of Re and ruler of Egypt. The palette of the scribe Itju from the Faiyum explicitly assigns to King Apophis mastery of the divine script under the aegis of the divinities Thoth and Seshat. Yet in script and monumental production, the Hyksos generated little more than their fourteenth dynasty predecessors and less than their seventeenth dynasty rivals. This is a question of quality as well as of scale, since the better preservation of evidence in Upper Egypt distorts the record. Fifteenth dynasty hieroglyphic inscriptions are almost entirely confined to their names on old sculpture, including one granite altar, and there is no evidence for original Hyksos sculpture or quarrying. The dedication by Apophis inscribed on a granite block found at Bubastis displays shallow and irregular carving. In this, the Hyksos remained alien to the Egyptian tradition of kingship. Near Eastern features at Tell ed-Dabʿa include religious mud-brick architecture and equine burials. Royal names and titles incised on unglazed steatite scarabs and scaraboids constitute the bulk of text from their rule; here the Hyksos use Egyptian script and language, drawing both on late Middle Kingdom tradition around the residence and on the first Levantine output of steatite scarabs. By contrast, there seems to be virtually no production of seal-amulets in the Theban area, and there are no certain royal name scarabs for the seventeenth dynasty before crude examples for Kamose. Only under Ahmose, perhaps following the reconquest of the Memphis and Delta areas, does Egyptian glazed steatite scarab production return to equal the highest quality of the Middle Kingdom.

Less monumental forms of communication and inscription are poorly attested in both parts of Egypt; there are no letters or administrative papyri surviving for the fifteenth or seventeenth dynasties. The most extensive literary manuscript of the period, the Westcar Papyrus, was probably drawn up and buried at Thebes under the seventeenth dynasty; its Hieratic handwriting continues a late Middle Kingdom development toward rounder, but now more precisely defined, signs and groups. The manuscript preserves an otherwise unattested series of tales of wonder set in the Old Kingdom's fourth dynasty court; its reference to the births of three future kings may draw from king-list data on the fifth dynasty, but it suggests the historical coincidence of three royal brothers in the mid-thirteenth dynasty as a possible date of composition. This leaves the Rhind Mathematical Papyrus as the principal Hieratic document associated with the Hyksos, dated by its copyist to Apophis as king of Egypt. The Second Kamose Stela reports interception on the Oasis Road of a letter in clay from the Hyksos king Apophis to a new ruler of Kush; this appears to imply another writing tradition, either an oasis custom or, more obviously to us, that of Mesopotamian cuneiform. In Upper Egypt, Hieratic ostraca from buildings near the palace at Deir el-Ballas record name lists for supplies or deliveries, including one with reference to pigs. This indicates that any alternative methods of communication in the Northern kingdom were not adopted in the South.

Developments in the South of Egypt, under the seventeenth dynasty, were conditioned by both the Hyksos occupation in the Delta and the growth in the power of Kush to the south. When Egyptian Middle Kingdom fortresses in Nubia were abandoned is not certain or whether the withdrawal was gradual, sudden, or dictated primarily by cost or by force. Current consensus places their gradual abandonment in the second half of the thirteenth dynasty. The garrison commanders in some instances transferred allegiance to the ruler of Kush, as attested at Buhen. They were reconquered under Kamose and Ahmose. Relations with the southern peoples may not have been as one-dimensional as the political history of war suggests. At Deir el-Ballas there were cooking pots of the type found at the Kushite capital, Kerma; this indicates a Kushite element at the seventeenth dynasty residence at exactly the time of the Egyptian reconquest of Lower Nubia, though one might posit war captives to explain the alien presence. Such southeastern desert nomads seem to have been known collectively in Egyptian texts as "Medjay." These appeared as security guards in the Egyptian Nile Valley from the late twelfth dynasty, when one Medjay was guard at the Illahun pyramid complex of Senwosret II. During the Second Intermediate Period, a Nubian-related strain becomes discernible in Egyptian cemeteries from a different burial shape (shallow and circular), goods, and pottery. These "Pan-Grave" people may be the Medjay of the texts. By the end of the Second Intermediate Period, their burial customs are no longer distinctive, indicating gradual Egyptianization of the group. The texts continue to distinguish them well into the late New Kingdom, when royal necropolis guards were still titled "Medjay."

In Egypt's Southern kingdom, administration at first continued the late Middle Kingdom pattern, with highly precise titles for officials. A key source is the Juridical Stela from Karnak, recording transfer of the office of mayor of Elkab under a seventeenth dynasty king Nebiryerau. This records inheritance of public office, within the constraints of royal approval, in a leading family of the day, where relatives and ancestors include viziers and princesses. Late Middle Kingdom titles persist in the surviving Elkab tombs, with a notable proportion of military officials, such as the "Commander of the Ruler's Crew."

SECOND INTERMEDIATE PERIOD. *Lid of a coffin from the Second Intermediate Period.* (The Metropolitan Museum of Art, Rogers Fund, 1912. [12.181.299])

The use of "King's Son" as a military title becomes evident, anticipating the New Kingdom title "Viceroy (literally "king's son") of Kush." In phase 3 of the Second Intermediate Period, administrative titles seem to have been swept away, and the latest Second Intermediate Period and earliest New Kingdom stelae either omit titles altogether before a personal name or give a simplified term such as "scribe." There is also a marked change in the cutting technique of stelae; crudely incised relief predominates in seventeenth dynasty stelae from Edfu, Thebes, and Abydos, often with a spiked lotus motif and awkward limb joins, whereas those from the period around reunification return to elegantly proportioned figures in raised relief. At a higher level, sculptors worked in limestone in both two and three dimensions throughout the period; the two sphinxes of Sankhenre Montuhotep from Edfu demonstrate the talents available, and competent temple reliefs are attested at various sites, notably for Nebkhepperre Intef. It is not clear that any seventeenth dynasty king commissioned work in hard stone. [*For difficulties in dating Sekhemrawadjkhau Sobekemsaf, see the article* Thirteenth Dynasty.]

As far as is known, all seventeenth dynasty kings were buried at Thebes, on the foothill facing Karnak across the river (Dra Abul Naga). Portions of their burials survive. Royal tombs outside the Valley of the Kings were vulnerable in the major breakdown in civil order under Ramesses IX in the twentieth dynasty; upon restoration of order, a royal commission inspected the tombs, as recorded in the Tomb Robbery Papyri. The burial of one king, Sobekemsaf, was found to have been looted; it is possible that the tombs outside the Valley of the Kings were already emptied under Ramesses IX, well before the caching of the royal mummies from the Valley of the Kings was begun at the end of the reign of Ramesses XI.

In the 1820s, royal coffins and other burial equipment were found, bearing the names of kings mentioned in the Tomb Robbery Papyri. The site was explored again in the 1859–1860 season, and these two early clearances indicate that the royal tomb was cut in the rock, and it had a frontal court, stone pyramidion, and small obelisks. In 1881, the body of King Sekenenre Ta'o, from phase 3 of the Second Intermediate Period was found with that of his son Ahmose and several royal women contemporary to his period in the cache of New Kingdom pharaohs. Burials may have been treated differently according to kinship, status, location, and date of the caching operation; the burial of Queen Ahhotep was discovered separately in 1859. Seventeenth dynasty royal burials contained a mummiform coffin of variable quality, with feathered decoration and royal headcloth. Canopic equipment was of painted wood. Burial goods included limited precious materials, notably the silver diadem said to have been found in the gilt coffin of King Intef, and a green jasper heart scarab set in gold, naming King Sobekemsaf and deriving in form from thirteenth dynasty human-faced heart scarabs. Funerary texts on these objects are sparse, but they also survive in fragments of a shroud in the gilt Intef coffin. The now-lost coffin of Queen Montuhotep contained the earliest full series of what became, in the New Kingdom, the *Book of Going Forth by Day* (*Book of the Dead*). There is no directly comparable late thirteenth dynasty royal material; the

edition of funerary texts from the Coffin Texts into the *Book of Going Forth by Day* might have been occasioned by the move of the royal court to Thebes, depriving access to ancient centers of learning at Heliopolis, Memphis, and Hermopolis.

The Ahhotep burial and mention of the Hyksos king's sisters anticipate the prominence of royal women in the early eighteenth dynasty (notably Ahmose Nefertari). Exceptional titles of Ahhotep, wife of Sekenenre and mother of Ahmose, perhaps reflect circumstances of royal succession and war, but they may have been composed after reunification. Retrospective elevation to special status is attested for Tetisheri, grandmother of Ahmose, in his stela establishing an ancestor cult for her.

The final phase of war is attested in detail for restricted episodes. Hostilities may have begun under Sekenenre Ta'o, whom a New Kingdom tale set in conflict with Apophis; his skull bears the imprint of a Near Eastern–style blade. The campaign of his successor Kamose is recounted on his two Karnak stelae and one contemporary Hieratic copy; the relation of Kamose to both predecessor and successor is unknown, as is the date of the conquest of Avaris (the Hyksos capital at Tell ed-Dab'a) by Ahmose. Sporadic detail on the expulsion of the Hyksos from the Delta and expansion into the Levant comes from the autobiography of Ahmose, son of Abana, in his tomb-chapel at Elkab. On the ground at Tell ed-Dab'a there is a gap in settlement after Ahmose. Possible references to reunification are obscure journal excerpts on the back of the Rhind Mathematical Papyrus, noting unusual climatic conditions that are interpreted by some historians as a byproduct of the Thera eruption. The nature of the departure of the Hyksos is unknown.

[*See also* Dab'a, Tell ed-; Fifteenth Dynasty; Hyksos; Kamose; Papyrus Westcar; Seventeenth Dynasty; Thirteenth Dynasty; *and* Yahudiyya, Tell el-.]

BIBLIOGRAPHY

Berlev, Oleg D. *Trudovoe naselenie Egipta v epokhu Srednego Tsarstva* [The working population of Egypt in the Middle Kingdom]. Moscow, 1972. Although not translated into English, this includes in chapter 4 (pp. 74–95) the only full study of Near Easterners in late Middle Kingdom funerary monuments and papyri, with the data cited above. Students of Egyptology will be able to consult the lists of conventionally transliterated names and titles of Near Eastern estate workers (pp. 89–93) and their masters (pp. 93–94).

Bietak, Manfred. *Avaris and Piramesse: Archaeological Exploration in the Eastern Nile Delta*. London, 1986. Revision of a 1981 monograph first published in 1979 in *Proceedings of the British Academy* 65 (1979), 225–289. Preliminary account by the excavator of the key Hyksos site Tell ed-Dab'a.

Bietak, Manfred. "Connections between Egypt and the Minoan World." In *Egypt, the Aegean and the Levant*, edited by W. V. Davies and L. Schofield, pp. 19–28. London, 1995. Includes examples of the Minoan fresco fragments unearthed at Tell ed-Dab'a.

Bourriau, Janine. "Nubians in Egypt during the Second Intermediate

Period: An Interpretation Based on the Egyptian Ceramic Evidence." In *Studien zur altägyptischen Keramik*, edited by Dorothea Arnold, pp. 25–41. Mainz am Rhein, 1981. A cogent example of archaeological correction of textual evidence.

Habachi, Labib. *The Second Stela of Kamose.* Abhandlungen des Deutschen Archäologischen Instituts, Kairo, 8. Glückstadt, 1972. The first edition of the most important royal text on the war against the Hyksos.

Hayes, W. C. *A Papyrus of the Late Middle Kingdom in the Brooklyn Museum (Brooklyn 35.1446)*. Brooklyn, 1955. The first edition, with historical interpretations different from those in Quirke (1990).

Kemp, Barry J. "Old, Middle and Second Intermediate Period c.2686–1552 bc." In *The Cambridge History of Africa*, edited by J. Desmond Clark, pp. 658–769. Cambridge, 1982. Represents the prevailing consensus on the history of the period. Ryholt (1997) has recently sought to redefine in particular the fourteenth and sixteenth dynasties; this contributor has retained the Kemp version.

Oren, Eliezer, ed., *The Hyksos: New Historical and Archaeological Perspectives.* Philadelphia, 1997.

Quirke, Stephen. *The Administration of Egypt in the Late Middle Kingdom: The Hieratic Documents.* New Malden, 1990. Discussion differs on some points from that of the first editor, Hayes (1955).

Redford, Donald B., "The Hyksos Invasion in History and Tradition." *Orientation* 39 (1970), 1–51.

Redford, Donald B. *Pharaonic King-lists, Annals and Day-Books.* Mississauga, Ont., 1986. The remarks on the Turin Canon should be read in conjunction with the recent reappraisal by Ryholt (1997).

Ryholt, Kim S. B. *The Political Situation in Egypt during the Second Intermediate Period c.1800–1550 b.c.* Carsten Niebuhr Institute Publications, 20. Copenhagen, 1997. A wide-ranging reevaluation of the archaeological and textual sources, with comprehensive bibliography and list of sources for kings. Note that definitions of dynasties differ from those in Kemp (1982), and archaeologists have yet to review several conclusions based on specific contexts. Still, the reappraisal includes invaluable discussions of key data such as royal scarabs and the Turin Canon.

Winlock, Herbert E. *The Rise and Fall of the Middle Kingdom in Thebes.* New York, 1947. This includes the principal discussion of the burial equipment of Theban kings of the Second Intermediate Period, with revisions of several points in his previous article on the subject, in *Journal of Egyptian Archaeology* 10 (1924), 217–277.

STEPHEN G. J. QUIRKE

SED FESTIVAL. *See* Festivals.

SEDMENT. *See* Herakleopolis.

SEKHMET. *See* Feline Deities.

SEMNA. *See* Forts and Garrisons.

SENENMUT, chief steward of Amun during the co-regency of Hatshepsut and Thutmose III (c. 1502–1482 BCE). Senenmut was one of the most influential officials of his day. His parents, Ramose and Hatnofer, were of common birth, and several of his early priestly titles link him to the town of Armant, south of Thebes, which may have been his place of origin. Senenmut probably began his career under Thutmose II (c. 1516–1504 BCE), with an appointment as the tutor of the royal princess Neferura and as steward of the estates of both Neferura and her mother, Queen Hatshepsut.

This early connection to the households of two royal women served him advantageously when, at the death of her husband, Hatshepsut became regent for the youthful Thutmose III. Early in the new reign, Senenmut carried out a commission for the queen to extract a pair of obelisks from the granite quarries at Aswan, where he inscribed a graffito in commemoration of his achievement. In accordance with contemporary practice, he also carved out a memorial chapel for himself at Gebel es-Silsila, the source of sandstone for Theban temples in the New Kingdom.

With the self-declared accession of Hatshepsut to the throne of Egypt several years into the reign of Thutmose III, Senenmut was awarded his most important title, that of great steward of Amun, giving him responsibility for administering the burgeoning wealth of the priesthood of the temple of Karnak. At the same time, he commenced construction on his tomb complex in Western Thebes, which consists of a decorated funerary chapel situated on the hill of present-day Sheikh Abd el-Qurna and a rock-cut burial chamber situated in the Asasif Valley near Hatshepsut's mortuary temple. The size of his chapel and the quality of its decoration are unsurpassed for their time; the burial chamber is adorned with funerary liturgies, chapters from the *Book of Going Forth by Day (Book of the Dead)*, and an astronomical ceiling that are unusual for a private tomb.

Twenty-five statues of Senenmut, or fragments thereof, have been identified. These show him in a large variety of poses and gestures, often representing original statue types that were to become part of the Egyptian sculptural repertoire: holding the princess Neferura, offering an oversize sistrum, embracing a votive representation of a serpent or a cryptogram of Hatshepsut's name, and presenting a surveyor's measure. These statues and other monuments are inscribed with a large number of administrative and honorary titles, many having to do with priestly duties and the stewardship of the temple of Amun at Karnak. One set of titles refers to functions, such as that of stolist, that Senenmut may have carried out at the coronation or *sed*-festival of Hatshepsut. Although he is frequently identified in modern literature as the architect of Hatshepsut's temple at Deir el-Bahri, his title as royal architect appears on just one statue and in his burial chamber.

Senenmut is last attested in the sixteenth year of the reign of Thutmose III and Hatshepsut. His burial chamber was left unfinished and was never used, while many of his monuments show the erasure of his name, signifying a somewhat haphazard posthumous attack. Although some scholars have seen this persecution as evidence of Senenmut's participation in contemporary palace intrigue or as punishment for the usurpation of royal prerogative, neither view can be substantiated. His fate remains, in the end, an abiding mystery.

BIBLIOGRAPHY

Dorman, Peter F. *The Monuments of Senenmut: Problems in Historical Methodology.* London, 1988. A reconsideration of Senenmut's career, introducing new evidence from his Theban tombs, with emphasis on the chronology of Hatshepsut's reign and Senenmut's posthumous name erasures.

Dorman, Peter F. *The Tombs of Senenmut: The Architecture and Decoration of Tombs 71 and 353.* Publications of the Metropolitan Museum of Art Egyptian Expedition, 24. New York, 1991. Excavation records of the funerary chapel and burial chamber of Senenmut.

Lansing, Ambrose, and William C. Hayes. "The Egyptian Expedition, 1935–1936," *Bulletin of the Metropolitan Museum of Art* 32 (January 1937), pt. 2: 3–39. Preliminary report on the excavation of the intact burials below Senenmut's funerary chapel (tomb 71), including those of his parents, Ramose and Hatnofer.

Meyer, Christine. *Senenmut: Eine prosopographische Untersuchung.* Hamburg Ägyptologische Studien, 2. Hamburg, 1982. A thorough analysis in German of Senenmut's monuments and a presentation of the major stages of his career.

Schulman, Alan R. "Some Remarks on the Alleged 'Fall' of Senmut," *Journal of the American Research Center in Egypt* 8 (1968–1970), 29–48. An objective evaluation of the evidence surrounding Senenmut's demise.

Simpson, William Kelly. "Senenmut." In *Lexikon der Ägyptologie,* 4:849–851. Wiesbaden, 1984. A brief and convenient summary of Senenmut's career.

Winlock, Herbert E. "The Egyptian Expedition, 1925–1927," *Bulletin of the Metropolitan Museum of Art* 23 (February 1928), pt. 2: 24–58. Preliminary report on the discovery and excavation of Senenmut's burial chamber (tomb 353) near Hatshepsut's temple.

PETER DORMAN

SENNEDJEM, important courtier of the late eighteenth dynasty. Although his tomb near Akhmim was desecrated in antiquity, later quarrying and treasure-seeking operations additionally destroyed evidence. The tomb can be dated to the reign of Tutankhamun of the eighteenth dynasty; its decoration shares themes found in the Amarna tombs (royal chariot procession and window of appearances scene). Sennedjem's titles are best preserved on the lintel over the portico of the tomb, which was difficult for desecrators to reach. His title of office was "Overseer of (male) Nurses," but his titles of rank indicate that he was an important person in his own right: "Prince," "Count," "Sole Companion," "Fan-bearer on the Right of the King." An archaic and, in the New Kingdom,

rare title "Judge and District Administrator," indicates that he played a central role at a king's (Amenhotep III or IV/Akhenaten) *sed*-festival. Immediately following the title "Count," the title "Father of the God, Beloved of the God," indicates that he participated in the royal coronation.

In a later alteration to the lintel inscription, the title "God's Father" was inserted in front of the title "Overseer of Nurses." Research since the 1980s indicates that this title—as distinct from "God's Father, Beloved of the God" earlier in the title sequence—was held by men related to the king. Since it was inserted secondarily, the king in question cannot have been Tutankamun, under whom the tomb was begun, or any of his predecessors. The obvious candidate is Ay, known also to have come from Akhmim. Unique to the chariot procession is the appearance of another person in the royal chariot; this person is arguably Ay (before he became king). That Sennedjem included Ay in this way in his tomb decoration is another indicator of the familial relationship between them. In the struggle for power at the end of the eighteenth dynasty, won by the general and later king Horemheb, the family of Ay and Sennedjem, including the general Nakhtmin and another "Overseer of (male) Nurses" Senqed (who shared Sennedjem's tomb), fell from power and their monuments were desecrated.

BIBLIOGRAPHY

Ockinga, Boyo G. *A Tomb from the Reign of Tutankhamun at Akhmim.* The Australian Centre for Egyptology Reports, 10. Warminster, 1997.

BOYO OCKINGA

SENWOSRET I (r. 1971–1928 or 1958–1913 BCE), second king of the twelfth dynasty, Middle Kingdom. Senwosret I established the power and prestige of the Middle Kingdom. The first-born son of Amenemhet I, he was informed of his father's death and a plot against himself on his return from an expedition into the Western Desert. Senwosret hastened to the palace at el-Lisht and seized possession of the throne (see the *Story of Sinuhe*). It has been said that Senwosret had been his father's co-regent in the last ten years of the latter's life, yet the documents cited in support of this thesis are not conclusive. The *Instructions of Amenemhet*, an apocryphal testament of the deceased king, denies the existence of such a co-regency by saying that Amenemhet descended in the solar bark after his assassination and expressed his regret for not having named his eldest son, Senwosret, as his legitimate successor before the court (Obsomer 1995, but cf. Jansen-Winkeln 1991).

Once established as king, Senwosret I continued to im-

SENWOSRET I. *Statue of Senwosret I in the Egyptian Museum, Cairo.* (Courtesy David P. Silverman)

plement his father's policies. He consolidated the power of the state by developing a central administration under the vizier's authority (see the Reisner Papyrus) and by ensuring the loyalty of the most powerful nomarchs, who were satisfied with basking in the favor of the king; these included Djefa-Hapy of Asyut, Ameny of Beni Hasan, and Sarenput I of Elephantine. In the *Story of Sinuhe* (Obsomer 1999), the monarch is glorified as benevolent toward his loyal servants and ruthless against his enemies. The writing of the *Loyalist Instruction* has been attributed to the reign of Senwosret I. The arts flourished during this period, and numerous royal construction projects were undertaken at Elephantine (Satis Temple, Sanctuary of Heqa-ib), Tod (Montu temple), Karnak (Amon temple, whose White Chapel preserves the register of lands of the thirty-six nomes), Coptos (Min Temple), Abydos (Osiris

Temple, which enjoyed an extremely popular cult, and the stela of the vizier Mentuhotep), Heliopolis, and other cities. After the completion of the funerary complex of Amenemhet I, his royal pyramid was erected at el-Lisht.

Shortly before his assassination, Amenemhet I dispatched the vizier Antefoqer with an army to conquer Lower Nubia (Wawat). This victorious campaign enabled the Egyptians to establish their presence north of the Second Cataract, where they erected the fortress of Buhen (according to stelae from the fifth year of reign). There they controlled the C-group of Nubians (at Ikkur and Aniba) and extracted the rich natural resources at Toshka (gneiss) and Wadi el-Hudi (amethyst). In Year 18, a major expedition was undertaken to the south: while the king remained at Buhen, General Mentuhotep led a military campaign in Upper Nubia, possibly as far as Kerma, which probably forced the land of Kush into paying tribute.

There is little evidence of relations with Asia. From documents discovered near the Red Sea (Wadi Gawasis) we know of an expedition to the land of Punt in Amenemhet's twenty-fourth regnal year. In Year 25 of the reign, hunger and starvation began after a poor harvest. Several expeditions were organized to the quarries of Hatnub (to acquire calcite [Egyptian alabaster]), to the Sinai (for turquoise and copper) and to the Wadi Hammamat (for graywacke); at the last site, in Year 38, the herald Ameny oversaw the transport of 210 stones by more than 18,000 men (Farout 1994).

Senwosret I died after a forty-five-year reign and was succeeded by his son Amenemhet II. He was subsequently deified at Buhen as the founder of the Egyptian empire in Nubia.

BIBLIOGRAPHY

Farout, D. *Bulletin de l'Institut français d'archéologie Orientale*, 94, 1994.
Jansen-Winkeln, K. *Studien zur Altägyptischen Kultur*, 18, 1991.
Obsomer, C. *Sésostris Ier: Étude chronologique et historique.* Brussels, 1995.
Simpson, W. K. "Sesostris." In *Lexikon der Ägyptologie*, 5:890–899. Wiesbaden, 1984.
Vandersleyen, C. *L'Egypte et la vallée du Nil.* Vol. 2. Paris, 1995. See pp. 57–75.

CLAUDE OBSOMER
Translated from French by Elizabeth Schwaiger

SENWOSRET III (r. 1878–1843? BCE), fifth king of the twelfth dynasty, Middle Kingdom. Senwosret III was best known for his military achievements, distinctive portraiture, imposing monuments, and administrative reforms; these inspired both deification and his later incorporation into the legendary King Sesostris of classical times. How long Senwosret III ruled and whether he shared his throne remain controversial topics.

After clearing the canal at the First Cataract of the Nile for his fleet, he led four campaigns into Nubia to oppose the power of the Kushites and to protect trade. He extended Egypt's southern boundary to Semna, at the southern end of the Nile's Second Cataract, beyond which Nubians were permitted to pass only to trade or on official business. Stelae at the boundary recorded that Senwosret III surpassed his forefathers, admonished the Egyptians to maintain "my boundary," and described himself as aggressive, thoughtful, and merciful, whereas he described the Nubians as avoiding confrontations—only to attack when he withdrew. He built or expanded fortresses along the Nile from Buhen to Semna South and his ships advanced at least as far as the Dal Cataract. In the Levant,

he captured a district called "Skmm," perhaps the biblical Shechem.

The pronounced facial features of his statues distinguished Senwosret III from previous Egyptian kings. With heavy eyelids, pouches under the eyes, lined brow and cheeks, and down-turned mouth, he was portrayed as thoughtful and weary, whether as a young or old man, depending on the severity of the modeling. Those images of a concerned king were reflected in hymns that praised Senwosret III for protecting Egypt and extending its boundaries.

Some of his monuments are exceptional. At Deir el-Bahri, statues of Senwosret III are the first that are known to represent an Egyptian king standing in a posture of prayer (with his hands flat on his kilt). A stela there also continued the eleventh dynasty funerary cult of King Nebhepetre Montuhotep. A relief in Senwosret III's temple at Medamud depicted him either anticipating or celebrating the rejuvenation *sed*-festival (usually after thirty years of rule). Aside from a limestone casing, his pyramid at Dahshur was the first constructed entirely of mud bricks— the complex has many parallels with Djoser's. Exquisite jewelry was discovered in the burials of the female members of his family. He also built a temple complex at Abydos, which included a tomb that was either a cenotaph or his burial place.

Senwosret III further consolidated Egypt's government by ending the authority of all but the last of the nomarchs (the governors of the nomes, or provinces), a process started earlier in the twelfth dynasty. The officials' sons were probably then brought into the bureaucracy at the capital, rather than confirmed in their fathers' local positions.

Senwosret III became a patron deity in Nubia during the Middle Kingdom. Later, during the New Kingdom, temples were dedicated to him there, and the Nubian king Taharqa had an altar erected in his memory. Greek and Roman authors, most notably Herodotus and Diodorus Siculus, combined recollections of Senwosret III, Senwosret I, and Ramesses II into accounts of a king Sesostris— a conqueror, builder, and lawgiver. The length of Senwosret III's reign is uncertain. Some sources indicate that he ruled as many as thirty-nine years and reliefs at Dahshur mention a first *sed*-festival, but the highest contemporary dates with his name are from the nineteenth year of his kingship. Although it is most unlikely that he was coregent with Senwosret II, he may have shared his throne with Amenemhet III.

BIBLIOGRAPHY

Arnold, D., and A. Oppenheim. "Reexcavating the Senwosret III Pyramid Complex at Dahshur." *KMT* 6.2 (1995), 44–56.
Bourriau, Janine. *Pharaohs and Mortals. Egyptian Art in the Middle Kingdom.* Cambridge, 1988.

Delia, Robert D. "A Study of the Reign of Senwosret III." Ph.D. diss., Columbia University. New York, 1980. The most complete biography of the king; it is being revised for publication.

Delia, Robert D. "Khakaure Senwosret III, King and Man," *KMT*, 6.2 (1995), 18–33. A more general account of the king.

Franke, Detlev. "The Career of Khnumhotep III of Beni Hasan and the so-called 'Decline of the Nomarchs.'" In *Middle Kingdom Studies*, edited by Stephen Quirke, pp. 51–67. New Malden, 1991.

Simpson, William Kelly. "Sesostris III." In *Lexikon der Ägyptologie*, 5: 03–906. Wiesbaden, 1984. The essentials of the king's reign.

Wegner, J. "Old and New Excavations at the Abydene Complex of Senwosret III." *KMT* 6.2 (1995), 59–71.

ROBERT D. DELIA

SESOSTRIS. *See* Senwosret.

SETH. The god of confusion, spirit of disorder and personification of violence, and bad faith was nevertheless venerated by the Egyptians as a god with whom one had to come to terms. Disorder, at least to a certain extent, was accepted as a reality of life and as essential to the living order.

Seth was also known as the god who brought death into the world by killing Osiris. Osiris had to die, but Seth gave him an untimely, sordid, and lamentable death.

Seth and Horus fought for the rulership of the world, the kingship of Egypt, and the function of Osiris. In this battle Horus lost the light of his eye, and Seth the semen of his testicles. Seth, god of exuberant male sexuality not yet channeled into fertility, induced Horus to take part in pederastic acts and homosexual violation. The fruit of their relationship was the moon god Thoth, the son of the two lords. This pair of gods could also be referred to as the "two combatants." When they are mentioned by name, Horus as the royal god and prototype of the Egyptian gentleman always comes first, and Seth as the spirit of disorder comes second, for Horus has the more central and Seth the more peripheral position. Although these two gods were the mythological symbols of all strife and the primal antagonists, they were separated, reunited, and reconciled. The justification of Horus in the verdict of the gods on their case always had an exclusive tendency; in chiefly later variants of the myth, Seth is punished and driven out. But as long as Horus and Seth are reconciled, they unite the two lands of Egypt by joining the sedge and papyrus so that pharaoh can rule over a country of order and peace. The pharaoh is a Horus reconciled to Seth, or a gentleman in whom the spirit of disorder has been integrated. Together these two gods rule over the world through the pharaoh whom they purify and crown, but still each one has his special half of the world: Horus has Lower Egypt and Seth has Upper Egypt, though this bipartition may also be reversed. During the New Kingdom,

Horus is lord of the Black Land, the fertile Nile Valley, and Seth is lord of the Red Land, the desert and foreign countries. Not only the bipartition of the world but also many other contrasts were connected with these gods: north and south, heaven and earth, earth and underworld, right and left, black and red, being born and being conceived, rulership and strength, life and dominion.

Seth was also famous in a third and more positive role, first noted in the Coffin Texts: standing on the prow of the boat of the sun god Re, he repelled the evil snake Apophis. This aggressive warrior god and powerful thunder god, with his mighty scepter weighing 4,500 pounds, was employed by the sun god to conquer the reptile. In the myths of many cultures worldwide, the figure of the trickster—as this Egyptian god of confusion may be called—not only tricks gods and men, but is also the slayer of monsters.

A fourth aspect of Seth is that of the divine foreigner. His identification with Baal, the god of the Semites, is connected with the vicissitudes of the history of Seth and his cult. The first certain attestation of Seth can be found on the protohistoric votive mace head of King Scorpion on which appear clear depictions of dog-, pig-, or ass-like so-called Seth animals with the typical long curved snout, truncated ears, and raised tails. In later artifacts Seth may be represented in animal form as a sitting, standing, or lying Seth-animal, but also in human form, often with the head of a Seth-animal. More than twenty different animals, and even a bird and a fish, have been suggested as the mysterious Seth-animal. It seems best to accept the old idea of Champollion that it is a fabulous animal, like the griffin, supposed to live in the desert. It is not impossible, however, that this fabulous animal had the body of a dog or ass and the head of a pig. In writing system, the Seth-animal served as a determinative classification sign for about twenty-five words denoting confusion in cosmic, social, and personal life, such as "storm," "tumult," and "illness."

The kings of the first dynasty and also of Dynasty "0" were associated with Horus-falcons, but king Peribsen of the second dynasty replaced the falcon with the Seth-animal, and King Khasekhemwy put both falcon and Seth-animal above the *serekh* in which his name was written. But whether this indicates a Seth rebellion, as Newberry suggests in *Ancient Egypt* (1922, pp. 40–46), remains to be proved. Neither can it be proved that Seth was the god of the original inhabitants of Upper Egypt, the predynastic Naqada I culture who were subjugated by the Horus worshipers. It is interesting to note that Naqada, or Ombos, was the most important cult center of Seth in later times. The belief that one religion's devil is the god of a conquered religion is not uncommon and is not to be rejected in itself, but there is not enough proof that this was the case for Seth in Egyptian religion.

Already in the Old Kingdom, but especially in the imperial Ramessid period of the nineteenth and twentieth dynasties, Seth was viewed as the lord of foreign countries. The Libyan god Ash, the Western Semites' god Baal, and the Hittite god Teshub were recognized as forms of Seth, although such identifications or even combinations with other Egyptian gods are rare. Seth remains a god apart (*wdˁ*), as he is called since the Coffin Texts. Nevertheless, he had his traditional place in the Ennead of Heliopolis up into the first millennium BCE. His marriage with Nephthys remains a rather formal affair and, atypically, does not produce a divine child. It is at least doubtful whether Seth was ever held to be the father of Anubis, the child of Nephthys. That the crocodile Maga is said to be a son of Seth accentuates its demonic nature. Seth, whose exuberant sexual activities result in his being invoked in love charms and whose testicles are a symbol as a pendant of the Eye of Horus, has relations with the goddesses Hathor and Neith, and especially with the foreign goddesses Anat and Astarte. In texts the name of Seth is often substituted by "son of Nut," as if this violent, noisy thunder god is still a big boy. He is, however, not depicted being tended by his mother, like Horus by Isis. The texts of the first millennium BCE cursing Seth do not forget to mention that his own mother has turned against him.

Special cults of Seth were established on the border of the desert and at the beginnings of caravan routes: at Ombos, Sepermeru, the oases in the Western Desert, Avaris, and Piramesse. The frontier god or disorderly foreigner became the equal of Re, Ptah, or Amun as a god of state, court, and army when the Ramessid pharaohs of the nineteenth and twentieth dynasties had their residence in Piramesse near the border in the northeastern Delta. Even pharaohs took their name from him: Sety ("man of Seth") and Sethnakht ("Seth-is-strong").

The remarkable reputation of Seth in mythology and his reputedly violent and disorderly character did not prevent some Egyptians from adopting him as their local or personal god. Personal names show that some did not hesitate to ascribe to Seth the same qualities that others assigned to more reputable gods: "Seth-is-great," "Seth-is-gracious," "Seth-is-kind," "Seth-is-content," "Seth-gives-salvation," "Seth-causes-to live."

One title of a high priest of Seth was *šd-ḥrw*, which means "he who raises the voice" or "who causes commotion" or "who kicks up a row." We do not know whether this expression indicates the social position and behavior of the priesthood of Seth, or whether it is simply a nickname given by outsiders who abhorred Seth.

In the first millennium BCE the Seth-animal disappeared from art and hieroglyphic writing. As an enemy of the gods, he was represented as an ass with a knife stuck in his head. In the western oases, where he was venerated

SETH. *Depiction of Seth at right, teaching Thutmose III to shoot with the bow, from a relief at Karnak.*

as a god until the end of Egyptian religion in the fourth century CE he was represented with a falcon's head, like Horus, his alter ego. The turning point from veneration to demonization of Seth in the Nile Valley must be dated shortly after 700 BCE, in the time of the pious Kushite pharaohs of the twenty-fifth dynasty.

BIBLIOGRAPHY

Barta, Wilfried. *Göttinger Miszellan* 129 (1992), 33–38.

Bietak, Manfred. "Zur Herkunft des Seth von Avaris." *Aegypten und Levante* 1 (1990), 9–17.

Broze, Michèle. *Mythe et roman en Égypte ancienne: Les aventures de Horus et Seth dans le papyrus Chester Beatty I.* Leuven, 1996. A dissertation on the late Egyptian story of Horus and Seth.

Goldwasser, Orly. *From Icon to Metaphor: Studies in the Semiotics of the Hieroglyphs.* Freiburg and Göttingen, 1995. Remarks on the Seth-animal, pp. 99–106.

Kaper, Olaf E. "The Statue of Penbast: On the Cult of Seth in the Dakhleh Oasis." In *Essays on Ancient Egypt in Honor of Herman te Velde*, edited by J. van Dijk, pp. 231–241. Gröningen, 1997. Discusses the ongoing veneration of Seth in the western oases in Greco-Roman times.

Kaper, Olaf E. *Temples and Gods in Roman Dakhleh.* Dissertation, Groningen, 1997. Remarks on the Seth cult, pp. 55–85.

Loprieno, Antonio. *Topos und Mimesis.* Wiesbaden, 1988. See especially pp. 73–84 on Seth as a foreigner.

Parkinson, Richard B. "Homosexual Desire and Middle Kingdom Literature." *Journal of Egyptian Archaeology* 81 (1995), 57–76. Discusses the "homosexuality" of Horus and Seth.

Soukiassian, Georges. "Une étape de la proscription de Seth." *Göttinger Miszellan* 44 (1981), 59–68. On the turning point from the veneration to the demonization of Seth.

te Velde, Herman. "Seth." In *Lexikon der Ägyptologie,* 5: 908–911. Wiesbaden, 1984.

te Velde, Herman. "Egyptian Hieroglyphs as Signs, Symbols and Gods." *Visible Religion* 4/5 (1985–1986), 63–72. Remarks on the Seth-animal in hieroglyphic script.

te Velde, Herman. *Seth, God of Confusion.* Leiden, 1967, 2d ed., 1977. Details of texts, iconographic material, and older literature. The second edition has an updated bibliography.

te Velde, Herman. "Some Egyptian Deities and Their Piggishness." In *The Intellectual Heritage of Egypt: Studies Presented to Laszlo Kakosy,* pp. 571–578. Budapest, 1992. Remarks on the identity of the Seth-animal.

van Dijk, Jacobus. "Anat, Seth and the Seed of Pre." In *Scriptum Signa Vocis: Presented to J. H. Hospers,* pp. 31–51. Gröningen, 1986. Discussion of Seth as a foreigner and his relation to Baal.

Westendorf, Wolfhart. *Göttinger Miszellen* 97 (1987), 71–79.

HERMAN TE VELDE

SETNA KHAEMWASE CYCLE. Among the Demotic literary texts of the Ptolemaic and Roman periods, there survive narratives belonging to two "cycles." Each text of the Setna Khaemwase cycle has as its main character the historical figure of Khaemwase, son of King Ramesses II, who bore the priestly title of *sm* or *stm,* the Demotic form of which has traditionally been rendered as "Setna." The individual texts do not make reference to one another or form a recognizable chronological sequence, but they all seem to follow the same pattern of plot, in which Setna comes face to face with the spirit of a powerful magician of the distant past. Two stories are relatively well preserved. One of these is often called simply "the first Setna story" (or "first Khaemwase"), but has the ancient title "The Story of Setna Khaemwase and Naneferkaptah and His Wife Ahweret and Her Son Merib." The second story tells of Setna and his son, Siosiris. Other, more fragmentary texts appear to belong to different stories, except that one of a number of brief passages of narrative inscribed on jars, published by Wilhelm Spiegelberg, *Demotische Texten auf Krügen* (Leipzig, 1912), tells of the birth and education of Siosiris, but in wording different from that in the second Setna story.

The date of composition of the stories remains a matter of conjecture. The earliest surviving manuscripts that certainly belong to the cycle are of Ptolemaic date. One of the North Saqqara papyri, possibly from the fourth century BCE, involves a character "Ptahhotpe the Setna," but there is no reason to see any link with the later Setna cycle. It is not yet clear whether the Setna stories stemmed from an oral tradition. It is conceivable that they belonged in a long-standing written tradition. However, one possible line of speculation is that the first story assumed its present written form within the Ptolemaic period, while the second did so in the early Roman period.

The beginning of the first story is lost, but it is evident that Setna Khaemwase has encountered the spirit of a magician of the remote past, Naneferkaptah, in his tomb. The spirit of the magician's wife explains how her son, she herself, and her husband all paid with their lives for the theft of a magical book that the god Thoth had written with his own hand. Setna accepts a challenge from the magician to gamble for the book. After Setna has lost three times, his amulets nevertheless allow him to escape from the tomb, taking the book with him. However, he is soon punished by a nightmare episode: at the temple of Ptah he catches sight of the beautiful daughter of a priest, and becomes so infatuated that he signs away all his possessions to her, disinheriting his existing children, and finally ordering their deaths. Awakening, he returns the book to Naneferkaptah, and is able to give the magician's family a proper burial together in one tomb.

In the second story, Setna's own son is the reincarnation of a magician who has begged Osiris to be allowed to return to earth in order to rescue Egypt from the threats of a Nubian sorcerer. Before unmasking and destroying his rival magician, he conducts his father Setna on a tour of the underworld, demonstrating that a poor but virtuous man may be honored there, while the rich may be punished.

The first story is remarkable for a subtlety of plot and of characterization beyond that of most Demotic literature, and happens to allude to a number of aspects of Egyptian society not mentioned elsewhere. The disputed magical book may seriously reflect Egyptian funerary concepts, and, despite evident touches of humor, the story makes a number of moral points. The underworld episode in the second story has been much discussed, both as showing the absorption of Greek ideas into an Egyptian view of the afterlife, and as revealing Egyptian ideas that may have passed into Christianity.

BIBLIOGRAPHY

Fowden, Garth. *The Egyptian Hermes: A Historical Approach to the Late Pagan Mind.* Cambridge, 1986. See pp. 59–68, on "Books of Thoth and Technical Hermetica."

Griffith, F. L. *Stories of the High Priests of Memphis: The Sethon of Herodotus and the Demotic Tale of Khamuas.* 2 vols. Oxford, 1900. Remains the standard edition of the two best-preserved texts.

Lichtheim, Miriam. *Ancient Egyptian Literature: A Book of Readings.* Vol. 2, *The Late Period.* Berkeley, 1980. The latest full English translations of the two best-preserved texts, with introduction and notes, pp. 125–151.

Piccione, P. A. "The Gaming Episode in the *Tale of Setna Khamwas* as Religious Metaphor." In *For His Ka: Essays Offered in Memory of Klaus Baer,* edited by D. P. Silverman, pp. 197–204. Chicago, 1994.

Tait, W. J. "P. Carlsberg 207: Two Columns of a Setna Text." In *The Carlsberg Papyri I: Demotic Texts from the Collection,* edited by P. J. Frandsen, pp. 19–46. Carsten Niebuhr Institute Publications, 15. Copenhagen, 1991.

JOHN TAIT

SETY I (r. 1314–1304), second king of the nineteenth dynasty, New Kingdom. Sety I's throne name was Menmaat-re "Enduring is the Divine Order of Re," and his birth name, Setekhy, means "he who belongs to the god Setekh." His Horus name, *wḥm-mswt*, "repeating the creation" alludes to the beginning of a new era after the disturbances of the Amarna period—Sety I was the first king to succeed legitimately to the throne after his father Ramesses I. It may also allude to the beginning of a new Sothis cycle that nearly coincided with the ascent of Ramesses I during his short reign of two years. There is no proof at all, however, for a coregency between the two, or for a coregency between Sety I and his son Ramesses II. Sety's mother was Queen Satre, owner of tomb 38 in the Valley of the Queens; she is not identical with the lady Tju of the Four Hundred Year Stela, nor are Ramesses I and Sety I identical with the viziers of the same name on this stela, who are probably their ancestors. Sety's queen, (Mut)-Tuya, was the mother of the future king Ramesses II and of a daughter, Tja.

Renowned as an extremely pious son and king, Sety I enclosed a large mortuary chapel in his own funerary temple in Thebes for his father Ramesses I and built another one at Abydos where he is depicted with two brothers and three or more sisters in front of Osiris and his deified father. Sety I reigned only about ten years, but his deeds and achievements equal those of a longer reign. Dynamic battle reliefs on the outer northern wall of the Great Hypostyle Hall in Karnak show him as a triumphant warrior-king in two campaigns: one occurred in southern Palestine against the Shasu-Bedouin, the other took place in the Orontes Valley in Syria, where he repelled Hittite troops and regained the town of Kadesh. His building activities included the restoration of temples, reliefs, and sculptures from Elephantine in the South to Heliopolis in the North. At Thebes, he constructed the Great Hypostyle Hall in front of the temple of Amun at Karnak and on the western side of the Nile River, he built a mortuary temple and spendid royal tomb (tomb 17 in the Valley of the Kings) with elegant, colorful reliefs and an astronomical ceiling. In Abydos, he constructed a mortuary temple for the great gods of Egypt and his royal ancestors, the kings of Egypt from Menes until his reign, which was a national shrine and the most beautiful temple of ancient Egypt. To secure the revenues of this temple, Sety I reopened and explored the gold mines of the Eastern Desert and Nubia, laying out caravan roads and drilling wells for expeditions into that wild and desolate region. In the eastern Delta he inaugurated a splendid summer residence that later, under his son Ramesses II, was to become the famous city of Piramesse. When Sety I died in his midforties, he was buried in a magnificent anthropoid sar-

SETY I. *Relief from Abydos depicting Sety I offering Maat.* (Courtesy David P. Silverman)

cophagus of calcite (Egyptian alabaster) that was decorated lavishly inside and outside with scenes and texts from the *Book of Gates*. His well-preserved mummy was later reburied in the cachette of Deir el-Bahri and recovered in 1881, revealing the impressive face of a great king.

BIBLIOGRAPHY

Kitchen, Kenneth A. *Pharaoh Triumphant: The Life and Times of Ramesses II*. Cairo, 1990.

Kitchen, Kenneth A. *Ramesside Inscriptions*. Vol. 1, *Translations*. Cambridge, Mass., 1995.

Murnane, William J. *Ancient Egyptian Coregencies*. Chicago, 1977.

Murnane, William J. *The Road to Kadesh*. 2d ed. Chicago, 1990.

Redford, Donald B. *Egypt, Canaan, and Israel in Ancient Times*. Cairo, 1993.

Reeves, Nicolas, and Richard H. Wilkinson. *The Complete Valley of the Kings*. Cairo, 1996.

Stadelmann, Rainer. "The Mortuary Temple of Seti I at Gurna: Excavation and Restoration." In *Fragments of a Shattered Visage*. Monographs of the Institute of Egyptian Art and Archaeology, 1. Memphis, Tenn., 1991.

Vandersleyen, Claude. *L'Egypte et la vallée du Nil*. Vol. 2, *L'Epoque Ramesside: La XIXe Dynastie*. Paris, 1995.

RAINER STADELMANN

SETY II (r. 1221–1215 BCE), fifth or sixth king of the nineteenth dynasty, New Kingdom. This pharoah, a son of Merenptah (r. 1237–1226 BCE), left as his most important monuments a three-chambered bark shrine just behind the first pylon at Karnak and a royal tomb in the Valley of the Kings (tomb 15). The exact chronological relationship of the reign of Sety II to that of Amenmesse is unclear; Amenmesse may have preceded Sety II, or he may have reigned independently in Upper Egypt and Nubia during Sety II's rule.

Sety II's principal wife was Tawosret. The extent to which she exercised actual authority during his reign is unknown, but it is plausibly conjectured that she governed Egypt as regent during the reign of Sety II's son Siptah, who died young, and she appears to have assumed sole power in Egypt after Siptah's death.

Aside from Sety II's monuments in Thebes, he is known from Hermopolis, and his reign apparently saw the production of Papyri Anastasi IV, V, and VI. Sety II's body was among those discovered in the royal mummy cache in the tomb of Amenhotpe II (of the eighteenth dynasty).

BIBLIOGRAPHY

Chevrier, Henri. *Le temple reposoir de Séti II*. Cairo, 1940.

STEVE VINSON

SEVENTEENTH DYNASTY. An Upper Egyptian succession (c.1665–1569) of local rulers in the Theban area. It is partially contemporaneous with the fifteenth dynasty of Lower Egypt. These two dynasties form the end of the Second Intermediate Period. In Manetho's history, the seventeenth dynasty consists of five kings and is erroneously labeled "Shepherd Kings again," a term referring to Manetho's fifteenth and sixteenth dynasties. The Turin Canon lists fifteen kings for the same period, which seems to be more in accordance with the number of kings known through contemporary inscriptions. Some of the these kings, however, are known only from the Turin Canon and left no monuments that have yet been identified.

Despite several earlier and recent attempts, there is still no clarity with regard to the genealogical relationship between the early kings of the seventeenth dynasty and the last kings of the (Upper Egyptian) thirteenth dynasty. There is also some doubt as to the sequence of kings during the seventeenth dynasty; only for the later part of the dynasty is the sequence of kings reasonably well established through inscribed monuments of the time.

Almost all the known monuments that mention kings of the seventeenth dynasty come from sites in Upper Egypt. The nature and context of sources reveal that the political influence of these kings did not extend beyond the area delimited by Abydos in the north and Edfu/Hierakonpolis in the south. It is, however, interesting to note that the finding-places of these monuments seem to indicate royal building and other activities in areas of considerable strategic, economic, or religious importance. Within the Nile Valley, these sites include Abydos, Deir el-Ballas, Coptos, Medamud, Elkab, and Edfu, and outside the Nile valley, the "Farshut Road," Wadi Hammamat, and Gebel el-Zeit. The main political center, at least at the end of the seventeenth dynasty, seems to have been a city in the vicinity of the modern village of Deir el-Ballas, rather than Thebes, the capital of the eighteenth dynasty. At Deir el-Ballas, on the western bank of the Nile, remains of a large city with two fortified "palaces" have been uncovered. Inscribed blocks indicate that the Theban rulers Djehuty, Sekenenre Ta'o, and Ahmose were involved in building activities in the city. Opposite Deir el-Ballas, on the eastern bank, lies the important city of Coptos, the point of departure for quarrying, expeditions to the eastern desert and caravans to the Red Sea. From here, the seventeenth dynasty rulers were able to control activities on both the river and the caravan routes.

Among the rulers of the early and middle parts of the Seventeenth dynasty, only a few have left important records: Nebkheperre Antef V is attested in various places throughout Upper Egypt, especially in Coptos, and probably also on a block from a small chapel on the Theban end of the Farshut Road, the main route to the oases of the Western Desert and the north–south caravan routes. More than any other ruler of this dynasty, Antef V is also known from numerous scarabs, both contemporary and later. King Sobekemsaf I is known for building activities of some scale; blocks and quarry inscriptions with his name are attested in Karnak, Medamud, and Wadi Hammamat.

From the middle of the dynasty comes a monument that sheds some light on the political situation in Upper Egypt. Created during the reign of Sewadjenre Nebiriaw I, the famous Juridical Stela (discovered in the temple of Amun in Karnak) commemorates a sale of the office of governor of Elkab between members of an important military family. Several members of this family held the position of vizier, while others seem to have been connected with the royal families of the thirteenth and seventeenth dynasties. The text of the stela demonstrates the relative independence and power of local clans.

For the rulers at the end of the dynasty, records are more numerous and diversified, granting us some understanding of the political situation as well as of the genealogical relations of the royal family of this and the early eighteenth dynasty. At least four consecutive kings of this period—Sekenenre Taʿo, Kamose, Ahmose, and Amenhotpe I—were members of the same family, despite the fact that in the Turin Canon the seventeenth dynasty ends with Kamose.

All these kings were to some extent involved in military campaigns against the contemporaneous rulers of the fifteenth dynasty, the Hyksos, who ruled the Nile Delta and parts of northern Egypt from their capital at Avaris (modern Tell ed-Dabʿa). A Ramessid literary text seems to indicate a major quarrel between Sekenenre Taʿo (c.1600–1571 BCE) and the Hyksos king Apophis. The fact that the skull of Sekenenre's well-preserved mummy shows several lethal wounds, some apparently inflicted by non-Egyptian weapons, has been interpreted as the result of the personal involvement of the king in a military clash with the Hyksos.

It is, however, more likely that Sekenenre Taʿo's son and successor, Kamose, started the so-called wars of liberation against the Asian rulers in the Nile Delta. Two royal stelae erected by Kamose in the temple of Karnak as well as the famous Carnarvon Tablet and several biographical private inscriptions, commemorate the king's raids against his northern opponent. Under Kamose's successors, Ahmose and Amenhotpe I, the wars continued, and the Hyksos were finally expelled from Avaris.

The royal cemetery of the seventeenth dynasty lies in the northern part of the Theban necropolis in an area called Dra Abul Naga, where a number of royal coffins (today in the Cairo Museum, the Louvre, and the British Museum) and other objects of royal burials were found. However, to date no royal tombs of this period have been positively identified. Dra Abul Naga is also the site of a large private cemetery of the period. During recent excavations there by a joint expedition of the German Archae-ological Institute and the University of California, Los Angeles, several rock-cut tomb shafts and mud-brick superstructures were discovered.

[*See also* Dra Abul Naga; Hyksos; Kamose; *and* Second Intermediate Period.]

BIBLIOGRAPHY

Beckerath, Jürgen von. *Untersuchungen zur politischen Geschichte der Zweiten Zwischenzeit in Ägypten.* Ägyptologische Forschungen, 23. Glückstadt, Hamburg, and New York, 1964. Comprehensive study of the topic, but partially outdated.

Bennett, Chris. "The Structure of the Seventeenth Dynasty." *Göttinger Miszellen* 149 (1995), 25–32. Detailed study of the genealogy of the kings of the seventeenth dynasty.

Habachi, Labib. *The Second Stela of Kamose and His Struggle against the Hyksos Ruler and His Capital.* Abhandlungen des Deutschen Archäologischen Instituts, Kairo, 8. Mainz am Rhein, 1972. First comprehensive publication of the Kamose Stelae; needs to be checked against more recent publications.

Polz, Daniel. "Excavations in Dra Abu el-Naga." *Egyptian Archaeology* 7 (1995), 6–8.

Redford, Donald B. *Egypt, Canaan and Israel.* Princeton, 1992.

Winlock, Herbert E. "The Tombs of the Kings of the Seventeenth Dynasty at Thebes." *Journal of Egyptian Archaeology* 10 (1924), 217–277. Although somewhat outdated and partially incorrect, still the most comprehensive account on the location of the royal tombs of the seventeenth dynasty.

DANIEL C. POLZ

SEXUALITY. Sexuality in the universe of the Egyptians can be assessed at different levels. It is interlinked with fertility and erotica in a common aim, the procreation of the species and the continuation of life, even after death. A primitive awareness of sexuality is apparent in Predynastic figurines, but it is only during the Old Kingdom that we find a more sophisticated approach to the subject, which during the entire pharaonic period was veiled in symbolic conventions.

The available evidence for the attitude of the Egyptians toward sexuality is literary and pictorial. The written sources are by no means abundant, and the interpretation of representations is far from straightforward. With the exception of certain unofficial depictions of sexual intercourse, in pictorial language the means of expression are restrained and often disguised in a coded language. In the corpus of literary texts, information must be gleaned from stray references.

Divine Sexuality. Few members of the Egyptian pantheon are specifically credited with a sexual identity, though some are placed in situations where this is implied, such as triads of gods united to conform to a conventional mother-father-child pattern. Though distinguished in appearance and grammatical gender as male or female, some deities appear almost asexual. An exceptional case is that of the Syrian goddess Anat, who is said to be "a woman acting as a warrior, clad as men and girt as women." When sexuality is emphasized in the world of the gods, it is seen not only as a natural characteristic distinguishing the two sexes, but also as a power, a weapon to be exploited for the benefit of some and the disadvantage of others.

Some deities, like Min or the composite god Min-Amun, display their male sex in no uncertain terms in order to emphasize their position as powerful fertility gods. Min is depicted with an erect phallus; the color of his skin is the deep black of the fertile Nile silt that contains the life-sustaining seeds; and his heraldic plant is the Cos lettuce, whose stem exudes a sap reminiscent of seminal fluid. Bes, the dwarf god, uses his disproportionate characteristics of short body and long phallus in order to establish his image as protector of the woman's world from the moment of conception to childbirth. His look-alike Nekhet, meaning "the strong one," appears in literature and art as a virile god: his iconography includes, in addition to his erect member, birds' wings and composite headgear made of the heads of animals.

Among goddesses whose sexuality is of prime importance, Hathor must be mentioned—goddess of love, fertility, music, joy, and inebriation. Although these goddesses sometimes have a companion of the opposite sex (Hathor of Dendera cohabits with Horus of Edfu once a year, for example), they preserve their individual sexual identity, which functions in relation to the public whether they are on their own or not. The case of Osiris and Isis is different, for their destinies are linked in their sexual embrace: the fate of one is the *raison d'être* of the other.

According to popular belief, Osiris, mythological king of Egypt, is overcome and murdered by his brother Seth in a struggle for the leadership of the world. His body is dismembered and scattered along the Nile. Knowing that a complete body was essential for survival in the afterworld, Isis, his sister and wife, painstakingly searches for and assembles the pieces of his body. But until she works her magic with him, it remains a dead body. By positioning herself over his abdomen she "revived what was faint for the Weary One," as it says in one of the many hymns in her honor. In pictorial representation Isis is usually performing this crucial act in the guise of a bird hovering over the corpse of Osiris. At this moment she conceives an heir, the young Horus, who is later to undertake a battle with Seth for the rulership of the world; finally, Horus is declared the winner. Osiris, fulfilling his destiny as a dead king, becomes king of the underworld. The miracle of conception, brought about entirely by the magical ministrations of Isis, became a beacon of hope for many Egyptians who aspired to achieving rebirth in the afterworld. This sexual concept is of vital importance for an understanding of Egyptian funerary beliefs.

In popular literature, Isis appears a number of times in a role where she makes specific use of her sexuality for her own ends. During the trial concerning the case of Horus and Seth, a number of amusing episodes take place, including one in which Isis transforms herself into a beautiful maiden and lures Seth to condemn himself and his vile acts. Seth, in turn, is seen in a homosexual encounter with Horus, whereby, through the intervention of Isis, Seth is made to eat Horus's sperm. This is seen as a sign of defeat for Seth and a triumph for Horus.

Female sexuality in the divine sphere is displayed when a new sacred bull is installed in the city of Memphis. According to Diodorus (I.85), when the new bull, recognized by its special markings, is carried in procession on a state barge and placed in its new abode in the temple, for forty days women stimulate its power by lifting up their skirts and displaying their genitals to it. The tale of the struggle of Horus and Seth contains a related incident: Re, who presides over the court, becomes angry and exhausted. Hathor, in this case playing the part of daughter of Re, "came and stood before her father, the master of the universe. She uncovered her vulva for his face, and the great god smiled at her."

Royal Sexuality. In the corpus of miscellaneous texts from the Old Kingdom known as the Pyramid Texts, the sexuality of the king is mentioned together with his other physical needs. Through recitation of spells, he is encouraged in general to be sexually active. When the dead king commutes in the universe, there are no moral limits, and he may cohabit with all the females available.

By the time of the New Kingdom, royal sexuality is described in a particular literary genre known as "theogamy," or divine marriage. This was created in order to legitimize the divine institution of royal marriage and succession. Here, the royal husband is watching from the sidelines while the mighty god Amun enters the stage, allegedly in the guise of the king, but with easily recognizable characteristics such as "the scent of god." According to divine plan, the queen is to submit herself to the god in order to conceive an heir to the throne of suitable divine parentage. The queen soon acknowledges the divine qualities of her partner and becomes the receptacle for his seed. This event was narrated first by Queen Hatshepsut (playing the part of the divine issue), then copied by Amenhotpe III and Ramesses II.

A related theme is reflected in the Greco-Roman birthhouses, the so-called *mammisi*, built at right angles to the main axis at the entrance of major temples (Dendera, Edfu, etc.). Here was celebrated the birth of the son of the resident divine pair, whose qualities are mirrored in the ruler. The world of the gods and the life of the king are interwoven.

Private Sexuality. In Egyptian nonroyal funerary belief, sexuality plays a crucial part. The way in which this was clad in metaphorical language was first understood by Desroches-Noblecourt in 1954, followed up by important discussions by Westendorf (1967) and by Derchain in the 1970s. Certain aspects of the pictorial repertory in tombs with wall decoration, particularly from the Middle and New Kingdoms, make sense only when interpreted in the total context of funerary beliefs concerned with a continued existence after death. Rebirth was seen as a re-enactment of birth, and so the necessary preliminaries for the miracle of conception had to be available, this time in the decoration and equipment of the tomb. The crucial concept of sexuality and the preamble to sexual intercourse were underlined by the presence of beds and headrests, and more subtly in certain of the scenes of daily life. The "banquet scene" abounds in erotic symbolism: heavily made-up participants, often wearing flimsy garments; the omnipresent lotus flower, a common symbol of rebirth; the unguent cone and garments soaked in scent; heavy wigs and jewelry; the presence of mandrake fruits and intoxicating beverages—all details that, along with other symbols of female sexuality such as vervet and duck, relate to sexuality. In the Theban tombs of the eighteenth dynasty, the framework of the banquet scene is the annual Valley festival, celebrated in honor of Amun of Karnak visiting Hathor of Thebes. In Roman times this was explicitly interpreted in terms of divine cohabitation. It was an occasion when, under the influence of intoxicating beverages originating at the offering tables of the gods, the participants gathered in the tombs to communicate both with the divine and with their deceased relatives "coming out." The sexual atmosphere of the occasion is suggested by the symbolic imagery of the representations.

The fishing and fowling scenes in tombs of Middle and New Kingdom date, and perhaps even of the Old Kingdom, refer not to the tomb owner's sporting activities but to his capacity for procreation; the scene showing him hunting game in the desert with bow and arrow points in the same direction. Many of these interpretations can be substantiated by plays on words, a common Egyptian device.

Looking back to the Old Kingdom, with the later representations and their interpretation in mind, it is possible to see a link. The prominence of the lotus flower in wall decoration is a case in point. The flower, later proved to be symbol of rebirth, a token of affection among lovers, and even a slightly narcotic remedy facilitating the lifting of the spirit, is prominent because of its exaggerated size in the representations. The motif of the bed and the conjugal pleasures enjoyed on it is referred to in some sixth dynasty tombs, where the tomb owner's wife plays the harp in bed. The fact that this is part of funerary decoration makes clear its role as a prerequisite for rebirth.

In Egypt, where death played such a prominent part in life, it was inconceivable in conventional funerary belief to foresee a continued existence without the essential ac-

tivities performed on earth to sustain life: breathing, eating, drinking, and copulating. These concepts were taken either literally or in sublimated form, the deceased person having been transformed to a glorified spirit.

Sexuality in Focus at Tell el-Amarna. Nowhere is the question of sexuality more in focus than in the brief reign of Akhenaten. In the Amarna period, concepts were reconsidered and openly displayed in a different form, although sometimes the essence of the message was unaltered. The canon of representation centered on the king's own physiognomy, carefully worked out with the artists to portray him as the fertile manifestation on earth of the solar disk (Aten), incorporating both the male and female creative principles—just as the solar deity had proceeded alone to create the world. Akhenaten's outward form was adapted to the female (narrow shoulders, broad hips, accentuated breasts): male characteristics were confined to codes of dress, such as his bare upper torso and king's crown. In one case (a colossus from Karnak, now in the Cairo Museum), he is shown without his kilt and with no genitals. In art, the king's subordinates are rendered with similar female contours. A final detail of what can best be termed "unisex" consists in abandoning the usual skin color of red for men and yellow for women for a more or less uniform dark orange for both sexes.

It is perhaps significant that in the Amarna period the conventional sexual symbolism in funerary art disappeared, in itself evidence that the so-called scenes of daily life were far more than representations of leisure activities.

[See also Children; Erotica; Family; Fertility; and Marriage and Divorce.]

BIBLIOGRAPHY

Derchain, Philippe. "Symbols and metaphors in literature and representations of private life." *Royal Anthropological Institute News* 15 (1976), 7–10. A summary of the interpretations of the so-called scenes of daily life.

Desroches-Noblecourt, Christiane. "Poissons, tabous et transformations du mort." *Kêmi* 13 (1954), 33–42. A pioneering article on sexual symbolism in funerary belief. The author expanded her ideas on sexual symbolism in interpreting the Valley of the Queens as a giant vulva in *Les dossiers d'archéologie* 149–150 (1990), 4ff.

Manniche, Lise. *Sexual Life in Ancient Egypt.* London and New York, 1987. The only monograph on the subject, presenting source texts in translation and numerous illustrations.

Troy, Lana. *Patterns of Queenship in Ancient Egyptian Myth and History.* Uppsala Studies in Ancient Mediterranean and Near Eastern Civilizations, 14. Uppsala, 1986. A fundamental study on the sexuality underlying Egyptian thought, with particular reference to the royal family.

Westendorf, Wolfhart. "Bemerkungen zur "Kammer der Wiedergeburt" im Tutankhamungrab." *Zeitschrift für Ägyptische Sprache und Altertumskunde* 94 (1967), 139–150. A crucial work for the understanding of the sexual symbolism of certain motifs in scenes of daily life.

Westendorf, Wolfhart. "Schiessen und Zeugen: Eine Gemeinschaftkeit afrikanischer und ägyptischer Vorstellungen." In *Festschrift Hintze: Ägypten und Kusch*, edited by E. Endesfelder et al., pp. 481–486. Berlin, 1977.

LISE MANNICHE

SHABAQA (r. 712–698 or 716–702 BCE), fourth king of the twenty-fifth or Kushite dynasty, Late period. In the second year of his reign, Neferkare Shabaqa invaded Egypt from Kush ending the western Delta-based regime of Bakenranef (Bocchoris). (The Apis bull embalmed in Bakenranef's Year 6 had its vault sealed in Year 2 of Shabaqa.) Shabaqa celebrated that conquest and the securing of his borders by issuing a commemorative scarab: "He has slain those who rebelled against him in both South and North, and in every foreign land. The [Near Eastern] sand-dwellers faint because of him, falling down through fear of him; they come of themselves as captives and each among them seized his fellow."

In 712 BCE or later, Shabaqa cooperated with Assyria by extraditing the fugitive Iamani, ruler of Ashdod, to Sargon II's army commander. In 706 BCE (or earlier), a text of Sargon II (Tang-i Var) shows that Iamani was handed back to the Assyrians by Shabtaka, perhaps as coregent with Shabaqa. The finding at Nineveh of clay bullae in Shabaqa's name (from long-lost missives) may also indicate the pharaoh's pacific policy regarding Assyria. Egyptian intervention (in the guise of Prince Taharqa) in Palestine against Assyria in 701 BCE, is less likely to have occurred during Shabaqa's reign than in that of Shabtaka, who caused Taharqa to bring an army some two thousand miles from Nubia and proclaimed his intentions by his militaristic titles. Under whichever reign, the Egyptian forces were defeated. Within Egypt, Shabaqa showed an interest in various temples: at Memphis he buried another Apis bull and had an ancient cosmogony of the god Ptah inscribed on a basalt slab; he is also mentioned at Dendera, Esna, and especially Thebes. His sister, Amenirdis I, served in priestly office as God's Wife of Amun at Thebes, while the high priesthood of Amun devolved on his son, Haremakhet. Other Kushite (Nubian) dignitaries were also given posts in Thebes. In Nubia, Shabaqa worked at Kawa and built his pyramid tomb at el-Kurru.

BIBLIOGRAPHY

Eide, Tormod, et al., eds. *Fontes Historiae Nubiorum, Textual Sources for the History of the Middle Nile Region between the Eighth Century* BC *and the Sixth Century* AD. Vol. 1, *From the Eighth to the Mid-Fifth Century* BC. Bergen, 1994. A comprehensive presentation in English of texts from, and concerning, Nubian rulers.

Kitchen, K. A. *The Third Intermediate Period in Egypt (1100–650* BC*)*. 2d ed. with suppl. Warminster, 1996. Standard work for its entire period; full documentation for the reign of Shabaqa, and discussion of varying views.

Redford, D. B. *Egypt, Canaan and Israel in Ancient Times*. Princeton, 1992. A different approach from the preceding.

KENNETH A. KITCHEN

SHABTIS. *See* Funerary Figurines.

SHADOW. One of the major components in the Egyptian concept of an individual was the shadow (*shut; šwt*), along with the body, the *ka* (*k₃*), the *ba* (*b₃*), and the name. Like the body, the shadow was seen as a physical entity, and its relationship to light was understood. The *Prophecy of Neferti*, describing the absence of sunlight, says "no one will distinguish his shadow." The term *šwt* is used not only with reference to the shadow of individuals but also for the shade cast by any object, such as trees and buildings: the Sphinx Stela of Thutmose IV describes how the king "rested in the shadow of this great god" at noon. The term is also employed as a metaphor for protection—understandable in Egypt's climate—both from the heat of the sun and in a broader sense, as that extended by a god over the king, by the king's arm over his subjects, or even by the king's sun-shade over bystanders.

In common with the other elements of an individual, the shadow was viewed both as a component of its owner and a separate mode of existence. The image of a god carved on a temple wall could be called the god's shadow, and the temple itself was sometimes known as the shadow of its deity.

Most references to the shadow of a human being occur in funerary texts dealing with the afterlife. The earliest instances appear in the Coffin Texts of the First Intermediate Period and Middle Kingdom, where the shadow is usually mentioned together with the *ba*. Like the latter, it can be viewed as a mode of existence after death. In some cases, however, the *ba* and shadow seem to be two parts of a single entity: "Go, my *ba* and my shadow, that you (singular) may see the sun." Since the deceased's *ba* is regularly said to possess physical powers such as eating, drinking, and copulating, the shadow in such cases may have been understood as that of the *ba* itself.

Other passages in the Coffin Texts present the *ba* and shadow as distinct entities. Both are closely associated with the body in the tomb: the *ba* is said to be "in the earth" while the shadow is "in the inaccessible places" (the burial chamber), and the deceased states that "my *ba* belongs to my body, my shadow belongs to its arm." Like the *ba*, the shadow returned to the mummy at night: the Coffin Texts speak of "my *ba* and my shadow going on their feet to the place where that man [the deceased] is." In some cases, however, the shadow is more closely allied than the *ba* to its body. This is reflected in a passage from the Pyramid Texts and Coffin Texts that describes the deceased's consumption of the gods' *ba*s "while their shadows remain with their owners."

Unlike the *ba*, the shadow was rarely depicted, but it occasionally appears in funerary literature as a human silhouette, sometimes with an eye.

[*See also* Ba; Ka; *and* Names.]

BIBLIOGRAPHY

George, Beate. *Zu den altägyptischen Vorstellungen vom Schatten als Seele.* Bonn, 1970. This is the only recent work that deals with the shadow in any detail.

JAMES P. ALLEN

SHAWABTIS. *See* Funerary Figurines.

SHEEP AND GOATS. The time of the introduction into Egypt of domestic sheep (*sr*) or (*wt hdt*) and goats (*w ty*) or (*r*) has long been debated by researchers. Like many other of Egypt's domesticates, the wild progenitors were not native to the Nile Valley. The earliest undisputed evidence for domestic sheep and goats in Egypt has been recovered from the Faiyum Oasis and the site of Merimda (c.5000 BCE). Because both domestic sheep and goats were known in the Near East by this time and the progenitor of the domestic sheep (*Ovis orientalis*) was indigenous to that area, domestic goats and sheep were probably herded by easy stages across the Sinai and the northern coast of Egypt into the Nile Valley and the Faiyum Oasis.

From known tomb wall scenes, Egypt possessed in succession two different types of sheep that were only once depicted together. Until the Middle Kingdom, there was a hairy, thin-tailed breed with twisted horns extending laterally from the head; this breed was kept mainly for its meat, milk, and hide. Later, there was a woolier breed, possessing a shorter, thicker tail and recurved horns. This was not the fat-tail sheep of the modern Middle East, which was introduced into Egypt no earlier than the Roman period: the ancient Greek historian Herodotus described fat-tail sheep in his travels, but he made no mention of them in Egypt.

The long, bristly outer hairs of earlier Old Kingdom and other similar breeds are known as kemps. In wild sheep and in primitive domestic breeds, the undercoat is shed each spring and falls in dense mats that can either be gathered or plucked from the animal and spun or made into felt (a matted fabric). In advanced domesticated forms of sheep, such as the Middle Kingdom breed, kemps are absent and the fleece consists entirely of the woolly undercoat. Woolen textiles were accordingly scarce in Egypt until the Middle Kingdom, when the woolier

breed was introduced. The Old Kingdom sheep showed an improvement over the wild ancestor, since the kemp was woolier, the hair grew all the year round, and it did not moult. The loss of the ability to shed was an advantageous trait, developed through domestication, to reduce wool loss; it does require an added investment, since such sheep must be sheared.

The benefits of sheep as providers of wool, butter, cheese, and milk undoubtedly made an impression on the ancient Egyptians, who kept them until their usefulness as a meat producer outweighed their ability to produce those secondary products. The large herds that were reported to have been kept during the New Kingdom probably served, therefore, as a source of wool and dairy products and only after productivity waned were they slaughtered for meat.

The virility and aggressive nature of the ram no doubt contributed to its role as a symbol of fertility and power. The ram was identified with the god Khnum at Elephantine and worshiped in at least six other Upper Egyptian nomes. In Lower Egypt, the ram was identified with Osiris at Mendes and worshiped in one other nome. Herodotus wrote that, on occasion, rams were sacrificed to Amun at Thebes; Amun was frequently represented as a ram, a ram-headed god, or a god with ram's horns.

Evidence for some restrictions on sheep consumption is recorded by ancient historians. Plutarch reported that priests shunned mutton, and he added that the inhabitants of Lycopolis (Asyut) were the only people to eat mutton because the wolf, whom they held to be a god, ate it. Plutarch also reported that the Egyptian priests did not wear woolen garments: "priests, because they revere the sheep, abstain from using wool as well as its flesh."

In external appearance, the ancient Egyptian goat resembled the sheep in many respects. It was high-legged, short-haired, and had a long face with a straight nose. Scimitar-horned goats existed in Old Kingdom times, but by the Hyksos period the horn appeared twisted, "corkscrew" in shape, and the profile of the goat's nasal area was straight. The angle between the horns varied a great deal, especially when the horns pointed toward the back of the animal. As a rule, the females were horned, although a few representations show hornless goats. The modern goat of Egypt with its convex nose, drooping ears, and long hair is not a descendant of the ancient forms, but rather is a more recent introduction.

Goats are browsers. Because of their adaptation to particularly harsh environments, goats are perhaps the most versatile of all ruminants in their feeding habits, a factor that has greatly affected their success as a domesticated animal. They also have, relative to sheep and cattle, a wider tolerance of habitat types: they are able to feed and breed on a minimum of food and under extremes of temperature and humidity. Goats complement a flock of

SHEEP AND GOATS. *Rams depicted on a relief from the tomb of Nefer at Saqqara.* (Courtesy David P. Silverman)

sheep by browsing on thorny scrubland while the sheep graze on grasses. Goats might even have been of assistance to farmers in helping to clear land.

Both the tomb illustrations depicting only short-haired varieties and the large number of goat remains recovered from excavations of all periods suggest that goats were raised primarily for their meat, skin, and possibly milk, and not for their wool. Goat meat was a common dish for the peasant and working class, and goat leather was used to produce a diverse number of objects. Although the goat did not attain the same level of adoration as the ram, it was used as a sacrificial animal. One text relates that 1,089 goats were sacrificed to the Nile god, and Herodotus wrote that goats, not sheep, were the preferred sacrifice at Thebes. Prices of sheep and goat are not as well documented as those of cattle, but nineteenth dynasty documents indicate that the price of "small cattle" (i.e., sheep, goats, and pigs) fluctuated between one and three *deben* (the monetary unit, presumably copper).

[*See also* Animal Husbandry.]

BIBLIOGRAPHY

Clutton-Brock, Juliet. *A Natural History of Domesticated Mammals.* Austin, 1987. Standard text for reviewing the origins of domestic animals.

Epstein, H. *The Origin of Domestic Animals in Africa.* 2 vols. New York, 1971. Unique work on the origin of African domesticates; certainly a must for those interested in the animals of this continent.

Janssen, Jac. J. *Commodity Prices from the Ramesside Period.* Leiden, 1975. Good source for reviewing the relative worth of Egyptian commodities, such as sheep, cattle, and other livestock and food stuffs.

Janssen, Rosalind and Jac. J. Janssen. *Egyptian Household Animals.* Haverfordwest, 1989. Laypersons' guide to the domesticated animals of Egypt; entertaining but poorly referenced.

Reed, Charles. "Animal Domestication in the Prehistoric Near East." *Science* 130 (1959), 1629–1639. An example of how domestic sheep and goats developed and reached Egypt.

DOUGLAS J. BREWER

SHENOUTE (fl. 370–465 CE), Upper Egyptian abbot and first major author in Coptic, known in Greek as Sinouthios and in Latin as Sinuthius. Few dates from Shenoute's career are known. He became a monk around 371 CE, abbot in 385, and in 431 attended the Council of Ephesos and perhaps traveled to Constantinople in the retinue of Archbishop Cyril of Alexandria (412–444 CE). Shenoute reported that Cyril offered him the episcopal office, which he refused. Shenoute died in 465 (based on S. L. Emmel's reconstruction [1993] of a date under discussion for a century). From his uncle Pgol, Shenoute took over the monastery of Atripe (Monastery of Apa

Shenoute, Dayr Anbā Shinūdah, and known in English as the "White Monastery") located on the western bank of the Nile, opposite the ancient nome capital of Panopolis (present-day Akhmim). Under his (modified Pachomian) rule, the monastery prospered; tradition mentions as many as four thousand monks and nuns in different houses. The monastery church, built around 440 CE as a three-aisle basilica with a triconch sanctuary, influenced later Egyptian church architecture. In early modern times, the monastery (well into the Middle Ages a center of monophysite spirituality and learning) had fallen into ruins. The large monastic library, where nearly all extant copies of Shenoute's work were preserved, was then dispersed into museums worldwide.

Shenoute was the first major writer in Coptic who nonetheless accepted Greek literary and rhetorical culture. Shenoute's work consists mainly of copies of the sermons preached in the monastery church, letters to monks and nuns on subjects of monastic discipline, and letters to other correspondents. As identified by Emmel (1993), they were transmitted in two major collections, the *Canons* (mainly on monastic life) and the *Discourses* (on various homiletic and pastoral themes). Shenoute's theology followed the position of Theophilus of Alexandria (385–412 CE) after the archbishop's anti-Origenist about-face in 399 CE. Shenoute's works mirror his greatest interests: theological–exegetical and homiletic–pastoral.

Shenoute's *Life* was composed by his successor Besa, and it survives in several non-Western versions, including in Sahidic (fragments) and Bohairic Coptic and in Arabic, Ethiopic, and Syriac; it stressed his charitable work—his assistance to the lay population during famines and nomadic incursions—and his crusades against the remaining Egyptian paganism of his day.

[*See also* Coptic Literature.]

BIBLIOGRAPHY

Besa. *The Life of Shenoute*. Introduction, translation, and notes by David N. Bells. Cistercian Studies Series, 73 Kalamazoo, 1983 Translation of the Bohairic Coptic Life of Shenoute, with a general introduction to his life and works.

Emmel, Stephen Lewis. "Shenoute's Literary Corpus." Ph.D. diss., Yale University, 1993. Painstaking reconstruction of Shenoute's literary legacy; the point of reference for any future research with an exhaustive bibliography of his writings.

Frandsen, Paul John, and Eva Richter Aere. "Shenoute: A Bibliography." In *Studies Presented to Hans Jakob Polotsky*. Edited by Dwight Wayne Young, pp. 145–176. East Gloucester, 1981.

Leipoldt, Johannes. *Schenute von Atripe und die Entstehung des national ägyptischen Christentums*. Texte und Untersuchungen, 25.1 Leipzig, 1903. Outdated, but still useful evaluation of Shenoute's personality, his theology, and the life of the monastery under his rule.

Shisha-Halevy, Ariel. *Coptic Grammatical Categories: Structural Studies in the Syntax of Shenoutean Sahidic*. Analecta Orientalia, 53. Rome, 1986. Corpus-based grammar of Shenoutean Coptic.

van der Vliet, Jacques. "Spätantikes Heidentum in Ägypten im Ägypten im Spiegel der koptischen Literatur." In *Begegnung von Heidentum und Christentum im spätantiken Ägypten*. Riggisberger Berichte, 1, pp. 99–130. Riggisberg, 1993. Discussion of Shenoute's antipagan polemic and activities.

HEIKE BEHLMER

SHESHONQ I (r. 931–910 BCE), first king of the twenty-second Bubastite or Libyan dynasty, Third Intermediate Period. Ramesses III settled Libyan prisoners as conscripted troops in the eastern Nile Delta around 1180–1174 BCE, and one family eventually emerged at Bubastis, as a local chiefdom of the Meshwesh, five generations before Sheshonq I. Bubastis was midway along the route between Memphis and Tanis, Egypt's capitals in the twenty-first dynasty, and Sheshonq's forebears forged family links with both the high priests of Ptah at Memphis and the royal family in Tanis. Thus, his uncle Osorkon (the Elder) ruled briefly as fifth king ("Osochor," r. 990–984 BCE) of the twenty-first dynasty. Sheshonq became the right-hand man of Psusennes II, whose daughter, Maatkare B, married Sheshonq's eldest son Osorkon (I). When Psusennes II died without an heir, Sheshonq I took the throne, beginning the twenty-second dynasty (c.945–725 BCE).

Sheshonq I tightened royal rule in Upper Egypt: he appointed his second son Iuput as high priest of Amun in Thebes and military governor of Upper Egypt, and he encouraged intermarriage of his family with those of Theban notables. To divide political power south of Memphis, he installed his third son Nimlot B as commander at Herakleopolis near the Faiyum. This king carried out modest construction at various temples: traces are known from Tanis, Bubastis, Tell el-Maskhuta (Pitham), and Memphis itself; his son Iuput built a tomb-chapel at Abydos. Much later, to celebrate his war in Palestine, Sheshonq I founded two great structures in Thebes and Memphis and a temple at el-Hiba. The structure in Thebes was the great colonnaded forecourt fronting Amun's Karnak temple, accompanied by the Bubastite Gate and triumphal victory scene. In Memphis, there was a parallel court and gateway at the temple of Ptah, seen by the Greek historian Herodotus (Kitchen 1988, 1991). El-Hiba produced parts of another finely carved triumph scene, but no place-names are preserved.

Abroad, Sheshonq I made an alliance with Abibaal, king of Byblos in Phoenicia, by sending a statue to which Abibaal added his name. Sheshonq I probably desired to secure timber through this relationship. In the twentieth or twenty-first year of his reign, he invaded Palestine, officially because of a border incident (noted on the Karnak Stela), and he left a triumphal monument at Megiddo.

The success of his campaign is admitted in *1 Kings* 14.25–26. He had earlier used the fugitive Jeroboam to help break Solomon's realm into two factional kingdoms that would be more easily conquered (*1 Kings* 11.40, 12.16). On his return, Sheshonq I ordered the major works at Karnak (Silsila Stela of Year 21), at Memphis, and at el-Hiba (temple with triumph scene), but these great works lay unfinished after his sudden death in Year 22.

BIBLIOGRAPHY

Edwards, I. E. S. "Egypt: From the Twenty-second to the Twenty-fourth Dynasty." In *The Cambridge Ancient History*, edited by John Boardman et al. Vol. 3, pt. 1, *The Prehistory of the Bolkons, The Middle East and the Aegean World, Tenth to Eighth Centuries B.C.*, pp. 534–549. Cambridge, 1982.

Kitchen, Kenneth A. "A Note on Asychis." In *Pyramid Studies and Other Essays Presented to I. E. S. Edwards*. London, 1988.

Kitchen, Kenneth A. *The Third Intermediate Period in Egypt (1100–650 BC)*. 2d ed. with suppl. Warminster, 1986. Standard work for its entire period, full documentation for the reign of Sheshonq I and discussion of varying views.

Kitchen, Kenneth A. "Towards a Reconstruction of Ramesside Memphis." In *Fragments of a Shattered Visage*. London, 1991.

Redford, Donald B. *Egypt, Canaan, and Israel in Ancient Times*. Princeton, 1992. A different approach from those of Edwards and Kitchen.

University of Chicago, Oriental Institute. Epigraphic Survey. *Reliefs and Inscriptions at Karnak III: The Bubastite Portal*. 4 vols. Chicago, 1953. The definitive publication (drawings and photographs) of the Karnak triumph scene of Sheshonq I.

KENNETH A. KITCHEN

SHIPS AND SHIPBUILDING.

SHIPS AND SHIPBUILDING. Thousands of models, texts, and representations testify to more than 120 types of ancient Egyptian watercraft in use for several thousand years. Even more important, however, are the twenty full-sized vessels that provide evidence about how the Egyptians built and used their boats. The vessels from Abydos, Khufu's pyramid, el-Lisht, Dahshur and Mataria fall into two main categories: (1) elegant, ceremonial hulls or (2) working boats, as simple as a papyrus skiff or as complex as a freighter that could carry hundreds of tons. Building wooden ships and boats in a land with few trees required a tremendous investment of labor and resources and provided the state with comparable, often intangible, rewards.

When the first bundles of reeds or logs were made into simple Nile rafts is not known, but boat models from the Badarian culture (c.5500–4000 BCE) indicate canoe-like craft, probably constructed of reed bundles that were tied together. Representations dating to the Naqada II period (c.3500 BCE) suggest that several kinds of wooden boats were being built, in addition to large papyrus rafts; although skilled woodworkers could produce thin, flat boards, the fastening techniques were then simple and unsuited to boatbuilding. By the beginning of the Early Dynastic period (c.3100 BCE), worked wood included timbers with all of the major fastening techniques later used to build boats. The introduction of copper tools at about that time accelerated the construction process. Egypt's increased societal demand for warships, freighters, and ritual craft in pharaonic times hastened the development of their nautical technology. The ancient Egyptians relied so completely on the Nile River for moving about that the symbols for "north" and "south" are simple glyphs that anyone could understand: a boat with its rigging collapsed on deck, riding with the Nile's current, symbolized "north"; a boat with an upright mast and billowed sail to catch the constant north wind meant "south." The first image of a sail in all the world comes from ancient Egypt. In their religious texts, boats were associated with regeneration and with the waters of the primitive and chaotic abyss. Watercraft also served as some of the earliest symbols for the nascent state and kingship, in part because until the Roman period, only a few roads extended more than a few kilometers beyond the Nile Valley. Therefore ships were used for taxation, redistributing goods, transporting warriors, and a hundred other sacred or mundane tasks. Even the dead depended on water transport to their tombs; then magical spells summoned a reluctant ferryman and his boat to carry the dead person to the gods in the sky.

Construction Techniques. Builders used a variety of tools including saws, axes, adzes, and chisels to work both imported and local woods. Imported cedar of Lebanon ('Š) was preferred for ceremonial and seagoing vessels, but abundant supplies of locally available tamarisk and acacia woods were used to build the more numerous and economically significant freighters. Ceremonial boats had long timbers sculpted and carved to precise curvatures, wasting at least half of the original wood, while freight boats depended on flatter and shorter planks and frames that were frugally sawn from trimmed trunks, seemingly in standardized shapes and sizes that took advantage of a tree's natural curvature. Like most watercraft in the world until about 1000 CE, ancient Egyptian examples were built shell first; after laying down a central plank or keel, shipwrights built the shell of planking, by fastening timbers together along their edges, inserting framing last. More labor efficient, modern boatbuilding is skeleton first, in which a keel is laid down, framing attached, and the planking shell added last. Egyptian ships and boats relied on thick planks with joggled edges, fastened by a combination of mortise-and-tenon joints and ligatures or lashing. Mortise-and-tenon joints, called *menkh*, provided the primary means to join plank edges, both in carpentry and in watercraft. Unlike later Mediterranean craft, the known ancient Egyptian rivercraft do not use pegs to lock the

SHIPS AND SHIPBUILDING. *The solar boat of King Khufu, late fourth dynasty.* (Courtesy Dieter Arnold)

tenons in place, perhaps to simplify the (documented) disassembly and reassembly of Egyptian ships.

Shallow-draft vessels were the rule on the Nile, with working boats about three times longer than they were wide. The known ceremonial boats are typically five to eight times longer than their maximum width. Both working and ceremonial hulls used framing, inserted after the planked shell was built, to support the vessel's sides. Longitudinal carlings and stringers, transverse beams and even the ultra-high ends of some ceremonial types were interlocked in an elaborate geometry, to create and maintain hull integrity. Freighters were built more sturdily and had added strength from hogging trusses, to balance massive loads—such as a 740-ton statue or a pair of 330-ton obelisks. When evaluating the technology of hull construction, it is important to remember that a thousand years of boatbuilding preceded the Old Kingdom. Although a number of boat graves (boat-shaped mud-brick structures) are documented outside the royal graves at Saqqara and Helwan, little is known beyond maximum possible dimensions for the vessels. In 1991, archaeologists at Abydos discovered the oldest known planked boats. Their initial investigations of the twelve boat graves (each 19–26 meters/60–80 feet in length) revealed flat-bottomed, canoe-like craft that date to the first dynasty.

The majestic royal ship of Khufu (c.2640 BCE) from late in the fourth dynasty (Old Kingdom) serves both to enchant and confound modern scholars. At more than 43 meters (135 feet) in length, its imported cedar hull is perhaps the most complex artifact of its time. Its shortest

SHIPS AND SHIPBUILDING. *A bark depicted in a wall painting from Abydos.* (Courtesy David P. Silverman)

plank is 7 meters (22 feet) long; hundreds of tenons and nearly 1.5 kilometers (1 mile) of rope were required to assemble it. By the time that models made to accompany Tutankhamun's body to the grave were carved during the New Kingdom, about 1325 BCE, the shape of the Khufu hull had become the standard form of solar boats. No one knows how early that association began, however, and it is likely that several meanings were conflated. The sun god Re possessed two watercraft: one for traversing the sky by day and one for night; that became an important part of divine mythology shortly after the fourth dynasty, according to the Pyramid Texts. Known today as solar boats (barks; in British English, barques), models of the long and narrow vessels included a specific roster of accessories—such as mats, a seat or throne, and hawks and other emblems. Khufu's reconstructed vessel shares general features (cabins, mats) but none of the specific items consistently associated with solar boats. It may be a vessel type strongly associated with the pharaoh, whose own association with Re was so strong that the boat became inseparable from the growing worship of the sun god.

Wooden hulls that imitated the shape of papyrus rafts came to play important roles in funerary practices, such as transporting the newly mummified person to Egypt's most holy pilgrimage sites. Gods had their own sacred boats, and the sacred boat could be a divine manifestation of the god. Almost 120 words for boats and ships exist, with 32 used in the Old Kingdom Pyramid Texts. "Byblos" ships (*kbn.t*) and "Cretan" ships (*kf.t.u*) were special terms for seagoing craft believed to reflect either the origin of the raw materials (e.g., cedar from Lebanon) or a style of building associated with that cultural group. Thutmose III used *jmw.w*-ships and Wenamun, a late New Kingdom priest, sailed to Lebanon in a traveling ship (*br.bjr*). The most common words are *jmw* (ship or boat) and *wj3*, used to designate ceremonial ships until the New Kingdom, when this word became used for warships and ships of the king. The general word for freight ship, or freighter, is *ḥʿw*.

The ancient Egyptians developed advanced nautical technology fairly early—to move people and royal officials from one place to another, as well as distribute raw materials and grain. Egyptian rivercraft seem always to have carried their loads on deck, as their method of construction relies on spreading the weight of cargo across the hull, rather than concentrating it in the hold. Some scholars suggest that artistic convention is responsible for the many images of deck cargo, but structural reasons make deck loads imperative for the river freighters. Seagoing hulls may have more closely resembled undecked

Mediterranean ships, but until one is found, it will be difficult to make accurate interpretations of the paintings showing sea travel.

During the fourth dynasty, the 4-ton granite plug for Khufu's pyramid had been loaded aboard a ship at Aswan and shipped down river. By the eighteenth dynasty, gigantic monoliths weighing 740 tons and more could be moved from one end of the country to another. In addition to such spectacular feats, the nation's food supplies moved up and down the Nile from field to town to temple, accompanied by scribes and officers of the pharaoh. Thousands of images and models of watercraft attest to both the expertise of ancient shipwrights and the importance of watercraft within the Egyptian economy, society, and culture—roles emphasized by any study of monumental art and architecture, international contact and exchange, and the administration and protection of the kingdom.

[*See also* Seafaring; *and* Transportation.]

BIBLIOGRAPHY

Jenkins, N. *Boat beneath the Pyramid.* New York, 1980. Dated but well-illustrated look at the royal ship of Khufu and cultural context for watercraft.

Jones, Dilwyn. *A Glossary of Ancient Egyptian Nautical Titles and Terms.* London, 1988. This volume collects references to watercraft, their operators, and their operation from ancient texts.

Jones, Dilwyn. *Egyptian Bookshelf: Boats.* London, 1995. General overview of evidence for Egyptian watercraft.

Landström, B. *Ships of the Pharaohs.* London, 1970. Unsurpassed collection of pictorial evidence for Egyptian watercraft, but the interpretations are dated.

Lipke, P. *The Royal Ship of Cheops.* Oxford, 1984. Detailed report on the reconstruction of the Khufu ship.

Patch, D.C., and C. Ward Haldane. *The Pharaoh's Boat at the Carnegie.* Pittsburgh, 1990. Investigation of the Middle Kingdom Egyptian boat at the Carnegie Museum.

Vinson, Steve. *Egyptian Boats and Ships.* Buckinghamshire, 1994. Specialist information in an accessible, well-illustrated format.

Ward, Cheryl. *Sacred and Secular: Ancient Egyptian Ships and Boats.* Boston, 1999. Examines cultural context, as well as physical characteristics, of twenty ancient hulls for specialists and nonspecialists.

CHERYL WARD

SHIPWRECKED SAILOR. The *Story of the Shipwrecked Sailor* is one of the most mysterious and inspiring of all Egyptian texts, as the many publications and variety of interpretations confirm.

Source of Attestation Date. The *Shipwrecked Sailor* is sourced in a single papyrus from the Middle Kingdom, the Papyrus Petersburg 1115. The period has now been widely established as most probably the twelfth dynasty. Less consensus exists with regard to the completeness of the papyrus and/or the account. While some scholars support the existence of an original, longer papyrus, much speaks for the completeness of the text itself, especially its contents and the logic of its composition.

Contents. The story occurred in Thebes. A naval expedition to the south has obviously returned without success. Its leader, a nomarch, nameless as all other protagonists in the story, is afraid of having to report to the king. A follower tries to console him by telling the story of his own experience, which takes up most of the account: sole survivor of a shipwrecked expedition, he reaches an island ruled by a huge, 30 meter (100 foot) snake deity. The situation, which appears dangerous at first, soon turns to the good and the snake deity prophesies a safe return home for the shipwrecked sailor. The deity then begins to tell of its own fate as the presumed sole survivor among seventy-five snake deities after a cosmic catastrophe. (The fate that befell his daughter, especially mentioned in the tale, remains unclear.) The prophecy is fulfilled; the story ends in a sentence whose meaning has not been clearly established, leaving the question of the nomarch's ultimate fate unanswered and the overall meaning of the story open to interpretation.

Meaning. The variety of interpretations reflects the puzzlement this story has generated: fairy tale, sailor's tale, teaching fable, eschatological story, allegory, royal propaganda writ, antiroyal opposition document, or text with esoteric knowledge. Accordingly, the island has been viewed as a real, fictional, or mythical place. The snake deity has been variously interpreted as a god of creation, a mythical creature, or even as an embodiment of the king, while the shipwrecked sailor has been seen as an anti-hero or as a genuine adviser. The conclusion has been understood partially as positive/optimistic but also as negative/pessimistic. The numbers mentioned in the story (e.g., seventy-five snakes, four months' residence on the island) have been assessed as being incidental, without meaning/significance, or strongly symbolic (e.g. seventy-five manifestations of the sun king, annual cycle of seasons in four months, and more).

Recent studies emphasize, above all, the ambiguity and many layers of the text, which allow for different approaches to interpretation that complement one another. In other words, the understanding of the text as a piece of entertaining literature or as a text with a "teaching character" (on whatever level and with whatever intention) would have depended on the education of the reader.

Form. The complexity, and thus the literary value, of the story is also discernible from its carefully crafted composition: its character of a "story within a story within a story" (i.e., functioning simultaneously on three levels in terms of time and logic) is generally recognized today as a structure that invests the story with a literary quality. Composed in verse and grouped in a first level as thought couplets, the whole text is clearly divided into twenty "chapters" which are in turn structured in four major contextually-coherent sections. Stylistic means such as *parallelismus membrorum* or centered structure (the whole story is roughly based on an A-B-C-D-C′-B′-A′ pattern) are clearly evident throughout.

BIBLIOGRAPHY

Baines, John. "Interpreting the Story of the Shipwrecked Sailor." *Journal of Egyptian Archaeology* 76 (1990), 55–72. In-depth discussion of the different options for interpretation.

Burkard, Günter. *Überlegungen zur Form der ägyptischen Literatur: Die Geschichte des Schiffbrüchigen als literarisches Kunstwerk. Ägypten und Altes Testament, 22.* Wiesbaden, 1993. Completely revised translation of the *Shipwrecked Sailor* in the context of studying the structures of Egyptian literary texts; the poetic (verse) form of the text is reconstructed.

Foster, John. "The Shipwrecked Sailor: Prose or Verse?" *Studien zur Altägyptischen Kultur* 15 (1988), 69–109. Overall convincing reconstruction of the verse structure of the text with English translation.

Kurth, Dieter. "Zur Interpretation der Geschichte des Schiffbrüchigen." *Studien zur Altägyptischen Kultur* 14 (1987), 167–179. Especially important for the elaboration of different levels of interpretation.

GÜNTER BURKARD
Translated from German by Elizabeth Schwaiger

SHU. *Blue glazed faience statuette of Shu, Ptolemaic period.* (The Metropolitan Museum of Art, Rogers Fund, 1953. [53.122])

SHU. As a member of the Heliopolitan Ennead, Shu was one of the eldest deities in the Egyptian pantheon. In the Heliopolitan cosmology, the creator god Atum created Shu and his female counterpart, Tefnut. This act of creation by Atum is described variously as having been accomplished by means of masturbation, by sneezing, or by spitting out these two deities. Thus, Shu and his sister-wife were the first sexually differentiated gods in the Egyptian pantheon. As the first male god, Shu had warlike traits like Onuris and became associated with the pharaoh.

Shu was a cosmic deity whose role in Egyptian religion, while hard to describe, was nevertheless essential for the existence of human life. Shu was the god of life; he was manifest in the wind, air, light, and water that were necessary for life to function. As a force of life, he was a creator who was present at birth. The acts of hearing and speaking were both associated with him. Typically, Shu was thought of as the god of dry air and represented as a man wearing a feather on his head.

In depictions of the Egyptian cosmos, Shu was shown kneeling and lifting up the sky goddess Nut, separating her from her husband, the god of the earth, Geb. Shu's role was to support the heavens and to provide the space for life to develop on earth. It was Shu who separated darkness from light, and he was often perceived as a column of air, or as the empty space between heaven and earth. Shu's name (*šw*) meant "dryness" or "emptiness."

This empty space was not considered as a void, but rather an arena for the possibility of activity. Shu might also be envisioned as the rays of the sun.

Shu was mentioned in his role as a creative life force in both the Pyramid Texts and the Coffin Texts, but is not well known outside these religious texts until after the New Kingdom, when Shu became connected with the gods Onuris, Khonsu, Horus, and Sopdu and was worshipped along with them in their local cults. He was listed in the Turin Canon of kings as one of the early divine rulers of Egypt before this role was assumed by a mortal man. A more detailed description of Shu's reign in Egypt was found on a shrine originally from Saft el-Henna that dates to the sixth to fourth centuries BCE. Shu was related to the ram-headed god of Mendes, Banebdjedet, whose identity incorporated the first four divine rulers of the world: Re, Shu, Geb, and Osiris.

The main cult center of Shu and his consort Tefnut was at Tell el-Yahudiyya. The Greek name for this city was Leontopolis (the city of the lion), and Shu and Tefnut were worshiped here in leonine form. The local version of the Heliopolitan creation myth describes Shu and Tefnut as lion cubs who, when grown, guarded the eastern and western horizons, thus protecting the rising and the setting of the sun. Shu was also thought of as the offspring of the sun god, Re.

BIBLIOGRAPHY

Hornung, Erik. *Idea into Image: Essays on Ancient Egypt Thought.* Translated by Elizabeth Bredeck. New York, 1992.

Morenz, Siegfried. *Egyptian Religion.* Translated by Ann E. Keep. Ithaca, 1992.

Quirke, Stephen. *Ancient Egyptian Religion.* London, 1992.

te Velde, Herman. "Schu." In *Lexikon der Ägyptologie,* 5: 735–737. Wiesbaden, 1984.

JENNIFER HOUSER-WEGNER

SHUPPILULIUMAS. Hittite king, contemporary with Amenhotpe III and the following era, under Akhenaten, the Amarna period. Shuppuluimas—roughly "he who originated in the pure pool"—was the son of the unfortunate Tudkhaliash III, during whose reign the Hittite state had suffered considerable setbacks. By contrast, the reign of Shuppuluimas is considered so successful as to represent the beginning of a new dynasty and the Hittite Empire. His accession date is uncertain but certainly falls in the last third of Amenhotpe III's reign (c.1380 BCE). Shuppuluimas is the author of an Amarna Letter of uncertain date (EA 34) which indicates that the two lands were initially friendly.

The first (and main) antagonist of Shuppuluimas was the Mitannian monarch Tushratta, with whom he contended for control of northern Syria. In much of the minor turmoil reported to the Egyptians in the Amarna Letters one can see the consequences of the Hittites' struggles with the Mitannians, which had rippled throughout Syria-Palestine. The Hittite defeat of Tushratta in the "Great Syrian War" made Hatti the dominant power in northern Syria. Yet the decline of Mitanni and its replacement by the rump state of Khanigalbat also had the unintended consequence of liberating Assyria, then probably under the rule of Adad-nirari (I). Shuppuluimas's Syrian ventures also brought Kadesh into the Hittite orbit. This town was to be a major focal point in later struggles between Egypt and Hatti.

Another interesting event in Shuppuluimas's reign was his marriage to a Babylonian princess, probably a daughter of Burnaburiash. She was given the name of Tawannannash and became the chief queen of the realm.

Perhaps the most fateful (and enigmatic) incident in Hittite-Egyptian relations during the reign of Shuppuluimas occurred when he dispatched his son Zannanash to Egypt at the request of an Egyptian queen, almost certainly Tutankhamun's widow, who wished to marry a Hittite prince. Unfortunately, Zannanash was assassinated en route, and in a letter found at Boghazköy, his father threatens the Egyptians with war over what he views as Egyptian treachery. This event apparently led to about fifty years of conflict between the two powers, eventually culminating in the Battle of Kadesh.

Shuppuluimas may have fallen victim to a plague, possibly brought back to Hatti by Egyptian prisoners seized at Amqa. He was immediately succeeded by the crown prince, his son Aranwandash, who reigned briefly before another son, Murshilis I, assumed the throne.

BIBLIOGRAPHY

Beckman, G. *Hittite Diplomatic Texts.* Edited by H. A. Hofner, Jr. (SBL Writings from the Ancient World, 7.) Atlanta, 1996. Contains a good selection from Hittite treaties and diplomatic correspondence, not only between Egypt and Hatti but also with other contemporary countries.

Goetze, A. "The Struggle for the Domination of Syria (1400–1300 B.C.)." In *Cambridge Ancient History,* vol. 2, pt. 2, pp. 1–20. 3d ed. Cambridge, 1975. A good description of the history and society of the Hittite nation and its empire during the time of Shuppuluimas.

Murnane, W. J. *The Road to Kadesh: A Historic Interpretation of the Battle Relief of King Sety I at Karnak.* 2d ed. Chicago, 1990. A wide-ranging study, primarily concerned with international affairs in the Near East at the time of Shuppuluimas and the Amarna period.

Moran, W. L. *The Amarna Letters.* Baltimore and London, 1992. The best translation of the Amarna correspondence, providing much indirect evidence for the results of Shuppuluimas's foreign policy.

OGDEN GOELET

SIHEIL. *See* Aswan.

SILVER. Although gold deposits from the Nile Valley contain relatively large amounts of silver, this prized metal was not available there in either the native state or in the high yield ores of silver sulfide or silver chloride. The silver-gold alloy called electrum, however, occurs naturally in both Egypt and Nubia, and this native alloy was often employed as a "white" metal. Such use is understandable since electrum visually mimics silver when the silver component approaches 20 percent of the alloy; it also darkens with age (oxidizes, as silver does), leading to the misidentification of much early silver-rich gold as pure silver. This confusion may also account for the Egyptian word for "silver" (*nbw ḥḏ*), which contains the hieroglyphs for both "gold" and "white." By the fifth dynasty (2510 BCE), the word was reduced to *ḥḏ*, and it clearly refers to "silver," while *ḏ₃m* came to designate all grades of "electrum."

The presence of small silver ornaments, notably beads, occurs in Neolithic archaeological finds from the Naqada II period. While some may have been imported, the majority were crafted in Egypt. The most likely source of imported silver was the Near East, an area rich in galena, an argentiferous lead ore. In the ancient Near East, silver was extracted from this lead ore through cupellation, a two-step process in which the lead was first separated from the ore, then silver extracted from the lead. The temperatures required were relatively low (800°C), as was the yield—a ton of smelted ore resulted in only a few ounces of silver. Egypt depended on foreign sources for work-ready silver, since in the Nile Valley silver refining did not occur until late in the first millennium BCE, with the adoption of coinage.

Both textual and archaeological evidence indicate that silver entered Egypt through trade or as tribute from the Levant, Turkey, and Greece. Silver technology had been developed in that region around the fourth millennium BCE, and Sumerian texts indicate that its value was considerably less than that of copper. John Harris suggested (1961) that in Egypt, silver was more valuable than gold until the middle of the second millennium BCE, and that the relative value was 2:1. Silver's value then diminished, a result perhaps of increased production and its consequent devaluation in the ancient world's trade market. The lack of native silver did not prevent Egyptian metalsmiths from developing special skills in working the material, since many of the techniques employed by goldsmiths found ready application in silversmithing—melting, hammering, annealing, soldering, chasing, repoussé, gilding, casting, wire making, and granulation. In wall scenes and other illustrations, workers of the prized "white" metal were often shown in tandem with other metalworkers, though not as frequently as goldsmiths were shown.

Twenty silver bangles were included among the funerary equipment of Queen Hetepheres (fourth dynasty, c.2550 BCE), which testifies to the artisanry of Egyptian metalsmiths, as well as the status afforded silver. Those sheet-metal bracelets, found enclosed in a custom-fitted box, were inlaid with thin slices of carnelian, turquoise, and lapis lazuli, colorfully arranged in a series of butterfly patterns. These stones were not set in the usual cloisonné manner (within thin wires), but were fitted into flat pockets made by depressing the silver sheet, after it was softened through annealing. As a result, the stones are flush with the surface—a feature often associated with inlays set into wood or stone. An analysis of the silver by Dr. H. E. Cox and A. Lucas in 1927 revealed: silver (90.1 percent), gold (8.9 percent), and copper (1.0 percent); there were trace amounts of lead. The burial goods of Queen Hetepheres included several exceptional gold vessels, as well as furniture lavishly decorated with gold sheet and appliqués, but the quantity of silver was minimal (a finding that supports the theory of silver's then high value). The Tod Treasure, a hoard that included 153 silver vessels and numerous silver and gold ingots, was found buried near the foundation of a Middle Kingdom temple in Upper Egypt. The treasure was contained in four bronze boxes bearing the name of Amenemhet II (r.1929–1895 BCE), and it may have included trade items or gifts from abroad. Vessels, crafted in the Syrian-Minoan style, were found folded or crushed, suggesting that such worked silver was regarded as a raw material, to be reworked.

The fact that silver was scarce and imported undoubtedly added to its allure, as did its symbolic associations. Linked with the moon, it was affiliated with the god Thoth and used to craft headdresses and amulets incorporating the lunar disk. Of even greater significance was silver's connection to "the bones of the gods," which may account for the large amount of the gilt silver (gold-coated silver) in Egypt (gold, "the flesh" of the gods would have covered "the bones"). An exceptional example of gilt silver is that of a royal pectoral, inlaid with glass and semiprecious stones, in the collection of the Museum of Fine Arts, Boston. Dated to the Second Intermediate Period (c.1750 BCE), the jewel has a sheet-metal silver framework that was hammered to a thinness of only 1 millimeter. Electron-beam microprobe analysis of the metal by Richard Newman in 1990 indicated that the silver, probably derived from lead sulfide ore, was relatively pure, with small amounts of copper (2.5 percent), gold (0.3 percent), and lead (0.1 percent). Included among the Third Intermediate Period royal tombs at Tanis were a number of exceptional silver vessels, stands, the hawk-headed coffin of Sheshonq (r.931–910 BCE), and four miniature coffins inscribed for King Sheshonq II (c.850 BCE). The sheer quantity of silver utilized in these funerary items is indicative of the quantity of silver that was available to these Delta kings.

Several silver vessels and implements from the Napatan burial of Queen Khensa, a sister and wife of King Piye (747–716 BCE), demonstrate the continued importance of silver in the Nile Valley during the first millennium BCE. One, a hemispherical container with half-covered top and twin spouts, while another, with vertical sides, is inscribed with the names of the queen. Somewhat later, in the twenty-fifth dynasty, the bejeweled alabastron of King Aspelta (593–568 BCE) was fashioned, a calcite vessel having a gilded silver collar with pendant drops and inlays of Egyptian blue and semiprecious stones. The jeweled decoration consists of a sheet-silver backplate with five ornamental registers fabricated from gilded silver strips that are soldered to the base. A microprobe analysis of the silver (base) revealed the following composition: silver (93.3–94.6 percent), gold (4.2–5.1 percent), and copper (1.8–1.9 percent). Throughout Greco-Roman Egypt, silver maintained its privileged status; like gold, it continued to be refined, made into coinage, and fabricated into luxury items.

BIBLIOGRAPHY

Gänsicke, J. "King Aspelta's Vessel Hoard from Nuri in the Sudan." *Journal of the Museum of Fine Arts, Boston* 6 (1994), 14–40.

Harris, John. *Lexicographical Studies in Ancient Egyptian Minerals.* Berlin, 1961.

Kemp, Barry, and Robert Merrillees. *Minoan Pottery in Second Millennium Egypt.* Mainz, 1980.

Kendall, Timothy. *Kush: Lost Kingdom of the Nile.* Brockton, 1981.

Lacovara, Peter. "An Ancient Egyptian Royal Pectoral." *Journal of the Museum of Fine Arts, Boston.* 2 (1990), 18–29.

Lucas, A., and J. R. Harris. *Ancient Egyptian Materials and Industries.* London, 1989.

Moorey, P. R. S. *Materials and Manufacture in Ancient Mesopotamia: The Evidence of Archaeology and Art.* BAR International Series, 237, 1985.

Ogden, Jack. *Jewellery of the Ancient World.* New York, 1981.

Scheel, Bernd. *Egyptian Metalworking and Tools.* Aylesbury, 1989. An excellent introduction to ancient Egyptian metalworking.

PETER LACOVARA AND
YVONNE J. MARKOWITZ

SINAI, a peninsula (including its eastern extension in the Negev) encompassing a triangular desert region, in which the Mediterranean coastal plain forms a land bridge that connects Africa and Western Asia. The peninsula's central continuous plateaus of Al-Tih and Egma and the southern mountainous region of Gebel Musa contain a mineral-bearing area bounded to the west by the Gulf of Suez, the Bitter Lakes, and the Wadi Tumilat, and to the east by the Gulf of Elat and the Rift Valley in southern Arabah (between Elat and the Dead Sea). In ancient times, the Nile River's annual inundation enabled the cultivation of cereal grains and other crops in the Nile Valley and the Nile Delta's flood plains, which supported a large population, in contrast to the neighboring Sahara and Sinai deserts; these became progressively more arid and less populated after the Predynastic period (4000–3050 BCE). The Sinai provided a geographic filter through which materials and sociocultural exchanges passed between Egypt and the Near East, but it also formed a sufficient barrier to allow for the early development of a distinct Nile Valley civilization, one which evolved throughout antiquity.

Despite the Sinai's desert terrain, greater precipitation and open mountain scrub forests occur near its southern end and many springs and oases (e.g., Wadi Feiran) have supported continuous, albeit small and fluctuating, nomadic and sedentary populations. Throughout antiquity, both Egyptians and bedouins mined turquoise and copper in the southern Sinai (including copper in southern Arabah). In contrast, the northern Sinai maintained relatively higher populations, and it became both a strategic region that protected Egypt from invasions and a military and commercial route that connected Egypt with Arabia and Palestine.

Historical Overview. The Sinai contains many seasonal campsites that have been dated to the Paleolithic (700,000–5500 BCE), the Neolithic (5500–4000 BCE; Egypt's Badarian and Faiyum A cultures), the Chalcolithic (4000–3300 BCE; Egypt's Naqada I and II), the Early Bronze I (3300–3050 BCE; Egypt's Naqada II and III), and the Early Bronze II (3050–2687 BCE; Egypt's first dynasty and second). Nevertheless, Egyptian contact with Western Asia (the Near East) is not well attested until the late Predynastic (Naqada II and III) and the first dynasty. During those periods, Egyptian artifacts (e.g., flint knives, ceramic vessels, stone vessels, and items with royal names in *serekh* frames) appeared in Palestine and at many of the 30 Chalcolithic and the 250 Early Bronze I and II campsites in the northern Sinai. In the southern Sinai, Egyptian Predynastic potsherds were about 1 percent of the pottery found at two Chalcolithic sites and seven Early Bronze I and II sites. In addition, the presence in Egypt of Syrian-Palestinian and Mesopotamian material culture (e.g., pottery, cylinder seals, and architectural and artistic elements), plus items of turquoise and of copper, confirm that Egypt maintained contact with the Near East (through the northern Sinai) and with the southern Sinai during the Predynastic period and the first dynasty. By the second dynasty, however, Near Eastern artifacts decreased in Egypt, paralleling the decline in Sinai sites of Egyptian pottery.

Old Kingdom. The nature and extent of early Old Kingdom relations with the northern Sinai await clarification, since few Early Bronze III (2687–2374 BCE) sites are attested in this region; sixth dynasty pottery (e.g., Late Meidum vessels) and First Intermediate Period activity occurred at many of the 280 Early Bronze IV to Middle Bronze I (2374–1991 BCE) sites in the northern Sinai. Some Egyptian accounts (e.g., the sixth dynasty Biography of Weni) refer to Old Kingdom raids across the northern Sinai into Palestine, while late First Intermediate Period texts (e.g., the *Admonitions of Ipuwer* and *Instructions for Merikare*) mention West Asian incursions into the Nile Delta after the Old Kingdom's collapse.

Old Kingdom activity has been well attested in the southern Sinai. The Wadi Mughara (termed the "terraces of the turquoise") contains camps, copper-smelting sites, turquoise mines, and rock tablets that were dated to the kings of the third dynasty to the sixth. The Mughara tablets depicted some Egyptian deities that were worshiped in Sinai: a goddess (possibly Hathor), a jackal figure (Wepwawet, "opener of the ways"), and an ibis-headed figure (Thoth, "lord of the foreign countries"). To the northeast, Wadi Kharig yields a mining camp and an inscription of Sahure from the fifth dynasty. Egyptian activity disappeared from the southern Sinai during the First Intermediate Period.

Middle Kingdom. In the Middle Kingdom and in the Second Intermediate Period, Egyptian pottery and some sherds of Tell el-Yahudiyya ware were found at five settle-

SINAI. *Remains of the temple of Hathor at Serabit el-Khadim in the Sinai.* Various stelae are still standing; mining expeditions dedicated them to the goddess Hathor, who was associated with turquoise. (Courtesy Dieter Arnold)

ments in northwestern Sinai and at many of some one hundred campsites in north-central and northeastern Sinai. Egyptian texts, such as the *Story of Sinuhe* and the *Prophecy of Neferti*, record Amenemhet I's establishment of fortifications ("The Wall of the Ruler") in northwestern Sinai, possibly at Tell Heboua and/or at Tell er-Retabeh in the Wadi Tumilat. Later Egyptian texts (e.g., the Kamose Stelae) mention the infiltration and control of the Delta and Middle Egypt by Near Easterners (the fifteenth dynasty Hyksos, called "foreign rulers"). The Hyksos controlled a fortress 350 by 400 metres (some 1,140 by 1,320 feet) at Tell Heboua, which produced two stelae of King Apophis (r. 1605–1565 BCE).

Middle Kingdom activity intensified in the southern Sinai. Mughara was found to contain rock inscriptions of Amenemhet III and IV near the turquoise mines. Wadi Kharig had an inscription of Senwosret I beside a camp and two turquoise mines. Wadi Nasb contained a stela of Amenemhet III and a possible thirteenth dynasty cartouche (of Sobekhotpe II?). Rod el-'Air yielded Middle Kingdom graffiti and a nearby campsite. Serabit el-Khadim contained statuary and inscriptions of Amenemhet I through Amenemhet IV from the turquoise mines and a temple to Hathor ("Lady of the turquoise").

During the Second Intermediate Period and early eighteenth dynasty, West Asian (Hyksos?) activity in the southern Sinai may be attested through the presence of some sherds of Tell el-Yahudiyya ware and some Hyksos-style scarab seals at Serabit el-Khadim. In addition, Mughara, Wadi Nasb, and Serabit el-Khadim have perhaps thirty-five undeciphered Proto-Sinaitic inscriptions, including one stela that depicts an Egyptian mummiform deity (Ptah). Proto-Sinaitic is a script used to write a Semitic language (with twenty-seven to twenty-nine consonantal, pictorial signs, of which twenty-three to twenty-six derive from Egyptian hieroglyphs); it resembles the Proto-Canaanite alphabet of 1800–1500 BCE.

New Kingdom. Early in the eighteenth dynasty, Ahmose captured the Sinai fortress of Tjaru, defeated the Hyksos at Avaris (Tell ed-Dab'a), and conducted three campaigns against Sharuhen (Tell el-'Ajjul?) in southwestern Palestine. Ahmose then initiated the New Kingdom "empire" (albeit in the form of raids rather than occupation forces prior to Thutmose III) in the northern Sinai and in Syria-Palestine, and he renewed Egyptian turquoise mining and copper smelting in the southern Sinai. New Kingdom texts designated the northern Sinai as the "Ways of Horus," which included a series of forts and reservoirs depicted by Sety I at Karnak Temple. More than one hundred and fifty New Kingdom sites are between el-Qantara and Raphia in northern Sinai and numerous sites in northeastern Sinai form ten clusters, with a central fortress or administrative structure, a reservoir, magazines, and satellite campsites. Three New Kingdom sites at Tell Heboua (I–III) straddle a causeway between the western and eastern lagoons (probably *T₃ dnit:* "the dividing waters"), possibly representing Tjaru (erroneously equated with Tell Abu Sefah, the Romans' Sile). The "eastern" canal, found several kilometers to the southeast, may also be dated to this period.

The eastern frontier fortifications included Ramessid forts at Tell er-Retabeh (Wadi Tumilat) and Kom el-Qulzoum (today's Port Suez; Ptolemaic Clysma). The Isthmus of Suez also contained *in situ*, albeit possibly reused, gateway blocks of Ramesses II at Serapeum; a stone shrine of Sety I and a stela of Ramesses II at Gebel Abu Hassa; a stela of Ramesses II at Gebel Mourr; and New Kingdom (?) or later (Roman) activity at Ain Moussa (e.g., a *shawabti* funerary figurine). Those sites facilitated maritime and overland expeditions to an eighteenth dynasty anchorage and pharaonic site (numbers 345 and 346) in el-Merkha Bay, from which ancient expeditions accessed Mughara and Serabit el-Khadim. Another route to el-Merkha Bay traversed the Eastern Desert via Wadi Araba to cross the Red Sea.

Later biblical texts recount the Exodus of the Hebrews (Israelites) from Egypt, a crossing of the "Reed-Sea" (the Bitter Lakes [?]), and a sojourn in the Sinai. Egyptian sources however, contain no references to the Exodus, and its date and details remain controversial there. The earliest reference to Israel and its destruction in Palestine (c.1232 BCE) is found on Merenptah's Hymn of Victory stela ("Israel Stela").

New Kingdom activity concentrated at Wadi Nasb and Serabit el-Khadim, in contrast to Mughara, which yielded one inscription dated to Queen Hatshepsut and Thutmose III, plus a reported, albeit unconfirmed, inscription of Ramesses II. Wadi Nasb contained a copper mine, two furnaces, *tuyères*, slag heaps with New Kingdom faience, and an inscription of Ramesses II. Rod el-'Air produced some graffiti. The plateau at Serabit el-Khadim yielded twenty turquoise mines with two inscriptions of Thutmose IV. Mines G and L contained copper-smelting tools (e.g., two stone foot-bellows and tuyères), forty-seven stone molds (for metal axes, adzes, knives, chisels, mirrors, and ingots), stone tools, stone containers, a faience bowl, and New Kingdom potsherds. The plateau also yielded a small shrine of Ptah (with three stelae dedicated to Hathor), the Hathor Temple, and five sandstone quarries used for this temple's construction.

New Kingdom expeditions repaired and embellished the Middle Kingdom shrines of Hathor ("Lady of the Turquoise") and Sopdu ("Lord of the East") and constructed a western series of chambers (with Hathor-headed columns and pairs of stelae) and an enclosure wall, during the reigns of Amenhotpe I, Hatshepsut and Thutmose III, Amenhotpe II, Thutmose IV, Amenhotpe III, Sety I, Ramesses II, Merenptah, Sethnakhte, and Ramesses III, IV, and VI. The temple yielded royal and private stelae and statuary, as well as votive items: beads (from necklaces), bracelets, scarabs, figurines, plaques, sistra, throw-sticks, and containers of alabaster (calcite), faience, glass, and pottery (including Mycenaean and Cypriot potsherds). Many votives bore the cartouches of most New Kingdom rulers from Ahmose through Ramesses VI (including an unpublished votive of Horemheb), but excluded were Amenhotpe IV (Akhenaten), Semkhkare, Tutankhamun, Ay, and Amenmesse.

From the nineteenth dynasty to the twentieth, expeditions initiated copper mining and smelting at Wadi Reqeita (in southeastern Sinai) and in southern Arabah. The Arabah contained a rock inscription at Timna, from the time of Ramesses II, and one from Ramesses III at Site 582, as well as a Hathor shrine at Site 200, which produced votives with the cartouches of Sety I, Ramesses II, Merenptah, Sety II, Queen Tawosret, and Ramesses III, IV, and V.

Late in the twentieth dynasty (in the time of Ramesses VII to XI) and in the twenty-first to twenty-fifth dynasty, evidence of Egyptian activity disappeared from the southern Sinai and declined in the northern Sinai, which retained settlement at Retabeh, at some sites in northwestern Sinai, and at thirty Iron Age sites between Wadi el-'Arish and Wadi Ghazzeh. The Negev and Gulf of Elat, however, became an important region that linked Syria-Palestine with the Arabian spice trade. Epigraphic evidence indicates that Egypt conducted military activity into Palestine during the reigns of Siamun, Sheshonq I (who also invaded the Negev), Osorkon I (biblical Zerah?), Osorkon II, Shabtaqa, and Taharqa.

Late period. The Assyrian kings Sargon II (722–705 BCE) and Sennacherib (705–681 BCE) expanded their empire into southern Palestine, subjugating Arab tribes in northeastern Sinai in 720, 716, and 701 BCE. They were succeeded by King Esarhaddon, who failed to invade Egypt in 674 BCE, but who in 671 BCE captured the Nile Delta as far south as Memphis. His successor, Ashurbanipal, invaded Egypt in 667 and 664 BCE, during which he restricted the Kushite kingdom to Nubia and established the vassal ruler Necho I at Sais in the Delta.

The Saite Dynasty rulers Psamtik I and Necho II renewed Egypt's domination of Syria-Palestine between 612 and 601 BCE, while, according to the Greek historian Herodotus, Necho built a trireme shipping base on the Red

Sea. Northwestern Sinai contained Saite forts at Tell Defenneh, Tell Qedwa, and Tell el-Maskhuta (Pithom), and occupation continued at thirty sites in northeastern Sinai. The aforementioned eastern canal may have been used in this period, since it connected Defenneh and Qedwa. In 601 and 568 BCE, the Babylonian empire destroyed the forts at Qedwa and Maskhuta but failed to capture the Delta.

King Cambyses crossed the northern Sinai and defeated Egypt in 525 BCE, initiating the First Persian Occupation of Egypt (the twenty-seventh dynasty, 525–405 BCE). The Persians established more than two hundred settlements in northern Sinai and extended a canal from Maskhuta to the Red Sea. Despite a renewal of Egyptian independence from the twenty-eighth to the thirtieth dynasty, the Persian Empire reoccupied Egypt from 343 BCE until Alexander the Great occupied it in 332 BCE.

Greco-Roman times. During Greco-Roman times (332 BCE–395 CE), settlements in the northern Sinai increased to more than three hundred sites (ports, fortresses, and waystations). The southern Sinai regained its importance as a source of turquoise and it has yielded numerous Nabataean and Aramaean inscriptions at places such as Wadi Mukhattab (near Mughara) and Wadi Hesif es-Seghair (near Serabit el-Khadim). The Hathor temple at Serabit el-Khadim produced some (probably) Late period amulets, a Roman potsherd, an early Roman glass sherd, and an inscribed Meroitic offering table (c.300 BCE–350 CE). By the fourth century CE, the southern Sinai had become a refuge for hermits and a destination for pilgrims visiting settlements in Wadi Feiran, the Monastery of Saint Catherine (Mount Sinai), and other sites ascribed to the Hebrew sojourn in the Sinai.

[See also Eastern Desert and Red Sea.]

BIBLIOGRAPHY

Andelkovic, Branislau. *The Relations between Early Bronze Age I: Canaanites and Upper Egyptians.* The University of Belgrade, Centre for Archaeological Research, 14. Belgrade, 1995. Examines the presence of imported Early Bronze I Egyptian and Canaanite artifacts in Palestine and Egypt; provides good bibliography, maps, site plans, and line drawings of artifacts. Also includes sites in the Nile Delta, the northern Sinai, and the Negev.

Beit-Arieh, Itzhaq. "Serâbît el-Khâdim: New Metallurgical and Chronological Aspects." *Levant* 17 (1985), 89–116. Deals with copper-smelting technology and artifacts from Mines G and L at Serabit el-Khadim; discusses the association between the Proto-Sinaitic inscriptions and copper-smelting activity.

Bowersock, Glen W. *Roman Arabia.* Cambridge, Mass., 1983. Includes Nabataean and Roman activity in the Sinai and Negev; has maps, site plans, photographs, and a good bibliography.

Chartier-Raymond, M., et al. "Les sites miniers pharaoniques du Sud-Sinaï: Quelques notes et observations de terrain." *Cahiers de recherches de l'Institut de papyrologie et d'Égyptologie de Lille* 16 (1994), 31–77. Concerns a 1991 survey of ancient Egyptian turquoise and copper-mining sites, with bibliographical entries in the footnotes;

also contains a report by D. Valbelle on a 1993 expedition to Serabit el-Khadim. Articles are summarized in English.

Fontaine, Alfred L. *Monographie cartographique de l'Isthme de Suez, de la Péninsule du Sinaï, du nord de la chaîne arabique suivie d'un catalogue raisonné sur les cartes de ces régions.* Mémoires de la société d'Études historiques et géographiques, de l'Isthme de Suez, 2. Cairo, 1955. Useful cataloging of published maps of the Sinai Peninsula; good bibliography, historical background to cartographic work in this region, descriptions of the sites on the maps, and an index to sites and explorers.

Gardiner, Alan H., and T. Eric Peet. *The Inscriptions of Sinai. Part II: Translations and Commentary.* Edited and completed by Jaroslav Černý. Memoir of the Egypt Exploration Society, 45. London, 1955. This publication provides a well-referenced study with ancient Egyptian names for Sinai, routes, the composition of expeditions, mining techniques, and a catalog of translated inscriptions from Magharah, Wadi Nasb, Wadi Kharig (Kharit), Rod el-'Air, and Serabit el-Khadim.

Gardiner, Alan H., and T. Eric Peet. *The Inscriptions of Sinai. Part I: Introduction and Plates.* 2d rev. ed. by Jaroslav Černý. Memoir of the Egypt Exploration Society, 36. London, 1952. Represents the correction of and addition to inscriptions illustrated in the first edition, during the 1930 and 1935 Harvard University expeditions to Serabit el-Khadim.

Giveon, Raphael. *The Stones of Sinai Speak.* Tokyo, 1978. Well-illustrated general treatment of the history of exploration and explorers in Sinai, Egyptian mining at Wadi Maghara and Serabit el-Khadim, Egyptian deities worshiped in Sinai, an overview of Giveon's survey and excavations, some new plans of Egyptian camps, and some new inscriptions.

Gophna, Ram. *Excavations at 'En Besor.* Tel Aviv, 1995. Republication of 16 articles written between 1976 and 1993; includes recent summary and some new discussions of the excavations of the Early Bronze I site of 'En Besor in southern Palestine on the northeastern edge of the Sinai; Egyptian activity is mentioned at this site. Good bibliographies deal with the First Dynasty in the Sinai and southern Palestine.

Pinch, Geraldine. *Votive Offerings to Hathor.* Oxford, 1993. Examines several categories of artifacts and aspects of the Hathor cult at sites in Egypt and Sinai (Timna and Serabit el-Khadim); incorporates many unpublished items (from Museum collections) excavated at Serabit el-Khadim.

Rainey, Anson F. *Egypt, Israel, Sinai: Archaeological and Historical Relationships in the Biblical Period.* Tel Aviv, 1987. Eight articles deal with Egyptian activity and interrelations with Canaanites, including two treatments of the Hebrew Exodus.

Redford, Donald B. *Egypt, Canaan, and Israel in Ancient Times.* Princeton, 1992. Provides a recent examination of archaeological and epigraphic evidence on the nature and extent of Egyptian contact with West Asia across the Sinai, from the Palaeolithic to 586 BCE: contains a new study on the Hebrew Exodus.

Rothenberg, Beno, et al. *The Egyptian Mining Temple at Timna.* Researches in the Arabah 1959–1984, 1. London, 1988. Well-illustrated publication of the excavations at an Egyptian New Kingdom shrine at Timna, with historical background, technical articles, special studies, and catalogs of the pottery, objects, textiles, wood, faunal, and floral remains. Extensive bibliography for each section.

Sass, Bejamin. *The Genesis of the Alphabet and Its Development in the Second Millennium B.C.* Ägypten und Altes Testament, 13. Wiesbaden, 1988. Includes an extensive examination of the Proto-Sinaitic inscriptions; has a good bibliography.

Stern, Ephraim, ed. *The New Encyclopedia of Archaeological Excavations in the Holy Land.* 4 vols. 2d rev. ed. New York, 1993. Extensively revised and many new detailed articles on the Paleolithic to the Arab eras, good bibliographies, maps, plans, and photographs for sites and region in Palestine and the Sinai Peninsula.

GREGORY D. MUMFORD

SINUHE. The *Story of Sinuhe* is preserved in five Middle Kingdom manuscripts, including two from Thebes, and more than twenty New Kingdom copies, including scribal exercises, which present slightly different versions of the text. The text is complete; the number of surviving manuscripts is high for a fictional narrative, suggesting that *Sinuhe* was highly regarded. The earliest manuscript is the Theban Papyrus Berlin 3022, from the second half of the twelfth dynasty. The story's setting and eulogistic elements may suggest that it was composed shortly after the end of the reign of Senwosret I. It is approximately 570 metrical lines of verse long.

The narrative is introduced as the funerary autobiography of Sinuhe, a courtier whose service began under Amenemhet I:

> The Patrician and Count,
> Governor of the Sovereign's Domains in the Lands of
>   the Asiatics [Near East]
> the True Acquaintance of the King, whom he loves,
> the Follower Sinuhe, says . . .

The following first-person narrative includes a particularly wide range of other genres, including ritual songs and dramatic monologues. It is written in verse, with high-flown diction, and in a self-consciously fine style which is consistently varied, subtle, and resonant. The forty stanzas can be divided into five thematic sections.

In the first section of the tale, the expected pattern of a courtier's ideal life is shattered when Sinuhe overhears of the sudden death of Amenemhet I, and he flees abroad, where he eventually establishes himself in the Palestinian kingdom of Retjenu. The second section is occupied by his conversation with the ruler of Retjenu, Amunenshi, in which he affirms and extols the glory of the new king, Senwosret I. In the central section he tells how success abroad under Amunenshi's favor failed to bring him happiness, and the fourth section comprises an exchange of letters between Senwosret I and Sinuhe, in which the latter is exonerated from blame for his flight and is summoned back to Egypt. The final section recounts his homecoming with a lyrical ritual in the royal court, in which he is reestablished and reborn as a true Egyptian. The mock-inscription concludes as he is buried in the royal necropolis.

There are touches of local color in Sinuhe's experiences abroad, and the tale presents the conflict between Egyptian and foreign values, which is articulated in the structurally central duel between Sinuhe and a Palestinian rival. With an emphasis on personal reflection, the tale offers an introspective assessment of Egyptian cultural values. Much of it centers on the question of Sinuhe's motivation, in particular what led him to flee—a question that is continually left unresolved and is developed with a theodic aspect.

Sinuhe has frequently been discussed in connection with propaganda, but the propagandistic elements are integrated into a complex and multivalent whole. The tale has been much anthologized and analyzed; originally regarded as a copy of a historical inscription, it is now widely valued as the masterpiece of Middle Kingdom fictional literature. It is the subject of an article that marked a turning point in the Egyptological analysis of literary texts: John Baines's "Interpreting Sinuhe" (1982).

BIBLIOGRAPHY

Baines, John. "Interpreting Sinuhe." *Journal of Egyptian* Archaeology 68 (1982), 31–44. A landmark in the study of Egyptian literature.

Barns, John W. B. *The Ashmolean Ostracon of Sinuhe.* London, 1952. Edition of one manuscript with philological commentary.

Blumenthal, Elke. "Die Erzählung des Sinuhe." In *Mythen und Epen,* vol. 3, edited by Elke Blumenthal et al., pp. 884–911. (Texte aus der Umwelt des Alten Testament, III.5.) Gütersloh, 1995. Translation with full bibliography.

Gardiner, Alan H. *Notes on the Story of Sinuhe.* Paris, 1916. Early philological commentary, still of value.

Koch, Roland. *Die Erzählung des Sinuhe.* (Bibliotheca Aegyptiaca, 17.) Brussels, 1990. Standard edition of the text.

Parkinson, R. B. *The Tale of Sinuhe and Other Ancient Egyptian Poems 1940–1640* BC. Oxford, 1997. Recent translation, pp. 21–53.

Simpson, William K. "Sinuhe." In *Lexicon der Ägyptologie* 5: 950–55.

R. B. PARKINSON

SISTRUM derives from Greek *seiein* ('to shake') and is a musical instrument, a rattle that is shaken. As a sacred rattle, it is used in the divine cult, in religious processions, and in funerary cults. It was used from the Old Kingdom and was still popular in Roman times, so its use spread with the cult of Isis wherever the Romans went.

The sound of the sistrum is metallic, produced by a number of metal disks, strung onto a set of transverse bars, set horizontally into a frame of varying design. Its sound was thought to echo that of a stem of papyrus being shaken. The papyrus plant is at the base of the mythological environment of the sistrum—the papyrus thicket from which, on the one hand, the cow-goddess Hathor is seen to emerge and where, on the other, the goddess Isis raised her infant son, Horus. Both goddesses are closely connected with the sistrum.

In addition to the symbolic significance of its sound, the shape and decoration of the sistrum relate it to the divine. The two main types are the arched sistrum, made of metal, and the *naos*-shaped sistrum, usually made of faience. The handle of the arched form is either plain, in the shape of a papyrus stem (most common), or in the shape of a miniature column adorned with the head of the goddess Hathor. The god Bes may also be molded as part of the handle. The frame holding the horizontal metal rods with their disks is a parabolic loop. Known from the eighteenth dynasty, yet based on earlier prototypes for which we have the hieroglyphic designation but no picture, the arched sistrum was called *sḥm* or *ib*.

In the *naos*-shaped sistrum, the upper portion is in the shape of a sanctuary or door, across which the metal rods are placed. The handle of this instrument usually has the decoration of a Hathor head, and the pair of volutes flanking the door are shaped like the cows' horns of the goddess. A vulture may crown the *naos*, and the handle may be covered with the incised plumage of the bird. This type of sistrum whose acoustic effects would be extremely limited, was known as *ss*, *ššst*, or *sššt*, reflecting its primeval musical roots.

The symbolic value of the sistrum far exceeded its musical potential. The decoration sometimes included the royal *uraeus* (cobra), referring to the myth of the Solar Eye. In this myth, Hathor is in her role as the rebellious daughter of Re, to be appeased by music and dance. Based on this proven effect of the instrument, the sistrum was, from the New Kingdom on, the instrument that pacified and satisfied any deity, whether female such as Hathor, or male. In the temple of Amun-Re at Karnak, a *naos*-shaped sistrum was a prime cult object, perhaps through its connections to Hathor, who sometimes represented the female procreative element needed to sustain his virility. In Late period representations, the sistrum was held by priestesses adoring the deity face to face; this intimacy was a female prerogative. Other deities, too, benefited from the presence of the sistrum.

As the sistrum reflected in such a visible manner the presence of the gods, it is no wonder that in the Amarna era, it was virtually deprived of decoration, except for the papyrus handle. But it is significant that it was held by the queen or the princesses during the cult of Aten, the sun disk. The instrument belonged in the realm of cosmic deities. According to the ancient Greek historian Plutarch, the sistrum's arch was the lunar cycle, the bars were the elements, the twin Hathor heads rendered life and death, and the cat—often included in the decoration—was the moon.

Many of these instruments carry the names of royal persons. When the sistrum is depicted, it was often in the hands of royal family members. In the *Story of Sinuhe* we learn that the princesses received him with music and song. The musical instruments were not refined wind or string instruments, but the sistrum. In the Westcar Papyrus, when the goddesses dress up as itinerant musicians

to gain access to the birth chamber of the mother of the children of Re, they, too, accompany themselves only by the sistrum.

The sistrum was suitable for beating a rhythmical accompaniment in open-air processions. Apuleius, the Roman philosopher, described a procession in honor of Isis, in *The Golden Ass*, where the rhythmic pattern was three beats followed by a pause on the fourth. In more remote times, such as the religious feasts celebrated in Thebes during the New Kingdom, we also find groups of women shaking sistrums in honor of the divine procession. These celebrations were for Amun-Re, such as the Opet festival depicted on the walls of the Luxor temple or the Valley Festival rendered in countless Theban tombs. The world of the funerary cult is depicted in the Valley Festival, for the sistrum is seen presented to the tomb owner and his wife by their daughters. In fact, "bringing" and "receiving" were the key words, rather than making music or maintaining a beat, for the blessings that Hathor bestowed were the focus of the ceremony: the feeling of well-being and eternal life. The scenes show the sistrum often carried by its loop, looking similar to the *ankh*, the sign of life, of which it may be seen to be an equivalent.

Closely connected with sistrum playing is Ihy, the infant born of the union between the sky goddess Hathor of Dendera and the god of light Horus of Edfu. Through his music he performed the part of intermediary between the adorer and the goddess.

The sistrum is frequently paired with the *menat*, a heavy necklace that when grasped by its inverted keyhole-shaped counterpoise, would produce a variant rattling sound. The use of the sistrum has survived in the Coptic church, where it is directed at the four cardinal points, to demonstrate the extent of God's creation.

BIBLIOGRAPHY

Manniche, Lise. *Music and Musicians in Ancient Egypt*. London, 1991. Chapter 3, "Music for the Gods," includes mention of the role of the sistrum.

Ziegler, Christiane. "Sistrum" in *Lexicon der Ägyptologie*, 5: 958–963. Wiesbaden, 1984.

LISE MANNICHE

SIXTH DYNASTY. *See* Old Kingdom, *article on* Sixth Dynasty.

SLAVES. In human society, everyone who has a master or a lord is the servant or slave of that master or that lord. Few are without a lord (human or divine), so everybody is basically someone's servant or slave. Typically, in ancient Egypt, a priest was a god's slave (*ḥm-nṯr*); a subordinate in a nobleman's domain was the servant or slave in the lord's private estate (*bȝk n pr-dt*); or the slave/servant of the lord's ka (*ḥm-kȝ*); and so on. Correspondingly, a social inferior when addressing a superior often used the polite circumlocution "the servant/slave here" (*bȝk im*), designating the speaker. Conspicuously, one important title of pharaoh is *ḥm* ("body"), which etymologically might mean the slave/servant *par excellence* (of the gods). Anyone might be called the slave/servant of a god.

The consequence of such usage was that native terminology may be misleading to scholars. In reading Egyptian texts, therefore, context is the only criterion for determinating connotation. While interpreting documents the different forms of servitude must be considered, according to the various rights and services of the human involved. Unfree people might include not only slaves but also, in fact, others with various degrees of encumbered liberty. Therefore, a slave was the person owned by a master, as was any other chattel—used as the master pleased—to the extent of being disposed of by inheritance, gift, sale and so forth.

In documents, groups have been recognizable by the collective noun *mr.(y)t* (written with the hoe-sign). Those groups belonged to individuals and institutions (e.g., temples). Since the Old Kingdom, they were frequently mentioned along with land and cattle. In the Middle Kingdom, they could be acquired by bequest or another arrangement. In the New Kingdom, they could be recruited from captives or given in an endowment. Their apparently permanent relationship to the land and their master suggests that they were a type of slave. A similar term, *mr.t* (written with the canal-sign), denoted other groups who were seemingly not in connection with land and cattle but who were assigned to individuals and institutions. Individuals from such groups have not been identified, unless they were identical with the king's slaves (*ḥm.w nswit*) who, during the Middle Kingdom, were often transferred to estates of priests, nobles, and officials. The king's slaves had to work for their master and were considered his property. Their occupations were not confined to agriculture, as they were also employed in households. With the passage of time, their children undoubtedly inherited their status of servitude.

The principal and oldest cause of slavery was capture in war. In ancient Egypt, the general rule was that all captives—not only those from fighting forces—become a royal resource. The king could then resettle them in colonies for labor; he had equally the right to grant some of them to temples and to meritorious individuals; also they might be booty for his soldiers who had showed bravery in the field. The captives thus assigned to an individual could be as many as nineteen slaves, both male and female. Temples might receive unlimited numbers—inscriptions abound in references to many thousands. (Al-

though the evidence dates to the New Kingdom, this state might have prevailed earlier).

In the Brooklyn Papyrus of the Middle Kingdom, Near Easterners (*ʿȝm*)—men and women—were interspersed with Egyptian servants, outnumbering them. They seem to have been more highly regarded than the Egyptians—a distinction stemming, perhaps, from the fact that as prisoners of war or descendants thereof they belonged to a social stratum superior to that of Egyptians servants, most of whom were probably people who had committed unlawful acts or their descendants. A trade in (possibly captured) people from foreign countries was also possible. The Bologna Papyrus of the New Kingdom reports that Near Eastern slaves (*ḥm w*) were brought to Egypt on a ship.

Another type of enslavement was that of the birth child of a slave mother, whether or not the father was free. Such slaves could have been the offspring of a union between master and slave. Fatal exposure of undesired newborn children was not infrequently practiced in Egypt and the Near East; it has also been attested in Greco-Roman Egypt. Foundlings were ownerless property who might be picked up to become slaves. Yet the extant documents afford no evidence of such a practice during pharaonic times.

Some slaves were originally free persons who, having committed illicit acts, were forced to forfeit their liberty, perhaps with spouse and children. The status of slavery could, moreover, be created through self-sale into servitude, as several Demotic papyri of the sixth century BCE illustrate. Some were drawn into contractual terms of sale, whereby the persons involved (man or woman) undertook to become (along with their children) the slave of a master. As this procedure was familiar in common law, such contracts are best explained as self-enslavements in satisfaction of debt. If the debtor was unable to pay off the debt, the creditor discharged the debt by acquiring the debtor as a slave. In fact, such contracts revealed the person giving up, in addition, all that he owned.

Information about slave-dealing in ancient Egypt is scanty, though sale of slaves was not an uncommon business. There was no public market but instead dealers appear to be itinerant, approaching their customers personally. The transaction itself, with a document containing clauses usually used in sales of valuable commodities, had to be performed before officials or a local council (*qnbt*). From an inscription narrating the acquisition of some fields with thirty-five slaves (men and women), the inference is that the administration held special registers for slaves. Furthermore, a special tax was probably paid on the occasion; one known transaction was negotiated before the treasury scribe (in the Leiden Papyrus; 727 BCE). The price of slaves varied. In the Leiden inscription, thirty-two slaves (privately handled) were valued at 1 *deben* and 1/3 *kite* in silver. During the twenty-fifth dynasty and the twenty-sixth, the average price was about 2.9 *debens*. In Ramessid times, a dealer received goods at 4 *debens* and 1 *kite* for a young Syrian girl (according to the Cairo Papyrus).

Although the slave is a personal chattel, forming part of the master's property and although the master enjoys a number of rights, she or he was under some obligations. So, upon acquiring a girl, her mistress gave her a name. The mistress nourished the slave children and brought them up. On a statue of a man with his wife was depicted, as a token of affection, their young slave (Theban tomb 216). From the contents of an eighteenth dynasty letter: child slaves were not allowed to be set to hard work. The master might exploit, at discretion, the abilities of the slave, employing the slave in domestic service (as guardian of children, cook, brewer, washer, etc.), as gardener or fieldhand, in a stable, as a craftsman or otherwise industrially (as weaver, sandalmaker, etc.). The master might also make the slave learn a trade so as to better benefit from any skill. One of the items in an inheritance consisted of some trade agents (*šwt.yw*), who presumably were trained slaves. When a master caused a servant/slave to learn to write, a slave could be promoted to a manager in the master's estate. As to the groups called *mr (y)t*, those were organized in fieldwork under the supervision of overseers. Captive slaves, however, were mostly assigned to the king and the temples, and their status entailed manual labor.

The master was also entitled to dispose of a slave by a legal act. It is significant that slave services were often transferred in favor of religious endowments. King Apries of the twenty-sixth dynasty, for example, decreed that a district near Memphis be dedicated to the god Ptah, together with its slaves (*mr t*), cattle, and their produce. An individual might also create an endowment and furnish it with resources, as did the eighteenth dynasty overseer of Amun's domain, Sen-mut, with respect to certain offerings. He ceded fields and at least two slaves (male and female *ḥm*) for baking bread and brewing beer. On an eleventh dynasty stela, Intef recorded two deeds that were made with two men for the celebration of certain ceremonies in his favor after his death: he gave twenty packages (?) of cloth to one man and ten to the other, besides a man and a maid (slaves) for each, along with other privileges. On his statue Amun-mes, the steward of Amun's temple, narrated the donation of all his property to the god Amun, consisting of male and female slaves (*ḥm*), houses, gardens, cattle, and all that he had obtained. In one Demotic contract of 516 BCE, concerning the transfer of a slave along with his children to a new master, a lady, that slave gave consent to the negotiation; furthermore, he declared himself, with children and belongings, slave vis-à-vis the new mistress.

The number of slaves owned by an individual varied considerably. An official of the thirteenth dynasty had well over forty Near Eastern servants in his personal possession. On one stela, its owner reports, "I have acquired three male slaves and seven females in addition to what my father granted me." On an eleventh dynasty stela, its owner recounted boastfully, "[Whereas] my father's people were house-born—as property [*ht*] of his father and his mother—my people are likewise [from] the property of my father and my mother [but also from] my own property, which I have acquired through my activity." In Demotic marriage settlements, the husband may promise his wife saying, "To the children you shall bear for me shall belong everything I own, [be it] a house, land, slaves, animals, chattels." As to the slaves, such an engagement was put into effect when a husband came (for example in the Turin Papyrus) to divide his estate, including thirteen slaves, men and women, among his presumptive heirs. In an inheritance, where slaves form part of the estate, there might be various ways to dispose of them: the co-ownership of the beneficiaries might be either maintained or distributed separately, eventually even by fractions in one and the same slave. In such a case, the slave got several masters, each entitled to a share in that slave's work; such a share was determined by a monthly number of the "slave's days" (*hrw n bȝk*). Subsequently, a master might sell or buy or otherwise transact merely a share in that slave's work. Differences arose when persons other than the master lay claim to the slave's services. In one case, the problem about a slave girl was looked into by the local authorities; it was settled, however, in the vizier's office, according to the Berlin and the Bologna Papyrus. In another text, the conflict about a woman slave was eventually decided by the municipal council (*qnbt*). Also, in claims to a woman slave with her son, some people opposed each other in yet another conflict; that woman was reported to have been abducted later.

The flight of slaves was a social phenomenon that affected the lower economic strata. When a slave escaped, the master's actual power ended; however, the master could pursue the fugitive and ask the authorities for assistance in the recapture of the runaway. If, during the New Kingdom, the slave was retrieved, the fugitive was to be given back to the master; if not, the person(s) suspected of having harbored the fugitive could be challenged to swear in the temple (according to the Strasburg Papyrus). The fugitive's best chance was to escape Egypt altogether. Yet, there might be conventions, with neighboring states or reciprocal clauses that provided for extradition. By the treaty of alliance between Ramses II and the Hittite king Ḥattušili, fugitives, even of humble birth, were bound to be restored to their native land.

As in many ancient legal systems, the Egyptian slave was capable not only of negotiating transactions but also of owning personal property. In the Wilbour Papyrus of the New Kingdom, not less than eleven slaves (*ḥm*) appear—on the same footing as others, as individual holders of agricultural land—though their status regarding the land property is not clear. An illuminating stela deals with, among other things, two slave women (*ḥm*), who each gave her own plot of land to the master/mistress in exchange for various commodities. They acted independently, as owners of property. If engaged in commerce on behalf of their mistress, slaves had to be competent to negotiate business with a third party. For example, a freeman was recorded in the Leopold Papyrus to be working under the supervision of a Nubian slave, who belonged to the high priest of Amun.

Regarding judicial procedure, the papyri that report the investigations of the New Kingdom tomb robberies shed particular light on slaves. In fact, they reveal, among other persons, several male slaves implicated in those crimes. During the hearings, slaves were not maltreated any more than other culprits—occasionally they had to undergo torture and swear not to speak falsely. Sometimes a slave denounced another. In most cases, however, the testimony was outright against the master, who was accused of robbery. Though many slaves acted as witnesses, only some were incriminated of complicity. While one was placed under arrest, another was found innocent and was set at liberty.

To date, no evidence exists relating to the marriage of slaves; seemingly a union of male and female was *contubernium* (cohabitation sanctioned by the master). Yet in the New Kingdom, a king's barber gave his own niece as wife to his own slave and a lady accepted as husband for her slave, her own younger brother. In either case, however, the slave (male or female) had first to be manumitted in public. In the latter case, the mistress extended freedom to all her child slaves, with the view of adopting them and thus bequeathing to them her estate. Furthermore, in a sixth-century BCE Demotic contract, one Hor engages himself—along with offspring and earnings—to become the son of another, who would then exercise authority over him. Presumably, Hor was the slave who was emancipated in return for continuing to look after his master, as a son caring for his father; Hor's children were then equally bound to that effect. In ancient Egypt, no case is yet known of a slave purchasing freedom or a master releasing the slave by ransom.

Finally, there was the small community of Deir el-Medineh, discussed in the Brooklyn Papyrus, in which some fifteen women slaves were attached to either of two departments of the workmen's gang. Possibly the women had to grind the supplied grain into flour for the workmen's families. They remained state property, since the administration provided them with sustenance (mainly grain and water). Besides, there were privately owned slaves, both men and women. The chief workman, Neferhotep, for example, possessed some "house-born" slaves; his father was said to have had at least five. Another inhabitant ascertained, "One took our twelve slaves in replacement for [some tools]." Several records also indicate that shares in a private slave's work could be transacted for bequests and other legal acts.

[*See also* Law; *and* Work Force.]

BIBLIOGRAPHY

Allam, S. "Ventes et cession de quotes-parts en esclaves." *Actes du Colloque "Le Commerce en Egypte ancienne."* Cairo, 1996.
Bakir, Abd-el-Mohsen. *Slavery in Pharaonic Egypt.* Cairo, 1952.
Helck, Wolfgang. *Materialien zur Wirtschaftsgeschichte des Neuen Reiches.* Vol. 3, p. 512 ff. Mainz, 1963.
Helck, Wolfgang. "Sklaven." In *Lexikon der Ägyptologie,* 5: 982–987. Wiesbaden, 1984.

S. ALLAM

SNAKES. Snakes (*ḥf3w* was the most common Egyptian term for the members of the suborder *Ophidia*) were found throughout Egypt—in the desert sands, in old walls, in fields, by the Nile and in its swamps, on threshing floors, in houses, and in livestock enclosures and pastures. Poisonous snakes would have posed a threat to humans and domestic animals alike. A papyrus in the Brooklyn Museum which served as a manual for a doctor treating snakebite reveals that the Egyptians had an intimate knowledge of their biology. Although the beginning of the papyrus is broken off, it would once have listed the names of thirty-seven types of snakes distinguished by the ancient Egyptians; at least thirty-six species have been identified in modern Egypt, but the ancient typology most likely did not correspond exactly to the modern one. The papyrus gives a physical description of each snake and its habitat, along with precise descriptions of the symptoms produced by each snake's venom, whether or not the wound is mortal, and the name of the god or goddess of which the snake is considered to be a manifestation. Following the list of snakes is a list of remedies to cure bite victims (some of which are specified for certain types of snakes, and some for specific symptoms); these remedies include emetics, compresses, unctions, massages, incision of wounds, and fumigations. Magical incantations were sometimes spoken over the remedies. The ingredients in the remedies include liquids and substances of mineral, animal and vegetable origin. The most common ingredient is onion, still used frequently in Egyptian folk medicine today to treat snakebite.

One of the poisonous snakes the Egyptians had to contend with was the horned viper (*Cerastes cornutus*). When the horned viper attacks, it rasps its coils together before springing forward. The rasping sounds like the letter *f*,

SNAKES. *Detail of a wall painting showing the deceased tomb owner adoring a huge serpent called "son of the earth."* A twentieth dynasty painting from the tomb of the foreman Inherka at Thebes, which portrays a vignette from Chapter 87 of *The Book of Going Forth by Day (Book of the Dead).* (© Patrick Francis Houlihan)

and the horned viper was used as the hieroglyph to write this sound (*fy* is the Egyptian word for "viper" as well).

The Pyramid Texts allude repeatedly to the menace of serpents, and they recur in religious texts throughout ancient Egyptian history. First attested in the First Intermediate Period, the snake god Apophis was considered the enemy of order, or Maat. As early as the reign of Ramesses III, Apophis became the subject of a ritual recorded in several magic books. During religious processions and lunar feasts, images of Apophis were fashioned from papyrus and wax and then subjected to various tortures, representing the triumph of Re and Maat over the chaos symbolized by Apophis.

Not all snakes were considered bad. Deities associated with poisonous snakes were sometimes considered beneficial. The goddess Renenutet often appeared in the form of a hooded cobra. Her name is derived from an Egyptian word meaning "to nurse," and she was closely associated with the fertility of fields, and consequently was considered the goddess of the granary. Offerings of the first fruits were made and hymns sung to a statue of Renenutet when grain was brought to the granary or when wine was stored in the cellar. She also had close ties with woven material and personified linen. Although her name first appears in the Old Kingdom in the Pyramid Texts, she is not depicted in art until the New Kingdom. She was worshipped throughout Egypt, but her cult was of particular significance in the Faiyum.

The snake goddess Meretseger personified the pyramid-shaped peak that rises above the Valley of the Kings. She may have been an object of a domestic cult in the nearby village of the royal tomb-builders and their families, Deir el-Medina, because snake figurines were found during excavations, many of which were covered with cooking soot, suggesting she provided protection for the kitchen. Certainly nonpoisonous snakes would have been considered beneficial to the household, as they are sometimes regarded today in Egypt, because they eat rodents.

SNAKES. *Limestone statuette of a female serpent deity, reign of Psamtik I, twenty-sixth dynasty.* (University of Pennsylvania Museum, Philadelphia. Neg. # S8–62621)

The *uraeus* was the image of the Egyptian cobra (*Naja haje*), worn in the front of the king's headdress. Here the snake represents the snake goddess Wadjet, associated with the Lower Egyptian sanctuary of Buto. Her counterpart was the vulture goddess Nekhbet of Hierakonpolis in Upper Egypt. Wadjet acted as a mythical mother and midwife of the king.

A creation myth explains how the *uraeus* came into being. The god Atum had created the god Shu and the goddess Tefnut, who represented air and moisture, and they had gone out into the world. Atum sent his eye out to fetch them, which it did, but when it saw that it had been replaced by the sun, it became furious and transformed itself into a cobra, which Atum appeased by placing it on his brow. Thus the *uraeus* came to be considered a protector of kingship.

Winged snakes are depicted in Egyptian art and are found frequently in religious texts painted in the royal tombs in the Valley of the Kings. Wadjet was sometimes depicted as a winged snake. The Greek author Herodotus claimed to have seen skeletons of flying snakes when he visited Egypt. It is not known how the idea of winged snakes originated, but among the suggestions that have been put forth are the resemblance of the posture of the snake's neck and anterior of its body to wings when it is excited, the fact that horned vipers throw themselves at their victims, or the resemblance of a shedding snakeskin to wings.

Snakes appear in several Egyptian literary works. A central character in the *Story of the Shipwrecked Sailor* is a cobra who saves the shipwrecked sailor and looks after him on his island in the midst of the sea for four months. At the birth of the eponymous character in the *Story of the Doomed Prince*, the fates decree that he will die as a victim of a snake, dog, or crocodile. He escapes the first of these fates after his wife puts out some beer to attract the dangerous snake out of its hole; the snake drinks it, passes out, and is hacked up by the woman.

[*See also* Amphibians and Reptiles.]

BIBLIOGRAPHY
Anderson, John. *Zoology of Egypt: Volume First, Reptilia and Batrachia.* London, 1898. Contains systematic descriptions of a number of snake species.
Broekhuis, Jan. *De Godin Renenwetet.* Bibliotheca Classica Vangorcumiana, 19. Assen, 1971. Publication of a dissertation in Dutch on the goddess Renenutet, with an English summary on pp. 149–152.
Johnson, Sally B. *The Cobra Goddess of Ancient Egypt.* London and New York, 1990. An overview of the *uraeus* and a typological study of *uraei* during the Predynastic through Old Kingdom periods.
Keimer, Ludwig. *Histoire de serpents dans l'Égypte ancienne et moderne.* Memoires de l'Institut de l'Égypte, 50. Cairo, 1947. About snake-charming and worship in ancient and modern Egypt.
Leitz, Christian. *Die Schlangennamen in den ägyptischen und griechischen Giftbüchern.* Mainz, 1997. Lexicographic study of names of Egyptian snakes in Egyptian and Greek.
Marx, Hymen. *Checklist of the Reptiles and Amphibians of Egypt.* Cairo, 1968. Includes the most complete list of snake species in Egypt published to date.
Sauneron, Serge. *Un traité égyptien d'ophiologie.* Cairo, 1989. Publication of the papyrus identifying snakes and the treatment of their bites.

NICOLE B. HANSEN

SNEFERU (r. 2649–2609 BCE), first king of the fourth dynasty, Old Kingdom. Sneferu's Horus-name Neb-ma'at, "lord of the cosmic order," alludes to the divine nature of the king as the sun god Re. His birth name, Sneferu, means "the one who performs perfection" or "the perfected one." During the Old Kingdom, the royal father of a king was never explicitly named as such, nor was a crown prince given this title during the reign of his father. It is believed however, that Sneferu was the son of his predecessor, Huny. At the end of the *Instructions of Kagemni*, we read: "Then the Majesty of King Huny died, and the Majesty of King Sneferu was elevated [to the position of] beneficent king of this entire land." Sneferu's mother was Queen Meresankh, who was venerated together with Sneferu at Meidum and is indicated as his mother on the Palermo Stone.

This fifth dynasty monument records the most important historical events of each reign on a year by year basis; the enumeration of the regnal years is given in terms of a biennial counting of revenue—the year of the first counting, the year after the first counting, the year of the eighth counting and so on. For Sneferu's reign, only the years of the sixth through the eighth counting are preserved, however, the year after the seventh counting is omitted. The main events of these years were the building of a large fleet of ships—including seagoing vessels made of cedar from Lebanon—a raid into Nubia during which Sneferu is alleged to have brought back thousands of people and cattle to be settled in Egypt, the establishment of fortified settlements, and the construction of a new palace, probably that at Dahshur. A monument at Wadi Mughara that shows him smiting a local chieftain implies that he was active in the Sinai as well.

The Turin Canon attributes only twenty-four years to Sneferu. This is in conflict with the contemporary year counts on quarry marks and building stones. On the blocks of the Meidum pyramid, the fifteenth, sixteenth, and seventeenth times of counting, corresponding to the twenty-ninth, thirtieth, and thirty-first years of his reign, are well attested; at Dahshur, the dates of a fifteenth, sixteenth, and even a twenty-fourth time of counting are frequently observed. According to the biennial counting system, these dates result in a reign of forty-six years; the twenty-four years of the Turin Canon should therefore be doubled. A long reign is evident from the building activities of Sneferu, including five pyramids: the small step pyramid at Seila, the Meidum pyramid, the Bent Pyramid at Dahshur/South with its cult pyramid, and the Red Pyramid at Dahshur/North, comprising altogether more than 3.6 million cubic meters of stone—one million more than the Great Pyramid of Khufu at Giza. All this construction notwithstanding, Sneferu was regarded throughout Egyptian history as the exemplar of the good king (for example, in the well-known Westcar Papyrus story), who was deified and identified with Horus as early as the Middle Kingdom at Sinai, as well as at his pyramids at Meidum and Dahshur.

His principal queen was Hetepheres I, the mother of Khufu. The elder branch of the family at Meidum included the prince buried in *mastaba* 17, perhaps the first crown prince, and the princes Nefermaat and Rahotep, together with their wives, Atet and Neferet.

BIBLIOGRAPHY
Fakhry, Ahmed. *The Monuments of Sneferu at Dahshur.* Vol. I, *The Bent Pyramid.* Cairo, 1959.
Smith, William Stevenson, and George Andrew Reisner. *A History of the Giza Necropolis,* vol. 2, *The Tomb of Hetep-heres, The Mother of Cheops.* Cambridge, Mass., 1955.
Stadelmann, Rainer. "Snofru und die Pyramiden von Meidum und

Dahschur." *Mitteilungen des Deutschen Archäologischen Instituts, Abteilung Kairo* 36 (1980), 437–49.

Stadelmann, Rainer. "Beiträge zur Geschichte des Alten Reichs: Die Länge der Regierung des Snofru." *Mitteilungen des Deutschen Archäologischen Instituts, Abteilung Kairo, B.* 43 (1986), 229–40.

RAINER STADELMANN

SOBEK. A crocodile god representing the Nile floods and fertility, Sobek (Eg., *Sbk;* Gr., Suchos) was also a symbol of royal power, leading several late Middle Kingdom pharaohs to incorporate his name into their own. Sobek became a primordial deity and creator god in the New Kingdom owing to his assimilation with Re. By the Ptolemaic period, he was identified with numerous deities, taking on the aspect of a universal god.

Sobek was depicted as a crocodile wearing a tall plumed headdress, or as a human with a crocodile's head. Among his earliest portrayals is an Early Dynastic cylinder seal showing a crocodile on a standard. He also appears as a crocodile in temple reliefs, seals, royal statuary, and papyri. Beginning in the Middle Kingdom, Sobek or Sobek-Re sometimes took the form of a ram or a ram-headed human; in the New Kingdom and later, he might appear in fully human form; in the Greco-Roman period, he took many different forms.

Sobek's characteristics were already partly established by the time of the Pyramid Texts, which portray him both as a benevolent god of the Nile floods and as potentially ferocious and destructive. The Coffin Texts associate him with the Nile and its floods, the riverbanks, and fertility. Both the Coffin Texts and Middle Kingdom hymns to Sobek assimilate him into the Osirian myth and associate him with Horus. The hymns also identify him with Re, with whom he was syncretized from the Middle Kingdom onward. Epithets of Sobek in the New Kingdom describe him as a creator god. During the Ptolemaic and Roman periods, he was depicted at the bow of the solar bark, defeating the enemies of Re. Ptolemaic hymns not only continue to demonstrate his role as a creator but also refer to him as the supreme universal deity.

The cult of Sobek originated in marshy areas where crocodiles were common and later became so widespread that evidence of it is found throughout Egypt. His most prominent and earliest documented sanctuary was at Shedet in the Faiyum, later called Krokodilopolis by the Greeks. During the twelfth dynasty, when the reigning kings focused great attention on the Faiyum, Sobek became one of Egypt's principal state gods, reaching partic-

SOBEK. *Stela featuring a representation of Sobek, now in the Brooklyn Museum of Art.* (Courtesy of Stephen Phillips)

ular prominence under Amenemhet III. Another major cult center was situated at Kom Ombo in Upper Egypt, where several New Kingdom pharaohs dedicated buildings. Sobek's cult at Gebel es-Silsila is particularly well attested during the nineteenth dynasty. In the Theban area, he was worshipped at Gebelein and Dehamsha, where the eighteenth dynasty sanctuary included a complex installation for housing and feeding sacred crocodiles. Roman sources relate accounts of priests feeding sacred crocodiles in the Faiyum, and Ptolemaic and Roman period crocodile cemeteries have been found at a number of sites.

Neith was the mother of Sobek, and his father was Senuwy (the Greek crocodile god Psosnaus). Although he was identified with a number of different deities in pharaonic times, including Hathor, Horus, Khnum, and Re, Sobek was not portrayed as having a wife or children until Greco-Roman times, when he was worshipped at Kom Ombo and Philae with Hathor as his consort and Khonsu as their child.

BIBLIOGRAPHY

Brovarski, Edward. "Sobek," In *Lexikon der Ägyptologie*, 5: 995–1031. Wiesbaden, 1984.

Dolzani, Claudia. *Il Dio Sobk*. Rome, 1961.

Hart, George. "Sobek." In *A Dictionary of Egyptian Gods and Goddesses*, pp. 201–202. London, 1986.

Quirke, Stephen. *Ancient Egyptian Religion*, pp. 51, 73, 75. London, 1992.

DENISE M. DOXEY

SOBEKNEFERU (r. 1790–1786 BCE), last ruler of the twelfth dynasty, Middle Kingdom. Her name was originally pronounced Nofrusobek, but it was later reinterpreted. The Greek form was Scemiophris, as preserved in a quotation from the Greek-speaking Egyptian historian Manetho of the third century BCE.

According to the Turin Canon, a papyrus in the Museo Egizio in Turin, Italy, she ruled for three years, ten months, and twenty-four days. Her reign has left few traces; apart from some small objects, there are a handful of architectural and statue fragments, three of which were found at Hawara and Herakleopolis. Like the earlier rulers of her family, Sobekneferu concentrated her building activities in the Faiyum. Three of her statues discovered near Tell ed-Dab'a in the Nile Delta were probably moved there in Ramessid times. That she exercised full dominion over her realm is shown by an inscription marking the height of the flood made at the Nubian frontier fort at Kumma during her third year.

Manetho stated that Sobekneferu was Amenemhet IV's sister, but her own inscriptions emphasized her relationship to her father, the illustrious Amenemhet III. Like some earlier female rulers of Egypt, she probably gained her position through the lack of a viable male heir; unlike the others, however, she assumed the full royal titulary, where her feminine gender was carefully noted. Two of her statues from the Delta show her in women's clothing, although in traditional male attitudes, trampling the Nine Bows (that represented the subdued enemies of Egypt) and kneeling before the gods. One (in the Louvre in Paris) has women's clothing with the royal costume worn over it. The persistance of her name in New Kingdom grafitti and on king lists show that she was regarded as a legitimate ruler. Nevertheless, her reign was brief and her burial place has never been identified, although the dismantled northern pyramid at Mazghunah in the Faiyum has been suggested.

BIBLIOGRAPHY

Berman, Lawrence, and Bernadette Letellier. *Pharaohs: Treasures of Egyptian Art from the Louvre*. Cleveland, 1996. Illustrates Sobekneferu's Louvre statue with its unique costume; includes discussion and bibliography.

Byran, Betsy. "In Women, Good and Bad Fortune Are on Earth: Status and Roles of Women in Egyptian Culture. Sobeknefru." In *Mistress of the House, Mistress of Heaven: Women in Ancient Egypt*, edited by Anne K. Capel and Glenn E. Markoe, pp. 29–30. New York, 1996. Summarizes what is known about this ruler.

ROBYN A. GILLAM

SOCIAL STRATIFICATION. Ancient Egypt often seems to have been a civilization obsessed with status. A characteristic feature of Egyptian art is the hierarchical scaling seen in relief and statuary, whereby the larger a figure is depicted, the greater is his or her relative status compared to other figures in the composition. Expressions of relative status are particularly noticeable in the sphere of mortuary provision: the size of a tomb, its location, and the wealth of its contents all indicate the social position of the tomb owner. In general, Egyptian art presents a world where status was reserved for a small elite of literate males clustered around the person of the king. However, other, more diverse sources suggest a rather more complex picture of social stratification. Certain social groupings cut across traditional class divisions; and, like all aspects of ancient Egyptian civilization, social stratification underwent significant changes over time.

Origins and Historical Overview. The earliest communities in Egypt for which we have archaeological evidence emerge as relatively egalitarian, without marked differences in status based on wealth or birth. In Lower Egypt an egalitarian social structure seems to have characterized local communities until the last third of the fourth millennium BCE, when the Nile Delta became intimately involved in the process of state formation. From the early fourth millennium BCE, the graves at sites such as Heliopolis South and Wadi Digla show a distinct lack of wealth differentiation, while the pattern of settlements at Merimda and Maadi suggests a simple social structure composed of family units. The first evidence of incipient social stratification is found farther south, in Upper Egypt. It was in this part of the country that the process of political and economic centralization, which ultimately led to state formation, had its origins. For the early fifth millennium BCE, Badarian graves show limited evidence of social inequality, suggesting the beginnings of a stratified society in Upper Egypt.

Differences in grave size and wealth become more marked in the following Naqada I period: burials of certain individuals are distinguished by special artifact types (such as mace heads or ivory tags) which seem to have served as badges of status. Wealthy child burials are also encountered, a sure sign of inherited status: greater expenditure on the burial of an infant than on those of adults from the same community clearly indicates that hereditary lineages had developed, whose authority depended on birth rather than achievements. Taken together, the mortuary evidence indicates the crystallization of social distinctions and the development of an increasingly stratified society in Upper Egypt during the Naqada I period. In the following Naqada II period, political and economic power seem to have become concentrated in the hands of a few hereditary lineages whose influence (if not authority) extended over sizeable territories. This trend accelerated in the final phase of the Predynastic period, Naqada III, reaching its culmination in the formation of the Egyptian state at the very end of the fourth millennium BCE. After the unification of Egypt, all political and economic power was concentrated in the hands of a small ruling elite, presided over by a king claiming divine authority.

Written records from the beginning of the first dynasty indicate that Egyptian society was divided into two groups: the small, ruling elite of royal kinsmen (*p't*) and the mass of the populace (*rhyt*). This distinction is reflected in mortuary archaeology in the area around Memphis, the first capital of Egypt: the royal relatives who occupied the highest offices of state were buried in huge, imposing tombs on the edge of the desert escarpment at North Saqqara, whereas the majority of the city's population was interred across the river at Helwan/el-Ma'asara. It has been suggested that, during the first few dynasties, a talented individual from outside the *p't* might achieve high office, since the administration was expanding as the early kings developed sophisticated mechanisms of rule. However, given the meager evidence for Early Dynastic administration, it seems more likely that political and economic power were restricted to the king and his imme-

diate circle. The populace was literally subject to the king: early royal art depicts the *rhyt* as subjugated peoples, almost on a par with Egypt's foreign enemies. Early Dynastic society seems, therefore, to have been characterized by a marked division between the governing and governed classes.

Only in the fourth dynasty is there evidence that the highest offices of state were opened up to persons of non-royal birth, giving individuals from humbler backgrounds the chance to better their social status. Nonetheless, there was probably little change in the overall structure of society, which remained basically pyramidal in form: at the apex there was the king, fount of all authority and channel of communication between the people and the gods; beneath him were the royal family and the literate officials who made up the government; forming the base of the pyramid was the bulk of the population, most of them illiterate agricultural workers. At all times, the political influence of the peasantry remained virtually nonexistent.

At the end of the Old Kingdom, the breakdown of central authority and the political fragmentation of the country brought a blurring of social distinctions; practices and beliefs previously restricted to the royal sphere were adopted by a broader section of society. This process is most noticeable in funerary religion, where it has been dubbed "the democratization of the afterlife." From the First Intermediate Period onward, it was acceptable for anyone at death to identify himself or herself with Osiris; correspondingly, anyone could now hope to participate in some sort of life after death, a promise that had been effectively the preserve of the king during the Early Dynastic period and Old Kingdom. It used to be thought that the images of national distress so vividly described in Middle Kingdom literature represented firsthand accounts of social turmoil during the First Intermediate Period. It is now widely accepted that they reflect, rather, a particular preoccupation of Middle Kingdom literate society. Nonetheless, the First Intermediate Period stands as something of a watershed in the development of Egyptian society.

The reestablishment of centralized government at the beginning of the Middle Kingdom was accompanied outwardly by a return to Old Kingdom social structures, but in practice society was somewhat more fluid, with limited opportunities for advancement, irrespective of birth (see below). This trend became more pronounced in the New Kingdom, which is distinguished from preceding periods by the appearance of a significant "middle class," comprising craftsmen, traders, and minor officials. These people provided a link between the traditional, polarized classes of ruling and ruled, as did the various occupational categories which began to emerge as social groupings in their own right. One of the late New Kingdom Tomb Robbery Papyri contains a list of households on the western bank of the Nile at Thebes. Most of the households were in the village of Maiunehes, a community that had grown up around the mortuary temple of Ramesses III. Different categories of householders include senior civil officials, priests, scribes, military personnel, junior officials, craftsmen, and agricultural workers: a representative cross-section of late Ramessid society. The list also reveals the relative social fluidity of New Kingdom Egypt, whereby a priest might also hold a civil appointment, bringing him into contact with a wider range of people. A further picture of late New Kingdom society is provided by the Wilbour Papyrus, which lists land holdings in a stretch of Middle Egypt during the reign of Ramesses V (c.1143 BCE). Among those renting fields from the large land-owning temples are temple personnel themselves, wealthier farmers, and military colonists. The military aspect of New Kingdom society is striking, and important for questions of social mobility (see below). The foreign campaigns waged by New Kingdom pharaohs affected Egyptian society in another important way: they resulted in large numbers of prisoners of war entering Egypt. From this time on, an underclass of slaves was to remain a feature of the Egyptian hierarchy.

Egyptian society in the Late period may be conveniently divided into six groups: slaves, who were the property of their masters and enjoyed few legal rights; serfs, who were tied to the land, and who formed a significant element of the population; and four occupational categories of free citizens (commoners—mostly agricultural workers—warriors, priests, and administrative officials). By comparison, the Greek historian Herodotus identifies seven principal occupations—priests, warriors, cowherds, swineherds, tradesmen, interpreters, and pilots. Many of the groups are the same; the fact that Herodotus recognized interpreters and pilots as separate groups probably reflects his own particular experiences when traveling in Egypt, rather than Egyptian society in general. As at all periods, most of the population remained tied to the land, either legally or by force of circumstances, with few opportunities for social advancement. By contrast, the warrior class enjoyed high standing in Late period Egypt; most "warriors" originated as Libyan mercenaries who had settled in Egypt during the New Kingdom and Third Intermediate Period. In common with the priests, they probably felt some degree of corporate identity, perhaps even communal interest.

Social Mobility. From the beginning of Egyptian history, authority and literacy were inextricably linked. The general designation "scribe" simply indicated an official, since the ability to read and write secured access to the administration and hence a degree of political influence. For most of Egyptian history (until the Late period), the proportion of the population who could read and write is unlikely to have exceeded 5 percent, effectively restricting the reins of power to a tiny minority. The Wisdom Literature of the New Kingdom makes passing reference to education, but it remains unlikely that scribal training (which must have formed the most important element of education) would have been accessible or available to any but a very few children from lowly backgrounds. The single factor of literacy must, therefore, have been a powerful impediment to significant social mobility in ancient Egypt.

Throughout much of Egyptian history, there was a tension between the hereditary principle—whereby important offices often passed from father to son within a family—and the theoretical right of the king to appoint all officials. At certain periods, for example the late New Kingdom and Late period, powerful families monopolized some of the highest civil and religious positions. The "Petition of Petiese," preserved on Papyrus Rylands IX, illustrates how one family monopolized the office of high priest of Amun-Re at Teudjoi during the twenty-sixth dynasty. Although royal ratification was required in theory for each new appointment, several generations of Petiese's family succeeded to the office following the hereditary principle. In periods of strong central government, the king exercised his right to make appointments; at other times, there was little royal control over who held the most important religious and civil offices.

The "Petition of Petiese" also illustrates how families worked together to promote the interests of their members. Thus, in difficult circumstances, Petiese II could turn for support to his relatives who held the office of high priest of Amun-Re at Thebes. Such family networks must have been an important feature of officialdom throughout Egyptian history. For example, in the late eighteenth dynasty, Yuya and Tuya—a couple of nonroyal birth from a relatively modest background—were accorded the exceptional privilege of a burial in the Valley of the Kings, entirely because of the fact that their daughter had married the king, Amenhotpe III. The accession of Ay, after the death of Tutankhamun, may have been eased by his apparent connection with the same family.

Birth into a noble family was not the only means of achieving high office, and from the early Middle Kingdom on there are examples of individuals from humble backgrounds who reached the higher echelons of the court through their own achievements. On his stela from Abydos, an eleventh dynasty official named Mentuhotep implies that he was a self-made man: he boasts of being "one whose [own] counsel replaced for him a mother . . . a father . . . and a son." In the New Kingdom, those brought up at court with the future king could expect to be appointed to high office when their childhood companion came to the throne. It was also possible for those from lowlier backgrounds to rise to prominence. For example, Ahmose, son of Abana, was the son of a simple soldier, but he succeeded in acquiring land and wealth through his valiant actions in the war of liberation against the Hyksos under King Ahmose. In a similar way, Amenhotep, son of Hapu, one of the most powerful officials in the reign of Amenhotpe III, boasts in one of his statue inscriptions of having built his career on personal qualities rather than high birth.

At times when the usual system of royal succession broke down, it seems to have been easier for men of humble birth to rise to positions of power. Thus, Senenmut, who probably began his career as a simple soldier, enjoyed rapid promotion when Hatshepsut became regent for the young Thutmose III. Although Senenmut never held one of the chief offices of state, his position as the queen's "chief spokesman" and intimate gave him tremendous authority. In a similar way, Akhenaten raised individuals from lowly backgrounds to high office. An official named May held the influential post of "fan bearer on the king's right hand," as well as being "royal chancellor," "overseer of all the king's works," and "overseer of the soldiery of the Lord of the Two Lands." In his tomb biography, May attributes his success to royal favor: "I was a man of low origin both on my father's and on my mother's side, but the ruler established me; he elevated me . . . he caused me to associate with nobles and companions [though] I had been one who held last place." At the end of the Amarna period, the extirpation of the Thutmosid royal line allowed two military men of nonroyal birth, Horemheb and his colleague Ramesses I, to gain the highest office in the land, the kingship. The military formed a powerful section of New Kingdom society, and there was the potential for a successful soldier to reach the highest echelons of government. As "chief army commander" under Tutankhamun, Horemheb had effectively been the king's deputy; he was thus well placed to claim the office of kingship on the death of Ay, Tutankhamun's ephemeral successor. Horemheb also drew on military discipline to restaff "with the finest of the army" the major temple priesthoods, demoralized after Akhenaten's religious reforms. Being childless, Horemheb appointed another trusted army officer, Ramesses, as his heir. The succession at the end of the eighteenth dynasty emphasizes the degree to which the military saw itself as a distinct social group with its own identity and interests.

With each break in dynastic succession throughout Egyptian history, it is possible that the figure who emerged as the new king came from outside the royal family. Not surprisingly, perhaps, there is little evidence for the family background of such rulers. It was considered inappropriate—and, no doubt, unwise—to refer openly to a king's origins if these might cast doubt on his legitimacy. For example, it is likely that Amenemhet I, first king of the twelfth dynasty, had been vizier under his predecessor; perceived illegitimacy may have been one reason behind his apparent assassination. Though hedged about with divinity and ritual, the kingship may always have been viewed by powerful and ambitious individuals as a goal, an opportunity for the ultimate in social advancement.

In the late Ramessid period (twentieth dynasty), society reverted to a more rigid structure, with fewer opportunities for social mobility. Important offices of state now became the prerogative of a few influential families and were passed down from generation to generation with little direct reference to the king. Texts from this period also suggest a resignation to one's social status; this change of tone contrasts sharply with the optimistic outlook of some of the wisdom literature from the earlier New Kingdom, which reflects a distinctly "middle-class" view of society and its opportunities.

Although Egyptians of the Middle and New Kingdoms might hope for social advancement if their skills and achievements gained official recognition, Egyptians of the Late period faced the opposite prospect: debt or punishment for a criminal offense could force an Egyptian into serfdom or slavery. As an underclass, slaves became a significant feature of Egyptian society only in the New Kingdom. At first, slavery was more or less restricted to foreigners, captured in battle or traded from abroad. However, during the Persian period, when slavery was recognized by law, we find Egyptians acting as slaves to Jewish mercenaries on the island of Elephantine.

Two aspects of social stratification that have generated much interest are the positions of women and foreigners in ancient Egyptian society. High-status tombs (which, with few exceptions, were built for male members of the government apparatus) present a male-oriented view of society—the man dominating his wife and children, both iconographically and ideologically—that may not accord with the reality of daily life in an average Egyptian home. Documentary evidence from the New Kingdom workmen's village of Deir el-Medina suggests that women took a leading role in the local economy, in addition to managing household activities. Although it was extremely rare for women to achieve high office in their own right, their political influence may have been significantly greater than the male-dominated sources would have us believe. Likewise, official Egyptian ideology (and the iconography by which it was expressed) despised foreigners as inferior barbarians. However, there is plentiful evidence for foreign mercenaries having been recruited into the Egyptian army throughout pharaonic history. As a general rule, foreigners settling in Egypt were accepted as long as they adopted Egyptian customs and conducted themselves—at least in public—as Egyptians. During the Third Intermediate Period, foreign dynasties (such as the twenty-third and twenty-fifth) were even able to claim the kingship, but made strenuous efforts to portray themselves as traditional Egyptian pharaohs.

[*See also* Administration, *article on* State Administration; Inheritance and Disenfranchisement; Military; Officials; Priesthood; Royalty; Scribes; Slaves; Women; *and* Work Force].

BIBLIOGRAPHY

Bard, Kathryn A. *From Farmers to Pharaohs: Mortuary Evidence for the Rise of Complex Society.* (Monographs in Mediterranean Archaeology, 2.) Sheffield, 1994. Mortuary data (grave size and contents) from two Predynastic cemeteries are used to chart the rise of social stratification in Upper Egypt.

Dorman, Peter F. *The Monuments of Senenmut: Problems in Historical Methodology.* London and New York, 1988. A detailed study of the career of Senenmut, including discussion of his family background and his sudden rise to power in the reign of Hatshepsut.

Helck, Wolfgang. "Die soziale Schichtung des ägyptischen Volkes im 3. und 2. Jahrtausend v. Chr." *Journal of the Economic and Social History of the Orient* 2 (1959), 1–36. A unique article commenting on the evidence for changes in social stratification during the historical periods of ancient Egyptian civilization.

Kemp, Barry J. *Ancient Egypt: Anatomy of a Civilization.* London, 1989. Chapter 7 of this general work includes a section discussing the composition of society in the New Kingdom.

Malek, Jaromir. *In the Shadow of the Pyramids: Egypt During the Old Kingdom.* London, 1986. A detailed examination of Egyptian civilization during the Old Kingdom. Chapter 6 looks at the structure of Egyptian society and the working of government.

Robins, Gay. *Women in Ancient Egypt.* London, 1993. The best treatment to date of the role and status of women in ancient Egypt.

Trigger, Bruce G., et al. *Ancient Egypt: A Social History.* Cambridge, 1983. Four chronologically based chapters cover the full span of Egyptian dynastic history. A large part of chapter 4 deals with social stratification in the Late period.

Vernus, Pascal. "Quelques examples du type du "parvenu" dans l'Égypte ancienne." *Bulletin de la Société Française d'Égyptologie de Genève* 59 (1970), 31–47. Probably the only discussion of social mobility in ancient Egypt.

TOBY A. H. WILKINSON

SOKAR. The name of this divinity (Eg., *skr*; Gr., Sokaris), according to a hypothetical etymology based on Coffin Text Spell 816 and a twelfth dynasty papyrus, is derived from *sk r* ("cleaning of the mouth"), a word used in the context of the Opening of the Mouth ceremony, in which Sokar plays a role. Such word play, does not, however, constitute a true etymology. Nor (*pace* Brovarski 1987) does the name appear to be related to "Saqqara," which probably comes from the name of a Berber tribe, the Beni Saqqar.

In iconography established by the Old Kingdom, Sokar is depicted as an anthropomorphic figure with the head of a falcon, evoking his earthly representation and his divine ability to fly in the underworld, on earth, and in the heavens. He is shown either standing or seated on a throne, garbed in the cloth of a funerary god. He wears a White Crown and holds a scepter and a whip, the regalia of Osiris. Sokar is also represented in predatory form, again enveloped in fabric. As a falcon, he can be related to Horus, and like him wears the Double Crown. His solar functions are indicated by the presence of the disk and the *uraeus*. When in human form, Sokar occasionally wears the *atef*-crown.

Sokar's emblems include a barge, onions, and geese. The barge, or *ḥnw*, represents solar triumphs and is set on a sledge. At its prow may be the head of an antelope or a bull, an *int*-fish, and birds (falcons or swallows) along the edge of the hull. The mound-shaped *štyt*-chapel at its center culminates in a falcon's head. At the stern are three or four rudder pins. On the night preceding the procession of this barge, the deceased wears an onion necklace to prepare for the solarization of Sokar-Osiris. A luminous rebirth occurs on the morning of the twenty-sixth day in the month of Khoiak in the *ḥnw*-barge, which is protected by five geese, daughters of Re, and their barges. The transport of the *ḥnw* was organized by the high priest of Ptah in Memphis.

In the Old Kingdom, the festival of Sokar was already an annual event in the fourth month of the *ꜣḥt* season, on the twenty-fifth and twenty-sixth days. It involved a visit to the royal necropolis and offerings to the dead. In the Middle Kingdom, it incorporated Osirian aspects of festivals in Abydos. Later it became a solemn occasion marked by a procession of Sokar's *ḥnw*-barge in the great temples of Egypt. It celebrated the continuity of the cult of the divine king linked to the resurrection of Sokar and to the revival of the great cosmic cycles.

Egyptological tradition, however, defines Sokar as an essentially chthonic deity acting in the funerary world of the Memphite necropolis. Funerary and offering formulae that mention Sokar appear only in the Middle Kingdom. The Pyramid Texts describe Sokar as a god active in the rebirth of the king and in the ceremonies of confirmation and transfer of royal power. In the Middle Kingdom, he assumes a specific role in the transfiguration at death and in the Opening of the Mouth ceremony. In his role in the rites of statues as a metallurgist, he resembles Ptah, who transforms stone and wood. The entity Ptah-Sokar associates the wealth of the soil and its power of growth. The *Book of Going Forth by Day* (*Book of the Dead*) in New Kingdom times presents Sokar as an image of the world unified in Osiris, linked to the aforementioned festivals or to foundation rituals. The terrestrial Ptah-Sokar becomes Sokar-Osiris, the nocturnal incarnation of the sun during the fourth and fifth hours of the *Book of That*

Which Is in the Underworld (Amduat). He enables the sun to complete its course during the night and to be reborn in the morning. In the New Kingdom, Priests of Sokar bear the same titles as the Memphite clergy of Ptah did in the Old Kingdom, but now they almost always refer to the high priests of Heliopolis. Henceforth, an entity reuniting the three divine forms, Ptah-Sokar-Osiris, expresses creation-metamorphosis-rebirth.

In the Late period, numerous tombs are equipped with Ptah-Sokar-Osiris wood statuettes in anthropomorphic form with a falcon's head or in full animal form as a falcon. This rests on a base containing the *Book of Going Forth by Day,* or a grain mummy reminiscent of the "beds of Osiris." In the Ptolemaic period, the Osirian form of Sokar reached its zenith, becoming the focus of the Osirian festivals in the month of Khoiak.

Sokar is related two groups of deities: the Memphite group formed by Khnum, Herremenuyfy, and Chesmu, and the solar group constituted by Nefertum and the five divine daughters of Re, all present at the feast of Sokar. The "Memphite" Khnum is among the Memphite divinities listed in the Sokar chapel and the hall of Sokar and Nefertum in the temple of Sety I at Abydos. Nephthys may be Sokar's companion, or, less often, Seshat. Called "father and mother," Sokar has no family as such, even though a grammatical doublet—Sokaret—appears; Redoudja is identified as "son of Sokar" in Spell 941 of the Coffin Texts.

In the Pyramid Texts, Sokar is called a native of Rosetjau, a site near the Sphinx of Giza, but ultimately indicating any necropolis, and of Pedju(-she), the lake of Abusir. He is also master of the *štyt,* which refers to the cabin of the *ḥnw*-barge, his sandy environment mentioned in the *Book of That Which Is in the Underworld,* and a chapel dedicated to him in the temple of Horus at Edfu. Two other names for the sanctuary of Sokar are *pr-ḥnw* ("house of *henu*") and *ḥwt-Skr* ("chapel of Sokar"), referring to the functions of housing the divine barge and the statue of the deity. There are also chapels dedicated to Sokarian aspects and integrated in a temple consecrated to a mother major divinity. There is still no archaeological evidence of a temple solely dedicated to Sokar; however, the deity is known from sites throughout Egypt, initially through textual documentation and later, from the Middle Kingdom onward, through iconographic sources. In the Old Kingdom, Sokar is present from the Memphite necropolises to Helwan. Already well established in the Faiyum during the Middle Kingdom, the deity appears in the tombs of Deir el-Bahri. It reaches Thebes with the declaration of that city as the new capital. From the beginning of the New Kingdom, the deity is found at Karnak; during the reign of Hatshepsut it occupies an important place in the chapel-cavern of Anubis on the second terrace, as well as in the Thutmose I chapel on the third terrace at Deir

el-Bahri. Thutmose III dedicated a suite of rooms to Sokar in Akh-menu. In the tombs of Western Thebes, Sokarian elements occur for the first time. Amenophis III consecrated to Sokar a monumental architectural ensemble in his temple of "millions of years" in Thebes. The well-established Sokar cult of Western Thebes continued to develop in the Ramessid period, with numerous representations of Sokarian rites in private and royal tombs. At Gurneh, the Hall IX of the temple of Sety I was dedicated to Sokar, who was also given a cult site in the temple constructed by the same king at Abydos. A group of rooms in the Ramesseum was consecrated to him by Ramesses II, who also had the deity represented on the peripheral wall of the temples of Amun-Re and of Re-Horakhty at Karnak. The most important source for the cult of Sokar exists in the second court of the temple of "millions of years" of Ramesses III at Medinet Habu; In addition, Room 4 of this complex is a chapel for the *ḥnw*-barge.

The *ḥnw*-barge becomes dominant in the late Sokarian iconography. Sources include a few Theban sarcophagi from the twenty-first dynasty; the silver sarcophagus of Sheshonq II (twenty-second dynasty) with falcon mask, discovered in Tanis; statues from the twenty-second and twenty-third dynasties; the chapel of Osiris Heqa-Djet at Karnak (twenty-third dynasty); Theban Tomb 32 from the Saite period in Western Thebes; and the temple of Hibis at Chargha (twenty-seventh dynasty).

The sanctuary of Alexander at Karnak and Louvre Papyrus N 3176(S) prove that Akh-menu was active until the Ptolemaic period. Sokar and his barge are, however, infrequently represented in Thebes during Ptolemaic times: on the propylaeum of Khonsu at Karnak; at the temple of Montu in North Karnak; in the temple of Hathor at Deir el-Medina; in the temple of Hatshepsut at Deir el-Bahri; and on the small temple at Medinet Habu. By that time the Sokarian cult had moved to the temple of Horus at Edfu (Halls XIII–XIV) and that of Hathor at Dendera (Hall XVI and the six roof chapels), in the context of the Osirian celebrations in the month of Khoiak. The last representation of Osiris-Sokar with a falcon's head was done under Emperor Caracalla at Philae.

BIBLIOGRAPHY

Brovarski, E. "Sokar." In *Lexikon der Ägyptologie,* 5: 1055–1074. Wiesbaden, 1984.

Gaballa, G. A., and K. A. Kitchen. "The Festival of Sokar." *Orientalia* 38 (1969), 1–76.

Graindorge, C. "Les oignons de Sokar." *Revue d'Égyptologie* 43 (1992), 87–102.

Graindorge, C. *Le dieu Sokar à Thèbes au Nouvel Empire.* Göttinger Orientforschungen, 4/28. 2 vols. Wiesbaden, 1994.

Graindorge, C. "La quête de la lumière au mois de Khoiak: une histoire d'oies." *Journal of Egyptian Archaeology* 82 (1996), 83–105.

Graindorge, C. "L'vignon, la magie et les dieux." *Encyclopédie religieuse de l'Univers végétal,* pp. 317–333. Orientalia Monspeliensia, 10. Montpellier, 1999.

Porter, B., and R. L. B. Moss. *Topographical Bibliography of Ancient Egyptian Hieroglyphic Texts, Reliefs, and Paintings*. Vol. 2, *Theban Temples*. Oxford, 1991. Source of the numbers of temple chambers cited in the present article.

CATHERINE GRAINDORGE
Translated from French by Elizabeth Schwaiger

SOMTUTEFNAKHT, son of Pediese, whom he followed in office as "Shipmaster of Herakleopolis" (an important city in northern Middle Egypt, near the Faiyum) during at least the fourth to thirty-first years of the reign of Psamtik I of the twenty-sixth dynasty, or c.661–643 BCE, and perhaps a little longer. His father, Pediese, son of a Theban priest, had been appointed by a Kushite ruler (probably Taharqa), and lived on in retirement during Years 4 to 18 of Psamtik I. Pediese became allied to the local dynasty at Sais, marrying a princess of their line (Takhered-en-ta-ihet-weret). She bore Somtutefnakht, his son, who was possibly brought up at Sais. Thus, Necho I and Psamtik I bound in alliance to themselves the main princedom of northern Middle Egypt.

When in Year 9 (656 BCE) Psamtik I induced the authorities in Thebes to recognize his rule, he sent his daughter Nitokris there to be the future "God's Wife of Amun." It was to Somtutefnakht that he entrusted her and the impressive fleet that went with her, as is clear from the wording of a magnificent granite stela (the Nitokris Stela), and from a series of damaged scenes (the "Piankhy blocks") found at the temple of the goddess Mut in southern Karnak, in which Somtutefnakht appears. Two statues that Somtutefnakht dedicated in the eastern Nile Delta attribute to him the important title of governor of Upper Egypt. A younger Pediese, Somtufnakht's cousin, is said to have served as assistant to both Pediese senior and Somtutefnakht.

BIBLIOGRAPHY

Bakry, H. S. K. "Two Saite Statues of Samtowetefnakhte from the Delta." *Kêmi* 20 (1970), 19–36.

Benson, M., and J. Gourlay. *The Temple of Mut in Asher*. London, 1899. Photographs of scenes showing Somtutefnakht, pp. 257–258 and plates 20–22.

Caminos, Ricardo A. "The Nitocris Adoption Stela." *Journal of Egyptian Archaeology* 50 (1964), 71–101. A definitive study of the stela recording the transfer of Psamtik I's daughter to Thebes as "God's Wife of Amun," in care of Somtutefnakht.

Griffith, F. Ll. *Catalogue of the Demotic Papyri in the John Rylands Library*, vol. 3. Manchester, 1909. Includes the basic publication of Papyrus Rylands IX, which offers a useful but lopsided account of the Pedieses and Somtutefnakht (stressing the former at the expense of the latter).

Kitchen, K. A. *The Third Intermediate Period in Egypt (1100–650 B.C.)*. 2d ed. with suppl. Warminster, 1996. Essential study of Pediese and Somtutefnakht, with appropriate sources and further references.

KENNETH A. KITCHEN

SOTHIC CYCLES. *See* Calendars.

SOUL. *See* Akh; Ba; *and* Ka.

SPHINX. The sphinx is a purely Egyptian creation, first attested in the early fourth dynasty, about 2575 BCE. Around the end of the second millennium BCE, Egyptian sphinx images were exported to Syria-Palestine, where local artists imitated them, mostly in bas-relief and especially as female figures. From there the idea and form of a female sphinx of malevolent character was transferred into Greek myths, such as that of Oedipus. In Egypt sphinxes were generally associated with the sun god and with the king as a "living image" (*šsp-'nḫ*); this word may well have been the origin of the Greek word *sphinx*, although in Greek this word had the meaning "strangler," perhaps in association with the Greek interpretation of the sphinx as a malign creature.

The Great Sphinx at Giza, the most immense sculpture ever made by men—73.5 meters (235 feet) long and over 20 meters (64 feet) high—is the earliest example of this type of statue: part lion and part man, a creature metamorphosed into a divine being combining the strength of the most powerful wild animal and the intelligence of a human being, it is a great intellectual innovation. Two-dimensional images on slate palettes of the Early Dynastic period, three hundred to four hundred years earlier, depict the king as a wild lion or griffin destroying his enemies; in the Great Sphinx, animal power is tamed by human intelligence and is thus transformed into a divine calm.

A fourth dynasty date for the creation of the Sphinx is certain, but there is some question as to which of the kings residing at Giza envisaged and commissioned this unique sculpture. The possibilities are four: Khufu, builder of the Great Pyramid, or his successors Djedefre, Khafre, and Menkaure. Djedefre, who constructed but did not complete a pyramid on top of the northern hill of Abu Roash, has been suggested because he may have had several sphinxes of lesser size in his pyramid complex, which would be the earliest known sphinxes besides the Great Sphinx but this is not a strong argument. The pyramid complex of Menkaure lies too far from the Sphinx. Hence both Djedefre and Menkaure can be eliminated, and only Khufu and Khafre remain.

Most Egyptologists prefer Khafre because his name is mentioned on the Dream Stela of Thutmose IV in a context that includes the Sphinx. However, this large and elaborate stela, found by Caviglia in 1818, was erected by Thutmose IV in front of the Sphinx after he had become king. In the long inscription, Thutmose reports that once, when he still was a prince and head of the royal charioteers, he was hunting in the desert of Memphis near the pyramids. At noon he fell asleep in the shadow of the Sphinx and was then told in a dream that if he cleared the sand away from the flanks of the Sphinx, he would become king of Egypt. Of course he obeyed, and after ascending the throne he asked the people of Egypt to praise "Osiris of Rasetau (which is the area of the pyramids), the goddess Bastet, and the gods and goddesses of the resting place or sanctuary of . . . khaef." The last name can be reconstructed as Khae [Re], or Khafre. This part of the inscription—which has now disappeared completely, eroded by subterranean water—is the only evidence for the identification of the Sphinx with Khafre. There exists an older stela, however, erected by Thutmose's father Amenhotpe II, on which the king reports a similar visit to the area of the pyramids, where he admired the wonderful buildings—and here the text is completely preserved—of the resting place, the sanctuary of Khufu and Khafre. Thus, in the same context, both kings are mentioned. The Dream Stela of Thutmose IV is therefore by no means clear inscriptional proof that Khafre was the creator of the Great Sphinx. In the upper register of each stela, Amenhotpe and Thutmose make offerings to images of the Sphinx, which is called Horemakhet (Gr., Harmachis, or "Horus in the horizon"). This name of the god Horus is an innovation of the New Kingdom; it retains, however, the old word *3ḥt* ("horizon") from the name of Khufu's pyramid, Akhet-Khufu.

It is frequently assumed that the Great Sphinx was carved from a single rock within the quarries of Khafre, but a careful investigation of the quarries at Giza contradicts this. According to the latest investigations, the quarries of the Great Pyramid of Khufu extend from the northern and eastern ridges of the Giza plateau in the area south of the Great Pyramid. The southern limit is marked by a rock face on which the causeway of Khafre is built. Recent excavations have brought to light the remains of a construction ramp leading to the south side of the Great Pyramid. This ramp is situated south of the Great Pyramid and north of the causeway of Khafre in a depression which was once part of Khufu's quarries.

The extension of Khufu's quarries is the reason that Khafre's causeway does not run perpendicular to the east side of the pyramid, and also the reason that his valley temple is not situated in the axis of the pyramid complex but displaced to the south. This means that Khafre had to take account of some earlier, very important structure that already stood there. This can only have been the Sphinx. Thus, the large rectangular ditch in the center of which the Sphinx was carved surely belongs to the quarries of Khufu, as can be demonstrated by comparison of the different components of the rock formation in the body of the Sphinx and the layers of core stones of Khufu's pyramid. The sequence of the stones quarried from the different strata and used in the pyramid can be determined by their degree of erosion. Khufu was a great innovator who chose the commanding position on the ridge above what is now Giza. Each of his creations is somehow new: his pyramid layout, his cult temple, the cemeteries, and even his statuary. As the surviving fragments show, Khufu utilized all types of Egyptian statues except the kneeling form; all are at once innovative and supreme achievements. It is thus reasonable to assume that the Sphinx, too, is his creation.

There are also firm stylistic and iconographic considerations that point to Khufu. The only attempt at such an iconographic investigation has been that of Mark Lehner (1997), in his painstaking excavations and restoration of the Sphinx. He tried to superimpose the contours of the head of Khafre's famous statue with the Horus falcon (Cairo Museum CG 14) on that of the Sphinx; however, neither the contours of the face nor those of the *nms*-wig fit, even though Lehner took the result as further support for his thesis that the Sphinx is a work of Khafre.

Most of Khufu's statuary is probably still hidden in his as yet unexcavated valley temple, so as a basis for comparison we have only a famous small ivory statue from Abydos bearing his name, and two heads ascribed to Khufu—one in red granite, with the White Crown, in the Brooklyn Museum, and another rather small one in limestone, in the Bavarian State Collection in Munich. Of Khafre, several life-size statues and hundreds of fragments are preserved, all together representing about sixty or seventy statues. It may be questionable to compare a colossal sculpture like the Sphinx with statues of normal or even very small size; on the other hand, art historians have dated some famous artworks by comparison with portraits on coins.

The overall form of the Sphinx's face is broad, almost square. The chin is broad. By contrast, the features of Khafre are long, and noticeably narrower, and the chin almost pointed. The Sphinx wears the earlier, fully pleated type of *nemes* headcloth, like that of Djoser's statue. The same *nemes* headcloth, also fully pleated, can be seen on a statue fragment from Khufu's pyramid temple now in the Boston Museum of Fine Arts. In one important detail, the *nemes* of the Sphinx has no band in the form of a raised hem over the brow—again, the older type of the *nemes* as on Djoser's statue. From Djedefre's statues onward, the raised hem band over the brows becomes the norm. Under Khafre, only the lappets of the *nemes* headcloth are pleated, never the *nemes* peak or the *nemes* hood as is attested on the Sphinx. The side wings of the *nemes* headcloth of the Great Sphinx are deeply hollowed, but on Khafre's statues hardly at all. On all of Khafre's statues

SPHINX. *Quartzite sphinx of Thutmose III, eighteenth dynasty.* (The Metropolitan Museum of Art, Rogers Fund, 1908. [08.202.6])

the headcloth corners curl up, but they do not do so on the Sphinx.

The Sphinx has a *uraeus* cobra on the lower edge of the headcloth. In contrast to those of Khafre and Menkaure, it shows high relief with naturalistic detailing of the serpent's neck and the scales of its hood. The eyebrows of the Sphinx bulge powerfully forward, and they are pitched high and slope down toward the temples. The eyes are deep-set but strongly modeled. They are large and wide open, typical of sculpted heads from the time of Khufu. The ears are fundamentally different: those of the Sphinx are very broad and folded forward, while those of Khafre are elongated and situated closer to the temples.

A decisive criterion is the absence of a beard. The Sphinx has no indications of hair on its chin, nor is there any trace of a break under the chin. The fragments of a pleated god's beard which are now in the British Museum and in the Cairo Museum are certainly of New Kingdom origin, added to the Sphinx when it was identified with the god Horemahket. The rounded divine beard is an innovation of the New Kingdom and did not exist in the Old or the Middle Kingdom. When this beard was added, a small platform was carved out of the Sphinx's chest on which the beard and a newly added royal statue rested. In the Old Kingdom there is a strict rule: if a king wears a beard, it appears in all his representations, round plastic and relief, in Upper as well as Lower Egypt, without exception. In the fourth dynasty one can observe that Sneferu never has a beard. Neither does Khufu, either on his small ivory statue or on the Brooklyn or the Munich head. From Djedefre on, however, all kings, including Khafre and Menkaure wear the ceremonial beard. The fact that the Sphinx had no beard is strong evidence that the Great Sphinx is an original creation of Khufu.

The Great Sphinx was carved out of a high rock, which dominated the southeastern corner of Khufu's quarries. We will perhaps never know how Khufu and his master artist envisaged the Great Sphinx. There must have been a prototype, perhaps in Heliopolis, the city of the sun god; later texts mention a great Sphinx of Heliopolis. Whenever sphinxes were placed in front of Egyptian temples, they had a solar aspect and connotation. Thus, the idea of a creature in the form of a sphinx which is the form of appearance—that is, the phenotype—of the sun god might already have existed in Heliopolis from the times of Djoser, who had a shrine in Heliopolis, and of Sneferu, who identified himself with the sun god as Nebmaat, Lord of the Right World Order.

In front of the Great Sphinx lie the architectural remains of a large but uncompleted temple. The design of this building with large niches to the east and west indicates a solar connection. The temple is surely of fourth dynasty date, but it is not certain who began it, Khufu or Khafre. The axis of the temple is not on the axis of the Great Sphinx, nor was there a direct exit from the temple to the Sphinx statue.

Pairs of sphinxes were found lying in front of each gate of the valley temple of Khafre. The traces of the plinths were clearly visible during the excavation of the temple. Fragments of the forelegs of a large sphinx of Khafre were found in front of his pyramid temple. In the Middle Kingdom, sphinxes become more numerous and new types appear. The great Louvre sphinx (A 23) of Amenemhet II is clearly inspired by the Great Sphinx of Giza. For the first time, powerful queens and princesses are depicted as female sphinxes. At the end of the Middle Kingdom, a group of sphinxes of Amenemhet III amplify the grandeur of this part-human part-lion creature by replacing the *nemes* headcloth with a lion's mane surrounding the royal face. None of these sphinxes were found in situ; they were certainly transported from different locations to royal residence cities of the New Kingdom—Memphis, Piramesse, and Tanis—and may even have been resituated several times. Originally they may have been present in the temples of the sun god in Heliopolis. In the New Kingdom, we find sphinxes with the heads of rams and hawks in front of the temples of Amun at Karnak and Re-Horahkty at El-Gebua in Nubia. In one mortuary temple, a sphinx with the head of a crocodile was unearthed. All these creations display a definite connection with a sun god, whether Amun-Re, Re-Horahkty, or Sobek-Re. Avenues of sphinxes line the processional ways leading to temples or even connect temples over long distances, as at Karnak and Luxor. Two large sphinxes were lying in the first court of the mortuary temple of Sety I at Gurneh. It is probably the carving of this pair of sphinxes that is illustrated in the tomb of Paser (tomb 106) at Western Thebes.

Sphinxes of various materials, including painted and gilded wood and metal, are a common decoration on processional barks of gods and kings in the New Kingdom. In decorative art a sphinx is often depicted fighting or trampling enemies, as on a shield of Tutankhamun, or in Middle Kingdom pectorals, where falcon-headed sphinxes are shown smashing enemies. In pictures on jewelry and ivories, the ancient tradition of the king as a violent lion or a fierce griffin remain alive.

Roman emperors brought Egyptian sphinxes to Europe to decorate their temples and palaces. In the palace of Spalato (Split) of Emperor Diocletian at least thirteen sphinxes were unearthed. The rediscovery of ancient Egypt resulted in a revival of ancient Egyptian motifs, especially the sphinx. Impressive male sphinxes now decorate entrances to castles and bridges, as in Saint Petersburg, while female sphinxes adorn gardens and pavilions in European cities or beautify furniture, fireplace surrounds, or even luxurious table services.

[*See also* Egyptomania; Khafre; *and* Sculpture, *articles on* Royal Sculpture *and* Divine Sculpture.]

BIBLIOGRAPHY

Dessenne, A. *Le Sphinx: Étude iconographique.* Paris, 1957. *Egypt: The World of the Pharoahs.* Köln, 1998. See pp. 73–75.
Esmael, F. A. *Book of Proceedings: The First International Symposium on the Great Sphinx.* Cairo, 1992.
Hassan, Selim. *The Sphinx: Its History in Light of Recent Excavations.* Cairo, 1949.
Lehner, M. "Reconstructing the Sphinx." *Cambridge Archaeological Journal* 1 (1992), 3–26.
Lehner, M. *The Complete Pyramids: Solving the Ancient Mysteries.* London, 1997.
Shaw, I., and P. Nicholson, eds. *The Dictionary of Ancient Egypt. In Association with the British Museum.* London, 1995.

RAINER STADELMANN

SPORTS. Although no word equivalent to "sport" existed in the ancient Egyptian language, there was clearly a cultural element that is best expressed by this modern word. The expressions *sḏꜣi-ḥr* and *swtwt* incorporate the idea of "active diversion" as an essential component. In Egypt is found one of history's oldest sports cultures, surpassing in age, scope, and depth of sources even the Sumerian sports culture. The rise of the sports culture in Egypt coincides with the height of ancient Egyptian civilization at the beginning of the third millennium BCE, some twenty-three hundred years before the first Olympic games in Greece. If such marginal areas are included as games, hunting, and dance, Egyptian sports are represented in about two thousand figurative documents over three thousand years—an amazing wealth of sources compared to other early high cultures. This is further enriched by many written documents, of which the inscriptions of the athletic kings of the eighteenth dynasty are the most interesting. The study of these rich sources has only begun in the past three decades, and today we can speak of the existence of an actual sports culture in ancient Egypt.

The Sports of Kings. Archaeological discoveries in Egypt may well provide evidence about the very origins of sports. At the tomb complex of King Djoser (third dynasty) in Saqqara, a running track has been preserved in the southern court of the Step Pyramid, the oldest pyramid in Egypt. The conception was that the track, outlined in durable stone, was used by the dead king for a ritual run, when he had to display his good physical condition as a guarantee that he was able to fulfill the duties of a king and ensure the safety of his people, even after a thirty-year reign. The run itself, which the king probably performed as an exhibition on the occasion of his *sed*-festival, is a relic of early hunting societies in which the chief would safeguard the survival of his tribe with a successful hunt. The fact that this demonstration of physical ability endured in ceremonies in the historic period—though it took on a more ritual character in which the king's physical strength and power were magically reaffirmed—does not obscure its prehistoric origin. In one of the three representations of the running king in Djoser's tomb, the runner is clothed only in a penis sheath and is accompanied by the standard of the god Wepwawet ("opener of the ways"), a figure interpreted by some as a deity derived from the pack of dogs that would have run with the hunter of earlier times.

The physical skills of the king do not become emphasized until the eighteenth dynasty, after the expulsion of the Hyksos invaders. The traumatic experience of the first foreign reign in Egypt would henceforth define the image of the hero-king, who began to display athletic traits, especially under Amenhotpe II. The text on his Sphinx Stela describes the king as not only an outstanding runner and skillful helmsman of a 200-man rowboat, but also as an unrivaled bowman whose arrows pierce copper ingots, trade currency in the Bronze Age. (This motif appears in altered form centuries later in Homer's *Odyssey*, in the competition held for Penelope's suitors, an event still linked to the legitimation of a ruler.) The archer king stands erect in a chariot drawn by two horses, a technical innovation whose introduction to Egypt in the Hyksos period had far-reaching social consequences. The role of king now requires proof of the ruler's ability to handle this status vehicle and the animals competently, an activity that required constant training of driver as well as horses. The Sphinx Stela clearly depicts the pharaoh's additional skill as charioteer and horse-trainer. Ramesses III (twentieth dynasty) had himself immortalized in his funerary temple in Medinet Habu in an image showing the pharaoh selecting a pair of horses for training.

The athleticism of the eighteenth dynasty Egyptian kings must be understood as a "sporting tradition" (Hayes) that was passed on from father (Thutmose III) to son (Amenhotpe II) to grandson (Thutmose IV), and shared by other kings. Not only is there impressive inscriptional and pictorial proof—for example, the panel showing the young Amenhotpe II at archery practice with Min, the mayor of Thinis (tomb 109 at Western Thebes)—but also original equipment (composite bows and six chariots from Tutankhamun's tomb) to give us a firm notion of the sporting practices of the time. The boundary between sport and hunt was very fluid, since this equipment could also be used for hunting.

Competition. With Amenhotpe II, even the strict rule that a pharaoh could not be a participant in a sporting competition was overthrown. The idea of a defeated pharaoh, as might happen in competition, had no place in the royal dogma. Therefore, the king's sporting exhibition is always presented as an athletic demonstration without adversaries. As an exception, adversaries are mentioned in an inscription in Medamud commemorating an archery competition involving Amenhotpe II, yet they seem to have stood little chance against this royal athlete, according to the fragments that remain of this text. Despite the exclusivity of royal sport founded in ideology, the concept of sports records developed during the eighteenth dynasty and is documented in a comparison of recorded quantities and norms of achievement in archery, for several kings. The reigning king, confronted with the task of "expanding that which exists," outperformed not only his own previous record but also those of his predecessors.

Historical reality differed from the dogma. Egyptians were familiar with the phenomenon of competition, as deduced from the many documents on combative sports, the use of the motif of the suitors' contest in the *Story of the Doomed Prince*, or in the evidence of sporting events. How strong the competitive element ultimately was is clear when the gods handle the dispute of who would succeed their deceased king. The *Contendings of Horus and Seth* recounts how Horus and Seth, both seeking the throne, agree to a diving competition, which fails and is followed by another competition in boating. The highest possible position in the Egyptian cosmos is therefore assigned by competition. Jacob Burckhardt, whose coining of the expression "the agonal Greek" placed Hellenic culture above all others in ancient history, was wrong when he maintained that only the Greeks had knowledge of athletic competition.

Sport Traditions among Commoners. At first glance, the sporting traditions of private individuals are less ideologically bound than sport in the royal milieu, although there too the royal dogma can bear some influence.

Running. For the common man, running was a popular sport, owing to its natural character and uncomplicated organization, as was indeed the case in Greece;

however, there were hardly any Egyptian sources attesting to running as a sport until the discovery of the "Running Stela" of King Taharqa (690–664 BCE). It provided a text of great importance, not only for the history of running but also for the hitherto sparse sporting history of the Late period. The stela (685/684 BCE) tells the story of a race among soldiers selected from Taharqa's forces, over a distance of approximately 100 kilometers (65 miles, from Memphis to the Faiyum and back), with a two-hour break at the turnaround point. The recorded time of four Egyptian hours for this distance is barely credible, in view of their daily training and modern performance levels. It was a great honor for the successful runners to attend a celebratory meal together with the royal bodyguards and to win prizes. Diodorus Siculus provides a further reference to a similar approach to long-distance training in the mention of a historically unidentifiable king who apparently ordered his sons and their contemporaries to run 180 stadia every day before breakfast.

Fighting sports. Sports based in combat are strongly represented in the form of wrestling, fencing with sticks, and boxing. Of the three, wrestling is most frequently attested and is found throughout Egyptian history. As a motif, wrestlers appear at the dawn of Egyptian history on the City Palette, and by the fifth dynasty the first full representation is known of a wrestling match in several rounds. In the vizier Ptahhotep's tomb in Saqqara, inscribed names clearly establish that the six pairs of wrestlers shown in various positions are in fact a single pair, whose fight is recorded in episodes. The same principle is perfected in the Middle Kingdom tombs of Beni Hasan. Of the thirty-three rock-cut tombs of the nomarchs (administrators) of the Oryx nome, no fewer than nine depict wrestling scenes, as Shedid's studies (1994) have shown. The images of wrestlers, usually on the tomb's eastern wall, stretch across several registers and may include multiple pairs. A count from the published tombs is given in Table 1.

Approximately 2 percent of the scenes are dedicated to fighting on the floor. The wrestlers in the Beni Hasan tombs are naked except for a girdle, which offers many possible grip variations (similar to Japanese Sumo wrestling or the Glima style practiced in Iceland). Because of the pictorial context (military scenes), the wrestlers may

TABLE 1. *Number of wrestling pairs in the published tombs of the nomarchs at Beni Hasan.*

Tomb no.	Tomb Owner	Number of Pairs
2	Amenemhet	59
15	Baqti III	220
17	Cheti	122
29	Baqti I	6

have been soldiers who used wrestling as a form of physical training. Wrestling is still in evidence in the New Kingdom in this context. A group of Nubian soldiers have a standard that identifies them clearly as wrestlers. It appears that the Nuba, who practice this sport today and whose dress even attests to continuity, can look back on a thirty-five-hundred-year tradition of wrestling prowess. The wrestling theme was also modeled on ostraca and in statuettes. Occasionally, a referee—once shown with a trumpet—supervised the contest, as in the tomb of Neheri in Bersheh, and in the depiction of wrestlers below Ramesses III's appearance window in Medinet Habu. Some scenes of wrestlers are accompanied by short inscriptions that prove to be boastful epithets (challenging speeches).

Despite the abundant visual material on wrestling, little is known about the rules that governed the sport. Aside from the fact that grips and reaches to all parts of the body were allowed, and that the match continued even after the contestants had hit the floor, one can only deduce from the frequent pose of a victor standing above his unconscious opponent that victory was gained by wrestling the opponent to the point of incapacity; the victor then assumed a pose of triumph before the spectators.

The sources on wrestling often appear in combination with depictions of stick-fencing, or *nabbût*, a sport still practiced today in the Nile Valley. Two contestants, often soldiers, stand face to face, holding short batons; each wears various protective gear, such as shieldlike boards on the lower arm, or shields made of leather worn on the chin and forehead. The baton-wielding hand is sometimes protected as well. If the fight takes place on the roof of a boat cabin, as in the example in the tomb of Khons (tomb 31 at Western Thebes), the limited space creates an effect similar to that of a modern boxing ring.

Illustrations of boxing matches in ancient Egypt are extremely rare. They are undoubtedly shown in the ritual erection of the *djed*-pillar in the context of the *sed*-festival of Amenhotpe III, depicted in the tomb of Kheruef (tomb 192 at Western Thebes), where six pairs of fighters box bare-fisted in dancelike poses. In another example, boxing (along with wrestling and fencing) seems to be illustrated in a festive offering of tributes to Amenhotpe IV in the tomb of Merire II in Tell el-Amarna.

Sporting Events. Competitive sports in Egypt sometimes occurred during festivals, in which context they would occupy a more or less fixed position in the program; this may have developed later into events exclusively dedicated to sports. Although the topic has not been systematically researched, in addition to the examples already given—the royal *sed*-festival with its ritual run, the ritual raising of the *djed*-pillar, and the three events in the tribute celebration to Amenhotpe IV—there is

. *Middle Kingdom wrestling scenes, from Beni Hasan.*

some evidence pointing in this direction. Below the appearance window in the tomb of Ramesses III in Medinet Habu is a depiction of a sporting event that gives an immediate impression of international character. Ten pairs of fighters contend in wrestling and fencing matches before an audience of Egyptians (including royal children) and foreign spectators. The unusual element is that each pair consists of an Egyptian and a foreigner (Near Easterner, Libyan, or Nubian), and that all the foreigners seem to be losing. No doubt the Egyptian royal dogma of the ever-victorious pharaoh dictated how the athletic event was depicted—in conformity with ideology, instead of with the open fairness essential in modern sports competitions.

A unique sporting event is jousting (no longer documented in the New Kingdom), which was practiced during a festival marking the end of the working season in the marshes. While this scene appears about fifty times in Egyptian sources, other sporting events are rare as a main theme. A possible rowing competition under Tutankhamun is notable, as is a still unconfirmed funeral game for Thutmose III, which may have been depicted four generations after his death in the tomb of Amenmose (tomb 19 at Western Thebes). Finally, there is the large celebration on the occasion of a completed pyramid-building project, discovered on the causeway to the pyramid temple of Sahure (fifth dynasty). On this occasion, elaborate games,

including wrestling, fencing, archery, and possibly rowing, were held in conjunction with the setting of the last stone (*bnbn*) on the royal funeral structure.

[*See also* Games; *and* Hunting.]

BIBLIOGRAPHY

Carrol, Scott T. "Wrestling in Ancient Nubia." *Journal of Sport History* 15 (1988), 121–137.

Decker, Wolfgang. *Annotierte Bibliographie zum Sport im alten Ägypten.* St. Augustin, 1978. This annotated bibliography, containing some 700 titles upon first publication, is updated in *Stadion* 5 (1979), 162–192; 7 (1981), 153–172; 8/9 (1982/83), 193–214, as well as *Nikephoros* 1 (1988), 245–268; 2 (1989), 185–215; 3 (1980), 237; 4 (1991), 224; 5 (1992), 221f.; 6 (1983), 210f.; 7 (1994), 257; 8 (1995), 208; 11 (1998), 195–197.

Decker, Wolfgang. "Die Lauf-Stele des Königs Taharka." *Kölner Beiträge zur Sportwissenschaft: Jahrbuch der Deutschen Sporthochschule Köln,* St. Augustin 13 (1984), 7–37.

Decker, Wolfgang. *Quellentexte zu Sport und Körperkultur im alten Ägypten.* St. Augustin, 1975. Contains all Egyptian texts on sports in German translation (with the exception of the Runner's Stela of Taharqa, discovered after publication).

Decker, Wolfgang. "The Record of the Ritual." In *Ritual and Record: Sports Records and Quantifications in Pre-Modern Societies,* edited by John Marshal Carter and Arnd Krüger, pp. 185–215. New York, 1990.

Decker, Wolfgang. *Sports and Games in Ancient Egypt.* Translated by Allen Guttmann. New Haven, 1992.

Decker, Wolfgang, and Michael Herb. *Bildatlas zum Sport im Alten Ägypten: Corpus der bildlichen Quellen zu Leibesübungen, Spiel, Jagd, Tanz und verwandten Themen.* Handbuch der Orientalistik, 1: Der

Nahe und Mittlere Osten 14, 1–2. 2 vols. Leiden, 1994. Inclusive and comprehensive source corpus on Egyptian sport and related topics, containing some 2,000 documents, described in detail (including location, date, material, image content, and bibliography); roughly half are illustrated in the second volume.

De Vries, Carl E. "Attitudes of the Ancient Egyptians toward Physical-Recreative Activities." Ph.D. diss., University of Chicago, 1960. First important monograph on Egyptian sport.

Hawass, Zahi, and Miroslav Verner. "Newly Discovered Blocks from the Causeway of Sahure." *Mitteilungen des Deutschen Archäologischen Instituts, Abteilung Kairo* (1996), 177–186.

Hayes, William C. "Egypt: Internal Affairs from Tuthmosis I to the Death of Amenophis III." In *Cambridge Ancient History*, vol. 2, pp. 313–416. 3d ed. Cambridge, 1973. Note especially the chapter on "The Sporting Tradition," pp. 333–338.

Littauer, M. A., and J. H. Crouwel. *Chariots and Related Equipment from the Tomb of Tut'ankhamun.* Tut'ankhamun's Tomb Series, 8. Oxford, 1985.

McLeod, Wallace. *Composite Bows from the Tomb of Tut'ankhamun.* Series Tut'ankhamun's Tomb Series, 3. Oxford, 1970.

McLeod, Wallace. *Self Bows and Other Archery Tackle from the Tomb of Tut'ankhamun.* Tut'ankhamun's Tomb Series, 4. Oxford, 1982.

Shedid, Abdel Ghaffar. *Die Felsgräber von Beni Hassan in Mittelägypten.* (Zaberns Bildbände zur Archäologie, 16.) Mainz, 1994.

Touny, Ahmed E. Demerdash, and Steffen Wenig. *Sport in Ancient Egypt.* Leipzig, 1969.

Van de Walle, Baudouin. "Les rois sportifs de l'ancienne Égypte." *Chronique d'Égypte* 13 (1938), 234–257.

WOLFGANG DECKER
Translated from German by Elizabeth Schwaiger

STATE. Ancient Egypt was the world's first nation-state, and the ideology of the state—its strengths, weaknesses, functions, and structures—lies at the heart of Egyptian history and civilization. The ancient Egyptian state was a multifaceted and complex creation, fashioned by Egypt's early rulers from the political fragmentation of the Predynastic period, then developed by subsequent generations of kings to suit particular circumstances of their own times. Like all aspects of ancient Egyptian culture, the state was an evolving concept that reflected the changing political and economic realities for the three millennia of dynastic history.

State: Definition and Functions. When referring to Egypt as a *state*, it is important to clarify the meaning of the term, but there is no definition generally accepted by political theorists, historians, archaeologists, and anthropologists alike. Nonetheless, the term as applied to ancient Egypt may be broadly defined as a territorial entity with a system of exercising recognized legal authority over its population. Anthropologist Elman Service, in his *Primitive Social Organization: An Evolutionary Perspective,* 2d ed. (New York, 1971) devised a fourfold classification of societies, based on a number of factors—including social, economic, and religious organization; settlement patterns; and architecture. According to his classification, the state is the most developed form of society, characterized by several key features: (1) a class-based hierarchy under the authority of a ruler; (2) a centralized bureaucracy that levies and collects taxation and that imposes laws on the population as a whole; (3) the existence of a priestly class; (4) the demarcation of political frontiers, often fortified; and (5) urban settlements, with palaces, temples, and other large public buildings.

From the beginning of the first dynasty, ancient Egypt demonstrated most, if not all, of those features, with the important addition of writing as an aid in administrative control. There can be little doubt that, throughout dynastic times, ancient Egypt met the present-day criteria for statehood, even if ancient Egyptian seems to have lacked a word for "state." Although it is often difficult to distinguish between "state" and "society," and "state" and "government," for present purposes, *society* may be defined as "the collective body over which the state exercises its authority," and *government* may be defined as "the apparatus with which that authority is exercised." The ancient Egyptian state may be appropriately described as a complex political and cultural organism, operating on a number of levels, but its role at the core of ancient Egyptian civilization may best be understood by examining its functions throughout Egyptian history. The principal function of the early Egyptian state was the location and collection of resources, to support the royal court and its projects. Large-scale construction programs were a major goal of the state administration, since they served to promote the power and prestige of the head of state. To finance the grandiose and labor-intensive schemes, the state needed to control the economy, to divert resources from the productive to the nonproductive sector, and this was achieved through taxation. According to this view, the Egyptian state may be characterized as essentially self-seeking; however, centralized control of the economic system incidentally benefited a large sector of the population. Many state employees worked only on a part-time basis, sharing their duties with others on a roster ("phyle") system, and by this means, the number of state employees receiving redistributed income was artificially inflated. Thus from the early dynasties, the state became a net provider for a significant number of people, balancing its role as the agency that levied taxation.

The second function of the state was to administer the law and dispense justice, in accordance with the Egyptian concept of *maat* ("fairness and balance"). As champion of *maat*, the king embodied the ideals of justice and truth, which lay at the ideological heart of the Egyptian state. In other words, the expectation of fairness and protection from the state—and, by extension, all state officials—lay at the very heart of the state's existence. As head of state, the king was the ultimate arbiter in legal cases, although in practice this role was delegated to the king's chief minister, his vizier. In particular, the state may have played an important role in safeguarding private property and in ensuring fairness in disputes over land rights (which seem to have been common concerns, at least in texts from the New Kingdom). Although in theory all land belonged to the king/the state, there is good evidence for private ownership of land in various periods, and private landholding was probably always a feature of the Egyptian economy. Security of another kind was provided by the state—defense against foreign aggression and the violent incursions of those who lived on Egypt's desert margins. Raids on the prosperous communities of the Nile Valley by jealous, hungry neighbors were a constant threat and are attested from periods of weak central government. Once again, as champion of *maat,* the king's sacred duty was to protect Egypt and defend its people from hostile attack. The defeat of Egypt's enemies forms a central element in state iconography, from the very earliest periods, and real coercive power may be assumed to lie behind the images of all-conquering might. In addition to legal and personal protection, the state provided its citizens with economic security. Part of the agricultural surplus received by the state as taxation would be retained at the royal residence, to be stored as "buffer stocks" of both food and seed. This grain represented vital insurance against years of poor harvests. Only the state, with its huge resources and facilities, could gather and store the necessary amounts to provide a viable economic "safety-net." For a base population of peasant farmers, almost entirely dependent on the land for subsistence, that type of security must have had real value. In return for ceding sovereignty to the state and recognizing it as the ultimate authority, the populace was guaranteed good security for both person and property. Here, then, is the essential contract between the government and the governed that formed the basis of the Egyptian state, and which may help to explain its longevity.

State Formation and Dissolution. State formation in Egypt (often referred to by Egyptologists as "the unification") was a gradual process that occurred during the latter half of the fourth millennium BCE (the Predynastic period), culminating in the foundation of the dynastic state with the beginning of the first dynasty. The development of Egypt's administrative structures and mechanisms that allowed the early kings to bolster their own authority continued at least until the beginning of the fourth dynasty, some five centuries later. Our understanding of state formation—which resulted in a unified state from a collection of competing Predynastic territories—has been radically enhanced by recent archaeological work in Egypt. The state-building process was characterized by two separate but related factors: cultural development and political development. The first involved the northward spread of advanced Upper Egyptian technologies into the Nile Delta, leading to a single cultural tradition throughout Egypt by the late Naqada II period; the second involved the consolidation of territories—whether by political alliance or military force—to create one united kingdom by the beginning of the first dynasty. The process of political consolidation soon extended Egyptian control north into the neighboring land of southern Palestine and south into Lower Nubia; but during the latter half of the first dynasty, direct control of sites in the Near East was abandoned in favor of loose trade agreements.

Various factors have been proposed to account for the process of state formation in Egypt. Single factors (or "prime movers")—such as irrigation, population pressure, or trade—were once stressed, but a multicausal explanation is now favored. The desire to gain access to, and ultimately to control, trade routes seems to have been an important motive for Upper Egyptian expansionism in the late Predynastic period. Palestine and, to a lesser extent, Nubia were sources of prestige commodities required by the elites of Upper Egypt to display their growing authority. Widespread climatic changes, the role of cult centers, the charisma of individual rulers, and the importance of writing in the centralization of political and economic power were all significant additional factors in the formation of the Egyptian state. The impetus for the process may also have been inherent within a settled agricultural society that had strong ties to the Nile Valley and its special ecology. "Game theory" has been suggested as a model, by which a sense of sovereignty and the competitive urge for greater control of resources may have set in train a sequence of events that culminated in the unification of Egypt under a single ruler (see Barry Kemp's *Ancient Egypt: Anatomy of a Civilization*, London, 1989).

Ideology was at the heart of the early Egyptian state, and theocracy (divine kingship) was promoted as the only acceptable form of government. The king's divine role in unifying the Two Lands (Upper and Lower Egypt) became the essential myth of the theocratic state. Some of the elements of royal ideology and iconography were derived from important regional centers, creating psychological ties that bound the provinces to the court. Craftsmen employed in the royal workshops created a "great tradition" of court culture, which aspiring individuals sought to emulate and which was actively disseminated through royal patronage of provincial temples. This distinctive cultural tradition became an important factor in promoting the stability of the state and the position of the king at its apex. The other key elements of the early state were the creation of a large, centralized bureaucracy and the instigation of administrative practices to supervise and control every aspect of the Egyptian economy. During periods of strong central rule, the apparatus of government developed by the early kings successfully balanced and restrained the potential sources of conflict within Egypt. In fact, the concept of the state that developed in the formative period of ancient Egyptian history may be justly regarded as the greatest achievement of dynastic civilization; it was certainly the most enduring.

Three thousand years of Egyptian history included periods of political instability, when a weak central government caused the state to fracture into competing territories. The three Intermediate Periods represent the temporary failure of Egypt's state apparatus to contain provincial aspirations and other potential sources of disunity. Such structural weaknesses may be a feature of any complex political system, and—with the exception of the Hyksos infiltration from the Near East at the end of the Middle Kingdom—the roots of state dissolution were to be found within Egypt itself. For example, the weakening of central authority that marks the end of the Old Kingdom is generally attributed to the state's inability to balance its competing centralizing and centrifugal forces. By the late fifth dynasty, central responsibility for provincial governments had already been diluted by the appearance of powerful local governors; economic stress caused by unusual Nile flood levels (which seem to coincide with the decline in pyramid building at the end of the sixth dynasty) may have placed too heavy a burden on an already weakened central administration. At the end of the Middle Kingdom, forces outside Egypt (increasingly powerful polities in both the Near East and Upper Nubia) took advantage of a second period of state weakness, once again marked by unusual Nile levels, exacerbated no doubt by a succession of short reigns that would have strained belief in the all-important doctrine of divine kingship. Egypt became prey to the expansionist ambitions of neighboring cultures, and disunity ensued. The integrity of the state depended on the king maintaining his supreme political, military, and religious authority. Toward the end of the New Kingdom, the military in general and certain ambitious individuals in particular (elements in society that the New Kingdom government had sought to keep in check) gained the coercive potential to threaten the kingship. The king seems to have become an increasingly remote figure, content to delegate executive authority to others. Eventually, the internal pressures on the state proved too great, and the government was formally divided in two along geographical lines. Unity was reestablished under the kings of the twenty-sixth dynasty, and, for most of the Late period, Egypt successfully maintained a centralized state based on earlier models (although Egyptians no longer ruled Egypt, but Persians, Greeks, and Romans).

State Structure. As both supreme secular authority and the gods' representative on earth, the king was the institutional and ideological pivot around which the Egyptian theocratic state revolved. In theory, all power was derived from the king (who, in turn, derived his power from the supernatural sphere), and it was the king who exercised all authority—political, religious, and military. In practice, some delegation of authority was essential and, by the Old Kingdom at the latest, the Egyptian state had developed a sophisticated apparatus of government, with a hierarchical structure and several branches. The complex interrelationships between these different branches combined with the limitations of the available evidence make it difficult to delineate the structure of the state accurately. Important structural changes did take place during the long course of Egyptian history, though the evidence is stronger for some periods than for others. Very few administrative documents have survived from the Old and Middle Kingdoms, so it is difficult to give a full picture of the early governmental apparatus, let alone chart changes over time. Even for the best-documented periods, such as the New Kingdom, the finer details of the administrative system remain unclear, although much is known about some individual departments and offices of state. The general paucity of documents written on papyrus means that researchers trying to explain the workings of the Egyptian state often have to rely on the titles borne by government officials. These titles are not always straightforward to interpret, since some indicated general rank within the government hierarchy rather than a particular administrative office. Throughout its history, Egypt was probably characterized by a certain flexibility of responsibility among its government personnel.

The structure of the state may be divided for convenience into three broad areas: the king and members of the royal family; the government of Egypt; and the government of Egypt's foreign possessions (when Egypt ruled an empire beyond its own borders). As close relatives of the king, members of the royal family probably shared some of his supernatural authority and so would have been in a position to wield considerable secular power. In practice, close members of the king's family were often appointed to senior positions within the government. This had the dual function of binding potentially ambitious individuals in loyalty to the king as it reinforced the king's grip on the levers of power. Another means by which centralized control was maintained was the practice of having each government department headed by a small group of officials who reported directly to the king. The danger of a reclusive state apparatus too remote from the people seems to have been offset, at least partially, by regular royal progresses (travels) throughout Egypt and by royal visits to major shrines on the occasion of important annual festivals. On such occasions, the king would no doubt dispense justice, and his visibility would help to strengthen the bonds between the court and the populace. The king would also be able to gather information unfiltered by his ministers, in an effort to maintain his personal command of the state apparatus.

Although the government of Egypt was centralized at the royal residence in Memphis, and important decisions of state would have been made in the palace, the day-to-day running of affairs was delegated to the provincial administrations. From the late Old Kingdom until the end of the Middle Kingdom, and again in the Late period, each region (nome) was governed by a single individual (nomarch), often exercising considerable power with little reference back to the court—the theoretical fount of all authority. The structure of provincial government for the New Kingdom is poorly documented; town mayors perhaps had an enhanced role in implementing the state's policies. Relations between the central government and the regions played a crucial role in determining the cohesion of the state; a breakdown in the equilibrium between the two invariably resulted in the dissolution of the unified state.

In most areas of government (except religious and military duties), the king's representative—and the effective head of the administrative and judicial systems—was the chief minister, the vizier. The vizierate is the most important constant feature of Egyptian internal government during the Old, Middle and New Kingdoms. In the Late period, despite substantial continuity from earlier periods in most aspects of government and state structure, the office of vizier, while still attested, may have ceased to exercise significant administrative responsibility. By contrast, during the Second Intermediate Period, the viziers seemed to have provided stability during a time of short reigns and weakened central authority. The increased administrative complexity that characterized the New Kingdom brought an enhancement of the vizier's role. From the reign of Thutmose III of the eighteenth dynasty until the end of the twentieth dynasty, the vizierate was divided in two: a Southern vizier based at Thebes exercised authority over Upper Egypt, while a Northern vizier based in Memphis—who must have been the more influential, given his daily access to the king at the royal residence—was responsible for Lower Egypt. Other offices of state with less sweeping powers remained intact.

The department at the heart of the Egyptian state was the treasury, responsible for assessing, collecting, storing, processing, and redistributing taxation in the form of agricultural produce. This income supported the royal court, royal building projects, and the legions of government employees. From the first dynasty, the state carried out a regular census of the country's agricultural wealth, and it maintained detailed records of Nile flood levels, to calculate both the productive capacity of the land and the appropriate level of taxation. The treasury was headed by the "Royal Chancellor," a central title within the administration, attested from the early first dynasty. In the Old Kingdom, state building projects—such as pyramid construction—were the responsibility of a separate official, the "Master of the King's Works," who ranked second only to the vizier; his duties would have included organizing the huge work force of corvée labor needed to build royal monuments. As well as deriving income and supplies from taxation, the state also engaged in foreign trade to acquire prestige commodities not available in Egypt. Although foreign trade is often stated to have been a royal (state) monopoly, there is in fact no evidence that this was the case throughout most of dynastic times. Private individuals may have engaged in small-scale trading ventures from time to time, although it is inconceivable that any individual would have had the resources to compete with the state in this sphere. State-sponsored expeditions, whether to Nubia (for example, the mission conducted by Harkhuf in the sixth dynasty) or to the turquoise mines of the Sinai (in particular during the twelfth dynasty), are well attested. The greatest proportion of imported goods that entered Egypt were channelled through the treasury, perhaps giving the king *de facto* monopoly of foreign trade.

Throughout dynastic times, the temples formed a crucially important part of the state structure. From the earliest dynasties, local temples seem to have been used as agents of the state, helping to propagate royal rule and court culture. As such, they were periodically subject to decrees issued by the king regarding their maintenance or granting exemptions from state taxes. Only in the New Kingdom was there an emergence of powerful, quasi-independent temple institutions, in particular the Great Temple at Karnak, presided over by the high priest of Amun. During the following Third Intermediate Period, the high priests of Amun (who temporarily combined the office with that of "Great Army Commander") exercised real political authority as rulers of an Upper Egyptian territory. At other periods of Egyptian history, the state–temple dichotomy was something of an illusion: the administration of temples was essentially part of civil government, even in economic matters (as the Wilbour Papyrus makes clear); and every religious office from the high priest down was theoretically subject to royal approval. Moreover, loyal officials and royal relatives were often appointed to religious positions, and the temples never gained any coercive power. Thus, although the high priests were high-ranking men of state, their potential political influence remained extremely limited.

Limited power was not true, however, for the men at the head of another branch of the New Kingdom state, the military. Whereas during the Old and Middle Kingdoms armies had been raised on an *ad hoc* basis for military campaigns, Egypt's involvement with the Near East during the New Kingdom—following the expulsion of the Hyksos—necessitated a permanent, professional army. The military arm of the state became increasingly important, and kings of the eighteenth and nineteenth dynasties were keen to be seen as war leaders, adopting military iconography and sometimes leading their armies into battle. The military was organized and despatched from the royal residence at Memphis, theoretically guaranteeing royal control. Moreover, the office of supreme military commander ("Great Army General") was often granted to the crown prince, to ensure the army's loyalty to the reigning king. Nonetheless, it was a military man, Horemheb, who was best placed to claim the throne after the final extirpation of the eighteenth dynasty royal line; Horemheb chose another military man, Ramesses I, as his successor; and it was General Herihor who played the decisive role in the break-up of the Egyptian state at the end of the twentieth dynasty.

The militaristic character of the New Kingdom state was reflected, too, in the conquest of foreign lands, to form what is often termed the "Egyptian Empire." The Middle Kingdom state had effectively annexed Lower Nubia, which it controlled by means of a series of huge forts, stretching as far south as the Second Cataract. Yet the foreign conquests of the New Kingdom were on an altogether larger scale, encompassing the whole of Nubia, as well as territories to the northeast in Syria and Palestine. In the governing of its foreign possessions, the New Kingdom state followed two radically different approaches. The northern lands, in Syria-Palestine, were never fully integrated into the Egyptian realm; each territory was ruled by a local governor who had sworn allegiance to the pharaoh (though this did not prevent political maneuvring at Egypt's expense, as illustrated in the diplomatic correspondence of the Amarna Letters). Fortresses were controlled by individual battalion commanders, with no unified military command structure. By contrast, the government of Egypt's southern conquests, Lower and Upper Nubia (or Wawat and Kush in Egyptian terminology), was based closely on the system used for Egypt itself. A single battalion commander controlled all the Egyptian troops stationed in Nubia, giving him considerable coercive power; the "Battalion Commander of Kush" was to play an important role in the internal power struggles that characterized the end of the twentieth dynasty. Civil authority in Egyptian-controlled Nubia was exercised by the "Viceroy (or King's Son) of Kush," assisted by two deputies, one for Wawat and one for Kush. The main duties of the viceroy were the collection of taxes and tribute and the organization of gold-mining activities, the latter being the main reason for New Kingdom involvement in Nubia.

Following the end of the New Kingdom, Egypt lost control of its foreign conquests. Nubia was to become important in its own right, the indigenous rulers of Kush temporarily conquering Egypt to rule as the twenty-fifth dynasty. Sporadic Egyptian campaigns went to the Near East during the Late period, but increasingly, Egypt was the object of imperial expansion by neighboring powers: Assyrians, Persians, and Macedonians. Alexander the Great's conquest of Egypt brought to an end the existence of the independent, indigenous Egyptian state.

[*See also* Administration, *articles on* State Administration *and* Provincial Administration; Imperialism; Kingship; Officials; Royal Roles; *and* Taxation.]

BIBLIOGRAPHY

Claessen, H. J. M., and P. Skalník, eds. *The Early State.* The Hague, 1978. Papers on the phenomenon of early states; part one contains an important essay discussing the different theories of state origins, and part two includes a contribution on the early state in Egypt.

Cruz-Uribe, E. "A Model for the Political Structure of Ancient Egypt." In *For His Ka: Essays Offered in Memory of Klaus Baer,* edited by David P. Silverman, pp. 45–53. Studies in Ancient Oriental Civilization, 55. Chicago, 1994. Proposes a new model for the organization of the state, based on the interconnecting spheres of influence of the king and a few significant families; the author argues that powerful families played an important role in all periods of Egyptian government.

Roth, Ann Macy. *Egyptian Phyles in the Old Kingdom: The Evolution of a System of Social Organization.* Studies in Ancient Oriental Civilization, 48. Chicago, 1991. A detailed discussion of the origins, early development, and significance of a key feature of the Egyptian state administrative apparatus.

Seidlmayer, Stephan Johannes. "Town and State in the Early Old Kingdom: A View From Elephantine." In *Aspects of Early Egypt,* edited by Jeffrey Spencer, pp. 108–127. London, 1996. The results of recent archaeological fieldwork are deployed in a case study of how the early Egyptian state exerted its authority over a local community geographically distant from the capital.

Strudwick, Nigel. *The Administration of Egypt in the Old Kingdom.* London, 1985. Exemplifies the technique of prosopography—the use of titles as a source for the study of ancient Egyptian administration; highlights the major offices of state in the Old Kingdom and charts changes in the structure of the administration.

Trigger, Bruce G., et al. *Ancient Egypt: A Social History.* Cambridge, 1983. Four chronologically based chapters cover the full span of Egyptian dynastic history.

Van den Boorn, G. P. F. *The Duties of the Vizier: Civil Administration in the Early New Kingdom.* London, 1988. Translation and commentary of the text from the eighteenth dynasty Theban tomb of the vizier Rekhmire, known as "The Duties of the Vizier." Includes the most comprehensive discussion of the vizier's role in the early New Kingdom.

Warburton, David A. *State and Economy in Ancient Egypt. Fiscal Vocabulary of the New Kingdom.* Orbis Biblicus et Orientalis, 151. Fribourg and Göttingen, 1997. Discusses the concept of the state— the different theories that have been offered to explain early state behavior; proposes a "general theory of war, custom, and technology." Also presents the theoretical aspects of economic systems and the interrelationship between state and economy during the New Kingdom.

Wilkinson, Toby A. H. *State Formation in Egypt: Chronology and Society.* BAR International Series, 651. Oxford, 1996. A useful summary of evidence and theories concerning the formation of the Egyptian state; favors a multicausal approach, stressing the importance of local factors to account for regional variation in the pace and effects of state formation.

TOBY A. H. WILKINSON

STATUARY. *See* Sculpture.

STELAE. The Latin word *stela* (pl. *stelae*) derives from the Greek *stele*, which means pillar or vertical tablet. (In English, the usual forms are "stele"/"steles.") In Egypt, stelae are slabs of stone or wood, of many different shapes, usually bearing inscriptions, reliefs, or paintings. Stelae were erected as tombstones and as boundary markers but also as votive and commemorative monuments. From the first dynasty onward—when the earliest stelae were used in Egypt—until Roman times, a considerable change in the shapes of stelae, their decoration, and their

types of inscriptions occurred. As tombstones, they were originally erected outside the tombs, to mark the offering place and to name the tomb owner. In temples and sanctuaries, they were set up by individuals to worship the gods but also to commemorate special events, such as successful expeditions to the mines in the desert or victories over foreign powers. In addition to their funerary and votive uses, stelae were also used as boundary markers for fields, estates, administrative districts, or even countries. There are several ancient Egyptian expressions for the term stela, which reflect its different purposes. *Wḏ* is the most general expression, and it means "monument of any kind," "tombstone," "boundary stone," "monument in a temple," and more, according to Adolf Erman and Hermann Grapow.

Origins and Chronology. The earliest stelae were erected in Egypt during the first dynasty to mark the tombs of the kings and their courtiers in the cemetery of Abydos in Upper Egypt. Royal stelae of the first and second dynasties consisted of large stone slabs with rounded

STELAE. *Painted limestone statuette of Roy, an eighteenth dynasty scribe and royal steward, holding a round-topped stela. The inscription on the stela is a hymn to the sun god Re.* (The Metropolitan Museum of Art, Gift of J. Pierpont Morgan, 1917. [17.190.1960])

tops, inscribed with the name of the ruler. They were always set up in pairs, but their original position within the royal funerary complex is still unclear. Herbert Ricke (1950, p. 15, fig. 2) believed that the stelae have marked the offering place outside the superstructure of the royal tomb; but as Günter Dreyer (1991, p. 104) has pointed out they could also have been placed on the roof of the superstructure. Certainly, they were not set up inside the burial chambers of the tombs.

The stelae of the courtiers in Abydos are much smaller and less carefully executed than those of the royal tombs. Unlike the royal stelae of the first and second dynasties, they were not set up in pairs and do not have rounded tops. They were probably inserted into the walls of the superstructures of the tombs or erected in front of them. Sometimes they do not bear just the name and title but also an image of the standing tomb owner. During the second dynasty, the use of tomb stelae gradually decreased. Owing to the enlargement of the tomb superstructures as the Old Kingdom progressed, the offering place was moved into a niche in the panel decoration that covered the façades of the tombs; the false door evolved from this niche. The false doors in the tombs of the third dynasty in Saqqara consist of a door niche as well as a rectangular slab stela, which shows the tomb owner in front of an offering table. Similar slab stelae have already been found in the tombs of the second dynasty in Helwan, a large cemetery on the eastern bank of the Nile River, near the modern city of Cairo. Although those slab stelae are closely connected with false doors, during the fourth dynasty such stelae also appeared detached from false doors in the Giza *mastaba* tombs. A direct connection between those slab stelae and the round-topped stelae from the first and second dynasties in Abydos cannot be established.

The so-called classical stelae of the Middle Kingdom had their origin in those stone slabs, which were set into the brick *mastaba*s of the provincial cemeteries of the late Old Kingdom and the First Intermediate Period. A considerable number of such stelae from the sixth to the twelfth dynasty were discovered in the cemeteries of Naga-ed-Deir and Dendera in Upper Egypt. They are rectangular or of irregular shape and were originally inserted into the walls of the cult chambers or the pits of the tombs. George A. Reisner (in Dows Dunham, *Naga-ed-Deir Stelae from the First Intermediate Period*, Museum of Fine Arts Boston, 1937, p. 120) differentiated between two types of stelae from the First Intermediate Period:

1. Almost square stone slabs decorated with a scene that shows the tomb owner in front of an offering table; this type resembles the slab stelae and false-door tablets of the Old Kingdom.

2. Vertical rectangular slabs with rounded tops that depict the standing tomb owner. During the eleventh and twelfth dynasty the so-called classical stela of the Middle Kingdom evolved from this type.

Most stelae of the Middle Kingdom were vertical rectangular slabs, with a rounded top that symbolized the firmament. There were also rectangular stelae with a torus roll and a *cavetto* cornice, two elements that also appear on false doors and derive from early reed-and-mud constructions.

In the New Kingdom, the shapes of stelae were very similar to those of the Middle Kingdom, apart from some few innovations: for example, round-topped stelae as well as rectangular stelae with a torus roll and a *cavetto* cornice also contained a triangle as the upper part, a reminder of a pyramidion (the tip or capstone of a pyramid). Another innovation was the kneeling statue that held stelae in front of them (known as stelophorous statues). Painted wooden stelae occurred for the first time during the New Kingdom, but they become more frequent from the Third Intermediate Period onward. They were usually of a vertical rectangular shape, with a rounded top, but compared to earlier stelae the rounded top was given a flatter curve.

Function of Stelae. Often, stelae were erected in front of tombs or inserted into the walls of *mastaba*s and rock-cut tombs to name the tomb owner; that had become common practice during the first and second dynasties, and was again common during the First Intermediate Period and thereafter.

In the rock-cut tombs of the New Kingdom, stelae were placed in the open courts to represent the owner; they were also found on the side walls of the transverse halls, where they were cut out of the bedrock. There, the stelae marked the secondary offering place in the tomb, while the main offering place in the longitudinal hall usually consisted of a statue niche. By the end of the eighteenth dynasty, stelae were increasingly inserted into the façades of the tombs. In the Late period, tomb stelae were not only placed in the superstructure of the tomb but also directly in the underground burial chamber.

Stelae also served as commemorative monuments. A large group of such stelae from the twelfth and thirteenth dynasties originated in Abydos. At the end of the Old Kingdom, Abydos developed into an important cult center for the god Osiris; it then became a famous place of pilgrimage, where festivals and processions were regularly held. Most of the stelae were erected along the procession roads, and some of them were also placed in small sanctuaries (cenotaphs), with statues and offering tables. Those stelae were established as substitutes, through which their dedicators could participate in the festivals and

TYPES OF STELAE

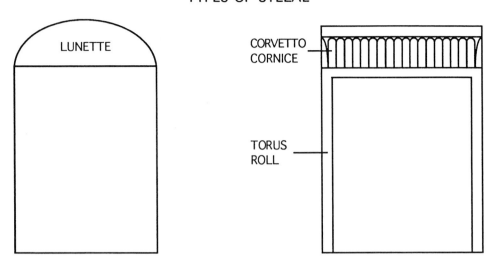

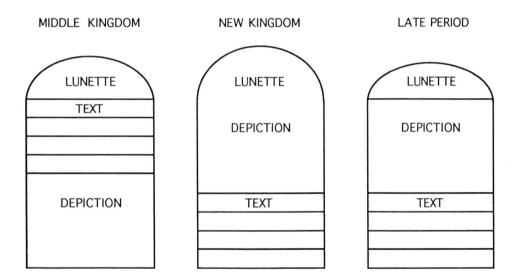

STELAE. *Arrangement of the sections of typical stelae.* (Courtesy Regina Hölzl)

might profit from the divine offerings. Sometimes commemorative stelae were set up in temples by kings or noblemen, to bear witness to successful military campaigns, royal building activities, dynastic marriages, and other official events, but they could also contain royal decrees.

A great number of votive stelae were dedicated to the gods. Presented to temples and sanctuaries by individuals, to express their personal devotion, they were also part of small altars erected in private homes, as was often the case in the houses of Deir el-Medina, a village in Western Thebes. There, from the eighteenth to the twentieth dynasty, lived the craftsmen engaged in the work at the royal tombs. "Magic" stelae were also erected in houses and

STELAE. *Painted wooden stela showing the singer of Amon playing a harp before the god Horus, twenty-second dynasty.* This stela is now in the Louvre, Paris. (Giraudon / Art Resource, NY)

tombs, as protection against dangerous animals, such as snakes or scorpions.

Stelae also marked the boundaries of fields, estates, administrative districts, and cities. For example, Akhenaten's newly founded capital of Amarna, in Middle Egypt, was marked by fifteen rock-cut boundary stelae on which the king explained why he had chosen that site for his new political and religious center. Also on Egypt's southern border with Nubia and in Egypt's newly conquered Near Eastern territories, the pharaohs were very eager to set up boundary stelae as a manifestation of their power.

Types of Decoration. Stelae usually have depictions and inscriptions, executed in raised or sunken relief, or painted onto the surface. The space within the top curve of a stela is called the lunette, and it is composed of special decorative elements. On Middle Kingdom stelae, the decoration of the lunette is clearly differentiated from the rest, the lower part of the stela, whereas in the New Kingdom the depictions in the lunette and those in the first register below it are blended into each other. In the Late period and also in the Ptolemaic period, a clear distinction was made between the lunette and the rectangular part of the stela, although some still follow the decorative scheme of New Kingdom stelae.

Typical elements used in decorating the lunettes were, for example, *udjat*-eyes and the winged sun disk—both symbols of protection and defense. *Udjat*-eyes have been interpreted as a combination of the eyes of a falcon and a wildcat. This image was also used as an amulet and was, for example, depicted on coffins and sarcophagi. The winged sun disk was originally a royal symbol and was usually depicted above temple entrances. Symbols for "life" and "regeneration," such as the *šn*-ring or the *'nḫ*-sign, as well as depictions of deities (especially the jackal god Wepwawet), have also appeared in the lunettes. Some additional decorative elements that were used during the Late period included barks with deities in them, scarabs, floral elements, and stars.

During the Middle Kingdom, the rectangular part of a stela usually contained several horizontal lines of inscription, above the depiction of the stela's owner and, occasionally, some of his relatives. On the so-called family stelae of the late twelfth and the thirteenth dynasties, from Abydos, a large number of figures were represented with the owner. Most of them were his relatives, but some might also be high officials, without any family connections, whose appearance on the stela raised the prestige of its owner.

In the New Kingdom, the first register of the rectangular part of a stela was decorated with adoration scenes, showing the owner and his family worshiping the gods. On tomb stelae of the Late period and the Ptolemaic period, the deceased was primarily shown among deities of the hereafter. The depictions were usually accompanied by short texts, but longer inscriptions were set below them. Votive stelae were often dominated by large images of the god to whom the stela was dedicated, and they contain very little text. Often the deities take the shape of animals, as was the case on the many stelae dedicated to the god Amun, on which he was depicted as a ram. Numerous stelae dedicated to the god Apis were found in the Serapeum, the tomb of the sacred Apis bulls in Saqqara; such stelae usually show the dedicator in adoration before the Apis bull.

During the nineteenth dynasty, votive stelae with depictions of large ears were used for the first time. The ears belonged to the gods, and they ensured that the prayers of the dedicators would be heard. Stelae with ears are classed as "magic" stelae, like the so-called *cippus* from the Late period, a type of stela with the image of the child god Horus standing on a crocodile and holding snakes, scorpions, and other dangerous animals; such stelae were thought to provide protection against harmful creatures.

Types of Inscriptions. Stelae inscriptions were usually written in hieroglyphs but occasionally also in Hieratic, the cursive writing of the ancient Egyptians. Late period stelae were also inscribed in Demotic, a written and spoken language that evolved during the twenty-sixth dynasty. Some stelae from the Ptolemaic period also have texts in Greek.

The earliest stelae of the first and second dynasties had only the name and title of the owner; by the Middle Kingdom, stelae were inscribed with various kinds of texts, the most common being the offering formula—a prayer through which the owner of a stelae expressed the wish to participate in the offerings that the king donated to the gods. Besides the offering formula, which remained the most common prayer on stelae throughout Egyptian history, stelae also had genealogies, dedication formulas, and other texts. Votive stelae were usually inscribed with hymns to the gods, while commemorative stelae had autobiographies or descriptions of certain important events.

For example, the Kamose stela was erected to commemorate the victory of the pharaoh Kamose over the Hyksos ruler, about 1570 BCE. Successful military campaigns were also mentioned on the boundary stelae that were set up by Senwosret III of the twelfth dynasty, in Semna and Uronarti, lower Nubia, and by Thutmose I and Thutmose III of the eighteenth dynasty, on the banks of the Euphrates River and on the Gebel Barkal in upper Nubia, respectively.

[*See also* False Door.]

BIBLIOGRAPHY

Bierbrier, Morris L., ed. *Hieroglyphic Texts from Egyptian Stelae, etc.* Vols. 10–12. London, 1982–1993. All three volumes contain descriptions, photographs and line drawings of stelae from the Ramessid period, many of them originating from the workmen's village of Deir el-Medina.

Dreyer, Gunter. "Zur Rekonstruktion der Oberbauten der Königsgräber der 1. Dynastie in Abydos." *Mitteilungen des Deutschen Archäologischen Instituts Kairo* 47 (1991).

Erman, Adolf, and Hermann Grapow, eds. *Wörterbuch der ägyptischen Sprache.* Berlin, 1926; reprinted 1971.

Eyre, Christopher J. "The Semna Stelae: Quotation, Genre, and Functions of Literature." *Studies in Egyptology: Presented to Miriam Lichtheim,* edited by Sarah Israelit-Groll, vol. 1, pp. 134–165. Jerusalem, 1990.

Habachi, Labib. *The Second Stela of Kamose and His Struggle against the Hyksos Ruler and His Capital.* Abhandlungen des Deutschen Archäologischen Instituts Kairo, 8. Glückstadt, 1972.

Hermann, Alfred. *Die Stelen der Thebanischen Felsgräber der 18. Dynastie.* Ägyptologische Forschungen, 11. Glückstadt, 1940. Still relevant study on eighteenth dynasty stelae from rock-cut tombs, including discussions on their purpose as well as their shapes, decorations, and inscriptions.

Khodzhash, Svetlana. *The Egyptian Reliefs and Stelae in the Pushkin Museum of Fine Arts, Moscow.* Translated from the Russian by Oleg Benlev. Leningrad, 1982. Offers explanations, descriptions, and photographs of nearly all types of stelae from the Old Kingdom to Roman times.

Müller, Hans W. "Die Totendenksteine des Mittleren Reiches, ihre Genesis, ihre Darstellung und ihre Komposition." *Mitteilungen des*

Deutschen Archäologischen Instituts, Abteilung Kairo 4 (1933), 165–206. Discusses origins and development of shapes of stelae as well as their purposes.

Munro, Peter. *Die spätägyptischen Totenstelen.* Ägyptologische Forschungen, 25. Glückstadt, 1973. Extensive study on funerary stelae from the Third Intermediate Period to the Ptolemaic era.

Murnane, William J., and Charles C. Van Siclen III. *The Boundary Stelae of Akhenaten.* London, 1993. New and complete edition of the boundary monuments of Tell el-Amarna, published in the fifth volume of Norman de Garis Davies's *The Rock Tombs of El-Amarna* (London, 1908).

Ricke, Herbert. *Bemerkungen zur ägyptischen Baukunst des Alten Reiches* 2, Beiträge zur ägyptischen Bauforschung und Altertumskunde Heft 5. Cairo, 1950.

Simpson, William K. *The Terrace of the Great God at Abydos: The Offering Chapels of Dynasties 12 and 13.* New Haven, 1974. Study on Middle Kingdom stelae from Abydos, their purpose and location.

Stewart, H. M. *Egyptian Stelae, Reliefs and Paintings from the Petrie Collection.* 3 vols. Warminster, 1976–1983. Publication on stelae from all periods now in the University College, London.

REGINA HÖLZL

STONEWORKING. In ancient Egypt, stone was used for building purposes as well as for utilitarian and revered objects; almost all kinds of available stone were used, both hard and soft. The relative hardness of stone can be described and compared to the Hardness Scale of Minerals devised by Friederich Mohs (1773–1839). Mohs arranged them in ten ascending degrees, from the softest (1, talc) to the hardest (10, diamond), with the rest listed between (2, gypsum; 3, calcite; 4, fluorite; 5, apatite; 6, orthoclase; 7, quartz; 8, topaz; and 9, corundum).

Two important tools for working hard stone (*rwdt*) were the tubular drill and the straight-edged saw, both of copper (*bỉȝ*) in use with a quartz sand (*šʿy*) abrasive. Before c.3500 BCE, some stones were drilled by the common marsh reed (*Phragmites communis*), rotated by a bow with dry quartz sand, but after that date, the Naqada II (c.3500–3150 BCE) stoneworker (*ḥm-inr*) copied the reed's tubular shape in copper and, later in dynastic times, in bronze. The reed effectively drilled hard limestone (*inr ḥḏ;* Mohs 3–5), calcite (often mistermed "Egyptian alabaster" or "alabaster," *šs;* Mohs 3–4), and marble (Mohs 3–5). Although pure calcite and pure limestone (both calcium carbonate) are usually of Mohs 3 hardness, variations in composition and/or mineral inclusions cause some varieties (particularly limestone which is usually combined with magnesium carbonate) to be harder—ranging between Mohs 3 and 5; modern-day drilling and cutting tests indicate this range for Egyptian calcite, limestone, and marble. Holes in harder stone—such as basalt (*bḫnw;* Mohs 7–8)—were made in ancient times by grinding with handheld borers of sandstone or borers of other stone material used with a quartz sand abrasive, continually twisted clockwise and counterclockwise. Perforations for stone beads were often made by similarly twisting borers of flint (*ds*) back and forth. [*See* Calcite *and* Limestone.]

The copper tube (which in use leaves a removable core) was sometimes driven by a bow, its string twisted around a tightly fitted wooden shaft and its top end rotated in a stone bearing-cap. For example, the perforated lug handles on Naqada II hard-stone vessels show striated tapered holes, typical of this drilling technique. Bow-driven copper tubes of 110 millimeters (6 royal fingers or 4.25 inches) in diameter were used to drill rows of adjacent touching holes in cutting out the center of Khufu's (Cheops') granite (*mȝt*) sarcophagus that is still inside the Great Pyramid at Giza. As long ago as 1883, W. M. Flinders Petrie discussed the dimensions of tubular-shaped holes and saw cuts in his *The Pyramids and Temples of Gizeh.*

Copper tubes varied from approximately 6 to 125 millimeters (0.25 to 5 inches) in diameter, with wall thicknesses of 1 to 5 millimeters (less than one-quarter inch), similar to saw-blade thicknesses. Small diameter, thin-walled tubes were created from beaten sheet copper, while large diameter, thick-walled tubes were probably cast in vertical sand molds. The weighted, straight-edged stone-cutting saw, cast horizontally (up to 2.5 meters [8 feet] in length with a thickness of about 5 millimeters), was employed to cut hard-stone architectural blocks and to roughly shape sculpture, beginning in the first dynasty (c.3050–2850 BCE). From the third dynasty onward (2687–2632 BCE), it was used to cut calcite and harder stone sarcophagi to size.

Present-day tests on granite, limestone, and calcite by drilling and sawing resulted in ratios of the weight of copper worn off the tools to the weight of the abraded stone removed—these were 1:0.9, 1:8, and 1:12, respectively; the usual consumption of sand and the amount of time for drilling or sawing 1 cubic centimeter of those stones were 250, 50, and 45 grams and 40, 5, and 2 minutes. That data allowed for some calculation of the approximate sand and copper consumption, as well as the manufacturing time, for a specific artifact. For example, the sawing, drilling, and finishing of Khufu's granite sarcophagus required about 37 metric tons (tonnes) of sand, 430 kilograms of copper, and 21 months of man-hour time to make. The finely ground resulting waste powders contained minute quartz, stone, and copper particles, quite dangerous to health (causing silicosis). In present-day tests, limestone and calcite powders were used to make faience cores, and granite powders created blue glazes that were similar to some ancient faience (*tḥnt*). The waste powders were also probably used to make a paste for drilling varieties of quartz (Mohs 7)—agate, amethyst, carnelian—and other stones for beads with a pointed,

STONEWORKING. Figure 1. *Mallet used in stoneworking, from Deir el-Bahri.* (University of Pennsylvania Museum, Philadelphia. Object # E 2434)

bow-driven copper drill. However, eighteenth and nineteenth dynasty (c.1569–1201 BCE) bead drillers at Thebes, Upper Egypt, each spun up to five bronze drills simultaneously with one bow. Present-day experiments confirmed the feasibility of that mass-production technique.

Vessels of breccia, diorite, basalt, porphyry, schist, and serpentine were made in large number in Naqada II times, because of the introduction of a combined drilling and boring tool; the vessels were always shaped before they were hollowed. Representations from dynastic times depicted a stone-weighted wooden shaft, angled at the top for a handle. The shaft was crafted from a forked branch, with its main stem cut away above the fork. A copper tube was forceably fitted onto the end of the shaft; the tool was moved back and forth, clockwise and counterclockwise, by wrist action. Several ever-widening tubes were worked

STONEWORKING. Figure 2. *Test* bas *relief in soft limestone, made by mallet-driven copper chisels.* The edges were scraped by flint tools. (Courtesy Denys A. Stocks)

at the same spot, to weaken the central mass safely, although in a large vessel adjacent holes were drilled around the mouth's perimeter to create the perforation effect. For a bulbous vessel, a forked shaft lashed to the main shaft drove a series of ever-larger figure eight-shaped stone borers, which widened the original drill hole. Vessels of gypsum (Mohs 2) were bored out by crescent-shaped flints that were on forked shafts, as were inverted, truncated-cone borers that shaped such gypsum vessels' mouths. Domestic trading in, for example, stone vessels, palettes, and flint knives, increased from Naqada II to Naqada III (c.3200–3050 BCE). In particular, Upper and Lower Egyptian Predynastic and later dynastic stone vessels were valuable trade objects, used in exchange for essential foreign raw materials, such as cedar wood from Lebanon.

Most stone types, including soft limestone and hard sandstone for building were quarried using picks and axes of granite, quartzite, chert, and flint. Very hard stone, however, such as granite, was detached by pounding with handheld dolerite balls. Conversely, the curved parts of sculptures were gently bruised into shape with hafted stone mauls. Limestone tomb walls were shaped and smoothed with flint and metal chisels and adzes; flat-tapered copper and/or bronze chisels fashioned soft limestone building blocks after their rough shaping by stone

tools. Present-day tests revealed that the copper or bronze chisel (*mḏꜣt*) and adze (*mšḫtyw*) were only effective for cutting the softer stones (Mohs 3 and 2)—limestone, red sandstone, and gypsum (Figure 2)—and so bas-reliefs and incised hieroglyphs in all other stones, including true calcite (a mineral with hexagonal crystallization), were necessarily worked by disposable (throw-away) flint tools. (Flint, although hard [Mohs 7], is brittle; it chips or flakes along a grain or cleavage line.) The shaping of hard-stone artifacts, such as vessels, and the cutting of hieroglyphs, was accomplished by driving rudimentary flint punches and chisels into the stone, thus chipping away small pieces (Figure 3). The tools suffered gradual destruction.

Occasionally, the hieroglyphs in harder stone were made smooth with stone grinders; but the hieroglyphs in softer stones, such as calcite and schist, were frequently scraped to a sharp edge with flint tools. After grinding, stone surfaces were polished with waste-drilling powders; flat surfaces were tested by three equal-length wooden rods. Two of the rods were joined by a length of string attached at the top of each. These were stood apart on the surface, with the string pulled taut. The third rod, held against the string and shifted along the surface, would then indicate high spots needing further work (marked by a finger coated in red ocher).

Stoneworkers lived in communities near the sites of

STONEWORKING. Figure 3. *The biliteral sign* nb *cut into granite by test flint punches and chisels.* The sign was polished by sandstone grinders and drilling powders of the waste material.

royal building and manufacture, for example, at Illahun in the Faiyum, Deir el-Medina at Thebes, and at Tell el-Amarna and Giza. Others toiled in palace, house, and temple workshops.

[*See also* Technology and Engineering; Tools; *and* Vessels.]

BIBLIOGRAPHY

Arnold, Dieter. *Building in Egypt: Pharaonic Stone Masonry.* New York, 1991. Discusses, in depth, all types of building in stone and the associated methods of stoneworking; there are extensive references.

Lucas, Alfred. *Ancient Egyptian Materials and Industries.* 4th rev. ed. by J. R. Harris. London, 1962. Offers a comprehensive appraisal of materials, including stone, worked by ancient Egyptians. A revised edition is presently in preparation.

Petrie, W. M. Flinders. *The Pyramids and Temples of Gizeh.* London, 1883.

Petrie, W. M. Flinders. *Tools and Weapons.* London, 1917. Describes and illustrates a large number of Egyptian tools, many of them excavated by Petrie.

Stocks, Denys A. "Ancient Factory Mass-Production Techniques: Indications of Large-Scale Stone Bead Manufacture during the Egyptian New Kingdom Period." *Antiquity* 63 (1989), 526–531. Describes the epigraphic evidence for ancient multiple-bead drilling and presents the results of tests on reconstructed tools.

Stocks, Denys A. "Making Stone Vessels in Ancient Mesopotamia and Egypt." *Antiquity* 67 (1993), 596–603. Gives the connections between stone vessel manufacture in ancient Egypt and Mesopotamia, in addition to a comprehensive description of Egyptian stone vessel production methods and tools.

Stocks, Denys A. "Technology and the Reed." *Manchester Archaeological Bulletin* 8 (1993), 58–68. Discusses the drilling capabilities of reed tubes, their adaptation and use as blowpipes and bellows equipment, and as a design pattern for the duplication of stone-cutting tubes manufactured in copper and bronze. (Available directly from the Department of Art History and Archaeology, University of Manchester, United Kingdom.)

Stocks, Denys A. "Derivation of Ancient Egyptian Faience Core and Glaze Materials." *Antiquity* 71 (1997), 179–182. Explains the possible use of waste powders, obtained from drilling and sawing stone with copper tools and sand, for making ancient faience cores and blue glazes.

DENYS A. STOCKS

STORAGE. Egypt's economy depended on collecting and redistributing grain, manufactured goods, and raw materials. Storage, therefore, played an integral role in the smooth functioning of the major institutions of state and temple. Palace, temples, and individuals all maintained "granaries" (*šnwt*) for food. Palaces and temples also established treasuries, each called the "House of Silver," that were intended to stockpile valuables. Workshops within a palace or temple were called the "House of the Plow"; there workers manufactured and stored finished goods including pottery, wooden furniture or even bread. The bureaucracies of the granary, treasury, and workshop were interconnected, although their relationships and the relative power of each of the bureaucracies shifted in response to the king's need to maintain control over Egypt's resources.

The Archaic Period and Old Kingdom. In the earliest periods, granaries are attested from archaeological examples, such as those excavated at Merimda-Beni Salama during the Badarian culture (c.5000 BCE), while treasuries are known from seals of officials who worked there as early as the first dynasty (c.3050–2825 BCE). Workshops located in the "House of the Plow" are represented on tomb walls by the fifth dynasty (c.2513–2374 BCE), though various kinds of industrial sites, such as those for manufacturing pottery and flint tools have been associated with earlier prehistoric periods. It is unclear when the "House of the Plow" was established to maintain them.

Models of granaries were found in tombs of the first two dynasties. They were shaped like cones on a round base or were domed with an opening for filling and emptying. The models resemble real granaries found throughout Egyptian history. Actual granaries were sometimes associated with tombs during this time, and they exhibit the same design as models, incorporating mud-brick vaulting coated with clay. Relief sculpture of granaries in tombs of the third and fourth dynasties show them filled with grain and fruit. By the sixth dynasty, granaries were represented alongside storage for manufactured goods. The proximity of food and manufactured items in those reliefs suggests a connection between granaries and the "House of the Plow" in this period.

The granary, however, had it's own bureaucracy in the Old Kingdom, headed by an overseer; scribes, inspectors, and chiefs were also assigned to work in the granary. Peh-

STORAGE. *A depiction of five granaries at Thebes, surrounded by a brick wall.* Three of the granaries have already been filled.

ernefer was both "Overseer of the Treasury" and "Overseer of All the Granaries of the King." This double appointment might indicate that both bureaucracies were sometimes controlled by the same individual; some scholars, however, believe that Pehernefer held these titles sequentially rather than simultaneously.

In the first and second dynasties, the treasury was directly connected to the palace as a subdivision of the "Council Chamber of Provisions." By the fourth dynasty, the treasury had become important enough that the council chamber was subordinate to it. The treasury controlled the collection, storage, and disbursement of taxes, income from the royal domains, goods manufactured and stored in the workshops, and raw materials from expeditions to Sinai. The granary and workshop were probably the actual sites of storage for the treasury.

Throughout Pharaonic Egypt, the "House of the Plow," or the workshop, was a place for food preparation, manufacturing of finished goods, and also storage of its creations. The "Overseer of the Workshop" was responsible for delivering the offerings to the temples from storage facilities and for the reversion of offerings to the priests. These workshops were attached both to the palace and to temples, though they were always founded and controlled by the king, even when used to meet cultic needs. By the reign of Pepy II (2300–2206 BCE), some workshops existed independently of other institutions. These workshops owned land attached to newly built towns.

The Middle Kingdom. From the Middle Kingdom, little evidence exists for a separate department of government that ran the granary. Though the titles "Overseer of the Granary," "Dragoman (Keeper) of the Granary," "Overseer of the Archive of the Granary," "Scribe of the Granary," and "Doorkeeper of the Granary" are all attested, the title "Overseer of the Granary" is much rarer than in the Old Kingdom. The functions of the department were possibly handled in this period by the vizier or the treasury department. In Papyrus Boulaq 18, dating to the thirteenth dynasty, there is no mention of a separate palace granary, though that document deals extensively with provisioning the palace. The sources of grain for the palace mentioned in the document are "Upper Egypt, the Treasury, and the Bureau of What the People Give."

The New Kingdom. Information on the granary, treasury, and workshops expands for the New Kingdom. From that period, detailed information for both royal and temple institutions is widely available.

Thutmose III (r. 1504–1452 BCE) centralized the administration of the granary under the direction of Yamunedjekh, "Overseer of the Granary of Upper and Lower Egypt"—the granaries were actually situated throughout the country. Papyrus Petersburg 1116A mentions granaries that provided provisions for the king, the "God's Wife of Amun" (referring to the Queen), and the Treasury, which controlled royal domains, fields of the pharaoh, and it's own fields. Each of these granaries controlled a large number of silos found throughout the country. The later Ramessid kings continued the practice of centralizing control of the granaries, though they moved the overseer's office from Thebes to Memphis and later, perhaps, to Tanis. In this period, scholars denote separate parts of the granary, since during the twentieth dynasty, a distinction was made between grain stored in the "magazine" and in the "corridor," yet the basic design of the granary remained unchanged; the meaning of this distinction is not understood.

In contrast to central control of the granary from Thebes, kings of the eighteenth dynasty maintained separate treasuries for Upper and for Lower Egypt. Both the overseers of the treasury were, however, located in Thebes in the eighteenth dynasty and reported to the vizier. The treasury's importance grew ever greater in this period because it was responsible for administrating products entering Egypt from both Syria and Nubia. The treasury also provisioned the workers in the Theban necropolis with both food and materials.

Reliefs at Medinet Habu supply an idea of the contents of an ideal treasury: room 10 held furniture and jars of ointment; room 11 held chests filled with precious metals, stones, and libation vases; room 12 held ritual staffs and various raw materials; and room 13 held libation vases, necklaces, statues, chests, and raw materials. Although the organizational principle is not clear, this depiction surely represented the ideal treasury of a temple.

The workshops of the New Kingdom are best known from documents and reliefs of the mortuary temples of kings. In Medinet Habu, for example, the workshop was clearly responsible for supplying offerings for daily rituals and for festivals. The workshop was divided into rooms, each of which was named for a specific kind of bread, beer or, sweet that was supplied to the cult. The rooms were sites both of production and storage. The rooms identified at Medinet Habu as "store rooms" would hold four times the 12,562 sacks (965,767 liters) needed for the ritual calendar at that temple. Thus, it seems likely that the rooms were also used for other functions, such as manufacture; this idea is confirmed by reliefs that show both storage and manufacturing in the same location.

The personnel of the workshop were either slaves or serfs. During the eighteenth dynasty, they were directed by the "Overseer of the Workshop," as can be observed in paintings in the tomb of Rekhmire at Qurna. By Ramessid times, the overseer's title had become honorary and the actual direction of this department was performed by a "Superior of the Workshop."

The hierarchy among granary, treasury, and workshop shifted from period to period and perhaps even from reign to reign. Papyrus Petersburg 1116A for example, speaks of a "workshop of the harem," which works for the granary of the treasury. Often, as here, the terms for "granary" or "workshop" are used without clear reference to its governing institution; but in such contexts the ancient reader would have known the bureaucratic structure. The assumption that the reader was aware of an understood meaning makes it difficult for modern scholars to ascertain many details of the bureaucracy of storage. Yet the fact of constant changes in those bureaucracies points to the central place that storage held in the Egyptian economy: no one person or bureaucracy was allowed to take complete control of the storage system in pharaonic Egypt, thus insuring that no real power base could be established that might threaten the royal house.

[*See also* Basketry, Matting, and Cordage; Taxation; Vessels; *and* Weights and Measures.]

BIBLIOGRAPHY

Andrassy, Petra. "Das *pr-šnˁ* in Alten Reich." *Studien zur Altägyptischen Kultur* 20 (1993), 17–35. Addresses the changes that occurred in the structure of the workshop during the reign of Pepy II.

Haring, B. J. J. *Divine Households: Administrative and Economic Aspects of the New Kingdom Royal Memorial Temples in Western Thebes*. Leiden, 1997. Contains the best up-to-date discussion of storage in granaries, workshops, and treasuries at mortuary temples during the New Kingdom.

Helck, Wolfgang. *Zur Verwaltung des Mittleren und Neuen Reichs*. Leiden, 1958. The classic study of the bureaucracy during the Middle and New Kingdoms.

Polz, Daniel. "Die *šnˁ*-Vorsteher des Neuen Reiches." *Zeitschrift für Ägyptische Sprache* 117 (1990), 43–60. Traces the changes in the title of the "Overseer of the Workshop" during the New Kingdom.

Schmitz, B. "Schatzhaus." In *Lexikon der Ägyptologie*, 5: 536–543. Wiesbaden, 1983. A good summary of the history of the treasury.

Schmitz, B. "Scheune, Scheunenvorsteher." In *Lexikon der Ägyptologie*, 5: 591–598. Wiesbaden, 1983. A good summary of the history of the granary.

EDWARD BLEIBERG

STRABO. *See* Ancient Historians.

SUN. *See* Astronomy; Hymns, *article on* Solar Hymns; *and* Myths, *article on* Solar Cycle.

SYMBOLS. By definition, symbols represent something other than what they actually depict. Generally, they are based on conventionally agreed-on meanings; but unlike signs, which usually stand for something quite concrete (as in the case of mathematical or linguistic signs), symbols usually stand for something less visible or tangible than the symbol itself—for example, in modern American culture the dove is used as a symbol of peace, and the hawk as a symbol of war. Symbols must frequently be differentiated from what Egyptologists call "attributes," which generally represent something by the display of one of its parts (as in the use of the crown for the king, the crook and flail for Osiris)—a case of synecdoche; and from emblems, which are distinctive badges that represent an individual, group, office, or nation (as in the use of the *serekh*, representing the palace façade, to display the Egyptian king's name). Of course, attributes and emblems often exhibit some of the characteristics of symbols.

Symbolic Expression in Egyptian Culture. The civilization of ancient Egypt was symbolically oriented to a degree rarely equaled by other cultures. It was through symbols that the Egyptians represented and affirmed many of their ideas, beliefs, and attitudes regarding the nature of life and reality. Symbols often depict aspects of reality that are difficult to represent through other modes of expression, and the ancient Egyptians used them constantly in this manner.

Symbolism, in fact, has been described as a primary form of ancient Egyptian thought, and it is necessary to understand the pervasive nature of this way of thinking in order to fully grasp the role of symbols in Egyptian society. Artists, architects, and craftspeople utilized symbols in the design and construction of objects ranging from temples, tombs, and other monuments to the smallest items of everyday life. Yet this constant incorporation of symbols was not merely a matter of decoration or playful visual punning. The use of symbolism allowed the ancient Egyptians to impose their view of life on the surface of perceived reality by incorporating or imagining symbols in the objects, forms, and activities that surrounded them.

This is not to say that symbols were employed only in the representational forms of art and architecture, for symbolism was manifested in many other areas of life, such as the practice of formal and informal magic, or religious ritual. Egyptian religion and magic both relied to a great extent on symbolism to accomplish their ends; as a result, the symbolism inherent in a given work is often an expression of underlying religious or magical beliefs that give the work life, meaning, and power.

Because symbols are different from the things they represent, some kind of association must always be present to link the symbol to its referent, the aspect of reality it represents. In Egyptian symbolism these associations are usually visual. In fact, the Egyptian language appears to have had no single word that exactly parallels our term "symbol"; the closest and most common approximation is probably *twt* ("image"), which underscores symbolism's largely visual basis. But symbols are not limited to the visual. Sounds (for example, the onomatopoeic equation of the ram's "baa" with the *ba* of the god) and perhaps even scents (incense offerings) and other sensory perceptions (perceived divine odors) could hold symbolic content for the Egyptians. But it is largely the expression of visual symbolism that has survived, and this provides the bulk of the evidence considered in this article.

In any type of symbolism, however, symbol and reality were inextricably intertwined in ancient Egypt. Thus, a person's name (both written and spoken) not only identified and represented that person as an individual but was also a veritable part of the individual's being, to the extent that to deface or destroy the name, and thus prevent its being spoken or seen, helped to destroy the existence of the person named. Once established, the symbolic aspect of an object became a part of its identity which was rarely ignored entirely, and frequently expressed to the full. Because light-reflecting mirrors shone like the sun, for example, for the Egyptians it was perhaps preferable that mirrors be circular, and that any decoration applied to them relate in some way to solar symbolism.

Not only were symbol and reality inextricably intertwined in Egyptian thought; symbols were also used to adjust perceived reality and to impose on it a meaningful and acceptable framework. This is seen especially in the fact that the Egyptian use of symbols represents a system in which the existence of conflicting facts was often successfully resolved by means of the ambivalent nature of the symbols themselves. Symbols frequently have several meanings and may openly contradict themselves in their expression, yet, in symbolic thought, the two opposing expressions may be viewed as complementary rather than contradictory. An animal such as the crocodile, for example, could symbolize not only death and destruction but also solar-oriented life and regeneration, because both appear to be true aspects of the creature's observed and mythical nature. Despite its fearsome and destructive aspects, the crocodile faces the morning sun as though in adoration and also hunts fish, the mythological enemies of the sun god. A similar polarity is seen in the Egyptian perception of many aspects of the natural world and in the character of many Egyptian gods. Osiris, for example, may be said to symbolize both death and regenerate life. Either meaning, or both, may be implicit to the use of a given symbol, depending on context.

The manipulation of contradictory facts through the use of symbols was not always complete, however, and in some cases symbols compete or consciously stress contradictions in the same setting. For example, the Egyptian king's position vis-à-vis that of the people is one of great power, and he is their protector, yet the king is at the same time dependent on the gods and receives their protection. Both aspects of reality are true, and both factors receive independent symbolic representation, though usually in different contexts.

To a certain extent, the function of symbols in Egyptian art, life, and thought was also contradictory. The symbols may be esoteric or exoteric—they may be utilized both to reveal and to conceal: to reveal by evoking important aspects of reality, and to conceal through limiting the audience that understands their message. Both aspects are integral parts of Egyptian symbolic expression and were employed according to context and need.

Aspects of Egyptian Visual Symbolism. In Egyptian culture the more important and frequently encountered aspects of visual symbolism are form, hieroglyphs, relative size, location, material, color, number, action, and gesture. These are considered separately below.

Form. Egyptian art utilizes form symbolism at two levels, which may be designated primary and secondary, or direct and indirect types of association. At the first level, objects are shown in the forms they are meant to repre-

SYMBOLS. *Emblematic purification dish from the Early Dynastic period.* This slate dish is a three-dimensional hieroglyphic inscription, in the form of an *ankh* surrounded by the symbol for *ka;* it can be read as "life to the *ka.*" (The Metropolitan Museum of Art, Rogers Fund, 1919. [19.2.16])

sent and gain symbolic significance through association and context—for example, the use of the *djed*-pillar as a symbol of support. At the secondary level, symbolic association occurs when significant forms are represented indirectly, as in the case of the clenched-hand amulets which represented sexual union.

In many cases, images that are widely disparate in form may actually relate to the same underlying symbolic theme; conversely, even small modifications of form may result in significant changes in symbolic meaning. The former may be seen in the array of symbols associated with the goddess Hathor, ranging from the papyrus plant to the cow; modification of a form is frequently seen in representations of the human figure, where different poses—kneeling, seated, standing, striding, etc.—may imply very different meanings. In formal architectural decoration, programmatic modification of forms—as in the location and color of solar disks in tombs, or the transition from plant bud to fully open capital forms of columns in temples—is frequently employed to symbolize spatial and temporal aspects of the cosmos.

Hieroglyphs. A specialized subset of form symbolism, hieroglyphic symbolism is one of the most frequent sources of symbols encountered in Egyptian art and may be expressed in several ways. In *ideographic* representa-tion (the depiction of a figure or object in the form of a hieroglyphic sign), hieroglyphic forms may function as representations of individuals and as manifestations of the gods themselves. *Rebus* representation (the spelling out of personal names or titles by combining hieroglyphic signs with syllabic values in the composition) was also commonly used for two- and three-dimensional representations of kings, and not infrequently for others.

While visual metaphor (the use of a sign to suggest something else with which it is somehow associated) is relatively infrequent, visual analogy (the use of hieroglyphic signs for things that they resemble) is particularly common in Egyptian art. In the latter type of representation, objects are made in the form of hieroglyphic signs they resemble—a mirror case or a vase in the shape of an *ankh* sign, or a headrest in the form of the horizon hieroglyph. This type of mimicking of forms is usually being tied in some way to the meaning or significance of the object.

The forms of hieroglyphs were also "projected" by the Egyptians onto actual objects in two ways. On the one hand, hieroglyphic forms were used in the design and production of various objects; on the other, natural objects were viewed and represented in the form of hieroglyphic signs which they resembled.

Only the educated elite of Egyptian society could properly write and read, and it was for them that most artworks were produced. Nevertheless, many people probably recognized at least some of the more common hieroglyphs and could understand common examples of hieroglyphic symbolism.

Size. The stratified sizes of god and human, king and subject, tomb owner and servant, or parent and child are usually symbolic of relative status and power within Egyptian compositions. This is particularly clear in scenes recorded on temple walls and in other settings which show the Egyptian king at a much larger scale than his enemies, heightening the hierarchical effect of the representation by emphasizing the helplessness of the enemy and the king's superhuman stature. In two- and three-dimensional colossal representations of kings and gods, the stratification is actually based on the relative scale of the colossus and the viewer. In a similar manner, even fully adult children are frequently depicted standing beside their parents as tiny figures, even though their figures, hair, and clothing leave no doubt as to their actual maturity. While Egyptian artists also used reduction of scale for purely artistic, compositional reasons, such instances are usually clearly discernible from symbolic ones.

The principle of same-sizing—to suggest equality or near-equality of status—may be achieved through both isocephaly and equality of scale. Isocephaly may indicate equality between subjects by placing heads of figures at the same level, or it may maintain a hierarchical difference by ensuring that an individual of lesser importance does not look down on a more important figure. Although isocephaly is frequently the result of use of the same drafting grid for both figures in Egyptian representations, many examples exist that indicate conscious same-sizing. Equality of scale does not always imply equality of status, however, and in New Kingdom battle scenes a single enemy figure may be depicted at the same scale as the Egyptian king in order to represent the enemy as a whole.

The adjusted size of individual body parts or areas for symbolic reasons must also be considered under this heading. Bodily proportions may be adjusted or emphasized as a means of suggesting maturity or status—as in the purposefully corpulent rendering of temple statues and tomb representations of private officials, and in some cases in royal representations. Many so-called fertility figurines clearly exaggerate male or female sexual characteristics for symbolic and magical purposes.

Location. The symbolism of location may be absolute or relative, referring on the one hand to the specific location of a representation, object, building, or place (such as a sacred site), and on the other to the positioning or alignment of something in relation to some other representation, object, building, or place. From very early times, funerary scenes depicting pilgrimages to sacred sites are clear indicators of the importance of locational aspects in ancient Egyptian religion. Even when the sites were not actually visited, they maintained a symbolic role that involved the spiritual continuity of the veneration of the sacred place. While locational symbolism thus frequently applies to actual specific sites, absolute locational symbols are often paired or juxtaposed as representatives of a more abstract geographic or cosmic dichotomy, such as Upper and Lower Egypt, east and west, or heaven and earth. This type of oppositional or symmetrical pairing is often expressed, in turn, through relative locational symbolism, which may range from the careful arrangement and alignment of elements within individual compositions or funerary (tomb goods) and religious (temple furniture) assemblages, to the architectural and decorative programs of whole buildings such as temples and tombs, and even the planning of groups of buildings and cities. Sometimes the orientation is according to a simple right/left, east/west, or north/south dichotomy; in other cases, it reflects subtler divisions within the structure of the individual composition or building.

Small-scale manifestations of this kind of relative placement may be seen, for example, in the "prepositional" placement of representations of kings before the figures of protective deities such as the overshadowing Horus falcon, the Hathor cow, and the sphinx in its various forms. This orientation implies the idea of protection for the king and is reflected in the hieroglyphic formula "protection behind him," commonly written behind the king. Similarly, to be "beneath" another figure might connote inferiority or subjugation, as may be seen in the carefully controlled relative placement of figures in scenes of victory over fallen enemies, and in the depiction of captives on the bases of royal thrones and footstools.

Material. Various materials held symbolic significance for the Egyptians, and not least of these were precious metals. Gold was regarded as divine on account of its color and brightness (symbolic of the sun) and its untarnishing nature (symbolic of eternal life). The flesh of the gods descended from the sun god Re was said to be of gold, and thus many images of deities were formed from this substance or gilded. Silver also had divine associations: the bones of the gods were said to be of this substance, and it was used extensively as a symbol of the moon in mirrors and in figures of lunar gods such as Khonsu and Thoth.

Many more common materials were also symbolically important. Among stones, for example, the black coloration of basalt gave it a natural association with the underworld, and lapis lazuli was symbolic of the heavens because of its blue ground color and starlike golden specks. Similarly, materials as diverse as wood, wax, and water could suggest one or more symbolic associations; water, for example, functioned as a symbol of purification and acceptance, and also of life, renewal, and fertility. The symbolic importance of a substance was often based on its natural color, but a substance might also be important because of some unusual characteristic or through mythological associations.

Color. This was one of the most important aspects of Egyptian symbolism and is the underlying reason for the symbolic associations of many materials. Individual colors could suggest different things according to context and use, however. Red, the color of fire, the sun, and blood, could symbolize any of these things, or the more abstract concepts of life and destruction associated with them. Blue was naturally associated with the heavens and water, and in the latter association could represent the concept of fertility. Yellow, a primary solar color, was used extensively for solar-related objects such as the scarab and the golden bodies of the gods. Black, although a color of the netherworld and its deities, could also be used in nonfunerary contexts and was symbolic of fertility through its associations with the rich black earth of the Nile Valley. Green, the color of luxuriant vegetation and thus of life itself, could signify health and vitality, and the sound or undamaged eye of Horus is often depicted in this color. White was sometimes used as a symbol of purity; but as a solar color, white could also be used as an alternative to yellow in some contexts.

The interchange of colors that exists in Egyptian art is partly a result of the somewhat different classification of colors used by the Egyptians, and partly of the principle of equivalence, whereby different colors were treated as one owing to physical similarities (for example, the white, yellow, and red appearances of the sun), or because of abstract, symbolic connections between them (e.g., black and green as colors of regeneration).

Number. Several numbers held symbolic significance for the Egyptians, especially the integers 2, 3, 4, 7, and their multiples—all of which are usually, in some way, expressions of unity in plurality. It is thus unity rather than diversity that is stressed in many of the dualities seen in Egyptian art. The phenomenon of duality pervades Egyptian culture and is at the heart of the Egyptian concept of the universe, which views the many evident dichotomies of light and dark, sun and moon, east and west, and so on, as expressions of the essential unity of existence. Similarly, while three was the number associated with the concept of plurality, three was also a number of unity inherent in plurality, as may be seen in the many divine families which Egyptian theology constructed of a god, his wife, and their child, or in the characterization of Amun, Re, and Ptah as the soul, face, and body of god. To a great extent, although they may often connote simple plurality, symbolic use of the numbers four, six, seven, nine, and twelve also follows this pattern of unity in plurality. Larger numbers, such as one thousand (as in the offering formula "a thousand loaves of bread") and greater, usually symbolize plurality alone.

Actions. Actions depicted in Egyptian art may be performed by gods, humans, or animals. They may be real, mythical, or iconographic, and may also be classed as ritual or nonritual. Any of these types of action may have symbolic significance.

Real actions are simply actions that take place in the real world. Many representations of the Egyptian king engaged in some kind of ritual activity depict real events in which the king actually participated. By contrast, images showing the king involved in mythically related activities may represent something that was acted out (as in certain temple rituals where costumed priests may have represented various deities), but these actions also appear to have been depicted largely for symbolic purposes. The motif of ritual slaying of enemies may well have been a real action at times, but it is frequently depicted in a mythical, generic manner. When actions in Egyptian art are of an apparently realistic nature but are depicted in an exaggerated or unrealistic manner for symbolic or propagandistic purposes, they may be described as *iconographic* actions.

The majority of formal actions depicted in Egyptian art are of a ritual nature; that is, most aspects of the activity—time, place, and manner—were carefully prescribed and conducted according to an established pattern or protocol. Each detail of such ritual actions may have specific symbolic significance. Nonritual actions, however, are the actions of everyday life, though these may sometimes have symbolic significance; thus, representations of pouring and throwing in some contexts may relate covertly to physical sexuality and hence to birth and the rebirth of the afterlife.

Gestures. A particular aspect of the symbolism of actions, gesture symbolism—using the positioning or movement of the body, head, arms or hands—is the most complex and least understood aspect of Egyptian visual symbolism. This is largely because Egyptian artists usually worked within established formulae for the depiction of the human body, and this conventional depiction serves both to obscure certain types of gestures and to summarize others, with gestures usually being "frozen" in the representations at a single characteristic point. Many, if not most, gestures depicted in Egyptian art functioned as nonverbal communication, however, and connoted general or specific meanings relating to themes such as greeting, asking, praising, offering, speaking, rejoicing, and so on. As a result, despite the frequent difficulty of analysis, many of these gestures may be observed in specific contexts and interpreted with some certainty.

Over all, two types of gestures can be differentiated: independent and sequential. Gestures such as that exhibited by mummiform representations of Osiris with the arms folded across the chest exist in isolation and have complete meaning in and of themselves without reference to any other gesture, action, or context, and may thus be termed "independent." More complex gesture patterns also exist, however, where a certain pose or gesture seen in representations actually occurred within a sequence of continuous action. These sequential gestures are found in contexts such as ritual funerary activities and formalized expressions of praise and offering and are understandably more difficult to reconstruct and interpret. It should also be remembered that a number of similar gestures actually represent different poses with different meanings; on the other hand, truly different gestures may sometimes function within the same range of meaning.

Interpretation of Symbols. In a given representation, artifact, or monument, one or several of the above symbolic dimensions may be present. In fact, it is rare that an Egyptian work has none of these elements; and the presence of symbolic aspects must be addressed in any thorough analysis of Egyptian artistic and architectural work.

Although different symbolic aspects may be emphasized in different settings or types of work, certain basic principles may be widely applied. Generally speaking, while a single, salient symbolic aspect is evident in a given representation or object, other aspects may reinforce this association or provide additional levels of meaning.

Once a symbolic association has been established between an object and its symbolic referent (e.g., the color red = sun), anything with the same characteristic may be said to be symbolic of that referent. Once an object or characteristic has become symbolic of a given referent, then its other characteristics may also be interpreted in terms of the same symbolic association. For example, the heron is associated with the Nile primarily because of its aquatic habits, but its blue coloration also ties into the same association. The swallow is associated with the sun primarily because it flies out from its nest in the ground at dawn and returns at dusk—and also because of its red coloring.

Interpreting the various types of symbols—discovering what they meant for the ancient Egyptians themselves—is not always a simple matter, however, and may be approached from a number of physical and psychological viewpoints. Even at a purely Egyptological level, the interpretation and understanding of symbols requires a careful approach. Primarily, we must beware of assuming that a given aspect of a two- or three-dimensional representational work or architectural structure had some symbolic significance for the Egyptians without reasonable indication that this was the case.

Because it developed in an open system of thought that allowed and encouraged the free association of ideas, Egyptian symbolism is easily misunderstood. This was as true for ancient and medieval observers as it is for us today, as we see, for example, in many of the "interpretations" of Egyptian symbols recorded by Plutarch. He tells us, for example, that the cat was regarded by the Egyptians as a symbol of the moon on account of its activity in the night and the "fact" that it produces increasing numbers of young (corresponding to the daily increase in the moon's light), and especially because its pupils expand and contract like the full and crescent moon. Yet how much, if any, of this reasoning was true for the ancient Egyptians' original association of the cat with the moon is difficult to ascertain. Even when care is taken in this regard, it must be remembered that symbols can be fluid things. Their meanings may certainly change over time, and it does not always follow that the symbolic significance of a given element in one composition will be identical in another work of earlier or later date.

The symbols utilized in Egyptian art may also exhibit different meanings in different contexts in the same period. In funerary contexts, feather patterning may be symbolic of the wings of certain protective goddesses, or of the avian aspects of the *ba* of the deceased. Textual evidence suggests even more possibilities, associating or identifying the deceased with a hawk, a swallow, or some other bird, so that in certain cases where context does not render a clear choice, it is difficult to decide on the specific significance of such a symbolic element—or if there could be some kind of generic symbolism meant to embrace many or all of these possible ideas. At the same time, many different symbols may be used for the same symbolic referent (e.g., the swallow, baboon, and *bulti*-fish, all used for the sun), but in many cases relatively little study has been devoted to the reasons for the choice of given symbols in different settings.

The Egyptians themselves were conscious of the ambiguity in their own symbolism and even seem to have encouraged it. Enigmatic statements in religious texts are not infrequently glossed with several divergent explanations, and the principle doubtless applies to representational as well as literary use of symbols. There is often a field or range of possible meanings for a given symbol, and while we may select a specific interpretation that seems most likely according to context, we must remember that other symbolic associations may also be involved.

This is not to say that ancient Egyptian symbolism is inchoate, inconsistent, or imprecise, but that a flexible approach must be maintained in attempting to understand its workings. Successful analysis must avoid unfounded speculation, yet at the same time it must attempt to incorporate the intellectual flexibility that the Egyptians themselves displayed.

[*See also* Amulets; Color Symbolism; Gesture; Insignias; *and* Scripts, *article on* Hieroglyphs.]

BIBLIOGRAPHY

Alleau, René. *La science des symboles.* Paris, 1976. Deals with the study of general symbolism and interpretive methodology.

Anthes, Rudolf. "Altägyptische Mythologie, Symbolon und Symbolik." *Grune Blätter, Mitteilungen und Aufsätze* 23.2 (1967), 1–20. Contains some interesting points.

Baines, John. "Temple Symbolism." *Royal Anthropological Institute News* 15 (1976), 3, 10–15. Surveys the programmatic use of symbolism in Egyptian temple architecture and decoration.

Biederman, Hans. *Dictionary of Symbolism: Cultural Icons and the Meanings behind Them.* New York, 1994. Instructive examples of symbolism in modern societies.

Bowra, C. M. *Heritage of Symbolism.* London, 1943. An older work which still provides some useful general discussions of symbolism.

Cooper, J. C. *An Illustrated Encyclopaedia of Traditional Symbols.* London, 1978. Compendium of general symbolism.

Derchain, Philippe. "Symbols and Metaphors in Literature and Representations of Private Life." *Royal Anthropological Institute News* 15 (1976), 7–10. Looks at aspects of the societal use of symbolism in ancient Egypt.

Dominicus, B. *Gesten und Gebärden in Darstellungen des Alten und Mittleren Reiches.* Heidelberg, 1994.

Goff, Beatrice L. *Symbols of Ancient Egypt in the Late Period: The Twenty-first Dynasty.* The Hague, 1979. Discussion of selected symbols used in funerary contexts; see also the review of this work in *Bibliotheca Orientalis* 39 (1982), 529–533.

Hornung, Erik. *Idea into Image: Essays on Ancient Egyptian Thought.* Translated by Elizabeth Bredeck. New York, 1992. Translation of *Geist der Pharaonenzeit* (Zürich, 1989). Provides good background to the Egyptian use of symbolism in various contexts.

Jung, Carl. *Man and His Symbols.* New York, 1964. The archetypal view, which has been widely influential in assessing symbolism from the psychological perspective.

Kendal, Timothy. "Kings of the Sacred Mountain: Napata and the Kushite Twenty-fifth Dynasty of Egypt." In *Sudan: Ancient Kingdoms of the Nile,* edited by Dietrich Wildung pp. 161–171. New York, 1997. The symbolic nature of Gebel Barkal, pp. 166–170, provides an excellent example of Egyptian visualization of symbolic forms in nature.

Lurker, Manfred, ed. *Bibliographie zur Symbolik, Ikonographie und Mythologie.* 4 vols. Baden-Baden, 1968–1971. Contains excellent bibliographies for the study of general symbolism.

Lurker, Manfred. *Symbole der Alten Ägypter.* Weilheim, 1964.

Needham, Rodney, ed. *Right and Left: Essays on Dual Symbolic Classification.* Chicago, 1973. Broad study of the symbolism of duality.

O'Connor, D. "Beloved of Maat: The Horizon of the Royal Palace in New Kingdom Egypt." In *Ancient Egyptian Kingship,* edited by D. O'Connor and D. Silverman, Leiden, 1995.

O'Connor, D. "Mirror of the Cosmos: The Palace of Merneptah." In *Fragments of a Shattered Visage: Proceedings of the International Symposium of Ramesses the Great,* edited by E. Bleiberg and R. Freed, Memphis, Tenn., 1991.

Raven, Marten J. "Magical and Symbolic Aspects of Certain Materials in Ancient Egypt." *Varia Aegyptiaca* 4 (1988), 237–242. Discusses many examples of nonvisual and nonauditory associated symbolism.

Schott, Siegfried. "Symbol und Zauber als Grundform altägyptischen Denkens." *Studium Generale* 6 (1953), 278–288. An older but still useful study of symbolism in Egyptian thought.

Westendorf, Wolfhart. "Symbol, Symbolik." In *Lexikon der Ägyptologie,* 6: 122–128. A short but useful survey linked to some, but not all, related articles in *L.Ä.*

Whitehead, Alfred North. *Symbolism: Its Meaning and Effect.* New York, 1927. Philosophical and semantic aspects of symbolism in its wider spheres of operation.

Wilkinson, Richard H. *Reading Egyptian Art: A Hieroglyphic Guide to Ancient Egyptian Painting and Sculpture.* London and New York, 1992. Focuses on the area of hieroglyphic symbolism.

Wilkinson, Richard H. *Symbol and Magic in Egyptian Art.* London and New York, 1994. Surveys the individual aspects of Egyptian symbolism.

RICHARD H. WILKINSON

SYRIA-PALESTINE. Since prehistory, the nature and extent of interactions between Egypt and Syria-Palestine (the Levant) had fluctuated across the North Sinai land bridge and through maritime contacts. Although Wadi el-Arish in North Sinai forms the traditional geopolitical and sociocultural border between Egypt and the Near East, Egyptian and Near Eastern raids and territorial expansion across this desert frontier periodically modified the political borders.

Late Predynastic (Early Bronze Age I). The late Predynastic (Naqada II–III; c.3500–3050 BCE) in Egypt corresponds to the Syria-Palestinian Early Bronze Age I (also termed EB IA-C, or Proto-Urban for EB IA-B). Although much of Syria-Palestine was inhabited by pastoralists and nomads, at this time settlements (mostly unfortified) and city-states began to emerge (e.g., Arad, Jericho, Megiddo, Beth Shan, and Tell Farah North). Syria and Palestine formed intermediaries for maritime and overland trade between Egypt and Mesopotamia, while maritime and overland routes may have connected Mesopotamia to Upper Egypt via the Red Sea and Eastern Desert (Quseir to Naqada, Coptos, and Hierakonpolis).

Near Eastern imports and influence appeared at this time in Egypt (e.g., at Maadi, Buto, Minshat Abu Omar, Giza, Abusir, Saqqara, Matmar, Naqada, and Abydos). They encompass lapis lazuli from Badakshan, pottery (late Uruk ware), cylinder seals (Protoliterate style), architecture (decorative wall cones at Buto), and artistic motifs (a "hero"-figure separating two animals; ship designs) from Mesopotamia; silver from Anatolia(?); pear-shaped mace heads, wood and resins (pine, cedar, and cypress or juniper), and pottery ('Amuq-style) from Syria; copper ores perhaps from Feinan (South Arabah); turquoise from Sinai; and olive oil, wine, salt, sulphur, bitumen (Dead Sea), resins, stone vessels, flints, and imported and locally copied pottery from Palestine. For instance, more than four hundred Palestinian pots appear in Tomb U-j at Abydos (Naqada IIIa2), while Palestinian pottery includes Red Polished ware ("Abydos ware"), Light Faced Painted ware, some Combed ware, and jars (with lug-handles, ledge-handles, and knobs), bowls, and loop-handled cups.

Egyptian items occur at more than thirty EB I sites in Palestine (e.g., 'Ein Besor, Arad, Lahav, 'Ereini, and Tel

Halif), reaching Megiddo to the north and Transjordan to the east. In North Sinai, the ratio of EB I–II Egyptian to Palestinian pottery is 80 percent to 20 percent. Yadin, Yeivin, Dessel, and Amiran/Ben-Tor hypothesize variously that the intense EB IB Egyptian material presence and influence in North Sinai and Palestine represent the product of an Egyptian invasion, a colony, a symbolic expression of sociopolitical power, or trade. Locally copied and imported Egyptian products include copper tools (axes, knives), flints (knives, sickle blades, chipped stones), stone palettes, pottery vessels (bowls, lotus-shaped bowls, bread molds, bottles, jugs, juglets, store jars, globular and drop-shaped jars, and cylindrical pots), clay sealings and vessels (with *serekh*s bearing the names of Ka, "Scorpion"?, and later kings). Imports from Egypt consist of alabaster mace heads, alabaster and faience vessels, pendants, beads (faience, calcite, carnelian, ostrich shell, and gold), Nile mollusks, catfish, and a faience baboon statuette. Egyptian construction techniques appear in mudbrick buildings, such as at EB IB 'Ereini, which contains much Egyptian influence and is interpreted by some as a colonial "capital." Some human remains from EB I burials are said to resemble "African" (i.e., Egyptian) populations. Egyptian pottery (e.g., possible Nubian ware) appears at Habuba Kabira in North Syria, while possible Egyptian gold occurs at Tepe Gawra (Mesopotamia).

Early Dynastic Period (Early Bronze Age II). The Early Dynastic (Archaic), Period (first–third dynasties, c.3050–2632 BCE) spans Early Bronze Age II. Settlement intensified in EB II Syria-Palestine, and many sites were fortified. Contemporary and later Egyptian texts, including the Palermo Stone, assert direct Egyptian contact with Palestine through the smiting of Near Easterners ("Asiatics") and the "east." King Khasekhemwy's statue base from Hierakonpolis records the exaggerated massacre of more than 48,000 northerners, reflecting intense military activity in Sinai and Palestine. Egyptian sculptures and other depictions display Near Easterners with beards, long hair, a headband, a short kilt, and arms often bound behind their backs. Redford (1992, pp. 32–33) lists the names applied to Near Easterners: "shoulder-knot people," "kilt-wearers," "kilties," "people of the bow," "archers," "the wild men of Asia," "northerners," "those-who-are-across-the-sand," and A'amu ('*ꜣmw*, a West Semitic-derived word for "Asiatics").

Egyptian products and influence continued in EB II South Palestine. Finds include imported and locally made pottery, stone vessels, a knife handle (at Ai), clay sealings and inscribed pots (some bear *serekh*-names of Narmer, Hor-Aha, and Den?), and architectural influences in mudbrick and stone buildings. Egyptian items also appear in Syria. A major port town in Lebanon, Byblos, yielded a stone vessel fragment of King Khasekhemwy and a sec-ond/third dynasty alabaster jar sherd naming Nefersesheshemre ("scribe of the royal tree-cutters"); Egyptian-style pottery occurs in the 'Amuq region of Syria.

Mesopotamian products and influence continued in Egypt during the first dynasty in the form of architecture with elaborate niches and buttresses, and cylinder seals, but these disappear by the second dynasty. Levantine products found in Egypt match the preceding period, but include seals with stylistic similarities to ones at Byblos, and cedar in royal burials at Abydos. Imported Red Polished ware becomes scarce in sites from the second and third dynasties: Red Polished ware continues, and Combed ware increases. Egyptian trade with the Near East appears in texts and jar sealings citing foreign items. One official is titled "Administrator of Foreign Lands." Texts term maritime ships "Byblos-ships." Late references note ship-building in Khasekhemwy's reign. Artistic motifs common to Egypt and the Levant include persons smiting prisoners and lions and bulls trampling foes.

Old Kingdom (Early Bronze Age III). The Old Kingdom (fourth–sixth dynasties, c.2632–2191 BCE) spans Early Bronze III. Although extensive urbanization continued in Palestine, many sites suffered abandonment, resettlement, or destruction, culminating in the termination of EB III. Egyptian activity and influence is less evident in North Sinai and Palestine, but continues in Syria.

Old Kingdom texts refer to the desert regions and possibly southwestern Palestine as Hariu-sha' (*ḥryw-šʿ*), "(the land of) the Sand Dwellers." Pyramid Text 716 alludes to Egypt's defense against Near Eastern incursions, mentioning the double-ram gate that repels the Fenkhu. Other texts locate the Fenkhu in West Syria and Lebanon, while the region to the east is termed Qedem, and the population is labeled A'amu. Mesopotamian texts from the third and second millennia BCE mention "the land of Amurru," which includes "the West," "the West-land," and all regions west of the Euphrates to the Mediterranean ("the sea of Amurru"). In another text, the Sumerian king of Lagash, Gudea (c.2100 BCE), obtains cedar from the mountains of Amana (Amanus) and stone from Basalla in the Amorite mountains in Syria-Palestine.

Imported Palestinian pottery appears in Egypt as late as the fourth dynasty, when Combed ware potsherds peak in quantity (one Combed ware pot yielded aromatic resin from a coniferous tree). The archaeological record, however, reveals decreasing Egyptian contact with EB III Palestine. The attribution of a cache of Early Dynastic calcite vessels from Ai ("Et Tell") to EB III is contested and otherwise placed in EB II; L. E. Stager notes that only one Egyptian drop-shaped pot is known from EB III Palestine. In contrast, the textual-pictorial record reveals Egyptian military activity against Near Easterners (A'amu), who are taken captive (*sqr.w-ʿnḫ*, "bound for life"). The fifth dynasty tomb of Yenty at Deshasheh depicts Egyptians besieging a fortified Near Eastern town. Sixth dynasty texts from Weni's tomb (reign of Pepy I) describe campaigns against "sand-dwellers" in Sinai and Palestine, during which Weni destroys villages, enclosures, and vineyards, and cuts down fig trees. Weni uses a ship to reach a place near "Gazelle-Nose," which is equated with Wadi Tumilat (eastern Delta), Mons Cassius, or Mount Carmel in northern Palestine (possibly reflecting Megiddo's destruction evident in level XVI).

Egyptian contact with northern Palestine and Syria is better known archaeologically. The EB III temple at Byblos contains fragments of architecture (*uraei* friezes, obelisks); Egyptian votive offerings for the "Mistress of Byblos" (Hathor/Ba'alat) include statuary, stone vessels, and artifacts of private and royal persons of the fourth, fifth, and sixth dynasties. Egyptian texts locate Byblos (*Kpny*), sometimes called "Fort Byblos" (*Wntt Kbn*), in the cedar-producing land of Negaw (Lebanon). Ebla, a major Syrian city, contains Egyptian artifacts.

Syrian imports and influence appear in Egypt (e.g., at Giza; Saqqara, Meidum, and Matmar) and include lumber, pottery (Red Polished ware, Metallic Combed ware, flasks), wine, olive oil, fruit, resins, animals, and people. By the late third dynasty, an increasing number of foreigners (captives or migrants) occur in texts listing laborers working on state construction projects. Texts mention Lebanese cedar for ship construction, palace doors, and masts. The Palermo Stone entry for Sneferu cites cedar from Lebanon. The remnants of Lebanese cedar, fir, cypress, and juniper occur throughout Egypt in funerary boats, sarcophagi, and beams in pyramids. Cedar resin is attested in embalming rituals. Texts cite Asiatic and other interpreters in Egypt, while relief fragments from Sahure's pyramid complex at Abusir illustrate the maritime transport from the Near East to Egypt of bears, pottery, and male and female persons of various ages, interpreted as merchants or captives.

First Intermediate Period (Middle Bronze Age I). The First Intermediate Period (seventh to early eleventh dynasties, c.2190–2040 BCE) parallels Middle Bronze I (elsewhere EB IV, EB-MB, EB IV/MB I, Caliciform, or Intermediate Bronze Age). Many EB III Palestinian towns were abandoned or destroyed, and shifting populations established new towns and seasonal camps elsewhere, including more than 390 new camps in the Negev. In contrast, settlements continued in Syria (e.g., Ebla and Byblos), and these yield evidence, albeit problematic, for some Egyptian trade or residual influence. The impoverishment, decentralization, and disintegration of Egypt's Memphite government in the late sixth dynasty coincided with the advent of widespread changes (c.2300–1950 BCE) in climate and vegetation: higher temperatures, droughts,

soil erosion, deforestation, and resulting low crop yields. This led to increased mortality rates in human and domestic and wild animal populations through famine and disease, as well as rising strife in the socio-cultural, economic, and political spheres, evident in corruption, reversals in social status, rising provincial centers, civil war and nomadic incursions from arid regions.

Although Egypt's destabilization coincided with a dramatic reduction in Egypto-Asiatic relations (imported Levantine pottery disappears from Egypt), North Sinai yields Palestinian "caliciform" pottery and Egyptian Red Sealing-Wax ware. A later text, the *Admonitions of Ipuwer*, mentions the cessation of contact with Byblos, but this text and others—the *Instructions for Merikare* and the *Prophecy of Neferty*—also report Near Eastern ("archers") incursions into the Nile Delta; this situation awaits confirmation by increasing archaeological work on this period in the Delta.

Middle Kingdom (Middle Bronze Age IIA). The Middle Kingdom (late eleventh and twelfth dynasties, c. 2040–1786 BCE) coincides with Middle Bronze IIA (elsewhere termed MB I). Around 2040 BCE, the Theban ruler Nebhepetre Montuhotpe I (mid-eleventh dynasty) reunified Egypt, defeating the tenth dynasty Herakleopolitan ruler in Middle Egypt, and other rulers and Asiatics in Lower Egypt. The stela of a contemporary official, Khety, at Deir el-Bahari, records expeditions to Sinai (*Bi3w*), activity against Asiatics, and the retrieval of turquoise, metals, and lapis lazuli. Other late eleventh dynasty texts note military and other contact with the Near East. A stela from Deir el-Ballas cites activity in the "Qedem-lands" (eastern Syria). A captioned head-smiting scene mentions using a throw-stick against "the eastern foreign lands." A king's steward, Henenu, is said to subdue "them-who-are-across-the-sand," and to obtain lumber from "the cedar slopes." General Antef's tomb displays Egyptians besieging a fortress defended by Asiatic-style persons. At Abisko near Aswan, a graffitto of Tjehemau mentions a campaign to kill the Asiatics of Djaty in Palestine.

After a brief resurgence of civil war in the late eleventh dynasty, the twelfth dynasty emerged under the leadership of Amenemhet I, who moved the capital to Itjtawy (el-Lisht) near Memphis. The *Prophecy of Neferty* and *Story of Sinuhe* indicate that he fortified the eastern Delta (the "wall of the ruler") to prevent incursions from Sinai and Palestine.

The Middle Kingdom state adopted magic—the so-called Execration Texts—to prevent internal and external threats to Egypt's security. This magic involved ritually cursing existing and potential enemies by writing names of Near Eastern and other chieftains, their personnel, regions, and cities on pottery vessels and clay figurines of bound captives, which were then broken and buried.

Weinstein, Redford, and others observe that these texts (Mirgissa, Berlin, and Brussels groups) display a reduction in names for Near Eastern regions and chieftains in contrast to increasing town names throughout the twelfth dynasty. At this time, MB IIA populations abandoned many MB I seasonal camps and resettled EB I–III towns, fortifying some towns but leaving many unfortified.

Middle Kingdom texts call Syria-Palestine "Retenu," which includes Upper Retenu (northern Palestine) and Lower Retenu (Syria). Late eighteenth-century BCE letters from Mari (Tell Hariri in Syria) locate the region of Amurru south of the city of Qatna in an area dominated by Hazor (northern Palestine). The toponym "Canaan," which usually encompasses Palestine, first appears in a Mari text that cites the "men of Canaan" in the town of Rahisum. Of interest, the Mari archives (c.1820–1760 BCE) contain 24,000 cuneiform tablets, some of which mention trade connections throughout the Levant, but they lack references to Egypt.

From the late eleventh dynasty, few Egyptian objects appear in Palestine, while the twelfth dynasty shows some increased contact and military activity in the Near East. The *Story of Sinuhe* relates the flight to Syria-Palestine of a royal bodyguard who is wrongfully implicated in the assassination of Amenemhet I. Sinuhe visits Byblos in Lebanon and Qedem in eastern Syria; he mentions a land called "Yaa," and finally settles in Upper Retenu (northern Palestine), which contains some Egyptian residents (fugitives?). One text, from the time of Senwosret I, asserts that the dangers—lions and Near Easterners ("Asiatics")—faced in travel abroad are sufficient for emissaries to will their belongings to their children. A stela of general Nesu-montu (reigns of Amenemhet I and Senwosret I) reports action against the "Sand-dwellers." Other early twelfth dynasty officials allude to Egyptian contact with Lebanon; for example a fleet of ships is built of Lebanese cedar. Redford and others list epithets of officials that detail military action against Near Easterners: throat-cutter of "them that are in Asia"; one who silenced "them-that-are-across-the-sand"; one who repressed "the enemies of Asia" and "rebels of the northern lands"; and one who destroyed "the wild bow-people, namely them-that-are-across-the-sand." A text from Saqqara, dated to Amenemhet II, documents the sending of an army in ten ships to Khenty-she (the Lebanese coast) to attack places in "Asia." A text of Khu-Sebek, dated to Senwosret III, records a campaign into Retenu to attack *Skmm* (Shechem?). A commander of troops under Amenemhet III has an epithet describing him as opening the land of the "Asiatics."

Archaeological evidence shows less definite Middle Kingdom contact with Palestine. Weinstein tallies fewer than fifty Egyptian and Egyptianizing items from secure MB IIA-A/B contexts: scarab and scaraboid seals, calcite and faience vessels, and carnelian jewelry. Other Egyptian products, such as stelae and statues of royalty and officials (e.g., Djehutihotep at Megiddo) occur in insecure contexts. In contrast, more Egyptian contact appears in Syria: The royal cemetery and temple at Byblos produce Egyptian-style architecture, statuary, stone vessels, and other artifacts with private and royal inscriptions (Amenemhet III–IV). Nine royal tombs at Byblos use Egyptian-style reliefs, hieroglyphic texts, and titles (*ḥȝty-ʿ*, "count"; *iry-pʿt*, "hereditary prince"). In the later tomb of King Antin, hieroglyphic texts call him "ruler of rulers" and "foreign ruler." Ugarit has a statue of one of Amenemhet II's daughters and two sphinxes of Amenemhet III.

Weinstein and others contest the various hypotheses claiming extensive Egyptian economic, diplomatic, and military activity (including a Middle Kingdom "empire" with garrison posts) in MB IIA Palestine, based on various texts and Middle Kingdom statuary and stelae found at Syrian-Palestinian sites. Most of the statuary cited as evidence for an empire is either ex situ (a later introduction) or could simply reflect contemporary royal gifts, votives, and other exports. One twelfth dynasty epithet describes an official accompanying the ruler's monuments to distant lands, but this may reflect reciprocal gift-giving rather than a marker of empire. Redford and others assert that the otherwise abundant Middle Kingdom texts lack evidence for the administrative infrastructure and garrison posts required to maintain an Egyptian empire in Palestine.

Near Eastern products and people appear in Egypt. Beni Hasan tomb 3, of Khnumhotep, depicts a caravan of Near Easterners on donkeys coming to Egypt from the land of Shut (Transjordan?). Archaeological and textual-pictorial sources reveal Canaanite imports of cattle, cedar, perhaps silver, olive oil, wine, and pottery. The Saqqara text of Amenemhet II lists several expeditions that bring Near Eastern tribute, booty, and prisoners to Egypt from *Ḫnty-š* (coastal Syria), *Ṯmpȝw* (western Syria), *Iwȝs* (Alshe), and *Iȝsy* (Alasiya, or Cyprus).

Late Middle Kingdom (Middle Bronze Age IIB). The late Middle Kingdom (thirteenth dynasty c. 1786–1665 BCE) spans Middle Bronze IIB (elsewhere MB II). Although an Egyptian votive of Neferhotpe I appears at Byblos, evidence of Egyptian activity decreases in MB IIB Syria-Palestine, which displays an increase in settlement size, fortifications, and destruction levels at many sites. In contrast, textual evidence shows many Near Easterners residing in Egypt during this period, prior to the "Hyksos" seizure of control in northern Egypt. The verso of Papyrus Brooklyn 35.1446, dated to Year 2 of Sobekhotpe III, reveals that Near Easterners formed as much as 56 percent of children and adult servants working in one Theban household. At this time, Tell ed-Dab'a (northeastern Delta) yields houses (with courtyards), funerary pottery, and other artifacts that match the architectural styles and material culture found throughout MB IIB-C Syria-Palestine.

Second Intermediate Period (Middle Bronze Age IIC). The Second Intermediate Period (fourteenth–seventeenth dynasties, c.1664–1569 BCE) encompasses Middle Bronze IIC (elsewhere termed MB III). Many scholars (e.g., Grimal, Ahlstrom) accept or reconstruct the fourteenth ("Xois"), fifteenth–sixteenth ("Hyksos"), and seventeenth ("Theban") dynasties as contemporary rivals ruling in the Delta and Nile Valley, based on surviving excerpts from classical treatises and Manetho's third-century BCE history of Egypt. Other scholars, however, assert that the fourteenth dynasty reflects a royal pedigree for and preceding the Hyksos rulers of the fifteenth, and place the sixteenth and seventeenth in a linear succession of Egyptian rulers centered at Thebes in Upper Egypt who inherit the remnants of the thirteenth dynasty's kingdom.

A Near Eastern invasion of Egypt probably occurred during the weakened rule of the late thirteenth dynasty, a time of the rise and fall of warring Amorite states throughout the Levant: Khana in the middle Euphrates, Yamkhad centered on Aleppo in Syria, Qatanum in the middle Orontes region, and Hazor in Galilee. Second Intermediate Period and later texts report an invasion and settlement of Near Easterners in the eastern Delta. The name "Hyksos" (Manetho's "shepherd kings") appears in later classical texts but is derived from a Middle Kingdom term, *ḥḳꜣ ḫꜣswt* ("rulers of foreign lands"), commonly applied to Palestinian rulers. A text of Kamose (seventeenth dynasty) defines these invaders as "Asiatics" (*ꜥꜣmw*), and calls King Apophis a "ruler of Retenu" and "a Syrian chief."

After invading the Delta, the Hyksos soon captured Memphis, removing statuary to Tell ed-Dab'a. They subsequently dominated Upper Egypt as far south as Thebes, which lies north of a Hyksos garrison post at Gebelein, and received taxes from Egyptian vassal nomes. A stela of Kamose and later texts note the establishment of Near Easterners in garrisons ("the places of the Asiatics") throughout northern Egypt. The late seventeenth dynasty Theban rulers fought the Hyksos: Seqenre-Ta'o's skull bears axe and dagger wounds that match Hyksos-style weaponry. Kamose erected two stelae detailing several campaigns, the last of which reached the Hyksos stronghold and capital at Avaris but failed to defeat or dislodge the Hyksos. Kamose indicates that the frontier between the Hyksos (fifteenth dynasty) and Egyptian (seventeenth dynasty) territories lay at Cusae in Upper Egypt (Nome 15).

The Hyksos material culture assemblage found at eastern Delta sites—Tell ed-Dab'a, Tell el-Maskhuta, and Tell el-Yahudiyya—is basically identical with the material found at MB IIB-C sites in Syria-Palestine. The presence of donkeys in some burials at Tell ed-Dab'a is also attested in Palestine. The Hyksos rulers and officials retained West Semitic names, which number a large proportion in epigraphic materials from the Delta. The Hyksos rulers also promoted Egyptian culture, however, commissioning statues copying Middle Kingdom styles, stelae, and buildings decorated with Egyptian art and hieroglyphic inscriptions. Their titulary retains the Egyptian title "son of Re," while their names contain the theophoric element -*re*'. Although Canaanite deities such as Ba'al, 'Anat, Ashtarte-Qudshu, Horon, and Resheph dominate the Hyksos pantheon, some of these Canaanite deities appear in their equivalent Egyptian forms: Seth represents Ba'al, and Hathor, "Mistress of the Two Trees," represents 'Anat. Further Canaanite influence in Hyksos religion is represented by a large Canaanite-style cultic precinct at Tell ed-Dab'a. Extensive maritime contact between the Hyksos and the Near East is attested in Kamose's second stela, which describes the harbor of Avaris as containing hundreds of cedar ships with cargoes of products from Retenu: gold, silver, turquoise, lapis, incense, fat, honey, moringa oil, willow, boxwood, sticks, fine woods, and numerous bronze axes.

Despite the early eighteenth dynasty kings' attempts to eradicate Hyksos monuments, the Hyksos and the Second Intermediate Period introduced many long-lived foreign innovations to Egypt: chariots and horses, composite bows, body armor, musical instruments (lutes, lyres), and game boards. Many West Semitic terms appear as loan words in hieroglyphs, such as names for military equipment (e.g., *markabata*, "chariot") and personnel (*kusina*, "charioteer"; *maryannu*, "chariot officers").

During MB IIC, large fortified towns appeared throughout Palestine, surrounded by huge ramparts and trenches. Although scholars debate the nature and extent of Hyksos influence in Palestine, the Hyksos probably either dominated or formed alliances with city-states in southwestern Palestine; at the time of their expulsion from Egypt, the Hyksos retained access to and control of Sharuhen (Tell el-'Ajjul?) in southwestern Palestine. The quantities of material wealth and the decrease in Palestinian sites yielding destruction layers suggest that MB IIC was a prosperous and relatively peaceful period. Extensive trade connections with Egypt are attested by Egyptian statuary, gold jewelry, amulets, scarabs, and calcite vessels at many Palestinian sites. Egyptian/Hyksos epigraphic material and artifacts occur in the MB IIC temple at Byblos. Small black/gray perfume juglets with white-filled punctate designs (commonly called "Tell el-Yehudiyya ware" after their original find spot) characterize the Hyksos period and occur throughout Palestine, Syria, Cyprus, Egypt, and Nubia.

Early Eighteenth Dynasty (Late Middle Bronze Age IIC and Late Bronze Age 1A). The reigns from Ahmose to Hatshepsut (c.1569–1482 BCE) span late Middle Bronze IIC and Late Bronze 1A occupation levels in northern Mesopotamia and Syria-Palestine. Many MB IIC Amorite sites and kingdoms were destroyed (Mari, Khana, Yamkhad) or reduced by Egyptian, Hittite, Hurrian, and Indo-Aryan invasions at different times between 1569 and 1482 BCE, and were replaced by new Aryian-Hurrian kingdoms and vassals in the Levant (Mitanni, Khanigalbat, Alalakh, Kadesh?) and southeastern Anatolia (Kizzuwadna in Cilicia).

King Ahmose (c.1569–1545 BCE) expelled the Hyksos from Egypt, capturing Tjaru (Tell Heboua) in Sinai and Avaris about his regnal years 11–12. He spent three years in defeating the Hyksos at Sharuhen and organized one campaign into Syria-Palestine as far as Byblos, initiating a policy of extending Egypt's frontiers northward to prevent future invasions. Amenhotpe I (c.1545–1525 BCE) sent an army into Syria, fighting at Tunip, Qedem, and other places near the Orontes River. Thutmose I (c.1525–1516 BCE) campaigned once in Retenu, fighting troops in "Naharin" (eastern Syria, locally called "Mitanni"): he reached the Euphrates, where he erected a boundary stela, and hunted elephants in Niya in the Orontes region. Thutmose II (c.1516–1504 BCE) subdued Shasu bedouin in the Sinai and possibly the Negev region, while Hatshepsut (coregent with Thutmose III, c.1502–1482 BCE) dispatched an expedition to Byblos for cedar.

Mid-Eighteenth Dynasty (Late Bronze Age 1B). The long reigns of Thutmose III and IV span Late Bronze 1B (c.1481–1410 BCE). Egyptian texts reflect ethnic and political changes in LB 1A Palestine, borrowing new names for Palestine (Kharu, or *Ḫ3rw*, derived from *Ḫurru*-land) and its inhabitants (Kharians, Kharu). Prior to Thutmose III's sole rule (c.1481–1452 BCE), the kingdom of Kadesh in the Orontes region formed an anti-Egyptian coalition of 330 Levantine princes, who gathered at Megiddo to confront Egypt. Thutmose III mobilized an army in his year 22/23 (c.1481 BCE) and traversed Palestine, rewarding loyal vassals; a later tale alludes to his capture of Joppa, which would become a major grain storage and chariot depot. Thutmose III held council at Yehem and decided to take the narrow and potentially disastrous 'Aruna Pass through the Carmel Range to Megiddo, bypassing the safer western and eastern routes via Yokoneam and Tanaach. His strategy worked: He outmaneuvered and dispersed the divided Near Eastern forces; however, a breakdown in Egyptian discipline allowed the enemy to reach Megiddo and resist for seven months before surrendering and swearing oaths of allegiance; the ruler of Kadesh evaded capture.

Despite this victory and the establishment of a fortress in Lebanon, Thutmose III led sixteen more expeditions into Syria-Palestine. He directed expeditions in Years 24, 25, and 26/28? to assert Egypt's authority and collect tribute. He quelled a rebellion in Syria in Year 29, capturing Wartet and Ardata. Further Syrian discontent necessitated a campaign in Years 30 against Kadesh, Sumur, and Ardata, and in Year 31 against Ullaza, collecting Near Eastern tribute. In Year 33, Thutmose fought and defeated an army of Naharin (Mitanni). He erected a boundary stela at the Euphrates adjacent to Thutmose I's stela, collected tribute, received gifts from Babylonia and Khatte (Anatolia), and hunted elephants in Niya. In Year 34 he toured Syria, receiving booty, tribute, and gifts from Retenu, Djahy, Nukhashshe, and Cyprus. Year 35 required a major campaign against Djahy, in which Thutmose captured Arayana and defeated a Mitannian army in Naharin. During five campaigns in Years 36 to 40, Thutmose fought Mitannians and others in the district of Nuges, placed a garrison at Ugarit (noted in a text dating to Amenhotpe II), toured Retenu, subdued Shasu bedouin, and received tribute from Retenu, Djahy, Alalakh, and other states), as well as gifts from Cyprus and Khatte. In Year 42 (or possibly Year 37), Thutmose III led a major campaign against Syria, capturing Arqata, Kadesh, their satellite towns, and Tunip, which contained an Egyptian base. He fought against the land of Takhsi and Naharin and received tribute.

Amenhotpe II (c.1454–1419 BCE) fought against Takhsi in his Year 3, during his coregency with Thutmose III. A renewal of Mitanni's domination and influence in Syria and a pending rebellion against Egypt's garrison in Ugarit precipitated Amenhotpe II's Year 7 suppression of rebels in Retenu and Syria, which culminated in the mass deportation of 89,600 people—Khurians, Nukhashsheans, bedouin, and 'Apiru. The capture of a Mitannian messenger in southern Palestine revealed Mitanni instigating unrest among Egypt's Palestinian vassals, who later rebelled and were subdued by Amenhotpe II in Year 9. Mitanni and Amenhotpe II later negotiated peace, possibly owing to Khatte's rising threat to Mitanni and Egypt's desire to stabilize its northern empire. The new frontier followed the Orontes River south to Kadesh and east to the Euphrates, officially distinguishing Egypt's northern vassals—Ugarit, Byblos, Beirut, Sidon, Tyre, Amki, Kadesh, the land of Upe, and Damascus—from Mitanni's vassals, Mukishe (Alalalkh), the Nukhashshe lands, Niya, Tunip, and Qatna. Despite the Egyptian-Mitannian peace, which brought exchanges of letters and gifts, and Thutmose IV's marriage to a Mitannian princess, Thutmose IV (c.1419–1410 BCE) still needed to suppress rebellions in Syria-Palestine and established a fort in Khurru, Syria. The northern empire now contained the provinces of Canaan (Palestine), Upe (Damascus region and Beka' Valley), and Amurru (western Syria), which were administered from Gaza, Kumudi, and Sumur (which replaced Ullaza), respectively. Each headquarters city had a commander, garrison, and storehouse.

Late Eighteenth Dynasty (Late Bronze Age 2A). The period from Amenhotpe III to Horemheb (c.1410–1323 BCE) covers LB 2A. Early in Amenhotpe III's reign (c.1410–1382 BCE), 'Apiru nomadic warriors infiltrated western Syria and created the militaristic kingdom of Amurru (an earlier indigenous name that now designated western Syria). Although it gained recognition as an Egyptian vassal, Amurru began expanding its territory, threatening neighboring vassals like Byblos; it was implicated in the seizure of Sumur, Egypt's northernmost headquarters city. Despite a campaign against Amurru by Amenhotpe III in his Year 5, by Mitanni—probably on Egypt's behalf—and by Amenhotpe IV (war scenes, Years 1–5?), Amurru continued its expansion, capturing Sumur, Tunip, and Byblos, and threatening Amki and Ugarit. 'Apiru disruptions in Palestine prompted Amenhotpe IV (c.1382–1365 BCE) to place a military governor in Jerusalem to secure this region.

In early LB 2A, Khatte (i.e., the Hittites, also rendered "Hatti") began fighting Mitanni for control of Aleppo in Syria, sending envoys to Egypt in Year 3 of Amenhotpe IV; later (c.1377 BCE) it successfully invaded, defeated, and seized Mitanni and its vassal territories of Aleppo, Mukishe, Nukhashshe, Niya, and Ishuwa. Although Khatte avoided attacking Egypt's territory, it defeated the troops of Kadesh and Abina, Egyptian vassals assisting Mitanni against Khatte, made a treaty with Egypt, and released the captured rulers of Kadesh and Abina. During Amenhotpe IV's reign, some former Mitannian vassals attempted—without success—to defect from Khatte to Egypt. Infighting expanded and intensified among Egypt's vassals, some of whom defected to Khatte, thereby placing Egypt's frontier south of Nahr el-Kelb (the Eleutheros Valley). Although Hittite texts mention rebellions by Kadesh, Amenhotpe IV failed to regain Kadesh in his Year 15. He was succeeded by Senkhkare (c.1365 BCE) and then Tutankhamun (c.1364–1355 BCE), the latter of whom also tried and failed to retake Kadesh. Tutankhamun's widow wrote to King Shuppiluliumas requesting marriage to a Hittite prince, but the prince was murdered en route by his Egyptian escort, thereby ending the eighteenth dynasty's royal line and allowing Ay to ascend the throne (c.1355–1352 BCE). An unprovenanced Egyptian text of contested authenticity records Horemheb (c.1352–1323 BCE) campaigning in Syria, where he briefly regained Ugarit and reached Carchemish.

Nineteenth Dynasty (Late Bronze Age 2B). This dynasty (c.1322–1149 BCE) encompasses Late Bronze 2B. During Ramesses I's reign (c.1322–1321 BCE), crown prince Sety campaigned in the "Fenkhu-lands," and re-

turned in his first regnal year to suppress a Shasu bedouin uprising in northern Sinai and Syria-Palestine. Sety I (c.1321–1304 BCE) defeated rebel vassals besieging Rehob and Egypt's garrison at Beth Shan. He received the submission of vassal princes in Lebanon, possibly visited Ullaza and Kumudi, and erected victory stelae at Beth Shan and Tyre. Although Sety I regained Amurru and Kadesh (where he erected a stela), the Hittites recaptured them, precipitating Ramesses II's (c.1304–1237 BCE) Year 4 campaign to secure Amurru, which defected to Egypt. In Year 5, Ramesses II attempted to retake Kadesh, failed, and returned to Egypt, leaving his Palestinian vassals in rebellion. He reasserted Egypt's suzerainty over Syria-Palestine in Year 6/7 (?), pacifying Canaan and Moab, in Year 8, fighting in Galilee and central Syria at Dapur; and in Year 10, attacking Dapur and erecting a stela at Nahr el-Kelb. Although rising tensions between Egypt and the Hittites led to an increase in Egyptian troops at Beth Shan in Year 18, later political developments culminated in a peace treaty between Egypt and Khatte in Year 21, fixing the Egyptian/Hittite border from Nahr el-Kelb to Damascus.

For the remainder of the nineteenth dynasty, Egyptian–Hittite relations grew friendlier: Ramesses II married a Hittite princess in Year 34; a Hittite prince, later King Tudkhalia IV, visited Egypt in Year 36/37; Ramesses II married another Hittite princess in Year 40/45; and the Hittite and Egyptian royal families corresponded frequently. Merenptah (c.1237–1226 BCE) provided Khatte with grain shipments during a famine. In his Year 5 he repulsed a Libyan invasion and reported peace with Khatte, the loss of Khurru (Syria now belonged to Khatte), the plundering of "the Canaan," and the capture and/or destruction of Ashkelon, Gezer, Yanoam, and Israel. (Since Sety I's reign "the Canaan" often referred to Gaza, the capital of the Egyptian province of Canaan, or Palestine). Information about Egyptian with the Near East relations is sparse for Amenmesse (c.1226–1222? BCE), Sety II (c.1222–1215 BCE), Siptah (c.1215–1209 BCE), and Tawosret (c.1209–1201 BCE), but their names, except perhaps Amenmesse, occur on items in Sinai and Palestine. Egyptian texts mention Syrians living in Egypt, including a Canaanite, Bay, who rose to vizier under Siptah and Tawosret.

Early Twentieth Dynasty (Iron Age 1A). The reigns of Sethnakhte and Ramesses III–VI (c.1200–1149 BCE) cover Iron Age 1A. The Elephantine Stela from Year 2 of Sethnakhte (c.1200–1198 BCE) mentions that he restored Egypt after Near Easterners—that is, the vizier Bay—had usurped the throne. Ramesses III (c.1198–1166 BCE) repulsed Libyan invasions in Years 5 and 11, and defeated an overland and maritime invasion by the Sea Peoples into Palestine and Egypt in Year 8; elsewhere, the Sea Peoples devastated Anatolia—including Khatte, Cyprus, and Syria. Ramesses III incorporated numerous captives into the army, stationing, clothing, and provisioning them in garrisons. Papyrus Harris I records that Ramesses III subjugated bedouin in Seir (Edom in South Arabah), established a temple in "the Canaan," and constructed many naval and cargo ships to transfer produce from Djahy to Egypt. The temples of Amun at Thebes, Re at Heliopolis, and Ptah at Memphis owned fleets to transport cattle, grain, oil, cedar, and personnel from more than 159 Palestinian towns belonging to them. Texts dating to Ramesses IV (c.1166–1160 BCE) note the receipt of Near Eastern livestock, products, tribute, and slaves. Ramesses IV's Wadi Hammamat stela of Year 3 calls him "a destroyer of foreign lands who rounds up Asiatics in their valleys." Deir el-Medina ostracon number 11 (reign of Ramesses V, c.1160–1156 BCE) mentions Syrians living in Egypt. Egypt's northern empire may have continued as late as Ramesses VI (c.1156–1149 BCE), whose name is the last one found at Serabit el-Khadim in the Sinai, and occurs on a ring from Deir el-Balah in the northeastern Sinai, on a bronze statue base at Megiddo, and on a scarab from Alalakh.

New Kingdom (Eighteenth–Twentieth Dynasties). Egypt obtained male and female Near Eastern slaves through warfare, royal gifts, annual vassal dues, and slave markets. Although many captives were branded and tattooed with the king's name, and communities of captives were often transplanted throughout Egypt's empire (e.g., Libyans placed in the Near East), the family members of rulers of conquered Levantine cities were taken as hostages to Egypt. Within Egypt, slave populations were replenished through the offspring of slaves or were redistributed throughout society as rewards, gifts, inheritance, or barter. Slaves had legal rights, owned property, and sometimes obtained freedom through adoption by owners, marriage to Egyptians, or royal or official intervention. Near Eastern slaves and residents mentioned in documents often bear names citing deities (Ishtar-ummi, "Astarte Is My Mother"; Pa-tjai-Baal), or their place of origin (Pen-Hazor, "the one from Hazor"; Pa-assur, "the Assyrian"), but frequently give their children Egyptian names (Pa-ameru, "the Amorite," calls his sons Merire and Useretmin).

Near Eastern personnel and slaves are recorded in the army, garrisons, temple and palace workshops, royal funerary temples, the royal harem, and in the *kȝp* or "royal nursery," an elite institution in which the sons of high-ranking officials and vassal rulers were educated in the Egyptian language and customs. These people appear as conscripts, mercenaries, laborers, brick-makers, doorkeepers, potters, masons, carpenters, shipwrights, vintners, concubines, maids, singers, dancers, weavers, interpreters, administrators, magicians, doctors, and cupbearers to the king. They may even attain viziership (like Aperia in the late nineteenth dynasty). Other Near Easterners were transient visitors, such as merchants,

messengers, emissaries, and the pastoralists who entered Egypt to water their flocks in the summer; the last are depicted arriving in Egypt by overland caravans and ships.

Near Eastern influence increased dramatically in the New Kingdom owing to massive influxes of slaves and migrants, as well as intense Egyptian contact with its Levantine vassals and neighbors. Near Eastern innovations, products, and influence appear in many forms: weaponry, such as composite bows, and chariotry; metallurgy, with new techniques of making jewelry; vertical looms; the production of glass; music and the new lyre and flutes; ship-building techniques; provisions like pomegranate wine; clothing and its decorative motifs—Egyptians, including Amenhotpe III, often wear Syrian wrap-around garments with fringes; vegetation, as Thutmose III imports and depicts exotic plants, art motifs and details; cuneiform script, used in international correspondence; foreign tales like *Astarte and the Sea* or *The Tale of ʿAnat and Seth;* and at least 391 Semitic loan words, which reflect many aspects of Egyptian society and culture. Egypt received large quantities of raw materials: lumber, metals and minerals, gems, glass, and incense; craft products including weaponry, jewelry, and metal vessels; provisions such as oil, wine, and honey; and domestic and wild animals—cattle, sheep, goats, Syrian elephants, and bears. Near Eastern deities, such as Resheph, Qudshu, Baʿal, ʿAnat, Horon (an Amorite god of shepherds), and Soped ("lord of the east"), were introduced or assumed greater importance in Egypt in this period. For instance, a temple to Baʿal existed at Memphis, while Amenhotpe III requested a visit by the cult statue of Ishtar of Nineveh to cure an ailment.

In return, archaeological and textual sources indicate that a broad range of Egyptian items, livestock, personnel, and influence were dispersed from Egypt to its vassals, garrisons, and Near Eastern neighbors. We find messages in Akkadian, ships, anchor stones with hieroglyphs, architectural elements, funerary and commemorative stelae, statues, statuettes, *ushabtis,* local figurines with Egyptian motifs and elements, and anthropoid coffins. Evidence exists for wrapped and perhaps mummified bodies at Tell el-Saidiyeh and Megiddo. Horses were traded, and provisions exchanged. A wide range of luxury goods and craft objects are also mentioned in inventories.

Egyptian and Kushite or Nubian residents, servants, traders, messengers, and members of military and other expeditions appeared throughout Syria-Palestine, while some Near Easterners married Egyptians. Many Levantine hostages were returned, after adopting Egyptian names, language, and customs, to inherit the rulership of vassal city-states. Near Eastern texts term these vassal rulers "mayors" (Akkadian, *ḫazanuti*), "supervisors" (Akkadian, *rabiṣu*), and "governors" (Canaanite, *šākin māti*).

Late Twentieth Dynasty (Iron Age 1B). The reigns of Ramesses VII–XI (c.1149–1076 BCE) cover early Iron Age 1B (c.1149–1000 BCE). An Assyrian text from the Year 3 (c.1071/70 BCE) of King Assur-bel-kala mentions a gift of a crocodile and an ape from an Egyptian king (Ramesses XI, c.1106–1076 BCE, or Smendes, c.1076–1050 BCE). A contemporary Egyptian text details the maritime journey of an Egyptian priest, Wenamun, to Byblos to obtain cedar for the divine boat of Amun, and reveals much information on postimperial Egyptian trade and other relations with Philistia and Phoenicia, especially Byblos.

[*See also* Byblos; Canaan; Gaza; Hyksos; Israel; Jerusalem; Joppa; Kadesh; Lebanon; Megiddo; Mitanni; *and* Sinai.]

BIBLIOGRAPHY

Aharoni, Y. *The Land of the Bible: A Historical Geography.* 2d ed. London, 1979. Contains many references and indexes for ancient Near Eastern toponyms.

Ahlström, G. W. *The History of Ancient Palestine.* Minneapolis, 1993. A comprehensive synthesis of the archaeology and history of Palestine, including Egypto-Asiatic relations.

Andelkovic, B. *The Relations between Early Bronze Age I Canaanites and Upper Egyptians.* Belgrade, 1995. A well-illustrated synthesis of imported EB Age I items and influences within the Egyptian and Palestinian material culture assemblages, arranged by region and site.

Ben-Tor, A. "New Light on the Relations between Egypt and Southern Palestine during the Early Bronze Age." *Bulletin of the American Schools of Oriental Research* 281 (Feb. 1991), 3–10.

Bietak, M. *Avaris the Capital of the Hyksos: Recent Excavations at Tell ed-Dab'a.* London, 1996. An overview of the Austrian excavations at Tell ed-Dab'a with many illustrations.

Bietak, M. "Egypt and Canaan During the Middle Bronze Age." *Bulletin of the American Schools of Oriental Research* 281 (Feb. 1991), 27–72.

Bleiberg, E. *The Official Gift in Ancient Egypt: Inw.* Norman, Okla., 1996. A study of 179 contexts for the official exchange of gifts (*inw*) between Egyptians, and Egyptians and foreigners, of different status.

Donadoni, S., ed. *The Egyptians.* Translated by R. Bianchi et al. Chicago, 1997. English translations of studies by various specialists, including sections on soldiers, slaves, and foreigners, by S. 'Ibada al-Nubi, A. Loprieno, and E. Bresciani, respectively.

Ehrich, R. W., ed. *Chronologies in Old World Archaeology.* 2 vols. 3d edn. Chicago, 1992. An invaluable synthesis and synchronizing of the prehistoric to 2000–1500 BCE material cultures of different regions and subregions of the world using sequence dating, relative dating, and absolute dating (calibrated radiocarbon dates).

Esse, D. L. *Subsistence, Trade, and Social Change in Early Bronze Age Palestine.* Studies in Ancient Oriental Civilization, 50. Chicago, 1991. A recent assessment of international relations between Palestine and neighboring regions, with illustrations, distribution maps, plans, photos, and an extensive bibliography.

Hayes, W. C. *A Papyrus of the Late Middle Kingdom in the Brooklyn Museum (Papyrus Brooklyn 35.1446).* Brooklyn, 1955. Translation and discussion of a late Middle Kingdom papyrus with information regarding Egypto-Asiatic relations and other matters, dating from Amenemhet III to Sobekhotpe III.

Hoch, J. *Semitic Words in Egyptian Texts of the New Kingdom and Third Intermediate Period.* Princeton, 1994. An extensive work with many references, a study of Egypto-Asiatic relations in the realm of language for the eighteenth to twenty-fourth dynasties.

Hoffmeier, J. K. *Israel in Egypt: The Evidence for the Authenticity of the Exodus Tradition.* Oxford, 1997. Although the main focus concerns the Exodus tradition, it also provides many references, an index, and a synthesis for "Asiatics" (Canaanites and Israelites) in Egypt before and after the Exodus period.

Kitchen, K. A. *Pharaoh Triumphant: The Life and Times of Ramesses II, King of Egypt.* Warminster, 1982. On events including a summary of the periods preceding and postdating this king.

Levy, T. E., ed. *The Archaeology of Society in the Holy Land.* New York, 1995. Articles by various authors with an up-to-date overview, references, and illustrations concerning different aspects of ancient society in Syria-Palestine from the prehistoric to Ottoman periods.

Malek, J., and S. Quirke. "Memphis, 1991: Epigraphy." *Journal of Egyptian Archaeology* 78 (1992), 13–18. The best facsimile copy of an important Middle Kingdom text concerning relations with the Near East.

Mark, S. *From Egypt to Mesopotamia: A Study of Predynastic Trade Routes.* Studies in Nautical Archeology, 4. London, 1997.

Mumford, G. D. "International Relations between Egypt, Sinai, and Syria-Palestine during the Late Bronze Age to Early Persian Period (Dynasties 18–26: c.1550–525 B.C.)." Ph.D. diss. University of Toronto, 1998.

O'Connor, D., and E. H. Cline. *Amenhotep III: Perspectives on His Reign.* Ann Arbor, 1998. For international relations, see chapter 7, which includes Egypt and the Levant, Anatolia, Aegean, Mesopotamia, and Nubia.

Oren, E. D., ed. *The Hyksos: New Historical and Archaeological Perspectives.* University Museum Monographs, 96; University Museum Symposium Series, 8. Philadelphia, 1997. This major work has the most up-to-date synthesis concerning the Hyksos and contains many articles by experts on this period of Levantine history, archaeology, and international relations.

Redford, D. B. *Egypt and Canaan in the New Kingdom.* Beer-Sheva, Studies by the Department of Bible and Ancient Near East, 4. Jerusalem, 1990. A synthesis of textual material regarding officials, administration, infrastructure, maintenance, taxation, Egyptian cultural impact, and other relations with the Near East by Egypt's New Kingdom empire in Canaan.

Redford, D. B. *Egypt, Canaan, and Israel in Ancient Times.* Princeton, 1992. A well-referenced synthesis from the Predynastic to the Saite period.

Ward, W. A. *Egypt and the East Mediterranean World 2200–1900 B.C.: Studies in Egyptian Relations During the First Intermediate Period.* Beirut, 1971. Although more material is becoming available for the First Intermediate Period from ongoing excavations, few treatments are devoted to relations with the Near East during this time period, and this remains an invaluable synthesis of material predating 1970.

Weinstein, J. M. "The Egyptian Empire in Palestine: A Reassessment," *Bulletin of the American Schools of Oriental Research* 241 (Winter 1981), 1–28. Although more recent studies have appeared regarding Egypt's New Kingdom empire, this article remains an invaluable contribution to our understanding of Egypt's relations with Palestine and provides a thorough assessment of archeological evidence.

Weinstein, J. M. "The Significance of Tell Areini for Egyptian-Palestinian Relations at the Beginning of the Bronze Age." *Bulletin of the American Schools of Oriental Research* 256 (Fall 1984), 61–69. In-depth treatment of Egypt's relations at Tell Areini and other sites in southwestern Palestine during the Early Bronze Age.

GREGORY D. MUMFORD

T

TABOO. In *Genesis* 3.1–7, all creation is divided into two categories, good and evil; the fruit from the tree in the middle of the garden would, if eaten, then provide the insight and means to distinguish between the two. The Egyptians looked on their universe in terms of a similar dichotomy. The concept *bwt*, which bears a certain resemblance to some definitions of the term "taboo," was the mechanism through which the two categories were differentiated.

"Taboo" is one of the few Polynesian words to be incorporated into European language and thought. Careful distinction must be made between at least three uses of the term. First, there is the everyday, casual application to various phenomena (things, persons, notions) that should be avoided. Those subject to the violation of this form of taboo may experience emotions ranging from offense to anger, while feelings of agonizing guilt may plague the perpetrator of the violation.

A second use of the term is found in the various technical definitions that historians of religion and anthropologists have worked out, based on comparative material from a great number of cultures. Here we find numerous reports on, and analyses of, prohibitions and "taboos," and even a cursory inquiry into the material will show clearly that there is a striking uniformity as to what is declared "taboo" in the most diverse societies at the most diverse times. The key words are "impurity," "contagion," "penalties," and similar expressions. Thus, for example, menstruation taboos are among the most universal, and the Egyptian material is no exception. The fate of the laundrymen is pitied in the *Instructions of Dua-Kheti;* their position in the social hierarchy is so humble that they have to wash the clothes of menstruating women. References to menstruation seem to show that contact with women during this time might even be dangerous. This would explain why the menstruation of wives or daughters was accepted as a legitimate cause for a worker to stay at home, as is documented in the well-known absentee lists from Deir el-Medina. The phenomena that form the substance of this group are prohibitions of which we are conscious. We know when we violate these taboos, and we know that their violation will make us "taboo" as well. Depending on the specific cultural circumstance, we may also be cleansed of our impurity. What may pass for a taboo in ancient Egypt often comes under this heading.

Third, there is the mechanism—prominent among the features known from the Polynesian material—whereby taboos are used as a means of establishing and maintaining social strata. Thus, appropriation of property and power was accomplished by declaring something taboo, and the political power of a person was delimited by the taboos he could impose. Taboos could be rendered invalid only if overruled by the taboos of a superior of the original instigator of the taboo. In Egypt things were different, but the king, as god, could make something *bwt*. He could not, however, exercise this power indiscriminately or at will, but only in order to reestablish the original, primeval order of the world (*maat*).

The development of the ancient concept *bwt* can be followed for more than two millennia. At the end of this time, which coincides with the Greco-Roman period, *bwt* is often used in a sense that comes close to some of the technical definitions of taboo produced by the historians of religion, but the core meaning of *bwt* was very different, because it was an integral part of the Egyptians view of the universe as the result of a process of differentiation. In Egypt, the world was created according to, and by means of, *maat*, a word that is often rendered as "world order" or "truth," but which also implies plenty and abundance—of food, for example. Creation resulted from the transformation of a part of nonexistence, or potential existence. In the Egyptian conception of being, the continuity of existence required repeated, cyclical contact with nonexistence. Yet at the same time, the latter had to be combatted, because it embraced not only potential being but also all the forces antagonistic to *maat* that were commonly part of true and immutable nonexistence. In theory, an Egyptian might commit acts that would cause him to die the "second death," which meant being forever associated with those same evil, uncreated, *maat*-antagonistic forces. Violating a *bwt* would bring this about, because *bwt* served to define all that was not of *maat*.

In order to understand better the nature of the Egyptian dichotomy between what might be labeled "good" and "evil," we must look at the earliest evidence for an expression of the opposition between *maat* and *bwt*. Here, at first it seems surprising to find hunger, thirst and feces as prototypes of things *bwt;* but on second thought, if in the earliest times the epitome of good, *maat*, was abundance of food, then lack of food would be bad. If nourishment is *maat*, then excretion becomes *bwt*. Further, these *bwt* things also applied to the realm of the dead and gods. The deceased declares in his funerary inscriptions that he has had no contact with feces, just as visitors to tombs and temples were admonished not to enter after having had contact with things which were *bwt*—not because this would be detrimental to the visitors themselves, but because of its harmful impact on the dead or the gods.

The ultimate concern of the Egyptians was salvation, which meant participation in the eternal cycle of life and death of the created world. Dying, in the normal sense of the word, led to other and more varied forms of existence. Death was an element of existence and, as such, it was within the realm of *maat*. Life emerged from death. However, in order to attain the desired state of a spirit or god in the afterworld, the deceased must have acquired a detailed knowledge of the essential properties of the hereafter. This implied a rejection of the idea of the afterworld as a reversed world—a world where, for instance, nourishment is feces and where the inhabitants move about upside down—as envisioned by demons representing the realm of nonexistence. In other words, the deceased must know the difference between what is of *maat* and the phenomena classified as *bwt*. And thus, whereas in Genesis knowledge was damning, in Egypt it was a prerequisite for salvation.

We may hypothesize that food and excrement played this role in the conception of the world because they are of such vital importance for life. These two categories further attained their status as prototypical symbols of good and evil because sharing food is the principal act of social incorporation in all societies. The dead is in a state of transition, and in that so-called liminal phase, he is subjected to a number of trials and tribulations. Interrogations are one of the ordeals that the dead must go through in order to prove himself a god. By virtue of its metonymic character, food is one of the principal means of putting his ability to the test. He is in a state of want and, still in terms of metonymy, hunger, and is therefore encouraged to eat what purports to be the lifegiving food of the afterworld. However, only by choosing the right kind of food in the afterworld could the dead become one of its blessed inhabitants.

The historical experience of the Egyptians, especially that of the painful transition between the Old and Middle kingdoms, provoked renewed reflections on the characteristics of evil, and the time-honored categories of excreta were inadequate to articulate the complex relationship between good and evil. During the Middle Kingdom, a process of rethinking was initiated. From the standpoint of the great dichotomy, the rest of the history of Egypt was a period of intensifying preoccupation with the problem of evil, reflected in the ever-increasing number of phenomena that were classified as *bwt*.

In this process, the contact with a *bwt* became harmful also to the living. The body's orifices and their counterpart, the thresholds of buildings, retained their status as being marked by *bwt*, and eventually the concept of *bwt* gave rise to numerous injunctions and prohibitions. Thus, access to temples required abstinence from sexual activity, observance of rules of cleanliness, and avoidance of certain types of food, such as pig, fish, or honey, depending mainly on the local cosmology (customs already seen inscribed on tomb walls of the Old Kingdom). In fact, each nome had its specific *bwt*, and each god had his *bwt*. The concept of *bwt* was further used to delimit acceptable moral standards, even to the extent that the Egyptians distinguished between various forms of dying and killing: a man could be killed and still be "alive," but if he died as a result of having been *sm3*-killed, he would be annihilated—that is, die the "second death." In the Late period there is finally some evidence that one could be cleansed of a *bwt*.

[*See also* Curses; Diet; Ethics and Morality; *and* Piety.]

BIBLIOGRAPHY

Douglas, Mary. *Purity and Danger: An Analysis of the Concepts of Pollution and Taboo.* London, 1966. Author of the hypothesis that taboo is a universal and indispensable means of establishing classificatory systems; the phenomena that are at the periphery of or fall between clear-cut categories are tabooed.

Frandsen, Paul John. "*BWT*—Divine Kingship and Grammar." In *Akten des Vierten Internationalen Ägyptologen Kongresses München 1985* Studien zur altägyptischen Kultur, Beihefte, 3, pp. 151–158. 1989. Works out the present definition of *bwt*.

Frandsen, Paul John. "Tabu." In *Lexikon der Ägyptologie*, 6: 135–142. Wiesbaden, 1985. Discusses major groups of taboos.

Kadish, Gerald E. "The Scatophagous Egyptian." *Journal of the Society of the Studies of Egyptian Antiquities* 9 (1979), 203–217. Follows Douglas in his interpretation of a certain type of texts.

Montet, Pierre. "Le fruit défendu." *Kêmi* 2 (1950), 85–116.

Steiner, Franz. *Taboo.* London, 1956. Excellent survey and critique of earlier research.

PAUL JOHN FRANDSEN

TAHARQA (r. 690–664 BCE), sixth king of the twenty-fifth or Kushite dynasty, Late period. Taharqa was the son of Piya (Piankhy) and was a younger brother of Shabtaqa, his immediate predecessor. Born late in Piya's reign, Taharqa was reared at Napata and came north to Egypt at age twenty, along with a party of royal siblings, at the behest of Shabtaqa early in the seventh century BCE. Controversy surrounds Taharqa's alleged participation in the Egyptian military intervention recorded in *2 Kings* 19.9, since it has sometimes been doubted that, in 701 BCE, he would have been old enough to go on campaign, even if the title "king" in the biblical passage is viewed as an anachronism. Moreover, a recently discovered stela of Sargon from Iran may further complicate the issue: it seems to imply that Shabtaqa was on the throne as early as 705 BCE.

Coming to the throne in 689 (backdated to 690) BCE, Taharqa enjoyed a successful decade and a half in power. He moved his residence to Memphis in the north and began a long-range program of rebuilding and temple endowment. His work is still visible in temple additions at Napata, Kawa, Edfu, Thebes, Abydos, and Memphis. In the sixth year of his reign (685–684 BCE), an especially high inundation of the Nile River brought an abundant crop and the annihilation of the rodent population. Seen as a gesture of divine favor, the miracles of that year were enhanced by the visit of the queen mother from Nubia to see her son ensconced on the throne of Egypt in the capital of the land.

A policy of foreign intervention was established at that time, directed against two of the traditional trouble spots for Egyptian hegemonic claims: the Levant and Libya. Taharqa astutely took advantage of the temporary weakness of the Assyrian Empire, attendant on the ineffectiveness and eventual assassination of Sennacherib. A series of little-known campaigns in Palestine and Lebanon (reflected only in the donation lists from the temple of Kawa in Nubia) is identified for the period extending to around 679 BCE. These resulted in a short-lived sphere of Egyptian influence along the coast from Ashkelon to Byblos. A major expedition into Libya achieved sufficient success that Taharqa could claim victory and transport booty and chattels back to Egypt, destined for the estate of Amun. These military accomplishments were celebrated to such an extent that later generations remembered Taharqa as one of the last great conquerors in the pharaonic tradition.

Taharqa's fortunes fell with the advent to power of the Assyrian king Esarhaddon (681–669 BCE). Whatever treaty or concordat Taharqa's predecessor had signed with Assyria was considered abrogated, and in 674 BCE the Assyrian army descended on the Nile Delta, intent on adding Egypt to the empire. Rebuffed on that occasion, Esarhaddon returned in 671 BCE and won the day. The Egyptian frontier defenses were outflanked, and Taharqa was forced to abandon Memphis and flee to the Sudan. Although he made a triumphal return to the north after the Assyrian troops withdrew, Taharqa was not to survive. The mere threat of a new invasion by the Assyrians was enough to drive him once again to Napata, where he died in 664 BCE.

BIBLIOGRAPHY

Grimal, Nicolas. *A History of Ancient Egypt.* Translated by Ian Shaw. Oxford, 1992.

Leclant, Jean. "Taharqa." In *Lexikon der Ägyptologie*, 6:156–184. Wiesbaden, 1986.

Onasch, Hans-Ulrich. *Die assyrischen Eroberungen Ägyptens.* Wiesbaden, 1994.

Redford, Donald B. "Taharqa in Western Asia and Libya." *Eretz Israel* 24 (Jerusalem, 1993), 188*–191*.

DONALD B. REDFORD

TAKING OF JOPPA. The modern name of a fragmentary tale preserved on the *verso* of Papyrus Harris 500 (Papyrus British Museum 10060). Written during the Ramessid period, the papyrus also contains the *Story of the Doomed Prince* and, on its *recto*, a series of love poems. Like these other works, *The Taking* (or *Capture*) *of Joppa* is written in literary Late Egyptian; it was probably composed not much earlier than the papyrus itself.

The story, whose beginning is lost, is set in the time of Thutmose III (eighteenth dynasty, c.1500 BCE). The surviving portion opens with the Egyptian army laying siege to the Palestinian coastal town of Joppa (modern Jaffa). A member of the Egyptian force named Thoth (or Djehuti) has apparently invited the ruler of Joppa (identified in the story only as "the enemy of Joppa") to a parley outside the walls of the town, where he plies the ruler and his retainers with food and drink. Once the retainers have lapsed into drunkenness, Thoth offers to surrender himself, his family, and goods. Perhaps misunderstanding the offer, the ruler asks to see the pharaoh's baton. Thoth first shows him the baton, then strikes the ruler senseless with it and has him manacled.

At this point Thoth conceals a force of Egyptian soldiers in two hundred large baskets. Word is sent to the ruler's wife that the baskets are part of the tribute of Thoth's surrender. The baskets are brought into Joppa, whereupon the Egyptian soldiers emerge and seize the town and its inhabitants. The story ends with Thoth sending word of his victory to the pharaoh in Egypt.

The extent to which *The Taking of Joppa* reflects historical events is uncertain. Thutmose III listed Joppa as one of the towns subjugated during his first military campaign, in Year 22–23 of his reign. In the story, however, the pharaoh is absent in Egypt when Joppa is taken. Assuming the story to have some basis in fact, it is possible that it reflects a subsequent rebellion of the city after the campaign of Year 22–23. This, in turn, may explain Joppa's status in the later eighteenth dynasty, when it was administered directly by Egypt rather than ruled as a semi-independent vassal state like most of its neighbors.

A general named Thoth, who was also "Overseer of Northern Countries," is known to have served under Thutmose III and was undoubtedly the model for the tale's hero.

The historicity of details in the story itself is purely conjectural. *The Taking of Joppa* is clearly a work of literature, like the other works preserved in Papyrus Harris 500. As such, its main literary interest lies in the ruse by which the Egyptians succeed in capturing the town, which prefigures the Trojan Horse of Homer's *Iliad*.

BIBLIOGRAPHY

Gardiner, Alan H. *Late-Egyptian Stories*. Bibliotheca Aegyptiaca, 1. Brussels, 1932. Publication of the ancient Egyptian text in hieroglyphic transcription, pp. 82–85a.
Goedicke, Hans. "The Capture of Joppa." *Chronique d'Égypte* 43 (1968), 219–233. Translation and commentary.
Wente, Edward F. "The Capture of Joppa." In *The Literature of Ancient Egypt*, edited by William Kelly Simpson, pp. 81–84. Rev. ed. New Haven and London, 1973. Translation.

JAMES P. ALLEN

TANIS, the capital, royal cemetery and principal Mediterranean port of Egypt (31°N, 32°E) during the Third Intermediate Period (c.1081–711 BCE). Its role as a great metropolis was brief, for it had little history before that period and declined thereafter. As an archaeological site, Tanis, in the northeastern Nile Delta, is characterized by an eclectic reuse of materials that were usurped from other locations and earlier reigns.

The village of San el-Hagar was built upon the western quay of Tanis, which occupied the eastern bank of the Tanite Nile distributary, the Bahr Saft, now only a small stream that dissipates into Lake Manzalla. The site of Tanis comprised two *geziras* (sandy hills above the flood plain); the southern hill is called Tulul el-Bid, and the northern Tell San el-Hagar. This northern tell, the largest in Egypt, comprises more than 177 hectares, and rises as high as 32 meters (100 feet). Its once fertile fields are now salty steppe, a condition that has prohibited modern occupation and preserved the site from recent destruction.

During the Old and Middle Kingdoms, the region was known as the Field of Dja'u and was considered a favorable fishing and fowling preserve. It belonged to various Lower Egyptian nomes; originally in the thirteenth nome, it fell within the fourteenth during the Middle Kingdom and ended as capital of the nineteenth in Ptolemaic times.

The first mention of the town is known from a nineteenth dynasty building block of Ramesses II (ruled c.1304–1237 BCE) used originally in Memphis. At Tanis, twentieth dynasty burials lie under an enclosure wall, indicating a settlement; however, the greater metropolis was not founded until the nineteenth year of the reign of Ramesses XI (c.1087 BCE), last king of the twentieth dynasty, when Egypt was divided between two potentates: High Priest Herihor took Upper Egypt, while Generalissimo Smendes seized Lower Egypt, and opened Tanis as a port, since Piramesse had ceased to function. The *Story of Wenamun*, a tale of trade in the Levant, depicted Wenamun embarking from Tanis on a mission for Herihor, under Smendes and his wife Tentamun, at the end of the twentieth dynasty. Smendes (r. 1081–1055 BCE) eventually founded the twenty-first dynasty. He was probably buried in Tanis, since one of his canopic jars, a funerary object, was found in the vicinity.

Smendes's successor, Psusennes I (r. 1055–1004 BCE), selected a depression of virgin sand some 8 meters (25.5 feet) above flood level, between four ranges of hills on Tanis's northern *gezira*, for the foundation of a temple to Amun; there a large brick enclosure wall was built from stone quarried from earlier structures at Piramesse. Joint inscriptions of Psusennes I and Pinudjem I within that temple indicate a reconciliation between the thrones of Tanis and Thebes. Psusennes I constructed a *mastaba* (tomb 3) at Tanis, in the southeastern corner of the enclosure, decorated with reliefs of himself offering to afterlife deities. He was interred there with rich furnishings, including usurped New Kingdom royal sarcophagi (one belonging to Merenptah of the nineteenth dynasty), a silver coffin, a gold death mask, and copious jewelry. General Wendjebaendjedet and Hornakht were also buried within the mausoleum of Psusennes I. Another king of the twenty-first dynasty, Amenemope (r. 1000–990 BCE), was buried in the adjacent structure (tomb 4), with another usurped sarcophagus, a gold death mask, some jewelry, and some objects of Siamun's, although this tomb was too small to have also contained his burial. Siamun (r. 984–965 BCE) built the temples of Mut and Khonsu in a southwestern enclosure, completing the ensemble of temples after the fashion of Karnak and making Tanis into a northern replica of Thebes. The kings of this dynasty whose burials have yet to be located are Smendes, Osochor (c.990–984 BCE), Siamun, and Psusennes II (c.965–931 BCE).

Sheshonq II (r. 931–910 BCE) of the twenty-second, or Libyan, dynasty, was buried intrusively in the antechamber of Psusennes I, with much finery, including a silver falcon-headed coffin, a gold death mask, jewelry, and silver canopic vessels. Osorkon I (r. 910–896 BCE) built a new four-chamber mausoleum (tomb 1) adjoining the southern wall of that of Psusennes I. It had scenes portraying funerary themes, but it was robbed in antiquity. Takelot I (r. 896–873 BCE) and Osorkon II (r. 873–844 BCE) were buried in Osorkon I's mausoleum. Osorkon II usurped many of the earlier monuments of the Amun temple and built the East Temple, using granite palmi-

TANIS. *The ruins of the temple of Amun.* (Courtesy Dieter Arnold)

form columns of Old Kingdom date, that were reinscribed by Ramesses II and himself.

Sheshonq III (r. 819–767 BCE) built the West Gate of the temple precinct, constructed out of reused obelisks and temple blocks (some from the Old and Middle Kingdoms). It was fronted by colossal statuary usurped from Ramesses II. He was buried to the north of Amenope in a separate structure (tomb 5), inscribed with royal mortuary books, but his tomb was robbed in antiquity. Two other destroyed tombs with unknown occupants were discovered—to the south of this structure (tomb 2) and to the west (tomb 6). Kings of the twenty-second dynasty whose burials have yet to be located are Takelot I (r. 896–873 BCE), Sheshonq IV (r. 763–725 BCE), and Sheshonq V, the blocks of whose kiosk were reused in a wall around the Sacred Lake.

The Late period Nubian king Piya (ruled c.731–712 BCE) of the twenty-fifth dynasty conquered Tanis and King Taharqa (r. 690–664 BCE) made it his royal residence for a brief time. Some archaizing reliefs of the dynasty have been found reused in the Sacred Lake's wall. Tanis then passed back and forth between the Nubians, the Assyrians, and the Saites until the twenty-sixth dynasty when Psamtik I (r. 664–610 BCE) built a kiosk at Tanis. It was adorned with a procession of nome gods but was dis-

mantled and reused in later structures. No significant work was then undertaken at Tanis during the ensuing First Persian Occupation. In the thirtieth dynasty, Nektanebo I (r. 380–363 BCE) probably erected the enormous outer enclosure wall of brick, as well as a temple to Khonsu that was annexed to the northern side of the Amun temple, near the North Gate; but it was not completed until the Ptolemaic period. The temple to Horus near the East Gate was also begun in the thirtieth dynasty and completed by the Ptolemies after the Second Persian Occupation. Ptolemy I (r. 305–282 BCE) built the East Gate of the precinct. Ptolemy II (r. 282–246 BCE) and Arsinoe dedicated a small brick chapel; some fine Ptolemaic statuary was also found in the vicinity. Ptolemy IV (c.222–205 BCE) built a temple in the southwestern Mut enclosure. Some Ptolemaic-era houses were built over the Amun temple, indicating that it was no longer in use.

By the Roman period (27 BCE–337 CE) the port of Tanis had silted up, and Tanis became a minor village. At that time, most of the temple limestone was burned for its lime. In Byzantine times (337–641 CE), Tanis served as a small bishopric, but it was eventually abandoned in Islamic times and was not resettled until the reign of Muhammad Ali, Pasha, under the Ottoman Empire.

Excavations at Tanis in the nineteenth century concerned the collection of statuary. In the late 1700s, Napoleon Bonaparte had the site of Tanis surveyed; in 1825, Jean-Jacques Rifaud sent two of its large pink granite sphinxes to Paris, to the Louvre Museum. Other statues soon went to Saint Petersburg and Berlin. Henry Salt excavated in Tanis during the British protectorate, and Bernardino Drovetti found eleven statues, which were sent to the Louvre, to Berlin, and to Alexandria (now lost). Auguste Mariette undertook the first large-scale excavations at Tanis from 1860 to 1864, discovering the Four Hundred Year Stela (with a Ramessid inscription in honor of Seth in Near Eastern garb) and several royal statues (many of Middle Kingdom date). Mariette identified Tanis with the Hyksos capital of Avaris on the basis of his unusual finds; moreover, the ubiquitous inscriptions of Ramesses II, naming the city of Piramesse, led Mariette to surmise that his site was also the Ramessid royal residence (most of his finds are now in the Egyptian Museum in Cairo).

M. W. Flinders Petrie dug at Tanis in 1884, and made a detailed plan of the temple precinct; he also copied inscriptions and excavated exploratory trenches. He found some Roman-era papyri that are now in the British Museum in London. Pierre Montet began working at Tanis in 1929. Just as World War II began, he discovered the royal tombs, which resulted in a severe lack of publicity (all those treasures reside today in the Egyptian Museum in Cairo). Pierre Montet's team conclusively proved that Tanis could not have been Avaris or Piramesse, but that inscribed materials from those cities had been moved to the site during the Third Intermediate Period. The French excavated at Tanis after the war, under Jean Yoyotte and Philippe Brissaud.

The site of Tanis is now characterized by large mounds of occupational debris, in the center of which lies the ruined temple precinct filled with scattered granite and sandstone blocks. The temple precinct, once enclosed within enormous brick walls, is entered through the remains of the pylon of Sheshonq III. The interior is strewn with fallen statuary, reused columns ranging in date from the Old through New Kingdoms, some fifteen or so reused obelisks of Ramesses II, and the reused temple blocks of all periods. At the center of the Amun temple are two deep wells that once served as Nilometers. The royal mausoleums are in the southwestern corner. In the northeastern corner is the Sacred Lake. At the southeastern corner, outside the main temple precinct, is a smaller precinct that houses the temples of Mut, Khonsu, and Astarte.

BIBLIOGRAPHY

Aldred, Cyril. *Jewels of the Pharaohs: Egyptian Jewellery of the Dynastic Period.* London, 1971. Detailed color photographs of certain objects found in the royal tombs of Tanis.

Baines, John, and Jaromir Málek. *Atlas of Ancient Egypt.* Oxford, 1980. A concise article on Tanis with a plan of the site's temple precinct and two illustrations of its statuary.

Brissaud, Philippe. *Cahiers de Tanis,* vol. I. Paris, 1987. First in an intended series on the on-going excavations at Tanis.

Goyon, Jean-Claude. *La decouverte des tresors de Tanis.* Paris, 1987. A brief French account of the discovery of the royal tombs at Tanis.

Kitchen, Kenneth. *The Third Intermediate Period in Egypt (1100–650 B.C.).* 2d ed. with suppl. Warminster, 1986. A detailed history of the Third Intermediate Period.

Montet, Pierre *Les nouvelles fouilles de Tanis (1929–1932).* Paris, 1933. A heavily illustrated French summary of the excavations at Tanis from 1904 to 1932.

Montet, Pierre. *Tanis: Douze annees de fouilles dans une capitale oubliee du delta egyptien.* Paris, 1942. A popular-style French book on the site and the discoveries of Montet's expedition, including line drawings and black-and-white photographs.

GEOFFREY GRAHAM

TAWERET. Depictions of the goddess Taweret depart sharply from the typically slim and beautiful female deities of ancient Egypt. In comparison with them, her image is frightful and grotesque: a composite deity with the head and body of a hippopotamus, the tail of a crocodile, and the hands and feet of a lioness. Most often she is shown standing upright on her hind legs. She usually carries or rests on the *s3* symbol, which means "protection," and she is often shown carrying a knife. The name Taweret (*T3-wrt*) means "the great one," and her frequent epithet is "Lady of Heaven."

Like those of the similarly strange-looking god Bes, images of the fearsome Taweret were used apotropaically by pregnant and nursing women, to keep evil away from their infants. Taweret has the rounded belly of a pregnant woman and the heavy breasts of a woman who is nursing. Her epithets include "Who Removes the Water," which may allude to the process of birth. Vessels from the New Kingdom in the shape of pregnant women echo the swollen form of the goddess, and there are also examples of "Taweret vessels" which have openings at the nipples, presumably for pouring milk.

From the Amarna period of the eighteenth dynasty—when worship of gods other than Aten was proscribed—there are even examples of Taweret images from the site of Tell el-Amarna, the center of the worship of the Aten. Taweret's presence emphasizes the importance of this protectress of pregnant woman in the lives of the common people, who did not cease their worship of this popular goddess.

Another epithet of Taweret is "She of the Pure Water," which may refer to her connection to the Nile River. Taweret was associated with the inundation because of her form as a riverine creature. She is called as "The One Who is in the Waters of Nun" in a shrine at Gebel es-Silsila. As a mother goddess, Taweret had associations with Hathor and Isis and was often depicted wearing the Hathor crown with a sun disk between two cow horns. Ostraca from the

TAWERET. *Glass figure of the goddess Taweret, on a pedestal, holding before her the symbol of Isis, Ptolemaic period.* (The Metropolitan Museum of Art, Purchase, Edward S. Harkness Gift, 1926. [26.7.1193])

site of Deir el-Medina indicate that Taweret could have had a demonic aspect, and her composition from ferocious creatures may have connected her with Seth, the god of chaos.

Taweret was a popular domestic goddess, and her image appears on household items such as beds, stools, and headrests. Her likeness also appears on magical wands made of hippopotamus ivory. Amulets of the goddess were very popular and appear into the Roman period (31 BCE– 395 CE). Stelae attest to her role as a healing deity. Much of her cult took place in domestic shrines, however, she may have had a sanctuary at Deir el-Medina. Apotropaic images of Bes and Taweret were placed on the outside of Ptolemaic temples to ward off evil. Taweret's popularity spread outside the borders of Egypt, and images of her have been found in Crete and at the sites of Kerma and Meroë in Nubia.

Taweret was one of several goddesses who could take the form of a hippopotamus, including Ipet ("the Nurse"), Reret ("the Sow"), and Hedjet ("the White One"). All these goddesses were associated with pregnancy and protection, and they are often difficult to distinguish from one another.

A constellation in the form of Taweret is depicted in the Theban tombs of Tharwas (tomb 353 in Western Thebes) and Senenmut (tomb 232 in Western Thebes), and in the Osiris Chapel in Medinet Habu as part of a scene showing the northern sky.

BIBLIOGRAPHY

Gundlach, Rolf. "Thoeris." In *Lexikon der Ägyptologie*, 6: 494–497. Wiesbaden, 1985.

Pinch, Geraldine. *Magic in Ancient Egypt.* London, 1994.

Sadek, Ashraf Iskander. *Popular Religion in Egypt during the New Kingdom.* Hildesheimer ägyptologische Beitrage, 27. Hildesheim, 1988.

JENNIFER HOUSER-WEGNER

TAXATION. Throughout Egyptian history, pharaoh's government taxed individual producers and officials alike in all sectors of the economy in a complex system of economic interdependency. As the incarnation of Horus, the king was the undisputed owner of all the land of Upper and Lower Egypt and was therefore entitled to bestow land and other property on whichever institutions, settlements, and individuals he chose. In return, the king reserved the right to require that the beneficiaries pay to the state various kinds of imposts, which might include a share in the produce of the land, cattle, and assorted products, as well as human labor for state projects.

Evidence for taxation is derived from administrative texts, literary texts, letters, and scenes from tombs that span the whole of pharaonic history and continue into Greco-Roman times. Administrative texts are often fragmentary and lack a clear context, and literary texts cannot always be taken at face value. To complicate matters, the Egyptians employed a variety of vague, nearly synonymous terms for "tax" more or less interchangeably. Moreover, they often used the same term with both a general and a technical meaning, sometimes in the same document. Taxes should be understood as contributions from individuals and institutions imposed by the state in fulfillment of its obligations to its own people, as well as to foreign countries, and to provide for the maintenance of pharaoh as head of state.

Old Kingdom. The fifth dynasty Palermo Stone provides the earliest details of taxation. These royal annals record, year by year, the reigns of individual kings nearly to the end of the fifth dynasty. Entries for the regnal years of pharaohs as early as the first dynasty identify a biennial event known as the "Following of Horus," a royal tour of inspection during which the king appeared before his people and collected revenues due him as the incarnation of Horus and head of state.

In the reign of Ninuter (second dynasty), the entries for the Following of Horus include references to what was evidently a biennial census or enumeration. In two instances late in the dynasty, this census is described as an "enumeration of gold and land." Therefore, toward the end of the second dynasty, the royal tour had become biennial and had expanded to include the counting of gold and land. In the reign of Sneferu (fourth dynasty), cattle are first mentioned as the subject of this count. By the reign of Neferirkare in the fifth dynasty, oxen and small livestock are included.

Supervision of the national revenue as early as the Predynastic period was under the authority of the chancellor in charge of the treasuries of Upper and Lower Egypt. By the reign of Ninuter, this responsibility included the biennial census as well as the collection and distribution of various commodities levied as taxes in kind in a nonmonetary economic system. Different commodities were under the charge of the appropriate departments. Grain, for example, was administered through the granaries, second in importance to the treasuries. Redistribution of tax revenues to their beneficiaries was handled by the "house of the master of largesse" linked to the palace.

Although these revenues funded ambitious royal building programs that often included temples, the temples and funerary endowments frequently sought exemption from dues imposed on them, especially compulsory labor. Royal charters of immunity which shelter the property and staffs of temples and foundations are first attested in the fourth dynasty with the fragmentary Exemption Decree of Shepseskaf, issued to protect the estate and staff of the pyramid of Menkaure. The fifth dynasty Decree of Neferirkare exempts staff and employees of the temple of Osiris at Abydos from compulsory labor and corvée in perpetuity under penalty of forfeiture of all property and freedom. The sixth dynasty Exemption Decree of Pepy I, concerning the *ka*-chapel of Queen Iput in the temple of Min at Coptos, protects the royal chapel and all its employees from the imposition of dues levied for the royal residence and from contribution to the Following of Horus.

Charters of immunity probably contributed to the demise of the Old Kingdom by reducing tax revenues and manpower available for public works projects. There is some evidence, however, that programs of government reforms at the end of the fifth dynasty and throughout the sixth attempted to address economic problems affecting the fiscal well-being of the state. Since exemption decrees continued to be enacted throughout Egyptian history, and it is not known to what extent or for how long they were enforced, the impact of these decrees on the economy has yet to be determined.

Scenes in the sixth dynasty Saqqara *mastaba* of the vizier Khentika reveal what could happen when officials failed to deliver their quota of taxes. One remarkable scene depicts the judgment and corporal punishment of five district governors brought before the vizier and charged with corruption in tax collection. Misappropriation of tax revenues was inexcusable, and punishment both swift and harsh.

Middle Kingdom. Knowledge of taxation during the Middle Kingdom is extremely limited. The Beni Hasan tomb autobiography of Amenemhat, a Middle Egypt nomarch in the reign of Senwosret I, identifies him as responsible for all dues (*b3kw*, "works") levied annually for the king's house, including the cattle census and taxes in grain. Amenemhat records that after "years of hunger," when he preserved his people from starvation, he refrained from exacting "the arrears of the land-tax."

A Middle Kingdom tax-assessor's journal from Harageh in the Faiyum details the measurement of agricultural land in the second month of the inundation. The assessor details time spent "measuring(?)" and "writing for him(?) the exaction of dues," as well as the registering of tenants or land-owners under the authority of the "royal treasurer and overseer of the land of the northern district." The date of these activities suggests the application of a fixed tax, which simplified work for the administrators but placed a heavy burden on the taxpayer in a year of poor harvest.

This journal recalls a later scene in the Theban tomb of Menna, scribe of the fields of the lord of the Two Lands under Thutmose IV, which depicts surveyors measuring a field in the company of scribes and an inspector. Scenes in the Elkab tomb of the mayor Paheri in Upper Egypt in the reign of Thutmose III depict the "scribe of counting grain" recording the harvest of Paheri's own estate with a coworker who tallies filled measures of grain. In another scene, laborers carry sacks of grain to barges in payment of the harvest-tax.

The recto of a late Middle Kingdom document (Papyrus Brooklyn 35.1446) concerns compulsory labor for state enterprises and lists seventy-six Upper Egyptian peasants who fled the compulsory labor they were required by the state to perform at regular intervals: tilling the fields, digging and repairing irrigation channels, and harvesting crops. When these men deserted their jobs, they became fugitives in violation of the corvée. Dereliction of duty could be punishable by permanent compulsory labor on government lands.

New Kingdom. Throughout the New Kingdom, temples were major beneficiaries of tax revenues generated by the general annual levy. Other beneficiaries were military garrisons and foreign settlements where war captives and mercenaries were quartered. Workers in the quarries and the accomplished artisans of the royal necropolis also required support from the general levy. In addition, the general levy had to provide for the upkeep of royal palaces and harems.

To raise the necessary revenues, a complex bureaucracy labored under the overseer of the granary of pharaoh, collecting taxes in grain, and the overseer of the treasury of pharaoh, collecting taxes on all other products. The vizier (or viziers, when there were two) coordinated these operations to ensure the efficient collection and redistribution of tax revenues.

A detailed account of the administration of tax collection and redistribution under the charge of the vizier is provided in the Theban tomb-chapel of Rekhmire, vizier of Upper Egypt under Thutmose III and Amenhotpe II. Prominent among the inscriptions is an enumeration of the duties of the vizier, together with the ethical principles that guided him in the execution of his office, material that goes back to a late Middle Kingdom original. Among Rekhmire's many responsibilities were the general maintenance of government records, the receipt of tax payments and foreign tribute from the officials responsible for their delivery, and supervision of the storehouses and estates of the temple of Amun. Scribes, heralds, and retainers served as his liaisons with provincial mayors, who were responsible for the collection and transport of taxes in grain and other products levied on their towns, outlying rural districts, and any harbors in their jurisdiction. Mayors also bore responsibility for the revenues of local temples.

There were also ad hoc levies that could be imposed when expenses of the state—such as those arising from military campaigns, the equipping of garrisons, or even work on the royal tomb—demanded more revenue than the general levy raised. The vizier was empowered to demand payment of ad hoc taxes wherever revenues could be obtained. It was not unusual for him to order the peremptory seizure of surplus revenues of one institution to meet a shortfall elsewhere in the system. This required familiarity with the budgets of all departments and institutions in the system and deft handling of their separate administrations.

Evidence for the abuse of authority and the unlawful expropriation of tax revenues comes from the late eighteenth dynasty Edict of Horemheb, a collection of royal decrees enacted by Horemheb to restore law and order following the troubled Amarna period. The edict addresses specific abuses on the part of soldiers and government officials who unscrupulously enriched themselves at the expense of the general populace and jeopardized state interests. It confirms the absolute right of the state to tax its citizens in both goods and services, in defiance of which it sets out harsh punishments. It is evident, however, that the edict is a set of ad hoc decrees necessitated by the fact that there was no codified system for revenue collection.

Although there are many New Kingdom documents concerning taxation, the terminology can be problematic. The common term *šmw* could have the meaning "harvest," "harvest-tax," or even "crop as rent," depending on context. The Wilbour Papyrus, a document detailing the assessment of agricultural land in Middle Egypt under the administration of temples and secular institutions in year 4 of Ramesses V, enumerates plots apportioned for smallholders, giving data that allow the calculation of a tax in grain (*šmw*) owing on their crops. These smallholders were assessed a tax calculated on only a very small portion of the plots at a fixed rate of one and one-half sacks per *aroura*. Most of their plots were either 3 or 5 *aroura* (1 *aroura* equals 0.27 hectare or 0.66 acre) of what was usually normal arable land in the "apportioning domain" of an institution.

The Wilbour Papyrus also provides data that enabled authorities to calculate the gross yield of relatively large plots of land, ascribed to temples and some secular institutions and cultivated by field laborers. These larger tracts, in the "normal domains" of institutions, were liable for a tax of 30 percent of their harvest based on a yield of five sacks per *aroura* of normal arable land. The remaining 70 percent was returned to the actual cultivators for their support. Rates of seven and a half and ten sacks per *aroura* also occur in these paragraphs levied on *tni* ("elevated?") land and *nhb* ("fresh") land, respectively.

The Wilbour Papyrus has been interpreted as evidence of an agrarian regime wherein temples and secular institutions (treasury of pharaoh, harems, or landing-places of pharaoh) administered land for cultivation as dependencies of the state. Temple-owned and administered fields were simply a special category of state land. It is irrelevant to debate whether the assessments detailed in the document should be understood as taxes payable to the state or rents accruing to institutions, since it would not be valid to distinguish temple property from state property. The temples constituted, in effect, a specialized department of the state organization. As a result, the "apportioning domains" of temples that enumerate plots of smallholders were often administered by local state officials, just as some of the "normal domains" were under the charge of high government officials. Temple lands and revenues accruing from them were at the disposal of the king, both as head of the state and as the chief high priest.

There are a number of Ramessid texts that detail the collection and transport of grain revenues as income accruing to the state from both temples and individuals for storage in both temple and city granaries for later redistribution. These include the Turin Taxation Papyrus, Amiens Papyrus, Papyrus Louvre 3171, British Museum Papyrus 10447, the Turin Indictment Papyrus (Papyrus Turin 1887), the Gurob Fragments, Turin Papyrus 1882 (*verso*), and the texts from the *verso* of Papyrus Sallier IV. The Turin Taxation Papyrus exemplifies the overlap in the activities and jurisdiction of temple and civil authorities. It records the collection of grain from crown land, temples, and individuals, by the scribe of the necropolis, in partial payment of the overdue wages of the necropolis workmen, and the receipt of the grain by the mayor of Thebes and chantresses (*šmꜥyt*) of Amun for deposition in Theban granaries.

Not all taxpayers accepted responsibility for the taxes for which they were held liable. Papyrus Valençay I (c. reign of Ramesses XI) is a letter of complaint from Meron, mayor of Elephantine, to the chief taxation master, concerning taxes the mayor allegedly owes on crown land in his charge. Meron denies all responsibility, ascribing liability to persons described as *nmḥw*—"private persons" or "freemen"—"who pay gold to the treasury of pharaoh." Thus, mayors were not responsible for the collection of taxes from *nmḥw* who remitted their taxes directly. Meron's complaint was not unique. In a model letter (Papyrus Bologna 1094), a priest protests "the excessive monies" (literally, "silver") he was ordered to remit, saying, "It is not my due tax at all!" If the responsible party failed to remit his taxes, he stood to forfeit his property, as depicted in the Theban tomb of Menna. Those with no property to forfeit were sentenced to compulsory labor.

The fragmentary tax lists on the recto of the Royal Canon of Turin may have been records of deliveries of various levies to the treasury, the temple of Amun, or a royal residence from a variety of persons, groups of individuals, institutions, and towns. Technical terms for different types of exactions include *bꜣkw*, *šꜣyt*, *šdyt*, *ḥtri*, and *tp-ḏrt*. *Bꜣkw* ("works," "labor," or even "dues") here applies to taxes on products outside of the agricultural sector of the economy, including the products of fishermen, natron-workers, and mat-makers, paid in kind. The many occurrences of *tp-ḏrt* ("head-hand") suggest a tax obligation incumbent on various lower officials. *Šdyt* occurs in the phrase "the precise exaction." *Šꜣyt* ("dues") occurs in such phrases as "dues of the staff" and "the exact dues." Occurrences of the term *ḥtr/ḥtri* include "exact levy" and "the levy that is upon them."

The badly damaged Bilgai Stela, which concerns a chapel dedicated to Amun of Usermare Setepenre (Ramesses II), provides evidence of the zeal with which some administrators executed their duties. An administrator of the estate connected with the chapel proudly boasts to Theban officials: "I am an officer advantageous to his lord, paying [his] harvest-tax (*šmw*) in full and [his] dues (*šꜣyt*) in full. Great was my surplus of harvest-tax and dues, ten times greater than my [annual] levy (*ḥtri*) of *šmw* and *šꜣyt*." Also mentioned are payments of honey and wine, the latter described as "the [assessed] labor (*bꜣkw*) of my people."

Bꜣkw and *šꜣyt* also occur together in the Great Harris Papyrus (12a,1; 32a,7; 51b,3) in the headings to sections of the document that enumerate items of the income of the separate and independent estates of Amun, Re, and Ptah. The headings read: "Property (*ḥt*), dues (*šꜣyt*), and labor (*bꜣkw*) of the people of every staff (*sdmt*) of (temple name) which [Ramesses III] gave to their treasuries, storehouses, and granaries as their annual levy (*ḥtri*)." The list that follows provides a precise accounting of all the metals, materials, agricultural produce, birds and animals, and ships accruing to the god's estate as the obligation of all who labored for or on behalf of the estate. These endowments may have been made by Ramesses III to compensate the temples for their contributions to his costly military campaigns in terms of men, cattle, and other necessities.

In the autobiographical inscription of the high priest Amenhotpe (c. reign of Ramesses IX), the terms *šmw*, *šꜣyt*, and *bꜣkw* occur together and appear to signify the most important revenues payable to the state as taxes under the authority of the high priest: "The harvest-tax (*šmw*), dues (*šꜣyt*), and labor (*bꜣkw*) of the people of the house of Amun-Re, King of the Gods, shall be under your authority. . . ." Also mentioned is the rarely occurring *tp-ḏrt*, which the high priest is said to have caused to be delivered to the estate of Amun. Thus, by the end of the twentieth dynasty, the high priest of Amun—whose family occupied many of the highest offices of the state including chief taxing-master (*ꜥꜣ n št*)—had some authority over tax revenues.

The right of the state to demand human labor is reflected in the term *bꜣkw*, which can mean a person's "work" or "labor." There is also the term *bḥ*, mentioned in the Nauri Exemption Decree of Sety I to denote compulsory labor, specifically for cultivating and harvesting fields. *Bḥ* might also apply to the work of weavers of a state institution, as well as quarry workers and construction laborers. The Nauri Decree also mentions *brt* as a type of compulsory labor. *Brt* also occurs in a model letter (Papyrus Anastasi II) where the plight of a stablemaster's maidservant made to serve in the *bryt* "hired gang" (?) suggests some kind of compulsory labor. In the same text, the stablemaster's retainer labors in Troia (modern Turah), where limestone was quarried, possibly in fulfillment of the corvée.

The term *inw* is usually translated as "tribute"—that is, the obligatory contribution of subject foreign governments to the annual general levy. Ineni, architect of Thutmose I, refers to *"inw* of all foreign lands which His Majesty gave to the temple of Amun as an annual levy." Although *inw* had flowed into Egypt as far back as the Old Kingdom, references to it as a rich source of revenue multiply during the New Kingdom, when the conquests of warrior pharaohs brought more and more foreign territory under Egypt's sway. Foreign lands were increasingly treated as part of Egypt herself, and their towns as Egyptian cities with an obligation to contribute to the annual levy administered by mayors and other officials. *inw* might consist of silver, gold, lapis, precious stones, chariots, horses, and cattle, as well as people to labor as servants and serfs; however, the word can also denote the "gift" or "special addition" given by kings or nomarchs to towns, as in the case of the nomarch Kheti I's gift of an irrigation system to Asyut in the First Intermediate Period.

Third Intermediate Period and Late Period. For the Third Intermediate Period there is sparse documentation of taxation. The annual general levy is described, however, in a stela of Sheshonq I, founder of the twenty-second dynasty, that celebrates the king's offerings to the temple of Harsaphes in Herakleopolis. Sheshonq restored the annual levy for the daily ox-offering on the towns and villages of the Herakleopolitan nome after the cult had fallen into neglect. A perpetual annual "quota"(?) of the levy (*tp n ḥtr*) consisting of 365 oxen is identified as the responsibility of individual Herakleopolitan towns and officials. The system of provisioning the temple bears striking similarities to that employed by Solomon, a near contemporary of Sheshonq I, and suggests that the Hebrew king utilized the system long employed by Egyptian kings to maintain various institutions under government authority.

Another reference to taxation comes in the twenty-fifth dynasty Piya Stela in the context of the offer by Peftjawybast, Libyan ruler of Herakleopolis in Middle Egypt, of his allegiance to the conquering Kushite pharaoh. This inscription, from Piya's temple at Gebel Barkal in Nubia, pledges that Herakleopolis will be taxed for the benefit of the house of Piya. This is an example of the use of the general annual levy for the maintenance of royal residences.

When the Kushite pharaoh Taharqa was crowned at Memphis, he restored the temples of Kawa in Nubia dedicated to Amun-Re, giving them gifts of "the wives of the princes of Lower Egypt" and the "children of the princes of the Tjehenu" to function as temple servants. Thus, conquests in the Nile Delta may have brought Libyan and other Lower Egyptian captives to the service of a Kushite pharaoh, much as pharaohs of the New Kingdom brought their foreign war captives to Egypt as prisoners to be supported by the general annual levy.

The Louvre Stela of Psamtek I, founder of the twenty-sixth dynasty, provides evidence of the levy placed on officials of occupied foreign territories for the benefit of the royal residence; it may be compared with the taxing of Herakleopolis for the benefit of the house of Piya. Both texts recall passages in the Edict of Horemheb where certain levies supplied royal residences, including harems, and the nineteenth dynasty Gurob Fragments, where levies may have supplied the harem of Mi-wer.

The Naukratis Stela of Nektanebo I, founder of the thirtieth dynasty, documents a 10 percent tax levied on imports from the Aegean to Naukratis, a city in the western Delta, for the benefit of the temple of Neith at Sais. The Saite pharaoh Amasis had shrewdly confined the activities of Greek merchants to Naukratis to exclude them from Egyptian-controlled ports in the eastern Delta. Revenue from a 10 percent tax on profits from the Greek monopoly at Naukratis was also given to the temple of Neith as payment for daily offerings. The Ptolemaic "Famine Stela" from the island of Sehel, at the First Cataract of the Nile, attributed to the third dynasty pharaoh Djoser, also describes a transit tax of 10 percent. The stela claims that after a seven-year famine, Djoser gave Khnum of Elephantine the gift of a large tract of land in Lower Nubia subject to various taxes, which added value to the donation. A 10 percent transit tax is also mentioned as levied on all gold, ivory, timber, and other goods imported into Egypt from southern regions and on any persons accompanying them.

Greco-Roman Period. The conquest of Egypt by Alexander in 332 BCE put the power to levy taxes in Egypt into the hands of Kleomenes of Naukratis. With the death of Alexander in 323 BCE, the administration of Egypt came under the Greek general Ptolemy, founder of the Ptolemaic dynasty. The Ptolemaic kings, who styled themselves pharaohs, won the support of the ancient priesthoods with donations of land and other wealth, the building of new temples, and the restoration of old foundations. These were wise policies in light of periodic rebellions against the foreign rulers. These donations and building activities, however, required the raising of sizable tax revenues.

Rulers such as Ptolemy II Philadelphus made certain that the monarchy benefited from the lucrative concessions and monopolies that privileged temples enjoyed, as well as from protective tariffs. The contemporary Zenon Archives provide figures for the port of Pelusium in the eastern Delta which indicate that protective tariffs on such imports as wool, oil, and wine, ranging from 20 to 50 percent, generated sizable revenue. A tax on ferries, one of the oldest sources of revenue for nomarchs, also enriched the central government.

When Egypt came under Roman rule in the time of

Augustus, a complex array of old and new taxes levied on such items as land, persons, occupations and services, sales and transfers, real and personal property, and the transit of goods and people was exacerbated by an increase in the efficiency of the system of tax collection. This system provided ample opportunity for rapacious officials to gouge a population resentful of corrupt administration but powerless to alter it. Finally, in 313 CE, following on the administrative reforms of Diocletian, a new system of calculating and collecting tax revenue was introduced that brought Egypt closer to the administrative structure of the Roman Empire.

[*See also* Administration, *articles on* State Administration *and* Provincial Administration; Economy; Kingship; *and* Officials.]

BIBLIOGRAPHY

Allam, Shafik. "Some Remarks on the Trial of Mose." *Journal of Egyptian Archaeology* 75 (1989), 123–156.

Baer, Klaus. "The Low Price of Land in Ancient Egypt." *Journal of the American Research Center in Egypt* 1 (1962), 25–45.

Caminos, Ricardo A. *Late-Egyptian Miscellanies.* London, 1954.

Edgerton, William F. "The Nauri Decree of Seti I: A Translation and Analysis of the Legal Portion." *Journal of Near Eastern Studies* 6 (1947), 219–230.

Gaballa, G. A. *The Memphite Tomb-chapel of Mose.* Warminster, 1977.

Gardiner, Alan H. "The Inscription of Mes: A Contribution to the Study of Egyptian Judicial Procedure." (Untersuchungen zur Geschichte und Altertumskunde Ägyptens, 4,3.) Leipzig, 1905.

Gardiner, Alan H. "The Stela of Bilgai." *Zeitschrift für Ägyptische Sprache und Altertumskunde* 50 (1912), 49–57.

Gardiner, Alan H. "Ramesside Texts Relating to the Taxation and Transport of Corn." *Journal of Egyptian Archaeology* 27 (1941), 19–73.

Gardiner, Alan H. "A Protest Against Unjustified Tax-Demands." *Revue d'Égyptologie* 6 (1951), 115–133.

Gardiner, Alan H. "Some Reflections on the Nauri Decree." *Journal of Egyptian Archaeology* 38 (1952), 24–33.

Gardiner, Alan H. *The Wilbour Papyrus.* 3 vols. Oxford, 1941–1948. Vol. 4, *Index*, by Raymond O. Faulkner. Oxford, 1952.

Gasse, Annie. *Données nouvelles administratives et sacerdotales sur l'organisation du domaine d'Amon, XXe–XXIe dynasties.* Cairo, 1988.

Goedicke, Hans. *Königliche Dokumente aus dem Alten Reich.* Wiesbaden, 1967.

Hayes, William C. "Royal Decrees from the Temple of Min at Coptus." *Journal of Egyptian Archaeology* 32 (1946), 3–23.

Helck, Wolfgang. "Abgaben und Steuern." In *Lexikon der Ägyptologie*, 1.1:3–12. Wiesbaden, 1972.

Janssen, Jac. J. "Prolegomena to the Study of Egypt's Economic History during the New Kingdom." *Studien zur Altägyptischen Kultur* 3 (1975), 127–185.

Janssen, Jac. J. "The Role of the Temple in the Egyptian Economy During the New Kingdom." In *State and Temple Economy in the Ancient Near East*, edited by E. Lipiński, vol. 2, pp. 505–515. Leuven, 1979.

Janssen, Jac. J. "Agrarian Administration in Egypt during the Twentieth Dynasty." *Bibliotheca Orientalis* 43 (1986), 351–366.

Katary, Sally L. D. *Land Tenure in the Ramesside Period.* London, 1989.

Kruchten, J.-M. *Le Décret d'Horemheb: Traduction, commentaire épigraphique, philologique et institutionel.* Brussels, 1981.

Menu, Bernadette. *Le régime juridique des terres et du personnel attaché à la terre dans le papyrus Wilbour.* Lille, 1970.

Menu, Bernadette. *Recherches sur l'historie juridique, économique et sociale de l'ancienne Égypte.* Versailles, 1982.

Quirke, Stephen. *The Administration of Egypt in the Late Middle Kingdom.* New Malden, 1990.

Redford, Donald B. "Studies in Relations Between Palestine and Egypt during the First Millennium B. C., I: The Taxation System of Solomon." In *Studies in the Ancient Palestinian World*, edited by J. W. Wevers and D. B. Redford, pp. 141–156. Toronto, 1972.

Smither, Paul C. "A Tax Assessor's Journal of the Middle Kingdom." *Journal of Egyptian Archaeology* 27 (1941), 74–76.

Strudwick, Nigel. *The Administration of Egypt in the Old Kingdom: The Highest Titles and Their Holders.* London, 1985.

Vleeming, Sven P. *Papyrus Reinhardt: An Egyptian Land List from the Tenth Century* B.C. Berlin, 1993.

Wente, Edward F. *Late Egyptian Letters.* Studies in Ancient Oriental Civilization, 33. Chicago, 1967.

SALLY L. D. KATARY

TECHNOLOGY AND ENGINEERING. Since the decipherment of hieroglyphs, Egyptologists have delineated the religion and customs of the ancient Egyptians, as well as their economic development. The mathematical level of the ancient Egyptians, basically a simple trigonometry, is apparent from a few documents containing mensuration problems. The relationship of astronomy to Egyptian religion, and the derivation of time-keeping and calendars from it, is relatively well understood. Insight into their technology and engineering, however, has been provided primarily by their monuments, ruins, and artifacts. The available evidence indicates that they were a practical people, very much directed to meeting daily needs. There is little confirmation, however, that they could also pursue the more abstract theoretical knowledge of science. The development of technology and engineering in Egypt was consequently rooted in practicality. Only the broadest outlines of these changes can be sketched here, by following the origin and spread of agriculture throughout the Nile Valley and the Delta, noting the structural use of mud bricks and stone, determining their capabilities in metalworking, and observing their use of wood, pottery, and ceramics.

Agricultural Origins in the Nile Valley and the Delta. The economic history of ancient Egypt has been said to be characterized as one continuous ecological adjustment to the available water supply, in an attempt to intensify productivity by increasing land area and use (Butzer 1976). Agriculture there is first known from about the fifth millennium BCE, at Merimde Beni Salama, to the northwest of present-day Cairo; in the Faiyum of northern Egypt; and in the Badarian communities to its south (Hassan 1997). Prior to 5000 BCE, there was possibly some domestication of local animals (e.g., cattle) and seed grasses; but the real beginnings of agriculture include the introduction of emmer wheat, barley, and herd animals (sheep, goats, pigs, cattle) from the Near East into Egypt.

In Predynastic Egypt, "natural irrigation" resulted from the annual flooding and draining of the Nile floodplain, providing sufficient crops to meet population demands. With an increase of population, however, an increase in food productivity could only be achieved with additional, or "artificial" irrigation, which would have increased the available arable cropland and given some water control, permitting a second or third crop during some years.

Artificial irrigation technology throughout the pharaonic period was geared toward the regulation of the annual "normal" Nile floods. The ability to control the effects of low or deficit flood levels was limited by the lack of an effective water-transport system; most of this time, water was hauled manually, using shoulder yokes—hardly sufficient for more than local horticultural-type plots. Even the late introduction of the *shaduf* water-lifting lever during the New Kingdom provided a practical use only in the local horticultural context. Butzer noted (1976) that such controls during the yearly flood stage consisted of improving natural levees; clearing natural overflow channels; damming natural drainage channels with earthen dams and gates; subdividing flood basins into smaller units; and controlling water access to those units. Although not centralized for the whole of Egypt, such efforts appear to have been locally administered from Predynastic times. Perennial irrigation and relatively sustainable cropping was a very late development, possible only after the introduction of the *saqiya*, an animal-turned water wheel, first used in the Faiyum during Ptolemaic times. The first archaeological evidence for artificial irrigation is a scene on the mace head attributed to the Predynastic King "Scorpion," dated to about 3100 BCE, which shows him ceremonially cutting an irrigation ditch. Major land-reclamation schemes, however, were probably first attempted only during Middle Kingdom times by the twelfth dynasty pharaoh, Amenemhet III, in the Faiyum. Such irrigation technology could not cope with excessive or deficit flood levels.

Because irrigation was only controlled locally, trends to higher or lower floods would have initiated significant modifications to the immediate topography, with concomitant economic pressures that might have affected the local political hierarchy. Some pressures might have spread enough to affect the central authority of the pharaoh. That the social fabric could be undone at such times is evident from the examples of both the mass deaths and the mass plundering and pillaging by gangs of looters, as attested in various documented famines. When such conditions lasted for several generations, life along the Nile was nothing less than brutal. Deficit floods were most probably the ultimate check on population expansion in dynastic Egypt. Population density appears never to have exceeded about three million through this period; it did not surpass five million until late Ptolemaic times (undoubtedly the result of significantly improved agriculture and trade arrangements).

Although irrigation technology improved throughout the pharaonic period, evidence for innovations in other agricultural methods seems to be lacking. For example, surviving tomb scenes all intimate that seeds were always broadcast onto unprepared (unplowed) soil. The use of the plow (for breaking, turning, and aerating) and the hoe (for weeding and cultivating) appears to have been limited only to drier locales or horticultural plots. Scenes with plows and hoes from various historical periods show the same basic wooden designs throughout dynastic times; surviving examples tend to verify a lack of design initiative.

Naturally, the fertile silt deposited as topsoil by the Nile floods would have required some preparation and added fertilizer in land areas higher than or beyond the floodplain periphery, because of nitrogenous losses. There is, however, no direct evidence that the Egyptians developed a systematic use of fertilizer; possibly, the keeping of dovecotes, a practice continued in some present-day Egyptian villages, provided a natural fertilizer in their collected bird droppings. Silt-laden topsoil would not have been depleted of nitrogen if the nitrogen-depleting grain and nitrogen-binding legume crops had been rotated; but nitrogen-binding fodder crops are not explicitly mentioned until Ptolemaic times and it is doubtful that the Egyptians recognized their practicality or potential as nitrogen-binding agents. The restoration of irrigated land by allowing it to lie fallow also does not seem to have been practiced in Egypt. The reliance was on fresh soil deposition by the annual flooding.

Agriculture in Egypt can therefore be summarized as a winter cultivation largely confined to the flood basins and dependent on the annual flood irrigation. Irrigation technology was rudimentary and was applied locally, rather than at the national level; this technology was designed to enhance acreage and winter-crop yield, to reduce the effects of short-term flood variability, and to protect settlements and fields from flood damage. It could neither cope with excessive or deficit floods nor with long-term trends of decreasing flood volume. The storage and distribution of food was administered for the most part by the nomes (regional governorships), through local temples that controlled vast estates, or through the royal residences by the pharaoh.

An important adjunct to food production was the making of beer and wine. In addition to their use as beverages, both were also frequently used as mortuary offerings, libations in religious ceremonies, and as a constituent in medicines. Beer residues have been detected in Predynastic and later period jars; analyses of such residues, studies of tomb scenes and models, and comparisons with the manufacture of present-day peasant beer, indicate that the ancient Egyptians understood well the key steps in brewing beer: the conversion of the starch of a cereal grain into sugar and the alteration of that sugar into alcohol and carbon dioxide by natural (biotic) fermentation (Lucas 1962). The cereal grain most commonly used appears to have been the barley *Hordeum distichum,* a shorter two-rowed version distinct from the modern, longer two- or six-rowed barley (*Hordeum vulgare*). The cereal grain known as emmer wheat (*Triticum dicoccum*), having a two-grained spikelet, was also used as a starch source. Both cereals have been found in dried residues from beer jars and from dried and exhausted grain left after mashing. A present-day beer made by Nubians from barley bread, strongly leavened millet bread, or wheat bread, called *bouza,* seems to be a close approximation to the ancient drink, a thin gruel-like concoction averaging about 7 percent alcohol content.

Wines in ancient Egypt were produced from grapes, dates, the myxa fruit, pomegranates, and the sap of the dom palm tree. The most frequently depicted in tomb scenes and found in wine jars is that made from grapes. Since tomb scenes do show dark-colored—blue and violet—as well as red, pink, green, and white grapes, it may be inferred that both white and red varietals were produced; however, there are no specific written references to the colors of wine. The depth of wine color is a function of whether and how long colored grape skins have been included in the fermentation process. For example, even the darkest grapes will produce only white wines if the skins have been strained out during juice production. The docket labels on many surviving wine jars form an important source of study, because they are not unlike modern wine labels, giving the vintner, vineyard, quality of wine, date of production, and reigning pharaoh (Lesko 1977). The latter two items sometimes form the only means of determining the length of a pharaoh's reign if a statistically significant sample of jar dockets have survived.

Structural Engineering. The first monumental architecture of the Early Dynastic period occurred at Hierakonpolis, Abydos, and Memphis—an indication of the presence of a viable, multitiered economy. The monumental building programs of the Old Kingdom pharaohs required large-scale labor input. Consequently, these programs probably contributed to the establishment of a stable social order because they involved not only *in situ* construction but also the large-scale transportation of agricultural products and materiel. Dieter Arnold (1991) has noted that the economic effects of this organizational effort to work and move stone permeated nearly the whole of the three thousand years of ancient Egypt. The zenith was reached with the New Kingdom constructions of many temples, palaces, massive obelisks, and gigantic statues.

The use of stone as a building material appeared late in Egyptian history. Predynastic structures were first made of dried reeds and twigs that were later plastered with clay. The first use of sun-dried mud bricks also dates to the Late Predynastic period (still commonly used today). Houses in villages and towns were all made of mud bricks coated with plaster; only the doorposts and jambs of upper-class houses were lined with stone. Stone was also used for support bases of pillars made of wood. Even pharaohs' palaces were usually made of mud bricks. The prime surviving example of urban planning is the New Kingdom city of Akhetaten, near the present-day village of El-Amarna. There all the temples, palaces, and houses of the bureaucracy, as well as those of the peasants, were made of mud bricks. The outer-wall plaster coatings of gypsum were of two types: a white surface, covered with polychrome artwork (Smith 1970); and a light brown or tan surface, mimicking the appearance of limestone (Wells 1989). In its pristine completed condition, the city must therefore have been an imposing sight.

The earliest uses of stone on a small scale all date to the first dynasty. By the third dynasty, increased use of stone is evident, mostly in mortuary complexes. The archetype of that dynasty is Djoser's Step Pyramid, the adjacent buildings, and the enclosure wall. This architectural complex at Saqqara represents an unparalleled transition in the use of stone for building purposes. Yet careful examination shows the still tentative nature of the construction, as for example in the use of support columns undetached from their wall matrix. These columns are little more than bas-reliefs in the walls—portraits of reed bundles and lotus plants frozen in stone. The principal types of stones used in ancient Egypt were limestone, granite, sandstone, basalt, calcite, and quartzite. Many quarries that were used to supply these building materials still exist, and studies of them have provided much information on the ancient Egyptian ability to cut and move large blocks.

No detailed architectural plans of houses, temples, or tombs have yet been discovered; however, there are a number of surviving sketch plans, or drafts, of architectural elements of such buildings on paving slabs, ostraca, and wooden panels. Some contain measurements, as though they were on-the-spot orders issued by an overseer, which were to be discarded after completion of the depicted task. The chief measuring unit was the cubit, which seems to have averaged about 52.5 centimeters (20 inches) in length (Arnold 1991). Measuring rods in cubit multiples—the square, the square level, the *bay,* and the *merkhet*—are the principal surviving surveyor's instruments. The square was used as it is today, for constructing walls at right angles. The square level, an A-frame with a plumbbob attached at the vertex of the A, was used to maintain level walls or foundations. The *bay* was a notched palm rib, probably used for sighting in the manner of a modern theodolite. The *merkhet* was essentially a plumb-bob device of various shapes. The most common was an L-shape with the bob hanging from the short vertical arm. The Egyptian sun clock evolved from this device by the addition of a T-bar to the short arm, for the casting of a shadow along the longer arm held horizontal as the sun moved across the sky, a natural development since the sun dial needed to be kept level.

Arnold (1991) reports that modern field tests suggest that a difference in height of about 1 centimeter could be recognized, albeit with some difficulty, at a distance of 40 to 45 meters (131 to 148 feet) using the simple square level. The accuracy in the leveling of the Great Pyramid indicates about 2 centimeters of difference in height between the casing stones at the foot of the pyramid on the northern and southern sides. This result is remarkable, considering the length of the sides at about 230 meters (541 feet), and there is a central bedrock mound about 7 meters (24 feet) high obstructing the diagonal sightlines. Thus field tests suggest that about three sequential forward/reverse measurements, at intervals of roughly 80 meters (262 feet), were made along the edge base length to level one side. Although it has been suggested that water-filled trenches were used to level the foundations of the Giza pyramids, that does not seem likely. Transporting the large quantities of water necessary to fill the trenches, uphill, over the long distances from the river, would have been difficult; and the water probably would have been absorbed into the surroundings before adequate measurements could have been made.

The cutting and transport of large stone blocks weighing tens or hundreds of tons does not appear to have imposed an insurmountable problem for the Egyptians, for whom time was a cheap commodity. The analysis of quarry marks indicates that blocks were cut with either copper chisels or stone implements, depending on the hardness of the stone; surviving small sledges and some tomb wall scenes show that they were moved overland or by water. The great engineering feat of the eighteenth dynasty (New Kingdom) was the cutting and overland transport, for a distance of some 700 kilometers (435 miles), of the blocks for the Colossi of Memnon—the seated statues of Amenhotpe III positioned at the entrance to his mortuary temple in Western Thebes. Each block weighed about 700 tons. The peak in stone transport, however, was reached by Ramesses II in the next dynasty, with the positioning of many colossal statues and obelisks around the country, including the 1,000-ton monolith of himself at the Ramesseum.

One of the most interesting of surviving structures is the Old Kingdom valley temple of Khafre's pyramid, considered extraordinary because of the polished calcite floors, red granite walls, and the four-sided, monolithic columns and lintels. These aspects alone would rank it among the finest of the ancient Egyptian constructions. Yet a special design element lends it unique character. Apart from two entrances into the temple, at the northern and southern extents of its eastern side, the building was originally completely enclosed and roofed with five terraces, the largest of which covered the main Hall of Columns. Consequently, without special provision, the interior of the temple would have been completely dark, making various ritual ceremonies impossible. The architect did, in fact, provide for natural sunlight illumination of the interior by a very clever design that utilized fourteen polished Egyptian alabaster (calcite) reflecting surfaces (as mirrors), with window slots cut into the walls at the roofline of the Hall of Columns in clerestory fashion. These surfaces would have scattered sunlight diffusely into the window slots and onto the ceiling (providing an illumination similar to modern fluorescent lighting behind milk-white Plexiglas panels). Predating Frank Lloyd Wright's indirect ceiling illumination by more than forty-five hundred years, this design feature must be ranked in the forefront of Egyptian technological achievements.

Metallurgy. The primary ancient Egyptian metals were copper, lead, gold, silver, iron, and tin. Four main alloys were also used: (1) bronze, a mixture of copper and tin; (2) a copper-lead alloy; (3) electrum, a native alloy, a mix of gold and silver; and (4) brass, very late in Egyptian history, a mix of copper and zinc.

Copper. The earliest known use of metal in Egypt was for copper beads, borers, and pins (found in tombs of the Badarian period). Some ornaments and small implements, such as needles and tweezers, also date to Predynastic times. Weapons of copper are known from Late Predynastic times and, in use during the first dynasties, were heavy axheads, adzes, knives, daggers, spears, chisels, ewers, and basins. Many copper vanity mirrors from all periods are known—some few mirrors were made of silver (Lilyquist 1979).

The well-known sixth dynasty statues of Pepy I (one small and one larger than life size) were made of beaten copper plates—they are the oldest known metal statues in Egypt. One of the most interesting examples of beaten copper, however, is the section of copper pipe found by Ludwig Borchardt (1910) in one of the causeway drains from the fifth dynasty mortuary temple of Sahure's pyramid. Along with Khafre's "alabaster [calcite] mirrors" of the previous dynasty, this unusual discovery must be ranked among the most innovative of ancient Egyptian architectural practices.

Although copper occurs as a native metal and was worked in the Paleolithic and Mesolithic like any other stone, the production of hardened copper was an Egyptian discovery undoubtedly related to their fabrication of copper weapons and edged tools. After such implements had been cast in molten copper, the cutting edges would have been cooled, then hammered for further shaping and thinning. Hammering produces a harder metal; if hammered too much, copper becomes brittle. Eventually, Egyptians discovered that reheating the copper for a short period restored the hardness, a process called annealing or tempering.

Bronze. The introduction of bronze into Egypt is presumed to have been from Mesopotamia or one of the other Near Eastern countries. There are a few bronze objects from the Old Kingdom of uncertain provenance or date. The beginning of the Bronze Age in Egypt is therefore usually attributed to Middle Kingdom times, from which there are a number of well-authenticated bronze items and tools. The hardness of the bronze alloy can also be increased by a hammering-annealing process. From the eighteenth dynasty onward, Egyptian use of bronze is extensive and, in later times, bronze was largely used for making statuettes. The addition of lead to copper (and later to bronze) seems to have resulted from their discovery that the melt was easier to cast, a desirable property in the production of statuary.

Gold. Metalworking in gold is almost as old as the Egyptians' use of copper. Small items of gold have been found in Predynastic graves. Native gold and gold ores were most often from alluvial sands and gravels or from veins in quartz rock of the Eastern Desert, between the Nile and the Red Sea. The only surviving ancient Egyptian map (a papyrus in the Museo Egitzio in Turin, Italy) dates to the twentieth dynasty reign of Ramesses IV (c.1150 BCE), showing the location of a gold-bearing region in the Wadi Hammamat of the Eastern Desert. Although Egyptian goldsmiths were fine craftsmen with a high degree of skill, it is of interest that they do not seem to have purified or refined gold until long after the close of the pharaonic period. According to data quoted by Lucas (1962), proportional variability of gold in Egyptian dynastic jewelry (70.8–99.8 percent) is similar to that shown by assays of gold samples from modern Egyptian mines (76.0–90.3 percent); such data indicate that ancient Egyptians worked with varying grades of native gold rather than refining it. Nevertheless, the gold was so skillfully worked that few modern practices in goldworking were unknown to them.

Electrum. The native alloy of gold and silver, electrum, was used in Egypt from Early Dynastic times through the end of the pharaonic period. Its silver content varies from about 20 to 30 percent, some as high as 40 percent. The more silver present, the lighter yellow the alloy appears. Electrum is harder than either gold or silver, so its primary use was for jewelry that had to withstand wear. In some instances, it was used for overlaying obelisks. The capstones of some pyramids may also have been made of electrum, with a low silver content, so that gold's bright, deep-yellow color could predominate.

Iron. The most controversial question about the Iron Age in Egypt is, how early were Egyptians able to smelt and produce iron implements for practical purposes? Iron occurs on Earth both as a native metal (from terrestrial sources and from meteorites) and in mineral ores. Meteoritic iron has a high nickel content, which makes it possible for analysts to distinguish it from any other iron. Iron minerals—hematite, magnetite, and limonite—are plentiful in Egypt and, as early as Predynastic times, all have been made into beads, small amulets, and statuettes. Although iron was worked in this way, the intentional smelting of iron from mineral ore was probably a very late development in Egypt. In fact, native iron cannot be easily shaped and manipulated by beating in the cold state, as can native copper or even bronze. The earliest iron implement known is the iron dagger found on the body of Tutankhamun (eighteenth dynasty), presumed to be a gift from a king of the Middle East (where the Iron Age had already begun). Because no large similar tool or weapon has yet been discovered for an earlier or immediately later Egyptian dynasty, the Iron Age in Egypt is usually ascribed to later times, around the twenty-fifth dynasty, when such tools began to proliferate. [*See* Iron.]

A controversy also surrounds a piece of an iron plate (26 × 8.6 × 0.3–0.5 cm/10.25 × 3.25 × 0.13–0.25 in.) found in a joint, in the interior of the southern airshaft exit of Khufu's pyramid at Giza, by J. R. Hill in 1837, after he had blasted off two tiers of overlying stone. The fragment is not of meteoritic iron, since it does not contain nickel (an elemental component of meteoritic iron). From a modern chemical analysis of a bit of this fragment, El Gayer and Jones (1989) concluded, however, that the metal object was indigenous to the fourth dynasty; the authors stated that the piece had been manufactured by a comparatively low temperature, solid-state-reduction of iron oxide with charcoal, which produced a porous, spongy mass of iron metal that had never passed through the molten state. It was then hammered into a number of thin layers. This description is not inconsistent with the metal-production technology of the Old Kingdom. For example, from Old Kingdom tomb scenes, Scheel (1985–1989) has described the use of charcoal fires and ovens; the specially designed clay blowpipes for elevating temperatures; the smelting of metal from ores; the refining process; the reheating of metal bars and ingots to glow with specific colors that indicate the relative ease of hammering into a variety of shapes; the hammering of the metal pieces into thin layers and plates; and the polishing of the finished products with various sizes of grit, leather, and polishing cloths. In the tomb scenes, the metals were copper, gold, silver, and electrum; in later periods, also lead, tin, and bronze. Although iron was not specifically recognized in any tomb inscriptions, if that metal had been available from some source, then these scenes show that working it could have resulted in a piece not unlike El Gayer and Jones's description. The lack of other such hammered pieces is difficult to explain. Craddock and Lang (1993), two British Museum metallurgists, dismissed this analysis primarily because El Gayer and Jones had reported the presence of gold on the outer layer; their own electron microscope scanning and X-ray fluorescence spectroscopic examination of both the bit examined by El Gayer and Jones and the larger fragment from which it came did not detect any traces of gold. They concluded that although the fragment exhibited a form of primitive metalworking, it was unnecessary to suppose that it was even of pharaonic origin, and they ascribed its production to post-medieval times. Although the sworn statement by J. R. Hill of the circumstances where he found the piece seems straightforward, precluding accidental or intentional insertion at some later date, the situation may never be definitively settled.

Wood, Pottery, Ceramics, and Glass. Large-scale use of wood for Egyptian construction depended mostly on imported timber, of better quality and larger size than available locally. The most famous surviving examples are the solar boats of Khufu made from the cedars of Lebanon. One such boat, found in 1954, in an east–west-oriented boat pit, consisted of more than twelve hundred pieces, measures 45 meters (145 feet) in length, and took nearly two decades to reconstruct. The second still lies disassembled, in a neighboring boat pit beside the Great Pyramid at Giza.

Woodworking and joinery were special skills that could not have developed until after suitable metal tools were available. From local woods—acacia, fruit wood, willow—a number of statues, carved panels, doors, and tomb furniture date to the Old Kingdom. Cedar coffins and canopic chests, as well as ebony boxes, date to the Middle Kingdom. Numerous wooden objects, furniture, boxes, gaming boards, bows, and chariots came from the tomb of Tutankhamun and other New Kingdom tombs. The shrines covering the sarcophagus of Tutankhamun were of wood covered by gesso, a type of plaster, overlain with gold. An unusual aspect of Egyptian woodworking was the development of patchwork joinery, because of the local lack of large straight planks—the trees of the Nile Valley were small and sparse. Irregular pieces were joined by means of dowels, flat tongues, and cramps. Metal nails were rarely used until the New Kingdom. The skillful use of veneer and inlay to cover inferior and patchwork woods was also practiced in all periods. In building construction, wood was limited to beams that provided lateral wall support or, sometimes, the vertical support of roofs in elite housing. Wood was also used for sledges and similar transport devices that aided the movement of large stone blocks.

Clay. In Egypt, the manipulation of clay into pottery vessels of various shapes dates to Neolithic times. Clay was also used to model small figures of animals and people in Predynastic times. The kneading, shaping, drying, and baking of clay into pots was portrayed in tomb scenes and in some wooden models of workshops. The introduction of the potters' wheel from the Near East is usually ascribed to the Old Kingdom; its use is illustrated in a fifth dynasty tomb scene, so it may have been in use even earlier. Categorized in considerable detail are the methods of manufacture, the materials, shapes, thicknesses, degree of firing, and surface decorations of many Egyptian wares. This work has enabled archaeologists to establish the provenance and dates of such pieces.

An interesting example of the many fragments of pottery found scattered at numerous sites in Egypt is a part of the neck of a water pot from Tell el-Amarna. Four fingerprints from the left hand of a potter can be seen on the inside. Although the ancient site is covered by potsherds from many periods, this piece is indigenous to the time of Nefertiti, because it is similar in material, thickness, and slip to broken pieces that can be seen in the matrix of many of the mud bricks used in constructing the houses there in her time.

Glaze. The development of vitreous glaze is also an early craft in Egypt, dating to Badarian times, when small soapstone (steatite) objects were covered by it. Later, in Predynastic times, the glazing of powdered quartz objects was used, which developed into the extensive Egyptian industry of faience—important in all periods, especially in the production of amulets, votive objects, *ushabtis*, and the like. Although faience has been particularly associated with Egyptian craftsmen it probably originated in Mesopotamia around the fifth millennium BCE, to appear in Egypt as the result of trade or invasions. The use of glaze on other materials was also common, such as the blue vitreous glaze on plastered ceilings in the Amarna housing.

Glass. The production of pure glass, as opposed to glaze from which it is derived, was a development of the early New Kingdom in Egypt. It may not have been a pure Egyptian invention, because trade relations with the Near East suggest more glass there than in Egypt. Objects have also been unearthed in Egyptian tombs that have glass jewels of both the Egyptian and Near Eastern styles—indicating the presence of Near Eastern craftsmen in Egypt. Lilyquist and Brill (1993) have presented some detailed compositional analyses of both glasses.

Conclusion. This brief survey of the development of technology and engineering in Egypt has focused on the practical necessities that led to some remarkable inventions, techniques, or skills. Most were used to promote the larger-than-life importance of the god-king to society; others to enhance the enjoyment of life, whether that be for the smaller proportion of the wealthier or the larger proportion of poorer inhabitants of the Nile Valley.

[*See also* Agriculture; Architecture; Bricks and Brick Architecture; Bronze; Ceramics; Copper; Glass; Gold; Iron; Leather; Silver; Stoneworking; Tools; *and* Woodworking.]

BIBLIOGRAPHY

Arnold, Dieter. *Building in Egypt: Pharaonic Stone Masonry.* New York, 1991. The best available modern treatment of the subject.

Borchardt, Ludwig. *Das Grabdenkmal des Königs Sahu-re.* Leipzig, 1910. The excavation report.

Butzer, Karl W. *Early Hydraulic Civilization in Egypt: A Study in Cultural Ecology.* Chicago, 1976. A dry, but thorough exposition on the subject.

Craddock, P. T., and J. Lang. "Gizeh Iron Revisited." *Journal of Historical Metallurgy* 27.2 (1993), 57–59.

Edwards, I. E. S. *The Pyramids of Egypt.* Rev. ed. Harmondsworth, 1993. The final edition of this classic work; the best treatment of the subject in English.

El Gayer, El Sayed, and M. P. Jones. "Metallurgical Investigation of an Iron Plate Found in 1837 in the Great Pyramid at Gizeh, Egypt." *Journal of Historical Metallurgy* 23.2 (1989), 75–83.

Hassan, Fekri. "The Wealth of the Land." In *Ancient Egypt,* edited by David P. Silverman. New York, 1997.

Hölscher, Uvo. *Das Grabdenkmal des Königs Chephren.* Leipzig, 1912. The excavation report.

Lesko, Leonard H. *King Tut's Wine Cellar.* Berkeley, 1977.

Lilyquist, Christine. *Ancient Egyptian Mirrors from the Earliest Times through the Middle Kingdom.* Münchner Ägyptologische Studien, 27. Munich, 1979. The surviving mirrors in various Egyptian museum collections; some study of shape and sizes.

Lilyquist, C., R. H. Brill, et al. *Studies in Early Egyptian Glass.* New York, 1993. The surviving glass objects in museum collections; some study of composition.

Lucas, A. *Ancient Egyptian Materials and Industries.* 4th ed., rev. and enl. by J. R. Harris. London, 1962. This postmortem revision of Lucas's work by J. R. Harris is one of the most detailed expositions available on materials in engineering technology of the ancient Egyptians.

Scheel, Bernd. *Egyptian Metalworking and Tools.* Aylesbury, England, 1989. More detailed treatment is available in three German articles entitled, "Studien zum Metallhandwerk im Alten Ägypten," in the journal *Studien zur altägyptischen Kultur,* 12 (1985), 117–177; 13 (1986), 181–205; 14 (1987), 247–264. The first covers material from Old Kingdom tombs; the second, from Middle Kingdom tombs; the third, from the New Kingdom and Late period.

Smith, R. W. "Computer Helps Scholars Re-create an Egyptian Temple." *National Geographic* 138 (1970), 634–655. A photographic and descriptive article on reconstructing a wall of the Aten temple of Akhenaten at Karnak; the illustration on pp. 646–647, of polychrome artwork on a white background, may be like many of the buildings at Akhetaten. Areas of white gypsum coating the mud bricks of Akhenaten's mortuary temple can still be seen.

Wells, R. A. "The Amarna M,X,K Boundary Stelae Date: *Hwt-itn* Ceremonial Altar Initial Results of a New Survey." *Studien zur Altägyptischen Kultur* 16 (1989), 289–327. Presents an engineering survey

study of part of Akhenaten's mortuary temple at Akhetaten and comments on nearby mud-brick structures.

RONALD A. WELLS

TEFNUT. In the tradition of the city of Heliopolis in the Nile Delta, the goddess Tefnut and her twin brother Shu were the offspring of Re-Atum and comprised the first generation of the Ennead. As a deity, Tefnut remains a vague figure and has little myth associated with her. The meaning of her name (*Tfnt*) is dubious, although there is a slight possibility that it was derived from the verb *tfn* ("to rise"). Tefnut's function is ambiguous, but as the twin of Shu she may have been a feminine deity of the air, balancing the similar masculine function of her brother and spouse and assisting him to support the sky. If this was her earliest significance, one might suggest that her function of personifying the moist air was a balance to that of Shu, who personified the dry air. Hence, Tefnut was more a mythologization of a theological concept, or a cosmic function, than a hypostatic deity.

In Heliopolitan tradition, Tefnut and Shu engendered Geb (Earth) and Nut (Sky), the two complementary elements of the cosmic structure. This relationship was more than a genealogical connection, for it meant that the abstract signification of Shu and Tefnut as the air evolved into a more concrete expression in the "tangible" deities Geb and Nut. Tefnut and Shu may thus be seen not simply as personifications of parts of the cosmos, but as integral elements upon which creation depended. In the later Memphite tradition, Tefnut was identified with the tongue of Ptah and became an instrument of divine creativity. Tefnut's association with Ptah is reflected in the temple at Hibis, where in front of the seated Ptah appear two *ba*-birds labeled Shu and Tefnut. Such a portrayal is not the iconography of popular belief but is symbolic of the theological function of the figures depicted.

Tefnut's antiquity is evident in her appearance in the Old Kingdom Pyramid Texts, but the Middle Kingdom Coffin Texts stress an important development in her signification. At an early stage she became identified with the goddess Maat, the principle of eternal order. This identification is expressed in Spell 80 of the Coffin Texts when Atum states, "Tefnut is my living daughter . . . Maat is her name." Atum is also described as kissing his daughter Maat "so that he may rise every day . . . so that the god may be born." Such a statement provides evidence of the central spiritual importance of the concept of Tefnut/Maat within the Egyptian theological synthesis.

Tefnut was frequently depicted as a lioness or a human female with the head of a lioness, sometimes wearing the solar disk and the *uraeus*. The solar function thus suggested was expressed in the myth that she and Shu received the sun god Re as he was reborn each morning. In her aspect as guardian of Re and of the pharaoh, she was also depicted as the *uraeus* alone. At times she was also said to be the wife of Thoth, a tradition connected with a legend of Tefnut's flight to Nubia, which states that she was brought back by Shu and Thoth, after which she became the wife of one of them. Although this tradition testifies to the flexibility of Egyptian myth, it appears to be a later reinterpretation of an original myth.

BIBLIOGRAPHY

Allen, James P. *Genesis in Egypt: The Philosophy of Ancient Egyptian Creation Accounts.* Yale Egyptological Studies, 2. New Haven, 1988. Contains some very interesting and useful interpretations of the nature and function of Tefnut.

Ions, Veronica. *Egyptian Mythology.* 2d ed., 1968. Contains a number of interesting references to Tefnut. The author does not undertake a detailed interpretation, but provides a good detailed account of the goddess.

Shirun-Grumach, I. "Remarks on the Goddess Maat," in *Pharaonic Egypt: The Bible and Christianity*, edited by Sarah Israelit-Groll, pp. 173–201. Jerusalem, 1985. pp. 173–201. A very fine study of Tefnut in her identification with Maat. Especially useful for its translation of relevant Egyptian texts.

VINCENT ARIEH TOBIN

TELL ED-DABʿA. *See* Dabʿa, Tell ed-.

TELL EL-AMARNA. *See* Amarna, Tell el-.

TELL EL-MASKHUTA. *See* Pithom.

TELL EL-YAHUDIYYA. *See* Yahudiyya, Tell el-.

TEMPLES. Egyptian temples existed from the middle of the fourth millennium BCE at the latest. According to tradition, the earliest were in the shape of reed huts. The last Egyptian temple built was a complex of buildings on Philae which ceased to be used in the mid-sixth century CE. After this, the existing structures were used as residences, vandalized or destroyed as pagan reminders, or exploited as quarries. However, the razing of temples for the last reason was already common in pharaonic times—to make room for a new building, to remodel a temple facility, or merely to reuse the materials on another site. Thus, out of the thousands of temples that once existed, only a fraction have been preserved for us. Most of these in exist today outline; the rest are almost all ruins, and only a few are intact to some extent. The extant temples are predominantly from the last millennium of Egyptian history, the Greco-Roman period (fourth century BCE to sixth century CE).

Egyptian temples are first and foremost objects of study for architectural and art history. They are also useful in efforts to reconstruct Egyptian religion and the history of the Egyptian state.

Egyptian temples were mostly erected by the state, at the head of which stood the pharaoh. Thus, the temples had a political function, which was expressed in both images and texts. In the foreground, because it was directly visible in the decoration, was the function of communication with the gods. Therefore, the temples are places of religious practice, though strongly influenced by political considerations. Just as the temples were state institutions, Egyptian religion was a state religion. The state is closely connected with two nonreligious aspects: first, temples had to be administered, a well-researched topic; and second, they required an economic base, which is apparent in many details, particularly lists of donors for its furnishing. The temple economy and administration as sectors belonging to the state had a life of their own, because they supported the regime in a purely practical sense (except in periods of unrest), and also because of the prominence of temples as a proportion of the overall economy. However, the primary function of the temples was worship directed to deities.

Egyptian Temples as Sacred Places. The gods are usually seen as the intended recipients of temple cults, but this view is not entirely accurate. Deceased and even living kings, as well as deceased private individuals (particularly officials and their households), could also be "looked after" in a cultic manner (the so-called mortuary cults). In the case of human subjects, it was their spiritual component (including the *ka*) that was tended and thought of as an active power. The same concept applied to gods, who were active powers with which one communicated by means of the cult ritual. The temple where living humans came in contact with these holy powers was thus a sacred place.

The sacred center. The initiation of communication between the performer of the cult and its recipient in temples of the gods (see the classification of temples below)— that is, the king (or his representative) and a deity—was made possible through sacrifices and was effected in the "sacred center" of a temple. This center is usually the so-called chamber of the cultic image. This chamber, or the place of the cultic image in smaller structures, includes a room or place of sacrifice. In temples whose cultic schedule included processions, there are also procession rooms, such as the hall of appearances and the festival court. The

TEMPLES. *Model of the fifth dynasty pyramid and mortuary temples of king Sahure at Abusir.* This model was made under the supervision of Ludwig Borchardt in the early twentieth century. (The Metropolitan Museum of Art, Dodge Fund, 1911. [11.165])

holiness, most intense in the chamber of the cultic image, decreased through this sequence of rooms until it terminated at the temple entrance.

The communication between performer and recipient of the cult took place through the medium of the cultic image. Through the sacrifice, the cultic image was "brought to life" and prepared to receive the sacred power. The deity entered the image, and then communication could proceed. The sacred power came from the "next world" or "beyond," which a human could not reach physically, but only by sending forth a spiritual power (as in the ritual of the Opening of the Mouth) or as a dead person.

The sacred center of a temple was therefore a point of transition between this world and the next. However, this opens up a fundamental problem: Such points of transition also existed outside temples; what then can actually be designated a temple? Sacred power might enters this world through any being or object, and foremost among these was the king. The sacred power was received by the king at his coronation, which took place in the chamber of the cultic image or antechamber of the temple. Once invested with the sacred power, the king entered the palace, which was therefore a sacred place, though not a point of transition. The king was purified for the performance of the cult in the sacristy of the temple, understood as a place of transition because the sacred power is conveyed by the water.

Another place with a point of transition from this world into the beyond is the tomb, which has sites for burial and cult. The burial chamber is separated from this world and belongs completely to the next. When the cult is performed, the *ka* of the deceased goes to the place of the cult to receive the offerings. The cult area is the place of transition—a symbolic door, a representation in relief of the deceased person, or a cultic statue. The cultic parts of tombs, strictly speaking, are therefore also temples. As complexes, tombs are distinguished from temples in that they contain sections that are architecturally designed as belonging to the next world. By contrast, in a temple the part belonging to the next world is not specified.

The points of connection between this world and the next world in a temple might be numerous. In addition to the chamber of the cultic image, every statue (of a deity, king, or private individual) in a temple was a potential point of transition because they could be animated through sacrifices, and in this sense the sacred power of the entity represented dwelled in the statue. Even relief images and textual mentions could be places of transition; the ritual invocation of a name implies a bringing to life. These additional points of transition are part of the inner periphery of the temple (see below).

Fundamental function. All the functions of a temple were dependent on the central point of transition between this and the next world, and enabling this was the fundamental function. This transition took place in the framework of ritual sequence and was thereby regulated. The regulation of the transition and the temporary sojourn of the sacred power in this world served to control the power and to achieve the intended purpose of the performance. The king was theoretically the performer of the cult, and thus he was given his power by the sun god. Communication between the deity and a private individual was possible only in exceptional cases—in the proclamation of an oracle, or in even in direct prayer to the deity, as was possible in Akhetaten. The royal performance of the cult, generally speaking, invoked the sacred power for the preservation of *maat*, the order of the world.

The performance of the cult by the king or his proxy, a priest, linked a temple with the sphere of the divine; thus, the land of Egypt was connected with the divine at as many points as there were temples. To structure this connection in a manner as extensive and secure as possible was one of the goals of the temple construction programs repeatedly implemented from the time of Senwosret I until they ceased with the thirtieth dynasty.

Inner periphery. An Egyptian temple complex is composed of sequences of spaces, of which the innermost consists of the dwelling spaces of the temple's main deity. Boundary walls surround the complex, in front of which there may be access roads, a residential area, and other elements. The area between the center and the (inner) temenos (see below) is called the "inner periphery" of the temple.

Cultic rooms. The dwelling spaces of the main deity are the primary rooms, in which the statue or statues of the main god are housed. First, there is the chamber where the cultic image more or less permanently remained. If the cult of the main god included a procession, there is a "bark chapel" with a pedestal to support the "bark" or ship-shaped litter with its cabin in which a separate cultic image of the god might be kept; in many cases the cultic statue from the central chamber was itself removed for processional display. There are several documented cases in which the two primary rooms are conjoined so that the cultic statue and the bark stood in the same space.

Particularly in temples of the Greco-Roman period, of but also in earlier ones, cultic rooms are also provided for other gods of the Ennead besides the temple's main deity. These may be arranged as a circle of cultic chambers or chapels around a primary room of the temple. These autonomous chambers of cultic images are designated "secondary rooms."

There are also cult places within temples which contain statues of the king or even of private individuals. These allowed the persons represented to partake in the sacrifices to the main deity in the form of offerings passed on to them, or to be given separate offerings. The statue of the king mediates between the one making the sacrifice and the main deity of the temple. On an economic level, the king or official offering the sacrifice is allowed to consume the offered goods himself, once he has placed them before the statue. The places where these statues are kept can be thought of as tertiary rooms. Statues of private individuals might also be placed in niches within primary rooms.

The whole cultic area frequently encompasses other separately constructed offering chambers and processional corridors, especially in later temples, but also in large complexes of the New Kingdom. The corridors are called "halls of appearances" and "festival halls." In the hall of appearances, the bark of the god "appeared" and moved out from the temple, frequently through the festival hall, in which a crowd of people greeted the deity. These spaces outside the immediate cultic spaces may be designated as "rooms of mediate connection with the cult."

Other sacred places include namely spaces for storing cultic objects and treasury chambers (frequently the same space), as well as chambers and halls for ritual slaughter and "sacristies" for the purification of the king or the priest acting in his place.

The sacred places are often separated from the rest of the temple precinct by an inner *temenos.* Around this wall there are administrative buildings, residences for the priests, and storage rooms and other economic units belonging to the temple. These buildings may or may not be delimited by an outer surrounding wall.

Ground plan, levels, and sequence in the inner periphery. Two principles alternate in the horizontal plan of temples: separation and connection. All the spaces of the sacred center and of the inner periphery are closed off from one another by walls. Since the sacred powers must be protected from other active magical powers, and also because the sacred powers must not be allowed to leave the inner periphery, all openings of these spaces must be secured with care. These powers were dangerous and had to be kept completely under control, an aim served by the spatial arrangement and decoration of a temple. The openings of sacred spaces are windows (rarely) and doors. The windows are not to let those within look out, but rather to let in light and air. In Ptolemaic temples, rays of the sun are frequently depicted on window frames, a sign that sunlight was allowed—indeed, magically compelled—to come in. Apotropaic signs on the outer walls prevent immaterial negative powers from passing through the opening. The doorways are secured by two means: materially by installing wooden doors, evident today (only by their accessories in the stone work), and magically by applying either apotropaic signs or representations of the king entering—showing that the king alone is entitled to pass. Doors are also magically secured through the king's titles

TEMPLES. *Model of the nineteenth dynasty Hypostyle Hall of the Temple of Amun at Karnak.* (The Metropolitan Museum of Art, Levi Hale Willard Bequest, 1890. [90.35.1])

depicted on their frames. The processional passages to the center are set off by pillars, columns, and/or statues and are thereby magically secured.

The vertical plan is expressed in the varied height of horizontal levels and in the walls. The placement of the walls has been discussed above. The most important horizontal levels are the floor and the roof, both of which may vary in elevation. The passage from the temple entrance to the chamber of the cultic image, for example, often slopes upward as either a ramp or a flight of stairs, so that the human approaches the enthroned deity from below. The parallel between sacred space and the heavens is also apparent, particularly in the bark room, which is designated as heaven, and its entrance doors as the gates of heaven.

The upward-sloping floor is often complemented by a downward slope of the roof. In the cross-section of a temple, this often produces the effect of shortening the perspective. The room that is farthest back in such a cross-section, the chamber of the cultic image, thus appears as a kind of cave, the prototype of a sacred place.

Two types of temples can be distinguished according to outward shape: free-standing temples and rock-cut temples. In the first group the separations are erected; in the second, the spaces that the separations are to enclose are negatively created. If one begins with the concept that the wall of living rock is a boundary between this world and the otherworld, then cutting a temple into the rock extends the realm of this world into the otherworld: the temple is thereby enclosed by the otherworld and in a certain sense belongs to it. In this way the Egyptians gave shape to a part of the otherworld and granted it a kind of order.

The inner periphery of a temple is structured as a series of stages, characterized by decreasing sacredness as one moves outward. With increasing sacredness coincides a lessening of the number of persons who perform service: in the cultic image and bark chambers, according to the iconography, only the king or his proxy is admitted.

Outer periphery. The center and the inner periphery form the temple itself, where the cult is performed. It is normally separated from its surroundings by a wall. Here,

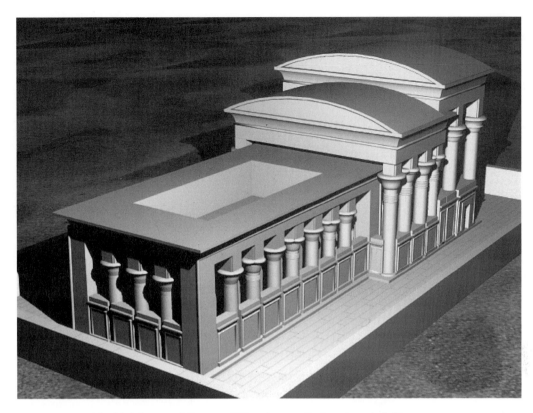

TEMPLES. *The birth house of Cleopatra VII at Armant, Ptolemaic period.* (Computer reconstruction by Barry Girsh; courtesy Dieter Arnold)

at the (inner, if an intermediate zone is provided) enclosing wall of the temple, chaos begins, according to the dualistic thought of the Egyptians. However, this chaos is stratified. If administrative, residential, and economic structures are arranged around the temple, then this area no longer belongs to the sacred place; however, if the entire complex is enclosed by another, outer wall, some of the sacredness of the inner temple diffuses into the area enclosed by the outer wall. This is an intermediate zone between the inner and outer periphery, which could be considered holy ground: in the twenty-sixth dynasty, for example, tombs of kings were erected here. Therefore, as seen from within, chaos begins on the boundary of the inner periphery; but, as seen from outside, the intermediate zone and the outer periphery are regarded as still sacred and within the protection of the temple. When they took over as heads of temples after the collapse of the Old Kingdom, district princes had the intention of cultically binding the entire district to the divine.

The conceptual model of the temple found application on larger scales. The space occupied by several temples (e.g., at Abu Simbel) could assume sacred status by virtue of the underground processional passages linking the temples. An entire region, for example the Faiyum, could acquire the character of a temple by imposing an appropriate exterior structure: the sacred center was Krokodilopolis, and at the outer boundary in Biahu, almost as the sign of an outer enclosing wall, an entrance with a double statue was erected by Amenemhet III. The next step consisted in conceiving Egypt in its entirety as a temple: its center was the palace of the king (as stated in a wisdom text of Amenemhet I); the outer periphery could consist of the entire realm. Thus, in the eighteenth dynasty, Thebes, with the Amun temple in Karnak, was the center to which the whole world had to pay tribute (Tomas inscription of Thutmose I). The basis for this conceptual model was the iconic character of temple.

The Temple Cult and Its Instruments. Egyptian temples, seen from the outside, are static and immovable structures; yet temples, like statues and mummies, were animated with the ritual of the Opening of the Mouth. In this manner, they took on the character of dynamic entities. Temples were inherently "living" by virtue of the fact that they were the dwelling places of sacred powers, but in order to keep a living temple viable, cultic instruments,—objects as well as rites—were necessary. Like location, architecture, decoration, and sacred transactions, they were components of the temple. The operation of a temple began with its erection and furnishing and was maintained through the ongoing performance of the cult.

Erection of temples. Two closely interwoven aspects of the erection of Egyptian temples can be distinguished: the cultic aspect, and the practical matters of building and furnishing. It is typical that Egyptian records deal almost exclusively with the cultic aspect; this is connected with the two Egyptian "realities" (see below).

Cultic founding. The erection of a temple began with its founding, the laying of the cornerstone. The first step of this ritual was the separation and bounding of the building site by means of stretching a cord. The effective inclusion of sacred powers during the separation was made possible through the cultic presence of Seshat, the goddess of calculation, represented by her priest. Thus, the foundation of a temple was an act of creating a sacred place.

The earliest depiction of a foundation ceremony comes from the sun temple of King Newoserre (fifth dynasty, second half of the twenty-fifth century BCE). The "stretching of the cord" was followed by the digging of earth from the foundation pit (scene 4); the "pouring of sand"—the ritual separation of the temple from the underground (scene 5); the laying of sacrificial animals in the foundation pit (scene 2); the scraping of the bricks (scene 3) and the laying of the bricks (scene 6), thus sealing the foundation pit. This concluded the foundation and was followed (in the case of Newoserre) by a visit by the king (scene 7). Particularly in temples from the Greco-Roman period, the dedication of the temple that follows its building is depicted as an offering of a representation of the temple (temple façade) to its main deity.

Building. Like the foundation phase, accounts of temple building and furnishing are limited to matters relating to the cult. A report to Sethos I on the building of the rock-cut temple of Kanais typifies this: "His Majesty commanded to give directions to the leader of the royal workers who were with him as stone cutters. By cutting into this mountain a temple was made for these gods. . . . When the monument had been finished and its inscriptions completed, His Majesty came to adore his fathers, all the gods" (Lichtheim, *Ancient Egyptian Literature,* vol. 2, (p. 54).

The description of the completion of a temple also concentrates on what is cultically necessary. The temple of dead of Amenophis III in west Thebes is described as "a monument of eternity and everlastingness, of fine sandstone worked with gold throughout. Its pavements were made pure with silver, all its doors with fine gold. It is very wide and great and decorated enduringly" (Lichtheim, p. 44). The so-called silver of the floor was in reality a layer of poured sand; only the sandstone may have actually been in the real temple.

The erection of a temple was accomplished in stages. The central rooms and inner periphery of temple structure itself were built, at least from the New Kingdom on, of limestone or sandstone, while the remainder was built of sun-dried mud bricks. On the walls, the reliefs and texts were first sketched, then chiseled into the walls, and then painted (these technical stages can be clearly distinguished in the royal tombs in the Valley of the Kings).

Components: Location, architecture, decoration, and action. The sacred center of a temple consists of the chamber of the cultic image and the bark sanctuary, surrounded by the inner periphery, outer periphery, outer enclosure wall, and environs. We have related the decreasing sacredness from center to environs to an increasing quality of chaos. This also means that the design of a temple had to consider its external situation or location. The site is the framework for the architecture of the shrine, which is divided into rooms and courts. Passageways and walls, the elements of the architecture, are decorated with pictorial works. This third component of a temple encompasses all two-dimensional decorations, including reliefs, paintings, and texts, as well as three-dimensional objects and also markers like obelisks. This completes the tally of the temple components that can be seen today. To perform the cult, however, cultic implements of various kinds were also necessary. Hardly any of these remain preserved today (at best, a few arm-shaped censers), but they included barks, the vehicles for processions of the divinities, and also (as depicted in the crypts of Dendera) important cultic instruments. The last included books in which the rituals were consigned in written form, so that they would be available to the lector-priests who performed the cult as guides and a basis for recitations. Finally, there were the actions themselves, the actual performance of the cult.

Location. A temple's designers faced two tasks in situating it: fitting the building into the surrounding landscape, and orienting it according to the directions of the compass. Here a distinction must be made between geographical and cultic orientation. Behind the latter stands the conceptual model of the sun's course, rising in the east and setting in the west; the former includes the seasonal shift of the sun's path from south to north. Therefore, sun temples are oriented with their sacred center pointing east; the back wall, the point of transition from the beyond into this world, is placed in the eastern part of the temple, and the access in the western part. All kinds of mortuary cult temples, particularly those of the kings of the New Kingdom, are oriented according to the setting phase of the sun, or westward, so that the sacred center is at the western edge of the temple. All other temples are oriented according to one of these two patterns. The path of the sun as it shifts toward the north or the south is reflected in temples that must make use of the spring and

TEMPLES. *Antique photograph (c.1885) of the Hypostyle Hall of the Temple of Amun at Karnak.* Photograph by the Bonfils family. (University of Pennsylvania Museum, Philadelphia. Neg. # T2–988)

autumn equinoxes—for example, the great temple of Abu Simbel and its typological forerunner, the temple of Horemheb in Gebel el-Silsilah. A southern orientation is found particularly in complexes that have the "return" of the eye of the sun as their theme. A northern orientation alludes to the night: the mortuary temple of Djoser in Saqqara is oriented toward the north. The theme here is the transfer of the deceased king to the northern sky, where he is to take over the guidance of Polaris, the North Star. The northern altar serves the cultic purpose of supporting this transfer of the king to the northern sky. This northern orientation is also apparent in the conception of the tomb pyramids of the Old Kingdom.

The actual placement of a temple building was often not selected according to the geographical cardinal points, but rather obeyed constraints of the landscape or other cultic requirements. However, even then the concept of east–west orientation was determinant, and this is shown by the cultic orientations of the compass. This requirement could be served by the manipulation of decorative elements; for example, on both sides of a passageway there are depictions of the king entering to perform the cult; on the cultic (though hot geographical) northern side he wears the Red Crown, which represents Lower Egypt and thus the north, while on the cultic southern side he wears the White Crown of Upper Egypt. The symbols of the two crown goddesses, Wadjyt for the north and Nekhbet for the south, can also be used. Thus, it is insignificant from a cultic standpoint whether the geographical cardinal directions are taken into account. Even tombs and other funerary cult structures, which according to the common conception belong on the western side of the Nile, could be placed on the eastern side, given appropriate defining decoration. For instance, in the private tombs of Tell el-

Amarna, hymns addressed to the rising sun are inscribed on the (geographical) western entrance.

Fitting the temple into the landscape basically followed a predetermined quality of sacredness of the place and was thus connected to tradition. It might serve to bind a political or economic center to the divine, or it might depend on a cult association. The Satet temple at Elephantine goes back to a prehistoric cultic niche in the corner of a rock cliff, the sacredness of which was continued in later millennia. The area of Abu Simbel must have been sacred even before the erection of the temple buildings of Ramesses II, judging by a reference in the temple of Horemheb at Abu Hoda, which is directly across the Nile. In contrast, the choice of Amarna as the place for the new capital under Akhenaten was dictated precisely by its lack of tradition.

The marking of political and economic centers and their cultic connection to the divine can frequently be recognized: the securing of the mining region of Serabit el-Chadim in the western Sinai Peninsula; the securing of access to the gold mines of Barramija by means of the temple of Kanais, built by Sethos I; the erection of the royal tomb buildings in the area of greater Memphis as funerary counterparts to the worldly capital; or the temple complexes in the eastern Delta, intended for the cultic connection of the Ramessid residence.

The idea of cult association can be clearly seen in all cult centers, which normally do not consist of a random accumulation of temples. Rather, they are characterized precisely by the cultic connection of individual complexes. Examples of such cultic places are Abydos, with its central Osiris temple and the peripheral individual royal temples that are arranged in an Osirian manner; Hermopolis; and Elephantine, whose temple complex follows the theological construction of the "Triad of Elephantine."—Khnum as the local god of the First Cataract, Satet, his consort, as the ruler of Elephantine, and her daughter Anuket as the rule of the island of Sehel. Accumulations of cultic places in turn form cultic districts, such as the association of Heliopolis–Memphis (Heliopolis for the cult of the rising sun, and Memphis with its royal tomb complexes and facilities for the cult of the setting sun) and, in particular, eastern and western Thebes, also connected to the rising and setting sun.

The distinction between free-standing temples and those hewn into living rock is also important in a discussion of architecture. Reference has been made to the positive/negative distinction between these two kinds of temples. What is more significant is that the choice of form seems not to have been guided by a need to adapt the structure to local features, but rather by conceptual distinctions. The rock wall is considered to be the boundary between this world and the next; therefore, temples hewn in the rock are ordered areas that have been thrust into realm of myth. Thus, the mythic Khemnis, where Isis or Hathor raises the boy Horus, is conjoined with the Hathor shrine of Hatshepsut in Deir el-Bahri and with the Small Temple of Abu Simbel by means of appropriate decoration. In contrast, the temple of Amenhotpe III at El-kab, though erected in a rocky wadi, is not hewn into the rock.

Natural and artificial architecture. Fitting a temple into the surrounding landscape could be accomplished in two ways. First, the outer periphery can be interrupted by an element of the inner periphery: in temples with a procession passage, which is externally delineated primarily by statues, this passage naturally continues outside the inner periphery, because the purpose of a procession is cultic contact with other shrines. This processional passage outside the temple precincts, as the way of the deity, is segregated from the outer periphery surrounding it. It may be marked out by avenues of sphinxes or even by station shrines (this is the case in Thebes, where a part of the path of the procession for the Opet festival passes through the Nile, which is a part of the temple complexes as "natural architecture"). Processional passages of this kind are mainly features of cultic complexes, but they can also occur in a temple that stands alone, particularly when they are access ways to the temple—for example, in Serabit el-Chadim, where private votive stelae line the "Sacred Way" to the Hathor temple.

However, fitting a temple into the landscape normally required taking the natural features into account in the design. Thus, the towering wall of rock behind the mortuary temple of Mentuhotep II in Deir el-Bahri should be viewed as part of the temple itself, because not only is the tomb of the king deeply thrust into the rock, but the cultic image chamber is also designed as a niche built into the rock. The same holds true for the Amun temple in Gebel Barkal, behind which rises a high promontory that can be interpreted as a statue of Amun on account of its natural shape. The mountain itself, called "pure (=holy) mountain," the bowels of which are reckoned to be in the otherworld, is the seat of sacred powers. This can be seen clearly in the main valley of the Wadi Hammamat, the southern wall of which is seen as the "palace" of the local god Min (time of Mentuhotep II). The goddess of the dead, Hathor, in Western Thebes is depicted stepping out of her house, the rock wall mentioned above.

In a further incorporation of a natural feature, temples to the sun god frequently do not possess a cultic image; rather, they are constructed as open courts to make direct cultic contact with the sun, which itself is the cultic image. In such places, the sun, along with the vault of the heavens, its dwelling place, can be considered as natural architecture that is part of the temple. This is particularly the case in Tell el-Amarna and in the sun shrines of the mortuary temples in Western Thebes.

The "artificial architecture" of a temple includes all its artificially constructed elements—everything that is situated within the outer enclosure wall, as well as separately constructed procession passages. The artificial architectural form of a temple is dependent on its function. For example, bark shrines occur only in temples that have the performance of processions as one of their functions. In cultic image chambers and bark shrines, side niches are built only where statues of a king are to be set up to partake of the sacrifices. We rarely see floor plans without corresponding functions; an exception is the mortuary temple of Hatshepsut in her Hathor temple, in which the side niches seem not to have been filled until her confidant, Senenmut, usurped them in order to install his own images and texts. Conventionalized floor plans emerged only relatively late; the temples of the Greco-Roman period had a canonical series of rooms (cultic image chamber, bark shrine, chapels of the Ennead hall of offerings, hall of appearances, festival court) and were therefore equipped for processions.

Along with the division and structuring of the temple complex, the architecture formed a framework for the decoration, providing spaces to erect demarcating obelisks, free-standing statues. Of greater importance, however, were the two-dimensional images applied to the walls (reliefs, paintings, and texts).

Decoration. Along with tombs, stelae, and papyri, temple decorations represent the most important sources of information on pharaonic Egypt. Their wonderful variety of themes includes not only cultic scenes but also depictions of the temple foundation, the subjection of foreign peoples, coronations of kings, and other activities. Along with iconography, we must note their relationship to their architectural framework on the one hand, and to the cult or function of the temple on the other. For the latter, the key concept is "interrelation between scene and place" (Arnold, 1992). For example, it is clear that battle scenes do not reflect actual events in the place where they were created; however, since the main function of a temple is performing the cult, such representations must be related to that. Thus, two categories of scenes and other decorative elements of decoration can be distinguished: those that depict cultic activities which were performed at the site, and scenes that support the cult by depicting the historic or mythological origin of these activities. The first category is exemplified by representations of caring for the cultic image or the bark. Images that support the cult include battle scenes, like those of the Battle of Qadesh in Ramesses II's temples in Luxor and Abu Simbel, as well as other scenes "slaying the enemy." These may demonstrate the winning of historical world dominance in relationship to the deity of the temple, or they may be intended to transpose imagined events into reality through divine assistance. An example of the latter concept is the representation of the slaughter of Lower Egypt in the chapel of Mentuhotep II in Dendera, in which the titles of the king unmistakably point back to the time before the subjection of the Northern Kingdom. Other examples of scenes that support the cult but refer only indirectly to its performance are the depictions of the deities of the temple god's entourage, which are regarded as their "dwellings," while their ongoing efficacy is guaranteed by the enlivening power of the temple. In Speos Artemidos near Beni Hasan, these depictions of deities are part of the representation of the coronation of Hatshepsut (or Sethos I), which did not take place in this temple. Likewise, the door guardians, the statues of the king that watch over the entrances of the temple, can be classified as supporting the cult. In contrast, statues of kings and of private individuals, as the secondary recipients of sacrifices, are directly relevant to the cult. A similar role was played by foundation texts, the written or pictorial identification of the temple with the cosmos (for example, the representations of birds on the ceiling of the temple of Dendera), or of the bark shrine with the heavens. In addition, we may note cultic scenes that are depicted in the temple but were certainly performed outside it (for example, the processional of the festival of Opet, which is represented in its entirety in the Red Chapel of Hatshepsut inside the Amun temple.

Activities: ritual and processional. The main task of temple personnel was the performance of the cult and the maintenance of its prerequisites. They were the instrument whereby the special functions which underlay the conception of a temple were carried out. Since everything hinged on communication with sacred powers, the care of the cultic image, through which the deity communicated with the one who performed the cult, was a crucial cultic action. Performed daily (or several time a day), it may be called "daily ritual." The most important sources for understanding daily ritual are the images in the deity chapels of the temple of Sethos I in Abydos, the depictions of the ritual of Amenhotpe I in Thebes, and the large number of depictions of the daily ritual in the "closed temple" of Luxor. These cultic actions include the opening of the deity's shrine, the enlivening of the cultic image so that the deity can "reside" in it, cleaning and dressing the cultic image, textually fixed dialogue with the deity (which endows the king with the ruling power) and finally the closing of the shrine.

In contrast to the daily ritual is the festival cult, which took place at certain times and had special functions (e.g., the coronation of a king), or made cultic contact with other temples possible through processions. In Thebes, the Opet festival was the occasion of the annual renewal of royal rule in a procession from the Amun temple in Karnak to the Amun temple in Luxor. During the Festival of the Valley, Amun and the other deities of the Triad of Karnak (Mut and Khons) moved from Karnak to the western side of Thebes to visit the dead kings in their mortuary temples (the kings were thereby identified with Amun). There was also a procession commemorating the sacred marriage between Horus of Edfu and Hathor of Dendera, represented and described in Ptolemaic temples.

Formal and iconic aspects. The sequence of the components was directed toward communication with the divine, magically established through the decoration which assigned the specific function to a temple room. The temple as a whole is structured into levels: action, decoration, and architecture, to which the external situation is added. This sequence from inside to outside can be summed up under the concept of "aspect of use."

This formal or material aspect of the temple is complemented by its iconic aspect, or the aspect of its contents. On every level of the temple, something is depicted. The temple is a depiction of the world: the wave-shaped structure of the enclosure wall is a representation of the opposition between dry land and the primeval ocean, while the pylon, with its two pylon towers and the recess between them within the gateway, represents the horizon (this is why a shrine to the sun is often found in this recess). The temple building itself is the cosmos: the temple ceiling with its depictions of birds, for instance, is the sky; the bark shrine and the cultic image chamber are identified as the vault of the heavens through textual definition. The decoration also lays down the iconic aspect of the architecture, thus interpreting it. Today we have only representations in pictures and texts of the cultic actions. The fact that such records often reveal logical breaks, suggesting that they were often no longer understood by the scribes who copied them, shows that there was a gap between the actual cultic action and its ideal depicted or textual description. It can be said that the decoration only interprets the action. The iconic aspect of the decoration, however, goes beyond this: for instance, if the representation of the *sed*-festival in the sun shrine of Newoserre (fifth dynasty) was painted several times, occasionally it signified only the ritual purification of the king who performed the cult. The repeated use of the "slaughter of the enemy" motif need not represent actual killing: it signifies only the magical extinction of hostile or chaotic elements, and thereby the establishment of the cosmic order. Such pictorial and textual compositions are to be regarded as insoluble hieroglyphs, almost as "ligatures," that signify something other than what they portray.

Static and dynamic aspect. The formal or material aspect of a temple seems to be static, since in all its components it stands before the beholder in an immovable state. However, apart from the fact that every sunrise enlivens a temple (as is depicted in the temple of Dendera), the pictures on the temples portray actions and the texts reflect, either directly or indirectly, such dynamic events, or else they are fragments of speeches of gods or kings. As a result, the temple is constantly in operation. A temple is only static in outward appearance; in fact, it is a dynamic structure. If no cult action is any longer being performed in a temple, its operation is still ensured by its decoration. If this decoration is also missing, it might still be assumed that the architectural shell had enough iconic power to secure the efficacy of the temple. Of course, this is only speculation; it is equally possible that this efficacy was ensured by a statue of the deity.

Realities, interpretation, sense. We owe to Eberhard Otto the distinction between empirical or "first" reality, and fiction or "second" reality. All the pictorial representations and texts in a temple are in principle "second reality," which has cleansed reality of everything that does not pertain to *maat*. In the end, this second reality replaces the first. Reality is modified and/or interpreted in all representations, and the resulting second reality is clearly a fiction. In the mortuary temple of Hatshepsut in Deir el-Bahri, for instance, her biography is depicted fictionally: the announcement of the decision of the sun god Amun-Re to establish her as queen in Egypt, her divine birth, the announcement by her father, Thutmose I, designating her as his successor, and finally her coming to rule. All of this is interpretation or even reinterpretation of the real history. In contrast to the generally accepted view that Hatshepsut intended this as propaganda, we must look at the function of this representation in the temple as a whole—its meaning or purpose (in the foundation text for the Speos Artemidos at Beni Hasan, the assumption of the reign is represented in a completely different manner). The central function in this case is the identification of the dead queen in the cultic image chamber with Amun-Re in the context of the Festival of the Valley. The fictionalized biography of Hatshepsut served as preparation for the queen's life in the hereafter, and it was the purpose of the Festival of the Valley forever to perpetuate this life. This sense, meaning, or purpose is a third reality, which was probably conceived when the planning for the temple began, and out of which the second reality, the fictional representation, arose. The purpose of the multiple representation of the *sed*-festival in the sun shrine of Newoserre to signify the purification of the king, must also be placed in the context of this third reality.

Recipients and Performers of the Cult. Communication between the beyond and this world grants central significance to two persons: the performer of the cult and its recipient. The performance of the cult serves the needs of the performer—the king—and through him the whole land and its inhabitants. By means of the cultic action the king (or, usually, his representative) causes the recipient to enter the cultic image magically and to be available for communication. The recipient was almost always a deity or a deified deceased king.

God and king. The duality of performer and recipient holds true for all sacred places, even tombs. Already in the earliest period, as documented by such cult instruments as the mace and palette of Narmer, the cult permitted communication between the king and the sun god. These cult instruments contained reports on the king's government, and when they were deposited in the temple of the sun god, these reports were transmitted culticly to the sun god in heaven and thereby made eternal. The king was legitimized for this communication by the fact that through his ascent to the throne and coronation, he was given the role of the sun god on earth. He received the magic powers of the sun god Horus along with the title of Horus. The magical power had to be regularly renewed, ideally every day after sunrise, every year following the rhythm of the sun's course, and after the passing of a generation in the *sed*-festival. This communication was maintained throughout the history of Egypt, and for all the gods.

The recipient of the cult could also be a deceased king, who in the afterworld assumed the role of the sun god of that world. This quality of the deceased king was still preserved even when the sun god role of the living king gradually faded. A deceased king could also be a recipient of the cult if he became a deity with influence in a particular locality; as did Unas in the area of his pyramid in Saqqara, or Senwosret III in Semnah at the Second Cataract.

A living king very seldom became a cult recipient, although, particularly in temples of the New Kingdom, the king's likeness could represent aspects of a god (such as the colossal statues of Ramesses II in Abu Simbel). When the king was depicted together with deities in the cultic image chamber, this meant that he was assumed into the community of gods (as in the temples of Thutmose III in Ellesija, of Horemheb in Gebel el-Silsila, or the great temple of Abu Simbel). It was in Abu Simbel that the divine birth of the king was ritually renewed through the semi-annual enlivening of the cult statue of Ramesses II by the sun's light.

Temples as political centers. The kingdom, at least from the Old Kingdom onward, was understood as the "kingship of Re," conveyed to the earthly king. And so, from the Middle Kingdom onward, Re or Amun-Re was also designated as king of Egypt. As the quality of sun god decreased in the earthly king, the heavenly sun god was brought more and more into the day-to-day policy of the kingdom. The intervention of the god was obtained by

means of an oracle: Hatshepsut I and her successor Thutmose III had themselves legitimated through oracles. In the Ramesside period, oracles were a common instrument of government in the framework of the temple cult. Eventually Amun-Re assumed the political leadership of the land as king of Egypt: the king in Tanis and the high priest in Thebes were then only his representatives and no longer sun gods on earth.

Kings and private individuals. In the Egyptian social structure three levels were distinguished: the gods, the king (who by his office was a god, though in other respects human), and the so-called private individuals. Officials, including those of a temple, held only delegated power. Only the king, had the ability and the right to maintain communication with the gods, and only in the temple, since it was here that this communications could be conducted in a protected and regulated manner. Communication with the gods was possible for private persons only under certain conditions: the formula of the sacrifice for the dead, "May the king be gracious and give the gods (so that they may given to the deceased person)," clearly shows his mediating role. In Tell el-Amarna, private persons might invoke the Aten, but only to ask his favor for the king. When, at the end of the Ramessid period, the high priest Herihor took the place of the king in the cult, he assumed the title of king in that context, within the Amun temple at Karnak. The giving of oracles to private persons took place in Karnak via statues of the king, intermediaries between god and man.

A high official, however, could sponsor a statue to be placed in the temple, allocating land the yield of which would pay for sacrifices. If an official set up a statue of the king, the king often supplemented the income of his statue, and the yield was credited to the official as a pension. In later times, this led to the temple of Karnak becoming so overfilled with statues that they had to be ritually removed and buried.

On rare occasions, the boundary between the royal and private spheres was blurred. For example, the favorite and high official under Amenhotpe III, Amenhotep son of Hapu, was allowed to build himself a mortuary temple in the royal style.

Temple and State. The identification between the king and the state, and the sole right of the king to perform the cult, clearly shows that temples were state institutions. The performance of the cult by priests was possible only by way of authority delegated from the king; therefore, in cult scenes only the king is portrayed as performer, even if he never entered the temple in question. A distinction between temple and state, and therefore a division between state and cult powers, can only be seen in certain indications after the end of the Ramessid period.

The central function of temples in royal policy made

building, expanding, and modifying temples important in the governing plans of kings. Witnesses to this are the so-called building inscriptions, in which the participation of a king in the construction of a temple is substantiated. The more important a deity and its temple complex were, the more they were cited in the titles of the king. The neglect of cultic buildings was frequently cited as evidence that things had gone badly for the country—for example, in texts of Hatshepsut or Tutanckamun. If the cult was neglected, the king no longer possessed magical divine power, and his rule could not succeed. This branch of royal policy is generally designated "cult policy," and most kings had a temple-building program.

Every king was expected to expand what existed and to surpass his predecessors, even though in theory these predecessors had already attained perfection. Thus, in the *Instructions of Amenemhet* (composed during the reign of his son, Senwosret I), Amenemhet I charges his successor to "pursue perfection even more." Thus, many temples were continually expanded, with a portico being added, or another temple room, or obelisks; or decorations were merely extended or modified. Even the substitution of royal names belongs in this context. Significant examples of this are the Amun temple of Karnak, the Small Temple of Medinet Habu on the western side of Thebes, the Luxor temple, and the Hathor temple of Serabit el-Chadim. The restoration inscriptions of Sethos I in many temples, which were demolished on the orders of Akhenaten, are also evidence of centrally planned cult policy.

Extensive, centrally planned erection of temple complexes throughout the land can almost never be documented with a text referring to a program, but it becomes clear through comprehensive interpretation of archaeological evidence. The first major temple-building program was initiated by Senwosret I in the first half of the twentieth century BCE. Apparently his goal was to connect the whole country to the divine by means of these royal communication centers. The next extensive program occurred under Amenhotpe III (fourteenth century BCE). He connected royal tomb buildings (royal tomb in Western Thebes, Apis tomb in Saqqara), royal mortuary temples (areas of Medinet Habu and Saqqara), temples of the sun god (Giza/Heliopolis/Memphis, Karnak temple and Luxor temple, Gebel Barkal in the vicinity of the Fourth Cataract, and temples for the *sed*-festival at Bubastis, Malqata, Elephantine, and Soleb) into a network of temples that spanned the country. The temple-building program of Ramesses II (thirteenth century BCE) included many rock-cut temples in Lower Nubia. It may also be assumed that the thirteenth dynasty (fourth century BCE) initiated a temple-building program, which was then carried out under the Ptolemies.

Classification of Temples. One can start from the assumption that it is the function of Egyptian temples that primarily determines their content and shape. Almost all previous attempts to classify Egyptian temples utilized groupings that overlapped as little as possible. The *Reallexikon der ägyptischen Religionsgeschichte* by Hans Bonnet lists "normal" temples dedicated to gods, mortuary temples, sun temples, birth-houses, temples for the New Year's festival and bark stations. The objection may be raised that mortuary temples, at least in Thebes, where the great majority of them are located, are temples to gods in the central area, with bark stations. They also contain sun temples. Dieter Arnold classifies temples into localities for divine cult, localities for royal cult, and so forth, correctly starting from function. Since the general function was communication, and the human partner in this dialogue, according to dogma, was always the king, a classification can be derived according to the central recipients of the cult. Beyond this, there is the perspective of the temple's location, architecture, and decoration. It is often not possible to classify whole temples, but only parts of temples: every Egyptian temple is a singular (and frequently complex) phenomenon. The central recipients of the cult were gods (including deceased kings who were equated with gods), living kings, deceased kings, and (if we include private mortuary cult complexes) deceased private individuals.

Temples dedicated to gods. These temples principally served the purpose of ensuring the rule of the reigning king. In them the cult was directed to a cultic image, a statue or a stela portraying the divinity. Examples are the closed temple in Luxor and some other smaller temple complexes in the area of Karnak. Very often temples dedicated to gods contain not only a central cultic image, but also a bark shrine with a processional bark, as at the Amun temple of Karnak. The barks were used in processions that carried the deity to other temples, which I would call "visitation temples." A significant portion of the temple complexes in Thebes are such visitation temples—for example, the open temple in Luxor (visited in connection with the festival of Opet), the Small Temple in Medinet Habu (for the festival of Amun), and the mortuary temple of Hatshepsut I in Deir el-Bahri, or its replacement which Thutmose III erected (in the context of the Festival of the Valley). All these temples are destination temples for processions that started in Karnak. In the Festival of the Valley, however, all the "mortuary temples" of the deceased kings were visited: the barks of the Triad of Thebes (Amun-Re, Mut, and Khons) each spent one night there, so that Amun could be "united" with the deceased king. The central sections of the mortuary temples provided for this purpose were thus station temples. From the depictions of the festival of Opet of Hatshepsut, we know that its procession also utilized station temples of this kind.

A special class of the temples dedicated to gods are the

sun courts. These were open courts with an altar from which cultic contract was established not with a particular cultic image, but with the sun in the sky. The sun itself almost certainly functioned as the cultic image. Examples include the sun temple in Heliopolis, the sun wings of the mortuary temples, and the Aten shrines in Tell el-Amarna.

Besides these, particular festival temples should be mentioned: the Osiris chapels on the roofs of Ptolemaic temple complexes; temples for the New Year's Festival in the same place; and the birth-houses (*mammisi*) from the Late and Greco-Roman periods, where the birth of the son of a god was celebrated.

Temples dedicated to a reigning king. These temples differ fundamentally from temples dedicated to gods, because here, rather than a god in the other world, the living king was both receiver and performer of the cult. These temples celebrate the stages of a king's coming to rule, particularly his begetting, birth, and nursing, the assumption of the throne, the *sed*-festival, and the king's capacity to rule. The birth-houses of the late period go back to the birth cycles that were documented from the eighteenth dynasty. In the so-called *mr.t* shrines of the Old Kingdom (known only from texts), the reigning king, as divine father, regularly celebrated the sacred wedding with the queen Kamut effect principle), in order to renew himself as the divine son. Birth temples or birth rooms certainly existed in the New Kingdom, for example in connection with the "house of princes" in the ritual palace of Hatshepsut, outside the temple of Karnak, and south of the Great Temple of Abu Simbel. The birth-houses of the Late period go back to the birth cycles connected with the so-called *mammisi*. The next stage in the cult consisted of a procession to a Khemnis sanctuary, in which the divine mother (Hathor or Isis) suckled and protected the new-born Horus. The Hathor sanctuary of Hatshepsut in Deir el-Bahri and the Small Temple of Abu Simbel are examples. The renewal of the kingdom after the passing of a generation was the purpose of the temples for the *sed*-festival; the earliest representation of such a complex is on the Narmer Mace, while the last trace is the Gate of Osorkon II in Bubastis. In the eighteenth and nineteenth dynasties there were temples hewn in the rock (e.g., the Ellesija temple of Thutmose III, or the Great Temple of Abu Simbel), in which the king is depicted as enthroned together with deities in the cultic image chamber, portraying the reception of the reigning king into the company of the gods. Since the decoration of these temples depicted this reception as following proof that king had ensured his domination over the world and the performance of the cult, I call them "royal maturity temples." Connected to this are cultic areas that combine the reception of the king into divine company with the theme of the homage of officials—for example, the grottos of Qasr Ibrim.

Temples dedicated to deceased kings. The most important temple complexes for kings in the afterworld are the royal funerary cult temples, which essentially consist of a funerary offering place and offering places for their statues. There is evidence of complexes of this kind going back to dynasty zero: in the U cemetery in Abydos, for the earlier kings there was apparently a common place for offerings, though without any particular architectural features. In the pyramid temples, a site in the outermost western position in front of the pyramid was the most important funerary offering place. It was supplemented with offering places for statues, particularly in the valley temples. The statues in the valley temples of Unas in Saqqara became the focal point for his cult after he became a local god. Pyramid complexes, especially of the Old Kingdom but also in the Middle Kingdom (e.g., the pyramid complex of Amenemhet III), contained *sed*-festival temples for the deceased king; the earliest examples are the large brick enclosures or valley districts in Abydos, and the Jubilee Court in the Enclosure of Djoser. In the pyramid complexes of the Old Kingdom there are offering places for statues (five shrines for statues) at the transition from the festival temple of the afterworld to the funerary offering temple.

Practically all the royal funerary cult complexes contain sun chapels, the purpose of which was to introduce the deceased king into the course of the sun, or else to bring the sun magically into the king's tomb. The best-known examples are the sun temples of the fifth dynasty in the area of Memphis and the sun courts in the mortuary temples of western Thebes. The former are also known as "mortuary temples of Re," which makes it clear that they can be seen as a form of divine image temple and also of the temple of the deceased king.

The cultic operation of the centers for the funerary cult was complemented by chapels for royal statues in the temples dedicated to gods. The significance of these cult chapels, as far as the king was concerned, was to allow him to partake in offerings to a god. In exceptional cases we find statue cult chapels of this kind even for a reigning king, such as the chapel of Mentuhotpe II in Dendera, through which a Horus statue of the king as conqueror of the Heracleopolitan Northern Kingdom was involved in the cult of Hathor. The purpose of this chapel was to ensure the subjugation of the Northern Kingdom, which had not yet actually taken place. The cultic statue chapels probably included the royal palaces adjacent to the mortuary temples (south of the forecourt): a statue of the king, present at the Window of Royal Appearances, would attend the processions of deities between the palace and the forecourt.

Alongside the complexes for the funerary cult were so-called memorial temples, which the Egyptians called "mansions of millions of years." These include the Hypostyle Hall of the Amun temple in Karnak, built by Sethos I, in which there was no particular cult for the king, but through which the processions of the major Theban festivals passed.

A particular type of temple for deceased kings is the predecessor chapel. These were located in the southern (Sokar-Osiris) sections of New Kingdom mortuary temples. Parallel to the places for the sun cult in the mortuary temples, which were erected north of the station temples, here on the western end were built places for the funerary cult, and the predecessor chapel was situated east of these. They are dedicated to the predecessor of the royal owner of the temple and also (in the temple of Ramesses II in Abydos, for example) to all legitimate predecessors, who are listed by name. The purpose of these chapels was to document the legitimacy of the royal builder—and, in the case of Ramesses II, to establish his connection with primeval times.

In the central station temple of mortuary temples of the New Kingdom, there is a special space provided for a ritual associating the deceased king with Amun-Re, performed during the Festival of the Valley (for example, room V of the mortuary temple of Sethos I in Gurneh). The statues of the god and of the king were purified or enlivened together.

Private cult complexes. Along with the cultic parts of tombs of private individuals, mention should be made of private statue cult spaces in temples (for participation in offerings), and especially of private chapels along processional routes. In the Middle Kingdom there were such chapels in Abydos on the path ("stairway of the Great God") taken by the burial and resurrection procession of Osiris; such a chapel featured a stela with a likeness of the deceased, through which he might participate in the processions. There are similar private chapels in Gebel el-Silsila, the Upper Egyptian stone quarry, to enable the chapel-owners to maintain contact with the Nile.

Classification according to site. The fact that the east bank of the Nile lies toward the sunrise, and the west bank toward the sunset, is the basic reason for the selection of burial sites. As noted above, however, there are many examples in which the cardinal directions east and west are redefined symbolically. The mortuary temple and tomb of Mentuhotpe II were fitted into the middle of the basin of Deir el-Bahri, on the west bank across from Karnak; Hatshepsut then inserted her mortuary temple into the middle of the remaining part of the valley. In the city of Akhetaten, we know that the basin of Amarna was seen as a reflection of the cosmos and interpreted as the "horizon of Aten." What was important in many cases was the proximity of the Nile, as in the case of the private chapels in Gebel el-Silsila, the South Temple of Buhen, or the rock-cut temple of Ramesses II in Lower Nubia. The Speos Artemidos at Beni Hassan is situated at the en-

trance to a wadi, which was interpreted as the gateway to the land of Punt. The temple of Amenhotpe III in Wadi Hellal east of Elkab has a similar relationship to the eastern desert. The temple of Kanais in the eastern desert secures access to the gold mines of Barramija, while the Hathor temple of Serabit el-Chadim secures the area of the turquoise mines in the western Sinai.

Classification according to structure. First, a distinction must be made between free-standing temples, to which the majority of Egyptian temples belong, and temples cut into living rock. I have noted that rock walls represent a boundary between this world and the next, and that the choice between a rock-cut or free-standing temple had nothing to do with the site (I cannot concur with the conjecture that rock-cut temples are mainly former stone quarries): the temple of Amenhotpe III in Wadi Hellal is free-standing, even though there are rock faces available, and the same holds for the Hathor temple in Serabit el-Chadim. The decision to built temples hewn in rock was certainly based on function; for example, Khemnis temples, as mythical localities, were built into rock walls. The Great Temple of Abu Simbel served the purpose of regenerating the reigning king through the light of the sun: here too, there is a mythical place involved. The principle that the function determines the shape accounts for the fact that from an architectural standpoint there are many kinds of temples: divine image temples provide for at least one room for the cultic image: temples for divine barks additionally have a bark shrine and places for the procession (hall of appearances, festival court): visitation temples may be limited to a bark room, and so forth.

History. A history of Egyptian temples has not yet been written, though Badway included them in his history of Egyptian architecture. Dieter Arnold has proposed some fundamental principles and presented an overview of individual temples. Here we can only describe their development in broad terms. Following are central perspectives and their application in various periods of Egyptian history.

Early period and Old Kingdom: Predominance of kingly recipients. There is evidence of sacred places in Egypt at a very early date. As soon as there existed an idea of sacred powers with which one might communicate—and here statuettes that date from the Badari an phase of the Predynastic period at the latest may stand as evidence—we can assume that there were places and sites where contact with those powers took place through cultic objects. Even before the origin of the Egyptian state, the magical influence of sacred powers was invoked: a famous bowl from the Naqada I period shows the rising and setting sun. An offering cult was certainly practiced at the tombs of kings (and, no doubt, private individuals), but we know nothing about it before the beginning of burials in the U cemetery in Abydos: however, we may conjecture

TEMPLES. *Antique photograph (c.1876) of a temple gateway at Medinet Habu.* Photograph by the Bonfils family. (University of Pennsylvania Museum, Philadelphia. Neg. # T2–958c)

that the temples had many forerunners. The earliest "temple" is the sanctuary in a rock niche at Elephantine, first used as early as the Naqada era and maintained almost without interruption into the Roman era. The sacred center of this cultic place was a crevice through which the divine could emerge. There is evidence not only of natural cultic structures of this kind, but also of buildings, in representations on D-ware pottery (Naqada II) and on tables of names from the Thinite period. These were found in huts made of perishable materials (wood and reed mats), built in Lower Egypt and probably elsewhere. We can already recognize the deities represented in these huts by cultic statues. A particular type is the Min sanctuary, the so-called *shn.t*, which may originally have been a temporary tent sanctuary in the eastern desert. Thus, by the Thinite period, two types of sanctuaries can be distinguished: small local temples dating back to the prehistoric period, and kings' tombs, which by then were certainly the primary cultic sites in Egypt. The distribution of tombs of kings and cenotaphs throughout Egypt (Abydos and Saqqara) already shows the intention to connect the land to the divine by means of cultic places. In the Old

Kingdom, the royal tomb districts, the pyramid complexes, must have been the central cultic places of Egypt, especially since the deceased king not only assumed the role of the sun god in the next world but also was responsible in this world to the cult and the welfare of his posterity. His leadership in the circle of Polaris, becomes evident in the third dynasty with the Djoser precinct, where the deceased king reigns over the night sky. This site is also valuable in that it contains tent sanctuaries reproduced in stone, confirming the earlier representations.

The most important temple dedicated to a god before the end of the Old Kingdom was the Horus temple of Hierakonpolis, where cultic contact was maintained between the king as sun god on earth and sun god who travels through the heavens, both identified with Horus (as shown by ornament incorporating reports on government). The outward form of this temple is unknown to us because it was torn down by the time of the New Kingdom and then rebuilt.

There was already a sun court in Heliopolis which functioned well into the Greco-Roman period. Among other things, it served as a cult center for the rising sun god, while the pyramid complexes (in the fifth dynasty the sun sanctuaries were specialized) on the west side were dedicated to the setting sun.

In many places in the land there were temple buildings in which the pantheon as related to the king was maintained—for example, the Min temple in Koptos, and in Abydos the Temple of Khontamenti, the "First of the Westerners," the first among the deceased kings who protects the royal necropolis. In the Old Kingdom he is still identified with Osiris, and out of this the central site of the Osiris cult for the whole land developed: Osiris as the father of the reigning king and the underworld equivalent of the sun god.

For Hathor, the divine mother of the reigning king, a temple was built in Dendera during the sixth dynasty at the latest. This temple continued to exist in changing architectural forms until Roman times.

The break of the First Intermediate Period: Creator god and moral renewal. The collapse of the rule of the kings in Memphis with the end of the sixth dynasty deprived the temples of their royal leadership, which was taken over by the nomarchs. The priests of this period turned to debate, holding the sun god to be the creator, and to the moral renewal of Egypt. New designs of temples from this period are unknown to us.

Middle Kingdom to New Kingdom: Predominance of the divine recipient. With the eleventh dynasty, a new era of Egyptian temple-building began, specifically with the takeover of the Hathor temple by the nomarchs of Thebes and the conception of Amun-Re as the sun god of Thebes. If we classify the Hathor temple of Dendera as a normal temple of the divine image (the statue cult center of Mentuhotpe II took part in the sacrificial procession of this temple), then the Amun temple in Karnak, in contrast, may have been conceived from the outset as part of the Thebian cult association. From the period preceding the twelfth dynasty there are hardly any remains of the temple at all. However, Intef II had Amun-Re conceived by combining aspects of Min and Re, in parallel to the Heliopolis-Memphis cultic association; and, at the latest, beginning from the time of Mentuhotpe II there is evidence of the cultic joining of Karnak and Deir el-Bahri with the ceremony of "Rowing for Amun." Remains of chapels from the eleventh dynasty under the Small Temple of Medinet Habu suggest that a parallel cultic association existed between Luxor and Medinet Habu (later documented as the Amun festival for the mortuary temple of Amun)—in other words, for the rectangular area that made up the cultic surroundings of Thebes. The Amun temple was then expanded by Senwosret I and retained this shape until the beginning of the eighteenth dynasty. This king undertook the first temple-building program intended to bind the whole land to the divine world. A feature of this program was the incorporation of a numerous

pantheon from Buhen in Lower Nubia to the Delta. The king, who was no longer the "sun god on earth" as in the Old Kingdom, gradually became identified with the most important gods and took over their roles.

In contrast to temples dedicated to gods, the royal tomb complexes decreased in importance. A kind of transition between these two groups of sacred places is represented by the cultic association of Osiris in Abydos with the royal tomb of Djer, which was interpreted as the tomb of Osiris. The burial and resurrection procession of Osiris up the "stairway of the Great God" is designated the "mysteries of Osiris."

The beginning of the eighteenth dynasty was also the start of great temple-building projects in Egypt. Thutmose I made Thebes the center of the world, renewed the Amun temple, and thus established its conception for a century. The determining principle was the rectangle, which was expanded through successive placement of the mortuary temples of the kings in the context of the Festival of the Valley (in their respective identification temples, each deceased king is identified with Amun). By the time of Hatshepsut, the cultic location of Karnak began to change through the introduction of the divine oracle and the ceremony of the divine birth of the king in the ritual palace in front of the entrance of the Amun temple. The cultic association between Karnak and Deir el-Bahri was expanded with the Khemnis procession to the Hathor temple on the west bank.

Thutmose III continued the temple-building program of Hatshepsut, extending it to Gebel Barkal, which was now the southern boundary of the kingdom. This was followed by an extensive new temple-building program under Amenhotpe III at the beginning of the fourteenth century BCE. This greatly altered the cultic conception of the Amun temple in terms of its construction and in terms of the rectangle: it encompassed the Heliopolis-Memphis parallel (each with a triad of a tomb, a mortuary temple, and a temple dedicated to a god) and covered the land with a series of temples for the *sed*-festival.

The Amarna period represents a temporary break, when a new capital was intended to effect the magical refounding of the state as a model of the world and of Egypt. The new capital, designed according to the cultic model of Thebes, complete with sun courts, was understood as the "horizon of Aten," the newly defined sun god (the concomitant closing of the earlier temples was reversed after Akhenaten's death).

In the Ramessid period, the cultic concept of the land remained essentially unchanged. However, the Amun temple with its many subsidiaries became the most important association of temples. There had been a gradual decline of the traditional royal ideology, which Ramesses II attempted to stop with a series of rock-cut temples in Lower Nubia, in which the reigning king is taken up into the world of the gods. The predominance of divine recipients of the cult ended with the assumption of the Egyptian kingship by the sun god; the earthly king was now merely his vicar.

Third Intermediate Period: God as the king of Egypt. In the centuries that followed, there was limited expansion of the temples which did not alter their design. The cultic principle of god as king of Egypt was determinant in some degree until the end of the ancient Egyptian civilization in the sixth century CE.

Late period and Greco-Roman period: The temple state under foreign rule. The most important temples of Egypt, with the exception of a few temples dedicated to gods, were expanded or modified before the Greco-Roman period and after the conquest of Egypt by Alexander the Great. The practice of including the king's tomb and placing the deceased king in the course of the sun was abandoned toward the beginning of the Third Intermediate Period. In a sense, the relationship is reversed: in many cases the king's tomb is moved into the temple area, and therefore belongs to the intermediate zone between the inner and the outer periphery. The continuing operation of the temples concentrated on the traditional divine image temples and divine bark temples (with the now canonical sequence of cultic image chamber, bark sanctuary, hall of the Ennead with chapels on the sides, hall of the offering table, hall of appearances, and festival court): from the Late period onward, we see the *mammisi* or birth-houses, situated outside the main temple in the intermediate zone and forming their own sacred centers with a periphery. It is from the main temple that the goddess (e.g., in Dendera) moves forward in procession to the birth-house in order to give birth to her son, who becomes king of Upper and Lower Egypt in the succession of pharaohs through history. This succession supersedes the earthly rule of the sun god (from the twenty-first dynasty) and continues the tradition of the birth cycles, as depicted in Deir el-Bahri and Luxor. The earthly vicar of the divine king—the Ptolemaic king or the Roman Caesar—is now only the pro forma leader of the cult and carries out the temple-building program. The last such project may have been planned by the thirtieth dynasty before Alexander the Great; it was carried out by the Ptolemies. Although the earthly king was the administrative superior of the temple personnel, the royal son of god magically exerted rule. However, in the Greco-Roman period, the actual pharaonic state in its traditional form existed only in the framework of the temple, as a "temple state," and then only as long as the temple cult endured. The cult ended long after the definitive closing of most of the temples by the Christian Roman emperors in the mid-sixth century, when the Byzantine commander Narses put an end the operation of the Isis temple on Philae, where the cult had survived for a time as a joint Egyptian-Meroitic enterprise.

[*See also* Abu Simbel; Administration, *article on* Temple Administration; Economy, *article on* Temple Economy; Karnak; Luxor; Medinet Abu; Mut Precinct; *and* Priesthood.]

BIBLIOGRAPHY

Arnold, Dieter. *Die Tempel Ägyptens: Götterwohnungen, Kultstätten, Baudenkmäler.* Zurich, 1992. The best survey of Egyptian temples.

Bonnet, Hans. *Reallexikon der ägyptischen Religionsgeschichte.* Berlin, 1952. "Tempel," pp. 778–788.

David, Rosalie. *A Guide to Religious Ritual at Abydos.* Warminster, 1981. A unique description of the significance of temple decoration.

Gundlach, Rolf, and Matthias Rochholz, eds. *Ägyptische Tempel: Struktur, Funktion und Programm.* (Hildesheimer Ägyptologische Beiträge, 37.) Hildesheim, 1994.

Kemp, Barry J. *Ancient Egypt: Anatomy of a Civilization.* London and New York, 1989.

Kurth, Dieter, ed. *Ägyptologische Tempeltagung: Systeme und Programme der ägyptischen Tempeldekoration.* (Ägypten und Altes Testament, 33.1). Wiesbaden, 1995.

Lauer, Jean-Philippe. *Saqqara, the Royal Cemetery of Memphis: Excavations and Discoveries since 1850.* London, 1976. A survey of one district of Old Kingdom pyramid complexes.

Lipinska, Jadwiga. *The Temple of Tuthmosis III: Architecture (Deir el Bahari II).* Warsaw, 1977.

Murnane, William J. *United with Eternity: A Concise Guide to the Monuments of Medinet Habu.* Chicago, 1980. A good introduction to the royal mortuary temples of the New Kingdom.

Nelson, Harold H. *Key Plans Showing Locations of Theban Temple Decorations.* (University of Chicago, Oriental Institute Publications, 56.) Chicago, 1941.

Porter, Bertha, and Rosalind Moss, eds. *Topographical Bibliography of Ancient Egyptian Hieroglyphic Texts, Reliefs, and Paintings.* Vol. 2, *Theban Temples.* 2d edn. Oxford, 1972. Many of Egypt's temples were built in Thebes, and this volume includes many plans.

Porter, Bertha, and Rosalind Moss, eds. *Topographical Bibliography of Ancient Egyptian Hieroglyphic Texts, Reliefs, and Paintings.* Vol. 6, *Upper Egypt: Chief Temples (Excluding Thebes).* Oxford, 1939.

Quirke, Stephen, ed. *The Temple in Ancient Egypt: New Discoveries and Recent Research.* London, 1997.

Reymond, E. A. E. *The Mythical Origin of the Egyptian Temple.* Manchester, 1969.

Shaw, Ian. "Balustrades, Stairs and Altars in the Cult of the Aten at El-Amarna." *Journal of Egyptian Archaeology* 80 (1994): 109–127. An introduction to temple implements at this site.

Simpson, William K. *The Terrace of the Great God at Abydos: The Offering Chapels of Dynasties 12 and 13.* (Publications of the Pennsylvania-Yale Expedition to Egypt, 5.) New Haven and Philadelphia, 1974.

Spencer, Patricia. *The Egyptian Temple: A Lexicographical Study.* London, 1984.

"Tempel (als Institution)" and related articles. In *Lexikon der Ägyptologie* 6: 355–420.

ROLF GUNDLACH
Translated from German by Robert E. Shillenn

TETI (r. 2374–2354 BCE), first king of the sixth dynasty, Old Kingdom. A change in dynasties at the beginning of Teti's reign is specified by the third-century BCE Egyptian historian Manetho, but there is no perceptible break be-

TETI. *Interior of the tomb of Teti at Saqqara, sixth dynasty.* (Courtesy Dieter Arnold)

tween the fifth and sixth dynasties in the archaeological record. Still, the Horus name of this king, Seheteptawi, "One Who Pacifies the Two Lands," implies the role of peacemaker, indicating a new era.

Like his predecessors, Teti ruled from the Memphite area, but during the sixth dynasty Upper Egypt became more prominent in written records. As settlements grew in areas away from the center of power, the king emphasized his sovereignty by connecting his name with those of local deities. For example, on a sistrum in The Metropolitan Museum of Art, New York, Teti's name is recorded alongside that of Hathor of Dendera. The prosperity of the temple of Osiris at Abydos was augmented by Teti: a stela in the British Museum records that the "fields and personnel" of that temple were exempted from taxes (fields were taxed according to their yield, and personnel were used as conscripted labor).

Abroad, there seems to have been no break in foreign relations during Teti's rule. Teti's name, together with those of other kings of the period appears on artifacts from Byblos, indicating a continuing trade with Syria. Expeditions to the south and west of Egypt were also conducted during Teti's reign: a number of graffiti carved during this time have been found at Tomas in Nubia, left by persons with titles that showed them to be leaders of cara-

vans. We have no evidence of mining expeditions to Sinai during Teti's reign.

Saqqara is the burial place of Teti, his family, and his officials. His pyramid, the "Pyramid Which Is Enduring of Places," was built at northern Saqqara. A ground-level entrance leads to the burial chamber, where the walls are inscribed with Pyramid Texts; the sarcophagus remains *in situ*. Little survives of Teti's mortuary temple; the causeway and valley temple are also lost. Two extant pyramids belonging to Teti's queens Iput mother of Pepy I, and Khuit, were built near his funerary complex. The existence of a third queen, Seshseshet, was discovered in 1988 on reused blocks bearing her name that were found in Teti's mortuary temple. Teti's officials were also buried near his pyramid, among them two of his viziers. The first was Kagemni, who was succeeded by Mereruka. Mereruka was married to a daughter of Teti, also named Seshseshet. His thirty-two chamber *mastaba* tomb is the largest at Saqqara.

Manetho records that Teti was murdered by his bodyguard. The validity of his account is uncertain, since there is no other evidence to verify the claim. It may, however, be a misplaced reference to the assassination of Amenemhet I.

The cult of Teti continued long after his death. It was

prominent in the First Intermediate Period and early Middle Kingdom, when officials of his cult were buried near his pyramid: the area around the pyramid is honeycombed with small tombs and shafts. Teti's pyramid may have provided a focal point for a nearby settlement, which accounts for the popularity of the area: his pyramid-town is mentioned in the tenth dynasty as a populous urban area.

BIBLIOGRAPHY

Fakhry, Ahmed. *The Pyramids*. Chicago and London, 1961. Contains a description of Teti's pyramid.

Helck, Wolfgang. "Gedanken zum Mord an König Teti." In *Essays in Egyptology in Honor of Hans Goedicke*, edited by B. M. Bryan and D. Lorton, pp. 103–112. San Antonio, 1994.

Lehner, Mark. *The Complete Pyramids*. London and New York, 1997.

Stadelmann, R. "König Teti und der Beginn der 6. Dynastie." In *Hommage à Jean Leclant*, edited by C. Berger et al., vol. 1, pp. 327–335. Paris, 1994.

DIANA MAGEE

TEXTILES. *See* Weaving, Looms, and Textiles.

THEBAN NECROPOLIS, a site that covers a 9-square-kilometer (5.5-square-mile) area of the western bank of the Nile River, at modern Luxor (24°44′ N, 32°36′ E). Best known as the site of New Kingdom royal mortuary complexes and hundreds of tombs for court officials and temple priests, it is one of the richest archaeological zones in the world and has been declared a World Heritage Site by UNESCO. In dynastic times, the area was called "The West of Thebes" (*W3st*), "The Great West," or "The Western Region of Thebes." Thebes is a Greek word, and it may have originated in a mishearing of Djeme, the name for the area around Medinet Habu.

Actually, the term *necropolis* is something of a misnomer; the area contains a much more diverse collection of ancient sites than just cemeteries, and our knowledge of its archaeological contents comes as much from ancient texts as from archaeological excavations. Even today, much of the Theban necropolis has been only cursorily examined and very few of its tombs, temples, and shrines have been properly studied, recorded, or conserved. No detailed and comprehensive map of the necropolis has been charted; archaeologists and tourism developers continue to rely on nineteenth-century sketch maps and a seriously incomplete 1:1,000 survey plan made in 1925. (The Theban Mapping Project, which is preparing detailed maps and plans of the entire necropolis, will rectify this, but it will be the new century before it is complete.)

Broadly speaking, the Theban Necropolis may be divided geographically and archaeologically into four sections. These include the following:

1. *The cultivable land between the Nile and the desert edge.* Today as a 3-kilometer-wide (1.8-mile-wide) agricultural zone with numerous modern villages, few archaeological sites are to be found, because the annual Nile floods from Paleolithic times until 1960 CE buried most of them under many meters of silt. Only a few sites are known today (see map): Birket Habu (*1*), an artificial lake created for the first and second *sed*-festivals of the New Kingdom ruler Amenhotpe III, lies at the southern end of the necropolis; and the same king's mortuary temple (*2*), of which little remains but the Colossi of Memnon to the north. At the northern end of the necropolis, beyond the temple of Sety I and presumably beneath the modern village of Nag' Geneina, there is said to have been a town called Khefet-her-nebes (*3*), the "Western Residence" of several eighteenth dynasty pharaohs (however, that name was sometimes applied to larger areas of the necropolis). Several ancient canals were dug across the flood plain to connect the Nile with various temples along the desert edge: one lay in the north (*4*), along an east-west line between Karnak and Deir el-Bahri; another, in the south (*5*), was dug on a line between Luxor temple and Medinet Habu. [*See* Deir el-Bahri; Karnak; *and* Medinet Habu.] They may have been connected by a north–south canal adjacent to the desert edge; these canals were used during various religious festivals. Undoubtedly, many small, ancient shrines and settlements dotted this landscape as well.

2. *The desert edge.* This is a low silt-and-sand-covered limestone plain that varies in width from 10 meters (about 30 feet) at the north–south midpoint of the necropolis to 3 kilometers (1.8 miles) at the southern end, where Amenhotpe III's *heb-sed* palace, Malqata (*6*), was located. [*See* Malqata.] At the northern end of the necropolis the desert plain is more than 2 kilometers (1.25 miles) wide and includes an area called el-Tarif (*7*), in which several hundred tombs from the end of the Old Kingdom through the Middle Kingdom have been found. In this low desert, immediately adjacent to cultivation (and in places overrun by it because of extensive modern irrigation schemes), the remains of more than two dozen mortuary temples and shrines of New Kingdom rulers and important commoners were found. From north to south, these include the following:

(*8*) the mortuary temple of Sety I; (*9*) the mortuary temple of Nebwenenef, a high priest of Onurus and Hathor at Dendera; the first prophet of Amun in the reign of Ramesses III; (*10*) the mortuary temple of Amenhotpe I; (*11*) the mortuary temple of Ahmose-Nefertari; (*12*) the valley temple of Hatshepsut; (*13*) several temples of the Ramessid Period; (*14*) the mortuary temple of Thutmose III; (*15*) the mortuary temple of Merenptah-Siptah; (*16*) the mortuary temple of Amenhotpe II; (*17*) the Chapel of

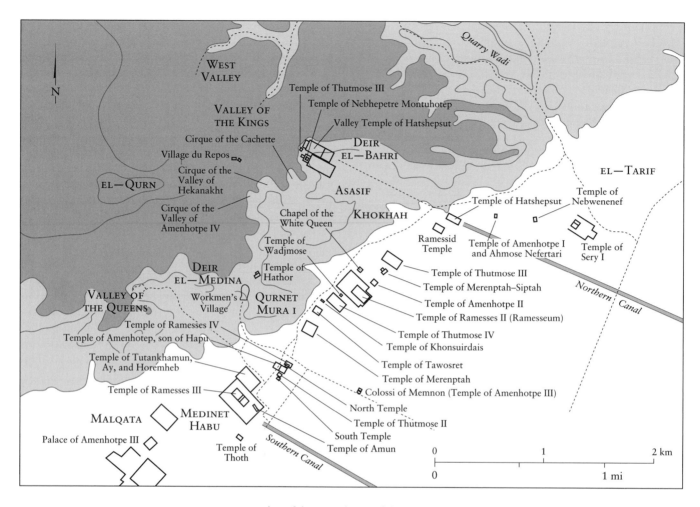

THEBAN NECROPOLIS. *Plan of the central area of the Theban necropolis, Western Thebes.*

the White Queen, named for a white limestone bust of a woman found on a wall there, which Petrie (1896) believed to be a daughter of Ramesses II, but which could also be much later; (*18*) the mortuary temple of Ramesses II, the Ramesseum, currently being studied by the Centre du Documentation; (*19*) the mortuary temple of Wadjmose, son of Thutmose I; (*20*) the mortuary temple of Thutmose IV; (*21*) the chapel of Khonsuirdais; (*22*) the mortuary temple of Tawosret, daughter of Merenptah; (*23*) the mortuary temple of Merenptah, much of it constructed from blocks taken from the mortuary temple of Amenhotpe III, recently studied by the Swiss Institute; (*24*) the mortuary temple of Ramesses IV; (*25*) the "North Temple" of an anonymous individual; (*26*) the mortuary temple of Amenhotep, son of Hapu (reign of Amenhotpe III); (*27*) the mortuary temple of Thutmose II, reused by Thutmose III; (*28*) the "South Temple" of an anonymous individual; (*29*) the mortuary temple of Ay, Tutankhamun, and Horemheb; (*30*) the mortuary temple of Ramesses III; a part of Medinet Habu, which also contains an early

eighteenth dynasty temple, the mortuary temple of Hatshepsut and Thutmose III; a tomb chapel of Saite princesses; a Ptolemaic temple to Thoth; and other buildings of dynastic, Roman and Christian times; (*31*) the Ptolemaic temple of Thoth at Qasr el-Aguz; and (*32*) the Roman temple of Isis at Deir es-Shelwit.

According to British Museum Papyrus 10068 (twentieth dynasty), dozens of New Kingdom houses lay at the edge of the cultivation, among these temples and shrines. The papyrus gives a house census with the names and titles of priests, officials, and scribes who lived there, side by side with the families of beekeepers, washermen, and brewers.

3. *Several small limestone hills rise from the desert plain.* They contain hundreds of small tombs of priests and noblemen, mostly of New Kingdom date, a few from the Old and the Middle Kingdom or the Late period. Many of the tombs were oriented to face the mortuary temple of their owner's pharaoh. More than four hundred finely decorated tombs have been assigned catalog numbers by

Egyptologists, but there are many hundreds more, still unexcavated and unstudied. The nobles' tombs were set from north to south in five general areas:

(*33*) Dra Abul Naga; seventeenth and eighteenth dynasty tombs and numerous tombs of Ramessid high priests; [*See* Dra Abul Naga.] (*34*) Asasif, with forty tombs, all but seven of them nineteenth dynasty or later; [*See* Asasif.] (*35*) Khokhah, with five Old Kingdom (sixth dynasty) tombs and fifty-three of the New Kingdom; [*See* Khokhah.] (*36*) Ilwet es-Sheikh Abd el-Qurna, divided into northern and southern parts—the northern, a long, narrow hill, has upper and lower sections. In the upper are sixty-nine tombs, fifty-five of them dating to the eighteenth dynasty; in the lower are sixteen tombs, eight of them eighteenth dynasty; outside these sections are another twenty-eight eighteenth dynasty tombs, three that are earlier than the eighteenth dynasty and thirty that are later. (*37*) Qurnet Murai has seventeen tombs, fourteen of Ramessid date, three of the eighteenth dynasty. The cliffs west of areas *35*, *36*, and *37* define the Deir el-Bahri cirque, in which lie the mortuary temples of (*38*) Hatshepsut (eighteenth dynasty), (*39*) Thutmose III (eighteenth dynasty), and (*40*) Montuhotep II (eleventh dynasty); and the so-called Wadi Habl (*41*), in which lie a mortuary temple of Montuhotep IV and the tomb of Meket-Re. Here, numerous hieroglyphic, Hieratic, and Demotic graffiti may be seen on the cliff faces, as they are here and elsewhere throughout the necropolis.

One kilometer (about a half-mile) north of Dra Abul Naga lies a narrow wadi (*42*) with an ancient quarry that served as the source of stone for Queen Hatshepsut's mortuary temple (and is the source of stone for its repair). The temple is the starting point of an ancient caravan route that went north to Farshut. Farther north, several other wadis adjacent to the desert plain contain seventh-century CE Coptic hermitages and, perhaps, the tombs of minor royalty.

South and west of Qurnet Murai, in a narrow passage between two hills, lies Deir el-Medina (*43*), a village and cemetery built for the artisans and quarrymen responsible for the digging and decoration of the New Kingdom royal tombs in the Valley of the Kings.

4. *Outlying wadis and the desert plateau.* Scattered across the desert plateau lie numerous Paleolithic work stations. Between Deir el-Medina and the Valley of the Kings stand the remains of dry-wall masonry huts built in the New Kingdom as a "village du repos" (*44*) for the workmen. North and west of the Valley of the Kings are traces of a low stone wall (*45*) that apparently defined the limits of the sacred necropolis during the New Kingdom. There are also scattered remains of Coptic monasteries, churches, and hermitages lying on or near map features (*33*), (*37*) and (*42*). The highest point on the plateau is a

hill called the Qurn (*46*) in Arabic, meaning "horn," or "crown of the head," which towers above the Valley of the Kings. Its northern slope is covered with scores of small stone shrines. At the northern limit of the necropolis, on Thoth Hill, atop the second-highest point on the western bank of the Nile, lie the remains of a mud-brick temple of the Middle Kingdom (*47*) dedicated to Thoth, which was constructed on the remains of an Old Kingdom or Early Dynastic structure (currently being studied by a Hungarian expedition). The two most famous wadis in the necropolis are the (*48*) East Valley of the Kings (called in Arabic, Biban el-Moluk) and the (*49*) West Valley of the Kings (called in Arabic, Wadyein). The East Valley is the best known and most extensively explored; it contains about sixty tombs of New Kingdom rulers and high officials. The West Valley contains only two (or possibly three) known royal tombs. Several small adjacent wadis also contain tombs, stelae, or graffiti (*50*). To the south of the Valley of the Kings lies (*51*), the Valley of the Queens (called in Arabic, Biban el-Harim), containing more than eighty tombs of queens, princesses, royal sons, and court officials.

Several wadis south and west of the Valley of the Queens and the Qurn were explored early in the twentieth century, by Howard Carter, and found to contain numerous small pit tombs, belonging in most cases to minor princesses of the New Kingdom. These wadis include Wadi Sikket Taqa el-Zeid (also called Wadi A) (*52*), where an early tomb of Hatshepsut was found, Wadi Qubbanat el-Qirud (with Wadi B and Wadi D) (*53*), and Wadi Gharbi (with Wadi F and Wadi G) (*54*).

[*See also* Asasif; Deir el-Bahri; Deir el-Medina; Karnak; Khokhah; Luxor; Qurna; Thebes; Tombs; Valley of the Kings; *and* Valley of the Queens.]

BIBLIOGRAPHY

Arnold, Dieter. *Gräber des Alten und Mittleren Reiches in El-Tarif.* Archäologische Veröffentlichungen; Deutsches Archäologisches Institut, Abteilung Kairo, 17. Mainz, 1976.

Gardiner, Alan H. and A. E. P. Weigall. *A Topographical Catalogue of the Private Tombs of Thebes.* London, 1913.

Haeny, Gerhard. "L'origine des traditions thébaines concernant Memnon." *Bulletin de l'Institute français d'archéologie Orientale* 64 (1966), 203–212.

Haeny, Gerhard, ed. *Untersuchungen im Totentempel Amenophis' III Beitrage zur ägyptischen Bauforschung und Altertumskunde*, 11. Wiesbaden, 1981.

Kemp, Barry, and David O'Connor. "An Ancient Nile Harbour: University Museum Excavations at the 'Birket Habu'." *International Journal of Nautical Archaeology* 3.1 (1974), 101–136.

Memnonia: Bulletin édité par l'Association pour la sauvegarde de Ramesseum. Cairo, 1990–.

Nims, Charles Francis. *Thebes of the Pharaohs: Pattern For Every City.* London, 1965.

Otto, Eberhard. *Topographie des thebanischen Gaues. Untersuchungen zur Geschichte und Altertumskunde Aegyptens*, 16. Berlin, 1952.

Peet, T. Eric. *The Great Tomb-Robberies of the Twentieth Egyptian Dynasty.* Oxford, 1930.

Petrie, W. M. Flinders. *Six Temples at Thebes.* London, 1897.

Riefstahl, Elizabeth. *Thebes in the Time of Amunhotep III.* Norman, Oklahoma, 1964.

Thomas, Elizabeth. *The Royal Necropoleis of Thebes.* Princeton, 1966.

University of Chicago. Oriental Institute, Epigraphic Survey. *Medinet Habu,* vol. 1, *Earlier Historical Records of Ramses III.* Oriental Institute Publications, 8. Chicago, 1930.

University of Chicago. Oriental Institute, Epigraphic Survey. *Medinet Habu,* vol. 2, *Later Historical Records of Ramses III.* Oriental Institute Publications, 9. Chicago, 1932.

University of Chicago. Oriental Institute, Epigraphic Survey. *Medinet Habu,* vol. 3, *The Calendar, the "Slaughterhouse," and Minor Records of Ramses III.* Oriental Institute Publications, 23. Chicago, 1940.

University of Chicago. Oriental Institute, Epigraphic Survey. *Medinet Habu,* vol. 4, *Festival Scenes of Ramses III.* Oriental Institute Publications, 51. Chicago, 1940.

University of Chicago. Oriental Institute, Epigraphic Survey. *Medinet Habu,* vol. 5, *The Temple Proper,* pt. 1: *The Portico, the Treasury, and Chapels Adjoining the First Hypostyle Hall with Marginal Material from the Forecourts.* Oriental Institute Publications, 83. Chicago, 1957.

University of Chicago. Oriental Institute, Epigraphic Survey. *Medinet Habu,* vol. 6, *The Temple Proper,* pt. 2: *The Re Chapel, the Royal Mortuary Complex, and Adjacent Rooms with Miscellaneous Material from the Pylons, the Forecourts, and the First Hypostyle Hall.* Oriental Institute Publications, 84. Chicago, 1963.

University of Chicago. Oriental Institute, Epigraphic Survey. *Medinet Habu,* vol. 7, *The Temple Proper,* pt. 3: *The Third Hypostyle Hall and All Rooms Accessible from It with Friezes of Scenes from the Roof Terraces and Exterior Walls of the Temple.* Oriental Institute Publications, 93. Chicago, 1964.

University of Chicago. Oriental Institute, Epigraphic Survey. *Medinet Habu,* vol. 8, *The Eastern High Gate with Translation of Texts.* Oriental Institute Publications, 94. Chicago, 1970.

Weeks, Kent R. *Atlas of the Valley of the Kings.* Cairo, 2000.

KENT R. WEEKS

THEBES (modern Luxor) ancient Greek name for the Upper Egyptian town of Waset (or Nut) and, from the end of the Old Kingdom, the main city of the fourth Upper Egyptian nome (25°43' N, 32°38' E). Thebes became the capital of Egypt during parts of the eleventh dynasty and during the New Kingdom. In the Greek sources (e.g., Homer's *Odyssey*), the Boeotian and the Egyptian Thebes were differentiated by the epithets *heptapyloios* ("seven-gated") and *hekatompyloi* ("hundred-gated"), respectively. *Hekatompyloi* may have referred to either the numerous doorways (pylons) in the temples on the eastern bank of the Nile River or to the tomb entrances on the western bank of the Nile. The site of Thebes includes areas on both sides of the Nile: On the eastern bank, the city of Waset had the two main temples of Upper Egypt during the New Kingdom, the temple of Karnak in the north and the temple of Luxor in the south; on the western bank, large private and royal cemeteries, as well as numerous temple complexes, extended over an area of more than 4 kilometers (2.4 miles) in length and 0.5–1 kilometer (about a quarter to a half mile) in width. The great number of monuments, many exceptionally well preserved, make the Theban area the largest and most important archaeological site in Egypt.

Eastern Bank of the Nile. A discussion of the principal archaeological features follows.

The temple of Karnak. Archaeologically, the eastern bank of Thebes is dominated by the gigantic temple complex of Karnak, the home of Egypt's main god Amun-Re from the time of the Middle Kingdom onward. The earliest known parts of the temple have been dated to the first half of the eleventh dynasty, when a presumably modest temple, or a chapel, for the god Amun was erected by King Antef II. The temple was substantially expanded in the twelfth dynasty, during the reign of Senwosret I. The temple, however, seems to have remained in this state for almost four hundred years. From the eighteenth dynasty until the Roman period, Karnak was a place of continuous building activity, but of varying intensity.

The temple of Luxor. The main part of the temple of Luxor was founded by Amenhotpe III (r. 1410–1372 BCE). An earlier triple shrine (bark-station), built by Queen Hatshepsut and Thutmose III (r. 1502–1452 BCE) north of the first pylon, remained in use at later times; then in the nineteenth dynasty, Ramesses II added an open court to the north of the existing Amenhotpe III building. Since the Ramessid addition respected the orientation of the axis of the earlier shrine, this caused a widening angle of orientation and therefore a significant deviation for the central axis of the temple complex. During New Kingdom times, the Luxor temple was one of the most important centers for, and a starting point of, numerous feasts, festivals, and ceremonies (e.g., the Valley and the Opet Festivals). The main temple was connected with the temples of Karnak and Mut by a paved avenue of sphinxes.

In 1989, the Egyptian Antiquities Organization discovered a major cache in the forecourt of the Amenhotpe III temple. This deposit, in the western part of the court, contained several statues of New Kingdom and later date gods and kings. All were in pristine condition, and they are now on permanent display in the Luxor Museum.

The ancient city. Little is known about life in the ancient metropolis of Thebes, although it must have been one of the largest cities of New Kingdom Egypt, with an estimated population of forty thousand to fifty thousand. The center of the city during New Kingdom and later times assumedly stretched between the two major temples of Karnak and Luxor, probably on both sides of the avenue of sphinxes that connected them. In the mid-1960s, an excavation by the Egyptian Antiquities Organization in the small suburb of Hod Abu el-Gud (300 me-

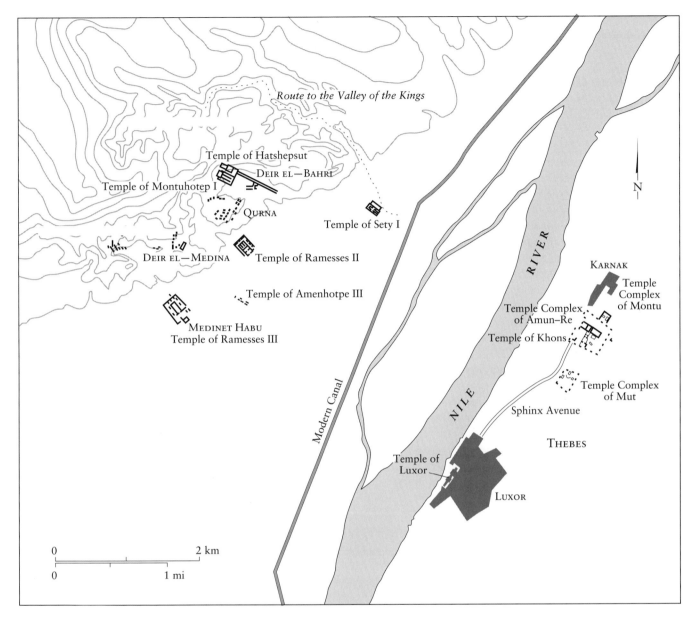

THEBES. *Plan of Thebes.*

ters/about 1,000 feet south of the Karnak enclosure wall) revealed part of a late New Kingdom town site, with mud-brick houses of modest size. If similar to other major cities of the New Kingdom—Tell el-Amarna, Malqata, and Deir el-Ballas—it is expected that royal palaces and large private houses also existed in the center of ancient Thebes, an area now almost entirely covered by modern-day Luxor.

Excavations by the Akhenaten Temple Project have revealed an extensive domestic quarter of Old Kingdom date that extends hundreds of meters east of the present Karnak *temenos*. To the southeast of the *temenos*, an ex-

tensive quarter of villas was uncovered that dated from the Ramessid Period, and belonged, according to door-post inscriptions, to officials of the treasury. Late period Demotic texts referred to several districts, such as "the north of the City" and "House of the Cow"; northeast of the *temenos*, excavation has uncovered a sector of town houses, that date from c.690 to 340 BCE. A fluctuation in Thebe's fortunes was suggested by the wholesale abandonment of vast tracts of housing at the close of the twentieth dynasty and again after 343 BCE.

Western Bank of the Nile. A discussion of the principal archaeological features follows.

Old Kingdom tombs. During the Old Kingdom, Thebes was no more than a small provincial town, although as early as the late fourth dynasty, it was the capital of the fourth Upper Egyptian (Theban) nome. Tombs from the later part of the Old Kingdom are known from two areas of the Theban necropolis: from el-Tarif and from Khokhah. In el-Tarif, the area opposite Karnak, remains of two large mud-brick *mastaba*s were unearthed, which may have belonged to local rulers or to nomarchs of the fourth and the fifth dynasty. The Khokhah area contains several small rock-cut tombs that were decorated with wall paintings. Three of these tombs were created for nomarchs of the Theban nome (tombs 186, 405, and 413). [*See* Khokhah.] Occasional finds of Old Kingdom objects in other areas of the Theban necropolis seem to indicate isolated (shaft?) burials rather than large cemeteries, for example, scattered pottery sherds of the fourth or the fifth dynasty from the Dra Abul Naga area. [*See* Dra Abul Naga.]

Middle Kingdom cemeteries. At the end of the First Intermediate Period, a family of local rulers from the Theban area gained power in Upper Egypt. The first three kings of the eleventh dynasty, Antef I to Antef III (r. 2134–2068 BCE), erected large tomb complexes in the area of el-Tarif. Each of these *saff*-tombs (the Arabic term *saff* means "row," referring to the rows of pillars in front of the tombs' façades) had an entrance building at the eastern end, followed by a gigantic 250–300 meter (750–900 foot) rectangular, sunken open court that was dug into the desert surface. At the western end of this open court, one or two rows of pillars (twenty to twenty-four pillars) were cut out of the rock. In the middle of the façade, a small passage led to one or two chambers of modest size, which in turn led to the royal burial shaft. The wall behind the façade, as well as both side walls of the long court, contained a large number of additional and subsidiary burial chambers, presumably for the members of the royal family and high officials of the court. These tomb complexes seem to have been undecorated, with the exception of the entrance buildings on the east, where, in the tomb of Antef II (died 2068 BCE), the famous Dog Stela was found. Other members of the court and some officials of the local administration erected their own private *saff*-tombs, of considerably smaller scale, in the vicinity of their ruler's tomb complex.

After the reunification of the country, Nebhepetre Montuhotep I (r. 2061–2011 BCE) moved the royal burial place to the valley of Deir el-Bahri, where he erected his huge tomb and temple complex. Although not a pyramid, the architectural layout of this complex clearly contained elements of the earlier Old Kingdom pyramid complexes—namely, a valley temple, at the edge of the cultivation, with a long causeway that led to the temple building. Courtiers and high officials of the time excavated their *saff*-tombs in the slope of the valley overlooking the royal temple and causeway. In a valley south of Deir el-Bahri (the so-called "Third Valley"), a similarly ambitious temple and tomb project was begun under one of Montuhotep I's successors. Although this complex was never finished or used, some of the high officials at that time had already built their own tombs in the vicinity of this ruler's unfinished tomb (e.g., the tomb of Meketra, tomb 280).

Very little is known about private burials in the Theban necropolis during the twelfth dynasty (1991–1786 BCE), since the royal tombs and cemeteries of the high officials were located in the northern part of the country (e.g., in el-Lisht, Dahshur, Hawara, and Illahun), after the first king of the dynasty, Amenemhet I, moved the country's capital to Itjtawy (perhaps today's el-Lisht). Only one decorated tomb of this period (tomb 60) is known to have been excavated in Sheikh Abd el-Qurna. Officials of the local Theban administration and some middle- and lower-class individuals continued to be buried in *saff*-tombs; however, none of the approximately ninety to one hundred tombs of this type in the Theban necropolis has been positively dated to the twelfth dynasty.

Cemeteries of the Second Intermediate Period. Until the 1980s, relatively little was known about burials and cemeteries of the Second Intermediate Period. Private burials were located all over the Theban necropolis: these included a unique and undisturbed burial of a woman in a *rishi*-coffin of the seventeenth dynasty in the northern part of the necropolis; mass burials at the eastern end of Asasif; and several burial shafts of high officials (including a princess and a vizier) that were dated to the same period in the Valley of the Queens. Yet excavations have also demonstrated that the area of Dra Abul Naga in the northern part of the Theben Necropolis was probably the main Theban cemetery during the second part of the Second Intermediate Period. Also in this area, parts of the burial equipment were discovered, including several coffins, of kings of the seventeenth dynasty. Therefore, the Dra Abul Naga region was, almost certainly, the location of the seventeenth dynasty royal burials, although none of the tombs has yet been positively identified.

New Kingdom cemeteries and mortuary temples. Changes in theological conceptions at the end of the Second Intermediate Period and during the first decades of the eighteenth dynasty also resulted in a new understanding of royal and private funerary architecture. The most visible result of this new architecture was the deliberate separation of the royal tomb from the temple for the funerary cult of the deceased king. The age-old practice of an architectural unity for the royal burial place and the place for the royal funerary cult, as realized in the sophisticated pyramid complexes of the Old and Middle Kingdoms, no longer existed. With only a few exceptions, throughout the New Kingdom, the tombs of the kings were placed in a remote valley in the mountains west of Thebes, which is known today as the Valley of the Kings. Their cult places, the mortuary temples, were erected at the border between the desert and the cultivated area, with no immediate connection to the tombs. Although Amenhotpe I (r. 1545–1525 BCE) is credited for having been the founder of the Valley of the Kings (and, therefore, for the separation of tomb and temple), there seem to be neither traces of his mortuary temple nor those of his immediate successors, Thutmose I and Thutmose II. The small structures usually attributed to those kings were, most probably, erected posthumously.

The first fully developed mortuary temple of the New Kingdom was that of Queen Hatshepsut (died 1482 BCE) at Deir el-Bahri. Architecturally, this unique temple combines elements of the nearby temple of Montuhotep I with those of the earlier royal *saff*-tombs of el-Tarif. For the following hundred and fifty years, virtually every king built a mortuary temple for his funerary cult. The most impressive was the temple of Amenhotpe III, which was presumably one of the largest buildings on the western bank; The Colossi of Memnon once flanked the entrance to this temple building and are now the only surviving, standing parts of the temple. For unknown reasons, the temple was dismantled during the New Kingdom and, today, little more than the foundation remains. In recent years, the Swiss Institute, Cairo, discovered a number of decorated limestone (calcite) blocks from a structure of the temple of Amenhotpe III that were being used as foundation blocks in the mortuary temple of Merenptah (died 1226 BCE).

The classical form of the New Kingdom mortuary temple on the Nile's western bank is represented by the nineteenth dynasty temples of Sety I, Ramesses II (the Ramesseum) and the twentieth dynasty temple of Ramesses III (Medinet Habu), the last being the best preserved. [*See* Sety I; Ramesses II; Ramesses III.] The political and economic crises at the end of the twentieth dynasty prevented the later Ramessid kings from erecting large temple complexes in the Theban area. The last known mortuary temple is that of Ramesses IV, located at the eastern end of Asasif; however, this ambitious building project was never finished. [*See* Asasif.]

For over four hundred years, the Valley of the Kings was the last resting place of the New Kingdom rulers. Which king of the early eighteenth dynasty was first to have a tomb there is still undetermined. The earliest positively identified eighteenth dynasty royal tombs are those of Thutmose III (tomb 34, died 1452 BCE) and Hatshepsut (tomb 20, died 1482 BCE). Similar uncertainty exists about the burial places of other female members of the royal family during the eighteenth dynasty. Although a number

of burial pits in remote areas of the Theban hills (e.g., the Valley of the Monkeys in the southern part of the necropolis) are known to have contained burials of royal princesses, no tombs there for the queens (except, perhaps, for the tomb of Queen Ahmose-Nefertari in Dra Abul Naga) or the princes have yet been identified. During Ramessid times, the Valley of the Kings was the only royal burial ground in Egypt; all the kings of this period are known to have built their own tombs there or usurped already existing tombs (the only "missing" royal tomb may be that of Ramesses VIII, if this king ever existed). A number of royal princes were also buried in the Valley of the Kings, whereas some of the queens and other princes of Ramessid times were buried in the Valley of the Queens.

The new conception of royal burials had an immediate impact on the location and general layout of nonroyal tombs. No longer could a high courtier or official have his private tomb erected in the vicinity of his king's tomb, as was the custom in the Old and Middle Kingdoms. The resulting, entirely new, conception of the private tomb led to the T-shaped basic form for private New Kingdom tombs at Thebes. From the beginning of the eighteenth dynasty and until the end of the twentieth dynasty, several hundred private tombs were cut out of the limestone hills and plains in various locations on the western bank of the Nile. The most important of them are the New Kingdom private cemeteries of Sheikh Abd el-Qurna, Khokhah, Dra Abul Naga, and the necropolis of the royal workmen in Deir el-Medina.

Later cemeteries. From the end of the New Kingdom to the twenty-fifth and the twenty-sixth dynasty, no substantial royal or private tombs are known on the western bank of the Nile at Thebes. The royal burial grounds were moved to other places outside Thebes (e.g., Tanis); officials of the Theban administration and the priests preferred to be buried in mass burials (e.g., the caches of the priests of Amun and Montu in Deir el-Bahri). All over the Theban necropolis, however, older tomb structures were extensively reused, often without disturbing or removing the original burials. During the twenty-fifth and the twenty-sixth dynasty, a number of exceptionally large tomb structures were erected in Thebes, in the Asasif (e.g. Harwa, tomb 37; Montuemhat, tomb 34; Pedamenophis, tomb 33; and Ibj, tomb 36); their owners belonged to the priestly and administrative elite of the theocracy of Amun in Thebes.

Other monuments. On the highest elevation of the western bank of Thebes, so-called Thoth Hill, in the northernmost part of the necropolis, there are substantial remains of a Middle Kingdom temple structure that, in its present form, was erected by Montuhotep II (r. 2011–2000 BCE) and presumably dedicated to the god Thoth. The remains consist of a massive mud-brick enclosure wall and an inner tripartite sanctuary. The entrance of the sanctuary was flanked by limestone jambs, decorated with sunken relief that mentions the royal titles and names of the king. Excavations by a Hungarian expedition have revealed foundation deposits at all four corners of the temple, as well as an earlier structure, below the Middle Kingdom level, which may be dated to the Old Kingdom.

Between the temples of Amenhotpe III and that of Ramesses III (Medinet Habu) are the scanty remains of a temple structure that, from the layout and ground plan, resembles the architecture of royal mortuary temples. It was erected by and probably used for the cult of the high Theban official—Amenhotep, son of Hapu—who was a "scribe of recruits" and an "overseer of works" during the reign of Amenhotpe III and who was credited with erecting the famous Colossi of Memnon of Amenhotpe III. [*See* Amenhotep, Son of Hapu.]

Halfway between the laborers' settlement of Deir el-Medina and the Valley of the Queens is a small rock-cut sanctuary, with several chapels that were dedicated to the god Ptah and the local Theban goddess Meretseger. Although royal stelae and inscriptions are known from the sanctuary, it was mainly used by the inhabitants of Deir el-Medina for the worship of the goddess, one of the patron deities of the village during the Ramessid period.

Approximately 2 kilometers (1 mile) south of the temple of Medinet Habu, and outside the borders of the Theban necropolis, is a small, unfinished temple that was founded in Roman times and dedicated to the worship of the goddess Isis. Only the propylon, the entrance to the main temple, and the inner sanctuary are decorated with raised relief; the outside and most of the inner walls were left plain.

[*See also* Asasif; Deir el-Bahri; Deir el-Medina; Dra Abul Naga; Karnak; Khokhah; Luxor; Mut Precinct; Theban Necropolis; Tombs; Valley of the Kings; *and* Valley of the Queens.]

BIBLIOGRAPHY

Abder Raziq, Mahmud. "Funde aus Abu El-Gud (Karnak)." *Annales du service des antiquités de l'Égypte* 70 (1984–85), 9–11. Short report on a settlement excavation in the city of Luxor.

Arnold, Dieter. *Der Tempel des Königs Mentuhotep von Deir el-Bahari.* vol. 1: *Architektur und Deutung.* Archäologische Veröffentlichungen, Deutsches Archäologisches Instituts, Abteilung Kairo, 8. Mainz, 1974.

Arnold, Dieter. *Gräber des Alten und Mittleren Reiches in El-Tarif.* Archäologische Veröffentlichungen, Deutsches Archäologisches Instituts, Abteilung Kairo, 17. Mainz, 1976.

Assmann, Jan, ed. *Theben,* vol. 1–13. Mainz am Rhein, 1983–1996. Publication series of mostly Ramesside private tombs in the Theban Necropolis.

Davies, Norman de Garis, and Alan H. Gardiner. *The Tomb of Antefoker.* Theban Tomb Series, 2. London, 1920.

Dziobek, Eberhard. "The Architectural Development of Theban Tombs in the Early Eighteenth Dynasty." In *Problems and Priorities in Egyptian Archaeology,* edited by Jan Assmann, Günter Burkard, and Vivian Davies, pp. 69–79. London, 1987.

University of Chicago, Oriental Institute, The Epigraphic Survey, *Medinet Habu.* Oriental Institute Publications, vols. 8, 9, 23, 51, 83, 84, 93, and 94. Chicago, 1930–70.

Kampp, Friederike. *Die thebanische Nekropole.* Theben, 13. Mainz, 1996. Standard publication of the private tombs of Thebes with up-to-date bibliography.

Nims, Charles F. "Places about Thebes." *Journal of Near Eastern Studies* 14 (1955), 110–121. Important additions and corrections to Otto (1952).

Nims, Charles F. *Thebes of the Pharaohs.* London, 1965.

Osing, Jürgen. *Der Tempel Sethos' I. in Gurna. Die Reliefs und Inschriften.* Vol. I. Archäologische Veröffentlichungen, Deutsches Archäologisches Instituts, Abteilung Kairo, 20. Mainz, 1977.

Otto, Eberhard. *Topographie des thebanischen Gaues.* Untersuchungen zur Geschichte und Altertumskunde Ägyptens, 16. Leipzig, 1952. Very detailed study of the topography of the eastern and western banks of the Nile at Thebes, although outdated. See also Nims (1955), important book review (see above).

Polz, Daniel. "The Location of the Tomb of Amenhotep I—A Reconsideration." *Valley of the Sun Kings: New Explorations in the Tombs of the Pharaohs,* edited by Richard H. Wilkinson, pp. 8–21. Tucson, 1995.

Polz, Daniel. "The Ramsesnakht Dynasty and the Fall of the New Kingdom." *Studien zur Altägyptischen Kultur* 25 (1998), 257–293.

Porter, Bertha, and Rosalind L. B. Moss. *Topographical Bibliography of Ancient Egyptian Hieroglyphic Texts, Reliefs and Paintings,* vols. I, 1 and 2. Oxford, 1960–1972.

DANIEL C. POLZ

THIRD DYNASTY. See Old Kingdom, *article on* Third Dynasty.

THIRD INTERMEDIATE PERIOD, the term generally used to describe the twenty-first through twenty-fifth dynasties. Like the previous two Intermediate Periods, it was an era of declining centralized power, a consequent splitting of the nation into a number of separate polities and the appearance of rulers of foreign extraction. The twenty-fifth dynasty, although of Nubian origin, marked a reversal of the disintegrative tendencies of the first four dynasties of the period, and in many of its political and cultural aspects it was more closely allied with the succeeding twenty-sixth dynasty.

Sources. There are a number of sources of data available for the study of the period, although far more scanty than those preserved from Ramesside times. The twenty-first dynasty is particularly poorly served, with almost no surviving administrative papyri or ostraca, private votive statuary, or stelae. This is very unfortunate, as twenty-second dynasty statuary has been very helpful in reconstructing the genealogies of this period. Royal texts are also rare.

For throughout the entire period, a series of carved documents in the temple of Amun at Karnak have provided useful primary data, including the remains of the Priestly Annals; records of Nile flood levels on the main quay; a series of hieroglyphic graffiti; a long chronicle text, and one major royal wall composition. Funerary material has also been helpful, in particular the notations on mummy bandages and other items bearing royal names. For the latter part of the Third Intermediate Period, numerous private stelae record pious donations, and there are a series of statues of private individuals, both of which frequently mention contemporary monarchs and dates.

Chronology and Dynastic Divisions. Although the broad thrust of developments during the period are generally agreed, there continues to be considerable debate as to the precise chronology and temporal and political relationships between the various royal lines. Although a standard chronology exists, primarily the work of Kenneth A. Kitchen, there is no unanimity among specialists, and significant revision remains possible, with a probable general lowering of dates prior to 800 BCE, by twenty-five to fifty years.

The main chronological peg of the period has been the Palestinian campaign of Sheshonq I, which has usually been dated, through its mention in 1 *Kings* 14.25, to 928 BCE. Unfortunately, it is not completely clear where in his reign this campaign should be placed. However, the Assyrian/biblical calculations that underpin that date are now being questioned. Other work also suggests that certain kings of Egypt, who were normally placed in the main succession should instead be regarded as local kings of Thebes only, raising further problems with the so-called standard chronology. These areas of difficulty will be highlighted below; two sets of regnal dates will accordingly be given for most monarchs, first the standard one and then, in square brackets, a revisionist version.

Twenty-first Dynasty. With the demise of Ramesses XI of the twentieth dynasty (r. 1111–1081 [1094–1064] BCE), the national throne passed to Smendes I (r. 1081–1055 [1064–1038] BCE), perhaps a son-in-law of the late king, who ruled from the Nile Delta city of Tanis (San el-Hagar). Earlier, while governor of the town, Smendes had been mentioned in the *Report of Wenamun*, an account (possibly fictionalized) of a voyage to Lebanon to purchase wood. Wenamun's misfortunes probably illustrated the fall in Egypt's international standing during the previous few decades.

South of el-Hiba, however, the country was controlled by Pinudjem I (r. 1076–1038 [1063–1026] BCE), probably a nephew of Smendes and the latest representative of a series of army commanders and high priests of Amun who had been established in authority at Thebes during the last decade of the New Kingdom. The existence of this Thebes-based military/priestly regime, in parallel with the monarchy, is a particular motif that continues throughout the Third Intermediate Period. During Smendes' reign, the high priest and general, Pinudjem, obtained pharaonic titles as local king in Thebes and was succeeded in his military and pontifical offices by, in turn, his sons Masaharta, Djedkhonsiufankh, and Menkheperre. This kind of priestly/kingly transition was to be not infrequent.

Another important offspring of Pinudjem I was his daughter Maetkare, who took the title "God's Wife of Amun." During the Early New Kingdom this had been a title held by the king's chief wife, but when resurrected during the twentieth dynasty it seems to have been held by a virgin princess, whose status appears to have paralleled that of the high priest of the god. Although the prominence of the office varied at times during the Third Intermediate Period, it was ultimately to eclipse and replace that of the high priest himself during the twenty-sixth dynasty.

There seems to have been some kind of violent outbreak in Thebes shortly before the end of Smendes' reign. Djedkhonsiufankh briefly followed Masaharta as high priest but, soon afterward, Menkheperre assumed the high priesthood and proceeded southward to Thebes to suppress some kind of disorder, which may have been linked with the extreme brevity of his predecessor's tenure.

Psusennes I, another son of Pinudjem I, took the Tanite throne (r. 1055–1004 [1038–984] BCE), followed by the short reign of Amenemnisu (r. 1004–1000 [984–981] BCE). Psusennes I and his brother Menkheperre were presumably of a similar age, for they were to hold their respective offices, essentially in parallel, for half a century. Psusennes I's tomb at Tanis was found intact in the 1939–1940 season; it also contained the body of his general, Wendjebaendjed, as well as those of his successor, Amenemhet and the later monarchs Siamun, Psusennes II, and Sheshonq II.

Although it is generally assumed that Amenemhet (r. 1000–990 [981–971] BCE) was Psusennes I's son, a clear break in the line of the dynasty seems to have occurred after Amenemhet's death, since his successor was Osochor (Osorkon the Elder, r. 990–984 [971–965] BCE), the son of the Libyan chief of the Ma (Meshwesh). His existence was only established in 1977. The significance of this Libyan appearance on the Tanite throne is unclear; Libyans had been among the foes of Merenptah and Ramesses III, but no evidence exists to indicate a violent takeover. Rather, the family in question seems to have been resident in Egypt for generations, although able to be distinguished by their ancestral Libyan names and titles. [See Libya.] Indeed, the line of Herihor may have included Libyans, since a number of its scions, from the priest-general's sons—Osorkon, Masaqaharta, and Masaharta—to the latter's namesake, Pinudjem I's son and successor as high priest of Amun, bore Libyan names.

Thus, it is possible that the death of Amenemhet's was followed by the assumption of the crown by a collateral line of the existing family, with the senior members of the dynasty retaining the Upper Egyptian command, in the form of Menkheperre's sons, the high priests Smendes II and Pinudjem II, and the latter's offspring and successor, Psusennes II. Osochor's successor, Siamun (r. 984–965 [965–945] BCE), is of unknown antecedents. His purely Egyptian name need not count against him being a member of the Libyan family, as the aforementioned family of Herihor contained a mixture of name types within a single generation; then, too, he may represent a member of the Theban branch taking back control after Osochor's death.

What happened at the end of Siamun's reign is uncertain. The conventional view is that he was followed in turn by the former high priest, Psusennes II (r. 965–931 BCE), and then Sheshonq I, but there are indications that Psusennes II, who had replaced Pinudjem II as high priest in the tenth year of Siamun, may have only held full royal names and titles as a junior coregent of Sheshonq I from about 945 to 940 BCE. Sheshonq I thus may well have been the direct successor of Siamun or, indeed, may have actually assumed power, at least in Thebes, before Siamun's death, to judge from a text in which Sheshonq's second regnal year was accompanied by his naming as a mere chief of the Ma.

The economy. A chronic shortage of funds has been suggested by the extensive recycling of building and other material at Tanis, Thebes, and other sites. Almost all the hard stone used at Tanis is reused stone, while it is now clear that the rewrapping and caching of the New Kingdom royal mummies during the period was accompanied by the stripping of all surviving material of value, in particular, the gold.

Twenty-second dynasty. Sheshonq I (r. 931–910 [945–924] BCE) was a nephew of Osochor, and the son of Nimlot A, chief of the Ma. He reimposed royal control over Upper Egypt through the appointment of his own son, Iuput, as high priest of Amun. Another son, known as Nimlot B, was appointed military governor of Herakleopolis. At Memphis, the high priesthood continued to be held by the incumbent family, in the person of Shedsunefertum A, who also held the distinction of being a king's brother-in-law, having married a daughter of a ruler of the twenty-first dynasty.

Apart from the possibility of some activity by Siamun, there is no real evidence for Egyptian military intervention in Palestine from the late Ramessid period until the reign of Sheshonq I. Then, the king penetrated into Palestine, at least as far north as Megiddo, where he erected a stela, before returning to Egypt. A large wall area at Karnak was dedicated to the depiction of the Palestinian campaign, and a long list of the towns attacked was provided, although some entries are unreadable.

This campaign is usually equated with the attack on Jerusalem by "King Shishak," related in the Bible's first book of *Kings* as taking place in the fifth regnal year of Judea's King Rehoboam. The equivalence of the names seems transparent, despite the recent chronologically inspired protests to the contrary. However, the relevant toponym is missing from the Karnak reliefs, and the itinerary of the campaign does not fit easily. Possibly, the attack on Jerusalem took place as part of an earlier or later second campaign, of which no monumental commemoration is extant.

On Sheshonq I's death, the throne passed to Osorkon I (r. 910–896 [924–889] BCE), whose wife Maetkare B was a daughter of Psusennes II. Soon after his accession, the new king's eldest son, Sheshonq C, succeeded as high priest of Amun. A statue of Osorkon I, with an added Phoenician inscription, has been found at Byblos on the Lebanese coast, attesting to continuing international relations at the time: another statue from the site belonged to Sheshonq I.

Toward the end of Osorkon I's long reign, Sheshonq became his father's coregent and was replaced as pontiff by a brother, Iuwlot. Unfortunately, Sheshonq II died shortly afterward, the result of an infected head wound.

When Osorkon I died soon afterward, he was followed by Takelot I (r. 896–873 [889–874] BCE), whose reign is particularly obscure. Thebes continued to be ruled by the high priest, Iuwlot, and then by his brother, Smendes III, but almost nothing else is known of the events during Takelot I's occupation of the throne.

Takelot I's son was Osorkon II (r. 873–844 [874–835] BCE), and around the time of his accession, Harsiese, apparently the son of Sheshonq II, was appointed high priest of Amun. Perhaps that was an unwise choice, given Harsiese's direct descent from the former twenty-first dynasty high priests. Giving such a man Egypt's southern command, rather than a son of Osorkon II, diluted the direct control of the Tanite king over Thebes. Furthermore, it may be that at some later time this Harsiese claimed royal titles, after the model of Pinudjem I, although an attempt has been made by Karl Jansen-Winkeln (1995) to make the high priest and King Harsiese different individuals.

Elsewhere in Egypt, during the Third Intermediate Period, the practice of installing royal sons in positions of power was continued from previous reigns, and extended at Memphis, where the old, established line of high priests was supplanted by the crown prince, Sheshonq D. The ap-

THIRD INTERMEDIATE PERIOD. *Victory relief of Sheshonq I, on the exterior wall of the Bubastite Portal, in the First Court of the Great Temple of Amun at Karnak.* The king was formerly modeled in plaster on the right-hand side of the scene, smiting his enemies before Amun. Behind Amun are the name-rings of the defeated Palestinian cities. (Courtesy Aidan Dodson)

proach was also readopted at Thebes after the end of the pontificate of King Harsiese's son, when Prince Nimlot C became high priest of Amun. Nimlot combined his high priesthood with his earlier post, the governorship of Hierakleopolis and Middle Egypt, in which he followed his earlier namesake, the son of Sheshonq I. Nimlot C predeceased his father, Osorkon II, and was followed in the pontificate by his own son, Takelot F. The female side of the Amun clergy was headed by the "God's Wife," Karomat G, who was a king's daughter, but the identity of her father is uncertain. Little is known of twenty-second dynasty "God's Wives," although a number were buried in the area of the Ramesseum at Western Thebes.

The only evidence for Osorkon II's foreign relations is the statue that was presented to the ruler of Byblos and also the remains of a vase from Samaria. In addition, he seems to have been the pharaoh who contributed a thousand troops to the coalition of the Syrian-Palestinian polities that opposed the Assyrian king, Shalmaneser III, at the Battle of Qarqar in 853 BCE. Later, he sent gifts of various exotic fauna to the Assyrian king, who was pleased to present them as "tribute from Egypt."

Late in the reign, the high priest of Amun, Takelot F, appears to have imitated Harsiese in taking kingly names and titles. As Takelot II, he was formerly regarded by Egyptologists as being Osorkon II's successor at Tanis from 850 to 825 (or 844–819) BCE, but evidence marshalled in 1989 by David A. Aston strongly points to his having been a Theban king, effectively founding the "Theban twenty-third dynasty" in 841 BCE (see below).

On this basis, Osorkon II's direct successor at Tanis was Sheshonq III (r. 819–767 [835–795] BCE), presumably his son, although no certain evidence survives. The new king had three known sons: his prematurely deceased heir, Bakennefi, Pashedbast, and his second successor, Pemay.

Sheshonq III's authority was acknowledged by the great array of "princedoms" and "chiefdoms" that had been established throughout the Nile Delta during the middle of the twenty-second dynasty. Based on each of the major cities of the area, this network of territories was to remain a key element in Egyptian politics for the remainder of pharaonic history.

Despite the number of local rulers in existence by the

latter part of his reign, Sheshonq III's position as nominal overlord of all Egypt does not seem to have been seriously challenged. Until the 1980s, it appeared that he was directly succeeded by his son, Pemay (r. 767–763 [786–780] BCE), but the 1980s reassessment indicated that a King Sheshonq IV probably interposed between the two (r. 785–773 [795–783] BCE).

The short reigns of these two kings are rather obscure, as is the much longer one of Sheshonq V (767–730 [780–743] BCE). All continued to rule from Tanis, but before the end of the latter's reign, the twenty-second dynasty monarch had become no more than a "first among equals" among the myriad local rulers in the Delta.

The *Theban twenty-third dynasty* is the term now used to describe a group of kings who ruled in Upper Egypt alongside the later Tanite kings. Considerable debate exists as to whether some should be regarded as being based at Leontopolis in the Delta, rather than at Thebes, but the consensus seems to be shifting toward the latter option.

The first king to be so classified could be either Harsiese or Takelot II, both of whom seem to have begun their careers as Theban high priests. Takelot II's activities were largely confined to the area of Thebes. The king had married Karomat D, daughter of the former high priest, Nimlot C; with her, and others, he had at least seven children, four sons and three daughters. The eldest son, Osorkon B, was appointed to the high priesthood of Amun, while at least two of the daughters married various Theban dignitaries. The northern part of what had been since the twenty-first dynasty part of the Theban polity was in the hands of Ptahudjankhef, another son of Nimlot C, based at Hierakleopolis.

Troubles seem to have begun in Takelot II's eleventh regnal year, when the high priest, Osorkon B, was forced to sail southward from el-Hiba toward Thebes to face some potential "enemy who will take hold of the office of the High Priest of Amun." This occurrence was recorded in the Chronicle of Prince Osorkon at Karnak, the major written source for the events that followed. Initial success was followed two years later by the appearance on the scene of Petubastis (King Pedubast I; r. 813–773 [830–799] BCE) as a direct rival to Takelot II, the expulsion of Prince Osorkon from his city, and a civil war.

This lasted some two decades, during which the Petubastis faction seems to have received support from Sheshonq III of Tanis. At one point, Osorkon resumed office, only to be expelled from Thebes once again; at length, he was able to find the wherewithal to finally defeat the opposition and resume his office. Within a short time of his return, the prince-priest became king at Thebes, as Osorkon III (r. 773–745 [799–769] BCE).

The king had a number of children, the eldest son being Takelot G, who served as high priest of Amun for the whole of Osorkon III's reign. He was also placed in charge of Hierakleopolis, which gave him undisputed operational control of the Theban realm. Takelot's sister, Shepenwepet (I), later became "God's Wife of Amun." It seems that the power of the "God's Wife" was henceforth increased at the expense of the high priest, later ladies appearing to be far more important than their male colleagues, some of whose very identities are today uncertain.

After a quarter-century as king, Osorkon appointed High Priest Takelot as coregent (c.750–c.720 [774–759] BCE). As high priest, the new king was replaced by his own son, Osorkon F. Takelot's place at Hierakleopolis was taken by Peftjauawybast, clearly a scion of the royal house, who would later be its final ruling representative.

After Takelot III and his brother and successor, Rudamun (757–754 [759–739] BCE), the succession at Thebes is somewhat obscure. Peftjauawybast, who ruled the northern part of the former Theban dominion (c.749–720 [734–724] BCE) seems to be classifiable as part of this line, until supplanted by the twenty-fifth dynasty. The later kings of the dynasty displayed a distinct archaism in their titulary, which was to be taken further during the later twenty-fifth dynasty and the twenty-sixth.

The *(Tanite) twenty-third dynasty* comprises a number of different groups of kings, including the Theban line, just described, and some at Leontopolis (Kitchen) in the Delta. The trend now seems to be to use the term to designate the rulers at Tanis who followed Sheshonq V on the throne at Tanis. The last of them is known to be Osorkon IV (730–715 BCE), with a predecessor probably being Pedubast II ([743–730] BCE), but little detail is available concerning them, apart from Osorkon's ultimate submission to the invading twenty-fifth dynasty.

The *twenty-fourth dynasty* is the designation used for two rulers of the west-Delta Principality of the West, based at Sais, who used pharaonic titles, named Tefnakhte (r. 724–717) and Bakenrenef (r. 717–711). It was entirely contemporary with the twenty-fifth dynasty, and according to Manetho, Bakenrenef was burned alive by its King Shabaqa.

Twenty-fifth dynasty. The kings of this dynasty were part of a line that had established itself in Upper Nubia (Kush) not long after the Egyptian withdrawal from south of Aswan, after the end of the New Kingdom; they were centered on Napata. (Gebel Barkal [*see* Napata; Twenty-fifth Dynasty]). Although the dynasty began with Alara in the early eighth century BCE, about 755 BCE, King Kashta assumed full pharaonic titles, and rapidly expanded his power into lower Nubia.

Kashta was succeeded by Piya (735–712 BCE). Early in his reign, Kushite influence was extended farther north, to Thebes. There, the king had his sister, Amenirdis I, adopted by the incumbent "God's Wife of Amun," Shepenwepet I, as her intended successor. The appearance of the regnal years of both Piya and his Theban twenty-third dynasty contemporary, Amunrud or Rudamun, in a graffito referring to their priestly sisters implies that both kings were recognized at Thebes. After Amunrud's death, Thebes seems to have effectively passed under Kushite rule.

Following southward expansion by Tefnakhte, the twenty-fourth dynasty Prince of the West, Piya undertook a campaign against Lower Egypt, capturing Memphis and accepting the submission of most of the local rulers of the Delta. The most notable of these were two who held pharaonic titles, Osorkon IV (twenty-third dynasty) and Iuput II of Leontopolis (754–720/715 BCE). In all, fifteen Delta rulers came to formally submit to him, the exception being Tefnakhte, who was only ultimately prevailed upon to submit, and then only by proxy.

Piya then withdrew back to Kush, leaving Egypt in the control of his new vassals; Nubian authority was not reasserted over Lower Egypt until after the accession of his brother and successor, Shabaqa (r. 712–698 BCE). He was followed on the throne by his nephew, Shabtaqa (r. 705–690 BCE), a son of Piya (Pi[ankh]ya). Since the late tenth-century BCE campaigns of Sheshonq I, Egypt had apparently kept herself largely apart from the politics of Syria–Palestine, but Egypt's troops were in 701 BCE unsuccessfully fighting against the Assyrians at the Battle of Eltekeh. Among the Egyptian–Nubian personnel was Taharqa, who was crowned king at Memphis in 690 BCE, following Shabtaqa's death.

At Thebes, the tradition of installing one of the reigning king's close female relations as the heir-apparent to the current "God's Wife of Amun" was continued, with Taharqa's daughter, Amenirdis (II), being adopted by her aunt, Shepenwepet II. Male priesthoods of Amun also remained in the royal family: the high priests Haremakhet and Harkhebi were, respectively, the son and grandson of Shabaqa.

An important figure at Thebes under Taharqa (r. 690–664 BCE) was Montuemhet, who combined the offices of mayor of the city with the fourth prophetship of Amun. [*See* Montuemhet.] Also key figures during the dynasty (and afterward) were the "stewards of the God's Wives of Amun," Akhamunru and Harua, who were responsible for major tombs in the Asasif area of Western Thebes.

The rule of the twenty-fifth dynasty was brought to an end by an Assyrian invasion, which led to Taharqa's flight back to Napata and the definitive departure of his successor, Tanutamun, after a short resurgence. Egypt's retreat was followed by an Assyrian sack of Thebes, and masses of loot were carried back to Assyria. Power in Egypt ultimately passed to the Assyrian vassal of Sais, Psamtik I, who became the founder of the twenty-sixth dynasty (r.

664–610 BCE), which is regarded either as a fresh period in itself (the Saite) or as the first dynasty of the Late period. [*See* Late Period.]

Sites and Settlement Patterns. The archaeological data for the Third Intermediate Period is fairly scrappy, as compared with some other periods, but is still significant. The poor excavation of many Delta sites has been unfortunate, given the political center of gravity, which had definitively shifted there. Elsewhere, a major growth in the number of fortified settlements in Middle Egypt reflected the breakdown in the conception of the unitary state; that was paralleled by the walled nature of the major Delta centers. There is evidence that more of the rural population was now to be found dwelling within those protected towns, sallying forth on a daily basis to till the fields.

Large amounts of material have survived at Tanis, however, including the royal tombs; the temple of Amun had been begun in the eleventh century BCE by Psusennes I, a court added by Siamun in the tenth century BCE, and a new forecourt and other outlying structures the responsibilities of Osorkon II and Sheshonq III in the ninth and the eighth century BCE. Major temple remains have been examined at Bubastis, where a Jubilee Hall was added by Osorkon II. Material from Memphis attests to work under the twenty-first dynasty and the twenty-second, including the high priests' necropolis, while out at Giza a small temple was erected by Psusennes I. After a break in the record between Smendes I and Osorkon II, burials of the Apis bulls were carried out at the Saqqara Serapeum; votive stelae left there are important historical documents for the latter part of the period. Spanish excavations at Ehnasiya [*see* Herakleopolis] have revealed significant twenty-second dynasty remains, including a necropolis.

The northern outpost of the Theban regime, el-Hiba, still awaits comprehensive attention, although a temple of Sheshonq I is known. Farther south, a considerable number of high-status burials, spanning the whole period, have been found at Abydos. At Thebes, the first courtyard of the Karnak temple was constructed by Third Intermediate Period kings, while the small chapel of Osiris-Ruler-of-Eternity was the eighth-century BCE joint work of Osorkon III and Takelot III. At Western Thebes, the center of administration was the temple complex at Medinet Habu, which also housed the tombs of the later "God's Wives" and at least one of the Theban kings, Harsiese. The tombs of lesser individuals clustered around Deir el-Bahri/Asasif and the Ramesseum; until the latter part of the twenty-fifth dynasty, these tombs were almost exclusively of simple design and housed the body and coffins, accompanied by minimal equipment.

Cultural and Artistic Traditions. During the first part of the period, there seems to be a clear attempt to continue the state traditions of the late New Kingdom. However, it has been suggested that transition of the twenty-second to the twenty-third dynasty, the Libyan cultural background of the royal house encouraged the breakdown of the state into separate polities. This non-Egyptian stratum might also explain the extreme banality of most royal titularies, which are extremely repetitive, reusing a very limited number of elements and making the positive identification of a number of kings rather difficult. For example, of a sample fifteen kings of this period, seven certainly bore the prenomen Usermare and another five bore Hedjkheperre.

For most of the period, the artistic norms closely followed New Kingdom prototypes. However, from around 800 BCE, there was an increasing move toward archaism, with the Old Kingdom then being viewed and emulated as the key prototype. This may be seen in the adoption of simple titular names by the kings of the late Theban twenty-third dynasty and the twenty-fifth and was also to be seen emerging in artistic styles. The archaism becomes particularly marked during the twenty-fifth dynasty, with the trend continuing into the twenty-sixth dynasty, of which it is often (wrongly) held to be characteristic.

[*See also* Bakenrenef; Osorkon; Petubastis; Piya; Shabaqa; Sheshonq I; Taharqa; Tanis; *and* Twenty-Fifth Dynasty.]

BIBLIOGRAPHY

Aston, David A. "Takeloth II—A King of the 'Theban Twenty-third Dynasty'?" *Journal of Egyptian Archaeology* 75 (1989), 139–153.

Bierbrier, Morris L. *The Late New Kingdom in Egypt (c. 1300–664 B.C.): A Genealogical and Chronological Investigation.* Warminster 1975.

Bonhême, Marie-Ange. *Les noms royaux dans l'Égypte de la troisième période intermédiere.* Cairo, 1987.

Caminos, Ricardo. *The Chronicle of Prince Osorkon.* Rome, 1958.

Dodson, Aidan M. "Psusennes II." *Revue d'Égyptologie* 38 (1987), 49–54.

Dodson, Aidan M. "Psusennes II and Shoshenq I." *Journal of Egyptian Archaeology* 79 (1993), 267–268. Two discussions of the possible contemporaneity of the last king of the Twenty-first and first king of the Twenty-second Dynasties.

Dodson, Aidan M. "A New King Shoshenq Confirmed?" *Göttinger Miszellen* 137 (1993), 53–58. A presentation of the evidence for a hitherto-unsuspected King Sheshonq (IV) as the direct successor of Sheshonq III.

Dodson, Aidan M. "Towards a Minimum Chronology of the New Kingdom and Third Intermediate Period." *Bulletin of the Egyptian Seminar* (forthcoming). A discussion of the chronological options for the late second and early first millennia BCE.

Fazzini, Richard A. *Egypt: Dynasty XXII–XXV (Iconography of Religions XVI/10).* Leiden, 1988. Deals with the art and iconography of the latter part of the Third Intermediate Period.

Heerma van Voss, M. *Ägypten, die 21. Dynastie (Iconography of Religions XVI/9).* Leiden 1982. Deals with the art and iconography of the earlier part of the Third Intermediate Period.

Jansen-Winkeln, Karl. "Thronname und Begräbnis Takeloths I." *Varia Aegyptiaca* 3 (1987), 253–258. The re-identification of the king who was classified as the first of the name Takelot.

Jansen-Winkeln, Karl. "Historische Probleme der 3. Zwischenzeit." *Journal of Egyptian Archaeology* 81 (1995), 129–149. A discussion of certain questions concerning the twenty-second and the twenty-third dynasties.

Kitchen, Kenneth A. *The Third Intermediate Period in Egypt (1100–650 B.C.).* 3d ed., with new preface and supplement. Warminster, 1995. The absolutely fundamental work on the period, first published in 1972, upon which all subsequent works were based although now dated in a number of areas.

Leahy, Anthony. "The Libyan Period in Egypt: An Essay in Interpretation." *Libyan Studies* 16 (1985), 51–65.

Leahy, Anthony, ed. *Libya and Egypt, c.1300–750 BC.* London, 1990. A collection of important papers dealing with aspects of the Third Intermediate Period.

Myśliwiec, Karol. *Royal Portraiture of the Dynasties XXI–XXX.* Mainz, 1988.

O'Connor, David. "The Third Intermediate Period." *Ancient Egypt: A Social History.* Cambridge 1983. pp. 232–249. A key summary of the social and political trends during the period.

Tanis: l'or des pharaons. Paris, 1987. The richly illustrated catalog of the exhibition of material from San el-Hagar. Abridged editions in English are *Gold of the Pharaohs* (Edinburgh 1988 and Victoria NSW 1988); the latter incorporates additional information not included in the other versions.

AIDAN DODSON

THIRTEENTH DYNASTY. Sources for the Hellenistic king list by the third-century BCE historian Manetho give a confused picture of the period between the twelfth and eighteenth dynasties. For convenience, four of the five intervening dynasties can be aligned with groups of kings attested in contemporary sources. [*See* Second Intermediate Period.] The term "thirteenth dynasty" may be applied to the long series of kings who ruled Egypt from the Residence at Itjtawy after the twelfth dynasty. At the beginning of the dynasty they seem to control all Egypt, but its end is marked by foreign rule of the north of the country. The dynasty thus straddles the Middle Kingdom (Egypt united) and Second Intermediate Period (Egypt divided). It is not clear when or how the period of unity ended. In the Ramessid king list papyrus known as the Turin Canon, the total for the twelfth dynasty is followed (col. 6, 4) by a broken heading for "kings [. . .] after [the House of ?] Sehetpibre" (Amenemhet I), a reference to the founder of the twelfth dynasty and of its royal residence at Itjtawy. Down to column 7, four of these kings are attested in both northern and southern Egypt, but the kings in the remainder of column 7 are known from contemporary monuments only in the South. In column 8, only kings Nehesy and Mersedjefare are otherwise attested, and their monuments are confined to the eastern Delta. They were perhaps contemporary with the later thirteenth dynasty, which would have ruled the rest of Egypt from Itjtawy. The latest source for Itjtawy as the royal residence is the late thirteenth dynasty stela of Horemkhauf, overseer of fields and high priest of Horus at Hierakonpolis. The long series of kings is characterized by short reigns, without a clear pattern of succession. After the fall of Itjtawy and the north to the Hyksos ("fifteenth dynasty"), the same series continues in the reduced southern kingdom centered on Thebes ("seventeenth dynasty").

Sources for the period include neither royal annals nor private autobiographies with information on military events. Instead, they are rich in more generic data on kingship and kinship, administration, religious and other literature, and funerary customs. All point to broad continuity in material culture over the period from Senwosret III to the middle of the thirteenth dynasty, after the reign of Khaneferre Sobekhotpe IV. Thereafter, differences between the Upper Egyptian and Memphite areas become more marked. The eastern Delta constitutes the exception to this cultural homogeneity, and already by the end of the twelfth dynasty may have had a substantial Western Asiatic population. During the thirteenth dynasty, eastern Delta sites seem to become entirely Western Asiatic in their material culture, and they presumably define the separate political unit ruled by the fourteenth dynasty. In the next phase of this demographic shift, Itjtawy was entirely eclipsed by foreign eastern Delta rulers, the "Hyksos" fifteenth dynasty, who replaced the thirteenth dynasty as the principal force in Egypt. One great difference between the twelfth and thirteenth dynasties lies in the scale of royal projects, echoing the shorter average length of reign. Reigns of a decade or less begin with Amenemhet IV and Sobekneferu, last two rulers of the twelfth dynasty. The known pyramids are on a small scale, and no new large temples survive. There are no expeditions to Sinai recorded for the thirteenth dynasty. In the Wadi Hammamat and Wadi el-Hudi, inscriptions attest to the brother kings Neferhotpe I and Sobekhotpe IV, and to the unplaced Sobekemsaf I. At Gebel Zeit (the galena mines on the Red Sea coast), stelae record kings who appear early in the thirteenth dynasty of the Turin Canon. Outside and inside Egypt, there are no surviving examples of royal jewelry of the quality and scale of the twelfth dynasty finds from Illahun, el-Lisht, Dahshur, and Byblos. Nevertheless, sculptors continued and developed the distinct tradition from Senwosret III and Amenemhet III, in which the king is portrayed as a grave and senior ruler, rather than only as the ideal youth. The first masterpiece in this sequence is the siltstone statue of Sekhemkare Amenemhet from Elephantine. Later examples in hard stone include the pairs of red granite colossi for Semenkhkare Mermesha (h. 3.62 and 3.67 meters/11.6 and 11.7 feet) and Khaneferre Sobekhotep IV (h. 2.68 and 2.71 meters/8 and 8.7 feet), which have been found at Tanis, and the red granite colossus of an otherwise unattested Sneferibre Senwosret at the Seventh Pylon at Karnak (h. 2.75

meters/3.8 feet). The lower part of a quartzite statue of Sehetepkare Intef (h. 0.84 meter/2.7 feet) was found at Medinet Maadi. This production in hard stone contrasts with the record for the seventeenth dynasty, securely represented only by the pair of limestone sphinxes of Sankhenre Montuhotep found at Edfu. There are also two statues of uncertain attribution, four statues of Sekhemrawadjkhau Sobekemsaf I, and two statues of the same or another King Sobekemsaf. Sekhemrawadjkhau Sobekemsaf I has been assigned by most commentators to the seventeenth dynasty, but the sculpture includes two red granite statues certainly inscribed for him (h. 1.64 and 1.5 meters/5.25 and 4.8 feet), and one large-scale red granite statue for an unspecified Sobekemsaf (h. 1.32 meters/4.25 feet). He is also one of the only kings of the period to be named in the Wadi Hammamat. It would be difficult to assign him securely to either the thirteenth or seventeenth dynasty. This case demonstrates the continuity in the kingship in Upper Egypt, as well as the gaps existing in the record. The production of hard stone royal sculpture may closely follow the contours of political history, because it required exceptional control of natural and human resources and the maintenance of centers of hieroglyphic inscription and art. The quality, material, and scale of royal monuments thus joins the pattern of their distribution as evidence for locating the principal point or points of rupture in the shift from unified Middle Kingdom to disunited Second Intermediate Period.

On present evidence, the thirteenth dynasty may be divided into three unequal parts. In the earlier phase, reigns seem to have been extremely short, on the evidence of both the Turin Canon and the contemporary monuments. This phase is characterized by continuity from the twelfth dynasty, and specifically from Amenemhet III, in sculpture, in position and type of royal tombs, and in administration, as reflected in both the Illahun legal papyri and the level marks at the Second Cataract of the Nile. The central phase presents a group of more widely and substantially attested rulers, from Sekhemrakhutawy Amenemhet Sobekhotpe II to Merneferre Aya, and including the brother kings Khasekhemre Neferhotpe I and Khaneferre Sobekhotpe IV. The latter is the best-attested king of the dynasty, and the only one to be honored into posterity in archaizing Late period scarabs and an unusual account by Artapanus placing Moses in his reign. The group from Sekhemrasewadjtawy Sobekhotpe III to Aya is well known from a particular form of royal name scarab, in some instances regularly including the name of a nonroyal parent of the king. The great rock inscriptions for Sekhemrasewadjtawy Sobekhotpe III and Khaneferre Sobekhotpe IV confirm an emphasis on family where the king is not himself of royal birth. The later phase of the dynasty covers kings attested only in Upper Egypt, sometimes in fine sculpture, but generally from small-scale soft stone products, not always of the highest quality. The effective secession of the eastern Delta may be dated to this period. This final phase closes under an unknown king with the retreat from Itjtawy to Thebes, where the line of Egyptian kings continues as the seventeenth dynasty. It is not known whether the departure from Itjtawy occurred as a gradual shift in royal residency from Itjtawy to Thebes, or as a single event. Nor is it known from contemporary sources whether the change was violent, as portrayed in the excerpt from Manetho in Josephus, the first-century CE historian's account.

The king lists and contemporary sources name fifty or more kings of the thirteenth dynasty, defined as rulers of Egypt from Itjtawy following the twelfth dynasty. The mechanisms for royal succession remain the greatest problem for our understanding of the period. The Egyptian theory of divine kingship casts each new king as son of the sun god, and therefore obscures the political aspect of succession. Historians have tended to assume that each king should be the son of his predecessor, on the model of European dynasties. Primogeniture is the social ideal in Egyptian texts, and family relations must have played a prominent part in succession to any office, but they seem not to have formed a requirement for kingship. In times of strong kingship, the reigning king would have been well placed to ensure that his eldest son followed him on the throne, and this seems to be the case for the twelfth dynasty and for much of the eighteenth. When there was no son, or when the kingship was weaker, the oligarchic structures of power may reveal themselves in a range of patterns of succession. For the thirteenth dynasty, father-to-son succession is implied by the titles of a woman named Nubhetepti, who is said to be king's wife and king's mother; brother-to-brother succession is documented for Neferhotpe I and Sobekhotpe IV, who record the same nonroyal parents. For instances of nonroyal parentage, it may be noted that the grandfather of Neferhotpe I and Sobekhotpe IV was a military officer. The influence of the military might be discerned in the personal name of one king, the previously mentioned Mermesha, literally "overseer of troops." This would be suitable for a military family, though the title can also apply to directors of work gangs. It is equally uncertain whether the names of kings Wegaf and Khendjer are foreign in origin. Foreigners and the military would doubtless always have had some role in court life, and their impact on royal succession would not be a purely thirteenth dynasty phenomenon.

Some have seen the bureaucracy as the guarantor of continuity, and its head, the vizier, as the power broker and kingmaker of the period. This rests in part on a misdating of the accounting document Papyrus Boulaq 18 to the reign of Sobekhotpe III. The document refers to the vizier Ankhu, also attested on Louvre stela C12 with King Khendjer. Since the two kings are separated on the Turin Canon by three others, it seemed as if Ankhu was in office for five reigns; however, the papyrus has now generally been redated to Sobekhotpe II, immediate predecessor of Khendjer in the Turin Canon. Ankhu's tenure of office therefore seems less extensive. Moreover, Ankhu appears not as a ruling official but as the regular executive arm of the crown on two royal decrees copied in Papyrus Brooklyn 35.1446. This removes all textual evidence for the hypothesis of a king dominated by bureaucracy.

The vizier Ankhu left a statue of himself and one of each parent at Karnak, and other leading officials are attested from equally impressive works. These indicate access to the finest sculptors, but, where they can be measured against exactly contemporary royal monuments, they are overshadowed in scale. Some statues and stelae bear a formula stating that the monument was set up in a temple by permission of the king. The most impressive sequence of sources comes from Iymeru Neferkare, whose second name might seem royal in pretension, but who served as vizier to the best-attested king of the dynasty, Sobekhotpe IV. Despite the reduction in scale of royal monuments in a time of short reigns, the relation between king and court seems comparable to that seen in monuments for periods of stronger kingship (Senwosret I and his vizier-treasurer Montuhotep; Amenhotpe III and his director of manpower and monuments, Amenhotep, son of Hapu). As for those periods, more precise family trees are needed to explore the relations between the holders of the highest offices in one reign, or across more than one. The web of kinship is documented from several sources well into the seventeenth dynasty for Nubkhas, wife of an unknown king of the middle phase of the dynasty. Her daughter married a mayor of Elkab from a family including viziers. In genealogical reconstruction, it is important to attempt full documentation of all higher positions across time, including gaps in the data—for example, where it is not known who held key positions or to which family they belonged. In most cases the relationships cannot be documented, and, if this is not taken into account, the partial data may give a false picture of the strength of influence of a family.

Two incomplete Hieratic documents, Papyri Boulaq 18 and Brooklyn 35.1446, provide an unusually detailed glimpse of the administration at work, complemented by the titles of officials recorded on their hieroglyphic monuments and in quarrying and mining inscriptions. The first largely comprises lists and tables of palace income and expenditure each day during a visit to Thebes by the king and his family. The second preserves a register summarizing, in geographical order from south to north, the thirteenth dynasty progress of legal cases in which an individual had failed to fulfill labor obligations during the reign of Amenemhet III of the twelfth dynasty. The register may have been lodged in the Main Enclosure, the bureaucratic institution attested for the system of enclosures for work gangs (Egyptian, *khenret*). In these sources the administration comprises discrete sections, coordinated by the bureau of the vizier. For Thebes, Papyrus Boulaq 18 specifies three sections (Egyptian *waret*) responsible for delivering income in kind: the Bureau for the Distribution of Manpower, the White House ("treasury"), and the Head of the South. It seems clear from the Brooklyn Papyrus, and the list of towns on the Ramesseum Onomasticon, that the Head of the South designated southern Upper Egypt, from Elephantine to Abydos. Thebes provided the operational center for this area and, according to the Semna Despatches on another Ramesseum papyrus, for occupied Lower Nubia. The Head of the South is already attested in the early twelfth dynasty under Senwosret I, and the treasury dominates twelfth dynasty quarrying and mining, as the department for valuable commodities. However, the specific coordination of departments, each as interlinked *waret*, may not have been finalized until later in the twelfth dynasty, or perhaps even the thirteenth, when administrative titles reached their most precise stage, with prefix and suffix titles to delineate scope. Papyrus Boulaq 18 presents in effect a banking system based on commodity value, with abstract calculation of income presumably according to a predetermined assessment of means, as later illustrated figuratively for the Head of the South in the tomb-chapel of the eighteenth dynasty vizier Rekhmire. The segmented system seems to have operated at the local level; a district could be divided into northern and southern *waret*, and the same word was used for smaller sections of dense occupation, such as part of a necropolis, or for the individual sectors of artistic production.

It is often difficult to distinguish between material of late twelfth and early to mid thirteenth dynasty date, so strong is the continuity between the two. In this larger period, the late Middle Kingdom, we first see the sporadic funerary custom of placing literary manuscripts with the dead in the burial chamber. No reason for this custom is ever made explicit. The largest surviving find is the contents of a chest found in 1899 in a reused late Middle Kingdom shaft tomb on the precinct that became the Ramesseum. This preserves, albeit imperfectly, one of the only private libraries from pharaonic Egypt. Its owner is unknown, but the contents are closely paralleled by two other survivals, the Deir el-Medina Library of a Ramessid scribe of royal craftsmen, and the Late period papyri collected by Charles Wilbour. These books of the literate class outside court show the same combination of instructions for conducting ritual, hymns to deities, literary nar-

ratives and discourses, incantations and prescriptions for good health, and technical texts such as the Ramesseum Onomasticon. For the literary texts, date of composition remains debated, and it is not possible to assign any work with confidence to the thirteenth dynasty. In general, longer compositions with later features might be dated to later in the Middle Kingdom; the *Instructions of Ipuwer* contains late grammatical constructions, as well as references to institutions not attested before the late Middle Kingdom, such as the great *khenret*. Another literary text with late grammatical features is the Westcar Papyrus, preserved in one Second Intermediate Period copy, and containing a sequence of tales focused on the court of King Khufu. The tales end with an account of the divine birth of three brother kings of the fifth dynasty, and this might be construed as an oblique reference to the three historically attested royal brothers in the mid-thirteenth dynasty: Neferhotpe I, Sihathor, and Sobekhotpe IV. If this reference was intended, it might provide a date of composition, but the contemporary situation could equally have stimulated a copy or reissue of an older text. Similarly, resonance in contemporary royal names could have affected Ramessid and Late period reissues of the Middle Egyptian narrative of King Neferkare (Pepy II of the late Old Kingdom) and his affair with his general, Sasenet. The thirteenth dynasty may therefore be characterized as a period of established literary manuscript production, but, on present evidence, the twelfth dynasty seems more plausibly the period of production of the surviving literary masterpieces in Middle Egyptian.

[*See also* Second Intermediate Period.]

BIBLIOGRAPHY

Davies, W. Vivian. *A Royal Statue Reattributed*. British Museum Occasional Paper 28. London, 1981. Discussion of sculpture of King Sobekemsaf, with a list of statues of Second Intermediate Period kings. The author places the king in the seventeenth dynasty, contrary to the discussion above.

Hayes, W. C. *A Papyrus of the Late Middle Kingdom in the Brooklyn Museum (Brooklyn 35.1446)*. Brooklyn, 1955. The first edition, with historical interpretations different from those in Quirke (1990).

Kemp, Barry J. "Old, Middle and Second Intermediate Period c.2686–1552 BC." In *The Cambridge History of Africa*, vol. 1, pp. 658–769. Cambridge, 1982. Reprinted in Bruce G. Trigger et al., *Ancient Egypt: A Social History*, pp. 71–182. Cambridge, 1982. Represents the prevailing consensus on the history of the period. Ryholt (1997) has recently sought to redefine in particular the fourteenth and sixteenth dynasties; this article retains the Kemp version.

Redford, Donald B. "The Hyksos Invasion in History and Tradition." *Orientalia* 39 (1970), 1–51.

Quirke, Stephen. *The Administration of Egypt in the Late Middle Kingdom: The Hieratic Documents*. New Malden, 1990. Discussion differs on some points from that of the first editor, Hayes.

Quirke, Stephen. "Royal Power in the 13th Dynasty." In *Middle Kingdom Studies*, edited by Stephen Quirke, pp. 123–139. New Malden, 1991.

Quirke, Stephen. "Archive." In *Ancient Egyptian Literature*, edited by

Antonio Loprieno, pp. 379–401. Leiden, New York, and Cologne, 1996. Includes discussion of the Ramesseum papyri in the context of other finds of groups of papyri.

Ryholt, Kim S. B. *The Political Situation in Egypt during the Second Intermediate Period c.1800–1550* B.C. Carsten Niebuhr Institute Publications, 20. Copenhagen, 1997. A wide-ranging reevaluation of the archaeological and textual sources, with comprehensive bibliography and list of sources for kings. Note that definitions of dynasties differ from those in Kemp, and archaeologists have yet to review several conclusions based on specific contexts. However, the reappraisal includes invaluable discussions of key data such as royal scarabs and the Turin Canon.

STEPHEN G. J. QUIRKE

THIRTIETH DYNASTY. *See* Late Period, *article on* Thirtieth Dynasty.

THIRTY-FIRST DYNASTY. *See* Late Period, *article on* Thirty-first Dynasty.

THOTH. A deity with a wide range of associations, including nature, cosmology, writing, science, medicine, and the afterlife, Thoth (Eg., *Dḥwty*) was worshiped throughout Egypt from the Early Dynastic period through Roman times. The meaning of his name is obscure. Because Thoth was the divine messenger, the Greeks associated him with Hermes, calling him Hermes Trismegistos ("thrice great Hermes"), a title probably derived from his Egyptian epithet *pȝ ʿȝ ʿȝ ʿȝ.*

Thoth takes two major iconographic forms. As a squatting dog-headed baboon, he appears in figurines as early as the first dynasty (c.3050–2850 BCE). Early Dynastic slate palettes show ibises on standards, an image clearly associated with Thoth by the Old Kingdom. In later periods, he is frequently depicted as an ibis or ibis-headed human, often carrying the palette and pen of a scribe. His headdresses include the crescent moon and disk, the *atef*-crown, and the crowns of Upper and Lower Egypt. In both baboon and ibis forms, Thoth is portrayed overseeing and protecting scribes. In scenes from temples, he and Horus anoint the king with water. They also pour libations over the deceased on cartonnage coffins of the Third Intermediate Period. In scenes of divine judgment, such as the vignettes accompanying chapter 125 of the *Book of Going Forth by Day (Book of the Dead)*, Thoth records and announces the verdict, typically appearing as an ibis-headed man, and sometimes as a baboon seated atop the scales of justice.

As a moon god, Thoth regulated the seasons and lunar phases and counted the stars. Hence, he was associated with astronomy, mathematics, and accounting. As the god

THOTH. *Basalt figure of a cynocephalus ("dog-headed") baboon, a species considered one of the principal manifestations of the god Thoth.* This statue dates from the twentieth dynasty, during the reign of Ramesses III. (University of Pennsylvania Museum, Philadelphia. Neg. # S8–47040)

of scribes and writing, Thoth, the "lord of the sacred word," personified divine speech. Seshat, the goddess of writing and literature, was said to be either his wife or daughter. By the Middle Kingdom Thoth, as a god of wisdom and justice, was connected with Maat, the personification of rightness and world order. The Greeks viewed him as the source of all wisdom and the creator of languages.

At Hermopolis, Thoth was worshipped as a cosmogenic deity, believed to have risen on a mound from the primeval chaos to create the Ogdoad consisting of Nun, Naunet, Heh, Heket, Kek, Keket, Amun, and Amaunet, coordinated male and female couplets representing various forces of nature. In solar religion, Thoth and Maat navigated the bark of Re. Some sources refer to him as the son of Re. The *Book of Going Forth by Day* describes him as returning Re's eye, which had wandered away. Ac-

THOTH. *Depiction of the weighing of the heart of the deceased in the hall of judgment, twenty-first dynasty.* Thoth, in his ibis-headed form, stands by the scales, along with the jackal-headed Anubis, while Horus sits in judgment. This image is executed in paint and stucco on a wooden casket for funerary figurines, now in the Louvre, Paris. (Giraudon / Art Resource, NY)

cording to Plutarch, after Re had forbidden Nut from giving birth during any month of the year, Thoth tricked the moon goddess Selene into giving him some of her light, which he used to create the five epagomenal days, on which Nut gave birth to the great Ennead. Texts from the Ptolemaic temples of Edfu and Dendera credit Thoth with traveling to Nubia on behalf of Re to pacify the raging Tefnut and persuade her to return to Egypt.

Textual evidence for Thoth and his cult is found throughout Egyptian history. The Pyramid Texts portray him as the advocate and protector of the deceased king, destroying his enemies and carrying him across the river if the ferryman refuses. The dead king may be transformed into a bird with the wings of Thoth. Thoth introduces the king to Re. He also appears as a lunar god, the nightly manifestation of Re, and as a god of thunder and rain. By the Old Kingdom, the festival of Thoth is regularly mentioned in funerary offering formulas. In the Middle Kingdom, the Coffin Texts associate Thoth with

divine justice, claiming that his verdict can satisfy both Horus and Seth. The *Book of Two Ways* refers to the deceased as stars which reside in the sky beside Thoth. Middle Kingdom instructions and tales regularly use Thoth as a metaphor for justice, and in funerary autobiographies, officials demonstrate their impartiality by claiming to be "truly precise like Thoth." In the New Kingdom, Thoth figures prominently in the *Book of Going Forth by Day*, of which he is said to be the author. He acts on behalf of the deceased before a series of divine tribunals; just as he had done for Osiris. He also conducts the interrogation, records the results of weighing the heart against *maat*, and announces the verdict. Hymns and prayers to Thoth, focusing on his role as patron of scribes, were used as school texts (as in Papyrus Anastasi V) and appear on statues of scribes. New Kingdom didactic literature, such as the *Instructions of Amenemope*, refers to Thoth as a symbol of justice. The *Book of Thoth*, believed to contain all knowledge of laws, magic, nature, and the afterlife, figures prominently in the Ptolemaic stories of Neferkap-tah and Setna Khaemwaset, both of whom seek to appropriate the book's information, only to suffer unforeseen consequences.

Thoth plays the role of aide and mediator in the Osiris legend. He assists Horus and Anubis in reconstructing the body of Osiris and teaches Isis the spells necessary to revive him. In one version, he heals the infant Horus after Isis finds him dead of a scorpion bite. He is a staunch advocate of Horus in his battle against Seth, finding and restoring Horus's eye after Seth casts it away. He replaces the head of Isis after Horus cuts it off in a rage, and after Seth has eaten lettuce containing Horus's semen, Thoth invokes the semen to appear as a sun disk from the head of Seth. Finally, he helps to bring the proceedings to a conclusion by suggesting that the Ennead contact Osiris for his opinion.

The principal cult center of Thoth was at Hermopolis, ancient Egyptian Khemenu, near the modern town of el-Ashmunein. This was the site of a major New Kingdom temple, at which Amenhotpe III claims to have dedicated a pair of thirty-ton quartzite baboons. The biography of the fourth-century BCE high priest of Thoth, Petosiris, from his tomb at Tuna el-Gebel, recounts his renovation of the temple, said to house the egg from which Thoth had hatched, following the Persian invasion. Tuna el-Gebel was also the site of a massive fifth-century BCE cemetery of sacrificed baboons and ibises, as well as a sacred lake around which the ibises lived. Saqqara was home to a similar cemetery at which more than five hundred thousand ibises and baboons were buried in subterranean passageways; it was also the site of an oracle of Hermes Trismegistos. The Ogdoad of Hermopolis, headed by Thoth, was worshiped at Thebes because of its association with Amun. Sanctuaries of Thoth existed at a number of other sites as well.

[*See also* Monkeys and Baboons.]

BIBLIOGRAPHY

Armour, Robert A. *Gods and Myths of Ancient Egypt.* Cairo, 1986.

Bleeker, Claas J. *Hathor and Thot.* Leiden, 1973.

Boylan, Patrick. *Thoth, the Hermes of Egypt: A Study of Some Aspects of Theological Thought in Ancient Egypt.* London, 1922.

Hart, George. *A Dictionary of Egyptian Gods and Goddesses.* London, 1986.

Kurth, Dieter. "Thoth." In *Lexikon der Ägyptologie* 6: 497–523. Wiesbaden, 1986.

Lurker, Manfred. *The Gods and Symbols of Ancient Egypt.* London, 1980.

Mercante, Anthony S. *Who's Who in Egyptian Mythology.* 2d ed., edited and revised by Robert S. Bianchi. Metuchen, N.J. and London, 1995.

Watterson, Barbara. *The Gods of Ancient Egypt.* New York and Bicester, 1984.

DENISE M. DOXEY

THUTMOSE I (ruled c.1525–1516 BCE), third king of the eighteenth dynasty, New Kingdom. Thutmose I was born to the "King's Mother," Seniseneb, and an unknown father. He married Ahmose, who was possibly his biological sister, and he is known to be the father of five children, although some are disputed by scholars. Of the five, his wife Mutnofret bore Amenmose, the "King's Eldest Son," who became commander of the army, as well as the little-known Wadjmose; Thutmose II followed his father to the throne, married to his sister Hatshepsut (she reigned after his death, acting as regent to Thutmose III); another of Thutmose I's daughters, Neferu-bity, is sometimes attributed to Thutmose II and Hatshepsut. Perhaps Thutmose I's most puzzling personal relationship is with Ahmose-Nefertari, mother of Amenhotpe I, who helped legitimate his reign; he built her tomb and provided a proper burial for her.

Thutmose I ruled for nine years, and no convincing evidence exists for a coregency with Amenhotpe I or with Hatshepsut (as she later claimed). He conducted three military campaigns and built extensively in Egypt.

Thutmose I conducted military campaigns in Kush and the Near East. The southern campaign to Kush occurred early in his reign and was described by his contemporary, Ahmose-si Ibana, as a policing action. In the Near East, Thutmose gave less clear reasons for the war, but as he told the priests of Abydos, he had "made the boundaries of Egypt as far as that which the sun disk encircles." Modern commentators, however, have understood these activities as raids designed to establish Egypt's place in the international power politics of the day. They resulted in booty and diplomatic gifts while they influenced local politics. Even if they were intended to colonize the Near East, no subsequent campaign enforced his claims until Thutmose III came into his inheritance.

Thutmose I added to the Middle Kingdom temple at Karnak, with the construction of two pylons, a hypostyle hall, two obelisks, a courtyard, and a *temenos* wall. In North Karnak, he sponsored the completion of the calcite (Egyptian alabaster) chapel of Amenhotpe I, a gateway, and a treasury. Those structures, along with the *išd*-tree scene that links him to Senwosret I, demonstrate his interest in building on the legacy of the Middle Kingdom. He founded the workmen's village of Deir el-Medina and a way-station in Deir el-Bahri, and he had his mortuary temple built. His numerous Nubian construction projects are known, and buildings near Memphis are attested by inscriptions (for example, at the House of Aakheperkare and on a foundation in Meidum that flourished in Hatshepsut's time).

According to inscriptions, Thutmose I was fifty at his death. The mummy attributed to him and reburied in the twenty-first dynasty in Deir el-Bahri, however, is that of an eighteen-year-old male—thus it is unlikely that he was correctly identified as the king. Thutmose I was the earliest known king to be buried in the Valley of the Kings, and a sarcophagus bearing his name is known from tomb 38 in the Valley of the Kings.

Thutmose I's reign set an important example for subsequent Egyptian rulers. Both Hatshepsut and Thutmose III derived the legitimacy of their rule from him. To honor him, Hatshepsut built a chapel to him in her mortuary temple, and Thutmose III implicitly compared his own military victories to his grandfather's, recounting that on the Euphrates River, his own victory stela was erected next to that of his royal ancestor.

Thutmose I set the pattern for the great kings of the eighteenth dynasty. His reign linked the glorious Middle Kingdom to the achievements of the New Kingdom.

[*See also* Hatshepsut; *and* Thutmose III.]

BIBLIOGRAPHY

Redford, Donald B. "A Gate Inscription from Karnak." *Journal of the American Oriental Society* 99.2 (1979), 270–287. On the wars with the Near East.

Redford, Donald B. *Egypt, Canaan, and Israel.* Princeton, 1992.

Robins, Gay. "Amenhotpe I and the Child Amenemhat." *Göttinger Miszellen* 30 (1978), 71–75.

Robins, Gay. "A Critical Examination of the Theory that the Right to the Throne of Ancient Egypt Passed through the Female Line in the 18th Dynasty." *Göttinger Miszellen* 62 (1983), 68–69. On the king's parents and family.

Romer, John. "Tuthmosis I and Bibân el-Molûk: Some Problems of Attribution." *Journal of Egyptian Archaeology* 60 (1974), 119–133. On the tomb of Thutmose I and whether it is tomb 38 in the Valley of the Kings.

EDWARD BLEIBERG

THUTMOSE III (r. 1504–1452 BCE), fifth king of the eighteenth dynasty, New Kingdom, son of Thutmose II and his lesser wife Isis. A text, preserved in Karnak and compiled later in his reign, describes a divine oracle proclaiming the child Thutmose as the rightful successor of his father. The young prince was established on the throne of his late father in 1504 BCE, but owing to his youth he was able to rule only under the tutelage of the dowager queen Hatshepsut. She kept him in the background for the next twenty years, but despite her formal usurpation of the throne, she never deprived him of his royal attributes. As he matured, more records bearing his name alone were made and some scholars believe that he undertook at least two military expeditions to Nubia and Syria on his own. From the twentieth year of Thutmose III's reign, two reliefs of the royal pair are known that represent both rulers with equal status for the first time. Two years later, Thutmose became the sole ruler.

For two decades Thutmose III was occupied with conducting military campaigns, described in his *Annals,* the longest (223 columns) and one of the most important historical inscriptions known from Egypt. Quite factual and less bombastic than other such texts—they derive from the prosaic journal genre—the *Annals* give the most complete account of Egyptian military achievements on Asian territory, and of the booty and tribute taken there. Also included are lists of imposts from Nubia.

Three centers of political power arose in western Asia against Egyptian supremacy: a strong coalition of rebellious townships and principalities, led by the city of Kadesh on the middle Orontes River; Tunip, occupying the basin of the lower Orontes; and Mitanni, beyond the Euphrates. Thutmose III led his first and most important campaign in his twenty-second to twenty-third regnal year against the fortified town of Megiddo, which belonged to the Kadesh coalition.

The campaign shattered the enemy forces, and Thutmose III's army captured the fortress. A list in the Karnak temple enumerates 119 towns that were conquered during the first campaign. Those defeats were not sufficient to subdue Kadesh; between Years 24 and 39, fourteen separate campaigns were made against the city, and only in Year 42 was Kadesh conquered and the entire territory subdued. During the last campaign, Tunip was also invaded and reduced, thus ending the wars in northwestern Syria.

In Thutmose's Year 33, after crossing the Euphrates and defeating the Mitanni, the king set a boundary stela that marked the northern limit of his empire. That campaign was made memorable by the unusual mode of transport of the Egyptian fleet from the coast to the Euphrates: the boats were moved over 250 miles by means of oxcarts.

Sources about the Nubian wars are meager, but the so-called Hymn of Victory and records on three pylons in Karnak, together with the inscriptions of Nehi, the viceroy of Nubia, provide information on Thutmose III's achievements in southern Egypt. He established the limit of his rule at the Fourth Cataract of the Nile.

Booty and tribute from the king's conquests enabled him to carry out an extensive building program and to establish new feasts and special offerings. He built more than fifty temples—some attested only by written sources—not only in Egypt but also in Nubia and Palestine. After the death of Hatshepsut, he first continued what she had initiated, but soon he began his own constructions. After Year 42, he ordered the erasure of her name from all the monuments and the removal or destruction of her images. The reason for this defamation is still a matter of dispute among scholars. In contrast, and evidently to justify his claim to the throne, Thutmose III demonstrated a great piety toward the monuments of his royal predecessors. In the Karnak temple, sixty-one kings are represented in a

THUTMOSE III. *Sculpted head of Thutmose III.* (University of Pennsylvania Museum, Philadelphia. Neg. # S4–143068)

special shrine, with Thutmose III making offerings to them. He rebuilt or restored the monuments of Senwosret I and III, Amenhotpe I, and his grandfather Thutmose I. In many cartouches where the name of Hatshepsut was inscribed originally, he ordered it changed to that of Thutmose I, or Thutmose II.

His greatest building activity was concentrated at Karnak, where his program established the basic design of the complex of religious architecture. He rebuilt the hypostyle hall of Thutmose I and covered it with a new ceiling—at the same time screening from view the obelisks

of Hatshepsut. He dismantled her "Red Chapel" and built a new pylon (VI) and a bark shrine of red granite there, preceded by a hall with a ceiling supported by a pair of monolithic pillars, now called *heraldic,* which are unique to Egyptian architecture. Around the central part of the temple, a massive *temenos* wall was constructed with rows of chapels, workshops, and stores adjoining its southern and northern sides. From the east, a large temple was founded for celebration of the royal jubilee. Its great hypostyle hall was the first to possess three aisles, the central aisle higher than the side ones. Windows between two levels of the hall's roof admitted light.

In the same jubilee temple, two chambers were unusually decorated: their walls were covered with reliefs depicting the flora and fauna seen by the Egyptian army in Syria. Farther to the east, behind the *temenos* wall, another sanctuary—probably founded by Hatshepsut—existed. In front of it a pedestal marks the place for the obelisk, which was later removed to Rome and still stands there as the Lateran Obelisk. This obelisk was intended to remain as a single monument contrary to the custom of erecting them as pairs. Three such pairs raised by Thutmose III adorned Amun's temple, and he sent another pair to Heliopolis.

Important additions were made south of the main part of the Karnak temple: a large sacred lake 80 by 130 meters (250 × 400 feet) was created, and a calcite (Egyptian alabaster) shrine for the sacred bark of Amun was situated nearby. Hatshepsut had founded a pylon (VIII) on the processional avenue leading to Luxor, and Thutmose III added another one (VII), along with a great court.

In Western Thebes, a mortuary temple was begun during the co-regency; a small temple at Medinet Habu also dates from that period. Works in both were continued after the death of the queen, and another temple, presumably a monumental kiosk to receive the bark of Amun during the Valley festival, was founded at Deir el-Bahri, possibly late in Thutmose III's reign.

Outside Thebes the king founded many temples, most of them known from texts—for example, the stela of Minmose, listing several destroyed sanctuaries—or from loose wall blocks or architraves. Examples of better-preserved temples include the restored temple of Satet (Elephantine), founded by Hatshepsut but enlarged by Thutmose III; the temple at Buhen, with a similar history; and, most important, the temple at Aniba, built by Thutmose III and enlarged by Amenhotpe II. The architects of Thutmose III are remembered for the invention of basilica hypostyles, and for two unique forms of pillars: heraldic and the so-called tent-pole columns in the jubilee temple.

All the preserved architectural monuments from the reign of Thutmose III were decorated richly with reliefs in a formal, classic style. The remains of a temple at Deir el-Bahri, that was built during the last decade of the reign, conforms to this style. Excavations there unearthed thousands of fragmentary, delicately carved raised reliefs with polychrome as fresh as when newly painted; large parts of the wall representations have been reconstructed from those fragments. Although most parts are missing from the original polychrome royal figures, it can be seen that Thutmose III is shown wearing a red *šndyt*-kilt together with the Red Crown of Lower Egypt, a previously unknown combination.

These excavations also yielded two three-dimensional portraits of Thutmose III, which are important for establishing the dating criteria for his royal portraiture because they definitely originate from the last decade of his reign and differ greatly from earlier portraits. The date of the new style of sculptures coincides with the defamation of Hatshepsut and can be dated to Year 42 of Thutmose's reign. D. Laboury has stated that the later portraits are facially similar to those of the king's ancestors, Thutmose I and II. All similarity to Hatshepsut's portraits had disappeared at this time though earlier it was so strong that without inscriptions containing the names it is almost impossible for scholars to know which of the co-regents is depicted.

Information on the family of Thutmose III is meager. His early marriage to Princess Neferure remains unconfirmed. His wife Sat-jah bore his eldest son, Amenemhet, who died prematurely. The ruler then married the nonroyal Meryetre-Hatshepsut II, who became the mother of the future king, Amenhotpe II. There were also a number of other children.

Several prominent officials served under Thutmose III. The vizier Rekhmire (owner of Theban tomb 100) was the most important; another was an officer, Amenemhab (tomb 85), who left a valuable supplementary account of seventeen of his master's Asian campaigns, including a description of an elephant hunt and an incident during the siege of Kadesh. The prince of Kadesh sent forth a mare to distract the Egyptian chariotry stallions; Amenemhab killed the animal, saving the cavalry from disaster. In the tombs of other high officials, such as Menkheperreseneb, Puemre, or Amunezeh, interesting scenes of the reception of Asian tribute are depicted. Three viziers of Thutmose III—Ahmose, his son Useramon, and the Useramon's nephew Rekhmire—had tomb chapels in Western Thebes that were painted rather than sculpted. The decoration of those tombs displays the remarkable development of the painter's art.

Thutmose III died at the end of his fifty-third regnal year and was succeeded by his son Amenhotpe II, whom he took as his co-regent during the last years of his life. He was buried in a beautifully decorated rock-cut tomb in the Valley of the Kings (tomb 34). Yellowish-brown and pink paintings in the cartouche-shaped burial chamber resemble a huge papyrus roll spread out on the walls. The texts of the *Book of That Which Is in the Underworld (Amduat)* are in cursive hieroglyphs, and the figures in a simplified, linear style.

"Tuthmosis III made so enormous an impression on the history of Egypt, that he seems to dominate it," wrote the early Egyptologist E. A. Wallis Budge. The posthumous cult of this great warrior and builder lasted until the Ptolemaic period; he was revered as a hero in numerous scenes of private devotion, and his name on scarabs and amulets was used to provide magical protection for their owners.

BIBLIOGRAPHY

Davies, B., and A. J. Peden. *Studies in the Reign of Thutmosis III*. In Archaeology and Oriental Studies. Liverpool (in preparation).

Della Monica, M. *Thoutmosis III, le plus grand des pharaons*. Paris, 1991.

Laboury, Dimitri. *La statuaire de Thoutmosis III*. Liege, 1998.

Lipińska, J., and G. B. Johnson. "Thutmose III at Deir el Bahari." *KMT: A Journal of Ancient Egypt* 3.3 (1992), 13–25.

Redford, D. B. "Thutmosis III." In *Lexikon der Ägyptologie*, 6: 540–548, Wiesbaden, 1986.

Vandersleyen, C. *L'Égypte et la vallée du Nil*. Vol. 2. Paris, 1995.

JADWIGA LIPIŃSKA

THUTMOSE IV (r. 1419–1410 BCE), eighth king of the eighteenth dynasty, New Kingdom. He ruled over Egypt at a turning point in the dynasty. Succeeding his father Amenhotpe II, Thutmose inherited political and economic dominance from Nubia to the south to Syria in the north. Thutmose IV needed only to conduct brief military demonstrations in Nubia and Syria to maintain this influence, and he guaranteed continued peace through a diplomatic relationship with the Mitanni ruler Artatama by marrying the Syrian king's daughter. During the decade of Thutmose's reign, peace and affluence encouraged a less military expression of Egypt's greatness than had been the norm under Amenhotpe II and his father, Thutmose III. Both had emphasized domination of Egypt's enemies in their monuments, but in his (admittedly fewer) constructions, Thutmose IV explored divine, particularly solar, associations of the king. Ultimately this led to a presentation of the kingship as particularly related to the sun god, as is seen in the reigns of Amenhotpe III and IV (known also as Akhenaten).

Thutmose IV was one of several princes of adult age when his father died, and mutilated monuments dedicated by several kings' sons at Giza, where Amenhotpe II had built a small temple to the Great Sphinx, have suggested a throne rivalry may have accompanied Thutmose's accession. In fact, Thutmose IV left a fictitious account of his accession on a stela erected between the paws of the

THUTMOSE IV. *Relief of Thutmose IV from Karnak.*
(Courtesy Donald B. Redford)

Great Sphinx. The inscription, dated in Year 1, tells how the Sphinx, the sun god Horemakhet, spoke to prince Thutmose, promising him the kingship of Egypt if he would clear the sand away from the great statue's body. The Sphinx stela's narrative was earlier interpreted to indicate that he had stolen the throne from one of his brothers. In the eighteenth dynasty, however, kings employed oracular tales that verified their fitness to rule whether they usurped the throne or not: both Hatshepsut and Thutmose III left such stories, as did Amenhotpe III.

Thutmose IV left small-scale monuments at many of the major temples in Egypt and in Nubia, including a festival court at the western entrance of the great Karnak temple to Amun and a calcite shrine set into a doorway in that same court. He completed the excavation of the Sphinx at Giza and built an enclosure wall to prevent further sand from encroaching. Both at Giza and in Nubia at the temple of Amanda, Thutmose IV linked himself to the sun god in the North, at Heliopolis, rather than to Amun-Re of Karnak. Some have thought that this presaged Akhenaten's repudiation of Amun, but Thutmose IV was otherwise more than loyal to the god of Karnak. The site of Giza became a popular place of pilgrimage during the later New Kingdom, and Thutmose IV was associated with the Great Sphinx on a number of Ramessid stelae left there.

Thutmose elevated his nonroyal mother to be his consort and highest priestess of Amun ("God's Wife"), but he also married a woman named Nefertiry, the Syrian princess referred to above, and a few years later, his sister or daughter Iaret. His heir was produced, however, by a non-royal woman, Mutemwia, not recognized during Thutmose's reign. The king's administration reflected the less military time in which Thutmose ruled, having many bureaucrats (royal scribes) and no known generals. Thutmose was buried in the Valley of the Kings (tomb 43), a large well-cut monument that was left only partially decorated. He also began the excavation of a second tomb, number 22 in the West Valley, where his son and successor Amenhotpe III was eventually buried. The king's funerary cult continued through the twentieth dynasty.

BIBLIOGRAPHY

Bryan, Betsy M. *The Reign of Thutmose IV.* Baltimore, 1991. An overall study of the reign.

Bryan, Betsy M. "Antecedents to Amenhotep III." In *Amenhotep III: Perspectives on His Reign*, edited by David O'Connor and Eric Cline, pp. 27–62. Ann Arbor, 1998. An overview of the reigns of Amenhotep II and Thutmose IV.

Dodson, Aidan. "Crown Prince Dhutmose and the Royal Sons of the Eighteenth Dynasty." *Journal of Egyptian Archaeology* 76 (1990), 87–96. Distinguishes between several like-named princes.

Letellier, Bernadette. "La cour à péristyle de Thoutmosis IV à Karnak (et la 'cour des fêtes' de Thoutmosis II)." In *Hommages à la mémoire de Serge Sauneron*. Bibliothêque d'Études, 81. Paris, 1979. Describes the blocks that made up this dismantled structure and the general shape of the original court, as well as its scene content.

BETSY M. BRYAN

TIGRIS RIVER. *See* Mesopotamia.

TIME. Hardly any aspect of life failed to impress upon Egyptians a sense of the pervasiveness and, often, the urgency of time: the natural patterns of years, the agricultural cycle (seasons), day and night, and the more or less regular flooding of the Nile, as well as the more formal constructs of living imposed by social, economic, and bureaucratic demands. The need to gratify the monarch by the prompt completion of delegated tasks produced a culture of timeliness, in which officials boasted—even in their tombs, where time no longer had quite the same urgency—how quickly they had carried out their assignments. The intense Egyptian reaction to temporal concerns led to the construction of a divine landscape and an afterlife in which change was annihilated, a world without history, illness, injury, or teleology. To understand the Egyptian view of eternity, it is first necessary to understand the role of time in the mundane world of pharaonic Egypt. No ancient Egyptian treatise on time has survived, so the full range of ancient texts must be exploited.

Measurement of Time. The earliest Egyptian calendar was lunar and continued in use for cultic circumstances. For the purposes of daily life, however, they devised, early in the third millennium BCE, a calendar consisting of 365 days, approximating the solar year. This "civil" calendar was divided into three seasons—Akhet ("Inundation"), Peret ("Growing"), and Shemu ("Lacking Water"?)—each consisting of four thirty-day months (rounding off the shorter lunar month). The final five days of the year were seen as anomalous—that is, they did not fit neatly into the monthly/seasonal structure—and were called the *ḥryw rnpt* "the days beyond the year" (Greek, "epagomenal"). Lacking the additional one-quarter day of the solar year, this civil calendar "wandered" and did not return to harmony with the actual seasons for about 1,461+ years, a "return" held to be of great significance. Apart from an occasional crabbiness about the discordance between the natural seasons and the artificial ones of the civil calendar, the matter seems not to have discomforted the Egyptians much.

This civil calendar was used mainly for dating official and private records. Thus a "historical," legal, administrative, or epistolary document might bear such a date formula as: "Regnal year 2, third month of Peret-season, day 1, under the Majesty of the King of Upper and Lower Egypt, Ni-ma'at-Re." The months of each season were numbered; although that convention continued throughout pharaonic history, the names of the lunar months came to be applied to those of the civil calendar; beginning in the New Kingdom and becoming common usage in later periods. Some religious festivals and priestly duty shifts were fixed according to the civil calendar; priestly income from temple property were sometimes calculated in terms of so many three hundred sixtieth shares.

The enumeration of years was tied to royal reigns, at first by reference to the year of a biennial cattle census and the year after such a count, but this system gave way late in the Old Kingdom to the simple counting of the regnal years of each pharaoh. Until the eighteenth dynasty, the regnal year count changed on the first day of the civil calendar, that is, on I *Akhet* 1. The fifth dynasty annals (the Palermo Stone) reflect the fact that kings did not conveniently die on the fifth epagomenal day of the civil year; consequently, the first year of a new king's reign included only as many days as he actually reigned. By the mid-eighteenth dynasty, the regnal year count changed on the anniversary date of the king's accession to the throne. Thus, the account of Thutmose III's first military campaign in western Asia reports that the army crossed the Egyptian frontier on "Year 22, IV *Peret* 25" and arrived at Gaza on "Year 23, I *Shemu* 4, the day of the Festival of the King's Accession." The year count had changed nine days after the first entry. Not all documents, however, were felt to require a date and many, presumably with short term value or to be entered under a particular year heading in an administrative log, have limited dating information, often merely the season, month, day indications, without a regnal year or the ruler's name.

The integrity of this temporal sequence of regnal years was felt to be so important for orderly administrative, legal, and economic life (especially rentals, contracts, and organization of labor) that the Egyptians were careful about maintaining it. For instance, despite the post–Amarna process of turning the "heretic" pharaoh Akhenaten into a non-person, the necessities of an early nineteenth dynasty legal case demanded that his regnal years not be overlooked, hence a temporal subterfuge was employed, supplying a reference to a "Year 3 of the Rebel (?)." Consequently, reign lengths, where they have survived, are usually trustworthy, even in the cases of long-lived monarchs, such as Pepy II (sixth dynasty) and Ramesses II (nineteenth dynasty), with the exception of errors that might have crept in due to careless copying and recopying of the records. Significantly no king was said to have lived to the ideal old age of 110 years. Despite the durability of the tradition that each king was the embodiment of the god Horus in this life and of Osiris in the next, each ruler was understood to have lived a historically unique life, even if their *res gestae* can now be shown to be fictions or imitations of the achievements of earlier rulers.

At least as early as the eighteenth dynasty, administrators divided the thirty-day month into three ten-day weeks, as with the workmen at Deir el-Medina who worked according to a schedule, with regularly specified days off each week, in addition to release from work at various points in the annual festival cycle and (perhaps) for birthdays.

In many daily administrative and economic activities, a precise scheme for the measurement of the parts of a day was of lesser urgency, but in those activities in which shifts of workers—for example, the temple staffs noted earlier or construction workers—it became important. The convention of twelve hours of the day and twelve hours of the night had its principle expression in religious texts, such as those detailing "life" in the netherworld. In the workaday world, from at least as early as the Middle Kingdom—in the Reisner papyri, for example—it is evident that the work day for nonagricultural labor was defined as ten hours long. Use was made of a water-clock (Greek, "*clepsydra*"): either one in which time was measured by markings revealed as the water flowed out (at the time of Amenhotpe I), or one in which a rod marked with units was immersed in the liquid to indicate the hour. Probably much older was the "shadow-clock," a simple device in which the shadow cast by a vertical element moved along a scale of hours on a horizontal piece

perpendicular to its base. Physicians used a crude temporal device—the pace of the pulse—as one index of a patient's health.

Navigating Time. The Egyptian sense of time in daily economic, social, and administrative life was without question linear. The performance of assignments, work, or contracts required a view that in this world, at least, there was a flow of time along which one's actions and needs could be plotted. Grain loans, labor contracts, or land rentals required a linear sense of time, since they involved some expectation of future outcome. As a result, the Egyptians were able to perform all the necessary manipulations of time: "event" definition, location, and association; the determination of duration and calculation of interval, and periodization (for example the historical introduction to Papyrus Harris I, in the time of Ramesses III). Farmers had limited need for all these trappings of time, apart from the demands of tax collectors and other bureaucrats.

In the Thutmose III inscription cited earlier, the stages of the campaign were located with a date. The Year 22/23 account of his first campaign—culled from the fuller log of the military scribes—goes further, in that it provided the means to determine issues of duration; it provides precise dates for the various stops along the line of march, for example. The intervals could also be calculated. In addition, the reference to the festival of the king's accession reflects the associative process that linked one time locus (the dated event in the annals) and some prior event (the king's ascent to the throne) and its recurrent celebration; contiguity—the association of an event with some simultaneous occurrence—is also attested. The Palermo Stone achieves this end by linking a particular regnal year with certain other events of that year, thereby establishing the uniqueness of that year. Likewise, they could readily compare two similar events widely separated in time, the young Pepy II (sixth dynasty) links the pygmy being brought to the capital by the official Horkhuf to the pygmy brought from Punt by an official of the reign of King Izezi about a century earlier.

Statements as to duration are fairly common. Assiduous officials report how long it took them to carry out their assignments, whether days or months. Sometimes such references are more explicit: "IV *Akhet* 18: the day of moistening the barley and spreading a (funerary) bed for the Osiris Neferhotep; this day forward until the twenty-fifth day, eight days in all." Similarly, in a work agreement one reads: "I will complete the six days which I have allotted to the supervisor Mesuamun, spending day after day until the fulfilling of the relevant price exchange agreement." Labor contractors or supervisors apparently kept elaborate rosters of work and workers on projects. Papyrus Reisner I contains the records of a twentieth century BCE construction project for a period of 122 consecutive days; it keeps track of man-days (one man working a ten-hour day) of labor, days going to and from the project, and, surprisingly, days of absenteeism. Scribes were expected to be able to draw up work rosters and the requisite food payments based on the specifications of the amount of stone, sand, and rubble to be moved, all in accordance with a set notion of the relationship between man-days and the quantity of work to be performed. Impatient overseers lodged complaints about the loss of work time occasioned by bureaucratic inefficiency in the distribution of food and clothing to the laborers.

Locating oneself or one's achievements in time was an important matter to those Egyptians who intended their tomb biographies to be read by future generations. Such texts were likely not to give specific dates, but typically reported that the author had lived "in the time of King N"; if his life span included several reigns, then it would be "in the time of King N, King X, and King Z," sometimes making the last reference current by saying something like "now, in the time of King Z, ..."

The lexicon of such references reveals the spatial underpinnings of some temporal terminology; in the phrase "in the time of King N," one of the commonly used words (*ḥꜣw*) means "vicinity," locating the writer in the temporal vicinity of the ruler in question. Occasionally the process is reversed and reference is made to the "king of your time (vicinity)," that is, the lifetime of the individual. Few references survive giving the specific date of an individual's birth; one person, for example, records that he was born in Year 27 of King Amenemhat II. Nonetheless, a number of Egyptians report their age in their inscriptions, mostly realistically. When Thutmose III asked his newly installed chief minister how long it had been since he was circumcised—presumably the latter's entry into adulthood—Weser replied that it was thirty years. In general, while the Egyptians marked some stages in their life cycles, they generally did not link these to precise temporal markers, but with general life stages. They did, however, sometimes identify themselves with generational cohorts.

Talking about Time. The vocabulary of time in Egyptian is enormous; its riches can only be hinted at here. No single Egyptian word conveyed the full range of "time." The various parts of the day (for example, dawn, morning, evening, or night) have distinct terms. The word *ḥꜣw* refers to a block of time. *Rk* has resisted any etymological analysis but seems to have the same significance, and the two words are used more or less interchangeably. A common word for "lifetime" or "period of time" is *ꜥḥꜥw*, "standing," that is, duration. *Rnpt* ("year") reflects the year as a thing that "becomes young (again)." *Tr* ("season") appears to reflect some notion of regular repetition. *Sp* signifies an "occurrence," that is, an event. The negative construction *n sp* ("never") denies some event (that is, "Never was there the occasion of.")

Scholars continue to debate whether Egyptian has, strictly speaking, a tense system or whether it is a language driven by the concept of aspect (Egyptian—an Afro-Asiatic language—was originally a more heavily inflected language than is evident from the earliest surviving texts; the existence of a stative form—the end state of an action—in early texts confirms that). The reality is likely a combination of the two. Some forms seem to have very specific time referents relative to the speaker, while others focus on the question of whether an action is complete or incomplete, and where in the temporal spectrum the action resided, resides, or will reside. The fact remains that Egyptians could identify grammatically and syntactically the relative past-ness, present-ness, or future-ness of events or circumstances.

Time in Egyptian Literature and Art. Time also figures importantly in Egyptian literature and in the representational arts. In seeking to fashion creditable, seemingly historical (even if fundamentally mythic) landscapes for their narratives, Egyptian writers often employed temporal devices and indicators. In some texts, such as the story of Wenamun's journey to Phoenicia, dates are supplied to create the impression that what unfolds is a genuine historical account. In narratives in which the characters are clearly divine or quasi-divine, the pseudo-historical effect is created both by specific and vague temporal devices. Thus, in the story of the conflict between the gods Horus and Seth over the succession to the throne, the author reports that the hearing of the dispute before a divine tribunal had already been going on for some eighty years when the narrative opens; no attempt is made to harmonize that time reference with the fact that Horus is labeled as being so young at one point that his mouth still smells from his mother's milk. Divine time is incomprehensible; the lifetime of a mortal is but an instant to the gods, but the use of human time indicators may help to bring it into some sort of appreciable scale. New Kingdom tales often include vague phrases like "Now many days after this" to convey the sense of the passage of time.

Of greater interest is the use of time as a structural device. In the well-known *Story of the Shipwrecked Sailor,* the narrative begins with the "voice" of an unidentified narrator, who tells us the story of a ship's captain whose return from an unsuccessful mission has him in fear of the king's wrath. One of the captain's men, to reassure his leader, tells him of an adventure of his own that had been a disaster but came out well in the end; in the course of that story, the sailor tells of encountering a fabulous serpent, evidently a divine being, who aids him and reassures him. The serpent, to while away the time until the sailor is destined to be rescued, then tells the sailor of an calamitous occurrence in his own life. The writer has regaled the audience with a set of stories in a temporal regression.

Another popular literary device of Middle Kingdom writers involves placing some events in the narrative in a much earlier period, principally to set the stage for some prognostications. In the Westcar Papyrus, a prediction about the replacement of the fourth dynasty line by that of the fifth dynasty is set back in the early part of the former period. The prophecy of Neferti, principally a piece of propaganda to bolster the legitimacy of the usurper/founder of the twelfth dynasty, has the emergence of that ruler to reestablish order foreseen by a priest early in the fourth dynasty, more than five centuries earlier.

In reliefs and paintings in Egyptian temples and tombs, artists frequently depicted events in a series of sequentially arranged vignettes, frequently illustrating the accompanying texts. These might include rituals, divine and royal processions and festivals (the *sed*-Festival, for example), the procession of the king through the various regions of the netherworld, or of the deceased commoner making his or her way to the tribunal of Osiris for judgment. In the mortuary temple of Queen Hatshepsut the events of the expedition she had sent to the distant land of Punt are presented in a clearly linear temporal sequence.

Eternity. It is not easy to say anything precise about the Egyptian conception of eternity, despite the immense literature on the subject, and the general inclination of Egyptologists to think that it is the primary component of the Egyptian view of time. Nonetheless, once having formed some idea of how the Egyptians thought about and manipulated time in the course of their daily lives, it becomes evident that whatever the philosophical/theological details might be, the Egyptians basically constructed their ideas of and responses to eternity as a way of surviving death, almost completely free from time and all those elements to which the Egyptians attached negative values, change, illness, injury, or aging. After all, the goal of much of the funerary literature for the use of the individual post-mortem Egyptian was, as the texts say "so as not to die a second time." The Egyptians hoped for the continuation of life after death, and they had no intention whatever to go through the cycles of life all over again. They intended to survive death in the full vigor of life—enjoying food, drink, and sex, and mingling with the gods—and, for all practical purposes, become a god. To be free from time is the problem, because in fact the Egyptian ability to conceptualize such an afterlife was wholly dependent on the notion that eternity would involve ahistorical time, that is, time without change, process without results, only enough of the signposts of time to create the "reality" of post-mortem life. The tomb is one's "House of Eternity," temples might be "Mansions of Eternity" (or the near equivalent "millions of years"). Eternity has no effect; it is a time sphere in which the appearance of the processes of daily life goes on just enough to prove to

them that they are actually living. Eternity, then, is a flight from time's effects. Even the thought of a final apocalypse that would bring the end of time was uncongenial; there is comparatively little textual material that projects or depicts an end to the world and to time. Not surprisingly—there are, after all, cynics in all cultures—some Egyptians had doubts about this afterlife. One ancient Egyptian poet reminded his listeners that "no one returns from over there to tell us of their circumstances."

The god Osiris, ruler and judge in the afterlife, bore epithets such as "Lord of Eternity" (*nb nḥḥ*) and "Ruler of Eternity" (*ḥḳ3 ḏt*). These epithets contain two words (*ḏt* and *nḥḥ*) that are often loosely translated as "eternity." Few lexical issues have led to so much scholarly literature, for the most part without resolution. Some have sought to understand one of the terms to mean "unendingness" and the other "everlastingness," clearly meanings that embody different ideas. Some scholars speak of the "two eternities," and it may well be that one refers to the time of this life, the other to the next. That the terms sometimes appear to be used interchangeably as well as together (to indicate a totality of concepts) does not help to clarify the matter. Nor do the periodic attempts of the Egyptians to rationalize the two terms inspire a great deal of confidence; in the *Book of Going Forth by Day* (*Book of the Dead*), the term *ḏt* is associated with Osiris, the earth, and the past, while *nḥḥ* is linked to Re, the sun, and the future. The later complementarity between Osiris and Re unified the two concepts at world's end.

A number of divinities were associated with time, notably Re, who, as creator of the ordered universe also created time. In other cultic centers, Ptah, Isis, Neith, Amun were associated with time and its various attributes. Thoth, as a result of his lunar associations, was later said to be the originator of the calendar and recorded the lengths of reign of the kings. In addition, a number of temporal concepts—the year, the Nile, the seasons, and the hours, to mention a few—were hypostatized as gods and goddesses.

[*See also* Astrology; Astronomy; Calendars; Chronology and Periodization; *and* Historiography.]

BIBLIOGRAPHY

Assmann, Jan. "Ewigkeit." In *Lexikon der Ägyptologie*, 2:47–254. Wiesbaden, 1974.

Assman, Jan. *Zeit und Ewigkeit im Alten Ägypten.* Heidelberg, 1975.

Bács, T. "Two Calendars of Lucky and Unlucky Days." *Studien zur Altägyptischen Kultur* 17(1990), 41–64.

Bakir, Abdel el-Mohsen. *The Cairo Calendar, No. 86637.* Cairo, 1966.

Bakir, Abdel el-Mohsen. "A Further Reappraisal of the Terms: Nhh and Dt." *Journal of Egyptian Archaeology* 60 (1974), 252–254.

Beckerath, Jürgen von. "Geburtstage." In *Lexikon der Ägyptologie*, 2:476–477. Wiesbaden, 1974.

Bochi, Patricia A. "Images of Time in Ancient Egyptian Art." *Journal of the American Research Center in Egypt* 31 (1994), 55–62.

Brunner, Hellmut, and S. Schoske. "Die Grenzen von Zeit und Raum bei den Ägyptern." *Archiv für Orientforschung* 17 (1984–1985), 141–145.

Depuydt, Leo. *Civil Calendar and Lunar Calendar in Ancient Egypt.* Leuven, 1977.

Depuydt, Leo. *Conjunction, Contiguity, Contingency.* New York and Oxford, 1993.

Gardiner, Alan H. "An Administrative Letter of Protest." *Journal of Egyptian Archaeology* 13 (1927), 75–78.

Gardiner, Alan H. "A Later Allusion to Akhenaten." *Journal of Egyptian Archaeology* 24 (1938), 124.

Helck, Wolfgang. "Feiertage und Arbeitstage in der Ramessidenzeit." *Journal of the Economic and Social History of the Orient* 7 (1964), 136–166.

Helck, Wolfgang. "Altersangaben." In *Lexikon der Ägyptologie,* 1:157–158. Wiesbaden, 1972.

Hornung, Erik. *Idea into Image: Essays on Ancient Egyptian Thought.* New York, 1992.

Hornung, Erik. "Zeitliches Jenseits im Alten Ägypten." *Eranos Jahrbuch* 47 (1978) 269–307.

Janssen, Rosalind M. *Growing Up in Ancient Egypt.* London, 1990.

Kadish, Gerald E. "Time and Work-Discipline in Ancient Egypt. In *Studies in Honor of William Kelly Simpson,* edited by P. der Manuelian, vol. 2, pp. 439–449. Boston, 1996.

Kákosy, Laszlo. "Einige Probleme des ägyptischen Zeitbegriffes." *Oikumene* (Budapest) 2 (1978), 95–111.

Kákosy, Laszlo. "Schöpfung und Weltuntergang in der ägyptischen Religion." *Acta Antiqua* (Budapest) 11 (1963), 17–30.

Kákosy, Laszlo. "Zeit." In *Lexikon der Ägyptologie,* 6:1361–1371. Wiesbaden, 1985.

Lichtheim, Miriam. *Ancient Egyptian Literature.* 3 vols. Berkeley, 1973–1980.

Niwinski, A. "Noch Einmal über zwei Ewigkeitsbegriffe: Ein Vorschlag der graphischen Lösung in Anlehnung an die Ikonographie der 21 Dynastie." *Göttinger Miszellen* 48 (1981), 41–53.

Posener-Kriéger, Paule. *Les archives du temple funéraire de Néferirkarê (Les papyrus d'Abousir).* Cairo, 1976.

Redford, Donald B. *Pharaonic King-lists, Annals and Day-books.* Publications of the Society for the Study of Egyptian Antiquities, 4. Mississauga, Ont. 1986.

Spalinger, Anthony J. *Revolutions in Time Studies in Ancient Egyptian Calendrics.* San Antonio, 1994.

Verner, Miroslav. "The Egyptian Confrontation of Man and Time." In *Aspects of Ancient Oriental Historiography.* Prague, 1973.

Westendorf, Wolfhart. "Die Geburt der Zeit aus dem Raum" *Göttinger Miszellen* 63 (1983), 71–76.

Westendorf, Wolfhart. "Raum und Zeit als Entsprechungen der Beiden Ewigkeiten." In *Fontes atque Pontes Ägypten und Altes Testament,* 5. Edited by M. Görg, pp. 422–435. Wiesbaden, 1983.

Zabkar, Louis V. "Some Observations on T. G. Allen's Edition of the Book of the Dead." *Journal of Near Eastern Studies* 24 (1965), 75–87.

GERALD E. KADISH

TITULARY. With origins in the close relationship between the king and the gods as well as in the unification of the two chiefdoms of Upper and Lower Egypt in the late Predynastic period, ancient Egyptian royal titulary was one of the rulers' most enduring symbols of power. The full five-part titulary consists of four names which the king assumed on the day of his accession, along with the name given to him at birth.

The Five Names of the King. The first name in the titulary is the so-called Horus name. It is always written within a *serekh,* a rectangle that contains the royal name. The *serekh* is bordered at the bottom by the kind of recessed paneling found on the façades of early mud-brick tombs and palaces and is often crowned with the figure of the falcon god Horus. At work here was the belief that the king was the physical embodiment of Horus on earth. Since the god Osiris, who was believed once to have been a king on earth, was considered by that time to be the king of the underworld, his son Horus was said to have inherited his father's place on earth and become the king of the living.

The Two Ladies name—literally. "He who belongs to the two ladies (actually the word "lord" in its feminine form)"—placed the king under the protection of the two goddesses Nekhbet and Wadjet. Nekhbet, in the form of a vulture, was the tutelary goddess of the city of Elkab in Upper Egypt, while Wadjet, represented as a cobra, came from the city of Buto in Lower Egypt. Because these two sites represented two of the most prominent cities from the Predynastic southern and northern chiefdoms respectively, the Two Ladies name symbolized the king's close association with both regions of Egypt. The name also underlined the ancient Egyptians' dualistic view of the world.

The third name, which should perhaps be referred to as the gold name, is more difficult to interpret. Because it was simply written with the hieroglyph for gold when it was introduced in the Early Dynastic period, it has been postulated that the name symbolized both the king's divinity—since gold is everlasting in its appearance—and the golden appearance of the rising sun. It is also possible that an association with the god Seth was understood, since Seth was the tutelary god of "Gold-town" (Egyptian *Nubet,* modern Naqada) in Upper Egypt. Such dualism between the two divine brothers Horus and Seth would have appealed to the Egyptians' understanding of their world. This interpetation may explain the writing of the name in the Middle Kingdom, when a falcon hieroglyph is consistently added over the hieroglyph for "gold," at which point the name may have been understood as the "Horus of gold."

The fourth and fifth entries in the titulary are sometimes referred to as the throne and birth names, respectively. Each is written inside an oval ring (called a "cartouche" today) that is a hieroglyph representing a length of rope folded and tied at one end. This hieroglyph symbolizes everything that the sun encircled and is thus an indication of the king's overlordship of the cosmos.

The throne name, often rendered as "King of Upper

and Lower Egypt" in modern translations, literally means "He who belongs to the sedge and the bee" (*nsw-bity* in Egyptian); the sedge plant (*sw*) is a symbol of Upper Egypt, and the bee (*bit*) represents Lower Egypt. This name is another symbol of the king's dominion over the southern and northern regions of Egypt. By the middle of the fourth dynasty, in the reign of King Djedefre, one of Khufu's sons, the throne name is almost always compounded with the divine name "Re." For example, Djedefre's name means "his strength is Re"; Khafre's name, "Re appears"; Menkaure's name, "The *ka*s of Re are firm," and so forth. From the Middle Kingdom onward, this is the name most often used to identify the king when only one of the five names is used in an inscription. When two names are used, the throne and the birth names are selected.

The last element, the birth name, was, as the modern appellation implies, the name given to the king at birth. It is sometimes referred to as the "Son of Re" name, since this epithet always precedes the cartouche inside which the birth name is written. The epithet symbolizes the filial relationship between the king and the creator god Re. This fifth name is the one modern scholars use when mentioning a specific king (for example, King Tutankhamun), often followed by a roman numeral to indicate which one of the similarly named kings is meant (for example, Amenhotpe III, Ramesses II).

Historical Development. Although all components of the five-fold titulary are attested by the end of the first dynasty, the most common name to appear in the earlier historical records is the Horus name. Kings of the first dynasty are usually referred to by compound names such as "the Horus Aha" or "the Horus Djer." One can see how such names, which have clearly aggressive tones at this time, were not chosen at random, and how they often indicate a king's desire to announce his political program. For example, the two names just mentioned mean "the fighter" and "the strong one," respectively. Other kings of this early period are similarly named the Horus Djet ("the cobra"), the Horus Den ("the [head] cutter"), and the Horus Adjib ("the slaughterer of hearts"). At this time the Two Ladies name should perhaps not be considered as part of an institutionalized royal titulary, since it mostly functions as an epithet forming part of the throne name.

Great changes in the royal titulary occurred during the Old Kingdom. The last king of the third dynasty, Huny, was the first to enclose his throne name in a cartouche. The use of the epithet "Son of Re" by the kings of the fourth dynasty has already been mentioned, but the other major development at this time was that henceforth, Egyptian kings would be mentioned more by their names within the cartouche than their Horus names. Another notable elaboration came with the kings of the fifth dy-

nasty, who were the first to distinguish between the throne and the birth names by using two cartouches in their titulary.

By the Middle Kingdom, the full five-fold royal titulary was clearly established, and kings henceforth used all five royal names regularly. By the New Kingdom, another significant change was the addition of epithets, such as "Strong Bull" to the Horus name to indicate military prowess, and "Ruler of Thebes" or "Beloved of (a given divinity)" to the cartouches containing the birth name. The last epithet was often used to honor the god of a particular site where the royal cartouche was carved. Another reason for the inclusion of an epithet within a cartouche name was to allow one king to differentiate himself from previous, similarly named rulers. For example, the throne name of the nineteenth dynasty king Ramesses II is Usermare Setepenre ("Powerful is the Cosmic Harmony of Re, Chosen by Re"). To distinguish himself from his illustrious predecessor, Ramesses III of the twentieth dynasty added the epithet "Mery-Amun" ("Beloved of Amun") to the Usermare portion of his throne name. The additional phrase was itself borrowed from Ramesses II's birth name, Ramesses Mery-Amun.

This borrowing of portions of a venerated ancestor's name was not a new phenomenon. The practice is attested as far back as the Middle Kingdom, when Amenemhet I, the first king of the twelfth dynasty, borrowed part of the titulary of King Tety, the founder of the sixth dynasty. Tety had called himself the Horus Sehetep-tawy ("He Who Pacifies the Two Lands"). Amenemhet I modified this into Sehetep-ib-tawy ("He Who Pacifies the Mind of the Two Lands") as his first Horus name; he would later change this to Wehem-mesut ("Repeating of Births"), an epithet that would be used by subsequent kings in their titulary to inaugurate new eras of their own. Similarly, King Tety had chosen Sema ("The Uniter") for his Golden Horus name—the same name Amenemhet I later chose for his own Golden Horus name.

Such borrowings became fairly commonplace when certain kings wished to look back to better times than their own, or simply to recall more illustrious ancestors. The first instance is clearly visible with certain rulers of thirteenth dynasty, who added the names Antef and Amenemhet to their cartouches, reminding their contemporaries of the great kings of the eleventh and twelfth dynasties. For the second case, we can look to King Thutmose I of the eighteenth dynasty, who simply added the adjective "great" to the throne name of King Senwosret I of the twelfth dynasty to form his own throne name. Similarly, when King Cambyses, a foreign ruler on the throne of Egypt, requested the help of an Egyptian priest to compose his royal titulary, the priest chose the Horus name Sematawy ("The Uniter of the Two Lands"), recalling that of the great eleventh dynasty ruler Nebhepetre Montuhotep I, who had ended the civil war of the First Intermediate Period to usher in the prosperous period of the Middle Kingdom. Similarly, when King Nektanebo I of the thirtieth dynasty established himself on the throne, he chose Kheperkare for his throne name, invoking the throne name of the great twelfth dynasty ruler Senwosret I.

[*See also* Names.]

BIBLIOGRAPHY

Gardiner, Alan H. *Egyptian Grammar.* 3d rev. ed. Oxford, 1957. Excursus A, pp. 71–76, is an excellent introduction to the royal titulary and its significance.

Quirke, Stephen. *Who Were the Pharaohs?: A History of their Names with a List of Cartouches.* New York, 1990. One of the most accessible and up-to-date studies of the topic.

RONALD J. LEPROHON

TIYE, the principal queen of Amenhotpe III (r. 1410–1372 BCE), eighth king of the eighteenth dynasty, New Kingdom. She was the mother of at least five of his daughters and of his successor Amenhotpe IV (called Akhenaten). Tiye's nonroyal parents, who were reburied in the Valley of the Kings, Western Thebes, are well documented; her brother Anen was Second Prophet of Amun. Some Egyptologists suspect that the "God's Father" Ay, who became king on the death of Tutankhamun (r. 1355–1346 BCE), was also her brother, but conclusive evidence is lacking. Both royal and nonroyal monuments signal Tiye's importance during the reigns of both her husband and her son. Numerous statues in various sizes and materials depicted her alongside Amenhotpe III, while reliefs showed her assisting him in the cult and participating in his *sed*-festival, where an associated caption described her as accompanying the king "like the [goddess] Maat in the following of the [sun god] Re."

A political role for Tiye has been inferred from her mention in the Amarna Letters; one letter was addressed to her by Tushratta, king of the Mitanni, and two others from Tushratta to Akhenaten advised him to consult her. The archaeological record confirms Tiye's presence at Akhenaten's new capital, Akhetaten (Tell el-Amarna), where he commissioned cult installations for her. When Tiye died, she was interred by her son in his own tomb there, yet the presence of objects bearing her name in tomb 55 in the Valley of the Kings at Thebes (in particular, a gilded shrine made at Akhenaten's order) has led to the supposition that her burial was transferred. Texts on two of Tiye's *shawabtis* call her "King's Mother," which dated their manufacture to her son's reign. They were found in Amenhotpe III's tomb in the western branch of the Valley of the Kings, suggesting that she ultimately reposed beside her husband. Objects inscribed with Tiye's name that were found among Tutankhamun's "treasure" represent her latest attestation.

BIBLIOGRAPHY

Kemp, Barry J., ed. *Amarna Reports,* vol. 6. Egypt Exploration Society Occasional Publication, 10. London, 1995. Pages 459 and 460 provide an update on the buildings at Tell el-Amarna associated with Tiye.

Kozloff, Arielle P., and Betsy M. Bryan, with Lawrence M. Berman. *Egypt's Dazzling Sun: Amenhotep III and His World.* Cleveland, 1992. Exhibition catalog with extensive bibliography; illustration and discussion of statuary and reliefs depicting Tiye.

Reeves, Nicholas. *The Complete Tutankhamun: The King, the Tomb, the Royal Treasure.* London, 1990. See pp. 163, 168, and 199 for objects from the tomb inscribed with Tiye's name.

Reeves, Nicholas, and Richard H. Wilkinson. *The Complete Valley of the Kings: Tombs and Treasures of Egypt's Greatest Pharaohs.* London, 1996. Includes comments on Tiye's burial in the Royal Tomb at Amarna and on the tombs of Tiye's parents (KV 46) and her husband (WV 22) at Thebes.

MARIANNE EATON-KRAUSS

TOD. The village of Tod is situated around an ancient mound (*kôm*), on the eastern bank of the Nile, approximately 20 kilometers (15 miles) south of Luxor. On the northern side of the *kôm*, Jean-François Champollion visited what was left of a high crypt, emerging from the temple that remained buried underneath the village. In 1934, Fernand Bisson de la Roque cleared the ruins of the first two halls, both from the Ptolemaic period: the first a hypostyle hall, and the other dominated by the high crypt. At the back, the far end of the temple revealed traces of a church, built directly on the limestone paving of the pharaonic sanctuary. The Ptolemaic eaves (*avancée*), made of sandstone, surround an ancient limestone wall, linked to this paving and carrying a lengthy historical inscription from Senwosret I.

Beneath the paving slabs lay blocks from previous construction phases of the temple, dating back to the reigns of Montuhotpe I and II and Amenemhet I. In the foundation sand, beneath a narrowed eave, were four copper chests, with the name of King Amenemhet II engraved on them. They were filled with lapis lazuli and silver, and included some gold objects. The lapis lazuli either remained uncut or consisted of fragments of beads or cylinder seals from the Near East, of various origins and dating back to the third and the beginning of the second millennium BCE. The silver came in flattened ingots, ingot chains and coiled cups. The origins of these cups are still disputed. The most consistent hypotheses identify these cups as Minoan or Syrian. A similar cup was discovered in a Mycenaean tomb; but this isolated find, perhaps more ancient than the tomb from which it came, does not call into question the date of burial of the treasure, under Amenemhet II.

The excavations carried out by the Musée du Louvre between 1981 and 1991 focused on the temple's surroundings. They revealed a terrace built at the beginning of the Middle Kingdom, which had private chapels that survived until the New Kingdom. There was no western entrance until the *dromos* was created in the third century BCE, likely under Ptolemy IV, at the same time as construction of the two Ptolemaic halls was undertaken, to replace halls dating back to the time of Thutmose III. The *dromos* was never completed, and the platform overlooking a pier was redesigned in the second or first century BCE, with the construction of a monumental door, which also remained unfinished.

Before the Ptolemaic period, access to the temple was limited to the north, as indicated by the placement of a wayside bark chapel begun by Thutmose III, and completed by Amenhotpe II. *Talatats*, standard blocks used in buildings during Amenhotpe IV's reign, were most likely brought over from Karnak, and possibly were used to complete the upper sections of the temple at the end of the Ptolemaic period (decorations are attributed to Ptolemy VIII Euergetes II and Ptolemy XII Auletes), or even during the Roman period (the most recent reliefs are dated to Antonius Pius). North of the two Ptolemaic halls a lake was dug, either while or shortly after the halls were built. To the south, the *kôm* indicates different stages of urban growth, and not of some other temple.

BIBLIOGRAPHY

Barbotin, C., and J.-J. Clère. "L'inscription de Sésostris Ier à Tôd." *Bulletin de l'Institut Français d'Archéologie Orientale* 91 (1991), 1–32.

Bisson de la Rocque, F. *Tod*. Fouilles de l'Institut Français d'Archéologie Orientale, 17. Cairo, 1937.

Bisson de la Rocque, F. *Catalogue général des Antiquités égyptiennes du Musée du Caire, Trésor de Tôd*. Cairo, 1950.

Bisson de la Rocque, F., Georges Contenau, and Fernand Chapouthier. *Le Trésor de Tôd*, Cairo, 1953.

Pierrat, G., et al. "Fouilles du Musée du Louvre à Tôd, 1988–1991." *Cahiers de Karnak* 10: 405–503.

GENEVIÈVE PIERRAT-BONNEFOIS

TOILETRIES AND COSMETICS. Cosmetics and perfumes were an important part of life for both sexes in ancient Egypt; they helped to create the desired body image. Perfumed salves were used daily, as was eye makeup, as part of a hygienic regimen designed to improve health as well as appearance. So important were these items that they were carried forth to the afterlife: cosmetic aids were applied to the bodies of the dead during mummification, and scents were a necessary part of the burial process. No Egyptian hoping for a complete and proper burial would have thought of entering the afterlife without the "seven sacred oils." When ancient thieves rifled the tomb of Tutankhamen, they took the unguents and left behind the calcite vases in which they had been stored. Mirrors, kohl holders, and perfume containers were standard burial equipment for both sexes. Formulas from medical and other texts also attest to the importance of personal appearance. For example, recipes have survived with instructions on how to prevent hair loss or remove wrinkles.

Personal Hygiene. The most important element of personal hygiene was always cleanliness, achieved by frequent washing or bathing. Priests had to wash daily, or more often, to remain ritually pure. Upper-class houses of the New Kingdom were equipped with bathrooms, usually consisting of a room or alcove equipped with a stone slab on which people might kneel or stand while water was poured over them from above.

Soap, as it is known today, did not exist. Modern soap is made of fat and lye obtained by pouring water over hardwood ash. Given the lack of hardwood trees in Egypt and surrounding countries, ancient inhabitants of the Nile Valley had to find other cleansers. Thus, instead of soap, ancient Egyptians compounded "body scrubs" of salt, natron, and honey to cleanse the body. Recipes for these cleansers are found in medical papyri. One such cleanser, from the back of the Edwin Smith Medical Papyrus, also includes calcite (Egyptian alabaster) granules. In the burial effects of the minor wives of Thutmose III, pots of "cleansing cream," consisting of vegetable oils or animal fat and lime (CaO), were found. Natron could also be used alone as a cleanser. (Although natron was used in mummification, its use as a skin cleanser is not as unlikely as it might seem: some modern bath cubes consist of talc, scent, calcium carbonate, and calcium bicarbonate, the latter two being the chief components of natron.) After cleansing, the skin would need to be moisturized with unguents and scented oils to keep it from drying out in Egypt's arid climate.

Perfumes and Unguents. In modern parlance, a "perfume" is made of essential oils in an alcohol base. Distillation of pure alcohol was unknown in pharaonic times; "perfume" or "cologne" as such did not exist in ancient Egypt. Instead, oils and fats were impregnated with the essences of various plants. It is almost impossible to tell from what substances these extracts were made, since the essential oils have not survived in extant samples of unguents. Scholars can only reconstruct the ingredients from images in tombs, recipes for scent from the Greco-Roman period, and knowledge of the raw materials available to pharaonic perfumers.

The plants used to scent pharaonic perfumed oils most likely included the water lily (lotus) and the flowers of the

TOILETRIES AND COSMETICS. *Various cosmetic items, including a princess's wig, a basket, a mirror, a razor, tweezers, and hair curlers.* (The Metropolitan Museum of Art, Museum Excavations, 1928–29 [30.3.35] and Rogers Fund, 1936 [36.3.189–203])

henna plant. Two varieties of water lily, (*Nymphaea caerulea* and *N. lotus*), are denoted (inaccurately) by Egyptologists with the single term "lotus." *Nymphaea* was a supremely important plant for the ancient Egyptians, used as decorative element, food, and medicine, and replete with religious symbolism. Its scent was supposedly that of the sweat of the gods; its opening and closing mimicked the pattern of life and rebirth. It has been suggested that plant's essence, dissolved in wine, was used as an intoxicant.

The flowers of the henna plant (*Lawsonia inermis*) also have a strong scent, which would have been used in perfumes, as might other fragrant flowers such as the Madonna lily (*Lilium candidum*). Representations of perfume-making from the Late period show a plant resembling the Madonna lily being picked and pressed to extract its essence.

Other scented substances—cedar wood, cinnamon bark, resins, herbs (such as thyme), and spices (such as coriander)—would have been used in the creation of unguents and perfumes. The resins in use no doubt included myrrh and frankincense, as well as ladanum or galbanum. Ladanum is derived from the leaves and branches of

shrubs of the genus *Cistus*, which grow in many locations around the Mediterranean. Galbanum, derived from *Ferula* (a large herb), would have been imported from Persia, possibly by the time of the New Kingdom.

Both the leaves and the bark of the various types of cinnamon tree (*Cinnamomum zeylanicum, C. camphora,* or *C. cassia*) may have been utilized in the preparation of unguents and perfumes, certainly by the Roman period, as the use of the term *kinamomon* in Coptic attests. During the Roman Empire, an extremely expensive scent called *malabathron*, made with cinnamon, was highly prized. The type of cinnamon bark used was probably *C. zeylanicum*, which is not native to Egypt but to Ceylon.

Perfume could be created by crushing the aromatic elements (seeds, bark, flowers, leaves, and so on) and infusing oil or fat with them. Three techniques seem to have been in use: enfleurage, in which layers of fat are saturated with perfume from flowers, which would be replaced from time to time; maceration, in which flowers or other plant materials are dipped into fats or oils heated to a temperature of about 65°C, and the mixture then sieved and allowed to cool; and expressing the perfume directly from flowers or fruit. Many types of oils derived from nuts and seeds were available for use as the base of perfumes and unguents, including balanos oil, linseed oil, olive oil, sesame oil, almond oil, and ben oil. Ben oil was derived from the horseradish tree (*Moringa oleifera*). Castor oil would also have been available, but as it has a strong smell, is unlikely to have been used. Olive oil and almond oil would have been among the most expensive since, although they can grow in Egypt, these trees were not native to the Nile Valley and would have required special cultivation. Almond oil has a particularly sweet smell which would have made it desirable as a base for scent or makeup.

With all of these varying types of vegetable oils available, it is interesting to note that of the thirty-five vases of perfumes found in Tutankhamun's tomb, the only one that had not been emptied was found to contain an unguent based on animal grease. The animal from which the fat came has not been determined. In medical texts from ancient Egypt, however, the fat of geese and the tallow of oxen are most often specified as a base for remedies applied externally. The fat of ducks, sheep, and goats, less expensive and thus more widely available, might also have been used. In one analyzed specimen of unguent, the fatty matter was mixed with another substance, which was tentatively identified as a balsam or resin (such as myrrh). This might have been included to add fragrance or to fix the scent already mixed. A few containers of perfumes from the tomb contained only resin, a Middle Kingdom sample also contained tiny splinters of wood. The latter were almost certainly from a fragrant tree such as cedar.

The sophistication of pharaonic perfumers in creating fragrances should not be underestimated. Both Pliny the Elder and Athenaeus, in fact, claim that Egyptian fragrance was the best in the world, because its scents were the longest lasting and it was the country best suited to the production of perfume (presumably owing to the great number of ingredients available there). A number of ancient authors, such as Pliny, Dioscorides, and Theophrastus, give recipes for perfumes which include several ingredients. For example, a famous perfume from Mendes, one of several mentioned by classical authors, contained balanos oil, cassia, myrrh, and aromatic resins. In his book *Concerning Odours*, Theophrastus mentions a scent made from cinnamon and myrrh mixed with other, unnamed substances.

One item of pharaonic perfumery that has created discussion among scholars is the cones which appear on the heads of banqueters and others in festive garb during the New Kingdom. These cones are usually believed to have been made of scented fat, probably ox tallow impregnated with myrrh, although there has been a recent suggestion that they were made of beeswax. Egyptologists have noted

that a similar custom survived among certain Bedouin tribes until the present century, and fat was worn as a hairdressing by Nubian tribes. Egyptologist Rita Freed has suggested that the custom originated as a means of counteracting the drying effect of the sun on hair.

Many unguents and oils were made from expensive or rare substances. Thus, in ancient Egypt most unguents and perfumes would have been easily available only to the rich. The importance of scent to personal hygiene and wellbeing, however, was universal. Unguents and scented oils were an essential part of the daily toilette for all classes throughout Egyptian history because oils and unguents were essential to protect and condition the skin in the dry climate. In fact, the striking workmen of Deir el-Medina listed body oil as one of their demands. Both sexes were advised to rub pellets of ground carob (or juniper) into the skin to act as a deodorant.

Cosmetics and Other Body Modifications. The use of makeup around the eyes was universal in pharaonic Egypt. Even statues of deities were given a fresh daily application of kohl (eye-paint; known in ancient Egypt as *msdmt*). The use of kohl was regarded as essential to ocular health as well as a necessary enhancement to beauty. Medical recipes often specify kohl, mixed with fat, as one of the remedies for inflamed eyes. So important was the proper application of eye-paint to the concept of beauty that one of the Egyptian words meaning "beautiful", 'n, is determined with the hieroglyph of an eye with *msdmt* applied to the lid.

The color of the kohl used and the areas of the eye to which it was applied varied over time. The oldest samples, found in graves of the Predynastic period, contain galena, a lead ore with a silvery-black sheen. In the Old Kingdom, a green eye-paint made from malachite was used. While black eyepaint was applied to the lashes and rims of the eyes, green eye makeup might be applied across the lids from the bridge of the nose to the outer tips of the eyebrows. By the New Kingdom, green eye-paint is rarely depicted, although samples of eye-paint made from malachite occur in the nineteenth dynasty.

Although galena and malachite were the usual substances, chemical analyses have shown that a variety of materials could be used in kohl: oxide of manganese, brown ocher, carbonate of lead, magnetic oxide of iron, black oxide of copper, and, very rarely, sulphide of antimony or chrysocolla (a copper ore of blue-green color). All of these, except antimony, were produced within Egyptian territories, including Sinai, the Red Sea coast, and Nubia.

The painting of lips and cheeks was another beauty enhancement practiced by ancient Egyptian women. Although the exact ingredients of pharaonic rouge and lip-color are unknown, it is usually thought that they were composed of red ocher in a base of oil or, more likely, animal fat. A paste made from the roots and leaves of henna has also been suggested as a possible colorant, and was also used on fingernails and toenails, a practice suggested by the presence of color on the nails of statues. A few statues of the New Kingdom have reddened nipples, which may represent another use of henna. The oldest representation of a person rouging her cheeks is probably from the eleventh dynasty. A unique representation of a woman painting her lips occurs in the Turin Erotic Papyrus, which dates to the New Kingdom. However, lip-color was probably available earlier and would have been used by women, and perhaps men, from at least the Middle Kingdom.

A number of recipes for wrinkle removal, or "transforming an old man into a youth," may be found in the Ebers Papyrus and other related medical texts. One of the more complicated preparations, found effective "millions of times," prescribes the oil from double-cooked fenugreek as a facial cream for men. Another preparation, found in the Ebers Papyrus, uses frankincense, balanos oil, and "rush-nut." "Gum"—that is, frankincense, balsam, or other tree gum—is a common ingredient in many of these recipes. Forbes (1965) compares some recipes to a modern cold cream containing wax, almond oil, and borax. There was also a preparation that seems to be for acne: it consisted of the fruit of the *ksbt*-tree and red ocher.

In addition to these temporary modifications of appearance, some ancient Egyptians were tattooed, although the practice seems to have been more or less restricted to women in the pharaonic period. Some predynastic statues also seem to represent tattoos. The hips and upper thighs of those often steatopygous females are covered with a pattern of dots, which may represent either beads or tattoos. A few mummies of later periods also show signs of a pattern of dots covering portions of the torso. The earliest example is the body of a woman called Amunet, priestess of Hathor, who lived during the Middle Kingdom. Other female mummies from the same time period also show tattooed patterns of dots on upper arms and chest. One of these also has a unique decorative scar across her abdomen just above the pubic area. While ornamental scarification was practiced in Nubia, it is not otherwise known in Egypt, and it is not surprising to find that these women were associated with Nubia. Tattoos are rarely represented in Middle Kingdom art, except for small stylized female figurines whose hips and torso are decorated with dots. New Kingdom female musicians depicted in wall paintings and on bowls are occasionally represented with an image of Bes on their thighs; this is presumably a tattoo, and, in fact, a mummified woman from a cemetery at Aksha in Nubia has an abstract image of Bes tattooed on

TOILETRIES AND COSMETICS. *Twelfth dynasty cosmetic jar in the form of a cynocephalus ("dog-headed") baboon.* This jar is made of blue-veined marble and is from Girgeh. The cynocephalus baboon was considered to be a manifestion of the god Thoth. (The Metropolitan Museum of Art, Rogers Fund, 1910. [10.176.54])

her body. It has been suggested that these are apotropaic markings, although it is equally likely that these musicians were associated with the cults of Bes or Hathor. From the Greco-Roman period, there are textual mentions of men and women with tattoos, but no depictions survive. The tradition of tattooing, however, survived among the Copts, and elderly women with a tattooed pattern of crosses on their foreheads may still be met in Egypt today. The tattoo in ancient Egypt, however, was not a regular feature of the beauty regime and seems to have had a particular association with cultic function.

Cosmetic and Perfume Containers and Implements. Cosmetic and unguent containers were made in almost every material imaginable: faience, glass, stone (especially calcite), clay, and even wood. The vessels that held perfumed ointments often took the form of figures carrying

TOILETRIES AND COSMETICS.
*Wood and ivory cosmetic box
and cosmetic vessels made of
anhydrite, twelfth dynasty.* The top
compartment of the box contains a
mirror. (The Metropolitan Museum
of Art, 26.7.1438; 26.7.1351;
26.7.1439–1442; 27.9.1; 10.176.54;
10.130.1269a-c)

jars or spoons in a variety of shapes. Perfume containers were also made in a variety of media, including glass, stone, and faience. Faience containers might be in the shape of the god Bes, monkeys, or round boxes with decorative lids embellished with figures of frogs or other creatures. A particularly popular form was the teardrop shape known in classical times as the alabastron, from the most popular material used, although glass was also popular. Some other glass perfume and unguent containers of the New Kingdom anticipate Greek vessel forms and can be conveniently called *amphoriskoi* or *krateriskoi*.

Cosmetic spoons are flat receptacles for wax or ointment, the exact nature of which has not been determined. They are attested in a bewildering variety of shapes, sizes, and materials. The decorative scheme for many of these spoons falls into one of the most common genres of embellishment for cosmetic items: the use of the nubile female form as a handle. Other cosmetic spoons may be in the form of bound animals, the hollowed-out body of the animal forming the bowl of the spoon. New Kingdom cosmetic spoons sometimes look like young girls swimming after birds or animals. Some scholars believe that these have a symbolic meaning: the girl represents the goddess Nut, and the animal in question symbolizes another deity. When the animal is a goose, Geb, the earth deity and husband of Nut, has been suggested as the deity. The term "cosmetic spoons" may be misnomer for these containers, since they are found in temples as well as tombs, and are not found in conjunction with other items of obvious cos-

metic use. According to Lise Manniche, cosmetic spoons are replete with erotic symbolism (as are some of the cosmetic boxes, especially those shaped like monkeys); depictions of naked girls, ducks, and lotus.

Containers for eye-paint often consist of multiple tubes linked together, although they also occur as lidded pots. The multiple-tube kohl containers are occasionally labeled as containing kohl specific to different seasons or "for every day." This, however, is not the norm. Inscriptions on certain multiple containers indicate that the eye-paints contained within are medicinal in nature and are specific to eye ailments common in certain seasons. Containers that may have held a single type of kohl are made in many materials, including faience, wood, pottery, calcite, diorite, serpentine, and just about every other variety of stone worked by the ancient Egyptians. Many are simple tubes; some have other shapes, such as palm columns. A few containers appear to have been made solely for decorative use, as no residue is found inside. In addition to the containers for eye-paint, shells were used to mix the ingredients, and palettes were made so that the kohl could be ground more finely. The palettes of the Predynastic period onward take a variety of shapes: some are rhomboidal, but others represent stylized flattened animals, such as fish, turtles, and hippopotami. The rhomboidal palettes often show evidence of considerable use, with hollows created by grinding on both sides. Kohl was usually applied with an applicator stick, which might be made of bronze, ivory, glass, stone, or wood.

Mirrors were made from polished metal, often bronze or gold, and were almost always supplied with decorated handles. Pillars, papyrus shapes, and young girls, often holding kittens or ducks, are common motifs for handle ornament. Sometimes the face of the goddess Hathor is incorporated into a handle. As in the case of representations of young girls as handles, the papyrus umbel is retained as the element just below the reflective surface. From Tutankhamun's tomb there is an *ankh*-shaped golden mirror with matching case. Most mirrors, however, seem to have been kept in linen bags, to judge by the impressions of fabric on the corroded metal of the disk. Because of their resemblance to the sun disk, mirrors were also highly symbolic items used in cultic practice. For example, a group of young girls shown in the Old Kingdom tomb of Mereruka performs a sort of dance in which they apparently attempt to reflect the sun's rays from mirror to mirror.

Professions Connected With Perfumery or Cosmetics. A few professions may be linked to the use and/or production of scent and makeup. Various reliefs show men and women making perfume. They are depicted gathering flowers and then putting them into large bags that are fitted over sticks at either end. The sticks are then turned so that the twisting bags squeeze the essence from the flowers. The earliest representation of perfume-making comes from a Middle Kingdom tomb at Beni Hasan, but most are of later date, from the New Kingdom, Saite period, and Ptolemaic era.

Another profession said to exist in pharaonic times is that of "cosmetician." There are a few mentions of the title *sšt n kdwt* attested for New Kingdom women. This is usually understood to mean that this woman applied eye-paint; however, it has recently been argued that other occurrences of this title are to be understood as "female scribe," which is how one would usually read the term. There are no depictions of women applying cosmetics to other women, although there are a number of reliefs of hairdressers, including a satirical cartoon showing a mouse mistress whose hair is dressed by a cat servant.

[*See also* Hygiene; Mirrors; *and* Oils and Fats.]

BIBLIOGRAPHY

Bianchi, Robert S. "Tattoo in Ancient Egypt." In *Marks of Civilization.* Los Angeles, 1988. A short overview of the tattoo in pharaonic Egypt.

Boston Museum of Fine Arts. *Egypt's Golden Age: The Art of Living in the New Kingdom, 1558–1085 B.C.* Boston, 1982. The catalog of this exhibit, which contained objects from dozens of museums, includes some excellent summaries and examples of ancient Egyptian cosmetic containers and implements.

Fletcher, Joanne. *Oils and Perfumes of Ancient Egypt.* London, 1998. A popular work which discusses the manufacture of perfumes in ancient Egypt and includes recipes for re-creating pharaonic un-guents. Samples of three "ancient" scents are included: cedarwood, cinnamon leaf, and water lily (lotus).

Forbes, R. J. *Studies in Ancient Technology.* Vol. 3. 3d ed. Leiden, 1965. Chapter 1 deals with cosmetics and perfumes in Greece and the Near East, as well as in Egypt.

Friedman, Florence Dunn, ed. *Gifts of the Nile: Ancient Egyptian Faience.* London, 1998. Catalog of an exhibition of Egyptian and Nubian faience, which although not specifically dealing with cosmetic and perfume containers, includes many examples of both.

Hepper, F. Nigel. *Pharaoh's Flowers: The Botanical Treasures of Tutankhamun.* London, 1990. An excellent supplement to Manniche's *Herbal*, offering photographs and botanical drawings of the plants discussed. Although restricted to plant species found in the tomb of Tutankhamun, it offers detailed discussions of the plants in question and, in chapter 2 ("Oils, Resins and Perfumes"), investigations of remains of unguents and related materials.

Lucas, A. *Ancient Egyptian Materials and Industries.* 4th ed., revised by J. R. Harris. London, 1989. Those interested in the results of chemical analyses of perfumes, cosmetics, and incenses will find chapter 6 most useful.

Manniche, Lise. *An Ancient Egyptian Herbal.* Rev. ed., London, 1999. Although a popular work on the plants used by the ancient Egyptians in medicine, cosmetics, etc., this lists the Latin, English, ancient Egyptian, Coptic, Greek, and modern Egyptian Arabic names for the plants.

LYN GREEN

TOMB ROBBERY PAPYRI. The Tomb Robbery Papyri are a group of documents (Papyrus Amherst/Leopold II, Papyrus Abbott, Papyrus Mayer A & B, Papyrus British Museum 10052, and a few others) concerned with the plunder of royal tombs and mortuary temples in Thebes at the end of the twentieth dynasty. The papyri date mostly to Years 19 and 20 of Ramesses XI (Years 1 and 2 of the "Renaissance Era"), although a few of them date to approximately thirty-five years earlier, in Years 16–18 of Ramesses IX. The designation "tomb robbery papyri" these documents have received is something of a misnomer, since much of the material actually deals with despoliation of temple property. As arbitrary as the resulting "trials" may seem by modern standards, it is important to note that not every person charged was found guilty, and that the degree of punishment varied widely. Furthermore, it is easy to forget amid the drama of the thefts themselves that the papyri provide evidence of an extensive cover-up of negligence, corruption, and even the complicity of high officials at Thebes. In the end, the authorities decided that the integrity of the royal tombs could no longer be maintained, and so they began removing the royal mummies from their tombs in both the Valley of Kings and the Valley of Queens for reburials in two large caches. A systematic removal of all valuables from the royal tombs probably followed soon thereafter.

Judging from the extant papyri, the three main targets of the thieves apparently had been the royal tombs of the seventeenth dynasty, chiefly along the cliffside at Dra Abul Naga, several mortuary temples, and the Valley of the Queens. It is not known whether any of the great royal tombs in the Valley of the Kings had been recently plundered as well, but in all likelihood they too had suffered. According to the papyri, most of the individuals involved in the robberies appear to have been members of the community of royal necropolis workers at Deir el-Medina, along with their associates scattered throughout other Western Thebes communities.

A papyrus recently discovered in Rochester, New York, describes the crimes of a certain Djehutihotep, the chief guard of the Karnak temple, arguably the most sacred place in Egypt. Access to the temple may have been restricted, but it was a far more public space than the royal tombs, so that this incident in particular provided unavoidable evidence of the extent of negligence and corruption at the highest levels of the Theban administration. It is not surprising that most of the investigation and subsequent measures had to be taken out of the hands of the now discredited former officials.

That there were several instances of major robberies underscores the extent of both corruption and economic distress in late Ramessid Egypt, eventually leading to the discredit and collapse of the royal house. The papyri reveal that the Theban populace suffered starvation, incursions of Libyan tribesmen, and a general breakdown in public order and safety. Although concerned mainly with the Theban region, the robbery papyri most likely reflect a nationwide state of turmoil, which was to result in the imposition of military rule under Herihor during the so-called Renaissance Era during the reign of Ramesses XI.

BIBLIOGRAPHY

Goelet, O. "A New 'Robbery' Papyrus: Rochester MAG 51.346.1." *Journal of Egyptian Archaeology* 82 (1996), 107–127. An account of a "robbery" papyrus that summarizes an investigation into the robberies of the chief doorkeeper at the Karnak temple, certainly the most public and embarrassing of all the thefts.

Kitchen, K. A. *The Third Intermediate Period in Egypt (1100–650* BC). 2d ed., with supplement and preface. Warminster, 1995. Recently updated, and by far the most comprehensive and accurate source for the history, genealogies, and dating systems of the late twentieth dynasty.

McDowell, A. G. *Jurisdiction in the Workmen's Community of Deir el-Medina* (Egyptologische Uitgaven, 5.) Leiden, 1990. A study of the legal procedures and terms in the robbery papyri and related documents.

Peet, T. E. *The Meyer Papyri A & B: Nos. M 11162 and M. 11186 of the Free Public Museums, Liverpool.* London, 1920. Publication of two of the most important robbery papyri.

Peet, T. E. *The Great Tomb-Robberies of the Twentieth Egyptian Dynasty.* Oxford, 1930. The fundamental publication and study of all the major papyri detailing the robberies; contains the hieroglyphic transcriptions of the texts and an extensive commentary.

OGDEN GOELET

TOMBS. [*This entry surveys the major types of ancient Egyptian tombs, with reference to their chronological development, architectural features, and their theological significance. It comprises three articles:*

An Overview
Royal Tombs
Private Tombs

For related discussions, see Necropolis *and* Pyramid.]

An Overview

Few ancient cultures have had their mortuary customs as intensively studied as ancient Egypt, but even today the origins of its remarkable dynastic burial practices are poorly understood. The earliest known burials come from the Nubian desert and date to about 12,000 to 14,000 years ago. They are simple pit graves, oval in plan, about 100 centimeters long and 50 centimeters wide, consisting of shallow depressions that were covered with large pieces of sandstone. The bodies—there could be several in a single grave—were tightly contracted and lay on the left side, head positioned to the east. There were no grave goods buried with them.

Except for these early finds, the archaeological record is virtually silent for the next seven or eight millenia, until the Neolithic period. In part, this is due to the fact that, with only localized exceptions (notably the work of Werner Kaiser in Upper Egypt and of Fred Wendorf in Nubia), no thorough or systematic archaeological surveys of Paleolithic and Epi-Paleolithic sites have yet been undertaken along the edges of the Nile Valley. Numerous Neolithic sites, however—particularly in Upper Egypt— have revealed scores of cemeteries, some of them large and used over long periods of time. They include such principal sites as Naqada, Abydos, Hierakonpolis, el-Ahaiwa, Nag el-Deir, el-Gerza, el-Amra, Mahasna, Mesaed, and many others. (I omit from lists of Neolithic cemeteries the burials at Merimda in Lower Egypt; the evidence from there of intra-village burials is now considered dubious.)

During the first millennium of the Upper Egyptian Neolithic, from roughly 5000 to 4000 BCE, graves of the Badarian culture continue to be small (c. 100–150 centimeters/3.2–4.8 feet in diameter), round or oval, shallow pits with single bodies lying in a contracted position, head to the south, face to the west. Yet there are now funerary goods in these graves—the earliest known in Egypt—and they attest to an already well-developed belief in the afterlife. Pottery is especially common, but we also find jewelry, flint tools, small slate cosmetic palettes, and ivory and bone figurines of women and animals. Bodies may be dressed in linen kilts or robes, wrapped in skins, or placed in basketry containers. In a few cases, graves are lined with reed matting, but as yet there is no solid evidence of superstructures over the pit.

A similar pattern of burial continues into the Naqada culture, but with some elaboration. For example, tombs are now often covered with branches or reed mats over which a small mound of gravel is placed. Grave goods are more numerous and varied and include black-topped red-ware pottery, stone vessels, slate palettes, bone and ivory figurines, combs, and small "tags" topped with carvings of human or animal heads.

During the next stage, burial patterns show an increasing degree of sophistication and complexity. In later phases of the Naqada culture, settlement sites in both the north and the south were becoming more urbanized, and the adjacent cemeteries exhibit increasing evidence of social differentiation. Graves are larger and often have a rectangular plan instead of an oval one. The substructure of the tomb is now constructed using a series of narrow walls to divide what formerly was a single pit into a series of rectangular cells, the centermost of which serves as a burial chamber. This relatively large cell is surrounded by a number of smaller ones in which increasingly large quantities of grave goods are placed. To the extent that the number and size of cells indicate quantities of funerary equipment, it is revealing that the tomb of Khasekhemwy has a burial chamber of less than 18 square meters (193 square feet), but surrounding cells cover more than 1,000 square meters (10,720 square feet). Some cells are lined with woven reed mats or wooden planks; a few have painted walls. At the site of Hierakonpolis, the famous Painted Tomb 100 has plaster walls decorated with scenes that have been interpreted as showing hunting, boating, fighting, and perhaps ritual dancing. Such a tomb is thought to have been intended for an individual of particularly high social rank. Grave goods in Naqada II become more elaborate and numerous, and include finely painted pottery, palettes and mace heads, stone vessels, jewelry (some of the pieces in gold and silver), and elegantly worked flint tools.

In very late Neolithic and Early Dynastic times, a series of dramatic changes in mortuary architecture undoubtedly reflect significant changes in funerary customs and religious beliefs. Some may have been influenced by western Asian (Near Eastern) cultures, but it is certainly appropriate to emphasize the indigenous character of Egyptian funerary customs and their architectural manifestations. Some were perhaps tied to regional Egyptian environmental and cultural differences; others were the outgrowth of dynastic Egypt's increasingly complex culture and stratified society.

In discussing changes in the mortuary architecture, it is convenient to deal separately with the superstructure and the substructure of the Egyptian tomb, because these followed relatively independent lines of development. The first typology of tomb architecture was developed in an elaborate 1936 study by George Andrew Reisner. Only recently, thanks in part to the important excavations at Abydos, have the general patterns layed out by Reisner been significantly expanded on.

At Abydos, from a period Egyptologists now call dynasty zero, elaborate burial complexes have been found lying in the western desert. In each complex, a large, multichambered substructure, apparently based on domestic architectural plans and filled with hundreds of local and imported pottery vessels, served as the tomb of an official of high social standing, probably a king. Above this large, central tomb lay a mound of sand, surrounded by small retaining walls. The top of the mound did not extend above the surrounding desert surface and was apparently covered by thin roof. The excavator, Gunther Dreyer, believes that this mound was of magical significance and that there was a second mound built above it, with a pair of stelae standing before it that gave the name of the deceased and served as a tomb marker. Near the superstructure lay hundreds of subsidiary graves, apparently of wives, family members, and servants. Some distance away, at the edge of cultivation, a large and apparently empty mud-brick rectangle (covering as much as 5,000 square meters/53,600 square feet) was constructed, perhaps to serve as an early form of the later valley temple that formed a part of the royal funerary complex.

In the first and second dynasties, the oval gravel or sand mounds that covered the tombs were made even larger and their plan became more nearly rectangular. Such mounds are known from Abydos and Hierakonpolis, but some believe that they might originally have been associated with the so-called Sand Mound of Heliopolis, a symbol of the island in the great primeval sea on which the first creation was said to have occurred. The mound was now built of mud brick, and some superstructures, particularly at Saqqara, measured up to 25 × 60 meters (80 × 192 feet) and stood 3 to 4 meters (10 to 13 feet) high. These flat-topped structures had outer walls constructed with an elaborate pattern of niching, a device sometimes referred to as a "palace façade." Early examples of this façade are complex examples of brickwork; later examples tend to be simpler; all seem intended to imitate the wooden paneling or woven reed matting associated with shrines representing Upper and Lower Egypt. Some early niched façades, such as that of Saqqara *mastaba* 3503, had hundreds of clay ox heads with real horns placed on a narrow, low platform within and in front of the niches.

By the end of the Early Dynastic period, the niched fa-

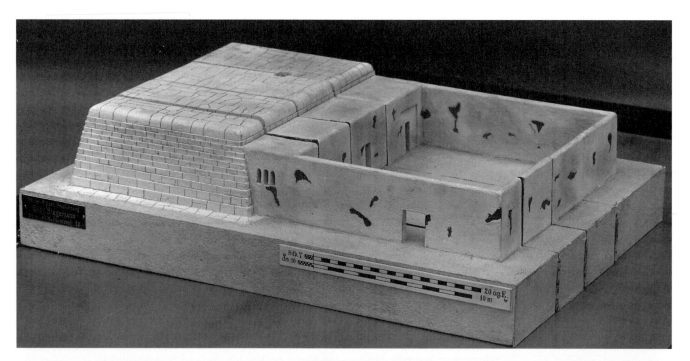

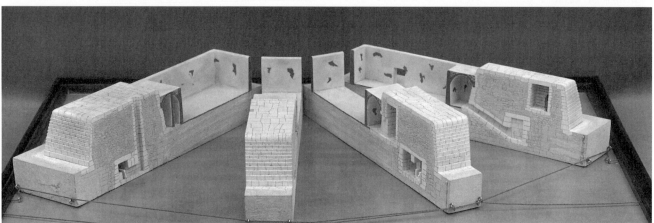

TOMBS: AN OVERVIEW. *Model of the fifth dynasty tomb of Userkafankh and his wife.* (The Metropolitan Museum of Art, Dodge Fund, 1913 [13.72])

çade had been reduced to two simple niches, one at each end of the superstructure's eastern wall; the remainder of the exterior had smooth, sloping-sided faces, giving the structure the appearance of an inverted bread pan, or a bench of the type that sits outside many modern Egyptian village houses. Such benches are called *mastaba*s in Arabic, and that word is used to describe this type of tomb superstructure. *Mastaba* tombs of substantial size and complexity are to be found at Saqqara, but they may never have been used for burials: many Egyptologists believe that the Saqqara structures were cenotaphs (dummy tombs), and that the actual burial place of Egypt's early royal families was Abydos.

The substructures of these tombs were also growing larger, and the number of cells a tomb might contain, their size, and their depth below ground also were increasing as offerings of food and drink, clothing, jewelry, games, and the like became more numerous. These cells were roofed with wooden boards and beams. Access to them initially was only through the top, prior to construction of the superstructure, until, in the mid-first dynasty, a staircase was added leading to the burial chamber. These tombs were surrounded by an enclosure wall and, beyond it, a series of subsidiary burials, a pit in which a model boat was placed and, in some instances, dummy buildings ("fictive architecture," it has been called) whose purpose can in most cases only be guessed.

During the Old Kingdom, *mastaba* tombs were built in great number for officials of the royal court and others of Egypt's upper class. At Giza, these *mastaba*s are laid out in large, well-ordered cemeteries that followed a carefully designed grid system. The substructures of these tombs are small because actual funerary offerings were now being replaced by representations on chapel walls. Often the substructure consists of little more than a vertical shaft leading to a single, undecorated burial chamber dug perhaps ten meters underground. The superstructure of these *mastaba*s, on the other hand, grew considerably, and often covers several hundred square meters. Instead of being solid stone structures, they now have within them numerous chambers, usually rectangular rooms laid out in a simple but seemingly meandering plan.

The southern of the two niches on the eastern wall of Early Dynastic *mastaba*s had evolved into a doorway by the late third dynasty, and it led into a chamber in which were placed decorated panels or stelae giving names and titles of the tomb owner. An early example is the tomb of Hesy-Re, in which elegantly carved wooden panels show the tomb owner and give his name and titles. During the fourth dynasty, the size and number of such chambers grew as their walls were decorated with increasingly large and elaborate scenes of offerings and rituals and long lists of names and titles. Such texts and scenes replaced actual offerings of food and drink that had formerly been placed in the substructure and the small, inscribed stelae set in niches. The types of scenes shown and their distribution apparently were subject to a number of rules that changed gradually during the Old Kingdom. Most frequently, the scenes depict activities involving the preparation of food—planting, harvesting, herding, slaughtering, cooking, storing, banqueting—and, a bit later, scenes of assorted craftsmen at work: carpenters, potters, leatherworkers, jewelers, and the like. Texts, originally little more than a name and a few titles, gradually grew to include elaborate offering lists, prayers, and autobiographies.

Two additional features also appeared within the superstructure: a *serdab* (cellar), a room in which, behind a slit window, was placed a statue of the deceased; and a "false door," through which the soul of the deceased could move between the burial chamber and the offering chapels. The earliest example of a *serdab* may be seen in the first dynasty tomb of Den at Abydos; an especially well-known example is that in Djoser's Step Pyramid complex.

The growing elaboration of both super- and substructures in Early Dynastic *mastaba* tombs laid the foundation for one of the most dramatic and sudden changes to be see in mortuary architecture: the appearance of the pyramid as the royal burial place, the earliest known example of which is the third dynasty Step Pyramid complex of Djoser (Netjerykhet) at Saqqara. Fortunately for Egyptology, for more than seventy years, since 1926, this remarkable monument has been carefully excavated and studied by an equally remarkable scholar, Jean-Philippe Lauer. It is to his work that we owe our picture of the Step Pyramid complex and the origin of Egyptian pyramids generally.

A pyramid, the elaborate complex of buildings that surrounded it, and the huge bureaucracy needed to maintain it and perform the functions it was intended to serve were of profound importance. A pyramid was intended as the burial place of the pharaoh, but the complex also served as a temple to the god Horus, with whom the pharaoh was identified in this life, and to Osiris, with whom he would be identified in the next. Thus, the pyramid was not merely a tomb; it was a physical and symbolic expression of the relationship Egyptians believed existed among ordinary humans, the pharaoh, and the gods. Its design and content were of such importance we must assume that its every aspect was the result of careful and regular deliberations about sacred beliefs and practices. Changes made in mortuary architecture or funerary cults were the result of rethinking the man–god relationship and speculating about the nature of the afterlife. Such changes would not have been made frivolously; they reflected the Egyptians constantly evolving ideas about life and death. To understand Egyptian mortuary architecture, we must therefore know as much as possible about Egyptian religious beliefs, kingship, folk traditions, and such secular matters as economics and politics. Unfortunately, we shall almost certainly never have enough data to be able to think like an ancient Egyptian or to explain fully the meaning of these monuments and their component parts. But we should remember that, for the Egyptians, there were compelling reasons for building mortuary monuments as they did. Tombs neither grew randomly nor changed form or content without reason.

The Step Pyramid changed dramatically throughout Djoser's reign. Later tradition says that it was the work of a great architect and wise man, Imhotep. If he actually existed, he is the first architect in history to whom we can give a name. In a series of six building phases, Imhotep took what had begun as a relatively small *mastaba* superstructure and changed it into a step pyramid that rose in six stages to a final height of more than 60 meters (192 feet). Its base covered over 12,000 square meters (128,640 square feet), and it contained over 330,000 cubic meters (10.6 million cubic feet) of limestone blocks. Beneath the pyramid, more than 30 meters (100 feet) below ground, workmen cut a labyrinthine series of corridors nearly 6 kilometers (4 miles) long, then filled them with more than forty thousand stone vessels and countless other funerary offerings, including objects of earlier kings, perhaps family heirlooms or historical reminders of Djoser's antecedents. A huge central shaft, measuring 7 × 7 × 28 meters (22 × 22 × 90 feet), led from the surface down to a granite burial chamber at the center of the subterranean complex. Above ground, surrounding the pyramid, a 10-meter-high (32-foot-high) stone enclosure wall with a simple niched facade extended 1,600 meters (5,120 feet) north to south and 300 meters (960 feet) east to west. Within it lay open courtyards, dummy buildings, courts for religious festivals, and mortuary temples—structures thought necessary not only for the requisite funeral ceremonies but also for the pharaoh's activities in the afterlife.

At the southern end of the Step Pyramid enclosure, a staircase descended more than 28 meters (90 feet) below the enclosure wall into a much smaller but no less complex series of corridors and chambers. Here, too, another huge shaft led to a granite chamber. This was Djoser's so-called Southern Tomb. It has been called the cenotaph of Djoser (especially by those who argue that the Early Dynastic tombs at Abydos were cenotaphs, while those at Saqqara were true royal burials, not the other way round). Others contend that it was the burial place of Djoser's *ka*.

Only two other certain stepped pyramid complexes were built after Djoser's: one by his successor, Horus Sekhemkhet, also at Saqqara; and another by the next king, Khaba, at Zawiyet el-Aryan, halfway between Saqqara and Giza. That of Sekhemkhet was intended to be larger than Djoser's, but it was never finished and, apparently, never used. The so-called Layer Pyramid of Khaba is smaller than Djoser's, and it too was unoccupied. Both of these step pyramids show subterranean chamber plans similar to each other but significantly different from that of the Djoser complex. (Seven other stepped pyramids, none more than about 15 meters [48 feet] high, were constructed late in the third dynasty at sites as far south as Elephantine; they seem to have been purely symbolic structures, erected near sites of religious or royal significance.)

Sneferu, first king of the fourth dynasty, may be credited as Egypt's greatest builder of pyramids and as builder both of the last step pyramid and the first "true" pyramid. His pyramid at Meidum was begun as a step pyramid of seven stages, then eight, then finally changed to a true pyramid with sides that sloped upward at an angle of 51° 50′. A 58-meter-long (185-foot-long) passage descends through the pyramid's north face to a horizontal, subterranean corridor, then extends vertically to a small, corbelled burial chamber, the floor of which lies at ground level. This basic plan, seen here for the first time, was to be followed by most later pyramid builders. So was Sneferu's addition of a small "satellite pyramid" adjacent to the main one, and his construction of a causeway reaching from the Nile Valley westward to the enclosure wall of the pyramid complex.

For reasons that are unclear, Sneferu also built two other pyramids, each substantially larger than that at Meidum, 25 kilometers (15.6 miles) to the north at the site of Dahshur. One is called the North (or Red) Pyramid, and the other is the Bent Pyramid; each has from two to three times the volume of the pyramid at Meidum. The variations in design of Sneferu's three pyramids suggest that his reign was a period of experimentation with pyramid design, and the variations were almost certainly due as much to theological considerations as to problems of engineering and stability.

The best-known pyramids, of course, are the three built in the fourth dynasty on the Giza Plateau: the Great Pyramid of Khufu, the Pyramid and Sphinx of Khafre, and the Pyramid of Menkaure. Between construction of the first and second of these, there also was a pyramid constructed by Djedefre, son of Khufu and his successor as pharaoh, at Abu Roash, about 10 kilometers (6.25 miles) north of Giza. The pyramids of Khufu and Khafre are the largest ever built: each contains more than 2 million cubic meters (64 million cubic feet) of stone. That of Menkaure has only a tenth as much; that of Djedefre only a twentieth.

By any standard, the Giza Pyramids are impressive, but each was just a part of what by the fourth dynasty had come to be a fairly standard complex that included the pyramid, a mortuary temple (although there is some question as to whether it was ever used as such), an enclosure wall and causeway, pits for sacred barks, a valley temple, smaller pyramids for principal wives, cemeteries for officials and noblemen, and extensive domestic buildings that housed the large number of priests, servants, craftsmen, and others needed to ensure the proper functioning of the royal funerary cult.

During the fifth and sixth dynasties, another dozen pyramids were constructed, but on a much smaller scale than those at Giza, and with rubble fill replacing the large cut limestone blocks used in earlier construction. The pyramid itself is of reduced size in these complexes, but there is greater emphasis on such other features as the mortuary temple. Most of these pyramids were built either at Abusir, a site just north of Saqqara, or at Saqqara itself. Thanks to the discovery of several very fragmentary papyri at Abusir, we know something about the economy and administration of such temple complexes. Pyramid

TOMBS: AN OVERVIEW. *The restored columned portico of the family tomb of Seshemnefer at Giza, late fifth or early sixth dynasty.* (Courtesy Dieter Arnold)

complexes and their mortuary cults were enormous, expensive institutions and clearly formed very significant components of the Egyptian economy and bureaucracy. Indeed, some Egyptologists have attributed the economic and political decline of Old Kingdom Egypt in part to the expense of maintaining these funerary endowments.

With the reign of Unas at the end of the fifth dynasty, royal pyramids came to include hieroglyphic religious texts, called Pyramid Texts, on the walls of the burial chamber and its antechamber. These texts provide us with important clues to the funerary, offering, and magical rituals associated with the burial of a pharaoh and his anticipated role in the afterlife. Pyramid Texts grew increasingly elaborate during the sixth dynasty; by the First Intermediate Period, they also came to be inscribed in nonroyal tombs. They were replaced in the Middle Kingdom by Coffin Texts, and in the New Kingdom by the *Book of Going Forth by Day (Book of the Dead)*.

During the First Intermediate Period, a few small pyramids were constructed—two at Saqqara and one in Middle Egypt; several so-called *saff* tombs at Ta'arif on the western bank of the Nile at Thebes apparently had small pyramids in their entrance courtyards. But except for these few examples, most tombs during this time were small rock-cut tombs laid out in varying provincial styles. These tombs, dependent on locally available materials and labor, varied greatly in size and quality, although their basic plan was the same as rock-cut tombs of the Old Kingdom, such as those at Giza or Aswan. Among the principal sites of First Intermediate Period and Middle Kingdom rock-cut tombs, one also should note Beni Hasan, Deshasheh, Sheikh Said, Meir, Bersheh, and Qaw.

The tradition of constructing large royal pyramids was revived during the Middle Kingdom. At el-Lisht, Amenemhet I and Senwosret I each built pyramids of, respectively, 55 and 61 meters (176 and 195 feet) in height; at Dahshur, their several successors built pyramids about 75 meters (240 feet) high. Surrounding Amenemhet I's pyramid was a series of twenty-two pit burials for royal women, and there were also small *mastaba*s within the enclosure. The pyramid of Senwosret, little more than a hill of rubble today, was a large structure surrounded by nine subsidiary pyramids, apparently for wives of the pharaoh. The Dahshur pyramid of Senwosret III also had six queens' pyramids within its enclosure. But in the pyramid complex of Amenemhet III, also at Dahshur, queens' pyramids were abandoned, and two suites of rooms within the king's pyramids were set aside for his principal wives. Several Middle Kingdom pyramids (that of Amenemhet III at Haware, for example) show experimentation with ways to thwart tomb robbers by installing sliding blocks, dummy chambers, blind alleys, and other techniques, but they were not successful.

Only a few pyramids or *mastaba*s were constructed after the Middle Kingdom. *Mastaba*s are found at level sites where cliffs are unavailable for rock-cut tombs and/or in districts where deliberately archaizing funerary customs were in favor. There are small pyramids associated with workmen's tombs in the New Kingdom Theban village of Deir el-Medina, and rather more impressive pyramid fields at such Nubian sites as el-Kurru, Nurri, and Meroë (which date to late dynastic times and continue into the fourth century CE). But for the most part, after the Middle Kingdom, both kings and noblemen were interred in rock-cut tombs.

Rock-cut tombs, sepulchers cut horizontally into a cliff face or hillside, appeared in Egypt in the third to fourth dynasties, perhaps first in quarries on the Giza Plateau, and slightly later at sites in Upper Egypt, where they became extremely common. At first, these rock-cut tombs were similar to small *mastaba*s in their interior plan, but the *serdab* was replaced by deeply cut relief figures of the deceased and his family carved in the tomb's rear wall. The burial chamber lay below, accessible down a vertical shaft. Later, the burial chamber might be found beneath the forecourt or even some distance from the tomb-chapel itself. By the fifth to sixth dynasties, the plans of rock-cut tombs were following their own line of development, a line that quickly led to more and larger chambers, a columned portico, and interior pillared halls.

By the Middle Kingdom rock-cut tombs had become common, and at several large necropolises—Beni Hasan, Nag el-Deir, Gebelein, and Asyut, for example—many superbly carved and decorated examples may be found. The tombs at these sites vary in size, chamber proportions, and plan, suggesting that different areas of Upper Egypt followed different mortuary traditions. Examples of such differences may be seen by comparing tombs at Deir Rifa, Nag el-Mashaykh, Abydos, Esna, Elkab, and Hierakonpolis.

One of the most important sites of rock-cut tombs is the Theban necropolis. Tombs may be found here from the later Old Kingdom onward, initially small and relatively isolated. Under the eleventh dynasty Inyotefs, the tombs were cut in clusters in the faces of large sunken courtyards—and hence are called "saff" or "row" tombs—and consisted of one to four small chambers in one or two of which pillars (one or two of them) were carved. By the New Kingdom, hundreds of rock-cut tombs were carved at Thebes, occupying virtually all of the hillsides (but few of the sheer cliffs) in the Theban necropolis.

Private rock-cut Theban tombs are of three general types: those with a rectangular façade and a central entrance; those with a pyramid in a courtyard at the front of the tomb; and those with columned or pillared porticos at their entrance. Generally, beyond the courtyard and doorway, there is a long, narrow chamber at right angles to the entry axis, called the *wsḫt* (broad hall); beyond that lies a long hallway, its axis at right angles to that of the *wsḫt*; at the end of the hallway is a small shrine or *naos*. It is a simple cruciform plan. Some tombs have an additional square chamber between the *wsḫt* and the long hallway, and sometimes that chamber contains a varying number of pillars.

The best-known rock-cut tombs are those of the New Kingdom pharaohs in the Valley of the Kings at Thebes. Their plans are more elaborate than private tombs, and they are substantially larger. Their chambers can occupy hundreds of cubic meters, and it is clear that they were not simply repositories for foodstuffs and funerary equipment but played a significant role in the processes intended to ensure the continued functioning of kingship and the balance of *maat* after the death of a pharaoh. Such important objectives demanded that the decoration of royal tombs be more formal and more focused on religious themes than that of private tombs. Especially good examples of the various plans and decorative programs of royal tombs may be seen in the tombs of Thutmose III and IV, Horemheb, Sety I, and Ramesses III. Tomb five in the Valley of the Kings, the burial place of several sons of Ramesses II, is the largest and most unusual tomb ever found in Egypt, boasting well over a hundred chambers and corridors.

Following the New Kingdom, royal tombs were built in the Nile Delta, where environmental conditions precluded the use of features common to tombs in Upper Egypt. It was not unusual for tombs to be built in courtyards cut beneath temple compounds. At Thebes, private tombs continued to be dug, some of them among the largest complexes of chambers and corridors to be found in Egypt (e.g., tomb 33, Pedamonopet; tomb 34, Montuemhet; tomb 37, Harwa). Many contain details taken from the architecture of earlier times (e.g., the use of the niched façade).

There are numerous other necropolises in Egypt from the Late period and from Greek and Roman times, including Coptos, Beni Hasan, el-Hiba, Giza, el-Fostat, and Alexandria. At Saqqara, the Serapeum, the burial place of sacred Apis bulls from the New Kingdom onward, must certainly rank as one of the most impressive examples of Egyptian rock-cut tombs.

[*See also* Burial Practices; Giza; Necropolis; Pyramid; Saqqara; *and* Theban Necropolis.]

BIBLIOGRAPHY

Badawy, Alexander. *A History of Ancient Egyptian Architecture.* 3 vols. Giza, 1954; Los Angeles, 1966, 1968.

Brunner, Hellmut. *Die Anlagen der ägyptischen Felsgräber bis zum Mittleren Reich.* Glückstadt, 1936.

Dodson, Aidan. *Egyptian Rock-Cut Tombs.* Princes Risborough, 1991.

Dreyer, Gunter. "A Hundred Years at Abydos." *Egyptian Archaeology: Bulletin of the Egypt Exploration Society* 3 (1993), 10–12.

Edwards, I. E. S. *The Pyramids of Egypt.* 5th ed. Harmondsworth, 1993.

Hornung, Erik. *Valley of the Kings.* New York, 1990.

Lehner, Mark. *The Complete Pyramids.* London, 1998.

Maragioglio, Vito, and C. A. Rinaldi. *L'architettura delle pyramidi memfite.* 8 vols. Turin, 1963; Rapallo, 1964–1977.

Reisner, George A. *The Development of the Egyptian Tomb Down to the Accession of Cheops.* Cambridge, Mass., 1936.

Smith, E. Baldwin. *Egyptian Architecture as Cultural Expression.* New York, 1938.

Smith, William Stevenson. *The Art and Architecture of Ancient Egypt.* Revised by William Kelly Simpson. New Haven, 1981.

Staedelmann, Rainer. *Die ägyptischen Pyramiden vom Ziegelbau zum Weltwunder.* Kulturgeschichte der antiken Welt, 10. Mainz, 1991.

Vandier, Jacques. *Manuel d'archéologie égyptienne.* Vol. 2, *Les grandes epoques l'architecture funéraire.* Paris, 1954.

KENT R. WEEKS

Royal Tombs

The Egyptian idea of kingship attributed divine spiritual qualities to the king, in addition to his mortal nature, but this divine aspect did not keep a pharaoh's human body from dying. In order to resolve this conflict between reality and theology, an enormous mechanism was created to explain and correct this calamity. Essentially, the king's body had to be properly buried like those of everyone else, but the body was understood not to be dead, and the burial place was not a tomb in the modern sense but rather a station for transitional or spiritual events. With the help of funerary rituals, rich grave goods, the magic of spells and pictures on the tomb walls, and a powerful symbolic architectural framework, the "dead" king was revived and his eternal life and rulership established. The ideas and methods changed over the course of the millenia, and the degree of material investment in this mechanism varied from kings of inferior status to rulers of high prestige and godlike qualities. Thus, the diminishing divine power of the king after the end of the New Kingdom is reflected in the royal tombs of the twenty-first and twenty-second dynasties at Tanis.

Burial. Several royal burials have been found intact, albeit of ephemeral kings: Tutankhamun, Amenemope, Psusennes, Sheshonq II, and Osorkon II. In several other royal tombs robbers overlooked or left parts of the burial and the grave goods. These objects, together with parallels from private tombs and representations in tomb paintings, help us to reconstruct the ideal contents of a royal funerary assemblage. The basic burial of a royal body was not much different from that of a wealthy private person, but ideally, it had to outshine private funerary equipment in both quantity and quality. The grave goods consisted of personal belongings—objects of daily use, weapons, and tools—and of the official regalia (crowns, scepters, jewelry, etc.). However, the divine aspect of the pharaoh also required magic objects that made his resurrection possible and protected him in the next life: for example, multitudes of shrines with images of deities, and huge ceremonial resurrection beds with the heads of Hathor, cheetah, and hippotamus. Vessels with food provisions, oils, and ointments, which predominated in the grave goods in early times, were gradually reduced in consequence of the development of daily offering ceremonies. The complete grave goods of one of the great kings must have been overwhelming.

During the first three dynasties, the royal body probably rested in a wooden coffin, of which no traces have survived. From Khufu on, the body was placed in a stone sarcophagus. During the Old Kingdom the royal sarcophagus is plain and box-shaped; it may have housed one or several inner wooden coffins. In the the Middle Kingdom the royal granite sarcophagus has the symbolic shape of a Lower Egyptian reed shrine standing inside a paneled enclosure with gates. Some early New Kingdom sarcophagi are of red quartzite and are made in the shape of a royal cartouche. The corners of those of the later eighteenth dynasty are sculpted with figures of the protective goddesses Isis, Nephthys, Neith, and Selket. On the lid of the sarcophagi of Merenptah and Tawosret, the figure of the deceased is shown in the round. From the twelfth dynasty on, the royal body was enclosed in an anthropoid coffin of gilded wood. Like the bark of the gods, the sarcophagus is sheltered by a huge gilded wooden shrine. Similarly the canopic chest receives, from the twelfth dynasty, a burial of its own in a separate chamber; accordingly the shape and size of the canopic box represent a smaller version of the sarcophagus.

Architecture. The royal tombs of the Early Dynastic period are clustered around the Umm el-Qa'ab at Abydos. They apparently reflected the dwelling aspect of the eternal existence in the afterworld. A huge, cabin-like wooden chamber is sunk under the desert surface and protected by a brick retaining wall with small, niche-like side chambers. Some walls seem to have been sheathed with green faience tiles depicting an otherworldly palace. Above ground, stelae with the royal name marked a flat, *mastaba*-like platform. The main tomb is surrounded by a considerable number of smaller tombs of servants, who may have been sacrificed at the king's death. In the second dynasty, more side chambers were added for the storage of the enormous quantities of grave goods, and access to

TOMBS: ROYAL TOMBS. *The fourth dynasty* mastaba *of Shepseskaf at Saqqara*. (Courtesy Dieter Arnold)

the tombs was provided by straight staircases. Also at Abydos, but at a distance from the actual burial tombs, monumental brick enclosures (known as "forts") supply the second important aspect of the royal afterlife. Completely above ground and without underground chambers, they seem to be models of palace-fortresses or arenas for the display of royal ceremonies in the afterlife. Table 1 lists the identified royal tombs of the Early Dynastic period.

Monumental, elaborate *mastaba*s of the first dynasty at Saqqara North, excavated by Walter B. Emery beginning in 1936, are no longer believed to be the tombs of kings. At least the kings Hotepsekhemwy, Ranebi, Ninuter (and perhaps Khasekhemwy) of the second dynasty built huge underground gallery tombs at Saqqara, and in the Western Desert vast stone enclosures seem to represent the associated "forts" or "palaces." The underground apartments still represent the tomb type of a residential palace surrounded by enormous galleries filled with supplies. The aboveground structures are lost.

A new type of otherworldly residence was designed for King Djoser at Saqqara. For the first time, a huge, multilayered superstructure was built in stone, representing a full-scale palace city. The complex contains two similar underground tombs under stone *mastaba*s, the northern one probably the tomb for the royal body. Later the north-

TABLE 1. *Royal Tombs of the Early Dynastic Period.*

Dynasty "0"	
Ka	Abydos B 7–9, 1–2
First dynasty	
Narmer	Abydos B 17–18
Aha	Abydos B 10–15–19
Djer	Abydos O (326); fort A (269)
Djet	Abydos Z (174); fort B (154)
Merneith	Abydos Y (41); fort C (?)
Den	Abydos T (121); fort C (?) (80)
Enedjib	Abydos X (63); fort D (?)
Semsem	Abydos U (69); fort D (?)
Ka'a	Abydos Q (26); fort at Deir Sitt Damiana
Second dynasty	
Hotepsekhemwy	Saqqara, near Unas
Ranebi	Saqqara?
Ninuter	Saqqara
Peribsen	Abydos P; "Middle Fort"
Khasekemwy	Abydos V; fort at Shunet el-Zebib

ern *mastaba* was transformed into a 60-meter-high (192-foot-high) step *mastaba*. The chambers are huge granite boxes surrounded by a system of corridors ornamented with a façade of reed palaces cased with green faience tiles. Enormous underground galleries were filled with pottery and stone vessels containing food.

Some ephemeral successors of Djoser began building similar complexes that were all to be provided with a step *mastaba*. They remained unfinished and display the gradual abandonment of the idea of a huge otherworldly residence.

A new building type, probably expressing a more heavenly aspect, appeared under Sneferu, culminating in the first true monumental pyramids. The burial apartments are partially elevated into the pyramid core, and the burial chambers, with the help of corbeled roof construction, achieve the enormous interior height of 15 meters (48 feet). The galleries for the grave goods have disappeared. These architectural features and the simultaneous appearance of a superstructure in pyramid shape suggest a reorientation of ideas about the royal afterlife under Sneferu, probably in consequence of the growing importance of the solar religion. The royal tombs of Khufu, Khafre, and Menkaure follow this tendency and are marked by the enormous size of their pyramids. The funerary apartments still show experimental changes and are marked by efforts to protect the roofs of the entrance passage and the crypt against structural damage. So-called air shafts in the pyramids of Khufu and Khafre were probably meant to permit communication between the royal chamber and heaven.

The long experimental period ended with Menkaure, and under Shepseskaf (in the Mastabat Fara'un), a scheme for the underground chambers emerges that would predominate in royal tombs of the Old and Middle Kingdoms. The burial crypts from Khufu on are dominated by the royal stone sarcophagus. The rectangular crypt is oriented east–west so that the sarcophagus can occupy the short western side, with its head to the north. The entrance opens opposite it from an antechamber to the east. From Khafre on, the ceiling of the chamber is usually saddle-shaped because of the efficiency of this building form in supporting the heavy pressure of the pyramid core, and also because of the symbolic, heavenlike tent shape of the ceiling. Additional granite beams or several layers of sloping limestone beams protect the interior ceiling slabs. A narrow, shallow, sloping passage enters the antechamber from the north. After the funeral, this passage was blocked with several huge portcullises. One or three chambers—probably wrongly termed *serdab*—branch off to the east of the antechamber; these may have contained grave goods. This type of underground apartment is closely connected with the aboveground form of the pyramid. Both architectural units seem to aim at the transformation of the king, apparently through permitting his participation in the daily voyage of the sun. He would leave his tomb through the top of the pyramid in the morning in order to join Re-Horakhty in his bark and return into the tomb at sunset. Table 2 lists known royal pyramids of the Old Kingdom.

TABLE 2. *Royal Pyramids of the Old Kingdom.* The dimensional measurements are given first in cubits (then in meters).

Pyramid	Angle	Base	Height
Meidum M3	51°51′	275 (144.32)	175 (92)
Bent Pyramid (Sneferu)	54°31′ (upper, 44°30′)	360 (189)	200 (105)
Dahshur North (Sneferu)	45°	420 (220)	200 (105)
Khufu	51°50′40″	440 (230.36)	280 (146.5)
Djedefre	60°	200 (105)	175 (92)
Zawiet el-Arjan		210 (110)	
Khafre	53°10′	410 (215.29)	275 (143.87)
Menkaure	51°	200 (105.5)	125 (65.55)
Userkaf	53°	140 (73.3)	94 (49)
Sahure	50°45′	150 (78.75)	–(50)
Neferefre		125 (65)	
Djedkare	52°	150 (78.75)	
Unas	56°	110 (57.70)	–(43)
Teti		150 (78.75)	100 (52.5)
Pepy I		150 (78.75)	100 (52.5)
Merenre		175 (90–95)	
Pepy II	53°13′	150 (78.75)	100 (52.5)

The crypts of the pyramids of the twelfth dynasty only partially follow the Old Kingdom pattern; one difference is the existence of a separate side chamber for the canopic burial. The crypt of Senwosret I, which is lost in the ground water, may have copied the Old Kingdom ground plan, as does the granite crypt of Senwosret III. However, the relatively modest tomb of Amenemhet I does not differ from contemporary private tombs. The crypts and passages in the tombs of Amenemhet II and Senwosret II develop unique plans of their own, without exact prototypes. The tomb of Amenemhet III at Dahshur has an enormous system of chambers and passages that may have housed grave goods or represented mythical localities. After structural damage, the pyramid was abandoned, and the underground apartment of Amenemhet III's second pyramid at Hawara reflects an overriding concern for basic safety principles: a monolithic crypt, and massive protective roof construction to resist pressure from above. Table 3 lists the known royal pyramids of the twelfth dynasty.

The tombs of the kings of the thirteenth dynasty also concentrate on the protection of the royal sarcophagus (which becomes one with the chamber) and on mechanisms for blocking the passages. The tombs of the seventeenth dynasty kings at Dra Abul Naga (Western Thebes) are relatively simple rock-cut tombs beneath a brick pyramid with a cult chapel. Their architectural remains were lost again after their discovery and robbing in 1827.

A new type of royal tomb appears only with the New Kingdom, influenced by local conditions in the Valley of the Kings at Thebes. Beneath the vertical limestone cliffs,

TABLE 3. *Royal Pyramids of the Twelfth Dynasty*. The dimensional measurements are given first in cubits (then in meters).

Pyramid	Angle	Base	Height
Amenemhet I	54°	160 (84)	112 (59)
Senwosret I	49°24'	200 (105.23)	116 (61.25)
Amenemhet II?		160 (84)	
Senwosret II	42°35'	200 (105.88)	–(48.65)
Senwosret III	50°	200 (105)	–(61.25)
Amenemhet III (Dahshur)	54–56°	200 (105)	143? (75?)
Amenemhet III (Hawara)	48–52°	200 (102)	110? (58?)

sloping passages and staircases lead into deeply hidden crypts. These rock-cut tombs have no superstructure, but their entrance sections seem to have been partially accessible for ceremonial purposes. The sloping access corridors and staircases of the tombs down to Amenhotpe III show a 90° bend or curve (in the case of Hatshepsut) that is considered to be characteristic of the tomb of Osiris at Abydos. Each corridor branch ends in a chamber; the upper one probably marks a ceremonial tomb, and the lower one is the burial crypt with the sarcophagus. Crypts from Thutmose I to Thutmose III have rounded corners; apparently their oval shape may represent a royal cartouche, or the twelfth nocturnal hour of the *Book of That Which Is in the Underworld* (*Amduat*). From Amenhotpe II on, the sarcophagus stands in the rear part of a huge pillared burial hall, and from Thutmose IV on, in a deeply recessed basin. A deep shaft, considered to be dedicated to Sokar, separates the sloping entrance passage from the interior of the tomb.

From Horemheb on, the axis of the tomb (except in the tomb of Ramesses II) is straight but splits into a second parallel section which leads to the actual lower crypt. The upper section is considered to be a secondary, symbolic tomb for the king as a personification of Osiris. The lower burial hall develops into an impressive architectural space. The roof of the crypt is slightly vaulted and supported by two rows of four pillars. The area between the pillars is lowered and contains the prominent sarcophagus. Here the Osiris king was thought to unite with the sun god. The crypt is surrounded by a number of side chapels, some for storage and some dedicated to deities of the underworld. During the Ramessid period, the entrance shaft and the steep staircases disappear and the originally considerable slope of the passages is flattened out, assimilating the tomb to the form of a rock-cut temple. An unusual feature is the very slight increase in the dimensions of the doors, passages, number of pillars, and size of the sarcophagus. The royal tombs in the main valley are as follows:

Thutmose I and Hatshepsut	KV 20 (KV = Valley of the Kings)
Thutmose II	KV 42
Thutmose III	KV 34
Amenhotpe II	KV 35
Thutmose IV	KV 43
Tutankhamun	KV 62
Ramesses I	KV 16
Sety I	KV 17
Ramesses II	KV 7
Sons of Ramesses II	KV 5
Merenptah	KV 8
Sety II	KV 15
Amenmesse	KV 10
Siptah	KV 47
Horemheb	KV 57
Twosret and Sethnakhte	KV 14
Ramesses III	KV 11
Ramesses IV	KV 2
Ramesses V and VI	KV 9
Ramesses VII	KV 1
Ramesses IX	KV 6
Ramesses XI	KV 4
Amenhotpe III	WV 22 (WV = Western Valley)
Ay	WV 23

The tombs of the kings of later periods were built as temple tombs in the residence cities of the Delta. Some of the royal tombs of the twenty-first and twenty-second dynasties were found by Pierre Montet in 1939 at Tanis. The 50 × 60-meter complex contains the tombs of Psusennes I, Amenemope, Osorkon II, Sheshonq III, and some other high-ranking persons. They stand in the forecourt of the temple of Amun. Because of the level of ground water, the chambers are situated close beneath the surface. They are massive stone constructions with a small antechamber and a niche for the sarcophagus. As an exception, the kings of the Kushite twenty-fifth dynasty were again buried in plain rock-cut chamber tombs beneath small, steep pyramids in the cemeteries of el-Kurru and Nuri at Napata. The tombs of the twenty-sixth dynasty (Apries, Amasis) in the temple of Neith at Sais are lost, but from descriptions by Herodotus (II.169), it is known that the sarcophagus stood in an aboveground shrine surrounded by palm columns. Some tombs of the twenty-ninth and thirtieth dynasties were situated in Mendes; they were destroyed by the Persians in 343 BCE. Remains of the tomb of Nepherites are preserved. The sarcophagus of Nektanebo II was found dislocated in Alexandria (Brit. Mus. EA 10).

The tombs of Alexander the Great and the Ptolemies were separate mausoleum buidings, probably in a mixed classical and pharaonic style, some topped with pyra-

TOMBS: ROYAL TOMBS. *Interior of the eighteenth dynasty tomb of Thutmose III in the Valley of the Kings.* (Photography by the Egyptian Expedition, The Metropolitan Museum of Art)

mids. They stood in the Sêma (Sôma) of the royal palace at Alexandria. Ptolemy VI built a common mausoleum for Alexander and the early Ptolemies; the precise location of the cemetery is unknown but is supposed to be in the quarter of the Nabi Danial mosque.

Decoration. The oldest example of decoration in a royal tomb is the depiction of the starry sky on the ceiling of Djoser's burial chamber. Tomb walls were inscribed from the time of King Unas on with the Pyramid Texts, covering the walls of the entrance passage, antechamber, and burial chamber (tombs of Unas, Tety, Pepy I, Merenre, Pepy II, and Ibi). The royal tombs of the Middle Kingdom all seem to be uninscribed; the texts may have been transferred onto the wooden coffins.

When decoration reappears in the eighteenth dynasty, the program has changed. All tombs from Thutmose I to Ramesses XI are decorated with religious texts and scenes, at first only painted, but from Horemheb on in relief. The decoration and text mainly address the extension of the king's life and rule in the netherworld. From relatively simple inscriptions in tombs from Thutmose I to III, which are restricted to the *Book of That Which Is in The Underworld*, more complicated textual programs develop, including the *Book of Gates* and *Book of Caverns*. The old motive of ensuring the king's participation in the daily journey of the sun is further developed, culminating in the hope that the king might not only travel through the realm of the underworld but also rise with the sun (the Solar Litany near the tomb entrance). Impressive are the huge astronomical representations in the vaults of Ramessid sarcophagus halls. The increasing decorative program of the New Kingdom seems to be one reason for the extension of the tomb chambers and walls.

Spiritual Tombs or Cenotaphs. The more spiritual, otherworldly aspects of the king also needed an architectural stage, and this was provided in the form of an empty tomb, or cenotaph. Such secondary royal tombs are known from all periods, but we do not understand with which property of the king they were associated, mainly because they are not inscribed or decorated. The difficulty is exacerbated by the fact that some kings have not just one but several cenotaphs. Were they meant for the *ka,* or for the official aspect of kingship, or were they intended as a god's tomb—perhaps Osiris or Sokar? Some are probably canopic burials; others may simply be abandoned tomb projects. Because the cenotaph is associated with the divine aspects of the king, it has almost no parallel in private tomb architecture. Following is a list of known cenotaphs of the Old Kingdom:

Djoser   1. Stepped Mastaba at Saqqara
         2. South tomb at Saqqara
Sneferu 1. Pyramid of Meidum
         2. Secondary Pyramid of Meidum
         3. Bent Pyramid of Dahshur north tomb
         4. Bent Pyramid at Dahshur western tomb
         5. Secondary pyramid at Bent Pyramid
         6. Pyramid of Seila
Khufu   1. Lower chamber of Giza Pyramid (?)
         2. Middle chamber of Giza Pyramid (?)
         3. Secondary pyramid at Giza
Khafre   1. Lower chamber of Giza Pyramid (?)
         2. Secondary pyramid south of Giza Pyramid
Menkaure 1. Upper chamber of Giza Pyramid (?)
         2. Secondary pyramid south of Giza Pyramid

All succeeding kings of the Old Kingdom have only one burial crypt and a smaller, secondary pyramid at the southeastern corner of the main pyramid, which certainly are symbolic tombs, because their chambers are too small for a regular coffin or burial. The last secondary pyramid is that of Senwosret I at el-Lisht.

Some royal tombs of the Middle Kingdom also show other installations for symbolic burials of unknown purpose. In the chamber of the Bab el-Hosan of Nebhepetre Mentuhotep at Deir el-Bahri, an empty coffin and a seated statue of the king colored black (as Osiris?) and wearing *sed*-festival dress were found (Egyptian Museum, Cairo, JE 36195). Senwosret III built a subsidiary tomb in the northeast of his pyramid at Dahshur. His main achievement was, however, his cenotaph at Abydos, comprising four different tomb sections. Finally, Amenemhet III apparently had a "south tomb" inside his Dahshur pyramid, in addition to numerous other chambers of unknown purpose.

Cenotaphs were not necessarily empty. They might incorporate a sarcophagus, as well as grave goods or a statue of the king (e.g., Mentuhotep), or perhaps a royal *ka*-statue (as for King Hor at Dahshur; Egyptian Museum, Cairo, JE 30948).

The royal tombs of the New Kingdom seem to have contained installations for a subsidiary burial. From Thutmose III on, an upper antechamber of the burial crypt develops into a separate tomb. During the nineteenth dynasty, royal tombs clearly show an independent upper tomb with a pillared chamber that did not, however, have a sarcophagus of its own. A staircase at its side leads into the real crypt at a lower level. Kings Ahmose and Sety I, following the prototype of Senwosret III, built enormous cenotaphs—or rather, Osiris tombs—at Abydos. The royal tombs of later periods no longer contain cenotaph-like features.

Cult Installations at Royal Tombs. The double nature of the king is also reflected in the two different types of post-mortem ceremonies carried out at the royal tombs relating to pyramid temples. From Sneferu on, buildings for these cults were erected in the pyramid enclosure, starting with modest stone buildings set against the east side of the pyramid (Meidum, Dahshur) and later developing into huge temples (Giza, Abusir, Saqqara). The divine aspect of the king is treated in the same way as that of the "real" gods. The king receives a statue cult similar to that of the gods; the earliest identifiable is located in the so-called valley temple of the Bent Pyramid. A much larger valley and pyramid temple was built for Khafre, dominated by huge installations for a royal statue cult. Simpler versions of this statue temple developed into the front part of the standard pyramid temples of the later Old Kingdom.

The second, inner part of the pyramid temple derives from a different source. With the gradual diminishing of divine powers and qualities at the end of the fourth dynasty, the dead king became a more human entity in need of the assistance of his surviving subjects. This resulted in a royal mortuary cult with features similar to those of private practice. From the time of Shepseskaf and Userkaf, offering halls for this mortuary cult were included in the pyramid temples of the fifth and sixth dynasties, and later in those of the twelfth. The last examples of this type of pyramid temple were built for Senwosret I at el-Lisht and Amenemhet II at Dahshur. A smaller secondary offering chapel was built in the center of the north side of the pyramids, covering the pyramid entrance. It might have originated in the secondary false door niche at the northern end of private *mastaba*s of the fourth dynasty.

During the Middle Kingdom the old forms were soon emptied of their original significance and the new situation met by the creation of a new type of royal cult temple that was separate from the pyramid and its cult. In these sanctuaries, cults of gods probably played a more significant role and served as a kind of support system for the

TOMBS: ROYAL TOMBS. *The nineteenth dynasty burial chamber of Sety I in the Valley of the Kings.* (Photography by the Egyptian Expedition, The Metropolitan Museum of Art)

cult of the king. The prototypes of this new cult form are the huge temple south of the pyramid of Senwosret III, and the so-called Labyrinth at the pyramid of Amenemhet III at Hawara.

These royal cult temples of the late twelfth dynasty seem to have developed into the so-called mortuary temples for the kings of the New Kingdom, most of which are situated on the western bank of the Nile at Thebes and are designated "mansions of millions of years." The main cultic feature seems to have been the linking of the cult of Amun-Re with that of the dead king. The temples are marked by a specific architectural program.

The royal tombs of the New Kingdom seem to have been accessible for some cultic activities even after the funeral but do not display specific installations for that purpose. The cult chapels of the kings of the Late period have disappeared but certainly included provisions for a funerary cult.

[*See also* Abydos; Cenotaphs; Coffins, Sarcophagi, and Cartonnages; Giza; Necropolis; Pyramid; Saqqara; Valley of the Kings; *and* Valley of the Queens.]

BIBLIOGRAPHY

General Works
Arnold, Dieter and Erik Hornung. "Königsgrab." In *Lexikon der Ägyptologie*, 3: 496–514. Wiesbaden, 1980.
Hornung, Erik. *The Valley of the Kings*. Translated from the German by David Warburton. New York, 1981.
Reeves, Nicholas. *The Complete Valley of the Kings*. New York, 1996.
Romer, John. *Valley of the Kings*. New York, 1981.

Early Period
Amélineau, Émile. *Les nouvelles fouilles d'Abydos*. 3 vols. Paris, 1899–1905.
Dreyer, Günter. "Umm el-Qaab. Nachuntersuchungen im frühzeitlichen Königsfriedhof." *Mitteilungen des Deutschen Archäologischen Instituts, Abteilung Kairo* 46 (1990), 53–90; 49 (1993), 23–62.
Dreyer, Günter. "Zur Rekonstruktion der Oberbauten der Königsgräber der 1. Dynastie in Abydos." *Mitteilungen des Deutschen Archäologischen Instituts, Abteilung Kairo* 47 (1991), 93–104.
Dreyer, Günter. "Recent Discoveries at Abydos Cemetery U." In *The Nile Delta in Transition: 4th.–3rd. Millennium B. C.*, edited by Edwin C. M. van den Brink, pp. 293–299. Tel Aviv, 1992.
Kaiser, Werner. "Zu den königlichen Talbezirken der 1. und 2. Dynastie in Abydos und zur Baugeschichte des Djoser-Grabmals." *Mitteilungen des Deutschen Archäologischen Instituts, Abteilung Kairo* 25 (1969), 1–21.
Kaiser, Werner, and Peter Grossmann. "Umm el-Qaab. Nachuntersuchungen im frühzeitlichen Königsfriedhof (1. Vorbericht)." *Mitteilungen des Deutschen Archäologischen Instituts, Abteilung Kairo* 35 (1979), 155–163.
Kaiser, Werner, and Günter Dreyer. "Umm el-Qaab. Nachuntersuchungen im frühzeitlichen Königsfriedhof (2. Vorbericht)." *Mitteilungen des Deutschen Archäologischen Instituts, Abteilung Kairo* 38 (1982), 211–269.
Kemp, Barry J. "Abydos and the Royal Tombs of the First Dynasty." *Journal of Egyptian Archaeology* 52 (1966), 13–22.
Kemp, Barry J. "The Egyptian 1st Dynasty Royal Cemetery." *Antiquity* 41 (1967), 22–32.
Lauer, Jean-Philippe. "Évolution de la tombe royale égyptienne jus-

qu'à la pyramide à degrés." *Mitteilungen des Deutschen Archäologischen Instituts, Abteilung Kairo* 15 (1957), 148–165.
Lauer, Jean-Philippe. "Le développement des complexes funéraires royaux en Égypte." *Bulletin de l'Institut français d'archéologie Orientale* 79 (1979), 355–394.
Mainz, R. "Sandtumulus oder Ziegelplatte?" *Discussions in Egyptology* 26 (1993), 25–46.
O'Connor, David. "New Funerary Enclosures (Talbezirke) of the Early Dynastic Period at Abydos." *Journal of the American Research Center in Egypt* 26 (1989), 51–86.
Petrie, William M. Flinders. *The Royal Tombs of the First Dynasty*. 2 vols. London, 1900–1901.

Old Kingdom
Brinks, Jürgen. *Die Entwicklung der Königlichen Grabanlagen des Alten Reiches: Eine strukturelle und historische Analyse altägyptischer Architektur*. Hildesheimer Ägyptologische Beiträge, 10. Hildesheim, 1979.
Dreyer, Günter, and W. Kaiser. "Zu den kleinen Stufenpyramiden Ober- und Mittelägyptens." *Mitteilungen des Deutschen Archäologischen Instituts, Abteilung Kairo* 36 (1980), 43–59.
Dunham, Dows. *The Royal Cemeteries of Kush*. 5 vols. Cambridge, Mass., 1950–1963.
Dziobek, Eberhard. "Eine Grabpyramide des frühen NR in Theben." *Mitteilungen des Deutschen Archäologischen Instituts, Abteilung Kairo* 45 (1989), 109–132.
Edwards, I.E.S. *The Pyramids of Egypt*. Rev. ed. Harmondsworth, 1985.
Fakhry, Ahmed. *The Pyramids*. Chicago, 1961.
Grinsell, Leslie. *Egyptian Pyramids*. Gloucester, 1947.
Helck, Wolfgang. "Pyramiden." In *Paulys Realencyclopädie der classischen Altertumswissenschaft*, edited by G. Wissowa, vol. 23, pp. 2167–2282. Stuttgart, 1959.
Hinkel, F. W. "Pyramiden im Sudan: Der Könligliche Nordfriedhof von Meroe." *Das Altertum* 26 (1980), 77–88.
Hinkel, F. W. "Pyramiden oder Pyramidenstumpf?" *Zeitschrift für Ägyptische Sprache und Alterumskunde* 108 (1981), 105–124.
Lauer, Jean-Philippe. *Histoire monumentale des pyramides d'Égypte*. Bibliothèque d'Étude, 39. Cairo, 1962.
Lauer, Jean-Philippe. *Le mystère des pyramides*. Paris, 1974.
Moret, A. "L'Influence du décor solaire sur la pyramide." In *Mélanges Maspero*, pp. 623–636. Mémoires publiés par les membres de l'Institut Français d'archéologie orientale du Caire, 66–68. Cairo, 1935–1938.
O'Connor, David. "Boat Graves and Pyramid Origins." *Expedition: The Bulletin of the University Museum of the University of Pennsylvania* 33 (1991), 5–17.
Speleers, L. "La signification des Pyramides." In *Mélanges Maspero*, pp. 603–621. Mémoires publiés par les membres de l'Institut Français d'archéologie orientale du Caire, 66–68. (Cairo, 1935–1938).
Stadelmann, Rainer. *Die grossen Pyramiden von Giza*. Graz, 1990.
Stadelmann, Rainer. *Die ägyptischen Pyramiden*. 2d ed., rev. & enl. Darmstadt, 1991.

Middle Kingdom
Arnold, Dieter. *Der Tempel des Königs Mentuhotep von Deir el-Bahari*. 3 vols. Archäologische Veröffentlichungen, Deutsches Archäologisches Institut, Abteilung Kairo, 8. Mainz, 1974–1981.
Arnold, Dieter. *The Temple of Mentuhotep at Deir el-Bahari*. Publications of The Metropolitan Museum of Art, The Egyptian Expedition, 21. New York, 1979.
Arnold, Dieter. *Der Pyramidenbezirk des Königs Amenemhet III. in Dahschur*. Archäologische Veröffentlichungen, Deutsches Archäologisches Institut, Abteilung Kairo, 53. Mainz, 1987.
Arnold, Dieter. *The South Cemeteries of Lisht*, vol. 1, *The Pyramid of*

Senwosret I. Publications of the Metropolitan Museum of Art, The Egyptian Expedition, 22. New York, 1988.

Arnold, Dieter. *The South Cemeteries of Lisht*, vol. 3, *The Pyramid Complex of Senwosret I.* Publications of the Metropolitan Museum of Art, The Egyptian Expedition, 25. New York, 1992.

Gautier, J.-E., and G. Jéquier. *Fouilles de Licht.* Cairo, 1902. *Herodotus*, Book II, 148–149. Translated by A. D. Godley. Loeb Classical Library. Cambridge, Mass., 1926.

Lythgoe, A. M. "The Egyptian Expedition." *Bulletin of the Metropolitan Museum of Art* 2 (April, 1907), 61–63; 2 (July, 1907), 113–117; 3 (May, 1908), 83–84.

Mace, C. "The Egyptian Expedition." *Bulletin of the Metropolitan Museum of Art* 3 (October, 1908), 184–188; (October, 1914), 207–222; 16 (November, 1921), 5–19; 17 (December, 1922), 4–18.

Morgan, Jacques D. *Fouilles à Dahchour en 1894–1895.* Vienna, 1903.

Morgan, Jacques D. *Fouilles à Dahchour Mars-Juin 1894.* Vienna, 1895.

Naville, Edouard. *The XIth Dynasty Temple at Deir el-Bahari.* 3 vols. London, 1907–1913.

Petrie, William M. Flinders. *Hawara, Biahmu and Arsinoe.* London, 1889.

Petrie, William M. Flinders. *Kahun, Gurob and Hawara.* London, 1890.

Petrie, William M. Flinders. *The Labyrinth, Gerzeh and Mazghuneh.* London, 1912.

New Kingdom

Abitz, Friedrich. *Die religiöse Bedeutung der sogenannten Grabräuberschächte in den ägyptischen Königsgräbern der 18. bis 20. Dynastie.* Ägyptologische Abhandlungen, 26. Wiesbaden, 1974.

Abitz, Friedrich. "The 'Well' in the King's Tombs of Bibân el-Moluk." *Journal of Egyptian Archaeology* 64 (1978), 80–83.

Abitz, Friedrich. *König und Gott.* Ägyptologische Abhandlungen, 40. Wiesbaden, 1984.

Abitz, Friedrich. *Baugeschichte und Dekoration des Grabes Ramses' VI.* Orbis biblicus et orientalis, 89. Freiburg, 1989.

Abitz, Friedrich. "Die Entwicklung der Grabachsen in den Königsgräbern im Tal der Könige." *Mitteilungen des Deutschen Archäologischen Instituts, Abteilung Kairo* 45 (1989), 1–25.

Altenmüller, Hartwig. "Bemerkungen zu den Königsgräbern des Neuen Reiches. *Studien zur Altägyptischen Kultur* 10 (1983), 25–61.

Dodson, Aidan. "The Tombs of the Kings of the Early Eighteenth Dynasty at Thebes." *Zeitschrift für Ägyptische Sprache und Alterumskunde* 115 (1988), 110–123.

Helck, Wolfgang. "Königsgräbertal." In *Lexikon der Ägyptologie*, 3: 514–526. Wiesbaden, 1980.

Hornung, Erik. "Struktur und Entwicklung der Gräber im Tal der Könige." *Zeitschrift für Ägyptische Sprache und Alterumskunde* 105 (1978), 59–66.

Hornung, Erik. *The Tomb of Pharaoh Seti I. Das Grab Sethos I.* Zurich and Munich, 1991.

Hornung, Erik. *Sethos, ein Pharaonengrab*, pp. 32–43. Basel, 1991.

Reeves, Nicholas. *Valley of the Kings: The Decline of a Royal Necropolis.* London and New York, 1991.

Romer, John. *Valley of the Kings.* New York, 1981.

Thomas, Elizabeth. *The Royal Necropoleis of Thebes.* Princeton, 1966.

Winlock, H. E. "The Tombs of the Kings of the Seventeenth Dynasty at Thebes." *Journal of Egyptian Archaeology* 10 (1924), 217–277.

Petrie, William M. Flinders, G. Brunton and M. A. Murray. *Lahun*, vol. 2. London, 1923.

Cenotaphs

Ayrton, Edward R., et al. *Abydos pt. 3, 1904.* London, 1904.

O'Connor, David. "The 'Cenotaphs' of the Middle Kingdom at Abydos." *Mélanges Gamal Eddin Mokhtar*, edited by Paule Posener-Kriéger, pp. 161–177. Cairo, 1985.

Simpson, William Kelly. *The Terrace of the Great God at Abydos: The Offering Chapels of Dynasties 12 and 13.* New Haven, 1974.

Wegner, J. "South Abydos: Burial Place of the Third Senwosret?" *KMT: A Modern Journal of Ancient Egypt* 6 (1995), 59–71.

Late Period

Badawy, A. Das Grab des Kronprinzen Scheschonk. Sohnes Osorkon's II. und Hohenpriesters von Memphis." *Annales du service des antiquités de l'Égypte* 54 (1956), 153–177.

Edinburgh City Art Centre. *Gold of the Pharaohs: Catalogue of the Exhibition of Treasures from Tanis.* Edinburgh, 1988.

Fraser, P. M. *Ptolemaic Alexandria*, vol. 1, pp. 15ff. Oxford, 1972.

Goyon, Georges. *La découverte des trésors de Tanis.* Persea, France, 1987.

Herodotus, Book 2, 169–175. Loeb Classical Library. Cambridge, Mass., 1946.

Jenni, Hanna. *Das Dekorationsprogramm des Sarkophages Nektanebos II.* Aegyptiaca Helvetica, 12. Geneva, 1986.

Montet, Pierre. *La nécropole royale de Tanis.* 3 vols. Paris, 1947–1960.

Stadelmann, Rainer. "Das Grab im Tempelhof: der Typus des Königsgrabes in der Spätzeit." *Mitteilungen des Deutschen Archäologischen Instituts, Abteilung Kairo* 27 (1971), 111–123.

Stadelmann, Rainer. "Tempelbestattung." In *Lexikon der Ägyptologie*, 6: 376–377. Wiesbaden, 1986.

Strabo, Book 17, 794, 802. Loeb Classical Library. Cambridge, Mass., 1949.

Thiersch, H. "Die alexandrinische Königsnekropole." *Jahrbuch des Deutschen Archäologischen Instituts* 25 (1910), 55–97.

DIETER ARNOLD

Private Tombs

Both royal and private tombs in ancient Egypt shared the ideal prototype of a sepulchre with two distinct elements, the below-ground closed burial chamber (the substructure) and the above-ground offering place (the superstructure). Yet only private individuals of the very highest status could afford fully fledged examples of both. For most of Egyptian history, the execution of both elements differed between those provided for kings and those for others. Behind that division was the divine status of the king, one who was regarded as taking his place alongside his fellow deities in death, in contrast to the private person, who would in some form continue to enjoy in the afterlife his or her mode of life on earth.

Thus, while the offering places (mortuary temples) of the pharaohs closely followed in decoration and function the cult-places of the gods, those attached to private tombs were usually adorned with scenes of life on earth, with a view to magically re-creating the terrestrial environment in the hereafter. Some scholars argue that many such vignettes actually hold some ritual significance, particularly those with a view to the rebirth of the dead in the next world though an erotic subtext. Although such implications are quite possible, one should probably see them as secondary developments, during the New Kingdom, overlain on the basic re-creation of the earthly environment and its food-production potentialities. That would also seem to lie behind the models of daily life scenes that are found within the burial chambers of First Intermediate Period and Middle Kingdom tombs. [*See* Models.]

Apart from the agricultural food-production category of depictions (together with the production of clothing and other items of personal adornment), a number of others were found fairly consistently through time, although there were changes in emphasis during the different historical periods. First, there was the motif of the tomb owner and his family, in particular his wife, who usually shared her spouse's tomb. Sepulchres belonging to nonroyal women were probably those of the unmarried or divorced.

In addition to simple scenes of the owner and family as recipients of offerings, there were sometimes scenes relating to the owner's role in relation to the king, the fundamental relationship in determining a person's status in ancient Egypt. For that reason, in a number of eighteenth dynasty chapels, relevant office-bearers preserved copies of the statement of "Duties of the Vizier." Officials who had served as tutors of royal children are shown with their charges upon their laps; when viewing such scenes it is important to realize that they may relate to periods of service that were far in their past at the time when the tomb was being decorated: an infant prince, in some cases, was actually the reigning sovereign by the time his image was inscribed upon a wall.

Hunting depictions are frequent from the Old through New Kingdoms, and they fall into four basic types. Three feature the tomb owner: fowling in the marshes on a light papyrus boat; hunting hippopotami in a similar manner; and hunting desert animals. The fourth comprises fishing or fowling by professionals, perhaps under the watchful gaze of the tomb owner. Sports and recreation were also shown; singing and dancing, perhaps in the context of a banquet, were most common, but there are Middle Kingdom examples of wrestling scenes, and others of board gaming, although the popular *senet* (*snt*) certainly had a significance in the struggle to pass to the afterlife.

The appearance of funerary rites in a tomb chapel is not surprising, although in general these avoid the mythological elements, the main motif being the procession of the body and its funerary equipment to the tomb, accompanied by wailing mourners; to this, the ceremony of Opening the Mouth was added in New Kingdom times.

Superstructures. A number of different forms were used in private tombs to incorporate the tomb chapel. All share the feature of an offering place, centered on a stela, that often took the form of a false door, which acted as the interface between this world and the next. The simplest examples have no more than this, but the most elaborate have whole series of vestibules, corridors, and chambers, often extensively decorated in relief and/or paint with the kinds of vignettes described above.

The offering place and any associated rooms could generally be housed according to one of three basic modes. The first mode is against, or within, a low, rectangular structure of brick or stone, known as a *mastaba;* while regarded as most characteristic of the Archaic Period and Old Kingdom, *mastaba*s are found throughout Egyptian history. The second mode is for rooms to be carved out of the rock, without any appreciable built element (known as a rock-cut tomb); such tombs began in the Old Kingdom, and they are then ubiquitous. The third mode is for the structure to be entirely free-standing, with particularly elaborate examples known as temple-tombs; this approach seems to begin in the Middle Kingdom and became much more frequent in the New Kingdom and later, when it was more widely used in locations that would have previously used the *mastaba* (i.e., in flat areas of desert without significant rock escarpments).

There are, of course, anomalous examples that combined features of more than one of those basic types, while each may be further subdivided into subcategories, which will be described below, where appropriate. The choice of chapel type seems usually to have been determined by the topography or geology of the chosen site.

Tomb Chambers. The actual burial place, or substructure, is always distinct from the chapel, although frequently closely associated with it. Many lower status burials are without any kind of offering place, or they may have a stela built into the entrance to the substructure.

In private tombs, the burial chamber itself is very seldom decorated and, with a handful of exceptions, any adornment is usually restricted to offering lists and/or to extracts from the various funerary books—the collections called the Pyramid Texts, Coffin Texts, *Book of Going Forth by Day* (*Book of the Dead*), *Book of That Which Is in the Underworld* (*Amduat*), and others. (Among the most elaborately decorated of all private burial chambers are those of the nineteenth dynasty necropolis workmen at Deir el-Medina. Tellingly, those were the very men who spent their time preparing the intricately decorated royal burial places in the Valley of the Kings.) The burial chamber's architecture was generally simple, as was that of any antechambers, although some very elaborate examples are known, particularly in the New Kingdom and Saite period, when a series of galleries and pillared halls could be used.

In parts of Lower Egypt, especially in the Nile Delta, owing to the proximity of ground water, or in locations elsewhere where the cutting of deep shafts was otherwise impracticable, substructures were constructed of stone or brick in large but shallow cuttings in the ground surface. Within such, one or more rooms could be constructed of stone or brick, and then covered over with soil. In the former case, flat stone roofs could be employed, but in

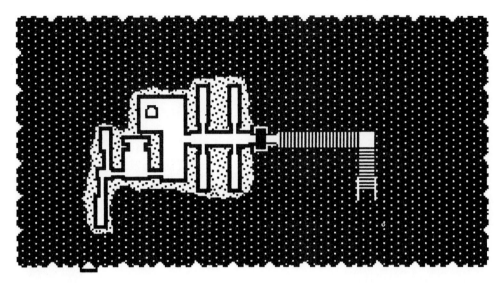

TOMBS: PRIVATE TOMBS. *Diagram of a typical second dynasty* mastaba. The superstructure is solid, and the burial apartments are deeply cut into the rock. They are approached by a stairway from the roof of the *mastaba* and blocked by a portcullis, sliding down a narrow shaft. (Courtesy Aidan Dodson)

most brick structures a vaulted roof was frequently used (known as a vaulted tomb).

The ideal form of substructure, however, was cut into the rock (rock-cut), approached by either a vertical shaft (a pit-tomb) or a sloping gallery (a corridor-tomb). In most private tombs, the substructure lay below, or in close association with, the chapel. In certain cases, however, it could be separated from it by some very considerable distance, good examples existing in the New Kingdom, when a very favored individual could be granted burial near the king's tomb, in the Valley of the Kings. In such an event, the chapel continued to be located on the other side of the Theban cliffs, alongside those of the owner's peers.

Early Dynastic Period. The first tombs differed little from those of late Predynastic times, being brick-lined cuttings in the desert gravel, roofed in wood and topped by little more than a sandy mound. During the first dynasty, however, substructures become more elaborate, more deeply cut, with greater subdivision and the addition of an access stairway. *Mastaba* superstructures, initially containing store-chambers, and with elaborately paneled outer surfaces, are found from the very beginning of the dynasty. Very large examples, excavated between 1935 and 1956 by W. B. Emery, are known at Saqqara and were formerly regarded as belonging to kings; however, their private nature was clearly demonstrated by Barry Kemp in the mid-1960s ("The First Dynasty Royal Cemetery" *Antiquity* 41 [1967], 22–32), although the debate continues in some circles.

During the second dynasty, *mastaba*s became solid, sometimes losing their paneling decoration to more closely resemble the plain brick benches that gave such tombs that Arabic appellation. Below ground, tomb-chambers are frequently to be found tunnelled deeply into the bedrock, approached by stairways, rather than being built in open cuttings. Such substructures are sometimes quite elaborate. Chapels, where identifiable, seem restricted to stelae inserted in the back of a niche at the southern end of the eastern wall of the *mastaba*, opposite the break in any enclosure wall.

Old Kingdom. Third dynasty tombs represented a further development of the immediately preceding types. Most notable was the expansion of the chapel, which was cut into the core of the *mastaba* and was frequently in cruciform shape. It may also be more intimately connected with the adjacent enclosure wall, producing a corridor parallel to the face of the *mastaba*. In the tomb of Hesyre at Saqqara, the chapel was decorated both in paint and by the insertion of relief-carved wooden panels.

During the fourth dynasty, the first stone-built *mastaba*s appeared. Paneling was by then restricted to the chapel areas. The principal offering place continued to be at the southern end of the eastern wall, but a second one, generally belonging to the wife, was sometimes made at the northern end. As time went by, the size and decoration of the offering place increased in size, penetrating deeper into the core of the *mastaba*, in some cases incorporating an open courtyard. The most elaborate of all *mastaba*

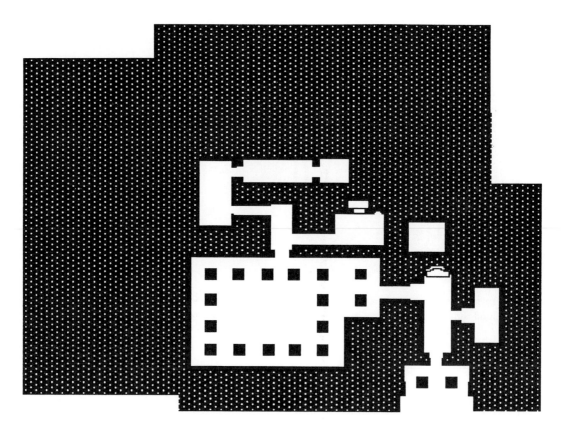

TOMBS: PRIVATE TOMBS. *Diagram of the interior of a* mastaba *from the fifth dynasty.*
A colonnaded court is incorporated into the plan. The exterior plan of a *mastaba* might be
modified to accommodate local features, such as earlier funerary monuments. (Courtesy
Aidan Dodson)

chapels is that of Mereruka (c.2360 BCE) at Saqqara, which has nearly thirty rooms that occupy most of the *mastaba*'s ground area.

An important element of most chapels was the *serdab,* a term derived from the Arabic word for "cellar." This was a room, usually near the stela, in which lay one or more statues of the deceased and his family—in some cases running into the tens. The only communication between the *serdab* and the outside world was one or two small apertures, through which the statues could "see" out or be reached by incense burned outside in the chapel.

From the fourth dynasty onward, most substructures were approached by vertical shafts beginning on the roof of the *mastaba* and penetrating deep into the bedrock, although in some (e.g., the tombs of Tiye at Saqqara and Ptahshepses at Abusir) the burial chamber was directly below the chapel floor, with access via a shallow sloping ramp. A number of tombs of the sixth dynasty had their burial chambers decorated with offering lists, arranged in the same way that such catalogs were placed on the interior of contemporary coffins and sarcophagi. A number of similarly decorated chambers have been found at Delta sites, for example at Tell Basta, where they were constructed in pits excavated only a little way below the surface. Stone sarcophagi are found in very many of the private tombs of the Old Kingdom, and in the succeeding Middle Kingdom, but the use of stone for the outer mortuary container was less frequent in other periods. The entrance to fourth dynasty burial chambers sometimes accommodated a so-called reserve head, a stone portrait of the deceased that seems to have been intended to replace the real head if it was damaged or destroyed.

While the *mastaba* remained the standard for cemeteries lying on the desert plain, such as Giza and Saqqara, rock-cut chapels were employed on the edge of escarpments at both sites, their form and decoration similar to what may be seen within contemporary *mastaba*s. Farther south, in the Nile Valley, the number of major private tombs increased as the period continued and were often built at sites unsuitable for *mastaba*s. The rock-cut chapels in those areas tended to use plans symmetrical about their main axis and, as such, provide prototypes for examples in later periods.

First Intermediate Period and Middle Kingdom.
Around the royal cemeteries of Lower Egypt, principally at el-Lisht and Dahshur, most private tombs took the form

of *mastaba*s. Others were built at Abydos and at other Middle Egyptian sites. As is the case with most Middle Kingdom sepulchres, their substructure designs varied considerably, with both shaft and corridor entries. Certain tombs incorporated features aimed at improving the security of the substructure, including large sliding portcullis-blocks and shafts arranged above corridors to shower a plunderer with large volumes of sand. The *mastaba* of Senwosret-ankh at el-Lisht had its substructure decorated with extracts from Old Kingdom Pyramid Texts.

At Western Thebes, beginning with the eleventh dynasty, the *saff*-type of rock-cut chapel is first found, with a very wide portico supported by rock-cut pillars, behind which a passage leads toward the offering place. Early examples open off the sunken courtyards of the tombs of kings Antef I, II, and III at el-Tarif; the later ones occupy high locations on the Sheikh Abd el-Qurna hill.

In the late First Intermediate Period/early Middle Kingdom a considerable devolution of power occurred for the provinces; hence there were built a number of very rich necropolises. The rock-cut tomb chapels had fairly standardized plans, although some had added structures on their exteriors (for example, at Qau el-Kebir, where some of the largest of all were created). Those high-status sepulchres were accompanied by large fields of middle-status burials, usually comprising simple shaft tombs without superstructures. The best recorded such site is Beni Hasan, where more than four hundred shafts, containing some one thousand burials, were opened by John Garstang from 1902 to 1904.

A series of governmental reforms carried out by Senwosret III, which concentrated far more power—and hence high-status individuals—at the national capital, resulted in a major reduction in the number of large private tombs built away from the royal necropolis after his reign. Aside from those directly adjacent to the royal pyramids, few significant private tombs of the late twelfth and thirteenth dynasties have been recorded.

Second Intermediate Period. Very few tombs of the end of the thirteenth and the seventeenth dynasties have been properly excavated, but those known at Thebes seem to have comprised little more than a small cavity in the rock, into which the coffin and a small quantity of funerary equipment were inserted. More substantial tombs may begin again in the late seventeenth dynasty, but are difficult to distinguish from those of the early eighteenth.

New Kingdom. Until the middle of the eighteenth dynasty, almost all known high-status tombs were rock-cut chapels at Western Thebes, with the exception of a few at Elkab and certain other southern locations. Earlier Theban chapels may have been reused Middle Kingdom structures; most follow the same T-shaped pattern, with a wide, but shallow, forehall or portico, and a passage leading back to the offering place. Most early tombs were

placed high up on the cliffs of the Sheikh Abd el-Qurna hill, to provide an imposing site. Since the rock at that elevation is fairly poor in quality, nearly all such chapels were decorated in paint only.

Access to the substructure was usually by means of a vertical shaft within the chapel or just outside, although some of the larger tombs had a ramp approach. Certain Sheikh Abd el-Qurna chapel owners, however, had their burial chambers some distance away. For example, Senenmut (c.1482 BCE) had his at Deir el-Bahri, and the vizier Amenemopet (c.1430 BCE) was interred over a kilometer (almost a mile) away in the Valley of the Kings. Some other nobles with Valley of the Kings burial chambers have not yet had their chapels identified (e.g., Yuya and Tjuiu, parents-in-law of Amenhotpe III).

Elaborations of the basic chapel and substructure plans are frequent in the later eighteenth dynasty, principally through the addition of one or more pillared halls. This is particularly the case during the reign of Amenhotpe III, the chapel of Amenemhat-Surero having no fewer than seventy columns supporting its roof. Some of the later tombs were constructed at a very low level on the Theban hillside, to allow access to rock suitable for relief decoration. Only a few burial chambers were decorated, usually with cursive renderings of the *Book of That Which Is in the Underworld* (*Amduat*), but that of the mayor Sennefer was given anomalous scenes and a roof painted with grapevines. Very few private tombs of the New Kingdom were equipped with stone sarcophagi, wooden examples being standard. Only under Amenhotpe III was stone once more used with any frequency for private mortuary containers, but then only for anthropoid (human-shaped) coffins, not normally rectangular sarcophagi. The stone anthropoid coffins are particularly characteristic of the first half of the Ramessid period.

During the Amarna period there was a major upheaval in tomb decoration. The private tombs at Amarna itself, together with a handful at Thebes, abandoned the scenes of daily life that were used in private tombs since Old Kingdom times. They were replaced with a decoration centered on the doings of the royal family, who became regarded as the sole interface between this world and that of the divine. In these chapels, the tomb owner was relegated to a subsidiary role; his main substantive depiction was on the jambs of the outermost doorway. Otherwise, he might be included as a minor figure in some scene or he might be receiving a reward from his monarch. Yet the plans of the tombs remained very similar to earlier tombs.

In the period immediately preceding the accession of Amenhotpe IV, major tombs can once more be easily identified away from Thebes, particularly at Saqqara, where was buried the vizier Aperel. His tomb was built on the escarpment at the edge of the plateau and is a conventional rock-cut chapel, with a fairly elaborate substruc-

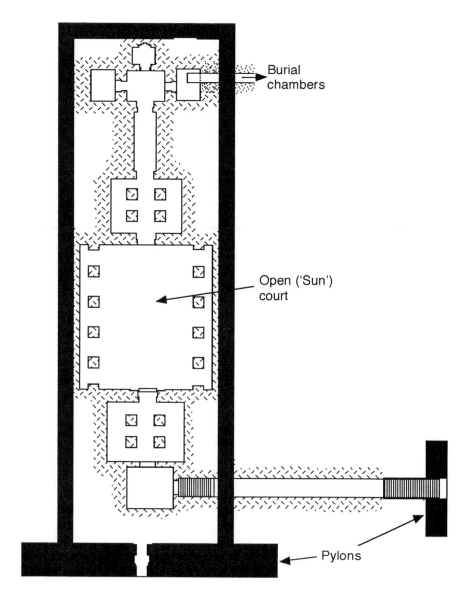

TOMBS: PRIVATE TOMBS. *Diagram of a monumental tomb of the twenty-fifth to twenty-sixth dynasty, typified by a series on the Asasif at Western Thebes.* A brick enclosure, fronted by a pylon, surrounds a rock-hewn open courtyard and inner chapel rooms, from which leads the superstructure. (Courtesy Aidan Dodson)

ture reached via shafts. As of 1999, much of the escarpment was still covered by debris to the depth of tens of meters, and a very extensive necropolis may lie farther down, probably including earlier tombs; excavations there are under the direction of Alain Zivie and may yet reveal a hillside of tomb-chapels akin to those seen at Thebes.

Following the return to orthodoxy, there was a major use of another area of Saqqara for private tombs, in that case an area of flat desert south of the causeway of Unas, unsuitable for rock-cut chapels. Instead, temple-tombs were constructed, the larger examples fronted by pylons and closely resembling the sanctuaries of gods. Complex substructures were approached by shafts, one example, belonging to the treasurer Maya (c.1340 BCE), being decorated with painted relief. The superstructures were elaborately decorated with scenes that were geared rather more toward ritual and the career of the deceased than in earlier private tombs. The finest example of all is the tomb of General Horemheb, who later became king. Much smaller freestanding chapels were also built in the area, sometimes comprising but one room. Similar structures were also built at Saqqara near the pyramid of Teti.

A similar shift in decorative themes in the post-Amarna era was noted in the rock-cut tombs at Thebes, and the chapels of the Ramessid period are distinctly different from those of the earlier eighteenth dynasty, with an almost total loss of daily-life depictions. Instead, the deceased were shown adoring deities, while elements of funerary books creep up from the burial chamber to take their place upon the chapel wall. Ground plans, however, continued to follow earlier norms in most cases.

An interesting group of tombs were those built for and by the Royal Necropolis workmen at Deir el-Medina, which have small decorated rock-cut chapels and substructures. They were adorned with small pyramids, which are also a feature of many Ramessid private tombs, in particular those on the Dra Abul Naga hill at Thebes. Pyramids had ceased to be used by kings at the end of the Second Intermediate Period, but were adopted by private individuals during the eighteenth dynasty.

In addition to the cemeteries at Thebes and Saqqara, high-status tombs were found at a variety of sites throughout Egypt, and even in Nubia, between the Amarna period and the end of the New Kingdom. Most are conventional rock-cut tomb-chapels, or freestanding chapels, but in the Delta they are brick-vaulted built structures that were erected in cuttings within or near temple precincts; the superstructures are almost universally lost, but they may have been small brick chapels directly above the burial chambers. Good examples are known at Tell Basta, including the tombs of the viceroys of Kush, Hori II and III (c.1200 and c.1160 BCE). Examples of such vaulted tombs are well known at Abydos, where the earliest specimens were dated to the first part of the eighteenth dynasty; they can be seen to have been surmounted by *mastaba*s.

Third Intermediate Period. Following the end of the New Kingdom, there were radical changes in private burial practice. Almost all recorded private burials of the period seem to come from Thebes, and tomb-chapels of any sort seem to have disappeared altogether, with the exception of one or two usurpations of earlier monuments. Instead, single or multiple burials were placed in superstructureless subterranean chambers, often appropriated from earlier owners in the area of the Asasif. In these, coffins were set without sarcophagi and with the most abbreviated of funerary equipment—occasionally a box of *shawabti*s and, even less regularly, a set of (empty) canopic jars.

The first part of the twenty-second dynasty continued late twenty-first dynasty norms. Under Osorkon I, however, there were changes in the forms of coffins and mummy adornment that seem to be coeval (at Thebes) with the center of burial being moved down to the locale of the Ramesseum. Small brick chapels, sometimes lined with sandstone reliefs, were built to surmount tombs in shallow shafts, giving access to chambers little larger than the contained coffin(s). Such coffins were accompanied by limited quantities of funerary equipment, principally dummy canopics and wooden funerary figures. Other twenty-second/third dynasty burials, under the eighteenth dynasty temple at Deir el-Bahri, featured the reintroduction of wooden sarcophagi into the private funerary record. Monumental private tombs were reintroduced at Thebes during the twenty-fifth dynasty, but their substantive development occurred in the first part of the next (Saite) dynasty.

In the north of Egypt, the built tomb that was sunk in the ground adjoining a major sanctuary continued in use, although only a few nonroyal Third Intermediate Period examples are known. In particular, a series belonging to high priests of Ptah under Osorkon II and Sheshonq III were found at Memphis by Ahmad Badawi in 1942, stone built and enclosing in one case a silver coffin.

Something akin to the New Kingdom temple-tombs were built during the Third Intermediate Period at Abydos, although these examples show a blurring between this type and the ancient *mastaba*. High status examples are that of Pasebakhanut, son of the twenty-first dynasty high priest of Amun, Menkheperre, and a whole series of those of female members of the twenty-fifth dynasty royal family. Substructures were often vaulted, directly supporting the superstructure, and were completely integrated with it during the twenty-fifth dynasty, when such tombs were often given multiple chambers and a superstructure with a circular, corbelled chamber, although the exact form of the exterior remains a matter for debate.

Saite Period. While the small-scale burials used at Thebes since the early years of the Third Intermediate Period persisted during the new period, huge rock-cut tombs and tomb-chapels were constructed once again both there and in northern cemeteries. The monumental Theban tombs were all set in the area of the Asasif; above ground, they comprise mud-brick enclosures, fronted by large pylons of the same material. They were centered on a large courtyard, sunk into bedrock, and approached by a sloping passage and vestibule. Chambers and chapels opened from the courtyard, while inner parts of the main chapel were cut in the rock behind it. The concealed substructure led on, deep into the rock, and in some cases continued for hundreds of feet before reaching the burial chamber, perhaps ultimately approached by shafts. In the largest of all, that of the lector-priest Petamenophis, the burial chamber was the twenty-second chamber or gallery beyond the courtyard, every room being decorated with funerary texts. [*See* Petamenophis.]

A very similar sepulchre was built at Saqqara for the vizier Bakenrenef, but most of the remainder of the Saite tombs at the site (and also at Abusir) apparently lacked superstructures other than walls; they also incorporated stelae, surrounding an extremely wide, deep, open shaft in the bedrock. The kernel of the tomb was a stone or brick-built burial chamber, in the form of a contemporary wooden sarcophagus, constructed at the bottom of the shaft. Such tombs were designed to be entirely filled with sand after the burial; temporarily closed holes in the chamber roof were opened after the funeral to allow sand

TOMBS: PRIVATE TOMBS. *A Ptolemaic "temple-tomb" at Tuna el-Gebel.* (Courtesy Aidan Dodson)

in from the main shaft, to engulf the sarcophagus and also to fill a parallel access shaft and connecting vestibules. Access to the burial was thereby impossible, unless almost every grain of sand had been removed from the tomb first (thousands of cubic meters). Certain tombs added to the effect by arranging a series of concentric sand-filled shafts around the perimeter of the tomb. The success of the design has been shown by the number that survived intact; another example, datable to the early twenty-seventh dynasty, was found by Ladislaw Beres at Abusir in 1995 and proved to contain the undisturbed burial of the priest Iufaa.

Other tombs of the period adopted the *mastaba* form. An example would be that of Tjery at Giza, where a symmetrical arrangement of rooms was enclosed.

Late Period. Very little is known of burials of the Persian twenty-seventh dynasty. Some of the shaft tombs at Saqqara and Abusir overlap the dynasty, but otherwise almost nothing can be attributed to the time. A funerary stela of an Egyptian-Persian was found at Saqqara in 1994 but in a reused context that tells little about its place of origin.

To the Egyptian twenty-eighth to thirtieth dynasties may be attributed a quantity of stone and wood coffins and sarcophagi, but only a handful of the tombs from which they come have been studied or published. They include free-standing chapels and *mastaba*s at Abydos, as well as various types of communal burial.

Ptolemaic Period. In early Ptolemaic times, in certain areas, the New Kingdom tradition of having the superstructure in the external form of a miniature contemporary temple was reintroduced; for example, the tomb of Petosiris at Tuna el-Gebel (c.300 BCE). Its inner room was decorated after the manner of a Ramessid royal tomb; burial chambers led off a shaft in the center of the chamber. The outer part was adorned with daily-life scenes, in an unusual composite Egyptian/Greek style. Other tombs at the same site are more akin to houses, with doors, windows, and drainspouts carved onto the exterior. Yet the majority of burials seem to have been in communal tombs, as seems to have been the case for most interments of the Third Intermediate Period.

Besides these Egyptian-derived tombs, purely classical sepulchres were constructed in some areas, in particular at Alexandria and in other then-newly founded cities. A good range of specimens have been excavated since 1987 at Marina el-Alamein, including column tombs of a type well known from Asia Minor, and elaborate hypogea, incorporating a banqueting hall, and burials within loculi and/or communal side chambers. While architectural detail was usually classical, quasi-Hellenized representations of Egyptian deities were sometimes used.

Roman Period. Hellenistic-style tombs were continued after the Roman occupation of the country, as well as more traditional types, with body treatments ranging from purely Egyptian to those with heavy Hellenistic influence. The major innovation of Roman times was the introduction of painted portraits into the mummy wrappings, particularly in the Faiyum region, while three-dimensional heads and hands became far less traditionally Egyptian in appearance.

In some regions, rather than being immediately buried, mummies apparently remained for considerable periods among the living, at home and/or in a public repository, in which homage could be offered to them, perhaps housed in some kind of wooden shrine. Many very finely adorned mummies, with painted portraits or gilded stucco masks, show signs of rough handling over a considerable period of time, and it has been noted that the foot and shin portions of some of them had scribbles and knocks that might be acquired by being left in an accessible place. Many also show weakness in the bandaging around the ankles that could have been caused by years of being propped upright. Groups of bodies would periodically be removed from homes or repositories to the cemetery, where they would be placed in mass burial pits, piled one atop another, presumably reflecting the need to make way for more recent dead among the living.

[See also Saqqara.]

BIBLIOGRAPHY

Badawy, Alexander. *A History of Egyptian Architecture.* 3 vols. Cairo and Berkeley, 1954–1968.

Bierbrier, Morris L., ed. *Portraits and Masks: Burial Customs in Roman Egypt.* London, 1997.

Blackman, Aylward M., and Michael A. Apted, *The Rock Tombs of Meir.* 6 vols. London, 1914–1953.

Bourriau, Janine D. *Pharaohs and Mortals: Egyptian Art in the Middle Kingdom.* Cambridge, 1988.

Carnarvon, Earl of, and Howard Carter. *Five Years' Explorations at Thebes.* London, 1912. Reprinted at Storrs-Mansfield/Brockton in 1996. The best published account of early New Kingdom private tombs at Thebes.

Davies, Norman de Garis. *The Rock Tombs of El Amarna.* 6 vols. London, 1903–1908.

Dodson, Aidan M. *Egyptian Rock-cut Tombs.* Princes Risborough, 1991.

Eigner, Diethelm. *Die monumentalen Grabbauten der Spätzeit in der Thebanischen Nekropole.* Vienna, 1984. The definitive work on the huge twenty-sixth dynasty tombs on the Asasif at Thebes.

Empereur, Jean-Yves. *Alexandria Rediscovered.* London, 1998. Contains two well-illustrated chapters on the necropolises of the Greco-Roman city of Alexandria.

Firth, Cecil M., and Battiscombe Gunn. *The Teti Pyramid Cemeteries.* Cairo, 1926. The publication of important necropolises, ranging in date from the Old to New Kingdoms.

Garstang, John. *The Burial Customs of Ancient Egypt.* London, 1907. A comprehensive account of the lower necropolis at Beni Hasan, a representative example of a middle-class cemetery of the Middle Kingdom.

Gardiner, Alan H. *The Tomb of Amenemhat.* London, 1915. Reprinted in 1973. The classic work on a typical eighteenth dynasty private tomb-chapel.

Habachi, Labib. *Tell Basta.* Cairo, 1957. An account of some typical Delta private tombs of the later New Kingdom.

Harpur, Yvonne. *Decoration of Private Tombs in the Old Kingdom.* London, 1987.

Hayes, William C. "The Tomb of Nefer-khewet and his Family." *Bulletin of the Metropolitan Museum of Art* 30, II (1935), 17–36. The preliminary report on the excavation of a typical middle-class tomb of the mid-eighteenth dynasty.

Ikram, Salima, and Aidan Dodson. *The Mummy in Ancient Egypt.* London, 1998. Contains a comprehensive description of the development of the Egyptian tomb and its contents.

Kampp, Friederike. *Die Thebanische Nekropole.* 2 vols. Mainz, 1996. An exhaustive and fundamental work on the architecture of the New Kingdom tombs at Thebes, listing every single known example, numbered or not.

Kanawati, Naguib. *The Tomb and Its Significance in Ancient Egypt.* Cairo, 1987.

Lauer, Jean-Phillippe. *Saqqara, Royal Necropolis of Memphis.* London, 1976. An account of the excavations at the site, including extensive descriptions of a number of private tombs, ranging from the first to twenty-sixth dynasties.

Manniche, Lise. *City of the Dead.* London, 1988. Also published as *The Tombs of the Nobles at Luxor.* Cairo, 1987.

Manniche, Lise. *Lost Tombs: A Study of Certain Eighteenth Dynasty Monuments in the Theban Necropolis.* London, 1988. An investigation into the original location of many decorative fragments now in various collections; it also provides important insights into the layout of typical tombs of the early New Kingdom.

Martin, Geoffrey T. *The Hidden Tombs of Memphis.* London, 1991. The New Kingdom private necropolis at Saqqara.

Muhammed, M. Abdul-Qader. *The Development of the Funerary Beliefs and Practices Displayed in the Private Tombs of the New Kingdom at Thebes.* Cairo, 1966. An exhaustive, well-illustrated, discussion of the decoration of many of the Theban private tombs.

Niwinski, Andrej. *21st Dynasty Coffins from Thebes: Chronological and Typological Studies.* Mainz, 1988. The definitive work on burials of the period.

Peet, T. Eric. "The Vaulted Tombs of Brick." *The Cemeteries of Abydos,* vol. 2, pp. 84–91. London, 1914.

Reisner, George A. *The Development of the Egyptian Tomb Down to the Accession of Cheops.* Oxford and Cambridge, Mass., 1936. Reprinted at Storrs-Mansfield/Brockton in 1996.

Reisner, George A. *A History of the Giza Necropolis,* I. Cambridge,

Mass., 1942. Reprinted at Storrs-Mansfield/Brockton in 1997. Together, Reisner's two volumes trace the basic evolution of Egyptian private tombs to the end of the fourth dynasty.

Sadeek, W. el-. *Twenty-sixth Dynasty Necropolis at Giza*. Vienna, 1984. Concentrates on the *mastaba* of Tjery.

Smith, Stewart Tyson. "Intact Tombs of the Seventeenth and Eighteenth Dynasties from Thebes and the New Kingdom Burial System." *Mitteilungen des Deutschen Archäologischen Instituts, Kairo* 48 (1992), 193–231. An important compendium of the available material for the study of private burials of the New Kingdom.

Spencer, A. Jeffrey. *Brick Architecture in Ancient Egypt*. Warminster, 1979.

Walker, Susan, and Morris L. Bierbrier. *Ancient Faces: Mummy Portraits from Roman Egypt*. London, 1997.

Winlock, Herbert E. *Excavations at Deir el Bahri 1911–1931*. New York, 1942. Includes accounts of burials from various periods found at the site.

Zivie, Alain-Pierre. *Decouverte à Saqqarah. Le vizir oublié*. Paris, 1990. Account of the discovery and contents of the tomb of Aperel at Saqqara.

AIDAN DODSON

TOOLS. About 3500 BCE, Egyptian metalworkers discovered the way to smelt copper ore and cast copper into sizeable and useful metal tools. At first, small adze blades, chisels, and ax heads were cast into open molds made in damp sand. Such metal tools—the chisel (*mdzt*) and the adze (*mshtyw*) evolved from earlier stone tools that had been driven by rudimentary mallets; or they were swung by hand in glancing blows against materials. The metal ax (*mibt*) and knife (*ds*) imitated earlier stone shapes. Sand molds are only used once, but at Illahun, a twelfth dynasty (c.1991–1786 BCE) manufacturing town in the Faiyum of Middle Egypt, workers cast chisels, knives, and ax heads in reusable open pottery molds. Such fired ceramic molds allowed the mass production of metal castings. The use of closed pottery and stone molds, in two halves, plus the lost-wax (*ciré pèrdue*) process created small, solid castings; large, lost-wax molds, with clay cores, produced hollow castings that consumed relatively less metal. Open wooden molds were used for making mud bricks; pottery molds were for shaping faience cores; and clay and limestone molds were for casting glass in dynastic times.

From Neolithic times or earlier, fire was created by bow-drilling—a long, waisted, hardwood drill-stick was spun by a bow (similar to a hunting bow) in a hole previously drilled into a softwood block by an auger. By the twelfth dynasty, a waisted drill-stock force-fitted with a short replaceable stick superseded the long drill-stick. An ejection hole in the stock let a worker remove worn sticks (Figure 1). Waisted drill-shafts allowed a stretched bowstring to engage on a wider diameter, automatically increasing its grip.

Predynastic and dynastic smelting furnaces were fired up and obtained their air through blowpipes. Between two and six blowpipe workers were illustrated in tomb scenes of the fifth dynasty (c.2513–2374 BCE) to the eighteenth dynasty (c.1569–1315 BCE). The furnace blowpipe, supplied with a nozzle of dried clay, was fashioned from the common marsh reed (*Phragmites communis*); it measured about 1 meter (3 feet) in length. Jewelers' blowpipes were about half as long. Reed stems were prepared by jabbing a thinner sharpened reed or stick through a reed's leaf-joint partitions, to open all the previously separate hollow sections. Present-day blowpipe experiments determined that four to six workers could supply enough air to melt up to 1.3 kilograms of copper or bronze in one crucible of fired clay and fused ash. Crucibles were also employed for melting the constituents of glass. In the sixth dynasty tomb of Mereruka at Saqqara, workers were shown manipulating crucibles with flat stones or pottery pads, but workers in the eighteenth dynasty tomb of the vizier Rekhmire held crucibles with withies (two freshly cut sticks). Foot-operated bellows were depicted in eighteenth dynasty Theban tombs. These consisted of two adjacently placed, flat-bottomed circular pottery bowls, each tightly fitted at the rim with a loose leather diaphragm. A worker alternately trod on one diaphragm and simultaneously pulled up the other with an attached string. A natural walking rhythm ensured a steady supply of air through attached reed tubes. Such large copper and bronze tools as stone-cutting saws needed the concurrent operation of several furnaces to melt sufficient metal for a single casting. Other cast metals were gold, silver, and lead.

Copper, bronze, gold, and silver plates—probably open cast to the thinnest dimension possible, 5 millimeters—were then beaten when cold into thinner sheets on a stone anvil set on a wooden block that was buried in the earth. The metalworker used a selection of hand-held spherical and hemispherical stone hammers that varied in size and

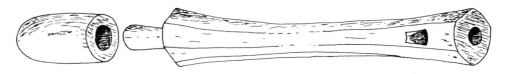

TOOLS. Figure 1. *Kahun bow-driven drill stock, with its wooden drill cap.* A tool can be removed by pushing a short stick into the ejection hole. (Drawn from Manchester Museum Catalogue number 23. Courtesy Denys A. Stocks)

weight. Gold leaf was beaten thin between skins that allowed a flexibility for application; and raised reliefs in metal (*repoussé*) were achieved with chisels and punches of bone, wood, stone, and metal.

Some long flat-edged, copper stone-cutting saws—used with quartz sand abrasive for cutting hard stone statuary, sarcophagi, and blocks—were cast and used at a 5 millimeter thickness, but others were beaten thinner. For cutting wood and soft limestone, the edges of thin copper saws were given serrations, by notching them on a hard, sharp object—probably inspired by the Mesolithic serrated flint sickles for cutting reeds and other stems in use before the introduction of copper casting (reconstructed stone-cutting saws and replica wood-cutting saws efficiently cut these materials). In Middle Kingdom tomb scenes, workers saw planks off timber lashed to sturdy posts that are partially buried in the ground. A metal or stone wedge probably kept a cut open in the wood. Inserted into the lashing is a short wooden rod with a stone counterweight hanging on its free end (tests with reconstructed equipment showed that the rod acts like a tourniquet, quickly tightening or loosening the lashing).

Spherical and hemispherical hammers were also used to shape gold and silver vessels, which were placed upside down on a tripod anvil. Smooth agate burnishers and leather balls were used to polish the finished vessels. The anvil consisted of a forked branch, set at an angle into the ground, with a long wooden or metal rod passing easily through an upward-slanting hole drilled into the upper part of the branch. Such a reconstructed anvil demonstrated that not only did the projecting rod function as the third leg of the tripod but also its length was adjustable for work on both large and small vessels (by sliding it through the hole). Weight on the anvil "locks" it into position.

Cast copper and bronze tools were shaped cold for maximum hardness; however, excessive hammering causes cracking. The Egyptians eventually found that some tools needed to be annealed—by heating and then cooling several times for multiple hammerings. The copper adze was developed from the slim, narrow Predynastic blade to the wider one of dynastic times. Some blades were cast with lugs, to aid their fastening by leather thong to wooden handles; others had a distinctive neck. Adze blades were used for skimming and shaping wood or soft limestone surfaces. Wooden mallets drove flat-tapered and crosscut-tapered chisels, but these were strongest in cross section and were sometimes fitted with wooden handles; they were used with mallets to cut and lever wood from deep mortises. Chisels were often held for carving wooden sculpture, and intricate carving could be achieved by flint as well as by metal tools. The shape of metal ax heads changed with time, but the ax's cutting edge—used by car-

TOOLS. Figure 2. *A reconstructed bow-driven drill shaft, fitted with its copper tube.* (Courtesy Denys A. Stocks)

penters and boat builders—was rounded in form, for splitting wood along the grain and chopping across the grain. The ax was sometimes supplied with lugs or a hole, for fastening the head to its wooden handle. Tool handles were made from branches that had the bark removed by flint scrapers and the surfaces smoothed by sandstone blocks.

Leatherworkers since Paleolithic times had used flint scrapers and flint knives for preparing and cutting hides; these tools were also used in Egypt for cutting and splitting reeds, papyrus, and other plant stems and were developed into metal scrapers and knives. The New Kingdom semicircular bronze leather-cutting knife was fitted into a wooden handle, and copper and bronze awls, bodkins, and needles were made to stitch leather pieces together (previously, they were made from bone or ivory).

Stone tools—for working calcite and harder stone vessels, for statuary, sarcophagi, palettes, stelae, and the cutting of bas reliefs and incised hieroglyphs—included chisels, punches, and scrapers of flint and hafted stone mauls. Some stones were shaped and smoothed by stone grinders—probably by a paste made from finely ground waste-drilling powders, and possibly a mud polishing medium,

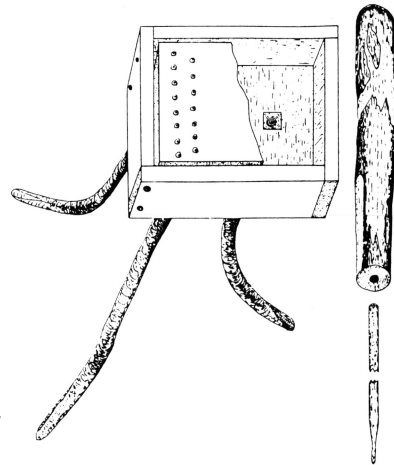

TOOLS. Figure 3. *(Left) A reconstructed three-legged New Kingdom drilling table, showing the probable way in which beads were located for drilling. (Right) A reconstructed stick handle and bronze drill rod.* (Courtesy Denys A. Stocks)

applied with leather balls. Picks and axes of granite, quartzite, chert, and flint were use to quarry the softer stones, like limestone and sandstone; dolerite pounders were used for detaching harder stone for construction, statuary, and obelisks. Flint adzes, chisels, and scrapers were used alongside copper and bronze adzes and chisels for smoothing and carving reliefs in soft limestone tomb walls, blocks, and other objects.

Egyptian workers possessed five types of bow-driven tools, including (1) the fire drill (d_3); (2) copper and bronze tubular drills (Figure 2); (3) copper and bronze single-bead drills; (4) bronze drill-rods for simultaneously perforating several stone beads; and (5) a wooden drill-stock that drove interchangeable tools, such as the fire stick or the metal auger (used to drill stringing holes in furniture and peg [dowel] holes for furniture joints). The bow-driven augers probably did not drill large holes in ships' timbers; instead, a copper auger attached to a handle was used, which gave great twisting power to its cutting edges.

For drilling the suspension lugs carved on stone vessels, statuary, sarcophagi, and their lids, bow-driven tubes were employed with dry quartz sand abrasive. These were formed from thin sheet copper for small tubes, but the large ones were probably cast in vertical molds. Reed tubes, rotated on sand, were used to drill calcite and hard limestone vessels before about 3500 BCE. After that date, Predynastic workers copied the hollow reed's shape in copper, and later, bronze. A stone vessel's interior was widened by a forked shaft lashed to a weighted shaft that drove circular, figure-eight, and conical-shaped stone borers, employing quartz sand as an abrasive. For boring soft gypsum, crescent-shaped flints were also driven by forked shafts. The single-bead drill was fitted with a waisted shaft, driven by a small bow; a stone drill-cap exerted pressure. Holes were begun with flint borers, exclusively used for perforation before the metal drills were employed. In Thebes, two-to-five bronze drill-rods were rotated, each in a hole drilled into the bottom of a stick handle; the drills were held in a straight line by an operator's free hand and simultaneously spun by a long bow. The beads were probably set into a mud block that rested in a hollow-topped, three-legged table (Figure 3). (Reconstructed drilling equipment has shown that the change to

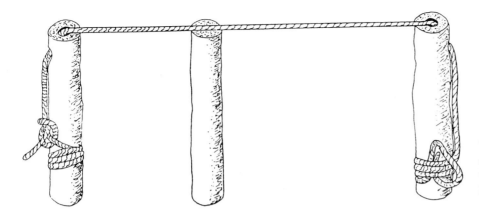

TOOLS. Figure 4. *A reconstructed surface-testing tool, consisting of two outer rods, taut string, and the third rod for revealing surface inaccuracies.* (Courtesy Denys A. Stocks)

mass-production drilling decreased perforation times for 10 millimeter-diameter amethyst beads from five hours to about one hour per bead.) Stone beads were polished by rubbing them along grooves in a wooden block filled with abrasive paste. Bow strings—or ropes if driving large-diameter tubes—were manufactured from halfa grass, flax fiber, woven linen, palm fiber, or papyrus.

For stone architecture, workers employed three vitally important tools for verifying horizontal and vertical planes and surface flatness: (1) An A-shaped wooden frame, for horizontal planes had originally been calibrated by making the bottom of the two legs just touch standing water—the only true horizontal in nature. The horizontal crosspiece was then marked where a plumb line, hung from the A's apex, passed it. (2) A vertical plane was checked by a wooden tool made from two accurately matched short pieces that were fastened at right angles (one above the other) to a longer, vertical piece; a freely hanging plumb line then just touched the end of both horizontal pieces when the plane was truly vertical. Tests with a modern spirit level found replicas of these to be accurate. (3) A stone surface-testing tool consisted of three wooden rods, accurately matched in length; two rods stood upright on the stone surface were joined at the top by a string, pulled taut; the third rod, when held against the string and shifted along the surface showed any unevenness (Figure 4). Replica rods can reveal surface inaccuracies as small as 0.25 millimeter (0.01 inch) along a length of 1.25 meters (4 feet) and therefore over an area of 1.25 meters squared (16 square feet). The joined rods, used as an inside caliper, may have verified parallelism between the end joints of blocks as the fitting progressed but before sliding them into position on gypsum mortar. Other important building tools included the wooden square, the lever, the roller, the plasterer's float, the cubit measure, a sledge for moving blocks, as well as measuring cords and leveling lines.

[*See also* Stoneworking; *and* Technology and Engineering.]

BIBLIOGRAPHY

Arnold, Dieter. *Building in Egypt: Pharaonic Stone Masonry.* New York, 1991. Discusses, in depth, all types of building in stone, together with associated methods of stoneworking.

Lucas, Alfred. *Ancient Egyptian Materials and Industries.* 4th rev. ed. by J. R. Harris. London, 1962. Offers a comprehensive appraisal of materials, including stone, worked by ancient Egyptians.

Petrie, W. M. Flinders. *Tools and Weapons.* London, 1917. Describes and illustrates a large number of Egyptian tools, many of them first excavated by Petrie.

Stocks, Denys A. "Ancient Factory Mass-Production Techniques: Indications of Large-Scale Stone Bead Manufacture during the Egyptian New Kingdom Period." *Antiquity* 63 (1989), 526–531. Describes the epigraphic evidence for ancient multiple-bead drilling; presents the results of tests on reconstructed tools.

Stocks, Denys A. "Making Stone Vessels in Ancient Mesopotamia and Egypt." *Antiquity* 67 (1993), 596–603. Gives the connections between stone-vessel manufacture in ancient Egypt and Mesopotamia, in addition to a comprehensive description of Egyptian stone-vessel production methods and tools.

DENYS A. STOCKS

TRADE AND MARKETS. Ancient Egypt was basically a "supply state." Products for consumption were delivered to state or temple institutions, which in turn distributed food supplies and other goods to the population. Allocation was based on a fair assessment of each person's requirements. People received as much as they needed. Surplus could be traded at local markets, a system which helped fill gaps in the flow of supply.

Trade among regions was always conducted by institutions, which bartered with the surplus from their own production. Merchants worked for these institutions, playing the role of agents in the exchange. Their task was to exchange the surplus of the institution they represented for as many valuable goods as possible. Generally speaking, merchants were therefore not working for their own personal profit. Merchants who worked for their own gain existed in ancient Egypt only during the New Kingdom.

Market Trade. The original and oldest form of trade is market trading in the form of barter. Many Old Kingdom tombs contain paintings that illustrate this type of trade and provide information about trading practices and goods. The images in the tomb of Niankhkhnum and Khnumhotep in Saqqara from the end of the fifth dynasty are especially expressive.

The bartered goods comprised surplus from state allocations, local food products, and homemade objects. The very nature of barter makes it difficult to tell "buyers" from "vendors," but some distinctions are possible. The suppliers are usually shown in front of their carefully arranged goods, sitting either on the ground or on low stools, while the "purchasers" are shown standing, frequently carrying a shopping bag slung over the shoulder. Bartering was generally carried out by the vendor calling out his goods, to which he referred in direct speech as "my thing"; the buyer responded and described what he was offering in exchange. The exchange was called "trade" (*swnt*); the act of bartering was described as "giving in substitution" (*rdit m isw*) or "giving in exchange" (*rdit m ḏbꜥw*).

Market goods. The goods exchanged at the market were usually basic staples, rarely luxury goods. Bread and beer were the most commonly traded items. Both were produced in most households. The second most frequently traded item was fish, caught in the Nile and in the canals. Because fish had such a short "shelf life," surplus from a catch had to be sold immediately. Only dried fish could be stored over longer periods. Fresh and dried fish are common commodities in Old Kingdom market scenes, which also show pieces of meat. The meat was probably surplus from the mortuary temples, where priests received meat as payment and then sold any surplus at the market. Vegetables were also very important: onions, leeks, lettuce, and melons traded at the market were both home-grown and surplus from payments received by priests. Again, these goods had to be traded quickly. There are some images of orchard fruit being offered for exchange—sycamore and other figs, and grapes. These were mostly surplus items from state allocations, since private orchards did not exist in the Old Kingdom.

The artifacts offered for exchange included leather or rush sandals, large fans for fanning fires, walking-sticks with ornate knobs, pieces of furniture, and headrests. These homemade objects would not have been made of valuable materials.

Ceramic containers were also brought to market, as were objects made of copper, such as mirrors, fish-hooks, and chisels, as well as salves and oils, which were prepared right at the market. All these goods held a special place in the trade, because raw materials from the king's property were needed to produce them and the vendor would have needed to purchase these in advance. The potential for trade in more valuable goods is illustrated by

the trade with linens. The cloth came from state-run weaving workshops and was sold at a fixed price based on a standard of value (*šꜥt*).

Prices. As goods were exchanged on the market, prices tended to be determined by supply and demand. Nevertheless, some barter transactions seem to have been subject to fixed "exchange rates." Two commonly used standards of value were applied to determine the price of goods. One was the *ḥḳꜣt* measure, which developed from cereal farming and was used to determine the amount of goods given in lieu of wages. The other was the *šꜥt*, which stood for an absolute standard of value.

The *ḥḳꜣt* cereal measure is frequently mentioned in the dialogues of Old Kingdom market scenes. The merchant offers his product at a price measured in *ḥḳꜣt*. Because the cereal measure asked for by the merchant is not shown in the hand of the potential buyer, we can assume that this was a fictitious standard of value in small units. This theory is also supported by the fact that the *ḥḳꜣt* measure was used for low values. In the tomb of Ti near Saqqara, the price of a walking-stick or pole is expressed by the vendor as follows: "My friend, see this beautiful stick that is dry. Three *ḥḳꜣt* corn for it!" Similarly, in the tomb of Niankhkhnum and Khnumhotep in Saqqara, we find: "See, these loaves of *šmḏw* bread. There are six (in exchange) for two *ḥḳꜣt* corn!"

Another unit, which comes closer to our notion of money, is the *šꜥt* of the market scenes. The tomb paintings of Niankhkhnum and Khnumhotep show scenes in which an indeterminate amount of cloth changes hands in exchange for six *šꜥt*. The same standard of value appears in other Old Kingdom texts. The so-called House-purchase Document from Giza uses *šꜥt* to determine the value of cloth and items of furniture: the house costs ten *šꜥt*; in exchange a four-ply cloth is given for three *šꜥt*, a two-ply cloth for three *šꜥt*, and a bed for four *šꜥt*. The same standard of value remained in use until the end of the nineteenth dynasty under the name *šnꜥt*; in the New Kingdom it is subordinated to other standards of value. In the late New Kingdom, one *šnꜥt* is the equivalent of one-twelfth of one "silver deben[?]," as noted by Jaroslav Černý (1953/1954). It is assumed that it was a "coin," frequently used by the public in the New Kingdom and possibly based on a unit of silver. Unfortunately, the hieroglyphic determinative for *šꜥt* cannot be identified, so we still do not know what kind of object a *šꜥt* may have been.

Market control. In a supply economy the market is supervised by state representatives. The market supervisor's task is to control type, volume, and quality of exchange goods and to prevent goods and raw materials that are the property of the state from being diverted from their intended routes to an illegal "black market." Furthermore, price controls protect customers from being cheated.

TRADE AND MARKETS. *Old Kingdom depiction of various activities at a market.*

However, the market supervisors are difficult to identify in Old Kingdom illustrations of market scenes. They may be represented by the figures shown walking through the market with monkeys or baboons on a leash, or sometimes swinging a scepter. A youthful man walking a baboon is once described as "supervisor" in the dialogue. However, we cannot exclude the possibility that the men seen walking with monkeys and baboons were offering the animals for barter, since baboons and monkeys were popular pets in ancient Egypt. The elders seen sitting on stools are apparently persons of respect and influence. A cloth covers their shoulders, and in the captions they are referred to as the "leaders of craftsmen." However, it is unlikely that they were market supervisors since they are usually shown to be bartering themselves.

Importance of local markets. The relief scenes give no clues about the location of the markets. It is reasonable to assume, however, that they were conveniently close to road intersections or on riverbanks near harbors. These advantageous sites would have made them into communication centers, where people of many different social classes would come together and enter into dialogue with one another as they bartered in the street. Because strangers from other towns as well as local inhabitants are shown in the market scenes, the markets were probably also important news centers. The sheer number of people who visited a market, also made it a good place for the service sector. Refreshments were sold in inns, and sealmakers and barbers offered their services in the market.

Because of their situation in towns at crossroads or

near the river, the marketplaces developed into trade centers which drew people from far away. This is evident in the *Story of the Eloquent Peasant* from the early Middle Kingdom. The story, which takes place during the Herakleopolitan period (c.2190–2040 BCE) after the Old Kingdom, recounts the fate of an oasis-dweller from the Wadi Natrun who sets out to market in Herakleopolis with a donkey caravan; en route, his donkeys and all his goods—natural products, salt, plants, wood, furs, and birds—are stolen. In the end he initiates a lawsuit to fight the injustice done to him. The arguments of this lawsuit are the core of this literary document.

The international significance of the market town is also evident in the New Kingdom. Its tomb paintings from Thebes show trading ships anchoring near the market of Thebes and trade goods being offered there. One case from the period of Amenhotpe III (1410–1372 BCE), documented by Davies and Faulkner (1947, pl. 8), is evidence that Asian merchants traded on the market in Thebes.

Thus, the market was an important center of local trade at all times. Texts from the Ramessid period indicate that shepherds sold surplus animals from their herds on the local market. Priests bartered with the surplus from the temple offerings which they received as payment. A good example for flourishing local trade is found in the nineteenth dynasty artisans' settlement of Deir el-Medina, where craftsmen manufactured beds, crates, sedan chairs, coffins, wood statues, and other items for tomb furnishings, to offer in exchange for goods they needed for their own use.

Domestic Trade. The mechanisms of barter trade portrayed in Old Kingdom market scenes also apply to trade between regions, but the latter was rarely effected on a person-to-person level. It was nearly always carried out between institutions. Private merchants, working on their own, are the exception.

An early indicator of interregional trade is contained in the inscription by the district chief Ankhtifi of Mo'alla in Upper Egypt from the First Intermediate Period (c.2190 BCE). Ankhtifi recounts how the good administration of the district under his leadership ensured an abundance of cereal at a time when the rest of Egypt was plagued by starvation. To help his contemporaries, he permitted local trade in which cereal was exchanged for valuable goods which were brought before him: "[The South arrived] with its people, the North came [with] his children. It brought best salve oil in exchange for my Upper Egyptian barley." More surplus cereal was used for interregional trade and sent south and north on freight ships: "This, my Upper Egyptian barley went upstream to Wawat [Lower Nubia] and downstream to the district of Thinis [Abydos]." The inscription is important because it clearly demonstrates that Ankhtifi sold his cereal on the local and on the interregional markets—that is, he traded.

The cereal was transported on freighters, which were indispensable for interregional trade. Domestic trade in Egypt was carried out almost exclusively on the Nile and depended on ships that navigated this natural traffic route. The ownership of ships was largely a privilege of civil administration and of the temples. Where private individuals are named as shipowners in New Kingdom papyri, they are invariably members of an institution, usually a temple. This was probably also the case in the Old Kingdom, whose private tombs often contain images of cargo ships. Because cargo ships were rarely privately owned, individuals could not readily participate in interregional trade.

The case is similar for transported goods that were not privately owned, but the property of institutions. As trade goods they were sold from institution to institution. The goods for sale, transported by ship, were mostly natural produce and products taken from the surplus of specific sectors in the economy in either civil or temple administrations. The freight lists, preserved in the logbooks, give us an idea of what they comprised. One such logbook is Papyrus Turin 2008+2016 (Janssen 1961); the list of transported goods in this log includes natural products such as oil, wine, cereal, salt, and fish, as well as papyrus products and different types of cloth.

The merchants who traded the surplus on behalf of the different institutions were called *šwti*. They were employed at the temples or were dependents of individuals who held high office in the temple. During the nineteenth and twentieth dynasties, some members of the military administration are named as superiors of these *šwti* merchants. There is abundant documentation from the late eighteenth dynasty onward that these merchants belonged mostly to temple institutions. An early source from c.1400 BCE identifies a *šwti* merchant from the Aten temple in Tell el-Amarna. During the Ramessid period, merchants from many other temples are identified: from the temple of Sobek in Crocodilopolis, the temple of Re in Karnak (?), the Ptah temple of Memphis (?), a temple of Sety I, and a Khnum temple in Elephantine.

The *šwti* merchants were interested in finding new trade sources for their temples and in gaining access to other temples by means of "fixed values," usually precious metals. The profit was used to buy temple utensils or statues and to finance buildings. It may also have been used for trade with foreign lands to the north, especially Lebanon, from which the much-sought cedar wood was imported.

The profession of the *šwti* merchant was considered difficult and unrewarding. The merchants were employed by the institutions or dependent on superiors who pocketed the profit as representatives of the institutions. It is therefore a logical development that some *šwti* merchants would take the step toward independence. A court case is documented about one of these independent merchants (see Gardiner, 1935). The lawsuit proves that independent merchants did exist in ancient Egypt. Thus an "itinerant huckster" (as Gardiner calls him), active in year 15 of Ramesses II's rule (1290 BCE), sold a Syrian woman as a slave in exchange for various objects (cloth, containers, and clothes), with the resulting difficulty that the woman who purchased the slave had to borrow from neighbors and friends to make the payment.

Toward the end of the Ramessid period, merchants played a somewhat disreputable role. Under Ramesses IV merchants took part in the misappropriation of temple cereal (Papyrus Turin 1887 *verso*, 1,7 ff.). Under Ramesses IX and XI, conditions were even worse. Under Ramesses IX (1139–1120 BCE), fourteen merchants from the Faiyum were implicated in the Theban tomb robberies (Papyrus British Museum 10053: British Museum 10068). A similar event occurred under Ramesses XI (1111–1081 BCE). Court protocols, preserved in Papyrus British Museum 10052 and in Papyrus Mayer A, reveal that the merchants participated in the tomb thefts as purchasers and receivers of stolen goods, for which they paid with food, cereal, and copper.

Foreign Trade. Little is known about foreign trade in ancient Egypt and about the export of Egyptian goods to neighboring states. Although the many Middle Kingdom statues found in Syria and Palestine are conclusive proof that there was indeed trade in Egyptian cultural objects during the Middle Kingdom, there are very few written records to support the idea. In general, the sources provide no information about the manner and practices of foreign trade even in the New Kingdom. The report of the expedition to the land of Punt under Hatshepsut, from the early New Kingdom (1502–1482 BCE), and the more or less contemporary report of Sennefer about his journey to Byblos, describe trade with foreign lands as if the Egyptians had simply gone to fetch whatever they required, and all they needed to give in return was a simple offering to a local deity. The reality was surely quite different. A good example is in the tale of Wenamun from the Third Intermediate Period. Wenamun was dispatched by his king to buy wood and paid a high price in cloth, parchment, rope, lentils, and dried fish, as well as gold and silver containers (*Wenamun* 2, 40 ff.).

We have much more information about imported goods. The main countries from which goods were imported were Syria-Palestine, Nubia, Cyprus, and Punt. The imported products were mostly raw materials and products of which the Egyptians themselves had very little or none, as well as luxury goods, which were especially sought in the Egyptian society of the New Kingdom. From Syria and Palestine slaves, horses, cattle, small livestock, wood, silver, copper, and valuable minerals were imported. Cyprus delivered copper and elephant tusks;

from the Aegean came luxury articles such as Minoan and Mycenaean oil containers. The south, especially Nubia, was rich in gold and mineral deposits, stone for statues and temple buildings, and valuable woods—among them ebony—as well as small livestock and cattle, which were imported to Egypt together with other goods from the South. From the land of Punt came myrrh and incense.

Foreign trade with the north was usually handled through Syrian merchants, who controlled most of the foreign trade in Egypt during the New Kingdom. The dominance of Syrian merchants is evident in their many Syrian names, as Helck (1971) has shown. It is also reflected in a special trade lexicon: thus, the expression for "trading" during the New Kingdom becomes "using the language of Syria." During the Late period foreigners were prohibited from trading in Egypt. The Saite kings of the eighth and seventh centuries BCE forced foreign merchants—at that time mostly Greeks—to cease all direct trade with Egyptians. The trading post of Naukratis was founded specifically for foreign merchants, who had to trade from there directly with the Egyptian state and its trading centers. However, these efforts proved largely unsuccessful; according to Herodotus (II, 39), Greek merchants were once again in evidence across Egypt during the Persian period.

Trade Routes. Egypt was far away from all the great international trade routes of the time and had to establish links to them. The caravan route to Palestine followed the "Ways of Horus" across the Isthmus of Qantara to Raphia. It was in use from Egyptian prehistory and corresponds to the "Way of the Land of the Philistines" of the Old Testament (*Ex.* 13, 17). We know from the polemical treatise in Papyrus Anastasi I that farther north in southern Palestine the route divided into one branch that followed the Mediterranean coast and another that led via Megiddo and Hazor upstream along the Litani River and downstream along the Orontes.

The caravan route to Nubia and to modern Sudan began in Asyut in Middle Egypt. The route, which is still used today, leads from Asyut via the oases of Kharga and Dungul to Tomas. Its ancient course was described in the biographical inscriptions of the tomb of Horkhuf from Aswan in the sixth dynasty (c.2300 BCE).

The Red Sea was reached via a caravan route that led from Coptos in Middle Egypt across the Eastern Desert. The end station lay at the exit of the Wadi Gawasis near a port where raw materials and products from the Sinai and from the land of Punt were unloaded. Punt, far to the south, was reached by sea following the coastline of the Red Sea. In the Late period the Red Sea was also navigable from Memphis via a precursor to the Suez Canal. This canal branched off from the Nile at a point south of the site of modern Cairo and led through the Wadi Tumilat all the way to the straits of Suez.

The sea route into the eastern Mediterranean was of great importance. It began on the Nile at the port of Memphis and led via the Pelusiac branch of the Nile to the large port centers in the eastern Mediterranean, where Egyptian trade could link up with overseas trade. In Ugarit at the mouth of the Orontes River, the Egyptian route crossed the frequently traveled east–west route which led from Cyprus to the southern coast of Asia Minor, as well as to the Aegean.

[See also Prices and Payment; Seafaring; and Weights and Measures.]

BIBLIOGRAPHY

Altenmüller, Hartwig. "Markt." In *Lexikon der Ägyptologie* 3: 1191–1194. Wiesbaden, 1976. Provides a summary of sources on the local market in ancient Egypt.

Černý, Jaroslav. "Prices and Wages in Egypt in the Ramesside Period." *Cahiers de l'histoire mondiale* 1 (1953/1954), 910–914.

Davies, Norman de G., and R. O. Faulkner. "A Syrian Trading Venture to Egypt." *Journal of Egyptian Archaeology* 33 (1947), 40–46.

Gardiner, Alan H. "A Lawsuit Arising from the Purchase of Two Slaves." *Journal of Egyptian Archaeology* 21 (1935), 140–146.

Helck, Wolfgang. *"Die Beziehungen Ägyptens zu Vorderasien im 3. und 2. Jahrtausend v. Chr."* Ägyptologische Abhandlungen 5 (1971), 428–431.

Janssen, Jac J. *Two Egyptian Ship's Logs: Papyrus Leiden I 350 Verso and Papyrus Turin 2008+2016.* Suppl. *Ondheidkundige Mededelingen iut het Rijksmuseum van Oudheden te Leuven 52.* Leiden, 1961.

Liverani, Mario. *Prestige and Interest. International Relations in the Near East ca. 1600–1100 B.C.* History of the Ancient Near East Studies, 1. Padua, 1990. A study devoted to gifts, commerce, and the ideological basis of international connections during the New Kingdom.

Römer, Malte. *Der Handel und die Kaufleute im Alten Ägypten.* Studien zur Altägyptischen Kultur, 19. Hamburg, 1992. Contains a well-researched analysis of trade in ancient Egypt and on the merchants connected with trade, pp. 257–284.

HARTWIG ALTENMÜLLER
Translated from German by Elizabeth Schwaiger

TRANSPORTATION. The people of the Nile Valley used many types of boats and barges as the principal means of transportation (until the advent of mechanized transport in the twentieth century). Roads in ancient Egypt have not been well researched; however, expeditions in the Western Desert near Luxor (ancient Thebes) suggest that much can be learned about the full extent of overland transportation routes.

Boats and Barges. As early as the Predynastic period, boats emerge as a major theme in Egyptian art. It is not always clear whether the boats portrayed are real or mythic craft, so it is not known how they were constructed. Nonetheless, archaeological evidence for woodworking techniques and for wood worked into planks suggests that wooden ships might have been constructed before the first dynasty. By the first dynasty, large wooden vessels were certainly being constructed, as is known from the boat graves near royal or elite tombs at Abydos and Saqqara. Although those vessels were ceremonial, from them it can be inferred that wooden vessels had become important to Egypt's social and economic development. A petroglyph of slain and captured prisoners near a boat dated to the reign of the first dynasty king Zer at Gebel Sheikh Sulliman, as well as a boat on the Narmer Palette, suggest that, in addition to whatever role ships may have played in the transportation of cargo, ships had also assumed a military role in the Early Dynastic period.

From the Old Kingdom, boats were essential to the transportation of bulk cargoes of all types, including, but not limited to, stone for major building projects. Transport ships were a common theme in the art of private tombs and public monuments; written texts (like the autobiography of the courtier Weni) record that the use and construction of wooden ships were essential to carrying out peaceful and military missions in the Nile Valley.

Mediterranean shipping to and from Egypt is suggested for the Early Dynastic period and is certain for the Old Kingdom. The importation of wood for ship construction during the first dynasty is suggested by a wooden label from the tomb of the Horus Aha at Abydos, showing ships accompanied by the Old Egyptian word *mr*, meaning "cedar." In the fourth dynasty, the Palermo Stone reports ships of pine being imported, presumably from Syria-Palestine, under the pharaoh Sneferu. From the Old Kingdom, the first mention was made of *kpn*, or "Byblos" vessels—ships that clearly have some sort of connection with the Syrian city of that name; the earliest attestation for an expedition to Punt may be sixth dynasty, in the autobiography of Pepy-nakht. Reliefs from the sun temple of Sahure show Near Easterners on seagoing vessels that, although unnamed, were very likely such ships.

The peculiarities of Egyptian ship construction, which used no nails or pegs but planks lashed together with ropes of papyrus or halfa grass, made it theoretically possible for vessels to be disassembled, transported, and reassembled elsewhere. While absolute proof is not forthcoming, such a process seems to be indicated in Egyptian texts from the Middle Kingdom, which refer to land expeditions traveling overland to the Red Sea, where fleets were constructed for expeditions to Arabia or East Africa. A similar hauling of prefabricated boat parts for later reassembly may be alluded to in the Gebel Barkal stela of Thutmose III, in which the pharaoh reports that, during his campaign in Syria, "I caused that many ships of cedar be built upon the mountains of God's Land, in the area called 'Mistress of Byblos'; [they were] placed on wagons, cattle dragging [them]; they proceeded before my majesty to cross this great river [i.e., the Euphrates]."

Typically, Egyptian transport vessels were approximately three times as long as they were broad, with a maximum width at midships about three times the depth of the hull. Although a summary of the great variety of names for ship types far exceeds the space available here, a few types should be mentioned. The *wsḥ* (feminine var. *wsḥ.t*) or "broad" vessel was the typical large bulk hauler. Papyri with accounts from the Ramessid period suggest that the largest such ships could hold almost 1,000 Ramessid *ḫȝr*-measures, or almost 50 metric tons (best information from the twentieth dynasty Amiens Papyrus). Dimensions for large *wsḥ*-vessels are given in the inscriptions of the "Piya (Piankhy) blocks" of the twenty-fifth dynasty; there it was recorded that *wsḥ*-vessels hauling cargo from Sais to Thebes were approximately 45 cubits in overall length and 15 cubits wide, or approximately 23.5 by 7.8 meters (75 by 25 feet). Other common ship types were the *mnš*-ships, known primarily from the New Kingdom in connection with shipping on the Mediterranean and Red Sea; *qr* or *kr*-ships were used from the New Kingdom into at least the Persian period and appear to have been typically smaller than *wsḥ*-vessels, at least in Ramessid documentation. The *byr*-vessels were a ship type that was in use during the New Kingdom; in New Kingdom documentation, *byr* typically refers to seagoing ships. By the Persian period, however, *byr* mainly refers to Nile River boats, and they were known to Herodotus and other Greek travelers, under the form *baris*, as the typical native Nile River craft.

Large building projects also created the need for special purpose barges. The autobiography of Weni records the building of an extraordinarily broad barge for the hauling of a stone altar from Hatnub to Memphis: 30 cubits in width by 60 in length, or a length-to-beam ratio of 2:1. From el-Lisht, fragments of twelfth-dynasty wooden transport ships, used as construction fill at the pyramid of Senwosret I, suggest the possibility of a vessel with an 8-meter (25.6-foot) maximum beam and a 1.5-meter (5-foot) hull depth, or a ratio of 5.3:1. The ships from which these timbers were taken were evidently strongly framed and strengthened longitudinally with a sort of keelson, or heavy internal beam low in the ship. The largest such barge known appears to have been the obelisk carrier of Hatshepsut, portrayed in a relief at her mortuary temple at Deir el-Bahri. If the relief is an accurate depiction of this vessel, the barge was more than long enough to hold both of Hatshepsut's Karnak obelisks end to end, and massively reinforced with three layers of through-beams. A written description of an obelisk-hauling barge from the earlier reign of Thutmose I is to be found in the autobiography of Ineni. Smaller ships were, of course, engaged in building projects as well, hauling cargoes of only a few blocks at a time. A number of ostraca preserve cargo lists for ships hauling stone during the construction of the Ramesseum. Similar ostraca are known for the construction of the temple of Sety I at Abydos.

In the Ptolemaic and Roman periods, a large variety of ship names appear in connection with cargo transportation. Aside from *byr*, Demotic documents record the far commoner *rms*- and *ḏy*-vessels, and perhaps also the *qr*, known from Ramessid documents. In Greek documentation from Ptolemaic Egypt, the largest-known vessels are called *kerkouros*-ships, which might hold up to 10,000 *artabas* (approximately 250 metric tons) of grain. In Roman documentation, common types are the *Hellenikon*, or "Greek" boat, and the *pakton*, possibly "lashed" boat; the contrast may be between ships built using Greco-Roman and indigenous Egyptian ship construction techniques.

While Egyptian sea connections with other Mediterranean lands seems assured from at least the Old Kingdom, the extent to which Egyptian ships sailed beyond the Red Sea is less clear. Sea travel to Punt, probably on the horn of Africa, is attested from at least the fifth dynasty, under Sahure. The suggestion of Predynastic or Early Dynastic sea connections with southern Mesopotamia seems dubious; the first actual proof of a sea route from Egypt to Mesopotamia comes in the Persian period, with the Red Sea canal stelas erected by Darius I documenting shipping to Persia. In the Greco-Roman period, however, sailors based in Red Sea ports routinely traveled to India.

Land Transportation. Trade connections between Egypt and neighboring lands in the Near East and southern Africa are known from at least the Predynastic period. A number of Egyptian sites in southern Palestine from the first dynasty of the Early Dynastic period are built inland, suggesting that they were reached by land rather than water. Whether Nubian settlements to the south of Egypt were at this period more often reached by land or by river is more difficult to say, but numerous petroglyphs of boats in Upper Egypt and Nubia, many of Predynastic date, suggest that boats were much used. Rock inscriptions from the Predynastic period in the Wadi Hammamat and at other desert sites confirm expeditions into the desert; Egyptian expeditions left inscriptions in the Sinai peninsula by the third dynasty. Certainly caravan routes were already well established in the Old Kingdom, when the autobiography of the sixth dynasty HorKhuf records expeditions along Elephantine and oasis roads; this last was a desert route connecting the oases of the Western Desert. Probably the same route figures in the Second Kamose Stela of the transition to the eighteenth dynasty, which reports the interception of a message being carried "beyond the oases" from the Hyksos ruler in the Egyptian delta to his Nubian allies.

A northern route from the Nile Delta into the Near East, called the "Ways of Horus," became the principal route by which Egpytian armies, traders, and diplomats entered Egyptian possessions in Syria-Palestine during the New Kingdom; the route was well equipped with fortifications, wells, and way-stations.

An extensive network of roads in the desert west of Thebes is being explored by the Luxor-Farshût Desert Road Survey, led by John Darnell of Yale University; the survey is beginning to yield a picture of the routes by which traders, pilgrims, and soldiers traveled by land from the Predynastic period onward. Throughout Egyptian history, mining and trading expeditions traveled through the Wadi Hammamat; vast expeditions are claimed, with one comprising as many as seventeen thousand men. Desert routes required regular watering stations, and the finding of wells might be portrayed as a miraculous event; likewise, the provision of wells can be advertised as an act of royal beneficence, as in the Wadi Mia inscription of Sety I. In the Ptolemaic and Roman periods, a desert route leading southeast, from Coptos to the port city of Berenice on the Red Sea coast, became active. Persons traveling through the Eastern Desert during the Roman period were at least occasionally taxed, evidently to support security forces in the area.

Land transportation was mainly carried out by donkey caravan. Wheeled transport vehicles are not attested before the eighteenth dynasty (i.e., the use of wagons to haul boats or boat components in Syria, under Thutmose III). The camel is not attested as a beast of burden in Egypt before the Ptolemaic period, and it becomes a true economic asset by the Roman period.

[*See also* Seafaring; *and* Ships and Shipbuilding.]

BIBLIOGRAPHY

Casson, L. *Ships and Seamanship in the Ancient World.* Princeton, 1971. The classic and indispensable introduction to the subject, although the discussion of ancient Egypt is not as strong as the discussion of the Greco-Roman world.

Casson, L. *The Periplus Maris Erythraei.* Princeton, 1989. A specialized but still accessible work on trade in the Greco-Roman Red Sea.

Gardiner, A. H. "Ramesside Texts Relating to the Taxation and Transport of Corn." *Journal of Egyptian Archaeology* 27 (1941). Classic contribution to the study of Egyptian grain transportation in the late New Kingdom.

Gophna, R. "Egyptian Trading Posts in Southern Canaan at the Dawn of the Archaic Period." *Egypt, Israel, Sinai, Archaeological and Historical Relationships in the Biblical Period,* edited by A. F. Rainey, chapter 1. Jerusalem, 1987.

Jones, D. *A Glossary of Ancient Egyptian Nautical Titles and Terms.* London, 1988. A specialist work, but the first place to begin building bibliography on most nautical subjects.

Jones, D. *Boats.* Austin, 1995. A popular introduction to boats and ships of ancient Egypt.

Lipke, P. *The Royal Ship of Cheops.* BAR International Series, 225. National Maritime Museum, Greenwich, Archaeological Series, 9. Oxford, 1984. A comprehensive and extremely useful archaeological and naval-architectural study of the fourth dynasty Khufu (Cheops) ship.

Oren, E. "The 'Ways of Horus' in North Sinai." In *Egypt, Israel, Sinai, Archaeological and Historical Relationships in the Biblical Period,* edited by A. F. Rainey, chapter 5. Jerusalem, 1987.

Partridge, Robert. *Transport in Ancient Egypt.* London, 1996.

Vinson, S. *The Nile Boatman at Work, 1200 BCE–400 CE.* Munich, 1998. A socioeconomic study of Nile boat captains and their crews.

Vinson, S. *Egyptian Boats and Ships,* Shire Egyptology Series, 20. Princes Risborough, 1994. A popular introduction to ships and boats in ancient Egypt.

STEVE VINSON

TREES. *See* Flora.

TUNA EL-GEBEL. *See* Hermopolis.

TURA. *See* Quarries and Mines.

TURIN CANON. *See* King Lists.

TURQUOISE. *See* Gems.

TUTANKHAMUN (r. 1355–1346 BCE) eleventh king of the eighteenth dynasty and the last of that dynasty whose consaguineous ties to the royal family are beyond doubt. Born at Amarna, he was first called Tutankhaten ("living image of [the sun god] Aten"), a name documenting an intimate association with Akhenaten (r. 1372–1355 BCE), who in all probability was his father. Information is lacking about Tutankhamun's mother, but since no document from his reign names her, she may be presumed to have died before his accession.

The suspicion that Tutankhamun could have been a usurper was dispelled in 1922 by the discovery of his tomb; the examination and analysis of his mummy revealed that he was a teenager when he died (and thus a child at his accession, since he reigned about a decade). Small-scale objects from his tomb, made for a child-king, confirm his tender age at accession.

The representations and texts on the gold throne found in the tomb prove that Tutankhamun's queen was Akhenaten's and Nefertiti's third daughter Ankhesenpaaten. The names of the royal couple in the inscriptions on the throne were altered in antiquity to read "Tutankhamun and Ankhesenamun," in conformity with the policy that restored Amun to the preeminence that he had enjoyed among the gods before Akhenaten's "revolution."

Tutankhamun has often been considered a relatively unimportant ruler and his reign has been dismissed, yet the monuments tell another story. During the decade in which he occupied the throne, extensive restoration was undertaken to repair damage inflicted on Amun's cult in the iconoclastic phase of Akhenaten's reign. Simultaneously, the first official attacks on Akhenaten's memory occurred. Such policy decisions, as reflected in the alteration of the king's name from Tutankhaten to Tutankhamun, were taken early in his reign, perhaps as early as the brief period between the death and burial of his predecessor, Smenkhkare. Tutankhamun's extreme youth precludes attributing the initiative for those moves to the king himself; undoubtedly, both the "God's Father" Ay (r. 1346–1343 BCE) and General Horemheb (r. 1343–1315 BCE), who succeeded Tutankhamun, played major roles in the politics of the period, but whether as allies or rivals is not known.

During Tutankhamun's first regnal year, the court and administration were moved from Akhetaten (Amarna) to Memphis. Tutankhamun was in residence there when a decree was issued in his name to refurbish and re-endow the temples neglected during Akhenaten's reign. The cult of the deified living ruler, as it was practiced before the Amarna period, was also revived for Tutankhamun. Pictorial references to military activity in the Near East and Nubia are preserved in reliefs at Karnak temple and in the tomb of Horemheb at Memphis, but the historicity of those events is problematic.

The cause of Tutankhamun's death is not known, despite repeated but unsubstantiated claims that he was assassinated. Ay, who survived him by only a few years, honored his memory, but under Horemheb, Tutankhamun's monuments were regularly usurped. His tomb, number 62 in the Valley of the Kings, however, remained inviolate. Howard Carter's discovery of it in 1922 was one of the most spectacular archaeological finds of the twentieth century. Seventy-five years later, the majority of the objects from the tomb still await study and publication.

[See also the entry on Howard Carter.]

BIBLIOGRAPHY

Eaton-Krauss, Marianne. "Neue Forschungen zum Schatz des Tutanchamun." *Antike Welt* 22.2 (1991), 97–105. Includes preliminary results of research on the thrones from the tomb.

Eaton-Krauss, Marianne. *The Sarcophagus in the Tomb of Tutankhamun.* Oxford, 1993. Publication on the sarcophagus, arguing that it was among the items of funerary equipment usurped from Tutankhamun's predecessor, Smenkhkare.

Eaton-Krauss, Marianne, and William J. Murnane. "Tutankhamun, Ay, and the Avenue of Sphinxes between Pylon X and the Mut Precinct at Karnak," *Bulletin de la Société d'égyptologie de Genève* 15 (1991), 31–38. Reviews the evidence for Ay's attitude toward Tutankhamun and for the persecution of Akhenaten's memory during Tutankhamun's reign.

Reeves, Nicholas. *The Complete Tutankhamun: The King, the Tomb, the Royal Treasure.* London, 1990. Retells the story of the tomb's discovery and surveys the equipment included with the burial; includes summary comments on the person of Tutankhamun (best consulted in conjunction with the review by M. Eaton-Krauss, *Journal of Egyptian Archaeology* 80 [1994], 253–256).

MARIANNE EATON-KRAUSS

TWELFTH DYNASTY. A period of slightly over two hundred years, was ruled by a single royal family in the Middle Kingdom. A sound administration was developed and foreign involvement was increased, so this dynasty represents a high point in social structure and the governance of the nomes (provinces), as well as in art, architecture, and literature. In the Turin Canon, a list of the pharoahs, this dynasty's rulers are designated as "[kings] of the Residence of Itj-tawy," followed by a summation as "kings of the Residence [of Itj-tawy] 8, amounting to 213 years, 1 month, and 17 days."

These achievements had ensued through a series of positive circumstances. The eleventh dynasty had benefited from the success of the previous Herakleopolitan dynasties' reconquest and consolidation of the Nile Delta, thus preventing foreign incursions. The rulers of the twelfth dynasty thereby profited from this situation and from the activities of the eleventh dynasty's rulers, the Montuhoteps of Thebes, who opened the quarries in the Eastern and Western Deserts, forged the route to the Red Sea through the Wadi Hammamat, and renewed control of Nubia, to the south.

The documentation for the twelfth dynasty is impressive and diverse, including autobiographies of the local governors in their rock-cut tombs, numerous stelae and royal stelae, letters, accounting ledgers, annals for part of one reign, and the propagandizing tendencies in the extensive literature developed during the dynasty.

The chronology of the dynasty has been in revision on the basis of several investigations. For many years, the accepted range was 1991–1786 BCE, but today three considerations have become pertinent: (1) the reevaluation of the existence or nonexistence of several coregencies; (2) the length of the reigns of Senwosret II and III; and (3) the validity of the astronomical reckoning of the heliacal rising of Sirius, in the seventh year of a ruler assumed to be Senwosret III, as observed in the North at Heliopolis-Memphis (a higher date) or in the South at Elephantine-Aswan (a lower date).

Evidence for the foundation of the twelfth dynasty rests on various sources of different nature and authority. In order of importance, they are dated contemporary documents, king lists, and literary compositions. The Turin Canon records a period of seven years after the end of the eleventh dynasty as a lacuna in its records. According to the Egyptian priest and historian, Manetho, an Amenemhet (I ?) is placed after the end of the eleventh dynasty and before the twelfth. Most scholars believe that the compilation in the Turin Canon reflects a gap in the source, which would be unusual. Rather, the lacuna may reflect a period of disturbance, anarchy, and lack of a recognized kingship. In those seven years of the Turin list, it is logical to fit the two-year reign of Montuhotep III, perhaps the last of his line, or else this last Montuhotep may have filled out the seven years. He is attested in inscriptions that record an expedition to the Wadi Hammamat to find a sarcophagus and lid for his burial—and the official in charge of this force of 10,000 men was his vizier, Amenemhet, whom scholars recognize as the founder of the twelfth dynasty, ruling as Amenemhet I. [*See* Amenemhet I.]

After assuming the kingship, Amenemhet recognized the necessity of ruling from the North, instead of from Thebes, and founded a new city in the vicinity of Memphis, named with due modesty, "Amenemhet takes possession of the two lands (Itj-tawy)." This capital has yet to be located, but it is assumed to lie in the neighborhood of the pyramids of the first rulers of the dynasty at el-Lisht, just south of Memphis. The name may in fact derive from the *Itj* of Itj-tawy. Of Amenemhet's ancestry, little is known, but a literary text, the *Prophecy of Neferti*, indicates that he was from the South and that his mother was from Ta-Seti (the First Cataract region). Curiously, few dated monuments (of officials or the kingship) have been attested for his reign. His twenty-ninth regnal year is known from Nubia and his death in his thirtieth is known from the *Story of Sinuhe*. He is known from his pyramid at el-Lisht and a few texts, reliefs, and statuary. Based in plan on the pyramid complexes of the Old Kingdom, and utilizing stone borrowed from their monuments, his pyramid has presented more problems than solutions. He and his successor are represented in the same scene on foundations blocks in his destroyed mortuary temple—a possible argument for their coregency. Surrounding his pyramid were the chapels and burials of his queens and officials, among which is the *mastaba* tomb of his well-attested vizier Intef-oker—who continued in office in the reign of his successor Senwosret I—and his steward Rohuerdjersen.

That a new era was at hand is clear from several sources. The literary composition known as the *Prophecy of Neferti* was set in the court of Sneferu, the founder of the fourth dynasty. It predicts a time of troubles, the Delta overrun by Asiatic infiltrators, the land governed by several rulers, the land subjected to anarchy and natural disasters but finally rescued by a savior king from the South, "Ameny," in whom we recognize Amenemhet I, evidently a usurper and not of the Montuhotep family. Later in his reign, he altered his titulary to include the name, "Repeater of Births (Manifestations)," perhaps thereby proclaiming a kind of Renaissance. [*See* Neferti.]

The circumstances surrounding the king's death in his thirtieth year were reflected in tradition through several literary texts. In the posthumous literary *Instructions* to his son, details were given of his assassination or attempted assassination. The king boasts of his regime but bewails the lack of appreciation of his followers and his harem, which resulted in the attack on his life. In the *Story of Sinuhe*, the protagonist flees in panic on overhearing the reporting of the king's death to his son and successor. Sinuhe flees, ends up in Palestine, is befriended by a local chief, given land and the hand of the chief's daughter, fights a local bully (a prototype of the David–Goliath battle), and returns to Egypt to be honored by Senwosret I. The depiction of the Egyptian royal court and the entourage of the queen and her children who remember Sinuhe and his desire to be buried properly at home and not abroad are rare details of life at that time. [*See* Sinuhe.]

On the basis of the text of the *Instructions* and the citation in Manetho of an assassination of a King Amenemhet, it is possible that an unsuccessful assassination attempt resulted in Amenemhet's decision to associate his son Senwosret with him, as joint king, in a coregency that spanned the latter part of Amenemhet's reign but not necessarily the traditional ten-year coregency that was, until recently, assumed by Egyptologists. Alternatively, the assassination may have been successful, inspiring Sinuhe's precipitous flight on hearing the news, a situation that argues against a coregency. The nature of these circumstances has been colored by the three literary, essentially nonhistorical texts: the *Prophecy of Neferti*, the *Instructions of Amenemhet*, and the *Story of Sinuhe*.

Amenemhet managed to control the infiltration of Asiatics into the eastern region of the Nile Delta by building of a line of forts, "the walls of the prince," to maintain a watch along the border. In the South, there is evidence of his campaigns in Nubia and control of the southern borders.

The second ruler of the dynasty was Senwosret I, in whose forty-five-year reign an extraordinary amount of building took place throughout the land, with major construction at many of the great temple sites. Particularly notable is the "white chapel," now in the open-air museum at Karnak, a peripteral barque-shrine of fine limestone, built on the occasion of his *sed*-festival; it has been reassembled from its blocks that were reused by a later ruler in one of the great pylons. The workmanship of the scenes and texts in relief is outstanding, with fine internal detail in the hieroglyphs. Around the base is a list of the nomes (provinces), with their local deities, and a record of the length of each nome of Upper Egypt along the Nile. The temple of Karnak was also rebuilt in his reign. According to a recent interpretation, it was founded on 21 December (Gregorian) in 1946 BCE, on the azimuth (a measurement of a heavenly body) of the sunrise. The deity Amun of Thebes was the southern counterpart of the Heliopolitan deity Re-Atum. [*See* Senwosret I.]

In both royal and nonroyal texts, mention was made of the refurbishing of temples after a period of neglect and destruction. Athough such statements were conventional, in the case of the twelfth dynasty, a period of destruction may well have occurred during the years just before its advent. At Elephantine, part of the temple has recently been restored, with its exceptional reliefs. The temple at Coptos has reliefs that show the king celebrating his *sed*-festival, which occurred in his thirty-first year. An important inscription from the temple at Tod also deserves mention.

At el-Lisht, the royal pyramid north of that of Senwosret I's father's was modeled on those of the sixth dynasty. Twelve life-size seated statues were originally placed around its court. The tomb of Senwosret I's important seal-bearer, Montuhotep, was built adjacent to the pyramid. Montuhotep had commissioned several statues of himself in the temple of Karnak, as well as a memorial chapel at Abydos, having a large stela with a lengthy text. He was the likely administrator of the vast temple and royal building projects carried out during the reign, supervising the construction, architecture, and art. Several rolls of papyri probably dating to this reign, found on a coffin in a tomb at a cemetery on the eastern bank of the Nile, opposite Abydos, preserve the accounting of the construction crews with their rations. The lists are arranged with the name of the foreman, followed by the names of the workmen. The men seem to be part of a permanent construction gang that was sent as far away as Coptos to carry out building projects. Some of the officials cited in this archive built memorial chapels west of the river at Abydos and are known from their stelae.

The thirty-five-year reign of Amenemhet II is the least known of the twelfth dynasty, with few datable sources. An exception is a large fragment of annals recorded on two blocks of granite at Memphis; the largest block was reused as the base for a statue of Ramesses II and was first noted in 1956 (but only fully published in 1991). It records a mixture of cult and political matters—religious events, festival celebrations, accounts of offerings, the sending of troops abroad, the mention of two previously unknown Near Eastern states, the tribute brought by Nubian princes, the gifts sent by Near Eastern princes, a bird-catching expedition of the king, some rewards to his officials, and other subjects. From his reign, a deposit of silver vessels and other precious objects of Aegean workmanship was discovered at the temple at Tod.

The following reign of Senwosret II has several dates in his sixth regnal year and a probable eighth year faintly inscribed on a stela from Nubia. So it is difficult to ascribe more than ten years to his reign. However, a diverse series of documents on papyrus comprises a vast amount of material from his pyramid temple and the pyramid townsite at Illahun, which extended into the following reigns and well into the thirteenth dynasty. These include conveyances of property, lists of goods, enumerations of households, pages from temple registers, lists of temple furniture, letters and model letters, mathematical exercises, accounts of laborers, a series of hymns to Senwosret III, medical texts on midwifery, and even a veterinary manual.

Senwosret II was succeeded by his son Senwosret III, whose last clearly recorded regnal year was his nineteenth. A recent hypothesis suggests that he may have lived into his fortieth regnal year; having been deified in his lifetime, he deserted his prepared pyramid site at Dahshur, created a vast burial (?) and funerary temple site at Abydos, and handed over the reins of administration to his son Amenemhet III as the active partner in a twenty-year-long coregency, with the years recorded in terms of the reign of the latter. One argument for this coregency is the attested forty-six-year-long reign of Amenemhet III, who built two pyramid complexes, one at Dahshur and one at Hawara. Senwosret III is particularly associated with Nubia, where he was depicted as a god in the temple reliefs of the New Kingdom. A boundary marker at the fortress of Semna records his boast that he extended his borders farther south than any of predecessors. In the text, he characterized the Nubians as base cowards, indicating that he captured their women and adherents, seized their cattle, and cut down and set fire to their grain. In a well-known passage at the end of the text, he indicated that any son of his who maintained this boundary is a real son, but any son who failed to fight for it was not his son: "he was not born to me." He also campaigned in Palestine, during the course of which one of his officers, named Khuwy-Sobek, cited a battle at Sekmem, possibly the biblical Shechem.

Among the papyri found at Illahun, mentioned above, was a cycle of songs or hymns to Senwosret III, which defined the nature of the kingship. The king is addressed as one:

> protecting the land, extending your borders,
> overwhelming the foreign lands with your crown, . . .
> The tongue of your Majesty restrains Nubia,
> and your words rout the Near Easterners. . . .
> letting men sleep until daybreak.
>
> How joyful are [your gods],
>   for you have reestablished their offerings.
> How joyful are your [people],
>   for you have fixed their boundaries. . . .
> How joyful are the Egyptians because of your might,
>   for you have protected [their] traditions.

These selected phrases from the text vaunt the ruler as a warrior who extended the borders, to dominate the Nubians and Near Easterners, as well as a benevolent, concerned protector of his own people, a shepherd of the citizens.

Many of the sites away from the main cities and temple areas are noted for the rock-cut tombs of the governors of the nomes (the provinces) of Upper Egypt. They essentially replaced the *mastaba* chapels and tombs of the Old Kingdom that were centered around the pyramid sites of the rulers of the fourth to the sixth dynasty at Giza and at Saqqara. The construction of these tombs entailed large expanses of wall painting or carved relief with many of the themes repeating the same subjects of the Old Kingdom tombs: the owner seated in front of offering breads, with other food and drink; daily life on his estate; viewing the census of cattle; scribes recording his income; the provision of food, drink, clothing, and oils; the ploughing and sowing of barley and emmer wheat; the threshing, winnowing, and delivery of the grain; the breeding and raising of cattle; milking; butchering; fowling and fishing; the raising of domesticated fowl; hunting in the desert and bringing the desert animals to the owner (oryx, antelope, hyena, etc.); food preparation—baking, brewing, cooking, and the activities of the kitchen; workshops with carpenters hewing timbers to construct boats, beds, chairs, and a variety of furniture; jewelers stringing necklaces and leatherworkers preparing their hides. The main sites for these rock-cut tombs were Elephantine-Aswan (in the first Upper Egyptian nome), Beni Hasan (in the sixteenth Upper Egyptian nome), Bersheh (in the fifteenth Upper Egyptian nome), Meir (in the fourteenth Upper Egyptian nome), and Asyut (in the thirteenth Upper Egyptian nome), as well as several other nomes.

In a tomb at Beni Hasan, dated in the sixth regnal year of Senwosret II, there is a scene of bedouin bringing products from the Eastern Desert, including galena (lead ore). They are shown in their colorful un-Egyptian dress, and a young member of the group is near a donkey laden with a bellows. The leader's name, Abi-Shar, is Semitic, and he is designated as a "chief of the desert lands," a term that was later represented by the designation Hyksos.

At Bersheh, there is a unique scene in the tomb chapel of Djehutyhotep of twenty-one pairs of men, with supervisors (more than fifty men), dragging a large statue of the tomb owner (or, less probably, the king) on a sledge, possibly from the travertine quarry to the local temple or to the man's tomb. The statue is estimated to be 7 meters (22 feet) high and 18 tons, and it may have been barged across the Nile. Even larger statues were known to have been barged in later times.

The twelfth dynasty came to an end with the short reigns of Amenemhet IV (nine years) and a ruling queen, Sobekneferu (four years). The Turin Canon then indicates a break. Amenemhet IV, having had a short coregency with his father, probably attained the throne at an advanced age. As in his father's reign, trade was continued with Byblos, on the coast of Lebanon, with the exchange of royal gifts to the local governors. The last ruler of this dynasty, Queen Sobekneferu, was recognized in the king lists and, like Nitokerty, the ruling queen at the end of the sixth dynasty, brought the twelfth dynasty to an end.

These rulers of the Middle Kingdom built pyramids in the style of their predecessors of the Old Kingdom, and their queens and officials built their tombs in the vicinity of the pyramids of the kings. The great pyramid sites of the Old Kingdom at Giza and Saqqara, but not Dahshur, were neglected in favor of burial sites at el-Lisht (Amenemhet I, Senwosret I), Dahshur (Amenemhet II, Senwosret III, Amenemhet III), Illahun (Senwosret II), and Hawara (a second site for Amenemhet III). The burials of the queens and princesses have yielded outstanding jewelry.

Abydos, in the eighth Upper Egyptian nome, was the sacred precinct of the god Osiris—and the original burial site of the rulers of the first two dynasties. In the twelfth dynasty, Abydos became a pilgrimage site. Officials from throughout the land set up memorial chapels on the processional route to the graves of the early kings. These chapels included inscribed stelae, offering tables, and statuary. Thousands of these elements were somewhat unsystematically removed at the end of the nineteenth century and are now in the Egyptian Museum in Cairo, as well as in museums in Europe and America. The text of one of the major stelae indicates that an official of Senwosret III, named Ikhernofret, was sent by the king to Abydos to fashion the ritual equipment and to conduct the great procession and the enactment of the "mysteries" of the worship of Osiris. The stelae of these officials attest to their loyalty to Osiris and to their hope for eternal favor in his following, the perpetual viewing of the rites, and the receiving of offerings and the inhaling of the incense. [*See* Ikhernofret.]

In the Old Kingdom, from the last king of the fifth dynasty onwards, a series of spells was inscribed in the underground chambers of the rulers. Known as the Pyramid Texts, they were composed to facilitate the king's ascent to the celestial regions and to join the gods. In the Middle Kingdom, these spells were revised, extended, and reinterpreted to benefit ordinary nonroyal mortals, and they were inscribed on the interior of the wooden coffins, hence their designation, the Coffin Texts. One of the more interesting set of spells is known as the *Book of the Two Ways*—it is essentially a map of the afterworld inscribed on the inside of the coffin, below the mummy. [*See* Coffin Texts *and* Pyramid Texts.]

The twelfth dynasty was characterized by accomplishments on several levels: the rise of a successful bureaucracy with professional administrators, including the viziers and army commanders; the development of the Faiyum basin for agriculture; the increased exploitation of quarries in the Sinai for turquoise and quarries in the Eastern Desert for the hard stone used in statuary and building and the gem-quality precious stones, such as amethyst, for jewelry; the control of trade with Nubia with the creation of a series of fortresses along the Nile in upper Nubia; and the establishment of Egyptian relations with the city-states of Palestine and Syria, during which the name of Jerusalem first appeared in documents.

It was the golden age of literature. Major compositions were *Sinuhe*, *The Man Who Was Weary of Life*, the *Satire on the Trades*, the *Book of Kemit*, and several compositions set in earlier times but now established as authored in the twelfth dynasty: The *Instructions for Merikare*, *The Eloquent Peasant*, as well as *The Story of King Cheops and the Magicians*. The *Instructions of Ptahhotep* is probably to be assigned to the dynasty.

It was also a golden age of art and architecture, both on the royal level—with the outstanding series of royal statues, pyramids, and temple components—and on the private level—with the painted tombs of the nomarchs in the provinces, the stelae and statuary of the officials of the bureaucracy, and the statuary in the sanctuary of the deified Heqaib at Elephantine.

[*See* Amenemhet III; Eloquent Peasant; Historical Sources, *articles on* Archaeological and Artistic Evidence *and* Textual Evidence; Instructions for Merikare; Kemit; King Lists; Man Who Was Weary of Life; Middle Kingdom; Senwosret III; *and* Sobekneferu.]

BIBLIOGRAPHY
Altenmüller Hartwig, and Ahmed Moussa, "Die Inschrift Amenemhets II. aus dem Ptah-Tempel von Memphis. Vorbericht," *Studien zur Altägyptischen Kultur* 18 (1991), 1–48, with folding plate. Important annals of an early year of the king.
Arnold, Dorothea. "Amenemhat I and the Early Twelfth Dynasty at Thebes," *Metropolitan Museum of Art Journal* 26 (1991), 5–48. Considers the activity in building at Thebes before the move north to Itj-tawy; dates the Hekanahkte archive to the time of Senwosret I, not to the Eleventh Dynasty.
Clère, J.-J. "Histoire des XIe et XIIe Dynasties égyptiennes," *Cahiers d'Histoire Mondiale I* (1954), 643–668.
Franke, Detlef. *Das Heiligtum des Heqaib im Elephantine: Geschichte eines Provinzheiligtums im Mittleren Reich*. Heidelberg, Studien zur Archäologie und Geschichte Altägyptens 9, 1994. Has translations of texts important for the study of the dynasty.
Gasse, Annie. "Améni, un porte-parole sous le règne de Sésostris Ier," *Bulletin de l'Institut Français d'Archéologie Orientale* 88 (1988), 83–94. Studies the career of this official based on a text from the Wadi Hammamat.
Hayes, William C. "The Middle Kingdom in Egypt: Internal History from the Rise of the Herakleopolitans to the Death of Ammenemes III," in: I.E.S. Edwards and others (eds.), *The Cambridge Ancient History*, 3d ed. vol. I, Part 2: *Early History of the Middle East*, 1971, pp. 464–531; "Egypt: From the Death of Ammenemes III to Seqene-
nre II," *The Cambridge Ancient History*, 3d ed., vol. II, Part 1, *History of the Middle East and the Aegean Region c. 1800–1380 B.C.* 1973, pp. 42–76. Still the most reliable and extensive treatment of the subject (and brought up to date by Vandersleyen in 1995).
Hirsch, Eileen. "Die Kultpolitik Amenemhets I. im Thebanischen Gau," in: Rolf Gundlach and Matthias Rochholz (eds.), *Ägyptische Tempel-Struktur, Funktion und Programm* (HÄB 37) Hildesheim (1994), 137–142.
Matzker, Ingo. *Die letzten Könige der 12. Dynastie*, Frankfurt am Main, 1986.
Obsomer, Claude. *Sésostris Ier: Étude Chronologique et Historique du Règne*, Brussels, 1995. Rejects the coregency of Amenemhet I and Senwosret I.
Parkinson, Richard. *Voices from Ancient Egypt: An Anthology of Middle Kingdom Writings.* London, 1991.
Quirke, Stephen. *The Administration of Egypt in the Late Middle Kingdom: The Hieratic Documents*, New Malden, Surrey, 1990.
Simpson, William K. "Mentuhotep, Vizier of Sesostris I, Patron of Art and Architecture," *Mitteilungen des Deutschen Archäologischen Instituts, Abteilung Kairo* 47 (1991), 331–340.
Simpson, William K. *The Terrace of the Great God at Abydos: The Offering Chapels of Dynasties 12 and 13*, Publications of the Pennsylvania–Yale Expedition to Egypt 5, New Haven, 1974.
Strauß-Seber, Christine. "Zu Bildprogramm und Funktion der Weißen Kapelle in Karnak," in: Rolf Gundlach and Matthias Rochholz (eds.), *Ägyptische Tempel-Struktur, Funktion und Programm* (HÄB 37) Hildesheim (1994), 287–318. Thorough analysis of the "kiosk" of Senwosret I at Karnak.
Vandersleyen, Claude. *L'Egypte et la Vallée du Nil*, Tome 2: *De la fin de l'Ancien Empire à la fin du Nouvel Empire*. Paris: La Nouvelle Clio, Presses Universitaires de France, 1995, 43–122. Up-to-date and thorough analysis of the dynasty, based on the 1971 and 1973 works of Hayes.
Wegner, Josef. "The Nature and Chronology of the Senwosret III-Amenemhat III Regnal Succession: Some Considerations Based on New Evidence from the Mortuary Temple of Senwosret III at Abydos," *Journal of Near Eastern Studies* 55 (1996), 249–279. A detailed study in which a long (twenty-year) coregency between these rulers is proposed, probably beginning after the nineteenth regnal year of Senwosret III.

WILLIAM KELLY SIMPSON

TWENTIETH DYNASTY. *See* New Kingdom, *article on* Twentieth Dynasty.

TWENTY-FIFTH DYNASTY. Traditionally, a series of four kings of Kush (Upper Nubia, in the northern Sudan) who ruled also as pharaohs of Egypt; two of their predecessors also intervened in Egypt but did not effectively rule north of Thebes. By the late ninth to early eighth centuries BCE at the latest, a line of local rulers ruled (apparently) from Napata (modern Gebel Barkal) below the Fourth Cataract of the Nile; they are known only from their burials at nearby el-Kurru. Later inscriptions name a ruler Alara who perhaps preceded the first historically known kings, Kashta and Piya. Through his intervention in Egypt, Piya can be shown to have ascended the throne of Kush quite soon after about 750 BCE, such that Kashta before him may have ruled in Kush from about 760 BCE. Kashta reoccupied the long, relatively poor valley of the Nile from the Second Cataract all the way north to the First, imposing his authority on Egypt's southernmost town, Aswan, where in pharaonic style he dedicated a stela in the temple of the local god, Khnum. As an adherent of Amun, god of Thebes, it is possible that Kashta thrust even farther north and sought to include Thebes itself within his domain; but this is very uncertain.

Kashta's successor Piya certainly laid claim to Thebes, and had troops and garrisons in place in Upper Egypt even before his great campaign through Egypt in his Year 20, about 728 BCE. As Theban Amun's fervent worshiper and defender, he was sensitive to anyone else's pretensions to rule over Amun's home domain. Thus, when Tefnakht, prince of the western Nile Delta, began steadily to take over one province after another in northern and middle Upper Egypt, moving steadily southward, Piya was evidently convinced that he might lose Thebes to the northern intruder if nothing were done. The inability of his local commanders to cope stirred him at last into mounting a full campaign, overcoming opposition all the way to Memphis, Egypt's traditional administrative capital and the junction-point of the Two Lands (like Cairo today). Thence, Tefnakht retreated to his own center at Sais, and to the security of his Delta swamplands. Piya had himself accepted by the sun god Re at Heliopolis, receiving the submission in person of all the Delta's local rulers other than Tefnakht, who simply sent his envoy. However, Piya did not stay to rule Egypt in person, but returned to Kush. Back in Napata, he added pylons and a great columned hall in front of Amun's venerable temple at the foot of the "holy mountain" (Gebel Barkal), to become a local equivalent of the pylons and pillared halls of Amun's home temple of Karnak in Thebes. A huge victory stela and scenes on temple walls proclaim his passing ascendancy in Egypt. Theban papyri were now dated by his reign; he had installed his sister (or half-sister) Amenirdis I as the next "God's Wife of Amun" (high priestess and king's representative) at Thebes. But otherwise Egypt was left to its own devices: to the local princes, and to Tefnakht, who declared himself king but wisely did not return south of Memphis.

Piya's successor Shabaqa was not content to rule only in Kush, and in his second year he swept down the Nile into Egypt, took Memphis, and (according to the tradition in Manetho) captured Tefnakht's successor Bakenrenef and "burned him alive." However that may be, an Apis bull, sacred to the god Ptah of Memphis, had just died. It was being prepared for burial in Year 6 of Bakenrenef, which became Year 2 of Shabaqa (by conquest) before the vault was closed upon the bull's mummy. In modern, absolute terms, the date of that eventful year is not generally agreed, but it certainly seems to belong bracketed within 715 and 712 BCE, with Shabaqa's accession in Kush falling within 716–713 BCE. In 716 BCE, the Assyrian record is very clear: Sargon II at el-Arish, uncomfortably near Egypt's eastern border, received a gift of twelve horses from Shilkanni, king of Egypt (*Musri*). Tanis was the seat of the princedom nearest to the northeastern border, and it is clear to most scholars that the name "Shilkanni" is shortened from *Ushilkanni, Usilkan/(O)sorkon. This would be the last explicit mention of that Osorkon IV who was ruling from Tanis and Bubastis only a dozen years before, and who had then submitted to Piya. In 712 BCE, Iamani, rebel ruler of Ashdod, fled to Egypt, only to be handed back to the Assyrians by a potentate who ruled not only Egypt but also Nubia. A newly published text (Frame 1999; Redford 1999) names Shabataqa as "king," returning Iamani to Sargon II in (only) 706 BCE. If so, then it is possible that Shabataqa was coregent with Shabaqa during at least 706–702 BCE. The term "pir'u of Musri" ("pharaoh of Egypt") had been thought to be exclusively used of Delta dynasts, rather than of Shabaqa from Nubia. But reconsideration of the full evidence shows that, right from the start, the Nubian rulers were themselves called "Pharaoh Piya," "Pharaoh Shabaqa," "Pharaoh Taharqa," etc., in the papyri of this period. So both "pir'u of Musri" ("pharaoh of Egypt") and "ruler of Nubia" (*Meluhha*) are valid cuneiform titles for Nubian kings ruling Egypt. Thus, Shabaqa took over Egypt either as early as 716 BCE, or as late as 712, or at some date in between. The minimum date for the fourteen or fifteen years of Shabaqa might (by some authorities) be set at about 713/712 to 698 BCE; the higher date according to other scholars would be about 716/715 to 702 BCE. The low date is probably concluded by the new text of Sargon II, mentioned above.

One more Assyrian historical datum intervenes here: Sennacherib's invasion of Palestine in 701 BCE, to suppress a revolt by Philistine and Hebrew vassals. The Assyrian account names the various Levantine dynasts, including "Hazakiau" the Judean, clearly the Hezekiah king of Judah of the biblical sources (*2 Kings* 18.17–19.37; *Isaiah* 36–37). Both Assyrian and biblical sources also agree that within a decade of this, Sennacherib was murdered (*2 Kings* 19.36–37, or *Isaiah* 37.37–38; A. L. Oppenheim, in Pritchard, 1950–1969, p. 288 § [b]). The biblical sources name Taharqa as present in the Palestinian conflict in 701 BCE, referring to him as a king. Since their mention of the murder of Sennacherib cannot predate its occurrence in 681 BCE, the present form of those narratives does not predate 681 either, by which time Taharqa had been king for a decade; hence, the (by then) familiar title was applied to him in such writings of 681 or later. This is exactly parallel to the way in which Taharqa (when king) referred back to himself as "His Majesty" when mentioning his activities while he was still a prince (in Kawa Stela IV). If a minimal chronology is adopted for Shabaqa, then he was reigning in 701 and sent Taharqa with the Egyptian force; if the higher dates are used, then it was the newly crowned Shabtaqa who did so. The latter option has advantages over the former, in that it is consistent with the friendly relations of Shabaqa with Assyria (returning the fugitive Iamani; exchanges of correspondence indicated by clay seals of Shabaqa from Nineveh), by contrast with the unusually bellicose titulary adopted by Shabtaqa, who also promptly summoned his younger brother Taharqa to bring an army some 3000 kilometers (2,000 miles), all the way from Upper Nubia to Lower Egypt. If the force was needed for use in the campaign of 701 BCE, this makes immediate sense, but not otherwise.

Leaving chronology's painful thorns aside, the history of the earlier twenty-fifth dynasty may now be sketched in its own right. Not too long after taking over Egypt, Shabaqa repatriated Iamani, rebel ruler of Ashdod, to Assyria; clay seals of Shabaqa from Nineveh demonstrate the continued good relations between the Nile monarchy and Assyria. Several datelined monuments punctuate the course of Shabaqa's rule over Egypt. These include Year 2 for both his first Apis burial at Memphis and a Nile flood text on the Karnak quay at Thebes, besides a donation stela at Pharbaithos in the Delta. At Bubastis, another stela is of Year 3, and at Buto is one of Year 6. Less certain is another Nile flood text of Year 4(?), while the Apis bull buried in a Year 14 was probably that installed in Shabaqa's Year 2. In Year 12, a graffito in Wadi Hammamat indicates that the Theban authorities were either quarrying stone or prospecting for minerals then. Finally, in Year 15 (Shabaqa's last) is dated the statue of a priest devoted to the cults of the gods Amun and Khons and of the late king Piya. In terms of public works (especially for the gods), Shabaqa made a modest but fresh start. At Memphis, he inscribed on a basalt block an ancient theological treatise written on a decayed papyrus. He also added minor shrines to Ptah's great precinct—one for the goddess Mut. At Thebes, he added minor chapels, and texts to Pylon IV at Karnak (refurbishing the "treasury" building), texts in the pylon gateway at Luxor, with a colonnade before it, and a new pylon gateway at the old temple in Medinet Habu, among other projects. In Nubia, his names occur at Kawa temple; at el-Kurru, he built a pyramid for his own burial.

Shabtaqa (or better, Shebitku; cf. Manetho's "Sebichos") followed his putative uncle Shabaqa either di-

rectly or after a brief coregency. Adopting bellicose titles (unlike any for seventy years past or almost any used later), it was most likely he who sent his younger brother Taharqa to join Philistia and Judah against Sennacherib, king of Assyria, in 701 BCE, especially considering that he caused Taharqa to bring an army almost 3000 kilometers (2,000 miles) from the depths of the Sudan, and no other war is known that would have required their deployment. The expedition failed, and the Kushite kings hesitated to intervene directly in Palestine thereafter. In internal matters, Shabtaqa's highest known dateline at present is Year 3 in a Nile flood text on Karnak quay in Thebes; a supposed "Year 10" (Leclant, *Lexikon der Ägyptologie*, 5: 515, 516 [n.1]), is a misunderstanding of Meek's cipher "Year *x*," meaning "year [*unknown/lost*]." In terms of monuments, it is often stated that Shabtaqa left almost no monuments as compared to Shabaqa, but this is a groundless exaggeration. Like Shabaqa, Shabtaqa worked at Memphis (blocks from buildings, statue, possibly at the Serapeum); he likewise worked at Karnak (as in the temple of Osiris Ruler of Eternity, and a chapel near the Sacred Lake), and at Luxor (new reliefs on the exterior southern wall). In Nubia, besides minor traces, he built his pyramid at el-Kurru, of almost the same dimensions (only 30 centimeters/10 inches shorter on each side) as that of Shabaqa. In Thebes, his aunt Amenirdis I was the reigning God's Wife of Amun, and might have already adopted Shabtaqa's sister Shepenupt II as her intended successor.

In 690 BCE, Taharqa duly ascended the thrones of Egypt and Kush, being crowned in Memphis. He did so, explicitly, "after the Falcon [Shabtaqa] had flown to heaven," that is, died; so there is no justification for inventing a coregency between Taharqa and his elder brother. Taharqa reigned for twenty-six years as the greatest and most active ruler of his line. The first half of his reign was a time of peace; the second half was troubled by Assyrian invasions, because the Assyrian kings suspected Taharqa of fomenting revolt among their Levantine vassals. During the peaceful years, most memorable was Year 6 (685 BCE) when an unusually high Nile flood inundated the Valley but brought the blessing of good crops, untainted by vermin, locusts, or wind-blight. As a youth, Taharqa had vowed to restore the Kawa temple in Kush; in his first ten years he achieved this, also endowing it richly, as his inscriptions there record. In Thebes he built on a truly monumental scale, adding noble colonnades in Karnak at the four cardinal points—in front of the temple of Amun (west), in front of the temple of Montu (north), in front of the East Temple (east), and in front of the temple of Khons (south). Within the Karnak precinct, he built a "high temple" with crypts just north of the sacred lake (replacing Shabaqa's work), and a series of minor chapels for

Osiris. Across the Nile, he erected a boundary wall around the Medinet Habu "old temple" and completed Shabaqa's pylon. In the deserts, a chapel of his stands in Bahria oasis to the west, and a text in Wadi Hammammat attests activity (quarrying?) in the Eastern Desert. In the North, Memphis had various minor works undertaken, and the care of the Apis bulls maintained (burial known from Year 24, 667 BCE). Nubia, too, benefited from his devotion, besides the Kawa temple. Taharqa built a new temple (B 300) at Gebel Barkal, added features to the Great Temple of Amun (B 500), and sculpted serpent figures on the mountain massif. Work was done northward at Buhen and Semna and by Kasr Ibrim. Tabo (Pnubs) and Sanam received temples, and southward some structure was built at Old Meroë. Taharqa built his pyramid at Nuri instead of el-Kurru; enigmatically, his name occurs in another pyramid up north at Sedeinga, but this may be a later work in which blocks of his were reused.

The clouds of war gathered in the 670s BCE. Esarhaddon, king of Assyria, defeated and executed the king of Sidon in 677 BCE, but saw Egypt as the source of disaffection. Therefore, he invaded Egypt in 674 BCE but was defeated, thanks doubtless to Egypto-Nubian mastery of the local topography unfamiliar to the Assyrians. But Esarhaddon returned in 671 BCE, when he was able to defeat Taharqa, sweep through to Memphis, and even capture members of the pharaoh's family there. However, this seemingly did not stop Taharqa's involvement in anti-Assyrian activity; Esarhaddon marched yet again on Egypt in 669 BCE but died on the way. His son Assurbanipal took up the challenge, invading Egypt in 667/666 BCE. The defeated Taharqa fled to Thebes, where Assurbanipal's forces followed him, but they did not pursue him when he fled onward into Kush. As total victor, Assurbanipal then imposed his formal overlordship on Egypt's local dynasts, taking their oaths and also leaving Assyrian governors in charge. But once the Great King was gone, many of the dynasts intrigued with the absent Taharqa. The Assyrian governorate arrested various dynasts for summary execution and sent some to Nineveh who suffered the same fate, except for Necho I of Sais, who pledged loyalty and was reappointed in Egypt by 665 BCE.

Shortly after this (in 664 BCE), Taharqa died, leaving the throne and the contest to his nephew Tanutamun. Inspired by a dream, the new king unwisely raised the standard of revolt, slaying Necho I, the leading Assyrian vassal. In vengeance, Assurbanipal yet again sent a punitive force (664/663 BCE) that soon took over Memphis, chasing up to Thebes after Tanutamun, who fled on into Kush. They sacked Thebes, and Tanutamun never ventured north again. The Nubian dominion was over, and the future of Egypt lay with the Delta princes, headed by Psam-

tik I, son of Necho. The real ruler of Thebes for much of this troubled period was its mayor, the redoubtable Montuemhat.

Historically and culturally, the twenty-fifth dynasty was a time of transition, a junction point between the Third Intermediate Period proper (twenty-first to twenty-fourth dynasties) and the Saite–Persian period that began with the twenty-sixth dynasty. Historically, there is an overlap. Superficially, the main Nubian rulers imposed an outward unity of rule, harbinger of the future under the twenty-sixth dynasty; they were full pharaohs of Egypt, by whose reigns all dates were reckoned, as well as being kings of Kush. But behind that façade, as in the late twenty-second/twenty-third dynasties, almost all the local dynasts stayed in power in their own fiefs; only the "crowned heads" in Sais, Tanis, and Leontopolis were removed for a time (Leontopolis, permanently). In administrative usage, the cursive script was evolving at this time: Hieratic into more cursive "Abnormal Hieratic," and into even more cursive Demotic, which became the principal script for use on secular papyri and ostraca with the twenty-sixth dynasty. In art, a return to models of the Old Kingdom had begun by the twenty-fifth dynasty's ascendancy, and developed on into the Saite age; in formal temple reliefs, we find high-quality, well-finished work using hieroglyphs that exhibit as much inner detail as fine Old and Middle Kingdom work. In royal titularies, the late twenty-second/twenty-third dynasties had already reverted to the simple style of the Horus, Twin-Goddess, and Golden Horus names typical of the Old and Middle Kingdoms, which continued in the twenty-fifth dynasty (with a return to cartouche names without secondary epithets) for the remainder of Egypt's indigenous dynasties; only Shabtaqa's use of the old "imperialist," New Kingdom-style titulary sticks out as different.

Finally, the fact remains that the twenty-fifth dynasty was by origin non-Egyptian. Before Piya's sweep through Egypt, its early kings had begun to use royal cartouches (Kashta); Piya's expedition brought him face to face with the full surviving architectural majesty of all Egypt, pyramids and huge temples alike, as well as into close contact with officials and priests who could explain Egyptian theology, ritual, and funeral usage to him. From his time, pyramids became the norm for royal tombs in Kush, even if burial modes inside them changed more slowly. Theban Amun probably provided the model for the worship of Amun at Napata and elsewhere, and indirectly for the rites of other gods by adaptation. As with the preceding Libyan dynasties, the Nubian rulers and their immediate families learned to revere Osiris for their hopes of an afterlife, and built appropriate chapels or cenotaphs at his holy city of Abydos. As Iuput, son of Sheshonq I, had done, so one of Piya's queens, Peksater, had a chapel built in Abydos. The lives, customs, and artifacts of Nubians below royal rank were probably much less affected for long enough; but Egyptian and Egyptianizing objects may have carried the nuance of prestige after Piya's odyssey.

[*See also* Napata; Piya; Shabaqa; *and* Taharqa.]

BIBLIOGRAPHY

Adams, William Y. *Nubia, Corridor to Africa.* London, 1977. Major survey of Nubian cultures from prehistory to medieval times, including the Napatan kingdom of the twenty-fifth dynasty.

Eide, Tormod, Tomas Hägg, Richard Holton Pierce, and László Török, eds. *Fontes Historiae Nubiorum: Textual Sources for the History of the Middle Nile Region between the Eighth Century BC and the Sixth Century AD*, vol. I, *From the Eighth to the Mid-Fifth Century BC.* Bergen, 1994. A comprehensive presentation in English of texts from, and concerning, Kushite rulers.

Frame, Grant. "The Inscription of Sargon II at Tang-i Var." *Orientalis* n.s. 68 (1999), 31–57.

James, T. G. H. "Egypt: the Twenty-fifth and Twenty-sixth Dynasties." In *The Cambridge Ancient History*, 2d ed., vol. 3, pt. 2, edited by John Boardman, I. E. S. Edwards, N. G. L. Hammond, E. Sollberger, C. B. F. Walker, pp. 677–708 (sections I–V). Cambridge, 1991. A critical appraisal of the sources for, and history of, the twenty-fifth dynasty.

Kendall, Timothy. "The Napatan Palace at Gebel Barkal, a First Look at B 1200." In *Egypt and Africa: Nubia from Prehistory to Islam*, edited by W. V. Davies, pp. 302–313. London, 1991. Provides a pioneer study of the building (B 1200) that was probably the Napatan palace of the twenty-fifth dynasty and its Kushite successors.

Kitchen, K. A. *The Third Intermediate Period in Egypt (1100–650 BC).* 2d ed. rev. Warminster, 1996. Includes full discussion of various views of the chronological and historical aspects of the dynasty in the light of the available facts.

Leclant, J. "Schabaka," "Schabataka," "Taharqa," "Tanutamun." In *Lexikon der Ägyptologie*, 5: 499–513, 514–519; 6: 155–184, 211–215. Wiesbaden, 1984–1986. Comprehensive surveys of these reigns (in French) with very detailed and valuable references.

Parker, Richard A. *A Saite Oracle Papyrus from Thebes in the Brooklyn Museum.* Brown Egyptological Studies, 4. Providence, 1962. Publicatuion of a remarkable document, including the "signatures" of the principal priests of Theban Amun at the change from the twenty-fifth to twenty-sixth dynasties.

Pritchard, James B., ed. *Ancient Near Eastern Texts Relating to the Old Testament*, 3d ed. Princeton, 1969. A long-established and valuable anthology of Egyptian and Near Eastern texts in English translation; the habit of not giving the complete text in many cases is its main drawback.

Redford, Donald B. "A Note on the Chronology of Dynasty 25 and the Inscription of Sargon II at Tang-i Var." *Orientalis* n.s. 68 (1999), 58–60.

Russmann, Edna R. *The Representation of the King in the XXVth Dynasty.* Brussels, 1974. A study of the styles of royal statuary during the twenty-fifth dynasty.

Welsby, Derek A. *The Kingdom of Kush: The Napatan and Meroitic Empires.* London, 1996. A new account of the Kushite civilization itself in Nubia, from the twenty-fifth dynasty onward.

Wenig, S., et al. *Africa in Antiquity.* 2 vols. New York, 1978. Catalog of a major exhibit on the civilizations of ancient Nubia, well illustrated, with comprehensive essays on several aspects at many periods including the twenty-fifth dynasty and Napatan epoch.

Wildung, Dietrich, ed. *Sudan: Ancient Kingdoms of the Nile.* New York and Paris, 1997. Well-illustrated work on ancient Nubian civilization, including the twenty-fifth dynasty.

KENNETH A. KITCHEN

TWENTY-SIXTH DYNASTY. *See* Late Period, *article on* Twenty-sixth Dynasty.

TWO BROTHERS. The late nineteenth dynasty narrative generally known as the *Tale of the Two Brothers*, found on the d'Orbiney Papyrus (British Museum 10183), and written in Late Egyptian, was first announced in 1852, exciting the interest of Egyptologists, biblical scholars, and folklorists virtually from the outset. At that time, no one dreamed that ancient Egypt could have produced a narrative such as *Two Brothers*, in which the hero is persecuted, exiled, and returned to heroic glory in a fashion similar to the European folktale or *märchen*. Furthermore, the existence of this narrative suggested strongly to nineteenth-century folklore scholars that *märchen* did not originate solely in the Indo-European arena, as then believed.

Biblical scholars were fascinated by the appearance in the first part of the story of the so-called "Potiphar's wife" episode that they knew from *Genesis* 39: the wife of the hero's older brother attempts unsuccessfully to seduce him. Egyptologists too were originally attracted to the biblical parallels present in the tale, but they were also interested in its Egyptian nature and origin. Unfamiliar with the study of folk narrative, however, Egyptologists have not generally viewed the story as a unity but rather as an awkward melding of disparate parts. In fact, a recent study of the narrative shows that it is structurally a well-integrated tale and that it, along with *Doomed Prince*, another Egyptian narrative from about the same period, presents the oldest example of *märchen* known to the world today. Because the protagonist and his brother in the *Story of the Two Brothers* carry gods' names, respectively Bata, an ancient mortuary deity, and Anubis, an even older mortuary deity related to royalty, one might question whether the narrative is truly *märchen*, but the actions of the tale suggest that it is, with at least eleven identifiable folktale motifs and four clear and different folktale types.

The multiple reincarnations and transformations of the hero, the location of the middle part of the tale in the Syrian-Palestinian area, where it appears as the Egyptian "otherworld," the similarities of parts of the narrative to the Osirian tale, and the reflection of various aspects of Egyptian life and kingship make this narrative a rewarding work to study. The inclusion of named deities suggests that tales about gods could degenerate into folk-tales, as some folklorists suggest, but it is more likely that his tale spoofs Egyptian deities and royalty. The *Tale of the Two Brothers* may also fill a political role, hinting at a royal transition that is less than regular, and placing the role of women in an unfavorable light. This narrative is, without question, a rich, complex, and unified tale.

BIBLIOGRAPHY

Goldman, S. *The Wiles of Women, The Wiles of Men: Joseph and Potiphar's Wife in Ancient Near Eastern, Jewish, and Islamic Folklore.* Albany, 1995. A discussion of the theme of attempted seduction, in its Near Eastern manifestations.

Hollis, S. T. *The Ancient Egyptian "Tale of Two Brothers": The Oldest Fairy Tale in the World.* Norman, Okla., 1990. Places the narrative in its ancient Near Eastern and Egyptian context, including discussions of characters, the relation of parts and motifs to their ancient Egyptian context, especially mortuary and other narrative materials, and its folkloristic implications; includes a translation and discussion of its relation to parts of the Ptolemaic Papyrus Jumilhac.

Hollis, S. T. "Ancient Israel as the Land of Exile and the 'Otherworld' in Ancient Egyptian Folktales and Narratives." In *Boundaries of the Ancient Near Eastern World. A Tribute to Cyrus H. Gordon—Four Score and Eight,* edited by M. Lubetski et al. Sheffield, 1997. Discusses the Syrian-Palestinian area as a site of exile and/or the "otherworld" in several Egyptian narratives, including *Two Brothers*.

Lichtheim, M. *Ancient Egyptian Literature: A Book of Readings.* Vol. 2, *The New Kingdom* Berkeley, 1976. A readily accessible translation of the narrative, but without commentary.

SUSAN TOWER HOLLIS

U

UGARIT. Modern Ras Shamra, a large (greater than 20 hectares [50 acres]) commercial entrepôt slightly inland from the Syrian coast, about 10 kilometers (6 miles) north of Latakia. Ugarit (Egyptian *'Ikrit,* Akkadian *U-ga-ri-it*) prospered during the second millennium BCE because of the agricultural richness of the large (greater than 2,000 square kilometers) kingdom of the same name that it controlled and its important role in maritime and overland trade. The palace archives of the fourteenth and thirteenth centuries BCE provide abundant evidence for the commercial, political, religious, and social history of the town. The port of ancient Ugarit is at nearby Minet el-Beidha, about 1 kilometer (0.6 mile) west of Ras Shamra; a second Ugaritic coastal settlement, founded in the mid thirteenth century BCE, lies about 5 kilometers (3 miles) to the southwest, at Ras Ibn Hani.

Following the accidental discovery of a burial cave at Minet el-Beidha in 1928, the French Archaeological Mission initiated excavations at Ugarit in 1929 and has continued working there almost every year since, under the direction of Claude F. A. Schaeffer, Henri de Contenson, Jean Margueron, and, most recently, Marguerite Yon. Ugarit's five major stratigraphic levels cover more than five thousand years of settlement history. The earliest evidence for occupation (Level VC = Pre-Pottery Neolithic B period) dates to the seventh millennium BCE, while the latest stratum (Level I = Late Bronze Age) ended in the early twelfth century BCE. The excavation of Minet el-Beidha was conducted by Schaeffer between 1929 and 1935, while that of the Late Bronze Age settlement at Ras Ibn Hani took place between 1975 and 1995 as a joint Franco-Syrian project headed by Jacques Lagarce and Adnan Bounni.

The early history of Egyptian relations with Ugarit is unclear. Several Egyptian stone vessels of late Predynastic and Early Dynastic period dates have been found at the site, but their find-spots (mostly Late Bronze Age contexts) suggest that they reached Ugarit long after their time of manufacture. Any commercial or political relationship between Ugarit and Egypt during the third millennium BCE (the time of Level IIIA) was probably of little significance, unlike that between Byblos and Egypt.

A variety of Egyptian Middle Kingdom objects have come from the excavations at Ugarit (or were purchased at Latakia) and are said to be from the site. The items containing royal names include a carnelian bead and a cylinder seal naming Senwosret I, a fragmentary seated statue of Princess Khnemetneferkhedjet, and fragments of a sphinx of Amenemhet III. Parts of several Egyptian nonroyal statues (including a statue group of the vizier Senwosretankh and his family) have also been found at Ugarit. Because the excavated items derive mostly from contexts after the early second millennium BCE, some of this material may have reached Ugarit later in the Middle Bronze Age or during the Late Bronze Age. The number of objects involved, combined with the occurrence of numerous Middle Kingdom royal-name objects at Byblos, make it more likely, however, that the royal finds represent diplomatic gifts from the Egyptian court to the local rulers of Ugarit. There is no mention of Ugarit in the Egyptian Execration Texts. The evidence for relations between Egypt and Ugarit during the Second Intermediate Period is limited to a few alabaster (calcite) vessels found in tombs dating to the second half of the Middle Bronze Age.

Connections between Egypt and Ugarit expanded significantly during the Late Bronze Age, when Ugarit became a major emporium for Egyptian maritime trade in the eastern Mediterranean, especially that with Cyprus. The name of the town first appears in New Kingdom topographical lists in the reign of Amenhotpe III (the long-supposed mention of Ugarit in the records of Amenhotpe II's Syrian campaign of his seventh year of reign is now generally dismissed). By the early fourteenth century BCE, the town and kingdom of Ugarit were already a vassal of Egypt.

Ugarit is the source of at least two cuneiform tablets in the diplomatic archive from Tell el-Amarna (Amarna Letters EA 45, 49); it probably is the source of three others (EA 46–48) and is mentioned in five additional letters (EA 1, 89, 98, 126, 151). In Letter 45, Ammistamru I, the ruler of Ugarit, professes his loyalty to the Egyptian king (evidently Amenhotpe III); in Letter 49, Ammistamru's successor, Niqmadu II, asks Amenhotpe IV to send him a physician. Niqmadu appears along with an Egyptian princess or noblewoman on a fragment of an alabaster vessel from the palace, suggesting a diplomatic marriage linking Egypt and its Ugaritan vassal kingdom late in the reign of Amenhotpe III or IV. Ugarit (especially the palace area of the site) has yielded Egyptian alabaster vase fragments containing the names of Amenhotpe II, Amenhotpe III, Queen Tiye, Nefertiti, and Horemheb, as well as many uninscribed alabaster vessels. A Ugaritic tablet from the palace mentions a king *Nmry*, a name some scholars identify with the prenomen of Amenhotpe III. Small scarabs of Thutmose IV and Amenhotpe III have also been found at Ugarit, as has one of the large marriage scarabs of Amenhotpe III and Tiye (the latter item coming from the palace). During the Amarna period, the Hittites moved down into Syria, and much of the northern Levant that had formerly been under Egyptian hegemony was lost. Ugarit was integrated into the Hittite Empire, which ruled the kingdom through its representative in Syria, the king of Carchemish.

Relations between Egypt and Ugarit probably continued through the late eighteenth dynasty and into the nineteenth, though at a reduced level of activity. Following the peace treaty that the Hittites and Egyptians signed in regnal year 21 of Ramesses II, contacts expanded substantially. Egyptian and Egyptianizing finds are numerous at Ugarit for the period covering the remainder of the thirteenth and early twelfth centuries BCE: several alabaster vessels inscribed with the names of Ramesses II, as well as many uninscribed alabaster vessels; a bronze sword containing the cartouche of Merenptah; several statues of nonroyal figures and gods; a nonroyal stela containing a dedication to the god Baal-Saphon; and various amulets, scarabs, and other small items. Close relations between Egypt and Ugarit are also attested by several letters found on cuneiform tablets: the earliest of these letters (tablet RS 20.182) was sent by the king of Ugarit to Ramesses II, while the latest (RS 86.2230) was sent by the well-known late nineteenth dynasty Egyptian official of Near Eastern origin, Bay, to the last ruler of Ugarit, Ammurapi. In addition, a cuneiform tablet found at Aphek near Tel Aviv contains a letter datable to the reign of Ramesses II from the governor of Ugarit, Takuḫlinu, to an Egyptian official, Ḥaya, regarding a transaction involving the purchase of wheat at Joppa for Ugarit.

The town of Ugarit suffered massive destruction early in the twelfth century BCE, probably at the hands of the Sea Peoples, and Ras Ibn Hani evidently was abandoned just shortly before Ugarit's demise. Following a brief reoccupation of the town, perhaps by squatters, Ugarit was left abandoned until the Persian period, while Ras Ibn Hani saw almost immediate resettlement.

BIBLIOGRAPHY

Giveon, Raphael. "Ugarit." In *Lexikon der Ägyptologie* 6: 838–842. Wiesbaden, 1986. History of Egyptian relations with Ugarit.

Helck, Wolfgang. "Ägyptische Statuen im Ausland—Ein Chronologisches Problem." *Ugarit-Forschungen* 8 (1976), 101–115. Author contends that the Middle Kingdom statuary found in various foreign places (including Ugarit) got there as a result of the looting of Egyptian sites during the early Hyksos period.

Lackenbacher, Sylvie. "Une correspondance entre l'administration du pharaon Merneptah et la roi d'Ougarit." In *Le pays d'Ougarit autour de 1200 av. J.-C.*, edited by Marguerite Yon et al., pp. 77–83. Ras Shamra-Ougarit, 11. Paris, 1995. Preliminary report on a letter sent from the Egyptian administration to the king of Ugarit.

Moran, William L. *The Amarna Letters*. Baltimore, 1992. Includes excellent translations of the letters pertaining to Ugarit.

Schaeffer, Claude F.-A. *Ugaritica III*. Mission de Ras Shamra, 8. Paris, 1956. Pp. 164–226 contain articles on the "Marriage Vase" of Niqmadu II, the bronze sword containing Merenptah's cartouche, and the marriage scarab of Amenhotpe III and Tiye.

Ward, William A. "Remarks on some Middle Kingdom Statuary found at Ugarit." *Ugarit-Forschungen* 11 (1979), 799–806. Author argues that some of the twelfth dynasty statuary found at Ugarit may come from contexts contemporary with that period.

Yon, Marguerite, ed. *Arts et industries de la pierre*. Ras Shamra-Ougarit, 6. Paris, 1991. Individual chapters contain much information on the Egyptian and egyptianizing alabaster vessels, stelae, sculpture, and other stone items from Ugarit.

Yon, Marguerite. "The End of the Kingdom of Ugarit." In *The Crisis Years: The 12th Century* B.C.: From Beyond the Danube to the Tigris, edited by William A. Ward and Martha Sharp Joukowsky. Dubuque, 1992. Study of the last years of Ugarit and the kingdom's relations with Egypt.

Yon, Marguerite. "Ugarit." In *The Anchor Bible Dictionary*, edited by David Noel Freedman, vol. 6, pp. 695–706. New York, 1992. Recent summary of the archaeological history of the site.

Young, Gordon Douglas, ed. *Ugarit in Retrospect: Fifty Years of Ugarit and Ugaritic*. Winona Lake, 1981. Proceedings of symposium honoring the fiftieth anniversary of the start of excavations at Ugarit; contains several essays relating to Egypt.

JAMES M. WEINSTEIN

UNDERWORLD. *See* Afterlife; Hell; *and* Paradise.

UPPER EGYPT. In the widest sense, Upper Egypt is the territory to the south of Giza province and as far south as Aswan. The region between Giza and Asyut is known as Middle Egypt, however, so strictly speaking, Upper Egypt is the Egyptian sector of the Nile Valley between Asyut in the north and in the south the First Cataract Nile River. In ancient times, Upper Egypt also included some lands to the south of Aswan, although the southern border of Egypt was originally north of that town. Upper Egypt is divided into two sectors: Southern Upper Egypt and Northern Upper Egypt. The southern region is from the First Cataract north to Luxor, and the northern region is from Luxor north to Asyut.

Upper Egypt is a narrow, fertile strip of land along the Nile River surrounded by deserts. The fertile part of the Nile Valley was called *kmt* ("the Black Land") by the Egyptians, and the deserts—both the Eastern and the West-

UPPER EGYPT. *Mo'alla, a rock-cut necropolis of the First Intermediate Period, about 24 kilometers (15 miles) to the south of Luxor.* (Courtesy Donald B. Redford)

ern—Deserts were known as *dšrt* ("the Red Land"). In Upper Egypt, the river flows through deserts parallel to the valley and also along cliffs; they are sometimes close to the river's edge and at other times away from the shore. Between Aswan and Luxor in particular, the escarpment east of the Nile is next to the river, and the water in places almost washes the base of the cliffs, except for the area east of Kom Ombo, where there is a wide plain. Rainfall over Upper Egypt is rare, so—because the economy of ancient Egypt was agricultural—the Nile and its annual flooding (in antiquity, between July and October) were important to the development of Egyptian civilization. The flood covered most of the land in the Nile Valley, but it was especially reliable on the lands closest to the river; the population has lived continuously on this flood plain bordering the river.

Upper Egypt has other resources that were important to the Egyptians—various stones and minerals—especially in the Eastern Desert. At the north end of the First Cataract and to the east of Aswan are the great quarries of red granite, used from the Early Dynastic period onward. Farther north, at Gebel es-Silsila, 20 kilometers (12.5 miles) north of Kom Ombo, the banks of the river are

sandstone cliffs, which were used as quarries from the New Kingdom onward. Basalt was quarried in the Eastern Desert, near Coptos, north of Luxor, and limestone was quarried from Esna in the south to Cairo in the north. Gold came from the Eastern Desert—at the latitude of Kom Ombo, Elkab, and Coptos—and Egypt exploited the region for this metal.

Upper Egypt was usually called "the Land of the South" or simply "the South." The area from Elephantine in the south to present-day Nag Hammadi (or a little to the north of it) was called *ḥn-nḥn*, which indicated the seven southernmost nomes (provinces) of Upper Egypt. The sector between Elephantine and Abydos was designated "the Head of the South."

Nomes of Upper Egypt. In the Early Dynastic period, around 2900 BCE, the state was founded; it was then organized by the kings of the first dynasty, who established administrative sectors known as *spꜣt* ("nomes" or "districts"). The nomes may have originally reflected the extent of the tribal areas of the independent states of the Predynastic period, each one governed by a local prince. After the unification of the country, the various nomes then retained a degree of independence from the central government, particularly in Upper Egypt. In the area from the First Cataract to the south of Memphis, there were more than twenty-two nomes. Each had its capital, the residence of the governors. During the fifth dynasty, the nomes were well established. Their lengths along the river are known from the Kiosk of King Sesostris I at Karnak (twelfth dynasty). The nomes were named and numbered from the south to the north (1–11).

History. As a region isolated by deserts to the east and west, Upper Egypt developed its own highly individual culture. The inhabitants had long been culturally distinct from the Lower Egyptians of the Delta region—as evidenced from earliest historical times. For example, in the prehistoric period the farmers of Upper Egypt buried their dead not within their villages, as was done in Lower Egypt, but in regular cemeteries at the desert's edge. The drying sand led to a sort of natural mummification. Upper Egypt was already settled by 4500 BCE, and it became a center of several cultures of the Neolithic and Predynastic periods, such as those called the Tasian and Badarian, found between Asyut and Akhmim, on the eastern bank of the Nile. Another culture that flourished in the region from about 4000 to 3000 BCE was the Naqada. It was named for the present-day village of Naqada on the western bank of the Nile, north of Luxor. The Naqada I culture, sometimes called the Amratian, spread from Deir Tasa in the north to Nubia in the south, with a large concentration of sites between Naqada and Abydos, and also at Hierakonpolis. At the time of the Naqada II culture, also called the Gerzean, about 3500 to 3000 BCE, some of the sites in Upper Egypt had become important population centers, such as Hierakonpolis (el-Kom el-Ahmar) and Abydos. Other sites are situated to the south and north of Thebes and the area of the First Cataract of the Nile near Aswan, but Hierakonpolis and Abydos were the two main centers of power in Upper Egypt.

Hierakonpolis ("the City of the Hawk," as the Greeks called it) was the Egyptian *Nekhen*, a religious capital of Upper Egypt. A Gerzean tomb of a prince with wall paintings was discovered there, as well as a temple. Objects with the names of some of the first-known kings of Egypt ("Scorpion" and Narmer), the immediate predecessors of the first dynasty, were found there. Their most notable monuments are the inscribed limestone ceremonial mace head of King "Scorpion" that depicts a temple-founding ceremony, and the famous slate palette of green schist of King Narmer, of whom a mace head has also been found. Both objects were designed for ceremonial use and bear important historical data. Narmer was one of the last Predynastic kings thought to have come from Hierakonpolis. Attempts were made by both kings, "Scorpion" and Narmer, to conquer the North (Lower Egypt); records of the war or the victory of the Upper Egyptian King-

dom over that of the North were carved on the above-mentioned objects from the first temple of Horus, the main deity of Hierakonpolis. Other monuments with the name of the second dynasty king Khasekhem have also been found at Hierakonpolis, two statues and three stone vessels. The statues, one of schist and one of limestone, represent the king seated on a throne, wearing the so-called *sed*-festival robe and also the White Crown of Upper Egypt.

Opposite Kom el-Ahmar/Hierakonpolis, on the other side of the Nile, is the archaeological site of Elkab, the Egyptian Nekheb, consisting of Predynastic and pharaonic settlements. The main deity of Elkab, the vulture goddess Nekhbet, played a dominant religious role in the institution of royalty. She took the form of a winged vulture holding the so-called Shen-rings (symbol of eternity) in her claws. She was known as the White One of Nekhen/Hierakonpolis and was the patron of Upper Egypt; she was also one of the deities who assisted at royal and divine births. Nekhbet and the cobra goddess Wadjet of Buto in the Delta were the protective deities of the Egyptian kings and the protectors of Upper and Lower Egypt. They were called the Two Ladies, *Nbti* in the name of the Egyptian kings, and they were depicted on the crowns of the kings. Nekhbet was later identified with Eileithyia, the Greek goddess of childbirth; for this reason, the Greeks gave the town of Elkab the name Eileithiaspolis.

Naqada is one of the largest archaeological sites of the Predynastic period in Egypt. An extensive area containing cemeteries near the villages of Tukh and Ballas, about 7 kilometers (4.5 miles) north of Naqada, has been excavated. A gigantic tomb with several objects belonging to Queen Nithotep, the mother of king Aha, a king of the first dynasty, was discovered near Naqada. The tomb contained fragments of stone vases, ivory tablets, and clay seals bearing the names of (Hor-) Aha and Nithotep.

At Tukh, north of Luxor, on the site of the Egyptian Nebut, "the Gold Town," the remains of a temple from the Predynastic period have been excavated, dedicated to the god Seth, the main deity of the Naqada-Tukh area. Seth is the god of the desert, so his cult centers, like the Predynastic city of Nebut, are along caravan routes. Seth, the god of Nebut, was called also Nebuty ("the one of the Nebut"). Religious texts say that Seth was born in the region of Naqada, that he was one of the oldest deities of Egypt, and that he was regarded as the Upper Egyptian god. Other texts say that the earth god, Geb, divided Egypt into two halves, giving the North to Horus and the South to Seth. Seth is also known from several objects from Upper Egypt; he is portrayed on the mace head of the Predynastic king "Scorpion" from Hierakonpolis, and also on a carved ivory artifact from el-Mahasna, north of Abydos, dating to Naqada I.

On the eastern side of the Nile, near Coptos, at the entrance to the Wadi Hammamat, there are also settlements and cemeteries dating to the late Predynastic and the Early Dynastic periods. The main deity of the site, Min, the god of fertility, was one of the most ancient of Egypt's deities. He was already worshiped at Coptos during the Early Dynastic period; his three colossal limestone statues, each over 4 meters (12.5 feet) high, perhaps from the Predynastic period, have been discovered there. He was considered the patron or protector of the workers of the mining expeditions in the Eastern Desert and was also the deity of the desert nomads. Since Predynastic times, Coptos, at the entrance to the Wadi Hammamat, was the starting point to the Eastern Desert's mines and quarries.

The third important site dating to the early history of Upper Egypt was Abydos, on the Nile's western bank, south of Suhag. Abydos was also a royal town at the time of the final unification of Egypt. The kings of the first and second dynasty and the members of their court were buried in tombs at a site called Um el-Qa'ab ("the Mother of potsherds"), which was the necropolis for the city of Abydos. The tomb of Aha, the first king to rule both Upper and Lower Egypt and the founder of the new capital of the united Egypt—known as "the White Wall," later Memphis—was also discovered at the site of Abydos. Since that time, Egypt became a centralized monarchy under a single king, later called "Pharaoh," which means "great house." Other tombs at the site of Abydos were dated to earlier Predynastic times. Abydos was also the most important cult center of Osiris in Upper Egypt. He was the Egyptian god of the dead and the king of the underworld. According to the later ancient Egyptians, the tomb of Osiris was to be found at Abydos; during the Middle Kingdom, the tomb of King Djer of the first dynasty at Umm el-Qa'ab was identified as the tomb of the god. From that time on, Abydos became an important sacred site in Egypt and also a place of pilgrimage. The pilgrimage to Abydos was the trip that every Egyptian aspired to make. A large number of tombs and offering chapels were constructed at the site in Abydos known as Kom el-Sultan, which contains a temple of the god Osiris, also called Osiris-Khentimentiu. Khentimentiu ("Foremost of the Westerners") was the original god of Abydos during the town's early history, and he had been early assimilated with Osiris. Thousands of stelae, offering tables, and other objects have been found at the site of the temple of Osiris-Khentimentiu; the inscribed artifacts give important information concerning the cult of Osiris. The cultures of the Predynastic and Early Dynastic periods were also found at other places in Upper Egypt: in the area of the First Cataract at the south border of Upper Egypt, near Edfu and Gebelein, and also between Dendera and Nag Hammadi.

The First Cataract, to the south of Aswan, stretches for about 10 kilometers (6.5 miles) along the course of the river and includes a number of large rocks and islands that divided the river into several streams. At the northern end (the head) of the cataract is the island of Elephantine, situated in the middle of the Nile, and facing the city of Aswan. A second island, Sehel, is about 3 kilometers (2 miles) south of Elephantine. A third and fourth, Philae and Bigga, are about 8 kilometers (5 miles) south of Aswan. A fifth island, near the end of the First Cataract, is el-Heise. From the Predynastic period onward, Khnum, the ram-headed god, was the main deity at the area of the First Cataract. He was called "the Lord of Qebehu," the Egyptian name of the First Cataract. Khnum was also the local god of the island Bigga (Eg., *Sn-mwt*), and he was worshiped on Elephantine with Satis and Anukis. Khnum was the god of the water and "Keeper of the Nile-sources," and he was also the god who brought the annual flood. Hapi, the Nile god, was believed to live in a cave in the region of the First Cataract. Elephantine, one of the most important islands of the First Cataract (Eg., *'bw*, "ivory" or "elephant"), was considered to be the southern frontier of Egypt during most of the history of the land; sometimes Senmut played the same role. On the southern part of Elephantine island, there are remains of an old town whose origins go back to the Early Dynastic period and which was almost continuously inhabited. A fortress at the same place dates to the Early Old Kingdom. Later, during the Old and Middle Kingdoms, Elephantine was the capital of the First Nome of Upper Egypt, and the seat of the governors, who were buried at the necropolis of Qubat el-Hawa, opposite Aswan. Elephantine was also the starting point for expeditions to Nubia.

Before Elephantine and Senmut were established as the southern frontier, the boundary between Egypt and Nubia is considered to have been at Gebel es-Silsila, north of Kom Ombo, a place called Kheny by the ancient Egyptians, which means "The Place of Rowing." The main deity here was the crocodile god Sobek. This deity was also worshipped at Nebyt, the modern Kom Ombo. There Sobek shared the temple of the town with the god Horus, or Haroeris, "Horus the Elder." In earliest times, Horus was worshiped at the First Nome; he was known there as the Lord of Ta-Seti, the Egyptian name of the First Nome. His cult center there was certainly the town of Nebyt (Kom Ombo), which may have been the capital of the First Nome before Elephantine later adopted this role. Horus of the First Nome may be the same god who was worshiped in Behedet, the modern Edfu, whose temple there, from Greco-Roman times, is one of the best-preserved temples of Egypt. Edfu was an important ancient site from the Early Dynastic period onward, and played a dominant role during the Old Kingdom. A necropolis of the Early Dynastic period and others from the Old Kingdom and the First Intermediate Period have been excavated at the site of Edfu. In earlier times, Behedet was considered to be the southern border of Egypt; this can be concluded from several stelae that mention two towns called Behedet, the northern one in Delta and the southern one at the site of Edfu. The borders of Egypt once lay between these two Behedets. Even earlier, in the prehistoric period, Hierakonpolis was considered the southern border of Egypt, before Behedet replaced it.

The god Horus was also worshiped at other places in Upper Egypt. He was the god of Nekhen (el-Kom el-Ahmar/Hierakonplois). The other cult center of Horus or Horus the Elder was the town of Gesa or Gesy—the Greco-Roman Appollonopolis Parva, north of Luxor. He was worshiped there with another old god named Neb-Shema'u, "The Lord of Upper Egypt," who is to be identified with the god Seth, the main deity in the area of Naqada/Tukh, north of Qus.

The other site with Early Dynastic remains to the north of Edfu was near present-day Gebelein, on the western bank. The town was called Enerti ("the two hills") or Per Hathor ("the house of Hathor"). Hathor was the main deity of the town, and her cult there goes back to the Early Dynastic period; from the ruins of her temple at the site there are also reliefs from the time of Djoser (third dynasty). To the west of the town are a great number of tombs from the late Predynastic period and others from the First Intermediate Period. Other cult centers of the goddess Hathor were in the area between Dendera and Nag Hammadi. At Dendera is the well-preserved temple of Hathor from Greco-Roman times but the site of the old town is much earlier. Near Dendera are extensive cemeteries with remains from the Early Dynastic period to the Middle Kingdom. Hathor was also worshiped in the area to the north of Dendera.

Upper Egypt in the Historical Period. After Egypt was united, the third to eighth dynasty kings chose the city of Memphis as their residence and as the capital of the whole of Egypt. At first, they were powerful enough to rule the whole land as their private estate. From the later years of the fourth dynasty, the highly centralized state gradually weakened. In Upper Egypt, the provincial governorships and other offices came to be regarded as hereditary appointments. In the neighborhood of the larger provincial towns or in the district capital, cemeteries were established for the local princes and their servants, like those near el-Hammamiya, Naga ed-Deir, Abydos, Dendera, Thebes, Edfu, and Elephantine. To counteract the growing power of the provincial nobles and to ensure the collection of taxes throughout the southern nomes, the post of the "Governor of Upper Egypt" was created, perhaps as early as the fifth dynasty, an important administrative office in the southern half of Egypt. The first one who had this title was Weni, an official of the sixth dynasty from Abydos, of humble birth; he won the confidence of the king and was elevated to that exalted position. He collected all the revenues due to the residence and exacted all the labor involved. The kings of the sixth dynasty were by any standard weak, so prominent provincials became great chieftains in their nomes and the provincial aristocracy took firm root in Upper Egypt. Toward the end of the sixth dynasty the title "Governor of Upper Egypt" was often a purely honorific one, and after the long rule of King Pepy II (2300–2206 BCE), the central authority of the pharaohs of the seventh and eighth dynasties became too weak to hold back the rising tide of anarchy. During the eighth dynasty, a strong family in Coptos played an important role in the politics of the land, but by the end of the eighth dynasty, the Old Kingdom collapsed, with the political system that it had created.

From the First Intermediate Period onward, then from the Second Intermediate Period until the end of the New Kingdom, Upper Egypt played a very important role. This role was played by the native princes and other rulers of Thebes. In early historical times, Thebes had not been an important city, and at the end of the Old Kingdom it was still an insignificant village on the eastern bank of the Nile, at the site of the modern Luxor. During the First Intermediate Period (2165–2040 BCE), Egypt was divided into two kingdoms, with the northern kingdom ruled by a dynasty known as the Herakleopolitan—the ninth and tenth dynasties. This kingdom was founded by a local prince called Akhtoy, governor of the twentieth nome of Upper Egypt, whose city was Nen-nesw, the Greek Herakleopolis, on the western side of the Nile, just south of the entrance to the Faiyum. The Herakleopolitans, or the House of Akhtoy, regarded themselves as legitimate successors to the pharaohs of the Old Kingdom. Their sphere of influence extended over the west and east of the Nile Delta, as well as Middle Egypt to the important eighth nome town of Abydos. The kings of Herakleopolis were supported by the strong nomarchs of the thirteenth nome, who resided at Asyut, its capital. One of them, Tefibi, invaded the eighth nome and captured it, but only for a short time.

At the end of the Old Kingdom and the beginning of the First Intermediate Period, the south of Egypt was first under the control of several nomarchs, two of whom are well known. The first is Ankhtifi, who resided at Hefat near the modern village el-Mo'alla, in the third nome of Upper Egypt; he also controlled the second and, for a short time, a part of the fourth. The other nomarch, Antef (Anyotef), resided at Waset—Thebes or Diospolis magna to the Greeks—which was also the metropolis of the fourth nome of Upper Egypt. The city is now the most important and the largest archaeological site of Upper Egypt, on both sides of the Nile, surrounding Luxor. Antef ruled over this nome until his death. One of his successors, called Antef I, the "Great Chief of Upper Egypt," succeeded in extending his power southward to the First Cataract and beyond it into the north of Nubia. After a long struggle he felt powerful enough to usurp a sort of kingship in the South. After he siezed the five southernmost nomes, he called himself Horus Sehertowy ("the pacifier of the Two Lands"), the son of Re Antef. His successor, Horus Wahankh ("established in life"), called Antef II, had the titles "King of Upper and Lower Egypt and the Son of Re." Antef II reigned for almost fifty years and fought with success against the pharaohs of the Herakleopolitan dynasty. First he extended his control northward to the important nome of This and thereby controlled Upper Egypt from Elephantine in the south to This in the north—a sector known as "The Head of Upper Egypt"—the geographic designation for the first eight nomes of Upper Egypt.

Antef II's expansion northward reached as far as the nome of Aphroditopolis, the tenth nome of Upper Egypt. Then one of his successors, Montuhotep I, continued the war of the southern kingdom, fighting northward; Asyut fell, as so did the fifteenth nome. Montuhotep marched toward Herakleopolis but the last of the Herakleopolitan kings, Merikare, died before the Theban reached Herakleopolis. During the fifty-year long reign of Montuhotep, the great Theban offensive continued until Herakleopolis fell. Finally, about 2040 BCE Montuhotep succeeded in uniting Egypt under his control and, from that date, Egypt remained under a single royal house until the Second Intermediate Period. By the victory of the Theban over the Herakleopolitan, the god Montu played a dominant role in his capacity as a mighty war god and as the patron of the eleventh dynasty. Four kings of the dynasty were called Montuhotep ("Montu-is-satisfied"). Montu, a falcon-headed god, was also worshiped in every important town of the fourth nome. The chief seat of the god was Armant, south of Luxor. Montu was also worshiped there as the sacred bull called Bekh, the Buchis Bull, who was ritually buried at the edge of the desert, north of Armant, in special catacombs known as the Bucheum. Montu was also the local god of the Egyptian Djerty, present-day el-Tud, opposite Armant. The other cult center of Montu in the fourth nome was at the town of Madu, present-day el-Medamud, about twenty kilometers (13 miles) north of Luxor. The sacred Bull of Montu at that site was kept in a special building or stable behind the main temple of the god. The kings of the eleventh dynasty may be the ones who brought Montu to Thebes, or he might be an old local god of the city, as in the other towns of the fourth nome. There he was called "Lord of Thebes and king of the gods, he who is on his throne in Karnak." Montu (since the Middle Kingdom also called Montu-Re) was worshiped in Thebes for a long time, even after the god Amun adopted his position at Thebes; Montu remained "the Lord of Thebes, the Bull of Armant, who came from Tud."

During the Second Intermediate Period, Thebes played the same role it had held in the First Intermediate Period. Egypt was again divided between the Hyksos, or the fifteenth and sixteenth dynasties in the North, and the seventeenth dynasty in the South. The Hyksos—from the Egyptian ḥḳ3-ḫ3swt ("the rulers of the foreign countries")—were from the Levant and of Semitic origin; they conquered the northeastern territories of Egypt. At the same time, also between about 1665 and 1555 BCE, another dynasty of native Egyptian kings ruled at Thebes and maintained a tight grip on Upper Egypt. They are known as the seventeenth dynasty. The border between the territories of the Hyksos rulers and the kings of the seventeenth dynasty expired at the town of Cusae, present-day el-Qusiyah in Middle Egypt. About 1570 BCE, when the Hyksos tried to penetrate into Theban territories, the kings of Thebes declared war on the Hyksos, but the Theban king at the time, Ta'o (also called Sekenenre), died in battle against the Hyksos. His son, Kamose, the last king of the seventeenth dynasty, took up the war with vigor; after his victories in Middle Egypt, Kamose was approaching the defenses of the Hyksos capital, Avaris, when he died. His brother, Ahmose I, then brought the war to a successful conclusion. He defeated the Hyksos and destroyed their capital. Ahmose succeeded in pushing the Hyksos out of Egypt, pursuing them to Sharuhen in southwestern Palestine. Ahmose later put down rebellions within Egypt and Nubia. He was honored as the founder of the eighteenth dynasty and of the New Kingdom. When Ahmose drove the Hyksos from Egypt, he chose Thebes as the capital of the newly unified Egypt.

From that time onward, the glory of Thebes grew, as did that of the god Amun—who became the state god of Egypt. In thanks for his victories, Ahmose made donations to the temple of Amun. In the Middle Kingdom, the ram-headed god Amun ("the invisible one") had become the main deity of Thebes. The founder of the twelfth dynasty had called himself Amenemhet ("Amun is at the Head"), and he and his successors had built a temple for Amun at Thebes, at the site of present-day Karnak. The New Kingdom rulers of the eighteenth and nineteenth dynasties showered the god Amun with costly gifts. As early as Thutmose III, Amun became the supreme god of the known world; Thebes, the town of Amun, became the capital of the mighty empire that he won for Egypt in the Near East. During the eighteenth dynasty, Amun was also worshiped in the mortuary temples of the kings buried at the necropolis of Thebes, on the western bank. Other temples and shrines were built for Amun throughout

Egypt. During the Amarna period, however, the temples of Amun were attacked and closed by order of King Akhenaten, who preferred the god Aten. Yet Amun was later worshiped by the Greeks, under the name Zeus-Ammon, and the Romans honored him as Jupiter-Ammon. Many festivals were celebrated in honor of Amun, one of which was the Valley festival, which included ritual meals and mortuary offerings before the tombs of Western Thebes. For the Opet festival, Amun's solar bark was carried in a ceremonial procession from Karnak to Luxor and back. Amun, his wife Mut, and their son Khons formed the great triad of Thebes. Mut was also honored with a temple at Thebes, complete with a sacred lake.

At the end of the twentieth dynasty, Thebes remained the administrative center of the South, and the high priests of Amun played an important political role. At that time, an official of the twentieth dynasty called Panehsi served Ramesses XI, the last king of the dynasty, as the viceroy of Nubia. When a revolt against the high priest of Amun took place in Thebes, Panehsi gathered up army units and marched to Thebes. He put down the rebellion, and he left one of his officers in charge of the city. This man, Herihor, made himself the high priest of Amun, portrayed himself as a king, and founded a dynasty of priest-kings at Thebes. He also put an end to the New Kingdom.

Herihor ruled most of Upper Egypt, while the kings of the twenty-first dynasty ruled from Tanis in the northeastern Delta. The importance of the high priests of Amun may be noticed during the twenty-second dynasty, when its first king, Sheshonq I, installed his son as high priest of Amun in Thebes. In the twenty-sixth dynasty, about 660 BCE, the Assyrian king, Assurbanipal, attacked Thebes and sacked it, carrying away a vast amount of treasure from its temples to his capital Nineveh. Then, during the thirtieth, last native Egyptian dynasty, king Nektanebo I linked Luxor with Karnak with the Avenue of Sphinxes.

[*See also entries on various Upper Egyptian sites mentioned in this article.*]

BIBLIOGRAPHY

Adams, B. *Ancient Hierakonpolis.* Warminster, 1974.
Aldred, C. *The Egyptians.* Rev. ed. London, 1984.
Baines, J., and J. Málek. *Atlas of Ancient Egypt.* New York, 1980.
Gardiner, A. H. *Egypt of the Pharaohs.* London, 1961.
James, T. G. H. *Ancient Egypt: The Land and Its Legacy.* London, 1988.
Thomas, A. *Egyptian Gods and Myths.* Aylesbury, 1986.
Winlock, H. E. *The Rise and Fall of the Middle Kingdom in Thebes.* New York, 1947.

FAROUK GOMAÀ

USHEBTIS. *See* Funerary Figurines.

V

VALLEY FESTIVAL. *See* Festivals.

VALLEY OF THE KINGS. The East and West Valleys of the Kings, to use the more correct names, were the burial places for the pharaohs of Egypt's eighteenth, nineteenth, and twentieth dynasties and for a small number of New Kingdom officials, priests, and royal family members. The East Valley of the Kings (abbreviated KV) is the better known of the two areas; the West Valley (abbreviated WV) contains only three royal tombs (WV 22, Amenhotpe III; WV 23, Ay; and WV 25, intended for a late eighteenth dynasty pharaoh), and perhaps four others. KV lies at 25°44′ north latitude, 32°36′ east longitude. It was called in antiquity "The Great, Noble Necropolis of Millions of Years of Pharaoh"; the name "Valley of the Kings" is a translation of its Arabic designation, Wadi el-Biban el-Mouluk, "The Valley of the Gates of the Kings."

The East Valley is a small wadi, or ravine, cut millions of years ago by rainfall and water runoff, defined by steep cliffs and, above them, by hill slopes that rise to nearly 500 meters (1,600 feet) above sea level. (Its floor lies at about 160 meters [500 feet] above sea level, and the cultivable land of the Nile Valley 1 kilometer [0.62 mile] east at about 80 meters [250 feet].) In plan, KV resembles a hand with fingers splayed: in the center of the palm lies the tomb of Tutankhamun (KV 62); most of the tombs lie along the edges of the low-lying paths that form the fingers. In total, the KV floor covers only about two hectares. Within this small area was dug so extensive an array of tombs that, in several instances, later tombs inadvertently ran into earlier ones—an indication that there was no "master plan" of KV available to ancient architects. This particular wadi was probably chosen as the place of royal burials from among the many wadis that lie on the western bank of the Nile because of its good-quality limestone bedrock, convenient location, and well-defined, easily protected topography, and perhaps because a mountain (called the Qurn in Arabic, meaning "horn" or "crown of the head") lying immediately south of KV looks from here very much like a pyramid, a form associated with the solar deity Re.

The KV tombs have fascinated travelers since dynastic times, but not until the eighteenth century did a few visitors record what they saw. There are a few graffiti of dynastic times, more than two thousand Greek graffiti left on cliff faces and tomb walls by ancient travelers, and several Coptic graffiti dating from the fourth through seventh centuries CE. None of these, however, offers much information except to indicate which parts of which KV tombs were accessible to visitors two millennia ago. From about the seventh century until 1739 CE, there are no records whatever of the East Valley. During the next century, the number of visitors increased greatly, and hundreds of nineteenth-century accounts reveal in considerable detail the condition of accessible tombs, the nature of their decoration, and their contents.

The disadvantage of this interest, of course, was that many visitors were anxious to rob KV tombs, not to study them. Pieces of decorated walls were carted off to European museums; thieves, both local and foreign, hacked through debris in frantic searches for gold; material, even if inscribed and of potentially great historical importance, was thrown away if it did not appear to have cash value. The result has been that most KV tombs have been hacked through and poorly studied; many, thought by thieves and early archaeologists to be unimportant pit tombs that contained no objects of value, have been left undug and unprotected. Only a handful of KV tombs have been adequately published; many are still only partially excavated; and none has yet received the conservation and protection that it deserves and, with increasing urgency, requires. Only recently have systematic studies of KV tombs and their condition been undertaken: the Theban Mapping Project is preparing a detailed database of KV and its tombs, and Erik Hornung is continuing an extensive study of their decoration. The publication by Elizabeth Thomas, *The Royal Necropoleis of Thebes* (Princeton, 1966), remains today, after three decades, still the most comprehensive and useful study available.

The condition of the KV tombs varies greatly. Some have been virtually destroyed by flash floods that occur every few decades, caused by torrential rains that strike the hills above the valley and pour thousands of tons of water and debris into low-lying tombs. The tomb of Bay (KV 13) was destroyed by such a flood in 1994, in a storm that also caused flooding in the tombs of Tawosret/Setnakhte (KV 14), Amenhotpe II (KV 35), and Horemheb (KV 57). Even Tutankhamun's tomb suffered water damage. Plans for the construction of flood barriers on the

Tomb No.	Tomb Owner	Type	History and Excavation
Eighteenth Dynasty Tombs			
KV 39	uncertain	odd	Loret, 1899, J. Rose, 1989–1992
KV 20	Thutmose I and Hatshepsut	odd	open at least 2 centuries; Burton, 1824, Carter, 1903–1904
KV 38	Thutmose I (reburial)		Loret, 1899
KV 34	Thutmose III	I	Loret, 1898
KV 35	Amenhotpe II	I	Loret, 1898; used in antiquity as a cache of royal mummies
KV 42	Hatshepsut-Merytre, wife of Thutmose III (not used by her)	I	Loret, 1898; Carter, 1900
KV 43	Thutmose IV	I	Carter, 1903
WV 22	Amenhotpe III	I	Carter, 1915
KV 46	Yuya and Thuya		Davis, 1905; substantial number of artifacts
KV 55	uncertain, perhaps from Amarna period		Ayrton, 1907
KV 62	Tutankhamun		Carter, 1922
WV 23	Ay	III	Belzoni, 1816; Schaden, 1972
KV 57	Horemheb	IV	Ayrton, 1908
Nineteenth Dynasty Tombs			
KV 16	Ramesses I	III	Belzoni, 1817
KV 17	Sety I	IV	Belzoni, 1817
KV 7	Ramesses II	II	open since antiquity, now being studied by French mission
KV 5	sons of Ramesses II		Burton, 1825; Weeks, 1989 on
KV 8	Merenptah	III	accessible since antiquity
KV 10	Amenmesse	III	accessible since antiquity; Schaden, 1992 on
KV 15	Sety II	III	accessible since antiquity; Carter, 1902–1904
KV 47	Siptah	III	Ayrton, 1905
KV 14	Tawosret and Sethnakhte		accessible since antiquity; Altenmüller, 1983–1987
Twentieth Dynasty Tombs			
KV 11	Sethnakhte/Ramesses III	III	accessible since antiquity; called "Bruce's Tomb" from his drawing of 1790
KV 2	Ramesses IV	III	accessible since antiquity; Ayrton, 1905; Carter, 1920
KV 9	Ramesses V and VI	III	accessible since antiquity, Burton, 1820s; Daressy, 1888
KV 1	Ramesses VII	III	open since antiquity; Brock, 1983
KV 6	Ramesses IX	III	open since antiquity; Daressy, 1888
KV 19	Montuherkhepeshef, son of Ramesses IX	III	Belzoni, 1817; Ayrton, 1905
KV 4	Ramesses XI	III	accessible since antiquity; Brooklyn Museum, 1980

hillsides have not yet materialized. Theft is no longer a problem, but tourism has taken its toll in some KV tombs, and vandalism and changing environmental conditions continue to be problems. Only two KV tombs have been found largely unplundered: KV 47, Yuya and Thuya, and KV 62, Tutankhamun; all others were vandalized in antiquity.

There are sixty-two numbered tombs in the East and West Valleys, plus another twenty unfinished pits and shafts designated A–T (WV and KV share a single numbering system). The first twenty-one tomb numbers were assigned by John Gardner Wilkinson in 1827. His system numbered tombs from the entrance of KV southward, then from west to east. Since then, tomb numbers 22 to 62 have been assigned in the approximate order of discov-

ery, with KV 62 (the tomb of Tutankhamun) being the most recently found.

Until late in the nineteenth century, most digging in the East Valley was illicit and incompetent. There were a few exceptions; one of the best known was the work of Giovanni Belzoni, who dug there in 1816. By modern standards, his work was poor, but it was significantly better than that of his colleagues. One of the tombs he uncovered was among the most spectacular ever found in the valley: KV 17, the nineteenth dynasty tomb of Sety I. The announcement of that discovery made headlines throughout Europe and encouraged an increasing number of Egyptological projects there and, indeed, throughout Egypt. The elaborate records published by Jean-François Champollion, Karl Richard Lepsius, and Ippolito Rosel-

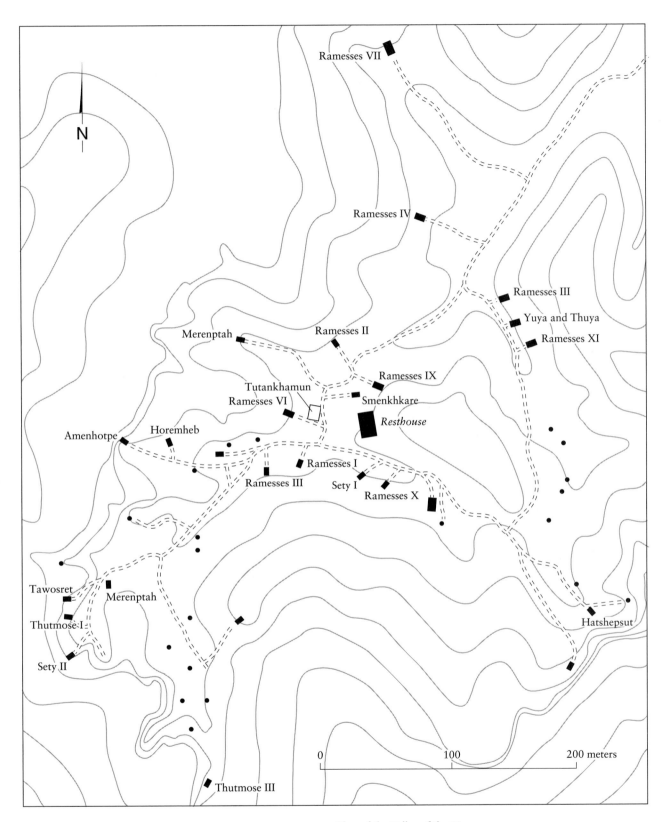

VALLEY OF THE KINGS. *Plan of the Valley of the Kings.*

lini are among the prime examples. Except for Belzoni, however, most KV projects continued to be amateurish and damaging to the monuments. It was not until 1883 that a systematic attempt was made (by Eugene Lefebure) epigraphically to record the KV tombs, and not until 1898 that excavations were undertaken (by Victor Loret, in KV 33–38) and their results published.

The most extensive and careful work in the East Valley was that conducted from about 1900 to 1922 by Howard Carter, first while he was an inspector of antiquities, then, after 1907, as director of archaeological excavations funded by Lord Carnarvon. It was Carter who in 1922 discovered the tomb of Tutankhamun (KV 62), but before that he was responsible for extensive exploration of the valley floor and for the discovery and recording of several KV and WV tombs.

It appears likely that every New Kingdom pharaoh at least began a tomb for himself in the Valley of the Kings, but not all tombs there can be assigned with certainty to individual rulers. The first pharaoh to have a KV tomb may have been Thutmose I (probably KV 20, later usurped by Hatshepsut); the last was Ramesses XI. Many tombs are uninscribed and can be roughly dated only by their architectural features; many others contain ambiguous inscriptions that make attribution difficult.

Broadly speaking, the KV royal tombs fall into four architectural and topographical categories which have only rough chronological significance, although there are many variations and alternative plans as well. One of the earliest types (I) consists of a level or sloping corridor that often makes one or two 90-degree turns to the left before reaching the burial chamber. These tombs are invariably cut into the base of the sheer cliffs that surround and define the East Valley. They date to the eighteenth dynasty. A second type (II) has a corridor that turns 90 degrees to the right and, in a chamber preceding the turn, has a pit cut into the floor, apparently meant to serve as a symbolic tomb of Sokar (not simply, as once was thought, as a device to prevent tomb robbery or keep floodborne debris from reaching the burial chamber). These tombs are not associated with any particular topographic features. They date to the eighteenth and nineteenth dynasties. A third type of royal tomb (III) is much larger than either types I or II; it consists of a long series of corridors that extend deeply into the hillside. Some of these tombs are dug along a single axis; others (type IV), including KV 57 (Horemheb) and KV 17 (Sety I), have a jog in their axis about halfway down their length. The long, relatively straight plan of this type of tomb caused early Greek travelers to label them *syringes*. The entrances of these tombs lie at the base of the Eastern Valley's sloping, debris-covered hillsides; they date to the nineteenth and twentieth dynasties.

Much is known about the techniques of digging and decorating the royal tombs. We have extensive documentation from Deir el-Medina, the nearby village in which the New Kingdom quarrymen and artisans lived. In such tombs as KV 57 (Horemheb), we find the decoration of chambers left in every conceivable stage of completeness, allowing a reconstruction of the cutting and decorative processes. Most commonly, the chamber walls are covered with scenes and texts from the principal religious texts, today collectively called the *Book of Going Forth by Day* (*Book of the Dead*). There are several such texts—the *Book of That Which Is in the Underworld*, the *Litany of Re*, the *Book of Gates*, and the books of *Caverns*, *Heavens*, and *Earth*—the last three of which are found only in the twentieth dynasty, but the first three in tombs throughout the New Kingdom.

The following is a table of the principal tombs in KV and WV, arranged in roughly chronological order. The name of the tomb owner, the tomb type, and the names and dates of excavators are given. Tombs not included here may be assumed to be small, unfinished, undecorated pits or other tombs of relatively minor interest.

[*See also* Theban Necropolis; *and* Valley of the Queens.]

BIBLIOGRAPHY

Hornung, Erik. *Das Grab des Haremhab in Tal der Könige*. Bern, 1971.

Hornung, Erik. *Tal der Könige. Die Ruhestatte der Pharaonen*. Zurich and Munich, 1982.

Hornung, Erik. *The Tomb of Pharaoh Seti I/Das Grab Sethos' I*. Zurich, 1991.

Reeves, Nicholas. *The Complete Tutankhamun: The King, The Tomb, The Royal Treasure*. Cairo, 1990.

Romer, John. *Valley of the Kings*. London, 1981.

Thomas, Elizabeth. *The Royal Necropoleis of Thebes*. Princeton, 1966.

Weeks, Kent R. "Recent Work in the Valley of the Kings." *Egyptian Archaeology, Bulletin of the Egypt Exploration Society* 4 (1994), 23–26.

Wilkinson, Richard H., and Nicholas Reeves. *The Complete Valley of the Kings, Tombs and Treasures of Egypt's Greatest Pharaohs*. London, 1996.

KENT R. WEEKS

VALLEY OF THE QUEENS. Designation introduced by Champollion in the nineteenth century for a pact of the Theban royal necropolis situated on the west bank of the Nile, opposite modern Luxor. The necropolis lies in a Y-shaped ravine which runs east–west, about 500 meters (1,600 feet) west of Deir el-Medina. Its Arabic names are Bibân el-Harîm and Bibân el-Malekat. Referred to by the ancients as *t₃ jnt 'ȝt* ("the Great Valley") and *t₃ jnt ršy* ("the Valley of the South"), the area was first utilized in the mid-eighteenth dynasty for burials of several high officials. Beginning in the nineteenth dynasty, it was used for the wives and children of the royal family.

VALLEY OF THE QUEENS. *Wall painting from the tomb of Nefertari, wife of Ramesses II, nineteenth dynasty.* (Courtesy Donald B. Redford)

From this point on it was called *t3 st nfrw* "the Place of Beauties," being described in the Abbot Papyrus as "the great (resting) places of the royal children, royal wives and royal mothers." It continued to fulfill this purpose in the twentieth dynasty, but afterward gradually fell into disuse. There are more than eighty tombs in the valley, of which twenty-one are inscribed to some extent; the others, except for one, are nothing more than single-chamber or pit tombs. Near the end of the northernmost arm of the wadi are vestiges of a dam built in the Ramessid period to divert runoff from flash flooding. Less than 40 meters (128 feet) away, situated between tombs 57 and 80, are the remains of a living installation for artisans, which also dates to the Ramessid period.

The tombs of Ramessid royals are the most impressive monuments of the site. Thus far identified as the earliest of these is tomb 38, that of Queen Sat-re, the wife of Ramesses I, the decoration of which never progressed beyond the stage of the draftsman's outlines. Female relatives of Ramesses II occupy seven substantial tombs, situated almost in a line along the northern flank of the valley. The tomb of the king's mother, Queen Tuya (tomb 80), is very poorly preserved, with only small remnants of decorated relief still adhering to the walls. The tombs of five

of the king's daughters—60 Queen Nebettawy, 68 Queen Meritamun, 71 Queen Bint-Anath, 73 Princess Henettawy, and 75 Queen Henumire—are strikingly similar in both design and decoration of religious motifs. The most important tomb of the group is that Nefertari (tomb 66), the king's principal wife for the first twenty-four years of his reign. Arguably the showpiece of the valley, the multi-chambered tomb is brightly decorated, with much of the color still pristine. Of the tomb's 520 square meters (5,600 square feet) of wall space, nearly 80 percent of the decoration is still intact. The wall scenes depict Nefertari's progression through the underworld, along with texts from the *Book of Gates*.

Along the far western fringe of the valley are five tombs (42, 43, 44, 53, and 55), and quite possibly a sixth (41), made for sons of Ramesses III. Four are outstanding in both decor and state of preservation: tomb 42, "First King's Son of His Majesty, Charioteer of the Royal Stable," Pareherwenemef; tomb 43, "Eldest King's Son, His Beloved, the Charioteer of the Royal Stable," Setiherkhopshef; tomb 44, "*Sem*-priest of Ptah, First King's Son of His Body," Khaemwaset; and tomb 55, "Hereditary Prince of the Two Lands, King's Son of His Body, His Beloved, Born of the God's Wife and God's Mother, the Great King's Wife,

King's Scribe, Overseer of Horses," Amenherkhopshef. In all four of these tombs, the princes are depicted as adolescents, with similar features and costume, in scenes of ritual with their father, the king. Moreover, in the tomb of Amenherkhopshef (tomb 55) is a text which states, "Given by favor of the King. . . . for the principal royal children," suggesting that tombs for the royal princes were commissioned in advance to be utilized when needed, with the name and titles of the recently deceased prince carved in just before burial.

There is indication that this was already the practice as early as the nineteenth dynasty to accommodate the female members of the royal family as well. Four tombs in the valley—31, 33, 36, and 40—were made for royal females, but except for one, the cartouches and titles were never filled in. These four lie along the southwestern fringe in proximity to one another. Tomb 33 was given over to Queen Tanedjmy, her name being painted in prior to her burial. Situated among the tombs of Ramesses III's sons along the western flank are tombs of two queens of the twentieth dynasty. Tomb 51 was made for "King's Mother, Isis," the mother of Ramesses VI. Although a matter of some debate, it is generally held that she is identical with Queen Isis Ta-Habadjilat, principal wife of Ramesses III. The fairly well-preserved tomb 52 belongs to "King's Daughter, Great King's Wife and King's Mother, Tyti," however, it is uncertain to whose reigns she is to be dated. A third queen of the period, "Great King's Wife and King's Mother, Tentopet," occupies tomb 74. Although not certain, it is most probable the Tentopet was wife to Ramesses IV and mother of Ramesses V. This tomb is one of a series of tombs set in a line along the valley's far northern flank; the others of this group are assigned to female members of the house of Ramesses II (see above). In the case of tomb 74, the location and similarity of design compare favorably with the tombs of the daughters of Ramesses II. There are other indications that this tomb was originally built for another daughter but was instead later taken over for the burial of Tentopet. Apart from pillars in the burial chamber on which her name is carved, Tentopet's name is simply painted in cartouches on the decorated walls; moreover, one scene in the tomb depicts a queenly figure above which is carved, "King's daughter of his body, his beloved, the mistress of the Two Lands," with columns for the name left blank.

The explorer and antiquarian Robert Hay first visited the necropolis in 1826, and he made extensive notes and plans, taking elevations of more than sixteen tombs. In 1828, John Gardner Wilkinson followed suit, copying twenty-four tombs. The following year, a joint French-Tuscan expedition brought Jean-François Champollion and Ippolito Rosellini to the site to carry out an epigraphic study of the principal monuments. Champollion

published his drawings in *Monuments del'Égypte et de la Nubie: Notices descriptives* (1844–1845), and Rosellini in *I Monumenti dell'Egitto e della Nubia, designati dalla Spedizione scientifico-letteraria Toscana in Egitto, I. Monumenti storici, III. Monumento del Culto* (1832, 1844). Karl Richard Lepsius conducted a scientific expedition to the Valley of the Queens in 1844, and Heinrich Brugsch in 1854. Commentaries and drawings by Lepsius appeared in *Denkmäler* in 1849 and 1900. In 1903, Ernesto Schiaparelli from the Turin Museum obtained an archaeological concession for the Valley of the Queens and undertook a program of exploration and study in 1903, 1904, and 1905. From 1971 until 1988, the Center of Study and Documentation for the Egyptian Antiquities Organization, together with the Centre National de la Recherche Scientifique (C.N.R.S.), under the direction of Christian Leblanc, completed a study and survey operation of the entire valley and immediate environs. In 1988, the Getty Conservation Institute carried out extensive restoration of tomb 66, of Nefertari, which consequently was opened to public viewing.

BIBLIOGRAPHY

Campbell, C. *Two Theban Queens, Nefert-ari and Ty-ti and Their Tombs.* London, 1909.

Campbell, C. *Two Theban Princes, Kha-em-Uast and Amen-khepshef, Sons of Ramesses III, Menna, A Land Steward, and Their Tombs.* London, 1910.

Hassanein, F., and M. Nelson. *La Tombe du prince Amon-(her)-khepchef.* Centre d' Études et de Documentation sur l'Ancienne Égypte, 71. Cairo, 1976.

Hassanein, F., and M. Nelson. *La Tombe du prince Khaemouaset.* Centre d'Études et de la Documentation sur l'Ancienne Égypte, 72. Cairo, 1992.

Leblanc, C. "Architecture et évolution chronologique des tombes de la Vallée des Reines." *Bulletin de l'Institut Français d'Archéologie Orientale* 89 (1989).

Leblanc, C. "Le dégagement de la tombe de Ta-nedjemy: Une contribution à l'histoire de la Vallée des Reines." *Bulletin de la-Société Française d'Égyptologie* 89 (1980), 32–49.

Leblanc, C. *Ta Set Neferou: Une Nécropole de Thebes-Ouest et Son Histoire.* Vol. 1. Cairo, 1989.

Leblanc, C. "La Vallée des Reines: Dégagement et publication des tombes; recherches sur l'histoire de la nécropole." In *Catalogue de l'exposition "Recherches sur les temples de Nubie—Histoire de la Montagne thébaine, du Ramesseum et de la Vallée des Reines,"* pp. 10–13. Cairo, 1982.

Siliotti, A., and C. Leblanc. *Nefertari e La Valle delle Regine.* Florence, 1993.

Schiaparelli, E. *Relazione sui lavori della Missione archeologica italiana in Egitto (anni 1903–1920).* Vol. 1, *Esplorazione della "Valle delle Regine" nella necropoli di Tebe.* Turin, 1924.

Thomas, E. *The Royal Necropoleis of Thebes.* Princeton, 1966.

Wall Paintings of the Tomb of Nefertari. Scientific Studies for their Conservation, *Annales du Service des Antiquités d'Égypte* (special edition). Cairo, 1987.

SUSAN REDFORD

VEGETABLES. In English, the term *vegetable* covers a range of widely differing plants that, cooked or raw, are used as food. In pharaonic Egypt, they formed an important part of the staple diet of the population, as indicated by both the representations of agricultural work and the lists of offerings. Texts also note the deliveries of numerous types of vegetables to the temples, even though it has not as yet proved possible to identify them all. The most important source for investigating vegetables are the remains from tombs and other archaeological sites. Tomb offerings were supplied for the eternal nourishment of the deceased. Not all the vegetables that were eaten were regarded as suitable for this ceremonial purpose, and special choices were made. For this reason, the vegetable remains found in settlement excavations, which have become known since the 1970s, are of particular interest; they reveal what was really consumed. Because of the dry climate, most of the plant remains in Egypt, although sometimes several thousand years old, have been so well preserved that botanical identification is possible.

Cultivated vegetables became important in pharaonic times, but in times of need, edible vegetables that grew wild were certainly collected as an important food reserve. Because wild vegetables were not employed as burial offerings, however, we do not know the extent to which they were used. Among them was the water caltrops (*Trapa natans*), which today occurs only in the upper reaches of the Nile River, in Ethiopia, but which is described as an Egyptian plant by classical authors. The lowermost stem of the papyrus (*Cyperus papyrus*) served as food and, usually bound together in bundles, can be seen among the offerings. The rhizomes of the two native Egyptian water lilies (*Nymphaea coerulea* and *Nymphaea lotus*) are also edible. In the drier areas of Egypt, the caper bush grew (*Capparis aegyptia*), whose elongated, green fruit can be eaten as a vegetable. (A leafy caper branch with a fruit is depicted on a faience tile from Tell el-Amarna.) It is not clear whether the Egyptians made use of the Abyssinian banana (*Ensete edule*), which now only grows to the south; some authors regard this as the inspiration for the "Naqada plant" painted on many prehistoric pots. The cooked inner part of the pseudo-trunk of the *ensete* was eaten as a vegetable, but no finds of *ensete* have yet been made.

Crucial for the nourishment of the large Egyptian population, however, were cultivated vegetables, which were usually grown in gardens and sometimes in the fields. The tomb paintings show these vegetable gardens—plots of land divided into small squares and watered by an agricultural worker, who wore a yoke with a pottery jug on each side.

Only a very few cultivated vegetables are descended from native Egyptian flora. Among them is the salad vegetable cos lettuce (*Lactuca sativa*), in Egyptian ꜥbw, whose parent plant *Lactuca seriola* grows throughout Egypt. There is evidence for lettuce from numerous Old Kingdom illustrations, which either show it as an offering or being cultivated in gardens. Substantial securely dated remains, however, are only available from the Roman period. The lettuce, whose stem and leaves contain a milky juice, was important in the cult of the ithyphallic god Min and was often depicted with him. Another cultivated vegetable indigenous to Egypt is the tiger nut (*Cyperus esculentus*), in Egyptian wꜥḥ. The rhizomes are about 1 to 1.5 centimeter (0.5 to 1 inch) in size and because of their high levels of sugar, starch, protein, and fat are particularly nourishing. They were often used as tomb offerings from Predynastic times onward.

All other vegetables used in pharaonic Egypt did not develop in the Nile Valley but were adopted from abroad, most often from the eastern Mediterranean region. Judging by present-day finds, the individual vegetables probably came to Egypt at different times. Yet it is only possible to say when this occurred for each with reservation, because archaeological excavations are always finding new plant material. Paleobotanical work in the Nile Valley is nowhere near complete.

At a very early stage, probably Predynastic, the Egyptians adopted the cultivation of alliaceous vegetables; onions (*Allium cepa*) were often depicted among the offerings, as was their cultivation in vegetable gardens. Actual finds, however, are first known only from the New Kingdom. In the cult of the Sokar festival, strings of onions had to be worn around the neck. Finds of garlic (*Allium sativum*) are also known only from the New Kingdom. Small Predynastic pottery models from el-Mahasna and Naqada, however, probably depict garlic bulbs and point to Predynastic cultivation. The third cultivated allium type was the leek. Finds dating from the New Kingdom do not enable differentiation to be made between *Allium porrum* (leek) or *Allium kurrath* (kurrat), which are botanically close.

Perhaps the most important cultivated vegetable in ancient Egypt were pulses (lentils, peas), numerous varieties of which were eaten. From Predynastic times, there are finds of lentils (*Lens culinaris*), everlasting pea (*Lathyrus sativus*), and fenugreek (*Trigonella foenum graecum*); from the Old Kingdom, the broad bean (*Vicia faba*), and from the New Kingdom, the chick pea (*Cicer arietinum*) and probably the pea (*Pisum sativum*). As yet, when the Egyptians began to cultivate the lupin (*Lupinus termis*) as a vegetable plant is unclear, possibly as early as the Middle Kingdom.

The cultivation of these pulses was adapted by the Egyptians from the Palestine region. They made use of two other types, however, whose native region was to the south of Egypt; they are the cow pea (*Vigna unguiculata*), known since the fifth dynasty, and the cajan or congo pea (*Cajanus cajan*), known from a seed find from the twelfth dynasty. Only in Roman times did the Egyptians first become acquainted with the cultivation of the vegetable types so widely known today: broccoli rape or rabe (*Brassica rapa*), kale (*Brassica oleracea*), and the common radish (*Raphanus sativus*).

[*See also* Agriculture; Diet; Flora; *and* Fruits.]

BIBLIOGRAPHY

Brewer, Douglas J., Donald B. Redford, and Susan Redford. *Domestic Plants and Animals.* Warminster, 1994.

Germer, Renate. *Flora des pharaonischen Ägypten,* Deutsches Archäologisches Institut, Abteilung Kairo, 14. Mainz, 1985.

Helck, Wolfgang. *Materialien zur Wirtschaftsgeschichte des Neuen Reiches.* 5 vols. Abhandlungen der Akademie der Wissenschaften und der Literatur in Mainz. Wiesbaden, 1961–1970.

Keimer, Ludwig. *Die Gartenpflanzen im Alten Ägypten,* vol. 1. Hamburg and Berlin, 1924; vol. 2, edited by Renate Germer. Deutsches Archäologisches Institut, Abteilung Kairo, 13. Mainz, 1984.

Zohary, Daniel, and Maria Hopf. *Domestication of Plants in the Old World.* 2d ed. Oxford, 1993.

RENATE GERMER
Translated from German by Julia Harvey
and Martha Goldstein

VESSELS for foods and liquids were made of a wide variety of materials, most commonly pottery, but also stone, metal, "Egyptian faience" (a quartz-bodied ceramic), "Egyptian blue" (a glass-frit), glass, wood, and other organic materials such as leather, shell, horn, ivory, and gourds. Vessel forms were often produced in more than one medium, and often technological features in one material would become decorative elements in another; for example, rivets and folded rims on metal vessels would be copied in ceramic ones.

Pottery. Ceramic pottery is the most abundant and archaeologically the most important of all the classes of vessels. It made its appearance in the Nile Valley very early in the Khartoum Mesolithic (c. 6000 BCE), and is part of a pan-African tradition of low-fired, black-surfaced wares with complex incised line-and-dot decoration, still to be found in parts of the continent today. Early Sudanese and Upper Egyptian pottery clearly belong to the same cultural esthetic, most notably the black-topped pottery characteristic of the Naqada I (Amratian) and Naqada II (Gerzean) periods of the later Neolithic (c. 4700–3500 BCE). The later Naqada sequence (Naqada II–III/Late Gerzean–Dynasty 0) saw the introduction of a new technology with built kilns, rather than the simple bonfire kilns of the preceding periods. This allowed a higher firing temperature that enabled the use of marl clays rather than

the riverine mud that had been used for the black-topped ceramics. These clays would fire with a buff surface and were decorated with red pigment, sometimes in imitation of stone vessels of the period.

Throughout the dynastic period both red-firing Nile silt clays and white to greenish or yellow marl clays were used. These different wares had subcategories that went in and out of fashion and were suitable for various purposes. For example, the whitish Qena clays are highly porous and make excellent jars for water, because they "sweat" and keep their contents cool. Nile silt clays, easily obtainable and low-fired, were ideal for cheap, utilitarian wares such as bread molds and offering vessels.

Decoration on pottery could be either naturalistic or abstract, and there have been suggestions that regional styles can be seen in the vase painting of the Predynastic period. By the end of this era, however, painting on pottery became rare and eventually disappeared altogether. Decorated ceramics appeared only sporadically throughout Egyptian history until the Coptic period. Instead, Egyptian artisans relied on shape and surface finish as the focus of their esthetic. For most periods, then, handles were rare, since they would break up the clean line of the vessel profile, and more often than not they are indicators of foreign influence. For much of the dynastic period, pottery styles are remarkably uniform all along the length of the Nile; even dimensions of certain types of vessels show little variation, some conforming to standard measures.

Fine polished wares made in white marl clay to imitate "Egyptian alabaster" (calcite), or red-surfaced to imitate copper, appear in the Early Dynastic period and Old Kingdom (3100–2250 BCE). At this point, the slow wheel was introduced, with only rims being thrown at first, and then entire vessels. Utilitarian wares such as beer and water jars and bread molds continued to be hand-built.

During the First Intermediate Period (2250–2061 BCE), along with the breakdown of classical style in art and architecture, pottery also became less finely finished, with greater regional diversity and added and incised ornament. The rise of the Middle Kingdom saw the return of the Memphite style in all the arts, including ceramic production. But the disorder of the Second Intermediate Period (1784–1570 BCE) brought on a period of local artistic innovation that again manifested itself in applied and etched elements on ceramic vessels.

Increased foreign contacts in the New Kingdom are manifest in new forms and painted decoration on pottery in Egypt, inspired by the ceramics of the Levant and the Aegean. Purely Egyptian styles can be seen in some elaborately painted vases with animal and hieroglyphic motifs, as well as a novel lotus-petal banding executed in a cobalt-derived blue pigment. While a few, more finely painted vases appeared in the Ramessid period, after the eigh-

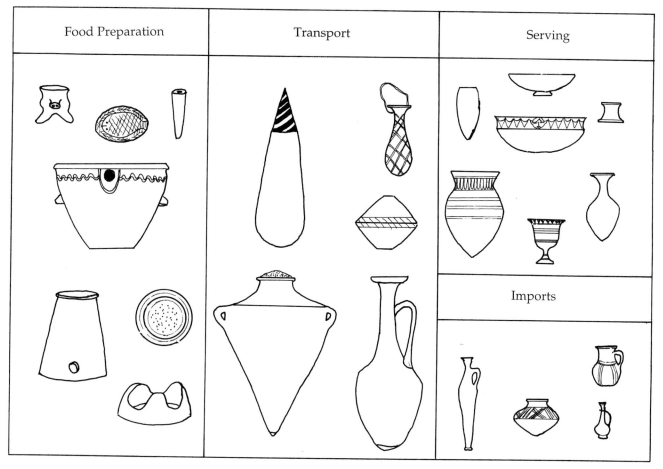

Food Preparation	Transport	Serving
		Imports

VESSELS. *Basic types of vessels used in everyday life.* (Courtesy Peter Lacovara)

teenth dynasty, most pottery returned to rather plain, utilitarian styles.

During the Persian period, the appearance of the faster-spinning kick wheel lent itself to decorative ribbed surfaces. It was not until the advent of the Ptolemaic period and increased outside contacts that Egyptian painted and decorated pottery reappeared.

Egyptian pottery seems to have had relatively little value for the ancients, and the few accounts that mention price underscore this. Imported foreign vessels seem to have had some keepsake value, and small examples, such as Cypro-Syrian "Spindle Bottles" and Cypriote base-ring wares (or *bilbils*) seem to be frequently reused. While some ancient Egyptian pottery vessels were made for everyday use, others seem to have been specifically meant for burials or offerings. Some vessel types also seem to have been put to a wide variety of uses. It is often difficult to gauge from representations what particular shapes of vessels were associated with which functions. Likewise, ancient Egyptian terminology is vague on the subject. Broken pots were sometimes mended, but this became

uncommon after the Predynastic period. Sherds, jar bases, and necks could be reused as tools, braziers and pot-stands, respectively.

Stone. Vessels in other media appear to have been more highly valued. Stone was used for vessels at the beginning of the Predynastic period, although these are rare and roughly made. Vases of patterned stone, such as fossiliferous limestone, breccia, and granite from the later Predynastic, were often imitated in pottery. With the advent of the dynastic period, the large tombs of high officials and members of the royal court were sometimes furnished with hundreds, if not thousands, of bowls, plates, and jars in stone—usually an attractive, banded calcite rock, often called "Egyptian alabaster." Some of these were produced by the finest court artisans and had paper-thin walls, and some were carved in two or more parts that could be fitted together perfectly. Examples were carved in the shape of baskets or pots and carried in string nets. Miniature versions of these forms were found in the tombs of the Old Kingdom, although full-size examples still were produced.

VESSELS. *Inscribed and painted hes-type wine jars with lids, late eighteenth to nineteenth dynasty.* They are made of painted Nile-silt ceramic and are 93.5 centimeters (36.75 inches) high with lid. (University of Pennsylvania, Philadelphia. Neg. # S8–31487)

Vessels of exotic stone appear in the Middle Kingdom, including obsidian and anhydrite, a type of gypsum, mistakenly called "blue marble." A favorite vessel form is the kohl pot, used for containing eye makeup. Other cosmetic jars appear in shapes derived from the cylinder jars of the Early Dynastic period and Old Kingdom. The New Kingdom saw an even greater variety of shapes and materials being used for stone vessels. Many forms derived from foreign vessels, and there seems to have been a demand for Egyptian stone vessels outside the Nile Valley. Sculptural forms, including plants, animals, and people, were used for containers throughout Egyptian history.

Stone vessels from Egypt were also exported to the Aegean, Syria-Palestine, Mesopotamia, and Nubia, and were copied by local craftsmen. A tall, slender vase with a wide, flat rim appeared in the Third Intermediate Period, and was exported throughout the Mediterranean world. It was called an "alabastron" by the Greeks, a term which later was applied to a type of rock not commonly used in Egypt, resulting in the confusion of "Egyptian alabaster" (a calcite rock, like travertine) with what is now called "alabaster" (an aggregate of gypsum).

Many stone vessels may have been produced solely for burial, since they show no sign of use and often appear to have been ritually smashed. Other stone vessels, however, served as containers for oils and unguents too rare to be left to leach out of porous pottery containers.

Metal. Metal vases appeared in the late Predynastic period. The earliest are simple forms hammered out of sheets of copper. The angular shapes of many Early Dynastic period pottery and stone vessels copy these simple forms. Spouts and handles were attached with rivets, and rims were usually folded over. Raising vessels from metal sheets was the primary manufacturing method for these containers, until bronze casting appeared. Casting allowed for the production of vessels with elaborate surface decoration in quantity, and far more easily than laboriously chasing the design by hand onto a metal surface. Precious-metal vessels were also produced, and the few that have survived are remarkable for their artistry; they range from simple cups and bowls to sumptuous creations with sculptural handles or inlaid decoration.

Faience and Glass. Faience, a glazed, quartz-bodied ceramic which usually is colored blue by the addition of copper, was also used for vessels from as early as the Early Dynastic period. This fragile material did not lend itself to everyday use, and most pieces seem to have been produced as grave goods or votive offerings. The most familiar forms are the bowls found in tombs of the New Kingdom, with lotuses, fish, and other symbols of rebirth. Faience vases with royal names appear in the furnishings of the royal tombs of the New Kingdom and as votive gifts to temples. Some faience kohl pots and cosmetic containers may actually have been used. "Egyptian blue" (a glass-frit, similar in composition to faience) was also used for vessels, but served mainly as a pigment in ground form.

True glass, probably an outgrowth of faience production, appeared in the eighteenth dynasty, largely associated with royal workshops. Most glass vessels are small and may have served as containers for precious oils and cosmetics. Egyptian kilns could barely melt glass, so the vessels were core-formed (made over a mud core dipped in the molten glass, much like a candy apple). The exterior surface could be decorated with melted rods of different-colored glass, applied to the surface and pushed and pulled to form different patterns.

Glass production declined after the end of the eighteenth dynasty, and it was not until later in the first millennium that it reappeared for vessels. The advent of higher-firing kilns in the Roman period allowed for mold-made wares and blown glass, which made glass vessels much easier to produce. Blown glass was cheap and efficient as a container and became enormously popular.

Organic Materials. Other materials employed for vessels included leather, usually in the form of a skin bag known as an *askos*, gourds decorated with incised motifs, and animal horn. Carved ivory was used for cosmetic containers, and shells could be utilized as shallow dishes for paints, ink, or cosmetics.

Utilitarian Vessels. Pottery vessels were used for food storage, preparation, and transport. Some conform to standard units of measure such as the *hin*, about one-half liter. Metal vessels may also have been used in cooking. Cooking pots in pottery occasionally show traces of burning, but often it is difficult to determine vessel function from use wear marks or residue. Egyptian texts and representations are often vague about which forms were being used. Vessel determinatives in inscriptions can also vary for the same word, suggesting that the Egyptians themselves used vessels of different shapes for the same function.

Vessels are frequently round or pointed on the bottom to sit in the sand or in ring stands, made of pottery or basketwork. Wooden stands were also made to hold vessels. Potstands would not only hold vessels but would also allow porous pottery containers to drip out their contents slowly and keep cool.

Special-Purpose Vessels. Containers of special form or with specific decoration often served ritual purposes. The *ḥs* vase, a slender elegant shape, was used for liquid offerings, and is found both in surviving examples and representations from the Early Dynastic period to the Roman period. *Ḥs* vases are found in pottery, copper, gilded, inlaid wood, faience, gold, and silver. Other ritual vases include the *situla*, used for pouring libations, *nmst* jars and *nw* jars for offerings, and canopic jars. Canopic jars were used to hold the internal organs after they were removed in the process of mummification. They first appeared in the Old Kingdom, invariably in sets of four, and by the New Kingdom, they were fitted with heads of the four sons of Horus, each designated to protect specific organs. During the Third Intermediate Period, when the entrails were placed back in the body, "dummy" jars (which did not open) were placed in the tomb to continue the tradition. Other imitation vessels made for burial included simulated stone vases (in wood or pottery), painted to look like stone.

[*See also* Basketry, Matting, and Cordage; Canopic Jars; Ceramics; Glass; Storage; *and* Weights and Measures.]

BIBLIOGRAPHY

Arnold, Dorothea, and Janine Bourriau. *An Introduction to Ancient Egyptian Pottery.* Mainz, 1993.

Aston, Barbara. *Ancient Egyptian Stone Vessels: Materials and Forms.* Heidelberg, 1994.

Friedman, Florence D., ed., *Gifts of the Nile: Ancient Egyptian Faience.* Providence, 1998.

PETER LACOVARA

VICEROY OF KUSH. *See* Nubia; Officials; *and* State, *overview article.*

VIZIER. *See* Officials; *and* State, *overview article.*

VOCABULARY. The discussion of vocabulary in ancient Egypt falls into several categories. First, we may examine the patterns of Egyptian lexical examples. As one might expect, the Egyptian language had a standard lexical inventory consistent with a preindustrial, agricultural society. Several areas of specialized knowledge, however, are well known. One is the medical sciences, an Egyptian realm of expertise: a number of texts survive that provide a wealth of information not only on the anatomical and physiological knowledge that the ancient Egyptians employed in the treatment of diseases, but also on the pharmaceutical properties of plants and minerals used in their prescriptions. Another area of lesser expertise is astronomy and mathematics, where again we have a number of documents that detail extensive terminologies for the subfields of practical geometry and practical star and moon observation. While most scholars of ancient science and technology consider the discoveries of Babylonian science to be at a higher developmental level, there is a clear local tradition that enriched the lexicon of Egyptian.

A second area that affected the lexical wealth of Egyptian was the exposure of ancient Egypt to a variety of other cultures throughout its history. As an Afro-Asiatic language, ancient Egyptian shared numerous traits with eastern, central, and northern African languages as well as with western Semitic languages. Thus, the standard vocabulary of these languages have numerous affinities from their developmental stages. Egyptian can be seen as a hybrid, utilizing elements from all these areas and thus sharing in their lexical roots.

After Egypt emerged as a unified country and after it had developed a unified script, it continued to interact with foreign countries through trade and warfare. These interactions inevitably provided the impetus to expand the lexical list through the introduction of trade goods not native to Egypt. One must note specific time periods where this happened. With the end of the Middle Kingdom, the invasion of the Hyksos compelled Egypt to absorb numerous people from Syria-Palestine. This was followed by Egyptian expansion to the northeast and south during the New Kingdom and the establishment of a foreign empire. This process had a dramatic effect on the culture of Egypt, and subsequently on the language. Numerous words from Semitic languages were added to the lexicon. Egyptian scribes developed a system known as "group writing" in order to accommodate the peculiar orthographies and sounds of foreign words. The early group writing styles from the late Old Kingdom and Middle Kingdom were refined during the New Kingdom, allowing scribes to deal with the approximately four hundred Semitic words introduced into Egyptian, as well as with foreign names.

A systematic examination of these foreign words shows that they cross the entire spectrum of Egyptian culture. They include military terms (*ti-ra-ya-na* "body armor), topographical items (*ka-ra-pa* "escarpment"), foods and beverages (*di-tu* "olives"), household objects (*ma-ša-di-di-t* "comb"), types of vessels (*ma-sa-ḫi-ta* "amphora"), medical terminology (*ga-ra-ta* "kidneys"), ideas of motion and emotion (*ha-s-t-ka-ta* "to swerve"), architecture (*mak-ta-ra* "tower"), tools (*bi-ša* "axe"), raw materials and minerals (*qa-ḏa* "gypsum"), occupations (*ku-ma-ru* "dancer"), political terms (*man-h-ta* "tribute"), flora and fauna (*'an-n-ru-na* "oak tree"), craft terminology (*ga-ra-ba* "to plane"), and numerous others. The attested vocabulary spans economic, legal, political, military, and religious categories. In one sense, the lexical items represent the broadest spectrum of cultural interaction during this period.

In the Late period, interactions between Egyptians and foreigners continued. Lexical borrowings were not as numerous, but a few can be noted: *mṯk* "wine merchant" as used in the name *p-s-n-mṯk* "Psammetichus," or *ḫstrpn* "satrap" (governor of Egypt during the Persian period). After the conquest of Egypt by Alexander the Great, Greek became the official language of the country for the next nine hundred years. Given this linguistic domination, one would expect that the native language would need to incorporate a series of lexical items that reflected the new political order and the concomitant social reorganization. However, most of the Greek words found in Demotic fall into a few limited categories: honorific titles of kings and deities, derivations of Greek proper names, administrative titles, and a limited number of technical terms. In fact, there seems to have been a tendency for Demotic scribes to translate Greek terms into Egyptian (for examples, *swtr* "Soter" is normally written in Demotic texts as *nty nḥm* "the one who saves"). As time progresses, there is no increase in the use of Greek words in Egyptian texts, even during the Roman period. This phenomenon suggests that the reaction to Greek was quite different from that to earlier Semitic influences.

The final phase of borrowing took place with the development of the Coptic stage of the Egyptian language. In this stage the Greek alphabetic script was adapted to Egyptian, with the addition of several signs representing sounds not found in Greek. With an artificial and foreign script now being used for the Egyptian language, and a whole new set of texts (Christian religious works), Coptic adopted numerous Greek words directly into the vocabulary. These lexical items came to permeate all aspects of Egyptian culture and thus reflect a gradual but accelerating diminution of the native language.

The last area to investigate is the influence of Egyptian

vocabulary on other languages. As an Afro-Asiatic language, Egyptian shared common roots with several other languages. Over time, some Egyptian vocabulary items were disseminated into contemporary cultures with whom they had contact, notably into Syria-Palestine. It is interesting to note that in the treaty between the Hittite king Hattusilis III and the Egyptian pharaoh Ramesses II there do not seem to be any Egyptian words in the Hittite version; it is possible that the Hittite version was written first, and a later Egyptian version derived from it as a direct translation.

When the occurrence of Egyptian loan words in cuneiform texts is analyzed, only a minuscule number are found. Most examples derive from the Amarna tablets found in Egypt, which represent letters exchanged between Egyptian vassals in Syria-Palestine and the Egyptian king. Numerous Egyptian names and some Egyptian toponyms are found, but the actual number of words that might be considered loan words is only about forty. These words are mainly found in lists of items wanted as tribute or as gifts, such as *a-zi-da* "drinking vessel" (Egyptian *ṯ3.t* "drinking vessel"), and *pa-qa* "linen" (Egyptian *p3q.t* "fine linen"). There are continuing discussions of how many of these words are actually Egyptian and how many are Semitic.

The absence of Egyptian words in foreign languages remains problematic. This may represent a lack of interest among the Egyptians in the cultures of their foreign neighbors. One could also speculate that since Akkadian was the *lingua franca* of the Near East during the New Kingdom and later, loan words normally came from the Akkadian into the receiving language (here, Egyptian), rather than vice versa.

By far the most common survival of ancient Egyptian words in modern languages is found in arabicized place names within Egypt. It is interesting to note that the words in English that we most associate with Egypt ("pyramid," "Cleopatra," "papyrus") are all derived from Greek. The Egyptian words *mr* "pyramid" and *ḏmʿ* "papyrus" have long passed out of use. The word "pharaoh," king of Egypt, survives and ultimately derives from the words *pr-ʿ3* "great house, palace," a designation used by the Egyptians to refer figuratively to the king. The word "Egypt" itself comes from the Greek "Aigyptos," which does derive (through Coptic) from the Egyptian toponym *ḥ.t k3 ptḥ*, a designation of the temple at Memphis, a major administrative center in Egypt.

The number of other words in English that might trace their roots back to ancient Egyptian is minimal. Some might argue that the proper name "Phineas" ultimately derives from the term *P3-nḥsy* "the Nubian," or that "Susan" may derive from the Egyptian *sšn* "lotus," though it is just as likely that the latter name derives from the Semitic root for "lotus." Through the medium of Arabic, it is likely that two terms come down to us: "adobe," perhaps derived from the Egyptian *idb/ḏb.t* "mud brick," and "ebony" from *hbny* "ebony."

[*See also* Language; *and* Names.]

BIBLIOGRAPHY

Clarysse, Willy. "Greek Loan Words in Demotic." In *Aspects of Demotic Lexicography*, edited by Sven Vleeming, pp. 9–33. Leuven, 1987.

Ellenbogen, M. *Foreign Words in the Old Testament, Their Origin and Etymology.* London, 1962.

Ghalioungui, P. *The Papyrus Ebers: A New English Translation.* Cairo, 1987.

Girgis, W., and A. Gregorius. "Greek Loanwords in Coptic." *Bulletin de la Société Archéologie Copte* 17 (1963–1964), 63–73; 18 (1965–1966), 71–96; 19 (1967–1968), 57–88; 20 (1969–1970), 53–68; 21 (1971–1973), 33–53; 23 (1976–1978), 199–222; 30 (1991), 77–92.

Helck, Wolfgang. *Die Beziehungen Ägyptens zu Vorderasien im 3. und 2. Jahrtausend v. Chr.* Wiesbaden, 1971.

Hoch, James. *Semitic Words in Egyptian Texts of the New Kingdom and Third Intermediate Period.* Princeton, 1994.

Lambdin, Thomas O. "Egyptian Loan Words in the Old Testament." *Journal of the American Oriental Society* 73 (1953), 145–155.

Lambdin, Thomas O. "Egyptian Words in Tell El Amarna Letter No. 14." *Orientalia* 22 (1953), 362–269.

Loprieno, Antonio. *Ancient Egyptian: A Linguistic Introduction.* Cambridge and New York, 1997.

Neugebauer, Otto, and Richard Parker. *Egyptian Astronomical Texts I–III.* London and Providence, 1960–1964.

Vycichl, Werner. *Dictionnaire étymologique de la langue Copte.* Leuven, 1983.

EUGENE CRUZ-URIBE

W

WEALTH. Knowledge of wealth in ancient Egypt is gleaned from a wide variety of autobiographical, documentary, and literary texts. These sources are supplemented by archaeological evidence from tombs and the remains of such New Kingdom settlements as Akhenaten's planned capital at Tell el-Amarna in Middle Egypt, the workmen's village at Deir el-Medina opposite Thebes, and the Middle Kingdom pyramid-town at Illahun at the edge of the Faiyum. Whereas autobiographical inscriptions and literary texts often represent an idealized view of wealth and privilege; documentary texts are often incomplete and lack context. Tomb size and decoration provide gauges of wealth and, if discovered intact, may contain artifacts of daily life, but the lack of well-preserved settlements prevents forming an overall picture of the distribution of wealth over time.

In the early Old Kingdom, the elite consisted primarily of close relatives of the pharaoh who held the highest offices in the land. In time, the burden of governing an increasingly complex state required the delegation of authority to officials with weaker ties to the king. Since there was no firmly established aristocratic class, new elites easily emerged in the provinces among capable individuals who personified the Old Kingdom virtues of vigor, pragmatism, and self-confidence. The state system of tax collection and redistribution afforded many administrators opportunities to gain personal wealth. Pragmatism, sanctioned by belief in a benevolent divine order that rewards excellence with wealth and prestige, gave Old Kingdom Egypt a strongly individualist ethos.

In the sixth dynasty, men of ability, such as the count and governor of Upper Egypt, Weni, charted paths from relative obscurity to national renown, partly through ambition and ability, partly through royal favor, and partly through the good fortune that brought them to the king's attention. Weni's claim that "never before had this office been held by any servant" suggests that never before had any commoner served as governor of Upper Egypt, an office introduced in the fifth dynasty. Thus, a hard-working commoner could secure great power and the wealth prominent officials enjoyed.

As early as the Old Kingdom, it was possible to gauge the wealth of an individual in terms of material possessions. Houses and outbuildings (sheds, barns), herds of livestock, surplus grain and other produce of the land, clothing and jewels, and boats were manifestations of wealth documented in inscriptions, tomb paintings, and artifacts, and sometimes in the meager remains of houses in the few surviving settlements that have been excavated.

The desire for greater control over the disposition of personal assets to benefit future generations led individuals to seek hereditary tenure of office, with acquired wealth, and to establish perpetual mortuary endowments that the eldest son maintained as "master of [his father's] possessions." Over time, considerable wealth was locked up in mortuary endowments; therefore, at the beginning of new dynasties, it was not uncommon for kings to terminate older endowments and redistribute their wealth. It was understood that as the source of all wealth, the pharaoh could unilaterally rescind the rights and privileges granted his subjects, constrained by some practical considerations.

Early on, men rich in material property (*rmṯ ḥwd*) were usually considered "great men" (*rmṯ wr, rmṯ ʿ3*) even though their wealth may have been inherited rather than earned. Thus, the expression *rmṯ ḥwd* eventually became synonymous with *rmṯ wr* or *rmṯ ʿ3*, regardless of how wealth was acquired. By the New Kingdom, *rmṯ-ʿ3* identified a "notable." In the Demotic of the Late period, *rmṯ-ʿ3* became the designation for a rich man.

Tomb autobiographies as early as the Old Kingdom praise not only the acquisition of wealth but also the exercise of social responsibility. The autobiographical inscription of Harkhuf, governor of Upper Egypt following Weni, is prefaced with the mortuary prayer in which the deceased claims that "[he] gave bread to the hungry, clothing to the naked, [and] brought the boatless to shore." Officials less renowned voiced similar, obviously formulaic claims that reflect popular piety. This is consistent with the expectation that successful men behave with generosity and benevolence toward their social and economic inferiors.

When the Old Kingdom collapsed and Egypt entered the turbulent First Intermediate Period, the system that promoted men of industry and intelligence was turned upside down. The prophet Neferti spoke of an age of violence in which everything was helter-skelter, the old social order was completely disrupted, and the underlying moral values were abandoned. Although this may exaggerate the historical reality, monarchs such as the Herakleopolitan king Merikare thought it politic to reward supporters with material wealth to ensure their loyalty. He also advised his son to advance a man because of his skills rather than his birth, because it is necessary to foster excellence wherever it is found. However, despite the egalitarian gospel promoted by rulers courting public favor, the First Intermediate Period did not usher in any kind of democracy, and wealth remained concentrated in a small elite.

During the Middle Kingdom, beginning with Senwosret I, foreign policy was aimed at the expansion and enrichment of Egypt through the mining of copper, gold, and precious stones, and the quarrying of alabaster and high-quality building stone in Egypt and Nubia, as well as through trade with western Asia. Land reclamation, initiated by Senwosret II in the Faiyum Basin, also enriched Egypt by making more agricultural land available to industrious farmers eager to become wealthy.

The Theban mortuary priest, farmer, and landlord Hekanakhte exemplifies the hard-working commoner who profited by the stable economic conditions of the early Middle Kingdom. Provided he could successfully juggle his responsibilities and pay his taxes, Hekanakhte was free to prosper by his farming and weaving enterprises in a barter economy where the products of the field, both grain and manufactured cloth, were the commodities most commonly traded.

By the reign of Senwosret III, a massive reorganization and expansion of the civil bureaucracy was aimed at limiting the wealth of feudal lords like those who had proved a threat to central authority in Herakleopolitan times. As provincial nobles and their once flourishing local courts were suppressed, a new middle class emerged that was comprised of small farmers, craftsmen, and tradesmen. Their prosperity is reflected in the numerous private monuments (statuettes, stelae) they erected near Osiris's Abydos temple. Thus, the national prosperity of Egypt was gradually spread over a larger proportion of the population than ever before.

The New Kingdom kings created an empire after the humiliation of the Second Intermediate Period, when foreigners briefly contested the rule of the Two Lands. Empire brought great wealth into Egypt under warrior-kings like Thutmose III, Sety I, and Ramesses II, but this wealth chiefly benefited particular groups of people.

Beginning with the eighteenth dynasty, an increasingly rich and influential military class flourished as a result of the system of rewarding veterans with real wealth: military honors (including gold); a share in pillage (slaves, cattle, weapons, and jewelry); and fields, servants, and livestock for their families, provided by the state. This taxable wealth was inheritable at the price of continued mili-

tary service. Prospects for wealth became a powerful attraction for increasing numbers of Egyptians seeking advancement through the military. The Ramessid *Inscription of Mose* from his Memphite tomb-chapel documents the conflict among three rival branches of the family over the trusteeship of such an estate, awarded to an ancestor centuries earlier. The fraud uncovered in the litigation of Mose's appeal indicates that compensation for military service was substantial and highly valued by veterans, their families, and descendants.

Pharaohs often appointed their personal favorites, as well as their most esteemed military veterans, to sensitive and prestigious positions within the royal establishment, which included royal tutor, honorary butler, fan-bearer, and steward of wealthy royal and temple estates. Social mobility increasingly became the prize of those willing to advance themselves through ruthless self-promotion and patronage politics (for example, Hatshepsut's favorite, the chief steward of Amun, Senenmut).

During the New Kingdom, temples controlled as much as a third of the agricultural land in Egypt, according to the Great Harris Papyrus of Ramesses III/IV, and they owned and/or administered much of the land in Middle Egypt, according to the Wilbour Papyrus of Ramesses V; in this, temples acted as a branch of the state administration. Astute priests in high ecclesiastical offices personally profited by the role of temples in the economy. For many, the priesthood served as a ladder to success.

From earliest times, pyramid complexes attracted tomb robbers whose activities spawned a black market in precious metals and luxury goods. Tomb robberies reached epidemic proportions during the twentieth dynasty, when government security failed to safeguard the Theban necropolis from the raids of foreign marauders and other criminals. Motivation for tomb robbery might be poverty, the settlement of debts, the purchase of "protection," the financing of a fine burial, or sheer avarice. A number of papyri survive detailing the arrest and prosecution of criminals who came from all levels of society. At the workmen's village at Deir el-Medina, Papyrus Salt 124 reveals that the foreman Paneb was charged with thefts from both royal and private tombs, the misappropriation of government equipment, and the misallocation of public labor for personal use. Although Paneb was probably the most notorious malefactor among the village's residents, he was not unique.

A different class of criminal was the employee who used knowledge of his employer's accounts to embezzle. The Turin Indictment Papyrus (Papyrus Turin 1887) documents the misappropriation of grain revenues by a priest of the temple of Khnum at Elephantine, in collusion with the ship's captain who transported the temple's grain to its granaries. Such crimes led Barry J. Kemp to comment that despite the superficial law-abiding exterior of Egyptian civilization, there "lurked a predatory instinct directed towards property rather than persons" (1991, 246). Such impulses emerged during periods of marked political, social, and economic instability, exemplified by the dissolution of the empire.

The major participants in the Late period agrarian economy were the state, the *machimoi* ("warriors") who included descendants of Libyan mercenaries, and the priests who consolidated a large proportion of Egypt's wealth in temple estates. Highly coveted priestly offices were usually hereditary; but sometimes a strong pharaoh intervened, as did Psamtik I (twenty-sixth dynasty), according to the petition of Petiese. Kinship ties, however, remained a significant factor in achieving wealth and status, and astute individuals did not hesitate to exploit them. Later on there were attempts to diminish temple wealth by the Persian rulers Cambyses, Xerxes, and Artaxerxes III.

In the Late period commerce was dominated by foreigners, especially the well-to-do Greek colonists at Naukratis in the western Nile Delta. Although some Egyptians reacted with hostility, others responded with characteristic pragmatism, finding comfort in the words of the Ramessid sage Amenemope:

> Better is praise [as] one beloved of people
> Than wealth in the storehouse;
> Better is bread with easy mind
> Than wealth with anxiety.

[*See also* Economy, *overview article and article on* Private Sector; *and* Social Stratification.]

BIBLIOGRAPHY

Baer, Klaus. "An Eleventh Dynasty Farmer's Letters to His Family." *Journal of the American Oriental Society* 83 (1963), 1–19. A review article that provides translations and considers problems in the interpretation of the correspondence of the early Middle Kingdom mortuary priest, farmer, and landlord Hekanakhte; discusses points of disagreement with James, 1962.

Bietak, Manfred. "Urban Archaeology and the 'Town Problem' in Ancient Egypt." In *Egyptology and the Social Sciences: Five Studies*, edited by Kent R. Weeks, pp. 97–144. Cairo, 1979. A description of the techniques utilized to study the archaeological remains of urban sites, which have much to offer the student of social and economic history.

Černý, Jaroslav. "Papyrus Salt 124 (Brit. Mus. 10055)." *Journal of Egyptian Archaeology* 15 (1929), 243–258. Translation and commentary concerning the papyrus that records the misdeeds of the Deir el-Medina foreman Paneb.

Gaballa, G. A. *The Memphite Tomb-chapel of Mose*. Warminster, 1977. Complete publication of the well-known Ramessid tomb-chapel of Mose. Gives attention to the legal text that describes the history of the legal wranglings over the estate of an early eighteenth dynasty soldier rewarded by pharaoh for military service with real estate.

James, T. G. H. *The Ḥekanakhte Papers and Other Early Middle Kingdom Documents*. New York, 1962. The complete publication of the correspondence of Hekanakhte and an evaluation of its place in the socio-economic documentation of the early Middle Kingdom.

Janssen, Jac. J. "Khaʿemtōre, A Well-to-do Workman." *Oudheidkundige Mededelingen uit het Rijksmuseum van Oudheden te Leiden* 58 (1977), 221–232. A valuable article about a Deir el-Medina workman by the contemporary authority on Deir el-Medina.

Kees, Hermann. *Ancient Egypt: A Cultural Topography*. London, 1961. A comprehensive geographical survey of ancient Egypt which explores the relationship between phases in Egyptian history and the distinct geographical features of the land.

Kemp, Barry J. *Ancient Egypt: Anatomy of a Civilization*. London and New York, 1991. A detailed examination of Egyptian society from an archaeological perspective, making use of recent excavation reports and reinterpreting older data; useful index and notes.

Kemp, Barry J. "The City of el-Amarna as a Source for the Study of Urban Society in Ancient Egypt." *World Archaeology* 9 (1977), 123–139.

Kemp, Barry J. "The Early Development of Towns in Egypt." *Antiquity* 51 (1977), 185–200. This and the previous article consider Egypt as an urbanized society in light of the excavation of town sites and what their valuable archaeological remains contribute to an understanding of social and economic history, emphasizing the inadequacy of inscriptional evidence in the early periods.

Kemp, Barry J. "Temple and Town in Ancient Egypt." In *Man, Settlement and Urbanism*, edited by Peter J. Ucko et al., pp. 657–680. London and Cambridge, Mass., 1972. Gives particular attention to the temple economy during the New Kingdom.

Lichtheim, Miriam. *Ancient Egyptian Literature*. 3 vols. Berkeley, 1973–1980. Includes modern translations of wisdom literature, tomb autobiographies, and literary texts relevant to the subject of wealth.

O'Connor, David. *Ancient Egyptian Society*. Pittsburgh, 1990. An introduction and brief overview of the structure of ancient Egyptian society, summarizing aspects of the socio-economic order, including the family, education, national security and internal order.

Peet, T. Eric. *The Great Tomb-Robberies of the Twentieth Egyptian Dynasty*. Vol. 1, *Text*; vol. 2, *Plates*. Oxford, 1930. A critical study with translations and commentary on the papyri that document the socio-economic phenomenon of tomb robbery during the twentieth dynasty.

Peet, T. Eric. "A Historical Document of Ramesside Age." *Journal of Egyptian Archaeology* 10, parts 1–2 (1924), 116–127. Translation of and commentary on Papyrus Turin 1887 (Turin Indictment Papyrus), concerning the fraud committed by a priest of the temple of Khnum at Elephantine and his accomplices.

Schenkel, Wolfgang. "Reichtum." In *Lexikon der Ägyptologie* 5:211–212. Wiesbaden, 1984.

Smith, H. S. "Society and Settlement in Ancient Egypt." In *Man, Settlement and Urbanism*, edited by Peter J. Ucko et al., pp. 705–719. London and Cambridge, Mass., 1972. An examination of documentary sources that illuminate aspects of life in ancient Egyptian towns and villages that grew up over time, in contrast to planned settlements such as Tell el-Amarna and the fortified Nubian towns.

Trigger, B. G., et al. *Ancient Egypt: A Social History*. Cambridge, 1983. Social, economic, and political history of Egypt from the Predynastic period down to the conquest of Alexander the Great, written by authorities on each period. Contains updated bibliographical essays for each chapter as well as a comprehensve bibliography.

SALLY L. D. KATARY

WEAPONS. *See* Military, *article on* Materiel.

WEAVING, LOOMS, AND TEXTILES. Thousands of ancient textiles have survived in Egypt, owing to the dry conditions and the practice of placing cloth in tombs. Pharaonic Egypt was famous throughout the ancient world for the production of linen. Well into Roman times, linen was regarded as a valuable commodity and was exported throughout the Mediterranean region.

Fibers. Although ancient Egypt is well known for the production of linen, flax was not the only textile fiber in use. Textiles have also been found made from sheep's wool, goat hair, and palm fibers.

There is a misconception that the Egyptians did not use wool, and the idea is based on comments by authors of the Classical era, notably the fifth-century BCE writer Herodotus, in his *Histories,* and by the first-century CE author Plutarch, in his *Isis and Osiris.* Examples of wool and woollen textiles have been found in Old and Middle Kingdom graves. Several examples of both woollen and goat-hair textiles were excavated at the mid-fourteenth-century BCE workmen's village at Tell el-Amarna. Several goat-hair textiles were also found at other ancient sites. Palm fiber is made from the bark of various types of palm trees; it is not commonly found, but at Tell el-Amarna one textile had a series of palm-fiber loops woven into it.

The majority of ancient Egyptian textiles were made from flax, of the genus *Linum,* but especially from *Linum usitatissimum.* Turning flax plants into a piece of cloth is an elaborate process; yet it can be shown from excavated Faiyum textiles that, during the Neolithic (c.5000 BCE), a variety of linen cloth types were being produced.

Flax is a member of the family Linaceae, order Linales. Although not native to Egypt, its use there dates to prehistoric times and, very possibly, it was imported into Egypt from the Levant.

Flax plants take about three months to mature. They are slender annuals with delicate blue flowers. Once the flowers have died away, the seedheads appear and the plants are ready to be harvested. Bundles of flax stems were grabbed and then pulled, rather than cut, out of the ground. After the flax plants were dried, the seedheads were removed, either by rippling (removing by hand) or by combing with a long, toothed board (the rippling comb). Exposure to water or to dew and sunlight loosens the fibers within the plant stems, in the process known as retting. After washing, drying, beating, and combing, the fibers are made ready for spinning.

Spinning. To produce long, useful threads, flax fibers are spun, that is twisted together. In doing so, a long, cohesive thread is produced that is slightly elastic. The technique of spinning in ancient Egypt is seen as two distinct but related processes. In the first stage, an initial and loose twist was given to the flax fibers; in the second stage, the actual spinning of the fibers occurred, to produce the thread. Then the spinning had three distinct stages: the drawing-out of the fibers; the twisting of the fibers; and the winding of the thread.

Once a spindle was set in motion, the spinner pulled or drew out (called "attenuation" or "drafting") a few fibers at a time from a mass. As the spindle turned the fibers, twist or spin was added. When there was sufficient twisted thread, the spindle was stopped and the thread wound onto the spindle shaft.

The most common form of spinning equipment to be used in ancient Egypt was the hand spindle. It was made of a stick (the shaft or spindle) with a weight (the whorl). The whorl acted like a flywheel, keeping the momentum of the spin regulated for speed and uniformity of motion. Three basic methods of spinning are known from both Middle and New Kingdom depictions: grasped-spindle spinning, support-spindle spinning, and drop-spindle spinning.

Preparing the Warp Threads. After the flax fibers were spun into a thread or yarn, they were ready to be woven into cloth. The first task was to remove the thread from the spindle and to warp the loom ("warping"), which involved placing the warp threads in position on the loom with the threads pulled tight ("tensioned"). Then the actual weaving commenced, with threads moved over and under the warp, row after row, in one of several patterns.

Looms. From a variety of ancient Egyptian written and representative sources, by the eighteenth dynasty of the New Kingdom two types of looms were in use—the ground, or horizontal, loom and the fixed-beam, or vertical, loom. The horizontal loom has a simple construction and consists of a horizontal warp stretched, over the length, between two beams, at top and bottom. The beams are generally kept in place by a pair or pegs driven into the ground. The weaver starts at one end of the warp and works until the other end is reached, moving the position of the heddle as needed. One of the oldest representations of the horizontal loom is on a Near Eastern Predynastic bowl (4500–4000 BCE), found in a woman's tomb (tomb 3802), at Badari, in Upper Egypt. A small amount of woven cloth can be seen at one end. One of the characteristic features of cloth woven on the ancient Egyptian horizontal loom is a selvedge edge, or weft-fringe, which is always on the left side of the cloth. Depictions of people wearing cloth with such a fringe are common in Middle Kingdom representations.

The second form of loom—the vertical, or fixed-beam—was depicted in various ancient tombs. As the name suggests, instead of the warp being stretched horizontally, the threads are pulled or tensioned vertically. The warp ends are wrapped around two beams (the upper, or warp, beam and the lower, or cloth, beam). The loom is placed upright or is leaned against something firm, such as a wall. Most depictions of ancient Egyptian vertical

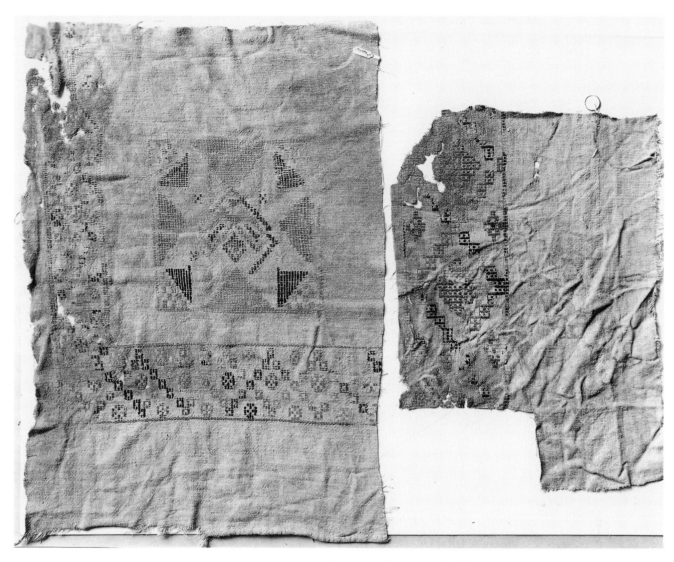

WEAVING, LOOMS, AND TEXTILES. *Two fragments of Coptic textiles from the Faiyum, made of linen, with inlaid woolen bands and panel.* (University of Pennsylvania Museum, Philadelphia. Neg. # S8–31736)

looms show the upright beams resting on blocks. Suitable stone blocks have been found both inside and outside some houses at the workmen's village of Tell el-Amarna. All are made of limestone, have a square shape with a large groove carved into them, and are extremely heavy. Weavers stood or sat at the base of the loom and worked upward. The warp was released during the weaving process, either by turning the warp beam or by lowering it.

The sizes of vertical looms varied. Two New Kingdom looms depicted in the eighteenth dynasty tomb of Thut-Nefer at Thebes are of different heights. Judging from the size of the weavers, the upright beams were 3–5 meters (10–16 feet) in height. This type of loom first appeared in Egyptian representations at the beginning of the New Kingdom, leading to scholarly speculation that the loom was introduced by the Hyksos, from the Near East. Since the range of looms used by the Hyksos is not known exactly, this attribution should be treated with caution.

Weave Forms. Weaving is the process of interlacing two or more sets of threads according to a predefined system, to produce all or part of a textile. In ancient Egypt, the range of weave forms, or patterns, seems to be limited to the following types: tabby, basket, tapestry, and warp-pattern weaves. The most common weave forms from ancient Egypt are the simple, or balanced, tabby weaves (with an equal number of warp to weft threads), the warp-

WEAVING, LOOMS, AND TEXTILES. *Depiction of textile manufacture, from Beni Hasan.* At the right, the flax is spun and unraveled. At the left, an obese supervisor oversees the workers at the loom.

faced tabby weaves, and weft-faced tabby weaves. A faced tabby weave has more threads in one system than the other. Thus a warp-faced tabby has more warp than weft threads per centimeter. The basket, or extended, weave is also a tabby weave, but the warp ends or the weft picks are in groups of two or more. Various types of basket weaves were used in ancient Egypt, including the half-basket and the warp-faced basket weaves.

Tapestry is a weave that comprises one warp with a weft having threads of different colors; these do not pass full width, from selvedge to selvedge, but are carried back and forth within the pattern, interweaving only with that part of the warp required for any one pattern area. Only a few examples of textiles woven in a tapestry weave have been found in Egypt, and all are associated with New Kingdom royal tombs. One of the textiles bears the cartouche of Amenhotpe II (r. 1454–1419). Several pieces were recorded by Howard Carter and Percy E. Newberry, from the tomb of Thutmose IV, who died c.1410 BCE. Several other examples, including a complete tunic in tapestry, were found in the tomb of Tutankhamun (r. 1355–1346 BCE).

A small number of textiles with warp-patterned designs—one of the most complex of the weaves used in Egypt during the ancient period—have been recorded from various New Kingdom sources. Relatively few details are known about the history of this type of weave, but in general, it is believed to be an imported form (perhaps from Syria), which came to Egypt at the beginning of the New Kingdom. One of the largest and most elaborate examples of this type of work is the so-called Girdle of Ramesses III (r. 1198–1166 BCE), now in the Liverpool Museum. The girdle measures 5.2 meters (16 feet) in length and tapers from 12.7 to 4.8 centimeters (5–1.8 inches) in width; it is decorated with zigzags, dots, and

rows of *ankh* signs in blue, red, yellow, green, and undyed flax (a light tan).

At the beginning of the Middle Kingdom, a form of weaving now called weft-looping started to be produced. The appearance of this cloth is similar to that of modern toweling. The Egyptians used the loops to create intricate patterns, including chevrons, diamonds, and bands. One of the earliest examples of this type of cloth came from the collective burial of sixty soldiers slain during the reign of Montuhotpe II (c.2000 BCE).

Various Egyptian texts refer to the different qualities of linens. One such text is in the eighteenth dynasty tomb of Rekhmire at Thebes (tomb 100) and there, references were made to "king's linen, bleached linen, fine linen, . . . linen, close-woven linen." The Egyptian appreciation of the various grades of linen can also be seen in the marks inked onto the cloth. In most cases, a temple or some other institution is marked, under which are various symbols. The symbols vary according to the quality of the cloth—thus, for example, a one-bag cloth is normally coarser than a two-bag cloth.

The difference between royal and nonroyal textiles is hard to define. As a generalization, the fineness of the cloth, the use of large areas of color, and the quantity of applied decoration (such as gold bracteates), all give an indication of a textile's rank. Some of the textiles from the tomb of Tutankhamun, for example, are so sheer that they are transparent when held up to light. Therefore, the tomb reliefs that show women wearing transparent clothing should be seen as a reflection of the truth.

Dyes. The use of dyed threads or dyed cloth can tentatively be traced back to the first dynasty, via a brownish piece of linen found at Tarkhan. Greater confidence about dyed cloth can be assigned to the late third or early fourth dynasty, based on a red cloth fragment from the site of

Meidum. In general, however, not until the New Kingdom was cloth frequently woven with colored threads. The ancient Egyptian dyestuffs can be divided into two basic types: ocher and plant dyes. Ocher is an earth that consists of hydrated oxide of iron (rust) mixed into clay. With heat, yellow iron oxide can be transformed by degree into red iron oxide; thus ocher can be used to create yellow, yellow-brown, and red colors. The dyeing of linen with iron oxide has a long tradition in Egypt, which may date back to the Early Dynastic period (as, for example, the first dynasty Tarkhan textile mentioned above). Linen that was colored red from iron oxide dyes was also found at various later sites, including the workmen's village at Tell el-Amarna.

Reds were not only produced by ochre, but also by plant dyes. Madder root (*Rubia tinctorum*) was one of the main sources; its main coloring agents are anthraquinones, most notably alizarin. Other known sources of red dyes used during pharaonic times are safflower (*Carthamus tinctorius*), henna (*Lawsonia alba* or *L. inermis*), and alkanet (*Anchusa tinctoria*).

The most common sources of the blue color in Egyptian textiles is indigotin, a substance found in plants of both the genus *Indigofera* (which includes indigo) and the genus *Isatis* (which includes woad, *I. tinctorum*). Although it is impossible to determine chemically the origin of the dyestuff, written sources from the period suggest that woad rather than indigo was the source.

A small number of textiles have a yellowish color, and they may have been dyed. So far, however, the actual dyestuffs have not been identified, but the potential sources of yellow dyes for ancient Egypt are safflower and pomegranate (*Punica granatum*).

The two most common dyestuffs associated with Egyptian textiles are indigotin blue and alizarin red. Both substances were obtained from plants that were, however, not native to Egypt. The plants (or the dyes) were imported, most probably from the Levant, beginning sometime during the early New Kingdom, as part of the commercial trade between the regions.

The Producers of Textiles. Certain jobs within Egyptian society were regarded as suitable for women, while others belonged to men. Yet it is not always easy for Egyptologists to establish which sex actually carried out some of the jobs, as there was some overlap of functions. Nevertheless, it is clear from both texts and depictions that the vast majority of those involved in the production of cloth were women. Although women were responsible for many aspects of cloth production, as well as its care, women never seem to be "in charge" of its production—all the major titles relating to cloth production belonged to men.

There was also a difference in which sex used what type of loom. Women were always shown using the horizontal loom, and most of the weavers depicted using the vertical loom were men. It may be that the "new" vertical loom had prestige or, perhaps, it was heavier and it therefore required more strength to work.

Finally, it should be noted that a number of textiles have yielded discrete marks that were woven into the selvedges. These are the marks of professional weavers, which identify a workshop or even a weaver. Textiles of varying qualities were uncovered at the workmen's village at Tell el-Amarna, all of which had the same mark woven into their selvedges.

Spinning and Weaving Workshops. From a variety of sources, it is known that there were at least four basic types of weaving workshops in ancient Egypt. For example, the study of domestic architecture has revealed details about the production of textiles within both small and large housing units. Numerous hand spindles mixed in with roofing material, for example, have been found at the Middle Kingdom site of Illahun (formerly called Kahun). Similar finds of spindles in roofing material were excavated at the New Kingdom site of the workmen's village at Tell el-Amarna. Evidence also exists for weaving within large housing units; for example, traces of a loom and weaving materials were found at a house in the main city at Tell el-Amarna.

Several letters were written during the Middle Kingdom that mention the production of cloth at home. In one letter, a house containing a loom was being sold, and the scribe Nakht wrote to a man called Aau that all had gone well with the sale of his house (Cairo Papyrus 91061). Nakht then noted that cloth was being woven on the loom and that some had already been sent to him: "Now as for the *mn*-cloth, it is set up [on the loom]. Now as for the bolt of cloth, it is woven; and in fact, I have sent you the bolt of cloth."

From several sources, it is known that large estates and palaces in ancient Egypt usually contained various workshops, including spinning and weaving ateliers, to provide the household with necessary items. The evidence would suggest that within such estate ateliers tens of people, usually women, were involved in the production of cloth. In the New Kingdom tomb of Djehutynefer at Thebes, a weaving workshop was depicted that shows numerous men and women busily at work preparing and spinning thread, as well as weaving it. A further indication of how many people may have been employed in a weaving workshop can be gained from a Middle Kingdom text (Brooklyn Papyrus 35.1446); it is a copy of a royal decree that authorized the transfer to a new owner of a group of ninety-six confiscated household servants. The list was badly damaged, so it is only possible to read the occupations of thirty-eight of the servants (twenty-nine women and nine men). Of the women, twenty were involved in the production of cloth, for example, as the "weaver of *h3tyw*-cloth" or the "weaver of *ssr*-cloth."

In addition to his chief queen, a pharoah had numerous other women within his court to whom he was married. Many would have had children and numerous servants around them. One of the solutions developed by the Egyptians to house these people was that of harem palaces in remote areas, such as that of Merwer at Abu Ghurob. One of the activities for the women was the production of cloth for the royal households, and it is likely that all those palaces contained spinning and weaving ateliers.

Cloth had an important role within the life of an Egyptian temple. Textiles were essential for various rituals in a temple, such as the dressing of statues of the gods. Cloth was used as part of the rations for priests and servants attached to the temple; it was also used to clothe them and to provide bedding. In some cases, the number of temple servants reached into the thousands, so the annual amount of cloth required would have been substantial. Sometimes cloth was given to the temples by wealthy or royal patrons. In the lists of goods given by Ramesses III to various temples throughout Egypt, records were kept of the quantities of garments, cloth, yarn, and flax donated by him on a yearly basis. Since yarn and flax were given to the temples, we learn that the temples had the means to turn such gifts into cloth. Was it done within the temple complexes or was it given out to women of the region, who would produce cloth for them? Most likely, both systems were used.

[*See also* Basketry, Matting, and Cordage; *and* Clothing and Personal Adornment.]

BIBLIOGRAPHY

Allgrove-McDowell, J. "Kahun: The Textile Evidence." In *The Pyramid Builders of Ancient Egypt,* edited by R. David, pp. 226–252. London, 1986. A general account of the textiles found at Kahun (now called Illahun).

Barber, E. J. W. *Prehistoric Textiles: The Development of Cloth in the Neolithic and Bronze Ages.* Princeton, 1991. A survey of the production of cloth in the ancient Eastern Mediterranean region.

Crowfoot, G. M., and de Garis Davies, N. "The Tunic of Toutankhamon." *Journal of Egyptian Archaeology* 27 (1941), 113–130. A detailed account of one of the garments from the tomb of Tutankhamun.

Germer, R. *Die Textilfärberei und die Verwendung gefärbter Textilien im Alten Ägypten.* Wiesbaden, 1992. A detailed description of dyes and dyeing techniques in ancient Egypt.

Hall, R. *Egyptian Textiles.* Aylesbury, 1986. A general introduction to the subject of Egyptian textiles.

Lucas, A., and J. R. Harris, *Ancient Egyptian Materials and Industries.* 4th ed. London, 1962. Numerous examples of and references to textiles and their production.

Riefstahl, E. *Patterned Textiles in Pharaonic Egypt.* Brooklyn, 1994. A detailed study of the various methods used to decorate textiles in ancient Egypt, based on actual examples and representations.

Roth, H. L. *Ancient Egyptian and Greek Looms.* Halifax, 1951. A study of looms and how they worked, based on ancient Egyptian and Greek representations.

Vogelsang-Eastwood, G. *De Kleren van de Farao.* Amsterdam, 1994. A general introduction to the production and use of textiles in ancient Egypt; with numerous illustrations.

GILLIAN M. VOGELSANG-EASTWOOD

WEDJAHORRESNE, a high-ranking official and priest who lived at Sais in the latter half of the sixth century BCE. The little that we know of him comes from texts inscribed on his naophorus statue now in the Vatican Museum. There we learn that he was a naval officer in the reigns of the twenty-sixth dynasty rulers Amasis and Psamtik III (569–525 BCE) and was raised to the rank of "Chief Physician and Controller of the Palace" after the Persian king Cambyses conquered Egypt in 525 BCE. His tomb was recently discovered at Abusir, although it remains unclear whether he was ever buried there.

Several intriguing questions surround this man. In one text on the Vatican Museum's statue, Wedjahorresne claims responsibility for creating the royal Egyptian titulary for Cambyses, who was the ruling pharaoh, and states that he was duly promoted to his new official positions as a result. These remarks have led a number of modern scholars to call him a traitor and collaborator. We should not necessarily brand Wedjahorresne with such modern and politically charged terms. There is much evidence that points to such "collaboration" as the norm during the Persian Empire; high-ranking officials in Persian-occupied foreign lands were usually retained in their posts, to promote peace and to preserve the ancient cultures of those lands. By the same standards, the biblical prophets Ezra and Nehemiah, both officials in the Persian Empire, would have to be termed "collaborators" as well. Furthermore, during their rule of Egypt as pharaohs, the Persian kings, for the most part, showed an interest in and respect for the Egyptian religion.

An additional point of interest stems from a fragmentary text, on the statue of another individual, which dates to the beginning of the Second Persian Occupation of Egypt (mid-fourth century BCE). It has been interpreted by several scholars as evidence that Wedjahorresne was revered as a holy man at Memphis 170 years after his death, a development that hardly points to belief in his behavior as treasonous, at least in the eyes of one of his countrymen who lived generations later.

BIBLIOGRAPHY

Baines, J. "On the Composition and Inscriptions of the Vatican Statue of Udjahorresne." In *Studies in Honor of William Kelly Simpson,* edited by P. Der Manuelian. Boston, 1996. Discusses the orientation and meaning of the texts on the Vatican Museum's statue, emphasizing their predominantly religious nature.

Holm-Rasmussen, T. "Collaboration in Early Achaemenid Egypt: A

New Approach." In *Studies in Ancient History and Numismatics.* Aarhus, 1988. Takes issue with the negative portrayal of Wedjahorresne as a collaborator.

Lloyd, A. B. "The Inscription of Udjahorresnet. A Collaborator's Testament." *Journal of Egyptian Archeology* 68 (1982), 166–180. Contains a full translation and discussion of the texts on the Vatican Museum's statue.

Posener, G. *La Première Domination Perse en Égypte. Bibliothéque d'Etude* 11 (1936), 1–26. Gives hieroglyphic texts, translations, and discussion of the texts of the statue at the Vatican Museum.

Verner, M. "La tombe d'Oudjahorresnet et le cimetière Saïto-Perse d'Abousir." *Bulletin de l'Institut Français d'archéologie orientale* 89 (1989), 283–290. Preliminary publication of the tomb of Wedjahorresne.

PAUL F. O'ROURKE

WEIGHTS AND MEASURES. True to the centralized and administrative nature of the pharaonic state, ancient Egypt had an official system of weights and measures, valid throughout the country, which did not show really significant changes until the Late period. This regulated system comprised three main subsystems that enforced capacity, length, and weight. Measures of capacity were the most complex, with regard to dry goods and fluids. For the food staples (bread and beer), a measure of "baking ratio" expressed the proportion between the fixed quantity of cereals and the size of loaves or the strength of beer. From the measures of length, the measures of area and volume were derived, as well as the more specific measure of a monument's external batter (upward and backward slope). Measures of weight (and some of capacity) were adapted for the valuation of goods, as a kind of notional "money."

The present-day equivalents of the measures in each category are known by calculating the average capacity, length, or weight of ancient measuring objects now in museums. This method is more accurate than trusting any one object, since many, worn with use, no longer retain their original length or shape; in fact, ancient technology was not always capable of manufacturing exact measures.

In ancient Egypt, some offices or temples retained "official" standard measures that could be checked when controversy arose—for example, stone rulers were less subject to contraction and expansion (from humidity) than their wooden counterparts of daily use. Apart from such natural factors as heat and humidity, measures were probably often altered deliberately or deemed to be unreliable. When collecting the grain due him in a distant village, a land proprietor of the eleventh dynasty felt it safer to send his own grain measure with his collectors, to prevent being cheated.

Before discussing the units of measures, it is important to say that an elementary universal measure is just the number resulting from counting goods. In fact, ancient Egyptian economic documents frequently record such figures, expressing quantities of a product counted either by the piece or by a usual grouping of pieces: bunches or garlands of flowers, clusters of dates, *mrw*-bundles of vegetables, *nḥ*-bundles of flax, handfuls of reeds, and even censerful or altarsful of incense.

Capacity. Ancient Egyptians had an elaborate system of measures of capacity, chiefly used, however, for measuring cereals and other dry goods, not fluids, as the very word "capacity" would seem to suggest.

Cereals. In this system, the basic unit was the *ḥḳзt* (or "bushel"), of 4.805 liters (about 5 quarts). In the Old and Middle Kingdoms, 10 *ḥзr* made the larger unit *khar* (or "sack"), of 48.05 liters (about 50 quarts). By the beginning of the New Kingdom, the value of the *khar* was increased to the equivalent of 16 *heqat* (76.88 liters or 80 quarts), expressed as 4 *fourfold-heqat*, each of 19.22 liters (20 quarts). This increase did not reflect an economic crisis, but the change of a decimal system to a binary system, which was probably intended to make accounting easier. Thenceforward, the *fourfold-heqat* was no more understood as being made up of four *heqat* but as a unit in its own right—the fourth of the *khar*, best known as an *ipt*, the Coptic form of ancient Egyptian *ipet* ("measure," whose name but not the value was borrowed in Hebrew as *ephah*). Smaller quantities were expressed as fractions of *oipe*, more precisely as one of the fractions of the geometric progression 1/2, 1/4 (the former *heqat*), 1/8, 1/16, 1/32, and 1/64. The latter quantity (0.30 liter, just under a pint) was divisible into 5 *rз* ("parts") of 0.06 liter each (3 ounces), reflecting the ancient division of the *heqat* into 80, and of the *fourfold-ḥḳзt* into 320 *rз*. Should the need arise, quantities even smaller could be expressed in fractions of *ro*. Contrary to these fractions, written in the ordinary Egyptian way (any given number under the hieroglyph figuring a mouth expresses a fraction, with this number as the denominator and 1 as the numerator), the fractions of *ipt* from 1/2 to 1/64 were written by the various parts of the hieroglyph *wḏзt* ("sound" or "complete eye," the symbol of completeness). Known as the "Horus Eye notation," it was obviously a mnemonic device and had for its basis the Egyptian myth in which the god Horus had had his eye taken out by his brother Seth, before it was restored to him by Thoth, god of knowledge, mathematics, and fair accounting. (See Figure 1.)

Fluids. The basic measure for fluids was the *ḥnw*, of 1/10 (1/40 *oipe*) or 0.48 liter (a pint), made up of 32 ("parts"), each of 0.06 liter (0.5 ounce). The name of this measure, the *ḥnw*, is best known under its Coptic form *hin*, later borrowed in Hebrew to name a measure of capacity about twelve times larger. Besides the *hin*, Egyptians used a large variety of vessels for specific products

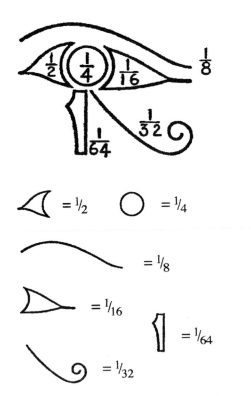

WEIGHTS AND MEASURES. *Figure 1. The Horus Eye notation of fractions.* (Courtesy Pierre Grandet)

(beer, wine, etc.) or specific kinds of products (liquids, oils, etc.), although each had a more or less fixed capacity (which we but rarely know), their diversity shows that these vessels were not true units of measure. In fact, their use indicates the mere counting pieces of a product, so economic records frequently express totals of products in "various vessels." Among the best known of such kinds of containers, one can quote the large storage vessel *mni* or *mnt* ("jar" of 20 or 30 *hin* [9.6 or 14.4 liters]), the small *mehtet* (of 1 *hin*), and the smaller *bas* (1/2 *hin*), a (1/4 *hin*), and *pg3* (1/8 *hin*) used for the presentation of offerings.

The "Baking Ratio." A measure called *psw* (from the Egyptian verb *pes*, "to cook"), commonly translated as "baking ratio," was used for expressing the number either of loaves or of *hin* of beer made from an *ipt* of grain. For loaves, this expressed a size (the greater the "baking ratio," the smaller the loaf) and for beer, a quality (the greater the "baking ratio," the weaker the beer). The purpose of this kind of measurement, which can be compared with our units for alcohol or our calories, was to allow the accountants to estimate the quantities of grain to be issued from the granaries either to prepare a divine offering or to feed a known number of people for a fixed period of time: the court, a party of workmen engaged in a monument's construction, or an army going abroad.

Length. The basic unit was the *cubit*, expressing the length of the forearm, from the elbow (Lat., *cubitus*) to the tip of the fingers (0.523 meter/18 inches). The measure was made up of 7 *palms* (the hand's width without the thumb), with each *palm* comprising 4 *fingers*, each of 1.86 centimeters (0.75 inch). Lesser lengths were measured in fractions of the finger. For the New Kingdom, votive *cubits* found in tombs bear inscriptions naming other measures not known elsewhere: apart from the *cubit* of 7 *palms*, here called *royal cubit*, there are the *small cubit* of 6 *palms* (44.82 cm), the *rmn* of 5 *palms* (37.35 cm), the *dsr* of 4 *palms* (29.88 cm), the *great span* of 3.5 *palms* (26.14 cm), the *small span* of 3 *palms* (22.41 cm), the *dopple* or *double palm* (14.94 cm), and the *fist* of 1.5 *palm* or 6 *fingers* (11.20 cm). Apart from the *cubit*, Egyptians of the New Kingdom sometimes used, for measuring the progress in the excavation of a tomb, a larger unit, called *nebi* ("pole"), a term that would survive in Egypt under its Greek transcription ναύβιον; its length has been estimated to 1 1/4 *cubits* (65.3 centimeters) by some but by others to about 70 centimeters divided in 7 parts of 10 centimeters each.

Land surveying needed a longer unit than the *cubit*, the *ht n nwh* ("rod of cord"), or more simply *ht* ("rod") of 100 cubits (52.30 meters/160 feet), since the measure of a land-measuring rope was 100 *cubits* long, stretched between two rods driven in the ground. Journeying needed a still larger unit, the *itrw* ("river"), which measured 20,000 cubits (10.46 kilometers/6.5 miles). As proven by a variant of its name, *itrw n skdwt* ("*itrw* of towing"), it originally expressed the length of a day's towing of a boat along the Nile. Modern scholarship sometimes translates *itrw* by *schoene*, since it is roughly equivalent to the Attic *schoene* of 10,656 meters or 10.656 kilometers. From the twelfth dynasty (Karnak White Chapel of Senwosret I), the Egyptians officially estimated the length of their country from Elephantine in the south to Behedet (Tell el-Balamun) at 106 *itrw* (1,108.76 kilometers/670 miles), divided into 86 *itrw* for Upper Egypt and 20 *itrw* for Lower Egypt—the border between the two being at the town of Per-Hapy (to the south of today's Old Cairo). Notwithstanding the etymology of *itrw*, which refers to the Nile as Egypt's primary route, the *itrw* also measured land distances.

Area. Ancient classical writers, such as Diodorus Siculus, expressed more than once an admiration for the Egyptians' geometrical knowledge, which was based on the need to take new measures of their fields each year, once the Nile flood retreated. The basic measure of area was the *stt*, commonly known as *aroura* (from the Greek ἄρουρα, "field," "land"), a square of land of 100 by 100 cubits or 1 *ht* by 1 *ht* (2,735.29 square meters). Multiples and submultiples were not defined by squaring multiples or submultiples (as we would do), but by multiplying or dividing the width, while retaining the length as 100 *cubits* (implying that fields were always thought to be set in rows, along a road or a canal, on which their widths abutted).

Volume. As a measure of volume proper, we know only of the *dnit*, which was a cubic *cubit* (0.143 cubic meters). This measure was used exclusively for measuring the progress made by workers in the excavation of a tomb. From such texts as the Rhind Mathematical Papyrus, scribes clearly knew how to calculate volumes from linear measures—even volumes like cylindrical granaries or truncated pyramids—but they neglected to give a name to the resulting cubic units.

Slope. The *sḳd* expressed the slope (or batter) of a masonry massive—like a pyramid—by giving the length in *palm*s of the horizontal basis of a right-angled triangle of 1 *cubit* height, whose hypotenuse was a section of the expected or measured slope. In Old Kingdom construction, there is an obvious trend to use mainly a *sḳd* of 5 1/2 *palm*s or 5 1/4 *palm*s, corresponding to slopes of 51°51' and 53°7' as exemplified, respectively, by the pyramids of Khufu and Khafre.

Weight. Ancient Egypt's basic unit of weight was the *dbn* (according to Akkadian sources, pronounced *tiban*). The etymology suggests it to have been originally a metal ring. From 13 grams during the Old Kingdom, its weight was increased to 91 grams (7 × 13 grams) during the Middle Kingdom. In the New Kingdom, it was divided into 10 *ḳdt* (Coptic, *qite*) of 9.1 grams each, with lesser weights expressed as fractions of *ḳdt*.

Value. Ancient Egyptians never used coins for exchanging goods. The first known coins in Egypt were made by the thirtieth dynasty pharaohs only to pay their Greek mercenaries. The *dbn* (see above) and other units of weight were used as notional units of value (similar to the term "pound"), allowing parity for the bartering of goods, by reducing them to a common scale. According to the value of the goods thus exchanged, these units (from the rarest to the commonest) could be a *dbn* of gold, silver, or copper. During the New Kingdom, gold was probably double the value of silver; and silver, originally one hundred times the value of copper in the nineteenth dynasty, became only sixty times its worth in the twentieth. As a standard of value, gold was never used at all, and silver was rarely used at Deir el-Medina, the community that provided most of this data. [*For an expanded discussion, see* Prices and Payment.]

BIBLIOGRAPHY

Gardiner, Alan H. *The Wilbour Papyrus*, vol. 2: *Commentary*. London, 1948, pp. 59–65. Assesses the measuring system in use at the end of the New Kingdom.

Gardiner, Alan H. *Egyptian Grammar. Being an Introduction to the Study of Hieroglyphs.* 3d ed. Oxford, 1973, section 266. The classical presentation of the ancient Egyptian system of weights and measures.

Helck, Wolfgang. "Maße und Gewichte (pharaonische Zt.)." In *Lexikon der Ägyptologie*, 3: 1199–1209. Wiesbaden, 1980. A short but comprehensive statement of the known facts.

James, T. G. H. *The Hekanakhte Papers and Other Early Middle Kingdom Documents.* Publications of the Metropolitan Museum of Art Egyptian Expedition, 19. New York, 1962. Appendix C, pp. 115–118, discusses the measurement system of a rural area in the eleventh dynasty.

Janssen, Jac. J. *Commodity Prices from the Ramessid Period. An Economic Study of the Village of Necropolis Workmen at Thebes.* Leiden, 1975. Presents the problem of ancient Egyptian "money" in chapter 1, pp. 101–111.

Robins, Gay, and Charles Shute. *The Rhind Mathematical Papyrus.* London, 1987. A short but comprehensive presentation of ancient Egyptian mathematics, geometry, and metrology, as expressed in the most important ancient Egyptian treatise on these matters (Rhind Mathematical Papyrus, British Museum 10057–10058).

PIERRE GRANDET

WENAMUN is the principal character of a literary text written in Late Egyptian (hereafter, *Wenamun*). The incomplete text is known from a Hieratic papyrus found at el-Hiba in Middle Egypt and kept in the Pushkin Museum, Moscow (Papyrus Moscow 120). On paleographic evidence, the manuscript dates from the twenty-first dynasty. The text itself was presumably composed early in that dynasty (mid-eleventh century BCE). Its literary character is apparent from the sophisticated plot, the rhetoric and irony of the dialogues, the imagery of the narrative, and the underlying reflection on political, theological, and cultural issues. Some stylistic features, for example, dates, lists, summations, and the appearance of historical personages, suggest an official report written in the first person singular, but I prefer to treat *Wenamun* as a work of literature cast in the form of a documentary text.

The report starts with the departure of Wenamun, an agent of the temple of Amun at Thebes acting on behalf of the high priest, Herihor, for the Phoenician harbor town of Byblos to procure timber for a new river bark of Amun. The date is placed within "Year 5," and is traditionally associated with the "Renaissance," which began in regnal year 19 of Ramesses XI, the last king of the twentieth dynasty. Alternatively, the date may belong to the fifth year of the twenty-first dynasty, if Herihor was the successor of Piankh (Egberts 1998, pp. 49–74). This sequence would account for the absence of an Egyptian pharaoh in *Wenamun*, because in the twenty-first dynasty, Egypt was divided into a southern entity with el-Hiba as northern outpost headed by the high priests of Amun, and a northern entity ruled by Smendes of Tanis and his successors. Smendes figures in *Wenamun* as the first sovereign visited by its protagonist. Wenamun's next stop is the harbor town of Dor (present Tell Dor, Israel), where he is robbed of his valuables. When he reaches Byblos, Wenamun is forced to stay there for nearly a year; after that he flees to Cyprus. At that point the text breaks off. The narrative's core is constituted of two disputes between Wenamun and Zakarbaal, the ruler of Byblos. In the first dispute, Zakarbaal is unwilling to deliver the timber without proper payment, dismissing Wenamun's demand for political obedience as a vassal of Egypt. Then Wenamun argues that Amun is the universal god, whose domain includes Byblos and the Lebanon. The second dispute involves, among other things, the issue of Egyptian ethnicity.

Wenamun is a work of fiction based on the historical circumstance of the construction of a new bark for Amun during the tenure of Herihor. Its theme, the vicissitudes of an Egyptian abroad, is familiar from earlier literary compositions. Like *Sinuhe*, *Wenamun* is a remnant of the ancient Egyptian discourse about cultural identity. At the same time, *Wenamun* constitutes a major source for the theocratic ideology of the twenty-first dynasty, in which the role of the pharaoh is assigned to Amun. By stressing the cross-cultural significance of Amun and integrating international politics into theology, the unknown author of *Wenamun* shows his audience a way of coping with the decline of the empire and the resulting division of Egypt.

BIBLIOGRAPHY

Egberts, Arno. "Hard Times: The Chronology of 'The Report of Wenamun' Revised." *Zeitschrift für Ägyptische Sprache und Altertumskunde* 125 (1998), 93–108. Revises the traditional understanding of the chronology of *Wenamun*.

Gardiner, Alan H. *Late Egyptian Stories*. Bibliotheca Aegyptiaca, 1. Brussels, 1932. The standard edition of *Wenamun* in hieroglyphic transcription on pages 61–76.

Lichtheim, Miriam. *Ancient Egyptian Literature*. Berkeley, 1976. Vol. 2, pp. 224–230, contains a good English translation of *Wenamun*.

ARNO EGBERTS

WENI. Born during the reign of Teti in the sixth dynasty and appointed to his first administrative position under that king, Weni (or Uni) enjoyed a long and distinguished career that likely ended during the reign of Merenre. His "autobiography," recorded on a limestone slab found at Abydos (now in the Cairo Museum), is the lengthiest such text of the period. It seems to have been known in later times. His career began under Pepy I in the palace bureaucracy, and he was soon in charge of the priests of the king's mortuary complex. He is mentioned in Pepy's Dashur decree, and the king's growing confidence in Weni brought him into sensitive judicial positions, both in the formal judicial apparatus (the "Six Great Mansions") and in the palace. He heard cases along with the vizier, and Weni claims to have been singled out to hear a confidential matter in the royal women's quarters that may have involved some accusation against one of Pepy I's queens—

all this, Weni says, despite his comparatively low rank at this time. At some point in Pepy I's reign, Weni had begun to prepare his own tomb (perhaps at Abydos) and, at his request, the king supplied some of its furnishings, notably the limestone sarcophagus, elements of the chapel doorway, and a libation table, further examples of the king's esteem. Weni, like many officials of that era, seeks to convince posterity of his singular achievements and preferments.

Pepy I charged Weni with the command of an Egyptian army levied from various parts of Egypt proper, which included Nubian and Libyan mercenaries, in order to deal with incursions by the "Near Eastern Sand-dwellers," either in the eastern Delta or southern Palestine. Weni boasts of his military dispositions and successes, launching into a remarkable fourteen-line poem of victory; this extraordinary literary piece consists of seven couplets, the first lines of which are identical, the second lines cataloging the destruction wrought on the "rebellious" Near Easterners. He claims to have been sent on a total of five such ventures.

Weni began the reign of Merenre as a senior palace official once more, but was soon appointed "Overseer of Upper Egypt," in which capacity he maintained civic order, saw to it that taxes were collected efficiently, assured the integrity of state property, and carried out various commissions of his sovereign relating to the latter's funerary establishment at Saqqara. The last included the capstone for the king's pyramid, a sarcophagus, various granite components of the offering chambers, and a great quartzite altar. Much of the stone had to be acquired far south of the capital, and Weni boasts of his efficient completion of his missions, which included the quarrying of the stone, the recruitment and organization of Nubian laborers to build the barges necessary to convey the stone to the pyramid site, and the clearing of channels at the First Cataract to facilitate the passage of the barges. Weni exemplifies the court officials of the sixth dynasty, closely tied to the royal establishment and to royal favor, and displaying considerable versatility.

BIBLIOGRAPHY

Baer, K. *Rank and Title in the Old Kingdom*. Chicago, 1960. See page 66 for the list of inscriptions. The autobiography text can be found at *Urk* 1: 98–110.

Lichtheim, M. *Ancient Egyptian Literature*. Berkeley, 1973.

Roccati, A. *La littérature historique sous l'Ancient Empire égyptien*. Paris, 1982.

GERALD E. KADISH

WEPWAWET was one of several ancient Egyptian deities who appeared in canine form. Usually depicted as a doglike creature with a gray or white head, Wepwawet is often incorrectly identified as a wolf, but the animal sacred to Wepwawet was most probably the jackal. The jackal was an appropriate representation for a funerary deity since the ancient Egyptians had no doubt observed the jackal's nocturnal activities in the desert areas used for cemeteries.

Like another jackal god, Anubis, Wepwawet was a funerary deity. He was one of the earliest deities worshiped at the cemetery site of Abydos in southern Egypt. The worship of Wepwawet at Abydos paralleled that of Khentyamentiu, yet another jackal god. When Osiris absorbed the characteristics of Khentyamentiu, Khentyamentiu's role as the lord of the cemetery at Abydos was filled by Anubis. With the rise of solar religion at the beginning of the twelfth dynasty, Osiris's role was limited to the underworld, and the position of local god and lord of the cemetery was in turn filled by Wepwawet, who bears the epithets "Lord of Abydos" and "Lord of the Necropolis." Wepwawet was also the local deity of the thirteenth nome of Upper Egypt, modern Asyut. The ancient Greeks called the town Lycopolis ("Town of the Wolf"), indicating early confusion about the original form of this god. Other cult centers of Wepwawet included Quban, el-Hargarsa, Memphis, and Sais.

Wepwawet's name (*Wp-w3.wt*) means "the opener of the ways" and refers to his role in leading the deceased through the paths of the underworld. In the funerary texts of the New Kingdom, such as the *Book of Going Forth by Day* (*Book of the Dead*) and the *Book of That Which Is in the Underworld* (*Amduat*), Wepwawet's role is that of a protective deity. In royal mythology, the king was accompanied by a fast, doglike creature while hunting, and the animal was referred to as the "the one with the sharp arrow who is more powerful than the gods." These arrows also "opened the way," and may be connected to the name of this deity.

Wepwawet is often depicted atop a standard. His image is accompanied by a *uraeus* and an enigmatic hieroglyph, which has been described as a representation of the placenta of the king. The standard of Wepwawet was carried preceding the king, and, in the Middle Kingdom, preceding Osiris in processions from the palace or temple. The Narmer mace head shows such a standard in use as early as the first dynasty. This use of the god's image on a standard may indicate his early role as a warlike deity. The jackal god Wepwawet symbolized Upper Egypt in royal processions, while Lower Egypt was represented by the Apis bull of Memphis. Wepwawet was thought of as the messenger and the champion of royalty. He is called the son of Isis, and has close connections with the deities Harendotes and Herishef. Like the god Shu, Wepwawet is referred to as "the one who has separated the sky from the earth."

BIBLIOGRAPHY

Graefe, Erhart. "Upaut." In *Lexikon der Ägyptologie* 6: 862–864. Wiesbaden, 1985.

Kees, Hermann. *Ancient Egypt: A Cultural Topography.* Edited by T. G. H. James. Chicago, 1961.

Spiegel, Joachim. *Die Götter von Abydos: Studien zum ägyptischen Synkretismus.* Wiesbaden, 1973.

JENNIFER HOUSER-WEGNER

WESTERN DESERT. At the eastern end of the great Sahara is the dry region called the Western Desert by the ancient Egyptians. With an area of some 680,000 square kilometers, the Western Desert covered about two-thirds of Egypt's land mass. It extended from the Nile Valley's agricultural strip west to the frontier between Egypt and Libya, and from just south of the Mediterranean littoral southward to the Sudan-Egypt frontier. It is an area of great sand plains, outcrops of sandstone, and limestone escarpments. There are areas of massive dune activity and areas of barren rock. It is an inhospitable region and one of the driest. It is generally low-lying, with the great Qattara Depression at the north being over 100 meters (320 feet) below mean sea level in places. Toward the south, in the Gilf Kebir and Gebel Uweinat regions, the land slowly rises, to a maximum at Gebel Uweinat of nearly 1900 meters (6,000 feet) above mean sea level. The climate of this region is extremely arid, although rainfall can be attracted to the highlands of Uweinat and the Gilf Kebir, where in good years it provides seasonal grazing for the animals of nomadic pastoralists. The winter Mediterranean rainfall seldom reaches southward far inland. Only where there are deposits of water underground may any life be supported in this vast waste; the water deposits were, during the geological past, rain fed—most recently ending about five thousand years ago. The underlying Nubian sandstones are porous enough to hold water, so the water deposits are kept intact by surrounding shales until a natural fault or a well is drilled to release it. Artesian pressure or pumping brings it to the surface for use. Day temperatures in this desert reach well over 50°C (122°F) in summer, while freezing temperatures are often encountered at night in December and January. The other constant feature of the desert climate is the prevailing wind, which blows from north-north-east; it creates spectacular landforms by its sculpting effects not only on sand but also on the rock formations.

During the Cretaceous era (some 100 million years ago), the great Tethys Sea covered most of the Sahara region, including the Western Desert. This created the limestone landforms of the region and left a legacy of salts in the geochemistry; these salts are still present in the soils and the water of the region. Within the limestone are the fossilized remains of a great variety of extinct marine and

WESTERN DESERT. *Kharga Oasis.* This shows the entry into the Kharga Depression. (Courtesy Donald B. Redford)

land-based animals. There are also cherts (a hard stone that fractures well), which have been raw material for the stone tools of Paleolithic and Neolithic peoples in the region. As might be expected, there is little wildlife in the desert. There are, however, some animals, particularly in the vicinity of wells. The populations are never great, so prey and predators both have a meager existence. There are mostly species that need little or no water, that derive enough liquid from their food to survive. Among them are the hare, fennic, fox, Dorcas gazelle, oryx, and various lizards, snakes, rodents, and insects. Virtually no plants are found, except where the roots can reach water.

There are water sources in a number of places in the Western Desert; most are small wells and springs, which may be dry at the surface and require some digging to reach the water. These small places may have some shrubs and a few trees, particularly palms, but are insufficiently watered to sustain human habitation on any viable basis. In addition, there are five major oases, where there has been permanent settlement for several millennia; from north to south, these are Siwa, Bahariya, Farafra, Dakhla, and Kharga. The Kharga Oasis is closest to the Nile River, while Siwa is the most distant from the river. These oases hold less than 1 percent of the total population of Egypt and are basically self-sufficient agricultural areas. Traditionally, the oases have been seen as having Greco-Roman period ruins and as having been at their most active at that time. Recent research, however, indicates otherwise. Whereas the Greco-Roman ruins are often visible, standing above ground, earlier remains dating back into prehistoric times are also present.

Modern explorations of the Western Desert began with the nineteenth-century European explorers and travelers, although there were some few pioneers in late medieval times. In 1819, F. Cailliaud traveled great distances over the oasis routes; A. Edmonstone traveled to Dakhla and Kharga in 1819; B. Drovetti went to Siwa Oasis and to the Kharga-Dakhla region around 1820; and the name of John Hyde (1819), can be found on many monuments. Others include J. G. Wilkinson, the pioneering Egyptologist; and Gerhardt Rohlfs, in 1875, with his great German geological expedition. In the twentieth century, W. Jennings-Bramley made a census of the desert Arabs, incidentally exploring a wide area; Ahmed Hassanein made pioneering traverses; there has also been an increasing number of European Egyptologists as interest in the antiquities of the oases has quickened; and such explorers as P. Clayton, R. Bagnold, W. B. K. Shaw, C. V. Haynes,

WESTERN DESERT. *Es-Smant, a village and Roman town site in the Dakhla Oasis.* (Courtesy Donald B. Redford)

and Ahmed Fakhry have all contributed to an increasing elaboration of knowledge of both the desert and the oases as natural phenomena and as places of habitation.

The Western Desert has always been a great natural protector of Egypt's western frontier. Since it had few people, it would not normally have been an area harboring a military threat in antiquity. It also had few mineral resources, unlike the mineral-rich Eastern Desert, so was not particularly attractive to the ancient Egyptians; it was considered an area apart, and although connected tenuously by settled populations, it was generally outside Egypt's mainstream. The Nile Valley was their home and they feared the deserts as strange places, full of evil. They seldom ventured into the deserts, unless there were good economic or military reasons. Officials in the Nile Valley were in charge of the oasis areas, keeping control over desert routes and collecting taxes. Yet the situation never seems to have been fraught with the military and bureaucratic personnel that other areas required.

When this part of the Sahara was more moist, during the earlier half of the Holocene, there was an extensive population. The work of the Combined Prehistoric Expedition, of the Beseidlungsgeschichte der Ost-Sahara project, and of the Dakhleh Oasis Project shows that there had been a viable population of hunters and gatherers, then pastoralists, and then, relatively settled peoples. With the higher rainfall pattern of ten thousand to six thousand years ago, humans and their prey were able to roam easily. As the humidity decreased, human activity became increasingly restricted to places of permanent water. Nabta Playa, west of Toshka, is an outstanding example of such habitations, at a shrinking water source, which continued in existence for several millennia before ending. The large oases, having permanent water, attracted increasingly settled populations.

The economic resources of the Western Desert are far fewer than those of the Eastern Desert. For example, away from the Nile the only significant quarries are the diorite quarries, west of Toshka, where Old Kingdom pharaohs, particularly Khafre (Chephren) gained this hard black stone for statuary. At the quarry, there is also a series of Middle Kingdom stelae. There are no mineral quarries elsewhere in the Western Desert. During pharaonic times, the five great oases of the desert each had its own connections with the cities of the Nile. They were particularly renowned for their various agricultural products, such as dates, olives, and wine. The only products of the oases, when depicted in tomb scenes or mentioned in texts, are agricultural products. In general, there is no known industry nor yet any mineral or other resources to have made them more economically important to the ancient Egyptians. The Kamose Stela (c.1570 BCE) does indicate the strategic importance of the four oases closest to the Nile—Bahariya, Farafra, Kharga, and Dakhla—particularly for defensive control of the western approaches to the river. The Libyan threat that occupied Egyptian international affairs in Ramessid times, was chiefly in the Mediterranean coastal region. The Libyan Desert, as the westward continuation of the Western Desert, was equally inhospitable and an equally effective barrier frontier. From the Libyan pre-desert, archaeological evidence shows no human inhabitants between the Old Stone Age and the Romans. Two hieratic stelae from Mut in the Dakhla Oasis, dating to the twenty-second dynasty and the twenty-fifth, attest to a community of Egyptians living there—as well as "Libyans"—and it seems likely that people known as Libyans to the Egyptians also lived in the other oases.

Several deities are associated with the western oases. The most important is the chief Theban god, Amun. With the Egyptian belief in the threatening deserts, however, it was natural that a number of desert deities became important in the oases. In the Dakhla Oasis, the major temple, at Mut, seems to have been dedicated to Seth, a deity of desert areas; there are also temples to the protective deity Tutu at Ismant el-Kharab and to Amun-nakht at Ein Birbiyeh. The Siwa Oasis is more closely connected to the Mediterranean coast than to the Nile Valley and so might be associated more closely with various Libyan tribes living to the west of Egypt. There are Egyptian references to the region and its peoples from the Early Dynastic period; while there is evidence for prehistoric occupation of Siwa, there are no Egyptian monuments earlier than the twenty-sixth dynasty in the oasis, and the inhabitants until then were probably Libyans. In the reign of Amasis (569–526 BCE) a temple dedicated to Amun was built at Aghurmi, and from the mid-sixth century it became renowned as an oracular center. The Greek historian Herodotus recounted that a large army was sent by Cambyses (525–522 BCE) to attack the oracle of Amun at Siwa; the force went from Thebes to Kharga and subsequently disappeared somewhere in the Western Desert in a sandstorm. Later known as the Oracle of Jupiter-Amun, the oracle was consulted and admired by many throughout the Mediterranean world, perhaps the most famous being Alexander the Great.

Bahariya Oasis is much closer to the Nile than Siwa, only 200 kilometers (125 miles) west of Beni Mazar. Being so much closer to ancient Egypt, it played a greater role in its history. As in all the oases, there is ample evidence at Bahariya for prehistoric occupation of the region. While no monuments earlier than the late eighteenth dynasty have been found there, its name, *dsds*, is known from Middle Kingdom times. This oasis may have been the residence of the Libyan group that eventually became the twenty-second dynasty (931–725 BCE). The smallest of the great Western Desert oases, Farafra, lies some 180 kilometers (115 miles) southwest of Bahariya and just over 300 kilometers (200 miles) west of the Nile Valley at Manfalut. In pharaonic times, it was termed the *Ta-iht* ("Land of the Cows"), an indication of a past richness that has since vanished.

The "Great Southern Oasis" *(Wh3.t rsy.t)* consists of both the Kharga Oasis and the Dakhla Oasis. Kharga, lying parallel to the Nile between Nagada and Edfu, and a maximum of 230 kilometers (145 miles) distant, was important as part of a second route into Sudan, the Darb el-Arbain. On it are many monuments and sites of Greco-Roman times, several of which are caravanserais. The capital of the region was at Hibis, present-day Kharga. The largest of all the oases, was Dakhla, farther to the west; it was occupied by the end of the sixth dynasty, and there was a major Egyptian settlement, not only at Ein Aseel, the capital, but throughout the oasis area. Although evidence suggests a continuous habitation by ancient Egyptians, after the initial settlement there was never a large population until the Roman period, when a number of temples were built, three major towns established, and the many smaller sites—all of which attests to the economic importance of the area to the Roman world market. After the collapse of that empire, the role of the Western Desert oases dwindled to one of local subsistence farming.

[*See also* Desert Environments; *and* Eastern Desert and Red Sea.]

BIBLIOGRAPHY

Beadnell, H. F. L. *An Egyptian Oasis: An Account of the Oasis Of Kharga in the Libyan Desert.* London, 1909. An account of life in the Kharga Oasis early in the twentieth century, with emphasis on water sources.

Bagnold, R. *Libyan Sands.* Bristol, 1935. An account of the Western Desert explorations by a world authority on sand and deserts.

Caton-Thompson, G. *Kharga Oasis in Prehistory.* London, 1952. The seminal work on Pleistocene prehistoric excavations at Kharga Oasis.

Churcher, C. S., and A. J. Mills, eds. *Reports from the Survey of Dakhleh Oasis. Western Desert of Egypt, 1977–1987.* Dakhleh Oasis Project Monograph, 2. Oxford, 1999. Essays concerning results from the survey of the oasis by members of the Dakhleh Oasis Project.

Edmonstone, A. *A Journey to Two of the Oases of Upper Egypt.* London, 1822. An account of the journey by the first European to visit Dakhla Oasis; also the first description of the oasis.

Fakhry, A. *The Necropolis of El-Bagawat in Kharga Oasis.* Cairo, 1951. An account of a well-preserved, large early-Christian cemetery at Kharga.

Fakhry, A. *The Oases of Egypt,* vol. 1: *Siwa Oasis.* Cairo, 1973. A description of the modern oasis, its people, customs, history, and monuments.

Fakhry, A. *The Oases of Egypt,* vol. 2: *Bahariya and Farafra Oases.*

Cairo, 1974. A description of the people and the monuments of these two oases.

Giddy, L. L. *Egyptian Oases.* Warminster, 1987. A compendium of the sources in the Nile Valley and in the oases for the oases of Bahariya, Dakhla, Farafra, and Kharga; also the account of some excavations at Ayn Asil, Dakhla Oasis.

Kuper, Rudolph. *Forschungen zur Umweltgeschichte der Ostsahara.* Cologne, 1989. First results of the environmental studies in the desert; English summaries.

Wendorf, Fred, R. Schild, and A. E. Close, eds. *Cattle Keepers of the Eastern Sahara.* Dallas, 1984. Contains a series of essays on prehistoric work in the southern Western Desert.

Winlock, H. E. *Ed Dakhleh Oasis: Journal of A Camel Trip Made in 1908.* New York, 1936. A brief account of the standing monuments of the Dakhleh Oasis.

Winkler, H. *Rock Drawings of Southern Upper Egypt.* London, 1939. Contains reproductions of and commentary on the petroglyphs of the Western Desert.

ANTHONY J. MILLS

WIGS. *See* Hairstyles.

WILBOUR PAPYRUS. This important document dates to regnal Year 4 of an unnamed king who, by internal evidence, must be Ramesses V. It is slightly more than 10 meters (33 feet) in length, with Hieratic text by two different scribes on both the *recto* (Text A) and *verso* (Text B). The records are entered into 127 columns and comprise a total of 5,200 lines of text, making it one of the longest of all ancient Egyptian nonfunerary papyri. Although the document can be described as a cadaster, or registry of land holdings for an approximately 145-kilometer (95-mile) stretch of Middle Egypt between the modern towns of Atfih and el-Minya, the purpose underlying these records—rental lists, land surveys, and taxation records have all been suggested—remains obscure. Whatever its overall intent may have been, the Wilbour Papyrus provides valuable information about late Ramessid administrative practices, temple economy, onomastics, population, occupations, toponyms, and many other topics. Taken together, these data offer a unique view of the political and economic forces that were to result in the divided and impoverished Egypt of the Third Intermediate Period. We must, however, always remember that this evidence may reflect only the situation prevailing in one small region and for a brief time.

Nevertheless, the stratification of society into roughly the same broad classifications mentioned by Herodotus (Book II, 14, 2) might already be reflected in the Wilbour Papyrus, in which the most common occupations encountered are priests, military men, "ladies," herdsmen, stablemasters, farmers, and scribes. It is striking that a substantial proportion of the people listed in the document were foreigners, mostly Libyan and Near Eastern, probably foreign mercenaries and their descendants who had been settled on farmland in reward for their military service. Other foreigners may represent the results of a longstanding policy of forcibly resettling prisoners of war on temple lands.

Oddly enough, Herodotus does not mention different classes of cultivators, a striking omission in a largely agricultural economy. By contrast, one of the most commonly encountered terms in the Wilbour Papyrus is *iḥwty*, which has usually been rendered as "farmer." The word *iḥwty* may actually mean something closer to "agent of the state treasury," and if so, this would have far-reaching consequences for interpretations of late Ramessid society and economy.

The Wilbour Papyrus seems particularly concerned with grain production and tax or rent collection on both state- and temple-owned lands, which account for a high percentage of the property listed. From the way certain entries are treated, it becomes apparent that modern distinctions between church, state, and crown were often blurred, if not nonexistent, in ancient Egypt. Within Egypt's distributive economy such institutional elements tended to be independent, yet they cooperated in land management. By the time the Wilbour Papyrus was written, the royal house had become increasingly enfeebled and economic power had shifted decisively in favor of the temples, which were probably not politically effective entities. Perhaps as part of the same process, the Wilbour Papyrus distinguished between those fields framed by cultivators attached to the state, that is, either the temples or the royal house, and properties worked by private individuals.

BIBLIOGRAPHY

Gardiner, A. H. *The Wilbour Papyrus.* 4 vols. Oxford, 1948. The original publication of the Wilbour Papyrus; a thorough study, including the hieroglyphic text, extensive commentary, and indices.

Haring, B. J. "The Administration of Temple Fields." In *Divine Households. Administrative and Economic Aspects of the New Kingdom Royal Memorial Temples in Western Thebes,* pp. 281–326. Leiden, 1997. The most recent examination of the economy of royal funerary estates, which play a paramount role in this document; provides up-to-date references on many of the terms and practices mentioned.

Janssen, Jac. J. "Agrarian Administration in Egypt during the Twentieth Dynasty." *BiOr* 43 (1986), 351–366. Another viewpoint on the nature of the Wilbour Papyrus, by an expert on Ramessid economics and administrative practices.

Katary, S. L. D., *Land Tenure in the Ramesside Period.* London, 1989.

O'Connor, D., "New Kingdom and Third Intermediate Period, 1552–664 BC." In *Ancient Egypt. A Social History,* edited by B. G. Trigger et al., pp. 183–278. Cambridge, 1983. Brings forth what the Wilbour Papyrus reveals about late New Kingdom society.

OGDEN GOELET

WINE. *Drawing of a Theban tomb picture depicting winemaking, from the New Kingdom.* On the top right is a small temple to the goddess of the harvest, before whom is placed an offering of grapes and wine. On the left, workers crush the grapes by foot. On the lower right, workers use jugs to fill large wine jars.

WINE.

WINE. The ancient Egyptians enjoyed two major kinds of alcoholic drinks in their daily lives: beer (*ḥnḳt*) and wine (*irp*). The term *irp* (Coptic, *erp, elp*) refers specifically to grape-based wine, which was already in existence in the Predynastic period, as testified by the wine jars found in sites of this period. As far as can be determined, based on the geographical distribution of wild grapevine, Egypt was not its original home. The technique of wine production was probably imported from Syria–Palestine during the prehistoric period, as suggested by a number of Syrian-style wine jars found in both prehistoric and Early Dynastic period sites.

Our knowledge of the production of wine in Egypt is assisted by a number of tomb paintings from the Old Kingdom onward, which depicted various vintage scenes. First the grapes (*i33rt*) were put into a large vat, made of clay, wood, or stone, and they were crushed by foot, much as they are today in some European vineyards. When the juice was collected, it was poured into a jar to ferment for a few days. A secondary fermentation followed; the jar would be sealed with rush bung-stoppers, and the entire mouth of the jar would be covered with mud capsules, leaving only a small hole to release the carbon dioxide that could still be produced during this second stage of fermentation. When this stage ended, the jar would then be sealed completely. The wine jars are usually amphora-like vessels, sometimes with two handles attached at the shoulder. Most vessels have pointed bottoms, presumably to gather the residue in the liquid. Thus they needed to be placed on a stand or suspended from a cord if an upright position was desired. Although for daily use wine cups were made in a variety of shapes and sizes, a special kind of round goblet (*nw*-pot) was proper for the wine-offering ceremony.

Speculations exist about the color of wine produced by the ancient Egyptians. The color of wine is determined by whether crushed red skin is allowed to be mixed with the grape juice and fermented together. In ancient Egypt, the residue in the vat, including the crushed skin, was put in a wine press (made of a sack and two poles) to extract the remaining liquid, and this extract was most certainly mixed with the first juice extracted by foot; the wine produced in this way would be "red"—with various degrees of redness. Mythological and literary allusions indicate that wine was considered red. The wine-press god Shesmu, for example, was depicted as a slaughterer who pressed human heads in the wine press. Undoubtedly, this was an allusion to a scene wherein grape juice was extracted from the wine press, and the red juice was likened to human blood. In an offering liturgy of the Greco-Roman period, the offering of wine symbolized the filling of the Eye of Horus with its blood. This, however, does not exclude the possibility that white wine could also be produced, but the only literary evidence for the existence of white wine in Egypt comes from the Greek author Athenaeus.

Since wine production involved intensive labor, the price of wine was considerably higher than that of beer. One source has it that in the Ramessid period the price of wine was five times that of beer. It was a drink consumed mostly by the elite upper class, in all kinds of festivals, banquets, and funerals. The offering lists in the tomb of wealthy Egyptians would usually list several kinds of wine as a standard offering. Among these are *irp Imt* (wine of Imet, eastern Delta), *irp mḥw* (wine of Lower Egypt), *irp Snw* (wine of Syene, i.e., Pelusium), and *irp Ḥ3m* (wine of Ham, probably in the western Delta). These geographical names are, presumably, the location of some famous vineyards. Although vineyards in Upper Egypt were mentioned, the majority were located in Lower Egypt and in some of the oases. Besides the royal house vineyards and the noble family estate vineyards, the temples often possessed large numbers of vineyards. Harris Papyrus I mentions that 433 vineyards were endowed to the Theban temples in the reign of Ramesses III. During the Greco-Roman period, the oases of Dakhleh, Kharga, Bahariya, and Farafra seemed to have been very prosperous in wine production. This might actually have been the policy of the Ptolemaic rulers, specifically Ptolemy II and Ptolemy III, who encouraged Greek mercenaries to settle in Egypt and become vintners.

Wine was a prestigious drink; it was used in religious rituals as an offering to Egyptian deities, and scenes of wine-offerings are ubiquitous on temple walls of all periods. In the Pyramid Texts, Osiris was mentioned as the "Lord of Wine," presumably from his relationship with the annual inundation of the Nile, the seasonal revival of vegetation in general, and the vine in particular. Many Greco-Roman authors noted that the color of the Nile was red during the inundation, and a story mentioned that the Nile water once turned into wine—most likely a mythological interpretation of a natural phenomenon caused by the iron-rich red alluvium washed into the Nile from the Atbara branch during the flood season. Among the deities who received wine as an offering was the goddess Hathor, who had a special relationship with wine. She was often referred to as the "Lady of Drunkenness." A festival of "the Drunkenness of Hathor" was celebrated at Dendera, and her coming to Egypt was mentioned as coincidental with the coming of the flood, which is another allusion to the wine color of the water, as well as the rejuvenating power of the flood. Wine in daily life was an enjoyable drink, whereas in myth and theology it was symbolic of blood and the power of rejuvenation.

[*See also* Beer; *and* Intoxication.]

BIBLIOGRAPHY

Lesko, Leonard H. *King Tut's Wine Cellar.* Berkeley, 1977. A popular account of wine production and some wine labels of the New Kingdom period. Richly illustrated.

Lucas, Alfred A. *Ancient Egyptian Materials and Industries.* 4th ed. rev. by J. R. Harris. London, 1962. Includes a technical discussion of the production of wine.

Lutz, H. F. *Viticulture and Brewing in the Ancient Orient.* Leipzig, 1922. A general account of wine production in the ancient Near East; dated but still useful.

Poo, Mu-Chou. *Wine and Wine Offering in the Religion of Ancient Egypt.* London, 1995.

MU-CHOU POO

WISDOM TEXTS. Applied to the literature of ancient Egypt, the term Wisdom texts is somewhat of a misnomer, for under this rubric are gathered several different types of literature. That is, *The Instructions of Amenemope* and *The Instruction of Amenemhet* are both wisdom texts but differ profoundly in their purposes, just as *The Prophecy of Neferti* and *The Man Who Was Weary of Life* also differ, both from each other and from the first two examples of this genre. Thus it might be better to gather them all under the heading of "didactic literature," which does better justice to their diversity. Didactic literature includes those pieces the purpose of which is to convey information, teach, or persuade. The Egyptian term *sbȝyt* (usually translated "instruction") does not cover all the pieces of literature that fit under the rubric of didactic literature. Various subdivisions of this kind of literature are the teachings, maxims, or instructions usually thought of as the central kind in this genre (*Ptahhotep, Anii*), the complaint (*Eloquent Peasant*), the lament (*Ipuwer*), the prophecy (*Neferti*), and the testament (*Amenemhet*). Sometimes the purpose seems to be simply the passing on of important information (*Amenemhet*).

Another feature of Egyptian didactic literature is what might be called "embeddedness." Many examples of this literature clearly have one purpose and yet offer aspects of other types of literature. *The Eloquent Peasant* is a clear example of this feature: it begins as a story with the oasis-dweller entering the Nile Valley with his goods and encountering a venal official. This is narrative, which continues until the peasant is provoked into making his complaints, each of which forms a short disquisition on the nature of "justice," and which collectively amount to a treatise on *maat* itself. The purpose of this text is actually to explore *maat;* and the narrative at beginning and end is to enhance both the character of the peasant and to emphasize the centrality of *maat* within ancient Egyptian civilization. That is, the purpose of the piece is didactic, not narrative; but both types of literature are employed to this one end. The most celebrated example of such embeddedness occurs in the genre of narrative, in the *Story of Sinuhe,* where several of the kinds of Egyptian literature appear, forming parts of the larger whole.

Background. Wisdom Literature is one of the richest and most varied kinds of literature to survive from ancient Egypt, appearing late in the Old Kingdom (though this has been disputed) and continuing through the New Kingdom and on to the end of pharaonic history. Wisdom texts in most cases, and unlike the other major types of literature, are signed—that is, they are attributed to an author who composed them, no matter when surviving copies were written by a given scribe; and there is evidence that such authors formed the company of "classical" writers and wise men of the Egyptian literary tradition. They are the authors recalled in the New Kingdom schoolrooms, who are held up as models by later dynasties. Ptahhotep, Hordjedef, Khety, Ipuwer, and Neferti—among others—are the immortals of Egyptian literature just as Shakespeare, Wordsworth, and Whitman are in the

Anglo-American tradition. Here and there one even finds earlier pieces quoted by later writers (as in the reference to the *Book of Kemit*, supposedly by Khety, in the so-called *Satire on the Trades*). This type of literature embodied the "wisdom" or practical philosophy of ancient Egypt.

The question arises, however, whether these writers ever wrote the Wisdom attributed to them. Attaching one's literary efforts to the name of an already famous author was common in the ancient world, and it is difficult to tell whether an attribution is accurate or not. Thus, because the *Instruction of Ptahhotep* is attributed to Ptahhotep, vizier of King Izezi in the fifth dynasty, this does not place the composition of the piece in the Old Kingdom. The *Instruction of Ptahhotep* could be a case of pseudepigraphy and even written later—as late as the Middle Kingdom, as some scholars have claimed. A cautious approach is required, though accepting the author and time named in the text is probably best until clear evidence undermines the attribution.

In addition, the Wisdom texts—and especially the maxim texts—are usually given a dramatic setting. The burden of the piece is conveyed within some sort of literary framework. There is a specific setting in time and place in which characters speak and interact to further the author's overall purpose. This framework can often provide details and clues as to the work's time of composition, milieu, and intent, as well as to the work's historical significance, which can be helpful in locating the work in history. Again, caution must be used since the author of a work of literary caliber is well able to imagine the "facts" of his work. How factual can one be about the itinerary in *The Shipwrecked Sailor* when the island is imaginary and a fifty-foot serpent appears? Yet the treasures from the serpent's storehouse are real-life commodities. Where in such presentations does fact end and fancy begin?

Maat, the Ideal. Disparate in content as the Wisdom texts are, most of them are concerned in one way or another with *maat*, that central concept of ancient Egyptian civilization variously translated (depending upon context) as "truth," "right," "justice," or "order." The maxim texts, in particular, hold up *maat* as the ideal to be striven for and followed by the son addressed in the maxims. The complaints, laments, and prophecies also give *maat* a central place—by its absence in the turmoils presented in the various texts (the topsy-turvy chaos of the social ruin and the disorder that Ipuwer portrays, or Neferti's comment on the golden age that will occur when Ameny—Amenemhet I—comes to the throne). Similarly, the theme to which the Eloquent Peasant continually returns, as he attempts to have his wrongs redressed, is *maat* (as "justice"). In the royal instructions, the king is to rule by *maat* (as political order mirroring the divine order instituted by the gods).

Even in *The Man Who Was Weary of Life*, the man agonizes over the absence of *maat* in his life.

The most common and characteristic situation occurs in the subdivision of the Wisdom texts called the maxims (*Ptahhotep, Hordjedef,* a portion of *Khety, Amenemope,* and *Anii*), where the dramatic situation portrays a father passing on his wisdom to his son. The father is depicted as old and famous, toward the end of a successful public career in the service of the king. He wants to perpetuate the knowledge he has gained as a guide to later generations; and he is seen in the act of communicating his wisdom to a son. In *Ptahhotep* the vizier stands before King Izezi to ask permission for someone to hear (i.e., be taught) the fruits of his wisdom; and the intent is clear that his experience is important enough to be taught to the sons of the nobles throughout the kingdom. No specific son, natural or adopted, is named here; but in the other maxim texts it is usually one of the wise man's actual sons who is the recipient of the wisdom.

These wise men vary in the offices they hold. Ptahhotep was a vizier; another maxim text simply reads "a man" (who is writing an instruction for his son); another, Amenemopet, is one of the highest officials in Egyptian agriculture, and the advice in his maxims is most often centered on agricultural matters. Generally speaking, these men have authority because they have been successful in the public life of their times. They have made a mark that is worth remembering, and they speak primarily of public matters: how to debate, how to conduct oneself at table, how be a successful courtier, how to get ahead, how to please a superior, and so on. In the earlier maxim texts like *Ptahhotep*, emphasis is primarily upon such public activities and conduct. In a New Kingdom example, *Amenemope* places a much greater emphasis upon moral qualities. The student is urged to pursue *maat* and the constellation of virtues that it entails. Whether this is a matter of evolution in the genre of the maxim text tradition, or simply a chance occurrence due to the lack of sufficient examples, it is impossible to tell. But there is no doubt that the *Amenemope* is a much richer piece of writing—or at least it attempts to integrate a much wider range of human experience into a recommended way of life. Indeed, Amenemopet speaks more than once specifically of his teaching as exactly that, "a way of life."

Of the various kinds of Wisdom texts, the maxim tradition in particular (and the last third of *Khety*) develops a portrait of the ideal man. He is, literally, the *gr* ("the silent man"). His antitype is the *šmm* ("the heated man"). Yet the traditional literal translation of *gr* does not do justice to the concept the Egyptian was trying to convey. For a gathering of contexts in which *gr* is used indicates that the "silent man" is in reality a thoughtful, temperate, judicious person, one who insists on having his moment to reflect before reacting to the words and actions of the "hothead" who confronts him. The figure of the *gr* is present in most of the maxim texts from *Ptahhotep* on, but it is seen at its fullest in the *Amenemope*, where the contrast between the two human types occurs several times. In fact, section 4 is devoted to a contrast between them: the intemperate man is like a tree growing within the darkness of a temple; it withers and dies and is thrown on the rubbish heap and burned. The temperate or thoughtful man is like a tree growing in the sunlight (under the eye of Re), which flourishes and continues to live in the garden. The judicious man (indeed, the ideal man, or scholar-official in this context) has the usual constellation of virtues: he is truthful, honest, straightforward, open, respectful, circumspect, diligent, generous, caring, sympathetic—all of which characteristics can be derived from the behavior recommended in *Amenemope*. Perhaps the only trait to provoke comment today is the seemingly excessive respect required toward superiors. Nevertheless, the maxim texts are, after all, aimed at priming the newcomer for his career in public service.

The *Instruction of Khety* adds significantly to this portrait of the ideal man. Khety is instructing his small son, Pepy, in the pleasures of education; and of course at the simplest level it is a matter of simply going to the scribal school and learning to read and write. But more is implied by Khety; his instruction widens into a consideration of the purpose of such training, and a defense of education and the territory such education opens up to the diligent student. In section 29, the reward is mentioned: Pepy should hold fast to the things he will learn at school, because as an educated man he will be able to set forth on the journey of life, following in the footsteps of the great men of the Egyptian tradition of wisdom and learning.

Survey of Wisdom Texts. A brief survey of the various didactic texts follows. The best represented of the subdivisions are the maxim texts: the *Hordjedef, Ptahhotep,* and *Kagemni* purportedly from the Old Kingdom; the *Man for His Son* and the *Loyalist Instruction* from the Middle Kingdom (both fragmentary); and *Ani, Amenemopet,* and *Khakheperresonb* from the New Kingdom.

1. *The Instructions of Ptahhotep.* This complete text (in at least two "editions") is the text to which all other Egyptian maxim collections are compared. It is complete, consisting of a prologue, thirty-seven maxims, and an epilogue. It is set in the reign of King Izezi of the fifth dynasty (though, to repeat, like all didactic texts it may be pseudepigraphous). Ptahhotep, the king's vizier, asks Izezi to appoint someone younger to act as his staff of life, his "son," so that he may pass on his wisdom for the next generation. In a moving speech, Ptahhotep speaks of the losses and frailties inherent in old age. The king grants the request, adding that such teaching will be a standard for the sons of the nobility. "No one is born wise." The individual maxims develop an approach to the ways and requirements of public life and suggest the conduct needed for success: honesty, judiciousness, respect for superiors, moderation, and other virtues. In the epilogue, Ptahhotep develops a portrait of the good son. He is a "hearing son"—that is, one who listens, digests, and follows what has been taught him. Doing so, he becomes a credit to his father and family; he is well known among the officials in public life and his actions approved; and he will, through deeds and his own teaching, become one who carries on the great tradition of Egyptian wisdom, "the teachings of the fathers of old."

2. *The Maxims of Hordjedef (Djedefhor).* This is a fragmentary text set in the time of the son of King Khufu, composed by the father for his son, Au-ib-rě. It is apparently a maxim text, although from what has been recovered thus far, little can be said about its content.

3. *The Instruction for Kagemni.* This apparently is also a maxim text, but only the conclusion survives. It is set in the time of kings Huny and Sneferu (of the third and fourth dynasties, respectively). A short epilogue describes the reception of the vizier's words by his children.

4. *The Instructions of a Man for His Son.* This fragmentary text is apparently from the Middle Kingdom. There is no prologue (other than the genre marker, *sbꜣyt*), and it either ends abruptly or its conclusion is missing. Since the author is not named, neither time nor occasion are clear. The surviving sections are a mingling of the maxim structuring and praise of the king, the latter reminding one of *The Loyalist Instruction.*

5. *Instructions of Anii.* These maxims derive from the eighteenth dynasty of the New Kingdom and are composed by a father who is probably not of noble birth. His advice to his son Khonshotep centers on concerns such as marrying, founding a household, and following the virtues. There is little of officialdom or public life in the admonitions. In addition to the interest engendered by a glimpse of a different social milieu, there is an interesting epilogue wherein father and son have an argument over the son's ability to absorb the father's words. Khonshotep respects Anii but does not feel that he can live up to what his father expects of him. The instruction ends with an uneasy *modus vivendi* between the two.

6. *The Instructions of Amenemope.* This piece is the richest of the surviving maxim texts. Attributed to a high official in the ministry of agriculture, the maxims were written during the New Kingdom, probably during the Ramessid period, by Amenemope for his smallest son, Hor-em-maa-kheru. The special value of this instruction lies in the depth of the father's words. He advocates a life of devotion to moral conduct and public service, grounded

in religious belief. There is a "way of truth" and the son is urged to seek it out and follow it as he pursues his career in agriculture. There are many passages that are genuinely moving, and many finely phrased passages that are distilled into epigrams of surprising force ("The mind of man is the breath of God—beware lest He turn his back.") And it is here that the contrast between the *gr* and the *šmm* (the judicious man and the hothead) is most fully formulated.

7. *The Instructions for Merikare.* Unlike the preceding six titles, this is a royal instruction, composed (presumably) by a king of the tenth dynasty of the First Intermediate Period (perhaps a later Khety) for his royal son, Merikarê. It is set in Herakleopolis, the center of the opponents of the Theban dynasts who soon were to unify the country and commence the Middle Kingdom. It is not a maxim text; rather, its structure is a mixture of advice for the royal son (in the form of maxims for good government), with historical narrative, and testament—that is, a kind of apologia for the father's actions and life. The piece ends with what may be called a "hymn" to the Creator God. The work has been taken as a major historical source for events just preceding the unification of the Middle Kingdom; and the personal advice for the son emphasizes developing good government after a time of turmoil for Herakleopolis.

8. *The Instructions of Amenemhet.* This too is a royal instruction, but it might be better termed a testament. The speaker is King Amenemhet I returning from the afterworld as a ghost to encourage his son, Senwosret I, to take the throne and govern well; however, the piece is largely taken up by a justification of the dead king's policies while alive, a warning to the son about the perfidies of courtiers ("Trust no one!"), and a brief description of a palace coup—presumably the one that took him off. The ghost urges the son to rule well and with a firm hand, for his father will in spirit be sitting at his side ruling with him.

9. *The Loyalist Instruction.* This didactic text of the Middle Kingdom is spoken by a high-ranking nobleman (whose name is unknown due to a lacuna in the text) for his children. It falls into two parts, the first a series of stanzas praising the king and advising the children to serve and follow him wholeheartedly, and the second a series of short sections providing advice on care and management of the servants and workers on the great estates. The fundamental theme of this piece is offering and receiving loyalty.

10. *The Instructions of Khety.* The text has often gone by the misleading title *The Satire on the Trades*. The father, Khety, delivers his words to his son, Pepy, as the two sail the Nile bound for the royal residence and the scribal school in which Pepy is about to be enrolled. Khety remarks on the value of education, and the piece as a whole

is a defense of education. There is a section in the final third of the piece structured in the maxim form, but more than half is composed of a series of portraits or vignettes of persons in various humble occupations (not "professions"). These people are examples of what may well happen to little Pepy if he does not apply himself to his studies—they are miserable, poverty-stricken, and terribly overworked. Pepy is encouraged, rather, to study the wisdom of the sages; then he will be able to set out on the path of wisdom, the path of the Friends of Mankind.

11. *The Admonitions of Ipuwer.* A different kind of didactic text is presented in *Ipuwer*, the lament. It is a long, confused, and repetitious text, at least in its surviving form. It is variously dated from the Old Kingdom to the Second Intermediate Period, although many place it to some time in the Middle Kingdom. Because of this wide range, historical conclusions are difficult to draw. A picture is painted of the land in chaos—usually in terms of the poorer exalted above the richer, and the lesser above the greater, in a topsy-turvy world of disorder—the antithesis of the *maat* needed to govern an ordered society. Toward the end of the surviving text, there seems to be some hope of better times; but since both the beginning and end are missing, it is difficult to determine what the author's solution is for the national unrest and distress.

12. *The Eloquent Peasant.* This Middle Kingdom piece is an interweaving of narrative and wisdom in the guise of a lament for the loss of "justice" (*maat*). In the narrative frame, a peasant from the Wadi Natrun is traveling to market in the Nile Valley with his donkey, which is loaded with goods to be sold. He is accosted by a venal bureaucrat, who seizes his goods and donkey for the trifling offense of trespassing on the latter's fields. All this is intended to provoke the peasant to protest his innocence and to insist upon justice against the trumped-up charges leveled at him. The core of the text is the peasant's nine carefully formulated and rhetorically complex appeals to Maat. The story is set in the time of Amenemhet II, for whom the peasant's disquisitions are set down in writing and who, at the end of the frame story, invites the peasant to the court for restitution of his goods and reward for his inconvenience.

13. *The Words of Khakheperresonb.* This also is a lament, more clearly of the kind seen in *Ipuwer*. Only the prologue of the presumed lament is given, wherein the author strains for novel words, phrases, and modes of expression in order to convey the enormity of the evils that have come upon society and himself. There is some similarity in tone to the despair of *The Man Who Was Weary of Life*, but the specifics of the author's situation are entirely missing.

14. *The Dispute Between a Man Who Was Weary of Life and His Soul.* This piece, in dialogue form, consists of an argument between Self and Soul—the man wanting to commit suicide and thus proceed immediately to the afterlife, and the soul (*ba*) trying to persuade the man to endure life until it concludes naturally. Life has been mortally oppressive to the man, and he despairs of righting it or repairing the disorder in it. The piece ends inconclusively, but the man is able to express his despair and longing for the next world in a series of exquisite lyrics. Although passages are difficult to interpret, the overall tone is one of oppressive and deadening loss of hope. The *Dispute* is one of the most profound and most philosophical pieces in ancient Egyptian literature.

15. *The Prophecy of Neferti.* This example of the didactic genre is pure prophecy. Set in a narrative framework and placed in the time of King Sneferu of the fourth dynasty, it presents a prophecy of the time of troubles in the First Intermediate Period, followed by the foretelling of the arrival of a prince from the southland, Ameny, or King Amenemhet I, who will restore order and force the Near Eastern interlopers back into their own lands. Egypt will be returned to the Egyptians, and the goddess Maat will be restored to her throne. The burden of the piece is the whole range of troubles that the invasion of the eastern Delta will bring: it is a time of disorder like that presented in *Ipuwer;* Re will have to create civilization again. The happy outcome of the story is obvious propaganda for the arrival of the Middle Kingdom, which is why the events and the prophecy are dramatically backdated to the fourth dynasty.

A few other examples of didactic literature exist, but they are fragmentary and of little consequence to date. There are the instructions of Amunnakht and Sisobek, both very fragmentary. There are also instructions attributed to Imhotep of the third dynasty and those attributed to Khety of Herakleopolis. Both are referred to in Egyptian literature but have not survived.

Style and Structure. It remains only to say a word about the style and structure of Egyptian didactic texts. Most of the material in the texts is grouped in pairs of clauses, which are best called couplets. This can be shown from what are called verse points, small dots in red ink on the copies, and placed there by the scribes who copied the texts. When these units are lined up, one below the other (as in modern verse), the sentence meanings usually occur after each two verse-pointed section: an Egyptian literary sentence takes two such clauses. This can be seen, for example, by applying the verse-point method to *The Instruction of Ptahhotep*, thus illustrating that whatever the verse points represented, it was there in antiquity. If the idea of verse points is applied to texts lacking verse points, the results seem to be the same. This can be seen from a text like *The Instructions of Amenemope*, where the verse points are lacking but where the individual clauses are laid out as lines of verse, still in couplet form, though at times offering a rare triplet or quatrain. (That is, Egyptian didactic texts are written in verse form, primarily in couplets.)

Interestingly, this couplet structure is the same throughout ancient Egyptian belles lettres: whether lyric or narrative or the various forms of didactic literature, all are composed with these two-line units. The differences of the genres occur at a different level of construction, but the building blocks for each are the same—the couplet—a verse form. While startling at first glance, this fact is not so strange if one considers the epigrammatic style of more modern poetry—say, eighteenth-century British poetry. Also, one is reminded that in antiquity, "verse" conveyed a much wider range of material than it does today. Instruction on agriculture as well as wisdom was composed in this manner.

[*See also* Eloquent Peasant; Hordjedef; Instructions of Amenemhet; Instructions of Amenemope; Instructions of Anii; Instructions of Kagemni; Instructions of Khety; Instructions of a Man for His Son; Instructions for Merikare; Instruction of Ptahhotep; Ipuwer; Man Who Was Weary of Life; *and* Neferti.]

BIBLIOGRAPHY

Assmann, Jan. *Ma'at: Gerechtigkeit und Unsterblichkeit im Alten Ägypten.* Munich, 1990.

Brunner, Helmut. *Altägyptische Weisheit.* Zurich, 1988.

Hornung, Erik, and Othmar Keel. *Studien zu altägyptischen Lebenslehren.* Orbis Biblicus et Orientalis, 28. Freiburg and Göttingen, 1979.

Lichtheim, Miriam. *Ancient Egyptian Literature.* 2 vols. Los Angeles, 1973, 1978.

Lichtheim, Miriam. *Late Egyptian Wisdom Literature in the International Context.* Göttingen, 1983.

Loprieno, Antonio, ed. *Ancient Egyptian Literature.* Leiden, 1996.

Parkinson, R. B. *The Tale of Sinuhe and Other Ancient Egyptian Poems 1940–1640 B.C.* Oxford, 1997.

Römheld, D. *Wege der Weisheit.* Berlin, 1989.

Simpson, William Kelly, ed. *The Literature of Ancient Egypt.* New ed. New Haven, 1973.

JOHN L. FOSTER

WISDOM TRADITION. In Mozart's opera, *The Magic Flute*, Sarastro—priest and philosopher—sings a solemn hymn to Isis and Osiris, asking the divine pair to grant "the spirit of wisdom" to the young couple before him. Such Masonic influences—as well as those of such Egyptophilic groups as the Rosicrucians, proponents of "pyramid power," various Afrocentrists, and groups of earnest tourists seeking mystical union with the imagined esoterica of ancient Egypt—provide continuing testimony to the durability of the long-held belief that the Egyptians were in possession of profound knowledge and wisdom. Over the millennia, the Egyptians have been thought of as great initiators in medicine, mathematics, engineering, art, and architecture, but particularly as more deeply versed in the mysteries of philosophy, religion, and magic than anyone else. The roots of this perception are several.

It may well be that the Egyptians themselves initiated the tradition. In the late New Kingdom pseudohistorical story of the journey of a Theban priest named Wenamun to Phoenicia, the Egyptian author of the narrative put into the mouth of Zakarbaal, the prince of Byblos, this sentiment: "It was in fact Amun who founded all lands; he founded them after he had founded that land of Egypt from which you have come. Subsequently, craftsmanship came from it to reach this place where I am, and wisdom (*sbȝiw*) came from it to reach this place where I am." This passage suggests at least one reason why many have attributed such wisdom to Egypt: the belief that Egypt was the oldest civilization, a notion that exerted power over at least some later Greek writers. After all, that is what ancient priests and dragomen told foreign visitors to their country. Some of this knowledge is of a rather mundane sort; we know, for example, that Egyptian physicians were sought after by such Near Eastern rulers as the prince of Ugarit, and that Egyptian physicians were at the Hittite court at least as early as the fourteenth century BCE. Similarly, the awareness in the ancient world of Egyptian geometry, sculptural styles, and architectural ideas contributed to the lore of Egyptian craftsmanship.

More important, however, was the sense among Greeks, Romans, Muslims, Renaissance Europeans, and assorted true believers in recent times that the ancient Egyptians had tapped into a hidden reservoir of knowledge, and, therefore, wisdom. This notion, too, is probably a reflection of attitudes that arose within Egyptian society. From at least as early as the Old Kingdom, the idea took hold that there were bodies of knowledge that were not to be given wide circulation—even among Egyptians—but were to be kept in the hands of a socially determined few, initiates in a general sense, who were subject to a kind of decorum whose purpose was to limit the dissemination of such knowledge. Such knowledge may well have been orally transmitted initially, but it was not long before it came to be written down; even so, it was not generally available to a wide audience. At the root of this tradition was the Egyptian belief in the power of utterance as a creative force. Even the carefully circumscribed materials inscribed or painted on the walls of temples and tombs were not, for the most part, accessible to the masses. The texts on papyrus kept in temple libraries would be even more restricted. The key to such knowledge was clearly thought to be literacy, an accomplishment that probably not more than 3–5 percent of the Egyptian population possessed. Lector-priests—those who read out the rituals—had access to and knowledge of restricted texts; not surprisingly,

these priests were thought of as magicians and prognosticators. The Hebrew scriptures make the connection, as in *Exodus* 7.8ff., for example, where pharaoh calls on his wise men and magicians; the former apparently were understood by the Israelites to be sacred scribes with the knowledge of written magic spells. No doubt this attitude intensified over time as the various priesthoods of the Late period became more influential and exercised control over the hieroglyphic writing system, making it more complex and inaccessible to the uninitiated.

Greeks, following their Minoan predecessors, were trading in Egypt at least as early as the fifteenth century BCE, but it was not until the seventh century BCE that they were permitted to establish a permanent trading entrepot in the Nile Delta. Greek travelers, such as Hecataeus of Miletus (late sixth–early fifth century BCE) and Herodotus (fifth century BCE), came and marveled over the wonders of Egypt, the latter taking in much of what the Egyptian priests told him. He came away regarding the Egyptians as the most religious of people, although he adopts the ploy that he should not say too much of what he has learned. Even so, the Egyptian priest Manetho (third century BCE) regarded Herodotus as quite ignorant of Egyptian ideas and practices. The fourth century BCE writer Eudoxus of Cnidus actually did study with Egyptian priests, to whom he ascribed a central role in Egyptian life and knowledge. This was not new, however. The Pythagorean tradition held that its founder had spent twenty years studying in Egypt, although little of the teachings ascribed to him, except perhaps mathematics, bears much resemblance to Egyptian thought. Likewise, Solon, the Athenian reformer, is reported to have traveled to Egypt and studied with an Egyptian priest. It is alleged that Plato, too, visited Egypt. Important in shaping the tradition about Egyptian wisdom during the Hellenistic period was Hecataeus of Abdera (c.300 BCE). His work, now known mostly through its later use by Diodorus Siculus (first century BCE), apparently contained more accurate information on Egypt than did the writings of his predecessors, but, more important, he portrayed Egyptian religion—as did Manetho—as a rational philosophical system rooted in the natural world, countering, at least for a time, the tendency to concentrate on the mysteries and wonders of Egypt.

Perhaps most influential, however, was Chaeremon of Alexandria (first century CE), who may have been a Hellenized Egyptian with a firsthand knowledge of Egyptian belief, although he himself was inclined toward Stoicism. With him came the clearest characterization of the Egyptian temples as universities of sorts, where priests studied both spiritual and mundane matters, a view that has gained a new lease on life among modern Afrocentrists and those seeking esoteric enlightenment. But Chaeremon was less interested in an accurate presentation of Egyptian beliefs than in showing that the results of the Egyptian priests' studies of texts and hieroglyphs were not in fact antithetical to Greek philosophy, and in countering the mockery and distaste that Egyptian worship of animals and animal-headed gods triggered in his audience. Chaeremon's emphasis on the allegorical interpretation of Egyptian hieroglyphics and myths, and his claims for Egyptian astrology in particular, were inadvertently to give rise to a major trend in Greco-Roman thought about Egypt, one that is still at the root of the "wisdom tradition." However rational his approach might have been, his work was used primarily as an access point to information about Egyptian esoterica, exemplified, for example, by Plutarch's essay "On Isis and Osiris" and by Iamblichus's *The Mysteries of Egypt* (second century CE). The *Hieroglyphika* of Horapollon, a fifth-century CE Hellenized Egyptian, building on Chaeremon's approach, taught that the Egyptian hieroglyphics could be studied at two levels: the surface meanings of daily language—some of which he got right—and the deeper allegorical meanings that provided the key to learning about the mysteries of the universe. This work remained immensely influential in the hands of many Renaissance writers; perhaps the most remarkable in this vein was the seventeenth-century Jesuit seeker of arcane knowledge and interpreter of ancient Egyptian hieroglyphics, Athanasius Kircher.

Yet another stream in this esoteric tradition is to be found in the Hermetic texts of the third and fourth centuries CE, which purport to be based on the teachings of a certain Hermes Trismegistus, interpreted as "Thoth the Thrice Great." This collection of Greek mystical and magical texts contains little of actual Egyptian origin, but it nonetheless sought to legitimize its alleged esoteric content by claiming to be essentially Egyptian. Egyptian magic had a long history, with many texts preserved from pagan and Coptic Christian Egypt. The Hermetic tradition is heavily shaped by astrological, alchemical, and magical notions, some of which became the remote ancestors of the modern theosophical movements. Gnosticism, in both non–Christian and Christian varieties, gives the impression of being based in the Egyptian religious tradition; in fact, little of it has been traced to earlier Egyptian belief and practice, the main source being Manichaeism.

The influence of Neoplatonism in the development of an Egyptocentric wisdom tradition is more difficult to characterize. Although the greatest exponent of this combination of mysticism and Platonism, Plotinus (third century CE), studied in Alexandria, he was generally opposed to astrology and magic. He may have had some gnostic leanings originally, but he became a strong opponent of that set of disparate beliefs. His successors, notably Por-

phyry and Iamblichus, turned back to theurgy, the practice of magic that became especially popular with Egyptian Neoplatonists. Among the uses of such magic was the alleged ability to contact spirits of the deceased to affect matters in this world, something that may have some Egyptian antecedents. In later times Neoplatonism gave way to a primarily magical system, cloaking itself in philosophy.

In modern times there has been a revival of interest in many of these trends, especially with a growing doubt in reason and greater interest in mysticism, astrology, and magic. Arising out of very different interests has been the Afrocentrist impulse. This corpus of twentieth-century literature has been largely a reaction against perceived European colonialist and Orientalist tendencies to claim priority of intellectual achievement in history. This has given rise to claims not only of the priority, but of the superiority of African—generally defined as ancient Egyptian—contributions to European culture, especially, but not exclusively, through ancient Greek philosophy. This has led to a resurgence of interest in the intellectual achievements of ancient Egypt.

[*See also* Afrocentrism; Allegory; Ancient Historians; *and* Egyptomania.]

BIBLIOGRAPHY

Baines, John. "Restricted Knowledge, Hierarchy, and Decorum: Modern Perceptions and Ancient Institutions." *Journal of the American Research Center in Egypt* 27 (1990), 1–23.

Behlmer, Heike. "Ancient Egyptian Survivals in Coptic Literature." In *Ancient Egyptian Literature. History and Forms*, edited by A. Loprieno, pp. 567–590. Leiden, 1996.

Burstein, Stanley M. "Images of Egypt in Greek Historiography." In *Ancient Egyptian Literature. History and Forms*, edited by A. Loprieno, pp. 591–604. Leiden, 1996.

Evangeliou, Christos. *The Hellenic Philosophy: Between Europe, Asia, and Africa*. Binghamton, 1997.

Iversen, Erik. "Egypt in Classical Antiquity: A Résumé." In *Hommages à Jean Leclant*, vol. 3, pp. 295–305. Cairo, 1994.

Iversen, Erik. *The Myth of Egypt and Its Hieroglyphs in European Tradition*. Copenhagen, 1961.

Lefkowitz, Mary, and Guy MacLean Rogers, eds. *Black Athena Revisited*. Chapel Hill, 1996. This book has the fullest bibliography and articles on the work of Martin Bernal, his supporters and critics.

Morenz, Siegfried. *Die Begegnung Europas mit Ägypten*. Zürich and Stuttgart, 1969.

Obsomer, Claude. "Hérodote et les prêtres de Memphis." In *Egyptian Religion: The Last Thousand Years*, edited by W. Clarysse et al., pp. 1423–1442. Leuven, 1998.

Preus, Anthony. "Greek Philosophy: Egyptian Origins." In *Research Papers on the Humanities and Social Sciences*. Binghamton, 1992.

Ray, John. "Ancient Egypt." In *Divination and Oracles*, edited by M. Loewe and C. Blacker, pp. 174–190. London, 1981.

Ritner, Robert K. "Egypt under Roman Rule: The Legacy of Ancient Egypt." In *The Cambridge History of Egypt*, edited by Carl F. Petry, vol. 1, pp. 1–33. Cambridge, 1998.

Ritner, Robert K. *The Mechanics of Ancient Egyptian Magical Practice*. Studies in Ancient Oriental Civilizations, 54. Chicago, 1993.

Thissen, H. J. "Ägyptologische Beiträge zu den griechischen magischen Papyri." In *Religion und Philosophie im Ägypten* edited by U. Verhoeven and Erhart Graefe, pp. 293–302. Leuven, 1991.

Wente, Edward F. "Mysticism in Egypt?" *Journal of Near Eastern Studies* 41 (1982), 161–179.

GERALD E. KADISH

WOMEN. Women in ancient Egypt did not form a single coherent group, since ancient Egyptian society was highly stratified. At the top of the social organization was the king, together with the royal family, followed by the ruling elite group. That group consisted of the literate male officials through whom the king governed the country, and their families. The illiterate, nonelite groups were at the bottom of ancient Egyptian society and formed the vast majority of the population. Those groups supplied food, goods, and services to the elite. The sources from which scholars can learn about women present a number of gaps and biases that make it difficult to obtain a complete picture of ancient Egyptian society and the place of women within it. Most of the extant evidence was produced by and for the king and the elite. Although textual and representational materials of the elite include images of the nonelite, those were produced specifically to serve the purposes of the elite and provide limited information about the nonelite.

A further problem in the study of ancient Egyptian women is that texts and monuments were produced by men. Although some elite women may have been literate, there are no surviving texts, except possibly some letters, that are known to have been written specifically by or for women. The images of women found on monuments were almost certainly produced by men, since no professional female artist is attested anywhere. Thus, what we know of women represents a male point of view, and women do not speak directly to us. In addition, textual sources make it clear that a major sphere of female activity and authority was the household, so that our general lack of knowledge concerning settlement sites and houses is also a severe handicap to the study of women.

Because ancient Egyptian civilization spans three millennia, it cannot be assumed that society remained unchanged. Evidence cannot be read backward and forward in time to fill the gaps found in one period with material from another. It is impossible, therefore, to produce a unified picture of women and their position in society that applies to all three millennia.

Royal Women. Royal women—mother, wives, and daughters—surrounded the king, but they did not all have equal status. The most important were the king's mother and his primary wife, who shared a ritual role as bearers of divine queenship, complementary to the divine aspect of the king. The king's consort was often his sister (or half-

WOMEN. *Statue of Nofret, wife of the high priest Rahotep, Old Kingdom.*

sister), but she could also be of nonroyal origins, as were most secondary wives, who had the potential to become king's mother if their sons succeeded to the throne. Scholars know little about the background of king's wives of nonroyal birth, but the available evidence suggests that they came from elite families. During the New Kingdom, kings also made diplomatic marriages with foreign princesses.

Although royal women potentially had access to the highest authority in the land, it is unclear whether they normally shared in or exercised any of that authority. Some queens, however, are known to have acted as regents for young kings, and King Ahmose's stela honoring his mother Ahhotep shows that she had wielded real authority. Otherwise, some king's mothers and consorts probably played an unofficial role by influencing the king in making decisions or formulating courses of action.

At certain periods, royal women also held the powerful office of "God's Wife of Amun" in the cult of Amun at Thebes. At the beginning of the eighteenth dynasty, King Ahmose bestowed the office, together with a considerable endowment, on his consort, Ahmose Nefertary. The title was also held by Merytamun, wife of Amenhotpe I, and then by Hatshepsut. When Hatshepsut ruled as regent for

Thutmose III, "God's Wife" was her most frequently used title, occurring more often than "King's Principal Wife," but after she became king, she passed on the office to her daughter, Neferura. Later, during the sole rule of Thutmose III, the title seems to have become less important and to have disappeared for royal women in the reign of Amenhotpe III, although an anonymous "God's Wife" is found twice in scenes in the Luxor temple. Royal "God's Wives" occurred again sporadically in the nineteenth and twentieth dynasties, but the title does not seem to have been particularly important for them. During the Third Intermediate Period through the twenty-sixth dynasty, the office of "God's Wife" once again became prominent. This time, however, it was held only by king's daughters, each of whom adopted her appointed successor.

What, then, was the role of the "God's Wife"? Eighteenth dynasty temple scenes show her participating in temple ritual; being purified in the sacred lake, along with male priests, before entering the temple; taking part in rituals to destroy Egypt's enemies; and summoning the gods to their evening meal. In temple scenes of the Third Intermediate Period through the twenty-sixth dynasty, the "God's Wife," now often called the "God's Adorer," is shown interacting directly with deities in scene types once limited to the king. In addition to offering directly to deities, she is also embraced, suckled, and crowned by them. It would seem, therefore, that the "God's Wife" had a priestly role within the cult of Amun at a time when priests were otherwise almost exclusively male.

It is important to ask what the basis was for the role and authority of the "God's Wife." How did she come to hold her position in relation to the god Amun? The answer lies in another title that these women held, that of "God's Hand." This title refers to the original act of masturbation by which the creator god set in motion the creation of the ordered universe. Because the word for "hand" in ancient Egyptian is grammatically feminine, it was easy to personify as a goddess the hand with which the creator god masturbated. The fact that the title "God's Hand" was linked to that of "God's Wife" shows that these women were enacting the role of the divine god's hand that stimulated the creator god in his act of creation. Exactly how this translated into specific temple ritual is unclear, but it is likely that the importance of these women derived from a role in which they were believed to stimulate the god Amun sexually, so that he would continually repeat the act of creation and thereby prevent the cosmos from being overwhelmed by chaos.

Elite Women. Women in elite families were concerned mostly with the management of the household and the bearing and rearing of children, since virtually all women would have been expected to get married and raise a family. Little is known about how marriages were arranged, or about prescribed, preferred, or proscribed marriage partners. Marriage was not a matter for the state with religious or legal sanctions, and it seems to have been constituted by a man and woman living together. Property was of primary concern in marriage, especially its division in the case of divorce. Women kept control of the property and goods they brought into a marriage and could dispose of them as they wished, although in normal circumstances they would pass them on equally to their children. On the death of her husband, a woman received one-third of their joint property, while the other two-thirds was divided equally among his children, male and female.

The chance survival of a document drawn up by a woman called Naunakht concerning the disposition of her property shows how a woman could favor some children over others and divide her property according to her own wishes rather than accepted custom. Naunakht lived during the twentieth dynasty in the workmen's village at Deir el-Medina. She was comparatively wealthy in her own right, having inherited property from her father and first husband, and being entitled to a third of the property she held jointly with her second husband. Her first marriage was childless, but she had eight children by her second, and normally her property would have been divided equally among them. However, she explains in the document she has had drawn up that some of her children are not behaving toward her in her old age as they should. Therefore, she disinherits these and divides her property among the offspring of whom she approves.

From the seventh century BCE, written contracts were drawn up between spouses concerning their economic rights and obligations. In the event of divorce, the man promised to give the woman a sum of money, her third share of their joint property, and the equivalent value of what the woman originally brought with her into the marriage. It is unclear whether such favorable conditions for the woman continued an earlier tradition, but they must have made divorce expensive for men, and perhaps protected women from being arbitrarily repudiated, or badly treated and driven out of the house.

Divorce was the reverse of marriage and occurred when one partner moved out of the marital home. Little is known about the reasons for divorce. A Late period contract states: "If I repudiate you as a wife, be it that I hate you, be it that I want another woman as wife instead of you." Some divorces were probably due to incompatibility or to the desire of one spouse to take a new partner. Lack of children, however, was surely a common cause, since the purpose of marriage was to have children; adultery on the part of the woman was certainly another. In fact, Late period contracts protected the husband if he wished to divorce his wife for adultery, for in such a case a woman lost her financial rights.

Because life expectancy for both partners was lower than it is today, many marriages were relatively short. Remarriage after death or divorce was possible for both men and women, so many individuals had more than one marriage partner in a lifetime. There is some evidence that wealthy men occasionally engaged in polygyny, but the practice does not seem to have been widespread.

From the Middle Kingdom forward, a married woman was called "mistress of the house," a title that implies she was in charge of running a household. This implication is supported by a section in the eighteenth dynasty *Instructions of Anii* that says: "Do not control your wife in her house, when you know she is efficient; don't say to her: 'Where is it? Get it!' when she has put it in the right place." It was a wife's job to manage the household, giving her an area of authority that, depending on her social status, could be quite extensive.

Women of the upper elite were responsible for running large establishments with numerous servants whose work they would organize and oversee, even if they did not themselves have to perform manual tasks. Wives of the lower elite would have overseen smaller households with fewer servants, and they would probably have performed a number of domestic tasks themselves. The grinding of grain, baking, spinning, and weaving were traditionally regarded as woman's work.

Central to most women's lives was the bearing and rearing of children. Infant mortality and death in childbirth were high, and houses contained a domestic shrine for the performance of rituals designed to promote the well-being of the family as well as successful conception and childbirth. The shrine was often decorated with images of the household god Bes, who protected women in childbirth and young children. In excavated settlement sites, common finds include small figurines of nude women, sometimes accompanied by a child. These probably relate to domestic cults and the promotion of female fertility. Also found in the houses of Deir el-Medina were stelae of deceased relatives and ancestor busts that formed focal points for ritual. The dead were thought to be able to influence the lives of the living, and deceased relatives could be asked to help with family problems and to aid in the conception of children. Because the household and childbirth were both areas of female authority, women probably played a major role in domestic ritual, a fact reflected in two unusual stelae that depict ancestral busts. In one, a woman kneels adoring a bust, and in the other she stands before a bust, burning incense and libating.

The concern with women's health and their ability to bear children is also reflected in sections of the medical papyri that are devoted to specifically female matters. These include tests to discover whether a woman is fertile, whether she is pregnant, and the sex of the unborn child.

They also deal with menstrual problems, prevention of miscarriage, hastening birth, ensuring milk supply, and protection of mother and child after birth. Motherhood was celebrated in the texts of the male elite, where it is made clear that a son was supposed to hold his mother in affection and honor.

Elite men provided for their dependents through government income. Although women could not hold government office, they could have independent means, and from as early as the Old Kingdom they could own land and other property. Goods and property were usually inherited equally by all children, and women could become (co-) owners of large estates that provided them with an income. Women retained ownership of goods and property after marriage. They could also generate income through cultivating land that they owned or rented. They could enter into business transactions, trading items like textiles and vegetables which they almost certainly produced themselves. A few scenes in tomb chapels show women in a market setting selling goods, in one case apparently exchanging perishable items such as bread, fish, and vegetables for grain. Women could own slaves and hire them out by the day. Women, like men, could draw up a document for the disposition of their property after death, if they wished to make other arrangements than the normal, equal division among all their children. Legally, women were treated as separate individuals responsible for their actions, whether married or not. They could go to court as plaintiff, defendant, or witness on an equal footing with men, but there is no evidence that women normally sat as members of the court, which may have worked to their disadvantage.

Most priests were men, but some women also served. During the Old and Middle Kingdoms, many high-ranking women were priestesses of Hathor, but few acted as priestesses of other deities. During the New Kingdom, the priesthood became a full-time occupation and a branch of the bureaucracy in which male officials made their careers. Women were musicians in the cults of deities, accompanying the performance of ritual by shaking the sacred sistrum. The musicians of a temple were headed by a superior who was often the wife of a senior priest in the cult.

The rituals performed inside temples functioned on a cosmic level and were closed to most people. The outer parts of temples were more accessible, and personal worship often focused on images in those areas. Both men and women visited temples to pray, and a text on the statue of an official set up in a shrine of Hathor is addressed specifically to women. In it, the official offers to intercede with the goddess on their behalf to obtain "a good husband" for them. The worship of Hathor was popular with women because of the goddess's connection

WOMEN. *Group of mourning women, eighteenth dynasty*. This wall painting is from the tomb of Ramose, one of Akhenaten's generals, at Qurna. The animated style is typical of the Amarna period. (© Photograph by Erich Lessing / Art Resource, NY)

with sexuality, fertility, and childbirth. Although the donors of votive offerings in temples are usually not known, some votive pieces presented to Hathor were undoubtedly dedicated by women because the donor is named or depicted.

Votive statues and stelae were set up in the outer areas of temples to associate the donor with the temple deity and rituals in perpetuity. Most of the statues belonged to men, whereas a portion of the stelae belonged to women. Although statues were more expensive items than stelae, it is unlikely that economic reasons alone account for this discrepancy; there must have been some other factor involved that virtually excluded women from owning temple statues.

Elite men and women shared the same funerary beliefs and practices, but at any given socioeconomic level, men's burials tend to be richer than those of women. The tomb-chapel was the most expensive item of funerary equipment, and only relatively high officials owned one. The decoration featured the male official as the primary figure, although he was often accompanied by his wife and other relatives in secondary positions, and family members were usually interred in the burial chambers associated with the chapel. In eighteenth dynasty burials of husbands and wives, the woman often has one coffin fewer than her husband, and may share some items with him, such as the *Book of Going Forth by Day* (*Book of the Dead*), where the husband is clearly the primary owner. The funerary rites performed over the deceased before the tomb chapel were the same for men and women. They were al-

ways carried out by male priests, whereas women were prominent as mourners. Two women played the roles of the goddesses Isis and Nephthys mourning the dead Osiris. In tomb chapels, the funerary cult focused on statues of the chapel's owner and his wife, so that a large number of funerary statues depict women. Although the funerary cult was ideally performed by the eldest son, stelae show other family members, including the wife and daughters of the deceased, performing some of the rituals.

The standard image used for elite women in art depicts them as being of childbearing age in order to stress their central role as childbearers—whatever their actual age—so that a man's mother, wife, and daughter may all be represented similarly. Women's fertility is often further emphasized through the manipulation of female dress to reveal the outline of the body and, at many periods, the pubic area. In contrast to women, men have a mature image in addition to a youthful one. The former shows them as successful government officials, an image not appropriate to women. Compared to men, women are generally depicted in a more passive manner, standing with their feet almost together, frequently doing nothing, whereas men stand with one leg well advanced, often performing an action. Gender is also distinguished by skin color, with men being depicted as reddish-brown and women as a lighter yellowish-brown. Many images, both two- and three-dimensional, depict couples and tell us something about how husbands and wives were perceived in relation to one another. Overall, there is a hierarchy of gender that privileges the male and subordinates the female through the use of one or more of a number of strategies: scale, compositional position, pose, and distribution of texts. The man is almost always identified by his official titles, but the woman is known simply by her relationship to her husband.

Nonelite Women. There is little information available about the families and households of the nonelite. As in Egypt today, much of the ancient population probably lived in mud-brick villages by the Nile River. Some of the men were engaged in the various nonscribal occupations known from elite sources, but the majority worked on the land. Most women were occupied with household duties and childbearing and rearing, which was as important to the nonelite as the elite, since children provided free labor in the fields and support for their aged parents.

Some women worked outside the home, although according to elite sources their work was more restricted than that of men. They were employed as household servants; eighteenth dynasty banquet scenes depict them waiting on the guests. Other evidence shows that they were employed as hairdressers, wet nurses, and possibly nannies. One of the most frequently represented tasks involving women is bread-making, a laborious process that involved breaking up the whole grains of wheat or barley by pounding them in a mortar with a long pestle, then grinding the result on a grindstone to make flour. The flour was then mixed with water to form dough and baked into loaves. Men are most frequently depicted pounding the whole grains in the mortar, while women grind flour. Women are also depicted watching the bread molds stacked on the fire, shielding their face from the heat with one hand and poking the fire with a stick held in the other. In model bakeries of the First Intermediate Period and the Middle Kingdom, often the only women included are those grinding grain; all the rest of the workers are men. Further evidence that grinding grain was especially associated with women comes from administrative documents dating to the reign of Sety I that relate to bread-making for the royal palace at Memphis. They list the amount of grain given to twenty-six women for grinding, together with the amount of flour produced. The government also provided households at Deir el-Medina with female slaves to grind grain.

Brewing was closely associated with baking, since beer was made from fermented grain, and bakeries and breweries are often depicted next to each other. The workers involved in brewing are most frequently men, although women are sometimes shown sieving the beer mash to extract the liquid. Other forms of food preparation, such as butchering; preparing and preserving meat, birds, and fish; and cooking are always depicted being done by men. This gender distinction was perhaps limited to large households with male servants. In nonelite families without ser-vants where male family members worked at occupations outside the house, women would surely have been responsible for food preparation.

Textile production was traditionally women's work, and in large households female servants were probably employed in the manufacture of cloth. Women were also trained as musicians and dancers, appearing in tomb scenes from the Old Kingdom to the eighteenth dynasty. Although music frequently had a ritual aspect, troupes of performers were employed by larger households as well as by temples. Dating to the end of the Old Kingdom, male musicians were also found, and men and women may have performed together.

The nonelite were also employed in craft production in the workshops of the king, temples, and great officials. The depictions and models show workshops for carpentry, jewelry-making and metal-working, sculpture, leather-working, and weaving. Women were excluded from all craft production except weaving. During the Old and Middle Kingdoms, only women were involved in textile production, but from the eighteenth dynasty, men are shown operating the newly introduced vertical loom.

The largest area in which the nonelite were employed was on the land, and scenes in tombs from the Old Kingdom to the eighteenth dynasty depict activities connected with the agricultural year, animal husbandry, and work in the marshes, some of which are also represented in three-dimensional models. Women are almost entirely absent from these activities, except when shown performing a few specific tasks at harvest time. In the Old Kingdom, women are shown winnowing the grain after threshing, although in later periods this appears to have been done by men. From the very end of the Old Kingdom forward, women are often shown following the male reapers to collect fallen ears of grain in small baskets. During the eighteenth dynasty, although not earlier, women are shown harvesting flax, which was pulled up by the roots rather than cut like grain. The preponderance of male workers on large estates is confirmed by a letter dating to the twenty-fourth year of Ramesses II's reign that lists the workers on an estate of Amun in the Delta—they are all male. We know from other documents that women were attached to temple estates, but it is not clear what their duties were.

The evidence shows that the ideal world of the elite included a division of labor among the nonelite, in which women were far more restricted than men in what they could do. It suggests that women were expected to be concerned mainly with household duties, either in their own homes or as servants in the houses of the elite. The question is how far this gender-based division of labor was in force outside the elite sphere. Women, like men, were liable for state labor, but it is unclear what duties they

WOMEN. *Upper-class women offering a lemon and a mandragora root to another woman during a banquet, eighteenth dynasty.* This detail of a wall painting is from the tomb of Nakht, a scribe and priest under Thutmose IV, at Qurna. (© Photograph by Erich Lessing / Art Resource, NY)

were assigned, although they may have been conscripted to work in state fields. In a New Kingdom copy of a Middle Kingdom text, women act as beaters to make birds rise in the marshes, although in tomb chapels only men are shown in marsh scenes. Two New Kingdom love poems use the image of girls netting birds, an occupation carried out in tomb scenes by men. The image would hardly be effective, however, if this was something that girls did not do. The discrepancy may be explained by the fact that in one poem the girl takes the birds home to her mother, suggesting that she is not working on the type of large estate depicted in tomb scenes, but is catching birds to support her family. It seems probable that the elite ideal was not universal.

In contrast to elite women, we have little evidence of the legal and economic situation of nonelite women, although we can be sure that it varied according to their position or that of their families in the social hierarchy. Subsistence-level income or even poverty may have been the lot of many nonelite women and men. In describing the life of a peasant farmer, an elite author recounts a series of disasters that result in the farmer being unable to pay his taxes. When the tax collectors come, he is beaten while his wife and children are tied up, and in the end they are left without any grain. Although exaggerated for the purposes of the text, such disasters undoubtedly occurred, and neither men nor women would have had much legal recourse against the state and other powerful institutions. Overbearing and dishonest officials could presumably make life difficult for the nonelite, although

in some Middle Kingdom texts officials deny that they have ever mistreated inferiors. In similar texts from all periods, officials claim to have looked after widows, and the New Kingdom *Instructions of Amenemope* warns officials not to cheat or harass widows, suggesting that some widows were liable to receive such treatment.

Conclusion. The fact that women were not part of the government bureaucracy reveals that ancient Egypt, like most societies, was male dominated. The source of all authority resided in the king, from whom it passed to his male officials. The exclusion of women from the kingship (apart from a few exceptional cases) and from the bureaucracy clearly limited their access to official authority, but this does not mean that they were without any authority or were dominated entirely by the male part of the population. Not only were there areas within society where women held authority or shared it with men, but the interactions of men and women were affected by status, so that, for instance, an elite woman no doubt had authority over male servants.

Not all authority in ancient Egypt was of the same type. Some was officially recognized as part of the public, legitimate structure of society, while other types existed through nonofficial channels. The first type formed part of the elite's ideal view of society recorded on the monuments. The second lay outside the ideal and is only occasionally glimpsed in nonmonumental documentation. Although women were excluded from direct access to the sources of authority enjoyed by male officials, they had indirect access through opportunities to influence their husbands and sons. Further, the ability of women to own or rent land, conduct business, and accumulate income in their own right would have given them a potential role in public life through their contributions to the economy of their community. Undoubtedly, women with wealth could achieve an independence impossible for those who had to rely on their husbands for support, and they would probably have been able to wield considerable power within the family and local community.

[*See also* Beauty; Birth; Children; Family; Inheritance; Marriage and Divorce; Priesthood; Queens; *and* Royal Family.]

BIBLIOGRAPHY

Allam, Schafik. "Women as Owners of Immovables in Pharaonic Egypt. In *Women's Earliest Records from Ancient Egypt and Western Asia,* edited by Barbara S. Lesko, pp. 123–135. Atlanta, 1989.

Bryan, Betsy M. "In Women Good and Bad Fortune are on Earth: Status and Roles of Women in Egyptian Culture." In *Mistress of the House, Mistress of Heaven: Women in Ancient Egypt,* edited by Anne K. Capel and Glenn E. Markoe, pp. 25–46. New York, 1996.

Černý, J. "The Will of Naunakhte and the Related Documents." *Journal of Egyptian Archaeology* 31(1945), 29–53. Publication of a document in which a woman disinherits some of her children.

Eyre, C. J. "Crime and Adultery in Ancient Egypt." *Journal of Egyptian Archaeology* (1984), 92–105.

Fischer, Henry G. "Priesterin." In *Lexikon der Ägyptologie* 4: 1100–1105. Wiesbaden, 1982. Important English-language article on priestesses.

Fischer, Henry G. "Women in the Old Kingdom and the Heracleopolitan Period." In *Women's Earliest Records from Ancient Egypt and Western Asia,* edited by Barbara S. Lesko, pp. 5–24. Atlanta, 1989.

Friedman, Florence D. "Aspects of Domestic Life and Religion." In *Pharaoh's Workers: The Villagers of Deir el Medina,* edited by Leonard H. Lesko, pp. 95–117. Ithaca and London, 1994. Explores domestic cult at Deir el-Medina, including its relation to women and childbirth.

Gardiner, A. H. "A Lawsuit arising from the Purchase of Two Slaves." *Journal of Egyptian Archaeology* 21(1935), 140–146. Publication of a document concerning the purchase of a female and a male slave by a woman.

Gardiner, A. H. "Adoption Extraordinary." *Journal of Egyptian Archaeology* 26(1940), 23–29. Publication of a document concerning the adoption of a woman by her husband as his heir, and the subsequent adoption of three slaves by the woman.

Johnson, Janet H. "The Legal Status of Women in Ancient Egypt." In *Mistress of the House, Mistress of Heaven: Women in Ancient Egypt,* edited by Anne K. Capel and Glenn E. Markoe, pp. 175–186. New York, 1996.

Lichtheim, Miriam. *Ancient Egyptian Literature.* Berkeley, 1976.

Pestman, P. W. *Marriage and Matrimonial Property in Ancient Egypt.* Leiden, 1961. A study of the so-called marriage contracts of the Late period.

Pinch, Geraldine. "Childbirth and Female Figurines at Deir el-Medina and el-Amarna." *Orientalia* 52(1983), 405–414.

Robins, Gay. *Women in Ancient Egypt.* London and Cambridge, Mass., 1993. Contains extensive bibliography.

Robins, Gay. "Some Principles of Compositional Dominance and Gender Hierarchy in Egyptian Art." *Journal of the American Research Center in Egypt* 31(1994), 33–40. Shows how husbands are normally given compositional precedence over their wives in two- and three-dimensional art.

Robins, Gay. "Women and Children in Peril: Pregnancy, Birth and Infant Mortality in Ancient Egypt." *KMT: A Modern Journal of Ancient Egypt* 54 (1994–1995), 24–35.

Robins, Gay. "Dress, Undress, and the Representation of Fertility and Potency in New Kingdom Egyptian Art." In *Sexuality in Ancient Art,* edited by Natalie Boymel Kampen, pp. 27–40. Cambridge, 1996. Discusses women as icons of fertility.

Roehrig, Catharine H. "Woman's Work: Some Occupations of Nonroyal Women as Depicted in Ancient Egyptian Art." In *Mistress of the House, Mistress of Heaven: Women in Ancient Egypt,* edited by Anne K. Capel and Glenn E. Markoe, pp. 13–24. New York, 1996.

Smith, Stuart Tyson. "Intact Tombs of the Seventeenth and Eighteenth Dynasties from Thebes and the New Kingdom Burial System." *Mitteilungen des Deutschen Archäologischen Instituts, Abteilung Kairo* 48(1992), 193–231. Shows tendency for husbands to have slightly wealthier burials than their wives.

Sweeney, Deborah. "Women's Correspondence from Deir el-Medineh." In *Atti Sesto Congresso Internazionale di Egittologia,* vol. 2, pp. 523–529. Turin, 1993. Discusses the possibility of female literacy in relation to material from Deir el-Medina.

Troy, Lana. *Patterns of Queenship in Ancient Egyptian Myth and History.* Uppsala, 1986.

Ward, William A. "Non-Royal Women and their Occupations in the Middle Kingdom." In *Women's Earliest Records from Ancient Egypt and Western Asia,* edited by Barbara S. Lesko, pp. 33–43. Atlanta, 1989.

GAY ROBINS

WOOD. *See* Flora; *and* Woodworking.

WOODWORKING. A small number of Old Kingdom tombs have scenes that show woodcutters using either the single-notch or double-notch methods to fell small indigenous trees. The Nile acacia, *šndt* (*Acacia nilotica*); sycomore fig, *nh* (*Ficus sycomorus*); sidder, *nabk* (*Ziziphus spina-christi*); and tamarisk *isr* (*Tamarix nilotica* and *Tamarix aphylla*), provided much of the timber used during both the Predynastic and Early Dynastic periods. These trees often produced poor quality wood of short length and small cross-sectional area, which limited the types of construction.

With the importation of large conifers (*ḳdtt*), such as cedar from Syria as early as the fourth dynasty, more ambitious works could be considered. On the northern exterior wall of the hypostyle hall within the Great Temple of Amun at Karnak is a wall carving that shows woodcutters felling a tall Lebanese cedar, *ꜣš* (*Cedrus libani*). One man cuts the base of the trunk with an ax, while others support the tree with ropes tied to the uppermost branches; this controlled the tree's fall, which prevented any damage to the grain on impact. For the New Kingdom, we have documents that record quantities of coniferous timber being imported. In an eight-month period, during the reign of Thutmose III, one shipyard procured 600 meters (2,000 feet) of planking. The exotic hardwood timbers used by Egyptian carpenters (*mdḥ*) to manufacture royal furniture and decorative inlays were imported from Egypt's southern border region. In the mortuary temple of Queen Hatshepsut, scenes show small logs of African ebony, *hbny* (*Dalbergia melanoxylon*), being loaded onto ships for transport on the Nile River to Egypt.

Once timber has been felled, it has to be cut into lumber, and then the boards are seasoned to reduce the moisture content. In the sixth dynasty tomb of Iteti at Dishasha, some illustrations show these processes. The technique of cleaving is seen, and two men are splitting a board from a log fixed to a trestle. Another carpenter is shown defining the edges of a board to be cleaved with an ax (*minb*). Cleaving began as early as the Predynastic period to obtain long boards. Better quality short boards were sawn; however, Egyptians did not use a saw pit (which is considered to be a Roman development). Instead, they tied the log against a short post and ripped it down with a pullsaw (*tf*); this is a long saw, with a sharp nose and large teeth that point toward its integral metal handle. Its development occurred at the time when better quality imported timber was made available. After the boards had been cut, they had to be seasoned, to reduce their moisture content; if seasoning is not done promptly, the boards will warp, check, and bow. Egyptians seasoned timber by stacking the boards, allowing air to circulate within the stack, which dried them naturally. They would have become experienced in estimating the moisture content to the point where timber with approximately 8 to 12 percent moisture would be suitable for most woodworking processes.

At the end of the Predynastic period, we learn about small copper tools made by smelting the metal from its ore. The metal would have been cast into ingots, from which the tools were hot forged. In a first dynasty tomb at Saqqara (tomb 3471), Walter B. Emery found a large cache of woodworking tools. Unlike Old Kingdom carpenters, those working before them in the Early Dynastic period used only short saws to convert timber to planks and to cut joints in it. Those early saws were similar in profile, the blade having a round blunt nose and curved edges. Forged from a bar of copper, it left a rib along the center of the blade, which extended into a tang that was located in a wooden handle. Along one of the curved edges were nibbled-out teeth, which were irregular in both shape and pitch, all bent to one side of the blade (unlike the set of a modern saw, where each tooth is bent to the right and left alternately). The ancient hand saw was difficult to use, since one side of the blade would have always been in contact with the wet, or resinous, kerf. On coffin boards discovered at Tarkhan, the problems carpenters encountered when using these short saws are visible; the saw lines run across the face of the board at many angles. This was overcome with the introduction of the pullsaw; however, the short saws remained in use but were steadily modified. The New Kingdom examples have a straight back and a molded handle and were used to cut boards to length, across the grain, and to cut the faces of joints.

The adze (*nwt* or *'nt*) was used to true and shape timber and, in the hands of an experienced carpenter, was a very versatile tool. At first, its blade was forged with straight edges; gradually it was developed to have side lugs and a rounded top. The sharpened blade was bound to a shaped wooden handle with wet leather thongs, which tightened the assembly as they dried. The adze blade would have been ground, or honed, against a slate with a little oil, which had been stored in a flask made from an animal horn.

Both mortise and firmer chisels have been found in tombs dating from the Early Dynastic period. The mortise chisel (*md3*) had a wooden handle with a flat top, indicating that it was struck with a mallet. The blade was also square and stout, which prevented it from bending as chips of timber were prised out of a deep mortise. The firmer chisel was used for finishing joints and for carving; it has a thin blade, while the top of the handle is rounded, allowing it to fit comfortably in the palm of the carpenter's hand.

In the fifth dynasty tomb of Ty are wall reliefs that show Old Kingdom carpenters engaged in a number of common woodworking processes. One is seen using a bowdrill to bore a hole in the lid of a box; two others are sanding a long box with sandstone rubbers, to smooth the grain. The New Kingdom carpenter continued to use these tools, as well as a try square and cubit rod, to test the accuracy of wooden elements. He also used a cutting aid to make mitered corners. Egyptian carpenters exploited the physical properties of timber and understood the concept of joinery. We see in their work the three conventional forms of construction: the frame, the stool, and the carcase. They realized that the strength of timber was along the grain, not across it, and that shrinkage was negligible along the grain. With the use of flint and other stone tools during the early Predynastic period, we see that carpenters used butt joints and edge joints that were always mechanically fastened together, either with leather thongs or with pegs. In later periods, loose tenons were used. With the introduction of the copper hand saw and the copper chisel, it became possible to cut joints in timber.

The simplest joint cut is the rebated butt, also known as a lap joint, and it was found holding together the corners of a pair of trays from a first dynasty tomb at Saqqara, excavated by Emery. The mortise-and-tenon joint was found on first dynasty bed-frame construction, where the tenon had either square or molded shoulders; this form of joint was used extensively in all fields of carpentry. New Kingdom examples were found with both bareface and stub tenons. Housing joints were used when a box was to be divided into compartments, using parti-

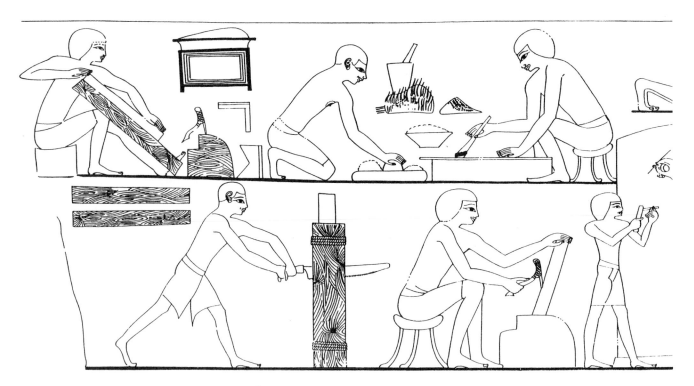

WOODWORKING. *New Kingdom carpenters.* This drawing is of an eighteenth dynasty wall painting from the tomb of the vizier Rekhmire at Thebes. (After Norman de Garis Davies, *The Tomb of Rekh-mi-re at Thebes.* New York, 1943, Plate LV; Courtesy Geoffrey Killen.)

tions. Halving joints were used for the stud work of a cabin wall on a model boat. While the blade and stock of try squares were fastened together with a bridle joint, barrels and corn measures were manufactured with a stave construction that had coopered joints.

The bed canopy of the fourth dynasty Queen Hetepheres I was constructed with a simple dovetail joint. Variants of this joint were used, such as the lapped dovetail on drawer construction and the through dovetail on both box and coffin construction. The miter joint was found on simple Early Dynastic frame construction. By the Middle Kingdom, a number of complex miter variants were used to join the corners of large rectangular coffins. Restricted by the conversion process, sawn timber could only be obtained in short lengths. If long lengths were required, then short boards were scarf jointed together. The faces in contact would be cut at an angle, and a double dovetail socket was cut across the splice into which was driven a butterfly-shaped wooden cramp. Boat builders used two other types of scarf joint, the tied hook and the spliced form.

The process of bending unseasoned timber was depicted in a wall relief in the Old Kingdom tomb of Ty at Saqqara. In the Middle Kingdom tombs at Beni Hasan, painted scenes show carpenters manufacturing bows (for arrows), by steam bending thin strips of timber. In a passage within the Step Pyramid complex at Saqqara, fragmentary parts of a plywood coffin were found. This example of six-ply wood, where the grain of each alternating sheet is at right angles to the adjacent sheets, was made from veneers of cypress, juniper, and Aleppo pine. The veneers were of different sizes, which resulted in a patchwork construction that was held together with small flat pegs. The surface of the coffin was carved into a corrugated pattern before being overlaid with a gold sheet, which was fixed to the plywood board with small gold pins. The tomb of Rekhmire at Thebes has a painted scene that shows a carpenter applying hot glue to a strip of decorative veneer with a brush. Glue was made by boiling down the skin and bones of animals, and it appears to have been used from as early as the fifth dynasty. The joints of small boxes have been found glued together; however, pegs and dowels continued to be used in preference to glue on large constructional pieces, where the joints might be stressed.

The art of turning, using a lathe, was first seen in the Macedonian tomb of Petosiris at Tuna el-Gebel. One man rotated the wooden workpiece with a rope twisted around it. The turner scraped the rotating timber into shape with a chisel, which he held against the bed of the lathe. Although turning is generally considered to be a Greco-Roman invention, we cannot entirely dismiss the possibility that it was known much earlier.

Carpenters worked in state and temple workshops (*wḫryt*), managed by an overseer, who would have been directed by an official. Illustrations in the tombs of Ty and Rekhmire and a model from the tomb of Meketra trace the developments made in tools and techniques throughout dynastic times. The Middle Kingdom carpenter worked in a formal workshop; he squatted on the floor and was shown to perform a process repeatedly. Scenes from the New Kingdom show that the carpenter had achieved the status of an artisan; he sits on a stool and works at a specially designed bench, which helped him cut and hold his work. New Kingdom wooden products were often elaborately embellished. They were recognized throughout the ancient world as objects of quality.

BIBLIOGRAPHY

Aldred, C., Holmyard, E. J., and Singer, C. "Fine Woodworking." *A History of Technology*. Vol. I, pp. 685–703. Oxford, 1954. An examination of the decorative techniques applied to furniture.

Baker, H. S. *Furniture of the Ancient World, Origins and Evolution 3100–475 BC*, London, 1966. A generalized history of furniture in the ancient world.

Killen, G. P. *Ancient Egyptian Furniture, 4000–1300 BC*. Vol. 1. Warminster, 1980. Describes in detail the wood, tools and techniques used by Egyptian carpenters; has a valuable list of furniture preserved in major world museums.

Killen, G. P. *Ancient Egyptian Furniture, Boxes, Chests and Footstools*. Vol. II. Warminster, 1994. Continues the theme of the first volume and contains a second list of furniture preserved in minor world museums.

Killen, G. P. *Egyptian Woodworking and Furniture*. Princes Risborough, 1994. A valuable pocket-sized book for those seeking more general information on woodworking.

Lucas, A., and J. R. Harris, eds. *Ancient Egyptian Materials and Industries*. London, 1962. Authoritative book with a chapter on wood and woodworking in ancient Egypt.

Petrie, W. M. Flinders. *Tools and Weapons*. London, 1917. An in-depth survey of the development of tools in ancient times.

Reisner, G. A., and W. S. Smith. *A History of the Giza Necropolis, Volume II. The Tomb of Hetep-heres the Mother of Cheops*. Cambridge, Mass. 1955. Excavation report contains excellent working drawings of the queen's furniture, with photographs before and after restoration.

Shaw, I., and P. T. Nicholson. *Ancient Egyptian Materials and Technology*. Cambridge, 1999.

GEOFFREY KILLEN

WORK FORCE. The prodigious building achievements of the ancient Egyptians are clear evidence of a well-organized and well-supplied work force. The labor recruitment and organizational skills that made these feats possible also supplied and allocated labor for other state and nonstate projects. However, as with all aspects of Egyptian society, it is the elite levels of administration that are most visible in the evidence; the character, origins, and experiences of the work force itself are rarely recorded.

Evidence. The widest variety of information about the organization of labor survives from the mortuary sphere. Both royal and nonroyal tombs sometimes contain archaeological evidence of the organization of their creators in the form of patterns in quarry marks or characteristic artistic styles. The numbers and hierarchy of a complement of tomb builders and cult functionaries can be seen in the distribution of house sizes in the planned towns that were built in or near cemeteries to accommodate them, and sometimes also in the architecture of the institutions that employed them. The so-called scenes of daily life found in tomb-chapels depict people working at a variety of tasks, although this evidence must be used carefully.

Textual sources give a different kind of detail. Tomb autobiographies and lists of titles found in tomb-chapels mention a few titles that can be related to labor organization. Legal texts that describe the construction of tombs and assert the satisfaction of the workers with their remuneration were sometimes recorded on chapel walls. Mortuary cult personnel were occasionally granted exemptions from taxes and corvée labor in decrees that specify the kinds of labor that might otherwise be required.

The evidence outside of cemeteries is scarcer. State-sponsored settlements for workers in remote areas have been excavated. Rare administrative papyri record names of workers, assignments of duties, or pay distributions. Literary works may, in passing, give information on labor and its typical organization. School texts often give exaggerated accounts of the horrors of manual labor in order to frighten students into studying for administrative positions. Quarry texts record the officials and sometimes also the workers who took part in such expeditions; isolated tools are inscribed with the names of the administrative units that used them.

Terminology for Work. Philology can also suggest patterns in the way work was viewed. Several Egyptian words for "work" are attested at different periods. The most basic appears to be *k3t*, which seems to have the same general application as the English term. It is often used for construction activities (as implied by its determinative, a man carrying a basket on his head), but it can also be applied to crafts, agriculture, and service, and the work it describes can be done by animals, gods, and the king, as well as ordinary people. The alternative term *b3k* seems to imply heavier physical labor and menial service, although in the abstract *b3k* can also be done to produce articles of craftsmanship. *B3k* can also be applied to taxes and foreign tribute, and hence may have overtones of labor that is owed; it was not done by kings or gods. The nouns *b3k* and *b3kt* ("male and female servants/slaves") exist; there are no corresponding nouns derived from *k3t*.

Rarer and possibly more specialized words include *pss*, which is used only in the New Kingdom. It is always written in group writing, and so may represent a foreign borrowing. The term *š* in one Old Kingdom text, and perhaps also in several titles, is used to describe stone-carving; it is unclear whether it has a wider application. *Sšr* also occurs in the Old Kingdom; its determinative suggests a connection with cloth, and it may refer to work paid for in that commodity.

Members of the Work Force. Work in the public sphere was generally done by men. Women took part in domestic and agricultural labor, but after the Old Kingdom they are rarely seen to work outside of the home except as weavers, as servants, or as musicians in temples or at private parties. Even during the Old Kingdom, when artwork and titles sometimes suggest more extensive work outside the home, women seem to have been employed mainly in service activities in the local economy, rather than being attached professionally to state institutions. In exceptional cases, women in the Old Kingdom filled such roles as stewards of the estates of other women, priestesses, and physicians. However, most work done by women was an extension of their traditional household activities: child care, weaving, sewing, and entertaining with music. There is no unambiguous evidence for prostitution in the pharaonic period, although it has generally been assumed that prostitutes existed. Lists of laborers recruited for state projects sometimes include women's names, but it is unclear what services they performed.

According to the Demotic wisdom text recorded on the Insinger Papyrus (17,22–18,3), a boy would begin to work when he was about ten years old, for a ten-year training period. The years from twenty to thirty would be spent accruing sufficient property to support himself and his family, and from thirty to forty gaining wisdom, leaving his last sixty years to enjoy the fruits of his labor and his knowledge. This chronology relates to professional and elite occupations (and is idealized as to the length of life expected); nonetheless, it suggests that the working life of most men was comparatively short, from twenty to forty. If a man followed the advice of other sages, he would marry at age twenty, so that by the time he was forty he would have a son nearing his prime working years, and so could retire.

Because of biblical references to the labors of the Hebrew people in Egypt, there has been considerable interest in the foreign component of the Egyptian work force. It is clear that foreign captives were brought to Egypt as early as the Old Kingdom, and the Palermo Stone records that Snefru brought back seven thousand Nubians and eleven hundred Libyans, presumably from military campaigns. At least in the New Kingdom, foreign captives were sometimes awarded to successful military men, for whom they presumably worked. Foreigners working for private individuals would mostly have been engaged in agricultural work, but the king may also have retained some captives for state labor. Other non–Egyptian laborers may have been voluntary immigrants, and among these there probably were craftsmen skilled in trades and methods unknown to the Egyptians. The foreign names appearing in some Middle Kingdom lists may also have belonged to voluntary immigrants. One particular class of foreign workers were the *md3y* (*medjay*) of Nubia, who seem to have served as policemen throughout Egypt in the Middle Kingdom and later. Although the word implies a Nubian origin, the term may have come to be a professional label, so that all members of it were called *medjay,* regardless of their ethnic origin.

Types of Labor. The following discussion deals with classes of workers as defined in the Egyptian socioeconomic system.

Scribal and administrative labor. The class of literate men formed the elite of Egyptian society. Scribal training was the principal engine of upward social mobility, and carried a great deal of prestige. The schools supplied the state, the temples, and the administrative levels of the army with their personnel, so training was broad and unspecialized. Advancement seems to have been to some extent merit-based, although family and social relationships were also important. Outside large institutions, scribes might also work for high officials as stewards or as officials in their mortuary cults. It is widely assumed that a class of independent scribes-for-hire was available to the general population for writing letters and dealing with legal documents; however, there is little evidence for scribes who were not attached to an institution.

Crafts and other skilled labor. The evidence for crafts labor and similar specialized nonagricultural labor is both limited and biased. Labor of this sort is often depicted in relief carvings and models placed in tombs and tomb-chapels. These figurines were meant to provide the deceased tomb owner with such labor and skills in the afterlife. Although these depictions are probably accurate as to the processes employed, the happiness of the laborers, their dress, and even their numbers may be distorted. The textual sources are even more biased, because they consist mainly of descriptions of crafts work intended to inspire students to study hard for a bureaucratic career in order to avoid such employment. Such texts as the *Satire on the Trades* (Papyrus Sallier II) emphasize the unpleasant nature of crafts work. The archaeological evidence for such work is less biased but scanty. At Giza, bakeries and other food-processing areas have been excavated, in addition to areas that may have been used for sculpture and other crafts connected with supplying tombs and mortuary cults. The short-lived New Kingdom site of Amarna has more extensive evidence of workshops, and smaller installations are known from the sites of el-Lisht, Malqata, and Kataana-Qantir.

Both the archaeological remains and the tomb models seem to indicate that most crafts production was done in small workshops. With larger institutions, these workshops were not enlarged, but duplicated many times to achieve the desired level of production. Such a modular system prevented any significant economies of scale, but it allowed a well-established system of training and administration to be adapted for the production of any quantity of goods desired. In addition to cemeteries, workshops might be found attached to temples, to the palace, and to other large institutions, as well as to the estates of elite officials. Depictions of people buying and selling crafts objects in markets suggest that workshops of this type also existed independently, supplying the crafts needed by the local population. These independent workshops were probably the model emulated by the larger state institutions.

Domestic crafts production also existed. In the Old Kingdom (and probably later periods as well), women could sell cloth produced in their homes, both in the open market and to large institutions. (The control of women over cloth and clothing is emphasized in two stories, the Webaoner story of the Westcar Papyrus and the *Story of the Two Brothers;* in both stories, women attempting to seduce men offer them clothing.) The textual evidence from Deir el-Medina also suggests that small-scale production of funerary equipment was done in the home by some state workers, as a sideline.

Agricultural labor. By far the largest component of the Egyptian labor force was involved in food production, mainly of wheat. Tomb scenes routinely depict the sowing of seed, plowing it under, harvesting, threshing with donkeys, and winnowing of grain. (This last task alone is usually shown being performed by women.) Most Egyptian accounts of this kind of labor (in satirical works, such as Papyrus Sallier I) depict it as undesirable, unrewarding work, although some account must be taken of the didactic purpose of such descriptions.

Most agricultural laborers were probably tenant farmers, who paid a part of their crops to a landlord and another part to tax collectors for the state. In some cases (for example, as reflected in the Old Kingdom exemption decree from Dahshur), cult functionaries and possibly other low-level officials themselves worked the lands of their institution's endowment (presumably rent-free), as remuneration for their nonagricultural work; such workers would have had to return a portion of their crops to their institutions, in addition to paying any taxes from which the cult had not been exempted.

Some agricultural workers may have worked for private entrepreneurs, as suggested by the letters of Hekanakhte, one such entrepreneur. He seems to have rented a variety of different types of land (to create a "diversified portfolio"), and then had them cultivated by a group of dependents. In exchange for providing the security of the rent, he presumably pocketed a large share of the proceeds. The details of this arrangement are, however, somewhat unclear. While texts like Papyrus Sallier I and the Hekanakhte papyri tend to depict farming as done by a single family or household, tomb depictions imply a more communal organization, with plowing, sowing, and reaping done by large groups of men working simultaneously. These scenes suggest that a different kind of farming was done on large estates, with the owner or lessor of the land providing a large number of workers to farm the land together.

It is unclear to what degree these workers, like medieval serfs, were tied to the land. Autobiographical texts of favored officials state that the king rewarded them with land and with people, presumably to work it. Many of the men so rewarded were soldiers, in which cases the people granted with the land were presumably captured foreigners, and tantamount to slave labor. It seems likely that even Egyptian peasants' choice of where or whether to farm was limited. A telling passage occurs in the story the *Eloquent Peasant* in which the complaints of the peasant against a powerful steward are dismissed because "perhaps it is one of his people who has gone to someone else besides him."

Corvée labor. Work for the state seems often to have been staffed by workers drafted from the general population. These groups were probably summoned for projects such as mining and quarrying, military expeditions, the building of pyramids and other state construction projects, and for domestic maintenance such as road-building and work on canals and the irrigation system. Corvée labor is attested by decrees exempting members of institutions such as temples from the draft and, rarely, by administrative texts listing the laborers.

To judge from the long list of official ranks to whom exemption decrees are addressed, it is clear that a variety of government departments had the authority to call up workers, although the actual recruitment (and sometimes the supervision) of these laborers seems to have been done by local officials. The recruits are often referred to as *nfrw,* "young men," so age may have been a criterion of selection for the draft.

The work of such conscripts is probably illustrated by the texts found on *shabtis,* tomb figures who are said to answer, should the tomb owner in the afterlife be drafted "to cultivate fields, to flood riverbanks, to carry sand from the east to the west." This text, from chapter 6 of the *Book of Going Forth by Day* (*Book of the Dead*) probably reflects the most common tasks assigned to corvée laborers: agricultural work, maintenance of the irrigation system, and transport of materials. That such substitute figures are provided in tombs implies that the tomb owner may have used similar substitutes during his lifetime to avoid these menial tasks. In the later New Kingdom, the large crews of *shabtis* provided in tombs were given overseers, one for every ten men. This suggests that close supervision was needed for this unwilling labor force.

It has often been thought, based on statements by Greek travelers, that state construction work, particularly on royal pyramids, was done only during the months of the inundation, when fields were flooded and agricultural laborers would be available. This assumption is not supported by the dates sometimes recorded in mason's marks (which seem to cluster in the other seasons) or by the system of rotating service that seems to have been in force. Moreover, the months of July, August, and September, during which the inundation occurred, would not be the most efficient months for hard physical labor in the desert.

Slave labor. As noted above, foreign captives were brought forcibly to Egypt, and formed a pool of slave labor available to the state and favored individuals whom the state wished to reward. The term *ḥm-nswt*, literally "king's slave," which was often used to describe agricultural workers, may refer to people so designated. It is unclear whether these people's servitude was permanent or more limited, and whether their children had similar status. Nor is it clear what rights, if any, they had. That maltreating them was seen as objectionable is clear from a passage in the "Negative Confession," given in chapter 125 of the New Kingdom *Book of Going Forth by Day.* There the deceased claims, "I have not denounced a slave (*ḥm*) to his supervisor." Nonetheless, the fact that this sin had to be denied indicates that it was sometimes committed.

Another type of laborer who had little control over the conditions of his labor was the peasant attached to a piece of land. In addition to being bestowed on a landlord to work a grant of land, laborers were sometimes given by the king to supply personnel for other gifts. An example is the Old Kingdom autobiography which records the gift of a carrying chair that includes the people to carry it. The rights of these laborers were presumably similarly limited.

The words *ḥm* and *ḥmt*, usually translated "male and female slaves," seem to have had a broad application. (The root is probably even related to the term used to refer to the king: *ḥm.f* "his majesty.") In many cases it may be wiser to translate the word "servant" rather than "slave," because the conditions of employment are so uncertain, and may differ significantly from better-known occurrences of slavery. This is particularly true of Egyptians who are assigned this status. Although legal texts of the late New Kingdom and later attest to cases where entire families were sold into perpetual slavery to pay off their debts, it is not clear to what extent this was an innovation, perhaps due to foreign influence. Earlier texts do not mention such sales, even though several classes of people with very limited autonomy clearly existed.

Administration of the Work Force. State labor of all kinds in Egypt tended to be closely supervised by a hierarchy of administrators extending from the lowest level supervisor of ten workers through the "overseer of works" of the central government, who was usually directly responsible to the king. Scribes painstakingly recorded the progress of the work, the presence or absence of the workmen, the distribution of rations and payment, and the breakage and replacement of equipment. Unfortunately, few of these records have survived, and the reconstruction of the organization of labor in different periods of Egyptian history depends on a few chance discoveries.

Old Kingdom. From the middle of the first dynasty through the end of the Old Kingdom, there are references to *phyles* (Egyptian *z3w*), a system of labor organization used to schedule several groups of workers, notably royal and nonroyal mortuary cult functionaries, construction crews, and possibly palace attendants. The system consisted of five named groups (*wr*, *st*, *w3dt*, *nds*, and *jmj-nfrt*) that worked in a repeating monthly rotation. (These names have suggested to some that phyles were originated as boat crews, but in fact the similarity of the terminologies seems to have been secondary.) In some cases, these groups were divided so that the cycle lasted ten rather than five months. It has been suggested (Roth, 1991) that these groups originated in predynastic clan groups that supported the king, and that membership remained kin-based even after the clans had evolved into a system of service that allowed the king to spread his patronage among a larger number of people. (The nonroyal applications of the system were presumably adopted as a status symbol; tomb owners borrowed the expensive royal system to display their wealth.)

In fourth dynasty construction crews, phyles were part of a more complex hierarchy. The smallest groups were probably called "tens," and were responsible for moving individual blocks of stone. They may have consisted of varying numbers of men, although it should be noted that *shabtis* were organized into groups of ten in later periods. There were apparently four or more such groups in each phyle, each of which was supervised by an "overseer of ten." The level of organization above the phyle was the *'pr*, or "gang," of which there were two for every large section of the project, possibly so that competition between them would maintain the most efficient pace of the work. These gangs had names built on the names of the reigning king, such as "the companions of Khufu," or "the drunkards of

Menkaure" (although joking names like the latter seem to have been confined to masons' marks, and do not appear in the monumental depictions). The titles *wr 10 šmʿw* ("chief of Upper Egyptian tens") and *jmj-r zȝw šmʿw* ("overseer of Upper Egyptian phyles") suggests that a similar system was used to administer corvée labor on state projects in Upper Egypt. (The five named phyles do not seem to have been used outside the Memphite region, except on projects organized from Memphis.) Other systems of rotating service are also known from the Old Kingdom. For his mortuary cult and the cult of Hathor of Tehne, the priest of Hathor, Nikaʿankh, organized a twelve-month rotation of his wife and children.

Quarry work during this period is attested by inscriptions left in quarries in the Sinai, the Wadi Hammamat, Aswan, and Hatnub. The work was directed by several different kinds of officials, including "god's treasurers," "captain of a boat," or "overseers of the army" (or "expedition"; see Eyre, 1987, pp. 10–11). Unlike the workmen in construction crews, the organization of these laborers is clearly connected to boats in some cases, presumably because boats were necessary to transport the finished product to its destination.

Middle Kingdom. Comparatively little is known about labor organization during the Middle Kingdom period. In royal mortuary temples, the phyle system survived in an altered form, as attested in the Illahun papyri. There, there were only four phyles, identified by numbers rather than names; their monthly periods of rotation thus occurred consistently from year to year. However, the system seems to have been less important during the Middle Kingdom, and was used only to organize the lower levels of the priesthood.

The Illahun papyri also include lists of construction workers, presumably employed in building the nearby pyramid of Senwosret II. One list mentioned at least twenty-nine different groups of workers, who seem to have been employed for periods of two months. Each gang had a foreman, and consisted of five or ten men. A higher official, assisted by a scribe, exercised authority over all the gangs working on the project.

The other principal source for labor organization during this period is the Reisner papyri, from Naga el-Deir in Upper Egypt. These four papyri list the personnel of three construction projects and a tool shop attached to a shipyard. They record the family connections of each corvée worker, the kinds of labor done, and the rations and other payments received. The workers are called *mnjw*, "laborers," or, more generally, *ḥsbw*, "those who are counted." They are divided into crews of variable size (between one and almost forty men) and work under the supervision of a foreman (*ḥrp*), a crew leader (*tzw*), or, in the case of some of the smaller crews, a scribe. The work force seems

to be under the control of the palace (*pr-ʿ3*). The tool shop accounts are somewhat different, consisting of orders sent by the vizier to the steward of the palace in the Thinite nome. These documents are particularly valuable because each records several aspects of the same project.

New Kingdom. There is considerably more information about workers and their organization from the New Kingdom. The most detailed information comes from the settlement of Deir el-Medina, which housed the workmen who built the royal tombs of the eighteenth, nineteenth, and twentieth dynasties. The crew of workmen on the royal tombs grew over time, as royal tombs became larger and more elaborately decorated, but it never numbered more than about 120 men. Documents recovered from the area reveal that the "crew" (*jst*) was divided into two roughly equal "sides" (*rjt*), called the "left" and the "right," which presumably corresponded to the two sides of the tomb on which the workmen worked. (See Černý 1973, pp. 100–103). Like phyles, "sides" have been associated with boat crews, but they seem better paralleled in temples by the "sides" of priests who bear the gods' carrying barks. The evidence of candle consumption suggests that both "sides" worked at the same time, rather than in rotation. Each side was directed by a chief workman, assisted by a deputy. Also organized into "sides" were several types of less skilled workers, who delivered messages, mixed plaster, carried water, and did other more menial tasks; women were responsible for grinding the grain that the workmen received as rations. In some periods, each "side" had a scribe assigned to it; however, more often a single scribe handled the administration of both "sides."

The personnel of the crew included ordinary workers, sculptors, and draftsmen; all three groups received the same pay, but it is from the latter group that the administrators were usually drawn. Work was conducted for eight of the ten days of the Egyptian "week," in two periods of equal (but unknown) length, probably divided by a break. Workers were provided with housing, rations, firewood, tools, and various services in exchange for their labor. Responsibility for the maintenance and direction of the crew was held by various high officials in the eighteenth dynasty, but by the Ramessid period it had been transferred to the vizier.

Other state labor in the New Kingdom seems to have been similarly organized, if less well documented. Overall administration was handled by an *js n kȝt*, "Department of Work," which controlled materials as well as the labor force. Its internal hierarchy is unknown. Specific projects could be directed by a variety of officials, particularly stewards of various institutions and overseers of the treasury. Less skilled labor in the New Kingdom was often supplied by the army, which was used for transport and other tasks similar to corvée labor. Workmen from the army were presumably supervised by the army administration.

Compensation of the Work Force. The way in which the work force was paid is difficult to determine. Even the elite classes have not left many records. The lower levels of scribes and officials may have been given a wage in addition to their rations, while the upper ranks probably lived on the rents collected from endowment lands attached to their positions. Craftspeople probably earned the selling price of their goods, less the cost of materials and, in the case of workshops, a share for the workshop administrator. Agricultural workers presumably were rewarded with a portion of the crop, although substantial taxes and rents would ensure that this compensation was far from generous. Corvée labor was provided with rations, and perhaps other payment; slave labor presumably received only rations.

For a few groups, partial evidence survives. Old Kingdom texts recording the wages of craftsmen who worked on private tombs suggest that payment was made in two parts: rations to support the workers during their labor, and a quantity of durable goods, usually cloth. Scenes in the Old Kingdom tomb of Akhethetep depict women receiving jewelry for the cloth that they have supplied. In neither case is the amount specified.

Two Middle Kingdom accounts of ration payments highlight a huge disparity between the ordinary laborers and their supervisors. In crew of tomb builders, the upper tier of supervisors received ten times the rations of ordinary laborers, while the more specialized workers and lower-level administrators got twice to five times as much. The bread and beer rations of a quarrying expedition to the Wadi Hammamat were even more unequal: the leader of the expedition received two hundred loaves of bread and five jars of beer daily, while most of the workers got only ten loaves and one-third of a jar of beer. Lower-level administrators were paid three to ten times as much as a worker, while skilled workers made less than twice as much (see D. Valbelle, in Donadoni, 1997, pp. 39–40).

The New Kingdom workmen at Deir el-Medina were provided with houses and other necessities of living, as well as a basic monthly ration of 150 kilograms of wheat and 56 kilograms of barley. They also regularly received fish, vegetables, pottery, and firewood. Payments in more durable goods, such as clothing, were made annually or during visits by high officials. Rations were often delayed or incomplete, and when long periods passed without delivery, as happened during times of political turmoil and economic scarcity in the late twentieth dynasty, the workmen would leave their village and descend upon the temple granaries, where they would refuse to leave until their rations were supplied. Allusions to workmen's demands in Middle Kingdom texts from the royal mortuary complex of Senwosret II at Illahun suggest that this kind of strike had a long history. Although strikes seem to have had some success among state workers, those by less privileged workers would have been less effective.

[*See also* Slaves.]

BIBLIOGRAPHY

Bakir, A. M. *Slavery in Pharaonic Egypt.* Cairo, 1952. The basic study on the question of slavery in Egypt.

Černý, Jaroslav. *A Community of Workmen at Thebes in the Ramesside Period.* Cairo, 1973. An excellent, concise summary of what is known about the workers and labor organization in the New Kingdom settlement of Deir el-Medina.

David, Rosalie. *The Pyramid Builders of Ancient Egypt: A Modern Investigation of Pharaoh's Workforce.* London, 1986. A popular account of the workers at the settlement of Illahun, near the Middle Kingdom pyramid of Senwosret II.

Donadoni, Sergio, ed. *The Egyptians.* Chicago, 1997. A collection of essays dealing with different classes of people in ancient Egypt: peasants, craftsmen, scribes, bureaucrats, priests, soldiers, slaves, foreigners, the dead, the king, and women. Although the authors' approaches differ, the essays are rich in information and bibliography.

Drenkhahn, R. *Die Händwerker und ihre Tätigkeiten im Alten Ägypten.* Wiesbaden, 1976. The basic study of crafts production in ancient Egypt.

Eyre, C. J. "Work and the Organisation of Work in the Old Kingdom" and "Work and the Organisation of Work in the New Kingdom." In *Labor in the Ancient Near East,* edited by M. Powell, pp. 5–47, 167–221. New Haven, 1987. Important general surveys of the Old and New Kingdom evidence, with extensive bibliography on both topics.

Kadish, Gerald E. "Observations on Time and Work-Discipline in Ancient Egypt." In *Studies in Honor of William Kelly Simpson,* edited by P. Der Manuelian and R. Freed, pp. 439–448. Boston, 1996.

Roehrig, Catharine. "Women's Work: Some Occupations of Nonroyal Women as Depicted in Ancient Egyptian Art." In *Mistress of the House, Mistress of Heaven: Women in Ancient Egypt,* edited by G. Markoe and A. Capel, pp. 13–24. New York, 1996.

Roth, Ann Macy. *Egyptian Phyles in the Old Kingdom: The Evolution of a System of Social Organization.* Studies in Ancient Oriental Civilizations, 48. Chicago, 1991.

Roth, Ann Macy. "The Practical Economics of Tomb Building in the Old Kingdom: A Visit to the Necropolis in a Carrying Chair." In *For His Ka: Essays Offered in Memory of Klaus Baer,* edited by D. Silverman, pp. 227–240. Chicago, 1994.

Simpson, William Kelly. *Papyrus Reisner I: The Records of a Building Project in the Reign of Sesostris I.* Boston, 1963. *Papyrus Reisner II. Accounts of the Dockyard Workshop at This in the in the Reign of Sesostris I.* Boston, 1965. *Papyrus Reisner III. The Records of a Building Project in the Early Twelfth Dynasty.* Boston, 1969. *Papyrus Reisner IV. Personnel Accounts of the Early Twelfth Dynasty.* Boston, 1986. The basic publication and translation of the Middle Kingdom Reisner Papyri.

ANN MACY ROTH

WRITING. *See* Language; Literacy; Scribes; *and* Scripts.

X

X-GROUP. With the collapse of Meroë in the mid-fourth century CE, the agricultural life of the small towns and villages continued with little change until about one hundred years later when a new group, with a slightly different assemblage of archaeological remains, came into that area. The term "X-Group" was applied to that culture by the continuation of the alphabetic system that George A. Reisner had developed during his survey of Nubia early in the twentieth century. Apart from the luxury materials found in the chiefs' graves—some imported from Egypt and the Byzantine world—the main items were pottery; also found in graves, they show some differences from the earlier Meroitic but no dramatic change of style. Other than cemeteries, some small X-Group villages, constructed of sun-dried brick, are known.

The X-Group is now often called the Ballana culture, after the name of the site in Egyptian Nubia where a number of richly furnished mound tombs were found. Much of the Ballana tomb equipment—and similar finds at Gemai, Firka, and Tanqasi in Sudan—suggests that they are of important kings or tribal chiefs. Though showing some resemblances to that of Meroë, the grave goods are sufficiently different to show that new rulers with new burial customs had arrived in the area; the same is true of the settlements and the commoners' graves.

From ancient texts, two groups were known to come into this area of Nubia—the Nobatae and the Blemmyes. The people of the Ballana tombs are usually identified with the Nobatae, whom Procopius (an early sixth century CE Byzantine writer) says were brought into the Nile Valley from the Western Desert oases by the Roman emperor Diocletian (r.285–305 CE). They were supposed to oppose and control the Blemmyes, inhabitants of the Eastern Desert, who were attacking settlements and monasteries in the Nile Valley. The Blemmyes are usually con-sidered the ancestors of the present-day Beja, who today inhabit the same area (perhaps the same area as the Medjay of pharaonic texts).

That there was an important cultural change in the Nile Valley is shown by the disappearance of inscriptions in the Meroitic language by the end of the fourth century CE. The few inscriptions known are in Greek. The most elaborate of the Greek inscriptions is that of Prince Silko, written at Kalabsha as a secondary inscription on the wall of a first century CE temple. In this inscription, Silko calls himself "prince" *(basiliskos)* of the Nobatae and claims to have defeated the Blemmyes on two occasions. It seems that the Nobatae were largely successful in their role as peacekeepers, as Diocletian had intended. If their identification with those who made the distinctive X-Group material is correct, they established themselves quickly throughout much of the territory previously controlled by Meroë. From the middle of the sixth century CE, the northernmost of the three known Nubian kingdoms was called Nobatia. Most likely, the Nobatae had settled permanently along the Nile and were the people who introduced the Nubian language to the area, where it continues to the present day.

BIBLIOGRAPHY

Adams, William Y. *Nubia: Corridor to Africa.* London, 1977. The best general account with full references.

Emery, W. B., and L. P., Kirwan. *The Royal Tombs of Ballana and Qustul.* Cairo, 1938. The excavation report of the major X-Group site.

Emery, W. B. *Nubian Treasure.* London, 1965. A shortened and popular version of the 1938 report, with commentary; the author believed the tombs were those of Blemmye chiefs.

Shinnie, P. L. *Ancient Nubia.* London, 1996. Useful for general background.

PETER L. SHINNIE

Y

YAHUDIYYA, TELL EL- (ancient names, *Nay Ta-Hut* and *Leontopolis*), 30°17′N, 31°31′E. The earliest known Hyksos site and the type-site for a group of small black ceramic juglets, variously polished and decorated, with incised lines and comb-made punctate zigzags filled with a white paste. Manufactured in both the Levant and Egypt during the late first and the second quarters of the second millennium BCE, the juglets' range and significance have generated much literature. If the site's rampart is of the type common to Syria-Palestine during the Middle Bronze IIA–B periods, it is the only example of such a fortification in Egypt; the Hyksos capital of Avaris has no such fortifications. Tell el-Yahudiyya is also the site of a mid-second century BCE expatriate Jewish temple.

First investigated by Heinrich Brugsch in the nineteenth century, the site and nearby tombs and burials were superficially excavated by Edouard Naville and F. Llewellyn Griffith in 1886–1887, prior to their 1890 publication of the ceramic chronology. Griffith's notes contain archaeologically useful information on virtually all periods of the site's occupation, from the Hyksos to the Roman. In 1905 and 1906, W. M. Flinders Petrie conducted what has proven to be the premier excavation at the site, aided by his already developed Egyptian and Palestinian ceramic chronology (1906). A short field season by Shehata Adam in the 1950s produced useful new materials but did not substantively alter understanding of the site. Adam (1958) did, however, witness its ruinous state of preservation.

During the Second Intermediate Period (Middle Bronze IIB), the site was occupied by non–Egyptian settlers, identified in 1906 by Flinders Petrie as the Hyksos. It was surrounded by a great rampart, some 460 meters (1470 feet) square, similar to slightly earlier ones in Syria (e.g., Tell Mardikh) and in Palestine (e.g., Hazor, Tel Dan). Anomalously, entry seems to have been via a long ramp stretching into the desert. Occupational layers inside the enclosure were either impossible to excavate with available techniques or deemed insignificant in an intellectual climate long centered on cemetery excavation. As a result, Petrie focused on data from graves and tombs within the enclosure and from the small cemetery east of "The Town of Onias," which had first been investigated by Naville and Griffith. A good summation of data from these contexts, concerning pottery and small finds—particularly scarabs—was published by Petrie. The materials were both excavated and purchased from locals, but local soil conditions precluded the excavation of human remains.

Even in Naville's day, these materials could be compared to those from his 1885 excavations and purchases at Kataana-Qantir. With present-day excavations at Tell ed-Dab'a and Pithom, more can be said. In general, the burials at Tell el-Yahudiyya paralleled those of the late Hyksos phases at both Pithom and Tell ed-Dab'a. Although it may be accidental, there appear to have been no donkey burials, even though daggers and a Near Eastern battle-axe were recovered; this would also correlate with late phases at Tell ed-Dab'a and Pithom. Based on the pottery (probably closer to c.1650–1550 BCE than earlier), the occupation at Tell el-Yahudiyya now can be shown to be roughly contemporary to that of Pithom.

From the eighteenth and nineteenth dynasties, ceramic, epigraphic, architectural, and small-object evidence indicates a flourishing settlement, probably lasting through both New Kingdom dynasties, with, at one time, a temple or palace of Ramesses II. By Brugsch's time at the site, only portions of a small "chamber" or "pavilion" of Ramesses III remained, decorated—as were the palace floors at Kataana-Qantir—with glazed tiles, otherwise extremely rare in pharaonic Egypt. The discovery of these tiles, now in several museums, caused yet more destruction even before Petrie's excavations. Although a large block of Ramessid occupation material still remained in the western part of the tell, Petrie's investigations were limited to the cemetery materials, organized under the "period" headings of pre–Thutmose III, Thutmose III, Amenophis II, and the eighteenth dynasty.

For the evidence from the twentieth dynasty to the Roman period, Petrie continued to publish on his work in the cemetery, along with other material (the partial statue of Admiral Hor-Psamtek, found in the temple of Onias). His publication was, for the time, splendidly done—even some, mostly undated, utilitarian stone tools are published—and, given Petrie's instincts for seriation and intelligent utilization of scarab data, the datings appear close to the broad temporal spans under which they are

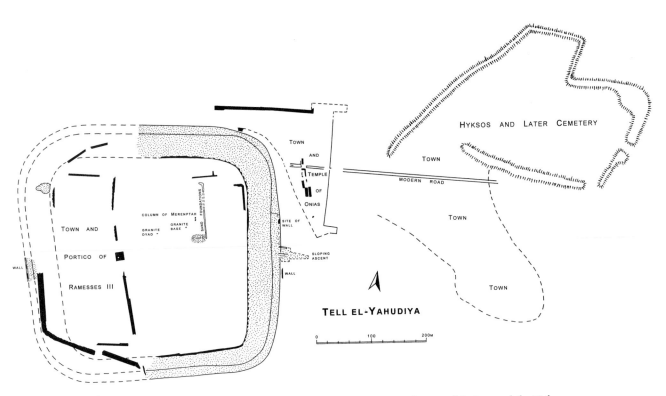

YAHUDIYYA, TELL EL-. *Composite plan of Tell el-Yahudiyya, the city of Onias, and the Hyksos and Later Cemetery.* (Loretta M. James after Petrie 1906, Plates 2 and 22. Courtesy Wadi Tumilat Project)

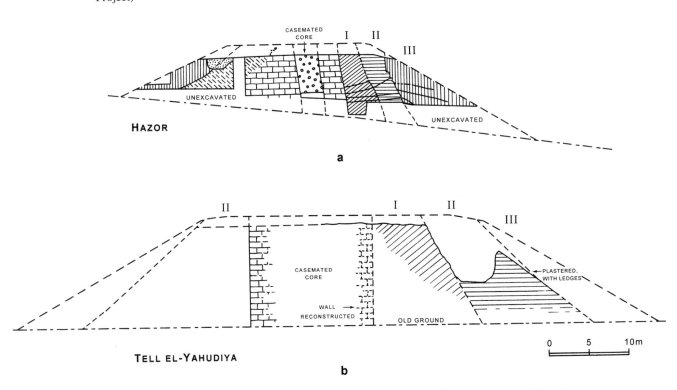

YAHUDIYYA, TELL EL-. *Comparative rampart sections: Tell el-Yahudiyya (reconstructed) and Hazor.* In each case, the exterior face of the rampart is to the right. The Roman numerals on the Tell el-Yahudiyya reconstruction correspond to the successive structural components of the Hazor rampart. (Loretta M. James after Petrie 1906, Plate 3 [cf. Plates 4 and 5], and Yadin 1972, Figure 11. Courtesy Wadi Tumilat Project and John S. Holladay)

grouped. As would be expected, his classifications are weak in those periods where there is now more detailed and accurate information, such as in the Saite through Ptolemaic periods, and this probably pertains to the other materials as well.

Apart from the as-yet undiscovered earlier Jewish temple at Elephantine, Tell el-Yahudiyya has the only Jewish temple from the Second Temple Period outside Jerusalem. While not positively identified—only architectural scraps and some foundational elements survived—the literary evidence from the first-century CE historian Flavius Josephus and the evidence of a nearby late Jewish cemetery make the location nearly certain. The temple was built on an artificial mound, roughly 20 meters (65 feet) high, with second-century BCE potsherds found throughout the fills. North of the temple foundations "heaps of potsherds" remained from the depredations of the local cotton farmers digging for phosphate-rich agricultural soil. Petrie reasonably interpreted this as the remains of the ancient town, presumably the homes of the elite, since he also assumed that a Jewish townsite underlay a modern village to the east of the mound. What remains of the temple and its courts are the foundations and a great staircase, its walls lime plastered, rising from east to west. "A great quantity of pieces of stucco lay round about here; it is hard, white, and smoothly faced, with a black dado and a line of red as a border for the white" (Petrie 1906, 24). The site was destroyed following an assault, probably that of 146 BCE, when Onias served as general for Cleopatra II. Roman-style tombs and materials were also in evidence (Naville and Griffith 1890).

BIBLIOGRAPHY

Adam, Shehata. "Recent Discoveries in the Eastern Delta." *Annales du Service des Antiquités de l'Égypte* 55 (1958), 301–324.

Bietak, Manfred. "Egypt and Canaan During the Middle Bronze Age." *Bulletin of the American Schools of Oriental Research* 281 (1991), 27–72.

Holladay, John S., Jr. "The Eastern Nile Delta During the Hyksos and Pre-Hyksos Periods: Toward a Systemic/Socioeconomic Understanding." In *The Hyksos: New Historical and Archaeological Perspectives*, edited by E. D. Oren, pp. 183–252. Philadelphia, 1997.

Holladay, John S., Jr. "Syro-Palestinian Ramparts and the 'Camp' at Tell-el Yahudiya." *Journal of the Society for the Study of Egyptian Antiquities* (n.d.).

Josephus, Flavius. *Josephus, with an English Translation by Ralph Marcus, Ph.D., in Nine Volumes.* Loeb Classical Library. London and Cambridge.

Kaplan, Maureen K. *The Origin and Distribution of Tell el-Yahudiyeh Ware.* Studies in Mediterranean Archeology, 42. Göteborg, 1980.

Lapp, Paul W. *Palestinian Ceramic Chronology: 200 B.C.–A.D. 70.* New Haven, 1961.

Merrilees, R. S. "El-Lisht and Tell el-Yahudiya Ware in the Archaeological Museum of the American University of Beirut." *Levant* 10 (1978), 75–98.

Naville, Edouard, and F. Ll. Griffith. *The Mound of the Jew and the City of Onias* (by Naville 1890) and *The Antiquities of Tell el Yahûdîyeh* (by Griffith 1887). Memoir of the Egypt Exploration Fund, 7. London.

Oren, Eliezer D., ed. *The Hyksos: New Historical and Archaeological Perspectives.* Philadelphia, 1997.

Petrie, W. M. Flinders. *Hyksos and Israelite Cities.* Publications of the Egyptian Research Account, 12. London, 1906.

Seger, Joe D. "The MB II Fortifications at Shechem and Gezer: A Hyksos Retrospective." *Eretz-Israel* 12 (1975), 34–45.

Yadin, Yigael. *Hazor: The Head of All Those Kingdoms.* The Schweich Lectures of the British Academy 1970. London, The British Academy, 1972.

JOHN S. HOLLADAY, JR.

Z

ZODIAC. *See* Astrology; Astronomy; *and* Calendars.

ZOOLOGICAL GARDENS. The ancient Egyptians derived considerable pleasure from viewing a variety of animals. Exotic birds and beasts, from distant lands, were avidly imported as marvels; they stirred wonder and excitement among royalty and members of the privileged classes, who took delight in their peculiar characteristics and behaviors. Although public zoological gardens as we know them did not exist in pharaonic Egypt, it is most probable that rare native and nonindigenous specimens were sometimes housed in menageries for display. Pictorial evidence suggests, and this has been corroborated by zooarchaeological findings, that some animals were used to stock hunting parks for sport. Of these extraordinary animals, some entered Egypt as highly appreciated political gifts, tribute from neighboring states. Fellow potentates in other ancient Near Eastern kingdoms were similarly inclined to occasionally keep an assortment of animals from far-flung regions both for show and hunting. Receiving and possessing rare creatures was always a matter of considerable royal prestige. An important underlying motivation for collecting such zoological treasures, beyond the general fascination with wildlife, was the symbolism—the royal display of personal, political, and militaristic mastery over remote countries through the domination of their fauna. The animals became living proof of a monarch's might and influence.

As Egypt's power and influence spread, particularly during the height of its empire, under the eighteenth dynasty, so did the procession of animals entering the Nile Valley from farther and farther away. The admiration of birds and beasts from the distant unknown was also duly celebrated in artistic works; it developed into a recurring theme in Egyptian iconography. Indeed, recording the arrival and inspection of those curiosities was accorded considerable space within the decorative program of both royal monuments and the grand private tomb-chapels of the core aristocracy. Several of those compositions, moreover, rank among the best known and greatest masterpieces of Theban tomb painting and provide the most vivid evocation of the dazzling variety of foreign animals that flowed into the country.

The Egyptian penchant for acquiring prestigious exotic creatures probably goes back before the emergence of pharaonic civilization, when nonnative species came into the Nile Valley from the tropical African hinterlands and from western Asia. The earliest-known occurrence of the importation of a rare foreign beast, preserved in art, comes from the fifth dynasty mortuary temple of Sahure at Abusir. The decoration of that edifice included a remarkable scene, featuring what is likely to have been the safe return home of an Egyptian trading expedition, sent under royal patronage to visit far-off Byblos on the Phoenician (eastern Mediterranean) coast. Part of the Egyptians' haul consisted of several delightful live Syrian bears (*Ursus arctos syriacus*), which were naturalistically portrayed in painted low relief; they were, likely, notable additions to the king's collection.

During the New Kingdom, there was a much expanded interest in the exotic, and this found one of its major expressions in the depiction of foreign fauna and flora. Egyptian trade with the African land of Punt is first attested in the Old Kingdom, but it is best known from the eighteenth dynasty, made famous by the great sea-borne expedition sent by Hatshepsut and immortalized in a series of spectacular painted reliefs on the walls of the southern half of the middle colonnade of her mortuary temple at Deir el-Bahari. Among the wealth of costly commodities from Punt, shown being triumphantly transported back to Egypt, are thirty-one myrrh trees (*Commiphora myrrha*), which were to be transplanted into the garden of her temple, as well as a collection of live creatures: among them were domestic cattle (*Bos taurus*), baboon (*Papio* sp.), green monkey (*Cercopithecus aethiops*), leopard (*Panthera pardus*), cheetah (*Acinonyx jubatus*), domestic dog (*Canis familiaris*), giraffe (*Giraffa camelopardalis*), and a long-legged bird, possibly an ostrich (*Struthio camelus*). Some of those prizes were surely displayed in Hatshepsut's menagerie.

Determined not to be outdone by Hatshepsut, his aunt and immediate predecessor, Thutmose III likewise exhibited a bent for acquiring natural history exotica. In two chambers set to the rear of his festival temple at Karnak, and conveniently referred to by Egyptologists as the "Botanical Garden," this warrior-king recorded in delicate, low relief some of the plants and animals he had gathered while on a military campaign into West Asia (the Near East) during the twenty-fifth year of this reign. This col-

ZOOLOGICAL GARDENS. *Nubians leading a giraffe, which is restrained by ropes tied to its forelegs.* This is a detail from a wall painting from the tomb-chapel of the eighteenth dynasty vizier Rekhmire at Thebes. Note the monkey scampering up the giraffe's long neck. (© Patrick Francis Houlihan)

lection of fauna and flora was presented as a tribute by Thutmose III to the powerful chief god of Thebes, Amun. While most of the 275 plants, shown complete with their root systems, adorning those walls may appear to be genuine botanical specimens and seem to form the world's oldest herbal, today's general consensus is that almost all are products of artisans' imaginations. They sought merely to indicate something as alien as possible. Several foreign species have been identified though: pomegranate (*Punica granatum*) and two plants from the Arum family (*Dracunculus vulgaris* and *Arum italicum*). Of the fifty-two animals extant on the walls of the chambers, thirty-eight are birds, and a few of these are unique in Egyptian iconogra-

phy: the darter (*Anhinga rufa*), diver (*Gavia* sp), and the great spotted cuckoo (*Clamator glandarius*). A small animal illustrated there has been tentatively identified as a Persian gazelle (*Gazella subgutturosa*), which, if correct, would make it another true import. Also prominently represented in the "Botanical Garden," as objects of wonder, were several head of cattle of the two-tailed and three-horned variety! Such oddities may be simple flights of creativity or, perhaps, even farmyard freaks, the kind well-known to herdsmen and veterinarians.

During the nineteenth dynasty, Ramesses II also demonstrated a predilection for obtaining exotic wildlife. His Nubian rock-cut temple at Beit el-Wali featured a scene of the importation of various wild and domestic animals, the spoils of Nubian war and tribute, which were shown paraded before the victorious king. These animals include the following: cattle, lion (*Panthera leo*), giraffe, monkeys, gerenuk (*Litocranius walleri*), Beisa oryx (*Oryx gazella beisa*), ostrich, cheetah, and leopard. Although often attributed to a pharaoh of the eighteenth dynasty, it was likely Ramesses II who had rendered in sunken relief, on a pylon of the temple of the war god Montu at Armant amid a frieze of Nubian booty, the transporting to Egypt of a live adult black or white rhinoceros (*Diceros bicornis* or *Ceratotherium simum*). The arrival of that huge creature from sub-Saharan Africa must have been hailed as a heroic feat, worthy of public commemoration. Archaeological excavations at Qantir, the Nile Delta residence of the Ramessid kings, have revealed the vestiges of a menagerie or a hunting park, although it might have served both purposes. The results are yet to be completely published, but preliminary zooarchaeological reports indicate the presence of many unusual game animals, some of them clearly nonindigenous species. From Assyrian sources, we know that during the Third Intermediate Period, Egyptian kings continued sending them diplomatic gifts of exotic wildlife.

The Greek-speaking rulers of the Ptolemaic dynasty in Egypt were concerned with amassing fine zoological collections of their own. Ptolemy I is reputed, for example, to have publicly exhibited, among the booty of his conquests, a rare Bactrian camel (*Camelus bactrianus*), from Asia. Ptolemy II established a great royal zoo in Alexandria, housing birds and beasts from all parts of the known world; his collection is famous for its appearance in his grand procession of extraordinary splendor, which was staged in Alexandria sometime in the early 270s BCE. A detailed account of that pageant by the historian Kallixeinos is preserved in the work of the Classical-era author Athenaeus (c.197–208). The Alexandrian zoo, or remnants of it, may have survived into the reign of Ptolemy VIII (51–47 BCE).

BIBLIOGRAPHY

Beaux, Nathalie. *Le cabinet de curiosités de Thoutmosis III: Plantes et animaux du "Jardin botanique" de Karnak* Leuven, 1990. The complete publication of the "Botanical Garden"; many of the proposed plant and bird identifications are speculative and should be approached with caution.

Boessneck, Joachim. *Die Tierwelt des alten Ägypten. Untersucht anhand kulturgeschichtlicher und zoologischer Quellen.* Munich, 1988. Provides authoritative discussion on some of the exotic animals represented in Egyptian art and brief reports on the animal remains recovered from the Ramessid menagerie or hunting park at Qantir.

Davies, Norman de Garis. *The Tomb of Rekh-mi-Re at Thebes.* Vols. 1–2 New York, 1943. Reprinted in the one volume by Arno in 1973. Publication of the famous tomb-chapel of the vizier Rekhmire at Thebes (tomb 100), with a magnificent scene showing the importing of animals and animal products from Nubia, Libya, Crete, and Syria.

Elat, Moshe. "The Economic Relations of the Neo-Assyrian Empire with Egypt." *Journal of the American Oriental Society* 98 (1978), 20–34. Discusses textual evidence for the exchange of exotic animals during the Third Intermediate Period.

Helck, Wolfgang, Eberhard Otto, and Wolfhart Westendorf, eds. *Lexikon der Ägyptologie.* Vols. 1–7. Wiesbaden, 1975–1992. Massive reference work, with articles in English, French, and German, on most topics relating to ancient Egypt, including zoological gardens.

Houlihan, Patrick F. *The Birds of Ancient Egypt.* Warminster, 1986. Contains discussions and illustrations of the identifiable birds pictured in the "Botanical Garden." (An edition of this book was also published in Cairo in 1988.)

Houlihan, Patrick F. *The Animal World of the Pharaohs.* London and New York, 1996. Handsomely illustrated book with extensive bibliography aimed at a general audience; considerable space is devoted to surveying exotic birds and beasts and the evidence for menageries in ancient Egypt.

Houlihan, Patrick F. "Birds, Beasts, and Bugs in Egyptian Art and Hieroglyphs." *A History of the Animal World in the Ancient Near East*, edited by Billie Jean Collins. Leiden, 2000. Provides extensive discussion of exotic animals represented in Egyptian iconography, with copious references.

Jennison, George. *Animals for Show and Pleasure in Ancient Rome.* Manchester, 1937. Chapter 2 is entitled "Zoological Magnificence in Egypt under the Ptolemies" and furnishes a good survey of our knowledge about the royal zoological garden at ancient Alexandria. For a more up-to-date translation of the text from Athenaeus, see Rice (1983) below.

Keimer, Louis. "Jardins zoologiques d'Égypte." *Cahiers d'histoire égyptienne* 6 (1954), 81–159. A brief but valuable history of menageries and zoological gardens in Egypt, from antiquity to the middle of the twentieth century.

Newton, F. G. "Excavations at El-'Amarnah, 1923–24." *Journal of Egyptian Archaeology* 10 (1924), 289–298; see also T. Whittemore, "The Excavations at El-'Amarnah, Season 1924–5." *The Journal of Egyptian Archaeology* 12 (1926) 3–23, and Henri Frankfort, *The Mural Painting of El-'Amarneh.* London, 1929. The excavators of Akhenaten's short-lived capital (Akhetaten) at Tell el-Amarna claimed that the North Palace contained a sort of zoological garden, with fish ponds, aviaries, and areas for viewing cattle, antelopes, and ibexes and consequently this view is frequently maintained in the Egyptological literature. This part of the city has been reinvestigated in recent years by Professor Barry J. Kemp of the University of Cambridge, who, in a personal communication, informs me that the old interpretation of the palace as having a zoological garden is almost certainly incorrect.

Osborn, Dale J., and Jana Osbornová. *The Mammals of Ancient Egypt.* Warminster, 1998. Contains useful information on exotic mammals imported into Egypt.

Pitsch, Helmut. "Zoologischer Garten." In *Lexikon der Ägyptologie*, 6: 1420–1423. Wiesbaden, 1986.

Rice, E. E. *The Grand Procession of Ptolemy Philadelphus.* Oxford, 1983. Up-to-date translation and commentary of the text dealing with Ptolemy II's great procession.

PATRICK F. HOULIHAN

DIRECTORY OF CONTRIBUTORS

Allam, S.
*Professor of Egyptology, Ägyptologisches Institut,
University of Tübingen, Germany*
Inheritance; Slaves

Allen, James P.
*Curator of the Department of Egyptian Art, The
Metropolitan Museum of Art, New York*
Ba; Grammar, *article on* Old Egyptian; Heliopolis;
Hymns, *article on* Solar Hymns; Pyramid Texts;
Ramesses I; Shadow; Taking of Joppa

Allen, Susan J.
*Research Associate, Department of Egyptian Art, The
Metropolitan Museum of Art, New York*
Archaeological and Research Institutions

Altenmüller, Hartwig
Professor of Egyptology, Universität Hamburg, Germany
Hunting; Mereruka; Old Kingdom, *articles on* Fifth
Dynasty *and* Sixth Dynasty; Trade and Markets

Andrews, Carol A. R.
*Assistant Keeper, Department of Egyptian Antiquities,
The British Museum, London, United Kingdom*
Amulets; Decipherment; Rosetta Stone

Arnold, Dieter
*Curator, Department of Egyptian Art, The Metropolitan
Museum of Art, New York*
Architecture; Lisht, el-; Meidum; Tombs, *article on*
Royal Tombs

Arnold, Felix
German Archaeological Institute, Cairo-Zamalek, Egypt
Houses

Ashton, Sally-Ann
*Research Assistant, The British Museum, London;
Honorary Research Assistant, University College
London, United Kingdom*
Portraiture

Astour, Michael C.
*Professor Emeritus of Historical Studies, Southern
Illinois University, Edwardsville*
Mitanni

Bagnall, Roger S.
*Professor of Classics and History, Columbia University,
New York*
Copts; Roman Occupation

Behlmer, Heike
*Lecturer in Egyptology and Coptic Studies, University of
Göttingen, Germany*
Shenoute

Berg, David A.
Independent Scholar, Toronto, Canada
Ahmose-Nefertari

Bianchi, Robert Steven
*Director of Academic and Cultural Affairs, Broughton
International, Inc., Lewiston, Idaho*
Champollion, Jean-François; Cleopatra VII; Esna;
Scarabs

Bietak, Manfred
*Professor of Egyptology, University of Vienna; Director of
the Austrian Archaeological Institute in Cairo; and
Research Director, SCIEM, Austrian Academy of
Sciences, Vienna, Austria*
Dab'a, Tell ed-; Hyksos

Bleiberg, Edward
Associate Curator, Egyptian, Classical, and Ancient Middle Eastern Art, The Brooklyn Museum of Art, New York
Amenhotpe I; Prices and Payment; Storage; Thutmose I

Bochi, Patricia A.
Independent Scholar, Washington, D.C.
Royal Tomb Painting

Bolshakov, Andrey O.
Curator of the Ancient Orient Section, Hermitage Museum, Saint Petersburg, Russia
Ka; Ka-Chapel; Offerings, *article on* Offering Tables

Bonhême, Marie-Ange
Paris, France
Divinity; Kingship; Royal Roles

Bonnet, Charles
Director of the Geneva University Mission in the Sudan; Former Associate Professor, University of Geneva, Switzerland
Kerma

Brand, Peter
Independent Scholar, Toronto, Canada
Sacred Barks

Bresciani, Edda
Professor of Egyptology, University of Pisa, Italy
Achaemenids; Late Period, *article on* Thirty-first Dynasty; Persia

Brewer, Douglas J.
Professor of Anthropology, Director of the Spurlock Museum, University of Illinois, Urbana-Champaign
Animal Husbandry; Cattle; Fauna; Fish; Sheep and Goats

Brunner-Traut, Emma
Professor of Egyptian Art, Language, and Culture; Professor of Classical Archaeology and Classical Science, Universität Tübingen, Germany
Crocodiles; Giraffes; Ichneumon

Bryan, Betsy M.
Alexander Badawy Professor of Egyptian Art and Archaeology, Johns Hopkins University, Baltimore, Maryland
Amarna, Tell el-; Amenhotpe III; Thutmose IV

Burkard, Günter
Professor of Egyptology, Ludwig-Maximilians-Universität, Munich, Germany
Shipwrecked Sailor

Butzer, Karl W.
Dickson Professor of Liberal Arts, University of Texas, Austin
Desert Environments; Irrigation; Nile

Callahan, Allen Dwight
Associate Professor of New Testament, Harvard Divinity School, Cambridge, Massachusetts
Scripts, *article on* Coptic

Cauville, Sylvie
Researcher, Centre National de la Recherche Scientifique, Paris, France
Dendera; Edfu

Chauvet, Violaine
Doctor of Philosophy Student, Johns Hopkins University, Baltimore, Maryland
Saqqara

Cialowicz, Krzysztof M.
Professor of Archaeology, Institute of Archaeology, Jagellonian University, Kraków
Ceremonial Mace Heads; Palettes; Predynastic Period

Cline, Eric H.
Adjunct Assistant Research Professor of Classics, University of Cincinnati, Ohio
Crete; Cyprus; Hittites; Mycenae

Corcoran, Lorelei H.
Associate Professor and Director, Institute of Egyptian Art and Archaeology, The University of Memphis, Tennessee
Masks

Cruz-Uribe, Eugene
Associate Professor of History, Northern Arizona University, Flagstaff
Scripts, *overview article*; Vocabulary

David, Ann Rosalie
Reader in Egyptology, University of Manchester, United Kingdom
Mummification

de Jong, Aleid
Independent Scholar, Utrecht, The Netherlands
Feline Deities; Hippopotami

Decker, Wolfgang
Professor of Sports History, Deutsche Sporthochschule, Cologne, Germany
Sports

Delia, Robert D.
Independent Scholar, Austin, Texas
Senwosret III

Derriks, Claire
Assistant, Egypt and Near Eastern Antiquities, Royal Museum of Mariemont, Belgium
Mirrors

Dodson, Aidan
Visiting Fellow, Department of Archaeology, University of Bristol, United Kingdom
Canopic Jars and Chests; Four Sons of Horus; Third Intermediate Period; Tombs, *article on* Private Tombs

Donadoni Roveri, Anna Maria
Chief Curator, Museo Egizio di Torino, Italy
Gebelein

Doret, Eric
Independent Scholar, Geneva, Switzerland
Ankhtifi of Mo'alla

Dorman, Peter
Associate Professor of Egyptology, Oriental Institute, University of Chicago, Illinois
Epigraphy; Rekhmire; Senenmut

Doxey, Denise M.
Assistant Curator, Ancient Egyptian, Nubian, and Near Eastern Art, Art of the Ancient World, Museum of Fine Arts, Boston, Massachusetts
Anubis; Epithets; Names; Nephthys; Priesthood; Sobek; Thoth

Dreyer, Günter
Director of the German Institute of Archaeology, Cairo, Egypt
Khasekhemwy; Merneith

Drower, Margaret S.
Honorary Visiting Professor, Insitute of Archaeology, University College, London, United Kingdom
Petrie, William Matthew Flinders

Eaton-Krauss, Marianne
Research Associate, Berlin-Brandenburgische Akademie der Wissenschaften, Germany
Akhenaten; Artists and Artisans; Nefertiti; Tiye; Tutankhamun

Egberts, Arno
Lecturer in Egyptology, Department of Near Eastern Studies, Leiden University, The Netherlands
Wenamun

Empereur, Jean-Yves
Director of Research, Centre National de la Recherche Scientifique, Centre d'Etudes Alexandrines, Alexandria, Egypt
Alexandria

Englund, Gertie
Senior Lecturer in Egyptology, Uppsala University, Sweden
Offerings, *overview article*

Favard-Meeks, Christine
Chef de Travaux, École Practique des Hautes Etudes, Section des Sciences Religieuses, Carnoules, France
Behbeit el-Hagar

Fazzini, Richard A.
Chairman, Department of Egyptian, Classical, and Ancient Middle Eastern Art, The Brooklyn Museum of Art, New York
Egyptomania; Mut Precinct

Feldman, Marian H.
Lecturer in Near Eastern Studies, University of California, Berkeley
Mesopotamia

Feucht, Erika
Professor of Egyptology, Ägyptologisches Institut der Universität Heidelberg, Germany
Birth; Childhood; Family

Filer, Joyce M.
Special Assistant for Human and Animal Remains, Department of Egyptian Antiquities, British Museum, London, United Kingdom
Hygiene

Fischer-Elfert, Hans-W.
Professor of Egyptology, Ägyptologisches Institut, Ägyptisches Museum, Leipzig, Germany
Education; Instructions of a Man for His Son; Instructions of Amenemope; Instructions of Anii

Foster, Ann L.
The Warburg Institute, London, United Kingdom
Forts and Garrisons

Foster, John L.
Research Associate, The Oriental Institute, University of Chicago, Illinois
Hymns, *article on* Osiris Hymns; Instructions of Amenemhet; Literature; Lyric; Narratives; Wisdom Texts

Frandsen, Paul John
Professor of Egyptology, The Carsten Niebuhr Institute of Near Eastern Studies, Copenhagen, Denmark
Taboo

Franke, Detlef
Privatdozent für Ägyptologie, Ägyptologisches Institut, Universität Heidelberg, Germany
Amenemhat of Beni Hasan; Amenemhet I; Elephantine; First Intermediate Period; Graffiti; Kinship; Middle Kingdom

Freed, Rita E.
Norma-Jean Calderwood Curator of Ancient Egyptian, Nubian, and Near Eastern Art, Museum of Fine Arts, Boston, Massachusetts
Art

Frey, Rosa A.
Independent Archaeologist, Cornwall, United Kingdom
Illahun

Friedman, Florence Dunn
Curator of Ancient Art, Museum of Art, Rhode Island School of Design, Providence
Akh

Friedman, Renée F.
Director of the Hierakonpolis Expedition, The British Museum, London, United Kingdom
Hierakonpolis

Gasse, Annie
Chargée de Recherche, Centre National de la Recherche Scientifique, Paris, France
Economy, *article on* Temple Economy

Germer, Renate
Egyptologist and Biologist, Archaeological Institute, University of Hamburg, Germany
Flora; Flowers; Fruits; Gardens; Vegetables

Gillam, Robyn A.
Lecturer in Classical Studies and Humanities, York University, Toronto, Ontario, Canada
Sobekneferu

Gnirs, Andrea M.
Postdoctoral Researcher of the German Research Foundation, University of Heidelberg, Germany; University of California, Los Angeles
Biographies; Military, *overview article*

Goebs, Katja
Research Fellow, Merton College, Oxford University, United Kingdom
Crowns

Goelet, Ogden
Research Professor of Egyptian Language and Culture, New York University, New York
Herihor; Ramesses XI; Ramesses-Hattusilis Correspondence; Shuppiluliumas; Tomb Robbery Papyri; Wilbour Papyrus

Goldwasser, Orly
Tel Aviv, Israel
Scripts, *article on* Hieroglyphs

Gomaà, Farouk
Doctor of Egyptian Art, Ägyptologisches Institut der Universität Tübingen, Germany
Khaemwaset; Upper Egypt

Gordon, Andrew
Independent Scholar, and Co-owner of Archaeologia Books, Oakland, California
Foreigners

Görg, Manfred
Professor of Old Testament Theology, Institut für Biblische Exegese, Munich, Germany
Biblical Tradition; Exodus

Graham, Geoffrey
Doctoral Candidate in Egyptology, Yale University, New Haven, Connecticut
Insignias; Tanis

Graindorge, Catherine
Lecturer in Egyptian Religion and Archaeology, Ägyptologisches Seminar der Freie Universität, Berlin, Germany
Sokar

Grandet, Pierre
Professor of Egyptian Language and Civilization,
Institut Khéops, Paris, France
New Kingdom, *article on* Twentieth Dynasty;
Ramesses III; Weights and Measures

Green, Lyn
Doctor, Royal Ontario Museum, Toronto, Canada
Beauty; Clothing and Personal Adornment;
Hairstyles; Toiletries and Cosmetics

Griffiths, J. Gwyn
Professor Emeritus of Classics and Egyptology,
University of Wales, Swansea, United Kingdom
Allegory; Isis; Myths, *articles on* Osiris Cycle *and*
Solar Cycle; Osiris; Plutarch

Guglielmi, Waltraud
Ausserplanmässiger Professor für Aegyptologie,
Universität Tübingen, Universität Marburg, Germany
Captions; Milk

Gundlach, Rolf
Professor of Egyptology, Institut für Ägyptologie der
Johannes Gutenberg-Universität, Mainz, Germany
Temples

Haarmann, Ulrich W.
Professor of Islamic Studies, and Director of the Center
for the Modern Orient, Free University, Berlin, Germany
Islam and Ancient Egypt

Hansen, Nicole B.
Egyptologist, University of Chicago, Illinois
Amphibians and Reptiles; Insects; Snakes

Harer, W. Benson, Jr.
Adjunct Professor, Department of Art, California State
University, San Bernardino
Lotus

Haring, Ben
Lecturer in Egyptology, Universiteit Leiden, The
Netherlands
Administration, *article on* Temple Administration;
Deir el-Medina

Harrell, James A.
Professor of Geology, The University of Toledo, Ohio
Calcite; Cartography; Diorite and Related Rocks

Harris, James E.
Independent Scholar, Ann Arbor, Michigan
Dental Care

Hartwig, Melinda K.
Doctor of Philosophy Candidate, Institute of Fine Arts,
New York University, New York
Painting

Harvey, Julia
Independent Scholar, Groningen, The Netherlands
Sculpture, *article on* Wood Sculpture

Haslauer, Elfriede
Curator of the Kunsthistorisches Museum Wien,
Ägyptisch-Orientalische Sammlung, Austria
Harem

Hassan, Fekri
Petrie Professor of Archaeology, University College
London, United Kingdom
Cities; Geography; Naqada; Natural Resources

Hawass, Zahi
Director, Giza Pyramids, Cairo, Egypt
Khafre; Khufu; Menkaure

Hill, Marsha
Associate Curator, Department of Egyptian Art, The
Metropolitan Museum of Art, New York
Bronze Statuettes

Hoffmann, Friedhelm
Wissenschaftlicher Assistent, Institut für Ägyptologie der
Universität Würzburg, Germany
Science

Hoffmeier, James K.
Professor of Old Testament and Near Eastern
Archaeology, Trinity International University,
Wheaton, Illinois
Fate; Israel; Military, *article on* Materiel

Hölbl, Günther
Extra-ordinary Professor of Egyptology, Curator,
Ägyptisch-Orientalische Sammlung, Kunsthistorisches
Museum, Wien, Austria
Ptolemaic Period

Holladay, John S., Jr.
Professor Emeritus of the Archaeology of Syria-Palestine,
University of Toronto, Ontario, Canada
Pithom; Yahudiyya, Tell el-

Hollis, Susan Tower
Visiting Associate Professor, State University of New York, Empire State College, Rochester, New York
Oral Tradition; Two Brothers

Hölzl, Regina
Research Associate, CAA-Project, Egyptian Department, Kunsthistorisches Museum, Vienna, Austria
Stelae

Houlihan, Patrick F.
Independent Scholar, Santa Rosa, California
Birds; Canines; Felines; Frogs; Hares; Hedgehogs; Pigs; Poultry; Rhinoceroses; Zoological Gardens

Houser-Wegner, Jennifer
Keeper, The Egyptian Section, University Museum, University of Pennsylvania, Philadelphia
Khonsu; Nefertum; Shu; Taweret; Wepwawet

Ikram, Salima
Assistant Professor of Egyptology, American University in Cairo, Egypt
Banquets; Diet

James, T. G. H.
Formerly Keeper of Egyptian Antiquities, The British Museum, London, United Kingdom
Carter, Howard

Jasnow, Richard
Assistant Professor of Egyptology, Johns Hopkins University, Baltimore, Maryland
Insinger Papyrus

Jeffreys, David G.
Lecturer in Egyptian Archaeology, Institute of Archaeology, University College London, United Kingdom
Memphis

Johnson, Janet H.
Professor of Egyptology, Oriental Institute, University of Chicago, Illinois
Grammar, *article on* Demotic; Scripts, *article on* Demotic

Josephson, Jack A.
Research Associate in the History of Egyptian Art, The Institute of Fine Arts of New York University, New York
Amasis; Archaism; Imhotep; Nektanebo

Junge, Friedrich
Professor of Egyptology, Universität Göttingen, Germany
Grammar, *overview article;* Language

Kadish, Gerald E.
Professor of History and Near Eastern Studies, State University of New York, Binghamton, New York
Historiography; Horkhuf; Karnak; New Kingdom, *article on* Amarna Period and the End of the Eighteenth Dynasty; Pepinakht Heqaib; Pylon; Time; Weni; Wisdom Tradition

Kahl, Jochem
Hochschuldozent of Egyptology, University of Münster, Germany
Old Kingdom, *article on* Third Dynasty

Kamrin, Janice
Independent Scholar, New York
Khnumhotep II of Beni Hasan

Kanawati, Naguib
Professor of History, Macquarie University, Australia
Akhmim

Känel, Frédérique von
Saint Médard-en-Jalles, France
Scorpions

Kaper, Olaf E.
Independent Scholar, Berlin
Myths, *article on* Lunar Cycle

Katary, Sally L. D.
Lecturer in Classical Studies, Thorneloe College, Laurentian University, Sudbury, Canada
Taxation; Wealth

Kendall, Timothy
Senior Scientist, Nubian Archaeology Project, EDC Inc., Newton, Massachusetts
Games; Kush; Napata

Kessler, Dieter
Professor of Egyptology, Institut für Ägyptologie, Ludwig-Maximilians-Universität, München, Germany
Bersheh; Bull Gods; Eastern Desert and Red Sea; Hermopolis; Middle Egypt; Monkeys and Baboons

Killen, Geoffrey
*Head of the Faculty of Design and Technology,
Statton School and Community College,
Biggleswade, United Kingdom*
    Furniture; Woodworking

Kitchen, Kenneth A.
*Brunner Professor Emeritus of Egyptology, School of
Archaeology, Classics, and Oriental Studies, Liverpool
University, United Kingdom*
    King Lists; New Kingdom, *article on* Nineteenth
    Dynasty; Osorkon; Petuabastis; Punt; Ramesses II;
    Shabaqa; Sheshonq I; Somtutefnakht; Twenty-fifth
    Dynasty

Kozloff, Arielle P.
*Independent Scholar; Vice President of The Merrin
Gallery, New York*
    Sculpture, *overview article and article on* Divine
    Sculpture

Kruchten, Jean-Marie
*Senior Lecturer in Egyptian Language, Université Libre
de Bruxelles, Belgium*
    Law; Oracles

Lacovara, Peter
*Curator of Ancient Art, Michael C. Carlos Museum,
Emory University, Atlanta, Georgia*
    Bricks and Brick Architecture; Bronze; Copper;
    Gold; Iron; Pan-Grave People; Silver; Vessels

Lapp, Günther
Arlesheim, Switzerland
    Coffins, Sarcophagi, and Cartonnages

Lawergren, Bo
*Professor of Physics, Hunter College, The City University
of New York*
    Music

Leach, Bridget
*Senior Conservator, Department of Conservation,
British Museum*
    Papyrus

Leahy, Anthony
*Senior Lecturer in Egyptology, University of
Birmingham, United Kingdom*
    Foreign Incursions; Libya; Sea Peoples

Lease, Gary
*Professor of History of Consciousness, University of
California, Santa Cruz*
    Nag Hammadi

Leclant, Jean
*Honorary Professor of Egyptian Civilization, Collège de
France; Permanent Secretary, Institut de France,
Académie des Inscriptions et Belles-Lettres, Paris, France*
    Harwa; Montuemhet; Pepy I; Pepy II

Leprohon, Ronald J.
*Professor of Egyptian Languages and Literature,
University of Toronto, Canada*
    Amenemhet III; Encomia; Ikhernofret; Offerings,
    article on Offering Formulas and Lists; Titulary

Lesko, Barbara S.
*Administrative Research Assistant, Department of
Egyptology, Brown University, Providence, Rhode Island*
    Cults, *article on* Private Cults

Lesko, Leonard H.
*Charles Edwin Wilbour Professor of Egyptology, Brown
University, Providence, Rhode Island*
    Book of Going Forth by Day; Book of That Which Is
    in the Underworld; Coffin Texts; Educational
    Institutions; Funerary Literature; Literacy; Nut

Limme, Luc J. H.
*Curator of the Egyptian Department, Musées Royaux
d'Art et d'Histoire, Brussels, Belgium*
    Elkab

Lipinska, Jadwiga
*Professor of Egyptian Art, and Curator of the National
Museum of Warsaw, Poland*
    Deir el-Bahri; Hatshepsut; Thutmose III

Lloyd, Alan B.
*Professor of Classics and Ancient History, University of
Wales, Swansea, United Kingdom*
    Ancient Historians; Apries; Herodotos; Necho I;
    Necho II; Philae

Luft, Ulrich H.
*Professor of Egyptology, University of Budapest,
Hungary*
    Religion

Magee, Diana
Research Assistant, Topographical Bibliography of Ancient Egyptian Hieroglyphic Texts, Reliefs, and Paintings, The Griffith Institute, Ashmolean Museum, Oxford, United Kingdom
Merikare; Teti

Malaise, Michel
Professor of Egyptology, University of Liège, Belgium
Bes

Manniche, Lise
External Lecturer in Egyptology, Carsten Niebuhr Institute of Near Eastern Studies, University of Copenhagen, Denmark
Erotica; Fertility; Funerary Cones; Royal Family; Sexuality; Sistrum

Manning, Joseph
Assistant Professor, Department of Classics, Stanford University, California
Crime and Punishment

Markowitz, Yvonne J.
Research Fellow, Art of the Ancient World, Museum of Fine Arts, Boston, Massachusetts
Bronze; Gold; Iron; Jewelry; Silver

McBride, Daniel R.
Cairo, Egypt
Nun

McDowell, A. G.
Visiting Assistant Professor of Law, The University of Pennsylvania, Philadelphia
Crime and Punishment

McKercher, Mary E.
Independent Scholar, Brooklyn, New York
Egyptomania

Meeks, Dimitri
Research Director of the Centre National de la Recherche Scientifique, Paris, France
Dance; Demons; Fantastic Animals

Meltzer, Edmund S.
Independent Scholar, Stevens Point, Wyoming
Egyptology; Horus

Menu, Bernadette M.
Research Director, CNRS (U.M.R. 5815)/Montpellier I University
Economy, *overview article and articles on* Royal Sector *and* Private Sector

Mills, Anthony J.
Independent Scholar, Wadebridge, United Kingdom
Lakes; Western Desert

Moran, William L.
Andrew W. Mellon Professor Emeritus of the Humanities, Harvard University
Amarna Letters

Morgenstein, Maury
Geoarchaeologist, and President, Geosciences Management Institute, Inc., Berkeley, California
Land and Soil

Morkot, Robert
Lecturer in Egyptology, University of Exeter, United Kingdom
Abu Simbel; Aswan; Ivory; Kom Ombo

Müller, Maya
Curator, Museum of Cultures, Basel, Switzerland
Afterlife; Re and ReHorakhty; Relief Sculpture

Mumford, Gregory D.
Visiting Assistant Professor of Egyptian Archaeology, University of California, Los Angeles
Mediterranean Area; Sinai; Syria-Palestine

Murnane, William J.
Professor of Ancient History, The University of Memphis, Tennessee
Battle of Kadesh; Coregency; Kadesh; Luxor; Medinet Habu; New Kingdom, *overview article*

Murray, Mary Anne
Department of Human Environment, Institute of Archaeology, University College London, United Kingdom
Agriculture

Myśliwiec, Karol
Professor of Ancient Egyptian Archaeology, and Director of the Research Centre for Mediterranean Archaeology, Polish Academy of Science, Warsaw, Poland
Atum; Sais; Sculpture, *article on* Royal Sculpture

Nicholson, Paul T.
Senior Lecturer in Archaeology, Cardiff University,
United Kingdom
Faience

Niwinski, Andrzej
Professor, Department of Egyptian Archaeology,
University of Warsaw, Poland
Coffins, Sarcophagi, and Cartonnages

Nordström, Hans-Åke
Retired Associate Professor of Archaeology,
Uppsala University, Sweden
A-Group

Nunn, John F.
Former Professor of Anesthesia, University of Leeds,
United Kingdom
Disease

Obsomer, Claude
Chargé de cours en langue et littérature égyptiennes,
Université Catholique de Louvain, Belgium; Institut
Catholique de Paris, France
Senwosret I

Ockinga, Boyo
Senior Lecturer in Egyptology, Macquarie University,
Sydney, Australia
Ethics and Morality; Piety; Sennedjem

Olson, Stacie L.
Independent Scholar, Sanatoga, Pennsylvania
Burial Practices

Orlandi, Tito
Professor of Coptic Literature, University of Rome "La
Sapienza," Italy
Grammar, *article on* Coptic; Manichaean Texts

O'Rourke, Paul F.
Research Associate, Department of Classical and Ancient
Middle Eastern Art, The Brooklyn Museum of Art,
New York
Coinage; Drama; Khnum; Wedjahorresne

Ossian, Clair R.
Professor of Geology, Tarrant County College,
Hurst, Texas
Granite; Limestone; Quartzite; Sandstone

Pardey, Eva
Lecturer in Egyptology, Research Assistant, University of
Hamburg, Germany
Administration, *article on* Provincial Administration

Parkinson, R. B.
Assistant Keeper, Department of Egyptian Antiquities,
The British Museum, London, United Kingdom
Eloquent Peasant; Hordjedef; Ipuwer; Papyrus
Westcar; Sinuhe

Peck, William H.
Curator of Ancient Art, The Detroit Institute of Arts,
Michigan
Historical Sources, *article on* Archaeological and
Artistic Evidence; Lepsius, Richard; Ostraka

Peden, Alex J.
Independent Scholar, Liverpool and Edinburgh,
United Kindgom
Ramesses IV; Ramesses IX

Piacentini, Patrizia
Professor of Egyptology, Università degli Studi di
Milano, Italia
Scribes

Pierrat-Bonnefois, Geneviève
Conservateur, Département des antiquités égyptiennes,
Museé du Louvre, Paris, France
Tod

Plas, Dirk van der
Centre for Computer-Aided Egyptological Research,
Faculty of Theology, Utrecht, The Netherlands
Hymns, *article on* Nile Hymns

Podzorski, Patricia V.
Assistant Director, Museum of Art and Archaeology,
University of Missouri, Columbia
Naga ed-Deir

Polz, Daniel C.
Associate Director, German Institute of Archaeology,
Cairo, Egypt
Asasif; Khokhah; Qurna; Seventeenth Dynasty;
Thebes

Poo, Mu-chou
Professor and Research Fellow, Institute of History and Philology, Academia Sinica, Taipei, Taiwan, Republic of China
Wine

Porter, Barbara A.
Independent Scholar, New York
Meir; Neithhotep

Pusch, Edgar B.
Egyptologist, Archaeologist, Roemer- und Pelizaeus-Museum, Hildesheim, Germany, and Field Director for Qantir-Piramesses, Egypt
Piramesse

Quirke, Stephen G. J.
Assistant Curator, The Petrie Museum of Egyptian Archaeology, University College London, United Kingdom
Administration, *article on* State Administration; Administrative Texts; Fifteenth Dynasty; Judgment of the Dead; Second Intermediate Period; Thirteenth Dynasty

Raver, Wendy
Adjunct Professor, Hunter College; New School University Library Collection Manager, The Brooklyn Museum of Art, New York
Instruction of Ptahhotep; Instructions for Merikare; Instructions of Hordjedef; Instructions of Kagemni; Man Who Was Weary of Life

Ray, John D.
Herbert Thompson Reader in Egyptology, Faculty of Oriental Studies, University of Cambridge, United Kingdom
Bakenrenef; Cults, *article on* Animal Cults; Late Period, *overview article and article on* Thirtieth Dynasty

Redford, Donald B.
Professor of Classics and Ancient Mediterranean Studies, The Pennsylvania State University, University Park
Annals; Contendings of Horus and Seth; Historical Sources, *article on* Textual Evidence; Joseph; Manetho; Mendes; Moses; Petosiris; Taharqa

Redford, Susan
Research Associate, Department of Classics and Ancient Mediterranean Studies, The Pennsylvania State University, University Park
Equines; Valley of the Queens

Redmount, Carol A.
Associate Professor of Egyptian Archaeology; Curator of Egyptian Archaeology, P. A. Hearst Museum of Anthropology, University of California, Berkeley
Ceramics; Land and Soil; Lower Egypt

Reeves, Nicholas
Honorary Fellow, Oriental Museum, University of Durham; Honorary Research Fellow, Institute of Archaeology, London
Kiya

Ritner, Robert K.
Associate Professor of Egyptology, The Oriental Institute, University of Chicago, Illinois
Dream Books; Magic, *overview article and articles on* Magic in Medicine, Magic in Daily Life, *and* Magic in the Afterlife; Medicine; Neferti

Robins, Gay
Professor of Ancient Egyptian Art, Emory University, Atlanta, Georgia
Color Symbolism; Gender Roles; Grid Systems; Legitimation; Queens; Women

Romanosky, Eugene
Project Editor, Oxford University Press, USA; Independent Scholar, New York
Ahmose; Min

Römer, Malte
Privatdozent für Ägyptologie, Freie Universität Berlin, Germany
Landholding

Roth, Ann Macy
Associate Professor of Egyptology, Howard University, Washington, D.C.
Afrocentrism; Funerary Ritual; Opening of the Mouth; Work Force

Ryan, Donald P.
Tacoma, Washington
Basketry, Matting, and Cordage

Sagrillo, Troy Leiland
Independent Scholar, Toronto, Canada
Bees and Honey

Sambin, Chantal
Independent Scholar, University of Lyon II, Neyron, France
Medamud

Samuel, Alan E.
Professor Emeritus of Greek and Roman History, University of Toronto, Ontario, Canada
Alexander

Samuel, Delwen
Wellcome Senior Research Fellow in Bioarchaeology, Institute of Archaeology, University College London, United Kingdom
Beer; Bread

Schenkel, Wolfgang
Professor of Egyptology, Eberhard-Karls-Universität Tübingen, Germany
Grammar, *article on* Middle Egyptian

Schlick-Nolte, Birgit
Independent Scholar, Liebieghaus—Museum alter Plastik, Frankfurt, Germany
Glass

Schlögl, Hermann A.
Professor of Egyptology, University of Fribourg, Switzerland
Aten

Schneider, Hans D.
Professor of Museological Aspects of Egyptian Archaeology, Rijksmuseum van Oudheden, Leiden, The Netherlands
Horemheb

Seidlmayer, Stephan J.
Altaegyptisches Woerterbuch, Section Director, Berlin-Brandenburg Academy of Sciences and Humanities, Berlin, Germany
Execration Texts; Necropolis

Serpico, Margaret T.
Wainwright Research Fellow, Oriental Institute, University of Oxford, United Kingdom
Oils and Fats

Shaw, Ian
Lecturer in Egyptian Archaeology, Institute of Archaeology, University College London, United Kingdom
Gems; Minerals; Quarries and Mines

Shinnie, Peter L.
Professor of Archaeology, University of Calgary, Alberta, Canada
Meroë; X-Group

Shubert, Steven Blake
Toronto, Ontario, Canada
Seals and Sealings

Shute, Charles (*deceased*)
Professor Emeritus of Histology, University of Cambridge, United Kingdom
Mathematics

Silverman, David P.
Curator in Charge, Egyptian Section, University of Pennsylvania Museum of Archaeology and Anthropology; Chair and Professor, Department of Asian and Middle Eastern Studies, University of Pennsylvania, Philadelphia
Curses; Deities; Humor and Satire; Scripts, *article on* Cryptography

Simon, Catherine
Curator, Shelby White and Leon Lery Collection, New York
Geb; Neith

Simpson, William Kelly
Professor of Egyptology, Yale University, New Haven, Connecticut
Instructions of Khety; Onomastica; Twelfth Dynasty

Smith, Mark
Reader in Egyptology, Oriental Institute, Oxford University, United Kingdom
Ankhsheshonqy; Papyrus Rylands IX

Smith, Stuart Tyson
Assistant Professor of Anthropology, University of California, Santa Barbara
Aniba; Imperialism; People; Race

Sourouzian, Hourig
Lecturer in Egyptian Art, University of Munich, Germany; American University of Cairo, Egypt
Merenptah

Spalinger, Anthony J.
Associate Professor of Egyptology, University of Auckland, New Zealand
Calendars; Chronology and Periodization; Festival Calendars; Festivals; Late Period, *article on* Twenty-sixth Dynasty; Piya; Psamtik I

Spanel, Donald B.
New York
Asyut; Beni Hasan; Funerary Figurines; Herakleopolis; Portraiture; Reference Works

Stadelmann, Rainer
Professor of Egyptian Art and Archaeology, Director Emeritus of the German Institute of Archaeology, Cairo, Egypt
Dahshur; Giza; Old Kingdom, *article on* Fourth Dynasty; Palaces; Sety I; Sneferu; Sphinx

Stocks, Denys A.
Research Associate, Department of Art History and Archaeology, University of Manchester, United Kingdom
Leather; Stoneworking; Tools

Störk, Lothar
Hamburg, Germany
Elephants

Strouhal, Eugen
Professor of Anthropology, First Medical Faculty, Prague, Czech Republic
Deformity

Tait, John
Edwards Professor of Egyptology, University of Texas, Austin; University College London, United Kingdom
Demotic Literature; Papyrus; Setna Khaemwase Cycle

Teeter, Emily
Associate Curator, Oriental Institute Museum, University of Chicago, Illinois
Cults, *article on* Divine Cults; Maat

Tefnin, Roland
Professor of Egyptian Art and Archaeology, Université Libre de Bruxelles, Belgium
Reserve Heads; Sculpture, *article on* Private Sculpture

Thomas, Angela P.
Senior Keeper of Human History, Bolton Museum and Art Gallery, United Kingdom
Abu Ghurob

Thomas, Nancy
Curator of the Department of Ancient and Islamic Art, Los Angeles County Museum of Art, California
Petamenophis

Thompson, Stephen E.
Independent Scholar, Coral Springs, Florida
Cults, *overview article*

Tietze, Christian
Field Archaeologist and Architect, University of Pottsdam, Institute of History
Bubastis

Tobin, Vincent Arieh
Professor of Classics, Saint Mary's University, Halifax, Canada
Amun and Amun-Re; Mythological Texts; Myths, *overview article and article on* Creation Myths; Tefnut

Tooley, Angela M. J.
Independent Scholar, Manchester, United Kingdom
Models

Traunecker, Claude
Strasbourg, France
Kamutef

Troy, Lana
Associate Professor of Egyptology, Uppsala University, Sweden
New Kingdom, *article on* Eighteenth Dynasty to the Amarna Period

Valloggia, Michel
Professeur Oridinaire d'Égyptologie, Faculté des Léttres de l'Université de Genève, Switzerland
Abu Rowash

van Dijk, Jacobus
Lecturer in Egyptology, University of Groningen, The Netherlands
Hell; Paradise; Ptah

Van Siclen, Charles C.
San Antonio, Texas
Amenhotpe II; Obelisk

Vandersleyen, Claude A. P.
Professor Emeritus of Egyptology, Université Catholique de Louvain, Belgium
Amenhotep, Son of Hapu; Kamose

Vassilika, Eleni
Keeper of Antiquities, The Fitzwilliam Museum, Cambridge, United Kingdom
Museums

Velde, Herman te
Professor Emeritus of Egyptology, University of Groningen, The Netherlands
Mut; Seth

Verner, Miroslav
Professor of Egyptology, Czech Institute of Egyptology,
Charles University, Prague-Cairo
Abusir; Old Kingdom, *overview article;* Pyramid

Vinson, Steve
Visiting Assistant Professor of History, The University of
Oregon, Eugene
Ay; Dra Abul Naga; Menes; Narmer; Ramesses VI;
Sety II; Transportation

Vischak, Deborah
Graduate Student, Institute of Fine Arts, New York
Hathor

Vogelsang-Eastwood, Gillian M.
Director, Stichting Textile Research Centre, Leiderdorp,
The Netherlands
Weaving, Looms, and Textiles

von der Way, Thomas
Professor of Egyptology, University of Mainz, Germany
Buto

Walsem, René van
University Lecturer of Egyptology, Leiden University, The
Netherlands
Interpretation of Evidence

Warburton, David A.
Research Assistant for Near Eastern Archaeology,
University of Aarhus, Denmark
Officials

Ward, Cheryl
Asssistant Professor of Nautical Archaeology, Texas A&M
University, Galveston
Seafaring; Ships and Shipbuilding

Weeks, Kent R.
Professor of Egyptology, American University in Cairo,
Egypt
Archaeology; Theban Necropolis; Tombs, *overview*
article; Valley of the Kings

Wegner, Josef W.
Assistant Professor of Egyptology, Department of Asian
and Middle Eastern Studies, University of Pennsylvania,
Philadelphia
Abydos; Cenotaphs; Cults, *article on* Royal Cults

Weinstein, James M.
Visiting Fellow in Classics, and Editor of the Bulletin
of the American Schools of Oriental Research,
Cornell University, Ithaca, New York
Byblos; Canaan; Foundation Deposits; Gaza;
Jerusalem; Joppa; Lebanon; Megiddo; Ugarit

Wells, Ronald A.
Independent Scholar, University of California, Berkeley
Astrology; Astronomy; Horoscopes; Technology and
Engineering

Welsby, Derek A.
Assistant Keeper of Egyptian Antiquities, The British
Museum, London, United Kingdom
C-Group; Kawa; Nubia

Wenke, Robert J.
Professor of Anthropology, University of Washington,
Seattle
Early Dynastic Period

Wente, Edward F.
Professor Emeritus of Egyptology, University of Chicago,
Illinois
Correspondence; Destruction of Mankind; Doomed
Prince; Grammar, *article on* Late Egyptian; Kemit;
Monotheism; Scripts, *article on* Hieratic

Werner, Edward K.
Independent Scholar, Jupiter, Florida
Armant; Montu; Montuhotep I, Nebhepetre

Wetterstrom, Wilma
Associate in Botany, Botanical Museum, Harvard
University, Cambridge, Massachussetts
Agriculture

Wiebach-Koepke, Silvia
Lecturer in Egyptology, University of Hamburg,
Germany
False Door

Wilfong, Terry G.
Assistant Professor of Egyptology, and Assistant Curator
for Greco-Roman Egypt, University of Michigan,
Ann Arbor
Coptic Literature; Faiyum; Intoxication; Journals;
Marriage and Divorce; Oxyrhynchus

Wilkinson, Richard H.
*Director of the University of Arizona Egyptian
Expedition, Tucson*
Gesture; Symbols

Wilkinson, Toby A. H.
*Fellow, Christ's College, University of Cambridge,
United Kingdom*
Social Stratification; State

Williams, Michael A.
*Professor and Chair, Near Eastern Languages and
Civilization, Seattle, Washington*
Nag Hammadi Codices and Related Texts

SYNOPTIC OUTLINE OF CONTENTS

The outline presented on the following pages is intended to provide a general view of the conceptual scheme of this encyclopedia. Entries are arranged in the conceptual categories listed below. Because the headings for these categories are not necessarily mutually exclusive, some entries in the encyclopedia are listed more than once.

Egyptology
Perceptions and Legacies of Ancient Egypt
History of the Field
Biographies

Land and Resources
Overviews
Historical Geography
Resources
Minerals and Metals
Flora and Fauna

Archaeological Sites
Overviews
Lower Egyptian Sites
Middle Egyptian Sites
Upper Egyptian Sites

History
Historiography
Historical Periods
Historical Figures

The State and Its Institutions
Monarchy
State Evolution and Administration

Foreign Relations
Overviews
Syria-Palestine
Mesopotamia
Persia
Mediterranean Area
Nubia
Other

Economy
General Essays
Subsistence Technologies and Occupations

Society and the Individual

Religion
Evolution, Levels, and Structures of Belief
Specific Deities
Burial and Afterlife
Rituals and Festivals
Symbols and Amulets

Arts and Sciences
Arts and Artifacts
Architecture
Language and Scripts
Literature
Science

INDEX

Note: The letters f and t in page numbers refer to figures and tables, respectively. Temples are typically listed under names of gods rather than locations. For example, the temple to Horus at Edfu is indexed under Horus. Page numbers for major discussions are given in bold.

EGYPTIAN KING LIST

Mesolithic Period (8500–5500 BCE)

PREDYNASTIC PERIOD

Neolithic Period (5500–3100 BCE)
Badarian	5500–4000 BCE
Amratian (Naqada I)	4000–3500 BCE
Gerzean (Naqada II)	3500–3150 BCE

Dynasty "0"
["Uj" occupant]	c.3150 BCE
Iry-Hor (?)	
Ka	c.3100–3050
"Scorpion"	

EARLY DYNASTIC PERIOD

First Dynasty (Thinite)
Narmer; Aha; Djer; Wadji;	c.3050–2850
Den; Enedjib; Semsem; Ka'a	

Second Dynasty (Thinite)
Hotepsekhemwy	c.2850–2820
Ranebi	c.2820–2790
Ninuter	c.2790–2754
Wadjnas	c.2754–2734
Senedy	
Peribsen	c.2734–2714
Khasekhemwy	c.2714–2687

OLD KINGDOM

Third Dynasty
Djoser	c.2687–2668
Nebka	c.2688–2682
Sekhemkhet	?
Khaba	?
Neferkare	c.2679–2673
Huny (?)	c.2673–2649

Fourth Dynasty
Sneferu	c.2649–2609
Khufu	c.2609–2584
Djedefre	c.2584–2576
Khafre	c.2576–2551
Menkaure	c.2551–2523
Shepseskaf	c.2523–2519
[2 unknown kings]	c.2519–2513

Fifth Dynasty
Userkaf	c.2513–2506
Sahure	c.2506–2492
Neferirkare Kakai	c.2492–2482
Shepseskare	c.2482–2475
Raneferef	c.2475–2474
Newoserre Any	c.2474–2444
Menkauhor	c.2444–2436
Djedkare Izezi	c.2436–2404
Unas	c.2404–2374

Sixth Dynasty
Teti	c.2374–2354
Userkare	?
Pepy I	c.2354–2310
Merenre Antyemsaf	c.2310–2300
Neferkare Pepy II	c.2300–2206
[Antyemsaf] II	c.2206
Nitokerty (Nitocris)	c.2205–2200
Neferka the child	[c.2200–2199]

Nefer	c.2199–2197
Aba	c.2197–2193
[. . .]	c. 2193–2191
[. . .]	c.2191

FIRST INTERMEDIATE PERIOD

Seventh Dynasty
Numerous ephemeral kings

Eighth Dynasty
"18 kings"　　c.2190–2165

Merenre Anty-emsaf II (sic)	Ny-kare
	Neferkare Terer
Neterkare	Neferkahor
Menkare	Neferkare
Neferkare	Pepysonby
Neferkare Neby	Sneferka-'anu
Djedkare Shemay	Kakaure
Neferkare Khenedy	Neferkaure
Merenhor	Neferkauhor
Sneferka	Neferirkare II

Ninth and Tenth Dynasties (Herakleopolitan)
"18 kings"　　c.2165–2040

Akhtoy I	Shed[. . .]
. . .	Hu-[. . .]
Neferkare	[6 kings]
Akhtoy II	Akhtoy III
Seneni (?)	Merikare
. . .	. . .
Mer[. . .]	

Early Eleventh Dynasty (Theban)
Antef I	2134–2118
Antef II	2118–2068
Antef III	2068–2061

MIDDLE KINGDOM

Late Eleventh Dynasty (All Egypt)
Nebhepetre Montuhotep I	2061–2011
Se'ankhibtowy Montuhotep II	2011–2000
Nebtowyre Montuhotep III	2000–1998
(Civil Strife 1998–1991)	

Twelfth Dynasty
Amenemhet I	1991–1962
Senwosret I	1971–1928
Amenemhet II	1929–1895
Senwosret II	1897–1877
Senwosret III	1878–1843
Amenemhet III	1843–1797
Amenemhet IV	1798–1790
Sobekneferu	1790–1786

Thirteenth and Fourteenth Dynasties
Khutowyre Sobekhotpe I	1786–1763
Sekhemkare Amenemhet-sonbef	1783–1780
(13 kings)	1780–1760
[. . .]	
Sekhemkare Amenemhet	
Sehtepibre	
Afni	
Seonkhibre Ameny-intef-Amenemhat	
Smenkare	

Sehtepibre Qemau si-Harendotes	
Sewadj-kare	
Nodjemibre	
Sobekhotep I	
Rensonbe	
Awibre Hor	
Sedjefakare Qay-Amenemhat	
Sobekhotpe II	1750–1756
Khendjer	1756–1751
(3 kings) [. . .]	1751–1749
Sekhemkare Sobekhotpe III	1749–1747
Khasekhemre Neferhotpe I	1747–1736
Sihathor	1735
Khaneferre Sobekhotpe IV	1734–1725
Khahetepre Sobekhotpe V	1725–1721
Wahibre Ya'ib	1721–1712
Merneferre Aya	1712–1700
Merhotepre An	1700–1698
Se'ankhenre Sewadjtu	1698–1695
Mersekhemre Neferhotpe	1695–1692
Sewadjkare Hori	1691
Merkare Sobekhotpe VI	1690–1688
(14 kings)	1688–c.1665

Merkheperre	Djedkherure
[3 or 4 kings]	Seonkhibre
Nehesy	Nefertumre
Khatire	Sekhem[. . .]re
Nebawre	Ka[. . .]re Kem
Sehebre	Neferibre
Merdjefare	[. . .]
Sewadjkare	Kha[. . .]re
Nebjefare	Akare
Webenre	Semen[. . .]re
[3 kings]	Djed[. . .]re
Awibre	[6 kings]
Heribre	Seneferre
Nebseure	Men[. . .]re
[. . .]	Djed[. . .]
Sekheperenre	

SECOND INTERMEDIATE PERIOD

Fifteenth Dynasty (Hyksos)
Maa-ibre Sheshy	c.1664–1662
Mer-userre Ya'akob-har	c.1662–1653
Seuserenre Khayan	c.1653–1614
[. . .] Yansas-adoen	c.1614–1605
Aa-woserre Apophis	c.1605–1565
[. . .] Hamudi	c.1565–1555

Early Sixteenth Dynasty (Hyksos)
22 kings+ 65+ years	c.1665–1600

Late Seventeenth Dynasty (Theban)
Sekenenre Ta'o	c.1600–1571
Senakhtenre Ta'o	
Kamose	c.1571–1569

NEW KINGDOM

Eighteenth Dynasty
Ahmose	c.1569–1545
Amenhotpe I	c.1545–1525
Thutmose I	c.1525–1516
Thutmose II	c.1516–1504
Thutmose III	1504–1452
Hatshepsut	1502–1482
Amenhotpe II	1454–1419
Thutmose IV	1419–1410